k_d Before-tax cost of debt
k_e Cost of newly issued common stock
k_M Required rate of return on "the market"
k_{ps} Cost of preferred stock
k_{RF} Rate of return on a riskless asset
k_s Cost of retained earnings, cost of common stock
k_{sL} Cost of equity of a levered firm
k_{sU} Cost of equity of an unlevered firm
M/B Market to book ratio
MIRR Modified internal rate of return
N Calculator key denoting number of periods
n (1) Life of a project (periods or years)
(2) Number of shares outstanding
MVA Market value added
NAL Net advantage to leasing
NOPAT Net operating profit after taxes
NOWC Net operating working capital
NPV Net present value
NWC Net working capital
P (1) Price of a share of stock; P_0 = price of stock today
(2) Price per unit of output
(3) Probability of occurrence
P/E Price/earnings ratio
PI Profitability index
PMT (1) Annuity payment
(2) Payment key on calculators
PV Present value
Q Unit sales
r Correlation coefficient
ROA Return on assets
ROE Return on equity
ROIC Return on invested capital
RP Risk premium
RP_M Market risk premium
S (1) Dollar sales
(2) Total market value of equity
SML Security Market Line
Σ Summation sign (capital sigma)
σ Standard deviation (lowercase sigma)
T Tax rate
t Time
TIE Times-interest-earned ratio
V (1) Value
(2) Variable cost per unit
V_L Total market value of a levered firm
V_U Total market value of an unlevered firm
w Proportion or weight
w_d Weight of debt
w_{ps} Weight of preferred stock
w_{ce} Weight of common equity
WACC Weighted average cost of capital
YTC Yield to call
YTM Yield to maturity

DANIEL PORCELY
MBA 03
404-321-4109

Financial Management

Theory and Practice

Tenth Edition

Financial Management

Theory and Practice

Tenth Edition

Eugene F. Brigham
University of Florida

Michael C. Ehrhardt
University of Tennessee

SOUTH-WESTERN
THOMSON LEARNING

Australia • Canada • Mexico • Singapore • Spain
United Kingdom • United States

SOUTH-WESTERN
THOMSON LEARNING

PUBLISHER: Mike Roche
EXECUTIVE EDITOR: Mike Reynolds
DEVELOPMENTAL EDITOR: Amy Holmes
MARKETING MANAGER: Charlie Stutesman
PROJECT MANAGER: Erin Gregg

COVER IMAGE: Stone/Bruce Rogovin
COVER PRINTER: Lehigh Press, Inc.
COMPOSITOR: Clarinda
PRINTER: R.R. Donnelley Willard

2 3 4 5 6 7 05 04 03 02 01

For more information about our products contact us at:
Thomson Learning Academic Resource Center
1-800-423-0563

For permission to use material from this text, contact us by:
Phone: 1-800-730-2214 **Fax:** 1-800-730-2215
Web: http://www.thomsonrights.com

Library of Congress Catalog Card Number: 00-111721
ISBN: 0-03-033561-2

Asia
Thomson Learning
60 Albert Street, #15-01
Albert Complex
Singapore 189969

Australia
Nelson Thomson Learning
102 Dodds Street
South Melbourne, Victoria 3205
Australia

Canada
Nelson Thomson Learning
1120 Birchmount Road
Toronto, Ontario M1K 5G4
Canada

Europe/Middle East/Africa
Thomson Learning
Berkshire House
168-173 High Holborn
London WC1 V7AA
United Kingdom

Latin America
Thomson Learning
Seneca, 53
Colonia Polanco
11560 Mexico D.F.
Mexico

Spain
Paraninfo Thomson Learning
Calle/Magallanes, 25
28015 Madrid, Spain

Financial Management

Theory and Practice

Tenth Edition

Preface

When we wrote the first edition of *Financial Management: Theory and Practice*, we had four goals: (1) to create a text that would help people make better financial decisions; (2) to provide a book that could be used in the introductory MBA course, but one that was complete enough for use as a reference text in follow-on case courses and after graduation; (3) to motivate students by demonstrating that finance is both interesting and relevant; and (4) to make the book clear enough so that students could go through the material without wasting time trying to figure out what we were saying.

WWW

For more information about this text be sure to visit the *Financial Management* web site at **http://www.harcourtcollege.com/finance/theory.**

As the title indicates, the book combines theory and practical applications. An understanding of finance theory is essential if students are to develop and implement effective financial strategies, and students also need a good working knowledge of the financial environment. Therefore, the book begins with some basic information and concepts, including background materials on the economic and financial environment, an overview of financial statement analysis, and the essentials of risk analysis and the valuation process. With this background, students can understand the specific techniques and decision rules that are used to help maximize the value of the firm. This structure has three important advantages:

1. Financial management is designed to help maximize the value of a firm. Value is determined by results as revealed in financial statements. Therefore, financial managers should understand how the decisions they make today will affect future financial statements, and our early coverage of this topic helps students see what financial management is all about. Also, most financial decisions are analyzed using spreadsheets, and if an instructor plans to have students use spreadsheets in the course, financial statement analysis provides an excellent starting point.
2. The early coverage of risk analysis, discounted cash flow techniques, and valuation permits us to use and reinforce these concepts throughout the book.
3. Students, even those who do not plan to major in finance, generally enjoy working with stock and bond valuation models, rates of return, and the like. Because the ability to learn a subject is a function of interest and motivation, and because *Financial Management* covers securities and markets early on, the book's organization is sound from a pedagogic standpoint.

Intended Market and Use

Financial Management is designed for use in a one-term introductory MBA course and as a reference for follow-on case courses and on the job. However, there is enough material for two terms, especially if supplemented with cases and/or selected readings. The book can also be used as an undergraduate introductory text with exceptionally good students, or where the introductory course is taught over two terms.

Major Changes in the Tenth Edition

As in every revision, we updated and clarified sections throughout the text. In addition, we made three major changes:

1. **Restructuring and Web/CD materials.** Over the years, financial researchers have developed new theories, the financial markets have spawned many new types of securities, consulting firms have developed new ways of thinking about financial practices, computers have facilitated better ways of analyzing decisions, and businesses have become increasingly global. Much of this new information simply must be added to the text, because without it students would be obsolete even before they graduate. However, this could result in a textbook that overwhelms students with more material than they can digest.

   The *Financial Management* web site is **http://www.harcourtcollege.com/finance/theory.**

   With this in mind, we reviewed every chapter to identify those core topics that are essential, those specialized topics that are important but not essential for every introductory finance course, and those topics that no longer warrant coverage. The core topics are covered in the text itself, as are some of the specialized but not essential materials. Other material deemed useful for reference purposes but not essential is now provided in four-color Adobe PDF files both on the CD-ROM that is packaged with the textbook and on the textbook's web site. Eleven chapters now have a "Web/CD Extension," and three entire chapters (Working Capital Management: Extensions, Pension Plan Management, and Financial Management in Not-for-Profit Businesses) were relegated to those media. This blending of a traditional textbook and an e-book results in a comprehensive introductory textbook plus easy access to additional specialized materials that the instructor may choose to cover. In addition, the Web/CD material gives students an enriched reference library that will be helpful in later courses and in their careers.
2. **New material.** Financial managers strive to maximize shareholder value, and this requires a focus on cash flow. Therefore, we wrote a new chapter that consolidates material on free cash flow, corporate valuation, value-based management, corporate governance, and incentive compensation. We also increased our coverage of real options and initial public offerings.
3. **Integration of spreadsheets and web-based data.** Proficiency with spreadsheets is an absolute necessity for all MBA students. With this in mind, we created an *Excel* spreadsheet, called a "Tool Kit," for each chapter to show how the calculations required in the chapter are done with *Excel.* The Tool Kit models include comments and screen shots that explain how to use many of the features and functions of *Excel;* thus, the Tool Kits also serve as self-taught tutorials on *Excel* itself.

In recent years the amount of useful financial data on the Web has grown exponentially. Unfortunately, so has the amount of not-so-useful Web material. This makes it difficult to determine which web site has the particular information we need, and even when we locate the right web site, navigating it is often difficult. To help others get to the information that is most relevant for financial management, we created a set of *Word* documents called "Web Safaris" that begin with a description of the data needed to solve a problem such as comparing a company's ratios with industry averages. The *Word* document has a hyperlink to the appropriate web site, along with a series of screen shots that take the user step-by-step through the site to the desired data.

The *Financial Management* web site is **http://www.harcourtcollege.com/finance/theory.**

The Tool Kits and Web Safaris are located on both the CD-ROM and the Instructor's portion of the text's web site.

Other Changes in the Tenth Edition

The entire book was reviewed for completeness, ease of exposition, and currency, and hundreds of small and not-so-small changes were made during this review. Some examples include the following.

The *Financial Management* web site is **http://www.harcourtcollege.com/finance/theory.**

1. **Improved linkage with the World Wide Web.** The rapid growth of the World Wide Web is creating almost limitless opportunities for improving financial education. We enhanced the web site for this Tenth Edition, and the site now provides teaching and learning tools for instructors and students. Students can access archived news summaries, use our database of financial research links, and more. Instructors have access to NewsWire, which provides summaries of recent articles from major business publications plus discussion questions and references to the text. Instructors can also download selected ancillaries, sample teaching materials, and share ideas with us and others who are using the book.

   We also incorporated additional links throughout the text in marginal notes entitled "On the WWW" to direct readers to web sites relevant to the subject being covered at that point. Also, as noted above, our "Web Safaris," with their hyperlinks and screen shots, guide readers to the data needed to deal with specific problems. Finally, we added some "Cyberproblems" to the end-of-chapter materials, which require students to track down and apply information from the Web.
2. **Placement of financial forecasting early in the book.** We moved forecasting from Part Five to Part One, and we now flow seamlessly from historical statements and ratios to forecasts of these items. Covering forecasting early helps students see how alternative strategies and decisions affect future financial statements, and thus the firm's value.
3. **Term structure of interest rates.** We clarified our somewhat confusing term structure discussion, and we now make a smooth transition from interest rate levels to the factors that influence the level and shape of the yield curve.
4. **Beta calculations.** Chapter 6, which introduces risk, return, and the CAPM, now shows how to calculate beta for an actual company, Wal-Mart. The calculation is discussed in the chapter, and the Tool Kit uses *Excel* to estimate the beta. We also include a Web Safari that shows how to obtain the returns needed for the calculation and another Safari that shows how to obtain published betas from the Web if you don't want to calculate your own.
5. **Beyond the CAPM.** We broadened the coverage of the second risk chapter to include asset pricing models that go beyond the CAPM. In particular, we added a detailed description of the Fama-French Three-Factor Model, plus a brief introduction to behavioral finance.
6. **Time value of money.** We broadened our discussion of spreadsheets for solving time value problems, and the chapter's Tool Kit provides annotations that explain how to use the key *Excel* financial functions. Also, we relegated the tabular approach to a Web/CD Extension to streamline the chapter.
7. **Value-based management and corporate governance.** We shifted the corporate valuation model from the stock chapter and combined it with some new material on value-based management and corporate governance to create a new chapter.
8. **Capital budgeting.** We reorganized and streamlined the three capital budgeting chapters. The first chapter still covers basic capital budgeting, but with more emphasis on spreadsheet solutions. The second chapter still covers cash flow estimation, but since cash flow estimation and risk analysis (sensitivity, scenario, and

simulation analysis) are typically done at the same time and within the same spreadsheet, we combined cash flow estimation and risk analysis.

We also developed a special Tool Kit for simulation analysis in capital budgeting, using an *Excel* Add-In graciously provided by Professor Roger Myerson of Northwestern University. If an instructor so chooses, he or she can have students simulate a capital budgeting project without the need for a proprietary software package.

The third major change in the capital budgeting section is the restructuring and reworking of the material on real options. We now begin this section with a discussion of financial options as a lead-in to real options, after which we discuss different procedures for bringing real options into the capital budgeting analysis.

11. **The Hamada model.** Capital structure decisions are always a bit nebulous, so to provide more structure to this discussion, we moved the Hamada model into the first chapter on capital structure.
12. **Initial public offerings (IPOs).** The IPO market has recently been one of the most exciting areas of finance, especially for people with an entrepreneurial bent, so we expanded and improved our coverage of investment banking in general and IPOs in particular.

The Instructional Package: An Integrated Approach to Learning

Financial Management includes a broad array of ancillary materials designed both to enhance students' learning and to help instructors prepare for and conduct classes. These ancillaries are included on both the Instructor's Resource CD-ROM and the textbook's web site.

1. ***Instructor's Manual.*** This comprehensive manual contains answers to all text questions and problems, plus detailed solutions to the end-of-chapter Mini Cases. It is available in print form as well as *Microsoft Word.*
2. ***PowerPoint* slides.** Each chapter has a Mini Case that covers all the essential issues presented in the chapters, and it can be used to provide structure for lectures. There are *PowerPoint* slides based on the Mini Case that present graphs, tables, lists, and calculations sequentially, much as one might present them on a blackboard or in transparencies. However, the slides are more crisp, clear, and colorful, and they use color coding to tie elements of a given slide together. Copies of these files are on the Instructor's Resource CD-ROM, the text's web site, and the Student CD-ROM. Also, to help students take notes, printed copies of the slides are available in the *Blueprints* ancillary, which is described later in this section.
3. **Mini Case spreadsheets.** In addition to the *PowerPoint* slides, we also provide *Excel* spreadsheets that do the calculations required in the Mini Cases. These are similar to the Tool Kits for the chapter, except (a) the numbers in the examples correspond to the Mini Case rather than the chapter per se, and (b) we added some features that make it possible to do what-if analysis on a real-time basis in class. We usually begin our lectures with the *PowerPoint* presentation, but after we have explained a basic concept we "toggle" to the *Excel* file and show how the case analysis is done in *Excel.*[1] For example, when teaching bond pricing, we begin with the *PowerPoint* show and cover the basic facts and calculations. Then we

[1]Note: To toggle between two open programs, such as *Excel* and *PowerPoint*, hold the Alt key down and hit the Tab key until you have selected the program you want to show.

toggle to the *Excel* sheet and use a graph to show how bond prices change as the interest rate varies. Many of our students also bring their laptops to class, and they follow along, doing the what-if analysis themselves.

4. **Web Safaris.** As noted earlier, we became frustrated with our own searches on the Internet, so we created a series of *Word* files that keep us from reinventing the wheel. Each Web Safari has a specific goal, such as finding the current spreads between government bonds and risky bonds with different ratings. The file has a hyperlink to the appropriate web site (**http://www.bondsonline.com** in this example) and screen shots that show how to navigate to the desired information. As noted earlier, we usually begin our lecture with the *PowerPoint* presentation, but we occasionally "toggle" to a Web Safari. When we teach in a wired classroom, we actually go on the Safari and bring up real-time data. When we aren't in a wired classroom, we just show the data from the file's screen shots.
5. ***Blueprints.*** As technological advances led lectures away from the blackboard, it became increasingly important to provide students with hard copies of the lecture materials. Students must have printed copies if they are to focus on the lecture yet still take useful notes. After some experimentation, we concluded that *Blueprints* would be most useful if it simply provided copies of the *PowerPoint* slides, along with space for notes and comments. Note too that since *Blueprints* covers the key points made in the chapters, it is not necessary for instructors to lecture on every single topic.

   When we teach the intro MBA course, we use a "course pack" that consists of our syllabus, a 10- to 12-page calculator tutorial (taken from the *Technology Supplement* described below), some old exams, and *Blueprints.* We can provide such a package to bookstores; for further information, contact your local sales representative. We also make the *PowerPoint* files available on our class web site for those students who prefer to work online.
6. ***Test Bank.*** Although some instructors don't like multiple-choice questions, they do provide a useful means for testing students on certain topics. If they are used, it is important that the questions be both unambiguous and consistent with the lectures and assigned readings. To meet this need, we developed a *Test Bank* that contains more than 1,200 class-tested questions and problems. It is available both in print and on the Instructor's Resource CD-ROM. A number of new and thoroughly class-tested conceptual questions and problems, which vary in level of difficulty, have been added to the *Test Bank.* Information regarding the topic and degree of difficulty, along with the complete solution for all numerical problems, is provided with each question.

   The *Test Bank* is available in book form, in *Microsoft Word* files, and in a computerized test bank, EXAMaster+, which has many features that make test preparation, scoring, and grade recording easy. For example, EXAMaster+ can automatically convert multiple-choice questions and problems into free-response questions, and it can alter the sequence of test questions to make different versions of a given test. The software also makes it easy to add to or edit the existing test items, or to compile a test that covers a specific set of topics. Of course, instructors who don't want to use EXAMaster+ can instead cut and paste questions from the *Word* files.
7. **End-of-chapter spreadsheet problems.** Most chapters have two types of spreadsheet problems. The first is a "Build a Model" problem, where students start with a spreadsheet that contains financial data plus instructions for solving a particular problem. The model is partially completed, with headings but no formulas, so the student must literally build the model. This structure guides the student through the problem, and it also makes it easier to grade the work, since all students' answers are in the same locations on the spreadsheet. The second

type of spreadsheet problem is called "What If Analysis." Here students start with a spreadsheet containing data, instructions, and a completed model, plus a series of questions that asks them to change certain inputs and to observe changes in the key outputs, which helps them become more aware of the risks inherent in most financial decisions. The "What If Analysis" spreadsheet and the partial spreadsheets for the "Build a Model" problems are on the Student CD-ROM. The solutions to the spreadsheet problems are in files on the Instructor's Resource CD-ROM and web site.

8. **End-of-chapter Cyberproblems.** Most chapters contain Cyberproblems that require students to go to specific web sites and answer a series of questions. The problems are located on the text's web site, and they are updated as needed to remain current. Answers are available to Instructors on the web site.
9. **Student CD-ROM.** The textbook comes with a CD-ROM that contains *PowerPoint* shows, *Excel* Tool Kits, *Excel* models for the end-of-chapter Mini Cases, *Word* files for the Web Safaris, *Excel* models for the end-of-chapter "What If Analysis" spreadsheet problems, partial *Excel* models for the end-of-chapter "Build a Model" spreadsheet problems, and chapter extension reference material.
10. **Instructor's Resource CD-ROM.** This CD contains all of the information on the student version (with the exception of the Web/CD Chapters and Extensions) plus *Word* files for the *Instructor's Manual* and the *Test Bank* and *Excel* files with the solutions to the "Build a Model" problems. This material is also available on the Instructor's portion of the web site.
11. **Transparencies.** About 250 lecture transparency acetates are available from South-Western.
12. **Digital Finance Case Library.** More than 100 cases written by Eugene F. Brigham and Linda Klein are now available via the Web, and new cases are added every year. These cases are in a customized case database that allows instructors to select cases and create their own customized casebooks. Most of the cases have accompanying spreadsheet models that, while not essential for working the case, do reduce number crunching and thus leave more time for students to consider conceptual issues. The models also show students how computers can be used to make better financial decisions. Cases that we have found particularly useful for the different chapters are listed in the end-of-chapter references.

    All of the cases, case solutions, and spreadsheet models can be previewed by professors from the Finance Case web site at **http://www.harcourtcollege.com/finance/fincase** with proper access. For professorial access contact your sales representative.
13. ***Technology Supplement.*** This ancillary contains tutorials for five commonly used financial calculators and for *Microsoft Excel*, *Lotus 1-2-3*, and *PowerPoint*. The calculator tutorials cover everything a student needs to know about calculators to work the problems in the text, and we provide the tutorials for selected calculators as a part of our course pack. The rather large manuals that accompany most calculators intimidate some students, and they find our 12-page, course-specific tutorials far easier to use. The spreadsheet tutorials teach students the basics plus some advanced spreadsheet features, and they prepare students to work with the specific finance models provided in the Tool Kits. Finally, the *PowerPoint* tutorial is useful to students who must make presentations or to instructors who want to make slides for use in their lectures.
14. **Finance NewsWire.** A problem inherent in printed textbooks is keeping them current in a constantly changing world. When Orange County goes bankrupt, or the Nasdaq crashes, it would be useful to relate these events to the textbook. However, the World Wide Web can help us keep up to date. Adopters of *Financial*

Management will have access to a South-Western web site that provides summaries of recent articles in *The Wall Street Journal*, *Business Week*, and other business publications, along with discussion questions and references to the text. This helps incorporate late-breaking news into classroom discussions. Instructors can also use the accompanying questions for quizzes and/or exams.

15. ***Study Guide.*** This supplement outlines the key sections of each chapter, and it provides students with a set of questions and problems similar to those in the text and in the *Test Bank*, along with worked-out solutions. Instructors seldom use the *Study Guide* themselves, but some students find it useful, so we recommend that instructors ask their bookstores to have copies available. Our bookstore generally has to reorder it, which attests to its popularity with students.

Acknowledgments

This book reflects the efforts of a great many people over a number of years. First, we would like to thank the following people who helped us with the Tenth Edition

Michael Barry	*Boston College*
Phil Gardial	*SMG Fairfax*
Janet Hamilton	*Portland State University*
Theodor Kohers	*Mississippi State University*
Frank O'Meara	*Keller School of Management*
David Overbye	*Keller School of Management*
Jay Ritter	*University of Florida*
Elizabeth Shields	*California State University–Fresno*
Mark Stohs	*California State University–Fullerton*

Second, earlier versions of individual chapters or groups of chapters were reviewed by professors and professionals who are experts on specific topics. We are grateful for the insights provided by

Edward I. Altman	*New York University*
Mary Schary Amram	*Analysis Group Economics*
Nasser Arshadi	*University of Missouri*
Abdul Aziz	*Humboldt State University*
William Beranek	*University of Georgia*
Gordon R. Bonner	*University of Delaware*
Ben S. Branch	*Bank of New England and University of Massachusetts*
David T. Brown	*University of Florida*
Mark Flannery	*University of Florida*
E. Bruce Frederickson	*Syracuse University*
Myron Gordon	*University of Toronto*
Hal Heaton	*Brigham Young University*
John Helmuth	*Rochester Institute of Technology*
Hugh Hunter	*Eastern Washington University*
James E. Jackson	*Oklahoma State University*
Vahan Janjigian	*Northeastern University*
Keith H. Johnson	*University of Kentucky*
Robert Kieschnick	*George Mason University*
Richard LeCompte	*Wichita State University*

Ilene Levin	*University of Minnesota–Duluth*
James T. Lindley	*University of South Mississippi*
R. Daniel Pace	*Valparaiso University*
Ralph A. Pope	*California State University–Sacramento*
Allen Rappaport	*University of Northern Iowa*
Michael Ryngaert	*University of Florida*
Fiona Robertson	*Seattle University*
James Schallheim	*University of Utah*
G. Bennett Stewart	*Stern Stewart & Co.*
Robert Strong	*University of Maine at Orono*
Eugene Swinnerton	*University of Detroit–Mercy*
Robert Taggart	*Boston College*
Jonathan Tiemann	*Wells Fargo Nikko Investment Advisors*
Sheridan Titman	*University of Texas at Austin*
Alan L. Tucker	*Temple University*
David Vang	*University of St. Thomas*
Gary R. Wells	*Idaho State University*
David Ziebart	*University of Illinois at Urbana*

In addition, we would like to thank the following people, whose reviews and comments on prior editions and companion books have contributed to this edition: Mike Adler, Syed Ahmad, Sadhana M. Alangar, Ed Altman, Bruce Anderson, Ron Anderson, Bob Angell, Vince Apilado, Henry Arnold, Bob Aubey, Gil Babcock, Peter Bacon, Kent Baker, Tom Bankston, Les Barenbaum, Charles Barngrover, Bill Beedles, Moshe Ben-Horim, Bill Beranek, Tom Berry, Bill Bertin, Roger Bey, Dalton Bigbee, John Bildersee, Russ Boisjoly, Keith Boles, Geof Booth, Kenneth Boudreaux, Helen Bowers, Oswald Bowlin, Don Boyd, G. Michael Boyd, Pat Boyer, Joe Brandt, Elizabeth Brannigan, Greg Brauer, Mary Broske, Dave Brown, Kate Brown, Bill Brueggeman, Kirt Butler, Robert Button, Bill Campsey, Bob Carleson, Severin Carlson, David Cary, Steve Celec, Don Chance, Antony Chang, Susan Chaplinsky, Jay Choi, S. K. Choudhury, Lal Chugh, Maclyn Clouse, Margaret Considine, Phil Cooley, Joe Copeland, David Cordell, John Cotner, Charles Cox, David Crary, John Crockett, Roy Crum, Brent Dalrymple, Bill Damon, Joel Dauten, Steve Dawson, Sankar De, Miles Delano, Fred Dellva, Anand Desai, Bernard Dill, Greg Dimkoff, Les Dlabay, Mark Dorfman, Gene Drycimski, Dean Dudley, David Durst, Ed Dyl, Dick Edelman, Charles Edwards, John Ellis, Dave Ewert, John Ezzell, Richard Fendler, Michael Ferri, Jim Filkins, John Finnerty, Susan Fischer, Steven Flint, Russ Fogler, Dan French, Tina Galloway, Michael Garlington, Jim Garvin, Adam Gehr, Jim Gentry, Philip Glasgo, Rudyard Goode, Walt Goulet, Bernie Grablowsky, Theoharry Grammatikos, Ed Grossnickle, John Groth, Alan Grunewald, Manak Gupta, Sam Hadaway, Don Hakala, Sally Hamilton, Gerald Hamsmith, William Hardin, John Harris, Paul Hastings, Bob Haugen, Steve Hawke, Del Hawley, Robert Hehre, George Hettenhouse, Hans Heymann, Kendall Hill, Roger Hill, Tom Hindelang, Linda Hittle, Ralph Hocking, J. Ronald Hoffmeister, Jim Horrigan, John Houston, John Howe, Keith Howe, Steve Isberg, Jim Jackson, Kose John, Craig Johnson, Keith Johnson, Ramon Johnson, Ray Jones, Manuel Jose, Gus Kalogeras, Mike Keenan, Bill Kennedy, Joe Kiernan, Rick Kish, Linda Klein, Don Knight, Dorothy Koehl, Jaroslaw Komarynsky, Duncan Kretovich, Harold Krogh, Charles Kroncke, Joan Lamm, P. Lange, Howard Lanser, Martin Laurence, Ed Lawrence, Wayne Lee, Jim LePage, Jules Levine, John Lewis, Chuck Linke, Bill Lloyd, Susan Long, Judy Maese, Bob Magee, Ileen Malitz, Phil Malone, Terry Maness, Chris Manning, Terry Martell, D. J.

Masson, John Mathys, John McAlhany, Andy McCollough, Bill McDaniel, Robin McLaughlin, Tom McCue, Jamshid Mehran, Ilhan Meric, Larry Merville, Rick Meyer, Jim Millar, Ed Miller, John Mitchell, Carol Moerdyk, Bob Moore, Barry Morris, Gene Morris, Fred Morrissey, Chris Muscarella, David Nachman, Tim Nantell, Don Nast, Bill Nelson, Bob Nelson, Bob Niendorf, Tom O'Brien, Dennis O'Connor, John O'Donnell, Jim Olsen, Robert Olsen, Coleen Pantalone, Jim Pappas, Stephen Parrish, Glenn Petry, Jim Pettijohn, Rich Pettit, Dick Pettway, Hugo Phillips, John Pinkerton, Gerald Pogue, R. Potter, Franklin Potts, R. Powell, Chris Prestopino, Jerry Prock, Howard Puckett, Herbert Quigley, George Racette, Bob Radcliffe, Bill Rentz, Ken Riener, Charles Rini, John Ritchie, Pietra Rivoli, Antonio Rodriguez, E. M. Roussakis, Dexter Rowell, Jim Sachlis, Abdul Sadik, Thomas Scampini, Kevin Scanlon, Frederick Schadler, Mary Jane Scheuer, Carl Schweser, John Settle, Alan Severn, Sol Shalit, Frederic Shipley, Dilip Shome, Ron Shrieves, Neil Sicherman, J. B. Silvers, Clay Singleton, Joe Sinkey, Stacy Sirmans, Jaye Smith, Steve Smith, Don Sorenson, David Speairs, Ken Stanly, Ed Stendardi, Alan Stephens, Don Stevens, Jerry Stevens, Glen Strasburg, Philip Swensen, Ernie Swift, Paul Swink, Gary Tallman, Dennis Tanner, Russ Taussig, Richard Teweles, Ted Teweles, Andrew Thompson, George Trivoli, George Tsetsekos, Mel Tysseland, David Upton, Howard Van Auken, Pretorious Van den Dool, Pieter Vanderburg, Paul Vanderheiden, Jim Verbrugge, Patrick Vincent, Steve Vinson, Susan Visscher, John Wachowicz, Mike Walker, Sam Weaver, Kuo Chiang Wei, Bill Welch, Fred Weston, Norm Williams, Tony Wingler, Ed Wolfe, Larry Wolken, Don Woods, Thomas Wright, Michael Yonan, Zhong-guo Zhou, Dennis Zocco, and Kent Zumwalt.

Special thanks are due to Fred Weston, Myron Gordon, Merton Miller, and Franco Modigliani, who have done much to help develop the field of financial management and who provided us with instruction and inspiration; to Roy Crum, who co-authored the multinational finance chapter; to Larry Wolken, who offered his hard work and advice for the development of the Lecture Presentation Software; to Dana Aberwald Clark, Susan Ball, and Chris Buzzard, who helped us develop the spreadsheet models; to Don Barksdale and Dana Aberwald Clark, who helped with the ancillaries; to Susan Whitman, who provided both word processing and editorial support, and to Joel Houston and Phillip Daves, whose work with us on other books is reflected in this text.

Both our colleagues and our students at the Universities of Florida and Tennessee gave us many useful suggestions, and the Harcourt and Elm Street Publishing Services staffs—especially Amy Holmes, Sue Nodine, Lauren Feldman, and Mike Reynolds—helped greatly with all phases of text development, production, and marketing.

Errors in the Text

At this point, authors generally say something like this: "We appreciate all the help we received from the people listed above, but any remaining errors are, of course, our own responsibility." And in many books, there are plenty of remaining errors. Having experienced difficulties with errors ourselves, both as students and as instructors, we resolved to avoid this problem in *Financial Management.* As a result of our error detection procedures, we are convinced that the book is relatively free of mistakes.

Partly because of our confidence that few such errors remain, but primarily because we want to detect any errors that may have slipped by so we can correct them in subsequent printings, we decided to offer a reward of $10 per error to the first person who reports it to us. For purposes of this reward, errors are defined as misspelled words, nonrounding numerical errors, incorrect statements, and any other error that inhibits comprehension. Typesetting problems such as irregular spacing and differences in opinion regarding grammatical or punctuation conventions do not qualify for this reward. Also, given the ever-changing nature of the World Wide Web, changes in web addresses do not qualify as errors. Finally, any qualifying error that has follow-through effects is counted as two errors only. Please report any errors to Michael C. Ehrhardt at the e-mail address given below.

Conclusion

Finance is, in a real sense, the cornerstone of the free enterprise system. Good financial management is therefore vitally important to the economic health of business firms, hence to the nation and the world. Because of its importance, financial management should be thoroughly understood. However, this is easier said than done—the field is relatively complex, and it is undergoing constant change in response to shifts in economic conditions. All of this makes financial management stimulating and exciting, but also challenging and sometimes perplexing. We sincerely hope that the Tenth Edition of *Financial Management* will help you understand the financial problems faced by businesses today, as well as the best ways to solve those problems.

Eugene F. Brigham
College of Business Administration
University of Florida
Gainesville, Florida 32611-7167
Brighaef@dale.cba.ufl.edu

Michael C. Ehrhardt
University of Tennessee
Ehrhardt@utk.edu

June 2001

Brief Contents

Contents

Web/CD Chapters (http://www.harcourtcollege.com/finance/theory10e/)

Web/CD Extensions (http://www.harcourtcollege.com/finance/theory10e/)

1

1

An Overview of Financial Management

In a beauty contest for companies, the winner is . . . General Electric.

Or at least General Electric is the most admired company in America, according to *Fortune* magazine's annual survey. The other top ten finalists are Microsoft, Dell Computer, Cisco Systems, Wal-Mart Stores, Southwest Airlines, Berkshire Hathaway, Intel, Home Depot, and Lucent Technologies. What do these companies have that separates them from the rest of the pack?

According to more than 10,000 executives, directors, and security analysts, these companies have the highest average scores across eight attributes: (1) innovativeness, (2) quality of management, (3) employee talent, (4) quality of products and services, (5) long-term investment value, (6) financial soundness, (7) social responsibility, and (8) use of corporate assets.

These companies also have an incredible focus on using technology to reduce costs, to reduce inventory, and to speed up product delivery. For example, workers at Dell previously touched a computer 130 times during the assembly process but now touch it only 60 times. Using point-of-sale data, Wal-Mart is able to identify and meet surprising customer needs, such as bagels in Mexico, smoke detectors in Brazil, and house paint during the winter in Puerto Rico. Many of these companies are changing the way business works by using the Net, and that change is occurring at a break-neck pace. For example, in 1999 GE's plastics distribution business did less than $2,000 per day of business online. In 2000 its web site did more than $2,000,000 per day in e-commerce.

With the unemployment rate so low, many companies now have a difficult time attracting employees. Not so for the most admired companies, which average 26 applicants for each job opening. This is because, in addition to their acumen with technology and customers, they are also on the leading edge when it comes to training employees and providing a workplace in which people can thrive.

In a nutshell, these companies reduce costs by having innovative production processes, they create value for customers by providing high-quality products and services, and they create value for employees through training and fostering an environment that allows employees to utilize all of their skills and talents.

Do investors benefit from this focus on processes, customers, and employees? During the most recent five-year period, these 10 companies posted an average annual stock return of 63.5 percent, more than double the S&P 500's average annual return of 28.3 percent. These exceptional returns are due to the ability of these companies to generate cash flow. But, as you will see throughout this book, a company can generate cash flow only if it also creates value for its customers, employees, and suppliers.

The purpose of this chapter is to give you an idea of what financial management is all about and what you will be studying in the rest of the book. Most issues in financial management revolve around these three questions: (1) What factors determine the price of a company's stock; (2) how can managers make choices that will add value to their companies; and (3) how can managers ensure that their companies don't run out of cash while executing their plans? If you learn how to answer these questions, and how to apply the answers at your company, then you will be well on your way to a great career.

Finance and Your Career

Suppose you don't plan to major in finance. Is the subject still important to you? Absolutely, for two reasons. First, you need a knowledge of finance to make many personal decisions, ranging from investing for your retirement to deciding whether to lease versus buy a car. Second, virtually all important business decisions have financial implications, so important decisions are generally made by teams from the finance, marketing, human resources, information technology, production, accounting, and legal departments. Therefore, if you want to succeed in the business arena, you must not only be highly competent in your own area but also must have a familiarity with the other business disciplines, especially finance.

Because there are financial implications in virtually all business decisions, nonfinancial executives definitely must know enough finance to work these implications into their own specialized analyses.[1] Because of this, finance is important for every business student, regardless of his or her major.

Visit **http://www.harcourtcollege.com/finance/theory** to see the web site accompanying this text. This ever-evolving site, for students and instructors, is a tool for teaching, learning, financial research, and job searches.

For those of you who do major in finance, your career will probably begin in one of these three areas: (1) *capital markets and institutions*, which deals with securities markets and financial institutions; (2) *investments*, which focuses on the decisions made by both individual and institutional investors as they choose securities for their investment portfolios; and (3) *financial management*, or "corporate finance," which involves decisions within firms. The career opportunities within each field are many and varied, but financial managers must have a knowledge of all three if they are to do their jobs well.

Capital Markets and Institutions

Many finance majors go to work for a financial institution, including banks, insurance companies, mutual funds, and investment banking firms. For success here, one needs a knowledge of valuation techniques, the factors that cause interest rates to rise and fall, the regulations to which financial institutions are subject, and the various types of financial instruments (stocks, bonds, mortgages, auto loans, certificates of deposit, and so on). One also needs a general knowledge of all aspects of business administration, because the management of a financial institution involves accounting, marketing, personnel, and computer systems, as well as financial management. An ability to communicate, both orally and in writing, is important, and "people skills," or the ability to deal with customers and to get others to do their jobs well, are critical.

One common entry-level job in this area is a bank officer trainee, where one goes into bank operations and learns about the business, from tellers' work, to cash

[1]It is an interesting fact the course "Financial Management for Nonfinancial Executives" has the highest enrollment in most executive development programs.

management, to making loans. One could expect to spend a year or so being rotated among these different areas, after which he or she would settle into a department, often as an assistant manager in a branch. Alternatively, one might become a specialist in some area such as real estate, and be authorized to make loans going into millions of dollars, or in the management of trusts, estates, and pension funds. Similar career paths are available with insurance companies, investment companies, credit unions, and consumer loan companies.

WWW

Consult **http://www.cob.ohio-state.edu/dept/fin/osujobs.htm** for an excellent site containing information on a variety of business career areas, listings of current jobs, and a variety of other reference materials.

Investments

Finance graduates who go into investments often work for a brokerage house such as Merrill Lynch, either in sales or as a security analyst. Others work for banks, mutual funds, or insurance companies in the management of their investment portfolios; for financial consulting firms advising individual investors or pension funds on how to invest their capital; for an investment bank, whose primary function is to help businesses raise new capital; or as financial planners who help individuals develop and achieve long-term financial goals. The three main functions in the investments area are sales, the analysis of individual securities, and determining the optimal mix of securities for a given investor.

Financial Management

Financial management is the broadest of the three areas, and the one with the greatest number of job opportunities. Financial management is important in all types of businesses, including banks and other financial institutions, as well as industrial and retail firms. Financial management is also important in governmental operations, from schools to hospitals to highway departments. The job opportunities in financial management range from making decisions regarding plant expansions to choosing what types of securities to issue when financing an expansion. Financial managers also have the responsibility for deciding the credit terms under which customers may buy, how much inventory the firm should carry, how much cash to keep on hand, whether to acquire other firms (merger analysis), and how much of the firm's earnings to plow back into the business versus pay out as dividends.

Regardless of which area a finance major goes into, he or she will need a knowledge of all three areas. For example, a bank lending officer cannot do his or her job well without a good understanding of financial management, because he or she must be able to judge how well a business is being operated. The same thing holds true for Merrill Lynch's security analysts and stockbrokers, who must have an understanding of general financial principles if they are to give their customers intelligent advice. Similarly, corporate financial managers need to know what their bankers are thinking, and they also need to know how investors judge a firm's performance and thus determine its stock price. So, if you decide to make finance your career, you will need to know something about all three areas.

Self-Test Questions

What three questions does financial management answer?

Why is it necessary for business students who do not plan to major in finance to understand the basics of finance?

What are the three main areas of finance?

If you have definite plans to go into one area, why is it necessary that you know something about the other areas?

How Are Companies Organized?

There are three main forms of business organization: (1) sole proprietorships, (2) partnerships, and (3) corporations. In terms of numbers, about 80 percent of businesses are operated as sole proprietorships, while most of the remainder are divided equally between partnerships and corporations. Based on dollar value of sales, however, about 80 percent of all business is conducted by corporations, about 13 percent by sole proprietorships, and about 7 percent by partnerships and hybrids. Because most business is conducted by corporations, we will concentrate on them in this book. However, it is important to understand the differences among the various forms.

Sole Proprietorship

A **sole proprietorship** is an unincorporated business owned by one individual. Going into business as a sole proprietor is easy—one merely begins business operations. However, even the smallest businesses normally must be licensed by a governmental unit.

The proprietorship has three important advantages: (1) It is easily and inexpensively formed, (2) it is subject to few government regulations, and (3) the business avoids corporate income taxes.

The proprietorship also has three important limitations: (1) It is difficult for a proprietorship to obtain large sums of capital; (2) the proprietor has unlimited personal liability for the business's debts, which can result in losses that exceed the money he or she invested in the company; and (3) the life of a business organized as a proprietorship is limited to the life of the individual who created it. For these three reasons, sole proprietorships are used primarily for small-business operations. However, businesses are frequently started as proprietorships and then converted to corporations when their growth causes the disadvantages of being a proprietorship to outweigh the advantages.

Partnership

A **partnership** exists whenever two or more persons associate to conduct a noncorporate business. Partnerships may operate under different degrees of formality, ranging from informal, oral understandings to formal agreements filed with the secretary of the state in which the partnership was formed. The major advantage of a partnership is its low cost and ease of formation. The disadvantages are similar to those associated with proprietorships: (1) unlimited liability, (2) limited life of the organization, (3) difficulty transferring ownership, and (4) difficulty raising large amounts of capital. The tax treatment of a partnership is similar to that for proprietorships, but this is often an advantage, as we demonstrate in Chapter 2.

Regarding liability, the partners can potentially lose all of their personal assets, even assets not invested in the business, because under partnership law, each partner is liable for the business's debts. Therefore, if any partner is unable to meet his or her pro rata liability in the event the partnership goes bankrupt, the remaining partners must make good on the unsatisfied claims, drawing on their personal assets to the extent necessary. The partners of the national accounting firm Laventhol and Horwath, a huge partnership that went bankrupt as a result of suits filed by investors who relied on faulty audit statements, learned all about the perils of doing business as a partnership. Thus, a Texas partner who audits a business that goes under can bring ruin to a millionaire New York partner who never went near the client company.

The first three disadvantages—unlimited liability, impermanence of the organization, and difficulty of transferring ownership—lead to the fourth, the difficulty partnerships have in attracting substantial amounts of capital. This is generally not a problem for a slow-growing business, but if a business's products or services really catch on, and if it needs to raise large sums of money to capitalize on its opportunities, the difficulty in attracting capital becomes a real drawback. Thus, growth companies such as Hewlett-Packard and Microsoft generally begin life as a proprietorship or partnership, but at some point their founders find it necessary to convert to a corporation.

Corporation

A **corporation** is a legal entity created by a state, and it is separate and distinct from its owners and managers. This separateness gives the corporation three major advantages: (1) *Unlimited life.* A corporation can continue after its original owners and managers are deceased. (2) *Easy transferability of ownership interest.* Ownership interests can be divided into shares of stock, which, in turn, can be transferred far more easily than can proprietorship or partnership interests. (3) *Limited liability.* Losses are limited to the actual funds invested. To illustrate limited liability, suppose you invested $10,000 in a partnership that then went bankrupt owing $1 million. Because the owners are liable for the debts of a partnership, you could be assessed for a share of the company's debt, and you could be held liable for the entire $1 million if your partners could not pay their shares. Thus, an investor in a partnership is exposed to unlimited liability. On the other hand, if you invested $10,000 in the stock of a corporation that then went bankrupt, your potential loss on the investment would be limited to your $10,000 investment.[2] These three factors—unlimited life, easy transferability of ownership interest, and limited liability—make it much easier for corporations than for proprietorships or partnerships to raise money in the capital markets.

The corporate form offers significant advantages over proprietorships and partnerships, but it also has two disadvantages: (1) Corporate earnings may be subject to double taxation—the earnings of the corporation are taxed at the corporate level, and then any earnings paid out as dividends are taxed again as income to the stockholders. (2) Setting up a corporation, and filing the many required state and federal reports, is more complex and time-consuming than for a proprietorship or a partnership.

A proprietorship or a partnership can commence operations without much paperwork, but setting up a corporation requires that the incorporators prepare a charter and a set of bylaws. Although personal computer software that creates charters and bylaws is now available, a lawyer is required if the fledgling corporation has any nonstandard features. The *charter* includes the following information: (1) name of the proposed corporation, (2) types of activities it will pursue, (3) amount of capital stock, (4) number of directors, and (5) names and addresses of directors. The charter is filed with the secretary of the state in which the firm will be incorporated, and when it is approved, the corporation is officially in existence.[3] Then, after the corporation is in operation, quarterly and annual employment, financial, and tax reports must be filed with state and federal authorities.

The *bylaws* are a set of rules drawn up by the founders of the corporation. Included are such points as (1) how directors are to be elected (all elected each year, or perhaps one-third each year for three-year terms); (2) whether the existing stockholders will have the first right to buy any new shares the firm issues; and (3) procedures for changing the bylaws themselves, should conditions require it.

---

[2]In the case of small corporations, the limited liability feature is often a fiction, because bankers and other lenders frequently require personal guarantees from the stockholders of small, weak businesses.

[3]Note that more than 60 percent of major U.S. corporations are chartered in Delaware, which has, over the years, provided a favorable legal environment for corporations. It is not necessary for a firm to be headquartered, or even to conduct operations, in its state of incorporation.

The value of any business other than a very small one will probably be maximized if it is organized as a corporation for these three reasons:

1. Limited liability reduces the risks borne by investors, and, other things held constant, *the lower the firm's risk, the higher its value.*
2. A firm's value depends on its *growth opportunities*, which, in turn, depend on the firm's ability to attract capital. Because corporations can attract capital more easily than unincorporated businesses, they are better able to take advantage of growth opportunities.
3. The value of an asset also depends on its *liquidity*, which means the ease of selling the asset and converting it to cash at a "fair market value." Because an investment in the stock of a corporation is much more liquid than a similar investment in a proprietorship or partnership, this too enhances the value of a corporation.

As we will see later in the chapter, most firms are managed with value maximization in mind, and this, in turn, has caused most large businesses to be organized as corporations. However, a very serious problem faces the corporation's stockholders, who are its owners. What is to prevent managers from acting in their own best interests, rather than in the best interests of the owners? This is called an **agency problem,** because managers are hired as agents to act on behalf of the owners. We will have much more to say about agency problems later in this chapter and throughout the book.

Hybrid Forms of Organization

Although the three basic types of organization—proprietorships, partnerships, and corporations—dominate the business scene, several hybrid forms are gaining popularity. For example, there are some specialized types of partnerships that have somewhat different characteristics than the "plain vanilla" kind. First, it is possible to limit the liabilities of some of the partners by establishing a **limited partnership,** wherein certain partners are designated **general partners** and others **limited partners.** In a limited partnership, the limited partners are liable only for the amount of their investment in the partnership, while the general partners have unlimited liability. However, the limited partners typically have no control, which rests solely with the general partners, and their returns are likewise limited. Limited partnerships are common in real estate, oil, and equipment leasing ventures. However, they are not widely used in general business situations because no one partner is usually willing to be the general partner and thus accept the majority of the business's risk, while the would-be limited partners are unwilling to give up all control.

The **limited liability partnership (LLP),** sometimes called a **limited liability company (LLC),** is a relatively new type of partnership that is now permitted in many states. In both regular and limited partnerships, at least one partner is liable for the debts of the partnership. However, in an LLP, all partners enjoy limited liability with regard to the business's liabilities, so in that regard they are similar to shareholders in a corporation. In effect, the LLP combines the limited liability advantage of a corporation with the tax advantages of a partnership. Of course, those who do business with an LLP as opposed to a regular partnership are aware of the situation, which increases the risk faced by lenders, customers, and others who deal with the LLP.

There are also several different types of corporations. One that is common among professionals such as doctors, lawyers, and accountants is the **professional corporation (PC),** or in some states, the **professional association (PA).** All 50 states have statutes that prescribe the requirements for such corporations, which provide most of the benefits of incorporation but do not relieve the participants of professional (malpractice) liability. Indeed, the primary motivation behind the professional corporation was to provide a way for groups of professionals to incorporate and thus avoid certain types of unlimited liability, yet still be held responsible for professional liability.

Finally, note that if certain requirements are met, particularly with regard to size and number of stockholders, one (or more) individuals can establish a corporation but elect to be taxed as if the business were a proprietorship or partnership. Such firms, which differ not in organizational form but only in how their owners are taxed, are called **S corporations.** Although S corporations are similar in many ways to limited liability partnerships, LLPs frequently offer more flexibility and benefits to their owners, and this is causing many S corporation businesses to convert to the LLP organizational form.

Self-Test Questions

What are the key differences between sole proprietorships, partnerships, and corporations?

Explain why the value of any business other than a very small one will probably be maximized if it is organized as a corporation.

Identify the hybrid forms of organization discussed in the text, and explain the differences among them.

Finance in the Organizational Structure of the Firm

Organizational structures vary from firm to firm, but Figure 1-1 presents a fairly typical picture of the role of finance within a corporation. The chief financial officer

FIGURE 1-1 Role of Finance in a Typical Business Organization

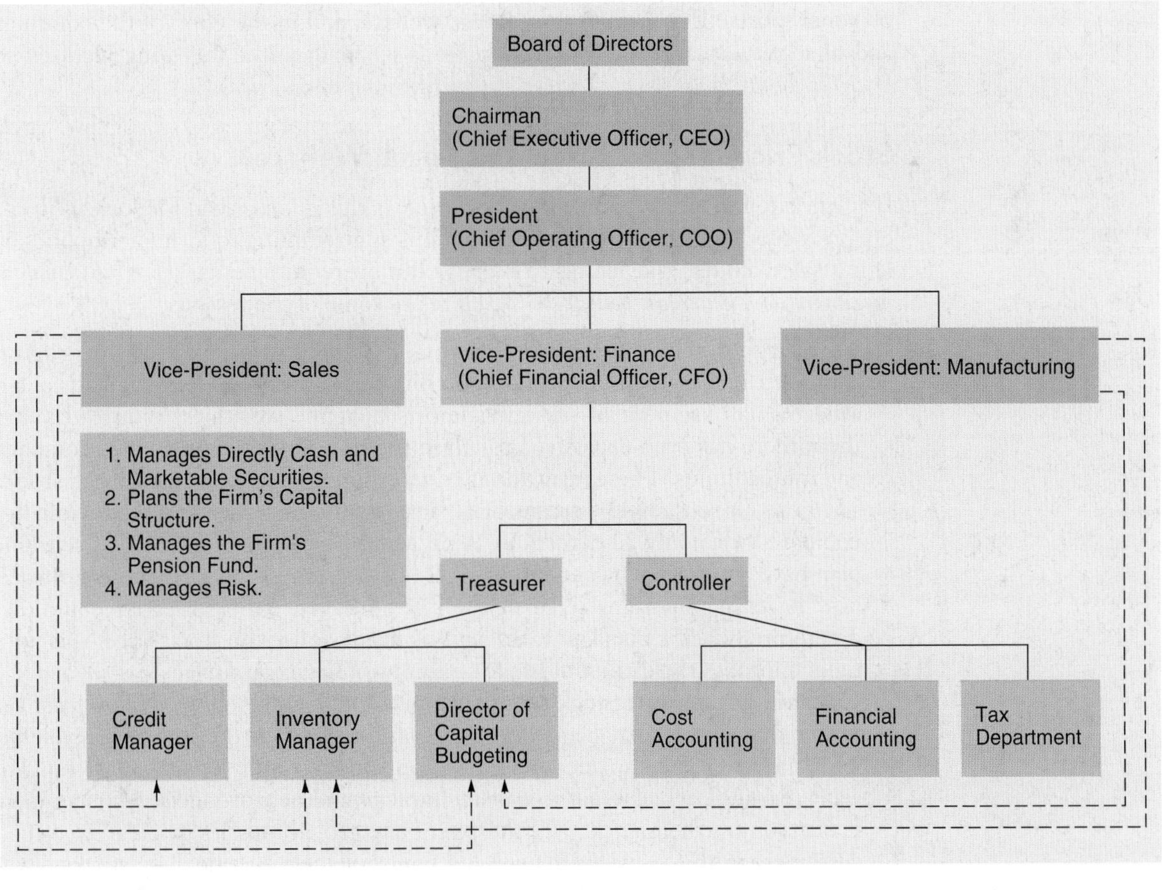

(CFO) generally has the title of vice-president: finance, and he or she reports to the president. The financial vice-president's key subordinates are the treasurer and the controller. In most firms the treasurer has direct responsibility for managing the firm's cash and marketable securities, for planning its capital structure, for selling stocks and bonds to raise capital, for overseeing the corporate pension plan, and for managing risk. The treasurer also supervises the credit manager, the inventory manager, the director of capital budgeting (who analyzes decisions related to investments in fixed assets), and the risk manager. The controller is typically responsible for the activities of the accounting and tax departments.

Self-Test Question

Identify the two primary subordinates who report to the firm's chief financial officer, and indicate the primary responsibilities of each.

The Goals of the Corporation

Shareholders are the owners of a corporation, and they purchase stocks because they want to earn a good return on their investment without undue risk exposure. In most cases, shareholders elect directors, who then hire managers to run the corporation on a day-to-day basis. Because managers are supposed to be working on behalf of shareholders, it follows that they should pursue policies that enhance shareholder value. Consequently, throughout this book we operate on the assumption that management's primary goal is **stockholder wealth maximization,** which translates into *maximizing the price of the firm's common stock.* Firms do, of course, have other objectives—in particular, the managers who make the actual decisions are interested in their own personal satisfaction, in their employees' welfare, and in the good of the community and of society at large. Still, for the reasons set forth in the following sections, *stock price maximization is the most important goal for most corporations.*

Stock Price Maximization and Social Welfare

If a firm attempts to maximize its stock price, is this good or bad for society? In general, it is good. Aside from such illegal actions as attempting to form monopolies, violating safety codes, and failing to meet pollution requirements, *the same actions that maximize stock prices also benefit society.* Here are some of the reasons:

1. **To a large extent, the owners of stock *are* society.** Seventy-five years ago this was not true, because most stock ownership was concentrated in the hands of a relatively small segment of society, comprised of the wealthiest individuals. Since then, there has been explosive growth in pension funds, life insurance companies, and mutual funds. These institutions now own more than 60 percent of all stock. In addition, more than 43 percent of all U.S. adults now own stock individually, as compared with only 22 percent in 1990. Moreover, most people with a retirement plan have an indirect ownership interest in stocks. Thus, most members of society now have an important stake in the stock market, either directly or indirectly. Therefore, when a manager takes actions to maximize the stock price, this potentially improves the quality of life for millions of ordinary citizens.
2. **Consumers benefit.** Stock price maximization requires efficient, low-cost businesses that produce high-quality goods and services at the lowest possible cost. This means that companies must develop products and services that consumers want and need, which leads to new technology and new products. Also, companies that maximize their stock price must generate growth in sales by creating value for customers in the form of efficient and courteous service, adequate stocks of merchandise, and well-located business establishments.

People sometimes argue that firms, in their efforts to raise profits and stock prices, increase product prices and gouge the public. In a reasonably competitive economy, which we have, prices are constrained by competition and consumer resistance. If a firm raises its prices beyond reasonable levels, it will simply lose its market share. Even giant firms such as General Motors lose business to Japanese and German firms, as well as to Ford and Chrysler, if they set prices above the level necessary to cover production costs plus a "normal" profit. Of course, firms *want* to earn more, and they constantly try to cut costs, develop new products, and so on, and thereby earn above-normal profits. Note, though, that if they are indeed successful and do earn above-normal profits, those very profits will attract competition, which will eventually drive prices down, so again, the main long-term beneficiary is the consumer.

3. **Employees benefit.** There are cases in which a stock increases when a company announces plans to lay off employees, but viewed over time this is the exception rather than the rule. In general, companies that successfully increase stock prices also grow and add more employees, thus benefiting society. Note too that many governments across the world, including U.S. federal and state governments, are privatizing some of their state-owned activities by selling these operations to investors. Perhaps not surprisingly, the sales and cash flows of recently privatized companies generally improve. Moreover, studies show that these newly privatized companies tend to grow and thus require more employees when they are managed with the goal of stock price maximization.

   Each year *Fortune* magazine conducts a survey of managers, analysts, and other knowledgeable people to determine the most admired companies. One of *Fortune*'s key criteria is a company's ability to attract, develop, and retain talented people. The results consistently show that there are high correlations among a company's being admired, its ability to satisfy employees, and its creation of value for shareholders. Employees find that it is both fun and financially rewarding to work for successful companies. So, successful companies get the cream of the employee crop, and skilled, motivated employees are one of the keys to corporate success.

Managerial Actions to Maximize Shareholder Wealth

What types of actions can managers take to maximize a firm's stock price? To answer this question, we first need to ask, "What determines stock prices?" In a nutshell, it is *a company's ability to generate cash flows now and in the future.*

While we will address this issue in detail in Chapter 10, we can lay out three basic facts here: (1) Any financial asset, including a company's stock, is valuable only to the extent that it generates cash flows; (2) the timing of cash flows matters—cash received sooner is better, because it can be reinvested in the company to produce additional income or else be returned to investors; and (3) investors generally are averse to risk, so all else equal, they will pay more for a stock whose cash flows are relatively certain than for one whose cash flows are more risky. Because of these three facts, managers can enhance their firms' stock prices by increasing the size of the expected cash flows, by speeding up their receipt, and by reducing their risk.

The three primary determinants of cash flows are (1) unit sales, (2) after-tax operating margins, and (3) capital requirements. The first factor has two parts, the *current level of sales* and their *expected future growth rate.* Managers can increase sales, hence cash flows, by truly understanding their customers and then providing the goods and services that customers want. Some companies may luck into a situation that creates rapid sales growth, but the unfortunate reality is that market saturation and competition will, in the long term, cause their sales growth rate to decline to a level that is limited by population growth and inflation. Therefore, managers must constantly strive to create new products, services, and brand identities that cannot be easily replicated by competitors, and thus to extend the period of high growth for as long as possible.

The second determinant of cash flows is the amount of after-tax profit that the company can keep after it has paid its employees and suppliers. One possible way to increase operating profit is to charge higher prices. However, in a competitive economy such as ours, higher prices can be charged only for products that meet the needs of customers better than competitors' products.

Another way to increase operating profit is to reduce direct expenses such as labor and materials. However, and paradoxically, sometimes companies can create even higher profit by spending *more* on labor and materials. For example, choosing the lowest-cost supplier might result in using poor materials that lead to costly production problems. Therefore, managers should understand *supply chain management*, which often means developing long-term relationships with suppliers. Similarly, increased employee training adds to costs, but it often pays off through increased productivity and lower turnover. Therefore, the *human resources staff* can have a huge impact on operating profits.

The third factor affecting cash flows is the amount of money a company must invest in plant and equipment. In short, it takes cash to create cash. For example, as a part of their normal operations, most companies must invest in inventory, machines, buildings, and so forth. But each dollar tied up in operating assets is a dollar that the company must "rent" from investors and pay for by paying interest or dividends. Therefore, reducing asset requirements tends to increase cash flows, which increases the stock price. For example, companies that successfully implement *just-in-time* inventory systems generally increase their cash flows, because they have less cash tied up in inventory.

As these examples indicate, there are many ways to improve cash flows. All of them require the active participation of many departments, including marketing, engineering, and logistics. One of the financial manager's roles is to show these other managers how their actions will affect the company's ability to generate cash flow.

Financial managers also must decide *how to finance the firm:* What mix of debt and equity should be used, and what specific types of debt and equity securities should be issued? Also, what percentage of current earnings should be retained and reinvested rather than paid out as dividends; this is the **dividend policy decision.**

Each of these investment and financing decisions is likely to affect the level, timing, and risk of the firm's cash flows, and, therefore, the price of its stock. Naturally, managers should make investment and financing decisions that are designed to maximize the firm's stock price.

Although managerial actions affect stock prices, stocks are also influenced by such external factors as legal constraints, the general level of economic activity, tax laws, interest rates, and conditions in the stock market. See Figure 1-2. Working within the set of external constraints shown in the box at the extreme left, management makes a set of long-run strategic policy decisions that chart a future course for the firm. These policy decisions, along with the general level of economic activity and the level of corporate income taxes, influence expected cash flows, their timing, and their perceived risk. These factors all affect the price of the stock, but so does another factor, the stock market's overall condition.

Does It Make Sense to Try to Maximize Earnings per Share?

In arguing that managers should take steps to maximize the firm's stock price, we indicated that managers should focus on increasing **cash flows** both now and in the

FIGURE 1-2 Summary of Major Factors Affecting Stock Prices

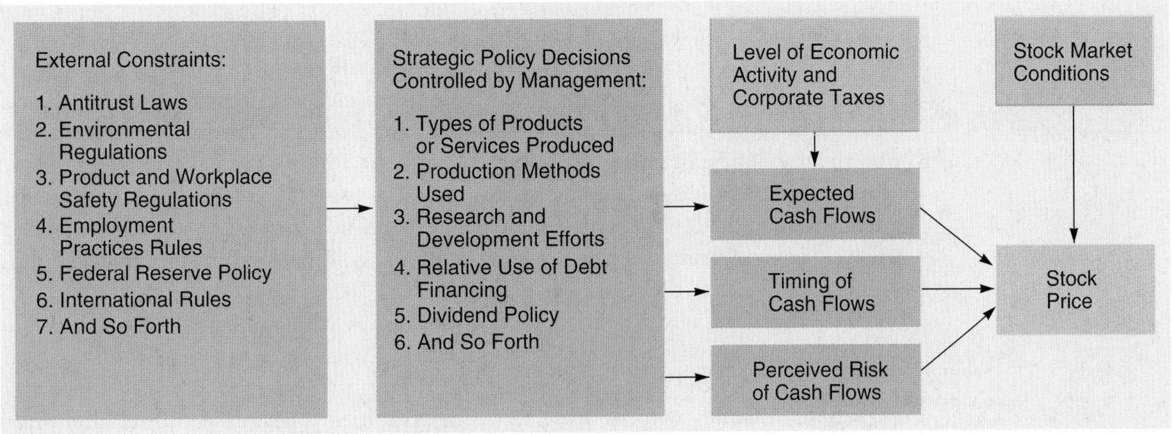

future. We have said nothing about maximizing **profit** or **earnings per share (EPS).** Although today most analysts rely primarily on cash flow to assess performance, attention still is paid to accounting measures, especially EPS. The accounting performance measures are appealing (1) because they are easy to use and understand; (2) because they are calculated on the basis of (more or less) standardized accounting principles, which reflect the accounting profession's efforts to measure financial performance on a consistent basis both across firms and over time; and (3) because net income is supposed to reflect the firm's potential for producing cash flows over time. Nevertheless, as we will see in the next chapter, there are important differences between earnings and cash flows.

Even though cash flows ultimately determine stockholder value, financial managers cannot ignore EPS, because earnings announcements send messages to investors. Say, for example, that a manager makes a decision that will greatly improve future cash flows and thus raise the stock price, yet the short-run effect will be a reduction in this year's EPS. Such a decision might be a change in inventory accounting policy that increases the reported cost of goods sold, hence lowers profits, but also increases cash flow because it reduces taxes. In this case, it makes sense for the manager to make the change because it increases cash flow, even though it reduces profits for this year. Note, though, that management must communicate the reason for the earnings decline, for otherwise the company's stock price would probably fall after the earnings announcement.

Self-Test Questions

What is management's primary goal?

How does stock price maximization benefit society?

What three basic factors determine the price of a stock?

What three factors determine cash flows?

Is profit maximization an appropriate goal for financial managers?

Should financial managers concentrate strictly on cash flow and ignore the effect of their decisions on EPS?

Financial Management in the New Millennium

When financial management emerged as a separate field of study in the early 1900s, the emphasis was on the legal aspects of mergers, the formation of new firms, and the various types of securities firms could issue to raise capital. During the Depression of the 1930s, the emphasis shifted to bankruptcy and reorganization, corporate liquidity, and the regulation of security markets. During the 1940s and early 1950s, finance continued to be taught as a descriptive, institutional subject, viewed more from the standpoint of an outsider than of a manager. However, a movement toward theoretical analysis began during the late 1950s, and the focus shifted to managerial decisions designed to maximize the value of the firm.

The focus on value maximization continues as we begin the 21st century. However, two other trends are becoming increasingly important: (1) the globalization of business and (2) the increased use of information technology. Both of these trends provide companies with exciting new opportunities to increase profitability and reduce risks. However, these factors are also leading to increased competition and to new risks. To emphasize these points throughout the book, we regularly provide "boxes" that describe how companies or industries have been affected by increased globalization and changing technology.

Globalization of Business

Check out **http://www.nummi.com/home.htm** to find out more about New United Motor Manufacturing, Inc. (NUMMI), the joint venture between Toyota and General Motors. Read about NUMMI's history and organizational goals.

Many companies today rely to a large and increasing extent on overseas operations. Table 1-1 summarizes the percentage of overseas revenues and profits for ten well-known corporations. Very clearly, these ten "American" companies are really "international" concerns.

Four factors have led to the increased globalization of businesses: (1) Improvements in transportation and communications, which lowered shipping costs and made international trade more feasible. (2) The increasing political clout of consumers, who desire low-cost, high-quality products. This has helped lower trade barriers designed to protect inefficient, high-cost domestic manufacturers and their workers. (3) As technology has become more advanced, the cost of developing new products has increased. These rising costs have led to joint ventures between such companies as

TABLE 1-1 Percentage of Revenue and Net Income from Overseas Operations for Ten Well-Known Corporations, 1999

Company	Percentage of Revenue Originated Overseas	Percentage of Net Income Generated Overseas
Chase Manhattan	27.8	26.6
Coca-Cola	62.3	64.6
Exxon	80.1	65.1
General Electric	23.9	31.1
General Motors	30.8	68.0
IBM	56.8	68.9
McDonald's	60.8	71.7
Merck	24.9	27.4
Minn. Mining & Mfg.	51.7	26.9
Walt Disney	16.7	18.9

Source: *Forbes* Magazine's 1999 Ranking of the 100 Largest U.S. Multinationals; *Forbes*, July 26, 1999, 202–206.

Coke Rides the Global Economy Wave

Over the past 20 years, Coca-Cola has created tremendous value for its shareholders. From the late 1970s through 1997, Coke's stock gained nearly $150 billion in market value, and it rose at a rate more than six times that of the Standard & Poor's 500 Index. A large part of that impressive growth was due to Coke's overseas expansion program. In recent years, nearly 75 percent of Coke's profit has come from overseas, and Coke sells roughly half of the world's soft drinks.

As Coke has discovered in recent years, however, risks arise when investing overseas. In the two-year period from June 1997 to June 1999, Coke's stock declined slightly, even as the overall market was increasing by more than 45 percent. Coke's poor performance during this period was due to troubles overseas. Weak economic conditions in Brazil, Germany, Japan, Southeast Asia, Venezuela, Colombia, and Russia, plus a quality scare in Belgium and France, hurt the company's bottom line.

Despite its recent difficulties, Coke remains committed to its global vision. In a recent annual report, Coke CEO Douglas Ivester stated, "We know that the global economy is here to stay. Troubled markets will improve. And people will still get thirsty." He pointed out that every day 47 billion drinks are consumed throughout the world, but only 1 billion of these drinks are Coke products. Ivester concluded, "We still have plenty of opportunity."

Unfortunately, Ivester will not have the opportunity to see his vision through. He was replaced shortly after his report was released.

General Motors and Toyota, and to global operations for many firms as they seek to expand markets and thus spread development costs over higher unit sales. (4) In a world populated with multinational firms able to shift production to wherever costs are lowest, a firm whose manufacturing operations are restricted to one country cannot compete unless costs in its home country happen to be low, a condition that does not necessarily exist for many U.S. corporations. As a result of these four factors, survival requires that most manufacturers produce and sell globally.

WWW

For more information about the Coca-Cola Company, go to **http://www.thecoca-colacompany.com/world/index.html,** where you can find profiles of Coca-Cola's presence in foreign countries. You may follow additional links to Coca-Cola web sites in foreign countries.

Service companies, including banks, advertising agencies, and accounting firms, are also being forced to "go global," because such firms can best serve their multinational clients if they too have worldwide operations. There will, of course, always be some purely domestic companies, but the most dynamic growth, and the best employment opportunities, are often with companies that operate worldwide.

Even businesses that operate exclusively in the United States are not immune to the effects of globalization. For example, the costs to a homebuilder in rural Nebraska are affected by interest rates and lumber prices—both of which are determined by worldwide supply and demand conditions. Furthermore, demand for the homebuilder's houses is influenced by interest rates and also by conditions in the local farm economy, which depend to a large extent on foreign demand for wheat. To operate efficiently, the Nebraska builder must be able to forecast the demand for houses, and that depends on worldwide events. So, at least some knowledge of global economic conditions is important to virtually everyone, not just to those involved with businesses that operate internationally.

Information Technology

As we advance into the new millennium, we will see continued advances in computer and communications technology, and this will continue to revolutionize the way financial decisions are made. Companies are linking networks of personal computers to one another, to the firms' own mainframe computers, to the Internet and the World Wide Web, and to their customers' and suppliers' computers. Thus, financial managers are increasingly able to share information and to have "face-to-face" meetings with distant colleagues through video teleconferencing. The ability to access and analyze data on a real-time basis also means that quantitative analysis is becoming more important, and "gut feel" less sufficient, in business decisions. As a result, the next generation of financial managers will need stronger computer and quantitative skills than were required in the past.

Changing technology provides both opportunities and threats. Improved technology enables businesses to reduce costs and expand markets. At the same time, however, changing technology can introduce additional competition, which may reduce profitability in existing markets.

The banking industry provides a good example of the double-edged technology sword. Improved technology has allowed banks to process information more efficiently, which reduces the cost of processing checks, providing credit, and identifying bad credit risks. Technology has also allowed banks to serve customers better. For example, today a bank's customers can use automatic teller machines (ATMs) everywhere, from the supermarket to the local mall. However, changing technology also threatens banks' profitability. Many customers no longer feel compelled to use a local bank, and the Internet allows them to shop worldwide for the best deposit and loan rates. An even greater threat is the continued development of electronic commerce. Electronic commerce allows customers and businesses to transact directly, thus reducing the need for intermediaries such as commercial banks. In the years ahead, financial managers must continue to stay abreast of technological developments, and they must be prepared to adapt to the changing environment.

Self-Test Questions

What two key trends are affecting financial management today?

How has financial management changed from the early 1900s to the present?

How might a person become better prepared for a career in financial management?

Business Ethics and Social Responsibility

Is the goal of maximizing stock prices consistent or inconsistent with high standards of ethical behavior and social responsibility? It is most definitely *consistent.* Many socially responsible firms have created enormous value for their owners, and many unethical firms now are bankrupt.

Business Ethics

The word *ethics* is defined in Webster's dictionary as "standards of conduct or moral behavior." **Business ethics** can be thought of as a company's attitude and conduct toward its employees, customers, community, and stockholders. High standards of ethical behavior demand that a firm treat each party that it deals with in a fair and honest manner. A firm's commitment to business ethics can be measured by the tendency of the firm and its employees to adhere to laws and regulations relating to such factors as product safety and quality, fair employment practices, fair marketing and selling practices, the use of confidential information for personal gain, community involvement, bribery, and illegal payments to obtain business.

There are many instances of firms engaging in unethical behavior. For example, in recent years the employees of several prominent Wall Street investment banking houses have been sentenced to prison for illegally using insider information on proposed mergers for their own personal gain, and E. F. Hutton, a large brokerage firm, lost its independence through a forced merger after it was convicted of cheating its banks out of millions of dollars in a check kiting scheme. Drexel Burnham Lambert, once the most profitable investment banking firm, went bankrupt, and its "junk bond king," Michael Milken, who had earned \$550 million in just one year, was sentenced to ten years in prison plus charged a huge fine for securities-law violations. Another investment bank, Salomon Brothers, was implicated in a Treasury bond scandal that resulted in the firing of its chairman and other top officers.

These cases received a lot of notoriety, and they made people wonder about the ethics of business in general. However, the results of a recent study indicate that the executives of most major firms in the United States do try to maintain high ethical standards in all of their business dealings. Furthermore, there is a positive correlation between ethics and long-run profitability. For example, Chase Bank suggested that ethical behavior has increased its profitability because such behavior helped it (1) avoid fines and legal expenses, (2) build public trust, (3) attract business from customers who appreciate and support its policies, (4) attract and keep employees of the highest caliber, and (5) support the economic viability of the communities in which it operates.

Most firms today have in place strong codes of ethical behavior, and they also conduct training programs designed to ensure that employees understand the correct behavior in different business situations. However, it is imperative that top management—the chairman, president, and vice-presidents—be openly committed to ethical behavior, and that they communicate this commitment through their own personal actions as well as through company policies, directives, and punishment/reward systems.

When conflicts arise between profits and ethics, sometimes the ethical considerations are so strong that they clearly dominate. However, in many cases the choice between ethics and profits is not clear cut. For example, suppose Norfolk Southern's managers know that its trains are polluting the air along its routes, but the amount of pollution is within legal limits and preventive actions would be costly. Are the managers ethically bound to reduce pollution? Similarly, suppose a medical products company's own research indicates that one of its new products may cause problems. However, the evidence is relatively weak, other evidence regarding benefits to patients is strong, and independent government tests show no adverse effects. Should the company make the potential problem known to the public? If it does release the negative (but questionable) information, this will hurt sales and profits, and possibly keep some patients who would benefit from the new product from using it. There are no obvious answers to questions such as these, but companies must deal with them on a regular basis, and a failure to handle the situation properly can lead to huge product liability suits and even to bankruptcy.

Social Responsibility

Another issue that deserves consideration is **social responsibility:** Should businesses operate strictly in their stockholders' best interests, or are firms also responsible for the welfare of their employees, customers, and the communities in which they operate? Certainly firms have an ethical responsibility to provide a safe working environment, to avoid polluting the air or water, and to produce safe products. However, socially responsible actions have costs, and not all businesses would voluntarily incur all such costs. If some firms act in a socially responsible manner while others do not, then the socially responsible firms will be at a disadvantage in attracting capital. To illustrate, suppose all firms in a given industry have close to "normal" profits and rates of return on investment, that is, close to the average for all firms and just sufficient to attract capital. If one company attempts to exercise social responsibility, it will have to raise prices to cover the added costs. If other firms in its industry do not follow suit, their costs and prices will be lower. The socially responsible firm will not be able to compete, and it will be forced to abandon its efforts. Thus, any voluntary socially responsible acts that raise costs will be difficult, if not impossible, in industries that are subject to keen competition.

What about oligopolistic firms with profits above normal levels—cannot such firms devote resources to social projects? Undoubtedly they can, and many large, successful firms do engage in community projects, employee benefit programs, and the like to a greater degree than would appear to be called for by pure profit or wealth maximization goals.[4] Furthermore, many such firms contribute large sums to charities. Still, publicly owned firms are constrained by capital market forces. To illustrate, suppose a saver who has funds to invest is considering two alternative firms. One devotes a substantial part of its resources to social actions, while the other concentrates on profits and stock prices. Many investors would shun the socially oriented firm, thus putting it at a disadvantage in the capital market. After all, why should the stockholders of one corporation subsidize society to a greater extent than those of other businesses? For this reason, even highly profitable firms (unless they are closely held rather than publicly owned) are generally constrained against taking unilateral cost-increasing social actions.

Does all this mean that firms should not exercise social responsibility? Not at all. But it does mean that most significant cost-increasing actions will have to be put on a *mandatory* rather than a voluntary basis to ensure that the burden falls uniformly on all businesses. Thus, such social benefit programs as fair hiring practices, minority training, product safety, pollution abatement, and antitrust actions are most likely to be effective if realistic rules are established initially and then enforced by government agencies. Of course, it is critical that industry and government cooperate in establishing the rules of corporate behavior, and that the costs as well as the benefits of such actions be estimated accurately and then taken into account.

In spite of the fact that many socially responsible actions must be mandated by government, in recent years numerous firms have voluntarily taken such actions, especially in the area of environmental protection, because they help sales. For example, many detergent manufacturers now use recycled paper for their containers, and food companies are packaging more and more products in materials that consumers can recycle or that are biodegradable. To illustrate, McDonald's replaced its Styrofoam boxes, which take years to break down in landfills, with paper wrappers that are less bulky and decompose more rapidly. Some companies, such as The Body Shop, go to great lengths to be socially responsible. According to the president of The Body Shop, the role of business is to promote the public good, not just the good of the firm's shareholders. Furthermore, she argues that it is impossible to separate business from social responsibility. Finally, for some firms socially responsible actions may not de facto be costly—the companies heavily advertise their actions, and many consumers prefer to buy from socially responsible companies rather than from those that shun social responsibility.

Self-Test Questions

How would you define "business ethics"?

Is "being ethical" good for profits in the long run? In the short run?

What would happen if one firm attempted to employ a costly socially responsible program but its competitors did not follow suit?

---

[4]Even firms like these often find it necessary to justify such projects at stockholder meetings by stating that these programs will contribute to long-run profit maximization.

Agency Relationships

Managers are empowered by the owners of the firm—its shareholders—to make decisions. However, managers may have personal goals that compete with shareholder wealth maximization, and *agency theory* deals with such potential conflicts of interest.

An *agency relationship* arises whenever one or more individuals, called a *principal,* (1) hires another individual or organization, called an *agent,* to perform some service and (2) then delegates decision-making authority to that agent. Within the financial management context, the primary agency relationships are those (1) between stockholders and managers and (2) between stockholders and creditors.[5]

Agency Conflict I: Stockholders versus Managers

A potential **agency problem** arises whenever the manager of a firm owns less than 100 percent of its common stock. If the firm is a proprietorship managed by its owner, the owner-manager will presumably operate so as to maximize his or her own welfare, with welfare measured in the form of increased personal wealth, more leisure, or perquisites.[6] However, if the owner-manager incorporates and then sells some of the stock to outsiders, a potential conflict of interests immediately arises. Now the owner-manager may decide to lead a more relaxed lifestyle and not work as strenuously to maximize shareholder wealth, because less of the incremental wealth will accrue to him or her. Also, the owner-manager may decide to consume more perquisites, because some of this cost will be borne by the outside shareholders. In essence, the fact that the owner-manager will neither gain all the benefits of the wealth created by his or her efforts nor bear all of the costs of perquisites will increase the incentive to take actions that are not in the best interests of other shareholders.

In most large corporations, potential agency conflicts are important, because large firms' managers generally own only a small percentage of the stock. In this situation, shareholder wealth maximization could take a back seat to any number of conflicting managerial goals. For example, people have argued that some managers' primary goal seems to be to maximize the size of their firms.[7] By creating a large, rapidly growing firm, managers may (1) increase their job security, because a hostile takeover may be less likely; (2) increase their own power, status, and salaries; and (3) create more opportunities for their lower- and middle-level managers. Furthermore, because the managers of most large firms own only a small percentage of the stock, it has been argued that they have a voracious appetite for salaries and perquisites, and that they generously contribute corporate dollars to their favorite charities because they get the glory but outside stockholders bear the cost.[8]

Obviously, managers can be encouraged to act in the stockholders' best interests through a set of incentives, constraints, and punishments. However, these tools are

---

[5]The classic work on the application of agency theory to financial management is Michael C. Jensen and William H. Meckling, "Theory of the Firm, Managerial Behavior, Agency Costs, and Ownership Structure," *Journal of Financial Economics,* October 1976, 305–360.

[6]*Perquisites* are executive fringe benefits such as luxurious offices, executive assistants, expense accounts, limousines, corporate jets, generous retirement plans, and the like.

[7]See J. R. Wildsmith, *Managerial Theories of the Firm* (New York: Dunellen, 1974).

[8]An excellent article that reviews the effectiveness of various mechanisms for aligning managerial and shareholder interests is Andrei Shleifer and Robert Vishny, "A Survey of Corporate Governance," *Journal of Finance,* June 1997, 737–783. Another paper that looks at managerial stockholding worldwide is Rafael La Porta, Florencio Lopez-De-Silanes, and Andrei Shleifer, "Corporate Ownership Around the World," *Journal of Finance,* April 1999, 471–517.

most effective if shareholders can observe all of the actions taken by managers. A potential *moral hazard* problem, wherein agents take unobserved actions in their own behalf, arises because it is virtually impossible for shareholders to monitor all managerial actions. In general, to reduce both agency conflicts and the moral hazard problem, stockholders must incur *agency costs,* which include all costs borne by shareholders to encourage managers to maximize the firm's stock price rather than act in their own self-interests. There are three major categories of agency costs: (1) expenditures to monitor managerial actions, such as audit costs; (2) expenditures to structure the organization in a way that will limit undesirable managerial behavior, such as appointing outside investors to the board of directors; and (3) opportunity costs that are incurred when shareholder-imposed restrictions, such as requirements for stockholder votes on certain issues, limit the ability of managers to take timely actions that would enhance shareholder wealth.

In the absence of any type of shareholder effort to affect managerial behavior, and hence with zero agency costs, there would almost certainly be some loss of shareholder wealth due to improper managerial actions. Conversely, agency costs would be unbearably high if shareholders attempted to ensure that every managerial action coincided exactly with shareholder interests. Thus, the optimal amount of agency costs to be borne by shareholders should be viewed like any other investment decision—agency costs should be incurred as long as each dollar spent returns more than a dollar in shareholder wealth.

There are two extreme positions regarding how to deal with shareholder-manager agency conflicts. At one extreme, if a firm's managers were compensated solely on the basis of stock price changes, agency costs would be low because managers would have a great deal of incentive to maximize shareholder wealth. However, it would be difficult if not impossible to hire competent managers under these terms, because the firm's earnings stream would be affected by economic events that were not under managerial control. At the other extreme, stockholders could monitor every managerial action, but this would be costly and inefficient. The optimal solution lies somewhere in the middle, where executive compensation is tied to performance but some monitoring is also done. Some specific mechanisms used to motivate managers to act in shareholders' best interests include (1) managerial compensation plans, (2) direct intervention by shareholders, (3) the threat of firing, and (4) the threat of takeover.

1. **Managerial compensation.** Managers obviously must be compensated, and the structure of the compensation package should be designed to meet two primary objectives: (a) to attract and retain able managers and (b) to align managers' actions as closely as possible with the interests of stockholders, who are primarily interested in stock price maximization. Different companies follow different compensation practices, but a typical senior executive's compensation is structured in three parts: (a) a specified annual salary, which is necessary to meet living expenses; (b) a cash or stock bonus paid at the end of the year, which depends on the company's profitability during the year; and (c) options to buy stock, or actual shares of stock, which reward the executive for long-term performance.

   Managers are more likely to focus on maximizing stock prices if they are themselves large shareholders. Often, companies grant senior managers **performance shares,** where the executive receives a number of shares dependent upon the company's actual performance and the executive's continued service. For example, Coca-Cola granted one million shares of stock worth \$81 million to its former CEO, Roberto Goizueta. The award was based on Coke's performance under Goizueta's leadership, but it also stipulated that Goizueta would receive the shares only if he stayed with the company for the remainder of his career.

Are CEOs Overpaid?

Business Week's annual survey of executive compensation recently reported that the average large-company CEO made $10.6 million in 1998, up from $2 million in 1990. This dramatic increase can be attributed to the fact that CEOs increasingly receive most of their compensation in the form of stock and stock options, which skyrocketed in value because of a strong stock market in the 1990s.

Heading the pack on the *Business Week* list was Disney's Michael Eisner, who in 1998 made $575.6 million, mostly from stock options. Rounding out the top five were Mel Karamazin of CBS ($201.9 million), Sanford Weill of Citigroup ($167.1 million), Stephen Case of America Online ($159.2 million), and Craig Barrett of Intel ($116.5 million). It is worth noting that these results occurred in large part because the executives exercised stock options that had been granted in earlier years. Thus, their 1998 reported compensation overstated their average compensation over time. Equally importantly, note that their stock options provided these CEOs with an incentive to raise their companies' stock prices. Indeed, most observers believe there is a strong causal relationship between CEO compensation procedures and stock price performance.

Note, though, that some critics argue that although performance incentives are entirely appropriate as a method of compensation, the overall level of CEO compensation is just too high. The critics ask such questions as these: Would CEOs like Eisner have been unwilling to take their jobs if they had been offered only half as many stock options? Would they have put forth less effort, and would their firms' stock prices have not gone up as much? It is hard to say. Other critics lament that the exercise of stock options has dramatically increased the compensation of not only truly excellent CEOs, but it has also dramatically increased the compensation of mediocre CEOs who were lucky enough to have had the job during a stock market boom that raised the stock prices of even companies with rather poor performance. Another problem is that the huge CEO salaries are widening the gap between top executives and middle manager salaries. This is leading to employee discontent and a decrease in employee morale and loyalty.

Most large corporations also provide **executive stock options,** which allow managers to purchase stock at some future time at a given price. Obviously, a manager who has an option to buy, say, 10,000 shares of stock at a price of $10 during the next five years will have an incentive to help raise the stock's value to an amount greater than $10.

The number of performance shares or options awarded is generally based on a set of objective criteria. Years ago, the primary criteria were accounting measures such as earnings per share (EPS) and return on equity (ROE). Today, though, the focus is more on the market value of the firm's shares or, better yet, on the performance of its shares relative to other stocks in its industry.

A relatively new measure of managerial performance, *economic value added (EVA)*, is being used by more and more firms to tie executive compensation to stockholder wealth maximization. EVA is a way to measure a firm's true profitability. The cost of debt capital (interest expense) is deducted when accountants calculate net income, but no cost is deducted to account for the cost of common equity. Therefore, in an economic sense, net income overstates "true" income. EVA overcomes this flaw in conventional accounting.

EVA is found by taking the after-tax operating profit and subtracting the annual cost of *all* the capital a firm uses. The higher its EVA, the more wealth the firm is creating for its shareholders. EVA and its companion measure, market value added (MVA), will be discussed in depth in Chapter 2.

Various procedures are used to structure compensation programs, and good programs are relatively complicated. Still, it has been thoroughly established that a well-designed compensation program can do wonders to improve a company's financial performance.

2. **Direct intervention by shareholders.** Years ago most stock was owned by individuals, but today the majority is owned by institutional investors such as insurance companies, pension funds, and mutual funds. Therefore, the institutional money managers have the clout, if they choose to use it, to exercise considerable influence over most firms' operations. First, they can talk with a firm's management and make suggestions regarding how the business should be run. In effect, institutional investors act as lobbyists for the body of stockholders. Second, any shareholder who has owned at least $1,000 of a company's stock for one year can sponsor a proposal that must be voted on at the annual stockholders' meeting, even if the proposal is opposed by management. Although shareholder-sponsored proposals are nonbinding and are limited to issues outside of day-to-day operations, the results of such votes are clearly heard by top management.

   Why are institutions now taking such an interest in the management of companies they own? The primary reason is that they no longer have an easy exit from the market. Their portfolios are so big that if they decided to dump a stock in a hurry, the stock's price would take a free-fall. Rather than throwing up their hands and selling the stock, many institutional investors have decided to stay and work with management. Also, there has been considerable pressure on pension fund managers from the Department of Labor, which supervises pension fund investment practices under the Employee Retirement Income Security Act (ERISA). Under ERISA, pension fund managers are required to vote in the best interests of the funds' beneficiaries, which often means voting against corporate management. Finally, the Securities and Exchange Commission (SEC) has been expanding the number of issues that shareholders can address in shareholder-sponsored proposals. In its latest move, the SEC ruled that executive compensation is a permissible topic for proposals. In the past, executive compensation was classified as a matter of "ordinary business," hence not addressable in shareholder proposals. Similarly, the SEC recently forced several companies to allow shareholders to vote on "golden parachute" executive retirement packages, which are contract provisions that give a corporate executive a large severance payment if the company is taken over by another company and the executive loses his or her job.

   The most fundamental change that institutional investors are lobbying for is a more independent board of directors—institutional investors see a management-controlled board as the weak link in the chain of managerial accountability to shareholders. Too often, according to most experts on corporate control, the directors are in management's hip pocket, which is why institutional investors are pressing for truly independent boards. In fact, many institutional investors would like to see an outside director installed as chairman of the board, as was done recently by General Motors, because they do not trust an inside chairman to serve the shareholders first and his or her management's interests second.[9]

3. **The threat of firing.** Until recently, the probability of a large firm's management being ousted by its stockholders was so remote that it posed little threat. This situation existed because the shares of most firms were so widely distributed, and management's control over the voting mechanism so strong, that it was almost impossible for dissident stockholders to get the votes needed to overthrow a management team. However, as noted above, that situation is changing.

   Consider the case of Baltimore Bancorp. Recently its chairman, Harry L. Robinson, spurned a friendly $17-per-share takeover offer from rival First Maryland

[9]A recent article that provides a detailed investigation of shareholder proposals during 1997 is Cynthia J. Campbell, Stuart L. Gillan, and Cathy M. Niden, "Current Perspectives on Shareholder Proposals: Lessons from the 1997 Proxy Season," *Financial Management*, Spring 1999, 89–98.

Bancorp. Dismayed stockholders saw the stock price drop to $5 a share, and, led by a Baltimore businessman, they revolted. A slate of dissident directors was nominated, and they lined up the support of T. Rowe Price, a Baltimore mutual fund management company that held about 9 percent of the stock. At Baltimore Bancorp's next annual meeting, shareholders elected the dissident directors, who won all six of the board seats that were up for election. Then the board ousted Robinson, and a new management team was put in place.

For every obvious case of shareholders' directly ousting current management, there have been dozens of indirect ousters. For example, the CEOs or other top executives at American Express, Goodyear, General Motors, Kodak, and AT&T all resigned recently amid speculation that their departures were due to their companies' poor performance. More and more, the reasons for executive departures are shifting from "poor health" and "personal reasons" to "at the request of the board."

4. **The threat of takeovers. Hostile takeovers** (when management does not want the firm to be taken over) are most likely to occur when a firm's stock is undervalued relative to its potential because of poor management. In a hostile takeover, the managers of the acquired firm are generally fired, and any who manage to stay on lose status and authority. Thus, managers have a strong incentive to take actions designed to maximize stock prices. In the words of one company president, "If you want to keep your job, don't let your stock sell at a bargain price."

Agency Conflict II: Stockholders versus Creditors

In addition to conflicts between stockholders and managers, there can also be conflicts between stockholders (through managers) and creditors. Creditors have a claim on part of the firm's earnings stream for payment of interest and principal on the debt, and they have a claim on the firm's assets in the event of bankruptcy. However, stockholders have control (through the managers) of decisions that affect the risk of the firm. Creditors lend funds at rates that are based on (1) the risk of the firm's existing assets, (2) expectations concerning the risk of future asset additions, (3) the firm's existing capital structure (that is, the amount of debt financing used), and (4) expectations concerning future capital structure decisions. These are the primary determinants of the riskiness of a firm's cash flows, hence the safety of its debt issues.

Now suppose stockholders, acting through management, cause a firm to sell some relatively safe assets and invest the proceeds in a large new project that is far riskier than the firm's old assets. This increased risk will cause the required rate of return on the firm's debt to increase, and that will cause the value of the outstanding debt to fall. If the risky project is successful, all the benefits go to the stockholders, because creditors' returns are fixed at the old, low-risk rate. However, if the project is unsuccessful, the bondholders may have to share in the losses. From the stockholders' point of view, this amounts to a game of "heads I win, tails you lose," which is obviously not good for the creditors. Similarly, suppose its managers borrow additional funds and use the proceeds to repurchase some of the firm's outstanding stock in an effort to "leverage up" stockholders' return on equity. The value of the debt will probably decrease, because now there will be more debt backed by an unchanged amount of cash flow and assets. In both the riskier asset and the increased leverage situations, stockholders tend to gain at the expense of creditors.

Can and should stockholders, through their managers/agents, try to expropriate wealth from creditors? In general, the answer is no, for there is no room for unethical behavior in the business world. Indeed, creditors attempt to protect themselves against stockholders by placing restrictive covenants in debt agreements. Moreover, if creditors perceive that a firm's managers are trying to take advantage of them, they will either refuse to deal further with it or else will charge a higher than normal interest rate to compensate for the risk of possible exploitation. Thus, firms that deal unfairly with creditors either lose access to the debt markets or are saddled with high interest rates and restrictive covenants, all of which are detrimental to shareholders.

In view of all this, it follows that to best serve their shareholders in the long run, managers must play fairly with creditors. Managers, as agents of both shareholders and creditors, must act in a manner that is fairly balanced between the interests of the two classes of security holders. Similarly, because of other constraints and sanctions, any management action that would expropriate wealth from any of the firm's other *stakeholders*, including its employees, customers, suppliers, and community, will ultimately be harmful to shareholders. In our society, stock price maximization requires fair treatment for all parties whose economic positions are affected by managerial decisions.

Self-Test Questions

What are agency costs, and who bears them?

What are some mechanisms that encourage managers to act in the best interests of stockholders? To not take advantage of bondholders?

Why should managers not take actions that are unfair to any of the firm's stakeholders?

Organization of the Book

The primary goal of a manager should be to maximize the value of his or her firm. To achieve this goal, managers must have a general understanding of how businesses are organized, how financial markets operate, how interest rates are determined, how the tax system operates, and how accounting data are used to evaluate a business's performance. In addition, managers must have a good understanding of such fundamental concepts as time value of money, risk measurement, asset valuation, and evaluation of specific investment opportunities. This background information is essential for anyone involved with the kinds of decisions that affect the value of a firm's securities.

The organization of this book reflects these considerations, so Part One presents some background material in five chapters. Chapter 1 discusses the goals of the firm and the "philosophy" of financial management. Chapter 2 describes the key financial statements, discusses what they are designed to do, and then explains how our tax system affects earnings, cash flows, stock prices, and managerial decisions. Chapter 3 shows how financial statements are analyzed, and Chapter 4 develops techniques for forecasting financial statements. Chapter 5 explains how financial markets operate and how interest rates are determined.

Part Two considers two of the most fundamental concepts in financial management—risk and the time value of money. First, Chapters 6 and 7 explain how risk is measured and how it affects security prices and rates of return. Next, Chapter 8 discusses the time value of money and its effects on asset values and rates of return.

Part Three covers issues related to financial assets, that is, stocks and bonds. Chapter 9 focuses on bonds, and Chapter 10 considers stocks. Both chapters describe the relevant institutional details, then explain how risk and time value jointly determine stock and bond prices.

Part Four shows how all the pieces of the puzzle fit together to affect the value of the firm. First, Chapter 11 explains how to measure the cost of capital, which is the rate of return that investors require to provide funding for fixed assets and working capital. Next, Chapter 12 shows how to use the cost of capital and the projected financial statements to determine the value of a corporation. Perhaps more importantly, this corporate valuation model allows managers to estimate the effects of proposed changes in operating strategies on the value of the corporation.

Part Five, "Strategic Investment Decisions," applies the concepts of corporate valuation to individual projects. Chapter 13 shows how to determine whether the cash flows of a potential capital investment will add value to the firm. Chapter 14 shows how to estimate the relevant cash flows that a project will produce, and how to assess the project's risk. Finally, many projects provide an opportunity for managers to make modifications if the environment changes after the project has been implemented. Such opportunities are called "real options," and Chapter 15 shows how to identify and then determine the value of real options.

Part Six discusses strategic financing decisions, which means how money should be raised. Chapters 16 and 17 examine capital structure theory, or the issue of how much debt versus equity the firm should use. Then, Chapter 18 considers the firm's distribution policy; that is, how much of the net income should be retained for reinvestment versus being paid out, either as a dividend or as a share repurchase?

Part Seven discusses some of the tactics involved in financing decisions. Chapter 19 describes how companies issue securities and how they refinance debt; Chapter 20 covers leasing; and Chapter 21 explains hybrid financing, including preferred stock, warrants, and convertible securities.

In Part Eight, our focus shifts from long-term, strategic decisions to short-term, day-to-day operating decisions. Chapter 22 explains how companies manage their current assets, especially inventories and accounts receivables. Chapter 23 addresses the ways companies use short-term credit to support daily operations.

Finally, in Part Nine, we address several special topics that draw upon the earlier chapters, including derivatives, risk management, bankruptcy, mergers, and multinational financial management.

It is worth noting that instructors may cover the chapters in a different sequence from the order in the book. The chapters are written in a modular, self-contained manner, so such reordering should present no major difficulties.

e-Resources

Your textbook comes with a CD-ROM containing several types of files:

1. It contains *Excel* files, called Tool Kits, that provide well documented models for almost all of the text's calculations. Not only will these Tool Kits help you with this finance course, but they will serve as tool kits for you in other courses and in your career.
2. There are problems at the end of the chapters that require spreadsheets, and the CD-ROM contains the models you will need to begin work on these problems.
3. The CD-ROM also contains *PowerPoint* files that correspond to the Mini Cases at the end of each chapter.

When we think it might be helpful for you to look at one of the CD-ROM's files, we'll show an icon in the margin like the one that is shown here.

These files and other resources can also be found on the textbook's Web page, **http://www.harcourtcollege.com/finance/theory.**

Summary

This chapter has provided an overview of financial management. The key concepts covered are listed below.

- Financial management answers these three questions: (1) **What causes a company to have a particular stock value?** (2) **How can managers make choices that will add value to their companies?** (3) **How can managers ensure that their companies don't run out of cash while executing their plans?**
- Finance consists of three interrelated areas: (1) **capital markets and institutions,** (2) **investments,** (3) and **financial management.**
- The three main forms of business organization are the **sole proprietorship,** the **partnership,** and the **corporation.**
- Although each form of organization offers advantages and disadvantages, **corporations conduct most business in the United States because this organizational form maximizes larger firms' values.**
- The primary goal of management should be to **maximize stockholders' wealth,** and this means **maximizing the stock price.** Legal actions that maximize stock prices usually increase social welfare.
- Firms increase cash flows by creating value for **customers, suppliers,** and **employees.**
- Three factors determine cash flows: (1) **sales,** (2) **after-tax operating profit margins,** and (3) **capital requirements.**
- The **price of a firm's stock** depends on the **size of the firm's cash flows,** the **timing of those flows,** and **their risk.** The size and risk of the cash flows are affected by the **financial environment** as well as the **investment, financing,** and **dividend policy decisions** made by financial managers.
- The two most important trends in finance are the **increased globalization of business** and the growing use of **computers and information technology.**
- An **agency problem** is a potential conflict of interests that can arise between a principal and an agent. The two most important agency relationships are (1) those between stockholders and management and (2) those between stockholders (acting through managers) and creditors.
- There are a number of ways to **motivate managers to act in the best interests of stockholders,** including (1) properly structured **managerial compensation,** (2) **direct intervention by stockholders,** (3) the **threat of firing,** and (4) the **threat of takeovers.**

Questions

1–1 Define each of the following terms:

a. Sole proprietorship; partnership; corporation
b. Limited partnership; limited liability partnership; professional corporation
c. Stockholder wealth maximization
d. Social responsibility; business ethics
e. Normal profits; normal rate of return
f. Agency problem
g. Economic value added (EVA)
h. Performance shares; executive stock options
i. Hostile takeover
j. Profit maximization
k. Earnings per share
l. Dividend policy

1–2 What are the three principal forms of business organization? What are the advantages and disadvantages of each?

1–3 Would the "normal" rate of return on investment be the same in all industries? Would "normal" rates of return change over time? Explain.

1–4 Would the role of the financial manager be likely to increase or decrease in importance relative to other executives if the rate of inflation increased? Explain.

1–5 Should stockholder wealth maximization be thought of as a long-term or a short-term goal—for example, if one action would probably increase the firm's earnings per share (EPS) from a current level of $41 to $51 in 6 months and then to $61 in 5 years, but another action would probably keep the EPS at $41 for several years but then increase it to $81 in 5 years, which action would be better? Can you think of some specific corporate actions that might have these general tendencies?

1–6 Drawing on your background in accounting, can you think of any accounting procedure differences that might make it difficult to compare the relative performance of different firms?

1–7 Would the management of a firm in an oligopolistic or in a competitive industry be more likely to engage in what might be called "socially conscious" practices? Explain your reasoning.

1–8 What is the difference between stock price maximization and profit maximization? Under what conditions might profit maximization not lead to stock price maximization?

1–9 If you were the president of a large, publicly owned corporation, would you make decisions to maximize stockholders' welfare or your own personal interests? What are some actions stockholders could take to ensure that management's interests and those of stockholders coincided? What are some other factors that might influence management's actions?

1–10 The president of International Microchips Inc. (IMI) made this statement in the company's annual report: "IMI's primary goal is to increase the value of the common stockholders' equity over time." Later on in the report, the following announcements were made:

a. The company contributed $2 million to the symphony orchestra in Seattle, its headquarters city.

b. The company is spending $600 million to open a new plant in Venezuela. No revenues will be produced by the plant for 4 years, so earnings will be depressed during this period versus what they would have been had the decision not been made to open the new plant.

c. The company is increasing its relative use of debt. Whereas assets were formerly financed with 30 percent debt and 70 percent equity, henceforth the financing mix will be 45/55.

d. The company uses a great deal of electricity in its manufacturing operations, and it generates most of this power itself. Plans are to utilize nuclear fuel rather than coal to produce electricity in the future.

e. The company has been paying out half of its earnings as dividends and retaining the other half. Henceforth, it will pay out only 40 percent as dividends.

Discuss how each of these actions would be reacted to by IMI's stockholders, customers, and labor force, and then how each action might affect IMI's stock price.

1–11 Assume that you are serving on the board of directors of a medium-sized corporation and that you are responsible for establishing the compensation policies of senior management. You believe that the company's CEO is very talented, but your concern is that she is always looking for a better job and may want to boost the company's short-run performance (perhaps at the expense of long-run profitability) to make herself more marketable to other corporations. What effect would these concerns have on the compensation policy you put in place?

1–12 If the overall stock market is extremely volatile, and if many analysts foresee the possibility of a stock market crash, how might these factors influence the way corporations choose to compensate their senior executives?

1–13 Teacher's Insurance and Annuity Association–College Retirement Equity Fund (TIAA–CREF) is the largest institutional shareholder in the United States, controlling $125 billion in pension funds. Traditionally, TIAA–CREF has acted as a passive investor. However, TIAA–CREF announced a tough new corporate governance policy beginning October 5, 1993.

In a statement mailed to all 1,500 companies in which it invests, TIAA–CREF outlined a policy designed to improve corporate performance, including a goal of higher stock prices for the $52 billion in stock assets it holds, and to encourage corporate boards to have a majority of independent (outside) directors. TIAA–CREF wants to see management more accountable to shareholder interests, as evidenced by its statement that the fund will vote against any director "where companies don't have an effective, independent board which can challenge the CEO."

Historically, TIAA–CREF did not quickly sell poor-performing stocks. In addition, the fund invested a large part of its assets to match performance of the major market indexes, locking TIAA–CREF into ownership of certain companies. Further complicating the problem, TIAA–CREF owns stakes of from 1 percent to 10 percent in several companies, and selling such large blocks of stock would depress their prices.

Common stock ownership confers a right to sponsor initiatives to shareholders regarding the corporation. A corresponding voting right exists for shareholders.

a. Is TIAA–CREF an ordinary shareholder?

b. Due to its asset size, TIAA–CREF assumes large positions with which it plans to actively vote. However, who owns TIAA–CREF?

c. Should the investment managers of a fund like TIAA–CREF determine the voting practices of the fund's shares, or should the voting rights be passed on to TIAA–CREF's stakeholders?

Cyberproblem

WWW

The information related to the cyberproblems is likely to change over time, due to the release of new information and the ever-changing nature of the World Wide Web. With these changes in mind, we will periodically update these problems on the textbook's web site.

1-1
OVERVIEW OF FINANCIAL MANAGEMENT

Management's primary goal is to maximize stockholder wealth. Firms often award stock options and bonuses on the basis of management performance, thus linking management's personal wealth with the firm's financial performance. The better the job managers do in maximizing share price, the greater their compensation.

Walt Disney's CEO, Michael Eisner, draws a compensation package in part based on the net income and return on shareholder equity of The Walt Disney Company. In 1994, he attracted a lot of attention when he exercised stock options on 5.4 million Disney shares for a net profit (after taxes and brokerage expenses) of around $127 million. At the time, he had also earned another 8 million stock options, then valued at about $161 million.

Let's see if Mr. Eisner deserves such generous bonuses and stock options. Look at the Cyberproblem on the textbook's web site and answer the questions shown there: **http://www.harcourtcollege.com/finance/theory/student/resources/cyberprob/ch01.html.**

Mini Case

CD

See ***Ch 01 Show.ppt*** for a *PowerPoint* presentation of the Mini Case.

Joe Birdsong opened Take A Walk on the Wild Side 17 years ago; the store is located in Nantahala, North Carolina, and it sells hiking, rafting, and kayaking equipment. Today, Joe has 50 employees including his daughter Anne, who works part time in the store to help pay for her college education.

Joe's business has boomed in recent years, and he is looking for new ways to take advantage of his increasing business opportunities. Although Joe's formal business training is limited, Anne will soon graduate with an MBA. Joe has offered her the opportunity to join the business as a full-fledged partner. Anne is interested, but she is also considering other career opportunities in finance.

Right now, Anne is leaning toward staying with the family business, partly because she thinks it faces a number of interesting challenges and opportunities. Anne is particularly interested in further expanding the business and then incorporating it. Joe is intrigued by her ideas, but he is also concerned that her plans might change the way in which he does business. In particular, Joe has a strong commitment to social activism, and he has always tried to strike a balance between work and pleasure. He is worried that these goals will be compromised if the company incorporates and brings in outside shareholders.

Anne and Joe plan to take a long weekend off to sit down and think about all of these issues. Anne, who is highly organized, has outlined a series of questions for them to address:

a. What three questions does financial management seek to answer?
b. What kinds of career opportunities are open to finance majors?
c. (1) What are the alternative forms of business organization?
   (2) What are their advantages and disadvantages?
d. What is the primary goal of the corporation?
   (1) Do firms have any responsibilities to society at large?
   (2) Is stock price maximization good or bad for society?
   (3) Should firms behave ethically?
e. What factors affect stock prices?
f. What determines cash flows?
g. What factors affect the level and risk of cash flows?
h. What are the most important financial management issues of the new millennium?
i. What is an agency relationship?
   (1) What agency relationships exist within a corporation?
   (2) What mechanisms exist to influence managers to act in shareholders' best interests?
   (3) Should shareholders (through managers) take actions that are detrimental to bondholders?

Selected Additional References

For alternative views on firms' goals and objectives, see the following articles:

Cornell, Bradford, and Alan C. Shapiro, "Corporate Stakeholders and Corporate Finance," *Financial Management,* Spring 1987, 5–14.

Donaldson, Gordon, "Financial Goals: Management versus Stockholders," *Harvard Business Review,* May–June 1963, 116–129.

Meckling, William H., and Michael C. Jensen, "Reflections on the Corporation as a Social Invention," *Midland Corporate Finance Journal,* Fall 1983, 6–15.

Seitz, Neil, "Shareholder Goals, Firm Goals and Firm Financing Decisions," *Financial Management,* Autumn 1982, 20–26.

The following articles extend our discussion of agency relationships:

Barnea, Amir, Robert A. Haugen, and Lemma W. Senbet, "Market Imperfections, Agency Problems, and Capital Structure: A Review," *Financial Management,* Summer 1981, 7–22.

Hand, John H., William P. Lloyd, and Robert B. Rogow, "Agency Relationships in the Close Corporation," *Financial Management,* Spring 1982, 25–30.

For a general review of academic finance, together with an extensive bibliography of key research articles, see

Brennan, Michael J., "Corporate Finance Over the Past 25 Years," *Financial Management,* Summer 1995, 9–22.

Cooley, Philip L., and J. Louis Heck, "Significant Contributions to Finance Literature," *Financial Management,* Tenth Anniversary Issue 1981, 23–33.

For more information on managerial compensation, see

Cooley, Philip L., and Charles E. Edwards, "Ownership Effects on Managerial Salaries in Small Business," *Financial Management,* Winter 1982, 5–9.

Hudson, Carl D., John S. Jahera, Jr., and William P. Lloyd, "Further Evidence on the Relationship between Ownership and Performance," *Financial Review,* May 1992, 227–239.

Lambert, Richard A., and David F. Larker, "Executive Compensation, Corporate Decision-Making and Shareholder Wealth: A Review of the Evidence," *Midland Corporate Finance Journal,* Winter 1985, 6–22. The Winter 1985 issue of the *Midland Corporate Finance Journal* contains several other articles pertaining to executive compensation.

Long, Michael S., "The Incentives Behind the Adoption of Executive Stock Option Plans in U.S. Corporations," *Financial Management,* Autumn 1992, 12–21.

Sridharan, Uma V., "CEO Influence and Executive Compensation," *Financial Review,* February 1996, 51–66.

"Stern Stewart Roundtable on Management Incentive Compensation and Shareholder Value," *Journal of Applied Corporate Finance,* Summer 1992, 110–130.

Stern, Joel M., G. Bennett Stewart III, and Donald H. Chew, "The EVA® Financial Management System," *Journal of Applied Corporate Finance,* Summer 1995, 32–46.

For more information on the role of corporate directors, see

"Corporate Governance: The Role of Boards of Directors in Takeover Bids and Defenses," *Journal of Applied Corporate Finance,* Summer 1989, 6–35.

2

Financial Statements, Cash Flow, and Taxes

Suppose you are a small investor who knows a little about finance and accounting. Could you compete successfully against large institutional investors with armies of analysts, high-powered computers, and state-of-the-art trading strategies?

The answer, according to one Wall Street legend, is a resounding yes! Peter Lynch, who had an outstanding track record as manager of the $10 billion Fidelity Magellan fund and then went on to become the best-selling author of *One Up on Wall Street* and *Beating the Street,* has long argued that small investors can beat the market by using common sense and information available to all of us as we go about our day-to-day lives.

For example, a college student may be more adept at scouting out the new and interesting products that will become tomorrow's success stories than is an investment banker who works 75 hours a week in a New York office. Parents of young children are likely to know which baby foods will succeed, or which diapers are best. Couch potatoes may have the best feel for which tortilla chips have the brightest future, or whether a new remote control is worth its price.

The trick is to find a product that will boom, yet whose manufacturer's stock is undervalued. If this sounds too easy, you are right. Lynch argues that once you have discovered a good product, there is still much homework to be done. This involves combing through the vast amount of financial information provided by companies. It also requires taking a closer and more critical look at how the company conducts its business—Lynch refers to this as "kicking the tires."

To illustrate his point, Lynch relates his experience with Dunkin' Donuts. As a consumer, Lynch was impressed with the quality of the product. This impression led him to take a closer look at the company's financial statements and operations. He liked what he saw, and Dunkin' Donuts became one of his all-time best investments.

The next two chapters discuss what financial statements are and how they are analyzed. Once you have identified a good product as a possible investment, the principles discussed in these chapters will help you "kick the tires."

A manager's primary goal is to maximize the value of his or her firm's stock. Value is based on the stream of cash flows the firm will generate in the future. But how does an investor go about estimating future cash flows, and how does a manager decide which actions are most likely to increase cash flows? The answers to both questions lie in a study of the financial statements that publicly traded firms must provide to investors. Here "investors" include both institutions (banks, insurance companies, pension funds, and the like) and individuals. Thus, this chapter begins with a discussion of what the basic financial statements are, how they are used, and what kinds of financial information users need.

The value of any business asset—whether it is a *financial* asset such as a stock or a bond, or a *real (physical) asset* such as land, buildings, and equipment—depends on the usable, after-tax cash flows the asset is expected to produce. Therefore, the chapter also explains the difference between accounting income and cash flow. Finally, since it is *after-tax* cash flow that is important, the chapter provides an overview of the federal income tax system.

CD

The textbook's CD-ROM contains an *Excel* file that will guide you through the chapter's calculations. The file for this chapter is ***Ch 02 Tool Kit.xls,*** and we encourage you to open the file and follow along as you read the chapter.

Much of the material in this chapter reviews concepts covered in basic accounting courses. However, the information is important enough to go over again. Accounting is used to "keep score," and if a firm's managers do not know the score, they won't know if their actions are appropriate. If you took midterm exams but were not told how you were doing, you would have a difficult time improving your grades. The same thing holds in business. If a firm's managers—whether they are in marketing, personnel, production, or finance—do not understand financial statements, they will not be able to judge the effects of their actions, and the firm will not be successful. Although only accountants need to know how to *make* financial statements, everyone involved with business needs to know how to *interpret* them.

A Brief History of Accounting and Financial Statements

WWW

Are you interested in learning more about the history of accounting? If so, take a tour through the "Virtual History of Accounting" organized by the Association of Chartered Accountants in the United States and located at **http://www.acaus.org/history/index.html.**

Financial statements are pieces of paper with numbers written on them, but it is important to also think about the real assets that underlie the numbers. If you understand how and why accounting began, and how financial statements are used, you can better visualize what is going on, and why accounting information is so important.

Thousands of years ago, individuals (or families) were self-contained in the sense that they gathered their own food, made their own clothes, and built their own shelters. Then specialization began—some people became good at making pots, others at making arrowheads, others at making clothing, and so on.

As specialization began, so did trading, initially in the form of barter. At first, each artisan worked alone, and trade was strictly local. Eventually, though, master craftsmen set up small factories and employed workers, money (in the form of clamshells) began to be used, and trade expanded beyond the local area. As these developments occurred, a primitive form of banking began, with wealthy merchants lending profits from past dealings to enterprising factory owners who needed capital to expand or to young traders who needed money to buy wagons, ships, and merchandise.

When the first loans were made, lenders could physically inspect borrowers' assets and judge the likelihood of the loan's being repaid. Eventually, though, lending became more complex—borrowers were developing larger factories, traders were acquiring fleets of ships and wagons, and loans were being made to develop distant mines and trading posts. At that point, lenders could no longer personally inspect the assets that backed their loans, and they needed some way of summarizing borrowers' assets. Also, some investments were made on a share-of-the-profits basis, and this meant that profits (or income) had to be determined. At the same time, factory owners and large merchants needed reports to see how effectively their own enterprises were being run, and governments needed information for use in assessing taxes. For all these reasons, a need arose for financial statements, for accountants to prepare those statements, and for auditors to verify the accuracy of the accountants' work.

The economic system has grown enormously since its beginning, and accounting has become more complex. However, the original reasons for financial statements still apply: Bankers and other investors need accounting information to make intelligent decisions, managers need it to operate their businesses efficiently, and taxing authorities need it to assess taxes in a reasonable way.

It should be intuitively clear that it is not easy to translate physical assets into numbers, which is what accountants do when they construct financial statements. The numbers shown on balance sheets generally represent the historical costs of assets. However, inventories may be spoiled, obsolete, or even missing; fixed assets such as machinery and buildings may have higher or lower values than their historical costs; and accounts receivable may be uncollectable. Also, some liabilities such as obligations to pay retirees' medical costs may not even show up on the balance sheet. Similarly, some costs reported on the income statement may be understated, as would be true if a plant with a useful life of 10 years were being depreciated over 40 years. When you examine a set of financial statements, you should keep in mind that a physical reality lies behind the numbers, and you should also realize that the translation from physical assets to "correct" numbers is far from precise.

As mentioned previously, it is important for accountants to be able to generate financial statements, while others involved in the business need to know how to interpret them. Effective financial managers must have a working knowledge of financial statements and what they reveal. Spreadsheets provide financial managers with a powerful and reliable tool to conduct financial analysis, and several different types of spreadsheet models are provided with the text. These models demonstrate how financial principles taught in this book are applied in practice. Readers are encouraged to use these models to gain insights into various concepts and procedures.

Financial Statements and Reports

WWW

For an excellent example of a corporate annual report, take a look at 3M's annual report found at **http://www.mmm.com/profile/finance/report.html.** Here you can find several recent annual reports in Adobe Acrobat and HTML formats.

Of the various reports corporations issue to their stockholders, the **annual report** is probably the most important. Two types of information are given in this report. First, there is a verbal section, often presented as a letter from the chairman, that describes the firm's operating results during the past year and discusses new developments that will affect future operations. Second, the annual report presents four basic financial statements—the *balance sheet*, the *income statement*, the *statement of retained earnings*, and the *statement of cash flows*. Taken together, these statements give an accounting picture of the firm's operations and financial position. Detailed data are provided for the two or three most recent years, along with historical summaries of key operating statistics for the past five or ten years.[1]

The quantitative and verbal materials are equally important. The financial statements report *what has actually happened* to assets, earnings, and dividends over the past

[1]Firms also provide quarterly reports, but these are much less comprehensive. In addition, larger firms file even more detailed statements, giving breakdowns for each major division or subsidiary, with the Securities and Exchange Commission (SEC). These reports, called *10-K reports*, are made available to stockholders upon request to a company's corporate secretary. Finally, many larger firms also publish *statistical supplements*, which give financial statement data and key ratios going back 10 to 20 years, and their reports are available on the World Wide Web.

few years, whereas the verbal statements attempt to explain why things turned out the way they did.

For illustrative purposes, we use data on MicroDrive Inc., a producer of disk drives for microcomputers. Formed in 1982, MicroDrive has grown steadily and has earned a reputation for being one of the best firms in the microcomputer components industry. MicroDrive's earnings dropped a bit in 2001, to $113.5 million versus $118 million in 2000. Management reported that the decline resulted from a three-month strike that kept the firm from fully utilizing a new plant that had been financed mostly with debt. However, management went on to paint a more optimistic picture for the future, stating that full operations had been resumed, that several new products had been introduced, and that 2002 profits were expected to rise sharply. Of course, the profit increase may not occur, and analysts should compare management's past statements with subsequent results when judging the credibility of the projected improvement. In any event, *the information contained in an annual report is used by investors to help form expectations about future earnings and dividends.* Therefore, the annual report is obviously of great interest to investors.

Self-Test Questions

What is the annual report, and what two types of information are given in it?

Why is the annual report of great interest to investors?

What four types of financial statements are typically included in the annual report?

The Balance Sheet

The left-hand side of MicroDrive's year-end 2001 and 2000 **balance sheets,** which are given in Table 2-1, shows the firm's assets, while the right-hand side shows the liabilities and equity, or the claims against these assets. The assets are listed in order of their "liquidity," or the length of time it typically takes to convert them to cash. The claims are listed in the order in which they must be paid: Accounts payable must generally be paid within 30 days, notes payable within 90 days, and so on, down to the stockholders' equity accounts, which represent ownership and need never be "paid off."

Some additional points about the balance sheet are worth noting:

1. **Cash versus other assets.** Although the assets are all stated in terms of dollars, only cash represents actual money. Note, though, that some types of marketable securities have a very short time until maturity and can also be converted very quickly into cash at prices close to their book values. These securities are called "cash equivalents," and they are included with cash. Other types of marketable securities have a longer time until maturity, and their market values are less predictable. These securities are classified as "short-term investments." Receivables are bills others owe MicroDrive, while inventories show the dollars the company has invested in raw materials, work-in-process, and finished goods available for sale. Finally, net plant and equipment reflect the amount of money MicroDrive paid for its fixed assets when it acquired those assets in the past, less accumulated depreciation.

   With $10 million of cash, MicroDrive can write checks for a total of $10 million (versus current liabilities of $310 million due within a year). The noncash assets should produce cash over time, but they do not represent cash in hand, and the amount of cash they would bring if they were sold today could be higher or lower than the values at which they are carried on the books.
2. **Liabilities versus stockholders' equity.** The claims against assets are of two types—liabilities (or money the company owes) and the stockholders' ownership

TABLE 2-1 MicroDrive Inc.: December 31 Balance Sheets (Millions of Dollars)

Assets	2001	2000	Liabilities and Equity	2001	2000
Cash and equivalents	$ 10	$ 15	Accounts payable	$ 60	$ 30
Short-term investments	0	65	Notes payable	110	60
Accounts receivable	375	315	Accruals	140	130
Inventories	615	415	Total current liabilities	$ 310	$ 220
Total current assets	$1,000	$ 810	Long-term bonds	754	580
Net plant and equipment	1,000	870	Total debt	$1,064	$ 800
			Preferred stock (400,000 shares)	40	40
			Common stock (50,000,000 shares)	130	130
			Retained earnings	766	710
			Total common equity	$ 896	$ 840
Total assets	$2,000	$1,680	Total liabilities and equity	$2,000	$1,680

NOTE: The bonds have a sinking fund requirement of $20 million a year. Sinking funds are discussed in Chapter 9, but in brief, a sinking fund simply involves the repayment of long-term debt. Thus, MicroDrive was required to pay off $20 million of its mortgage bonds during 2001. The current portion of the long-term debt is included in notes payable here, although in a more detailed balance sheet it would be shown as a separate item under current liabilities.

See *Ch 02 Tool Kit.xls* for details.

position.[2] The **common stockholders' equity,** or **net worth,** is a residual. For example, at the end of 2000,

$$\begin{array}{ccccccc} \text{Assets} & - & \text{Liabilities} & - & \text{Preferred stock} & = & \text{Common stockholders' equity.} \\ \$2{,}000{,}000{,}000 & - & \$1{,}064{,}000{,}000 & - & \$40{,}000{,}000 & = & \$896{,}000{,}000. \end{array}$$

Suppose assets decline in value; for example, suppose some of the accounts receivable are written off as bad debts. Liabilities and preferred stock remain constant, so the value of the common stockholders' equity must decline. Therefore, the risk of asset value fluctuations is borne primarily by the common stockholders. Note, however, that if asset values rise (perhaps because of inflation), these benefits will accrue exclusively to the common stockholders.

3. **Preferred versus common stock.** Preferred stock is a hybrid, or a cross between common stock and debt. In the event of bankruptcy, preferred stock ranks below debt but above common stock. Also, the preferred dividend is fixed, so preferred stockholders do not benefit if the company's earnings grow. Finally, many firms do not use any preferred stock, and those that do generally do not use much of it. Therefore, when the term "equity" is used in finance, we generally mean "common equity" unless the word "total" is included.
4. **Breakdown of the common equity accounts.** The common equity section is divided into two accounts—"common stock" and "retained earnings." The **retained earnings** account is built up over time as the firm "saves" a part of its earnings

[2]One could divide liabilities into (1) debts owed to someone and (2) other items, such as deferred taxes, reserves, and so on. Because we do not make this distinction, the terms *debt* and *liabilities* are used synonymously. It should be noted that firms occasionally set up reserves for certain contingencies, such as the potential costs involved in a lawsuit currently in the courts. These reserves represent an accounting transfer from retained earnings to the reserve account. If the company wins the suit, retained earnings will be credited, and the reserve will be eliminated. If it loses, a loss will be recorded, cash will be reduced, and the reserve will be eliminated.

rather than paying all earnings out as dividends. The common stock account arises from the issuance of stock to raise capital, as discussed in Chapter 10.

The breakdown of the common equity accounts is important for some purposes but not for others. For example, a potential stockholder would want to know whether the company actually earned the funds reported in its equity accounts or whether the funds came mainly from selling stock. A potential creditor, on the other hand, would be more interested in the total equity the owners have in the firm and would be less concerned with the source of the equity. In the remainder of this chapter, we generally aggregate the two common equity accounts and call this sum *equity*, *common equity*, or *net worth*.

5. **Inventory accounting.** MicroDrive uses the FIFO (first-in, first-out) method to determine the inventory value shown on its balance sheet ($615 million). It could have used the LIFO (last-in, first-out) method. During a period of rising prices, by taking out old, low-cost inventory and leaving in new, high-cost items, FIFO will produce a higher balance sheet inventory value but a lower cost of goods sold on the income statement. (This is strictly accounting; companies actually use older items first.) Since MicroDrive uses FIFO, and since inflation has been occurring, (a) its balance sheet inventories are higher than they would have been had it used LIFO, (b) its cost of goods sold is lower than it would have been under LIFO, and (c) its reported profits are therefore higher. In MicroDrive's case, if the company had elected to switch to LIFO in 2001, its balance sheet figure for inventories would have been $585,000,000 rather than $615,000,000, and its earnings (which will be discussed in the next section) would have been reduced by $18,000,000. Thus, the inventory valuation method can have a significant effect on financial statements. This is important when an analyst is comparing different companies.
6. **Depreciation methods.** Most companies prepare two sets of financial statements—one for tax purposes and one for reporting to stockholders. Generally, they use the most accelerated method permitted under the law to calculate depreciation for tax purposes, but they use straight line, which results in a lower depreciation charge, for stockholder reporting. However, MicroDrive has elected to use rapid depreciation for both stockholder reporting and tax purposes. Had MicroDrive elected to use straight line depreciation for stockholder reporting, its 2001 depreciation expense would have been $25,000,000 less, so the $1 billion shown for "net plant" on its balance sheet would have been $25,000,000 higher. Its net income and its retained earnings would also have been higher.
7. **The time dimension.** The balance sheet may be thought of as a snapshot of the firm's financial position *at a point in time*—for example, on December 31, 2000. Thus, on December 31, 2000, MicroDrive had $15 million of cash and marketable securities, but this account had been reduced to $10 million by the end of 2001. The balance sheet changes every day as inventories are increased or decreased, as fixed assets are added or retired, as bank loans are increased or decreased, and so on. Companies whose businesses are seasonal have especially large changes in their balance sheets. For example, most retailers have large inventories just before Christmas but low inventories and high accounts receivable just after Christmas. Therefore, firms' balance sheets change over the year, depending on when the statement is constructed.

Self-Test Questions

What is the balance sheet, and what information does it provide?

How is the order of the information shown on the balance sheet determined?

Why might a company's December 31 balance sheet differ from its June 30 balance sheet?

The Income Statement

Table 2-2 gives the 2001 and 2000 **income statements** for MicroDrive. Net sales are shown at the top of each statement, after which various costs are subtracted to obtain the net income available to common shareholders, which is generally referred to simply as net income. These costs include operating costs, interest costs, and taxes. A report on earnings and dividends per share is given at the bottom of the income statement. Earnings per share (EPS) is called "the bottom line," denoting that of all the items on the income statement, EPS is the most important. MicroDrive earned \$2.27 per share in 2001, down from \$2.36 in 2000, but it still raised the dividend from \$1.06 to \$1.15.[3]

Taking a closer look at the income statement, we see that depreciation and amortization are important components of total operating costs. Depreciation and amortization are similar in that both represent allocations of the costs of assets over their useful lives; however, there are some important distinctions. Recall from accounting that **depreciation** is an annual charge against income that reflects the estimated dollar cost of the capital equipment used up in the production process. Depreciation applies to **tangible assets,** such as plant and equipment, whereas **amortization** applies to **intangible assets** such as patents, copyrights, trademarks, and goodwill. Some companies use amortization to write off research and development costs, or the accounting goodwill that is recorded when one firm purchases another for more than its book value. Because they are similar, depreciation and amortization are often lumped together on the income statement.

Managers, security analysts, and bank loan officers often calculate **EBITDA,** which is defined as earnings before interest, taxes, depreciation, and amortization. MicroDrive currently has no amortization charges, so the depreciation and amortization on its income statement comes solely from depreciation. In 2001, MicroDrive's EBITDA was \$383.8 million. Subtracting the \$100 million of depreciation expense from its EBITDA leaves the company with \$283.8 million in operating income (EBIT). After subtracting \$88 million in interest expense and \$78.3 million in taxes, we obtain net income before preferred dividends of \$117.5 million. Finally, we subtract \$4 million of preferred dividends, which leaves MicroDrive with \$113.5 million of net income available to common stockholders. When analysts refer to a company's net income, they generally mean net income available to common shareholders. Likewise, throughout this book unless otherwise indicated, net income means net income available to common stockholders.

While the balance sheet can be thought of as a snapshot in time, the income statement reports on operations *over a period of time*, for example, during the calendar year 2001. During 2001 MicroDrive had sales of \$3 billion, and its net income available to common stockholders was \$113.5 million. Income statements can cover any period of time, but they are usually prepared monthly, quarterly, or annually. Of course, sales, costs, and profits will be larger the longer the reporting period, and the sum of the last 12 monthly (or four quarterly) income statements should equal the values shown on the annual income statement.

[3]After December 15, 1997, companies have had to report "comprehensive income" as well as net income. Comprehensive income is equal to net income plus several comprehensive income items. One example of comprehensive income is the unrealized gain or loss that occurs when a marketable security, classified as available for sale, is marked-to-market. For our purposes in this introductory finance text, we will assume that there are no comprehensive income items, so we will present only basic income statements throughout the text.

TABLE 2-2 MicroDrive Inc.: Income Statements for Years Ending December 31 (Millions of Dollars, Except for Per-Share Data)

	2001	2000
Net sales	$3,000.0	$2,850.0
Operating costs excluding depreciation and amortization	2,616.2	2,497.0
Earnings before interest, taxes, depreciation, and amortization (EBITDA)	$ 383.8	$ 353.0
Depreciation	100.0	90.0
Amortization	0.0	0.0
Depreciation and amortization	$ 100.0	$ 90.0
Earnings before interest and taxes (EBIT, or operating income)	$ 283.8	$ 263.0
Less interest	88.0	60.0
Earnings before taxes (EBT)	$ 195.8	$ 203.0
Taxes (40%)	78.3	81.2
Net income before preferred dividends	$ 117.5	$ 121.8
Preferred dividends	4.0	4.0
Net income	$ 113.5	$ 117.8
Common dividends	$ 57.5	$ 53.0
Addition to retained earnings	$ 56.0	$ 64.8
Per-Share Data		
Common stock price	$23.00	$26.00
Earnings per share (EPS)[a]	$ 2.27	$ 2.36
Dividends per share (DPS)[a]	$ 1.15	$ 1.06
Book value per share (BVPS)[a]	$17.92	$16.80
Cash flow per share (CFPS)[a]	$ 4.27	$ 4.16

[a]There are 50,000,000 shares of common stock outstanding. Note that EPS is based on earnings after preferred dividends—that is, on net income available to common stockholders. Calculations of EPS, DPS, BVPS, and CFPS for 2001 are as follows:

$$\text{Earnings per share} = \text{EPS} = \frac{\text{Net income}}{\text{Common shares outstanding}} = \frac{\$113{,}500{,}000}{50{,}000{,}000} = \$2.27.$$

$$\text{Dividends per share} = \text{DPS} = \frac{\text{Dividends paid to common stockholders}}{\text{Common shares outstanding}} = \frac{\$57{,}500{,}000}{50{,}000{,}000} = \$1.15.$$

$$\text{Book value per share} = \text{BVPS} = \frac{\text{Total common equity}}{\text{Common shares outstanding}} = \frac{\$896{,}000{,}000}{50{,}000{,}000} = \$17.92.$$

$$\text{Cash flow per share} = \text{CFPS} = \frac{\text{Net income} + \text{Depreciation} + \text{Amortization}}{\text{Common shares outstanding}} = \frac{\$213{,}500{,}000}{50{,}000{,}000} = \$4.27.$$

See *Ch 02 Tool Kit.xls* for details.

For planning and control purposes, management generally forecasts monthly (or perhaps quarterly) income statements, and it then compares actual results to the budgeted statements. If revenues are below and costs above the forecasted levels, then management should take corrective steps before the problem becomes too serious.

Self-Test Questions

What is an income statement, and what information does it provide?

Why is earnings per share called "the bottom line"?

Differentiate between amortization and depreciation.

What is EBITDA?

Regarding the time period reported, how does the income statement differ from the balance sheet?

TABLE 2-3 MicroDrive Inc.: Statement of Retained Earnings for Year Ending December 31, 2001 (Millions of Dollars)

See *Ch 02 Tool Kit.xls* for details.

Balance of retained earnings, December 31, 2000	\$710.0
Add: Net income, 2001	113.5
Less: Dividends to common stockholders	(57.5)[a]
Balance of retained earnings, December 31, 2001	\$766.0

[a]Here, and throughout the book, parentheses are used to denote negative numbers.

Statement of Retained Earnings

Changes in retained earnings between balance sheet dates are reported in the **statement of retained earnings.** Table 2-3 shows that MicroDrive began the year with \$710 million of retained earnings, earned \$113.5 million during 2001, paid out \$57.5 million in common dividends, and plowed \$56 million back into the business. Thus, the balance sheet item "Retained earnings" increased from \$710 million at the end of 2000 to \$766 million at the end of 2001.

Note that "Retained earnings" represents a *claim against assets,* not assets per se. Moreover, firms retain earnings primarily to expand the business, and this means investing in plant and equipment, in inventories, and so on, *not* piling up cash in a bank account. Changes in retained earnings occur because common stockholders allow the firm to reinvest funds that otherwise could be distributed as dividends. *Thus, retained earnings as reported on the balance sheet do not represent cash and are not "available" for the payment of dividends or anything else.*[4]

Self-Test Questions

What is the statement of retained earnings, and what information does it provide?

Why do changes in retained earnings occur?

Explain why the following statement is true: "Retained earnings as reported on the balance sheet do not represent cash and are not 'available' for the payment of dividends or anything else."

Net Cash Flow

Many financial analysts focus on **net cash flow.** A business's *net cash flow* generally differs from its **accounting profit** because some of the revenues and expenses listed on the income statement were not paid in cash during the year. The relationship between net cash flow and net income can be expressed as follows:

$$\text{Net cash flow} = \text{Net income} - \text{Noncash revenues} + \text{Noncash charges.} \quad \textbf{(2-1)}$$

The primary examples of noncash charges are depreciation and amortization. These items reduce net income but are not paid out in cash, so we add them back to net income

[4]The amount reported in the retained earnings account is *not* an indication of the amount of cash the firm has. Cash (as of the balance sheet date) is found in the cash account, an asset account. A positive number in the retained earnings account indicates only that in the past the firm has earned some income, but its dividends have been less than its earnings. Even though a company reports record earnings and shows an increase in the retained earnings account, it still may be short of cash.

The same situation holds for individuals. You might own a new BMW (no loan), lots of clothes, and an expensive stereo, hence have a high net worth, but if you had only 23 cents in your pocket plus \$5 in your checking account, you would still be short of cash.

Financial Analysis on the Internet

A wide range of valuable financial information is available on the Internet. With just a couple of clicks, an investor can easily find the key financial statements for most publicly traded companies.

Say, for example, you are thinking about buying Disney stock, and you are looking for financial information regarding the company's recent performance. Here's a partial (but by no means a complete) list of places you can go to get started:

- One source is Yahoo's finance web site, **finance.yahoo.com.**[a] Here you will find updated market information along with links to a variety of interesting research sites. Enter a stock's ticker symbol, click on Get Quotes, and you will see the stock's current price, along with recent news about the company. Click on Profile (under More Info) and you will find a report on the company's key financial ratios. Links to the company's income statement, balance sheet, and statement of cash flows can also be found. The Yahoo site also has a list of insider transactions, so you can tell if a company's CEO and other key insiders are buying or selling their company's stock. In addition, there is a message board where investors share opinions about the company, and there is a link to the company's filings with the Securities and Exchange Commission (SEC). Note that, in most cases, a more complete list of the SEC filings can be found at **www.sec.gov** or at **www.edgar-online.com.**
- Other sources for up-to-date market information are **www.cnnfn.com** and **www.cbs.marketwatch.com.** Each also has an area where you can obtain stock quotes along with company financials, links to Wall Street research, and links to SEC filings.
- Another good source is **www.quicken.com.** Enter the ticker symbol in the area labeled quotes and research. The site will take you to an area where you can find a link to the company's financial statements, along with analysts' earnings estimates and SEC filings. This site also has a section where you can estimate the stock's intrinsic value. (In Chapter 10 we will discuss various methods for calculating intrinsic value.)
- If you are looking for charts of key accounting variables (for example, sales, inventory, depreciation and amortization, and reported earnings), along with the financial statements, take a look at **www.smartmoney.com.**
- Another good place to look is **www.marketguide.com.** Here you find links to analysts' research reports along with the key financial statements.
- Two other places to consider: **www.hoovers.com** and **www.zacks.com.** Each has free research available along with more detailed information provided to subscribers.

Once you have accumulated all of this information, you may be looking for sites that provide opinions regarding the direction of the overall market and views regarding individual stocks. Two popular sites in this category are The Motley Fool's web site, **www.fool.com,** and the web site for The Street.com, **www.thestreet.com.**

Keep in mind that this list is just a small subset of the information available online. You should also realize that a lot of these sites change their content over time, and new and interesting sites are always being added to the Internet.

[a]To avoid redundancy, we have intentionally left off **http://** in all web addresses given here. A quick way to change an address is to highlight the portion of the address that is different and type in the appropriate letters of the new address. Once you're finished just press Enter.

when calculating net cash flow. Another example of a noncash charge is deferred taxes. In some instances, companies are allowed to defer tax payments to a later date even though the tax payment is reported as an expense on the income statement. Therefore, deferred tax payments would be added to net income when calculating net cash flow.[5] At the same time, some revenues may not be collected in cash during the year, and these items must be subtracted from net income when calculating net cash flow.

Typically, depreciation and amortization are by far the largest noncash items, and in many cases the other noncash items roughly net out to zero. For this reason, many analysts assume that net cash flow equals net income plus depreciation and amortization:

$$\text{Net cash flow} = \text{Net income} + \text{Depreciation and amortization.} \qquad \textbf{(2-2)}$$

[5]Deferred taxes may arise, for example, if a company uses accelerated depreciation for tax purposes but straight-line depreciation for reporting its financial statements to investors.

To keep things simple, we will generally assume that Equation 2-2 holds. However, you should remember that Equation 2-2 will not accurately reflect net cash flow in those instances where there are significant noncash items beyond depreciation and amortization.

We can illustrate Equation 2-2 with 2001 data for MicroDrive taken from Table 2-2:

$$\text{Net cash flow} = \$113.5 + \$100.0 = \$213.5 \text{ million.}$$

To illustrate depreciation's effect, suppose a machine with a life of five years and a zero expected salvage value was purchased in 2000 for $100,000 and placed into service in 2001. This $100,000 cost is not expensed in the purchase year; rather, it is charged against production over the machine's five-year depreciable life. If the depreciation expense were not taken, profits would be overstated, and taxes would be too high. So, the annual depreciation charge is deducted from sales revenues, along with such other costs as labor and raw materials, to determine income. However, because the $100,000 was actually expended back in 2000, the depreciation charged against income in 2001 and subsequent years is not a cash outlay, as are labor or raw materials charges. *Depreciation is a noncash charge, so it must be added back to net income to obtain the net cash flow.* If we assume that all other noncash items (including amortization) sum to zero, then net cash flow is simply equal to net income plus depreciation.

Self-Test Questions

Differentiate between net cash flow and accounting profit.

In accounting, the emphasis is on net income. What is emphasized in finance, and why is that item emphasized?

Assuming that depreciation is its only noncash cost, how can someone calculate a business's net cash flow?

Statement of Cash Flows

Even if a company reports a large net income during a year, the *amount of cash* reported on its year-end balance sheet may be the same or even lower than its beginning cash. The reason is that its net income can be used in a variety of ways, not just kept as cash in the bank. For example, the firm may use its net income to pay dividends, to increase inventories, to finance accounts receivable, to invest in fixed assets, to reduce debt, or to buy back common stock. Indeed, the company's *cash position* as reported on its balance sheet is affected by a great many factors, including the following:

1. **Net income.** Other things held constant, a positive net income will lead to more cash in the bank. However, as we discuss below, other things generally are not held constant.
2. **Noncash adjustments to net income.** To calculate cash flow, it is necessary to adjust net income to reflect noncash revenues and expenses, such as depreciation and deferred taxes, as shown above in the calculation of net cash flow.
3. **Changes in working capital.** Increases in current assets other than cash, such as inventories and accounts receivable, decrease cash, whereas decreases in these accounts increase cash. For example, if inventories are to increase, the firm must use some of its cash to acquire the additional inventory. Conversely, if inventories decrease, this generally means the firm is selling inventories and not replacing all of them, hence generating cash. On the other hand, if payables increase, the firm has received additional credit from its suppliers, which saves cash, but if payables decrease, this means it has used cash to pay off its suppliers. Therefore, increases in current liabilities such as accounts payable increase cash, whereas decreases in current liabilities decrease cash.

4. **Fixed assets.** If a company invests in fixed assets, this will reduce its cash position. On the other hand, if it sells some fixed assets this will increase cash.
5. **Security transactions.** If a company issues stock or bonds during the year, the funds raised will increase its cash position. On the other hand, if the company uses cash to buy back outstanding stock or to pay off debt, or if it pays dividends to its shareholders, this will reduce cash.

Each of the above factors is reflected in the **statement of cash flows,** which summarizes the changes in a company's cash position. The statement separates activities into three categories, plus a summary section:

1. **Operating activities,** which includes net income, depreciation, and changes in current assets and liabilities other than cash, short-term investments, and short-term debt.
2. **Investing activities,** which includes investments in or sales of fixed assets.
3. **Financing activities,** which includes raising cash by selling short-term investments or by issuing short-term debt, long-term debt, or stock. Also, because both dividends paid and cash used to buy back outstanding stock or bonds reduce the company's cash, such transactions are included here.

Accounting texts explain how to prepare the statement of cash flows, but the statement is used to help answer questions such as these: Is the firm generating enough cash to purchase the additional assets required for growth? Is the firm generating any extra cash that can be used to repay debt or to invest in new products? Such information is useful both for managers and investors, so the statement of cash flows is an important part of the annual report. Financial managers generally use this statement, along with the cash budget, when forecasting their companies' cash positions. This issue is considered in more detail in Chapter 4.

Table 2-4 shows MicroDrive's statement of cash flows as it would appear in the company's annual report. The top section shows cash generated by and used in operations—for MicroDrive, operations provided net cash flows of *minus* \$2.5 million. This subtotal, the minus \$2.5 million net cash flow provided by operating activities, is in many respects the most important figure in any of the financial statements. Profits as reported on the income statement can be "doctored" by such tactics as depreciating assets too slowly, not recognizing bad debts promptly, and the like. However, it is far more difficult to simultaneously doctor profits and the working capital accounts. Therefore, it is not uncommon for a company to report positive net income right up to the day it declares bankruptcy. In such cases, however, the net cash flow from operations almost always began to deteriorate much earlier, and analysts who kept an eye on cash flow could have predicted trouble. Therefore, if you are ever analyzing a company and are pressed for time, look first at the trend in net cash flow provided by operating activities, because it will tell you more than any other number.

The second section shows long-term fixed-asset investing activities. MicroDrive purchased fixed assets totaling \$230 million; this was the only long-term investment it made during 2001.

The third section, financing activities, includes borrowing from banks (notes payable), selling new bonds, and paying dividends on common and preferred stock. MicroDrive raised \$289 million by borrowing and by selling off its short-term investments, but it paid \$61.5 million in preferred and common dividends. Therefore, its net inflow of funds from financing activities was \$227.5 million.

In the summary, where all of these sources and uses of cash are totaled, we see that MicroDrive's cash outflows exceeded its cash inflows by \$5 million during 2001; that is, its net change in cash was a *negative* \$5 million.

See ***Ch 02 Tool Kit.xls*** for details.

TABLE 2-4 MicroDrive Inc.: Statement of Cash Flows for 2001 (Millions of Dollars)

	Cash Provided or Used
Operating Activities	
Net income	$117.5
Adjustments:	
Noncash adjustments:	
Depreciation[a]	100.0
Due to changes in working capital:[b]	
Increase in accounts receivable	(60.0)
Increase in inventories	(200.0)
Increase in accounts payable	30.0
Increase in accruals	10.0
Net cash provided by operating activities	($ 2.5)
Long-Term Investing Activities	
Cash used to acquire fixed assets[c]	($230.0)
Financing Activities	
Sale of short-term investments	$ 65.0
Increase in notes payable	50.0
Increase in bonds outstanding	174.0
Payment of dividends	(61.5)
Net cash provided by financing activities	227.5
Summary	
Net change in cash	($ 5.0)
Cash at beginning of year	15.0
Cash at end of year	$ 10.0

[a]Depreciation is a noncash expense that was deducted when calculating net income. It must be added back to show the correct cash flow from operations.
[b]An increase in a current asset *decreases* cash. An increase in a current liability *increases* cash. For example, inventories increased by $200 million, so that reduced cash by a like amount.
[c]The net increase in fixed assets is $130 million; however, this net amount is after a deduction for the year's depreciation expense. Depreciation expense would have to be added back to find the increase in gross fixed assets. From the company's income statement, we see that the 2001 depreciation expense is $100 million; thus, expenditures on fixed assets were actually $230 million.

MicroDrive's statement of cash flows should be worrisome to its managers and to outside analysts. The company had a $2.5 million cash shortfall from operations, it spent an additional $230 million on new fixed assets, and it paid out another $61.5 million in dividends. It covered these cash outlays by borrowing heavily and by selling $65 million of short-term investments. Obviously, this situation cannot continue year after year, so something will have to be done. Later in the chapter we will consider some of the actions MicroDrive's financial staff might recommend to ease the cash flow problem.

Self-Test Questions

What is the statement of cash flows, and what types of questions does it answer?

Identify and briefly explain the three different categories of activities shown in the statement of cash flows.

Modifying Accounting Data for Managerial Decisions

Thus far in the chapter we have focused on financial statements as they are presented in the annual report. However, these statements are designed more for use by creditors and tax collectors than for managers and equity (stock) analysts. Therefore, certain modifications are needed for use in corporate decision making. In the following sections we discuss how financial analysts combine stock prices and accounting data to make the statements more useful.

Operating Assets and Operating Capital

Different firms have different financial structures, different tax situations, and different amounts of nonoperating assets. These differences affect traditional accounting measures such as the rate of return on equity. They can cause two firms, or two divisions within a single firm, that actually have similar operations to appear to be operated with different efficiency. This is important, because if managerial compensation systems are to function properly, operating managers must be judged and compensated for those things that are under their control, not on the basis of things outside their control. Therefore, to judge managerial performance, we need to compare managers' ability to generate *operating income* (or *EBIT*) with the *operating assets* under their control.

The first step in modifying the traditional accounting framework is to divide total assets into two categories, **operating assets,** which consist of the assets necessary to operate the business, and **nonoperating assets,** which would include cash and short-term investments above the level required for normal operations, investments in subsidiaries, land held for future use, and the like. Moreover, operating assets are further divided into **operating current assets,** such as inventory, and **long-term operating assets,** such as plant and equipment. Obviously, if a manager can generate a given amount of profit and cash flow with a relatively small investment in operating assets, that reduces the amount of capital investors must put up and thus increases the rate of return on that capital.

Most capital used in a business is supplied by investors—stockholders, bondholders, and lenders such as banks. Investors must be paid for the use of their money, with payment coming as interest in the case of debt and as dividends plus capital gains in the case of stock. So, if a company buys more assets than it actually needs, and thus raises too much capital, then its capital costs will be unnecessarily high.

Must all of the capital used to acquire assets be obtained from investors? The answer is no, because some of the funds are provided as a normal consequence of operations. For example, some funds will come from suppliers and be reported as *accounts payable*, while other funds will come as *accrued wages and accrued taxes*, which amount to short-term loans from workers and tax authorities. Such funds are called **operating current liabilities.** Therefore, if a firm needs \$100 million of assets, but it has \$10 million of accounts payable and another \$10 million of accrued wages and taxes, then its *investor-supplied capital* would be only \$80 million.[6]

[6]Note that the term "capital" can be given two meanings. First, when accountants use the term "capital," they typically mean the sum of long-term debt, preferred stock, and common equity, or perhaps those items plus interest-bearing short-term debt. However, when economists use the term, they generally mean assets used in production, as in "labor plus capital." If all funds were raised from long-term sources, and if all assets were operating assets, then money capital would equal operating assets, and the accountants' capital would always equal the economists' capital. When you encounter the term "capital" in the business and financial literature, it can mean either asset capital or money capital. For example, in Coca-Cola's operating manuals, which explain to its employees how Coke wants the company to be operated, capital means "assets financed by investor-supplied capital." However, in most accounting and finance textbooks, and in the traditional finance literature, "capital" means investor-supplied capital, not assets. It might be easier if we picked one meaning and then used it consistently in this book. However, that would be misleading, because both meanings are encountered in practice. Therefore, we shall use the term "capital" in both ways. However, you should be able to figure out which definition is implied from the context in which the term is used.

Those current assets used in operations are called **operating working capital,** and operating working capital less operating current liabilities is called **net operating working capital.** Therefore, net operating working capital is the working capital acquired with investor-supplied funds. Here is the definition in equation form:

$$\begin{aligned}\text{Net operating working capital} &= \text{All current assets that do not pay interest} \\ &\quad - \text{All current liabilities that do not charge interest} \\ &= \text{Operating current assets} - \text{Operating current liabilities.}\end{aligned} \quad \textbf{(2-3)}$$

Now think about how these concepts can be used in practice. First, all companies must carry some cash to "grease the wheels" of their operations. Companies continuously receive checks from customers and write checks to suppliers, employees, and so on. Because inflows and outflows do not coincide perfectly, a company must keep some cash in its bank account. In other words, some cash is required to conduct operations. The same is true for most other current assets, such as inventory and accounts receivable, which are required for normal operations. However, any short-term securities the firm holds generally result from investment decisions made by the treasurer, and they are not used in the core operations. Therefore, short-term investments are normally excluded when calculating net operating working capital.[7]

Some current liabilities—especially accounts payable and accruals—arise in the normal course of operations. Moreover, each dollar of such current liabilities is a dollar that the company does not have to raise from investors to acquire current assets. Therefore, to calculate net operating working capital, we deduct these operating current liabilities from the operating current assets. Other current liabilities that charge interest, such as notes payable to banks, are treated as investor-supplied capital and thus are not deducted when calculating net working capital. If you are ever uncertain about an item, ask yourself whether it is a natural consequence of operations or if it is a discretionary choice by management. If it is discretionary, it is not an operating asset or liability.

We can apply these definitions to MicroDrive, using the balance sheet data given in Table 2-1. Here is the net operating working capital for 2001:

$$\begin{aligned}\text{Net operating working capital} &= (\text{Cash} + \text{Accounts receivable} + \text{Inventories}) \\ &\quad - (\text{Accounts payable} + \text{Accruals}) \\ &= (\$10 + \$375 + \$615) - (\$60 + \$140) \\ &= \$800 \text{ million.}\end{aligned}$$

MicroDrive's total operating capital at year-end 2001 was

$$\begin{aligned}\text{Total operating capital} &= (\text{Net operating working capital}) \\ &\quad + (\text{Operating long-term assets})\end{aligned} \quad \textbf{(2-4)}$$

$$\begin{aligned}&= \$800 + \$1{,}000 \\ &= \$1{,}800 \text{ million.}\end{aligned}$$

Note that MicroDrive's only operating long-term assets are net plant and equipment.

[7]If the marketable securities are held as a substitute for cash, and therefore reduce the cash requirements, then they may be classified as part of operating working capital. Generally, though, large holdings of marketable securities are held as a reserve for some contingency or else as a temporary "parking place" for funds prior to an acquisition, a major capital investment program, or the like.

Now note that MicroDrive's net operating working capital a year earlier, at year-end 2000, was

$$\text{Net operating working capital} = (\$15 + \$315 + \$415) - (\$30 + \$130) = \$585 \text{ million.}$$

Adding the $870 million of fixed assets, its total operating capital at year-end 2000 was

$$\text{Total operating capital} = \$585 + \$870 = \$1{,}455 \text{ million.}$$

Therefore, MicroDrive increased its operating capital to $1,800 from $1,455 million, or by $345 million, during 2001. Furthermore, most of this increase went into working capital, which rose from $585 to $800 million, or by $215 million. This 37 percent increase in net operating working capital versus a sales increase of only 5 percent (from $2,850 to $3,000 million) should set off warning bells in your head: Why did MicroDrive tie up so much additional cash in working capital? Is the company gearing up for a big increase in sales, or are inventories not moving and receivables not being collected? We will address this question in detail in the next chapter.

Net Operating Profit after Taxes (NOPAT)

If two companies have different amounts of debt, hence different amounts of interest charges, they could have identical operating performances but different net incomes—the one with more debt would have a lower net income. Net income is certainly important, but it does not always reflect the true performance of a company's operations or the effectiveness of its operating managers. A better measurement for comparing managers' performance is **net operating profit after taxes,** or **NOPAT,** which is the amount of profit a company would generate if it had no debt and held no financial assets. NOPAT is defined as follows:[8]

$$\text{NOPAT} = \text{EBIT}(1 - \text{Tax rate}). \tag{2-5}$$

Using data from the income statements in Table 2-2, MicroDrive's 2001 NOPAT is found to be

$$\text{NOPAT} = \$283.8(1 - 0.4) = \$283.8(0.6) = \$170.3 \text{ million.}$$

In 2001 MicroDrive generated an after-tax operating profit of $170.3 million. This was actually a little better than the 2000 NOPAT of $263(0.6) = $157.8 million. However, the income statements in Table 2-2 show that MicroDrive's earnings per share declined from 2000 to 2001. This decrease in EPS was caused by an increase in interest expense, and not by a decrease in operating profit. Moreover, the balance sheets in Table 2-1 show that debt increased from 2000 to 2001. But why did MicroDrive increase its debt? As we just saw, its investment in operating capital increased dramatically during 2001, and that increase was financed primarily with debt.

---

[8]For firms with a more complicated tax situation, it is better to define NOPAT as follows: NOPAT = (Net income before preferred dividends) + (Net interest expense)(1 − Tax rate). Also, if firms are able to defer paying some of their taxes, perhaps by the use of accelerated depreciation, then NOPAT should be adjusted to reflect the taxes that the company actually paid on its operating income. The Copeland et al. and Stewart books listed in the references at the end of the chapter explain in detail these and other adjustments.

Free Cash Flow

Earlier in this chapter, we defined net cash flow as net income plus noncash adjustments, which typically means net income plus depreciation. Note, though, that cash flows cannot be maintained over time unless depreciated fixed assets are replaced, so management is not completely free to use its cash flows however it chooses. Therefore, we now define another term, **free cash flow (FCF),** which is the cash flow actually available for distribution to investors *after the company has made all the investments in fixed assets and working capital necessary to sustain ongoing operations.*

When you studied income statements in accounting, the emphasis was probably on the firm's net income, which is its **accounting profit.** However, the value of a company's operations is determined by the stream of cash flows that the operations will generate now and in the future. As the statement of cash flows shows, accounting profit and cash flow can be quite different.

To be more specific, the value of operations depends on all the future expected free cash flows (FCF), defined as after-tax operating profit minus the amount of new investment in working capital and fixed assets necessary to sustain the business. Thus, free cash flow represents the cash that is actually available for distribution to investors. *Therefore, the way for managers to make their companies more valuable is to increase their free cash flow.*

Calculating Free Cash Flow

As shown earlier in the chapter, MicroDrive had a 2001 NOPAT of \$170.3 million. Its **operating cash flow** is NOPAT plus any noncash adjustments as shown on the statement of cash flows. For MicroDrive, where depreciation is the only noncash charge, the 2001 operating cash flow is \$270.3 million:

$$\text{Operating cash flow} = \text{NOPAT} + \text{Depreciation} \tag{2-6}$$

$$= \$170.3 + \$100$$
$$= \$270.3 \text{ million.}$$

As shown earlier in the chapter, MicroDrive had \$1,455 million of operating assets, or operating capital, at the end of 2000, but \$1,800 million at the end of 2001. Therefore, during 2001, it made a **net investment in operating assets** of

$$\text{Net investment in operating assets} = \$1{,}800 - \$1{,}455 = \$345 \text{ million.}$$

Net fixed assets rose from \$870 to \$1,000 million, or by \$130 million. However, MicroDrive reported \$100 million of depreciation, so its gross investment in fixed assets was \$130 + \$100 = \$230 million for the year. With this background, we find the **gross investment in operating assets** as follows:

$$\text{Gross investment} = \text{Net investment} + \text{Depreciation}$$

$$= \$345 + \$100 = \$445 \text{ million.}$$

MicroDrive's free cash flow in 2001 was

$$\text{FCF} = \text{Operating cash flow} - \text{Gross investment in operating assets} \tag{2-7}$$

$$= \$270.3 - \$445$$
$$= -\$174.7 \text{ million.}$$

An algebraically equivalent equation is

$$\text{FCF} = \text{NOPAT} - \text{Net investment in operating assets} \tag{2-7a}$$

$$= \$170.3 - \$345$$
$$= -\$174.7 \text{ million.}$$

Equations 2-7 and 2-7a are equivalent because depreciation is added to both NOPAT and net investment.

The Uses of FCF

Recall that free cash flow (FCF) is the amount of cash that is available for distribution to all investors, including both shareholders and debtholders. There are five good uses for FCF:

1. Pay interest to debtholders, keeping in mind that the net cost to the company is the after-tax interest expense.
2. Repay debtholders, that is, pay off some of the debt.
3. Pay dividends to shareholders.
4. Repurchase stock from shareholders.
5. Buy marketable securities or other nonoperating assets.

Recall that the company does not have to use FCF to acquire operating assets, since by definition FCF already takes into account the purchase of all operating assets needed to support growth. Unfortunately, there is evidence to suggest that some companies with high FCF tend to make unnecessary investments that don't add value, such as paying too much to acquire some other company. Thus, high FCF can lead to agency costs, as discussed in Chapter 1, if managers fail to act in the best interest of shareholders. We discuss agency costs and ways to control them throughout the book, especially in Chapter 12, where we discuss value-based management, and in Chapter 16, where we discuss the choice of capital structure.

In practice, most companies combine these five uses in such a way that the net total is equal to FCF. For example, a company might pay interest and dividends, issue new debt, and also sell some of its marketable securities. Some of these activities are cash outflows (for example, paying interest and dividends) and some are cash inflows (for example, issuing debt and selling marketable securities), but the net cash flow from these five activities is equal to FCF.

FCF and Corporate Value

FCF is the amount of cash available for distribution to investors, and, as a result, the value of a company depends on its expected future FCFs. Subsequent chapters will develop the tools needed to forecast FCFs, to evaluate their risk, and to calculate the value of a company given the size and risk of its expected cash flows. Chapter 12 ties all this together with a model that is used to calculate the value of a company. Even though you do not yet have the tools to apply the model, it's important that you understand this basic concept: *FCF is the cash available for distribution to investors. Therefore, the value of a firm is primarily dependent on its expected future FCFs.*

Evaluating FCF, NOPAT, and Operating Capital

Even though MicroDrive had a positive NOPAT, its very high investment in operating assets resulted in a negative free cash flow. Because free cash flow is what is available for distribution to investors, not only was there nothing for investors, but investors actually had to provide *additional* money to keep the business going. Investors provided most of this new money as debt.

Is a negative free cash flow always bad? The answer is, "Not necessarily. It depends on why the free cash flow was negative." If FCF was negative because NOPAT was negative, that is a bad sign, because then the company is probably experiencing operating problems. However, many high-growth companies have positive NOPAT but negative free cash flow because they are making large investments in operating assets to support growth. There is nothing wrong with profitable growth, even if it causes negative cash flows.

One way to determine whether growth is profitable is by examining the return on invested capital (ROIC), which is the ratio of NOPAT to total operating capital. For MicroDrive, it is \$170.3/\$1,800 = 9.5%. If the ROIC exceeds the rate of return required by investors, then a negative free cash flow caused by high growth is nothing to worry about. Chapters 11 and 12 discuss this in detail.

To calculate the ROIC, we first calculate NOPAT and operating capital. The return on invested capital (ROIC) is a performance measure that indicates how much NOPAT is generated by each dollar of operating capital:

$$\text{ROIC} = \frac{\text{NOPAT}}{\text{Operating capital}}. \tag{2-8}$$

If ROIC is greater than the rate of return investors require, then the firm is adding value. This required rate of return is found as the weighted average cost of capital (WACC). We explain the exact calculation of the WACC in Chapter 11, but for now you should note that a company's WACC depends jointly on its risk and the overall level of interest rates in the economy. The higher its risk, and the higher the general level of interest rate, the higher the WACC.

As noted earlier, a negative current FCF is not necessarily bad, provided it is due to high growth. For example, Home Depot has negative FCF due to its rapid growth, but it also has a very high ROIC (18.3 percent for 1999), and this high ROIC results in a high market value for the stock.

MicroDrive had an ROIC in 2001 of 9.46 percent (\$170.3/\$1,800 = 0.0946). Is this enough to cover its cost of capital? We'll answer that question in the next section.

Self-Test Questions

What is net operating working capital? Why does it exclude most short-term investments and also notes payable?

What is total operating capital, or, equivalently, total operating assets? Why is it important for managers to calculate a company's capital requirements?

What is NOPAT? Why might it be a better performance measure than net income?

What is free cash flow? Why is free cash flow the most important determinant of a firm's value?

MVA and EVA

Neither traditional accounting data nor the modified data discussed in the preceding section bring in stock prices, even though the primary goal of management is to maximize the firm's stock price. Financial analysts have therefore developed two new performance measures, MVA, or Market Value Added, and EVA, or Economic Value Added. These concepts are discussed in this section.[9]

Market Value Added (MVA)

The primary goal of most firms is to maximize shareholders' wealth. This goal obviously benefits shareholders, but it also helps to ensure that scarce resources are allocated efficiently, which benefits the economy. Shareholder wealth is maximized by

[9]The concepts of EVA and MVA were developed by Joel Stern and Bennett Stewart, co-founders of the consulting firm Stern Stewart & Company. Stern Stewart copyrighted the terms "EVA" and "MVA," so other consulting firms have given other names to these values. Still, EVA and MVA are the terms most commonly used in practice.

maximizing the *difference* between the market value of the firm's stock and the amount of equity capital that was supplied by shareholders. This difference is called the **Market Value Added (MVA):**

$$\begin{aligned}\text{MVA} &= \text{Market value of stock} - \text{Equity capital supplied by shareholders}\\ &= \text{(Shares outstanding)(Stock price)} - \text{Total common equity.} \qquad \textbf{(2-9)}\end{aligned}$$

To illustrate, consider Coca-Cola. Early in 2000, its total market equity value was \$139 billion, while its balance sheet showed that stockholders had put up only \$9.5 billion. Thus, Coca-Cola's MVA was \$139 − \$9.5 = \$129.5 billion. This \$129.5 billion represents the difference between the money that Coca-Cola's stockholders have invested in the corporation since its founding—including retained earnings—versus the cash they could get if they sold the business. The higher its MVA, the better the job management is doing for the firm's shareholders.

MVA sometimes is defined as the total market value of the company minus the total amount of investor-supplied capital. For most companies, the total amount of investor-supplied capital is the sum of equity, debt, and preferred stock. We can calculate the total amount of investor-supplied capital directly from their reported values in the financial statements. The total market value of a company is the sum of the market values of common equity, debt, and preferred stock. It is easy to find the market value of equity, since stock prices are readily available, but it is not always easy to find the market value of debt. Hence, many analysts use the value of debt that is reported in the financial statements, or the debt's book value, as an estimate of its market value.

For Coca-Cola, the total amount of reported debt was \$7.6 billion, and Coca-Cola had preferred no stock. Using this as an estimate of the market value of debt, Coke's total market value was \$139 + \$7.6 = \$146.6 billion. The total amount of investor-supplied funds was \$9.5 + \$7.6 = \$17.1 billion. Using these total values, the MVA was \$146.6 − \$17.1 = \$129.5 billion. Note that this is the same answer that we got using the previous definition of MVA. Both methods will give the same results if the market value of debt is approximately equal to its book value. But, as we will see in Chapter 9, the market value of debt is sometimes quite different from its book value, and this can have a big effect on MVA.

Economic Value Added (EVA)

Whereas MVA measures the effects of managerial actions since the very inception of a company, **Economic Value Added (EVA)** focuses on managerial effectiveness in a given year. The EVA basic formula is as follows:

$$\begin{aligned}\text{EVA} &= \text{Net operating profit after taxes, or NOPAT}\\ &\quad - \text{After-tax dollar cost of capital used to support operations}\\ &= \text{EBIT}(1 - \text{Corporate tax rate})\\ &\quad - \text{(Operating capital)(WACC).} \qquad \textbf{(2-10)}\end{aligned}$$

Operating capital is the sum of the interest-bearing debt, preferred stock, and common equity used to acquire the company's net operating assets, that is, its net operating working capital plus net plant and equipment. Operating assets by definition equals the capital used to buy operating assets.

We can also calculate EVA in terms of ROIC:

$$\text{EVA} = \text{(Operating capital)(ROIC} - \text{WACC).} \qquad \textbf{(2-10a)}$$

As this equation shows, a firm adds value—that is, has a positive EVA—if its ROIC is greater than its WACC. If WACC exceeds ROIC, then new investments in operating capital will reduce the firm's value.

WWW

If you want to read more about EVA and MVA, surf over to **http://www.sternstewart.com** and learn about it from the people who invented it, Stern Stewart & Co. While you are there, you may like to take a look at a video of executives describing how EVA has helped them, which can be found at **http://www.sternstewart.com/evaabout/comments.shtml.** To see the video, you will need Real Player, which can be downloaded for free from **http://www.realplayer.com.**

EVA is an estimate of a business's true economic profit for the year, and it differs sharply from accounting profit.[10] EVA represents the residual income that remains after the cost of *all* capital, including equity capital, has been deducted, whereas accounting profit is determined without imposing a charge for equity capital. As we will discuss more completely in Chapter 11, equity capital has a cost, because funds provided by shareholders could have been invested elsewhere, where they would have earned a return. Shareholders give up the opportunity to invest elsewhere when they provide capital to the firm. The return they could earn elsewhere in investments of equal risk represents the cost of equity capital. This cost is an *opportunity cost* rather than an *accounting cost*, but it is quite real nevertheless.

Note that when calculating EVA we do not add back depreciation. Although it is not a cash expense, depreciation is a cost, and it is therefore deducted when determining both net income and EVA. Our calculation of EVA assumes that the true economic depreciation of the company's fixed assets exactly equals the depreciation used for accounting and tax purposes. If this were not the case, adjustments would have to be made to obtain a more accurate measure of EVA.

EVA measures the extent to which the firm has added to shareholder value. Therefore, if managers focus on EVA, this will help to ensure that they operate in a manner that is consistent with maximizing shareholder wealth. Note too that EVA can be determined for divisions as well as for the company as a whole, so it provides a useful basis for determining managerial performance at all levels. Consequently, EVA is being used by an increasing number of firms as the primary basis for determining managerial compensation.

Table 2-5 shows how MicroDrive's MVA and EVA are calculated. The stock price was \$23 per share at year-end 2001, down from \$26 per share at the end of 2000. Its WACC, which is the percentage after-tax cost of capital, was 10.8 percent in 2000 and 11.0 percent in 2001, and its tax rate was 40 percent. Other data in Table 2-5 were given in the basic financial statements provided earlier in the chapter.

Note first that the lower stock price and the higher book value of equity (due to retaining earnings during 2001) combined to reduce the MVA. The 2001 MVA is still positive, but \$460 − \$254 = \$206 million of stockholders' value was lost during 2001.

EVA for 2000 was just barely positive, and in 2001 it was negative. Operating income (NOPAT) rose, but EVA still declined, primarily because the amount of capital rose more sharply than NOPAT—by about 26 percent versus 8 percent—and the cost of this increased capital pulled EVA down.

Recall also that net income fell somewhat from 2000 to 2001, but not nearly so dramatically as the decline in EVA. Net income does not reflect the amount of equity capital employed, but EVA does. Because of this omission, net income is not as useful as EVA for setting corporate goals and measuring managerial performance.

We will have more to say about both MVA and EVA later in the book, but we can close this section with two observations. First, there is a relationship between MVA and EVA, but it is not a direct one. If a company has a history of negative EVAs, then its MVA will probably be negative, and vice versa if it has a history of positive EVAs. However, the stock price, which is the key ingredient in the MVA calculation, depends more on expected future performance than on historical performance. Therefore, a

[10]The most important reason EVA differs from accounting profit is that the cost of equity capital is deducted when EVA is calculated. Other factors that could lead to differences include adjustments that might be made to depreciation, to research and development costs, to inventory valuations, and so on. These other adjustments also can affect the calculation of investor supplied capital, which affects MVA. See Stewart, *The Quest for Value*, listed in the Selected Additional References at the end of the chapter.

TABLE 2-5 MVA and EVA for MicroDrive (Millions of Dollars)

See ***Ch 02 Tool Kit.xls*** for details.

	2001	2000
MVA Calculation		
Price per share	$ 23.0	$ 26.0
Number of shares (millions)	50.0	50.0
Market value of equity	$1,150.0	$1,300.0
Book value of equity	$ 896.0	$ 840.0
MVA = Market value − Book value	$ 254.0	$ 460.0
EVA Calculation		
EBIT	$ 283.8	$ 263.0
Tax rate	40%	40%
NOPAT = EBIT(1 − T)	$ 170.3	$ 157.8
Total investor-supplied operating capital[a]	$1,800.0	$1,455.0
After-tax cost of capital, WACC (%)	11.0%	10.8%
Dollar cost of capital = Capital (WACC)	$ 198.0	$ 157.1
EVA = NOPAT − Capital cost	($27.7)	$ 0.70
ROIC = NOPAT/Operating capital	9.46%	10.85%
ROIC − Cost of capital = ROIC − WACC	(1.54%)	0.05%
EVA = Operating capital(ROIC − WACC)	($27.7)	$ 0.7

[a]Investor-supplied operating capital equals the sum of notes payable, long-term debt, preferred stock, and common equity. It could also be calculated as total liabilities and equity minus accounts payable, accruals, and short-term investments.

company with a history of negative EVAs could have a positive MVA, provided investors expect a turnaround in the future.

The second observation is that when EVAs or MVAs are used to evaluate managerial performance as part of an incentive compensation program, EVA is the measure that is typically used. The reasons are (1) EVA shows the value added during a given year, whereas MVA reflects performance over the company's entire life, perhaps even including times before the current managers were born, and (2) EVA can be applied to individual divisions or other units of a large corporation, whereas MVA must be applied to the entire corporation.

Self-Test Questions

Define the terms "Market Value Added (MVA)" and "Economic Value Added (EVA)."

How does EVA differ from accounting profit?

The Federal Income Tax System

The value of any financial asset (including stocks, bonds, and mortgages), as well as most real assets such as plants or even entire firms, depends on the stream of cash flows produced by the asset. Cash flows from an asset consist of *usable* income plus depreciation, and usable income means income *after taxes.*

Our tax laws can be changed by Congress, and in recent years changes have occurred frequently. Indeed, a major change has occurred, on average, every three to

A web site of interest concerning federal tax law is **http://www.taxsites.com/federal.html.** From this home page one can visit other sites that provide summaries of recent tax legislation or current information on corporate and individual tax rates.

four years since 1913, when our federal income tax system began. Further, certain parts of our tax system are tied to the inflation rate, so changes occur automatically each year, depending on the rate of inflation during the previous year. Therefore, although this section will give you a good background on the basic nature of our tax system, you should consult current rate schedules and other data published by the Internal Revenue Service (available in U.S. post offices) before you file your personal or business tax returns.

Currently (early 2001), federal income tax rates for individuals go up to 39.6 percent, and, when Social Security, Medicare, and state and city income taxes are included, the marginal tax rate on an individual's income can easily exceed 50 percent. Business income is also taxed heavily. The income from partnerships and proprietorships is reported by the individual owners as personal income and, consequently, is taxed at federal-plus-state rates going up to 50 percent or more. Corporate profits are subject to federal income tax rates of up to 39 percent, plus state income taxes. Furthermore, corporations pay taxes and then distribute after-tax income to their stockholders as dividends, which are also taxed. So, corporate income is really subject to double taxation. *Because of the magnitude of the tax bite, taxes play a critical role in many financial decisions.*

As this text is being written, Congress and the administration are debating the merits of different changes in the tax laws. Even in the unlikely event that no explicit changes are made in the tax laws, changes will still occur because certain aspects of the tax calculation are tied to the inflation rate. Thus, by the time you read this chapter, tax rates and other factors will almost certainly be different from those we provide. Still, if you understand this section, you will understand the basics of our tax system, and you will know how to operate under the revised tax code.

Taxes are so complicated that university law schools offer master's degrees in taxation to lawyers, many of whom are also CPAs. In a field complicated enough to warrant such detailed study, only the highlights can be covered in a book such as this. This is really enough, though, because business managers and investors should and do rely on tax specialists rather than trusting their own limited knowledge. Still, it is important to know the basic elements of the tax system as a starting point for discussions with tax experts.

Individual Income Taxes

Individuals pay taxes on wages and salaries, on investment income (dividends, interest, and profits from the sale of securities), and on the profits of proprietorships and partnerships. Our tax rates are **progressive**—that is, the higher one's income, the larger the percentage paid in taxes. Table 2-6 gives the tax rates for single individuals and married couples filing joint returns under the rate schedules that were in effect for the 2000 tax year.

1. **Taxable income** is defined as gross income less a set of exemptions and deductions that are spelled out in the instructions to the tax forms individuals must file. When filing a tax return in 2001 for the tax year 2000, each taxpayer receives an exemption of $2,800 for each dependent, including the taxpayer, which reduces taxable income. However, this exemption is indexed to rise with inflation, and the exemption is phased out (taken away) for high-income taxpayers. Also, certain expenses including mortgage interest paid, state and local income taxes, and charitable contributions, can be deducted and thus be used to reduce taxable income, but again, high-income taxpayers lose most of these deductions.
2. The **marginal tax rate** is defined as the tax rate on the last unit of income. Marginal rates begin at 15 percent and rise to 39.6 percent. Note, though, that when

See *Ch 02 Tool Kit.xls* for details.

TABLE 2-6 Individual Tax Rates for the 2000 Tax Year

SINGLE INDIVIDUALS

If Your Taxable Income Is	You Pay This Amount on the Base of the Bracket	Plus This Percentage on the Excess Over the Base	Average Tax Rate at Top of Bracket
Up to $26,250	$ 0	15.0%	15.0%
$26,250–$63,550	3,937.50	28.0	22.6
$63,550–$132,600	14,381.50	31.0	27.0
$132,600–$288,350	35,787.00	36.0	31.9
Over $288,350	91,857.00	39.6	39.6

MARRIED COUPLES FILING JOINT RETURNS

If Your Taxable Income Is	You Pay This Amount on the Base of the Bracket	Plus This Percentage on the Excess Over the Base	Average Tax Rate at Top of Bracket
Up to $43,850	$ 0	15.0%	15.0%
$43,850–$105,950	6,577.50	28.0	22.6
$105,950–$161,450	23,965.50	31.0	25.5
$161,450–$288,350	41,170.50	36.0	30.1
Over $288,350	86,854.50	39.6	39.6

NOTES:

a. These are the tax rates for the 2000 tax year. The income ranges at which each tax rate takes effect, as well as the ranges for the additional taxes discussed below, are indexed with inflation each year, so they will change from those shown in the table.

b. The average tax rate approaches 39.6 percent as taxable income rises without limit. At $1 million of taxable income, the average tax rates for single individuals and married couples filing joint returns are 37.4 percent and 36.9 percent, respectively, while at $10 million they are 39.4 and 39.3 percent, respectively.

c. In 2000, a *personal exemption* of $2,800 per person or dependent could be deducted from gross income to determine taxable income. Thus, a husband and wife with two children would have a 2000 exemption of 4 × $2,800 = $11,200. The amount of the exemption is scheduled to increase with inflation. However, if gross income exceeds certain limits ($193,400 for joint returns and $128,950 for single individuals in 2000), the exemption is phased out, and this has the effect of raising the effective tax rate on incomes over the specified limit by about 0.5 percent per family member, or 2.0 percent for a family of four. In addition, taxpayers can claim *itemized deductions* for charitable contributions and certain other items, but these deductions are reduced if the gross income exceeds $128,950 (for both single individuals and joint returns), and this raises the effective tax rate for high-income taxpayers by another 1 percent or so. The combined effect of the loss of exemptions and the reduction of itemized deductions is about 3 percent, so the marginal federal tax rate for high-income individuals goes up to about 42.6 percent.

In addition, there is the Social Security tax, which amounts to 6.2 percent (12.4 percent for a self-employed person) on up to $76,200 of earned income, plus a 1.45 percent Medicare payroll tax (2.9 percent for self-employed individuals) on *all* earned income. Finally, older high-income taxpayers who receive Social Security payments must pay taxes on 85 percent of their Social Security receipts, up from 50 percent in 1994. All of this pushes the effective tax rate up even further.

consideration is given to the phase-out of exemptions and deductions, to Social Security and Medicare taxes, and to state taxes, the marginal tax rate can exceed 50 percent.

3. One can calculate **average tax rates** from the data in Table 2-6. For example, if Jill Smith, a single individual, had taxable income of $35,000, her tax bill would be $3,937.50 + ($35,000 − $26,250)(0.28) = $3,937.50 + $2,450 = $6,387.50. Her *average tax rate* would be $6,387.50/$35,000 = 18.3% versus a *marginal rate* of 28 percent. If Jill received a raise of $1,000, bringing her income to $36,000, she would have to pay $280 of it as taxes, so her after-tax raise would be $720. In addition, her Social Security and Medicare taxes would increase by $76.50, which would cut her net raise to $643.50.

4. As indicated in the notes to the table, the tax code indexes tax brackets to inflation to avoid the **bracket creep** that occurred several years ago and that in reality raised tax rates substantially.[11]

Taxes on Dividend and Interest Income Dividend and interest income received by individuals is added to their other income and thus is taxed at rates going up to about 50 percent.[12] Because corporations pay dividends out of earnings that have already been taxed, there is *double taxation* of corporate income—income is first taxed at the corporate rate, and when what is left is paid out as dividends, it is taxed again at the personal rate.

It should be noted that under U.S. tax laws, interest on most state and local government bonds, called *municipals* or *"munis,"* is not subject to federal income taxes. Thus, investors get to keep all of the interest received from most municipal bonds but only a fraction of the interest received from bonds issued by corporations or by the U.S. government. This means that a lower-yielding muni can provide the same after-tax return as a higher-yielding corporate bond. For example, a taxpayer in the 39.6 percent marginal tax bracket who could buy a muni that yielded 5.5 percent would have to receive a before-tax yield of 9.11 percent on a corporate or U.S. Treasury bond to have the same after-tax income:

$$\text{Equivalent pre-tax yield on taxable bond} = \frac{\text{Yield on muni}}{1 - \text{Marginal tax rate}}$$

$$= \frac{5.5\%}{1 - 0.396} = 9.11\%.$$

If we know the yield on the taxable bond, we can use the following equation to find the equivalent yield on a muni:

$$\text{Equivalent yield on muni} = \left(\begin{array}{c}\text{Pre-tax yield}\\ \text{on taxable}\\ \text{bond}\end{array}\right)(1 - \text{Marginal tax rate})$$

$$= 9.11\%(1 - 0.396) = 9.11\%(0.604) = 5.5\%.$$

The exemption from federal taxes stems from the separation of federal and state powers, and its primary effect is to help state and local governments borrow at lower rates than they otherwise could.

Munis always yield less than corporate bonds with similar risk, maturity, and liquidity. Because of this, it would make no sense for someone in a zero or very low tax bracket to buy munis. Therefore, most munis are owned by high-bracket investors.

---

[11]For example, if you were single and had a taxable income of \$26,250, your tax bill would be \$3,937.50. Now suppose inflation caused prices to double and your income, being tied to a cost-of-living index, rose to \$52,500. Because our tax rates are progressive, if tax brackets were not indexed, your taxes would jump to \$11,287.50. Your after-tax income would thus increase from \$22,312.50 to \$41,212.50, but, because prices have doubled, your real income would *decline* from \$22,312.50 to \$20,606.25 (calculated as one-half of \$41,212.50). You would be in a higher tax bracket, so you would be paying a higher percentage of your real income in taxes. If this happened to everyone, and if Congress failed to change tax rates sufficiently, real disposable incomes would decline because the federal government would be taking a larger share of the national product. This is called the federal government's "inflation dividend." However, because tax brackets are now indexed, if your income doubled due to inflation, your tax bill would double, but your after-tax real income would remain constant at \$22,312.50. Bracket creep was a real problem until the 1980s, when indexing put an end to it.

[12]You do not pay Social Security and Medicare taxes on interest, dividends, and capital gains, only on earned income, but state taxes are generally imposed on dividends, interest, and capital gains.

Capital Gains versus Ordinary Income Assets such as stocks, bonds, and real estate are defined as *capital assets.* If you buy a capital asset and later sell it for more than your purchase price, the profit is called a **capital gain;** if you suffer a loss, it is called a **capital loss.** An asset sold within one year of the time it was purchased produces a *short-term gain or loss* and one held for more than a year produces a *long-term gain or loss.* Thus, if you buy 100 shares of Disney stock for $42 per share and sell it for $52 per share, you make a capital gain of 100 × $10, or $1,000. However, if you sell the stock for $32 per share, you will have a $1,000 capital loss. Depending on how long you held the stock, you will have a short-term or long-term gain or loss.[13] If you sell the stock for exactly $42 per share, you make neither a gain nor a loss; you simply get your $4,200 back, and no tax is due.

Short-term capital gains are added to such ordinary income as wages, dividends, and interest and are then taxed at the same rate as ordinary income. However, long-term capital gains are taxed differently. The top rate on long-term gains is 20 percent. Thus, if in 2000 you were in the 39.6 percent tax bracket, any short-term gains you earned would be taxed just like ordinary income, but your long-term gains would be taxed at 20 percent. Thus, capital gains on assets held for more than 12 months are better than ordinary income for many people because the tax bite is smaller.[14]

Capital gains tax rates have varied over time, but they have generally been lower than rates on ordinary income. The reason is simple—Congress wants the economy to grow, for growth we need investment in productive assets, and low capital gains tax rates encourage investment. To see why, suppose you owned a company that earned $1 million after corporate taxes. Because it is your company, you could have it pay out the entire $1 million profit as dividends, or you could have it retain and reinvest all or part of the income to expand the business. If it paid dividends, they would be taxable to you at a rate of 39.6 percent. However, if the company reinvests its income, that reinvestment should cause the company's earnings and stock price to increase. Then, if you wait for one year and one day and then sell some of your stock at a now-higher price, you will have earned a capital gain, but it will be taxed at only 20 percent. Further, you can postpone the capital gains tax indefinitely by simply not selling the stock.

It should be clear that the lower tax rate on capital gains encourages investment. The owners of small businesses will want to reinvest income to get capital gains, as will stockholders in large corporations. Individuals with money to invest will understand the tax advantages associated with investing in newly formed companies versus buying bonds, so new ventures will have an easier time attracting equity capital. All in all, lower capital gains tax rates stimulate capital formation and investment.[15]

---

[13] If you have a net capital loss (capital losses exceed capital gains) for the year, you can currently deduct only up to $3,000 of this loss against your other income (for example, salary, interest, and dividends). This $3,000 loss limitation is not applicable to losses on the sale of business assets, which by definition are not capital assets.

[14] For assets acquired after December 31, 2000, and held for more than five years, the capital gains rate is 18 percent. The Tax Code governing capital gains is very complex, and we have illustrated only the most common provision.

[15] Fifty percent of any capital gains on the newly issued stock of certain small companies is excluded from taxation, provided the small-company stock is held for five years or longer. The remaining 50 percent of the gain is taxed at a rate of 20 percent for most taxpayers. Thus, if one bought newly issued stock from a qualifying small company and held it for at least five years, any capital gains would be taxed at a maximum rate of 10 percent for most taxpayers. This provision was designed to help small businesses attract equity capital.

TABLE 2-7 Corporate Tax Rates as of January 2000

If a Corporation's Taxable Income Is	It Pays This Amount on the Base of the Bracket	Plus This Percentage on the Excess over the Base	Average Tax Rate at Top of Bracket
Up to $50,000	$ 0	15%	15.0%
$50,000–$75,000	7,500	25	18.3
$75,000–$100,000	13,750	34	22.3
$100,000–$335,000	22,250	39	34.0
$335,000–$10,000,000	113,900	34	34.0
$10,000,000–$15,000,000	3,400,000	35	34.3
$15,000,000–$18,333,333	5,150,000	38	35.0
Over $18,333,333	6,416,667	35	35.0

CD

See ***Ch 02 Tool Kit.xls*** for details.

Corporate Income Taxes

The corporate tax structure, shown in Table 2-7, is relatively simple. To illustrate, if a firm had $65,000 of taxable income, its tax bill would be

$$\begin{aligned}\text{Taxes} &= \$7{,}500 + 0.25(\$15{,}000)\\ &= \$7{,}500 + \$3{,}750 = \$11{,}250,\end{aligned}$$

and its average tax rate would be $11,250/$65,000 = 17.3%. Note that corporate income above $18,333,333 has an average and marginal tax rate of 35 percent.[16]

Interest and Dividend Income Received by a Corporation Interest income received by a corporation is taxed as ordinary income at regular corporate tax rates. *However, 70 percent of the dividends received by one corporation from another is excluded from taxable income, while the remaining 30 percent is taxed at the ordinary tax rate.*[17] Thus, a corporation earning more than $18,333,333 and paying a 35 percent marginal tax rate

[16]Prior to 1987, many large, profitable corporations such as General Electric and Boeing paid no income taxes. The reasons for this were as follows: (1) expenses, especially depreciation, were defined differently for calculating taxable income than for reporting earnings to stockholders, so some companies reported positive profits to stockholders but losses—hence no taxes—to the Internal Revenue Service; and (2) some companies that did have tax liabilities used various tax credits to offset taxes that would otherwise have been payable. This situation was effectively eliminated in 1987.

The principal method used to eliminate this situation is the Alternative Minimum Tax (AMT). Under the AMT, both corporate and individual taxpayers must figure their taxes in two ways, the "regular" way and the AMT way, and then pay the higher of the two. The AMT is calculated as follows: (1) Figure your regular taxes. (2) Take your taxable income under the regular method and then add back certain items, especially income on certain municipal bonds, depreciation in excess of straight line depreciation, certain research and drilling costs, itemized or standard deductions (for individuals), and a number of other items. (3) The income determined in (2) is defined as AMT income, and it must then be multiplied by the AMT tax rate to determine the tax due under the AMT system. An individual or corporation must then pay the higher of the regular tax or the AMT tax. In 2000, there were two AMT tax rates for individuals (26 percent and 28 percent, depending on the level of AMT income and filing status). Most corporations have an AMT of 20 percent. However, there is no AMT for very small companies, defined as those that have had average sales of less than $5 million for the last three years and whose average sales continue to be less than $7.5 million.

[17]The size of the dividend exclusion actually depends on the degree of ownership. Corporations that own less than 20 percent of the stock of the dividend-paying company can exclude 70 percent of the dividends received; firms that own more than 20 percent but less than 80 percent can exclude 80 percent of the dividends; and firms that own more than 80 percent can exclude the entire dividend payment. We will, in general, assume a 70 percent dividend exclusion.

would pay only (0.30)(0.35) = 0.105 = 10.5% of its dividend income as taxes, so its effective tax rate on dividends received would be 10.5 percent. If this firm had $10,000 in pre-tax dividend income, its after-tax dividend income would be $8,950:

$$\begin{aligned}\text{After-tax income} &= \text{Before-tax income} - \text{Taxes}\\ &= \text{Before-tax income} - (\text{Before-tax income})(\text{Effective tax rate})\\ &= \text{Before-tax income}(1 - \text{Effective tax rate})\\ &= \$10{,}000[1 - (0.30)(0.35)]\\ &= \$10{,}000(1 - 0.105) = \$10{,}000(0.895) = \$8{,}950.\end{aligned}$$

If the corporation pays its own after-tax income out to its stockholders as dividends, the income is ultimately subjected to *triple taxation:* (1) the original corporation is first taxed, (2) the second corporation is then taxed on the dividends it received, and (3) the individuals who receive the final dividends are taxed again. This is the reason for the 70 percent exclusion on intercorporate dividends.

If a corporation has surplus funds that can be invested in marketable securities, the tax factor favors investment in stocks, which pay dividends, rather than in bonds, which pay interest. For example, suppose GE had $100,000 to invest, and it could buy either bonds that paid interest of $8,000 per year or preferred stock that paid dividends of $7,000. GE is in the 35 percent tax bracket; therefore, its tax on the interest, if it bought bonds, would be 0.35($8,000) = $2,800, and its after-tax income would be $5,200. If it bought preferred (or common) stock, its tax would be 0.35[(0.30)($7,000)] = $735, and its after-tax income would be $6,265. Other factors might lead GE to invest in bonds, but the tax factor certainly favors stock investments when the investor is a corporation.[18]

Interest and Dividends Paid by a Corporation A firm's operations can be financed with either debt or equity capital. If it uses debt, it must pay interest on this debt, whereas if it uses equity, it is expected to pay dividends to the equity investors (stockholders). The interest *paid* by a corporation is deducted from its operating income to obtain its taxable income, but dividends paid are not deductible. Therefore, a firm needs $1 of pre-tax income to pay $1 of interest, but if it is in the 40 percent federal-plus-state tax bracket, it must earn $1.67 of pre-tax income to pay $1 of dividends:

$$\frac{\text{Pre-tax income needed}}{\text{to pay \$1 of dividends}} = \frac{\$1}{1 - \text{Tax rate}} = \frac{\$1}{0.60} = \$1.67.$$

Working backward, if a company has $1.67 in pre-tax income, it must pay $0.67 in taxes [(0.4)($1.67) = $0.67]. This leaves it with after-tax income of $1.00.

Table 2-8 shows the situation for a firm with $10 million of assets, sales of $5 million, and $1.5 million of earnings before interest and taxes (EBIT). As shown in Column 1, if the firm were financed entirely by bonds, and if it made interest payments of $1.5 million, its taxable income would be zero, taxes would be zero, and its investors would receive the entire $1.5 million. (The term *investors* includes both stockholders and bondholders.) However, as shown in Column 2, if the firm had no debt and was therefore financed only by stock, all of the $1.5 million of EBIT would be taxable

[18]This illustration demonstrates why corporations favor investing in lower-yielding preferred stocks over higher-yielding bonds. When tax consequences are considered, the yield on the preferred stock, [1 − 0.35(0.30)](7.0%) = 6.265%, is higher than the yield on the bond, (1 − 0.35)(8.0%) = 5.200%. Also, note that corporations are restricted in their use of borrowed funds to purchase other firms' preferred or common stocks. Without such restrictions, firms could engage in *tax arbitrage*, whereby the interest on borrowed funds reduces taxable income on a dollar-for-dollar basis, but taxable income is increased by only $0.30 per dollar of dividend income. Thus, current tax laws reduce the 70 percent dividend exclusion in proportion to the amount of borrowed funds used to purchase the stock.

TABLE 2-8 Returns to Investors under Bond and Stock Financing

See ***Ch 02 Tool Kit.xls*** for details.

	Use Bonds (1)	Use Stock (2)
Sales	$ 5,000,000	$ 5,000,000
Operating costs	3,500,000	3,500,000
Earnings before interest and taxes (EBIT)	$1,500,000	$1,500,000
Interest	1,500,000	0
Taxable income	$ 0	$1,500,000
Federal-plus-state taxes (40%)	0	600,000
After-tax income	$ 0	$ 900,000
Income to investors	$1,500,000	$ 900,000
Rate of return on $10 million of assets	15.0%	9.0%

income to the corporation, the tax would be $1,500,000(0.40) = $600,000, and investors would receive only $0.9 million versus $1.5 million under debt financing. The rate of return to investors on their $10 million investment is therefore much higher if debt is used.

Of course, it is generally not possible to finance exclusively with debt capital, and the risk of doing so would offset the benefits of the higher expected income. *Still, the fact that interest is a deductible expense has a profound effect on the way businesses are financed—our corporate tax system favors debt financing over equity financing.* This point is discussed in more detail in Chapters 11 and 16.

Corporate Capital Gains Before 1987, corporate long-term capital gains were taxed at lower rates than corporate ordinary income, so the situation was similar for corporations and individuals. Under current law, however, corporations' capital gains are taxed at the same rates as their operating income.

Corporate Loss Carry-Back and Carry-Forward Ordinary corporate operating losses can be carried back **(carry-back)** to each of the preceding 2 years and forward **(carry-forward)** for the next 20 years and used to offset taxable income in those years. For example, an operating loss in 2002 could be carried back and used to reduce taxable income in 2000 and 2001, and forward, if necessary, and used in 2003, 2004, and so on, to the year 2022. The loss is typically applied first to the earliest year, then to the next earliest year, and so on, until losses have been used up or the 20-year carry-forward limit has been reached.

To illustrate, suppose Apex Corporation had $2 million of *pre-tax* profits (taxable income) in 2000 and 2001, and then, in 2002, Apex lost $12 million. Also, assume that Apex's federal-plus-state tax rate is 40 percent. As shown in Table 2-9, the company would use the carry-back feature to recompute its taxes for 2000, using $2 million of the 2002 operating losses to reduce the 2000 pre-tax profit to zero. This would permit it to recover the taxes paid in 2000. Therefore, in 2002 Apex would receive a refund of its 2000 taxes because of the loss experienced in 2002. Because $10 million of the unrecovered losses would still be available, Apex would repeat this procedure for 2001. Thus, in 2002 the company would pay zero taxes for 2002 and also would receive a refund for taxes paid in 2000 and 2001. Apex would still have $8 million of unrecovered losses to carry forward, subject to the 20-year limit. This $8 million could be used to offset taxable income. The purpose of this loss treatment is to avoid penalizing corporations whose incomes fluctuate substantially from year to year.

TABLE 2-9 Apex Corporation: Calculation of Loss Carry-Back and Carry-Forward for 2000–2001 Using a $12 Million 2002 Loss

	2000	2001
Original taxable income	$2,000,000	$ 2,000,000
Carry-back credit	– 2,000,000	– 2,000,000
Adjusted profit	$ 0	$ 0
Taxes previously paid (40%)	800,000	800,000
Difference = Tax refund	$ 800,000	$ 800,000
Total refund check received in 2002: $800,000 + $800,000 =	$1,600,000	
Amount of loss carry-forward available for use in 2003–2022:		
2002 loss		$12,000,000
Carry-back losses used		4,000,000
Carry-forward losses still available		$ 8,000,000

CD

See *Ch 02 Tool Kit.xls* for details.

WWW

To learn more about tax havens, check out **http://www.escapeartist.com** for an in-depth analysis into tax havens, including country profiles and indexes of offshore banks and foreign markets.

Improper Accumulation to Avoid Payment of Dividends Corporations could refrain from paying dividends and thus permit their stockholders to avoid personal income taxes on dividends. To prevent this, the Tax Code contains an **improper accumulation** provision that states that earnings accumulated by a corporation are subject to penalty rates *if the purpose of the accumulation is to enable stockholders to avoid personal income taxes.* A cumulative total of $250,000 (the balance sheet item "retained earnings") is by law exempted from the improper accumulation tax for most corporations. This is a benefit primarily to small corporations.

The improper accumulation penalty applies only if the retained earnings in excess of $250,000 are *shown by the IRS to be unnecessary to meet the reasonable needs of the business.* A great many companies do indeed have legitimate reasons for retaining more than $250,000 of earnings. For example, earnings may be retained and used to pay off debt, to finance growth, or to provide the corporation with a cushion against possible cash drains caused by losses. How much a firm should be allowed to accumulate for uncertain contingencies is a matter of judgment. We shall consider this matter again in Chapter 18, which deals with corporate dividend policy.

Consolidated Corporate Tax Returns If a corporation owns 80 percent or more of another corporation's stock, it can aggregate income and file one consolidated tax return; thus, the losses of one company can be used to offset the profits of another. (Similarly, one division's losses can be used to offset another division's profits.) No business ever wants to incur losses (you can go broke losing $1 to save 35¢ in taxes), but tax offsets do help make it more feasible for large, multidivisional corporations to undertake risky new ventures or ventures that will suffer losses during a developmental period.

Taxation of Small Businesses: S Corporations

The Tax Code provides that small businesses that meet certain restrictions as spelled out in the code may be set up as corporations and thus receive the benefits of the corporate form of organization—especially limited liability—yet still be taxed as proprietorships or partnerships rather than as corporations. These corporations are called **S corporations.** ("Regular" corporations are called C corporations.) If a corporation elects S corporation status for tax purposes, all of the business's income is reported as personal income by its stockholders, on a pro rata basis, and thus is taxed at the rates

Tax Havens

Many multinational corporations have found an interesting but controversial way to reduce their tax burdens: By shifting some of their operations to countries with low or nonexistent taxes, they can significantly reduce their total tax bills. Over the years, several countries have passed tax laws that make the countries *tax havens* designed to attract foreign investment. Notable examples include the Bahamas, Grand Cayman, and the Netherlands Antilles.

Rupert Murdoch, chairman of global media giant News Corporation, has in some years paid virtually no taxes on his U.S. businesses, despite the fact that these businesses represent roughly 70 percent of his total operating profit. How has Murdoch been able to reduce his tax burden? By shifting profits to a News Corp. subsidiary that is incorporated in the Netherlands Antilles. As Murdoch puts it, "Moving assets around like that is one of the advantages of being global."

While activities such as Murdoch's are legal, some have questioned their ethics. Clearly, shareholders want corporations to take legal steps to reduce taxes. Indeed, many argue that managers have a fiduciary responsibility to take such actions whenever they are cost effective. Moreover, citizens of the various tax havens benefit from foreign investment. Who loses? Obviously, the United States loses tax revenue whenever a domestic corporation establishes a subsidiary in a tax haven. Ultimately, this loss of tax revenue either reduces services or raises the tax burden on other corporations and individuals. Nevertheless, even the U.S. government is itself somewhat ambivalent about the establishment of off-shore subsidiaries—it does not like to lose tax revenues, but it does like to encourage foreign investment.

that apply to individuals. This is an important benefit to the owners of small corporations in which all or most of the income earned each year will be distributed as dividends, because then the income is taxed only once, at the individual level.

Self-Test Questions

Explain what is meant by this statement: "Our tax rates are progressive."

Are tax rates progressive for all income ranges?

Explain the difference between marginal tax rates and average tax rates.

What is a "municipal bond," and how are these bonds taxed?

What are capital gains and losses, and how are they taxed relative to ordinary income?

How does the federal income tax system treat dividends received by a corporation versus those received by an individual? Why is this distinction made?

What is the difference in the tax treatment of interest and dividends paid by a corporation? Does this factor favor debt or equity financing?

Briefly explain how tax loss carry-back and carry-forward procedures work.

Depreciation

Depreciation plays an important role in income tax calculations—the larger the depreciation, the lower the taxable income and thus the lower the tax bill, hence the higher the cash flow from operations. Congress specifies, in the Tax Code, both the life over which assets can be depreciated for tax purposes and the methods of depreciation that can be used. We will discuss in detail how depreciation is calculated, and how it affects income and cash flows, when we take up capital budgeting in Chapters 13, 14, and 15.

Summary

The primary purposes of this chapter were (1) to describe the basic financial statements, (2) to present some background information on cash flows, and (3) to provide an overview of the federal income tax system. The key concepts covered are listed below.

- The four basic statements contained in the **annual report** are the balance sheet, the income statement, the statement of retained earnings, and the statement of cash flows. Investors use the information provided in these statements to form expectations about the future levels of earnings and dividends, and about the firm's riskiness.
- The **balance sheet** shows assets on the left-hand side and liabilities and equity, or claims against assets, on the right-hand side. (Sometimes assets are shown at the top and claims at the bottom of the balance sheet.) The balance sheet may be thought of as a snapshot of the firm's financial position at a particular point in time.
- The **income statement** reports the results of operations over a period of time, and it shows earnings per share as its "bottom line."
- The **statement of retained earnings** shows the change in retained earnings between balance sheet dates. Retained earnings represent a claim against assets, not assets per se.
- The **statement of cash flows** reports the effect of operating, investing, and financing activities on cash flows over an accounting period.
- **Net cash flow** differs from **accounting profit** because some of the revenues and expenses reflected in accounting profits may not have been received or paid out in cash during the year. Depreciation is typically the largest noncash item, so net cash flow is often expressed as net income plus depreciation. Investors are at least as interested in a firm's projected net cash flow as in reported earnings because it is cash, not paper profit, that is paid out as dividends and plowed back into the business to produce growth.
- **Operating current assets** are the current assets that are used to support operations, such as cash, inventory, and accounts receivable. They do not include short-term investments.
- **Operating current liabilities** are the current liabilities that occur as a natural consequence of operations, such as accounts payable and accruals. They do not include notes payable or any other short-term debts that charge interest.
- **Net operating working capital** is the difference between operating current assets and operating current liabilities. Thus, it is the working capital acquired with investor-supplied funds.
- **Operating long-term assets** are the long-term assets used to support operations, such as net plant and equipment. They do not include any long-term investments that pay interest or dividends.
- **Total operating assets** (or **capital**), or just **operating assets** (or **capital**), is the sum of net operating working capital and operating long-term assets. It is the total amount of capital needed to run the business.
- **NOPAT** is net operating profit after taxes. It is the after-tax profit a company would have if it had no debt and no investments in nonoperating assets. Because it excludes the effects of financial decisions, it is a better measure of operating performance than is net income.
- **Operating cash flow** arises from normal operations, and it is the difference between cash revenues and cash costs, including taxes on operating income. Operating cash flow differs from net cash flow because operating cash flow does not include either interest income or interest expense. It is equal to NOPAT plus any noncash adjustments.

- **Free cash flow (FCF)** is the amount of cash flow remaining after a company makes the asset investments necessary to support operations. In other words, FCF is the amount of cash flow available for distribution to investors, *so the value of a company is directly related to its ability to generate free cash flow.* It is defined as NOPAT minus the net investment in operating capital.
- **Market Value Added (MVA)** represents the difference between the total market value of a firm and the total amount of investor-supplied capital. If the market values of debt and preferred stock equal their values as reported on the financial statements, then MVA is the difference between the market value of a firm's stock and the amount of equity its shareholders have supplied.
- **Economic Value Added (EVA)** is the difference between after-tax operating profit and the total dollar cost of capital, including the cost of equity capital. EVA is an estimate of the value created by management during the year, and it differs substantially from accounting profit because no charge for the use of equity capital is reflected in accounting profit.
- The value of any asset depends on the stream of **after-tax cash flows** it produces. Tax rates and other aspects of our tax system are changed by Congress every year or so.
- In the United States, tax rates are **progressive**—the higher one's income, the larger the percentage paid in taxes.
- Assets such as stocks, bonds, and real estate are defined as **capital assets.** If a capital asset is sold for more than its cost, the profit is called a **capital gain.** If the asset is sold for a loss, it is called a **capital loss.** Assets held for more than a year provide **long-term** gains or losses.
- Operating income paid out as dividends is subject to **double taxation:** the income is first taxed at the corporate level, and then shareholders must pay personal taxes on their dividends.
- Interest income received by a corporation is taxed as **ordinary income;** however, 70 percent of the dividends received by one corporation from another are excluded from **taxable income.** The reason for this exclusion is that corporate dividend income is ultimately subjected to **triple taxation.**
- Because interest paid by a corporation is a **deductible** expense while dividends are not, our tax system favors debt over equity financing.
- Ordinary corporate operating losses can be **carried back** to each of the preceding 2 years and **forward** for the next 20 years and used to offset taxable income in those years.
- **S corporations** are small businesses that have the limited-liability benefits of the corporate form of organization yet are taxed as a partnership or a proprietorship.

Questions

2–1 Define each of the following terms:

a. Annual report; balance sheet; income statement
b. Common stockholders' equity, or net worth; retained earnings
c. Statement of retained earnings; statement of cash flows
d. Depreciation; amortization; EBITDA
e. Operating current assets; operating current liabilities; net operating working capital; operating capital
f. Accounting profit; net cash flow; operating cash flow; NOPAT; free cash flow
g. Market Value Added; Economic Value Added
h. Progressive tax; taxable income
i. Marginal and average tax rates

j. Bracket creep
k. Capital gain or loss
l. Tax loss carry-back and carry-forward
m. Improper accumulation
n. S corporation

2–2 What four statements are contained in most annual reports?

2–3 If a "typical" firm reports $20 million of retained earnings on its balance sheet, could its directors declare a $20 million cash dividend without any qualms whatsoever?

2–4 Explain the following statement: "While the balance sheet can be thought of as a snapshot of the firm's financial position *at a point in time*, the income statement reports on operations *over a period of time*."

2–5 Differentiate between accounting income and net cash flow. Why might these two numbers differ?

2–6 Differentiate between operating cash flow and net cash flow. Why might these two numbers differ?

2–7 What do the numbers on financial statements actually represent?

2–8 Who are some of the basic users of financial statements, and how do they use them?

2–9 What is operating capital, and why is it important?

2–10 Explain the difference between NOPAT and net income. Which is a better measure of the performance of a company's operations?

2–11 What is free cash flow? Why is it the most important measure of cash flow?

2–12 In what way does the Tax Code discourage corporations from paying high dividends to their shareholders?

2–13 What does *double taxation of corporate income* mean?

2–14 If you were starting a business, what tax considerations might cause you to prefer to set it up as a proprietorship or a partnership rather than as a corporation?

2–15 Explain how the federal income tax structure affects the choice of financing (use of debt versus equity) of U.S. business firms.

2–16 For someone planning to start a new business, is the average or the marginal tax rate more relevant?

Self-Test Problems (Solutions Appear in Appendix A)

ST–1 *NET INCOME, CASH FLOW, AND EVA*

Last year Rattner Robotics had $5,000,000 in operating income (EBIT). The company had a Net depreciation expense of $1,000,000 and an interest expense of $1,000,000; its corporate tax rate was 40 percent. The company has $14,000,000 in non-interest-earning current assets and $4,000,000 in non-interest-bearing current liabilities; it has $15,000,000 in net plant and equipment. It estimates that it has an after-tax cost of capital of 10 percent. Assume that Rattner's only noncash item was depreciation.

a. What was the company's net income for the year?
b. What was the company's net cash flow?
c. What was the company's net operating profit after taxes (NOPAT)?
d. What was the company's operating cash flow?
e. If capital in the previous year was $24,000,000, what was the company's free cash flow (FCF) for the year?
f. What was the company's Economic Value Added (EVA)?

ST–2 *EFFECT OF FORM OF ORGANIZATION ON TAXES*

Mary Henderson is planning to start a new business, MH Enterprises, and she must decide whether to incorporate or to do business as a sole proprietorship. Under either form, Henderson will initially own 100 percent of the firm, and tax considerations are important to her. She plans to finance the firm's expected growth by drawing a salary just sufficient for her family living expenses, which she estimates will be about $40,000, and by retaining all other income in the business. Assume that as a married woman with one child, she files a joint return. She has income tax exemptions of 3 × $2,800 = $8,400, and she estimates that her itemized deductions for each of the 3 years will be $9,700. She expects MH Enterprises to grow and to earn income of $52,700 in 2002, $90,000 in 2003, and $150,000 in 2004. Which form of business organization will allow Henderson to pay the lowest taxes (and retain the most income) during the period from 2002 to 2004? Assume that the tax rates given in the chapter are applicable for all future years. (Social Security taxes would also have to be paid, but ignore them.)

Problems

Note: By the time this book is published, Congress might have changed rates and/or other provisions of current tax law—as noted in the chapter, such changes occur fairly often. Work all problems on the assumption that the information in the chapter is applicable.

2–1 INCOME STATEMENT

Little Books Inc. recently reported net income of $3 million. Its operating income (EBIT) was $6 million, and the company pays a 40 percent tax rate. What was the company's interest expense for the year? [Hint: Divide $3 million by (1 − T) = 0.6 to find taxable income.]

2–2 NET CASH FLOW

Kendall Corners Inc. recently reported net income of $3.1 million. The company's depreciation expense was $500,000. What is the company's approximate net cash flow?

2–3 AFTER-TAX YIELD

An investor recently purchased a corporate bond which yields 9 percent. The investor is in the 36 percent tax bracket. What is the bond's after-tax yield?

2–4 PERSONAL TAXES

Joe and Jane Keller are a married couple who file a joint income tax return. The couple's taxable income was $97,000. Ignoring exemptions and deductions, how much federal taxes did they owe? Use the tax tables given in the chapter.

2–5 AFTER-TAX YIELD

Corporate bonds issued by Johnson Corporation currently yield 8 percent. Municipal bonds of equal risk currently yield 6 percent. At what tax rate would an investor be indifferent between these two bonds?

2–6 CORPORATE TAX LIABILITY

The Talley Corporation had a taxable income of $365,000 from operations after all operating costs but before (1) interest charges of $50,000, (2) dividends received of $15,000, (3) dividends paid of $25,000, and (4) income taxes. What is the firm's income tax liability and its after-tax income? What are the company's marginal and average tax rates on taxable income?

2–7 CORPORATE TAX LIABILITY

The Wendt Corporation had $10.5 million of taxable income from operations in 2001.

a. What is the company's federal income tax bill for the year?

b. Assume the firm receives an additional $1 million of interest income from some bonds it owns. What is the tax on this interest income?

c. Now assume that Wendt does not receive the interest income but does receive an additional $1 million as dividends on some stock it owns. What is the tax on this dividend income?

2–8 AFTER-TAX YIELD

The Shrieves Corporation has $10,000 that it plans to invest in marketable securities. It is choosing between AT&T bonds, which yield 7.5 percent, state of Florida muni bonds, which yield 5 percent, and AT&T preferred stock, with a dividend yield of 6 percent. Shrieves' corporate tax rate is 35 percent, and 70 percent of the dividends received are tax exempt. Assuming that the investments are equally risky and that Shrieves chooses strictly on the basis of after-tax returns, which security should be selected? What is the after-tax rate of return on the highest-yielding security?

2–9 AFTER-TAX YIELD

Your personal tax rate is 36 percent. You can invest in either corporate bonds that yield 9 percent or municipal bonds (of equal risk) that yield 7 percent. Which investment should you choose? (Ignore state income taxes.)

2–10 CASH FLOW

The Klaven Corporation has operating income (EBIT) of $750,000. The company's depreciation expense is $200,000. Klaven is 100 percent equity financed, and it faces a 40 percent tax rate. What is the company's net income? What is its net cash flow? What is its operating cash flow?

2–11 BALANCE SHEET

Which of the following actions will, all else equal, increase the amount of cash on a company's balance sheet?

a. The company issues $2 million in new common stock.
b. The company invests $3 million in new plant and equipment.
c. The company generates negative net income and negative net cash flow during the year.
d. The company increases the dividend paid on its common stock.

2–12 FINANCIAL STATEMENTS

The Smythe-Davidson Corporation just issued its annual report. The current year's balance sheet and income statement as they appeared in the annual report are given below. Answer the questions that follow based on information given in the financial statements.

a. Assume that all of the firm's revenues were received in cash during the year and that all costs except depreciation were paid in cash during the year. What is the firm's net cash flow available to common stockholders for the year? How is this number different from the accounting profit reported by the firm?
b. Construct the firm's Statement of Retained Earnings for December 31, 2001.
c. How much money has the firm reinvested in itself over the years instead of paying out dividends?
d. At the present time, how large a check could the firm write without it bouncing?
e. How much money must the firm pay its current creditors within the next year?

Smythe-Davidson Corporation: Balance Sheet as of December 31, 2001
(Millions of Dollars)

Assets		*Liabilities and Equity*	
Cash and equivalents	$ 15	Accounts payable	$ 120
Accounts receivable	515	Notes payable	220
Inventories	880	Accruals	280
Total current assets	$1,410	Total current liabilities	$ 620
Net plant and equipment	2,590	Long-term bonds	1,520
		Total debt	$2,140
		Preferred stock (800,000 shares)	80
		Common stock (100 million shares)	260
		Retained earnings	1,520
		Common equity	$1,780
Total assets	$4,000	Total liabilities and equity	$4,000

Smythe-Davidson Corporation: Income Statement for Year Ending December 31, 2001
(Millions of Dollars)

Sales	$6,250
Operating costs excluding depreciation	5,230
Depreciation	220
EBIT	$ 800
Less: Interest	180
EBT	$ 620
Taxes (40%)	248
Net income before preferred dividends	372
Preferred dividends	8
Net income available to common stockholders	$ 364
Common dividends paid	$ 146
Earnings per share	$ 3.64

2–13 INCOME AND CASH FLOW ANALYSIS

The Menendez Corporation expects to have sales of $12 million in 2002. Costs other than depreciation are expected to be 75 percent of sales, and depreciation is expected to be $1.5 million. All sales revenues will be collected in cash, and costs other than depreciation must be paid for during the year. Menendez's federal-plus-state tax rate is 40 percent.

a. Set up an income statement. What is Menendez's expected net cash flow?

b. Suppose Congress changed the tax laws so that Menendez's depreciation expenses doubled. No changes in operations occurred. What would happen to reported profit and to net cash flow?

c. Now suppose that Congress, instead of doubling Menendez's depreciation, reduced it by 50 percent. How would profit and net cash flow be affected?

d. If this were your company, would you prefer Congress to cause your depreciation expense to be doubled or halved? Why?

e. In the situation in which depreciation doubled, would this possibly have an adverse effect on the company's stock price and on its ability to borrow money?

2–14 INCOME STATEMENT

Last year Martin Motors reported the following income statement:

Sales	$2,000,000
Cost of goods sold	1,200,000
Depreciation	500,000
Total operating costs	$1,700,000
Operating income (EBIT)	$ 300,000
Interest expense	100,000
Taxable income (EBT)	$ 200,000
Taxes (40%)	80,000
Net income	$ 120,000

The company's CEO, Joe Lawrence, was unhappy with the firm's performance. This year, he would like to see net income doubled to $240,000. Depreciation, interest expense, and tax rate will all remain constant, and the cost of goods sold will also remain at 60 percent of sales. How much sales revenue must the company generate to achieve the CEO's net income target?

2–15 FREE CASH FLOW

You have just obtained financial information for the past 2 years for Powell Panther Corporation. Answer the following questions.

a. What is the net operating profit after taxes (NOPAT) for 2001?

b. What are the amounts of net operating working capital for 2000 and 2001?

c. What are the amounts of total operating capital for 2000 and 2001?

d. What is the free cash flow for 2001?

e. How can you explain the large increase in dividends in 2001?

Powell Panther Corporation: Income Statements for Year Ending December 31 (Millions of Dollars)

	2001	2000
Sales	$1,200.0	$1,000.0
Operating costs excluding depreciation	1,020.0	850.0
Depreciation	30.0	25.0
Earnings before interest and taxes	$ 150.0	$ 125.0
Less interest	21.7	20.2
Earnings before taxes	$ 128.3	$ 104.8
Taxes (40%)	51.3	41.9
Net income available to common stockholders	$ 77.0	$ 62.9
Common dividends	60.5	4.4

Powell Panther Corporation: Balance Sheets as of December 31 (Millions of Dollars)

	2001	2000
Assets		
Cash and equivalents	$ 12.0	$ 10.0
Short-term investments	0.0	0.0
Accounts receivable	180.0	150.0
Inventories	180.0	200.0
Total current assets	$372.0	$360.0
Net plant and equipment	300.0	250.0
Total assets	$672.0	$610.0
Liabilities and Equity		
Accounts payable	$108.0	$ 90.0
Notes payable	67.0	51.5
Accruals	72.0	60.0
Total current liabilities	$247.0	$201.5
Long-term bonds	150.0	150.0
Total debt	$397.0	$351.5
Common stock (50 million shares)	50.0	50.0
Retained earnings	225.0	208.5
Common equity	$275.0	$258.5
Total liabilities and equity	$672.0	$610.0

2–16 LOSS CARRY-BACK, CARRY-FORWARD

The Herrmann Company has made $150,000 before taxes during each of the last 15 years, and it expects to make $150,000 a year before taxes in the future. However, in 2001 the firm incurred a loss of $650,000. The firm will claim a tax credit at the time it files its 2001 income tax return, and it will receive a check from the U.S. Treasury. Show how it calculates this credit, and then indicate the firm's tax liability for each of the next 5 years. Assume a 40 percent tax rate on *all* income to ease the calculations.

2–17 LOSS CARRY-BACK, CARRY-FORWARD

The projected taxable income of the McAlhany Corporation, formed in 2002 is indicated in the table below. (Losses are shown in parentheses.) What is the corporate tax liability for each year? Assume a constant federal-plus-state tax rate of 40 percent.

Year	Taxable Income
2002	($95,000,000)
2003	70,000,000
2004	55,000,000
2005	80,000,000
2006	(150,000,000)

2–18 FORM OF ORGANIZATION

Susan Visscher has operated her small restaurant as a sole proprietorship for several years, but projected changes in her business's income have led her to consider incorporating. Visscher is married and has two children. Her family's only income, an annual salary of $52,000, is from operating the business. (The business actually earns more than $52,000, but Susan reinvests the additional earnings in the business.) She itemizes deductions, and she is able to deduct $8,600. These deductions, combined with her four personal exemptions for 4 × $2,800 = $11,200, give her a taxable income of $52,000 − $8,600 − $11,200. (Assume the personal exemption remains at $2,800.) Of course, her actual taxable income, if she does not incorporate, would be higher by the amount of reinvested income. Visscher estimates that her business earnings before salary and taxes for the period 2002 to 2004 will be:

Year	Earnings before Salary and Taxes
2002	$ 70,000
2003	95,000
2004	110,000

a. What would her total taxes (corporate plus personal) be in each year under
(1) A non-S corporate form of organization? (2002 tax = $7,530.)
(2) A proprietorship? (2002 tax = $8,355.50.)
b. Should Visscher incorporate? Discuss.

2–19 *PERSONAL TAXES*

Mary Jarvis, a single individual, has this situation for the year 2001: salary of $82,000; dividend income of $12,000; interest on Disney bonds of $5,000; interest on state of Florida municipal bonds of $10,000; proceeds of $22,000 from the sale of Disney stock purchased in 1984 at a cost of $9,000; and proceeds of $22,000 from the November 2001 sale of Disney stock purchased in October 2001 at a cost of $21,000. Jarvis gets one exemption ($2,800), and she has allowable itemized deductions of $4,900; these amounts will be deducted from her gross income to determine her taxable income.

a. What is Jarvis's federal tax liability for 2001?
b. What are her marginal and average tax rates?
c. If she had $5,000 to invest and was offered a choice of either state of Florida bonds with a yield of 6 percent or more Disney bonds with a yield of 8 percent, which should she choose, and why?
d. At what marginal tax rate would Jarvis be indifferent in her choice between the Florida and Disney bonds?

Spreadsheet Problems

2–20 *BUILD A MODEL: FINANCIAL STATEMENTS, EVA, AND MVA*

Start with the partial model in the file ***Ch 02-20 Build a Model.xls*** from the textbook's CD-ROM. Cumberland Industries' 2000 and 2001 balance sheets (in thousands of dollars) are shown below and in the partial model in the file:

	2001	2000
Cash	$ 91,450	$ 74,625
Short-term investments	11,400	15,100
Accounts receivable	103,365	85,527
Inventories	38,444	34,982
Total current assets	$244,659	$210,234
Net fixed assets	67,165	42,436
Total assets	$311,824	$252,670
Accounts payable	$ 30,761	$ 23,109
Accruals	30,477	22,656
Notes payable	16,717	14,217
Total current liabilities	$ 77,955	$ 59,982
Long-term debt	76,264	63,914
Total liabilities	$154,219	$123,896
Common stock	100,000	90,000
Retained earnings	57,605	38,774
Total common equity	$157,605	$128,774
Total liabilities and equity	$311,824	$252,670

a. The company's sales for 2001 were $455,150,000, and EBITDA was 15 percent of sales. Furthermore, depreciation amounted to 11 percent of net fixed assets, interest charges were $8,575,000, the state-plus-federal corporate tax rate was 40 percent, and Cumberland pays 40 percent of its net income out in dividends. Given this information, construct Cumberland's 2001 income statement. (Hint: Start with the partial model in the file.)

b. Next, construct the firm's statement of retained earnings for the year ending December 31, 2001, and then its 2001 statement of cash flows.

c. Calculate net operating working capital, total operating capital, net operating profit after taxes, operating cash flow, and free cash flow for 2001.

d. Calculate the firm's EVA and MVA for 2001. Assume that Cumberland had 10 million shares outstanding, that the year-end closing stock price was $17.25 per share, and its after-tax cost of capital was 12 percent.

2–21 *WHAT IF ANALYSIS: FORM OF ORGANIZATION*

Start with the model in the file ***Ch 02-21 What If Analysis.xls*** from the textbook's CD-ROM and answer the questions shown there.

Cyberproblem

The information related to the cyberproblems is likely to change over time, due to the release of new information and the ever-changing nature of the World Wide Web. With these changes in mind, we will periodically update these problems on the textbook's web site.

2–22 *FINANCIAL STATEMENTS, CASH FLOW, AND TAXES*

A manager's primary goal is to maximize the value of his or her firm's stock. The stock's value is calculated as the present value of the firm's future cash flow stream. A study of a firm's financial statements provides clues to its past, present, and likely future performance. Managers must understand financial statements because their actions have a direct impact on them. Managers and investors alike need to know how to read and interpret financial statements.

Let's examine Minnesota Mining and Manufacturing (otherwise known as 3M) Company's financial statements. Take a look at the Cyberproblem on the textbook's web site **http://www.harcourtcollege.com/finance/theory/student/resources/cyberprob/Ch02.html,** and answer the questions shown there.

Mini Case

See ***Ch 02 Show.ppt*** for a *PowerPoint* presentation of the Mini Case and ***Ch 02 Mini Case.xls*** for detailed calculations.

Donna Jamison, a 1997 graduate of the University of Tennessee with four years of banking experience, was recently brought in as assistant to the chairman of the board of Computron Industries, a manufacturer of electronic calculators.

The company doubled its plant capacity, opened new sales offices outside its home territory, and launched an expensive advertising campaign. Computron's results were not satisfactory, to put it mildly. Its board of directors, which consisted of its president and vice-president plus its major stockholders (who were all local businesspeople), was most upset when directors learned how the expansion was going. Suppliers were being paid late and were unhappy, and the bank was complaining about the deteriorating situation and threatening to cut off credit. As a result, Al Watkins, Computron's president, was informed that changes would have to be made, and quickly, or he would be fired. Also, at the board's insistence Donna Jamison was brought in and given the job of assistant to Fred Campo, a retired banker who was Computron's chairman and largest stockholder. Campo agreed to give up a few of his golfing days and to help nurse the company back to health, with Jamison's help.

Jamison began by gathering financial statements and other data.

BALANCE SHEETS

	2001	2000
Assets		
Cash	$ 7,282	$ 9,000
Short-term investments	0	48,600
Accounts receivable	632,160	351,200
Inventories	1,287,360	715,200
Total current assets	$1,926,802	$1,124,000
Gross fixed assets	1,202,950	491,000
Less accumulated depreciation	263,160	146,200
Net fixed assets	$ 939,790	$ 344,800
Total assets	$2,866,592	$1,468,800

BALANCE SHEETS

	2001	2000
Liabilities and Equity		
Accounts payable	$ 524,160	$ 145,600
Notes payable	720,000	200,000
Accruals	489,600	136,000
Total current liabilities	$1,733,760	$ 481,600
Long-term debt	1,000,000	323,432
Common stock (100,000 shares)	460,000	460,000
Retained earnings	(327,168)	203,768
Total equity	$ 132,832	$ 663,768
Total liabilities and equity	$2,866,592	$1,468,800

INCOME STATEMENTS

	2001	2000
Sales	$5,834,400	$3,432,000
Cost of goods sold	5,728,000	2,864,000
Other expenses	680,000	340,000
Depreciation	116,960	18,900
Total operating costs	$6,524,960	$3,222,900
EBIT	($ 690,560)	$ 209,100
Interest expense	176,000	62,500
EBT	($ 866,560)	$ 146,600
Taxes (40%)	(346,624)	58,640
Net income	($ 519,936)	$ 87,960
EPS	($ 5.199)	$ 0.880
DPS	$ 0.110	$ 0.220
Book value per share	$ 1.328	$ 6.638
Stock price	$ 2.25	$ 8.50
Shares outstanding	100,000	100,000
Tax rate	40.00%	40.00%
Lease payments	40,000	40,000
Sinking fund payments	0	0

STATEMENT OF RETAINED EARNINGS, 2001

Balance of retained earnings, 12/31/00	$ 203,768
Add: Net income, 2001	(519,936)
Less: Dividends paid	(11,000)
Balance of retained earnings, 12/31/01	($ 327,168)

STATEMENT OF CASH FLOWS, 2001

Operating Activities	
Net Income	($ 519,936)
Adjustments:	
Noncash adjustments:	
Depreciation	116,960
Changes in working capital:	
Change in accounts receivable	(280,960)
Change in inventories	(572,160)
Change in accounts payable	378,560
Change in accruals	353,600
Net cash provided by operating activities	($ 523,936)
Long-Term Investing Activities	
Cash used to acquire fixed assets	($ 711,950)
Financing Activities	
Change in short-term investments	$ 48,600
Change in notes payable	520,000
Change in long-term debt	676,568
Payment of cash dividends	(11,000)
Net cash provided by financing activities	$1,234,168
Sum: Net change in cash	(1,718)
Plus: Cash at beginning of year	$ 9,000
Cash at end of year	$ 7,282

Assume that you are Jamison's assistant, and you must help her answer the following questions for Campo. (Note: We will continue with this case in Chapter 3, and you will feel more comfortable with the analysis there, but answering these questions will help prepare you for Chapter 3. Provide clear explanations, not just yes or no answers!)

a. What effect did the expansion have on sales, net operating profit after taxes (NOPAT), net operating working capital, capital, and net income?

b. What effect did the expansion have on net cash flow, operating cash flow, and free cash flow?

c. Jamison also has asked you to estimate Computron's EVA. She estimates that the after-tax cost of capital was 11 percent in 2000 and 13 percent in 2001.

d. Looking at Computron's stock price today, would you conclude that the expansion increased or decreased MVA?

e. Computron purchases materials on 30-day terms, meaning that it is supposed to pay for purchases within 30 days of receipt. Judging from its 2001 balance sheet, do you think Computron pays suppliers on time? Explain. If not, what problems might this lead to?

f. Computron spends money for labor, materials, and fixed assets (depreciation) to make products, and still more money to sell those products. Then, it makes sales that result in receivables, which eventually result in cash inflows. Does it appear that Computron's sales price exceeds its costs per unit sold? How does this affect the cash balance?

g. Suppose Computron's sales manager told the sales staff to start offering 60-day credit terms rather than the 30-day terms now being offered. Computron's competitors react by offering similar terms, so sales remain constant. What effect would this have on the cash account? How would the cash account be affected if sales doubled as a result of the credit policy change?

h. Can you imagine a situation in which the sales price exceeds the cost of producing and selling a unit of output, yet a dramatic increase in sales volume causes the cash balance to decline?

i. In general, could a company like Computron increase sales without a corresponding increase in inventory and other assets? Would the asset increase occur before the increase in sales, and, if so, how would that affect the cash account and the statement of cash flows?

j. Did Computron finance its expansion program with internally generated funds (additions to retained earnings plus depreciation) or with external capital? How does the choice of financing affect the company's financial strength?

k. Refer to the income statements and the statement of cash flows. Suppose Computron broke even in 2001 in the sense that sales revenues equaled total operating costs plus interest charges. Would the asset expansion have caused the company to experience a cash shortage which required it to raise external capital?

l. If Computron started depreciating fixed assets over 7 years rather than 10 years, would that affect (1) the physical stock of assets, (2) the balance sheet account for fixed assets, (3) the company's reported net income, and (4) its cash position? Assume the same depreciation method is used for stockholder reporting and for tax calculations, and the accounting change has no effect on assets' physical lives.

m. Explain how (1) inventory valuation methods, (2) the accounting policy regarding expensing versus capitalizing research and development, and (3) the policy with regard to funding future retirement plan costs (retirement pay and retirees' health benefits) could affect the financial statements.

n. Computron's stock sells for $2.25 per share even though the company had large losses. Does the positive stock price indicate that some investors are irrational?

o. Computron followed the standard practice of paying dividends on a quarterly basis. It paid a dividend during the first two quarters of 2001, then eliminated the dividend when management realized that a loss would be incurred for the year. The dividend was cut before the losses were announced, and at that point the stock price fell from $8.50 to $3.50. Why would an $0.11, or even a $0.22, dividend reduction lead to a $5.00 stock price reduction?

p. Explain how earnings per share, dividends per share, and book value per share are calculated, and what they mean. Why does the market price per share *not* equal the book value per share?

q. How much new money did Computron borrow from its bank during 2001? How much additional credit did its suppliers extend? Its employees and the taxing authorities?

r. If you were Computron's banker, or the credit manager of one of its suppliers, would you be worried about your job? If you were a current Computron employee, a retiree, or a stockholder, should you be concerned?

s. The 2001 income statement shows negative taxes, that is, a tax credit. How much taxes would the company have had to pay in the past to actually get this credit? If taxes paid within the last 2 years had been less than $346,624, what would have happened? Would this have affected the statement of cash flows and the ending cash balance?

t. Working with Jamison has required you to put in a lot of overtime, so you have had very little time to spend on your private finances. It's now April 1, and you have only two weeks left to file your income tax return. You have managed to get all the information together that you will need to complete your return. Computron paid you a salary of $45,000, and you received $3,000 in dividends from common stock that you own. You are single, so your personal exemption is $2,800, and your itemized deductions are $4,550.

(1) On the basis of the information above and the individual tax rate schedule shown in the chapter, what is your tax liability?

(2) What are your marginal and average tax rates?

u. Assume that a corporation has $100,000 of taxable income from operations plus $5,000 of interest income and $10,000 of dividend income. What is the company's tax liability?

v. Assume that after paying your personal income tax as calculated in part t, you have $5,000 to invest. You have narrowed your investment choices down to California bonds with a yield of 7 percent or equally risky Exxon Mobil bonds with a yield of 10 percent. Which one should you choose and why? At what marginal tax rate would you be indifferent to the choice between California and Exxon Mobil bonds?

Selected Additional References

The effects of alternative accounting policies on financial statements are discussed in the investment textbooks referenced in Chapter 5 and also in the many excellent texts on financial statement analysis. For example, see

Fraser, Lyn M., *Understanding Financial Statements* (Englewood Cliffs, NJ: Prentice-Hall, 1992).

Gibson, Charles H., and Patricia A. Frishkoff, *Financial Statement Analysis* (Boston: Kent, 1986).

Hawkins, David E., *Corporate Financial Reporting and Analysis* (Homewood, IL.: Irwin, 1986).

For an excellent treatment of the relationship between free cash flows and the value of a company, see

Copeland, Tom, Tim Koller, and Jack Murrin, *Valuation: Measuring and Managing the Value of Companies* (New York: John Wiley & Sons, Inc., 1992).

Stewart, G. Bennett, *The Quest for Value* (New York: Harper Collins, 1991). Stewart is a founding partner of the consulting firm Stern Stewart & Co.

The following articles provide additional information on the effect of corporate taxes on business behavior:

Angell, Robert J., and Tony Wingler, "A Note on Expensing versus Depreciating under the Accelerated Cost Recovery System," *Financial Management*, Winter 1982, 34–35.

Comiskey, Eugene E., and James R. Hasselback, "Analyzing the Profit and Tax Relationship," *Financial Management*, Winter 1973, 57–62.

McCarty, Daniel E., and William R. McDaniel, "A Note on Expensing versus Depreciating under the Accelerated Cost Recovery System: Comment," *Financial Management*, Summer 1983, 37–39.

For a good reference guide to tax issues, see

Federal Tax Course (Englewood Cliffs, NJ: Prentice-Hall, published annually).

3

Analysis of Financial Statements

On May 19, 1999, Dell Computer Corp. announced that its first quarter earnings were 42 percent higher than those reported one year earlier. This dramatic increase in earnings was roughly in line with Wall Street projections. Nevertheless, Dell's stock fell nearly $4 a share immediately after the announcement.

At first glance, the market's response appears puzzling. However, analysts zeroed in on the fact that Dell's profit margin in the first quarter had fallen considerably. In recent months the computer business had become a lot more competitive, and this increased competition had pushed down computer prices. Dell's earnings report indicated that lower prices for consumers had lowered margins for Dell's shareholders.

Still, Dell stockholders have done fantastically well over the past ten years. A $10,000 investment in Dell in early 1989 would be worth over $5 million today. So, while Dell's increased earnings might suggest that the stock will continue to do well, the lower margins raised concerns that earnings growth in the years ahead might be lower than previously expected.

Wall Street's response to Dell's announced earnings brings home several important points. First, investors and others outside the company use reported earnings and other financial statement data to determine a company's value. Second, analysts are primarily concerned about *future* performance—past performance is useful only to the extent that it provides information about the company's future. Finally, analysts go beyond reported profits—they dig into the financial statements.

So, while many people regard financial statements as "just accounting," they are really much more. As you will see in this chapter, the statements provide a wealth of information that is used by managers, investors, lenders, customers, suppliers, and regulators. An analysis of its statements can highlight a company's strengths and shortcomings, and this information can be used by management to improve performance and by others to predict future results. Financial analysis can be used to predict how such strategic decisions as the sale of a division, a major marketing program, or expanding a plant are likely to affect future financial performance.

The primary goal of financial managers is to maximize the stock price, not ac measures such as net income or EPS. However, accounting data do influence stoc prices, and to understand why a company is performing the way it is and to forecast where it is heading, one needs to evaluate the accounting statements. Chapter 2 described the primary financial statements and showed how they change as a firm's operations undergo change. Now, in Chapter 3, we show how financial statements are used by managers to improve performance, by lenders to evaluate the likelihood of collecting on loans, and by stockholders to forecast earnings, dividends, free cash flow, and stock prices.

CD

The textbook's CD-ROM contains an *Excel* file that will guide you through the chapter's calculations. The file for this chapter is ***Ch 03 Tool Kit.xls,*** and we encourage you to open the file and follow along as you read the chapter.

If management is to maximize a firm's value, it must take advantage of the firm's strengths and correct its weaknesses. Financial statement analysis involves (1) comparing the firm's performance with that of other firms in the same industry and (2) evaluating trends in the firm's financial position over time. These studies help managers identify deficiencies and then take actions to improve performance. In this chapter, we focus on how financial managers (and investors) evaluate a firm's current financial position. Then, in the remaining chapters, we examine the types of actions managers can take to improve future performance and thus increase a firm's stock price.

This chapter should, for the most part, be a review of concepts you learned in accounting. However, accounting focuses on how financial statements are *made*, whereas our focus is on how they are *used* by management to improve performance and by investors when they evaluate the firm's stock and bonds.

Ratio Analysis

Financial statements report both on a firm's position at a point in time and on its operations over some past period. However, the real value of financial statements lies in the fact that they can be used to help predict future earnings, dividends, and free cash flow. From an investor's standpoint, *predicting the future is what financial statement analysis is all about*, while from management's standpoint, *financial statement analysis is useful both to help anticipate future conditions and, more important, as a starting point for planning actions that will improve the firm's future performance.*

Financial ratios are designed to help evaluate a financial statement. For example, Firm A might have debt of $5,248,760 and interest charges of $419,900, while Firm B might have debt of $52,647,980 and interest charges of $3,948,600. Which company is stronger? The burden of these debts, and the companies' ability to repay them, can best be evaluated by comparing (1) each firm's debt to its assets and (2) the interest it must pay to the income it has available for payment of interest. Such comparisons are made by *ratio analysis.*

We will calculate the Year 2001 financial ratios for MicroDrive Inc., using data from the balance sheets and income statements given in Tables 2-1 and 2-2 back in Chapter 2. We will also evaluate the ratios in relation to the industry averages. Note that dollar amounts are in millions.

Liquidity Ratios

A **liquid asset** is one that trades in an active market and hence can be quickly converted to cash at the going market price, and a firm's "liquidity ratios" deal with this question: Will the firm be able to pay off its debts as they come due over the next year or so? As shown in Table 2-1 in Chapter 2, MicroDrive has debts totaling $310 million that must be paid off within the coming year. Will it have trouble satisfying those obligations? A full liquidity analysis requires the use of cash budgets, but by relating the amount of cash and other current assets to current obligations, ratio analysis provides a quick, easy-to-use measure of liquidity. Two commonly used **liquidity ratios** are discussed in this section.

Ability to Meet Short-Term Obligations: The Current Ratio

The **current ratio** is calculated by dividing current assets by current liabilities:

$$\text{Current ratio} = \frac{\text{Current assets}}{\text{Current liabilities}}$$

$$= \frac{\$1{,}000}{\$310} = 3.2 \text{ times.}$$

$$\text{Industry average} = 4.2 \text{ times.}$$

Current assets normally include cash, marketable securities, accounts receivable, and inventories. Current liabilities consist of accounts payable, short-term notes payable, current maturities of long-term debt, accrued taxes, and other accrued expenses (principally wages).

MicroDrive has a lower current ratio than the average for its industry. Is this good or bad? Sometimes the answer depends on who is asking the question. For example, suppose a supplier is trying to decide whether to extend credit to MicroDrive. In general, creditors like to see a high current ratio. If a company is getting into financial difficulty, it will begin paying its bills (accounts payable) more slowly, borrowing from its bank, and so on, so its current liabilities will be increasing. If current liabilities are rising faster than current assets, the current ratio will fall, and this could spell trouble. Because the current ratio provides the best single indicator of the extent to which the claims of short-term creditors are covered by assets that are expected to be converted to cash fairly quickly, it is the most commonly used measure of short-term solvency.

MicroDrive's current ratio is well below the average for its industry, 4.2, so its liquidity position is relatively weak. Still, since current assets are scheduled to be converted to cash in the near future, it is likely that they could be liquidated at close to their stated value. With a current ratio of 3.2, MicroDrive could liquidate current assets at only 31 percent of book value and still pay off current creditors in full.[1]

Now consider the current ratio from the perspective of a shareholder. A high current ratio could mean that the company has a lot of money tied up in nonproductive assets, such as excess cash or marketable securities, or in inventory. In fact, it was Chrysler's buildup of marketable securities that led to a confrontation between management and Kirk Kerkorian, who owned 15 percent of Chrysler's stock. Kerkorian and Lee Iacocca, Chrysler's former CEO, said that funds should be reinvested in the company's operations or else returned to shareholders. Chrysler's management disagreed, arguing that funds were needed to weather possible future economic downturns. While the situation was not resolved to the complete satisfaction of Kerkorian and Iacocca, Chrysler did reduce its security holdings, and its stock rose.

Although industry average figures are discussed later in some detail, it should be noted that an industry average is not a magic number that all firms should strive to maintain—in fact, some very well-managed firms will be above the average while other good firms will be below it. However, if a firm's ratios are far removed from the averages for its industry, this is a red flag, and analysts should be concerned about why the variance occurs. For example, suppose a low current ratio is traced to low inventories. Is this a competitive advantage resulting from the firm's mastery of just-in-time inventory management, or an Achilles heel that is causing the firm to miss shipments

[1] 1/3.2 = 0.31, or 31 percent. Note that 0.31($1,000) = $310, the amount of current liabilities.

and lose sales? Ratio analysis doesn't answer such questions, but it does point to areas of potential concern.

Quick, or Acid Test, Ratio

The **quick, or acid test, ratio** is calculated by deducting inventories from current assets and then dividing the remainder by current liabilities:

$$\text{Quick, or acid test, ratio} = \frac{\text{Current assets} - \text{Inventories}}{\text{Current liabilities}}$$

$$= \frac{\$385}{\$310} = 1.2 \text{ times.}$$

$$\text{Industry average} = 2.1 \text{ times.}$$

Inventories are typically the least liquid of a firm's current assets, hence they are the current assets on which losses are most likely to occur in a bankruptcy. Therefore, a measure of the firm's ability to pay off short-term obligations without relying on the sale of inventories is important.

The industry average quick ratio is 2.1, so MicroDrive's 1.2 ratio is low in comparison with other firms in its industry. Still, if the accounts receivable can be collected, the company can pay off its current liabilities without having to liquidate its inventory.

Self-Test Questions

Identify two ratios that are used to analyze a firm's liquidity position, and write out their equations.

What are the characteristics of a liquid asset? Give some examples.

Which current asset is typically the least liquid?

Asset Management Ratios

The second group of ratios, the **asset management ratios,** measure how effectively the firm is managing its assets. These ratios are designed to answer this question: Does the total amount of each type of asset as reported on the balance sheet seem reasonable, too high, or too low in view of current and projected sales levels? If a company has excessive investments in assets, then its operating assets and capital will be unduly high, which will reduce its free cash flow and its stock price. On the other hand, if a company does not have enough assets, it will lose sales, which will hurt profitability, free cash flow, and the stock price. Therefore, it is important to have the *right* amount invested in assets. Ratios that analyze the different types of assets are described in this section.

Evaluating Inventories: The Inventory Turnover Ratio

The **inventory turnover ratio** is defined as sales divided by inventories:

$$\text{Inventory turnover ratio} = \frac{\text{Sales}}{\text{Inventories}}$$

$$= \frac{\$3{,}000}{\$615} = 4.9 \text{ times.}$$

$$\text{Industry average} = 9.0 \text{ times.}$$

As a rough approximation, each item of MicroDrive's inventory is sold out and restocked, or "turned over," 4.9 times per year. "Turnover" is a term that originated many years ago with the old Yankee peddler, who would load up his wagon with goods, then go off to peddle his wares. The merchandise was called "working capital" because it was what he actually sold, or "turned over," to produce his profits, whereas his "turnover" was the number of trips he took each year. Annual sales divided by inventory equaled turnover, or trips per year. If he made 10 trips per year, stocked 100 pans, and made a gross profit of \$5 per pan, his annual gross profit would be (100)(\$5)(10) = \$5,000. If he went faster and made 20 trips per year, his gross profit would double, other things held constant. So, his turnover directly affected his profits.

MicroDrive's turnover of 4.9 times is much lower than the industry average of 9 times. This suggests that MicroDrive is holding too much inventory. Excess inventory is, of course, unproductive, and it represents an investment with a low or zero rate of return. MicroDrive's low inventory turnover ratio also makes us question the current ratio. With such a low turnover, we must wonder whether the firm is actually holding obsolete goods not worth their stated value.[2]

Note that sales occur over the entire year, whereas the inventory figure is for one point in time. For this reason, it is better to use an average inventory measure.[3] If the firm's business is highly seasonal, or if there has been a strong upward or downward sales trend during the year, it is especially useful to make some such adjustment. To maintain comparability with industry averages, however, we did not use the average inventory figure.

Evaluating Receivables: The Days Sales Outstanding

Days sales outstanding (DSO), also called the "average collection period" (ACP), is used to appraise accounts receivable, and it is calculated by dividing accounts receivable by average daily sales to find the number of days' sales that are tied up in receivables. Thus, the DSO represents the average length of time that the firm must wait after making a sale before receiving cash, which is the average collection period. MicroDrive has 45 days sales outstanding, well above the 36-day industry average:

$$\text{DSO} = \begin{matrix}\text{Days}\\ \text{sales}\\ \text{outstanding}\end{matrix} = \frac{\text{Receivables}}{\text{Average sales per day}} = \frac{\text{Receivables}}{\text{Annual sales/360}}$$

$$= \frac{\$375}{\$3{,}000/360} = \frac{\$375}{\$8.333} = 45 \text{ days.}$$

$$\text{Industry average} = 36 \text{ days.}$$

Note that in this calculation we assumed a 360-day year. This convention is still followed by many in the financial community. However, if MicroDrive had calculated its DSO using a 365-day year, its DSO would have been 45.63 days.[4]

[2]A problem arises calculating and analyzing the inventory turnover ratio. Sales are stated at market prices, so if inventories are carried at cost, as they generally are, the calculated turnover overstates the true turnover ratio. Therefore, it would be more appropriate to use cost of goods sold in place of sales in the formula's numerator. However, established compilers of financial ratio statistics such as Dun & Bradstreet use the ratio of sales to inventories carried at cost. To develop a figure that can be compared with those published by Dun & Bradstreet and similar organizations, it is necessary to measure inventory turnover with sales in the numerator, as we do here.

[3]Preferably, the average inventory value should be calculated by summing the monthly figures during the year and dividing by 12. If monthly data are not available, one can add the beginning and ending figures and divide by 2. Both methods adjust for growth but not for seasonal effects.

[4]It would be better to use *average* receivables, either an average of the monthly figures or (Beginning receivables + Ending receivables)/2 = (\$315 + \$375)/2 = \$345 in the formula. Had the annual average receivables been used, MicroDrive's DSO on a 360-day basis would have been \$345.00/\$8.333 = 41 days. The 41-day figure is the more accurate one, but because the industry average was based on year-end receivables, we used 45 days for our comparison. The DSO is discussed further in Chapter 22.

The DSO can also be evaluated by comparison with the terms on which the firm sells its goods. For example, MicroDrive's sales terms call for payment within 30 days, so the fact that 45 days' sales, not 30 days', are outstanding indicates that customers, on the average, are not paying their bills on time. This deprives MicroDrive of funds that it could use to invest in productive assets. Moreover, in some instances the fact that a customer is paying late may signal that the customer is in financial trouble, in which case MicroDrive may have a hard time ever collecting the receivable. Therefore, if the trend in DSO over the past few years has been rising, but the credit policy has not been changed, this would be strong evidence that steps should be taken to expedite the collection of accounts receivable.

Evaluating Fixed Assets: The Fixed Assets Turnover Ratio

The **fixed assets turnover ratio** measures how effectively the firm uses its plant and equipment. It is the ratio of sales to net fixed assets:

$$\text{Fixed assets turnover ratio} = \frac{\text{Sales}}{\text{Net fixed assets}}$$

$$= \frac{\$3{,}000}{\$1{,}000} = 3.0 \text{ times.}$$

$$\text{Industry average} = 3.0 \text{ times.}$$

MicroDrive's ratio of 3.0 times is equal to the industry average, indicating that the firm is using its fixed assets about as intensively as are other firms in its industry. Therefore, MicroDrive seems to have about the right amount of fixed assets in relation to other firms.

A potential problem can exist when interpreting the fixed assets turnover ratio. Recall from accounting that fixed assets reflect the historical costs of the assets. Inflation has caused the value of many assets that were purchased in the past to be seriously understated. Therefore, if we were comparing an old firm that had acquired many of its fixed assets years ago at low prices with a new company that had acquired its fixed assets only recently, we would probably find that the old firm had the higher fixed assets turnover ratio. However, this would be more reflective of the difficulty accountants have in dealing with inflation than of any inefficiency on the part of the new firm. The accounting profession is trying to devise ways to make financial statements reflect current values rather than historical values. If balance sheets were actually stated on a current value basis, this would help us make better comparisons, but at the moment the problem still exists. Because financial analysts typically do not have the data necessary to make adjustments, they simply recognize that a problem exists and deal with it judgmentally. In MicroDrive's case, the issue is not a serious one because all firms in the industry have been expanding at about the same rate, hence the balance sheets of the comparison firms are reasonably comparable.[5]

Evaluating Total Assets: The Total Assets Turnover Ratio

The final asset management ratio, the **total assets turnover ratio,** measures the turnover of all the firm's assets; it is calculated by dividing sales by total assets:

$$\text{Total assets turnover ratio} = \frac{\text{Sales}}{\text{Total assets}}$$

$$= \frac{\$3{,}000}{\$2{,}000} = 1.5 \text{ times.}$$

$$\text{Industry average} = 1.8 \text{ times.}$$

[5]See FASB #89, *Financial Reporting and Changing Prices* (December 1986), for a discussion of the effects of inflation on financial statements.

MicroDrive's ratio is somewhat below the industry average, indicating that the company is not generating a sufficient volume of business given its total asset investment. Sales should be increased, some assets should be sold, or a combination of these steps should be taken.

Self-Test Questions

Identify four ratios that are used to measure how effectively a firm is managing its assets, and write out their equations.

How might rapid growth distort the inventory turnover ratio?

What potential problem might arise when comparing different firms' fixed assets turnover ratios?

Debt Management Ratios

The extent to which a firm uses debt financing, or **financial leverage,** has three important implications: (1) By raising funds through debt, stockholders can maintain control of a firm without increasing their investment. (2) Creditors look to the equity, or owner-supplied funds, to provide a margin of safety, so the higher the proportion of total capital provided by stockholders, the less the risk faced by creditors. (3) If the firm earns more on investments financed with borrowed funds than it pays in interest, the return on the owners' capital is magnified, or "leveraged."

To understand better how financial leverage affects risk and return, consider Table 3-1. Here we analyze two companies that are identical except for the way they are financed. Firm U (for "unleveraged") has no debt, whereas Firm L (for "leveraged") is financed with half equity and half debt that costs 15 percent. Both companies have \$100 of assets and \$100 of sales, and their expected operating income (also called earnings before interest and taxes, or EBIT) is \$30. Thus, both firms *expect* to earn \$30, before taxes, on their assets. Of course, things could turn out badly, in which case EBIT would be lower. Thus, in the second column of the table, we show EBIT declining from \$30 to \$2.50 under bad conditions.

Even though both companies' assets produce the same expected EBIT, under normal conditions Firm L would provide its stockholders with a return on equity of 27 percent versus only 18 percent for Firm U. This difference is caused by Firm L's use of debt, which "leverages up" its expected rate of return to stockholders. There are two reasons for the leveraging effect: (1) Because interest is deductible, the use of debt lowers the tax bill and leaves more of the firm's operating income available to its investors. (2) If operating income as a percentage of assets exceeds the interest rate on debt, as it generally does, then a company can use debt to acquire assets, pay the interest on the debt, and have something left over as a "bonus" for its stockholders. For our hypothetical firms, these two effects combine to push Firm L's expected rate of return on equity, defined as Net income/Common equity, up far above that of Firm U. Thus, debt can "leverage up" the rate of return on equity.

However, financial leverage can cut both ways. As we show in Column 2, if sales are lower and costs are higher than were expected, the return on assets will also be lower than was expected. Under these conditions, the leveraged firm's return on equity falls especially sharply, and losses occur. Under the "bad conditions" in Table 3-1, the debt-free firm still shows a profit, but Firm L shows a loss and thus has a negative return on equity. This occurs because Firm L needs cash to service its debt, while Firm U does not. Firm U, because of its strong balance sheet, could ride

See *Ch 03 Tool Kit.xls* for details.

TABLE 3-1 Effects of Financial Leverage on Stockholders' Returns

FIRM U (UNLEVERAGED)

Current assets	$ 50	Debt	$ 0
Fixed assets	50	Common equity	100
Total assets	$100	Total liabilities and equity	$100

	Expected Conditions (1)	Bad Conditions (2)
Sales	$100.00	$82.50
Operating costs	70.00	80.00
Operating income (EBIT)	$ 30.00	$ 2.50
Interest	0.00	0.00
Earnings before taxes (EBT)	$ 30.00	$ 2.50
Taxes (40%)	12.00	1.00
Net income (NI)	$ 18.00	$ 1.50
ROE_U = NI/Common equity = NI/$100 =	18.00%	1.50%

FIRM L (LEVERAGED)

Current assets	$ 50	Debt (interest = 15%)	$ 50
Fixed assets	50	Common equity	50
Total assets	$100	Total liabilities and equity	$100

	Expected Conditions (1)	Bad Conditions (2)
Sales	$100.00	$82.50
Operating costs	70.00	80.00
Operating income (EBIT)	$ 30.00	$ 2.50
Interest (15%)	7.50	7.50
Earnings before taxes (EBT)	$ 22.50	($ 5.00)
Taxes (40%)	9.00	(2.00)
Net income (NI)	$ 13.50	($ 3.00)
ROE_L = NI/Common equity = NI/$50 =	27.00%	(6.00%)

out the recession and be ready for the next boom. Firm L, on the other hand, must pay interest of $7.50 regardless of its level of sales. Since in the recession its operations do not generate enough income to meet the interest payments, cash would be depleted, and the firm probably would need to raise additional funds. Because it would be running a loss, Firm L would have a hard time selling stock to raise capital, and its losses would cause lenders to raise the interest rate, increasing L's problems still further. As a result, Firm L just might not survive to enjoy the next boom.

We see, then, that firms with relatively high debt ratios have higher expected returns when the economy is normal, but they are exposed to risk of loss when the economy goes into a recession. Therefore, decisions about the use of debt require firms to balance higher expected returns against increased risk. Determining the optimal amount of debt is a complicated process, and we defer a discussion of this topic until

Chapter 16. For now, we simply look at two procedures analysts use to examine the firm's debt: (1) They check the balance sheet to determine the proportion of total funds represented by debt, and (2) they review the income statement to see how well fixed charges are covered by operating profits.

How the Firm Is Financed: Total Debt to Total Assets

The ratio of total debt to total assets, generally called the **debt ratio,** measures the percentage of funds provided by creditors:

$$\text{Debt ratio} = \frac{\text{Total debt}}{\text{Total assets}}$$

$$= \frac{\$310 + \$754}{\$2{,}000} = \frac{\$1{,}064}{\$2{,}000} = 53.2\%.$$

$$\text{Industry average} = 40.0\%.$$

Total debt includes both current liabilities and long-term debt. Creditors prefer low debt ratios because the lower the ratio, the greater the cushion against creditors' losses in the event of liquidation. Stockholders, on the other hand, may want more leverage because it magnifies expected earnings.

MicroDrive's debt ratio is 53.2 percent, which means that its creditors have supplied more than half the total financing. As we will discuss in Chapter 16, a variety of factors determine a company's optimal debt ratio. Nevertheless, the fact that MicroDrive's debt ratio exceeds the industry average raises a red flag and may make it costly for MicroDrive to borrow additional funds without first raising more equity capital. Creditors may be reluctant to lend the firm more money, and management would probably be subjecting the firm to the risk of bankruptcy if it increased the debt ratio by borrowing additional funds.[6]

Ability to Pay Interest: Times Interest Earned

The **times-interest-earned (TIE) ratio** is determined by dividing earnings before interest and taxes (EBIT in Table 2-2) by the interest charges:

$$\text{Times-interest-earned (TIE) ratio} = \frac{\text{EBIT}}{\text{Interest charges}}$$

$$= \frac{\$283.8}{\$88} = 3.2 \text{ times.}$$

$$\text{Industry average} = 6.0 \text{ times.}$$

The TIE ratio measures the extent to which operating income can decline before the firm is unable to meet its annual interest costs. Failure to meet this obligation can bring legal action by the firm's creditors, possibly resulting in bankruptcy. Note that earnings before interest and taxes, rather than net income, is used in the numerator. Because interest is paid with pre-tax dollars, the firm's ability to pay current interest is not affected by taxes.

[6]The ratio of debt to equity is also used in financial analysis. The debt-to-assets (D/A) and debt-to-equity (D/E) ratios are simply transformations of each other:

$$D/E = \frac{D/A}{1 - D/A}, \text{ and } D/A = \frac{D/E}{1 + D/E}.$$

MicroDrive's interest is covered 3.2 times. Since the industry average is 6 times, MicroDrive is covering its interest charges by a relatively low margin of safety. Thus, the TIE ratio reinforces the conclusion from our analysis of the debt ratio that MicroDrive would face difficulties if it attempted to borrow additional funds.

Ability to Service Debt: EBITDA Coverage Ratio

The TIE ratio is useful for assessing a company's ability to meet interest charges on its debt, but this ratio has two shortcomings: (1) Interest is not the only fixed financial charge—companies must also reduce debt on schedule, and many firms lease assets and thus must make lease payments. If they fail to repay debt or meet lease payments, they can be forced into bankruptcy. (2) EBIT does not represent all the cash flow available to service debt, especially if a firm has high depreciation and/or amortization charges. To account for these deficiencies, bankers and others have developed the **EBITDA coverage ratio,** defined as follows:[7]

$$\text{EBITDA coverage ratio} = \frac{\text{EBITDA} + \text{Lease payments}}{\text{Interest} + \text{Principal payments} + \text{Lease payments}}$$

$$= \frac{\$283.8 + \$100 + \$28}{\$88 + \$20 + \$28} = \frac{\$411.8}{\$136} = 3.0 \text{ times.}$$

$$\text{Industry average} = 4.3 \text{ times.}$$

MicroDrive had $283.8 million of operating income (EBIT), presumably all cash. Noncash charges of $100 million for depreciation and amortization (the DA part of EBITDA) were deducted in the calculation of EBIT, so they must be added back to find the cash flow available to service debt. Also, lease payments of $28 million were deducted before getting the $283.8 million of EBIT.[8] That $28 million was available to meet financial charges, hence it must be added back, bringing the total available to cover fixed financial charges to $411.8 million. Fixed financial charges consisted of $88 million of interest, $20 million of sinking fund payments, and $28 million for lease payments, for a total of $136 million.[9] Therefore, MicroDrive covered its fixed financial charges by 3.0 times. However, if operating income declines, the coverage will fall, and operating income certainly can decline. Moreover, MicroDrive's ratio is well below the industry average, so again, the company seems to have a relatively high level of debt.

[7]Different analysts define the EBITDA coverage ratio in different ways. For example, some would omit the lease payment information, and others would "gross up" principal payments by dividing them by (1 − T) because these payments are not tax deductions, hence must be made with after-tax cash flows. We included lease payments because, for many firms, they are quite important, and failing to make them can lead to bankruptcy just as surely as can failure to make payments on "regular" debt. We did not gross up principal payments because, if a company is in financial difficulty, its tax rate will probably be zero, hence the gross up is not necessary whenever the ratio is really important.

[8]Lease payments are included in the numerator because, unlike interest, they were deducted when EBITDA was calculated. We want to find *all* the funds that were available to service debt, so lease payments must be added to the EBIT and DA to find the funds that could be used to service debt and meet lease payments. To illustrate this, suppose EBIT before lease payments was $100, lease payments were $100, and DA was zero. After lease payments, EBIT would be $100 − $100 = $0. Yet lease payments of $100 were made, so obviously there was cash to make those payments. The available cash was the reported EBIT of $0 plus the $100 of lease payments.

[9]A sinking fund is a required annual payment designed to reduce the balance of a bond or preferred stock issue. A sinking fund payment is like the principal repayment portion of the payment on an amortized loan, but sinking funds are used for publicly traded bond issues, whereas amortization payments are used for bank loans and other private loans.

The EBITDA coverage ratio is most useful for relatively short-term lenders such as banks, which rarely make loans (except real estate-backed loans) for longer than about five years. Over a relatively short period, depreciation-generated funds can be used to service debt. Over a longer time, those funds must be reinvested to maintain the plant and equipment or else the company cannot remain in business. Therefore, banks and other relatively short-term lenders focus on the EBITDA coverage ratio, whereas long-term bondholders focus on the TIE ratio.

Self-Test Questions

How does the use of financial leverage affect current stockholders' control position?

In what way do taxes influence a firm's willingness to finance with debt?

In what way does the use of debt involve a risk-versus-return trade-off?

Explain the following statement: "Analysts look at both balance sheet and income statement ratios when appraising a firm's financial condition."

Name three ratios that are used to measure the extent to which a firm uses financial leverage, and write out their equations.

Profitability Ratios

Profitability is the net result of a number of policies and decisions. The ratios examined thus far provide useful clues as to the effectiveness of a firm's operations, but the **profitability ratios** go on to show the combined effects of liquidity, asset management, and debt on operating results.

Profit Margin on Sales

The **profit margin on sales,** calculated by dividing net income by sales, gives the profit per dollar of sales:

$$\text{Profit margin on sales} = \frac{\text{Net income available to common stockholders}}{\text{Sales}}$$

$$= \frac{\$113.5}{\$3{,}000} = 3.8\%.$$

$$\text{Industry average} = 5.0\%.$$

MicroDrive's profit margin is below the industry average of 5 percent. This sub-par result occurs because costs are too high. High costs, in turn, generally occur because of inefficient operations. However, MicroDrive's low profit margin is also a result of its heavy use of debt. Recall that net income is income *after interest.* Therefore, if two firms have identical operations in the sense that their sales, operating costs, and EBIT are the same, but if one firm uses more debt than the other, it will have higher interest charges. Those interest charges will pull net income down, and since sales are constant, the result will be a relatively low profit margin. In such a case, the low profit margin would not indicate an operating problem—rather, it would indicate a difference in financing strategies. Thus, the firm with the low profit margin might end up with a higher rate of return on its stockholders' investment due to its use of financial leverage. We will see exactly how profit margins and the use of debt interact to affect the return on stockholder's equity later in the chapter, when we examine the Du Pont model.

International Accounting Differences Create Headaches for Investors

You must be a good financial detective to analyze financial statements, especially if the company operates overseas. Despite attempts to standardize accounting practices, there are many differences in the way financial information is reported in different countries, and these differences create headaches for investors trying to make cross-border company comparisons.

A study by two Rider College accounting professors demonstrated that huge differences can exist. The professors developed a computer model to evaluate the net income of a hypothetical but typical company operating in different countries. Applying the standard accounting practices of each country, the hypothetical company would have reported net income of $34,600 in the United States, $260,600 in the United Kingdom, and $240,600 in Australia.

Such variances occur for a number of reasons. In most countries, including the United States, an asset's balance sheet value is reported at original cost less any accumulated depreciation. However, in some countries, asset values are adjusted to reflect current market prices. Also, inventory valuation methods vary from country to country, as does the treatment of goodwill. Other differences arise from the treatment of leases, research and development costs, and pension plans.

These differences arise from a variety of legal, historical, cultural, and economic factors. For example, in Germany and Japan large banks are the key source of both debt and equity capital, whereas in the United States public capital markets are most important. As a result, U.S. corporations disclose a great deal of information to the public, while German and Japanese corporations use very conservative accounting practices that appeal to the banks.

Source: "All Accountants Soon May Speak the Same Language," *The Wall Street Journal*, August 29, 1995, A15.

Basic Earning Power (BEP)

The **basic earning power (BEP) ratio** is calculated by dividing earnings before interest and taxes (EBIT) by total assets:

$$\text{Basic earning power ratio (BEP)} = \frac{\text{EBIT}}{\text{Total assets}}$$

$$= \frac{\$283.8}{\$2,000} = 14.2\%.$$

$$\text{Industry average} = 17.2\%.$$

This ratio shows the raw earning power of the firm's assets, before the influence of taxes and leverage, and it is useful for comparing firms with different tax situations and different degrees of financial leverage. Because of its low turnover ratios and low profit margin on sales, MicroDrive is not getting as high a return on its assets as is the average company in its industry.[10]

[10]Notice that EBIT is earned throughout the year, whereas the total assets figure is an end-of-the-year number. Therefore, it would be conceptually better to calculate this ratio as EBIT/Average assets = EBIT/[(Beginning assets + Ending assets)/2]. We have not made this adjustment because the published ratios used for comparative purposes do not include it. However, when we construct our own comparative ratios, we do make the adjustment. Incidentally, the same adjustment would also be appropriate for the next two ratios, ROA and ROE.

Return on Total Assets

The ratio of net income to total assets measures the **return on total assets (ROA)** after interest and taxes:

$$\text{Return on total assets} = \text{ROA} = \frac{\text{Net income available to common stockholders}}{\text{Total assets}}$$

$$= \frac{\$113.5}{\$2,000} = 5.7\%.$$

$$\text{Industry average} = 9.0\%.$$

MicroDrive's 5.7 percent return is well below the 9 percent average for the industry. This low return results from (1) the company's low basic earning power plus (2) high interest costs resulting from its above-average use of debt, both of which cause its net income to be relatively low.

Return on Common Equity

Ultimately, the most important, or "bottom line," accounting ratio is the ratio of net income to common equity, which measures the **return on common equity (ROE):**

$$\text{Return on common equity} = \text{ROE} = \frac{\text{Net income available to common stockholders}}{\text{Common equity}}$$

$$= \frac{\$113.5}{\$896} = 12.7\%.$$

$$\text{Industry average} = 15.0\%.$$

Stockholders invest to get a return on their money, and this ratio tells how well they are doing in an accounting sense. MicroDrive's 12.7 percent return is below the 15 percent industry average, but not as far below as the return on total assets. This somewhat better result is due to the company's greater use of debt, a point that is analyzed in detail later in the chapter.

Self-Test Questions

Identify and write out the equations for four ratios that show the combined effects of liquidity, asset management, and debt management on profitability.

Why is the basic earning power ratio useful?

Why does the use of debt lower the ROA?

What does ROE measure? Since interest expense lowers profits, does using debt lower ROE?

Market Value Ratios

A final group of ratios, the **market value ratios,** relates the firm's stock price to its earnings, cash flow, and book value per share. These ratios give management an indication of what investors think of the company's past performance and future prospects. If the liquidity, asset management, debt management, and profitability ratios all look good, then the market value ratios will be high, and the stock price will probably be as high as can be expected.

Price/Earnings Ratio

The **price/earnings (P/E) ratio** shows how much investors are willing to pay per dollar of reported profits. MicroDrive's stock sells for $23, so with an EPS of $2.27 its P/E ratio is 10.1:

$$\text{Price/earnings (P/E) ratio} = \frac{\text{Price per share}}{\text{Earnings per share}}$$

$$= \frac{\$23.00}{\$2.27} = 10.1 \text{ times.}$$

$$\text{Industry average} = 12.5 \text{ times.}$$

As we will see in Chapter 10, P/E ratios are higher for firms with strong growth prospects, other things held constant, but they are lower for riskier firms. Because MicroDrive's P/E ratio is below the average for other food processors, this suggests that the company is regarded as being somewhat riskier than most, as having poorer growth prospects, or both.

Price/Cash Flow Ratio

In some industries, stock price is tied more closely to cash flow rather than net income. Consequently, investors often look at the **price/cash flow ratio:**

$$\text{Price/cash flow} = \frac{\text{Price per share}}{\text{Cash flow per share}}$$

$$= \frac{\$23.00}{\$4.27} = 5.4 \text{ times.}$$

$$\text{Industry average} = 6.8 \text{ times.}$$

The calculation for cash flow per share was shown in Chapter 2, but just to refresh your memory, cash flow per share is calculated as net income plus depreciation and amortization divided by common shares outstanding.

MicroDrive's price/cash flow ratio is also below the industry average, once again suggesting that its growth prospects are below average, its risk is above average, or both.

Note that some analysts look at multiples beyond just the price/earnings and the price/cash flow ratios. For example, depending on the industry, some may look at measures such as price/sales, price/customers, or price/EBITDA per share. Ultimately, though, value depends on earnings and cash flows, so if these "exotic" ratios do not forecast future EPS and cash flow, they may turn out to be misleading. This was true in the case of the dot-com retailers before they crashed and burned in 2000, costing investors many billions.

Market/Book Ratio

The ratio of a stock's market price to its book value gives another indication of how investors regard the company. Companies with relatively high rates of return on equity generally sell at higher multiples of book value than those with low returns. First, we find MicroDrive's book value per share:

$$\text{Book value per share} = \frac{\text{Common equity}}{\text{Shares outstanding}}$$

$$= \frac{\$896}{50} = \$17.92.$$

TABLE 3-2 MicroDrive Inc.: Summary of Financial Ratios (Millions of Dollars)

Ratio	Formula for Calculation	Calculation	Ratio	Industry Average	Comment
Liquidity					
Current	$\frac{\text{Current assets}}{\text{Current liabilities}}$	$\frac{\$1,000}{\$310}$	= 3.2×	4.2×	Poor
Quick, or acid, test	$\frac{\text{Current assets} - \text{Inventories}}{\text{Current liabilities}}$	$\frac{\$385}{\$310}$	= 1.2×	2.1×	Poor
Asset Management					
Inventory turnover	$\frac{\text{Sales}}{\text{Inventories}}$	$\frac{\$3,000}{\$615}$	= 4.9×	9.0×	Poor
Days sales outstanding (DSO)	$\frac{\text{Receivables}}{\text{Annual sales/360}}$	$\frac{\$375}{\$8.333}$	= 45 days	36 days	Poor
Fixed assets turnover	$\frac{\text{Sales}}{\text{Net fixed assets}}$	$\frac{\$3,000}{\$1,000}$	= 3.0×	3.0×	OK
Total assets turnover	$\frac{\text{Sales}}{\text{Total assets}}$	$\frac{\$3,000}{\$2,000}$	= 1.5×	1.8×	Somewhat low
Debt Management					
Total debt to total assets	$\frac{\text{Total debt}}{\text{Total assets}}$	$\frac{\$1,064}{\$2,000}$	= 53.2%	40.0%	High (risky)
Times-interest-earned (TIE)	$\frac{\text{Earnings before interest and taxes (EBIT)}}{\text{Interest charges}}$	$\frac{\$283.8}{\$88}$	= 3.2×	6.0×	Low (risky)
EBITDA coverage	$\frac{\text{EBITDA} + \text{Lease payments}}{\text{Interest} + \text{Principal payments} + \text{Lease payments}}$	$\frac{\$411.8}{\$136}$	= 3.0×	4.3×	Low (risky)
Profitability					
Profit margin on sales	$\frac{\text{Net income available to common stockholders}}{\text{Sales}}$	$\frac{\$113.5}{\$3,000}$	= 3.8%	5.0%	Poor
Basic earning power (BEP)	$\frac{\text{Earnings before interest and taxes (EBIT)}}{\text{Total assets}}$	$\frac{\$283.8}{\$2,000}$	= 14.2%	17.2%	Poor
Return on total assets (ROA)	$\frac{\text{Net income available to common stockholders}}{\text{Total assets}}$	$\frac{\$113.5}{\$2,000}$	= 5.7%	9.0%	Poor
Return on common equity (ROE)	$\frac{\text{Net income available to common stockholders}}{\text{Common equity}}$	$\frac{\$113.5}{\$896}$	= 12.7%	15.0%	Poor
Market Value					
Price/earnings (P/E)	$\frac{\text{Price per share}}{\text{Earnings per share}}$	$\frac{\$23.00}{\$2.27}$	= 10.1×	12.5×	Low
Price/cash flow	$\frac{\text{Price per share}}{\text{Cash flow per share}}$	$\frac{\$23.00}{\$4.27}$	= 5.4×	6.8×	Low
Market/book (M/B)	$\frac{\text{Market price per share}}{\text{Book value per share}}$	$\frac{\$23.00}{\$17.92}$	= 1.3×	1.7×	Low

Now we divide the market price by the book value to get a **market/book (M/B) ratio** of 1.3 times:

$$\text{Market/book ratio} = \text{M/B} = \frac{\text{Market price per share}}{\text{Book value per share}}$$

$$= \frac{\$23.00}{\$17.92} = 1.3 \text{ times.}$$

$$\text{Industry average} = 1.7 \text{ times.}$$

Investors are willing to pay relatively little for a dollar of MicroDrive's book value.

The average company followed by the *Value Line Investment Survey* had a market/book ratio of about 4.0 in 1999. Since M/B ratios typically exceed 1.0, this means that investors are willing to pay more for stocks than their accounting book values. This situation occurs primarily because asset values, as reported by accountants on corporate balance sheets, do not reflect either inflation or "goodwill." Thus, assets purchased years ago at preinflation prices are carried at their original costs, even though inflation might have caused their actual values to rise substantially, and successful going concerns have a value greater than their historical costs.

If a company earns a low rate of return on its assets, then its M/B ratio will be relatively low versus an average company. Thus, some airlines, which have not fared well in recent years, sell at M/B ratios below 1.0, while very successful firms such as Microsoft (which makes the operating systems for virtually all PCs) achieve high rates of return on their assets, causing their market values to be well in excess of their book values. In March 2000, Microsoft's book value per share was $6.68 versus a market price of $100, so its market/book ratio was $100/$6.68 = 14.97 times. Note, though, that high M/B (and P/E) ratios may also signal "irrational exuberance," or excessively high stock prices. Microsoft's M/B dropped sharply after its stock price was cut in two in 2000.

CD

See ***Ch 03 Tool Kit.xls*** for details.

Table 3-2 summarizes MicroDrive's financial ratios. As the table indicates, the company has many problems.

Self-Test Questions

Describe three ratios that relate a firm's stock price to its earnings, cash flow, and book value per share, and write out their equations.

How do market value ratios reflect what investors think about a stock's risk and expected rate of return?

What does the price/earnings (P/E) ratio show? If one firm's P/E ratio is lower than that of another, what are some factors that might explain the difference?

How is book value per share calculated? Explain how inflation and "goodwill" could cause book values to deviate from market values.

Trend Analysis, Common Size Analysis, and Percent Change Analysis

It is important to analyze trends in ratios as well as their absolute levels, for trends give clues as to whether a firm's financial condition is likely to improve or to deteriorate. To do a **trend analysis,** one simply plots a ratio over time, as shown in Figure 3-1. This graph shows that MicroDrive's rate of return on common equity has been declining since 1998, even though the industry average has been relatively stable. All the other ratios could be analyzed similarly.

Common size analysis and **percent change analysis** are two other techniques that can be used to identify trends in financial statements. Common size analysis is

FIGURE 3-1 Rate of Return on Common Equity, 1997–2001

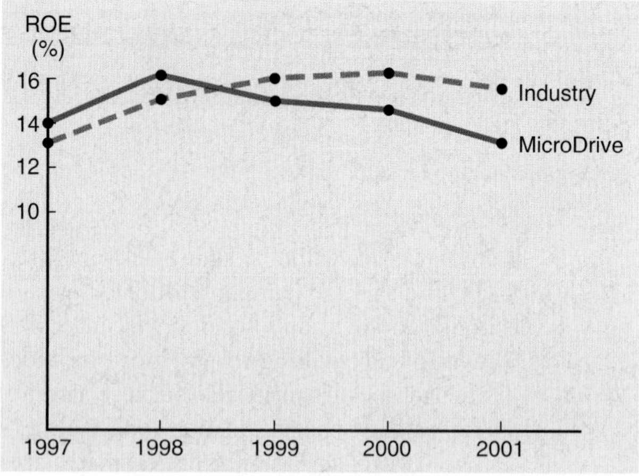

also useful in comparative analysis, and some sources of industry data, such as Robert Morris Associates, are presented exclusively in common size form.

In a common size analysis, all income statement items are divided by sales, and all balance sheet items are divided by total assets. Thus, a common size income statement shows each item as a percentage of sales, and a common size balance sheet shows each item as a percentage of total assets. The advantage of common size analysis is that it facilitates comparisons of balance sheets and income statements over time and across companies.

Table 3-3 contains MicroDrive's 2000 and 2001 common size income statements, along with the composite statement for the industry. (Note: Rounding may cause addition/subtraction differences in Tables 3-3 and 3-4.) MicroDrive's operating costs are slightly above average, as are its interest expenses, but its taxes are relatively low because of its low EBIT. The net effect of all these forces is a relatively low profit margin.

Table 3-4 shows MicroDrive's common size balance sheets, along with the industry average. Its accounts receivable are significantly higher than the industry average,

TABLE 3-3 MicroDrive Inc.: Common Size Income Statements

CD

See ***Ch 03 Tool Kit.xls*** for details.

	2000	2001	2001 Industry Composite
Net sales	100.0%	100.0%	100.0%
Costs excluding depreciation	87.6	87.2	87.6
Depreciation	3.2	3.3	2.8
Total operating costs	90.8%	90.5%	90.4%
Earnings before interest and taxes (EBIT)	9.2%	9.5%	9.6%
Less interest	2.1	2.9	1.3
Earnings before taxes (EBT)	7.1%	6.5%	8.3%
Taxes (40%)	2.8	2.6	3.3
Net income before preferred dividends	4.3%	3.9%	5.0%
Preferred dividends	0.1	0.1	0.0
Net income available to common stockholders (profit margin)	4.1%	3.8%	5.0%

TABLE 3-4 MicroDrive Inc.: Common Size Balance Sheets

	2000	2001	2001 Industry Composite
Assets			
Cash and equivalents	0.9%	0.5%	3.2%
Short-term investments	3.9	0.0	0.0
Accounts receivable	18.8	18.8	17.8
Inventories	24.7	30.8	19.8
Total current assets	48.2%	50.0%	40.8%
Net plant and equipment	51.8	50.0	59.2
Total assets	100.0%	100.0%	100.0%
Liabilities and Equity			
Accounts payable	1.8%	3.0%	1.8%
Notes payable	3.6	5.5	4.4
Accruals	7.7	7.0	3.6
Total current liabilities	13.1%	15.5%	9.8%
Long-term bonds	34.5	37.7	30.2
Total debt	47.6%	53.2%	40.0%
Preferred equity	2.4	2.0	0.0
Common equity	50.0	44.8	60.0
Total liabilities and equity	100.0%	100.0%	100.0%

its inventories are significantly higher, and it uses far more fixed charge capital (debt and preferred) than the average firm.

A final technique used to help analyze a firm's financial statements is percentage change analysis. In this type of analysis, growth rates are calculated for all income statement items and balance sheet accounts. To illustrate, Table 3-5 contains MicroDrive's income statement percentage change analysis for 2001. Sales increased at a 5.3 percent rate during 2001, while total operating costs increased at a slower 5.0 percent rate, leading to 7.9 percent growth in EBIT. The fact that sales increased faster than operating

TABLE 3-5 MicroDrive Inc.: Income Statement Percentage Change Analysis (Millions of Dollars)

See ***Ch 03 Tool Kit.xls*** for details.

	2000	2001	Percent Change
Net sales	$2,850	$3,000.0	5.3%
Costs excluding depreciation	$2,497	$2,616.2	4.8%
Depreciation	90	100.0	11.1
Total operating costs	$2,587	$2,716.2	5.0%
Earnings before interest and taxes (EBIT)	$ 263	$ 283.8	7.9%
Less interest	60	88.0	46.7
Earnings before taxes (EBT)	$ 203	$ 195.8	(3.5%)
Taxes (40%)	81	78.3	(3.3)
Net income before preferred dividends	$ 122	$ 117.5	(3.7%)
Preferred dividends	4	4.0	0
Net income available to common stockholders	$ 118	$ 113.5	(3.8%)

costs is positive, but this "good news" was offset by a 46.7 percent increase in interest expense. The significant growth in interest expense caused growth in both earnings before taxes and net income to be negative. Thus, the percentage change analysis points out that the decrease in reported income in 2001 resulted almost exclusively from an increase in interest expense. This conclusion could be reached by analyzing dollar amounts, but percentage change analysis simplifies the task. The same type of analysis applied to the balance sheets would show that assets grew at a 19.0 percent rate, largely because inventories grew at a whopping 48.2 percent rate. With only a 5.3 percent growth in sales, the extreme growth in inventories should be of great concern to MicroDrive's managers.

The conclusions reached in common size and percentage change analyses generally parallel those derived from ratio analysis. However, occasionally a serious deficiency is highlighted by only one of the three analytical techniques. Also, it is often useful to have all three and to drive home to management, in slightly different ways, the need to take corrective actions. Thus, a thorough financial statement analysis will include ratio, percentage change, and common size analyses, as well as a Du Pont analysis as described next.

Self-Test Questions

How does one do a trend analysis?

What important information does a trend analysis provide?

What is common size analysis?

What is percent change analysis?

Tying the Ratios Together: The Du Pont Chart and Equation

Table 3-2 summarized MicroDrive's ratios, and now Figure 3-2 shows how the return on equity is affected by asset turnover, the profit margin, and leverage. The chart depicted in Figure 3-2 is called a modified **Du Pont chart** because that company's managers developed this approach for evaluating performance. Working from the bottom up, the left-hand side of the chart develops the *profit margin on sales.* The various expense items are listed and then summed to obtain MicroDrive's total cost, which is subtracted from sales to obtain the company's net income. When we divide net income by sales, we find that 3.8 percent of each sales dollar is left over for stockholders. If the profit margin is low or trending down, one can examine the individual expense items to identify and then correct problems.

The right-hand side of Figure 3-2 lists the various categories of assets, totals them, and then divides sales by total assets to find the number of times MicroDrive "turns its assets over" each year. The company's total assets turnover ratio is 1.5 times.

The profit margin times the total assets turnover is called the **Du Pont equation,** and it gives the rate of return on assets (ROA):

$$\begin{aligned}\text{ROA} &= \text{Profit margin} \times \text{Total assets turnover}\\ &= \frac{\text{Net income}}{\text{Sales}} \times \frac{\text{Sales}}{\text{Total assets}} \qquad \textbf{(3-1)}\\ &= 3.8\% \times 1.5 = 5.7\%.\end{aligned}$$

MicroDrive made 3.8 percent, or 3.8 cents, on each dollar of sales, and its assets were "turned over" 1.5 times during the year. Therefore, the company earned a return of 5.7 percent on its assets.

If the company were financed only with common equity, the rate of return on assets (ROA) and the return on equity (ROE) would be the same because the total assets would equal the common equity:

FIGURE 3-2 Modified Du Pont Chart for MicroDrive Inc. (Millions of Dollars)

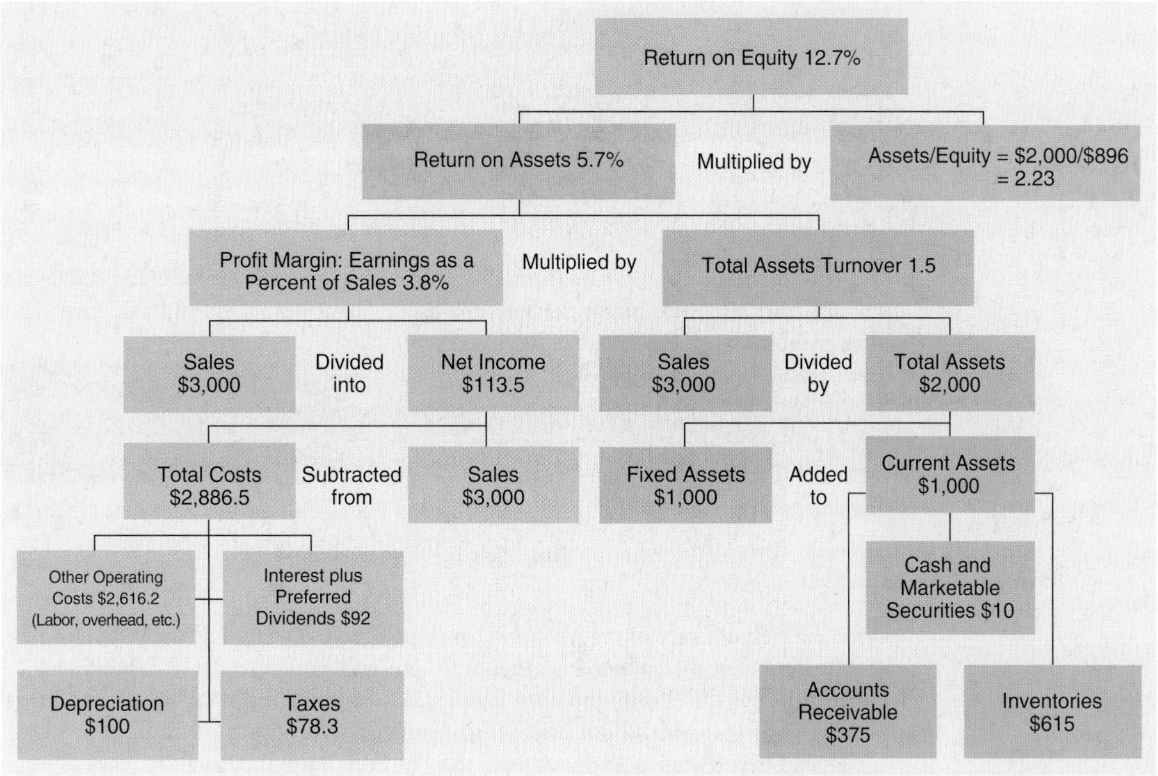

$$\text{ROA} = \frac{\text{Net income}}{\text{Total assets}} = \frac{\text{Net income}}{\text{Common equity}} = \text{ROE}.$$

This equality holds if and only if Total assets = Common equity, that is, if the company uses no debt. MicroDrive does use debt, so its common equity is less than total assets. Therefore, the return to the common stockholders (ROE) must be greater than the ROA of 5.7 percent. To find the ROE, multiply the rate of return on assets (ROA) by the *equity multiplier*, which is the ratio of assets to common equity:

$$\text{Equity multiplier} = \frac{\text{Total assets}}{\text{Common equity}}.$$

Firms that use a large amount of debt financing (a lot of leverage) will necessarily have a high equity multiplier—the more the debt, the less the equity, hence the higher the equity multiplier. For example, if a firm has $1,000 of assets and is financed with $800, or 80 percent debt, then its equity will be $200, and its equity multiplier will be $1,000/$200 = 5. Had it used only $200 of debt, then its equity would have been $800, and its equity multiplier would have been only $1,000/$800 = 1.25.[11]

[11]Expressed algebraically,

$$\text{Debt ratio} = \frac{D}{A} = \frac{A - E}{A} = \frac{A}{A} - \frac{E}{A} = 1 - \frac{1}{\text{Equity multiplier}}.$$

Here D is debt, E is equity, A is total assets, and A/E is the equity multiplier. This equation ignores preferred stock.

MicroDrive's return on equity (ROE) depends on its ROA and its use of leverage:[12]

$$\begin{aligned} \text{ROE} &= \text{ROA} \times \text{Equity multiplier} \\ &= \frac{\text{Net income}}{\text{Total assets}} \times \frac{\text{Total assets}}{\text{Common equity}} \end{aligned} \quad \text{(3-2)}$$

$$\begin{aligned} &= 5.7\% \times \$2{,}000/\$896 \\ &= 5.7\% \times 2.23 \\ &= 12.7\%. \end{aligned}$$

Now we can combine Equations 3-1 and 3-2 to form the *extended Du Pont equation,* which shows how the profit margin, the assets turnover ratio, and the equity multiplier combine to determine the ROE:

$$\begin{aligned} \text{ROE} &= (\text{Profit margin})(\text{Total assets turnover})(\text{Equity multiplier}) \\ &= \frac{\text{Net income}}{\text{Sales}} \times \frac{\text{Sales}}{\text{Total assets}} \times \frac{\text{Total assets}}{\text{Common equity}}. \end{aligned} \quad \text{(3-3)}$$

For MicroDrive, we have

$$\begin{aligned} \text{ROE} &= (3.8\%)(1.5)(2.23) \\ &= 12.7\%. \end{aligned}$$

The 12.7 percent rate of return could, of course, be calculated directly: both Sales and Total assets cancel, leaving Net income/Common equity = \$113.5/\$896 = 12.7%. However, the Du Pont equation shows how the profit margin, the total assets turnover, and the use of debt interact to determine the return on equity.

MicroDrive's management can use the Du Pont system to analyze ways of improving performance. Focusing on the left, or "profit margin," side of its modified Du Pont chart, MicroDrive's marketing people can study the effects of raising sales prices (or lowering them to increase volume), of moving into new products or markets with higher margins, and so on. The company's cost accountants can study various expense items and, working with engineers, purchasing agents, and other operating personnel, seek ways to hold down costs. On the "turnover" side, MicroDrive's financial analysts, working with both production and marketing people, can investigate ways to reduce the investment in various types of assets. At the same time, the treasury staff can analyze the effects of alternative financing strategies, seeking to hold down interest expense and the risk of debt while still using leverage to increase the rate of return on equity.

As a result of such an analysis, Ellen Jackson, MicroDrive's president, recently announced a series of moves designed to cut operating costs by more than 20 percent per year. Jackson and MicroDrive's other executives have a strong incentive for improving the company's financial performance, because their compensation is based to a large extent on how well the company does. MicroDrive's executives receive a salary that is sufficient to cover their living costs, but their compensation package also includes "performance shares" that will be awarded if and only if the company meets or exceeds target levels for earnings and the stock price. These target levels are based on MicroDrive's performance relative to its competitors. So, if MicroDrive does well, then Jackson and the other executives—and the stockholders—will also do well. But if things deteriorate, Jackson could be looking for a new job.

[12]Note that we could also find the ROE by "grossing up" the ROA, that is, by dividing the ROA by the common equity fraction: ROE = ROA/Equity fraction = 5.7%/0.448 = 12.7%. The two procedures are algebraically equivalent.

Self-Test Questions

Explain how the extended, or modified, Du Pont equation and chart can be used to reveal the basic determinants of ROE.

What is the equity multiplier?

How can management use the Du Pont system to analyze ways of improving the firm's performance?

Comparative Ratios and "Benchmarking"

Ratio analysis involves comparisons—a company's ratios are compared with those of other firms in the same industry, that is, with industry average figures. However, like most firms, MicroDrive's managers go one step further—they also compare their ratios with those of a smaller set of the leading computer companies. This technique is called **benchmarking,** and the companies used for the comparison are called **benchmark companies**. For example, MicroDrive benchmarks against Apex Systems, Cablenet, Carter Controls, BMR Corporation, Magnetic Sciences, and Luxor Corporation. MicroDrive's management considers these to be the best-managed companies with operations similar to its own. Here is the comparison of MicroDrive's ROE versus those of the benchmark firms:

	ROE
Cablenet	28%
Carter	26
BMR	22
Magnetic Sciences	19
Luxor	16
MicroDrive	**13**
Apex	9

Similar comparisons are made for the other key ratios, and this procedure allows management to see, on a company-by-company basis, how it stacks up against its major competitors.

Many companies also benchmark various parts of their overall operation against top companies, whether they are in the same industry or not. For example, MicroDrive has a division that sells hard drives directly to consumers through catalogs and the Internet. This division's shipping department benchmarks against L.L. Bean, even though they are in different industries, because L.L. Bean's shipping department is one of the best. MicroDrive wants its own shippers to strive to match L.L. Bean's record for on-time shipments.

Comparative ratios are available from a number of sources, including *Value Line.* Table 3-6 presents a list of key ratios for a variety of industries covered by *Value Line.* Useful ratios are also compiled by Dun and Bradstreet (D&B) and the *Annual Statement Studies* published by Robert Morris Associates, which is the national association of bank loan officers. Also, financial statement data for thousands of publicly owned corporations are available on magnetic tapes and CD-ROMs, and because brokerage houses, banks, and other financial institutions have access to these data, security analysts can and do generate comparative ratios tailored to their specific needs.

Each of the data-supplying organizations uses a somewhat different set of ratios designed for its own purposes. For example, D&B deals mainly with small firms, many of which are proprietorships, and it sells its services primarily to banks and other

TABLE 3-6 Key Financial Ratios for Selected Industries[a]

Industry Name	Current Ratio	Quick Ratio	Inventory Turnover[b]	Fixed Assets Turnover	Total Assets Turnover	Debt Ratio[c]	Days Sales Outstanding[d]	Profit Margin	Return on Assets	Return on Equity
Advertising	0.96	0.94	47.96	4.47	0.69	73.47%	184.39	4.46%	3.10%	14.51%
Aerospace/defense	1.21	0.66	4.94	6.19	1.01	58.81	47.08	4.02	4.05	13.39
Auto and truck	1.41	1.27	13.39	4.19	0.77	64.89	163.15	3.95	3.05	17.06
Beverage (soft drink)	1.00	0.84	19.88	3.70	0.94	53.65	36.67	10.59	9.91	33.26
Computer software	1.62	1.56	53.36	6.86	1.01	47.78	72.30	8.06	8.13	17.05
Educational services	1.90	1.77	34.51	5.95	1.02	31.89	50.79	6.48	6.61	11.01
Electronics	2.16	1.39	6.40	5.82	1.37	46.75	59.42	3.40	4.66	9.78
Entertainment	1.37	0.98	7.81	3.11	0.45	49.15	61.23	2.95	1.31	3.49
Environmental	1.37	1.19	22.38	1.73	0.75	53.67	70.92	3.32	2.49	6.78
Food processing	1.53	1.00	9.37	4.59	1.36	47.30	33.30	5.03	6.86	17.33
Grocery	1.04	0.33	12.51	5.37	2.69	64.05	6.90	1.81	4.88	17.66
Healthcare information systems	1.88	1.84	112.11	5.65	0.97	34.05	83.06	9.94	9.61	16.91
Home appliance	1.40	0.95	7.12	4.35	1.09	53.73	61.20	2.40	2.62	9.08
Homebuilding	2.18	0.69	2.80	4.35	1.04	58.14	26.79	3.17	3.30	9.81
Hotel/gaming	1.13	1.05	59.42	1.01	0.64	49.23	26.96	5.52	3.54	8.57
Industrial services	1.76	1.57	28.84	7.10	1.49	49.66	52.25	3.56	5.31	12.20
Internet	1.58	1.52	38.51	7.62	1.18	51.32	82.67	−6.67	−7.89	−17.67
Medical services	1.60	1.54	80.11	4.78	0.51	25.24	61.26	3.21	1.63	8.34
Newspaper	1.14	1.01	27.39	2.77	0.62	50.77	57.63	7.05	4.39	13.91
Paper and forest products	1.56	0.88	8.02	1.35	0.83	50.24	40.02	1.93	1.61	4.88
Restaurant	0.73	0.61	53.46	1.61	1.13	50.45	7.68	5.10	5.76	15.10
Retail store	1.77	0.82	6.32	4.86	1.83	58.59	38.87	2.78	5.10	15.02
Telecommunications services	0.86	0.83	74.00	1.08	0.56	53.23	76.22	7.17	4.01	13.09
Textile	2.41	1.16	5.32	3.11	1.23	59.12	50.02	3.30	4.06	12.59
Tobacco	1.18	0.56	7.23	6.35	0.92	40.46	24.24	7.01	6.48	35.71
Water utilities	0.52	0.46	35.75	0.32	0.26	52.63	31.68	11.97	3.07	10.59

[a]The ratios presented are averages for each industry. Ratios for the individual companies are also available.
[b]The inventory turnover ratio in this table is calculated as sales divided by inventory.
[c]The debt ratio in this table is calculated as the sum of all debt (current liabilities, deferred taxes, long-term debt, and preferred stock) divided by total assets.
[d]The days sales outstanding ratio in this table is calculated assuming a 360-day accounting year.
Source: *Value Line*, March 1999.

Ratio Analysis in the Internet Age

A great source for comparative ratios is **http://finance.yahoo.com.** About halfway down this web page is a field to enter a company's ticker symbol. Do this and click the "Get Quotes" button. This brings up a table whose last column is "More Info." In this column, select "Profile," which brings up a page with detailed information on the company. About halfway down the left side is a section called "More from Market Guide." Select the item "Ratio Comparisons." This brings up a detailed ratio analysis for the company and includes comparative ratios for other companies in the same sector, the same industry, and the S&P 500.

lenders. Therefore, D&B is concerned largely with the creditor's viewpoint, and its ratios emphasize current assets and liabilities, not market value ratios. So, when you select a comparative data source, you should be sure that your emphasis is similar to that of the agency whose ratios you plan to use. Additionally, there are often definitional differences in the ratios presented by different sources, so before using a source, be sure to verify the exact definitions of the ratios to ensure consistency with your own work.

Self-Test Questions

Differentiate between trend analysis and comparative ratio analysis.

Why is it useful to do a comparative ratio analysis?

What is benchmarking?

Uses and Limitations of Ratio Analysis

WWW

To find quick information about a company, link to **http://www.marketguide.com.** Here you can find company profiles, stock price and share information, and several key ratios.

As noted earlier, ratio analysis is used by three main groups: (1) *managers*, who employ ratios to help analyze, control, and thus improve their firms' operations; (2) *credit analysts*, including bank loan officers and bond rating analysts, who analyze ratios to help ascertain a company's ability to pay its debts; and (3) *stock analysts*, who are interested in a company's efficiency, risk, and growth prospects. In later chapters we will look more closely at the basic factors that underlie each ratio, which will give you a better idea about how to interpret and use ratios. Note, though, that while ratio analysis can provide useful information concerning a company's operations and financial condition, it does have limitations that necessitate care and judgment. Some potential problems are listed below:

1. Many large firms operate different divisions in different industries, and for such companies it is difficult to develop a meaningful set of industry averages. Therefore, ratio analysis is more useful for small, narrowly focused firms than for large, multidivisional ones.
2. Most firms want to be better than average, so merely attaining average performance is not necessarily good. As a target for high-level performance, it is best to focus on the industry leaders' ratios. Benchmarking helps in this regard.
3. Inflation may have badly distorted firms' balance sheets—recorded values are often substantially different from "true" values. Further, because inflation affects both depreciation charges and inventory costs, profits are also affected. Thus, a ratio analysis for one firm over time, or a comparative analysis of firms of different ages, must be interpreted with judgment.

4. Seasonal factors can also distort a ratio analysis. For example, the inventory turnover ratio for a food processor will be radically different if the balance sheet figure used for inventory is the one just before versus just after the close of the canning season. This problem can be minimized by using monthly averages for inventory (and receivables) when calculating turnover ratios.
5. Firms can employ **"window dressing" techniques** to make their financial statements look stronger. To illustrate, a Chicago builder borrowed on a two-year basis on December 29, 2000. Because the loan was for more than one year, it was not included in current liabilities. The builder held the proceeds of the loan as cash for a few days, and then paid off the loan ahead of time on January 2, 2001. This improved his current and quick ratios, and made his year-end 2000 balance sheet look good. However, the improvement was strictly window dressing; a week later the balance sheet was back at the old level.
6. Different accounting practices can distort comparisons. As noted earlier, inventory valuation and depreciation methods can affect financial statements and thus distort comparisons among firms. Also, if one firm leases a substantial amount of its productive equipment, then its assets may appear low relative to sales because leased assets often do not appear on the balance sheet. At the same time, the liability associated with the lease obligation may not be shown as a debt. Therefore, leasing can artificially improve both the turnover and the debt ratios. However, the accounting profession has taken steps to reduce this problem, as we discuss in Chapter 20.
7. It is difficult to generalize about whether a particular ratio is "good" or "bad." For example, a high current ratio may indicate a strong liquidity position, which is good, or excessive cash, which is bad (because excess cash in the bank is a nonearning asset). Similarly, a high fixed assets turnover ratio may denote either that a firm uses its assets efficiently or that it is undercapitalized and cannot afford to buy enough assets.
8. A firm may have some ratios that look "good" and others that look "bad," making it difficult to tell whether the company is, on balance, strong or weak. However, statistical procedures can be used to analyze the *net effects* of a set of ratios. Many banks and other lending organizations use discriminant analysis, a statistical technique, to analyze firms' financial ratios, and then classify the firms according to their probability of getting into financial trouble. See the Web/CD Extension to Chapter 25 for a description of discriminant analysis and its application to bankruptcy prediction.

Ratio analysis is useful, but analysts should be aware of these problems and make adjustments as necessary. Ratio analysis conducted in a mechanical, unthinking manner is dangerous, but used intelligently and with good judgment, it can provide useful insights into a firm's operations. Your judgment in interpreting a set of ratios is bound to be weak at this point, but it will improve as you go through the remainder of the book.

Self-Test Questions

List three types of users of ratio analysis. Would the different users emphasize the same or different types of ratios?

List several potential problems with ratio analysis.

Problems with ROE

In Chapter 1 we said that managers should strive to maximize shareholder wealth. If a firm takes steps to improve its ROE, does this mean that shareholder wealth will also increase? Not necessarily, for despite its widespread use and the fact that ROE and shareholder wealth are often highly correlated, serious problems can arise when firms use ROE as the *sole* measure of performance.

First, ROE does not consider risk. While shareholders clearly care about returns, they also care about risk. To illustrate this point, consider two divisions within the same firm. Division S has very stable cash flows and a predictable 15 percent ROE. Division R, on the other hand, has a 16 percent expected ROE, but its cash flows are very risky, so the expected ROE may not materialize. If managers were compensated solely on the basis of ROE, and if the expected ROEs were actually achieved, then Division R's manager would receive a higher bonus than Division S's manager, even though Division S may actually create more value for shareholders as a result of its lower risk.

Second, ROE does not consider the amount of invested capital. To illustrate, consider a rather extreme example. A large company has $1 invested in Project A, which has an ROE of 50 percent, and $1 million invested in Project B, which has a 40 percent ROE. The projects are equally risky, and the two returns are both well above the cost the company had to pay for the capital invested in the projects. In this example, Project A has a higher ROE, but because it is so small, it does little to enhance shareholder wealth. Project B, on the other hand, has the lower ROE, but it adds much more to shareholder value.

Consider one last problem with ROE. Assume that you manage a division of a large firm. The firm uses ROE as the sole measure of performance, and it determines bonuses on the basis of ROE. Toward the end of the fiscal year, your division's ROE is an impressive 45 percent. Now you have an opportunity to invest in a large, low-risk project that has an estimated ROE of 35 percent, which is well above the cost of the capital you need to make the investment. Even though this project is profitable, you might be reluctant to make the investment because it would reduce your division's average ROE, and therefore reduce the size of your year-end bonus.

These three examples suggest that a project's return must be combined with its risk and size to determine its effect on shareholder value. To the extent that ROE focuses only on rate of return, increasing ROE may in some cases be inconsistent with increasing shareholder wealth. With this in mind, academics, practitioners, and consultants have tried to develop alternative measures that overcome ROE's potential problems when it is used as the sole gauge of performance. One such measure is Economic Value Added (EVA), as discussed in Chapter 2. Chapter 12 provides a more detailed description of the relationship between ratios and shareholder value.

Self-Test Question

If a firm takes steps to improve its ROE, does this mean that shareholder wealth will also increase? Explain.

Looking Beyond the Numbers

WWW

Students might want to refer to AAII's educational web site at **http://www.aaii.org.** The site provides information on investing basics, financial planning, portfolio management, and the like, so individuals can manage their own assets more effectively.

Hopefully, working through this chapter has helped your understanding of financial statements and improved your ability to interpret accounting numbers. These important and basic skills are necessary when making business decisions, evaluating performance, and forecasting likely future developments.

Sound financial analysis involves more than just calculating numbers—good analysis requires that certain qualitative factors be considered when evaluating a company. These factors, as summarized by the American Association of Individual Investors (AAII), include the following:

1. **Are the company's revenues tied to one key customer?** If so, the company's performance may decline dramatically if the customer goes elsewhere. On the other hand, if the relationship is firmly entrenched, this might actually stabilize sales.

2. **To what extent are the company's revenues tied to one key product?** Companies that rely on a single product may be more efficient and focused, but a lack of diversification increases risk. If revenues come from several different products, the overall bottom line will be less affected by a drop in the demand for any one product.
3. **To what extent does the company rely on a single supplier?** Depending on a single supplier may lead to unanticipated shortages and thus to lower profits.
4. **What percentage of the company's business is generated overseas?** Companies with a large percentage of overseas business are often able to realize higher growth and larger profit margins. However, firms with large overseas operations also find that the value of their operations depends in large part on the value of the local currency. Thus, fluctuations in currency markets create additional risks for firms with large overseas operations. In addition, the political stability of the region is important.
5. **Competition.** Generally, increased competition lowers prices and profit margins. In forecasting future performance, it is important to assess both the likely actions of the current competition and the likelihood of new competitors in the future.
6. **Future prospects.** Does the company invest heavily in research and development? If so, its future prospects may depend critically on the success of new products in the pipeline. For example, the market's assessment of a computer company depends on how next year's products are shaping up. Likewise, investors in pharmaceutical companies are interested in knowing whether the company has developed any potential blockbuster drugs that are doing well in the required tests.
7. **Legal and regulatory environment.** Changes in laws and regulations have important implications for many industries. For example, when forecasting the future of tobacco companies, it is crucial to factor in the effects of proposed regulations and pending or likely lawsuits. Likewise, when assessing banks, telecommunications firms, and electric utilities, analysts need to forecast both the extent to which these industries will be regulated in the years ahead, and the ability of individual firms to respond to changes in regulation.

Self-Test Question

What are some qualitative factors analysts should consider when evaluating a company's likely future financial performance?

Summary

The primary purpose of this chapter was to discuss techniques used by investors and managers to analyze financial statements. The key concepts covered are listed below.

- **Financial statement analysis** generally begins with a set of **financial ratios** designed to reveal a company's strengths and weaknesses as compared with other companies in the same industry, and to show whether its financial position has been improving or deteriorating over time.
- **Liquidity ratios** show the relationship of a firm's current assets to its current liabilities, and thus its ability to meet maturing debts. Two commonly used liquidity ratios are the **current ratio** and the **quick,** or **acid test, ratio.**
- **Asset management ratios** measure how effectively a firm is managing its assets. These ratios include **inventory turnover, days sales outstanding, fixed assets turnover,** and **total assets turnover.**
- **Debt management ratios** reveal (1) the extent to which the firm is financed with debt and (2) its likelihood of defaulting on its debt obligations. They include the **debt ratio, times-interest-earned ratio,** and **EBITDA coverage ratio.**

- **Profitability ratios** show the combined effects of liquidity, asset management, and debt management policies on operating results. They include the **profit margin on sales,** the **basic earning power ratio,** the **return on total assets,** and the **return on common equity.**
- **Market value ratios** relate the firm's stock price to its earnings, cash flow, and book value per share, thus giving management an indication of what investors think of the company's past performance and future prospects. These include the **price/earnings ratio, price/cash flow ratio,** and the **market/book ratio.**
- **Trend analysis,** where one plots a ratio over time, is important, because it reveals whether the firm's condition has been improving or deteriorating over time.
- The **Du Pont system** is designed to show how the profit margin on sales, the assets turnover ratio, and the use of debt interact to determine the rate of return on equity. The firm's management can use the Du Pont system to analyze ways of improving performance.
- **Benchmarking** is the process of comparing a particular company with a group of "benchmark" companies.
- ROE is important, but it does not take account of either the amount of investment or risk. **Economic Value Added (EVA)** brings these factors into the analysis.

Ratio analysis has limitations, but used with care and judgment, it can be very helpful.

Questions

3–1 Define each of the following terms:

a. Liquidity ratios: current ratio; quick, or acid test, ratio

b. Asset management ratios: inventory turnover ratio; days sales outstanding (DSO); fixed assets turnover ratio; total assets turnover ratio

c. Financial leverage: debt ratio; times-interest-earned (TIE) ratio; coverage ratio

d. Profitability ratios: profit margin on sales; basic earning power (BEP) ratio; return on total assets (ROA); return on common equity (ROE)

e. Market value ratios: price/earnings (P/E) ratio; price/cash flow ratio; market/book (M/B) ratio; book value per share

f. Trend analysis; comparative ratio analysis; benchmarking

g. Du Pont chart; Du Pont equation

h. "Window dressing"; seasonal effects on ratios

3–2 Financial ratio analysis is conducted by four groups of analysts: managers, equity investors, long-term creditors, and short-term creditors. What is the primary emphasis of each of these groups in evaluating ratios?

3–3 Why would the inventory turnover ratio be more important when analyzing a grocery chain than an insurance company?

3–4 Over the past year, M. D. Ryngaert & Co. has realized an increase in its current ratio and a drop in its total assets turnover ratio. However, the company's sales, quick ratio, and fixed assets turnover ratio have remained constant. What explains these changes?

3–5 Profit margins and turnover ratios vary from one industry to another. What differences would you expect to find between a grocery chain such as Safeway and a steel company? Think particularly about the turnover ratios, the profit margin, and the Du Pont equation.

3–6 How does inflation distort ratio analysis comparisons, both for one company over time (trend analysis) and when different companies are compared? Are only balance sheet items or both balance sheet and income statement items affected?

3–7 If a firm's ROE is low and management wants to improve it, explain how using more debt might help.

3-8 How might (a) seasonal factors and (b) different growth rates distort a comparative ratio analysis? Give some examples. How might these problems be alleviated?

3-9 Why is it sometimes misleading to compare a company's financial ratios with other firms that operate in the same industry?

3-10 Indicate the effects of the transactions listed in the following table on total current assets, current ratio, and net income. Use (+) to indicate an increase, (−) to indicate a decrease, and (0) to indicate either no effect or an indeterminate effect. Be prepared to state any necessary assumptions, and assume an initial current ratio of more than 1.0. (Note: A good accounting background is necessary to answer some of these questions; if yours is not strong, just answer the questions you can handle.)

	Total Current Assets	Current Ratio	Effect on Net Income
a. Cash is acquired through issuance of additional common stock.	____	____	____
b. Merchandise is sold for cash.	____	____	____
c. Federal income tax due for the previous year is paid.	____	____	____
d. A fixed asset is sold for less than book value.	____	____	____
e. A fixed asset is sold for more than book value.	____	____	____
f. Merchandise is sold on credit.	____	____	____
g. Payment is made to trade creditors for previous purchases.	____	____	____
h. A cash dividend is declared and paid.	____	____	____
i. Cash is obtained through short-term bank loans.	____	____	____
j. Short-term notes receivable are sold at a discount.	____	____	____
k. Marketable securities are sold below cost.	____	____	____
l. Advances are made to employees.	____	____	____
m. Current operating expenses are paid.	____	____	____
n. Short-term promissory notes are issued to trade creditors in exchange for past due accounts payable.	____	____	____
o. Ten-year notes are issued to pay off accounts payable.	____	____	____
p. A fully depreciated asset is retired.	____	____	____
q. Accounts receivable are collected.	____	____	____
r. Equipment is purchased with short-term notes.	____	____	____
s. Merchandise is purchased on credit.	____	____	____
t. The estimated taxes payable are increased.	____	____	____

Self-Test Problems (Solutions Appear in Appendix A)

ST–1 *DEBT RATIO* K. Billingsworth & Co. had earnings per share of $4 last year, and it paid a $2 dividend. Total retained earnings increased by $12 million during the year, while book value per share at year-end was $40. Billingsworth has no preferred stock, and no new common stock was issued during the year. If Billingsworth's year-end debt (which equals its total liabilities) was $120 million, what was the company's year-end debt/assets ratio?

ST–2 *RATIO ANALYSIS* The following data apply to A.L. Kaiser & Company (millions of dollars):

Cash and marketable securities	$100.00
Fixed assets	$283.50
Sales	$1,000.00
Net income	$50.00
Quick ratio	2.0×
Current ratio	3.0×
DSO	40 days
ROE	12%

Kaiser has no preferred stock—only common equity, current liabilities, and long-term debt.

a. Find Kaiser's (1) accounts receivable (A/R), (2) current liabilities, (3) current assets, (4) total assets, (5) ROA, (6) common equity, and (7) long-term debt.

b. In part a, you should have found Kaiser's accounts receivable (A/R) = $111.1 million. If Kaiser could reduce its DSO from 40 days to 30 days while holding other things constant, how much cash would it generate? If this cash were used to buy back common stock (at book value), thus reducing the amount of common equity, how would this affect (1) the ROE, (2) the ROA, and (3) the total debt/total assets ratio?

Problems

3–1 *LIQUIDITY RATIOS*
Ace Industries has current assets equal to $3 million. The company's current ratio is 1.5, and its quick ratio is 1.0. What is the firm's level of current liabilities? What is the firm's level of inventories?

3–2 *DAYS SALES OUTSTANDING*
Baker Brothers has a DSO of 40 days. The company's average daily sales are $20,000. What is the level of its accounts receivable? Assume there are 360 days in a year.

3–3 *DEBT RATIO*
Bartley Barstools has an equity multiplier of 2.4. The company's assets are financed with some combination of long-term debt and common equity. What is the company's debt ratio?

3–4 *DU PONT ANALYSIS*
Doublewide Dealers has an ROA of 10 percent, a 2 percent profit margin, and a return on equity equal to 15 percent. What is the company's total assets turnover? What is the firm's equity multiplier?

3–5 *RATIO CALCULATIONS*
Assume you are given the following relationships for the Brauer Corporation:

Sales/total assets	1.5×
Return on assets (ROA)	3%
Return on equity (ROE)	5%

Calculate Brauer's profit margin and debt ratio.

3–6 *LIQUIDITY RATIOS*
The Petry Company has $1,312,500 in current assets and $525,000 in current liabilities. Its initial inventory level is $375,000, and it will raise funds as additional notes payable and use them to increase inventory. How much can Petry's short-term debt (notes payable) increase without pushing its current ratio below 2.0? What will be the firm's quick ratio after Petry has raised the maximum amount of short-term funds?

3–7 *RATIO CALCULATIONS*
The Kretovich Company had a quick ratio of 1.4, a current ratio of 3.0, an inventory turnover of 6 times, total current assets of $810,000, and cash and marketable securities of $120,000. What were Kretovich's annual sales and its DSO?

3–8 *TIMES-INTEREST-EARNED RATIO*
The H.R. Pickett Corporation has $500,000 of debt outstanding, and it pays an interest rate of 10 percent annually. Pickett's annual sales are $2 million, its average tax rate is 30 percent, and its net profit margin on sales is 5 percent. If the company does not maintain a TIE ratio of at least 5 times, its bank will refuse to renew the loan, and bankruptcy will result. What is Pickett's TIE ratio?

3–9 *RETURN ON EQUITY*
Midwest Packaging's ROE last year was only 3 percent, but its management has developed a new operating plan designed to improve things. The new plan calls for a total debt ratio of 60 percent, which will result in interest charges of $300,000 per year. Management projects an EBIT of $1,000,000 on sales of $10,000,000, and it expects to have a total assets turnover ratio of 2.0. Under these conditions, the tax rate will be 34 percent. If the changes are made, what return on equity will the company earn?

3–10 *RETURN ON EQUITY*
Central City Construction Company, which is just being formed, needs $1 million of assets, and it expects to have a basic earning power ratio of 20 percent. Central City will own no securities, so all of its income will be operating income. If it chooses to, Central City can finance up to 50 percent of its assets with debt, which will have an 8 percent interest rate. Assuming a 40 percent federal-plus-state tax rate on all taxable income, what is the *difference* between its expected ROE if Central City finances with 50 percent debt versus its expected ROE if it finances entirely with common stock?

3–11 CONCEPTUAL: RETURN ON EQUITY

Which of the following statements is most correct? (Hint: Work Problem 3-10 before answering 3-11, and consider the solution setup for 3-10 as you think about 3-11.)

a. If a firm's expected basic earning power (BEP) is constant for all of its assets and exceeds the interest rate on its debt, then adding assets and financing them with debt will raise the firm's expected rate of return on common equity (ROE).
b The higher its tax rate, the lower a firm's BEP ratio will be, other things held constant.
c. The higher the interest rate on its debt, the lower a firm's BEP ratio will be, other things held constant.
d. The higher its debt ratio, the lower a firm's BEP ratio will be, other things held constant.
e. Statement a is false, but b, c, and d are all true.

3–12 RETURN ON EQUITY

Lloyd and Daughters Inc. has sales of $200,000, a net income of $15,000, and the following balance sheet:

Cash	$ 10,000	Accounts payable	$ 30,000
Receivables	50,000	Other current liabilities	20,000
Inventories	150,000	Long-term debt	50,000
Net fixed assets	90,000	Common equity	200,000
Total assets	$300,000	Total liabilities and equity	$300,000

a. The company's new owner thinks that inventories are excessive and can be lowered to the point where the current ratio is equal to the industry average, 2.5×, without affecting either sales or net income. If inventories are sold off and not replaced so as to reduce the current ratio to 2.5×, if the funds generated are used to reduce common equity (stock can be repurchased at book value), and if no other changes occur, by how much will the ROE change?
b. Now suppose we wanted to take this problem and modify it for use on an exam, that is, to create a new problem that you have not seen to test your knowledge of this type of problem. How would your answer change if (1) We doubled all the dollar amounts? (2) We stated that the target current ratio was 3×? (3) We stated that the target was to achieve an inventory turnover ratio of 2× rather than a current ratio of 2.5×? (Hint: Compare the ROE obtained with an inventory turnover ratio of 2× to the original ROE obtained before any changes are considered.) (4) We said that the company had 10,000 shares of stock outstanding, and we asked how much the change in part a would increase EPS? (5) What would your answer to (4) be if we changed the original problem to state that the stock was selling for twice book value, so common equity would not be reduced on a dollar-for-dollar basis?
c. Now explain how we could have set the problem up to have you focus on changing accounts receivable, or fixed assets, or using the funds generated to retire debt (we would give you the interest rate on outstanding debt), or how the original problem could have stated that the company needed *more* inventories and it would finance them with new common equity or with new debt.

3–13 RATIO ANALYSIS

Data for Barry Computer Company and its industry averages follow.

a. Calculate the indicated ratios for Barry.
b. Construct the extended Du Pont equation for both Barry and the industry.
c. Outline Barry's strengths and weaknesses as revealed by your analysis.
d. Suppose Barry had doubled its sales as well as its inventories, accounts receivable, and common equity during 2001. How would that information affect the validity of your ratio analysis? (Hint: Think about averages and the effects of rapid growth on ratios if averages are not used. No calculations are needed.)

Barry Computer Company: Balance Sheet as of December 31, 2001 (In Thousands)

Cash	$ 77,500	Accounts payable	$129,000
Receivables	336,000	Notes payable	84,000
Inventories	241,500	Other current liabilities	117,000
Total current assets	$655,000	Total current liabilities	$330,000
Net fixed assets	292,500	Long-term debt	256,500
		Common equity	361,000
Total assets	$947,500	Total liabilities and equity	$947,500

Barry Computer Company: Income Statement for Year Ended December 31, 2001 (In Thousands)

Sales		$1,607,500
Cost of goods sold		
Materials	$717,000	
Labor	453,000	
Heat, light, and power	68,000	
Indirect labor	113,000	
Depreciation	41,500	1,392,500
Gross profit		$ 215,000
Selling expenses		115,000
General and administrative expenses		30,000
Earnings before interest and taxes (EBIT)		$ 70,000
Interest expense		24,500
Earnings before taxes (EBT)		$ 45,500
Federal and state income taxes (40%)		18,200
Net income		$ 27,300

Ratio	Barry	Industry Average
Current assets/current liabilities	______	2.0×
Days sales outstanding[a]	______	35 days
Sales/inventory	______	6.7×
Sales/fixed assets	______	12.1×
Sales/total assets	______	3.0×
Net income/sales	______	1.2%
Net income/total assets	______	3.6%
Net income/common equity	______	9.0%
Total debt/total assets	______	60.0%

[a]Calculation is based on a 360-day year.

3–14 *BALANCE SHEET ANALYSIS*

Complete the balance sheet and sales information in the table that follows for Hoffmeister Industries using the following financial data:

Debt ratio: 50%
Quick ratio: 0.80×
Total assets turnover: 1.5×
Days sales outstanding: 36 days[a]
Gross profit margin on sales: (Sales − Cost of goods sold)/Sales = 25%
Inventory turnover ratio: 5×

[a]Calculation is based on a 360-day year.

BALANCE SHEET

Cash	______	Accounts payable	______
Accounts receivable	______	Long-term debt	60,000
Inventories	______	Common stock	______
Fixed assets	______	Retained earnings	97,500
Total assets	$300,000	Total liabilities and equity	______
Sales	______	Cost of goods sold	______

3–15 *DU PONT ANALYSIS*

The Ferri Furniture Company, a manufacturer and wholesaler of high-quality home furnishings, has been experiencing low profitability in recent years. As a result, the board of directors has replaced the president of the firm with a new president, Helen Adams, who has asked you to make an analysis of the firm's financial position using the Du Pont chart. The most recent industry average ratios, and Ferri's financial statements, are as follows:

INDUSTRY AVERAGE RATIOS

Current ratio	2×	Sales/fixed assets	6×
Debt/total assets	30%	Sales/total assets	3×
Times-interest-earned	7×	Profit margin on sales	3%
EBITDA coverage	9×	Return on total assets	9%
Sales/inventory	10×	Return on common equity	12.9%
Days sales outstanding[a]	24 days		

[a]Calculation is based on a 360-day year.

Ferri Furniture Company: Balance Sheet as of December 31, 2001 (Millions of Dollars)

Cash	$ 45	Accounts payable	$ 45
Marketable securities	33	Notes payable	45
Net receivables	66	Other current liabilities	21
Inventories	159	Total current liabilities	$111
Total current assets	$303	Long-term debt	24
		Total liabilities	$135
Gross fixed assets	225		
Less depreciation	78	Common stock	114
Net fixed assets	$147	Retained earnings	201
		Total stockholders' equity	$315
Total assets	$450	Total liabilities and equity	$450

Ferri Furniture Company: Income Statement for Year Ended December 31, 2001 (Millions of Dollars)

Net sales	$795.0
Cost of goods sold	660.0
Gross profit	$135.0
Selling expenses	73.5
Depreciation expense	12.0
Earnings before interest and taxes	$ 49.5
Interest expense	4.5
Earnings before taxes (EBT)	45.0
Taxes (40%)	18.0
Net income	$ 27.0

a. Calculate those ratios that you think would be useful in this analysis.
b. Construct an extended Du Pont equation for Ferri, and compare the company's ratios to the industry average ratios.
c. Do the balance sheet accounts or the income statement figures seem to be primarily responsible for the low profits?
d. Which specific accounts seem to be most out of line in relation to other firms in the industry?

e. If Ferri had a pronounced seasonal sales pattern, or if it grew rapidly during the year, how might that affect the validity of your ratio analysis? How might you correct for such potential problems?

3–16 *RATIO ANALYSIS* The Corrigan Corporation's forecasted 2002 financial statements follow, along with some industry average ratios.

a. Calculate Corrigan's 2002 forecasted ratios, compare them with the industry average data, and comment briefly on Corrigan's projected strengths and weaknesses.

b. What do you think would happen to Corrigan's ratios if the company initiated cost-cutting measures that allowed it to hold lower levels of inventory and substantially decreased the cost of goods sold? No calculations are necessary. Think about which ratios would be affected by changes in these two accounts.

Corrigan Corporation: Forecasted Balance Sheet as of December 31, 2002

Cash	$ 72,000
Accounts receivable	439,000
Inventories	894,000
Total current assets	$1,405,000
Land and building	238,000
Machinery	132,000
Other fixed assets	61,000
Total assets	$1,836,000
Accounts and notes payable	$ 432,000
Accruals	170,000
Total current liabilities	$ 602,000
Long-term debt	404,290
Common stock	575,000
Retained earnings	254,710
Total liabilities and equity	$1,836,000

Corrigan Corporation: Forecasted Income Statement for 2002

Sales	$4,290,000
Cost of goods sold	3,580,000
Gross operating profit	$ 710,000
General administrative and selling expenses	236,320
Depreciation	159,000
Miscellaneous	134,000
Earnings before taxes (EBT)	$ 180,680
Taxes (40%)	72,272
Net income	$ 108,408

Per-Share Data

EPS	$4.71
Cash dividends	$0.95
P/E ratio	5×
Market price (average)	$23.57
Number of shares outstanding	23,000

Industry Financial Ratios (2002)[a]

Quick ratio	1.0×
Current ratio	2.7×
Inventory turnover[b]	7.0×
Days sales outstanding[c]	32 days
Fixed assets turnover[b]	13.0×
Total assets turnover[b]	2.6×
Return on assets	9.1%
Return on equity	18.2%
Debt ratio	50.0%
Profit margin on sales	3.5%
P/E ratio	6.0×
P/cash flow ratio	3.5×

[a]Industry average ratios have been constant for the past 4 years.
[b]Based on year-end balance sheet figures.
[c]Calculation is based on a 360-day year.

Spreadsheet Problems

3–17 BUILD A MODEL: RATIO ANALYSIS

Start with the partial model in the file ***Ch 03-17 Build a Model.xls*** from the textbook's CD-ROM. This problem requires you to further analyze the financial data given for Cumberland Industries in the Build a Model problem for Chapter 2.

Cumberland Industries' common stock has increased in price from $14.75 to $17.25 from the end of 2000 to the end of 2001, and its shares outstanding increased from 9 to 10 million shares during that same period. Cumberland has annual lease payments of $75,000 (which is included in operating costs on the income statement), but no sinking fund payments are required. Now answer the following questions.

Using Cumberland's financial statements as given in the Chapter 2 Build a Model problem, perform a ratio analysis for 2000 and 2001. Consider its liquidity, asset management, debt management, profitability, and market value ratios.

a. Has Cumberland's liquidity position improved or worsened? Explain.
b. Has Cumberland's ability to manage its assets improved or worsened? Explain.
c. How has Cumberland's profitability changed during the last year?
d. Perform an extended Du Pont analysis for Cumberland for 2000 and 2001.
e. Perform a common size analysis. What has happened to the composition (that is, percentage in each category) of assets and liabilities?
f. Perform a percent change analysis. What does this tell you about the change in profitability and asset utilization?

3–18 WHAT IF ANALYSIS: RATIO ANALYSIS

Start with the model in the file ***Ch 03-18 What If Analysis.xls*** from the textbook's CD-ROM and answer the questions shown there.

Cyberproblem

The information related to the cyberproblems is likely to change over time, due to the release of new information and the ever-changing nature of the World Wide Web. With these changes in mind, we will periodically update these problems on the textbook's web site.

3–19 USING RATIO ANALYSIS AS A TOOL

Chapter 3 demonstrates the various ways that managers and investors use financial statements. The following cyberproblem addresses the financial statement analysis of Brady Corporation, a leader in identification, safety, and material solutions. In 1998, the firm was hit hard by faltering foreign markets, so it embarked upon an aggressive campaign to redesign its cost structure. The firm believes this will help it to enhance future stockholder value. Brady follows the concept of Shareholder Value Enhancement (SVE), which is improved through increased sales, cost control, and effective use and control of assets. Take a look at the cyberproblem on the textbook's web site, **http://www.harcourtcollege.com/finance/theory/student/resources/cyberprob/ch03.html.**, and answer the questions shown there.

Mini Case

CD

See ***Ch 03 Show.ppt*** for a *PowerPoint* presentation of the Mini Case and ***Ch 03 Mini Case.xls*** for detailed calculations.

The first part of the case, presented in Chapter 2, discussed the situation that Computron Industries was in after an expansion program. Thus far, sales have not been up to the forecasted level, costs have been higher than were projected, and a large loss occurred in 2001, rather than the expected profit. As a result, its managers, directors, and investors are concerned about the firm's survival.

Donna Jamison was brought in as assistant to Fred Campo, Computron's chairman, who had the task of getting the company back into a sound financial position. Computron's 2000 and 2001 balance sheets and income statements, together with projections for 2002, are shown in the following tables. Also, the tables show the 2000 and 2001 financial ratios, along with industry average data. The 2002 projected financial statement data represent Jamison's and Campo's best guess for 2002 results, assuming that some new financing is arranged to get the company "over the hump."

	2002E	2001	2000
BALANCE SHEETS			
Assets			
Cash	$ 14,000	$ 7,282	$ 9,000
Short-term investments	71,632	0	48,600
Accounts receivable	878,000	632,160	351,200
Inventories	1,716,480	1,287,360	715,200
Total current assets	$2,680,112	$1,926,802	$1,124,000
Gross fixed assets	1,197,160	1,202,950	491,000
Less accumulated depreciation	380,120	263,160	146,200
Net fixed assets	$ 817,040	$ 939,790	$ 344,800
Total assets	$3,497,152	$2,866,592	$1,468,800
Liabilities and Equity			
Accounts payable	$ 436,800	$ 524,160	$ 145,600
Notes payable	600,000	720,000	200,000
Accruals	408,000	489,600	136,000
Total current liabilities	$1,444,800	$1,733,760	$ 481,600
Long-term debt	500,000	1,000,000	323,432
Common stock	1,680,936	460,000	460,000
Retained earnings	(128,584)	(327,168)	203,768
Total equity	$1,552,352	$ 132,832	$ 663,768
Total liabilities and equity	$3,497,152	$2,866,592	$1,468,800

NOTE: "E" indicates estimated. The 2002 data are forecasts.

	2002E	2001	2000
INCOME STATEMENTS			
Sales	$7,035,600	$5,834,400	$3,432,000
Cost of goods sold	6,100,000	5,728,000	2,864,000
Other expenses	312,960	680,000	340,000
Depreciation	120,000	116,960	18,900
Total operating costs	$6,532,960	$6,524,960	$3,222,900
EBIT	$ 502,640	($ 690,560)	$ 209,100
Interest expense	80,000	176,000	62,500
EBT	$ 422,640	($ 866,560)	$ 146,600
Taxes (40%)	169,056	(346,624)	58,640
Net income	$ 253,584	($ 519,936)	$ 87,960
EPS	$1.014	($5.199)	$0.880
DPS	$0.220	$0.110	$0.220
Book value per share	$6.209	$1.328	$6.638
Stock price	$12.17	$2.25	$8.50
Shares outstanding	250,000	100,000	100,000
Tax rate	40.00%	40.00%	40.00%
Lease payments	40,000	40,000	40,000
Sinking fund payments	0	0	0

NOTE: "E" indicates estimated. The 2002 data are forecasts.

	2002E	2001	2000	Industry Average
RATIO ANALYSIS				
Current		1.1×	2.3×	2.7×
Quick		0.4×	0.8×	1.0×
Inventory turnover		4.5×	4.8×	6.1×
Days sales outstanding (DSO)		39.0	36.8	32.0
Fixed assets turnover		6.2×	10.0×	7.0×
Total assets turnover		2.0×	2.3×	2.5×
Debt ratio		95.4%	54.8%	50.0%
TIE		−3.9×	3.3×	6.2×
EBITDA coverage		−2.5×	2.6×	8.0×
Profit margin		−8.9%	2.6%	3.6%
Basic earning power		−24.1%	14.2%	17.8%
ROA		−18.1%	6.0%	9.0%
ROE		−391.4%	13.3%	18.0%
Price/earnings		−0.4×	9.7×	14.2×
Price/cash flow		−0.6×	8.0×	7.6×
Market/book		1.7×	1.3×	2.9×
Book value per share		$1.33	$6.64	n.a.

NOTE: "E" indicates estimated. The 2002 data are forecasts.

Jamison examined monthly data for 2001 (not given in the case), and she detected an improving pattern during the year. Monthly sales were rising, costs were falling, and large losses in the early months had turned to a small profit by December. Thus, the annual data looked somewhat worse than final monthly data. Also, it appears to be taking longer for the advertising program to get the message across, for the new sales offices to generate sales, and for the new manufacturing facilities to operate efficiently. In other words, the lags between spending money and deriving benefits were longer than Computron's managers had anticipated. For these reasons, Jamison and Campo see hope for the company—provided it can survive in the short run.

Jamison must prepare an analysis of where the company is now, what it must do to regain its financial health, and what actions should be taken. Your assignment is to help her answer the following questions. Provide clear explanations, not yes or no answers.

a. Why are ratios useful? What are the five major categories of ratios?
b. Calculate the 2002 current and quick ratios based on the projected balance sheet and income statement data. What can you say about the company's liquidity position in 2000, 2001, and as projected for 2002? We often think of ratios as being useful (1) to managers to help run the business, (2) to bankers for credit analysis, and (3) to stockholders for stock valuation. Would these different types of analysts have an equal interest in the liquidity ratios?
c. Calculate the 2002 inventory turnover, days sales outstanding (DSO), fixed assets turnover, and total assets turnover. How does Computron's utilization of assets stack up against other firms in its industry?
d. Calculate the 2002 debt, times-interest-earned, and EBITDA coverage ratios. How does Computron compare with the industry with respect to financial leverage? What can you conclude from these ratios?
e. Calculate the 2002 profit margin, basic earning power (BEP), return on assets (ROA), and return on equity (ROE). What can you say about these ratios?
f. Calculate the 2002 price/earnings ratio, price/cash flow ratio, and market/book ratio. Do these ratios indicate that investors are expected to have a high or low opinion of the company?
g. Perform a common size analysis and percent change analysis. What do these analyses tell you about Computron?
h. Use the extended Du Pont equation to provide a summary and overview of Computron's financial condition as projected for 2002. What are the firm's major strengths and weaknesses?
i. Use the following simplified 2002 balance sheet to show, in general terms, how an improvement in the DSO would tend to affect the stock price. For example, if the company could improve its collection procedures and thereby lower its DSO from 44.9 days to the 32-day industry average without affecting sales, how would that change "ripple through" the financial statements (shown in thousands below) and influence the stock price?

Accounts receivable	$ 878	Debt	$1,945
Other current assets	1,802		
Net fixed assets	817	Equity	1,552
Total assets	$3,497	Liabilities plus equity	$3,497

j. Does it appear that inventories could be reduced, and, if so, how should that adjustment affect Computron's profitability and stock price?
k. In 2001, the company paid its suppliers much later than the due dates, and it was not maintaining financial ratios at levels called for in its bank loan agreements. Therefore, suppliers could cut the company off, and its bank could refuse to renew the loan when it comes due in 90 days. On the basis of data provided, would you, as a credit manager, continue to sell to Computron on credit? (You could demand cash on delivery, that is, sell on terms of COD, but that might cause Computron to stop buying from your company.) Similarly, if you were the bank loan officer, would you recommend renewing the loan or demand its repayment? Would your actions be influenced if, in early 2002, Computron showed you its 2002 projections plus proof that it was going to raise over $1.2 million of new equity capital?
l. In hindsight, what should Computron have done back in 2000?
m. What are some potential problems and limitations of financial ratio analysis?
n. What are some qualitative factors analysts should consider when evaluating a company's likely future financial performance?

Selected Additional References and Cases

The effects of alternative accounting policies on both financial statements and ratios based on these statements are discussed in the investment textbooks referenced in Chapter 6, and also in the many excellent texts on financial statement analysis. For example, see

Fraser, Lyn M., *Understanding Financial Statements* (Englewood Cliffs, NJ: Prentice-Hall, 1992).

Gibson, Charles H., and Patricia A. Frishkoff, *Financial Statement Analysis* (Boston: Kent, 1986).

Hawkins, David F., *Corporate Financial Reporting and Analysis* (Homewood, IL: Irwin, 1986).

For further information on the relative usefulness of various financial ratios, see

Chen, Kung H., and Thomas A. Shimerda, "An Empirical Analysis of Useful Financial Ratios," *Financial Management*, Spring 1981, 51–60.

Considerable work has been done to establish the relationship between bond ratings and financial ratios. For one example, see

Belkaoui, Ahmed, *Industrial Bonds and the Rating Process* (London: Quorum Books, 1983).

For sources of ratios and common size statements, see the following:

Dun & Bradstreet, *Key Business Ratios* (New York: Updated annually).

Financial Research Associates, *Financial Studies of the Small Business* (Arlington, VA: Updated annually).

Robert Morris Associates, *Annual Statement Studies* (Philadelphia: Updated annually).

The following cases from the Cases in Financial Management: Dryden Request *series focus on financial analysis:*

Case 35, "Mark X Company (A)," which illustrates the use of ratio analysis in the evaluation of a firm's existing and potential financial positions.

Case 36, "Garden State Container Corporation," which is similar in content to Case 35.

Case 36A, "Safe Packaging Corporation," which updates Case 36.

4

Financial Planning and Forecasting Financial Statements

For executives at Walt Disney, 1998 was a particularly difficult year. After several years of outstanding performance, Disney's earnings fell, causing a sharp drop in its stock price. Trying to address investors' concerns, Disney's Chairman and Chief Executive, Michael Eisner, began his annual letter to shareholders with the following words:

> To Disney Owners and Fellow Cast Members:
>
> I am looking out the window and can see the seasons change (yes, the seasons do change in Los Angeles—the eucalyptus leaves droop more and the sprinklers go on less often). I am reminded that our rhythms are set by the seasons and that any number of human endeavors are ruled by the calendar. Such as this annual report. Every 12 months we compile it, and every 12 months I sit down to write you this letter.
>
> There's just one problem with this annual exercise: It implies that businesses can be run in neat 12-month chunks of time. Unfortunately, the business cycle has its own seasons, which are not ruled by the orderly and predictable orbit of the earth around the sun. Indeed, at Disney we live by a 60-month calendar. We set our goals over rolling five-year timelines. In this context, each year is more like a season. Some are sunny and some are overcast, but each is merely a period of passage and not a destination. Our five-year calendars force us to think long-term. They make us devise strategies that add value, not squeeze profits.

Eisner went on to tell shareholders that the company's long-run forecast remained promising. After acknowledging that Disney had problems in its entertainment and broadcasting divisions, he went on to state that the company was taking steps to cut costs and to improve operations. Eisner also stated that Disney's earnings had been hampered because it had begun a series of expensive new projects, including Disney's Animal Kingdom, its Cruise Line, the launching of *ESPN Magazine*, and the renovation of Anaheim Stadium. However, he argued that they were laying the groundwork for future profitability.

In spite of Eisner's assurances, many analysts were doubtful about Disney's prospects, although others were betting that given its track record, the stock would rebound in the future. Unfortunately, no crystal ball exists for predicting the future. Instead, both corporate insiders and investors must base decisions on their own financial forecasts. While forecasting is necessarily somewhat subjective, we discuss in this chapter some basic principles that will improve financial forecasts. By the time you finish the chapter, you will have a good idea about how to forecast future results for Disney or any other company.

Source: Walt Disney Co.'s 1998 Annual Report.

Chapters 2 and 3 described what financial statements are and showed how both managers and investors analyze them to evaluate a firm's past performance. While this is clearly important, it is even more important to look ahead and to anticipate what is likely to happen in the future. So, both managers and investors need to understand how to forecast future results.

Managers make **pro forma,** or **projected, financial statements** and then use them in four ways: (1) By looking at projected statements, they can assess whether the firm's anticipated performance is in line with the firm's own general targets and with investors' expectations. For example, if the projected financial statements indicate that the forecasted return on equity is well below the industry average, managers should investigate the cause and then seek a remedy. (2) Pro forma statements can be used to estimate the effect of proposed operating changes. Therefore, financial managers spend a lot of time doing "what if" analyses. (3) Managers use pro forma statements to anticipate the firm's future financing needs. (4) Projected financial statements are used to estimate future free cash flows, which determine the company's overall value. Thus, managers forecast free cash flows under different operating plans, forecast their capital requirements, and then choose the plan that maximizes shareholder value.

The textbook's CD-ROM contains an Excel file that will guide you through the chapter's calculations. The file for this chapter is ***Ch 04 Tool Kit.xls*** and we encourage you to open the file and follow along as you read the chapter.

Security analysts make the same types of projections, forecasting future earnings, cash flows, and stock prices. Of course, managers have more information about the company than security analysts, and managers are the ones who make the decisions that determine the future. However, analysts influence investors, and investors determine the future of managers. To illustrate, suppose an influential analyst at a firm such as Goldman Sachs concludes, on the basis of a comparative financial analysis, that a particular firm's managers are less effective than others in the industry. The analyst's negative report could lead stockholders to revolt and replace management. Or, the report might lead a firm that specializes in taking over underperforming firms to buy stock in the company and then launch a hostile takeover designed to change management, improve cash flows, and give it a large capital gain.

We will have more to say about investors' and analysts' use of projections in Chapters 10 and 12, when we discuss how stock prices are determined. First, though, in this chapter we explain how to create and use pro forma financial statements. We begin with the strategic plan, which provides a foundation for pro forma statements.

Strategic Plans

Our primary objective in this book is to explain what managers can do to make their companies more valuable. Managers must understand how investors determine the values of stocks and bonds if they are to identify, evaluate, and implement projects that meet or exceed investor expectations. However, value creation is impossible unless the company has a well-articulated plan. As Yogi Berra once said, "You've got to be careful if you don't know where you're going, because you might not get there."

Companies begin with a **mission statement,** which is in many ways a condensed version of their strategic plan. Figure 4-1 shows the mission statement of Coca-Cola, which illustrates some key elements in all strategic plans.

Corporate Purpose

Both mission statements and strategic plans usually begin with a statement of the overall *corporate purpose.* Coca-Cola is very clear about its corporate purpose: "Our mission is to maximize shareowner value over time."

FIGURE 4-1 The Mission Statement of the Coca-Cola Company (http://www.thecoca-colacompany.com/tccc/index.html)

OUR MISSION

Our mission is to maximize shareowner value over time.

In order to achieve this mission, we must create value for all the constituents we serve, including our consumers, our customers, our bottlers, and our communities. The Coca-Cola Company creates value by executing a comprehensive business strategy guided by six key beliefs:

1. Consumer demand drives everything we do.
2. Brand Coca-Cola is the core of our business.
3. We will serve consumers a broad selection of the nonalcoholic ready-to-drink beverages they want to drink throughout the day.
4. We will be the best marketers in the world.
5. We will think and act locally.
6. We will lead as a model corporate citizen.

The ultimate objectives of our business strategy are to increase volume, expand our share of worldwide nonalcoholic ready-to-drink beverage sales, maximize our long-term cash flows, and create economic-value-added by improving economic profit.

The Coca-Cola system has more than 16 million customers around the world that sell or serve our products directly to consumers. We keenly focus on enhancing value for these customers and helping them grow their beverage businesses. We strive to understand each customer's business and needs, whether that customer is a sophisticated retailer in a developed market or a kiosk owner in an emerging market.

There are nearly 6 billion people in the world who are potential consumers of our Company's products. Ultimately, our success in achieving our mission depends on our ability to satisfy more of their beverage consumption demands and our ability to add value for our customers. We achieve this when we place the right products in the right markets at the right time.

This same corporate purpose is increasingly common for U.S. companies, but that has not always been the case. For example, Varian Associates, Inc., a New York Stock Exchange company with sales of almost $2 billion, was, in 1990, regarded as one of the most technologically advanced electronics companies. However, Varian's management was more concerned with developing new technology than with marketing it, and its stock price was lower than it had been ten years earlier. Some of the larger stockholders were intensely unhappy with the state of affairs, and management was faced with the threat of a proxy fight or forced merger. In 1991, management announced a change in policy and stated that it would, in the future, emphasize both technological excellence *and* profitability, rather than focusing primarily on technology. Earnings improved dramatically, and the stock price rose from $6.75 to more than $60 within four years of that change in corporate purpose. To improve its focus and thus increase shareholder wealth, Varian later split itself into three separate companies whose share price totaled to $120 in early 2001.

A corporate focus on creating wealth for the company's owners is not yet as common abroad as it is in the United States. For example, Veba AG, one of Germany's largest companies, created a stir in 1996 when it stated in its annual report that "Our commitment is to create value for you, our shareholders." This was quite different from the usual German model, in which companies have representatives from labor on their boards of directors and which explicitly state their commitments to a variety of stakeholders. As one might expect, Veba's stock has consistently outperformed the average German stock. As the trend in international investing continues, more and more non-U.S. companies are adopting a corporate purpose similar to that of Coke and Veba.

Corporate Scope

Its *corporate scope* defines a firm's lines of business and geographic area of operations. As Coca-Cola's mission statement indicates, the company limits its products to soft drinks, but on a global scale. Pepsi-Cola recently followed Coke's lead—it restricted its scope by spinning off its food service businesses.

Several recent studies have found that the market tends to value focused firms more highly than diversified firms.[1] The steel industry provides a study in contrasts. USX Corporation (formerly U.S. Steel) has diversified widely while Nucor Corporation (the second largest steel company) has stuck closely to the basic steel business. Here is Nucor's position:

> We are a manufacturing company producing primarily steel products. Nucor's major strength is constructing plants economically and operating them efficiently.

During the last two decades, an investment in Nucor's stock has increased by more than 16 percent per year versus 4 percent for USX. Many factors caused these results, but scope and focus certainly played an important role.

Corporate Objectives

The corporate purpose states the general philosophy of the business, but it does not provide managers with operational objectives. The *statement of corporate objectives* sets forth specific goals to guide management. Most organizations have both qualitative and quantitative objectives. For example, Coca-Cola's mission statement lists several corporate objectives, including "increase volume" and "create economic-value-added." However, these statements are qualitative, hence hard to measure, so the objectives need to be restated in quantitative terms, such as attaining a 50 percent market share, a 20 percent ROE, a 10 percent earnings growth rate, or a $100 million economic value added (EVA). Coca-Cola doesn't list its quantitative objectives in its mission statement, but it has them in its detailed strategic plan. Moreover, executive bonuses are based on achieving the quantitative objectives.

Corporate Strategies

Once a firm has defined its purpose, scope, and objectives, it must develop a strategy for achieving its goals. *Corporate strategies* are broad approaches rather than detailed plans. For example, one airline may have a strategy of offering no-frills service between a limited number of cities, while another's strategy may be to offer "staterooms in the sky." Strategies should be both attainable and compatible with the firm's purpose, scope, and objectives.

Some of the most interesting strategies developed in recent years are those of the Bell operating companies in the wake of the forced breakup of AT&T. The seven regional telephone holding companies that emerged from the breakup all provided basic local telephone service, but beyond that, they had different strategies that took them in different directions. Some now sell a broad array of telecommunications equipment, while others have more limited offerings. Some are rapidly diversifying into nonregulated lines of business—Bell Atlantic has spent more than $2 billion for this purpose—while others are diversifying at a much slower pace. Others are moving abroad; for example, BellSouth recently won a $220 million contract to build a mobile phone system in Argentina. Even more surprising, two separate mergers between the

[1]See, for example, Philip G. Berger and Eli Ofek, "Diversification's Effect on Firm Value," *Journal of Financial Economics*, Vol. 37, No. 1, 39–66 (1995); and Larry Lang and René Stulz, "Tobin's Q, Corporate Diversification, and Firm Performance," *Journal of Political Economy*, Vol. 102, Issue 6, 1248–1280 (1994).

operating companies—Bell Atlantic with NYNEX and SBC with Pacific Telesis and Ameritech—have recently been announced, and all of the "local service" companies are trying to get into the long-distance business in competition with former parent AT&T, so to some extent the breakup is being reversed.

Self-Test Questions

What are pro forma financial statements?

What are four ways that pro forma financial statements are used by managers?

Briefly describe the nature and use of the following corporate planning terms: (1) corporate purpose, (2) corporate scope, (3) corporate objectives, and (4) corporate strategies.

Operating Plans

Operating plans provide detailed implementation guidance, based on the stated corporate strategy, to help meet the corporate objectives. These plans can be developed for any time horizon, but like Disney, most companies use a five-year horizon. A five-year plan is most detailed for the first year, with each succeeding year's plan becoming less specific. The plan explains in considerable detail who is responsible for each particular function, when specific tasks are to be accomplished, sales and profit targets, and the like.

It should be noted that large, multidivisional companies such as General Electric break down their operating plans by divisions. Thus, each division has its own goals, mission, and plan for meeting its objectives, and these plans are then consolidated to form the corporate plan.[2]

Self-Test Questions

What is the purpose of a firm's operating plan?

What is the most common time horizon for operating plans?

Briefly describe the contents of a typical operating plan.

The Financial Plan

The financial planning process can be broken down into six steps:

1. Project financial statements and use these projections to analyze the effects of the operating plan on projected profits and financial ratios. The projections can also be used to monitor operations after the plan has been finalized and put into effect. Rapid awareness of deviations from the plan is essential in a good control system, which, in turn, is essential to corporate success in a changing world.
2. Determine the funds needed to support the five-year plan. This includes funds for plant and equipment as well as for inventories and receivables, R&D programs, and major advertising campaigns.
3. Forecast funds availability over the next five years. This involves estimating the funds to be generated internally as well as those to be obtained from external sources. Any constraints on operating plans imposed by financial restrictions must be incorporated into the plan. Constraints include restrictions on the debt ratio, the current ratio, and the coverage ratios.
4. Establish and maintain a system of controls to govern the allocation and use of funds within the firm. In essence, this involves making sure the basic plan is carried out properly.

[2]For more on the corporate planning process, see Benton E. Gup, *Guide to Strategic Planning* (New York: McGraw-Hill, 1980).

Financial Planning in the New Millennium

Many managers compare the current financial planning process with having a root canal: time-consuming and painful. Even worse, they are left with the nagging doubt that the results might not be completely reliable. According to a recent survey of finance professionals, only 45 percent are satisfied with their current planning process, and 90 percent believe it is too cumbersome. Nevertheless, 71 percent of the finance professionals believe long-term strategic planning is the single most critical activity for future success.

What's wrong with the current planning process? First, it's too slow. The process typically starts in July and ends in December. Given the ever-shortening life cycles of many products, plans are often out of date before they are completed. This creates implementation problems, and it also reduces the accuracy of earnings projections as reported to Wall Street. Second, it requires a considerable amount of managerial effort. On average, five full-time finance employees plus eight full-time nonfinance employees each spend four person-months on planning, equivalent to 4.33 person-years.

The process begins with gathering data. This includes past financial results, such as sales revenues, costs, and inventory levels. But it also includes nonfinancial data, which are often called "drivers." The drivers vary from business to business, but they include operating data such as batch size, defect rates, and the time it takes to serve a customer. Also, customer data (such as the number of customers who make repeat purchases, the time a customer spends viewing a web page, or the product mix a particular type of customer orders) and employee data (such as the absentee rate of employees and the degree of training that employees receive) must be collected. These drivers are the same ones being used by many companies in "Balanced Scorecard" management systems.

Gathering such data should be fairly easy, but often it is not. Only 24 percent of the surveyed companies have a single planning and reporting system—most have stand-alone software packages and spreadsheets that vary from division to division, and the different divisions use differing terminology. All this makes gathering data time-consuming and prone to mistakes.

The next step is to set targets for growth and financial results. Instead of being based on analysis, these targets are often set through negotiations between staff managers who make the budgets and line managers who must execute them. Fully 66 percent of managers believe planning is influenced more by politics than strategy.

The final step is to link compensation to the plan. Unfortunately, many companies either don't link managers' compensation to the plan or else link it to factors in the plan that are outside the managers' control.

Given the importance of financial planning, it's not surprising that many companies are reengineering their planning processes. Moreover, plenty of help is available for such reengineering. All of the Big Five accounting firms have consulting groups for financial planning, and all enterprise resource planning (ERP) software providers, such as SAP and PeopleSoft, have added financial planning modules. In addition, other specialized software leaders including SAS, Hyperion, Comshare, and Oracle provide financial planning software.

Information technology (IT) is revolutionizing data acquisition. For example, Owens Corning recently spent one year and $75 million implementing ERP software from SAP. Owens Corning had been closing its books and then spending five or six days analyzing the data to spot what needed to be changed and to update its forecasts. Now this is done automatically by the software. Sprint has now standardized its data across its enterprise, which allows its planners to directly access the company's data warehouse. In short, companies are standardizing data, linking data throughout the organization, and pulling this data directly into the planning process.

Better data access enables companies to dramatically shorten the planning cycle. Sprint has replaced annual budgets with quarterly reviews of a six-quarter rolling budget. Nortel reviews a rolling four-quarter budget twice a year instead of creating just one annual budget. Xilinx Inc., a developer of programmable semiconductors, reduced its budget cycle from five to three weeks. Nationwide Financial Services has reduced its budget cycle from four months to a few weeks.

Similar revolutions are occurring in forecasting. For example, Xilinx previously had to wait until the quarterly books were closed before it could update its forecast; now it can continuously update forecasts. Better forecasting technology is replacing political negotiations. A recent survey of companies reveals that 81 percent use trend-based projections, 65 percent use scenario evaluation, 41 percent use activity-based management (that is, linking the financial forecasts to the drivers), and 22 percent use simulations. Many companies are also streamlining the output of the planning process. For example, Nortel's old forecasted income statement had 100 line items. After realizing that managers focused on only a small number of these items, it consolidated many items, and now its projected income statement has only eight. Sprint's new planning process is much more accurate, with an error margin of 3 percent versus 10 percent previously.

As a result of better data, better forecasting techniques, shorter planning cycles, and streamlined planning processes, companies now have more accurate and useful financial plans.

Sources: Fritz McCormick, "Fewer and Fewer Beans," *CFO*, October 1999, 18; Susan Arterian, "Sprint Retools the Budget Process," *CFO*, September 1997, 88–91; Russ Banham, "The Revolution in Planning," *CFO*, August 1999, 46–56; and Cathy Lazere, "All Together Now," *CFO*, February 1998, 28–36.

5. Develop procedures for adjusting the basic plan if the economic forecasts upon which the plan was based do not materialize. For example, if the economy turns out to be stronger than was forecasted, then these new conditions must be recognized and reflected in higher production schedules, larger marketing quotas, and the like, and as rapidly as possible. Thus, Step 5 is really a "feedback loop" that triggers modifications to the financial plan.
6. Establish a performance-based management compensation system. It is critically important that firms reward managers for doing what stockholders want them to do—maximize share prices.

In the remainder of this chapter, we discuss how firms use computerized financial planning models to implement the three key components of the financial plan: (1) the sales forecast, (2) pro forma financial statements, and (3) the external financing plan.

Self-Test Question

What are the six steps of the financial planning process?

Computerized Financial Planning Models

Although financial forecasting as described in this chapter can be done with a calculator, virtually all corporate forecasts are made using computerized forecasting models. Most forecasting models are based on a spreadsheet program such as *Microsoft Excel*. Spreadsheets have two major advantages over pencil-and-paper calculations. First, we can develop a forecast much faster with a spreadsheet than a calculator if the forecast period extends beyond a year or two. Second, and more important, with a spreadsheet model you can change inputs and instantaneously recompute the projected financial statements and ratios, thus making it easy for managers to determine the effects of changes in variables such as unit sales, labor costs, and sales prices.

For this chapter, we forecasted financial statements for MicroDrive with an *Excel* model. The model is provided on the CD-ROM for the book, under the file name ***Ch 04 Tool Kit.xls***. You do not have to understand the model to understand the chapter, but working through the model will give you a better feel for the forecasting process.[3]

Self-Test Question

What are the two major advantages of spreadsheet models over pencil-and-paper calculations?

Sales Forecasts

The **sales forecast** generally starts with a review of sales during the past five to ten years, expressed in a graph such as that in Figure 4-2. The first part of the graph shows five years of historical sales for MicroDrive. The graph could have contained 10 years of sales data, but MicroDrive typically focuses on sales figures for the latest five years because the firm's studies have shown that its future growth is more closely related to recent events than to the distant past.

MicroDrive had its ups and downs during the period from 1997 to 2001. In 1999, poor performance of one of its drives led to bad publicity, which caused sales to fall

[3]There are small rounding differences between "by-hand" answers and those obtained using the spreadsheet. The spreadsheet carries calculations out to more decimal places and thus is somewhat more accurate than "by-hand" calculations.

FIGURE 4-2 MicroDrive Inc.: 2001 Sales Projection (Millions of Dollars)

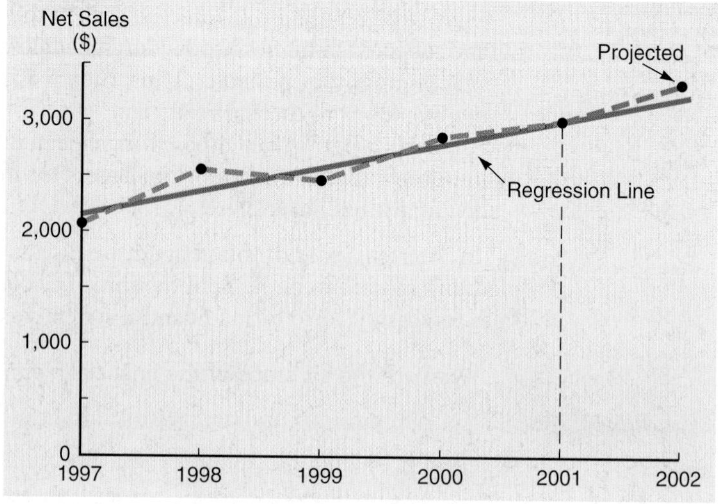

Year	Sales
1996	$2,058
1997	2,534
1998	2,472
1999	2,850
2000	3,000
2001	$3,300 (Projected)

below the 1998 level. Then, a banner year for microcomputer sales in 2000 pushed MicroDrive's sales up by 15 percent, an unusually high growth rate for the company. Based on a regression analysis, MicroDrive's forecasters determined that the average annual growth rate over the past five years was 9.1 percent. On the basis of this historical sales trend, on planned new-product introductions, and on MicroDrive's forecast for the economy, the planning committee projects 10 percent sales growth during 2001, to $3,300 million. Here are some of the factors MicroDrive considered in its sales forecast:

1. MicroDrive has two divisions: standard drives and custom drives. The standard drive division produces large quantities of standardized disk drives, generally having capacities of less than 20,000 megabytes (20 gigabytes) and selling for less than $500. The custom division manufactures high-capacity, super-fast drives with capacities greater than 100 gigabytes; they sell for as much as $3,000 and are produced in relatively small quantities. Sales growth is seldom the same for each division, so to begin the forecasting process, independent divisional forecasts are made on the basis of historical growth, and then the divisional forecasts are combined to produce a "first approximation" corporate sales forecast.
2. Next, the level of economic activity and the overall demand for microcomputers are forecasted. Here MicroDrive's planners must recognize that the firm's products are sold in two vastly different markets. Most drives are sold directly to personal computer manufacturers such as Dell, Gateway, and Compaq. Such sales are high volume, and their prices are negotiated. In addition, a significant percentage of

sales is made through wholesalers to individuals or small firms who are either making their own microcomputers or replacing failed disk drives.

3. Then, the forecasters must estimate MicroDrive's market share for each product line in each market, considering both the overall demand for disk drives and competition from other manufacturers. Consideration must be given to the firm's production capacity, to its competitors' capacities, and to new-product introductions both by microcomputer manufacturers and disk drive producers. Pricing strategies must also be considered—for example, should the company raise prices to boost margins, or should it lower prices to build market share and gain economies of scale in production?
4. MicroDrive sells all over the world. Its European sales represent about 20 percent of total sales, and Asian sales, which are currently only 4 percent of the total, were growing rapidly but have recently slumped. MicroDrive's foreign sales present unique forecasting problems. In particular, its planners must consider how exchange rate fluctuations might affect sales, trade agreements, governmental policies, and the like.
5. Inflation will also affect the firm's prices. Over the next five years, the inflation rate is expected to average 3 to 4 percent, and MicroDrive would like to increase prices, on average, by a like amount. In addition, the firm expects to expand its market share in certain products, resulting in a 4 percent growth rate in unit sales. The combination of unit sales growth and increases in sales prices has resulted in historical revenue growth rates in the 8 to 10 percent range, and this same situation is expected in the future.
6. Advertising campaigns, promotional discounts, credit terms, and the like also affect sales, so probable developments for these items are also factored in.
7. Forecasts are made for each division, both in the aggregate and on an individual product basis. The individual product sales forecasts are summed, and this sum is compared with the aggregated divisional forecasts. Differences are reconciled, and the end result is a sales forecast for the company as a whole but with breakdowns by the two divisions and by individual products.

If the sales forecast is off, the consequences can be serious. First, if the market expands by *more* than MicroDrive has prepared for, the company will not be able to meet demand. Its customers will end up buying competitors' products, and MicroDrive will lose market share. On the other hand, if its projections are overly optimistic, MicroDrive could end up with too much plant, equipment, and inventory. That would mean low turnover ratios, high costs for depreciation and storage, and write-offs of obsolete inventory. All of this would result in low profits, a low rate of return on equity, low free cash flows, and a depressed stock price. If MicroDrive had financed an unnecessary expansion with debt, high interest charges would compound its problems. Thus, an accurate sales forecast is critical to the firm's well-being.[4]

Self-Test Questions

List some factors that should be considered when developing a sales forecast.

Explain why an accurate sales forecast is critical to profitability.

[4]A sales forecast is actually the *expected value of a probability distribution*, so there are many possible levels of sales. Because any sales forecast is subject to uncertainty, financial planners are just as interested in the degree of uncertainty inherent in the sales forecast, as measured by the standard deviation, as in the expected level of sales.

Financial Statement Forecasting: The Percent of Sales Method

Once sales have been forecasted, we must forecast future balance sheets and income statements. The most commonly used technique is the **percent of sales method,** which begins with the sales forecast, expressed as an annual growth rate in dollar sales revenues. Many items on the income statement and balance sheets are assumed to increase proportionally with sales. For example, the inventories-to-sales ratio might be 20 percent, receivables/sales might be 15 percent, and so forth, for certain assets, liabilities, and costs. Then, as sales increase, those items also increase, and their values for a particular year are estimated as percentages of the forecasted sales for that year. The remaining items on the forecasted statements—items that are not tied directly to sales—depend on the company's dividend policy and its relative use of debt and equity financing.

If the forecasted percentage of sales for each item is the same as the percentage for the year preceding the forecast period, then each item will grow at the same rate as sales. This approach is called the **constant ratio method.** The advantage of this method is that it is easy to implement. The disadvantage is that it is not especially useful to managers, because one of the goals of operating managers is to limit the growth of certain items, such as costs and inventory, in order to improve profitability. In other words, *managers should strive to have improving, not constant, ratios!*

In the following sections we explain the percent of sales method, in both its constant and variable forms, and use it to forecast MicroDrive's financial statements.

Step 1. Analyze the Historical Ratios

The first step is to analyze the historical ratios. This differs somewhat from the ratio analysis of Chapter 3, since the objective here is to forecast the future, or pro forma, financial statements. The percent of sales method assumes that costs in a given year will be some specified percentage of that year's sales. Thus, we begin our analysis by calculating the ratio of costs to sales for several past years. We illustrate the method using only two years of data for MicroDrive, but a thorough analysis should have at least five years of historical data. Table 4-1 shows MicroDrive's ratio of cost to sales for the past two years for MicroDrive. In 2000, MicroDrive had an 87.6 percent ratio of cost to sales, and the ratio dropped to 87.2 percent in 2001. The table also shows the historical average, which in this case is the average of the two prior years. The last column shows the ratio of cost to sales for the industry composite, which is the sum of the financial statements for all firms in the industry. Note that MicroDrive has improved its cost/sales ratio, but it still is higher than the industry average.

The table also shows the ratio of depreciation to net plant and equipment. Because depreciation depends on the asset base, it is more reasonable to forecast depreciation as a percent of net plant and equipment rather than of sales.

Many other items on MicroDrive's balance sheets will also increase with sales. The company writes and deposits checks every day. Because managers don't know exactly when all of the checks will clear, they can't predict exactly what the balance in their checking accounts will be on any given day. Therefore, they must maintain a balance of cash and cash equivalents (such as very short-term marketable securities) to avoid overdrawing their accounts. We discuss the issue of cash management in Chapter 22, but for now we simply assume that the cash required to support the company's operations is proportional to its sales. Table 4-1 shows the ratio of cash to sale for the past two years, as well as the historical average and the industry composite ratio. All of the remaining pro forma balance sheet ratios, which we discuss below, also are shown in Table 4-1.

See *Ch 04 Tool Kit.xls* for details.

TABLE 4-1 Historical Ratios for MicroDrive Inc.

	Actual 2000	Actual 2001	Historical Average	Industry Average
Costs to sales	87.6%	87.2%	87.4%	87.1%
Depreciation to net plant and equipment	10.3	10.0	10.2	10.2
Cash to sales	0.5	0.3	0.4	1.0
Accounts receivable to sales	11.1	12.5	11.8	10.0
Inventory to sales	14.6	20.5	17.5	11.1
Net plant and equipment to sales	30.5	33.3	31.9	33.3
Accounts payable to sales	1.1	2.0	1.5	1.0
Accruals to sales	2.1	4.7	3.4	2.0

Unless a company changes its credit policy or has a change in its customer base, accounts receivable should be proportional to sales. Furthermore, as sales increase, firms generally must carry more inventories. Chapter 22 and Web/CD Chapter 28 discuss inventory management in detail, but for now we assume that inventory will also be proportional to sales.

It might be reasonable to assume that cash, accounts receivable, and inventories will be proportional to sales, but will the amount of net plant and equipment go up and down as sales go up and down? The correct answer could be either yes or no. When companies acquire plant and equipment, they often install more capacity than they currently need due to economies of scale in building capacity. For example, it was economically better for GM to build its Tennessee Saturn plant with a capacity of about 320,000 cars per year than to build a plant with a capacity equal to the initial projected sales of 50,000 and then add capacity as sales expanded. Saturn's sales were far below 320,000 units for the first few years of production, so it was possible to increase sales during those years without increasing plant and equipment. Moreover, even if a plant is operating at its maximum rated capacity, most companies can produce additional units by reducing downtime for scheduled maintenance, by running machinery at a higher than optimal speed, or by adding a second or third shift. Therefore, at least in the short run, companies may not have a very close relationship between sales and net plant and equipment.

However, some companies do have a fixed relationship between sales and plant and equipment, even in the short term. For example, new stores in many retail chains achieve the same sales during their first year as the chain's existing stores. The only way such retailers can grow (beyond inflation) is by adding new stores. Such companies therefore have a strong proportional relationship between fixed assets and sales.

Finally, in the long term there is a strong relationship between sales and net plant and equipment for virtually all companies: Few companies can continue to increase sales unless they eventually add capacity. Therefore, as a first approximation it is reasonable to assume that the long-term ratio of net plant and equipment to sales will be constant.

For the first years in a forecast, managers generally build in the actual planned expenditures on plant and equipment. If those estimates are not available, it is generally best to assume a constant ratio of net plant and equipment to sales.

Some items on the liability side of the balance sheet can be expected to increase spontaneously with sales, producing what are called **spontaneously generated funds.** The two primary types of spontaneous funds are accounts payable and accruals. Regarding payables, as sales increase, so will purchases of raw materials, and those larger purchases will spontaneously lead to a higher level of accounts payable. Similarly, more sales will require more labor, while higher sales normally result in higher taxable income and thus taxes. Therefore, accrued wages and taxes both increase.

All of the historical ratios are shown in Table 4-1. Using these ratios, along with the industry composite ratios and a knowledge of MicroDrive's operating plans and industry trends, its managers are ready to begin forecasting the projected, or pro forma, financial statements.

Step 2. Forecast the Income Statement

First, we forecast the income statement for the coming year. This statement is needed to estimate both income and the addition to retained earnings. Table 4-2 shows the forecast for 2002. Sales are forecasted to grow by 10 percent. The forecast of sales for 2002, shown in Row 1 of Column 3, is calculated by multiplying 2001 sales, shown in Column 1, by (1 + growth rate) = 1.1. The result is a 2002 forecast of $3,300 million.

As shown in Table 4-1, MicroDrive's ratio of costs to sales in 2001 was 87.2 percent ($2,616/$3,000 = 0.872). Thus, for each dollar of sales in 2001, MicroDrive incurred 87.2 cents of costs. Initially, the company's managers assume that the cost structure will remain unchanged in 2002. Later in the chapter we explore the impact of an improvement in the cost structure, but for now we assume that costs will equal 87.2 percent of sales. See Column 3, Row 2, of Table 4-2.

For 2001, the ratio of depreciation to net plant and equipment was 10 percent ($100/$1,000 = 0.10), and MicroDrive's managers believe that this is a good estimate of future depreciation. As we discuss in the next section, the forecasted net plant and equipment for 2002 is $1,100. Therefore, the forecasted depreciation for 2001 is 0.10($1,100) = $110.

Total operating costs, shown in Row 4, are the sum of other costs and depreciation. EBIT is found by subtraction, while the interest charges shown in Column 3 are simply carried over from Column 1. The final interest charge will depend on the debt in 2002, which we discuss in the next section.

See *Ch 04 Tool Kit.xls* for details.

TABLE 4-2 MicroDrive Inc.: Actual 2001 and Projected 2002 Income Statements (Millions of Dollars)

	Actual 2001[a] (1)	Forecast Basis (2)	First Pass 2002 Forecast (3)
1. Sales	$3,000	1.1 × 2001 Sales =	$3,300
2. Costs except depreciation	2,616	87.2% × 2002 Sales =	2,878
3. Depreciation	100	10.0% × 2002 Net plant =	110
4. Total operating costs	$2,716		$2,988
5. EBIT	$ 284		$ 312
6. Less interest	88	⟶	88[b]
7. Earnings before taxes (EBT)	$ 196		$ 224
8. Taxes (40%)	78		89
9. NI before preferred dividends	$ 118		$ 135
10. Dividends to preferred	4	⟶	4[b]
11. NI available to common	$ 114		$ 131
12. Dividends to common	$ 58		$ 63[c]
13. Addition to retained earnings	$ 56		$ 68

[a]To reduce clutter, the income statement as shown previously in Chapter 2 is rounded to whole numbers.
[b]Indicates a 2001 amount carried over for the 2002 forecast. Indicated in Column 2 by an arrow.
[c]See the text for explanation of dividends.

Earnings before taxes (EBT) is then calculated, as is net income before preferred dividends. Preferred dividends are carried over from the 2001 column, and they will remain constant unless MicroDrive decides to issue additional preferred stock. Net income available to common is then calculated, after which the 2002 dividends are forecasted as follows. The 2001 dividend per share was \$1.15, and this dividend is expected to increase by about 8 percent, to \$1.25. Since there are 50 million shares outstanding, the projected dividends are \$1.25(50) = \$62.5 million, rounded to \$63 million.

To complete the forecasted income statement, the \$63 million of projected dividends are subtracted from the \$131 million projected net income, and the result is the first-pass projection of the addition to retained earnings, \$131 − \$63 = \$68 million.

Step 3. Forecast the Balance Sheet

The assets shown on MicroDrive's balance sheet must increase if sales are to increase. MicroDrive's 2001 ratio of cash to sales was approximately 0.33 percent (\$10/\$3,000 = 0.003333), and its managers believe this ratio will remain constant in 2002. Therefore, the forecasted cash balance for 2002, shown in Column 3 of Table 4-3, is 0.003333(\$3,300) = \$11 million. MicroDrive's managers don't plan to add any short-term investments in 2002, so the amount in Column 1 of Row 2 is simply carried over to Column 3.

MicroDrive's 2001 ratio of accounts receivable to sales was \$375/\$3,000 = 0.125 = 12.5%. Later, we examine the effect of a change in credit policy, but for now we assume a constant credit policy and customer base. Therefore, the forecasted accounts receivable for 2002 is 0.125(\$3,300) = \$412.5 million, rounded to \$412 million as shown in Column 3 of Table 4-3.

The 2001 ratio of inventory to sales is \$615/\$3,000 = 20.5%. Assuming no change in MicroDrive's inventory management, the forecasted inventory for 2002 is 0.205(\$3,300) = \$676.5 million, rounded to \$677 million as shown in Column 3 of Table 4-3.

The ratio of net plant and equipment to sales for 2001 was \$1,000/\$3,000 = 33.33%. MicroDrive's net plant and equipment have grown fairly steadily in the past, and its managers expect steady future growth. Therefore, they forecast net plant and equipment for 2002 to be 0.3333(\$3,300) = \$1,100 million.

Once the individual asset accounts have been forecasted, they can be summed to complete the asset section of the balance sheet. For MicroDrive, the total current assets forecasted for 2002 are \$11 + \$0 + \$412 + \$677 = \$1,100 million, and fixed assets add another \$1,100 million. Therefore, as Table 4-3 shows, MicroDrive will need a total of \$2,200 million in assets to support \$3,300 million of sales in 2002.

If assets are to increase, liabilities and equity must also increase—the additional assets must be financed. For MicroDrive, the 2001 ratio of accounts payable to sales was \$60/\$3,000 = 0.02 = 2%. Its managers assume that the payables policy will not change, so the forecasted accounts payable for 2002 is 0.02(\$3,300) = \$66 million.

The 2001 ratio of accruals to sales was \$140/\$3,000 = 0.0467 = 4.67%. If this ratio does not change, then the forecasted level of accruals for 2002 will be 0.0467(\$3,300) = \$154 million.

Retained earnings will also increase, but not at the same rate as sales: The new amount of retained earnings will be the old amount plus the addition to retained earnings, which we calculated in Step 2. Also, notes payable, long-term bonds, preferred stock, and common stock will not rise spontaneously with sales—rather, the projected levels of these accounts will depend on financing decisions, as we discuss later.

In summary, (1) higher sales must be supported by additional assets, (2) some of the asset increases will be financed by spontaneous increases in accounts payable and

TABLE 4-3 MicroDrive Inc.: Actual 2001 and Projected 2002 Balance Sheets (Millions of Dollars)

	Actual 2001 (1)	Forecast Basis (2)	2002 Forecast First Pass (3)	AFN[a] (4)	Second Pass (5)
1. Cash and equivalents	$ 10	0.33% × 2002 Sales =	$ 11	→	$ 11
2. Short-term investments	0	→	0	→	0
3. Accounts receivable	375	12.5% × 2002 Sales =	412	→	412
4. Inventories	615	20.5% × 2002 Sales =	677	→	677
5. Total current assets	$1,000		$1,100		$1,100
6. Net plant and equipment	1,000	33.33% × 2002 Sales =	1,100	→	1,100
7. Total assets	$2,000		$2,200		$2,200
8. Accounts payable	$ 60	2% × 2002 Sales =	$ 66	→	$ 66
9. Notes payable	110	→	110[b]	+28	138
10. Accruals	140	4.67% × 2002 Sales =	154	→	154
11. Total current liabilities	$ 310		$ 330		$ 358
12. Long-term bonds	754	→	754[b]	+28	782
13. Total debt	$1,064		$1,084		$1,140
14. Preferred stock	40	→	40[b]	→	40
15. Common stock	130	→	130[b]	+56	186
16. Retained earnings	766	+68[c]	834	→	834
17. Total common equity	$ 896		$ 964		$1,020
18. Total liabilities and equity	$2,000		$2,088	+112	$2,200
19. Additional funds needed (AFN)			$ 112		

[a]AFN stands for "Additional Funds Needed." This figure is determined at the bottom of Column 3. Then, Column 4 shows how the required $112 of AFN will be raised.
[b]Indicates a 2001 amount carried over as the first-pass forecast. Arrows also indicate items whose values are carried over from one pass to another.
[c]From Line 13 in Column 3 of Table 4-2.

CD

See ***Ch 04 Tool Kit.xls*** for details.

accruals, and by retained earnings, but (3) any shortfall must be financed from external sources, using some combination of debt, preferred stock, and common stock.

The spontaneously increasing liabilities (accounts payable and accruals) are forecasted and shown in Column 3 of Table 4-5, the first-pass forecast. Then, those liability and equity accounts whose values reflect conscious management decisions—notes payable, long-term bonds, preferred stock, and common stock—are initially set at their 2001 levels. Thus, 2002 notes payable are initially set at $110 million, the long-term bond account is forecasted at $754 million, and so on. The 2002 value for the retained earnings (RE) account is obtained by adding the projected addition to retained earnings as developed in the 2002 income statement (see Table 4-2) to the 2001 ending balance:

$$\begin{aligned}\text{2002 RE} &= \text{2001 RE} + \text{2002 forecasted addition to RE}\\ &= \$766 + \$68 = \$834 \text{ million.}\end{aligned}$$

The forecast of total assets as shown in Column 3 (first-pass forecast) of Table 4-3 is $2,200 million, which indicates that MicroDrive must add $200 million of new assets in 2002 to support the higher sales level. However, the forecasted liability and equity accounts as shown in the lower portion of Column 3 rise by only $88 million, to $2,088 million. Because the balance sheet must balance, MicroDrive must raise an additional $2,200 − $2,088 = $112 million, which we define as **Additional Funds Needed (AFN).** The AFN will be raised by some combination of borrowing from the bank as notes payable, issuing long-term bonds, and issuing new common stock.

Step 4. Raising the Additional Funds Needed

MicroDrive's financial staff will decide how to raise the needed funds based on several factors, including the firm's target capital structure, the effect of short-term borrowing on the current ratio, conditions in the debt and equity markets, and restrictions imposed by existing debt agreements. After considering all of the relevant factors, the staff decided on the following financing mix:

	Amount of New Capital		
	Percent	Dollars (Millions)	Interest Rate
Notes payable	25%	$ 28	8%
Long-term bonds	25	28	10
Common stock	50	56	—
	100%	$112	

These amounts, which are shown in Column 4 of Table 4-3, are added to the initially forecasted amounts as shown in Column 3 to generate the second-pass balance sheet. Thus, in Column 5 notes payable increase to $110 + $28 = $138 million, long-term bonds rise to $754 + $28 = $782 million, and common stock increases to $130 + $56 = $186 million. At that point, the balance sheet is in balance.

Step 5: Financing Feedbacks

Our projected financial statements are incomplete because they do not reflect the fact that interest must be paid on the debt used to help finance the AFN, and that dividends will be paid on the new shares of common stock part. Those payments, which are called **financing feedbacks,** will lower the net income and retained earnings shown in the projected statements. There are two ways to incorporate feedbacks into the forecasted statements, the **manual approach** and the **automatic approach.** We explain both approaches below.

Manual Approach To use the manual approach, we first forecast the additional interest expense and dividends that result from external financings. New short-term debt costs 8 percent, so the $28 million of new notes payable will increase MicroDrive's projected 2002 interest expense by 0.08($28) = $2.24 million. Similarly, new long-term bonds will add 0.10($28) = $2.80 million in interest expense, so the total increase in interest expense will be $5.04 million. When these feedbacks are considered, interest expense as shown in the projected 2002 second-pass income statement in Column 4 of Table 4-4 increases to $88 + $5 = $93 million. These higher interest charges will, of course, also affect the remainder of the income statement. In particular, taxes will decrease by 0.40($5) = $2 million, since taxable income falls by $5 million.

The financing plan also calls for issuing $56 million of new common stock. MicroDrive's stock price was $23 at the end of 2001, and if we assume that new shares will be sold at this price, then $56/$23 = 2.4 million shares of new stock will have to be sold. Further, MicroDrive's 2002 dividend payment is projected to be $1.25 per share, so the 2.4 million shares of new stock will require 2.4($1.25) = $3 million of additional dividend payments. Thus, dividends to common stockholders as shown in the second-pass income statement increase to $63 + $3 = $66 million.

The net effect of the financing feedbacks is to reduce the addition to retained earnings by $6 million, from $68 million to $62 million. This reduces the balance sheet forecast of retained earnings by a like amount, so in Table 4-3 the second-pass 2002 balance sheet projection for retained earnings would fall by \$6 million. Thus, a shortfall of \$6 million will still exist as a result of financing feedback effects.

How will the second-pass shortfall be financed? In MicroDrive's case, 25 percent of the \$6 million will be obtained as short-term debt, 25 percent as long-term bonds, and 50 percent as new common stock.

Table 4-5 in the next section shows a third-pass balance sheet reflecting the \$6 million shortfall. We could create a fourth-pass balance sheet by using this financing mix to add another \$6 million to the liabilities and equity side. Would the fourth pass balance? No, because the additional \$6 million in capital would require another increase in interest and dividend payments, and this would affect the fourth-pass income statement. There would still be a shortfall, although it would be much smaller than the \$6 million shortfall on the third pass. We could continue repeating the process. In each iteration, the additional financing would become smaller and smaller, and after about five iterations, the AFN would be essentially zero. We do not show the additional iterations, but the final results are shown in Column 5 of Table 4-4 and Column 7 of Table 4-5.

Automatic Approach Spreadsheets can be used to automate the balancing process. *Excel* and other spreadsheets have a feature that causes worksheets to iterate until balancing criteria have been satisfied, thus almost instantly going through enough "passes" to cause the balance sheet to balance. The file ***Ch 04 Tool Kit.xls*** on the textbook's CD-ROM illustrates this with MicroDrive. We encourage you to open the file, select the AUTOMATIC FEEDBACK tab, and follow along as we explain how *Excel* handles the automatic balancing process.

See ***Ch 04 Tool Kit.xls*** for details.

As we demonstrated in the last section, adding debt reduces net income, which, in turn, reduces additions to retained earnings, which reduces the amount of internally generated financing, which increases the amount of required external financing from

TABLE 4-4 MicroDrive Inc.: Actual 2001 and Projected 2002 Income Statements with Financing Feedbacks (Millions of Dollars)

	Actual	2002 Forecast			
	2001 (1)	First Pass (2)	Feedback (3)	Second Pass (4)	Final[a] (5)
1. Sales	\$3,000	\$3,300		\$3,300	\$3,300.00
2. Costs except depreciation	\$2,616	\$2,878		\$2,878	\$2,877.82
3. Depreciation	100	110		110	110.00
4. Total operating costs	\$2,716	\$2,988		\$2,988	\$2,987.82
5. EBIT	\$ 284	\$ 312		\$ 312	\$ 312.18
6. Less interest	88	88[a]	+5	93	93.31
7. Earnings before taxes (EBT)	\$ 196	\$ 224		\$ 219	\$ 218.87
8. Taxes (40%)	78	89	−2	87	87.55
9. NI before preferred dividends	\$ 118	\$ 135		\$ 132	\$ 131.32
10. Dividends to preferred	4	4[a]		4	4.00
11. NI available to common	\$ 114	\$ 131		\$ 128	\$ 127.32
12. Dividends to common	\$ 58	\$ 63[b]	+3	\$ 66	\$ 65.28
13. Addition to retained earnings	\$ 56	\$ 68	−6	\$ 62	\$ 62.04

[a]If the dollars were taken out to several more digits, we would see differences between the "Second Pass" and "Final" columns due to successive feedbacks. But, as the data show, by the second pass most feedback effects have already been reflected.

the initially forecasted amount. Then, this second round of financing again reduces the addition to retained earnings, and thus starts the cycle again. However, one can create formulas in the spreadsheet that automatically add the additional financing and the additional interest and dividend payments. This involves a circular reference in which formulas indirectly refer to themselves. Because circular references often are the result of errors, *Excel* may flash a warning message. However in our model, we actually want the circular formulas, and we want *Excel* to automatically iterate through as many balancing passes as it takes to force the balance sheets to balance.

To start this process, click Tools > Options and then click on the Calculation tab. Then, check the box for Iteration. By default, *Excel* will automatically go through 100 iterations, which is enough to make the balance sheet balance. The end result includes just enough new external financing to support the specified growth in assets.

Analysis of the Forecast

See ***Ch 04 Tool Kit.xls*** for details.

The 2002 forecast as developed above is only the first part of MicroDrive's total forecasting process. We must next examine the projected statements and determine whether the forecast meets the financial targets as set forth in the five-year financial plan. If the statements do not meet the targets, then elements of the forecast must be changed.

TABLE 4-5 MicroDrive Inc.: Actual 2001 and Projected 2002 Balance Sheets with Financing Feedback (Millions of Dollars)

		2002 Forecast					
	Actual 2001 (1)	First Pass (2)	AFN (3)	Second Pass (4)	Feed-back[a] (5)	Third Pass (6)	Final[b] (7)
1. Cash	$ 10	$ 11		$ 11		$ 11	$ 10.98
2. Short-term investments	0	0		0		0	0.00
3. Accounts receivable	375	412		412		412	412.50
4. Inventories	615	677		677		677	676.50
5. Total current assets	$1,000	$1,100		$1,100		$1,100	$1,099.98
6. Net plant and equipment	1,000	1,100		1,100		1,100	1,000.00
7. Total assets	$2,000	$2,200		$2,200		$2,200	$2,199.98
8. Accounts payable	$ 60	$ 66		$ 66		$ 66	$ 66.00
9. Notes payable	110	110	+28	138		138	139.48
10. Accruals	140	154		154		154	154.00
11. Total current liabilities	$ 310	$ 330		$ 358		$ 358	$ 359.48
12. Long-term bonds	754	754	+28	782		782	783.48
13. Total debt	$1,064	$1,084		$1,140		$1,140	$1,142.97
14. Preferred stock	40	40		40		40	40.00
15. Common stock	130	130	+56	186		186	188.97
16. Retained earnings	766	834		834	−6	828	828.04
17. Total common equity	$ 896	964		$1,020		$1,020	$1,017.01
18. Total liabilities and equity	$2,000	$2,088		$2,200		$2,194	$2,199.98
19. Additional funds needed (AFN)		$ 112		$ 0		$ 6	$ 0.00

[a]Feedback is the net reduction in additions to retained earnings shown in Column 3 of Table 4-4.

[b]If the dollars were taken out to several more digits, we would see more differences between the "Third Pass" and "Final" columns due to successive feedbacks. But as the data show, by the third pass most feedback effects have been incorporated. After the iterations performed in the automated process, we cannot go out enough decimal places to find a difference.

Table 4-6 shows MicroDrive's actual ratios for 2001, its projected 2002 ratios, and the latest industry average ratios. (The table also shows a "Revised Forecast for 2002" in the third column, which we will discuss later. Disregard the revised data for now.) The firm's financial condition at the close of 2001 was weak, with many ratios being well below the industry averages. For example, MicroDrive's current ratio, based on Column 1 of Table 4-3, was only 3.2 versus 4.2 for an average competitor.

The "Inputs" section shown on the top three rows of the table provides data on three of the model's key drivers: (1) costs (excluding depreciation) as a percentage of sales, (2) accounts receivable as a percentage of sales, and (3) inventory as a percentage of sales. The preliminary forecast in Column 2 assumes these variables remain constant. While MicroDrive's cost-to-sales ratio is only slightly worse than the industry average, its ratios of accounts receivable to sales and inventory to sales are significantly higher than those of its competitors. Its investment in inventories and receivables is too high, causing its returns on assets, equity, and invested capital as shown in the lower part of the table to be too low. Therefore, MicroDrive should make operational changes designed to reduce its current assets.

The "Ratios" section of Table 4-6 provides more details regarding the firm's weaknesses. MicroDrive's asset management ratios are much worse than the industry averages. For example, its total assets turnover ratio is 1.5 versus an industry average of 1.8. Its poor asset management ratios drag down the return on invested capital (9.5 percent for MicroDrive versus 11.4 percent for the industry average). Furthermore, MicroDrive must carry more than the average amount of debt to support its excessive assets, and the extra interest expense reduces its profit margin to 3.9 percent versus 5.0 percent for the industry. Much of the debt is short term, and this results in a current ratio of 3.1 versus the 4.2 industry average. These problems will persist unless management takes action to improve things.

After reviewing its preliminary forecast, management decided to take three steps to improve its financial condition: (1) It decided to lay off some workers and close certain operations. It forecasted that these steps would lower operating costs (excluding depreciation) from the current 87.2 to 86 percent of sales as shown in Column 3 of Table 4-6. (2) By screening credit customers more closely and being more aggressive in collecting past-due accounts, the company believes it can reduce the ratio of accounts receivable to sales from 12.5 to 11.8 percent. (3) Finally, management thinks it can reduce the inventory-to-sales ratio from 20.5 to 16.7 percent through the use of tighter inventory controls.[5]

These projected operational changes were then used to create a revised set of forecasted statements for 2002. We do not show the new financial statements, but the revised ratios are shown in the third column of Table 4-6. You can see the details in the chapter spreadsheet model, ***Ch 04 Tool Kit.xls.*** Here are the highlights of the revised forecast:

1. The reduction in operating costs improved the 2002 NOPAT, or net operating profit after taxes, by $23.9 million. Even more impressive, the improvements in the receivables policy and in inventory management reduced receivables and inventories by $148.5 million. The net result of the increase in NOPAT and the reduction of current assets was a very large increase in free cash flow for 2002, from a previously estimated $7.3 million to $179.7 million. Although we do not show it, the improvements in operations also led to significantly higher free cash flow for each year in the whole forecast period.

[5]We will discuss receivables and inventory management in detail in Chapter 22.

TABLE 4-6 Model Inputs, AFN, and Key Ratios

	Actual 2001 (1)	Preliminary Forecast for 2002[a] (2)	Revised Forecast for 2002[a] (3)	Industry Average 2001 (4)
Model Inputs				
Costs (excluding depreciation) as percentage of sales	87.2%	87.2%	86.0%	87.1%
Accounts receivable as percentage of sales	12.5	12.5	11.8	10.0
Inventory as percentage of sales	20.5	20.5	16.7	11.1
Model Outputs				
NOPAT (net operating profit after taxes)	$170.3	$187.3	$211.2	
Net operating working capital	$800.0	$880.0	$731.5	
Total operating capital	$1,800.0	$1,980.0	$1,831.5	
Free cash flow (FCF)	($175.0)	$7.3	$179.7	
AFN		$117.9	($64.3)	
Ratios				
Current ratio	3.2×	3.1×	3.0×	4.2×
Inventory turnover	4.9×	4.9×	6.0×	9.0×
Days sales outstanding	45.0×	45.0×	42.5×	36.0×
Total assets turnover	1.5×	1.5×	1.6×	1.8×
Debt ratio	53.2%	52.0%	51.3%	40.0%
Profit margin	3.8%	3.9%	4.7%	5.0%
Return on assets	5.7%	5.8%	7.6%	9.0%
Return on equity	12.7%	12.5%	16.3%	15.0%
Return on invested capital (NOPAT/Total operating capital)	9.5%	9.5%	11.5%	11.4%

[a]All forecasts are based on the final revised projections as shown in Tables 4-4 and 4-5.

See ***Ch 04 Tool Kit.xls*** for details.

2. The profit margin improved to 4.7 percent. However, the firm's profit margin still lagged the industry average because its high debt ratio results in higher-than-average interest payments.
3. The increase in the profit margin resulted in an increase in projected retained earnings. More importantly, by tightening inventory controls and reducing the days sales outstanding, MicroDrive projected a reduction in inventories and receivables. Taken together, these actions resulted in a *negative* AFN of $64.3 million, which means that MicroDrive would actually generate $64.3 million more from internal operations during 2002 than it needs for new assets. This $64.3 million of surplus funds would be used to reduce debt, which would lead to a decrease in the forecasted debt ratio from 52.0 to 51.3 percent. The debt ratio would still be well above the industry average, but this is a step in the right direction.
4. These actions would also raise the rate of return on assets from 5.8 to 7.6 percent, and they would boost the return on equity from 12.5 to 16.3 percent, which is even higher than the industry average.

Although MicroDrive's managers believed that the revised forecast is achievable, they were not sure of this. Accordingly, they wanted to know how variations in sales would affect the forecast. Therefore, a spreadsheet model was run using several different sales growth rates, and the results were analyzed to see how the ratios would change under different growth scenarios. To illustrate, if the sales growth rate increased from 10 to 20 percent, the additional funding requirement would change dramatically, from a \$64.3 million *surplus* to a \$91.4 million *shortfall* because more assets would be required to finance the additional sales.

The spreadsheet model was also used to evaluate dividend policy. If MicroDrive decided to reduce its dividend growth rate, then additional funds would be generated, and those funds could be invested in plant, equipment, and inventories; used to reduce debt; or used to repurchase stock.

The model was also used to evaluate financing alternatives. In the previous revised forecasts, MicroDrive used 25 percent of the \$64.3 million surplus to reduce notes payable, 25 percent to reduce long-term bonds, and 50 percent to repurchase stock. If instead it used all 100 percent of the surplus to reduce short-term debt, then the current ratio would improve from 3.0 to 3.6. However, this would reduce the ROE from 16.3 to 15.9. If MicroDrive used all of the surplus to repurchase stock, the current ratio would fall from 3.0 to 2.9 and the ROE would increase from 16.3 percent to 16.6 percent. None of these changes in financing affect the ROIC or the free cash flow, but they might well have an effect on the risk of the stock.

We see, then, that forecasting is an iterative process. For planning purposes, the financial staff develops a preliminary forecast based on a continuation of past policies and trends. This provides a starting point, or "baseline" forecast. Next, the projections are modified to see what effects alternative operating plans would have on the firm's earnings and financial condition. This results in a revised forecast. Then alternative operating plans are examined under different sales growth scenarios, and the model is used to evaluate both dividend policy and capital structure decisions.

The spreadsheet model can be used to analyze alternative working capital policies—that is, to see the effects of changes in cash management, credit policy, inventory policy, and the use of different types of short-term credit. We will examine MicroDrive's working capital policy within the framework of the company's financial model later, but in the remainder of this chapter, we consider some other aspects of the financial forecasting process. Finally, the projected statements can be used to estimate the effect of different plans on MicroDrive's stock price. This is called value-based management, and is covered in Chapter 12.

Self-Test Questions

What is the AFN, and how is the percent of sales method used to estimate it?

Why do accounts payable and accruals provide "spontaneous funds" to a growing firm?

Would payables and accruals provide spontaneous funds to a no-growth firm? One that is declining?

Why do retained earnings not grow at the same rate as sales? In answering this question, think about a firm whose sales are not growing (g = 0%), but that is profitable and does not pay out all of its earnings as dividends.

The AFN Formula

Most firms forecast their capital requirements by constructing pro forma income statements and balance sheets as described above. However, if the ratios are expected to remain constant, then the following formula can be used to forecast financial requirements. Here we apply the formula to MicroDrive based on the 2001 data, not the revised data, as the revised data do not assume constant ratios.

Additional funds needed	=	Required increase in assets	−	Spontaneous increase in liabilities	−	Increase in retained earnings	
AFN	=	$(A^*/S_0)\Delta S$	−	$(L^*/S_0)\Delta S$	−	$MS_1(RR)$.	**(4-1)**

Here

AFN = additional funds needed.

A^* = assets that are tied directly to sales, hence must increase if sales are to increase. Note that A designates total assets and A^* designates those assets that must increase if sales are to increase. When the firm is operating at full capacity, as is the case here, $A^* = A$. Often, though, A^* and A are not equal, and either the equation must be modified or we must use the projected financial statement method.

S_0 = sales during the last year.

A^*/S_0 = percentage of required assets to sales, which also shows the required dollar increase in assets per \$1 increase in sales. $A^*/S_0 = \$2{,}000/\$3{,}000 = 0.6667$ for MicroDrive. Thus, for every \$1 increase in sales, assets must increase by about 67 cents.

L^* = liabilities that increase spontaneously. L^* is normally much less than total liabilities (L). Spontaneous liabilities include accounts payable and accruals, but not bank loans and bonds.

L^*/S_0 = liabilities that increase spontaneously as a percentage of sales, or spontaneously generated financing per \$1 increase in sales. $L^*/S_0 = (\$60 + \$140)/\$3{,}000 = 0.0667$ for MicroDrive. Thus, every \$1 increase in sales generates about 7 cents of spontaneous financing.

S_1 = total sales projected for next year. Note that S_0 designates last year's sales, and S_1 = \$3,300 million for MicroDrive.

ΔS = change in sales = $S_1 - S_0$ = \$3,300 million − \$3,000 million = \$300 million for MicroDrive.

M = profit margin, or profit per \$1 of sales. M = \$114/\$3,000 = 0.0380 for MicroDrive. So, MicroDrive earns 3.8 cents on each dollar of sales.

RR = retention ratio, which is the percentage of net income that is retained. For MicroDrive, RR = \$56/\$114 = 0.491. RR is also equal to 1 − payout ratio, since the retention ratio and the payout ratio must total to 1.0 = 100%.

Inserting values for MicroDrive into Equation 4-1, we find the additional funds needed to be \$118 million:

$$
\begin{aligned}
\text{AFN} &= \begin{bmatrix}\text{Required}\\ \text{asset}\\ \text{increase}\end{bmatrix} - \begin{bmatrix}\text{Spontaneous}\\ \text{liability}\\ \text{increase}\end{bmatrix} - \begin{bmatrix}\text{Increase}\\ \text{in retained}\\ \text{earnings}\end{bmatrix}\\
&= 0.667(\Delta S) - 0.067(\Delta S) - 0.038(S_1)(0.491)\\
&= 0.667(\$300\text{ million}) - 0.067(\$300\text{ million}) - 0.038(\$3{,}300\text{ million})(0.491)\\
&= \$200\text{ million} - \$20\text{ million} - \$62\text{ million}\\
&= \$118\text{ million.}
\end{aligned}
$$

To increase sales by \$300 million, the formula suggests that MicroDrive must increase assets by \$200 million. The \$200 million of new assets must be financed in some manner. Of the total, \$20 million will come from a spontaneous increase in liabilities, while another \$62 million will be obtained from retained earnings. The remaining

\$118 million must be raised from external sources. This value is an approximation, but it is only slightly different from the first-pass AFN figure (\$112 million) we developed in Table 4-3. It is virtually identical to the final AFN of \$117.9 million shown in Table 4-6.

Factors That Affect External Financial Requirements

This equation shows that external financing requirements depend on five key factors:

- **Sales growth (ΔS).** Rapidly growing companies require large increases in assets, other things held constant.
- **Capital intensity (A^*/S_0).** The amount of assets required per dollar of sales, A^*/S_0 in Equation 4-1, is called the **capital intensity ratio.** This ratio has a major effect on capital requirements. Companies with higher assets-to-sales ratios require more assets for a given increase in sales, hence a greater need for external financing.
- **Spontaneous liabilities-to-sales ratio (L^*/S_0).** Companies that spontaneously generate a large amount of liabilities from accounts payable and accruals will have a relatively small need for external financing.
- **Profit margin (M).** The higher the profit margin, the larger the net income available to support increases in assets, hence the lower the need for external financing.
- **Retention ratio (RR).** Companies that retain more of their earnings as opposed to paying them out as dividends will generate more retained earnings and thus have less need for external financing.

Note that Equation 4-1 provides an accurate forecast only for companies whose ratios are all expected to remain constant. It is useful to obtain a quick "back of the envelope" estimate of external financing requirements for nonconstant ratio companies, but in the planning process one should calculate the actual additional funds needed by the projected financial statement method.

Relationship between Sales Growth and Financial Requirements

The faster MicroDrive's growth rate in sales, the greater its need for additional financing. We can use Equation 4-1, which is plotted in Figure 4-3, to demonstrate this relationship. The tabular data show MicroDrive's additional financial requirements at various growth rates, and these data are plotted in the graph. The figure illustrates four important points:

1. **Financial feasibility.** At low growth rates, MicroDrive needs no external financing, and it even generates surplus cash. However, if the company grows faster than 3.21 percent, it must raise capital from outside sources. We found the 3.21 percent growth rate by setting AFN equal to zero, substituting gS_0 for ΔS and $S_0 + g(S_0)$ for S_1 in the AFN equation, and then solving the equation $0 = 0.667(g)(S_0) - 0.067(g)(S_0) - 0.038(S_0 + gS_0)(1 - 0.509)$ for g. The g that solved this equation was about 0.0321, or 3.21 percent.

   Further, the faster the growth rate, the greater the capital requirements. If management foresees difficulties in raising the required capital, it should reconsider the feasibility of the expansion plans.
2. **Effect of dividend policy on financing needs.** Dividend policy as reflected in the payout ratio (d in Equation 4-1) also affects external capital requirements—the

higher the payout ratio, the smaller the addition to retained earnings, hence the greater the need for external capital. Therefore, if MicroDrive foresees difficulties in raising capital, it should consider reducing the dividend payout ratio. This would lower (or shift to the right) the line in Figure 4-3, indicating smaller external capital requirements at all growth rates. However, before changing its dividend policy, management should consider the effects of such a decision on the stock price, as discussed in Chapter 18.

Note that the line in Figure 4-3 does *not* pass through the origin. Thus, at low growth rates (below 3.21 percent), surplus funds will be produced, because new retained earnings plus spontaneous funds will exceed the required asset increases. Only if the dividend payout ratio were 100 percent, meaning that the firm did not retain any of its earnings, would the "funds needed" line pass through the origin.

3. **Capital intensity.** If the capital intensity ratio is low, sales can grow rapidly without much outside capital. However, if the firm is capital intensive, even a small growth in output will require a great deal of new outside capital.

FIGURE 4-3 Relationship between Growth in Sales and Financial Requirements, Assuming S_0 = \$3,000 (Millions of Dollars)

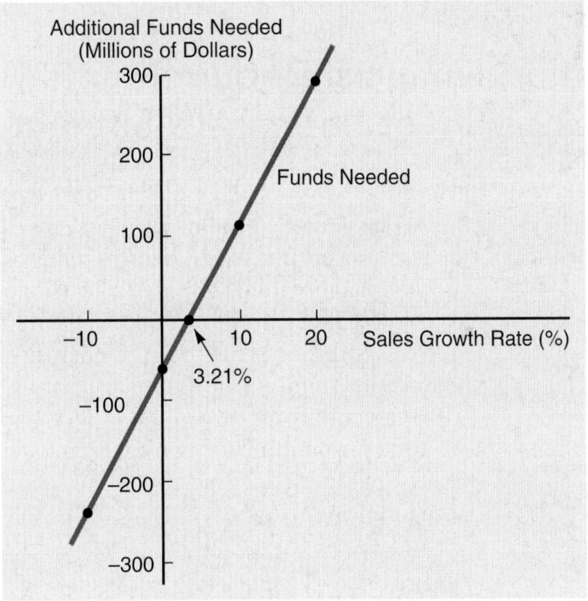

Growth Rate in Sales (1)	Increase (Decrease) in Sales, ΔS (2)	Forecasted Sales, S_1 (3)	Additional Funds Needed (4)
20%	\$600	\$3,600	\$293
10	300	3,300	118
3.21	96	3,096	0
0	0	3,000	−56
−10	−300	2,700	−230

Explanation of Columns:
Column 1: Assumed growth rate in sales, g.
Column 2: Increase (decrease) in sales, $\Delta S = g(S_0) = g(\$3{,}000)$.
Column 3: Forecasted sales, $S_1 = S_0 + g(S_0) = S_0(1 + g) = \$3{,}000(1 + g)$.
Column 4: Additional funds needed $= 0.667(\Delta S) - 0.067(\Delta S) - 0.019(S_1)$.

4. **Profit margin.** The profit margin, M, is also an important determinant of the funds-required equation—the higher the margin, the lower the funds requirements. In terms of the graph, an increase in the profit margin would cause the line to shift down, and its slope would also become less steep. Because of the relationship between profit margins and additional capital requirements, some very rapidly growing firms do not need much external capital. For example, for many years Xerox grew at a rapid rate with very little borrowing or stock sales. However, as the company lost patent protection and as competition intensified in the copier industry, Xerox's profit margin declined, its needs for external capital rose, and it began to borrow from banks and other sources.

Self-Test Questions

If all ratios are expected to remain constant, a formula can be used to forecast AFN. Give the formula and briefly explain it.

How do the following factors affect external capital requirements?

(1) Retention ratio.

(2) Capital intensity.

(3) Profit margin.

(4) Dividend payout ratio.

Forecasting Financial Requirements When the Balance Sheet Ratios Are Subject to Change

Both the AFN formula and the projected financial statement method as we initially used it assume that the ratios of assets and liabilities to sales (A^*/S_0 and L^*/S_0) remain constant over time. This, in turn, requires the assumption that each "spontaneous" asset and liability item increases at the same rate as sales. In graph form, this implies the type of relationship shown in Panel a of Figure 4-4, a relationship that is (1) linear and (2) passes through the origin. Under those conditions, if the company's sales increase from \$200 million to \$400 million, or by 100 percent, inventory will also increase by 100 percent, from \$100 million to \$200 million.

The assumption of constant ratios and identical growth rates is appropriate at times, but there are times when it is incorrect. Three such conditions are described in the following sections.

Economies of Scale

There are economies of scale in the use of many kinds of assets, and when economies occur, the ratios are likely to change over time as the size of the firm increases. For example, retailers often need to maintain base stocks of different inventory items, even if current sales are quite low. As sales expand, inventories may then grow less rapidly than sales, so the ratio of inventory to sales (I/S) declines. This situation is depicted in Panel b of Figure 4-4. Here we see that the inventory/sales ratio is 1.5, or 150 percent, when sales are \$200 million, but the ratio declines to 1.0 when sales climb to \$400 million.

The relationship in Panel b is linear, but nonlinear relationships often exist. Indeed, if the firm uses one popular model for establishing inventory levels (the EOQ model), its inventories will rise with the square root of sales. This situation is shown in Panel c of Figure 4-4, which shows a curved line whose slope decreases at higher sales levels. In this situation, very large increases in sales would require very little additional inventory.

FIGURE 4-4 Four Possible Ratio Relationships (Millions of Dollars)

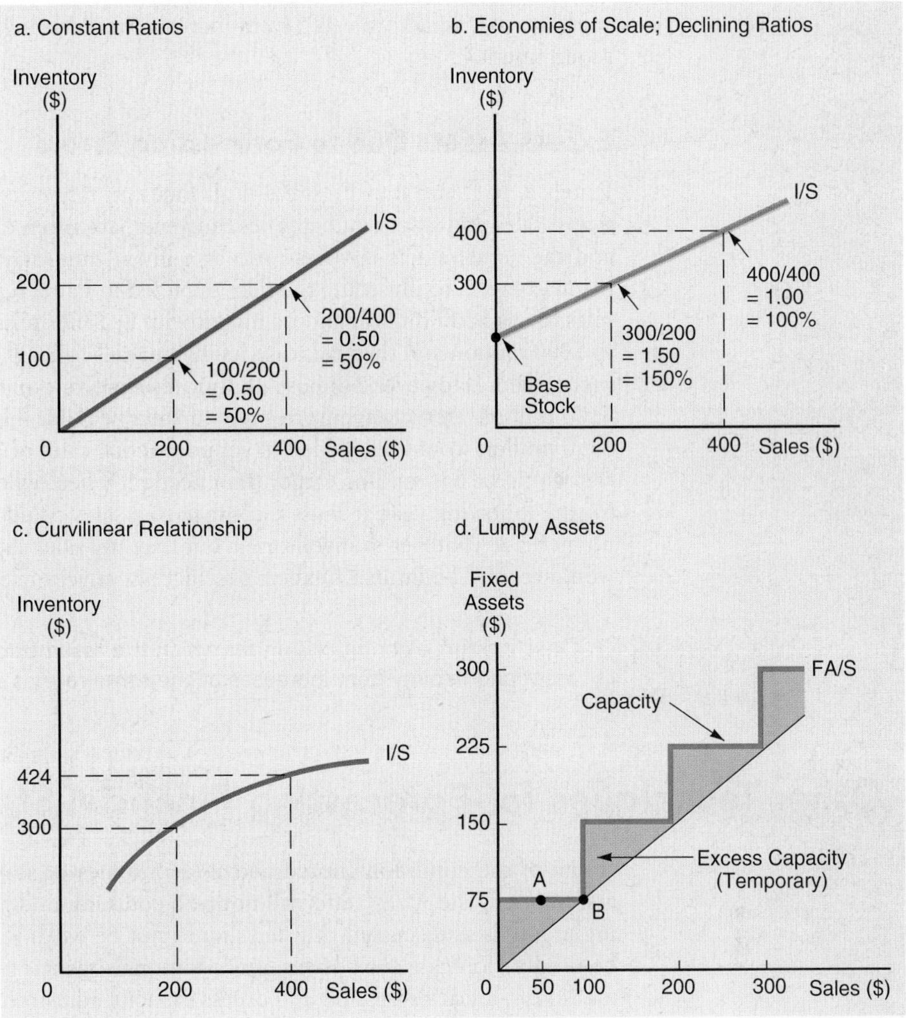

Lumpy Assets

In many industries, technological considerations dictate that if a firm is to be competitive, it must add fixed assets in large, discrete units; such assets are often referred to as **lumpy assets.** In the paper industry, for example, there are strong economies of scale in basic paper mill equipment, so when a paper company expands capacity, it must do so in large, lumpy increments. This type of situation is depicted in Panel d of Figure 4-4. Here we assume that the minimum economically efficient plant has a cost of $75 million, and that such a plant can produce enough output to reach a sales level of $100 million. If the firm is to be competitive, it simply must have at least $75 million of fixed assets.

Lumpy assets have a major effect on the fixed assets/sales (FA/S) ratio at different sales levels and, consequently, on financial requirements. At Point A in Panel d, which represents a sales level of $50 million, the fixed assets are $75 million, so the ratio FA/S = $75/$50 = 1.5. Sales can expand by $50 million, out to $100 million, with no additions to fixed assets. At that point, represented by Point B, the ratio

FA/S = \$75/\$100 = 0.75. However, since the firm is operating at capacity (sales of \$100 million), even a small increase in sales would require a doubling of plant capacity, so a small projected sales increase would bring with it a very large financial requirement.[6]

Excess Assets Due to Forecasting Errors

Panels a, b, c, and d of Figure 4-4 all focus on target, or projected, relationships between sales and assets. Actual sales, however, are often different from projected sales, and the actual assets-to-sales ratio at a given time may be quite different from the planned ratio. To illustrate, the firm depicted in Panel b of Figure 4-4 might, when its sales are at \$200 million and its inventories at \$300 million, project a sales expansion to \$400 million and then increase its inventories to \$400 million in anticipation of the higher sales. However, suppose an unforeseen economic downturn held sales to only \$300 million. Actual inventories would then be \$400 million, but inventories of only \$350 million would be needed to support actual sales of \$300 million. Thus, inventories would be \$50 million larger than needed. Then, when the firm makes its forecast for the following year, it must recognize that sales could expand by \$100 million with no increase whatever in inventories, but that any sales expansion beyond \$100 million would require additional financing to increase inventories.

Self-Test Question

Describe three conditions under which the assumption that each "spontaneous" asset and liability item increases at the same rate as sales is *not* correct.

Other Techniques for Forecasting Financial Statements

If any of the conditions noted above (economies of scale, excess capacity, or lumpy assets) apply, the A^*/S_0 ratio will not be a constant, and the constant growth forecasting methods as discussed thus far should not be used. Rather, other techniques must be used to forecast asset levels and additional financing requirements. Two of these methods—linear regression and excess capacity adjustments—are discussed in the following sections.

Simple Linear Regression

If we assume that the relationship between a certain type of asset and sales is linear, then we can use simple linear regression techniques to estimate the requirements for that type of asset for any given sales increase. For example, MicroDrive's sales, inventories, and receivables during the last five years are shown in the lower section of Figure 4-5, and both of these current asset items are plotted in the upper

[6]Several other points should be noted about Panel d of Figure 4-4. First, if the firm is operating at a sales level of \$100 million or less, any expansion that calls for a sales increase above \$100 million would require a *doubling* of the firm's fixed assets. A much smaller percentage increase would be involved if the firm were large enough to be operating a number of plants. Second, firms generally go to multiple shifts and take other actions to minimize the need for new fixed asset capacity as they approach Point B. However, these efforts can only go so far, and eventually a fixed asset expansion will be required. Third, firms often make arrangements to share excess capacity with other firms in their industry. For example, the situation in the electric utility industry is very much like that depicted in Panel d. However, electric companies often build jointly owned plants, or else they "take turns" building plants, and then they buy power from or sell power to other utilities to avoid building new plants that would be underutilized.

FIGURE 4-5 MicroDrive Inc.: Linear Regression Models (Millions of Dollars)

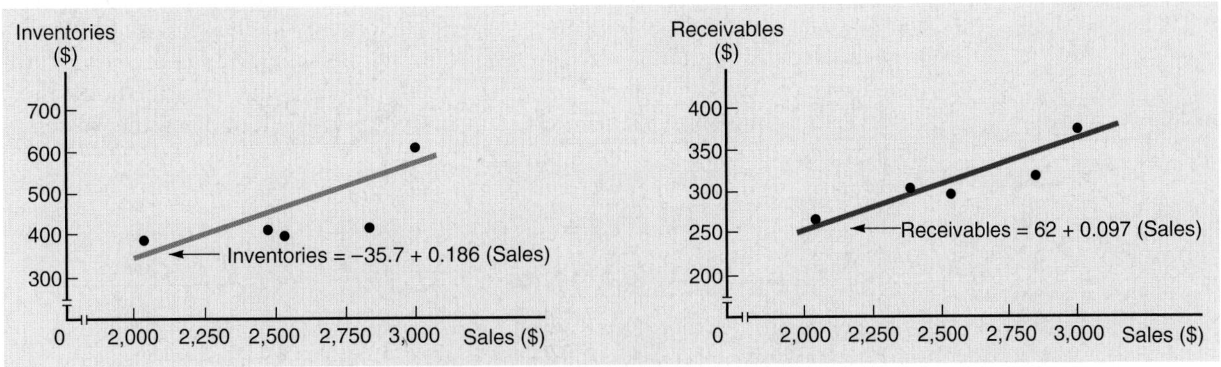

Year	Sales	Inventories	Accounts Receivable
1997	$2,058	$387	$268
1998	2,534	398	297
1999	2,472	409	304
2000	2,850	415	315
2001	3,000	615	375

section as scatter diagrams versus sales. Estimated regression equations, determined using a financial calculator or a spreadsheet, are also shown with each graph. For example, the estimated relationship between inventories and sales (in millions of dollars) is

$$\text{Inventories} = -\$35.7 + 0.186(\text{Sales}).$$

The plotted points are not very close to the regression line, which indicates that changes in inventory are affected by factors other than changes in sales. In fact, the correlation coefficient between inventories and sales is only 0.71, indicating that there is only a moderate linear relationship between these two variables. Still, the regression relationship is strong enough to provide a reasonable basis for forecasting the target inventory level, as described below.

We can use the regression relationship between inventories and sales to forecast 2002 inventory levels. Since 2002 sales are projected at $3,300 million, 2002 inventories should be $578 million:

$$\text{Inventories} = -\$35.7 + 0.186(\$3{,}300) = \$578 \text{ million}.$$

This is $99 million less than the preliminary forecast based on the projected financial statement method. The difference occurs because the projected financial statement method assumed that the ratio of inventories to sales would remain constant, when in fact it will probably decline. Note also that although our graphs show linear relationships, we could have easily used a nonlinear regression model had such a relationship been indicated.

After analyzing the regression results, MicroDrive's managers decided that a new forecast of AFN should be developed assuming a lower days sales outstanding and a higher inventory turnover ratio. Management recognized that the 2002 levels of these accounts were above the industry averages, hence that the preliminary results projected for 2002 back in Table 4-3 were unnecessarily high. When simple linear regression was used to forecast the receivables and inventories accounts, this caused the 2002 levels to reflect both the average relationships of these accounts to sales over the five-year period and the trend in the variables' values. In contrast, the projected financial statement method we developed earlier assumed that the nonoptimal 2001 relationships would remain constant in 2002 and beyond. These new assumptions were largely responsible for the improved forecasts shown in Column 3 of Table 4-6.

Excess Capacity Adjustments

Consider again the MicroDrive example set forth in Tables 4-2 and 4-3, but now assume that excess capacity exists in fixed assets. Specifically, assume that fixed assets in 2001 were being utilized to only 96 percent of capacity. If fixed assets had been used to full capacity, 2001 sales could have been as high as \$3,125 million versus the \$3,000 million in actual sales:

$$\text{Full capacity sales} = \frac{\text{Actual sales}}{\text{Percentage of capacity at which fixed assets were operated}} \tag{4-2}$$

$$= \frac{\$3{,}000 \text{ million}}{0.96} = \$3{,}125 \text{ million.}$$

This suggests that MicroDrive's target fixed assets/sales ratio should be 32 percent rather than 33.3 percent:

$$\text{Target fixed assets/Sales} = \frac{\text{Actual fixed assets}}{\text{Full capacity sales}} \tag{4-3}$$

$$= \frac{\$1{,}000}{\$3{,}125} = 0.32 = 32\%.$$

Therefore, if sales are to increase to \$3,300 million, then fixed assets would have to increase to \$1,056 million:

$$\text{Required level of fixed assets} = (\text{Target fixed assets/Sales})(\text{Projected sales}) \tag{4-4}$$

$$= 0.32(\$3{,}300) = \$1{,}056 \text{ million.}$$

We previously forecasted that MicroDrive would need to increase fixed assets at the same rate as sales, or by 10 percent. That meant an increase from \$1,000 million to \$1,100 million, or by \$100 million. Now we see that the actual required increase is only from \$1,000 million to \$1,056 million, or by \$56 million. Thus, the capacity-adjusted forecast is \$100 million − \$56 million = \$44 million less than the earlier forecast. With a smaller fixed asset requirement, the projected AFN would decline from an estimated \$118 million to \$118 million − \$44 million = \$74 million.

Note also that when excess capacity exists, sales can grow to the capacity sales as determined above with no increase whatever in fixed assets, but sales beyond that level will require fixed asset additions as calculated in our example. The same situation could occur with respect to inventories, and the required additions would be determined in exactly the same manner as for fixed assets. Theoretically, the same situation could occur with other types of assets, but as a practical matter excess capacity normally exists only with respect to fixed assets and inventories.

Self-Test Questions

If sales are expected to double, would it be more important to use the regression method of forecasting asset requirements if the true situation were like that in Panel a or that in Panel b of Figure 4-4?

If excess capacity exists, how will that affect the AFN?

Summary

This chapter described techniques for forecasting financial statements, which is a crucial part of the financial planning process. As we will see throughout the rest of the book, both investors and corporations regularly use forecasting techniques to help value a company's stock, to estimate the benefits of potential projects, and to estimate how changes in capital structure, dividend policy, and working capital policy will influence shareholder value. The key concepts covered are listed below:

- **Financial forecasting** generally begins with a forecast of the firm's sales, in terms of both units and dollars.
- Either the **projected,** or **pro forma, financial statement method** or the **AFN formula method** can be used to forecast financial requirements. The financial statement method is more reliable, and it also provides ratios that can be used to evaluate alternative business plans.
- A firm can determine its **additional funds needed (AFN)** by estimating the amount of new assets necessary to support the forecasted level of sales and then subtracting from that amount the spontaneous funds that will be generated from operations. The firm can then plan how to raise the AFN most efficiently.
- The **higher a firm's sales growth rate,** the **greater** will be its need for additional financing. Similarly, the **smaller its retention ratio,** the **greater** its need for additional funds.
- Adjustments must be made if **economies of scale** exist in the use of assets, if **excess capacity** exists, or if assets must be added in **lumpy increments.**
- **Linear regression** and **excess capacity adjustments** can be used to forecast asset requirements in situations where assets are not expected to grow at the same rate as sales.

The type of forecasting described in this chapter is important for several reasons. First, if the projected operating results are unsatisfactory, management can "go back to the drawing board," reformulate its plans, and develop more reasonable targets for the coming year. Second, it is possible that the funds required to meet the sales forecast simply cannot be obtained. If so, it is obviously better to know this in advance and to scale back the projected level of operations than to suddenly run out of cash and have operations grind to a halt. And third, even if the required funds can be raised, it is desirable to plan for their acquisition well in advance.

Questions

4–1 Define each of the following terms:

a. Operating plan; five-year plan
b. Financial plan
c. Sales forecast

d. Percent of sales method
e. Spontaneously generated funds
f. Dividend payout ratio
g. Pro forma financial statement
h. Additional funds needed (AFN); AFN formula
i. Capital intensity ratio
j. Lumpy assets
k. Financing feedback
l. Simple linear regression

4–2 Certain liability and net worth items generally increase spontaneously with increases in sales. Put a check (√) by those items that typically increase spontaneously:

Accounts payable	______
Notes payable to banks	______
Accrued wages	______
Accrued taxes	______
Mortgage bonds	______
Common stock	______
Retained earnings	______

4–3 The following equation can, under certain assumptions, be used to forecast financial requirements:

$$AFN = (A^*/S_0)(\Delta S) - (L^*/S_0)(\Delta S) - MS_1(1 - d).$$

Under what conditions does the equation give satisfactory predictions, and when should it *not* be used?

4–4 Assume that an average firm in the office supply business has a 6 percent after-tax profit margin, a 40 percent debt/assets ratio, a total assets turnover of 2 times, and a dividend payout ratio of 40 percent. Is it true that if such a firm is to have *any* sales growth ($g > 0$), it will be forced either to borrow or to sell common stock (that is, it will need some nonspontaneous, external capital even if g is very small)?

4–5 Suppose a firm makes the following policy changes. If the change means that external, nonspontaneous financial requirements (AFN) will increase, indicate this by a (+); indicate a decrease by a (−); and indicate indeterminate or no effect by a (0). Think in terms of the immediate, short-run effect on funds requirements.

a. The dividend payout ratio is increased. ______
b. The firm contracts to buy, rather than make, certain components used in its products. ______
c. The firm decides to pay all suppliers on delivery, rather than after a 30-day delay, to take advantage of discounts for rapid payment. ______
d. The firm begins to sell on credit (previously all sales had been on a cash basis). ______
e. The firm's profit margin is eroded by increased competition; sales are steady. ______
f. Advertising expenditures are stepped up.
g. A decision is made to substitute long-term mortgage bonds for short-term bank loans. ______
h. The firm begins to pay employees on a weekly basis (previously it had paid at the end of each month). ______

Self-Test Problems (Solutions Appear in Appendix A)

ST–1
GROWTH RATE
Weatherford Industries Inc. has the following ratios: $A^*/S_0 = 1.6$; $L^*/S_0 = 0.4$; profit margin = 0.10; and dividend payout ratio = 0.45, or 45 percent. Sales last year were $100 million. Assuming that these ratios will remain constant, use the AFN formula to determine the

maximum growth rate Weatherford can achieve without having to employ nonspontaneous external funds.

ST–2
ADDITIONAL FUNDS NEEDED

Suppose Weatherford's financial consultants report (1) that the inventory turnover ratio is sales/inventory = 3 times versus an industry average of 4 times and (2) that Weatherford could reduce inventories and thus raise its turnover to 4 without affecting sales, the profit margin, or the other asset turnover ratios. Under these conditions, use the AFN formula to determine the amount of additional funds Weatherford would require during each of the next 2 years if sales grew at a rate of 20 percent per year.

ST–3
EXCESS CAPACITY

Van Auken Lumber's 2001 financial statements are shown below.

Van Auken Lumber:
Balance Sheet as of December 31, 2001
(Thousands of Dollars)

Cash	$ 1,800	Accounts payable	$ 7,200
Receivables	10,800	Notes payable	3,472
Inventories	12,600	Accruals	2,520
Total current assets	$25,200	Total current liabilities	$13,192
Net fixed assets	21,600	Mortgage bonds	5,000
		Common stock	2,000
		Retained earnings	26,608
Total assets	$46,800	Total liabilities and equity	$46,800

Van Auken Lumber:
Income Statement for December 31, 2001
(Thousands of Dollars)

Sales	$36,000
Operating costs	30,783
Earnings before interest and taxes	$ 5,217
Interest	1,017
Earnings before taxes	$ 4,200
Taxes (40%)	1,680
Net income	$ 2,520
Dividends (60%)	$ 1,512
Addition to retained earnings	$ 1,008

a. Assume that the company was operating at full capacity in 2001 with regard to all items *except* fixed assets; fixed assets in 2001 were being utilized to only 75 percent of capacity. By what percentage could 2002 sales increase over 2001 sales without the need for an increase in fixed assets?

b. Now suppose 2002 sales increase by 25 percent over 2001 sales. How much additional external capital will be required? Assume that Van Auken cannot sell any fixed assets. (Hint: Use the percent of sales method to develop a pro forma balance sheet and income statement as in Tables 4-2 and 4-3.) Assume that any required financing is borrowed as notes payable. Do not include any financing feedbacks, and use a pro forma income statement to determine the addition to retained earnings. (Another hint: Notes payable = $6,021.)

c. Use the financial statements developed in part b to incorporate the financing feedback that results from the addition to notes payable. (That is, do the next financial statement iteration.) For purposes of this part, assume that the notes payable interest rate is 12 percent. What is the AFN for this iteration?

d. Suppose the industry average DSO and inventory turnover ratio are 90 days and 3.33, respectively, and that Van Auken Lumber matches these figures in 2002 and then uses the funds released to reduce equity. (It pays a special dividend, which reduces retained earnings.) What would this do to the rate of return on year-end 2002 equity? Use the second-pass balance sheet and income statement as developed in part c, and assume that the additional AFN amount calculated in that iteration is added to notes payable. (Hint: Notes payable is now $6,094.)

Problems

Carter Corporation's sales are expected to increase from $5 million in 2001 to $6 million in 2002, or by 20 percent. Its assets totaled $3 million at the end of 2001. Carter is at full capacity, so its assets must grow at the same rate as projected sales. At the end of 2001, current liabilities were $1 million, consisting of $250,000 of accounts payable, $500,000 of notes payable, and $250,000 of accruals. The after-tax profit margin is forecasted to be 5 percent, and the forecasted payout ratio is 70 percent. Use this information to answer Problems 4-1, 4-2, and 4-3.

4–1 *AFN FORMULA* Use the AFN formula to forecast Carter's additional funds needed for the coming year.

4–2 *AFN FORMULA* What would the additional funds needed be if the company's year-end 2001 assets had been $4 million? Assume that all other numbers are the same. Why is this AFN different from the one you found in Problem 4-1? Is the company's "capital intensity" the same or different?

4–3 *AFN FORMULA* Return to the assumption that the company had $3 million in assets at the end of 2001, but now assume that the company pays no dividends. Under these assumptions, what would be the additional funds needed for the coming year? Why is this AFN different from the one you found in Problem 4-1?

4–4 *SALES INCREASE* Pierce Furnishings generated $2.0 million in sales during 2001, and its year-end total assets were $1.5 million. Also, at year-end 2001, current liabilities were $500,000, consisting of $200,000 of notes payable, $200,000 of accounts payable, and $100,000 of accruals. Looking ahead to 2002, the company estimates that its assets must increase by 75 cents for every $1 increase in sales. Pierce's profit margin is 5 percent, and its payout ratio is 60 percent. How large a sales increase can the company achieve without having to raise funds externally?

4–5 *PRO FORMA STATEMENTS AND RATIOS* Upton Computers makes bulk purchases of small computers, stocks them in conveniently located warehouses, and ships them to its chain of retail stores. Upton's balance sheet as of December 31, 2001, is shown here (millions of dollars):

Cash	$ 3.5	Accounts payable	$ 9.0
Receivables	26.0	Notes payable	18.0
Inventories	58.0	Accruals	8.5
Total current assets	$ 87.5	Total current liabilities	$ 35.5
Net fixed assets	35.0	Mortgage loan	6.0
		Common stock	15.0
		Retained earnings	66.0
Total assets	$122.5	Total liabilities and equity	$122.5

Sales for 2001 were $350 million, while net income for the year was $10.5 million. Upton paid dividends of $4.2 million to common stockholders. The firm is operating at full capacity. Assume that all ratios remain constant.

a. If sales are projected to increase by $70 million, or 20 percent, during 2002, use the AFN equation to determine Upton's projected external capital requirements.

b. Construct Upton's pro forma balance sheet for December 31, 2002. Assume that all external capital requirements are met by bank loans and are reflected in notes payable. Do not consider any financing feedback effects.

c. Now calculate the following ratios, based on your projected December 31, 2002, balance sheet. Upton's 2001 ratios and industry average ratios are shown here for comparison:

	Upton Computers		Industry Average
	12/31/02	12/31/01	12/31/01
Current ratio	______	2.5×	3×
Debt/total assets	______	33.9%	30%
Rate of return on equity	______	13%	12%

d. Now assume that Upton grows by the same $70 million but that the growth is spread over 5 years—that is, that sales grow by $14 million each year. Do not consider any financing feedback effects.

(1) Calculate total additional financial requirements over the 5-year period. (Hint: Use 2001 ratios, ΔS = $70, but total sales for the 5-year period.)

(2) Construct a pro forma balance sheet as of December 31, 2006, using notes payable as the balancing item.

(3) Calculate the current ratio, total debt/total assets ratio, and rate of return on equity as of December 31, 2006. [Hint: Be sure to use *total sales*, which amount to $1,960 million, to calculate retained earnings but 2006 profits to calculate the rate of return on equity—that is, return on equity = (2006 profits)/(12/31/06 equity).]

e. Do the plans outlined in parts b and/or d seem feasible to you? That is, do you think Upton could borrow the required capital, and would the company be raising the odds on its bankruptcy to an excessive level in the event of some temporary misfortune?

4–6 *ADDITIONAL FUNDS NEEDED*

Stevens Textile's 2001 financial statements are shown below.

Stevens Textile:
Balance Sheet as of December 31, 2001
(Thousands of Dollars)

Cash	$ 1,080	Accounts payable	$ 4,320
Receivables	6,480	Accruals	2,880
Inventories	9,000	Notes payable	2,100
Total current assets	$16,560	Total current liabilities	$ 9,300
Net fixed assets	12,600	Mortgage bonds	3,500
		Common stock	3,500
		Retained earnings	12,860
Total assets	$29,160	Total liabilities and equity	$29,160

Stevens Textile:
Income Statement for December 31, 2001
(Thousands of Dollars)

Sales	$36,000
Operating costs	32,440
Earnings before interest and taxes	$ 3,560
Interest	560
Earnings before taxes	$ 3,000
Taxes (40%)	1,200
Net income	$ 1,800
Dividends (45%)	$ 810
Addition to retained earnings	$ 990

a. Suppose 2002 sales are projected to increase by 15 percent over 2001 sales. Determine the additional funds needed. Assume that the company was operating at full capacity in 2001, that it cannot sell off any of its fixed assets, and that any required financing will be borrowed as notes payable. Also, assume that assets, spontaneous liabilities, and operating costs are expected to increase by the same percentage as sales. Use the percent of sales method to develop a pro forma balance sheet and income statement for December 31, 2002. (Do not incorporate any financing feedback effects. Use the pro forma income statement to determine the addition to retained earnings.)

b. Use the financial statements developed in part a to incorporate the financing feedback as a result of the addition to notes payable. (That is, do the next financial statement iteration.) For the purpose of this part, assume that the notes payable interest rate is 10 percent. What is the AFN for this iteration?

4–7 *ADDITIONAL FUNDS NEEDED* Garlington Technologies Inc.'s 2001 financial statements are shown below.

Garlington Technologies Inc.: Balance Sheet as of December 31, 2001

Cash	$ 180,000	Accounts payable	$ 360,000
Receivables	360,000	Notes payable	156,000
Inventories	720,000	Accruals	180,000
Total current assets	$1,260,000	Total current liabilities	$ 696,000
Fixed assets	1,440,000	Common stock	1,800,000
		Retained earnings	204,000
Total assets	$2,700,000	Total liabilities and equity	$2,700,000

Garlington Technologies Inc.: Income Statement for December 31, 2001

Sales	$3,600,000
Operating costs	3,279,720
EBIT	$ 320,280
Interest	20,280
EBT	$ 300,000
Taxes (40%)	120,000
Net income	$ 180,000

Per Share Data

Common stock price	$24.00
Earnings per share (EPS)	$1.80
Dividends per share (DPS)	$1.08

a. Suppose that in 2002 sales increase by 10 percent over 2001 sales and that 2002 DPS will increase to $1.12. Construct the pro forma financial statements using the percent of sales method. How much additional capital will be required? Assume the firm operated at full capacity in 2001. Do not include any financing feedbacks.

b. Now assume that 50 percent of the additional capital required will be financed by selling common stock and the remainder by borrowing as notes payable. Assume that the interest rate on notes payable is 13 percent. Do the next iteration of financial statements incorporating financing feedbacks. What is the AFN for this iteration?

c. If the profit margin were to remain at 5 percent and the dividend payout rate were to remain at 60 percent, at what growth rate in sales would the additional financing requirements be exactly zero? (Hint: Set AFN equal to zero and solve for g.)

4–8 *EXTERNAL FINANCING REQUIREMENTS*

The 2001 balance sheet and income statement for the Damon Company are shown below.

Damon Company:
Balance Sheet as of December 31, 2001
(Thousands of Dollars)

Cash	$ 80	Accounts payable	$ 160
Accounts receivable	240	Accruals	40
Inventories	720	Notes payable	252
Total current assets	$1,040	Total current liabilities	$ 452
Fixed assets	3,200	Long-term debt	1,244
		Total debt	$1,696
		Common stock	1,605
		Retained earnings	939
Total assets	$4,240	Total liabilities and equity	$4,240

Damon Company:
Income Statement for December 31, 2001
(Thousands of Dollars)

Sales	$8,000
Operating costs	7,450
EBIT	$ 550
Interest	150
EBT	$ 400
Taxes (40%)	160
Net income	$ 240

Per Share Data

Common stock price	$16.96
Earnings per share (EPS)	$1.60
Dividends per share (DPS)	$1.04

a. The firm operated at full capacity in 2001. It expects sales to increase by 20 percent during 2002 and expects 2002 dividends per share to increase to $1.10. Use the percent of sales method to determine how much outside financing is required, developing the firm's pro forma balance sheet and income statement, and use AFN as the balancing item.
b. If the firm must maintain a current ratio of 2.3 and a debt ratio of 40 percent, how much financing, after the first pass, will be obtained using notes payable, long-term debt, and common stock?
c. Make the second-pass financial statements incorporating financing feedbacks, using the ratios in part b. Assume that the interest rate on debt averages 10 percent.

4–9 *LONG-TERM FINANCING NEEDED*

At year-end 2001, total assets for Bertin Inc. were $1.2 million and accounts payable were $375,000. Sales, which in 2001 were $2.5 million, are expected to increase by 25 percent in 2002. Total assets and accounts payable are proportional to sales and that relationship will be maintained. Bertin typically uses no current liabilities other than accounts payable. Common stock amounted to $425,000 in 2001, and retained earnings were $295,000. Bertin plans to sell new common stock in the amount of $75,000. The firm's profit margin on sales is 6 percent; 40 percent of earnings will be paid out as dividends.

a. What was Bertin's total debt in 2001?

b. How much new, long-term debt financing will be needed in 2002? (Hint: AFN − New stock = New long-term debt.) Do not consider any financing feedback effects.

4–10
ADDITIONAL FUNDS NEEDED

The Booth Company's sales are forecasted to increase from $1,000 in 2001 to $2,000 in 2002. Here is the December 31, 2001, balance sheet:

Cash	$ 100	Accounts payable	$ 50
Accounts receivable	200	Notes payable	150
Inventories	200	Accruals	50
Net fixed assets	500	Long-term debt	400
		Common stock	100
		Retained earnings	250
Total assets	$1,000	Total liabilities and equity	$1,000

Booth's fixed assets were used to only 50 percent of capacity during 2001, but its current assets were at their proper levels. All assets except fixed assets increase at the same rate as sales, and fixed assets would also increase at the same rate if the current excess capacity did not exist. Booth's after-tax profit margin is forecasted to be 5 percent, and its payout ratio will be 60 percent. What is Booth's additional funds needed (AFN) for the coming year? Ignore financing feedback effects.

Spreadsheet Problems

4–11
BUILD A MODEL: FORECASTING FINANCIAL STATEMENTS

Start with the partial model in the file ***Ch 04-11 Build a Model.xls*** from the textbook's CD-ROM. Cumberland Industries' financial planners must forecast the company's financial results for the coming year. The forecast will be based on the percent of sales method, and any additional funds needed will be obtained by using a mix of notes payable, long-term debt, and common stock. No preferred stock will be issued. Data for the problem, including Cumberland Industries' balance sheet and income statement, can be found in the spreadsheet problem for Chapter 2. Use these data to answer the following questions.

a. Cumberland Industries has had the following sales since 1996. Assuming the historical trend continues, what will sales be in 2002?

Year	Sales
1996	$129,215,000
1997	180,901,000
1998	235,252,000
1999	294,065,000
2000	396,692,000
2001	455,150,000

Base your forecast on a spreadsheet regression analysis of the 1996–2001 sales, and include the summary output of the regression in your answer. By what percentage are sales predicted to increase in 2002 over 2001? Is the sales growth rate increasing or decreasing?

b. Cumberland's management believes that the firm will actually experience a 20 percent increase in sales during 2002. Use the Chapter 2 spreadsheet problem to obtain the company's 2001 financial statements, then use those statements to construct 2002 pro forma financial statements. Assume that any additional funds needed (AFN) will be raised as follows: notes payable, 25 percent; long-term debt, 50 percent; and new common stock, 25 percent.

c. Now create a graph that shows the sensitivity of AFN to the sales growth rate. To make this graph, compare the AFN at sales growth rates of 5, 10, 15, 20, 25, and 30 percent.

d. Calculate net operating working capital (NOWC), total operating capital, NOPAT, and operating cash flow (OCF) for 2001 and 2002. Also, calculate the free cash flow (FCF) for 2002.

e. Based on the forecasted data for 2002, calculate Cumberland's sustainable growth rate, that is, the maximum growth rate without issuing new common stock.

f. Suppose Cumberland's management does not believe that accounts receivable and inventories should remain as a constant percentage of sales. Rather, they think that current assets should be predicted by using a regression analysis of recent levels versus sales. Use the following data on accounts receivable, inventories, and sales to run regressions to estimate the necessary levels of accounts receivable and inventories for 2002.

Year	Sales[a]	Inventories[a]	A/R[a]
1996	$129,215	$12,341	$24,764
1997	180,901	16,763	39,589
1998	235,252	20,564	53,764
1999	294,065	25,324	64,864
2000	396,692	35,997	98,568
2001	455,150	38,444	103,365

[a] In thousands of dollars.

4–12 WHAT IF ANALYSIS: ADDITIONAL FUNDS NEEDED

Start with the model in the file ***Ch 04-12 What If Analysis.xls*** from the textbook's CD-ROM and answer the questions shown there.

Cyberproblem

The information related to the cyberproblems is likely to change over time, due to the release of new information and the ever-changing nature of the World Wide Web. With these changes in mind, we will periodically update these problems on the textbook's web site.

4–13 FINANCIAL FORECASTING—USING ANALYSTS REPORTS

A sales forecast usually begins with a forecast of a firm's unit and dollar sales for some future period, and it is generally based on recent sales trends plus forecasts of the economic prospects for the nation, region, industry, and so forth. Analysts at investment research firms also make forecasts of companies' current and likely future financial performances. These analysts must piece together information that includes forecasts of the overall economy and the level and direction of interest rates. Moreover, they must examine economic and competitive conditions in specific industries including sales, costs, margins, profits, and cash flows for specific firms. In this cyberproblem, you will look at analysts' forecasts of earnings and recommendations about the investment potential of specific firms based on their forecasts of the firms' performances. The Zacks Investment Research web site, which can be found at **www.zacks.com,** is an excellent source of analysts' forecasts. Take a look at the cyberproblem on the textbook's web site, **http://www.harcourtcollege.com/finance/theory/student/resources/cyberprob/ch04.html,** and answer its questions about Sun Microsystems.

Mini Case

Sue Wilson, the new financial manager of Northwest Chemicals (NWC), an Oregon producer of specialized chemicals for use in fruit orchards, must prepare a financial forecast for 2002. NWC's 2001 sales were $2 billion, and the marketing department is forecasting a 25 percent increase for 2002. Sue thinks the company was operating at full capacity in 2001, but she is not sure about this. The 2001 financial statements, plus some other data, are shown below.

A. 2001 BALANCE SHEET (MILLIONS OF DOLLARS)

		Percent of Sales			Percent of Sales
Cash and securities	$ 20	1%	Accounts payable and accruals	$ 100	5%
Accounts receivable	240	12%	Notes payable	100	
Inventories	240	12%	Total current liabilities	$ 200	
Total current assets	$ 500	25%	Long-term debt	100	
Net fixed assets	500	25%	Common stock	500	
Total assets	$1,000		Retained earnings	200	
			Total liabilities and equity	$1,000	

B. 2001 INCOME STATEMENT (MILLIONS OF DOLLARS)

		Percent of Sales
Sales	$2,000.00	
Cost of goods sold (COGS)	1,200.00	60%
Sales, general, and administrative costs (SGA)	700.00	35%
Earnings before interest and taxes	$ 100.00	
Interest	16.00	
Earnings before taxes	$ 84.00	
Taxes (40%)	33.60	
Net income	$ 50.40	
Dividends (30%)	15.12	
Addition to retained earnings	$ 35.28	

C. KEY RATIOS

	NWC	Industry
Basic earnings power	10.00%	20.00%
Profit margin	2.52	4.00
Return on equity	7.20	15.60
Days sales outstanding (360 days)	43.20 days	32.00 days
Inventory turnover	8.33×	11.00×
Fixed assets turnover	4.00	5.00
Total assets turnover	2.00	2.50
Debt/assets	30.00%	36.00%
Times interest earned	6.25×	9.40×
Current ratio	2.50	3.00
Payout ratio	30.00%	30.00%
Operating profit margin after taxes (NOPAT/Sales)	3.00%	5.00%
Operating capital requirement (Operating capital/Sales)	45.00%	35.00%
Return on invested capital (NOPAT/Operating capital)	6.67%	14.00%

See **Ch 04 Show.ppt** for a *PowerPoint* presentation of the Mini Case and **Ch 04 Mini Case.xls** for detailed calculations.

Assume that you were recently hired as Wilson's assistant, and your first major task is to help her develop the forecast. She asked you to begin by answering the following set of questions.

a. Assume (1) that NWC was operating at full capacity in 2001 with respect to all assets, (2) that all assets must grow proportionally with sales, (3) that accounts payable and accruals will also grow in proportion to sales, and (4) that the 2001 profit margin and dividend payout will be maintained. Under these conditions, what will the company's financial requirements be for the coming year? Use the AFN equation to answer this question.

b. Now estimate the 2002 financial requirements using the percent of sales approach, making an initial forecast plus one additional "pass" to determine the effects of "financing feedbacks." Assume (1) that each type of asset, as well as payables, accruals, and fixed and variable costs, will be the same percent of sales in 2002 as in 2001; (2) that the payout ratio is held constant at 30 percent; (3) that external funds needed are financed 50 percent by notes payable and 50 percent by long-term debt (no new common stock will be issued); and (4) that all debt carries an interest rate of 8 percent.

c. Why do the two methods produce somewhat different AFN forecasts? Which method provides the more accurate forecast?

d. Calculate NWC's forecasted ratios, and compare them with the company's 2001 ratios and with the industry averages. How does NWC compare with the average firm in its industry, and is the company expected to improve during the coming year?

e. Calculate NWC's free cash flow for 2002.

f. Suppose you now learn that NWC's 2001 receivables and inventories were in line with required levels, given the firm's credit and inventory policies, but that excess capacity existed with regard to fixed assets. Specifically, fixed assets were operated at only 75 percent of capacity.

(1) What level of sales could have existed in 2001 with the available fixed assets? What would the fixed assets/sales ratio have been if NWC had been operating at full capacity?

(2) How would the existence of excess capacity in fixed assets affect the additional funds needed during 2002?

g. Without actually working out the numbers, how would you expect the ratios to change in the situation where excess capacity in fixed assets exists? Explain your reasoning.

h. Based on comparisons between NWC's days sales outstanding (DSO) and inventory turnover ratios with the industry average figures, does it appear that NWC is operating efficiently with respect to its inventories and accounts receivable? If the company were able to bring these ratios into line with the industry averages, what effect would this have on its AFN and its financial ratios? What effect would this have on free cash flow? (Note: Inventories and receivables will be discussed in detail in Chapter 22.)

i. The relationship between sales and the various types of assets is important in financial forecasting. The percent of sales approach, under the assumption that each asset item grows at the same rate as sales, leads to an AFN forecast that is reasonably close to the forecast using the AFN equation. Explain how each of the following factors would affect the accuracy of financial forecasts based on the AFN equation: (1) excess capacity, (2) base stocks of assets, such as shoes in a shoe store, (3) economies of scale in the use of assets, and (4) lumpy assets.

j. **(1)** How could regression analysis be used to detect the presence of the situations described above and then to improve the financial forecasts? Plot a graph of the following data, which is for a typical well-managed company in NWC's industry, to illustrate your answer.

Year	Sales	Inventories
1999	$1,280	$118
2000	1,600	138
2001	2,000	162
2002 (est.)	2,500	192

(2) On the same graph that plots the above data, draw a line that shows how the regression line must appear to justify the use of the AFN formula and the percent of sales forecasting procedure. As a part of your answer, show the growth rate in inventories that results from a 10 percent increase in sales from a sales level of (a) $200 and (b) $2,000 based on both the actual regression line and a *hypothetical* regression line that is linear and that goes through the origin.

k. How would changes in these items affect the AFN? (1) The dividend payout ratio, (2) the profit margin, (3) the capital intensity ratio, and (4) NWC begins buying from its suppliers on terms which permit it to pay after 60 days rather than after 30 days. (Consider each item separately and hold all other things constant.)

Selected Additional References and Cases

The heart of successful financial planning is the sales forecast. On this key subject, see

Pan, Judy, Donald R. Nichols, and O. Maurice Joy, "Sales Forecasting Practices of Large U.S. Industrial Firms," *Financial Management*, Fall 1977, 72–77.

Hirschey, Mark, and James L. Pappas, *Managerial Economics* (Fort Worth, TX: The Dryden Press, 1996).

Computer modeling is becoming increasingly important. For general references, see

Carleton, Willard T., Charles L. Dick, Jr., and David H. Downes, "Financial Policy Models: Theory and Practice," *Journal of Finance*, December 1973, 691–709.

Francis, Jack Clark, and Dexter R. Rowell, "A Simultaneous Equation Model of the Firm for Financial Analysis and Planning," *Financial Management*, Spring 1978, 29–44.

Grinyer, P. H., and J. Wooller, *Corporate Models Today—A New Tool for Financial Management* (London: Institute of Chartered Accountants, 1978).

Pappas, James L., and George P. Huber, "Probabilistic Short-Term Financial Planning," *Financial Management*, Autumn 1973, 36–44.

Traenkle, J. W., E. B. Cox, and J. A. Bullard, *The Use of Financial Models in Business* (New York: Financial Executives' Research Foundation, 1975).

Considerable effort has been expended to develop integrated financial planning models that identify optimal policies. For one example, see

Myers, Stewart C., and Gerald A. Pogue, "A Programming Approach to Corporate Financial Management," *Journal of Finance*, May 1974, 579–599.

For an article on control, see

Bierman, Harold, "Beyond Cash Flow ROI," *Midland Corporate Finance Journal*, Winter 1988, 36–39.

The Dryden Press Cases in Financial Management: Dryden Request *series contains the following applicable cases:*

Case 37, "Space-Age Materials, Inc.," Case 38, "Automated Banking Management, Inc.," Case 38A, "Expert Systems," Case 38B, "Medical Management Systems, Inc.," and Case 63, "Dental Records, Inc.," which all focus on using the percent of sales forecasting method to forecast future financing requirements.

5

The Financial Environment: Markets, Institutions, and Interest Rates

Financial managers and investors don't operate in a vacuum—they make decisions within a large and complex financial environment. This environment includes financial markets and institutions, tax and regulatory policies, and the general economy. These conditions both define the available financial alternatives and affect the outcomes of various decisions. Therefore, it is crucial that financial managers and investors have a good understanding of the environment in which they operate.

Good financial decisions require an understanding of the current direction of the economy, the level of interest rates, and the stock market—but figuring out what's likely to happen is no trivial matter. Going into the new millenium, the financial environment had been extraordinarily favorable to financial managers and investors: The economy had not seen a recession for nearly ten years; interest rates and inflation had remained relatively low; and the stock market had boomed throughout most of the past decade. At the same time, the financial environment had undergone tremendous changes, presenting financial managers and investors with both opportunities and risks.

Consider Charles Schwab and Merrill Lynch. Benefiting from the strong stock market, traditional brokerage powerhouse Merrill Lynch had seen its stock rise more than 250 percent over the past five years. During this same period, Charles Schwab, the leader in online trading, had seen its stock rise by nearly 1,800 percent! The Internet has enabled online brokers such as Schwab, E*Trade, DLJDirect, and Datek to offer investors the opportunity to trade stocks at a small fraction of the price traditionally charged by full-service firms such as Merrill Lynch. While online trading was virtually nonexistent just a couple of years ago, there are now an estimated 100 online brokers serving more than 4 million customers. Some estimate that by 2003 there will be more than 20 million online accounts.

Schwab's and Merrill Lynch's recent stock market performances indicate that the market is increasingly concerned about online trading's effect on full-service brokers. Despite a recent 30 percent pullback in its stock price, Schwab's stock has risen more than 260 percent over the past two years. During this same period, Merrill Lynch's stock price has actually declined. Recognizing this changing environment, Merrill Lynch has taken steps toward offering its customers the opportunity to trade online.

WWW

To take a look at the online ventures of Charles Schwab and Merrill Lynch, check out their web sites at **http://www.schwab.com** and **http://askmerrill.ml.com**. You can test the Schwab customer experience or take a tour of Merrill Lynch Online.

The same forces that dramatically affected the brokerage industry have had similar effects on other industries. Companies such as Barnes and Noble and Toys Я Us have been presented with new and aggressive competition from the likes of Amazon.com and eToys Inc. Likewise, changing technology has altered the way millions of consumers purchase airline tickets, hotel rooms, and automobiles. Consequently, financial managers must understand today's technological environment and be ready to change operations as the environment evolves.

In earlier chapters we discussed financial statements and showed how financial managers and others analyze them to see where their firms have been and are headed. Financial managers also need to understand the environment and markets within which businesses operate. This chapter describes the markets where capital is raised, securities are traded, and stock prices are established, as well as the institutions that operate in these markets. In the process, we also explore the principal factors that determine the level of interest rates.

The Financial Markets

The textbook's CD-ROM contains an *Excel* file that will guide you through the chapter's calculations. The file for this chapter is ***Ch 05 Tool Kit.xls,*** and we encourage you to open the file and follow along as you read the chapter.

Businesses, individuals, and governments often need to raise capital. For example, suppose Carolina Power & Light (CP&L) forecasts an increase in the demand for electricity in North Carolina, and the company decides to build a new power plant. Because CP&L almost certainly will not have the $1 billion or so necessary to pay for the plant, the company will have to raise this capital in the financial markets. Or suppose Mr. Fong, the proprietor of a San Francisco hardware store, decides to expand into appliances. Where will he get the money to buy the initial inventory of TV sets, washers, and freezers? Similarly, if the Johnson family wants to buy a home that costs $100,000, but they have only $20,000 in savings, how can they raise the additional $80,000? If the city of New York wants to borrow $200 million to finance a new sewer plant, or the federal government needs money to meet its needs, they too need access to the capital markets.

On the other hand, some individuals and firms have incomes that are greater than their current expenditures, so they have funds available to invest. For example, Carol Hawk has an income of $36,000, but her expenses are only $30,000, and Ford Motor Company has accumulated roughly $23 billion of cash and marketable securities, which it has available for future investments.

Types of Markets

People and organizations who want to borrow money are brought together with those with surplus funds in the *financial markets.* Note that "markets" is plural—there are a great many different financial markets in a developed economy such as ours. Each market deals with a somewhat different type of instrument in terms of the instrument's maturity and the assets backing it. Also, different markets serve different types of customers, or operate in different parts of the country. Here are some of the major types of markets:

1. **Physical asset markets** (also called "tangible" or "real" asset markets) are those for such products as wheat, autos, real estate, computers, and machinery. **Financial asset markets,** on the other hand, deal with stocks, bonds, notes, mortgages, and other **financial instruments.** All of these instruments are simply pieces of paper with contractual provisions that entitle their owners to specific rights and claims on real assets. For example, a corporate bond issued by IBM entitles its owner to a specific claim on the cash flows produced by IBM's physical assets, and a share of IBM stock entitles its owner to a different set of claims on IBM's cash flows. Unlike these conventional financial instruments, the contractual provisions of **derivative securities** are not direct claims on either real assets or their cash flows. Instead, derivatives are claims whose values depend on what happens to the value of some other asset. Futures and options are two important types of derivatives, and their values depend on what happens to the prices of other assets, say, IBM stock, Japanese yen, or pork bellies. Therefore, the value of a derivative security is *derived* from the value of an underlying real asset.

2. **Spot markets** and **futures markets** are terms that refer to whether the assets are being bought or sold for "on-the-spot" delivery (literally, within a few days) or for delivery at some future date, such as six months or a year into the future.
3. **Money markets** are the markets for short-term, highly liquid debt securities. The New York and London money markets have long been the world's largest, but Tokyo is rising rapidly. **Capital markets** are the markets for intermediate- or long-term debt and corporate stocks. The New York Stock Exchange, where the stocks of the largest U.S. corporations are traded, is a prime example of a capital market. There is no hard and fast rule on this, but when describing debt markets, "short term" generally means less than one year, "intermediate term" means one to five years, and "long term" means more than five years.
4. **Mortgage markets** deal with loans on residential, commercial, and industrial real estate, and on farmland, while **consumer credit markets** involve loans on autos and appliances, as well as loans for education, vacations, and so on.
5. **World, national, regional,** and **local markets** also exist. Thus, depending on an organization's size and scope of operations, it may be able to borrow all around the world, or it may be confined to a strictly local, even neighborhood, market.
6. **Primary markets** are the markets in which corporations raise new capital. If Microsoft were to sell a new issue of common stock to raise capital, this would be a primary market transaction. The corporation selling the newly created stock receives the proceeds from the sale in a primary market transaction.
7. The **initial public offering (IPO) market** is a subset of the primary market. Here firms "go public" by offering shares to the public for the first time. Microsoft had its IPO in 1986. Previously, Bill Gates and other insiders owned all the shares. In many IPOs, the insiders sell some of their shares plus the company sells newly created shares to raise additional capital.
8. **Secondary markets** are markets in which existing, already outstanding, securities are traded among investors. Thus, if Jane Doe decided to buy 1,000 shares of AT&T stock, the purchase would occur in the secondary market. The New York Stock Exchange is a secondary market, since it deals in outstanding, as opposed to newly issued, stocks. Secondary markets also exist for bonds, mortgages, various other types of loans, and other financial assets. The corporation whose securities are being traded is not involved in a secondary market transaction and, thus, does not receive any funds from such a sale.
9. **Private markets,** where transactions are worked out directly between two parties, are differentiated from **public markets,** where standardized contracts are traded on organized exchanges. Bank loans and private placements of debt with insurance companies are examples of private market transactions. Since these transactions are private, they may be structured in any manner that appeals to the two parties. By contrast, securities that are issued in public markets (for example, common stock and corporate bonds) are ultimately held by a large number of individuals. Public securities must have fairly standardized contractual features, both to appeal to a broad range of investors and also because public investors cannot afford the time to study unique, nonstandardized contracts. Their diverse ownership also ensures that public securities are relatively liquid. Private market securities are, therefore, more tailor-made but less liquid, whereas public market securities are more liquid but subject to greater standardization.

Other classifications could be made, but this breakdown is sufficient to show that there are many types of financial markets. Also, note that the distinctions among markets are often blurred and unimportant, except as a general point of reference. For example, it makes little difference if a firm borrows for 11, 12, or 13 months, hence, whether we have a "money" or "capital" market transaction. You should recognize the

WWW

Students can access current and historical interest rates and economic data as well as regional economic data for the states of Arkansas, Illinois, Indiana, Kentucky, Mississippi, Missouri, and Tennessee from the Federal Reserve Economic Data (FRED) site at **http://www.stls.frb.org/fred/**.

big differences among types of markets, but don't get hung up trying to distinguish them at the boundaries.

A healthy economy is dependent on efficient transfers of funds from people who are net savers to firms and individuals who need capital. Without efficient transfers, the economy simply could not function: Carolina Power & Light could not raise capital, so Raleigh's citizens would have no electricity; the Johnson family would not have adequate housing; Carol Hawk would have no place to invest her savings; and so on. Obviously, the level of employment and productivity, hence our standard of living, would be much lower. Therefore, it is absolutely essential that our financial markets function efficiently—not only quickly, but also at a low cost.[1]

Table 5-1 gives a listing of the most important instruments traded in the various financial markets. The instruments are arranged from top to bottom in ascending order of typical length of maturity. As we go through the book, we will look in much more detail at many of the instruments listed in Table 5-1. For example, we will see that there are many varieties of corporate bonds, ranging from "plain vanilla" bonds to bonds that are convertible into common stocks to bonds whose interest payments vary depending on the inflation rate. Still, the table gives an idea of the characteristics and costs of the instruments traded in the major financial markets.

Recent Trends

Financial markets have experienced many changes during the last two decades. Technological advances in computers and telecommunications, along with the globalization of banking and commerce, have led to deregulation, and this has increased competition throughout the world. The result is a much more efficient, internationally linked market, but one that is far more complex than existed a few years ago. While these developments have been largely positive, they have also created problems for policy makers. At a recent conference, Federal Reserve Board Chairman Alan Greenspan stated that modern financial markets "expose national economies to shocks from new and unexpected sources, and with little if any lag." He went on to say that central banks must develop new ways to evaluate and limit risks to the financial system. Large amounts of capital move quickly around the world in response to changes in interest and exchange rates, and these movements can disrupt local institutions and economies.

With globalization has come the need for greater cooperation among regulators at the international level. Various committees are currently working to improve coordination, but the task is not easy. Factors that complicate coordination include (1) the differing structures among nations' banking and securities industries, (2) the trend in Europe toward financial service conglomerates, and (3) a reluctance on the part of individual countries to give up control over their national monetary policies. Still, regulators are unanimous about the need to close the gaps in the supervision of worldwide markets.

Another important trend in recent years has been the increased use of **derivatives.** A derivative is any security whose value is *derived* from the price of some "underlying" asset. An option to buy IBM stock is a derivative, as is a contract to buy Japanese yen six months from now. The value of the IBM option depends on the price of IBM's stock, and the value of the Japanese yen "future" depends on the exchange rate between yen and dollars. The market for derivatives has grown faster than any other

[1]As the countries of the former Soviet Union and other Eastern European nations move toward capitalism, just as much attention must be paid to the establishment of cost-efficient financial markets as to electrical power, transportation, communications, and other infrastructure systems. Economic efficiency is simply impossible without a good system for allocating capital within the economy.

TABLE 5-1 Summary of Major Market Instruments

			Security Characteristics		
Instrument (1)	**Market (2)**	**Major Participants (3)**	**Risk (4)**	**Original Maturity (5)**	**Interest Rate on 5/22/00[a] (6)**
U.S. Treasury bills	Money	Sold by U.S. Treasury to finance government	Default-free	91 days to 1 year	6.1%
Banker's acceptances	Money	A firm's promise to pay, guaranteed by a bank	Low degree of risk if guaranteed by a strong bank	Up to 180 days	6.9
Commercial paper	Money	Issued by financially secure firms to large investors	Low default risk	Up to 270 days	6.6
Negotiable certificates of deposit (CDs)	Money	Issued by major money-center commercial banks to large investors	Default risk depends on the strength of the issuing bank	Up to 1 year	7.0
Money market mutual funds	Money	Invest in short-term debt; held by individuals and businesses	Low degree of risk	No specific maturity (instant liquidity)	5.6
Eurodollar market time deposits	Money	Issued by banks outside U.S.	Depends on the strength of issuing bank	Up to 1 year	7.0
Consumer credit loans	Money	Loans by banks/credit unions/finance companies	Risk is variable	Variable	Variable
U.S. Treasury notes and bonds	Capital	Issued by U.S. government	No default risk, but price will decline if interest rates rise	2 to 30 years	6.5
Mortgages	Capital	Loans secured by property	Risk is variable	Up to 30 years	8.6
State and local government bonds	Capital	Issued by state and local governments to individuals and institutional investors	Riskier than U.S. government securities, but exempt from most taxes	Up to 30 years	6.0
Corporate bonds	Capital	Issued by corporations to individuals and institutional investors	Riskier than government debt, but less risky than stocks; risk depends on strength of issuer	Up to 40 years[b]	8.1
Leases	Capital	Similar to debt in that firms can lease assets rather than borrow and then buy the assets	Risk similar to corporate bonds	Generally 3 to 20 years	Similar to bond yields
Preferred stocks	Capital	Issued by corporations to individuals and institutional investors	Riskier than corporate bonds, less risky than common stock	Unlimited	7 to 9%
Common stocks[c]	Capital	Issued by corporations to individuals and institutional investors	Risky	Unlimited	10 to 15%

[a]The yield reported on money market mutual funds is from *The Wall Street Journal*. All other data are from the *Federal Reserve Statistical Release*, **http://www.federalreserve.gov/releases/H15/update.** Money market rates assume a 3-month maturity. The corporate bond rate is for AAA-rated bonds.

[b]Just recently, a few corporations have issued 100-year bonds; however, the majority have issued bonds with maturities less than 40 years.

[c]Common stocks are expected to provide a "return" in the form of dividends and capital gains rather than interest. Of course, if you buy a stock, your *actual* return may be considerably higher or lower than your *expected* return. For example, Nasdaq stocks on average provided a return of about −39 percent in 2000, but that was well below the return most investors expected.

market in recent years, providing corporations with new opportunities but also exposing them to new risks.

Derivatives can be used either to reduce risks or to speculate. As an example of a risk-reducing usage, suppose an importer's net income tends to fall whenever the dollar falls relative to the yen. That company could reduce its risk by purchasing derivatives that increase in value whenever the dollar declines. This would be called a *hedging operation*, and its purpose is to reduce risk exposure. Speculation, on the other hand, is done in the hope of high returns, but it raises risk exposure. For example, Procter & Gamble lost $150 million on derivative investments, and Orange County (California) went bankrupt as a result of its treasurer's speculation in derivatives.

The size and complexity of derivatives transactions concern regulators, academics, and members of Congress. Fed Chairman Greenspan noted that, in theory, derivatives should allow companies to manage risk better, but that it is not clear whether recent innovations have "increased or decreased the inherent stability of the financial system."

Another major trend involves stock ownership patterns. The number of individuals who have a stake in the stock market is increasing, but the percentage of corporate shares owned by individuals is decreasing. How can both of these two statements be true? The answer has to do with institutional versus individual ownership of shares. More than 48 percent of all U.S. households now have investments in the stock market, compared with only 22 percent in 1990. However, more than 60 percent of all stock is now owned by pension funds, mutual funds, and life insurance companies. Thus, more and more individuals are investing in the market, but they are doing so indirectly, through retirement plans and mutual funds. In any event, the performance of the stock market now has a greater effect on the U.S. population than ever before. Also, the direct ownership of stocks is being concentrated in institutions, with professional portfolio managers making the investment decisions and controlling the votes. Note too that if a fund holds a high percentage of a given corporation's shares, it would probably severely depress the stock's price if it tried to sell out. Thus, to some extent, the larger institutions are "locked into" many of the shares they own. This has led to a phenomenon called **relationship investing,** where portfolio managers think of themselves as having an active, long-term relationship with their portfolio companies. Rather than being passive investors who "vote with their feet," they are taking a much more active role in trying to force managers to behave in a manner that is in the best interests of shareholders.

Self-Test Questions

Distinguish between physical asset markets and financial asset markets.

What is the difference between spot and futures markets?

Distinguish between money and capital markets.

What is the difference between primary and secondary markets?

Differentiate between private and public markets.

Why are financial markets essential for a healthy economy?

What are derivatives, and how is their value related to that of an "underlying asset"?

What is relationship investing?

Financial Institutions

Transfers of capital between savers and those who need capital take place in the three different ways diagrammed in Figure 5-1:

FIGURE 5-1 Diagram of the Capital Formation Process

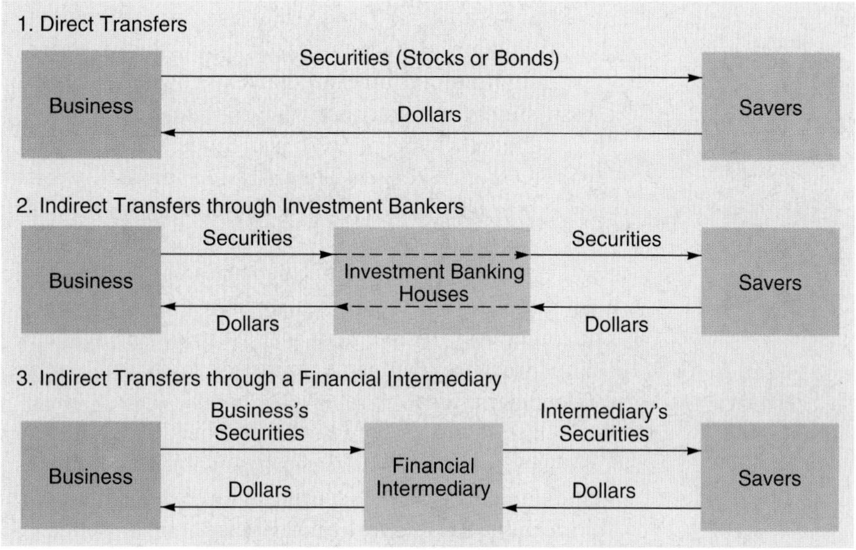

1. *Direct transfers* of money and securities, as shown in the top section, occur when a business sells its stocks or bonds directly to savers, without going through any type of financial institution. The business delivers its securities to savers, who in turn give the firm the money it needs.
2. As shown in the middle section, transfers may also go through an *investment banking house* such as Merrill Lynch, which *underwrites* the issue. An underwriter serves as a middleman and facilitates the issuance of securities. The company sells its stocks or bonds to the investment bank, which in turn sells these same securities to savers. The businesses' securities and the savers' money merely "pass through" the investment banking house. However, the investment bank does buy and hold the securities for a period of time, so it is taking a risk—it may not be able to resell them to savers for as much as it paid. Because new securities are involved and the corporation receives the proceeds of the sale, this is a primary market transaction.
3. Transfers can also be made through a *financial intermediary* such as a bank or mutual fund. Here the intermediary obtains funds from savers in exchange for its own securities. The intermediary then uses this money to purchase and then hold businesses' securities. For example, a saver might give dollars to a bank, receiving from it a certificate of deposit, and then the bank might lend the money to a small business in the form of a mortgage loan. Thus, intermediaries literally create new forms of capital—in this case, certificates of deposit, which are both safer and more liquid than mortgages and thus are better securities for most savers to hold. The existence of intermediaries greatly increases the efficiency of money and capital markets.

In our example, we assume that the entity needing capital is a business, and specifically a corporation, but it is easy to visualize the demander of capital as a home purchaser, a government unit, and so on.

Direct transfers of funds from savers to businesses are possible and do occur on occasion, but it is generally more efficient for a business to enlist the services of an **investment banking house** such as Merrill Lynch, Salomon Smith Barney, Morgan Stanley Dean Witter, or Goldman Sachs. Such organizations (1) help corporations design securities with features that are currently attractive to investors, (2) then buy these securities from the corporation, and (3) resell them to savers. Although the securities are sold twice, this process is really one primary market transaction, with the investment banker acting as a facilitator to help transfer capital from savers to businesses.

The **financial intermediaries** shown in the third section of Figure 5-1 do more than simply transfer money and securities between firms and savers—they literally create new financial products. Since the intermediaries are generally large, they gain economies of scale in analyzing the creditworthiness of potential borrowers, in processing and collecting loans, and in pooling risks and thus helping individual savers diversify, that is, "not putting all their financial eggs in one basket." Further, a system of specialized intermediaries can enable savings to do more than just draw interest. For example, individuals can put money into banks and get both interest income and a convenient way of making payments (checking), or put money into life insurance companies and get both interest income and protection for their beneficiaries.

In the United States and other developed nations, a set of specialized, highly efficient financial intermediaries has evolved. The situation is changing rapidly, however, and different types of institutions are performing services that were formerly reserved for others, causing institutional distinctions to become blurred. Still, there is a degree of institutional identity, and here are the major classes of intermediaries:

1. *Commercial banks*, the traditional "department stores of finance," serve a wide variety of savers and borrowers. Historically, commercial banks were the major institutions that handled checking accounts and through which the Federal Reserve System expanded or contracted the money supply. Today, however, several other institutions also provide checking services and significantly influence the money supply. Conversely, commercial banks are providing an ever-widening range of services, including stock brokerage services and insurance.

   Note that commercial banks are quite different from investment banks. Commercial banks lend money, whereas investment banks help companies raise capital from other parties. Prior to 1933, commercial banks offered investment banking services, but the Glass-Steagall Act, which was passed in 1933, prohibited commercial banks from engaging in investment banking. Thus, the Morgan Bank was broken up into two separate organizations, one of which is now the Morgan Guaranty Trust Company, a commercial bank, while the other is Morgan Stanley Dean Witter, a major investment banking house. Note also that Japanese and European banks can offer both commercial and investment banking services. This hindered U.S. banks in global competition, so in 1999 Congress basically repealed the Glass-Steagall Act.
2. *Savings and loan associations (S&Ls)*, which have traditionally served individual savers and residential and commercial mortgage borrowers, take the funds of many small savers and then lend this money to home buyers and other types of borrowers. Because the savers obtain a degree of liquidity that would be absent if they made the mortgage loans directly, perhaps the most significant economic function of the S&Ls is to "create liquidity" which would otherwise be lacking. Also, the S&Ls have more expertise in analyzing credit, setting up loans, and making collections than individual savers, so S&Ls can reduce the costs of processing loans, thereby increasing the availability of real estate loans. Finally, the S&Ls hold large, diversified portfolios of loans and other assets and thus spread risks in a manner that would be impossible if small savers were making mortgage loans directly. Because of these factors, savers benefit by being able to invest in more liquid, better managed, and less risky assets, whereas borrowers benefit by being able to obtain more capital, and at a lower cost, than would otherwise be possible.

In the 1980s, the S&L industry experienced severe problems when (1) short-term interest rates paid on savings accounts rose well above the returns being earned on the existing mortgages held by S&Ls and (2) commercial real estate suffered a severe slump, resulting in high mortgage default rates. Together, these events forced many S&Ls to either merge with stronger institutions or close their doors.

3. *Mutual savings banks*, which are similar to S&Ls, operate primarily in the northeastern states, accept savings primarily from individuals, and lend mainly on a long-term basis to home buyers and consumers.
4. *Credit unions* are cooperative associations whose members are supposed to have a common bond, such as being employees of the same firm. Members' savings are loaned only to other members, generally for auto purchases, home improvement loans, and home mortgages. Credit unions are often the cheapest source of funds available to individual borrowers.
5. *Life insurance companies* take savings in the form of premiums; invest these funds in stocks, bonds, real estate, and mortgages; and finally make payments to the beneficiaries of the insured parties. In recent years, life insurance companies have also offered a variety of tax-deferred savings plans designed to provide benefits to the participants when they retire.
6. *Mutual funds* are corporations that accept money from savers and then use these funds to buy stocks, long-term bonds, or short-term debt instruments issued by businesses or government units. These organizations pool funds and thus reduce risks by diversification. They also achieve economies of scale in analyzing securities, managing portfolios, and buying and selling securities. Different funds are designed to meet the objectives of different types of savers. Hence, there are bond funds for those who desire safety, stock funds for savers who are willing to accept significant risks in the hope of higher returns, and still other funds that are used as interest-bearing checking accounts (the **money market funds**). There are literally thousands of different mutual funds with dozens of different goals and purposes.
7. *Pension funds* are retirement plans funded by corporations or government agencies for their workers and administered generally by the trust departments of commercial banks or by life insurance companies. Pension funds invest primarily in bonds, stocks, mortgages, and real estate.

Changes in the structure of pension plans over the last decade have had a profound effect on both individuals and financial markets. Historically, most large corporations and governmental units used *defined benefit* plans to provide for their employees' retirement. In a defined benefit plan, the employer guarantees the level of benefits the employee will receive when he or she retires, and it is the employer's responsibility to invest funds to ensure that it can meet its obligations when its employees retire. Under a defined benefit plan, employees have little or no say about how the money in the pension plan is invested—this decision is made by the corporate employer. Note that employers, not employees, bear the risk that investments held by the plan will not perform well.

In recent years many companies (including virtually all new companies, especially those in the rapidly growing high-tech sector) have begun to use *defined contribution* plans, under which employers make specified, or defined, payments into the plan. Then, when the employee retires, his or her pension benefits are determined by the amount of assets in the plan. Therefore, in a defined contribution plan the employee has the responsibility for making investment decisions and bears the risks inherent in investments.

The most common type of defined contribution plan is the *401(k)* plan, named after the section in the federal act that established the legal basis for the plan. Governmental units, including universities, can use *403(b)* plans, which operate

Mutual Fund Mania

Americans love mutual funds. Just ten years ago, Americans had invested about $810 billion in mutual funds, which is not exactly chicken feed. Today, however, they have more than $5 trillion in mutual funds!

Not only has the amount of money invested in mutual funds skyrocketed, but the variety of funds is astounding. Thirty years ago there were just a few types of mutual funds. You could buy a growth fund (composed of stocks that paid low dividends but that had been growing rapidly), income funds (primarily composed of stocks that paid high dividends), or a bond fund. Now you can buy funds that specialize in virtually any type of asset. There are funds that own stocks only from a particular industry, a particular continent, or a particular country, and money market funds that invest only in Treasury bills and other short-term securities. There are funds that have municipal bonds from only one state. You can buy socially conscious funds that refuse to own stocks of companies that pollute, sell tobacco products, or have work forces that are not culturally diverse. You can buy "market neutral funds," which sell some stocks short, invest in other stocks, and promise to do well no matter which way the market goes. There is the Undiscovered Managers Behavioral fund that picks stocks by psychoanalyzing Wall Street analysts. And then there is the Tombstone fund that owns stocks only from the funeral industry.

How many funds are there? One urban myth is that there are more funds than stocks. But that includes bond funds, money market funds, and funds that invest in non-U.S. stocks. It also includes "flavors" of the same fund. For example, some funds allow you to buy different "share classes" of a single fund, with each share class having different fee structures. So even though there are at least 10,000 different funds of all types, there are only about 2,000 U.S. equity mutual funds. Still, that's a lot of funds, since there are only about 8,000 regularly traded U.S. stocks.

Sources: "The Many New Faces of Mutual Funds," *Fortune*, July 6, 1998, 217–218; "Street Myths," *Fortune*, May 24, 1999, 320.

essentially like 401(k) plans. In all of these plans, employees must choose from a set of investment alternatives. Typically, the employer agrees to make some "defined contribution" to the plan, and the employee can also make a supplemental payment. Then, the employer contracts with an insurance company plus one or more mutual fund companies, and then employees choose among investments ranging from "guaranteed investment contracts" to government bond funds to domestic corporate bond and stock funds to international stock and bond funds. Under most plans, the employees can, within certain limits, shift their investments from category to category. Thus, if someone thinks the stock market is currently overvalued, he or she can tell the mutual fund to move the money from a stock fund to a money market fund. Similarly, employees may choose to gradually shift from 100 percent stock to a mix of stocks and bonds as they grow older.

These changes in the structure of pension plans have had two extremely important effects. First, individuals must now make the primary investment decisions for their pension plans. Because such decisions can mean the difference between a comfortable retirement and living on the street, it is important that people covered by defined contribution plans understand the fundamentals of investing. Second, whereas defined benefit plan managers typically invest in individual stocks and bonds, most individuals invest 401(k) money through mutual funds. Since 401(k) defined contribution plans are growing rapidly, the result is rapid growth in the mutual fund industry. This, in turn, has implications for the security markets, and for businesses that need to attract capital.

Financial institutions have historically been heavily regulated, with the primary purpose of this regulation being to ensure the safety of the institutions and thus to protect investors. However, these regulations—which have taken the form of prohibitions on nationwide branch banking, restrictions on the types of assets the institutions

TABLE 5-2 Ten Largest U.S. Bank Holding Companies and World Banking Companies, and Top Ten Leading Underwriters

PANEL A *U.S. Bank Holding Companies*[a]	**PANEL B** *World Banking Companies*[b]	**PANEL C** *Leading Underwriters*[c]
Citigroup Inc.	Deutsche Bank AG (Frankfurt)	Merrill Lynch
Bank of America Corp.	UBS Group (Zurich)	Salomon Smith Barney
Chase Manhattan Corp.	Citigroup (New York)	Morgan Stanley Dean Witter
J. P. Morgan & Co.	Bank of America (Charlotte)	Goldman Sachs
Bank One Corp.	Bank of Tokyo (Tokyo)	Credit Suisse First Boston
First Union Corp.	HypoVereinsbank AG (Munich)	Lehman Brothers
Wells Fargo & Co. Inc.	ABN-AMRO Bank NV (Amsterdam)	Deutsche Bank
Fleet Financial Group	HSBC Holdings PLC (London)	J. P. Morgan
SunTrust Banks Inc.	Credit Suisse Group (Zurich)	Chase Manhattan
National City Corp.	ING Group (Amsterdam)	ABN-AMRO

NOTES:
[a]Ranked by total assets as of June 30, 1999. **Source:** Compiled by *American Banker* from bank holding company second quarter 1999 reports.
[b]Ranked by total assets as of December 31, 1998. **Source:** "Top 100 World Banking Companies in Assets," *American Banker,* August 5, 1999, 7.
[c]Ranked by dollar amount raised through new issues in 1999. For this ranking, the lead underwriter (manager) is given credit for the entire issue. **Source:** *The Wall Street Journal,* January 3, 2000, R24.

can buy, ceilings on the interest rates they can pay, and limitations on the types of services they can provide—have tended to impede the free flow of capital and thus have hurt the efficiency of our capital markets. Recognizing this fact, Congress has authorized some major changes, and more are on the horizon.

The result of the ongoing regulatory changes has been a blurring of the distinctions between the different types of institutions. Indeed, the trend in the United States today is toward huge **financial service corporations,** which own banks, S&Ls, investment banking houses, insurance companies, pension plan operations, and mutual funds, and which have branches across the country and around the world. Examples of financial service corporations, most of which started in one area but have now diversified to cover most of the financial spectrum, include Merrill Lynch, American Express, Citigroup, Fidelity, and Prudential.

Panel a of Table 5-2 lists the ten largest U.S. bank holding companies, and Panel b shows the leading world banking companies. Among the world's ten largest, only two (Citigroup and Bank of America) are from the United States. While U.S. banks have grown dramatically as a result of recent mergers, they are still small by global standards. Panel c of the table lists the ten leading underwriters in terms of dollar volume of new issues. Six of the top underwriters are also major commercial banks or are part of bank holding companies, which confirms the continued blurring of distinctions among different types of financial institutions.

Self-Test Questions

Identify three ways capital is transferred between savers and borrowers.

What is the difference between a commercial bank and an investment bank?

Distinguish between investment banking houses and financial intermediaries.

List the major types of intermediaries and briefly describe the primary function of each.

Online Trading Systems

The forces that led to online trading have also promoted online trading systems that bypass the traditional exchanges. These systems, known as electronic communications networks (ECNs), use technology to bring buyers and sellers together electronically. Bob Mazzarella, president of Fidelity Brokerage Services Inc., estimates that ECNs have already captured 20 to 35 percent of Nasdaq's trading volume. Instinet, the first and largest ECN, has a stake with Goldman Sachs, J. P. Morgan, and E*Trade in another network, Archipelago, which recently announced plans to form its own exchange. Likewise, Charles Schwab recently announced plans to join with Fidelity Investments, Donaldson, Lufkin & Jenrette, and Spear, Leeds & Kellogg to develop another ECN.

ECNs are accelerating the move toward 24-hour trading. Large clients who want to trade after the other markets have closed may utilize an ECN, bypassing the NYSE and Nasdaq.

In fact, Eurex, a Swiss-German ECN for trading futures contracts, has virtually eliminated futures activity on the trading floors of Paris, London, and Frankfurt. Moreover, it recently passed the Chicago Board of Trade (CBOT) to become the world's leader in futures trading volume. The threat of a similar ECN in the United States has undoubtedly contributed to the recent 50 percent decline in the price of a seat on the CBOT.

The move toward faster, cheaper, 24-hour trading obviously benefits investors, but it also presents regulators, who try to ensure that all investors have access to a "level playing field," with a number of headaches.

Because of the threat from ECNs and the need to raise capital and increase flexibility, both the NYSE and Nasdaq plan to convert from privately held, member-owned businesses to stockholder-owned, for-profit corporations. This suggests that the financial landscape will continue to undergo dramatic changes in the upcoming years.

Sources: Katrina Brooker, "Online Investing: It's Not Just for Geeks Anymore," *Fortune*, December 21, 1998, 89–98; "Fidelity, Schwab Part of Deal to Create Nasdaq Challenger," *The Milwaukee Journal Sentinel*, July 22, 1999, 1.

The Stock Market

As noted earlier, secondary markets are those in which outstanding, previously issued securities are traded. By far the most active secondary market, and the most important one to financial managers, is the *stock market*, where the prices of firms' stocks are established. Because the primary goal of financial management is to maximize the firm's stock price, a knowledge of the stock market is important to anyone involved in managing a business.

While the two leading stock markets today are the New York Stock Exchange and the Nasdaq stock market, stocks are actually traded using a variety of market procedures. However, there are just two basic types of stock markets: (1) *physical location exchanges*, which include the New York Stock Exchange (NYSE), the American Stock Exchange (AMEX), and several regional stock exchanges, and (2) electronic dealer-based markets that include the Nasdaq stock market, the less formal over-the-counter market, and the recently developed electronic communications networks (ECNs). (See the accompanying box entitled, "Online Trading Systems.") Because the physical location exchanges are easier to describe and understand, we consider them first.

The Physical Location Stock Exchanges

The **physical location exchanges** are tangible physical entities. Each of the larger ones occupies its own building, has a limited number of members, and has an elected governing body—its board of governors. Members are said to have "seats" on the exchange, although everybody stands up. These seats, which are bought and sold, give the holder the right to trade on the exchange. There are currently 1,366 seats on the

New York Stock Exchange, and in August 1999, a seat on the NYSE sold for $2.65 million. This is up from a price of $35,000 in 1977. As of September 2000, the asking price for a seat was about $2 million.

Most of the larger investment banking houses operate *brokerage departments*, and they own seats on the exchanges and designate one or more of their officers as members. The exchanges are open on all normal working days, with the members meeting in a large room equipped with electronic equipment that enable each member to communicate with his or her firm's offices throughout the country.

Like other markets, security exchanges facilitate communication between buyers and sellers. For example, Merrill Lynch (the largest brokerage firm) might receive an order in its Atlanta office from a customer who wants to buy shares of AT&T stock. Simultaneously, Morgan Stanley Dean Witter's Denver office might receive an order from a customer wishing to sell shares of AT&T. Each broker communicates electronically with the firm's representative on the NYSE. Other brokers throughout the country are also communicating with their own exchange members. The exchange members with *sell orders* offer the shares for sale, and they are bid for by the members with *buy orders*. Thus, the exchanges operate as *auction markets*.[2]

You can access the home pages of the major U.S. stock markets by typing **http://www.nyse.com** or **http://www.nasdaq.com**. These sites provide background information as well as the opportunity to obtain individual stock quotes.

The Over-the-Counter and the Nasdaq Stock Markets

While the stocks of most large companies trade on the NYSE, most stocks actually trade off the exchange in what has traditionally been referred to as the **over-the-counter market (OTC).** An explanation of the term "over-the-counter" will help clarify how this term arose. As noted earlier, the exchanges operate as auction markets—buy and sell orders come in more or less simultaneously, and exchange members match those orders. If a stock is traded infrequently, perhaps because the firm is new or small, few buy and sell orders come in, and matching them within a reasonable amount of time would be difficult. To avoid this problem, some brokerage firms maintain an inventory of such stocks and stand prepared to make a market for these stocks. These "dealers" buy when individual investors want to sell, and then sell part of their inventory when investors want to buy. At one time, the inventory of securities was kept in a safe, and the stocks, when bought and sold, were literally passed over the counter.

Today, these markets are often referred to as **dealer markets.** A dealer market is defined to include all facilities that are needed to conduct security transactions not

[2]The NYSE is actually a modified auction market, wherein people (through their brokers) bid for stocks. Originally—about 200 years ago—brokers would literally shout, "I have 100 shares of Erie for sale; how much am I offered?" and then sell to the highest bidder. If a broker had a buy order, he or she would shout, "I want to buy 100 shares of Erie; who'll sell at the best price?" The same general situation still exists, although the exchanges now have members known as *specialists* who facilitate the trading process by keeping an inventory of shares of the stocks in which they specialize. If a buy order comes in at a time when no sell order arrives, the specialist will sell off some inventory. Similarly, if a sell order comes in, the specialist will buy and add to inventory. The specialist sets a *bid price* (the price the specialist will pay for the stock) and an *asked price* (the price at which shares will be sold out of inventory). The bid and asked prices are set at levels designed to keep the inventory in balance. If many buy orders start coming in because of favorable developments or sell orders come in because of unfavorable events, the specialist will raise or lower prices to keep supply and demand in balance. Bid prices are somewhat lower than asked prices, with the difference, or *spread*, representing the specialist's profit margin.

Special facilities are available to help institutional investors such as mutual funds or pension funds sell large blocks of stock without depressing their prices. In essence, brokerage houses that cater to institutional clients will purchase blocks (defined as 10,000 or more shares) and then resell the stock to other institutions or individuals. Also, when a firm has a major announcement that is likely to cause its stock price to change sharply, it will ask the exchanges to halt trading in its stock until the announcement has been made and digested by investors. Thus, when Texaco announced that it planned to acquire Getty Oil, trading was halted for one day in both Texaco and Getty stocks.

Measuring the Market

A *stock index* is designed to show the performance of the stock market. The problem is that there are many stock indexes, and it is difficult to determine which index best reflects market actions. Some are designed to represent the whole equity market, some to track the returns of certain industry sectors, and others to track the returns of small-cap, mid-cap, or large-cap stocks. "Cap" is short for capitalization, which means the total market value of a firm's stock. We discuss below four of the leading indexes.

Dow Jones Industrial Average

Unveiled in 1896 by Charles H. Dow, the Dow Jones Industrial Average (DJIA) provided a benchmark for comparing individual stocks with the overall market and for comparing the market with other economic indicators. The industrial average began with just 10 stocks, was expanded in 1916 to 20 stocks, and then to 30 in 1928. Also, in 1928 *The Wall Street Journal* editors began adjusting it for stock splits, and making substitutions. Today, the DJIA still includes 30 companies. They represent almost a fifth of the market value of all U.S. stocks, and all are both leading companies in their industries and widely held by individual and institutional investors.

Wilshire 5000 Total Market Index

The Wilshire 5000, created in 1974, measures the performance of all U.S. headquartered equity securities with readily available prices. It was originally composed of roughly 5,000 stocks, but as of August 1999, it included more than 7,000 publicly traded securities with a combined market capitalization in excess of $14 trillion. The Wilshire 5000 is unique because it seeks to reflect returns on the entire U.S. equity market.

S&P 500 Index

Created in 1926, the S&P 500 Index is widely regarded as the standard for measuring large-cap U.S. stock market performance. The stocks in the S&P 500 are selected by the Standard & Poor's Index Committee for being the leading companies in the leading industries, and for accurately reflecting the U.S. stock market. It is value weighted, so the largest companies (in terms of value) have the greatest influence. The S&P 500 Index is used as a comparison benchmark by 97 percent of all U.S. money managers and pension plan sponsors, and approximately $700 billion is managed so as to obtain the same performance as this index (that is, in indexed funds).

Nasdaq Composite Index

The Nasdaq Composite Index measures the performance of all common stocks listed on the Nasdaq stock market. Currently, it includes more than 5,000 companies, and because many of the technology-sector companies are traded on the computer-based Nasdaq exchange, this index is generally regarded as an economic indicator of the high-tech industry. Microsoft, Intel, and Cisco Systems are the three largest Nasdaq companies, and they comprise a high percentage of the index's value-weighted market capitalization. For this reason, substantial movements in the same direction by these three companies can move the entire index.

Recent Performance

Go to the web site **http://finance.yahoo.com/.** Enter the symbol for any of the indices (^DJI for the Dow Jones, ^WIL5 for the Wilshire 5000, ^SPC for the S&P 500, and ^IXIC for the Nasdaq) and click the Get Quotes button. This will bring up the current value of the index, shown in a table. Click Chart (under the table heading "More Info"), and it will bring up a chart showing the historical performance of the index. Immediately below the chart is a series of buttons that allows you to choose the number of years and to plot the relative performance of several indices on the same chart. You can even download the historical data in spreadsheet form.

made on the physical exchanges. These facilities include (1) the relatively few *dealers* who hold inventories of these securities and who are said to "make a market" in these securities; (2) the thousands of brokers who act as *agents* in bringing the dealers together with investors; and (3) the computers, terminals, and electronic networks that provide a communication link between dealers and brokers. The dealers who make a market in a particular stock quote the price they will pay for the stock (the *bid price*) and the price at which they will sell shares (the *ask price*). Each dealer's prices, which are adjusted as supply and demand conditions change, can be read off computer screens all across the world. The *bid-ask spread*, which is the difference between bid and ask prices, represents the dealer's markup, or profit. The dealer's risk increases if the stock is more volatile, or if the stock trades infrequently. Generally, we would expect volatile, infrequently traded stocks to have wider spreads in order to compensate the dealers for assuming the risk of holding them in inventory.

Brokers and dealers who participate in the over-the-counter market are members of a self-regulatory body known as the *National Association of Securities Dealers (NASD),* which licenses brokers and oversees trading practices. The computerized network used by the NASD is known as the NASD Automated Quotation System, or Nasdaq.

Nasdaq started as just a quotation system, but it has grown to become an organized securities market with its own listing requirements. Over the past decade the competition between the NYSE and Nasdaq has been fierce. In an effort to become more competitive with the NYSE and with international markets, the Nasdaq and the AMEX merged in 1998 to form the Nasdaq-Amex Market Group, which might best be referred to as an *organized investment network.* This investment network is often referred to as Nasdaq, but stocks continue to be traded and reported separately on the two markets. Increased competition among global stock markets assuredly will result in similar alliances among other exchanges and markets in the future.

Since most of the largest companies trade on the NYSE, the market capitalization of NYSE-traded stocks is much higher than for stocks traded on Nasdaq (about $12.0 trillion compared with $3.8 trillion in late 2000). However, reported volume (number of shares traded) is often larger on Nasdaq, and more companies are listed on Nasdaq.[3]

Interestingly, many high-tech companies such as Microsoft and Intel have remained on Nasdaq even though they easily meet the listing requirements of the NYSE. At the same time, however, other high-tech companies such as Gateway 2000, America Online, and Iomega have left Nasdaq for the NYSE. Despite these defections, Nasdaq's growth over the past decade has been impressive. In the years ahead, the competition will no doubt remain fierce.

Self-Test Questions

What are the differences between the physical exchanges and the Nasdaq stock market?

What is the bid-ask spread?

The Cost of Money

Capital in a free economy is allocated through the price system. *The interest rate is the price paid to borrow debt capital. With equity capital, investors expect to receive dividends and capital gains, whose sum is the cost of equity money.* The factors that affect supply and demand for investment capital, hence the cost of money, are discussed in this section.

The four most fundamental factors affecting the cost of money are (1) **production opportunities,** (2) **time preferences for consumption,** (3) **risk,** and (4) **inflation.** To see how these factors operate, visualize an isolated island community where the people live on fish. They have a stock of fishing gear that permits them to survive reasonably well, but they would like to have more fish. Now suppose Mr. Crusoe had a bright idea for a new type of fishnet that would enable him to double his daily catch. However, it would take him a year to perfect his design, to build his net, and to learn how to use it efficiently, and Mr. Crusoe would probably starve before he could put his new net into operation. Therefore, he might suggest to Ms. Robinson, Mr. Friday, and several others that if they would give him one fish each day for a year, he would return two fish a day during all of the next year. If someone accepted the offer, then the fish that Ms. Robinson or one of the others gave to Mr. Crusoe would constitute *savings;*

---

[3]One transaction on Nasdaq generally shows up as two separate trades (the buy and the sell). This "double counting" makes it difficult to compare the volume between stock markets.

these savings would be *invested* in the fishnet; and the extra fish the net produced would constitute a *return on the investment.*

Obviously, the more productive Mr. Crusoe thought the new fishnet would be, the more he could afford to offer potential investors for their savings. In this example, we assume that Mr. Crusoe thought he would be able to pay, and thus he offered, a 100 percent rate of return—he offered to give back two fish for every one he received. He might have tried to attract savings for less—for example, he might have decided to offer only 1.5 fish next year for every one he received this year, which would represent a 50 percent rate of return to potential savers.

How attractive Mr. Crusoe's offer appeared to a potential saver would depend in large part on the saver's *time preference for consumption.* For example, Ms. Robinson might be thinking of retirement, and she might be willing to trade fish today for fish in the future on a one-for-one basis. On the other hand, Mr. Friday might have a wife and several young children and need his current fish, so he might be unwilling to "lend" a fish today for anything less than three fish next year. Mr. Friday would be said to have a high time preference for current consumption and Ms. Robinson a low time preference. Note also that if the entire population were living right at the subsistence level, time preferences for current consumption would necessarily be high, aggregate savings would be low, interest rates would be high, and capital formation would be difficult.

The *risk* inherent in the fishnet project, and thus in Mr. Crusoe's ability to repay the loan, would also affect the return investors would require: the higher the perceived risk, the higher the required rate of return. Also, in a more complex society there are many businesses like Mr. Crusoe's, many goods other than fish, and many savers like Ms. Robinson and Mr. Friday. Therefore, people use money as a medium of exchange rather than barter with fish. When money is used, its value in the future, which is affected by *inflation*, comes into play: the higher the expected rate of inflation, the larger the required return. We discuss this point in detail later in the chapter.

Thus, we see that the interest rate paid to savers depends in a basic way (1) on the rate of return producers expect to earn on invested capital, (2) on savers' time preferences for current versus future consumption, (3) on the riskiness of the loan, and (4) on the expected future rate of inflation. Producers' expected returns on their business investments set an upper limit on how much they can pay for savings, while consumers' time preferences for consumption establish how much consumption they are willing to defer, hence how much they will save at different rates of interest offered by producers.[4] Higher risk and higher inflation also lead to higher interest rates.

Self-Test Questions

What is the price paid to borrow money called?

What are the two items whose sum is the "price" of equity capital?

What four fundamental factors affect the cost of money?

Interest Rate Levels

Capital is allocated among borrowers by interest rates: Firms with the most profitable investment opportunities are willing and able to pay the most for capital, so they tend to attract it away from inefficient firms or from those whose products are not in

[4]The term "producers" is really too narrow. A better word might be "borrowers," which would include corporations, home purchasers, people borrowing to go to college, or even people borrowing to buy autos or to pay for vacations. Also, the wealth of a society and its demographics influence its people's ability to save and thus their time preferences for current versus future consumption.

demand. Of course, our economy is not completely free in the sense of being influenced only by market forces. Thus, the federal government has agencies that help designated individuals or groups obtain credit on favorable terms. Among those eligible for this kind of assistance are small businesses, certain minorities, and firms willing to build plants in areas with high unemployment. Still, most capital in the U.S. economy is allocated through the price system.

Figure 5-2 shows how supply and demand interact to determine interest rates in two capital markets. Markets A and B represent two of the many capital markets in existence. The going interest rate, which can be designated as either k or i, but for purposes of our discussion is designated as k, is initially 10 percent for the low-risk securities in Market A.[5] Borrowers whose credit is strong enough to borrow in this market can obtain funds at a cost of 10 percent, and investors who want to put their money to work without much risk can obtain a 10 percent return. Riskier borrowers must obtain higher-cost funds in Market B. Investors who are more willing to take risks invest in Market B, expecting to earn a 12 percent return but also realizing that they might actually receive much less.

If the demand for funds declines, as it typically does during business recessions, the demand curves will shift to the left, as shown in Curve D_2 in Market A. The market-clearing, or equilibrium, interest rate in this example declines to 8 percent. Similarly, you should be able to visualize what would happen if the Federal Reserve tightened credit: The supply curve, S_1, would shift to the left, and this would raise interest rates and lower the level of borrowing in the economy.

Capital markets are interdependent. For example, if Markets A and B were in equilibrium before the demand shift to D_2 in Market A, then investors were willing to accept the higher risk in Market B in exchange for a *risk premium* of 12% − 10% =

[5]The letter "k" is the traditional symbol for interest rates and the cost of equity, but "i" is used frequently today because this term corresponds to the interest rate key on financial calculators. Therefore, in Chapter 8, when we discuss calculators, the term "i" will be used for interest rate.

FIGURE 5-2 Interest Rates as a Function of Supply and Demand for Funds

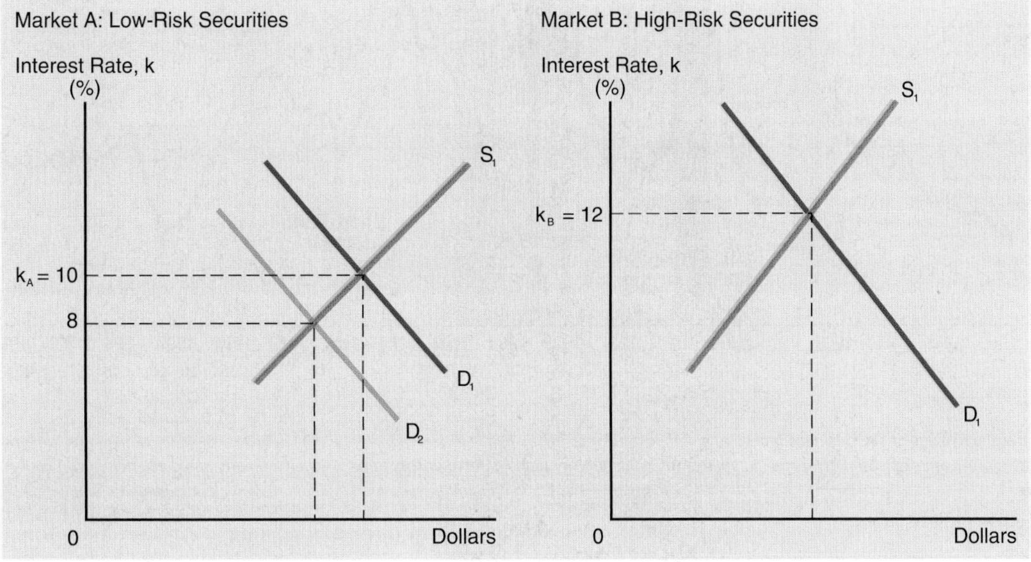

2%. After the shift to D_2, the risk premium would initially increase to 12% − 8% = 4%. Immediately, though, this much larger premium would induce some of the lenders in Market A to shift to Market B, which would, in turn, cause the supply curve in Market A to shift to the left (or up) and that in Market B to shift to the right. The transfer of capital between markets would raise the interest rate in Market A and lower it in Market B, thus bringing the risk premium back closer to the original 2 percent.

There are many capital markets in the United States. U.S. firms also invest and raise capital throughout the world, and foreigners both borrow and lend in the United States. There are markets for home loans; farm loans; business loans; federal, state, and local government loans; and consumer loans. Within each category, there are regional markets as well as different types of submarkets. For example, in real estate there are separate markets for first and second mortgages and for loans on single-family homes, apartments, office buildings, shopping centers, vacant land, and so on. Within the business sector there are dozens of types of debt and also several different markets for common stocks.

There is a price for each type of capital, and these prices change over time as shifts occur in supply and demand conditions. Figure 5-3 shows how long- and short-term interest rates to business borrowers have varied since the early 1960s. Notice that short-term interest rates are especially prone to rise during booms and then fall during recessions. (The shaded areas of the chart indicate recessions.) When the economy

FIGURE 5-3 Long- and Short-Term Interest Rates, 1962–2000

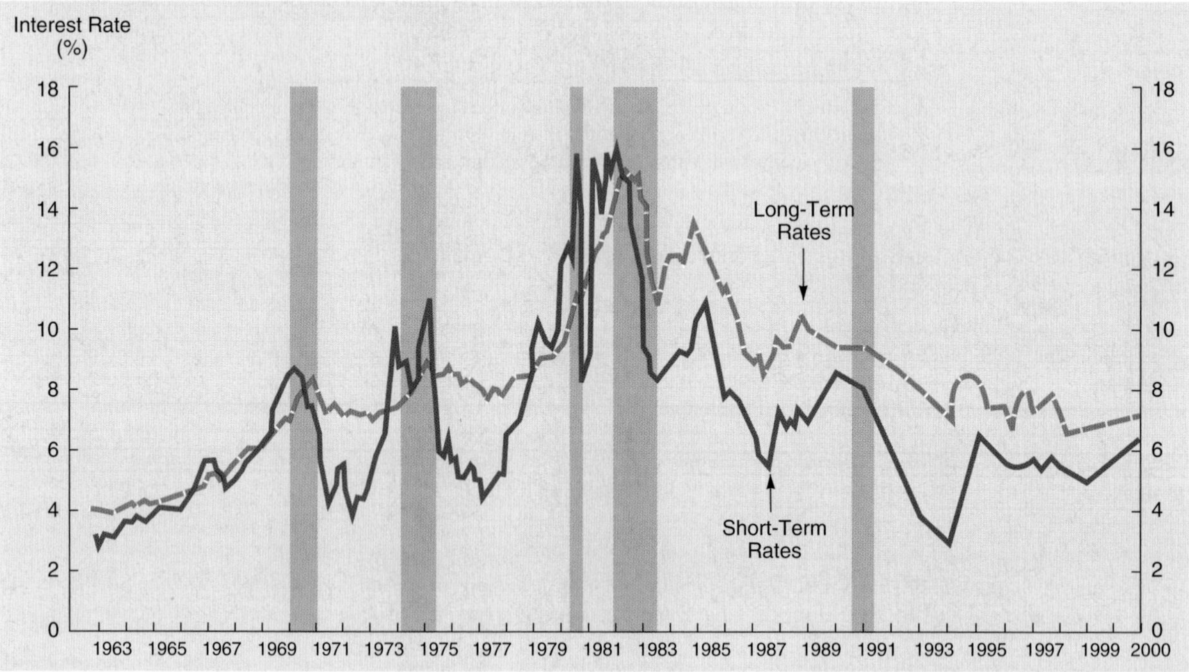

Notes:

a. The shaded areas designate business recessions.

b. Short-term rates are measured by three- to six-month loans to very large, strong corporations, and long-term rates are measured by AAA corporate bonds.

Source: *Federal Reserve Bulletin.*

is expanding, firms need capital, and this demand for capital pushes rates up. Also, inflationary pressures are strongest during business booms, and that also exerts upward pressure on rates. Conditions are reversed during recessions such as the one in 1991 and 1992. Slack business reduces the demand for credit, the rate of inflation falls, and the result is a drop in interest rates. Furthermore, the Federal Reserve deliberately lowers rates during recessions to help stimulate the economy and tightens during booms.

These tendencies do not hold exactly—the period after 1984 is a case in point. The price of oil fell dramatically in 1985 and 1986, reducing inflationary pressures on other prices and easing fears of serious long-term inflation. Earlier, those fears had pushed interest rates to record levels. The economy from 1984 to 1987 was strong, but the declining fears of inflation more than offset the normal tendency of interest rates to rise during good economic times, and the net result was lower interest rates.[6]

The effects of inflation on long-term interest rates is highlighted in Figure 5-4, which plots rates of inflation along with long-term interest rates. In the early 1960s, inflation averaged 1 percent per year, and interest rates on high-quality, long-term bonds averaged 4 percent. Then the Vietnam War heated up, leading to an increase in inflation, and interest rates began an upward climb. When the war ended in the early

[6]Short-term rates are responsive to current economic conditions, whereas long-term rates primarily reflect long-run expectations for inflation. As a result, short-term rates are sometimes above and sometimes below long-term rates. The relationship between long-term and short-term rates is called the *term structure of interest rates*, and it is discussed later in the chapter.

FIGURE 5-4 Relationship between Annual Inflation Rates and Long-Term Interest Rates, 1962–2000

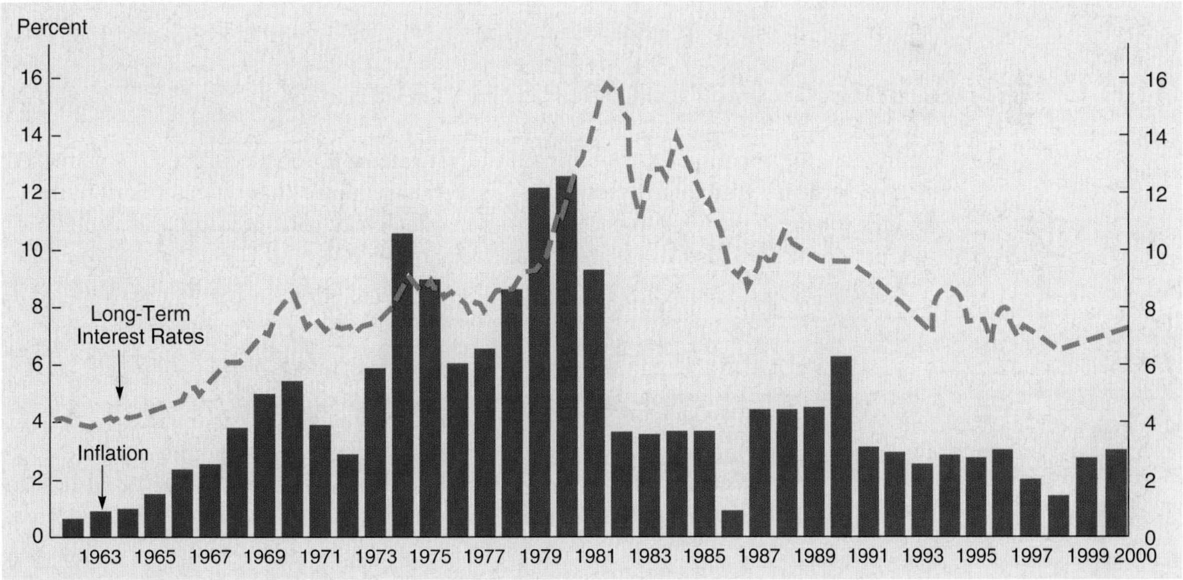

Notes:

a. Interest rates are those on AAA long-term corporate bonds.

b. Inflation is measured as the annual rate of change in the Consumer Price Index (CPI).

Source: *Federal Reserve Bulletin.*

1970s, inflation dipped a bit, but then the 1973 Arab oil embargo led to rising oil prices, much higher inflation and sharply higher interest rates.

Inflation peaked at about 13 percent in 1980, but interest rates continued to increase into 1981 and 1982, and they remained quite high until 1985, because people were afraid inflation would start to climb again. Thus, the "inflationary psychology" created during the 1970s persisted to the mid-1980s.

Gradually, though, people began to realize that the Federal Reserve was serious about keeping inflation down, that global competition was keeping U.S. auto producers and other corporations from raising prices as they had in the past, and that constraints on corporate price increases were diminishing labor unions' ability to push through cost-increasing wage hikes. As these realizations set in, interest rates declined. The gap between the current interest rate and the current inflation rate is defined as the "current real rate of interest." It is called the "real rate" because it shows how much investors really earned after taking out the effects of inflation. The real rate was extremely high during the mid-1980s, but it averaged about 4 percent during the 1990s.

In recent years, inflation has been running at about 3 percent a year. However, long-term interest rates have been volatile, because investors are not sure if inflation is truly under control or is getting ready to jump back to the higher levels of the 1980s. In the years ahead, we can be sure that the level of interest rates will vary (1) with changes in the current rate of inflation and (2) with changes in expectations about future inflation.

Self-Test Questions

How are interest rates used to allocate capital among firms?

What happens to market-clearing, or equilibrium, interest rates in a capital market when the demand for funds declines? What happens when inflation increases or decreases?

Why does the price of capital change during booms and recessions?

How does risk affect interest rates?

The Determinants of Market Interest Rates

In general, the quoted (or nominal) interest rate on a debt security, k, is composed of a real risk-free rate of interest, k*, plus several premiums that reflect inflation, the riskiness of the security, and the security's marketability (or liquidity). This relationship can be expressed as follows:

$$\text{Quoted interest rate} = k = k^* + IP + DRP + LP + MRP. \quad \textbf{(5-1)}$$

Here

k = the quoted, or nominal, rate of interest on a given security.[7] There are many different securities, hence many different quoted interest rates.

k* = the real risk-free rate of interest. k* is pronounced "k-star," and it is the rate that would exist on a riskless security if zero inflation were expected.

[7]The term *nominal* as it is used here means the *stated* rate as opposed to the *real* rate, which is adjusted to remove inflation effects. If you bought a 10-year Treasury bond in January 2001, the quoted, or nominal, rate would be about 6.4 percent, but if inflation averages 3 percent over the next 10 years, the real rate would be about 6.4% − 3% = 3.4%. To be technically correct, we should find the real rate by solving for k* in the following equation: $(1 + k^*)(1 + 0.03) = (1 + 0.064)$. If we solved the equation, we would find k* = 3.3%. Since this is very close to the 3.4 percent calculated above, we will continue to approximate the real rate by subtracting inflation from the nominal rate.

$k_{RF} = k^* + IP$, and it is the quoted risk-free rate of interest on a security such as a U.S. Treasury bill, which is very liquid and also free of most risks. Note that k_{RF} includes the premium for expected inflation, because $k_{RF} = k^* + IP$.

IP = inflation premium. IP is equal to the average expected inflation rate over the life of the security. The expected future inflation rate is not necessarily equal to the current inflation rate, so IP is not necessarily equal to current inflation as reported in Figure 5-4.

DRP = default risk premium. This premium reflects the possibility that the issuer will not pay interest or principal at the stated time and in the stated amount. DRP is zero for U.S. Treasury securities, but it rises as the riskiness of issuers increases.

LP = liquidity, or marketability, premium. This is a premium charged by lenders to reflect the fact that some securities cannot be converted to cash on short notice at a "reasonable" price. LP is very low for Treasury securities and for securities issued by large, strong firms, but it is relatively high on securities issued by very small firms.

MRP = maturity risk premium. As we will explain later, longer-term bonds, even Treasury bonds, are exposed to a significant risk of price declines, and a maturity risk premium is charged by lenders to reflect this risk.

As noted above, since $k_{RF} = k^* + IP$, we can rewrite Equation 5-1 as follows:

$$\text{Nominal, or quoted, rate} = k = k_{RF} + DRP + LP + MRP.$$

We discuss the components whose sum makes up the quoted, or nominal, rate on a given security in the following sections.

The Real Risk-Free Rate of Interest, k*

The **real risk-free rate of interest, k***, is defined as the interest rate that would exist on a riskless security if no inflation were expected, and it may be thought of as the rate of interest on *short-term* U.S. Treasury securities in an inflation-free world. The real risk-free rate is not static—it changes over time depending on economic conditions, especially (1) on the rate of return corporations and other borrowers expect to earn on productive assets and (2) on people's time preferences for current versus future consumption. Borrowers' expected returns on real asset investments set an upper limit on how much they can afford to pay for borrowed funds, while savers' time preferences for consumption establish how much consumption they are willing to defer, hence the amount of funds they will lend at different interest rates. It is difficult to measure the real risk-free rate precisely, but most experts think that k* has fluctuated in the range of 1 to 5 percent in recent years.[8] The best estimate of k* is the rate of return on indexed Treasury bonds, which was about 2.4 percent in February 2001.

[8]The real rate of interest as discussed here is different from the *current* real rate as discussed in connection with Figure 5-4. The current real rate is the current interest rate minus the current (or latest past) inflation rate, while the real rate, without the word "current," is the current interest rate minus the *expected future* inflation rate over the life of the security. For example, suppose the current quoted rate for a one-year Treasury bill is 5 percent, inflation during the latest year was 2 percent, and inflation expected for the coming year is 4 percent. Then the *current* real rate would be 5% − 2% = 3%, but the *expected* real rate would be 5% − 4% = 1%. The rate on a 10-year bond would be related to the expected inflation rate over the next 10 years, and so on. In the press, the term "real rate" generally means the current real rate, but in economics and finance, hence in this book unless otherwise noted, the real rate means the one based on *expected* inflation rates.

The Nominal, or Quoted, Risk-Free Rate of Interest, k_{RF}

The **nominal,** or **quoted, risk-free rate, k_{RF},** is the real risk-free rate plus a premium for expected inflation: $k_{RF} = k^* + IP$. To be strictly correct, the risk-free rate should mean the interest rate on a totally risk-free security—one that has no risk of default, no maturity risk, no liquidity risk, no risk of loss if inflation increases, and no risk of any other type. There is no such security, hence there is no observable truly risk-free rate. However, there is one security that is free of most risks—an indexed U.S. Treasury security. These securities are free of default, maturity, and liquidity risks, and also of risk due to changes in the general level of interest rates.[9]

If the term "risk-free rate" is used without either the modifier "real" or the modifier "nominal," people generally mean the quoted (nominal) rate, and we will follow that convention in this book. Therefore, when we use the term risk-free rate, k_{RF}, we mean the nominal risk-free rate, which includes an inflation premium equal to the average expected inflation rate over the life of the security. In general, we use the T-bill rate to approximate the short-term risk-free rate, and the T-bond rate to approximate the long-term risk-free rate. So, whenever you see the term "risk-free rate," assume that we are referring either to the quoted U.S. T-bill rate or to the quoted T-bond rate.

Inflation Premium (IP)

Inflation has a major impact on interest rates because it erodes the purchasing power of the dollar and lowers the real rate of return on investments. To illustrate, suppose you saved $1,000 and invested it in a Treasury bill that matures in one year and pays a 5 percent interest rate. At the end of the year, you will receive $1,050—your original $1,000 plus $50 of interest. Now suppose the inflation rate during the year is 10 percent, and it affects all items equally. If gas had cost $1 per gallon at the beginning of the year, it would cost $1.10 at the end of the year. Therefore, your $1,000 would have bought $1,000/$1 = 1,000 gallons at the beginning of the year, but only $1,050/$1.10 = 955 gallons at the end. In *real terms,* you would be worse off—you would receive $50 of interest, but it would not be sufficient to offset inflation. You would thus be better off buying 1,000 gallons of gas (or some other storable asset such as land, timber, apartment buildings, wheat, or gold) than buying the Treasury bill.

Investors are well aware of all this, so when they lend money, they build in an **inflation premium (IP)** equal to the average expected inflation rate over the life of the security. As discussed previously, for a short-term, default-free U.S. Treasury bill, the actual interest rate charged, $k_{T\text{-bill}}$, would be the real risk-free rate, k^*, plus the inflation premium (IP):

$$k_{T\text{-bill}} = k_{RF} = k^* + IP.$$

Therefore, if the real risk-free rate of interest were $k^* = 2.5\%$, and if inflation were expected to be 2.7 percent (and hence $IP = 2.7\%$) during the next year, then the quoted rate of interest on one-year T-bills would be $2.5\% + 2.7\% = 5.2\%$. Indeed, in January 2001, the expected one-year inflation rate was about 2.7 percent, and the yield on one-year T-bills was about 6.2 percent, so the real risk-free rate on short-term securities at that time was 2.5 percent.

---

[9]Indexed Treasury securities are the closest thing we have to a riskless security, but even they are not totally riskless, because k^* itself can change and cause a decline in the prices of these securities. For example, between October 1998 and January 2000, the price of one indexed Treasury security declined from 98 to 89, or by almost 10 percent. The cause was an increase in the real rate from 3.7 percent to 4.4 percent.

It is important to note that the inflation rate built into interest rates is the *inflation rate expected in the future*, not the rate experienced in the past. Thus, the latest reported figures might show an annual inflation rate of 2 percent, but that is for the *past* year. If people on average expect a 6 percent inflation rate in the future, then 6 percent would be built into the current interest rate. Note also that the inflation rate reflected in the quoted interest rate on any security is the *average rate of inflation expected over the security's life*. Thus, the inflation rate built into a one-year bond is the expected inflation rate for the next year, but the inflation rate built into a 30-year bond is the average rate of inflation expected over the next 30 years.[10]

Expectations for future inflation are closely, but not perfectly, correlated with rates experienced in the recent past. Therefore, if the inflation rate reported for last month increased, people would tend to raise their expectations for future inflation, and this change in expectations would cause an increase in interest rates.

Note that Germany, Japan, and Switzerland have over the past several years had lower inflation rates than the United States, hence their interest rates have generally been lower than ours. Italy and most South American countries have experienced high inflation, and that is reflected in their interest rates.

Default Risk Premium (DRP)

The risk that a borrower will *default* on a loan, which means not pay the interest or the principal, also affects the market interest rate on a security: the greater the default risk, the higher the interest rate. Treasury securities have no default risk, hence they carry the lowest interest rates on taxable securities in the United States. For corporate bonds, the higher the bond's rating, the lower its default risk, and, consequently, the lower its interest rate.[11] Here are some representative interest rates on long-term bonds during January 2001:

	Rate	DRP
U.S. Treasury	5.4%	—
AAA	6.5	1.1%
AA	6.9	1.5
A	7.4	2.0
BBB	8.2	2.8
BB+	9.7	4.3

The difference between the quoted interest rate on a T-bond and that on a corporate bond with similar maturity, liquidity, and other features is the **default risk premium (DRP).** Therefore, if the bonds listed above were otherwise similar, the default

[10]To be theoretically precise, we should use a *geometric average*. Also, because millions of investors are active in the market, it is impossible to determine exactly the consensus expected inflation rate. Survey data are available, however, that give us a reasonably good idea of what investors expect over the next few years. For example, in 1980 the University of Michigan's Survey Research Center reported that people expected inflation during the next year to be 11.9 percent and that the average rate of inflation expected over the next 5 to 10 years was 10.5 percent. Those expectations led to record-high interest rates. However, the economy cooled in 1981 and 1982, and, as Figure 5-4 showed, actual inflation dropped sharply after 1980. This led to gradual reductions in the *expected future* inflation rate. In January 2001, as we write this, the expected inflation rate for the next year is about 2.7 percent, and the expected long-term inflation rate is about 2.5 percent. As inflationary expectations change, so do quoted market interest rates.

[11]Bond ratings, and bonds' riskiness in general, are discussed in detail in Chapter 9. For now, merely note that bonds rated AAA are judged to have less default risk than bonds rated AA, while AA bonds are less risky than A bonds, and so on. Ratings are designated AAA or Aaa, AA or Aa, and so forth, depending on the rating agency. In this book, the designations are used interchangeably.

risk premium would be DRP = 6.5% − 5.4% = 1.1 percentage point for AAA corporate bonds, 6.9% − 5.4% = 1.5 percentage points for AA, 7.4% − 5.4% = 2.0 percentage points for A corporate bonds, and so forth. Default risk premiums vary somewhat over time, but the January 2001 figures are representative of levels in recent years.

Liquidity Premium (LP)

A "liquid" asset can be converted to cash quickly and at a "fair market value." Financial assets are generally more liquid than real assets. Because liquidity is important, investors include **liquidity premiums (LPs)** when market rates of securities are established. Although it is difficult to accurately measure liquidity premiums, a differential of at least two and probably four or five percentage points exists between the least liquid and the most liquid financial assets of similar default risk and maturity.

Maturity Risk Premium (MRP)

U.S. Treasury securities are free of default risk in the sense that one can be virtually certain that the federal government will pay interest on its bonds and will also pay them off when they mature. Therefore, the default risk premium on Treasury securities is essentially zero. Further, active markets exist for Treasury securities, so their liquidity premiums are also close to zero. Thus, as a first approximation, the rate of interest on a Treasury bond should be the risk-free rate, k_{RF}, which is equal to the real risk-free rate, k*, plus an inflation premium, IP. However, an adjustment is needed for long-term Treasury bonds. The prices of long-term bonds decline sharply whenever interest rates rise, and since interest rates can and do occasionally rise, all long-term bonds, even Treasury bonds, have an element of risk called **interest rate risk.** As a general rule, the bonds of any organization, from the U.S. government to Continental Airlines, have more interest rate risk the longer the maturity of the bond.[12] Therefore, a **maturity risk premium (MRP),** which is higher the longer the years to maturity, must be included in the required interest rate.

The effect of maturity risk premiums is to raise interest rates on long-term bonds relative to those on short-term bonds. This premium, like the others, is difficult to measure, but (1) it varies somewhat over time, rising when interest rates are more volatile and uncertain, then falling when interest rates are more stable, and (2) in recent years, the maturity risk premium on 30-year T-bonds appears to have generally been in the range of one or two percentage points.[13]

We should mention that although long-term bonds are heavily exposed to interest rate risk, short-term bills are heavily exposed to **reinvestment rate risk.** When short-term bills mature and the funds are reinvested, or "rolled over," a decline in interest rates would necessitate reinvestment at a lower rate, and this would result in a decline in interest income. To illustrate, suppose you had $100,000 invested in one-year T-bills, and you lived on the income. In 1981, short-term rates were about 15 percent, so your income would have been about $15,000. However, your income would have

---

[12]For example, if someone had bought a 30-year Treasury bond for $1,000 in 1998, when the long-term interest rate was 5.25 percent, and held it until 2000, when long-term T-bond rates were about 6.6 percent, the value of the bond would have declined to about $830. That would represent a loss of 17 percent, and it demonstrates that long-term bonds, even U.S. Treasury bonds, are not riskless. However, had the investor purchased short-term T-bills in 1998 and subsequently reinvested the principal each time the bills matured, he or she would still have had $1,000. This point will be discussed in detail in Chapter 9.

[13]The MRP for long-term bonds has averaged 1.4 percent over the last 73 years. See *Stocks, Bonds, Bills, and Inflation: Valuation Edition 2000 Yearbook* (Chicago: Ibbotson Associates, 2000).

declined to about $9,000 by 1983, and to just $5,700 by 2001. Had you invested your money in long-term T-bonds, your income (but not the value of the principal) would have been stable.[14] Thus, although "investing short" preserves one's principal, the interest income provided by short-term T-bills is less stable than the interest income on long-term bonds.

Self-Test Questions

Write out an equation for the nominal interest rate on any debt security.

Distinguish between the *real* risk-free rate of interest, k*, and the *nominal,* or *quoted,* risk-free rate of interest, k_{RF}.

How is inflation dealt with when interest rates are determined by investors in the financial markets?

Does the interest rate on a T-bond include a default risk premium? Explain.

Distinguish between liquid and illiquid assets, and identify some assets that are liquid and some that are illiquid.

Briefly explain the following statement: "Although long-term bonds are heavily exposed to interest rate risk, short-term bills are heavily exposed to reinvestment rate risk. The maturity risk premium reflects the net effects of these two opposing forces."

The Term Structure of Interest Rates

WWW

Students can find current U.S. Treasury yield curve graphs and other global and domestic interest rate information at Bloomberg markets' site at **http://www.bloomberg.com/markets/index.html.**

The **term structure of interest rates** describes the relationship between long- and short-term rates. The term structure is important to corporate treasurers who must decide whether to borrow by issuing long- or short-term debt and to investors who must decide whether to buy long- or short-term bonds. Thus, it is important to understand (1) how long- and short-term rates relate to each other and (2) what causes shifts in their relative positions.

Interest rates for bonds with different maturities can be found in a variety of publications, including *The Wall Street Journal* and the *Federal Reserve Bulletin,* and on a number of web sites, including Bloomberg, Yahoo, and CNN Financial. From interest rate data obtained from these sources, we can construct the term structure at a given point in time. For example, the tabular section below Figure 5-5 presents interest rates for different maturities on three different dates. The set of data for a given date, when plotted on a graph such as that in Figure 5-5 is called the **yield curve** for that date.

The yield curve changes both in position and in slope over time. In March 1980, all rates were relatively high, and since short-term rates were higher than long-term rates, the yield curve was *downward sloping.* However, by August 1999, all rates had fallen, and because short-term rates were lower than long-term rates, the yield curve was *upward sloping.* Six months later, in February 2000, all rates were higher, and the yield curve had become *humped*—medium-term rates were higher than both short- and long-term rates.

Figure 5-5 shows yield curves for U.S. Treasury securities, but we could have constructed curves for corporate bonds issued by Exxon Mobil, IBM, Delta Airlines, or

[14]Long-term bonds also have some reinvestment rate risk. If one is saving and investing for some future purpose, say, to buy a house or for retirement, then to actually earn the quoted rate on a long-term bond, the interest payments must be reinvested at the quoted rate. However, if interest rates fall, the interest payments must be reinvested at a lower rate; thus, the realized return would be less than the quoted rate. Note, though, that reinvestment rate risk is lower on a long-term bond than on a short-term bond because only the interest payments (rather than interest plus principal) on the long-term bond are exposed to reinvestment rate risk. Zero coupon bonds, which are discussed in Chapter 9, are completely free of reinvestment rate risk during their life.

FIGURE 5-5 U.S. Treasury Bond Interest Rates on Different Dates

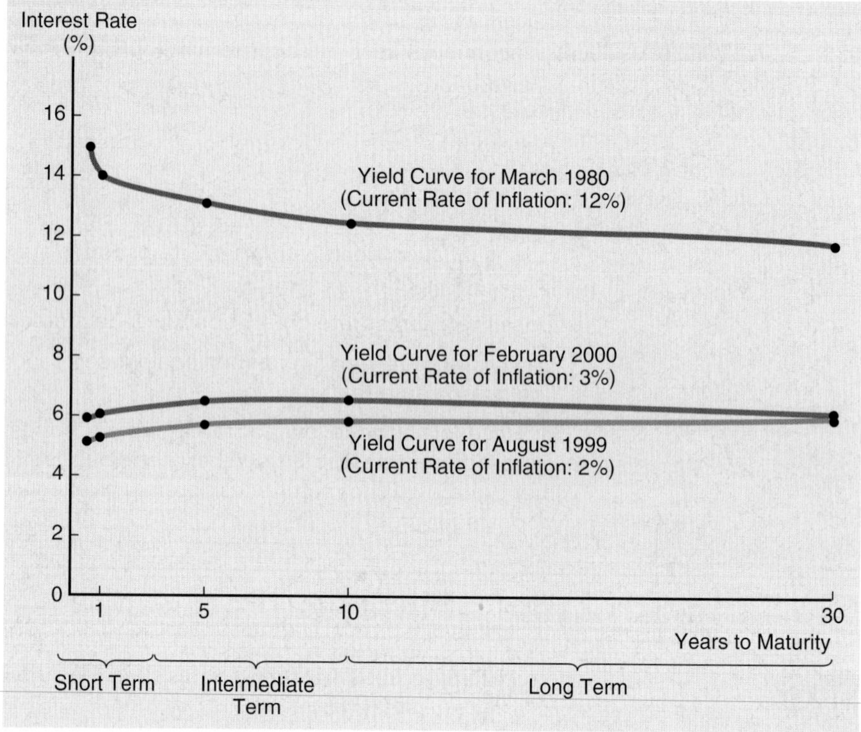

	Interest Rate		
Term to Maturity	**March 1980**	**August 1999**	**February 2000**
6 months	15.0%	5.1%	6.0%
1 year	14.0	5.2	6.2
5 years	13.5	5.8	6.7
10 years	12.8	5.9	6.7
30 years	12.3	6.0	6.3

any other company that borrows money over a range of maturities. Had we constructed corporate curves and plotted them on Figure 5-5, they would have been above those for Treasury securities because corporate yields include default risk premiums. However, the corporate yield curves would have had the same general shape as the Treasury curves. Also, the riskier the corporation, the higher its yield curve, so Delta Airlines, which has a lower bond rating than either Exxon Mobil or IBM, would have a higher yield curve than those of Exxon Mobil and IBM.

Historically, in most years long-term rates have been above short-term rates, so the yield curve usually slopes upward. For this reason, people often call an upward-sloping yield curve a **"normal" yield curve** and a yield curve that slopes downward an **inverted,** or **"abnormal," curve.** Thus, in Figure 5-5 the yield curve for March 1980 was inverted and the one for August 1999 was normal. However, the February 2000 curve is **humped,** which means that interest rates on medium-term maturities are higher than rates on both short- and long-term maturities. We explain in detail in the next section why an upward slope is the normal situation, but briefly, the reason is that short-term securities have less interest rate risk than longer-term securities, hence smaller MRPs. Therefore, short-term rates are normally lower than long-term rates.

Self-Test Questions

What is a yield curve, and what information would you need to draw this curve?

Explain the shapes of a "normal" yield curve, an "abnormal" curve, and a "humped" curve.

What Determines the Shape of the Yield Curve?

Since maturity risk premiums are positive, then if other things were held constant, long-term bonds would have higher interest rates than short-term bonds. However, market interest rates also depend on expected inflation, default risk, and liquidity, and each of these factors can vary with maturity.

Expected inflation has an especially important effect on the yield curve's shape. To see why, consider U.S. Treasury securities. Because Treasuries have essentially no default or liquidity risk, the yield on a Treasury bond that matures in t years can be found using the following equation:

$$k_t = k^* + IP_t + MRP_t.$$

While the real risk-free rate, k*, may vary somewhat over time because of changes in the economy and demographics, these changes are random rather than predictable, so it is reasonable to assume that k* will remain constant. However, the inflation premium, IP, does vary significantly over time, and in a somewhat predictable manner. Recall that the inflation premium is simply the average level of expected inflation over the life of the bond. Thus, if the market expects inflation to increase in the future, the inflation premium will be higher the longer the bond's maturity. On the other hand, if the market expects inflation to decline in the future, long-term bonds will have a smaller inflation premium than short-term bonds. Finally, if investors consider long-term bonds riskier than short-term bonds, the maturity risk premium will increase with maturity.

Panel a of Figure 5-6 shows the yield curve when inflation is expected to increase. Here long-term bonds have higher yields for two reasons: (1) Inflation is expected to be higher in the future, and (2) there is a positive maturity risk premium. Panel b of Figure 5-6 shows the yield curve when inflation is expected to decline, causing the yield curve to be downward sloping. Downward sloping yield curves often foreshadow economic downturns, because weaker economic conditions tend to be correlated with declining inflation, which in turn leads to lower long-term rates.

Now let's consider the yield curve for corporate bonds. Recall that corporate bonds include a default-risk premium (DRP) and a liquidity premium (LP). Therefore, the yield on a corporate bond that matures in t years can be expressed as follows:

$$k_{Ct} = k^* + IP_t + MRP_t + DRP_t + LP_t.$$

A corporate bond's default and liquidity risks are affected by its maturity. For example, the default risk on Coca-Cola's short-term debt is very small, since there is almost no chance that Coca-Cola will go bankrupt over the next few years. However, Coke has some 100-year bonds, and while the odds of Coke defaulting on these bonds still might not be that high, the default risk on these bonds is considerably higher than that on its short-term debt.

Longer-term corporate bonds are also less liquid than shorter-term debt, hence the liquidity premium rises as maturity lengthens. The primary reason for this is that, for the reasons discussed earlier, short-term debt has less default and interest rate risk,

FIGURE 5-6 Illustrative Treasury Yield Curves

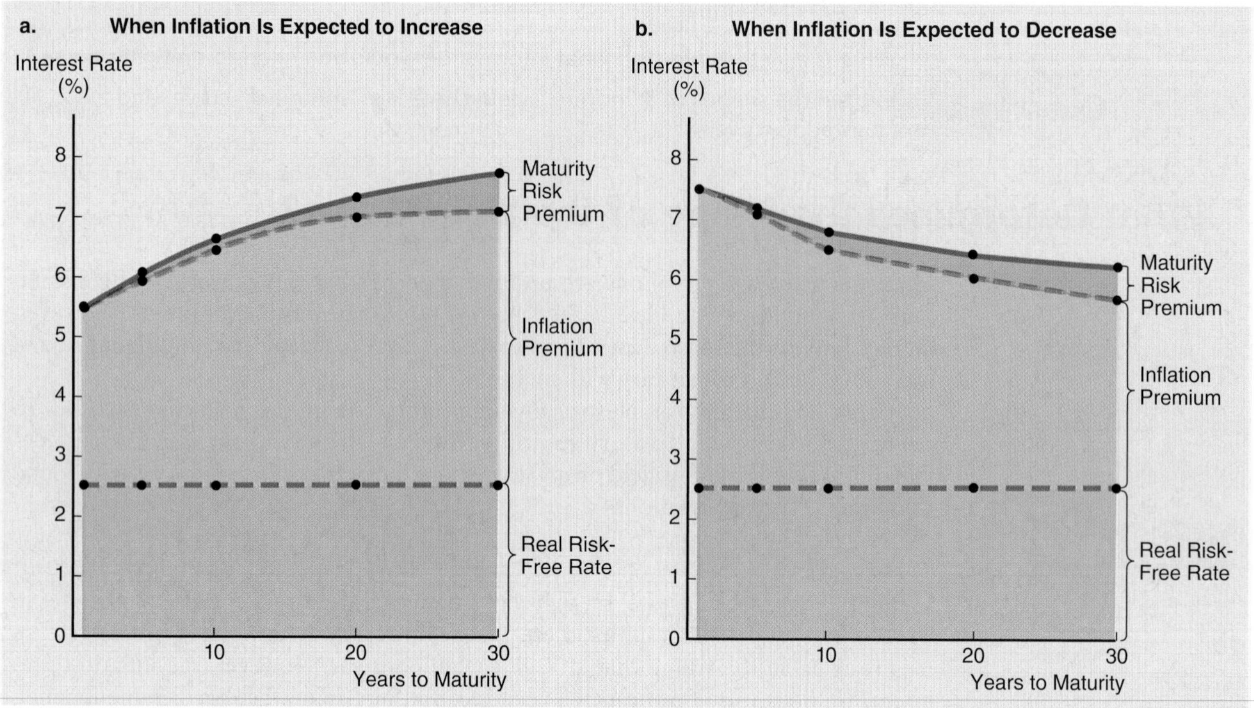

	With Increasing Expected Inflation					With Decreasing Expected Inflation			
Maturity	k*	IP	MRP	Yield	Maturity	k*	IP	MRP	Yield
1 year	2.50%	3.00%	0.00%	5.50%	1 year	2.50%	5.00%	0.00%	7.50%
5 years	2.50	3.40	0.18	6.08	5 years	2.50	4.60	0.18	7.28
10 years	2.50	4.00	0.28	6.78	10 years	2.50	4.00	0.28	6.78
20 years	2.50	4.50	0.42	7.42	20 years	2.50	3.50	0.42	6.42
30 years	2.50	4.67	0.53	7.70	30 years	2.50	3.33	0.53	6.36

so a buyer can buy short-term debt without having to do as much credit checking as would be necessary for long-term debt. Thus, people can move into and out of short-term corporate debt much more rapidly than long-term debt. The end result is that short-term corporate debt is more liquid, hence has a smaller liquidity premium than the same company's long-term debt.

Figure 5-7 shows yield curves for two hypothetical corporate bonds, an AA-rated bond with minimal default risk and a BBB-rated bond with more default risk, along with the yield curve for Treasury securities as taken from Panel a of Figure 5-6. Here we assume that inflation is expected to increase, so the Treasury yield curve is upward sloping. Because of their additional default and liquidity risk, corporate bonds always trade at a higher yield than Treasury bonds with the same maturity, and BBB-rated bonds trade at higher yields than AA-rated bonds. Finally, note that the yield spread between corporate bonds and Treasury bonds is larger the longer the maturity. This occurs because longer-term corporate bonds have more default and liquidity risk than shorter-term bonds, and both of these premiums are absent in Treasury bonds.

FIGURE 5-7 Corporate and Treasury Yield Curves

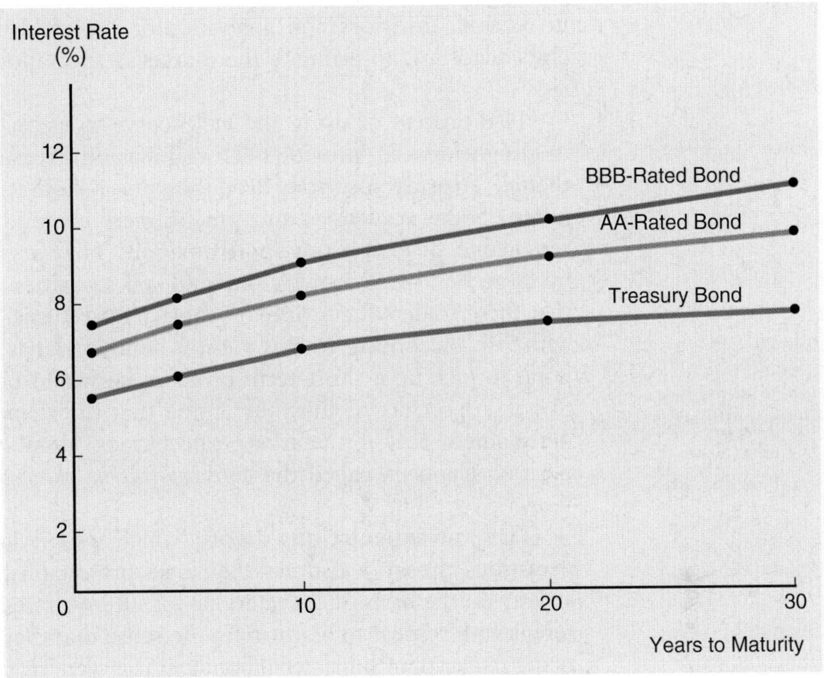

	Interest Rate		
Term to Maturity	**Treasury Bond**	**AA-Rated Bond**	**BBB-Rated Bond**
1 year	5.5%	6.7%	7.4%
5 years	6.1	7.4	8.1
10 years	6.8	8.2	9.1
20 years	7.4	9.2	10.2
30 years	7.7	9.8	11.1

Self-Test Questions

How do maturity risk premiums affect the yield curve?

If the rate of inflation is expected to increase, would this increase or decrease the slope of the yield curve?

If the rate of inflation is expected to remain constant in the future, would the yield curve slope up, down, or be horizontal?

Explain why corporate bonds' default and liquidity premiums are likely to increase with maturity.

Explain why corporate bonds always trade at higher yields than Treasury bonds and why BBB-rated bonds always trade at higher yields than otherwise similar AA-rated bonds.

Using the Yield Curve to Estimate Future Interest Rates[15]

In the last section we saw that the shape of the yield curve depends primarily on two factors: (1) expectations about future inflation and (2) the relative riskiness

[15]This section is relatively technical, but instructors can omit it without loss of continuity.

of securities with different maturities. We also saw how to calculate the yield curve, given inflation and maturity-related risks. In practice, this process often works in reverse: Investors and analysts plot the yield curve and then use information embedded in it to estimate the market's expectations regarding future inflation and risk.

This process of using the yield curve to estimate future expected interest rates is straightforward, provided (1) we focus on Treasury securities, and (2) we assume that all Treasury securities have the same risk; that is, there is no maturity risk premium. Some academics and practitioners contend that this second assumption is reasonable, at least as an approximation. They argue that the market is dominated by large bond traders who buy and sell securities of different maturities each day, that these traders focus only on short-term returns, and that they are not concerned with risk. According to this view, a bond trader is just as willing to buy a 30-year bond to pick up a short-term profit as he would be to buy a three-month security. Strict proponents of this view argue that the shape of the yield curve is therefore determined only by market expectations about future interest rates, and this position has been called the *pure expectations theory* of the term structure of interest rates.

The pure **expectations theory** (which is sometimes simply referred to as the "expectations theory") assumes that investors establish bond prices and interest rates strictly on the basis of expectations for interest rates. This means that they are indifferent with respect to maturity in the sense that they do not view long-term bonds as being riskier than short-term bonds. If this were true, then the maturity risk premium (MRP) would be zero, and long-term interest rates would simply be a weighted average of current and expected future short-term interest rates. For example, if 1-year Treasury bills currently yield 7 percent, but 1-year bills were expected to yield 7.5 percent a year from now, investors would expect to earn an average of 7.25 percent over the next two years:[16]

$$\frac{7\% + 7.5\%}{2} = 7.25\%.$$

According to the expectations theory, this implies that a 2-year Treasury note purchased today should yield 7.25 percent. Similarly, if 10-year bonds yield 9 percent today, and if 5-year bonds are expected to yield 7.5 percent 10 years from now, then investors should expect to earn 9 percent for 10 years and 7.5 percent for 5 years, for an average return of 8.5 percent over the next 15 years:

$$\frac{9\% + 9\% + \cdot\cdot\cdot + 9\% + 7.5\% + \cdot\cdot\cdot + 7.5\%}{15} = \frac{10(9\%) + 5(7.5\%)}{15} = 8.5\%.$$

Consequently, a 15-year bond should yield this same return, 8.5 percent.

To understand the logic behind this averaging process, ask yourself what would happen if long-term yields were *not* an average of expected short-term yields. For example, suppose 2-year bonds yielded only 7 percent, not the 7.25 percent calculated

[16]Technically, we should be using geometric averages rather than arithmetic averages, but the differences are not material in this example. In this example, we would set up the following equation: $(1 + 0.07)(1.075) = (1 + X)^2$. The left side is the amount we would have if we invested \$1 at 7 percent for one year and then reinvested the original \$1 and the \$0.07 interest for an additional year at the rate of 7.5 percent. The right side is the total amount we would have if instead we had invested \$1 at the rate X percent for two years. Solving for X, we find that the true two-year yield is 7.2497 percent. Since this is virtually identical to the arithmetic average of 7.25 percent, we simply use arithmetic averages. For a discussion of this point, see Robert C. Radcliffe, *Investment: Concepts, Analysis, and Strategy*, 5th ed. (Reading, MA: Addison-Wesley, 1997), Chapter 5.

above. Bond traders would be able to earn a profit by adopting the following trading strategy:

1. Borrow money for two years at a cost of 7 percent.
2. Invest the money in a series of 1-year bonds. The expected return over the 2-year period would be $(7.0 + 7.5)/2 = 7.25\%$.

In this case, bond traders would rush to borrow money (demand funds) in the 2-year market and invest (or supply funds) in the 1-year market. Recall from Figure 5-2 that an increase in the demand for funds raises interest rates, whereas an increase in the supply of funds reduces interest rates. Therefore, bond traders' actions would push up the 2-year yield but reduce the yield on 1-year bonds. The net effect would be to bring about a market equilibrium in which 2-year rates were a weighted average of expected future 1-year rates.

Under these assumptions, we can use the yield curve to "back out" the bond market's best guess about future interest rates. If, for example, you observe that Treasury securities with 1- and 2-year maturities yield 7 percent and 8 percent, respectively, this information can be used to calculate the market's forecast of what 1-year rates will yield one year from now. If the pure expectations theory is correct, the rate on 2-year bonds is the average of the current 1-year rate and the 1-year rate expected a year from now. Since the current 1-year rate is 7 percent, this implies that the 1-year rate one year from now is expected to be 9 percent:

$$\text{2-year yield} = 8\% = \frac{7\% + X\%}{2}$$

$$X = 16\% - 7\% = 9\% = \text{1-year yield expected next year.}$$

The preceding analysis was based on the assumption that the maturity risk premium is zero. However, most evidence suggests that there is a positive maturity risk premium, so the MRP should be taken into account.

For example, assume once again that 1- and 2-year maturities yield 7 percent and 8 percent, respectively, but now assume that the maturity risk premium on the 2-year bond is 0.5 percent. This maturity risk premium implies that the expected return on 2-year bonds (8 percent) is 0.5 percent higher than the expected returns from buying a series of 1-year bonds (7.5 percent). With this background, we can use the following two-step procedure to back out X, the expected 1-year rate one year from now:

Step 1: $\text{2-year yield} - \text{MRP on 2-year bond} = 8.0\% - 0.5\% = 7.5\%.$

Step 2: $7.5\% = (7.0\% + X\%)/2$

$X = 15.0\% - 7.0\% = 8.0\%.$

Therefore, the yield next year on a 1-year T-bond should be 8 percent, up from 7 percent this year.

Self-Test Questions

What key assumption underlies the pure expectations theory?

Assuming that the pure expectations theory is correct, how are long-term interest rates calculated?

According to the pure expectations theory, what would happen if long-term rates were *not* an average of expected short-term rates?

Investing Overseas

Investors should consider additional risk factors before investing overseas. First there is **country risk,** which refers to the risk that arises from investing or doing business in a particular country. This risk depends on the country's economic, political, and social environment. Countries with stable economic, social, political, and regulatory systems provide a safer climate for investment, and therefore have less country risk, than less stable nations. Examples of country risk include the risk associated with changes in tax rates, regulations, currency conversion, and exchange rates. Country risk also includes the risk that property will be expropriated without adequate compensation, as well as new host country stipulations about local production, sourcing or hiring practices, and damage or destruction of facilities due to internal strife.

WWW

Euromoney magazine publishes ranking, based on country risk. Students can access the home page of *Euromoney* magazine by typing **http://www.euromoney.com**. Although the site requires users to register, the site is free to use (although some data sets and articles are available only to subscribers.)

A second thing to keep in mind when investing overseas is that more often than not the security will be denominated in a currency other than the dollar, which means that the value of your investment will depend on what happens to exchange rates. This is known as **exchange rate risk.** For example, if a U.S. investor purchases a Japanese bond, interest will probably be paid in Japanese yen, which must then be converted into dollars if the investor wants to spend his or her money in the United States. If the yen weakens relative to the dollar, then it will buy fewer dollars, hence the investor will receive fewer dollars when it comes time to convert. Alternatively, if the yen strengthens relative to the dollar, the investor will earn higher dollar returns. It therefore follows that the effective rate of return on a foreign investment will depend on both the performance of the foreign security and on what happens to exchange rates over the life of the investment.

Self-Test Questions

What is country risk?

What is exchange rate risk?

Other Factors That Influence Interest Rate Levels

In addition to inflationary expectations, other factors also influence both the general level of interest rates and the shape of the yield curve. The four most important factors are (1) Federal Reserve policy; (2) the federal budget deficit or surplus; (3) international factors, including the foreign trade balance and interest rates in other countries; and (4) the level of business activity.

Federal Reserve Policy

WWW

The home page for the Board of Governors of the Federal Reserve System can be found at **http://www.federalreserve.gov**. You can access general information about the Federal Reserve, including press releases, speeches, and monetary policy.

As you probably learned in your economics courses, (1) the money supply has a major effect on both the level of economic activity and the inflation rate, and (2) in the United States, the Federal Reserve Board controls the money supply. If the Fed wants to stimulate the economy, as it did in 1995, it increases growth in the money supply. The initial effect of such an action is to cause interest rates to decline. However, a larger money supply may also lead to an increase in the expected inflation rate, which, in turn, could push interest rates up. The reverse holds if the Fed tightens the money supply.

To illustrate, in 1981 inflation was quite high, so the Fed tightened up the money supply. The Fed deals primarily in the short-term end of the market, so this tightening had the direct effect of pushing short-term rates up sharply. At the same time, the very fact that the Fed was taking strong action to reduce inflation led to a decline in expectations for long-run inflation, which led to a decline in long-term bond yields.

In 1991, the situation was just the reverse. To combat the recession, the Fed took steps to reduce interest rates. Short-term rates fell, and long-term rates also dropped, but not as sharply. These lower rates benefitted heavily indebted businesses and individual borrowers, and home mortgage refinancings put additional billions of dollars into consumers' pockets. Savers, of course, lost out, but the net effect of lower interest rates was a stronger economy. Lower rates encourage businesses to borrow for investment, stimulate the housing market, and bring down the value of the dollar relative to other currencies, which helps U.S. exporters and thus lowers the trade deficit.

During periods when the Fed is actively intervening in the markets, the yield curve may be temporarily distorted. Short-term rates will be temporarily "too low" if the Fed is easing credit, and "too high" if it is tightening credit. Long-term rates are not affected as much by Fed intervention. For example, the fear of rising inflation led the Federal Reserve to increase short-term interest rates six times during 1994. While short-term rates rose by nearly 4 percentage points, long-term rates increased by only 1.5 percentage points.

Budget Deficits or Surpluses

If the federal government spends more than it takes in from tax revenues, it runs a deficit, and that deficit must be covered either by borrowing or by printing money (increasing the money supply). If the government borrows, this added demand for funds pushes up interest rates. If it prints money, this increases expectations for future inflation, which also drives up interest rates. Thus, the larger the federal deficit, other things held constant, the higher the level of interest rates. Whether long- or short-term rates are more affected depends on how the deficit is financed, so we cannot state, in general, how deficits will affect the slope of the yield curve.

Over the past several decades, the federal government routinely ran large budget deficits. However, in 1999, for the first time in recent memory, the government had a budget surplus, and further surpluses are projected on into the future. As a result, the government is now paying back existing debt faster than it is issuing new debt. The net result is a decrease in the national debt. If these surpluses continue, the government will continue to be a net supplier of funds rather than a net borrower. All else equal, this will reduce interest rates.

International Factors

Businesses and individuals in the United States buy from and sell to people and firms in other countries. If we buy more than we sell (that is, if we import more than we export), we are said to be running a *foreign trade deficit.* When trade deficits occur, they must be financed, and the main source of financing is debt. In other words, if we import $200 billion of goods but export only $100 billion, we run a trade deficit of $100 billion, and we would probably borrow the $100 billion.[17] Therefore, the larger our trade deficit, the more we must borrow, and as we increase our borrowing, this drives up interest rates. Also, foreigners are willing to hold U.S. debt if and only if the rate paid on this debt is competitive with interest rates in other countries. Therefore, if the Federal Reserve attempts to lower interest rates in the United States, causing our rates to fall below rates abroad, then foreigners will sell U.S. bonds, those sales will depress bond prices, and that in turn will result in higher U.S. rates. Thus, if the trade deficit is large relative to the size of the overall economy, it will hinder the Fed's ability to combat a recession by lowering interest rates.

The United States has been running annual trade deficits since the mid-1970s, and the cumulative effect of these deficits is that the United States has become the

[17]The deficit could also be financed by selling assets, including gold, corporate stocks, entire companies, and real estate. The United States has financed its massive trade deficits by all of these means in recent years, but the primary method has been by borrowing from foreigners.

largest debtor nation of all time. As a result, our interest rates are very much influenced by interest rates in other countries around the world (higher rates abroad lead to higher U.S. rates). Because of all this, U.S. corporate treasurers—and anyone else who is affected by interest rates—must keep up with developments in the world economy.

Business Activity

Figure 5-3, presented earlier, can be examined to see how business conditions influence interest rates. Here are the key points revealed by the graph:

1. Because inflation increased from 1961 to 1981, the general tendency during that period was toward higher interest rates. However, since the 1981 peak, the trend has generally been downward.
2. Until 1966, short-term rates were almost always below long-term rates. Thus, in those years the yield curve was almost always "normal" in the sense that it was upward sloping.
3. The shaded areas in the graph represent recessions, during which (a) both the demand for money and the rate of inflation tend to fall and (b) the Federal Reserve tends to increase the money supply in an effort to stimulate the economy. As a result, there is a tendency for interest rates to decline during recessions. For example, on three different occasions in 1998 the Fed lowered rates by 25 basis points to combat the deepening global economic and financial crisis. When the economy is growing rapidly and inflation threatens, the Fed raises interest rates, as it did six times in 1999 and 2000. The Fed gave four reasons for the rate hikes: healthy financial markets, a persistent strength in domestic demand, firmer foreign economies, and a tight labor market. Currently, in early 2001, we are in a period of relatively stable, steady growth, while inflation remains at bay.
4. During recessions, short-term rates decline more sharply than long-term rates. This occurs because (a) the Fed operates mainly in the short-term sector, so its intervention has the strongest effect there, and (b) long-term rates reflect the average expected inflation rate over the next 20 to 30 years, and this expectation generally does not change much, even when the current inflation rate is low because of a recession or high because of a boom. So, short-term rates are more volatile than long-term rates.

Self-Test Questions

Other than inflationary expectations, name some additional factors that influence interest rates, and explain the effects of each.

How does the Fed stimulate the economy? How does the Fed affect interest rates? Does the Fed have complete control over U.S. interest rates; that is, can it set rates at any level it chooses?

Interest Rates and Business Decisions

The yield curve for February 2000, shown earlier in Figure 5-5, indicates how much the U.S. government had to pay in 2000 to borrow money for one year, five years, ten years, and so on. A business borrower would have had to pay somewhat more, but assume for the moment that we are back in February 2000 and that the yield curve for that year also applies to your company. Now suppose your company has decided (1) to build a new plant with a 30-year life that will cost $1 million and (2) to raise the $1 million by selling an issue of debt (or borrowing) rather than by selling stock. If you borrowed in 2000 on a short-term basis—say, for one year—your interest cost for that year would be only 6.0 percent, or $60,000. On the other hand, if you used long-term (30-year) financing, your cost would be 6.3 percent, or $63,000. Therefore, at first glance, it would seem that you should use short-term debt.

However, this could prove to be a horrible mistake. If you use short-term debt, you will have to renew your loan every year, and the rate charged on each new loan will reflect the then-current short-term rate. Interest rates could return to their previous highs, in which case you would be paying 14 percent, or $140,000, per year. Those high interest payments would cut into, and perhaps eliminate, your profits. Your reduced profitability could easily increase your firm's risk to the point where its bond rating would be lowered, causing lenders to increase the risk premium built into the interest rate they charge. That would force you to pay an even higher rate, which would further reduce your profitability, worrying lenders even more, and making them reluctant to renew your loan. If your lenders refused to renew the loan and demanded its repayment, as they would have every right to do, you might have to sell assets at a loss, which could lead to bankruptcy.

On the other hand, if you used long-term financing in 2000, your interest costs would remain constant at $63,000 per year, so an increase in interest rates in the economy would not hurt you. You might even be able to buy up some of your bankrupt competitors at bargain prices—bankruptcies increase dramatically when interest rates rise, primarily because many firms do use too much short-term debt.

Does all this suggest that firms should always avoid short-term debt? Not necessarily. If inflation falls over the next few years, so will interest rates. If you had borrowed on a long-term basis for 6.3 percent in February 2000, your company would be at a major disadvantage if it were locked into 6.3 percent debt while its competitors (who used short-term debt in 2000 and thus rode interest rates down in subsequent years) had a borrowing cost of only 3 or 4 percent.

Financing decisions would be easy if we could make accurate forecasts of future interest rates. Unfortunately, predicting interest rates with consistent accuracy is somewhere between difficult and impossible—people who make a living by selling interest rate forecasts say it is difficult, but many others say it is impossible.

Even if it is difficult to predict future interest rate *levels*, it is easy to predict that interest rates will *fluctuate*—they always have, and they always will. This being the case, sound financial policy calls for using a mix of long- and short-term debt, as well as equity, to position the firm so that it can survive in any interest rate environment. Further, the optimal financial policy depends in an important way on the nature of the firm's assets—the easier it is to sell off assets to generate cash, the more feasible it is to use large amounts of short-term debt. This makes it more feasible for a firm to finance its current assets such as inventories than its fixed assets such as buildings with short-term debt. We will return to this issue later in the book, when we discuss working capital policy.

Changes in interest rates also have implications for savers. For example, if you had a 401(k) plan—and someday you almost certainly will—you would probably want to invest some of your money in a bond mutual fund. You could choose a fund that had an average maturity of 25 years, 20 years, and so on, down to only a few months (a money market fund). How would your choice affect your investment results, hence your retirement income? First, your annual interest income would be affected. For example, if the yield curve were upward sloping, as it normally is, you would earn more interest if you choose a fund that held long-term bonds. Note, though, that if you choose a long-term fund and interest rates then rose, the market value of the bonds in the fund would decline. For example, as we will see in Chapter 9, if you had $100,000 in a fund whose average bond had a maturity of 25 years and a coupon rate of 6 percent, and if interest rates then rose from 6 percent to 10 percent, the market value of your fund would decline from $100,000 to about $64,000. On the other hand, if rates declined, your fund would increase in value. In any event, your choice of maturity would have a major effect on your investment performance, hence your future income.

Self-Test Questions

If short-term interest rates are lower than long-term rates, why might a borrower still choose to finance with long-term debt?

Explain the following statement: "The optimal financial policy depends in an important way on the nature of the firm's assets."

Summary

In this chapter, we discussed the nature of financial markets, the types of institutions that operate in these markets, how interest rates are determined, and some of the ways interest rates affect business decisions. In later chapters we will use this information to help value different investments, and to better understand corporate financing and investing decisions. The key concepts covered are listed below:

- There are many different types of **financial markets.** Each market serves a different region or deals with a different type of security.
- **Physical asset markets,** also called tangible or real asset markets, are those for such products as wheat, autos, and real estate.
- **Financial asset markets** deal with stocks, bonds, notes, mortgages, and other claims on real assets.
- **Spot markets** and **futures markets** are terms that refer to whether the assets are bought or sold for "on-the-spot" delivery or for delivery at some future date.
- **Money markets** are the markets for debt securities with maturities of less than one year.
- **Capital markets** are the markets for long-term debt and corporate stocks.
- **Primary markets** are the markets in which corporations raise new capital.
- **Secondary markets** are markets in which existing, already outstanding, securities are traded among investors.
- A **derivative** is a security whose value is derived from the price of some other "underlying" asset.
- Transfers of capital between borrowers and savers take place (1) by **direct transfers** of money and securities; (2) by transfers through **investment banking houses,** which act as middlemen; and (3) by transfers through **financial intermediaries,** which create new securities.
- The major intermediaries include **commercial banks, savings and loan associations, mutual savings banks, credit unions, pension funds, life insurance companies,** and **mutual funds.**
- One result of ongoing regulatory changes has been a blurring of the distinctions between the different financial institutions. The trend in the United States has been toward **financial service corporations** that offer a wide range of financial services, including investment banking, brokerage operations, insurance, and commercial banking.
- The **stock market** is an especially important market because this is where stock prices (which are used to "grade" managers' performances) are established.
- There are two basic types of stock markets—the **formal exchanges** (primarily the NYSE and Nasdaq markets) and the **over-the-counter market.**
- Capital is allocated through the price system—a price must be paid to "rent" money. Lenders charge **interest** on funds they lend, while equity investors receive **dividends and capital gains** in return for letting firms use their money.

- Four fundamental factors affect the cost of money: (1) **production opportunities,** (2) **time preferences for consumption,** (3) **risk,** and (4) **inflation.**
- The **risk-free rate of interest, k_{RF},** is defined as the real risk-free rate, k*, plus an inflation premium, IP, hence $k_{RF} = k^* + IP$.
- The **nominal** (or **quoted**) **interest rate** on a debt security, **k,** is composed of the real risk-free rate, k*, plus premiums that reflect inflation (IP), default risk (DRP), liquidity (LP), and maturity risk (MRP):

$$k = k^* + IP + DRP + LP + MRP.$$

- If the **real risk-free rate of interest and the various premiums were constant over time,** interest rates would be stable. However, both the real rate and the premiums—especially the premium for expected inflation—**do change over time, causing market interest rates to change.** Also, Federal Reserve intervention to increase or decrease the money supply, as well as international currency flows, lead to fluctuations in interest rates.
- The relationship between the yields on securities and the securities' maturities is known as the **term structure of interest rates,** and the **yield curve** is a graph of this relationship.
- The shape of the yield curve depends on two key factors: (1) **expectations about future inflation** and (2) **perceptions about the relative riskiness of securities with different maturities.**
- The yield curve is normally **upward sloping**—this is called a **normal yield curve.** However, the curve can slope downward (an **inverted yield curve**) if the inflation rate is expected to decline. The yield curve can be **humped,** which means that interest rates on medium-term maturities are higher than rates on both short- and long-term maturities.
- Because interest rate levels are difficult if not impossible to predict, **sound financial policy** calls for using a mix of short- and long-term debt, and also for positioning the firm to survive in any future interest rate environment.

Questions

5–1 Define each of the following terms:

a. Money market; capital market
b. Primary market; secondary market
c. Private markets; public markets
d. Derivatives
e. Investment banker; financial service corporation
f. Financial intermediary
g. Mutual fund; money market fund
h. Organized security exchanges; over-the-counter market
i. Production opportunities; time preferences for consumption
j. Real risk-free rate of interest, k*; nominal risk-free rate of interest, k_{RF}
k. Inflation premium (IP)
l. Default risk premium (DRP)
m. Liquidity; liquidity premium (LP)
n. Interest rate risk; maturity risk premium (MRP)
o. Reinvestment rate risk
p. Term structure of interest rates; yield curve
q. "Normal" yield curve; inverted ("abnormal") yield curve
r. Expectations theory
s. Foreign trade deficit

5–2 What are financial intermediaries, and what economic functions do they perform?

5–3 Suppose interest rates on residential mortgages of equal risk were 7 percent in California and 9 percent in New York. Could this differential persist? What forces might tend to equalize rates? Would differentials in borrowing costs for businesses of equal risk located in California and New York be more or less likely to exist than differentials in residential mortgage rates? Would differentials in the cost of money for New York and California firms be more likely to exist if the firms being compared were very large or if they were very small? What are the implications of all this for the pressure now being put on Congress to permit banks to engage in nationwide branching?

5–4 What would happen to the standard of living in the United States if people lost faith in the safety of our financial institutions? Why?

5–5 How does a cost-efficient capital market help to reduce the prices of goods and services?

5–6 Which fluctuate more, long-term or short-term interest rates? Why?

5–7 Suppose you believe that the economy is just entering a recession. Your firm must raise capital immediately, and debt will be used. Should you borrow on a long-term or a short-term basis? Why?

5–8 Suppose the population of Area Y is relatively young while that of Area O is relatively old, but everything else about the two areas is equal.

a. Would interest rates likely be the same or different in the two areas? Explain.

b. Would a trend toward nationwide branching by banks and savings and loans, and the development of nationwide diversified financial corporations, affect your answer to part a?

5–9 Suppose a new process was developed that could be used to make oil out of seawater. The equipment required is quite expensive, but it would, in time, lead to very low prices for gasoline, electricity, and other types of energy. What effect would this have on interest rates?

5–10 Suppose a new and much more liberal Congress and administration were elected, and their first order of business was to take away the independence of the Federal Reserve System, and to force the Fed to greatly expand the money supply. What effect would this have

a. On the level and slope of the yield curve immediately after the announcement?

b. On the level and slope of the yield curve that would exist two or three years in the future?

5–11 It is a fact that the federal government (1) encouraged the development of the savings and loan industry; (2) virtually forced the industry to make long-term, fixed-interest-rate mortgages; and (3) forced the savings and loans to obtain most of their capital as deposits that were withdrawable on demand.

a. Would the savings and loans have higher profits in a world with a "normal" or an inverted yield curve?

b. Would the savings and loan industry be better off if the individual institutions sold their mortgages to federal agencies and then collected servicing fees or if the institutions held the mortgages that they originated?

5–12 Suppose interest rates on Treasury bonds rose from 7 to 14 percent as a result of higher interest rates in Europe. What effect would this have on the price of an average company's common stock?

Self-Test Problem (Solutions Appear in Appendix A)

ST–1 *INFLATION RATES*

Assume that it is now January 1, 2002. The rate of inflation is expected to be 4 percent throughout 2002. However, increased government deficits and renewed vigor in the economy are then expected to push inflation rates higher. Investors expect the inflation rate to be 5 percent in 2003, 6 percent in 2004, and 7 percent in 2005. The real risk-free rate, k*, is expected to remain at 2 percent over the next 5 years. Assume that no maturity risk premiums are required on bonds with 5 years or less to maturity. The current interest rate on 5-year T-bonds is 8 percent.

a. What is the average expected inflation rate over the next 4 years?

b. What should be the prevailing interest rate on 4-year T-bonds?

c. What is the implied expected inflation rate in 2006, or Year 5, given that Treasury bonds which mature in that year yield 8 percent?

Problems

5–1
EXPECTED RATE OF INTEREST

The real risk-free rate of interest is 3 percent. Inflation is expected to be 2 percent this year and 4 percent during the next 2 years. Assume that the maturity risk premium is zero. What is the yield on 2-year Treasury securities? What is the yield on 3-year Treasury securities?

5–2
DEFAULT RISK PREMIUM

A Treasury bond that matures in 10 years has a yield of 6 percent. A 10-year corporate bond has a yield of 8 percent. Assume that the liquidity premium on the corporate bond is 0.5 percent. What is the default risk premium on the corporate bond?

5–3
EXPECTED RATE OF INTEREST

One-year Treasury securities yield 5 percent. The market anticipates that 1 year from now, 1-year Treasury securities will yield 6 percent. If the pure expectations hypothesis is correct, what should be the yield today for 2-year Treasury securities?

5–4
MATURITY RISK PREMIUM

The real risk-free rate is 3 percent, and inflation is expected to be 3 percent for the next 2 years. A 2-year Treasury security yields 6.2 percent. What is the maturity risk premium for the 2-year security?

5–5
EXPECTED RATE OF INTEREST

Interest rates on 1-year Treasury securities are currently 5.6 percent, while 2-year Treasury securities are yielding 6 percent. If the pure expectations theory is correct, what does the market believe will be the yield on 1-year securities 1 year from now?

5–6
EXPECTED RATE OF INTEREST

Interest rates on 4-year Treasury securities are currently 7 percent, while interest rates on 6-year Treasury securities are currently 7.5 percent. If the pure expectations theory is correct, what does the market believe that 2-year securities will be yielding 4 years from now?

5–7
EXPECTED RATE OF INTEREST

The real risk-free rate is 3 percent. Inflation is expected to be 3 percent this year, 4 percent next year, and then 3.5 percent thereafter. The maturity risk premium is estimated to be $0.0005 \times (t - 1)$, where t = number of years to maturity. What is the nominal interest rate on a 7-year Treasury security?

5–8
EXPECTED RATE OF INTEREST

Suppose the annual yield on a 2-year Treasury security is 4.5 percent, while that on a 1-year security is 3 percent. k^* is 1 percent, and the maturity risk premium is zero.

a. Using the expectations theory, forecast the interest rate on a 1-year security during the second year. (Hint: Under the expectations theory, the yield on a 2-year security is equal to the average yield on 1-year securities in Years 1 and 2.)

b. What is the expected inflation rate in Year 1? Year 2?

5–9
EXPECTED RATE OF INTEREST

Assume that the real risk-free rate is 2 percent and that the maturity risk premium is zero. If the nominal rate of interest on 1-year bonds is 5 percent and that on comparable-risk 2-year bonds is 7 percent, what is the 1-year interest rate that is expected for Year 2? What inflation rate is expected during Year 2? Comment on why the average interest rate during the 2-year period differs from the 1-year interest rate expected for Year 2.

5–10
MATURITY RISK PREMIUM

Assume that the real risk-free rate, k^*, is 3 percent and that inflation is expected to be 8 percent in Year 1, 5 percent in Year 2, and 4 percent thereafter. Assume also that all Treasury securities are highly liquid and free of default risk. If 2-year and 5-year Treasury notes both yield 10 percent, what is the difference in the maturity risk premiums (MRPs) on the two notes; that is, what is MRP_5 minus MRP_2?

5–11
INTEREST RATES

Due to a recession, the inflation rate expected for the coming year is only 3 percent. However, the inflation rate in Year 2 and thereafter is expected to be constant at some level above 3 percent. Assume that the real risk-free rate is $k^* = 2\%$ for all maturities and that the expectations theory fully explains the yield curve, so there are no maturity premiums. If 3-year Treasury notes yield 2 percentage points more than 1-year notes, what inflation rate is expected after Year 1?

5–12
YIELD CURVES

Suppose you and most other investors expect the inflation rate to be 7 percent next year, to fall to 5 percent during the following year, and then to remain at a rate of 3 percent thereafter. Assume that the real risk-free rate, k^*, will remain at 2 percent and that maturity risk premiums on Treasury securities rise from zero on very short-term securities (those that mature in a few days) to a level of 0.2 percentage point for 1-year securities. Furthermore, maturity risk premiums increase 0.2 percentage point for each year to maturity, up to a limit of 1.0 percentage point on 5-year or longer-term T-notes and T-bonds.

a. Calculate the interest rate on 1-, 2-, 3-, 4-, 5-, 10-, and 20-year Treasury securities, and plot the yield curve.
b. Now suppose Exxon, an AAA-rated company, had bonds with the same maturities as the Treasury bonds. As an approximation, plot an Exxon yield curve on the same graph with the Treasury bond yield curve. (Hint: Think about the default risk premium on Exxon Mobil's long-term versus its short-term bonds.)
c. Now plot the approximate yield curve of Long Island Lighting Company, a risky nuclear utility.

5–13 *YIELD CURVES* The following yields on U.S. Treasury securities were taken from *Federal Reserve Statistical Release* in May 2000:

Term	Rate
6 months	6.4%
1 year	6.3
2 years	6.9
3 years	6.8
5 years	6.7
10 years	6.5
20 years	6.6
30 years	6.2

Plot a yield curve based on these data.

5–14 *INFLATION AND INTEREST RATES* In late 1980, the U.S. Commerce Department released new figures that showed that inflation was running at an annual rate of close to 15 percent. At the time, the prime rate of interest was 21 percent, a record high. However, many investors expected the new Reagan administration to be more effective in controlling inflation than the Carter administration had been. Moreover, many observers believed that the extremely high interest rates and generally tight credit, which resulted from the Federal Reserve System's attempts to curb the inflation rate, would shortly bring about a recession, which, in turn, would lead to a decline in the inflation rate and also in the interest rate. Assume that at the beginning of 1981, the expected inflation rate for 1981 was 13 percent; for 1982, 9 percent; for 1983, 7 percent; and for 1984 and thereafter, 6 percent.

a. What was the average expected inflation rate over the 5-year period 1981–1985? (Use the arithmetic average.)
b. What average *nominal* interest rate would, over the 5-year period, be expected to produce a 2 percent real risk-free rate of return on 5-year Treasury securities?
c. Assuming a real risk-free rate of 2 percent and a maturity risk premium which starts at 0.1 percent and increases by 0.1 percent each year, estimate the interest rate in January 1981 on bonds that mature in 1, 2, 5, 10, and 20 years, and draw a yield curve based on these data.
d. Describe the general economic conditions that could be expected to produce an upward-sloping yield curve.
e. If the consensus among investors in early 1981 had been that the expected inflation rate for every future year was 10 percent (that is, $I_t = I_{t+1} = 10\%$ for $t = 1$ to ∞), what do you think the yield curve would have looked like? Consider all the factors that are likely to affect the curve. Does your answer here make you question the yield curve you drew in part c?

Spreadsheet Problem

5–15 *BUILD A MODEL: ANALYZING INTEREST RATES*

CD

a. Start with the partial model in the file ***Ch 05-15 Build a Model.xls*** from the textbook's CD-ROM. Suppose you are considering two possible investment opportunities: a 12-year Treasury bond and a 7-year, A-rated corporate bond. The current real risk-free rate is 4 percent, and inflation is expected to be 2 percent for the next two years, 3 percent for the following four years, and 4 percent thereafter. The maturity risk premium is estimated by this formula: MRP = 0.1% (t − 1). The liquidity premium for the corporate bond is estimated to be 0.7 percent. Finally, you may determine the default risk premium, given the company's bond rating, from the default risk premium table in the text. What yield would you predict for each of these two investments?

b. Given the following Treasury bond yield information from the May 22, 2000, *Federal Reserve Statistical Release*, construct a graph of the yield curve as of that date.

Maturity	Yield
3 months	5.89%
6 months	6.40
1 year	6.32
2 years	6.86
3 years	6.80
5 years	6.71
10 years	6.51
20 years	6.64
30 years	6.22

c. Based on the information about the corporate bond that was given in part a, calculate yields and then construct a new yield curve graph that shows both the Treasury and the corporate bonds.

d. Using the Treasury yield information above, calculate the following forward rates:

(1) The 1-year rate, one year from now.
(2) The 5-year rate, five years from now.
(3) The 10-year rate, ten years from now.
(4) The 10-year rate, twenty years from now.

Cyberproblem

The information related to the cyberproblems is likely to change over time, due to the release of new information and the ever-changing nature of the World Wide Web. With these changes in mind, we will periodically update these problems on the textbook's web site.

5–16 *FINANCIAL ENVIRONMENT*

The yield curve is a graph of the term structure of interest rates, which is the relationship of yield and maturity for securities of similar risk. When we think of the yield curve we typically think of the Treasury yield curve as found each day in financial publications such as *The Wall Street Journal.* The yield curve changes in both level and shape due to a variety of monetary, economic, and political factors that were discussed in Chapter 5. The Federal Reserve is a useful site for obtaining actual economic and monetary data. Along with other data, you can obtain historical interest rates at this site to construct a yield curve and analyze changes in interest rates.

To access information from the Federal Reserve, you will be using FRED (the Federal Reserve Economic Database). First, you must connect to the textbook's web site, **http://www.harcourtcollege.com/finance/theory/student/resources/cyberprob/ch05.html.** Answer the questions given at the cyberproblem.

Mini Case

CD

See ***Ch 05 Show.ppt*** and ***Ch 05 Mini Case.xls.***

Assume that you recently graduated with a degree in finance and have just reported to work as an investment advisor at the brokerage firm of Balik and Kiefer Inc. Your first assignment is to explain the nature of the U.S. financial markets to Michelle DellaTorre, a professional tennis player who has just come to the United States from Chile. DellaTorre is a highly ranked tennis player who expects to invest substantial amounts of money through Balik and Kiefer. She is also very bright, and, therefore, she would like to understand in general terms what will happen to her money. Your boss has developed the following set of questions which you must ask and answer to explain the U.S. financial system to DellaTorre.

a. What is a market? How are physical asset markets differentiated from financial markets?
b. Differentiate between money markets and capital markets.

c. Differentiate between a primary market and a secondary market. If Apple Computer decided to issue additional common stock, and DellaTorre purchased 100 shares of this stock from Merrill Lynch, the underwriter, would this transaction be a primary market transaction or a secondary market transaction? Would it make a difference if DellaTorre purchased previously outstanding Apple stock in the Nasdaq market?
d. Describe the three primary ways in which capital is transferred between savers and borrowers.
e. Securities can be traded on organized exchanges or in the over-the-counter market. Define each of these markets, and describe how stocks are traded in each of them.
f. What do we call the price that a borrower must pay for debt capital? What is the price of equity capital? What are the four most fundamental factors that affect the cost of money, or the general level of interest rates, in the economy?
g. What is the real risk-free rate of interest (k^*) and the nominal risk-free rate (k_{RF})? How are these two rates measured?
h. Define the terms inflation premium (IP), default risk premium (DRP), liquidity premium (LP), and maturity risk premium (MRP). Which of these premiums is included when determining the interest rate on (1) short-term U.S. Treasury securities, (2) long-term U.S. Treasury securities, (3) short-term corporate securities, and (4) long-term corporate securities? Explain how the premiums would vary over time and among the different securities listed above.
i. What is the term structure of interest rates? What is a yield curve?
j. Suppose most investors expect the inflation rate to be 5 percent next year, 6 percent the following year, and 8 percent thereafter. The real risk-free rate is 3 percent. The maturity risk premium is zero for securities that mature in 1 year or less, 0.1 percent for 2-year securities, and then the MRP increases by 0.1 percent per year thereafter for 20 years, after which it is stable. What is the interest rate on 1-year, 10-year, and 20-year Treasury securities? Draw a yield curve with these data. What factors can explain why this constructed yield curve is upward sloping?
k. At any given time, how would the yield curve facing an AAA-rated company compare with the yield curve for U.S. Treasury securities? At any given time, how would the yield curve facing a BB-rated company compare with the yield curve for U.S. Treasury securities? Draw a graph to illustrate your answer.
l. What is the pure expectations theory? What does the pure expectations theory imply about the term structure of interest rates?
m. Suppose that you observe the following term structure for Treasury securities:

Maturity	Yield
1 year	6.0%
2 years	6.2
3 years	6.4
4 years	6.5
5 years	6.5

Assume that the pure expectations theory of the term structure is correct. (This implies that you can use the yield curve given above to "back out" the market's expectations about future interest rates.) What does the market expect will be the interest rate on 1-year securities one year from now? What does the market expect will be the interest rate on 3-year securities two years from now?
n. Finally, DellaTorre is also interested in investing in countries other than the United States. Describe the various types of risks that arise when investing overseas.

Selected Additional References

Textbooks that focus on interest rates and financial markets include

Fabozzi, Frank J., *Bond Markets: Analysis and Strategies* (Englewood Cliffs, NJ: Prentice-Hall, 1992).

Johnson, Hazel J., *Financial Institutions and Markets: A Global Perspective* (New York: McGraw-Hill, 1993).

Kidwell, David S., Richard Peterson, and David Blackwell, *Financial Institutions, Markets, and Money* (Fort Worth, TX: The Dryden Press, 1993).

Kohn, Mier, *Money, Banking, and Financial Markets* (Fort Worth, TX: The Dryden Press, 1993).

Livingston, Miles, *Money and Capital Markets* (Cambridge, MA: Blackwell, 1996).

Smith, Stephen D., and Raymond E. Spudeck, *Interest Rates: Theory and Application* (Fort Worth, TX: The Dryden Press, 1993).

For current empirical data and a forecast of monetary conditions, see the most recent edition of this annual publication:

Salomon Smith Barney, *Supply and Demand for Credit* (New York).

The classic works on term structure theories include the following:

Culbertson, John M., "The Term Structure of Interest Rates," *Quarterly Journal of Economics*, November 1957, 489–504.

Fisher, Irving, "Appreciation and Interest," *Publications of the American Economic Association*, August 1986, 23–29 and 91–92.

Hicks, J. R., *Value and Capital* (London: Oxford University Press, 1946).

Lutz, F. A., "The Structure of Interest Rates," *Quarterly Journal of Economics*, November 1940, 36–63.

Modigliani, Franco, and Richard Sutch, "Innovations in Interest Rate Policy," *American Economic Review*, May 1966, 178–197.

For additional information on financial institutions, see

Greenbaum, Stuart I., and Anjan V. Thakor, *Contemporary Financial Intermediation* (Fort Worth, TX: The Dryden Press, 1995).

Kaufman, George G., *The U.S. Financial System* (Englewood Cliffs, NJ: Prentice-Hall, 1995).

CHAPTER 6
Risk and Return: The Basics

CHAPTER 7
Risk and Return: Portfolio Theory and Asset Pricing Models

CHAPTER 8
Time Value of Money

6

Risk and Return: The Basics

If someone had invested $1,000 in a portfolio of large-company stocks in 1925 and then reinvested all dividends received, his or her investment would have grown to $2,845,697 by 1999. Over the same period, a portfolio of small-company stocks would have grown far more rapidly, to $6,641,505. However, if instead he or she had invested in long-term government bonds, the $1,000 would have grown to only $40,219, and to a measly $15,642 in short-term bonds.

Given these numbers, why would anyone invest in bonds? The answer is, "Because bonds are less risky." Although common stocks over the past 74 years have produced considerably higher returns, (1) we cannot be sure that the past is a prologue to the future, and (2) stock values are more likely to experience sharp declines than bonds, so one has a greater chance of losing money on a stock investment. For example, in 2000 the average Nasdaq stock lost 39.3 percent of its value, and many individual stocks dropped by more than 95 percent. Bonds, though, provided positive returns that year, as they almost always do.

Of course, some stocks are riskier than others, and even in years when the overall stock market goes up, many individual stocks go down. Therefore, putting all your money in one stock is extremely risky. According to a *Business Week* article, the single best weapon against risk is diversification: "By spreading your money around, you're not tied to the fickleness of a given market, stock, or industry. . . . Correlation, in portfolio-manager speak, helps you diversify properly because it describes how closely two investments track each other. If they move in tandem, they're likely to suffer from the same bad news. So, you should combine assets with low correlations."

U.S. investors tend to think of "the stock market" as the U.S. stock market. However, U.S. stocks amount to only 35 percent of the value of all stocks. Foreign markets have been quite profitable, and they are not perfectly correlated with U.S. markets. Therefore, global diversification offers U.S. investors an opportunity to raise returns and at the same time reduce risk. However, foreign investing brings some risks of its own, most notably "exchange rate risk," which is the danger that exchange rate shifts will decrease the number of dollars a foreign currency will buy.

Although the central thrust of the *Business Week* article was on ways to measure and then reduce risk, it did point out that some recently created securities that are actually extremely risky have been marketed to naive investors as low-risk investments. For example, several mutual funds have advertised that their portfolios "contain only securities backed by the U.S. government" but then failed to highlight that the funds themselves are using financial leverage, are investing in "derivatives," or are taking some other action that boosts short-term returns but exposes investors to huge risks.

When you finish this chapter, you should understand what risk is, how it is measured, and what actions can be taken to ensure that you are adequately compensated for bearing it.

Sources: "Figuring Risk: It's Not So Scary," *Business Week,* November 1, 1993, 154–155; "T-Bill Trauma and the Meaning of Risk," *The Wall Street Journal,* February 12, 1993, C1; *Stocks, Bonds, Bills, and Inflation: Valuation Edition 2000 Yearbook* (Chicago: Ibbotson Associates, 2000).

The textbook's CD-ROM contains an *Excel* file that will guide you through the chapter's calculations. The file for this chapter is ***Ch 06 Tool Kit.xls***, and we encourage you to open the file and follow along as you read the chapter.

In this chapter, we start from the basic premise that investors like returns and dislike risk. Therefore, people will invest in risky assets only if they expect to receive higher returns. We define precisely what the term *risk* means as it relates to investments. We examine procedures managers use to measure risk, and we discuss the relationship between risk and return. Chapter 7 then goes on to study risk in more depth, and in Chapters 8, 9, and 10, we extend these relationships to show how risk and return interact to determine security prices. Managers must understand these concepts and think about them as they plan the actions that will shape their firms' futures.

As you will see, risk can be measured in different ways, and different conclusions about an asset's risk can be reached depending on the measure used. Risk analysis can be confusing, but it will help if you remember the following:

1. All financial assets are expected to produce *cash flows*, and the risk of an asset is judged in terms of the risk of its cash flows.
2. The risk of an asset can be considered in two ways: (1) on a *stand-alone basis*, where the asset's cash flows are analyzed by themselves, or (2) in a *portfolio context*, where the cash flows from a number of assets are combined and then the consolidated cash flows are analyzed.[1] There is an important difference between stand-alone and portfolio risk, and an asset that has a great deal of risk if held by itself may be much less risky if it is held as part of a larger portfolio.
3. In a portfolio context, an asset's risk can be divided into two components: (a) *diversifiable risk*, which can be diversified away and thus is of little concern to diversified investors, and (b) *market risk*, which reflects the risk of a general stock market decline and which cannot be eliminated by diversification, hence *does* concern investors. Only market risk is *relevant*—diversifiable risk is *irrelevant* to rational investors because it can be eliminated.
4. An asset with a high degree of relevant (market) risk must provide a relatively high expected rate of return to attract investors. Investors in general are *averse to risk*, so they will not buy risky assets unless those assets have high expected returns.
5. In this chapter, we focus on *financial assets* such as stocks and bonds, but the concepts discussed here also apply to *physical assets* such as computers, trucks, or even whole plants.

Investment Returns

With most investments, an individual or business spends money today with the expectation of earning even more money in the future. The concept of *return* provides investors with a convenient way of expressing the financial performance of an investment. To illustrate, suppose you buy 10 shares of a stock for $1,000. The stock pays no dividends, but at the end of one year, you sell the stock for $1,100. What is the return on your $1,000 investment?

One way of expressing an investment return is in *dollar terms*. The dollar return is simply the total dollars received from the investment less the amount invested:

$$\begin{aligned}\text{Dollar return} &= \text{Amount received} - \text{Amount invested}\\ &= \$1{,}100 - \$1{,}000\\ &= \$100.\end{aligned}$$

[1] A *portfolio* is a collection of investment securities. If you owned some General Motors stock, some Exxon Mobil stock, and some IBM stock, you would be holding a three-stock portfolio. Because diversification lowers risk, most stocks are held in portfolios.

If at the end of the year you had sold the stock for only \$900, your dollar return would have been −\$100.

Although expressing returns in dollars is easy, two problems arise: (1) To make a meaningful judgment about the return, you need to know the scale (size) of the investment; a \$100 return on a \$100 investment is a good return (assuming the investment is held for one year), but a \$100 return on a \$10,000 investment would be a poor return. (2) You also need to know the timing of the return; a \$100 return on a \$100 investment is a very good return if it occurs after one year, but the same dollar return after 20 years would not be very good.

The solution to the scale and timing problems is to express investment results as *rates of return,* or *percentage returns.* For example, the rate of return on the 1-year stock investment, when \$1,100 is received after one year, is 10 percent:

$$\begin{aligned}\text{Rate of return} &= \frac{\text{Amount received} - \text{Amount invested}}{\text{Amount invested}}\\ &= \frac{\text{Dollar return}}{\text{Amount invested}} = \frac{\$100}{\$1{,}000}\\ &= 0.10 = 10\%.\end{aligned}$$

The rate of return calculation "standardizes" the return by considering the return per unit of investment. In this example, the return of 0.10, or 10 percent, indicates that each dollar invested will earn 0.10(\$1.00) = \$0.10. If the rate of return had been negative, this would indicate that the original investment was not even recovered. For example, selling the stock for only \$900 results in a minus 10 percent rate of return, which means that each invested dollar lost 10 cents.

Note also that a \$10 return on a \$100 investment produces a 10 percent rate of return, while a \$10 return on a \$1,000 investment results in a rate of return of only 1 percent. Thus, the percentage return takes account of the size of the investment.

Expressing rates of return on an annual basis, which is typically done in practice, solves the timing problem. A \$10 return after one year on a \$100 investment results in a 10 percent annual rate of return, while a \$10 return after five years yields only a 1.9 percent annual rate of return. We will discuss all this in detail in Chapter 8, which deals with the time value of money.

Although we illustrated return concepts with one outflow and one inflow, in later chapters we demonstrate that rate of return concepts can easily be applied in situations where multiple cash flows occur over time. For example, when Intel makes an investment in new chip-making technology, the investment is made over several years and the resulting inflows occur over even more years. For now, it is sufficient to recognize that the rate of return solves the two major problems associated with dollar returns—size and timing. Therefore, the rate of return is the most common measure of investment performance.

Self-Test Questions

Differentiate between dollar return and rate of return.

Why is the rate of return superior to the dollar return in terms of accounting for the size of investment and the timing of cash flows?

Stand-Alone Risk

Risk is defined in *Webster's* as "a hazard; a peril; exposure to loss or injury." Thus, risk refers to the chance that some unfavorable event will occur. If you engage in skydiving, you are taking a chance with your life—skydiving is risky. If you bet on the horses, you are risking your money. If you invest in speculative stocks (or, really, *any* stock), you are taking a risk in the hope of making an appreciable return.

An asset's risk can be analyzed in two ways: (1) on a stand-alone basis, where the asset is considered in isolation, and (2) on a portfolio basis, where the asset is held as one of a number of assets in a portfolio. Thus, an asset's **stand-alone risk** is the risk an investor would face if he or she held only this one asset. Obviously, most assets are held in portfolios, but it is necessary to understand stand-alone risk in order to understand risk in a portfolio context.

To illustrate the risk of financial assets, suppose an investor buys \$100,000 of short-term Treasury bills with an expected return of 5 percent. In this case, the rate of return on the investment, 5 percent, can be estimated quite precisely, and the investment is defined as being essentially *risk free.* However, if the \$100,000 were invested in the stock of a company just being organized to prospect for oil in the mid-Atlantic, then the investment's return could not be estimated precisely. One might analyze the situation and conclude that the *expected* rate of return, in a statistical sense, is 20 percent, but the investor should recognize that the *actual* rate of return could range from, say, +1,000 percent to −100 percent. Because there is a significant danger of actually earning much less than the expected return, the stock would be relatively risky.

No investment should be undertaken unless the expected rate of return is high enough to compensate the investor for the perceived risk of the investment. In our example, it is clear that few if any investors would be willing to buy the oil company's stock if its expected return were the same as that of the T-bill.

Risky assets rarely produce their expected rates of return—generally, risky assets earn either more or less than was originally expected. Indeed, if assets always produced their expected returns, they would not be risky. Investment risk, then, is related to the probability of actually earning a low or negative return—the greater the chance of a low or negative return, the riskier the investment. However, risk can be defined more precisely, and we do so in the next section.

Probability Distributions

An event's *probability* is defined as the chance that the event will occur. For example, a weather forecaster might state, "There is a 40 percent chance of rain today and a 60 percent chance that it will not rain." If all possible events, or outcomes, are listed, and if a probability is assigned to each event, the listing is called a **probability distribution.** For our weather forecast, we could set up the following probability distribution:

Outcome (1)	Probability (2)
Rain	0.4 = 40%
No rain	0.6 = 60
	1.0 = 100%

The possible outcomes are listed in Column 1, while the probabilities of these outcomes, expressed both as decimals and as percentages, are given in Column 2. Notice that the probabilities must sum to 1.0, or 100 percent.

Probabilities can also be assigned to the possible outcomes (or returns) from an investment. If you buy a bond, you expect to receive interest on the bond plus a return of your original investment, and those payments will provide you with a rate of return on your investment. The possible outcomes from this investment are (1) that the issuer will make the required payments or (2) that the issuer will default on the payments. The higher the probability of default, the riskier the bond, and the higher the

TABLE 6-1 Probability Distributions for Martin Products and U.S. Water

		Rate of Return on Stock if This Demand Occurs	
Demand for the Company's Products	Probability of This Demand Occurring	Martin Products	U.S. Water
Strong	0.3	100%	20%
Normal	0.4	15	15
Weak	0.3	(70)	10
	1.0		

risk, the higher the required rate of return. If you invest in a stock instead of buying a bond, you will again expect to earn a return on your money. A stock's return will come from dividends plus capital gains. Again, the riskier the stock—which means the higher the probability that the firm will fail to perform as you expected—the higher the expected return must be to induce you to invest in the stock.

With this in mind, consider the possible rates of return (dividend yield plus capital gain or loss) that you might earn next year on a $10,000 investment in the stock of either Martin Products Inc. or U.S. Water Company. Martin manufactures and distributes routers and equipment for the rapidly growing data transmission industry. Because it faces intense competition, its new products may or may not be competitive in the marketplace, so its future earnings cannot be predicted very well. Indeed, some new company could develop better products and literally bankrupt Martin. U.S. Water, on the other hand, supplies an essential service, and because it has city franchises that protect it from competition, its sales and profits are relatively stable and predictable.

The rate-of-return probability distributions for the two companies are shown in Table 6-1. There is a 30 percent chance of strong demand, in which case both companies will have high earnings, pay high dividends, and enjoy capital gains. There is a 40 percent probability of normal demand and moderate returns, and there is a 30 percent probability of weak demand, which will mean low earnings and dividends as well as capital losses. Notice, however, that Martin Products' rate of return could vary far more widely than that of U.S. Water. There is a fairly high probability that the value of Martin's stock will drop substantially, resulting in a 70 percent loss, while there is no chance of a loss for U.S. Water.[2]

Expected Rate of Return

If we multiply each possible outcome by its probability of occurrence and then sum these products, as in Table 6-2, we have a *weighted average* of outcomes. The weights are the probabilities, and the weighted average is the **expected rate of return, $\hat{k}$**, called "k-hat."[3] The expected rates of return for both Martin Products and U.S. Water are shown in Table 6-2 to be 15 percent. This type of table is known as a *payoff matrix.*

[2]It is, of course, completely unrealistic to think that any stock has no chance of a loss. Only in hypothetical examples could this occur. To illustrate, the price of Columbia Gas's stock dropped from $34.50 to $20.00 in just three hours a few years ago. All investors were reminded that any stock is exposed to some risk of loss, and those investors who bought Columbia Gas learned that lesson the hard way.

[3]In Chapters 9 and 10, we will use k_d and k_s to signify the returns on bonds and stocks, respectively. However, this distinction is unnecessary in this chapter, so we just use the general term, k, to signify the expected return on an investment.

TABLE 6-2 Calculation of Expected Rates of Return: Payoff Matrix

		Martin Products		U.S. Water	
Demand for the Company's Products (1)	Probability of This Demand Occurring (2)	Rate of Return if This Demand Occurs (3)	Product: (2) × (3) = (4)	Rate of Return if This Demand Occurs (5)	Product: (2) × (5) = (6)
Strong	0.3	100%	30%	20%	6%
Normal	0.4	15	6	15	6
Weak	0.3	(70)	(21)	10	3
	1.0		$\hat{k}$ = 15%		$\hat{k}$ = 15%

The expected rate of return calculation can also be expressed as an equation that does the same thing as the payoff matrix table:[4]

$$\text{Expected rate of return} = \hat{k} = P_1k_1 + P_2k_2 + \cdots + P_nk_n = \sum_{i=1}^{n} P_ik_i. \quad \textbf{(6-1)}$$

Here k_i is the *i*th possible outcome, P_i is the probability of the *i*th outcome, and n is the number of possible outcomes. Thus, $\hat{k}$ is a weighted average of the possible outcomes (the k_i values), with each outcome's weight being its probability of occurrence. Using the data for Martin Products, we obtain its expected rate of return as follows:

$$\begin{aligned}\hat{k} &= P_1(k_1) + P_2(k_2) + P_3(k_3)\\ &= 0.3(100\%) + 0.4(15\%) + 0.3(-70\%)\\ &= 15\%.\end{aligned}$$

U.S. Water's expected rate of return is also 15 percent:

$$\begin{aligned}\hat{k} &= 0.3(20\%) + 0.4(15\%) + 0.3(10\%)\\ &= 15\%.\end{aligned}$$

We can graph the rates of return to obtain a picture of the variability of possible outcomes; this is shown in the Figure 6-1 bar charts. The height of each bar signifies the probability that a given outcome will occur. The range of probable returns for Martin Products is from −70 to +100 percent, with an expected return of 15 percent. The expected return for U.S. Water is also 15 percent, but its range is much narrower.

Thus far, we have assumed that only three situations can exist: strong, normal, and weak demand. Actually, of course, demand could range from a deep depression to a fantastic boom, and there are an unlimited number of possibilities in between. Suppose we had the time and patience to assign a probability to each possible level of demand (with the sum of the probabilities still equaling 1.0) and to assign a rate of return to each stock for each level of demand. We would have a table similar to Table 6-1, except that it would have many more entries in each column. This table could be used to

[4]The second form of the equation is simply a shorthand expression in which sigma (Σ) means "sum up," or add the values of n factors. If i = 1, then $P_ik_i = P_1k_1$; if i = 2, then $P_ik_i = P_2k_2$; and so on until i = n, the last possible outcome. The symbol $\sum_{i=1}^{n}$ in Equation 6-1 simply says, "Go through the following process: First, let i = 1 and find the first product; then let i = 2 and find the second product; then continue until each individual product up to i = n has been found, and then add these individual products to find the expected rate of return."

FIGURE 6-1 Probability Distributions of Martin Products' and U.S. Water's Rates of Return

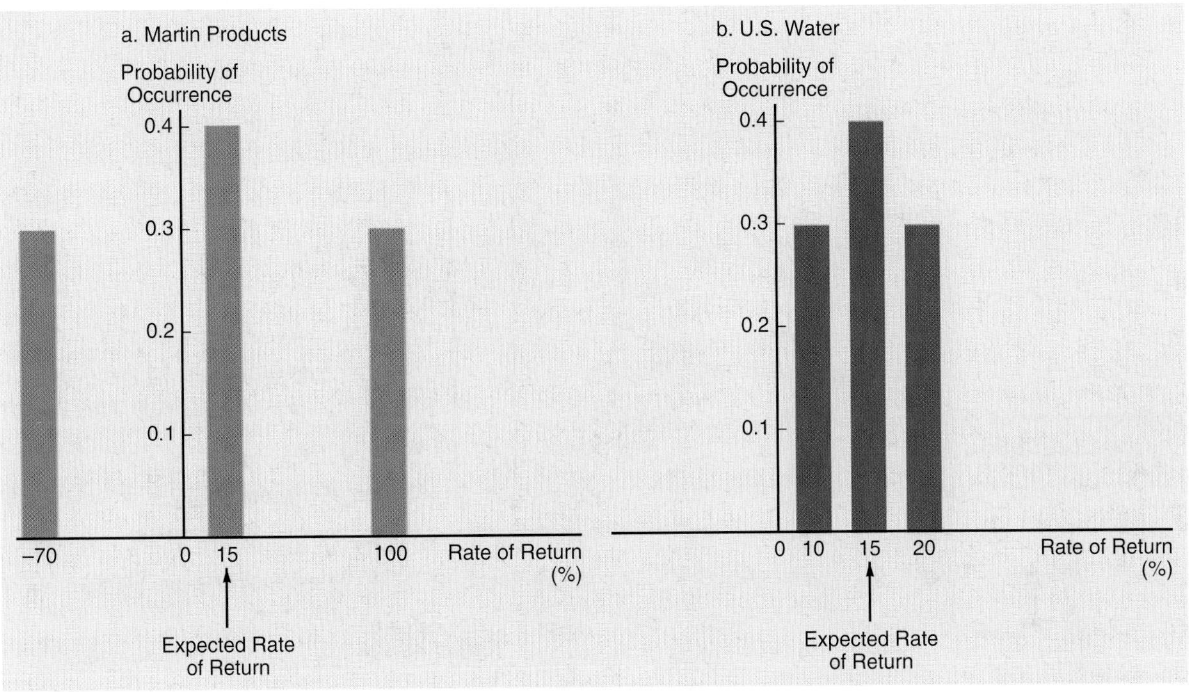

calculate expected rates of return as shown previously, and the probabilities and outcomes could be approximated by continuous curves such as those presented in Figure 6-2. Here we have changed the assumptions so that there is essentially a zero probability that Martin Products' return will be less than −70 percent or more than 100 percent, or that U.S. Water's return will be less than 10 percent or more than 20 percent, but virtually any return within these limits is possible.

The tighter, or more peaked, the probability distribution, the more likely it is that the actual outcome will be close to the expected value, and, consequently, the less likely it is that the actual return will end up far below the expected return. Thus, the tighter the probability distribution, the lower the risk assigned to a stock. Since U.S. Water has a relatively tight probability distribution, its *actual return* is likely to be closer to its 15 percent *expected return* than is that of Martin Products.

Measuring Stand-Alone Risk: The Standard Deviation

Risk is a difficult concept to grasp, and a great deal of controversy has surrounded attempts to define and measure it. However, a common definition, and one that is satisfactory for many purposes, is stated in terms of probability distributions such as those presented in Figure 6-2: *The tighter the probability distribution of expected future returns, the smaller the risk of a given investment.* According to this definition, U.S. Water is less risky than Martin Products because there is a smaller chance that its actual return will end up far below its expected return.

To be most useful, any measure of risk should have a definite value—we need a measure of the tightness of the probability distribution. One such measure is the **standard deviation,** the symbol for which is σ, pronounced "sigma." The smaller the standard deviation, the tighter the probability distribution, and, accordingly, the lower

FIGURE 6-2 Continuous Probability Distributions of Martin Products' and U.S. Water's Rates of Return

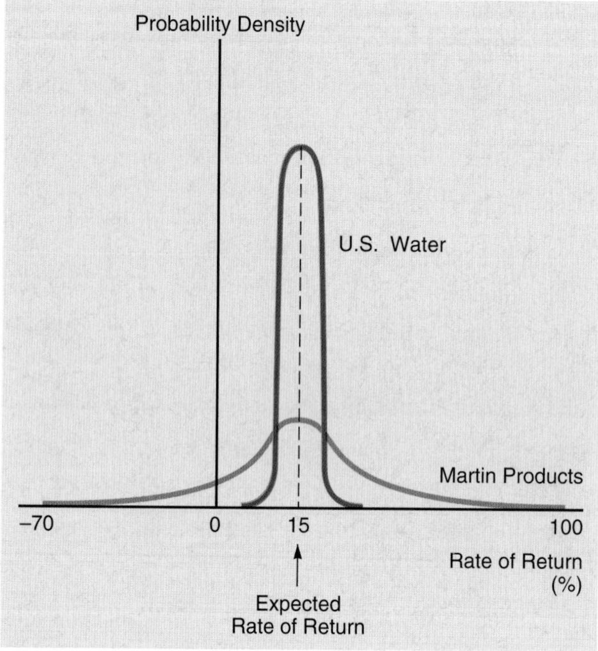

NOTE: The assumptions regarding the probabilities of various outcomes have been changed from those in Figure 6-1. There the probability of obtaining exactly 15 percent was 40 percent; here it is *much smaller* because there are many possible outcomes instead of just three. With continuous distributions, it is more appropriate to ask what the probability is of obtaining at least some specified rate of return than to ask what the probability is of obtaining exactly that rate. This topic is covered in detail in statistics courses.

the riskiness of the stock. To calculate the standard deviation, we proceed as shown in Table 6-3, taking the following steps:

1. Calculate the expected rate of return:

$$\text{Expected rate of return} = \hat{k} = \sum_{i=1}^{n} P_i k_i.$$

For Martin, we previously found $\hat{k} = 15\%$.

2. Subtract the expected rate of return ($\hat{k}$) from each possible outcome (k_i) to obtain a set of deviations about $\hat{k}$ as shown in Column 1 of Table 6-3:

$$\text{Deviation}_i = k_i - \hat{k}.$$

TABLE 6-3 Calculating Martin Products' Standard Deviation

$k_i - \hat{k}$ (1)	$(k_i - \hat{k})^2$ (2)	$(k_i - \hat{k})^2 P_i$ (3)
100 − 15 = 85	7,225	(7,225)(0.3) = 2,167.5
15 − 15 = 0	0	(0)(0.4) = 0.0
−70 − 15 = −85	7,225	(7,225)(0.3) = 2,167.5
		Variance = σ^2 = 4,335.0

Standard deviation = $\sigma = \sqrt{\sigma^2} = \sqrt{4,335} = 65.84\%$.

3. Square each deviation, then multiply the result by the probability of occurrence for its related outcome, and then sum these products to obtain the **variance** of the probability distribution as shown in Columns 2 and 3 of the table:

$$\text{Variance} = \sigma^2 = \sum_{i=1}^{n} (k_i - \hat{k})^2 P_i. \quad \textbf{(6-2)}$$

4. Finally, find the square root of the variance to obtain the standard deviation:

$$\text{Standard deviation} = \sigma = \sqrt{\sum_{i=1}^{n} (k_i - \hat{k})^2 P_i}. \quad \textbf{(6-3)}$$

Thus, the standard deviation is essentially a weighted average of the deviations from the expected value, and it provides an idea of how far above or below the expected value the actual value is likely to be. Martin's standard deviation is seen in Table 6-3 to be $\sigma = 65.84\%$. Using these same procedures, we find U.S. Water's standard deviation to be 3.87 percent. Martin Products has the larger standard deviation, which indicates a greater variation of returns and thus a greater chance that the expected return will not be realized. Therefore, Martin Products is a riskier investment than U.S. Water when held alone.

If a probability distribution is normal, the *actual* return will be within ± 1 standard deviation of the *expected* return 68.26 percent of the time. Figure 6-3 illustrates this point, and it also shows the situation for $\pm 2\sigma$ and $\pm 3\sigma$. For Martin Products, $k = 15\%$ and $\sigma = 65.84\%$, whereas $\hat{k} = 15\%$ and $\sigma = 3.87\%$ for U.S. Water. Thus, if

For more discussion of probability distributions, see the Chapter 6 Web/CD Extension on the textbook's CD-ROM. It is also available on the book's web site, **http://www.harcourtcollege.com/finance/theory.**

FIGURE 6-3 Probability Ranges for a Normal Distribution

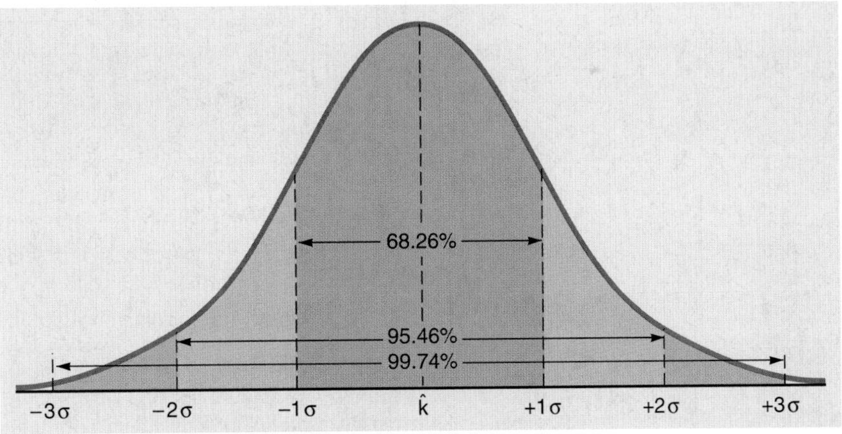

NOTES:

a. The area under the normal curve always equals 1.0, or 100 percent. *Thus, the areas under any pair of normal curves drawn on the same scale, whether they are peaked or flat, must be equal.*

b. Half of the area under a normal curve is to the left of the mean, indicating that there is a 50 percent probability that the actual outcome will be less than the mean, and half is to the right of $\hat{k}$, indicating a 50 percent probability that it will be greater than the mean.

c. Of the area under the curve, 68.26 percent is within $\pm 1\sigma$ of the mean, indicating that the probability is 68.26 percent that the actual outcome will be within the range $k - 1\sigma$ to $k + 1\sigma$.

d. Procedures exist for finding the probability of other ranges. These procedures are covered in statistics courses.

e. For a normal distribution, the larger the value of σ, the greater the probability that the actual outcome will vary widely from, and hence perhaps be far below, the expected, or most likely, outcome. *Since the probability of having the actual result turn out to be far below the expected result is one definition of risk, and since σ measures this probability, we can use σ as a measure of risk.* This definition may not be a good one, however, if we are dealing with an asset held in a diversified portfolio. This point is covered later in the chapter.

the two distributions were normal, there would be a 68.26 percent probability that Martin's actual return would be in the range of 15 ± 65.84 percent, or from −50.84 to 80.84 percent. For U.S. Water, the 68.26 percent range is 15 ± 3.87 percent, or from 11.13 to 18.87 percent. With such a small σ, there is only a small probability that U.S. Water's return would be significantly less than expected, so the stock is not very risky. For the average firm listed on the New York Stock Exchange, σ has generally been in the range of 35 to 40 percent in recent years.

Using Historical Data to Measure Risk

In the previous example, we described the procedure for finding the mean and standard deviation when the data are in the form of a known probability distribution. If only sample returns data over some past period are available, the standard deviation of returns can be estimated using this formula:

$$\text{Estimated } \sigma = S = \sqrt{\frac{\sum_{t=1}^{n}(\bar{k}_t - \bar{k}_{Avg})^2}{n-1}} \qquad \textbf{(6-3a)}$$

Here $\bar{k}_t$ ("k bar t") denotes the past realized rate of return in Period t, and $\bar{k}_{Avg}$ is the average annual return earned during the last n years. Here is an example:

Year	$\bar{k}_t$
1999	15%
2000	−5
2001	20

$$\bar{k}_{Avg} = \frac{(15 - 5 + 20)}{3} = 10.0\%.$$

$$\text{Estimated } \sigma \text{ (or S)} = \sqrt{\frac{(15-10)^2 + (-5-10)^2 + (20-10)^2}{3-1}}$$

$$= \sqrt{\frac{350}{2}} = 13.2\%.$$

The historical σ is often used as an estimate of the future σ. Much less often, and generally incorrectly, $\bar{k}_{Avg}$ for some past period is used as an estimate of $\hat{k}$, the expected future return. Because past variability is likely to be repeated, S may be a good estimate of future risk. But it is much less reasonable to expect that the past *level* of return (which could have been as high as +100% or as low as −50%) is the best expectation of what investors think will happen in the future.[5]

Measuring Stand-Alone Risk: The Coefficient of Variation

If a choice has to be made between two investments that have the same expected returns but different standard deviations, most people would choose the one with the lower standard deviation and, therefore, the lower risk. Similarly, given a choice between two investments with the same risk (standard deviation) but different expected

[5]Equation 6-3a is built into all financial calculators, and it is very easy to use. We simply enter the rates of return and press the key marked S (or S_x) to get the standard deviation. Note, though, that calculators have no built-in formula for finding S where probabilistic data are involved; there you must go through the process outlined in Table 6-3 and Equation 6-3. The same situation holds for computer spreadsheet programs.

returns, investors would generally prefer the investment with the higher expected return. To most people, this is common sense—return is "good," risk is "bad," and consequently investors want as much return and as little risk as possible. But how do we choose between two investments if one has the higher expected return but the other the lower standard deviation? To help answer this question, we often use another measure of risk, the **coefficient of variation (CV),** which is the standard deviation divided by the expected return:

$$\text{Coefficient of variation} = \text{CV} = \frac{\sigma}{\hat{k}}. \tag{6-4}$$

The coefficient of variation shows the risk per unit of return, and it provides a more meaningful basis for comparison when the expected returns on two alternatives are not the same. Since U.S. Water and Martin Products have the same expected return, the coefficient of variation is not necessary in this case. The firm with the larger standard deviation, Martin, must have the larger coefficient of variation when the means are equal. In fact, the coefficient of variation for Martin is 65.84/15 = 4.39 and that for U.S. Water is 3.87/15 = 0.26. Thus, Martin is almost 17 times riskier than U.S. Water on the basis of this criterion.

For a case where the coefficient of variation is necessary, consider Projects X and Y in Figure 6-4. These projects have different expected rates of return and different standard deviations. Project X has a 60 percent expected rate of return and a 15 percent standard deviation, while Project Y has an 8 percent expected return but only a 3 percent standard deviation. Is Project X riskier, on a relative basis, because it has the larger standard deviation? If we calculate the coefficients of variation for these two projects, we find that Project X has a coefficient of variation of 15/60 = 0.25, and Project Y has a coefficient of variation of 3/8 = 0.375. Thus, we see that Project Y actually has more risk per unit of return than Project X, in spite of the fact that X's standard deviation is larger. Therefore, even though Project Y has the lower standard deviation, according to the coefficient of variation it is riskier than Project X.

Project Y has the smaller standard deviation, hence the more peaked probability distribution, but it is clear from the graph that the chances of a really low return are higher for Y than for X because X's expected return is so high. Because the coefficient

FIGURE 6-4 Comparison of Probability Distributions and Rates of Return for Projects X and Y

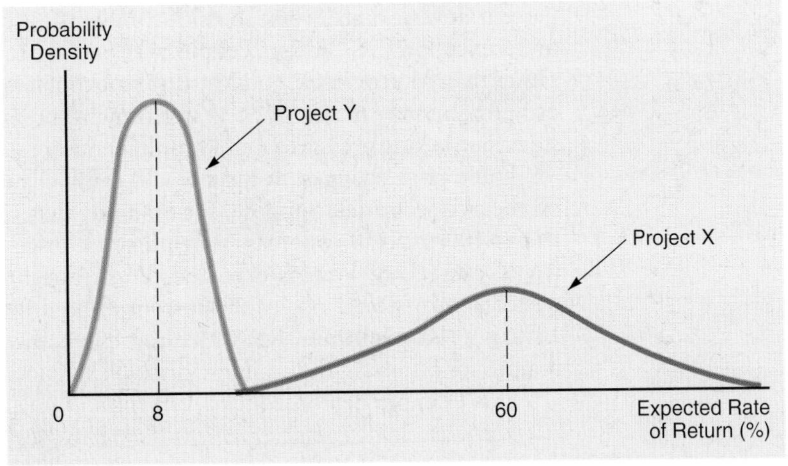

of variation captures the effects of both risk and return, it is a better measure for evaluating risk in situations where investments have substantially different expected returns.

Risk Aversion and Required Returns

Suppose you have worked hard and saved \$1 million, which you now plan to invest. You can buy a 5 percent U.S. Treasury security, and at the end of one year you will have a sure \$1.05 million, which is your original investment plus \$50,000 in interest. Alternatively, you can buy stock in R&D Enterprises. If R&D's research programs are successful, your stock will increase in value to \$2.1 million. However, if the research is a failure, the value of your stock will go to zero, and you will be penniless. You regard R&D's chances of success or failure as being 50-50, so the expected value of the stock investment is 0.5(\$0) + 0.5(\$2,100,000) = \$1,050,000. Subtracting the \$1 million cost of the stock leaves an expected profit of \$50,000, or an expected (but risky) 5 percent rate of return:

$$\text{Expected rate of return} = \frac{\text{Expected ending value} - \text{Cost}}{\text{Cost}}$$
$$= \frac{\$1{,}050{,}000 - \$1{,}000{,}000}{\$1{,}000{,}000}$$
$$= \frac{\$50{,}000}{\$1{,}000{,}000} = 5\%.$$

Thus, you have a choice between a sure \$50,000 profit (representing a 5 percent rate of return) on the Treasury security and a risky expected \$50,000 profit (also representing a 5 percent expected rate of return) on the R&D Enterprises stock. Which one would you choose? *If you choose the less risky investment, you are risk averse. Most investors are indeed risk averse, and certainly the average investor is risk averse with regard to his or her "serious money." Because this is a well-documented fact, we shall assume* **risk aversion** *throughout the remainder of the book.*

What are the implications of risk aversion for security prices and rates of return? The answer is that, other things held constant, the higher a security's risk, the lower its price and the higher its required return. To see how risk aversion affects security prices, look back at Figure 6-2 and consider again U.S. Water and Martin Products stocks. Suppose each stock sold for \$100 per share and each had an expected rate of return of 15 percent. Investors are averse to risk, so under these conditions there would be a general preference for U.S. Water. People with money to invest would bid for U.S. Water rather than Martin stock, and Martin's stockholders would start selling their stock and using the money to buy U.S. Water. Buying pressure would drive up U.S. Water 's stock, and selling pressure would simultaneously cause Martin's price to decline.

These price changes, in turn, would cause changes in the expected rates of return on the two securities. Suppose, for example, that U.S. Water's stock price was bid up from \$100 to \$150, whereas Martin's stock price declined from \$100 to \$75. This would cause U.S. Water's expected return to fall to 10 percent, while Martin's expected return would rise to 20 percent. The difference in returns, 20% − 10% = 10%, is a **risk premium, RP,** which represents the additional compensation investors require for assuming the additional risk of Martin stock.

This example demonstrates a very important principle: *In a market dominated by risk-averse investors, riskier securities must have higher expected returns, as estimated by the marginal investor, than less risky securities. If this situation does not exist, buying and selling in the market will force it to occur.* We will consider the question of how much higher the returns on risky securities must be later in the chapter, after we see how diversification

The Trade-Off between Risk and Return

The table accompanying this box summarizes the historical trade-off between risk and return for different classes of investments from 1926 through 1999. As the table shows, those assets that produced the highest average returns also had the highest standard deviations and the widest ranges of returns. For example, small-company stocks had the highest average annual return, 17.6 percent, but their standard deviation of returns, 33.6 percent, was also the highest. By contrast, U.S. Treasury bills had the lowest standard deviation, 3.2 percent, but they also had the lowest average return, 3.8 percent.

When deciding among alternative investments, one needs to be aware of the trade-off between risk and return. While there is certainly no guarantee that history will repeat itself, returns observed over a long period in the past are a good starting point for estimating investments' returns in the future. Likewise, the standard deviations of past returns provide useful insights into the risks of different investments. For T-bills, however, the standard deviation needs to be interpreted carefully. Note that the table shows that Treasury bills have a positive standard deviation, which indicates some risk. However, if you invested in a one-year Treasury bill and held it for the full year, your realized return would be the same regardless of what happened to the economy that year, and thus the standard deviation of your return would be zero. So, why does the table show a 3.2 percent standard deviation for T-bills, which indicates some risk? In fact, a T-bill is riskless *if you hold it for one year*, but if you invest in a rolling portfolio of one-year T-bills and hold the portfolio for a number of years, your investment income will vary depending on what happens to the level of interest rates in each year. So, while you can be sure of the return you will earn on a T-bill in a given year, you cannot be sure of the return you will earn on a portfolio of T-bills over a period of time.

Distribution of Realized Returns, 1926–1999

	Small-Company Stocks	Large-Company Stocks	Long-Term Corporate Bonds	Long-Term Government Bonds	U.S. Treasury Bills	Inflation
Average return	17.6%	13.3%	5.9%	5.5%	3.8%	3.2%
Standard deviation	33.6	20.1	8.7	9.3	3.2	4.5
Excess return over T-bonds[a]	12.1	7.8	0.4			

[a]The excess return over T-bonds is called the "historical risk premium." If and only if investors expect returns in the future that are similar to returns earned in the past, the excess return will also be the current risk premium that is reflected in security prices.

Source: Based on *Stocks, Bonds, Bills, and Inflation: Valuation Edition 2000 Yearbook* (Chicago: Ibbotson Associates, 2000).

affects the way risk should be measured. Then, in Chapters 9 and 10, we will see how risk-adjusted rates of return affect the prices investors are willing to pay for different securities.

Self-Test Questions

What does "investment risk" mean?

Set up an illustrative probability distribution for an investment.

What is a payoff matrix?

Which of the two stocks graphed in Figure 6-2 is less risky? Why?

How does one calculate the standard deviation?

Which is a better measure of risk if assets have different expected returns: (1) the standard deviation or (2) the coefficient of variation? Why?

Explain the following statement: "Most investors are risk averse."

How does risk aversion affect rates of return?

Risk in a Portfolio Context

In the preceding section, we considered the risk of assets held in isolation. Now we analyze the risk of assets held in portfolios. As we shall see, an asset held as part of a portfolio is less risky than the same asset held in isolation. Accordingly, most financial assets are actually held as parts of portfolios. Banks, pension funds, insurance companies, mutual funds, and other financial institutions are required by law to hold diversified portfolios. Even individual investors—at least those whose security holdings constitute a significant part of their total wealth—generally hold portfolios, not the stock of only one firm. This being the case, from an investor's standpoint the fact that a particular stock goes up or down is not very important; *what is important is the return on his or her portfolio, and the portfolio's risk. Logically, then, the risk and return of an individual security should be analyzed in terms of how that security affects the risk and return of the portfolios in which it is held.*

To illustrate, Pay Up Inc. is a collection agency company that operates nationwide through 37 offices. The company is not well known, its stock is not very liquid, its earnings have fluctuated quite a bit in the past, and it doesn't pay a dividend. All this suggests that Pay Up is risky and that the required rate of return on its stock, k, should be relatively high. However, Pay Up's required rate of return in 2001, and all other years, was quite low in relation to those of most other companies. This indicates that investors regard Pay Up as being a low-risk company in spite of its uncertain profits. The reason for this counterintuitive fact has to do with diversification and its effect on risk. Pay Up's earnings rise during recessions, whereas most other companies' earnings tend to decline when the economy slumps. It's like fire insurance—it pays off when other things go badly. Therefore, adding Pay Up to a portfolio of "normal" stocks tends to stabilize returns on the entire portfolio, thus making the portfolio less risky.

Portfolio Returns

The **expected return on a portfolio, $\hat{k}_p$,** is simply the weighted average of the expected returns on the individual assets in the portfolio, with the weights being the fraction of the total portfolio invested in each asset:

$$\hat{k}_p = w_1\hat{k}_1 + w_2\hat{k}_2 + \cdots + w_n\hat{k}_n \qquad \text{(6-5)}$$

$$= \sum_{i=1}^{n} w_i\hat{k}_i.$$

Here the $\hat{k}_i$'s are the expected returns on the individual stocks, the w_i's are the weights, and there are n stocks in the portfolio. Note (1) that w_i is the fraction of the portfolio's dollar value invested in Stock i (that is, the value of the investment in Stock i divided by the total value of the portfolio) and (2) that the w_i's must sum to 1.0.

Assume that in August 2001, a security analyst estimated that the following returns could be expected on the stocks of four large companies:

	Expected Return, $\hat{k}$
Microsoft	12.0%
General Electric	11.5
Pfizer	10.0
Coca-Cola	9.5

If we formed a \$100,000 portfolio, investing \$25,000 in each stock, the expected portfolio return would be 10.75%:

$$\begin{aligned}\hat{k}_p &= w_1\hat{k}_1 + w_2\hat{k}_2 + w_3\hat{k}_3 + w_4\hat{k}_4\\ &= 0.25(12\%) + 0.25(11.5\%) + 0.25(10\%) + 0.25(9.5\%)\\ &= 10.75\%.\end{aligned}$$

Of course, after the fact and a year later, the actual **realized rates of return, $\bar{k}$**, on the individual stocks—the $\bar{k}_i$, or "k-bar," values—will almost certainly be different from their expected values, so $\bar{k}_p$ will be different from $\hat{k}_p = 10.75\%$. For example, Coca-Cola might double and provide a return of +100%, whereas Microsoft might have a terrible year, fall sharply, and have a return of −75%. Note, though, that those two events would be somewhat offsetting, so the portfolio's return might still be close to its expected return, even though the individual stocks' actual returns were far from their expected returns.

Portfolio Risk

As we just saw, the expected return on a portfolio is simply the weighted average of the expected returns on the individual assets in the portfolio. However, unlike returns, the risk of a portfolio, σ_p, is generally *not* the weighted average of the standard deviations of the individual assets in the portfolio; the portfolio's risk will be *smaller* than the weighted average of the assets' σ's. In fact, it is theoretically possible to combine stocks that are individually quite risky as measured by their standard deviations to form a portfolio that is completely riskless, with $\sigma_p = 0$.

To illustrate the effect of combining assets, consider the situation in Figure 6-5. The bottom section gives data on rates of return for Stocks W and M individually, and also for a portfolio invested 50 percent in each stock. The three top graphs show plots of the data in a time series format, and the lower graphs show the probability distributions of returns, assuming that the future is expected to be like the past. The two stocks would be quite risky if they were held in isolation, but when they are combined to form Portfolio WM, they are not risky at all. (Note: These stocks are called W and M because the graphs of their returns in Figure 6-5 resemble a W and an M.)

The reason Stocks W and M can be combined to form a riskless portfolio is that their returns move countercyclically to each other—when W's returns fall, those of M rise, and vice versa. The tendency of two variables to move together is called **correlation,** and the **correlation coefficient, r,** measures this tendency.[6] In statistical terms, we say that the returns on Stocks W and M are *perfectly negatively correlated,* with r = −1.0.

The opposite of perfect negative correlation, with r = −1.0, is *perfect positive correlation,* with r = +1.0. Returns on two perfectly positively correlated stocks (M and M′) would move up and down together, and a portfolio consisting of two such stocks would be exactly as risky as each individual stock. This point is illustrated in Figure 6-6, where we see that the portfolio's standard deviation is equal to that of the individual stocks. *Thus, diversification does nothing to reduce risk if the portfolio consists of perfectly positively correlated stocks.*

Figures 6-5 and 6-6 demonstrate that when stocks are perfectly negatively correlated (r = −1.0), all risk can be diversified away, but when stocks are perfectly positively correlated (r = +1.0), diversification does no good whatsoever. In reality, most

[6]The *correlation coefficient, r,* can range from +1.0, denoting that the two variables move up and down in perfect synchronization, to −1.0, denoting that the variables always move in exactly opposite directions. A correlation coefficient of zero indicates that the two variables are not related to each other—that is, changes in one variable are *independent* of changes in the other.

It is easy to calculate correlation coefficients with a financial calculator. Simply enter the returns on the two stocks and then press a key labeled "r." For W and M, r = −1.0. *Excel* has a similar function.

FIGURE 6-5 Rate of Return Distributions for Two Perfectly Negatively Correlated Stocks (r = −1.0) and for Portfolio WM

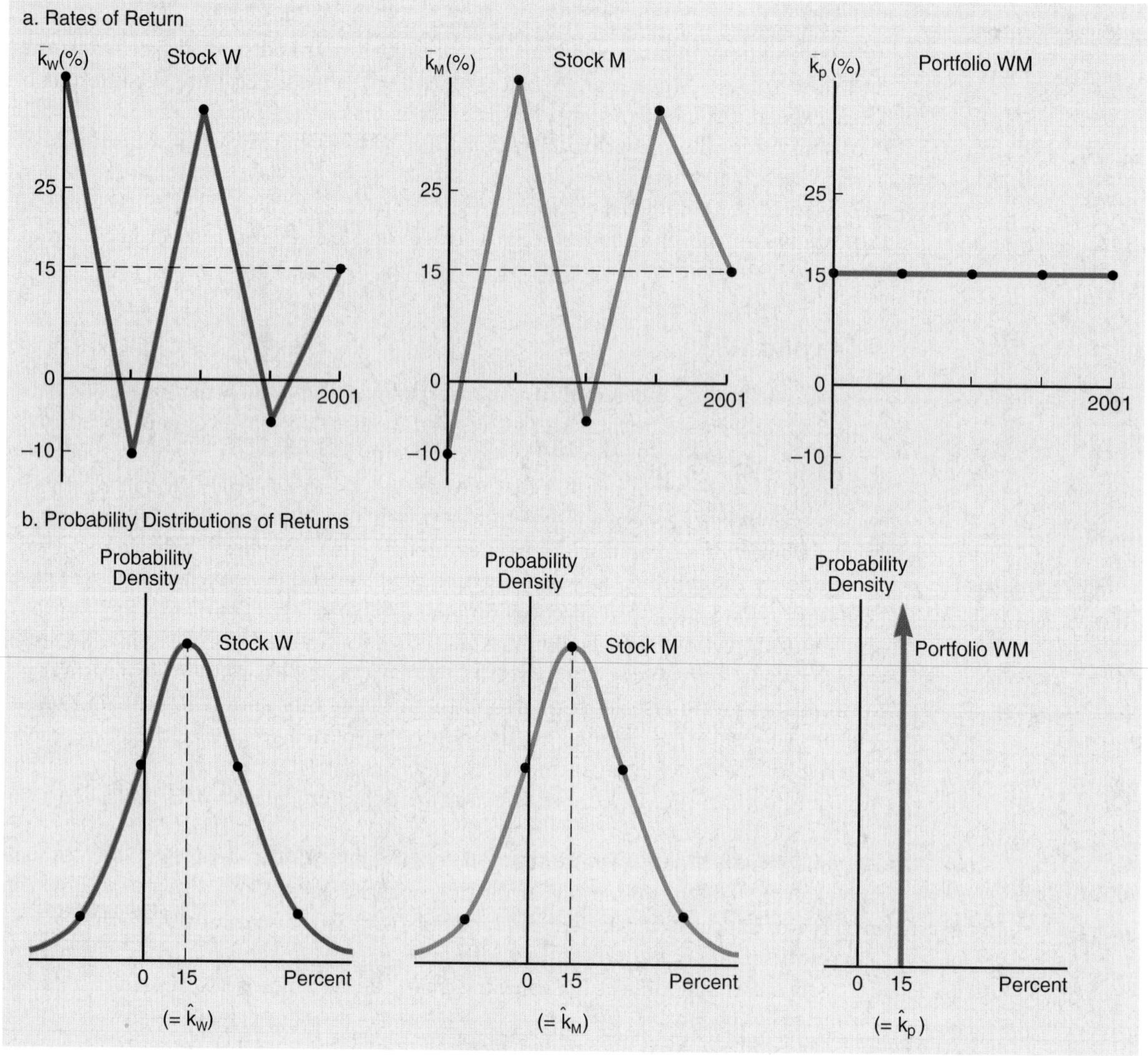

Year	Stock W ($\bar{k}_W$)	Stock M ($\bar{k}_M$)	Portfolio WM ($\bar{k}_p$)
1997	40.0%	(10.0)%	15.0%
1998	(10.0)	40.0	15.0
1999	35.0	(5.0)	15.0
2000	(5.0)	35.0	15.0
2001	15.0	15.0	15.0
Average return	15.0%	15.0%	15.0%
Standard deviation	22.6%	22.6%	0.0%

FIGURE 6-6 Rate of Return Distributions for Two Perfectly Positively Correlated Stocks (r = +1.0) and for Portfolio MM′

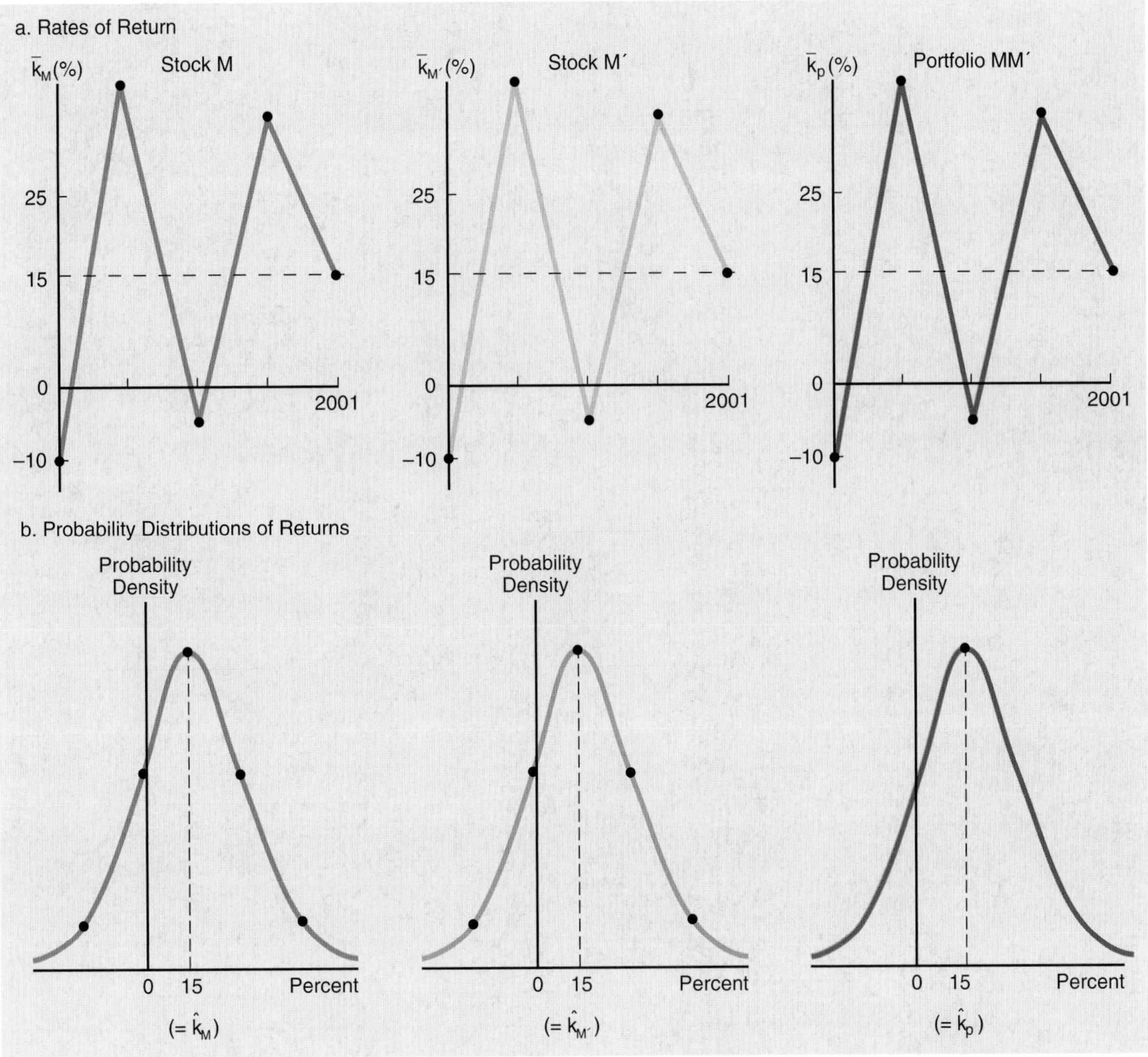

Year	Stock M ($\bar{k}_M$)	Stock M′ ($\bar{k}_{M'}$)	Portfolio MM′ ($\bar{k}_p$)
1997	(10.0%)	(10.0%)	(10.0%)
1998	40.0	40.0	40.0
1999	(5.0)	(5.0)	(5.0)
2000	35.0	35.0	35.0
2001	15.0	15.0	15.0
Average return	15.0%	15.0%	15.0%
Standard deviation	22.6%	22.6%	22.6%

FIGURE 6-7 Rate of Return Distributions for Two Partially Correlated Stocks (r = +0.67) and for Portfolio WY

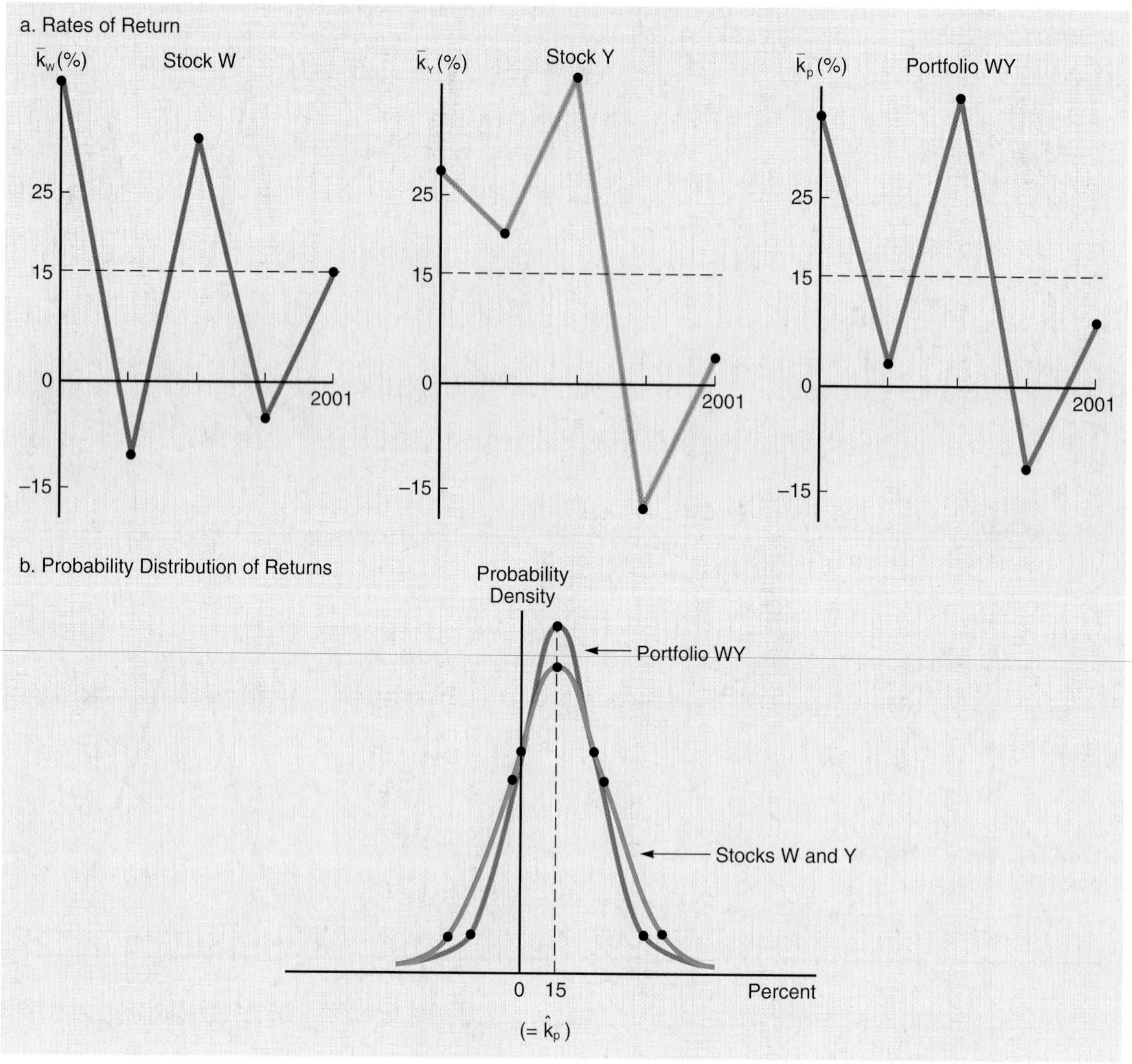

Year	Stock W ($\bar{k}_W$)	Stock Y ($\bar{k}_Y$)	Portfolio WY ($\bar{k}_p$)
1997	40.0%	28.0%	34.0%
1998	(10.0)	20.0	5.0
1999	35.0	41.0	38.0
2000	(5.0)	(17.0)	(11.0)
2001	15.0	3.0	9.0
Average return	15.0%	15.0%	15.0%
Standard deviation	22.6%	22.6%	20.6%

stocks are positively correlated, but not perfectly so. On average, the correlation coefficient for the returns on two randomly selected stocks would be about +0.6, and for most pairs of stocks, r would lie in the range of +0.5 to +0.7. *Under such conditions, combining stocks into portfolios reduces risk but does not eliminate it completely.* Figure 6-7 illustrates this point with two stocks whose correlation coefficient is r = +0.67. The portfolio's average return is 15 percent, which is exactly the same as the average return for each of the two stocks, but its standard deviation is 20.6 percent, which is less than the standard deviation of either stock. Thus, the portfolio's risk is *not* an average of the risks of its individual stocks—diversification has reduced, but not eliminated, risk.

From these two-stock portfolio examples, we have seen that in one extreme case (r = −1.0), risk can be completely eliminated, while in the other extreme case (r = +1.0), diversification does nothing to limit risk. The real world lies between these extremes, so in general combining two stocks into a portfolio reduces, but does not eliminate, the risk inherent in the individual stocks.

What would happen if we included more than two stocks in the portfolio? *As a rule, the risk of a portfolio will decline as the number of stocks in the portfolio increases.* If we added enough partially correlated stocks, could we completely eliminate risk? In general, the answer is no, but the extent to which adding stocks to a portfolio reduces its risk depends on the *degree of correlation* among the stocks: The smaller the positive correlation coefficients, the lower the risk in a large portfolio. If we could find a set of stocks whose correlations were −1.0, all risk could be eliminated. *In the real world, where the correlations among the individual stocks are generally positive but less than +1.0, some, but not all, risk can be eliminated.*

To test your understanding, would you expect to find higher correlations between the returns on two companies in the same or in different industries? For example, would the correlation of returns on Ford's and General Motors' stocks be higher, or would the correlation coefficient be higher between either Ford or GM and AT&T, and how would those correlations affect the risk of portfolios containing them?

Answer: Ford's and GM's returns have a correlation coefficient of about 0.9 with one another because both are affected by auto sales, but their correlation is only about 0.6 with AT&T.

Implications: A two-stock portfolio consisting of Ford and GM would be less well diversified than a two-stock portfolio consisting of Ford or GM, plus AT&T. Thus, to minimize risk, portfolios should be diversified across industries.

Before leaving this section we should issue a warning—in the real world, it is *impossible* to find stocks like W and M, whose returns are expected to be perfectly negatively correlated. *Therefore, it is impossible to form completely riskless stock portfolios.* Diversification can reduce risk, but it cannot eliminate it. The real world is closer to the situation depicted in Figure 6-7.

Diversifiable Risk versus Market Risk

As noted above, it is difficult if not impossible to find stocks whose expected returns are negatively correlated—most stocks tend to do well when the national economy is strong and badly when it is weak.[7] Thus, even very large portfolios end up with a

[7]It is not too hard to find a few stocks that happened to have risen because of a particular set of circumstances in the past while most other stocks were declining, but it is much harder to find stocks that could logically be *expected* to go up in the future when other stocks are falling.

However, note that derivative securities (options) can be created with correlations that are close to −1.0 with stocks. Such derivatives can be bought and used as "portfolio insurance." We discuss this further in Chapter 24.

substantial amount of risk, but not as much risk as if all the money were invested in only one stock.

To see more precisely how portfolio size affects portfolio risk, consider Figure 6-8, which shows how portfolio risk is affected by forming larger and larger portfolios of randomly selected New York Stock Exchange (NYSE) stocks. Standard deviations are plotted for an average one-stock portfolio, a two-stock portfolio, and so on, up to a portfolio consisting of all 2,000-plus common stocks that were listed on the NYSE at the time the data were graphed. The graph illustrates that, in general, the riskiness of a portfolio consisting of large-company stocks tends to decline and to approach some limit as the size of the portfolio increases. According to data accumulated in recent years, σ_1, the standard deviation of a one-stock portfolio (or an average stock), is approximately 35 percent. A portfolio consisting of all stocks, which is called the **market portfolio,** would have a standard deviation, σ_M, of about 20.1 percent, which is shown as the horizontal dashed line in Figure 6-8.

Thus, almost half of the riskiness inherent in an average individual stock can be eliminated if the stock is held in a reasonably well-diversified portfolio, which is one containing 40 or more stocks in a number of different industries. Some risk always remains, however, so it is virtually impossible to diversify away the effects of broad stock market movements that affect almost all stocks.

FIGURE 6-8 Effects of Portfolio Size on Portfolio Risk for Average Stocks

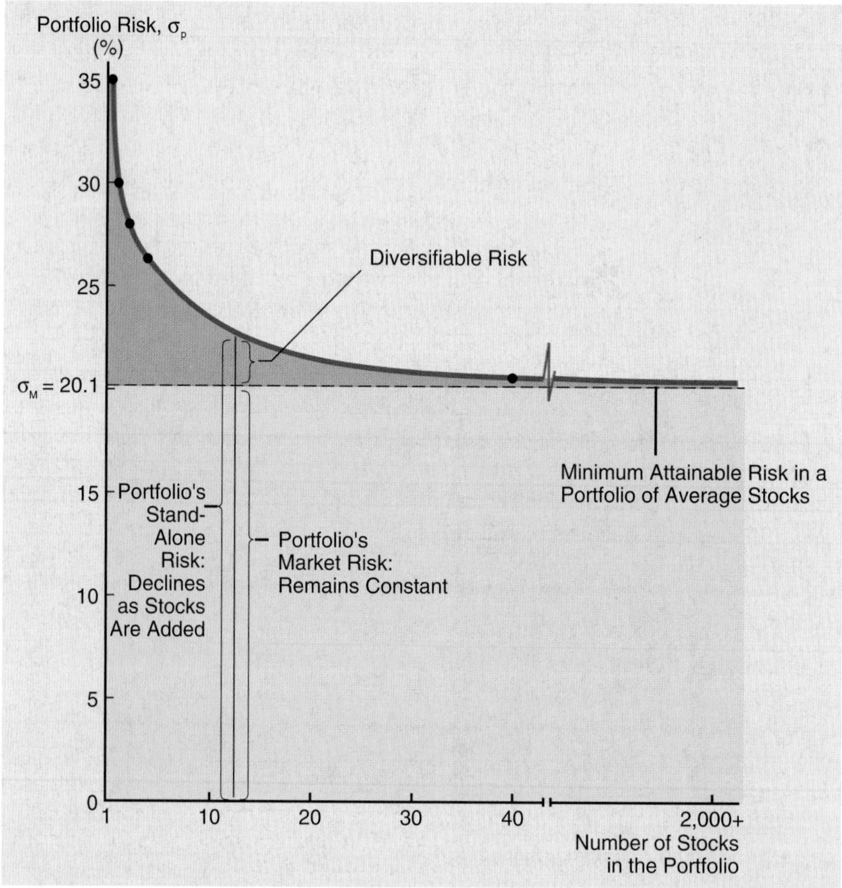

The part of a stock's risk that *can* be eliminated is called *diversifiable risk*, while the part that *cannot* be eliminated is called *market risk*.[8] The fact that a large part of the risk of any individual stock can be eliminated is vitally important, because rational investors *will* eliminate it and thus render it irrelevant.

Diversifiable risk is caused by such random events as lawsuits, strikes, successful and unsuccessful marketing programs, winning or losing a major contract, and other events that are unique to a particular firm. Because these events are random, their effects on a portfolio can be eliminated by diversification—bad events in one firm will be offset by good events in another. **Market risk,** on the other hand, stems from factors that systematically affect most firms: war, inflation, recessions, and high interest rates. Since most stocks are negatively affected by these factors, market risk cannot be eliminated by diversification.

We know that investors demand a premium for bearing risk; that is, the higher the risk of a security, the higher its expected return must be to induce investors to buy (or to hold) it. However, if investors are primarily concerned with the risk of their *portfolios* rather than the risk of the individual securities in the portfolio, how should the risk of an individual stock be measured? One answer is provided by the **Capital Asset Pricing Model (CAPM),** an important tool used to analyze the relationship between risk and rates of return.[9] The primary conclusion of the CAPM is this: *The relevant risk of an individual stock is its contribution to the risk of a well-diversified portfolio.* In other words, the risk of General Electric's stock to a doctor who has a portfolio of 40 stocks or to a trust officer managing a 150-stock portfolio is the contribution the GE stock makes to the portfolio's riskiness. The stock might be quite risky if held by itself, but if half of its risk can be eliminated by diversification, then its **relevant risk,** which is its *contribution to the portfolio's risk*, is much smaller than its stand-alone risk.

A simple example will help make this point clear. Suppose you are offered the chance to flip a coin once. If a head comes up, you win \$20,000, but if a tail comes up, you lose \$16,000. This is a good bet—the expected return is 0.5(\$20,000) + 0.5(−\$16,000) = \$2,000. However, it is a highly risky proposition, because you have a 50 percent chance of losing \$16,000. Thus, you might well refuse to make the bet. Alternatively, suppose you were offered the chance to flip a coin 100 times, and you would win \$200 for each head but lose \$160 for each tail. It is theoretically possible that you would flip all heads and win \$20,000, and it is also theoretically possible that you would flip all tails and lose \$16,000, but the chances are very high that you would actually flip about 50 heads and about 50 tails, winning a net of about \$2,000. Although each individual flip is a risky bet, collectively you have a low-risk proposition because most of the risk has been diversified away. This is the idea behind holding portfolios of stocks rather than just one stock, except that with stocks all of the risk cannot be eliminated by diversification—those risks related to broad, systematic changes in the stock market will remain.

Are all stocks equally risky in the sense that adding them to a well-diversified portfolio would have the same effect on the portfolio's riskiness? The answer is no. Different stocks will affect the portfolio differently, so different securities have different

---

[8]Diversifiable risk is also known as *company-specific*, or *unsystematic*, risk. Market risk is also known as *nondiversifiable*, or *systematic*, or *beta*, risk; it is the risk that remains after diversification.

[9]Indeed, the 1990 Nobel Prize was awarded to the developers of the CAPM, Professors Harry Markowitz and William F. Sharpe. The CAPM is a relatively complex subject, and only its basic elements are presented in this chapter. For a more detailed discussion, see Chapter 7.

The basic concepts of the CAPM were developed specifically for common stocks, and, therefore, the theory is examined first in this context. However, it has become common practice to extend CAPM concepts to capital budgeting and to speak of firms having "portfolios of tangible assets and projects." Capital budgeting is discussed in Chapters 13, 14, and 15.

The Benefits of Diversifying Overseas

The size of the global stock market has grown steadily over the last several decades, and it passed the $15 trillion mark during 1995. U.S. stocks account for approximately 41 percent of this total, whereas the Japanese and European markets constitute roughly 25 and 26 percent, respectively. The rest of the world makes up the remaining 8 percent. Although the U.S. equity market has long been the world's biggest, its share of the world total has decreased over time.

The expanding universe of securities available internationally suggests the possibility of achieving a better risk-return trade-off than could be obtained by investing solely in U.S. securities. So, investing overseas might lower risk and simultaneously increase expected returns. The potential benefits of diversification are due to the facts that the correlation between the returns on U.S. and international securities is fairly low, and returns in developing nations are often quite high.

Figure 6-8, presented earlier, demonstrated that an investor can significantly reduce the risk of his or her portfolio by holding a large number of stocks. The figure accompanying this box suggests that investors may be able to reduce risk even further by holding a large portfolio of stocks from all around the world, given the fact that the returns of domestic and international stocks are not perfectly correlated.

Despite the apparent benefits from investing overseas, the typical U.S. investor still dedicates less than 10 percent of his or her portfolio to foreign stocks—even though foreign stocks represent roughly 60 percent of the worldwide equity market. Researchers and practitioners alike have struggled to understand this reluctance to invest overseas. One explanation is that investors prefer domestic stocks because they have lower transaction costs. However, this explanation is not completely convincing, given that recent studies have found that investors buy and sell their overseas stocks more frequently than they trade their domestic stocks. Other explanations for the domestic bias focus on the additional risks from investing overseas (for example, exchange rate risk) or suggest that the typical U.S. investor is uninformed about international investments and/or views international investments as being extremely risky or uncertain. More recently, other analysts have argued that as world capital markets have become more integrated, the correlation of returns between different countries has increased, and hence the benefits from international diversification have declined. A third explanation is that U.S. corporations are themselves investing more internationally, hence U.S. investors are de facto obtaining international diversification.

Whatever the reason for the general reluctance to hold international assets, it is a safe bet that in the years ahead U.S. investors will shift more and more of their assets to overseas investments.

Source: Kenneth Kasa, "Measuring the Gains from International Portfolio Diversification," *Federal Reserve Bank of San Francisco Weekly Letter*, Number 94-14, April 8, 1994.

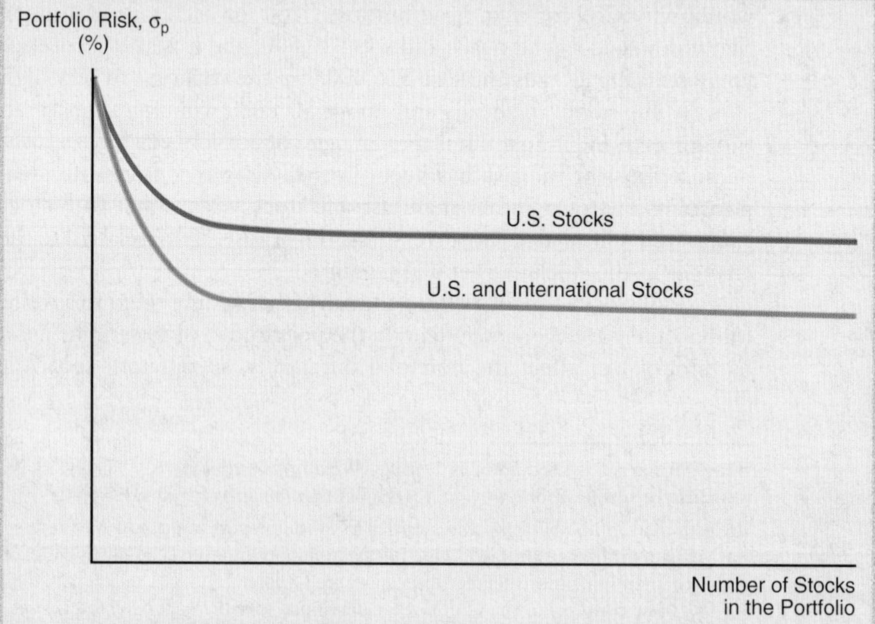

degrees of relevant risk. How can the relevant risk of an individual stock be measured? As we have seen, all risk except that related to broad market movements can, and presumably will, be diversified away. After all, why accept risk that can be easily eliminated? *The risk that remains after diversifying is market risk, or the risk that is inherent in the market, and it can be measured by the degree to which a given stock tends to move up or down with the market.* In the next section, we develop a measure of a stock's market risk, and then, in a later section, we introduce an equation for determining the required rate of return on a stock, given its market risk.

The Concept of Beta

As we noted above, the primary conclusion of the CAPM is that the relevant risk of an individual stock is the amount of risk the stock contributes to a well-diversified portfolio. The benchmark for a well-diversified stock portfolio is the market portfolio, which is a portfolio containing all stocks. Therefore, the relevant risk of an individual stock, which is called its **beta coefficient,** is defined under the CAPM as the amount of risk that the stock contributes to the market portfolio. In CAPM terminology, r_{iM} is the correlation between the i'th stock's expected return and the expected return on the market, σ_i is the standard deviation of the i'th stock's expected return, and σ_M is the standard deviation of the market's expected return. In the literature on the CAPM, it is proved that the beta coefficient of the i'th stock, denoted by b_i, can be found as follows:

$$b_i = \left(\frac{\sigma_i}{\sigma_M}\right) r_{iM}. \qquad \textbf{(6-6)}$$

This tells us that a stock with a high standard deviation, σ_i, will tend to have a high beta. This makes sense, because if all other things are equal, a stock with high stand-alone risk will contribute a lot of risk to the portfolio. Note too that a stock with a high correlation with the market, r_{iM}, will also have a large beta, hence be risky. This also makes sense, because a high correlation means that diversification is not helping much, hence the stock contributes a lot of risk to the portfolio.

Calculators and spreadsheets use Equation 6-6 to calculate beta, but there is another way. Suppose you plotted the stock's returns on the y-axis of a graph and the market portfolio's returns on the x-axis, as shown in Figure 6-9. The tendency of a stock to move up and down with the market is reflected in its beta coefficient. An *average-risk stock* is *defined* as one that tends to move up and down in step with the general market as measured by some index such as the Dow Jones Industrials, the S&P 500, or the New York Stock Exchange Index. Such a stock will, *by definition,* be assigned a beta, b, of 1.0, which indicates that, in general, if the market moves up by 10 percent, the stock will also move up by 10 percent, while if the market falls by 10 percent, the stock will likewise fall by 10 percent. A portfolio of such b = 1.0 stocks will move up and down with the broad market indexes, and it will be just as risky as the indexes. If b = 0.5, the stock is only half as volatile as the market—it will rise and fall only half as much—and a portfolio of such stocks will be half as risky as a portfolio of b = 1.0 stocks. On the other hand, if b = 2.0, the stock is twice as volatile as an average stock, so a portfolio of such stocks will be twice as risky as an average portfolio. The value of such a portfolio could double—or halve—in a short time, and if you held such a portfolio, you could quickly go from millionaire to pauper.

Figure 6-9 graphs the relative volatility of three stocks. The data below the graph assume that in 1999 the "market," defined as a portfolio consisting of all stocks, had a total return (dividend yield plus capital gains yield) of $\bar{k}_M = 10\%$, and Stocks H, A, and L (for High, Average, and Low risk) also all had returns of 10 percent. In 2000, the

FIGURE 6-9 Relative Volatility of Stocks H, A, and L

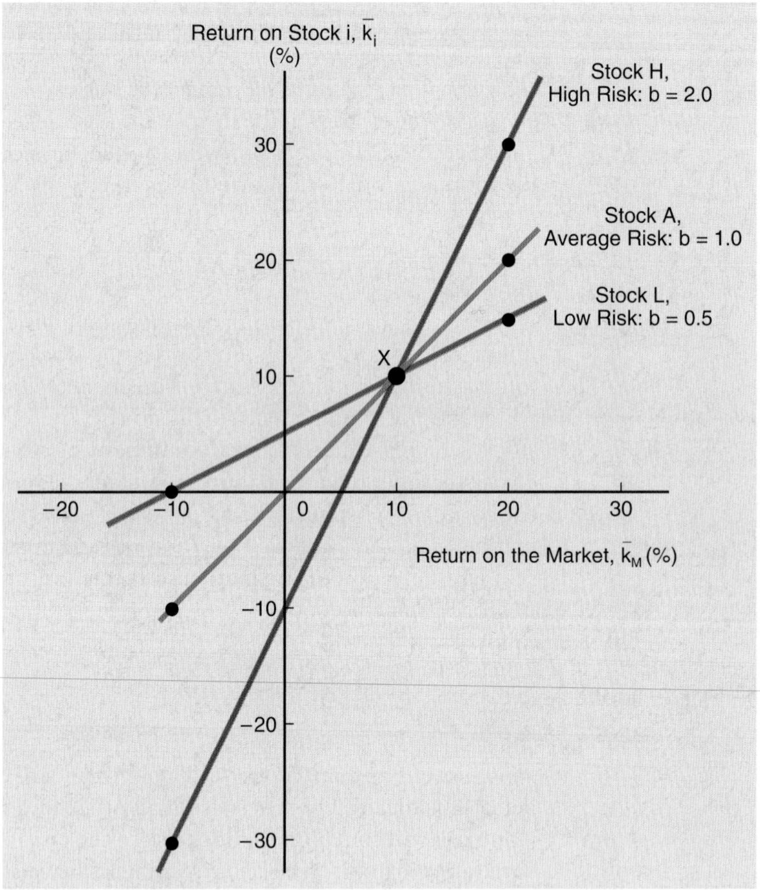

Year	$\bar{k}_H$	$\bar{k}_A$	$\bar{k}_L$	$\bar{k}_M$
1999	10%	10%	10%	10%
2000	30	20	15	20
2001	(30)	(10)	0	(10)

NOTE: These three stocks plot exactly on their regression lines. This indicates that they are exposed only to market risk. Mutual funds that concentrate on stocks with betas of 2, 1, and 0.5 would have patterns similar to those shown in the graph.

market went up sharply, and the return on the market portfolio was $\bar{k}_M = 20\%$. Returns on the three stocks also went up: H soared to 30 percent; A went up to 20 percent, the same as the market; and L only went up to 15 percent. Now suppose the market dropped in 2001, and the market return was $\bar{k}_M = -10\%$. The three stocks' returns also fell, H plunging to −30 percent, A falling to −10 percent, and L going down to $\bar{k}_L = 0\%$. Thus, the three stocks all moved in the same direction as the market, but H was by far the most volatile; A was just as volatile as the market; and L was less volatile.

Beta measures a stock's volatility relative to an average stock, which by definition has b = 1.0. As we noted above, a stock's beta can be calculated by plotting a line like those in Figure 6-9. The slopes of the lines show how each stock moves in response to a movement in the general market—*indeed, the slope coefficient of such a "regression line" is defined as a beta coefficient.* (Procedures for actually calculating betas are described later in this chapter.) Betas for literally thousands of companies are calculated and published by

TABLE 6-4 Illustrative List of Beta Coefficients

Stock	Beta
Merrill Lynch	1.85
America Online	1.60
General Electric	1.25
Microsoft Corp.	1.00
Coca-Cola	1.00
Procter & Gamble	0.85
Energen Corp.	0.80
Heinz	0.70
Empire District Electric	0.45

Source: *Value Line*, September 2000, CD-ROM.

Merrill Lynch, Value Line, Yahoo!, and numerous other organizations. The beta coefficients of some well-known companies are shown in Table 6-4. Most stocks have betas in the range of 0.50 to 1.50, and the average for all stocks is 1.0 by definition.

Theoretically, it is possible for a stock to have a negative beta. In this case, the stock's returns would tend to rise whenever the returns on other stocks fall. In practice, we have never seen a stock with a negative beta. For example, *Value Line* follows more than 1,700 stocks, and not one has a negative beta. Keep in mind, though, that a stock in a given year may move counter to the overall market, even though the stock's beta is positive. If a stock has a positive beta, we would *expect* its return to increase whenever the overall stock market rises. However, company-specific factors may cause the stock's realized return to decline, even though the market's return is positive.

If a stock whose beta is greater than 1.0 is added to a $b = 1.0$ portfolio, then the portfolio's beta, and consequently its risk, will increase. Conversely, if a stock whose beta is less than 1.0 is added to a $b = 1.0$ portfolio, the portfolio's beta and risk will decline. *Thus, since a stock's beta measures its contribution to the risk of a portfolio, beta is the theoretically correct measure of the stock's risk.*

The preceding analysis of risk in a portfolio context is part of the Capital Asset Pricing Model (CAPM), and we can summarize our discussion to this point as follows:

1. A stock's risk consists of two components, market risk and diversifiable risk.
2. Diversifiable risk can be eliminated by diversification, and most investors do indeed diversify, either by holding large portfolios or by purchasing shares in a mutual fund. We are left, then, with market risk, which is caused by general movements in the stock market and which reflects the fact that most stocks are systematically affected by events like war, recessions, and inflation. Market risk is the only relevant risk to a rational, diversified investor because such an investor would eliminate diversifiable risk.
3. Investors must be compensated for bearing risk—the greater the risk of a stock, the higher its required return. However, compensation is required only for risk that cannot be eliminated by diversification. If risk premiums existed on stocks due to diversifiable risk, well-diversified investors would start buying those securities (which would not be especially risky to such investors) and bidding up their prices, and the stocks' final (equilibrium) expected returns would reflect only nondiversifiable market risk.

   If this point is not clear, an example may help clarify it. Suppose half of Stock A's risk is market risk (it occurs because Stock A moves up and down with the market), while the other half of A's risk is diversifiable. You hold only Stock A, so you are exposed to all of its risk. As compensation for bearing so much risk, you want a risk premium of 8 percent over the 10 percent T-bond rate. Thus, your required return is $k_A = 10\% + 8\% = 18\%$. But suppose other investors, including your professor, are well diversified; they also hold Stock A, but they have eliminated its diversifiable risk and thus are exposed to only half as much risk as you. Therefore, their risk premium will be only half as large as yours, and their required rate of return will be $k_A = 10\% + 4\% = 14\%$.

If the stock were yielding more than 14 percent in the market, diversified investors, including your professor, would buy it. If it were yielding 18 percent, you would be willing to buy it, but well-diversified investors would bid its price up and drive its yield down, hence you could not buy it at a price low enough to provide you with an 18 percent return. In the end, you would have to accept a 14 percent return or else keep your money in the bank. Thus, risk premiums in a market populated by rational, diversified investors reflect only market risk.

4. The market risk of a stock is measured by its beta coefficient, which is an index of the stock's relative volatility. Some benchmark betas follow:

$b = 0.5$: Stock is only half as volatile, or risky, as an average stock.
$b = 1.0$: Stock is of average risk.
$b = 2.0$: Stock is twice as risky as an average stock.

5. A portfolio consisting of low-beta securities will itself have a low beta, because the beta of a portfolio is a weighted average of its individual securities' betas:

$$b_p = w_1b_1 + w_2b_2 + \cdots + w_nb_n = \sum_{i=1}^{n} w_ib_i. \quad \text{(6-7)}$$

Here b_p is the beta of the portfolio, and it shows how volatile the portfolio is in relation to the market; w_i is the fraction of the portfolio invested in the *i*th stock; and b_i is the beta coefficient of the *i*th stock. For example, if an investor holds a \$100,000 portfolio consisting of \$33,333.33 invested in each of three stocks, and if each of the stocks has a beta of 0.7, then the portfolio's beta will be $b_p = 0.7$:

$$b_p = 0.3333(0.7) + 0.3333(0.7) + 0.3333(0.7) = 0.7.$$

Such a portfolio will be less risky than the market, so it should experience relatively narrow price swings and have relatively small rate-of-return fluctuations. In terms of Figure 6-9, the slope of its regression line would be 0.7, which is less than that for a portfolio of average stocks.

Now suppose one of the existing stocks is sold and replaced by a stock with $b_i = 2.0$. This action will increase the beta of the portfolio from $b_{p1} = 0.7$ to $b_{p2} = 1.13$:

$$b_{p2} = 0.3333(0.7) + 0.3333(0.7) + 0.3333(2.0) = 1.13.$$

Had a stock with $b_i = 0.2$ been added, the portfolio beta would have declined from 0.7 to 0.53. Adding a low-beta stock, therefore, would reduce the risk of the portfolio. Consequently, adding new stocks to a portfolio can change the riskiness of that portfolio.

6. *Since a stock's beta coefficient determines how the stock affects the risk of a diversified portfolio, beta is the most relevant measure of any stock's risk.*

Self-Test Questions

Explain the following statement: "An asset held as part of a portfolio is generally less risky than the same asset held in isolation."

What is meant by *perfect positive correlation, perfect negative correlation,* and *zero correlation?*

In general, can the risk of a portfolio be reduced to zero by increasing the number of stocks in the portfolio? Explain.

What is an average-risk stock? What will be its beta?

Why is beta the theoretically correct measure of a stock's risk?

If you plotted the returns on a particular stock versus those on the Dow Jones Index over the past five years, what would the slope of the regression line you obtained indicate about the stock's market risk?

Calculating Beta Coefficients

The CAPM is an *ex ante* model, which means that all of the variables represent before-the-fact, *expected* values. In particular, the beta coefficient used by investors should reflect the expected volatility of a given stock's return versus the return on the market during some *future* period. However, people generally calculate betas using data from some *past* period, and then assume that the stock's relative volatility will be the same in the future as it was in the past.

To illustrate how betas are calculated, consider Figure 6-10. The data at the bottom of the figure show the historical realized returns for Stock J and for the market over the last five years. The data points have been plotted on the scatter diagram, and a regression line has been drawn. If all the data points had fallen on a straight line, as they did in Figure 6-9, it would be easy to draw an accurate line. If they do not, as in Figure 6-10, then you must fit the line either "by eye" as an approximation, with a calculator, or with a computer.

Recall what the term *regression line,* or *regression equation,* means: The equation $Y = a + bX + e$ is the standard form of a simple linear regression. It states that the dependent variable, Y, is equal to a constant, a, plus b times X, where b is the slope coefficient and X is the independent variable, plus an error term, e. Thus, the rate of return on the stock during a given time period (Y) depends on what happens to the general stock market, which is measured by $X = \bar{k}_M$.

Once the data have been plotted and the regression line has been drawn on graph paper, we can estimate its intercept and slope, the a and b values in $Y = a + bX$. The intercept, a, is simply the point where the line cuts the vertical axis. The slope coefficient, b, can be estimated by the "rise-over-run" method. This involves calculating the amount by which $\bar{k}_J$ increases for a given increase in $\bar{k}_M$. For example, we observe in Figure 6-10 that $\bar{k}_J$ increases from −8.9 to +7.1 percent (the rise) when $\bar{k}_M$ increases from 0 to 10.0 percent (the run). Thus, b, the beta coefficient, can be measured as follows:

$$b = \text{Beta} = \frac{\text{Rise}}{\text{Run}} = \frac{\Delta Y}{\Delta X} = \frac{7.1 - (-8.9)}{10.0 - 0.0} = \frac{16.0}{10.0} = 1.6.$$

Note that rise over run is a ratio, and it would be the same if measured using any two arbitrarily selected points on the line.

The regression line equation enables us to predict a rate of return for Stock J, given a value of $\bar{k}_M$. For example, if $\bar{k}_M = 15\%$, we would predict $\bar{k}_J = -8.9\% + 1.6(15\%) = 15.1\%$. However, the actual return would probably differ from the predicted return. This deviation is the error term, e_J, for the year, and it varies randomly from year to year depending on company-specific factors. Note, though,

FIGURE 6-10 Calculating Beta Coefficients

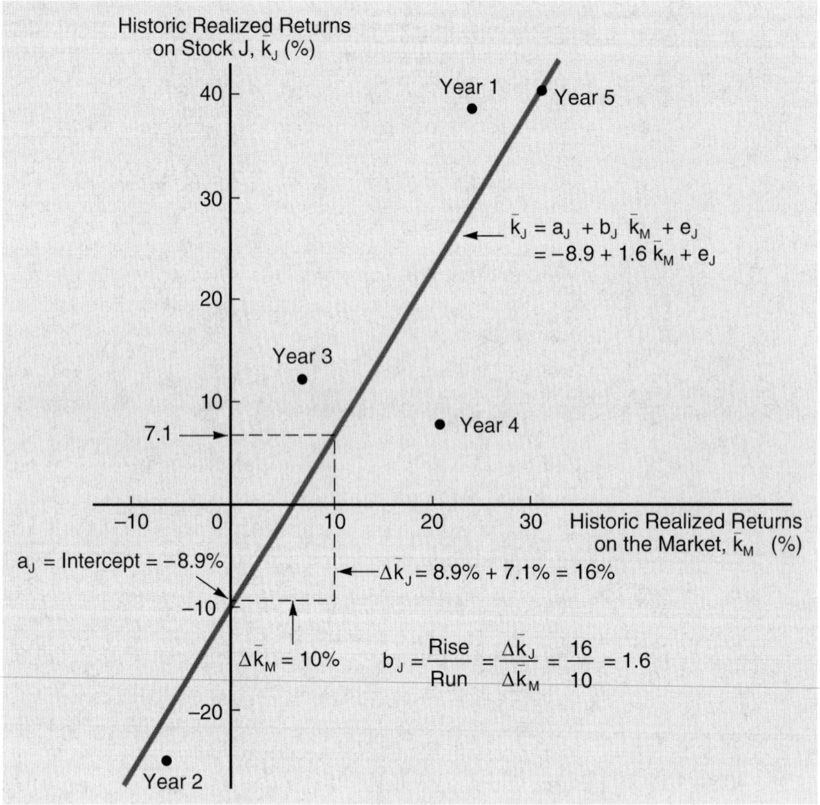

Year	Market ($\bar{k}_M$)	Stock J ($\bar{k}_J$)
1	23.8%	38.6%
2	(7.2)	(24.7)
3	6.6	12.3
4	20.5	8.2
5	30.6	40.1
Average $\bar{k}$	14.9%	14.9%
$\sigma_{\bar{k}}$	15.1%	26.5%

that the higher the correlation coefficient, the closer the points lie to the regression line, and the smaller the errors.

In actual practice, one would use the *least squares method* for finding the regression coefficients a and b. This procedure minimizes the squared values of the error terms, and it is discussed in statistics courses. However, the least squares value of beta can be obtained quite easily with a financial calculator.

Although it is possible to calculate beta coefficients with a calculator, they are usually calculated with a computer, either with a statistical software program or a spreadsheet program. The file ***Ch 06 Tool Kit.xls*** on your textbook's CD-ROM shows an application in which the beta coefficient for Wal-Mart Stores is calculated using *Excel*'s regression function.

The first step in a regression analysis is compiling the data. Most analysts use four to five years of monthly data, although some use 52 weeks of weekly data. We decided to use four years of monthly data, so we began by downloading 48 months of stock prices and dividend payments for Wal-Mart from the finance section of the Yahoo! web site. We decided to use the Wilshire 5000 Index as the market portfolio because this index contains most actively traded stocks. Table 6-5 shows a portion of this data; the full data set is in the file ***Ch 06 Tool Kit.xls*** on your textbook's CD-ROM.

The second step is to convert the stock prices and dividends to rates of return. For example, to find the March 2000 return, we add the March 2000 price of \$56.500 to the March 2000 dividend of \$0.06 to get the total ending dollar wealth for March 2000. We then subtract the starting investment for March 2000, which is the ending stock price of February 2000 of \$48.689. This results in the monthly value change for the stock, which we divide by the starting investment of \$48.689 to obtain the March 2000 return: 16.2% = 0.162 = (\$56.500 + \$0.06 − \$48.689)/\$48.689. We also find the percent change of the Wilshire 5000 Index level, and use this as the market return. For example, in March 2000 this is: 7.5% = 0.075 = (14,296.2 − 13,294.6)/13,294.6.

As Table 6-5 shows, Wal-Mart stock had an average annual return of 45.3 percent during this four-year period, while the market had an average annual return of 19.8 percent. As we noted before, it is usually unreasonable to think that the future expected return for a stock will equal its average historical return over a relatively short period, such as four years. However, we might well expect past volatility to be a reasonable estimate of future volatility, at least during the next couple of years. Note that the standard deviation for Wal-Mart's return during this period was 32.3 percent versus 16.6 percent for the market. Thus, the market's volatility is about half that of Wal-Mart. This is what we would expect, since the market is a well-diversified portfolio, in which much risk has been diversified away. The correlation between Wal-Mart's stock returns and the market returns is about 54 percent, which is close to the correlation for an average stock.

Check out **http://finance.Yahoo.com** for Wal-Mart using its ticker symbol of WMT. You can also download data for the Wilshire 5000 index using its symbol of ^WIL5.

TABLE 6-5 Stock Return Data for Wal-Mart Stores

Date	Market Level (Wilshire 5000 Index)	Market Return	Wal-Mart Stock Price[a]	Wal-Mart Dividend	Wal-Mart Return
April 2000	13,541.7	−5.3%	55.375	0	−2.0%
March 2000	14,296.2	7.5	56.500	0.06	16.2
February 2000	13,294.6	0.5	48.689	0	−11.0
January 2000	13,230.6	−4.2	54.681	0	−20.8
December 1999	13,812.7	5.6	69.038	0.05	20.1
November 1999	13,078.0	5.0	57.510	0	2.3
. . .	. . .	. . .	. . .	. . .	. . .
. . .	. . .	. . .	. . .	. . .	. . .
. . .	. . .	. . .	. . .	. . .	. . .
July 1996	6,247.0	−5.5	11.735	0	−5.4
June 1996	6,612.8	−1.0	12.407	0.025	−1.5
May 1996	6,677.4	2.5	12.626	0	8.4
April 1996	6,514.8	NA	11.650	0	NA
Average return (annual)		19.8%			45.3%
Standard deviation (annual)		16.6%			32.3%
Correlation between Wal-Mart and the market return		54%			

[a]Wal-Mart's stock prices are adjusted for a 2 for 1 stock split that occurred in April 1999.

Figure 6-11 shows a plot of Wal-Mart's stock returns against the market returns. As you will notice if you look in the file ***Ch 06 Tool Kit.xls***, we used the *Excel* Chart feature to add a trend line and to display the equation and R^2 value on the chart itself. Alternatively, we could have used the *Excel* regression analysis feature, which would have provided more detailed data.

Figure 6-11 shows that Wal-Mart's beta is about 1.05, as shown by the slope coefficient in the regression equation displayed on the chart. This means that Wal-Mart's beta is about equal to the 1.0 average beta. Thus, Wal-Mart moves up and down by roughly the same percent as the market. Note, however, that the points are not clustered very tightly around the regression line. Sometimes Wal-Mart does much better than the market, while at other times it does much worse. The R^2 value shown in the chart measures the degree of dispersion about the regression line. Statistically speaking, it measures the percentage of the variance that is explained by the regression equation. An R^2 of 1.0 indicates that all points lie exactly on the line, hence that all of the variance of the y-variable is explained by the x-variable. Wal-Mart's R^2 is about 0.29, which is typical for most individual stocks. This indicates that about 29 percent of the variance in Wal-Mart's returns is explained by the market returns. If we had done a similar analysis for portfolios of 20 randomly selected stocks, then the points would on average

FIGURE 6-11 Calculating a Beta Coefficient for Wal-Mart Stores

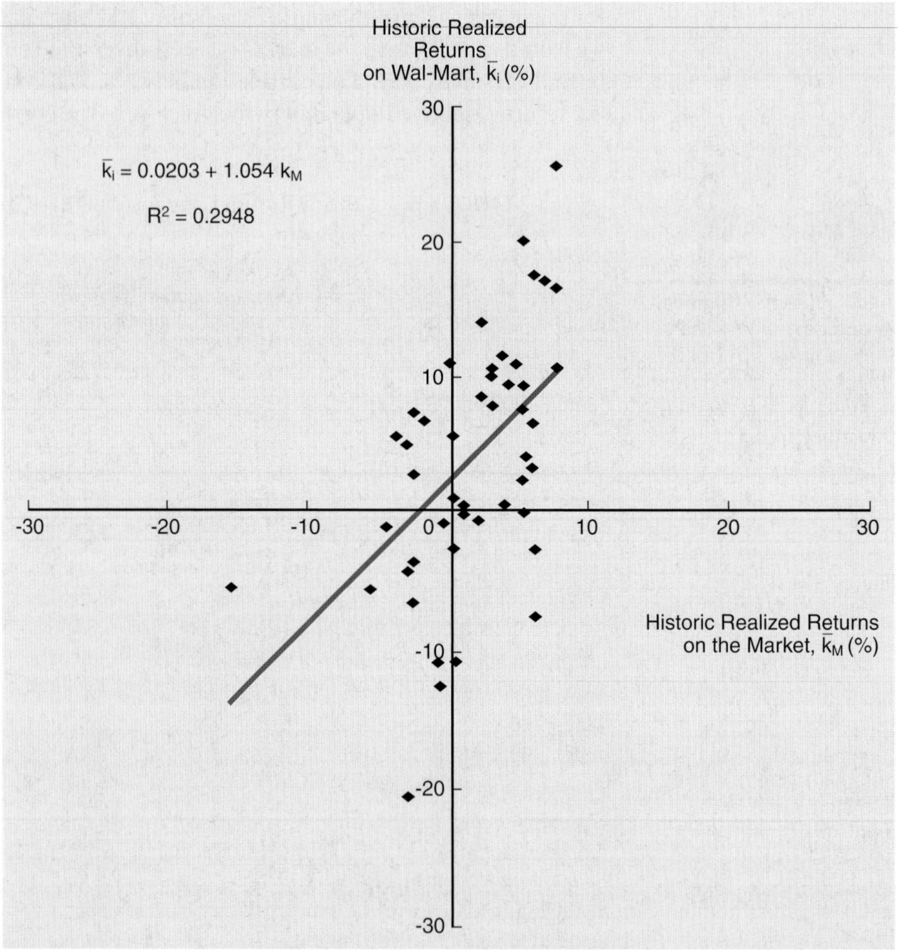

have been clustered tightly around the regression line, and the R^2 would have averaged over 0.9.

Finally, note that the intercept shown in the regression equation on the chart is about 0.02. Since the regression equation is based on monthly data, this means that over this period Wal-Mart's stock earned 2 percent more per month than an average stock as a result of factors other than a general increase in stock prices.

Self-Test Questions

What types of data are needed to calculate a beta coefficient for an actual company?

What does the R^2 measure? What is the R^2 for a typical company?

The Relationship between Risk and Rates of Return

In the preceding section, we saw that under the CAPM theory, beta is the appropriate measure of a stock's relevant risk. Now we must specify the relationship between risk and return: For a given level of risk as measured by beta, what rate of return should investors require to compensate them for bearing that risk? To begin, let us define the following terms:

$\hat{k}_i$ = *expected* rate of return on the *i*th stock.

k_i = *required* rate of return on the *i*th stock. Note that if $\hat{k}_i$ is less than k_i, you would not purchase this stock, or you would sell it if you owned it. If $\hat{k}_i$ were greater than k_i, you would want to buy the stock, because it looks like a bargain. You would be indifferent if $\hat{k}_i = k_i$.

$\bar{k}$ = realized, after-the-fact return. One obviously does not know what $\bar{k}$ will be at the time he or she is considering the purchase of a stock.

k_{RF} = risk-free rate of return. In this context, k_{RF} is generally measured by the return on long-term U.S. Treasury bonds.

b_i = beta coefficient of the *i*th stock. The beta of an average stock is $b_A = 1.0$.

k_M = required rate of return on a portfolio consisting of all stocks, which is called the *market portfolio.* k_M is also the required rate of return on an average ($b_A = 1.0$) stock.

$RP_M = (k_M - k_{RF})$ = risk premium on "the market," and also on an average ($b = 1.0$) stock. This is the additional return over the risk-free rate required to compensate an average investor for assuming an average amount of risk. Average risk means a stock whose $b_i = b_A = 1.0$.

$RP_i = (k_M - k_{RF})b_i = (RP_M)b_i$ = risk premium on the *i*th stock. The stock's risk premium will be less than, equal to, or greater than the premium on an average stock, RP_M, depending on whether its beta is less than, equal to, or greater than 1.0. If $b_i = b_A = 1.0$, then $RP_i = RP_M$.

The **market risk premium, RP_M,** shows the premium investors require for bearing the risk of an average stock, and it depends on the degree of risk aversion that investors on average have.[10] Let us assume that at the current time, Treasury bonds yield $k_{RF} = 6\%$ and an average share of stock has a required return of $k_M = 11\%$. Therefore, the market risk premium is 5 percent:

$$RP_M = k_M - k_{RF} = 11\% - 6\% = 5\%.$$

It follows that if one stock were twice as risky as another, its risk premium would be twice as high, while if its risk were only half as much, its risk premium would be half as large. Further, we can measure a stock's relative riskiness by its beta coefficient. If we know the market risk premium, RP_M, and the stock's risk as measured by its beta coefficient, b_i, we can find the stock's risk premium as the product $(RP_M)b_i$. For example, if $b_i = 0.5$ and $RP_M = 5\%$, then RP_i is 2.5 percent:

$$\text{Risk premium for Stock i} = RP_i = (RP_M)b_i \quad \textbf{(6-8)}$$
$$= (5\%)(0.5)$$
$$= 2.5\%.$$

As the discussion in Chapter 5 implied, the required return for any investment can be expressed in general terms as

$$\text{Required return} = \text{Risk-free return} + \text{Premium for risk.}$$

Here the risk-free return includes a premium for expected inflation, and we assume that the assets under consideration have similar maturities and liquidity. Under these conditions, the relationship between the required return and risk is called the **Security Market Line (SML).** The required return for Stock i can be written as follows:

$$\text{SML Equation:} \quad \begin{matrix}\text{Required return}\\ \text{on Stock i}\end{matrix} = \begin{matrix}\text{Risk-free}\\ \text{rate}\end{matrix} + \begin{pmatrix}\text{Market risk}\\ \text{premium}\end{pmatrix}\begin{pmatrix}\text{Stock i's}\\ \text{beta}\end{pmatrix}$$
$$k_i = k_{RF} + (k_M - k_{RF})b_i$$
$$= k_{RF} + (RP_M)b_i \quad \textbf{(6-9)}$$
$$= 6\% + (11\% - 6\%)(0.5)$$
$$= 6\% + 5\%(0.5)$$
$$= 8.5\%.$$

If some other Stock j were riskier than Stock i and had $b_j = 2.0$, then its required rate of return would be 16 percent:

$$k_j = 6\% + (5\%)2.0 = 16\%.$$

An average stock, with $b = 1.0$, would have a required return of 11 percent, the same as the market return:

$$k_A = 6\% + (5\%)1.0 = 11\% = k_M.$$

As noted above, Equation 6-9 is called the Security Market Line (SML) equation, and it is often expressed in graph form, as in Figure 6-12, which shows the SML when $k_{RF} = 6\%$ and $k_M = 11\%$. Note the following points:

[10] This concept, as well as other aspects of the CAPM, is discussed in more detail in Chapter 7. It should be noted that the risk premium of an average stock, $k_M - k_{RF}$, cannot be measured with great precision because it is impossible to obtain precise values for the expected future return on the market, k_M. However, empirical studies suggest that where long-term U.S. Treasury bonds are used to measure k_{RF} and where k_M is an estimate of the expected (not historical) return on the S&P 500 Industrial Stocks, the market risk premium varies somewhat from year to year, and it has generally ranged from 4 to 6 percent during the last 20 years.

FIGURE 6-12 The Security Market Line (SML)

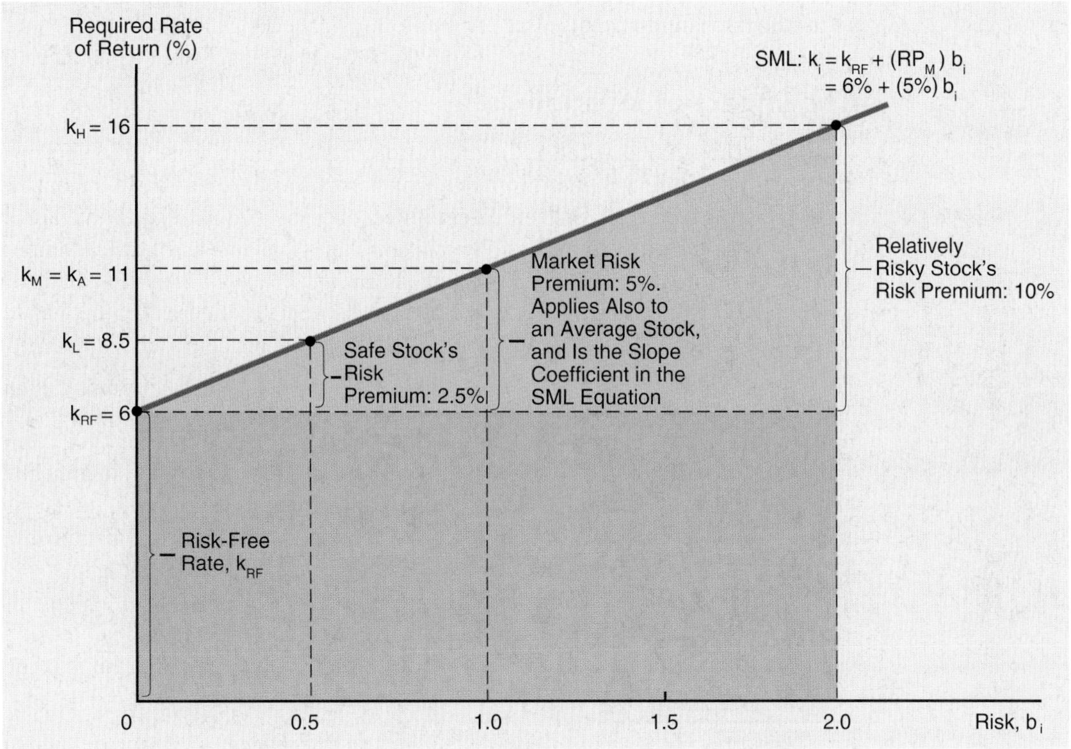

1. Required rates of return are shown on the vertical axis, while risk as measured by beta is shown on the horizontal axis. This graph is quite different from the one shown in Figure 6-9, where the returns on individual stocks were plotted on the vertical axis and returns on the market index were shown on the horizontal axis. The slopes of the three lines in Figure 6-9 were used to calculate the three stocks' betas, and those betas were then plotted as points on the horizontal axis of Figure 6-12.
2. Riskless securities have $b_i = 0$; therefore, k_{RF} appears as the vertical axis intercept in Figure 6-12. If we could construct a portfolio that had a beta of zero, it would have an expected return equal to the risk-free rate.
3. The slope of the SML (5% in Figure 6-12) reflects the degree of risk aversion in the economy—the greater the average investor's aversion to risk, then (a) the steeper the slope of the line, (b) the greater the risk premium for all stocks, and (c) the higher the required rate of return on all stocks.[11] These points are discussed further in a later section.
4. The values we worked out for stocks with $b_i = 0.5$, $b_i = 1.0$, and $b_i = 2.0$ agree with the values shown on the graph for k_L, k_A, and k_H.

[11]Students sometimes confuse beta with the slope of the SML. This is a mistake. The slope of any straight line is equal to the "rise" divided by the "run," or $(Y_1 - Y_0)/(X_1 - X_0)$. Consider Figure 6-12. If we let Y = k and X = beta, and we go from the origin to b = 1.0, we see that the slope is $(k_M - k_{RF})/(b_M - b_{RF}) = (11\% - 6\%)/(1 - 0) = 5\%$. Thus, the slope of the SML is equal to $(k_M - k_{RF})$, the market risk premium. In Figure 6-12, $k_i = 6\% + 5\% b_i$, so a doubling of beta (for example, from 1.0 to 2.0) would produce a 5 percentage point increase in k_i.

Both the Security Market Line and a company's position on it change over time due to changes in interest rates, investors' aversion to risk, and individual companies' betas. Such changes are discussed in the following sections.

The Impact of Inflation

As we learned in Chapter 5, interest amounts to "rent" on borrowed money, or the price of money. Thus, k_{RF} is the price of money to a riskless borrower. We also learned that the risk-free rate as measured by the rate on U.S. Treasury securities is called the *nominal*, or *quoted, rate*, and it consists of two elements: (1) a *real inflation-free rate of return, k**, and (2) an *inflation premium, IP,* equal to the anticipated rate of inflation.[12] Thus, $k_{RF} = k^* + IP$. The real rate on long-term Treasury bonds has historically ranged from 2 to 4 percent, with a mean of about 3 percent. Therefore, if no inflation were expected, long-term Treasury bonds would yield about 3 percent. However, as the expected rate of inflation increases, a premium must be added to the real risk-free rate of return to compensate investors for the loss of purchasing power that results from inflation. Therefore, the 6 percent k_{RF} shown in Figure 6-12 might be thought of as consisting of a 3 percent real risk-free rate of return plus a 3 percent inflation premium: $k_{RF} = k^* + IP = 3\% + 3\% = 6\%$.

If the expected inflation rate rose by 2 percent, to $3\% + 2\% = 5\%$, this would cause k_{RF} to rise to 8 percent. Such a change is shown in Figure 6-13. Notice that under the CAPM, the increase in k_{RF} leads to an *equal* increase in the rate of return on all

[12]Long-term Treasury bonds also contain a maturity risk premium, MRP. Here we include the MRP in k* to simplify the discussion.

FIGURE 6-13 Shift in the SML Caused by an Increase in Inflation

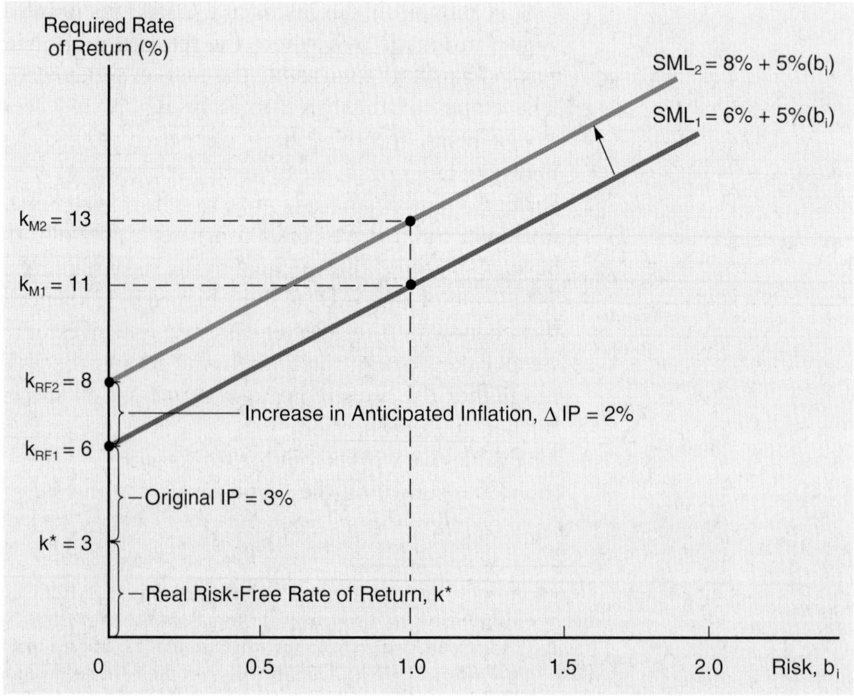

risky assets, because the same inflation premium is built into the required rate of return of both riskless and risky assets.[13] For example, the rate of return on an average stock, k_M, increases from 11 to 13 percent. Other risky securities' returns also rise by two percentage points.

Changes in Risk Aversion

The slope of the Security Market Line reflects the extent to which investors are averse to risk—the steeper the slope of the line, the greater the average investor's risk aversion. Suppose investors were indifferent to risk; that is, they were not risk averse. If k_{RF} were 6 percent, then risky assets would also provide an expected return of 6 percent, because if there were no risk aversion, there would be no risk premium, and the SML would be plotted as a horizontal line. As risk aversion increases, so does the risk premium, and this causes the slope of the SML to become steeper.

Figure 6-14 illustrates an increase in risk aversion. The market risk premium rises from 5 to 7.5 percent, causing k_M to rise from $k_{M1} = 11\%$ to $k_{M2} = 13.5\%$. The returns on other risky assets also rise, and the effect of this shift in risk aversion is more

[13]Recall that the inflation premium for any asset is equal to the average expected rate of inflation over the asset's life. Thus, in this analysis we must assume either that all securities plotted on the SML graph have the same life or else that the expected rate of future inflation is constant.

It should also be noted that k_{RF} in a CAPM analysis can be proxied by either a long-term rate (the T-bond rate) or a short-term rate (the T-bill rate). Traditionally, the T-bill rate was used, but in recent years there has been a movement toward use of the T-bond rate because there is a closer relationship between T-bond yields and stocks than between T-bill yields and stocks. See *Stocks, Bonds, Bills, and Inflation: 2000 Valuation Edition Yearbook* (Chicago: Ibbotson Associates, 2000) for a discussion.

FIGURE 6-14 Shift in the SML Caused by Increased Risk Aversion

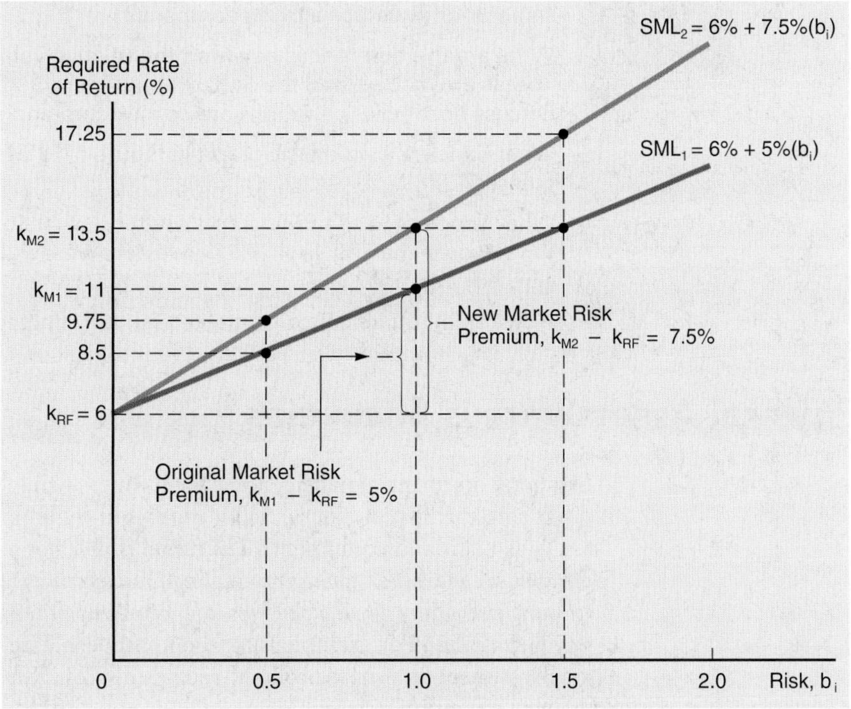

pronounced on riskier securities. For example, the required return on a stock with b_i = 0.5 increases by only 1.25 percentage points, from 8.5 to 9.75 percent, whereas that on a stock with b_i = 1.5 increases by 3.75 percentage points, from 13.5 to 17.25 percent.

Changes in a Stock's Beta Coefficient

As we shall see later in the book, a firm can influence its market risk, hence its beta, through changes in the composition of its assets and also through its use of debt. A company's beta can also change as a result of external factors such as increased competition in its industry, the expiration of basic patents, and the like. When such changes occur, the required rate of return also changes, and, as we shall see in Chapter 10, this will affect the firm's stock price. For example, consider MicroDrive Inc., with a beta of 1.40. Now suppose some action occurred that caused MicroDrive's beta to increase from 1.40 to 2.00. If the conditions depicted in Figure 6-12 held, MicroDrive's required rate of return would increase from 13 to 16 percent:

$$\begin{aligned} k_1 &= k_{RF} + RP_M b_i \\ &= 6\% + (5\%)1.40 \\ &= 13\% \end{aligned}$$

to

$$\begin{aligned} k_2 &= 6\% + (5\%)2.0 \\ &= 16\%. \end{aligned}$$

As we shall see in Chapter 10, this change would have a dramatic effect on MicroDrive's stock.

Self-Test Questions

Differentiate among the expected rate of return ($\hat{k}$), the required rate of return (k), and the realized, after-the-fact return ($\bar{k}$) on a stock. Which would have to be larger to get you to buy the stock, $\hat{k}$ or k? Would $\hat{k}$, k, and $\bar{k}$ typically be the same or different for a given company?

What are the differences between the relative volatility graph (Figure 6-9), where "betas are made," and the SML graph (Figure 6-12), where "betas are used"? Discuss both how the graphs are constructed and the information they convey.

What happens to the SML graph in Figure 6-12 when inflation increases or decreases?

What happens to the SML graph when risk aversion increases or decreases? What would the SML look like if investors were indifferent to risk, that is, had zero risk aversion?

How can a firm influence its market risk as reflected in its beta?

Physical Assets versus Securities

In a book on financial management for business firms, why do we spend so much time discussing the risk of stocks? Why not begin by looking at the risk of such business assets as plant and equipment? *The reason is that, for a management whose primary goal is stock price maximization, the overriding consideration is the risk of the firm's stock, and the relevant risk of any physical asset must be measured in terms of its effect on the stock's risk as seen by investors.* For example, suppose Goodyear Tire Company is considering a major investment in a new product, recapped tires. Sales of recaps, hence earnings on the new operation, are highly uncertain, so on a stand-alone basis the new venture appears to be quite risky. However, suppose returns in the recap business are negatively correlated with Goodyear's regular operations—when times are good and people have plenty of money, they buy new tires, but when times are bad, they tend to buy more recaps. Therefore, returns would be high on regular operations and low on the recap division during good times, but the opposite would occur during recessions. The result might be a pattern like that shown earlier in Figure 6-5 for Stocks W and M. Thus, what appears to be a risky investment when viewed on a stand-alone basis might not be very risky when viewed within the context of the company as a whole.

This analysis can be extended to the corporation's stockholders. Because Goodyear's stock is owned by diversified stockholders, the real issue each time management makes an asset investment should be this: How will this investment affect the risk of our stockholders? Again, the stand-alone risk of an individual project may be quite high, but viewed in the context of the project's effect on stockholders' risk, it may not be very large. We will address this issue again in Chapter 14, where we examine the effects of capital budgeting on companies' beta coefficients and thus on stockholders' risks.

Self-Test Questions

Explain the following statement: "The stand-alone risk of an individual project may be quite high, but viewed in the context of a project's effect on stockholders, the project's true risk may not be very large."

How would the correlation between returns on a project and returns on the firm's other assets affect the project's risk?

Some Concerns about Beta and the CAPM

The Capital Asset Pricing Model (CAPM) is more than just an abstract theory described in textbooks—it is also widely used by analysts, investors, and corporations. However, despite the CAPM's intuitive appeal, a number of recent studies have raised concerns about its validity. In particular, a study by Eugene Fama of the University of Chicago and Kenneth French of Yale cast doubt on the CAPM.[14] Fama and French found two variables that are consistently related to stock returns: (1) the firm's size and (2) its market/book ratio. After adjusting for other factors, they found that smaller firms have provided relatively high returns, and that returns are relatively high on stocks with low market/book ratios. At the same time, and contrary to the CAPM, they found no relationship between a stock's beta and its return.

As an alternative to the traditional CAPM, researchers and practitioners have begun to look to more general multi-beta models that expand on the CAPM and address its shortcomings. The multi-beta model is an attractive generalization of the traditional CAPM model's insight that market risk, or the risk that cannot be diversified away underlies the pricing of assets. In the multi-beta model, market risk is measured relative to a set of risk factors that determine the behavior of asset returns, whereas the CAPM gauges risk only relative to the market return. It is important to note that the risk factors in the multi-beta model are all nondiversifiable sources of risk. Empirical research investigating the relationship between economic risk factors and security returns is ongoing, but it has discovered several risk factors, including the bond default premium, the bond term structure premium, and inflation, that affect most securities.

Practitioners and academicians have long recognized the limitations of the CAPM, and they are constantly looking for ways to improve it. The multi-beta model is a potential step in that direction. In the next chapter we discuss some of the newer theories and evidence.

---

[14]See Eugene F. Fama and Kenneth R. French, "The Cross-Section of Expected Stock Returns," *Journal of Finance*, Vol. 47, 1992, 427–465; and Eugene F. Fama and Kenneth R. French, "Common Risk Factors in the Returns on Stocks and Bonds," *Journal of Financial Economics*, Vol. 33, 1993, 3–56.

Self-Test Question

Are there any reasons to question the validity of the CAPM? Explain.

Volatility versus Risk

Before closing this chapter, we should note that volatility does not necessarily imply risk. For example, suppose a company's sales and earnings fluctuate widely from month to month, from year to year, or in some other manner. Does this imply that the company is risky in either the stand-alone or portfolio sense? If the earnings follow seasonal or cyclical patterns, as for an ice cream distributor or a steel company, they can be predicted, hence volatility would not signify much in the way of risk. If the ice cream company's earnings dropped about as much as they normally did in the winter, this would not concern investors, so the company's stock price would not be affected. Similarly, if the steel company's earnings fell during a recession, this would not be a surprise, so the company's stock price would not fall nearly as much as its earnings. Therefore, earnings volatility does not necessarily imply investment risk.

Now consider some other company, say, Wal-Mart. In 1995 Wal-Mart's earnings declined for the first time in its history. That decline worried investors—they were concerned that Wal-Mart's era of rapid growth had ended. The result was that Wal-Mart's stock price declined more than its earnings. Again, we conclude that while a downturn in earnings does not necessarily imply risk, it could, depending on conditions.

Now let's consider stock price volatility as opposed to earnings volatility. Is stock price volatility more likely to imply risk than earnings volatility? The answer is a loud yes! Stock prices vary because investors are uncertain about the future, especially about future earnings. So, if you see a company whose stock price fluctuates relatively widely (which will result in a high beta), you can bet that its future earnings are relatively unpredictable. Thus, biotech companies have less predictable earnings than water companies, biotechs' stock prices are volatile, and they have relatively high betas.

To conclude, keep two points in mind: (1) Earnings volatility does not necessarily signify risk—you have to think about the cause of the volatility before reaching any conclusion as to whether earnings volatility indicates risk. (2) However, stock price volatility *does* signify risk.

Self-Test Questions

Does earnings volatility necessarily imply risk? Explain.

Why is stock price volatility more likely to imply risk than earnings volatility?

Summary

In this chapter, we described the trade-off between risk and return. We began by discussing how to calculate risk and return for both individual assets and portfolios. In particular, we differentiated between stand-alone risk and risk in a portfolio context, and we explained the benefits of diversification. Finally, we developed the CAPM, which explains how risk affects rates of return. In the chapters that follow, we will give you the tools to estimate the required rates of return for bonds, preferred stock, and common stock, and we will explain how firms use these returns to develop their costs of capital. As you will see, the cost of capital is an important element in the firm's capital budgeting process. The key concepts covered in this chapter are listed below.

- **Risk** can be defined as the chance that some unfavorable event will occur.
- The risk of an asset's cash flows can be considered on a **stand-alone basis** (each asset by itself) or in a **portfolio context,** where the investment is combined with other assets and its risk is reduced through **diversification.**
- Most rational investors hold **portfolios of assets,** and they are more concerned with the riskiness of their portfolios than with the risk of individual assets.
- The **expected return** on an investment is the mean value of its probability distribution of returns.
- The **greater the probability** that the actual return will be far below the expected return, the **greater the stand-alone risk** associated with an asset.
- The average investor is **risk averse,** which means that he or she must be compensated for holding risky assets. Therefore, riskier assets have higher required returns than less risky assets.
- An asset's risk consists of (1) **diversifiable risk,** which can be eliminated by diversification, plus (2) **market risk,** which cannot be eliminated by diversification.
- The **relevant risk** of an individual asset is its contribution to the riskiness of a well-diversified **portfolio,** which is the asset's **market risk.** Since market risk cannot be eliminated by diversification, investors must be compensated for bearing it.
- A stock's **beta coefficient, b,** is a measure of its market risk. Beta measures the extent to which the stock's returns move relative to the market.
- A **high-beta stock** is more volatile than an average stock, while a **low-beta stock** is less volatile than an average stock. An average stock has $b = 1.0$.
- The **beta of a portfolio** is a **weighted average** of the betas of the individual securities in the portfolio.
- The **Security Market Line (SML)** equation shows the relationship between a security's market risk and its required rate of return. The return required for any security i is equal to the **risk-free rate** plus the **market risk premium** times the security's beta: $k_i = k_{RF} + (RP_M)b_i$.
- Even though the expected rate of return on a stock is generally equal to its required return, a number of things can happen to cause the required rate of return to change: (1) **the risk-free rate can change** because of changes in either real rates or anticipated inflation, (2) **a stock's beta can change,** and (3) **investors' aversion to risk can change.**
- Because returns on assets in different countries are not perfectly correlated, **global diversification** may result in lower risk for multinational companies and globally diversified portfolios.

In the next chapter, we will examine the CAPM and some newer theories of risk and return in more detail. Then, in the following three chapters, we will see how a security's expected rate of return affects its value. Finally, in the remainder of the book, we will examine the ways in which a firm's management can influence a stock's riskiness and hence its price.

Questions

6–1 Define the following terms, using graphs or equations to illustrate your answers wherever feasible:

a. Stand-alone risk; risk; probability distribution
b. Expected rate of return, $\hat{k}$
c. Continuous probability distribution
d. Standard deviation, σ; variance, σ^2; coefficient of variation, CV

e. Risk aversion; realized rate of return, $\bar{k}$
f. Risk premium for Stock i, RP_i; market risk premium, RP_M
g. Capital Asset Pricing Model (CAPM)
h. Expected return on a portfolio, $\hat{k}_p$; market portfolio
i. Correlation coefficient, r; correlation
j. Market risk; diversifiable risk; relevant risk
k. Beta coefficient, b; average stock's beta, b_A
l. Security Market Line (SML); SML equation
m. Slope of SML as a measure of risk aversion

6–2 The probability distribution of a less risky expected return is more peaked than that of a riskier return. What shape would the probability distribution have for (a) completely certain returns and (b) completely uncertain returns?

6–3 Security A has an expected return of 7 percent, a standard deviation of expected returns of 35 percent, a correlation coefficient with the market of −0.3, and a beta coefficient of −1.5. Security B has an expected return of 12 percent, a standard deviation of returns of 10 percent, a correlation with the market of 0.7, and a beta coefficient of 1.0. Which security is riskier? Why?

6–4 Suppose you owned a portfolio consisting of $250,000 worth of long-term U.S. government bonds.

a. Would your portfolio be riskless?
b. Now suppose you hold a portfolio consisting of $250,000 worth of 30-day Treasury bills. Every 30 days your bills mature, and you reinvest the principal ($250,000) in a new batch of bills. Assume that you live on the investment income from your portfolio and that you want to maintain a constant standard of living. Is your portfolio truly riskless?
c. Can you think of any asset that would be completely riskless? Could someone develop such an asset? Explain.

6–5 A life insurance policy is a financial asset. The premiums paid represent the investment's cost.

a. How would you calculate the expected return on a life insurance policy?
b. Suppose the owner of a life insurance policy has no other financial assets—the person's only other asset is "human capital," or lifetime earnings capacity. What is the correlation coefficient between returns on the insurance policy and returns on the policyholder's human capital?
c. Life insurance companies have to pay administrative costs and sales representatives' commissions; hence, the expected rate of return on insurance premiums is generally low, or even negative. Use the portfolio concept to explain why people buy life insurance in spite of negative expected returns.

6–6 If investors' aversion to risk increased, would the risk premium on a high-beta stock increase more or less than that on a low-beta stock? Explain.

6–7 If a company's beta were to double, would its expected return double?

6–8 Is it possible to construct a portfolio of stocks which has an expected return equal to the risk-free rate?

Self-Test Problems (Solutions Appear in Appendix A)

ST–1 Stocks A and B have the following historical returns:
REALIZED RATES OF RETURN

Year	Stock A's Returns, k_A	Stock B's Returns, k_B
1997	(10.00%)	(3.00%)
1998	18.50	21.29
1999	38.67	44.25
2000	14.33	3.67
2001	33.00	28.30

a. Calculate the average rate of return for each stock during the period 1997 through 2001. Assume that someone held a portfolio consisting of 50 percent of Stock A and 50 percent of Stock B. What would have been the realized rate of return on the portfolio in each year from 1997 through 2001? What would have been the average return on the portfolio during this period?

b. Now calculate the standard deviation of returns for each stock and for the portfolio. Use Equation 6-3a.

c. Looking at the annual returns data on the two stocks, would you guess that the correlation coefficient between returns on the two stocks is closer to 0.9 or to −0.9?

d. If you added more stocks at random to the portfolio, which of the following is the most accurate statement of what would happen to σ_p?

(1) σ_p would remain constant.

(2) σ_p would decline to somewhere in the vicinity of 21 percent.

(3) σ_p would decline to zero if enough stocks were included.

ST–2 *BETA AND REQUIRED RATE OF RETURN*

ECRI Corporation is a holding company with four main subsidiaries. The percentage of its business coming from each of the subsidiaries, and their respective betas, are as follows:

Subsidiary	Percentage of Business	Beta
Electric utility	60%	0.70
Cable company	25	0.90
Real estate	10	1.30
International/special projects	5	1.50

a. What is the holding company's beta?

b. Assume that the risk-free rate is 6 percent and the market risk premium is 5 percent. What is the holding company's required rate of return?

c. ECRI is considering a change in its strategic focus; it will reduce its reliance on the electric utility subsidiary, so the percentage of its business from this subsidiary will be 50 percent. At the same time, ECRI will increase its reliance on the international/special projects division, so the percentage of its business from that subsidiary will rise to 15 percent. What will be the shareholders' required rate of return if they adopt these changes?

Problems

6–1 *EXPECTED RETURN*

A stock's expected return has the following distribution:

Demand for the Company's Products	Probability of this Demand Occurring	Rate of Return if This Demand Occurs
Weak	0.1	(50%)
Below average	0.2	(5)
Average	0.4	16
Above average	0.2	25
Strong	0.1	60
	1.0	

Calculate the stock's expected return, standard deviation, and coefficient of variation.

6–2 PORTFOLIO BETA

An individual has \$35,000 invested in a stock which has a beta of 0.8 and \$40,000 invested in a stock with a beta of 1.4. If these are the only two investments in her portfolio, what is her portfolio's beta?

6–3 EXPECTED AND REQUIRED RATES OF RETURN

Assume that the risk-free rate is 5 percent and the market risk premium is 6 percent. What is the expected return for the overall stock market? What is the required rate of return on a stock that has a beta of 1.2?

6–4 REQUIRED RATE OF RETURN

Assume that the risk-free rate is 6 percent and the expected return on the market is 13 percent. What is the required rate of return on a stock that has a beta of 0.7?

6–5 EXPECTED RETURNS

The market and Stock J have the following probability distributions:

Probability	k_M	k_J
0.3	15%	20%
0.4	9	5
0.3	18	12

a. Calculate the expected rates of return for the market and Stock J.
b. Calculate the standard deviations for the market and Stock J.
c. Calculate the coefficients of variation for the market and Stock J.

6–6 EXPECTED RETURNS

Stocks X and Y have the following probability distributions of expected future returns:

Probability	X	Y
0.1	(10%)	(35%)
0.2	2	0
0.4	12	20
0.2	20	25
0.1	38	45

a. Calculate the expected rate of return, $\hat{k}$, for Stock Y. ($\hat{k}_x = 12\%$.)
b. Calculate the standard deviation of expected returns for Stock X. (That for Stock Y is 20.35 percent.) Now calculate the coefficient of variation for Stock Y. Is it possible that most investors might regard Stock Y as being *less* risky than Stock X? Explain.

6–7 REQUIRED RATE OF RETURN

Suppose $k_{RF} = 5\%$, $k_M = 10\%$, and $k_A = 12\%$.
a. Calculate Stock A's beta.
b. If Stock A's beta were 2.0, what would be A's new required rate of return?

6–8 REQUIRED RATE OF RETURN

Suppose $k_{RF} = 9\%$, $k_M = 14\%$, and $b_i = 1.3$.
a. What is k_i, the required rate of return on Stock i?
b. Now suppose k_{RF} (1) increases to 10 percent or (2) decreases to 8 percent. The slope of the SML remains constant. How would this affect k_M and k_i?
c. Now assume k_{RF} remains at 9 percent but k_M (1) increases to 16 percent or (2) falls to 13 percent. The slope of the SML does not remain constant. How would these changes affect k_i?

6–9 PORTFOLIO BETA

Suppose you hold a diversified portfolio consisting of a \$7,500 investment in each of 20 different common stocks. The portfolio beta is equal to 1.12. Now, suppose you have decided to sell one of the stocks in your portfolio with a beta equal to 1.0 for \$7,500 and to use these proceeds to buy another stock for your portfolio. Assume the new stock's beta is equal to 1.75. Calculate your portfolio's new beta.

6–10 PORTFOLIO REQUIRED RETURN

Suppose you are the money manager of a $4 million investment fund. The fund consists of 4 stocks with the following investments and betas:

Stock	Investment	Beta
A	$400,000	1.50
B	600,000	(0.50)
C	1,000,000	1.25
D	2,000,000	0.75

If the market required rate of return is 14 percent and the risk-free rate is 6 percent, what is the fund's required rate of return?

6–11 PORTFOLIO BETA

You have a $2 million portfolio consisting of a $100,000 investment in each of 20 different stocks. The portfolio has a beta equal to 1.1. You are considering selling $100,000 worth of one stock which has a beta equal to 0.9 and using the proceeds to purchase another stock which has a beta equal to 1.4. What will be the new beta of your portfolio following this transaction?

6–12 REQUIRED RATE OF RETURN

Stock R has a beta of 1.5, Stock S has a beta of 0.75, the expected rate of return on an average stock is 13 percent, and the risk-free rate of return is 7 percent. By how much does the required return on the riskier stock exceed the required return on the less risky stock?

6–13 EXPECTED RETURNS

Suppose you won the Florida lottery and were offered (1) $0.5 million or (2) a gamble in which you would get $1 million if a head were flipped but zero if a tail came up.

a. What is the expected value of the gamble?
b. Would you take the sure $0.5 million or the gamble?
c. If you choose the sure $0.5 million, are you a risk averter or a risk seeker?
d. Suppose you actually take the sure $0.5 million. You can invest it in either a U.S. Treasury bond that will return $537,500 at the end of a year or a common stock that has a 50-50 chance of being either worthless or worth $1,150,000 at the end of the year.
  (1) What is the expected dollar profit on the stock investment? (The expected profit on the T-bond investment is $37,500.)
  (2) What is the expected rate of return on the stock investment? (The expected rate of return on the T-bond investment is 7.5 percent.)
  (3) Would you invest in the bond or the stock?
  (4) Exactly how large would the expected profit (or the expected rate of return) have to be on the stock investment to make *you* invest in the stock, given the 7.5 percent return on the bond?
  (5) How might your decision be affected if, rather than buying one stock for $0.5 million, you could construct a portfolio consisting of 100 stocks with $5,000 invested in each? Each of these stocks has the same return characteristics as the one stock—that is, a 50-50 chance of being worth either zero or $11,500 at year-end. Would the correlation between returns on these stocks matter?

6–14 SECURITY MARKET LINE

The Kish Investment Fund, in which you plan to invest some money, has total capital of $500 million invested in 5 stocks:

Stock	Investment	Stock's Beta Coefficient
A	$160 million	0.5
B	120 million	2.0
C	80 million	4.0
D	80 million	1.0
E	60 million	3.0

The beta coefficient for a fund like Kish Investment can be found as a weighted average of the fund's investments. The current risk-free rate is 6 percent, whereas market returns have the following estimated probability distribution for the next period:

Probability	Market Return
0.1	7%
0.2	9
0.4	11
0.2	13
0.1	15

a. What is the estimated equation for the Security Market Line (SML)? (Hint: First determine the expected market return.)
b. Compute the fund's required rate of return for the next period.
c. Suppose Bridget Nelson, the president, receives a proposal for a new stock. The investment needed to take a position in the stock is $50 million, it will have an expected return of 15 percent, and its estimated beta coefficient is 2.0. Should the new stock be purchased? At what expected rate of return should the fund be indifferent to purchasing the stock?

6–15 *REALIZED RATES OF RETURN*

Stocks A and B have the following historical returns:

Year	Stock A's Returns, k_A	Stock B's Returns, k_B
1997	(18.00%)	(14.50%)
1998	33.00	21.80
1999	15.00	30.50
2000	(0.50)	(7.60)
2001	27.00	26.30

a. Calculate the average rate of return for each stock during the period 1997 through 2001.
b. Assume that someone held a portfolio consisting of 50 percent of Stock A and 50 percent of Stock B. What would have been the realized rate of return on the portfolio in each year from 1997 through 2001? What would have been the average return on the portfolio during this period?
c. Calculate the standard deviation of returns for each stock and for the portfolio.
d. Calculate the coefficient of variation for each stock and for the portfolio.
e. If you are a risk-averse investor, would you prefer to hold Stock A, Stock B, or the portfolio? Why?

6–16 *FINANCIAL CALCULATOR NEEDED; EXPECTED AND REQUIRED RATES OF RETURN*

You have observed the following returns over time:

Year	Stock X	Stock Y	Market
1997	14%	13%	12%
1998	19	7	10
1999	−16	−5	−12
2000	3	1	1
2001	20	11	15

Assume that the risk-free rate is 6 percent and the market risk premium is 5 percent.
a. What are the betas of Stocks X and Y?
b. What are the required rates of return for Stocks X and Y?
c. What is the required rate of return for a portfolio consisting of 80 percent of Stock X and 20 percent of Stock Y?
d. If Stock X's expected return is 22 percent, is Stock X under- or overvalued?

Spreadsheet Problems

6–17 BUILD A MODEL: EVALUATING RISK AND RETURN

Start with the partial model in the file ***Ch 06-17 Build a Model.xls*** from the textbook's CD-ROM. Bartman Industries' and Reynolds Incorporated's stock prices and dividends, along with the Wilshire 5000 Index, are shown below for the period 1996-2001. The Wilshire 5000 data are adjusted to include dividends.

	Bartman Industries		Reynolds Incorporated		Wilshire 5000
Year	Stock Price	Dividend	Stock Price	Dividend	Includes Divs.
2001	$17.250	$1.15	$48.750	$3.00	11,663.98
2000	14.750	1.06	52.300	2.90	8,785.70
1999	16.500	1.00	48.750	2.75	8,679.98
1998	10.750	0.95	57.250	2.50	6,434.03
1997	11.375	0.90	60.000	2.25	5,602.28
1996	7.625	0.85	55.750	2.00	4,705.97

a. Use the data given to calculate annual returns for Bartman, Reynolds, and the Wilshire 5000 Index, and then calculate average returns over the 5-year period. (Hint: Remember, returns are calculated by subtracting the beginning price from the ending price to get the capital gain or loss, adding the dividend to the capital gain or loss, and dividing the result by the beginning price. Assume that dividends are already included in the index. Also, you cannot calculate the rate of return for 1996 because you do not have 1995 data.)

b. Calculate the standard deviations of the returns for Bartman, Reynolds, and the Wilshire 5000. (Hint: Use the sample standard deviation formula given in the chapter, which corresponds to the STDEV function in *Excel.*)

c. Now calculate the coefficients of variation for Bartman, Reynolds, and the Wilshire 5000.

d. Construct a scatter diagram graph that shows Bartman's and Reynolds' returns on the vertical axis and the market index's returns on the horizontal axis.

e. Estimate Bartman's and Reynolds' betas by running regressions of their returns against the Wilshire 5000's returns. Are these betas consistent with your graph?

f. The risk-free rate on long-term Treasury bonds is 6.04 percent. Assume that the market risk premium is 5 percent. What is the expected return on the market? Now use the SML equation to calculate the two companies' required returns.

g. If you formed a portfolio that consisted of 50 percent of Bartman stock and 50 percent of Reynolds stock, what would be its beta and its required return?

h. Suppose an investor wants to include Bartman Industries' stock in his or her portfolio. Stocks A, B, and C are currently in the portfolio, and their betas are 0.769, 0.985, and 1.423, respectively. Calculate the new portfolio's required return if it consists of 25 percent of Bartman, 15 percent of Stock A, 40 percent of Stock B, and 20 percent of Stock C.

6–18 WHAT IF ANALYSIS: REALIZED RATES OF RETURN

Start with the model in the file ***Ch 06-18 What If Analysis.xls*** from the textbook's CD-ROM and answer the questions shown there.

Cyberproblem

The information related to the cyberproblems is likely to change over time, due to the release of new information and the ever-changing nature of the World Wide Web. With these changes in mind, we will periodically update these problems on the textbook's web site.

6–20 RISK AND RATES OF RETURN

The tendency of a stock's price to move up and down with the market is reflected in its beta coefficient. Therefore, beta is a measure of an investment's market risk and is a key element of the CAPM.

In this exercise you will find betas using Yahoo!Finance, located at **http:// finance.yahoo.com.** Go to the cyberproblem on the textbook's web site, **http://www.harcourtcollege.com/theory/student/resources/cyberprob/ch06.html,** and answer the questions shown there.

Mini Case

See *Ch 06 Show.ppt* and *Ch 06 Mini Case.xls*.

Assume that you recently graduated with a major in finance, and you just landed a job as a financial planner with Merrill Finch Inc., a large financial services corporation. Your first assignment is to invest \$100,000 for a client. Because the funds are to be invested in a business at the end of 1 year, you have been instructed to plan for a 1-year holding period. Further, your boss has restricted you to the following investment alternatives, shown with their probabilities and associated outcomes. (Disregard for now the items at the bottom of the data; you will fill in the blanks later.)

Returns on Alternative Investments

		Estimated Rate of Return					
State of the Economy	**Probability**	**T-Bills**	**High Tech**	**Collections**	**U.S. Rubber**	**Market Portfolio**	**2-Stock Portfolio**
Recession	0.1	8.0%	(22.0%)	28.0%	10.0%*	(13.0%)	3.0%
Below average	0.2	8.0	(2.0)	14.7	(10.0)	1.0	
Average	0.4	8.0	20.0	0.0	7.0	15.0	10.0
Above average	0.2	8.0	35.0	(10.0)	45.0	29.0	
Boom	0.1	8.0	50.0	(20.0)	30.0	43.0	15.0
$\hat{k}$				1.7%	13.8%	15.0%	
σ		0.0		13.4	18.8	15.3	
CV				7.9	1.4	1.0	
b				−0.86	0.68		

*Note that the estimated returns of U.S. Rubber do not always move in the same direction as the overall economy. For example, when the economy is below average, consumers purchase fewer tires than they would if the economy was stronger. However, if the economy is in a flat-out recession, a large number of consumers who were planning to purchase a new car may choose to wait and instead purchase new tires for the car they currently own. Under these circumstances, we would expect U.S. Rubber's stock price to be higher if there is a recession than if the economy was just below average.

Merrill Finch's economic forecasting staff has developed probability estimates for the state of the economy, and its security analysts have developed a sophisticated computer program which was used to estimate the rate of return on each alternative under each state of the economy. High Tech Inc. is an electronics firm; Collections Inc. collects past-due debts; and U.S. Rubber manufactures tires and various other rubber and plastics products. Merrill Finch also maintains an "index fund" which owns a market-weighted fraction of all publicly traded stocks; you can invest in that fund, and thus obtain average stock market results. Given the situation as described, answer the following questions.

a. What are investment returns? What is the return on an investment that costs \$1,000 and is sold after 1 year for \$1,100?

b. (1) Why is the T-bill's return independent of the state of the economy? Do T-bills promise a completely risk-free return? (2) Why are High Tech's returns expected to move with the economy whereas Collections' are expected to move counter to the economy?

c. Calculate the expected rate of return on each alternative and fill in the blanks on the row for $\hat{k}$ in the table above.

d. You should recognize that basing a decision solely on expected returns is only appropriate for risk-neutral individuals. Because your client, like virtually everyone, is risk averse, the riskiness of each alternative is an important aspect of the decision. One possible measure of risk is the standard deviation of returns. (1) Calculate this value for each alternative, and fill in the blank on the row for σ in the table above. (2) What type of risk is measured by the standard deviation? (3) Draw a graph that shows *roughly* the shape of the probability distributions for High Tech, U.S. Rubber, and T-bills.

e. Suppose you suddenly remembered that the coefficient of variation (CV) is generally regarded as being a better measure of stand-alone risk than the standard deviation when the alternatives being considered have widely differing expected returns. Calculate the missing CVs, and fill in the blanks on the row for CV in the table above. Does the CV produce the same risk rankings as the standard deviation?

f. Suppose you created a 2-stock portfolio by investing \$50,000 in High Tech and \$50,000 in Collections. (1) Calculate the expected return ($\hat{k}_p$), the standard deviation (σ_p), and the coefficient of variation (CV_p) for this portfolio and fill in the appropriate blanks in the table above. (2) How does the risk of this 2-stock portfolio compare with the risk of the individual stocks if they were held in isolation?

g. Suppose an investor starts with a portfolio consisting of one randomly selected stock. What would happen (1) to the risk and (2) to the expected return of the portfolio as more and more randomly selected stocks were added to the portfolio? What is the implication for investors? Draw a graph of the two portfolios to illustrate your answer.

h. (1) Should portfolio effects impact the way investors think about the risk of individual stocks? (2) If you decided to hold a 1-stock portfolio, and consequently were exposed to more risk than diversified investors, could you expect to be compensated for all of your risk; that is, could you earn a risk premium on that part of your risk that you could have eliminated by diversifying?

i. How is market risk measured for individual securities? How are beta coefficients calculated?

j. Suppose you have the following historical returns for the stock market and for another company, K. W. Enterprises. Explain how to calculate beta, and use the historical stock returns to calculate the beta for KWE. Interpret your results.

Year	Market	KWE
1	25.7%	40.0
2	8.0	−15.0
3	−11.0	−15.0
4	15.0	35.0
5	32.5	10.0
6	13.7	30.0
7	40.0	42.0
8	10.0	−10.0
9	−10.8	−25.0
10	−13.1	25.0

k. The expected rates of return and the beta coefficients of the alternatives as supplied by Merrill Finch's computer program are as follows:

Security	Return ($\hat{k}$)	Risk (Beta)
High Tech	17.4%	1.29
Market	15.0	1.00
U.S. Rubber	13.8	0.68
T-bills	8.0	0.00
Collections	1.7	(0.86)

(1) Do the expected returns appear to be related to each alternative's market risk? (2) Is it possible to choose among the alternatives on the basis of the information developed thus far?

l. (1) Write out the Security Market Line (SML) equation, use it to calculate the required rate of return on each alternative, and then graph the relationship between the expected and required rates of return. (2) How do the expected rates of return compare with the required rates of return? (3) Does the fact that Collections has an expected return that is less than the T-bill rate make any sense? (4) What would be the market risk and the required return of a 50-50 portfolio of High Tech and Collections? Of High Tech and U.S. Rubber?

m. (1) Suppose investors raised their inflation expectations by 3 percentage points over current estimates as reflected in the 8 percent T-bill rate. What effect would higher inflation have on the SML and on the returns required on high- and low-risk securities? (2) Suppose instead that investors' risk aversion increased enough to cause the market risk premium to increase by 3 percentage points. (Inflation remains constant.) What effect would this have on the SML and on returns of high- and low-risk securities?

Selected Additional References and Cases

Probably the best sources of additional information on probability distributions and single-asset risk measures are statistics textbooks. For example, see

Kohler, Heinz, *Statistics for Business and Economics* (New York: HarperCollins, 1994).

Mendenhall, William, Richard L. Schaeffer, and Dennis D. Wackerly, *Mathematical Statistics with Applications* (Boston: PWS, 1996).

Probably the best place to find an extension of portfolio theory concepts is one of the investments textbooks. These are some good ones:

Francis, Jack C., *Investments: Analysis and Management* (New York: McGraw-Hill, 1991).

Radcliffe, Robert C., *Investment: Concepts, Analysis, and Strategy* (New York: HarperCollins, 1994).

Reilly, Frank K., and Keith C. Brown, *Investment Analysis and Portfolio Management* (Fort Worth, TX: The Dryden Press, 1997).

Sharpe, William F., *Investments* (Englewood Cliffs, NJ: Prentice-Hall, 1995).

Those who want to start at the beginning in studying portfolio theory should see

Markowitz, Harry M., "Portfolio Selection," *Journal of Finance*, March 1952, 77–91.

———, "Foundations of Portfolio Theory," *Journal of Finance*, June 1991, 469–477.

The following case from the Cases in Financial Management: Dryden Request *series covers many of the concepts discussed in this chapter as well as concepts to be covered in Chapter 7: Case 2, "Peachtree Securities, Inc. (A)."*

7

Risk and Return: Portfolio Theory and Asset Pricing Models

Skill or luck? That's the question *The Wall Street Journal's* Investment Dartboard Contest seeks to answer by pitting the stock-picking ability of professional analysts against both amateurs and stocks chosen by throwing darts at tables of stock listings.

Here's how the contest works. *The Wall Street Journal (WSJ)* picks four professional analysts, and each of those pros forms a portfolio by picking four stocks. The stocks must be traded on the NYSE, AMEX, or Nasdaq; have a market capitalization of at least \$50 million and a stock price of at least \$2; and have average daily trades of at least \$100,000. Amateurs can enter the contest by e-mailing their pick of a single stock to the *WSJ*, which then picks four amateurs at random and combines their choices to make a four-stock portfolio. Finally, a group of *WSJ* editors throws four darts at the stock tables. At the beginning of the contest, the *WSJ* announces the pros' picks, and at the end of six months, the paper announces the results. The top two pros are invited back for another six months.

The *WSJ* actually has six separate contests running simultaneously, with a new one beginning each month; since 1990 there have been 119 completed contests. The pros have beaten the darts 73 times and lost 46 times. Although they haven't been competing as long, readers are ahead of the pros by 4 to 3. The pros also beat the Dow Jones Industrial Average in 54 percent of the contests. However, the pros have an average six-month portfolio return of 12.4 percent, much higher than the DJIA six-month average of 6.9 percent and the darts' return of only 5.7 percent.

Do these results mean that skill is more important than luck when it comes to investing in stocks? Not necessarily, according to Burton Malkiel, an economics professor at Princeton and the author of the widely read book, *A Random Walk Down Wall Street*. Since the dart-selected portfolios consist of randomly chosen stocks, they should have betas that average close to 1.0, and hence be of average risk. However, the pros have consistently picked high-beta stocks. Because we have enjoyed a bull market during the last decade, one would expect high-beta stocks to outperform the market. Therefore, according to Malkiel, the pros' performance could be due to a rising market rather than superior analytical skills.

WWW

To enter the contest, send your choice of a stock to **dartboard@interactive.wsj.com.** You must provide your name, home address, e-mail address, and home and work phone numbers. You must also be willing to be interviewed. If you are a subscriber to the *Interactive WSJ* (see **http://wsj.com** for more information on subscribing), then you can check the performance of the pros, amateurs, and darts on a regular basis.

In Chapter 6 we presented the key elements of risk and return analysis. There we saw that much of the risk inherent in a stock can be eliminated by diversification, so rational investors should hold portfolios of stocks rather than just one stock. We also introduced the Capital Asset Pricing Model (CAPM), which links risk and required rates of return, using a stock's beta coefficient as the relevant measure of risk. In this chapter, we extend the Chapter 6 material by presenting an in-depth treatment of portfolio concepts and the CAPM, including a more detailed look at how betas are calculated. In addition, we discuss two other asset pricing models, the Arbitrage Pricing Theory model and the Fama-French three-factor model.

Measuring Portfolio Risk

CD

The textbook's CD-ROM contains an *Excel* file that will guide you through the chapter's calculations. The file for this chapter is ***Ch 07 Tool Kit.xls,*** and we encourage you to open the file and follow along as you read the chapter.

In the preceding chapter, we examined portfolio risk at an intuitive level. We now describe how portfolio risk is actually measured and dealt with in practice. First, the risk of a portfolio, which may itself be considered as a single asset held in isolation, is measured by the standard deviation of its returns. Equation 7-1 is used to calculate this standard deviation:[1]

$$\text{Portfolio standard deviation} = \sigma_p = \sqrt{\sum_{i=1}^{n} (k_{pi} - \hat{k}_p)^2 P_i}. \qquad \textbf{(7-1)}$$

Here σ_p is the portfolio's standard deviation; k_{pi} is the return on the portfolio under the *i*th state of the economy; $\hat{k}_p$ is the expected rate of return on the portfolio; P_i is the probability of occurrence of the *i*th state of the economy; and there are n economic states. This equation is exactly the same as the one for the standard deviation of a single asset, except that here the asset is a portfolio of assets (for example, a mutual fund).

Covariance and the Correlation Coefficient

Two key concepts in portfolio analysis are (1) covariance and (2) the correlation coefficient. **Covariance** is a measure that combines the variance (or volatility) of a stock's returns with the tendency of those returns to move up or down at the same time other stocks move up or down. For example, the covariance between Stocks A and B tells us whether the returns of the two stocks tend to rise and fall together, and how large those movements tend to be. Equation 7-2 defines the covariance (Cov) between Stocks A and B:

$$\text{Covariance} = \text{Cov}(AB) = \sum_{i=1}^{n} (k_{Ai} - \hat{k}_A)(k_{Bi} - \hat{k}_B)\, P_i. \qquad \textbf{(7-2)}$$

The first term in parentheses after the Σ is the deviation of Stock A's return from its expected value under the *i*th state of the economy; the second term is Stock B's deviation under the same state; and P_i is the probability of the *i*th state occurring. Before going through an example, note these points:

1. If the returns on A and B tend to move together, the terms in parentheses will both be positive or negative for each state of the economy; that is, if k_{Ai} is above its expected value, $\hat{k}_A$, then k_{Bi} will generally be above $\hat{k}_B$, and vice versa. Therefore, if the returns

[1]Other risk measures such as the coefficient of variation or semivariance could also be used to measure the risk of a portfolio, but since portfolio returns (1) are approximately normally distributed and (2) have reasonably similar expected values, these refinements are not necessary and hence are not used.

move together, the terms in parentheses will both be positive or both be negative, hence the product $(k_{Ai} - \hat{k}_A)(k_{Bi} - \hat{k}_B)$ will be positive, while if the returns move counter to one another, the products will tend to be negative. However, if the two stocks' returns fluctuate randomly, then the products will sometimes be positive and sometimes be negative, and the sum of the products will be close to zero because the positives and negatives will tend to cancel out. Therefore, if Stocks A and B tend to move together, their covariance, Cov(AB), will be positive, while if they tend to move counter to one another, Cov(AB) will be negative. If they fluctuate randomly, Cov(AB) could be either positive or negative, but, in either event, it will be close to zero.

2. If the return on either A or B is highly uncertain, then it will have a high standard deviation, its deviations as shown in the parenthetical terms will tend to be large, the products will tend to be large, and the absolute size of Cov(AB) will also tend to be large. However, Cov(AB) will be small, even if σ_A and/or σ_B is large, if A and B move randomly, because the plus and minus terms will cancel out.
3. If either stock has a zero standard deviation, hence is riskless, then all of its deviations $(k_i - \hat{k})$ will be zero, and Cov(AB) also will be zero. Similarly, if one asset is not completely riskless, but it has a relatively low risk, then its deviations will tend to be small, and this, too, will produce a small Cov(AB).
4. Therefore, Cov(AB) will be large and positive if two assets have large standard deviations and tend to move together; it will be large and negative for two high σ assets that move counter to one another; and it will be small if the two assets' returns move randomly, rather than up or down with one another, or if either of the assets has a small standard deviation.

To illustrate the calculation process, first look at Table 7-1, which presents the probability distributions of the rates of return on four stocks, and at Figure 7-1, which plots scatter diagrams between returns on several pairs of the stocks. We can use Equation 7-2 to calculate the covariance between Stocks F and G as follows:

$$\begin{aligned}\text{Cov(FG)} &= \sum_{i=1}^{5} (k_{Fi} - \hat{k}_F)(k_{Gi} - \hat{k}_G)P_i \\ &= (6 - 10)(14 - 10)(0.1) + (8 - 10)(12 - 10)(0.2) \\ &\quad + (10 - 10)(10 - 10)(0.4) + (12 - 10)(8 - 10)(0.2) \\ &\quad + (14 - 10)(6 - 10)(0.1) \\ &= -4.8.\end{aligned}$$

The negative sign indicates that the rates of return on Stocks F and G tend to move in opposite directions, which is consistent with the pattern shown in Panel b of Figure 7-1.

TABLE 7-1 Probability Distributions of Stocks E, F, G, and H

Probability of Occurrence	Rate of Return Distribution: E	F	G	H
0.1	10.0%	6.0%	14.0%	4.0%
0.2	10.0	8.0	12.0	6.0
0.4	10.0	10.0	10.0	8.0
0.2	10.0	12.0	8.0	15.0
0.1	10.0	14.0	6.0	22.0
	$\hat{k}$ = 10.0%	10.0%	10.0%	10.0%
	σ = 0.0%	2.2%	2.2%	5.3%

FIGURE 7-1 Scatter Diagrams

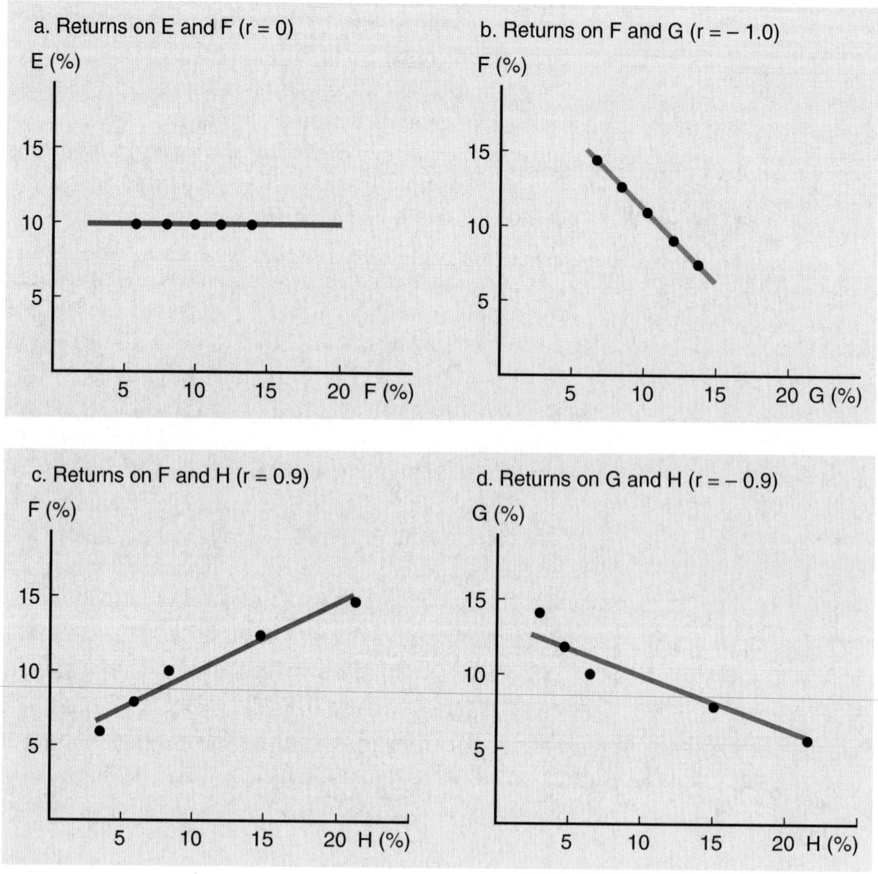

NOTES:
a. The lines shown in each graph are called *regression lines;* they will be discussed in detail in a later section.
b. These graphs are drawn as if each point had an equal probability of occurrence.

If we calculated the covariance between Stocks F and H, we would find Cov(FH) = +10.8, indicating that these assets tend to move together, as indicated by the positive slope in Panel c. A zero covariance, as between Stocks E and F, indicates that there is no relationship between the variables; that is, the variables are independent. (E's return is always 10 percent, so $\sigma_E = 0\%$, and the covariance of E with any asset must be zero.)

It is difficult to interpret the magnitude of the covariance term, so a related statistic, the **correlation coefficient,** is generally used to measure the degree of comovement between two variables. The correlation coefficient standardizes the covariance by dividing by a product term, which facilitates comparisons by putting things on a similar scale. The correlation coefficient, r, is calculated as follows for variables A and B:

$$\text{Correlation coefficient(AB)} = r_{AB} = \frac{\text{Cov(AB)}}{\sigma_A \sigma_B}. \quad (7\text{-}3)$$

The sign of the correlation coefficient is the same as the sign of the covariance, so a positive sign means that the variables move together, a negative sign indicates that they move in opposite directions, and if r is close to zero, they move independently of one another. Moreover, the standardization process confines the correlation coefficient to values between -1.0 and $+1.0$. Finally, note that Equation 7-3 can be solved to find the covariance:

$$\text{Cov(AB)} = r_{AB}\sigma_A\sigma_B. \quad \textbf{(7-3a)}$$

Using Equation 7-3, we find the correlation coefficient between Stocks F and G to be -1.0 (except for a rounding error):

$$r_{FG} = \frac{-4.8}{(2.2)(2.2)} \approx -1.0.$$

These two stocks are said to be perfectly negatively correlated. As Panel b of Figure 7-1 shows, the regression line for these two assets' rates of return is negatively sloped, and all points lie exactly on the line. Whenever the points are all on the regression line, r must be equal to 1.0 if the line slopes up and equal to -1.0 if the line slopes down.

The correlation coefficient between Stocks F and H is $+0.9$. Thus, there is a strong positive relationship—their regression line is upward sloping, but all points in Panel c are not exactly on the line. Generally, the closer the points are to the regression line, the higher the absolute value of the correlation coefficient.

The Two-Asset Case

Under the assumption that the distributions of returns on the individual securities are normal, a complicated looking but operationally simple equation can be used to determine the risk of a two-asset portfolio:[2]

$$\text{Portfolio SD} = \sigma_p = \sqrt{w_A^2\sigma_A^2 + (1 - w_A)^2\sigma_B^2 + 2w_A(1 - w_A)r_{AB}\sigma_A\sigma_B}. \quad \textbf{(7-4)}$$

Here w_A is the fraction of the portfolio invested in Security A, so $(1 - w_A)$ is the fraction invested in Security B. We illustrate the equation in the next section.

Self-Test Questions

How is the risk of a portfolio measured?

What does the correlation coefficient measure?

Efficient Portfolios

One important use of portfolio risk concepts is to select **efficient portfolios,** defined as those portfolios that provide the highest expected return for any degree of risk, or the lowest degree of risk for any expected return. To illustrate the concept, assume that two securities, A and B, are available, and we can allocate our funds between them in any proportion. Suppose Security A has an expected rate of return of $\hat{k}_A = 5\%$ and a standard deviation of returns $\sigma_A = 4\%$, while $\hat{k}_B = 8\%$ and $\sigma_B = 10\%$. Our first task is to determine the set of *attainable* portfolios, and then from this attainable set to select the *efficient* subset.

To construct the attainable set, we need data on the degree of correlation between the two securities' expected returns, r_{AB}. Let us work with three different assumed degrees of correlation, $r_{AB} = +1.0$, $r_{AB} = 0$, and $r_{AB} = -1.0$, and use them to develop the portfolios' expected returns, $\hat{k}_p$, and standard deviations, σ_p. (Of course, only one

[2]Equation 7-4 is derived from Equation 7-1 in standard statistics books. Notice that if $w_A = 1$, all of the portfolio is invested in Security A, and Equation 7-4 reduces to σ_A:

$$\sigma_p = \sqrt{\sigma_A^2} = \sigma_A.$$

The portfolio contains but a single asset, so the risk of the portfolio and that of the asset are identical. Equation 7-4 could be expanded to include any number of assets by adding additional terms, but we shall not do so here.

correlation can exist; our example simply shows three alternative situations that might exist.)

To calculate $\hat{k}_p$, we use a modified version of Equation 6-5 from Chapter 6, substituting the given values for $\hat{k}_A$ and $\hat{k}_B$, and then solving for $\hat{k}_p$ at different values of w_A. For example, when w_A equals 0.75, then $\hat{k}_p = 5.75\%$:

$$\begin{aligned}\hat{k}_p &= w_A\hat{k}_A + (1 - w_A)\hat{k}_B \\ &= 0.75(5\%) + 0.25(8\%) = 5.75\%.\end{aligned} \qquad \textbf{(6-5a)}$$

Other values of $\hat{k}_p$ were found similarly, and they are shown in the $\hat{k}_p$ column of Table 7-2.

Next, we use Equation 7-4 to find σ_p. Substitute the given values for σ_A, σ_B, and r_{AB}, and then solve for σ_p at different values of w_A. For example, in the case where $r_{AB} = 0$ and $w_A = 0.75$, then $\sigma_p = 3.9\%$:

$$\begin{aligned}\sigma_p &= \sqrt{w_A^2\sigma_A^2 + (1 - w_A)^2\sigma_B^2 + 2w_A(1 - w_A)r_{AB}\sigma_A\sigma_B} \\ &= \sqrt{(0.5625)(16) + (0.0625)(100) + 2(0.75)(0.25)(0)(4)(10)} \\ &= \sqrt{9.00 + 6.25} = \sqrt{15.25} = 3.9\%.\end{aligned}$$

Table 7-2 gives $\hat{k}_p$ and σ_p values for $w_A = 1.00, 0.75, 0.50, 0.25$, and 0.00, and Figure 7-2 plots $\hat{k}_p$, σ_p, and the attainable set of portfolios for each correlation. In both the table and the graphs, note the following points:

1. The three graphs across the top row of Figure 7-2 designate Case I, where the two assets are perfectly positively correlated, that is, $r_{AB} = +1.0$. The three graphs in the middle row are for the zero correlation case, and the three in the bottom row are for perfect negative correlation.
2. All three cases are more theoretical than realistic because we would rarely encounter $r_{AB} = -1.0$, 0.0, or +1.0. Generally, in the real world r_{AB} would be in the range of +0.5 to +0.7 for most stocks. Case II (zero correlation) produces graphs which, pictorially, most closely resemble real-world examples.
3. The left column of graphs shows how the *expected portfolio returns* vary with different combinations of A and B. We see that these graphs are identical in each of the three cases: The portfolio return, $\hat{k}_p$, is a linear function of w_A, and it does not depend on the correlation coefficients. This is also seen from the single $\hat{k}_p$ column back in Table 7-2.
4. The middle column of graphs shows how risk is affected by the portfolio mix. Starting from the top, we see that portfolio risk, σ_p, increases linearly in Case I, where $r_{AB} = +1.0$; it is nonlinear in Case II; and Case III shows that risk can be completely diversified away if $r_{AB} = -1.0$. Thus σ_p, unlike $\hat{k}_p$, *does* depend on correlation.

TABLE 7-2 $\hat{k}_p$ and σ_p under Various Assumptions

Proportion of Portfolio in Security A (Value of w_A)	Proportion of Portfolio in Security B (Value of $1 - w_A$)	$\hat{k}_p$	σ_p: Case I ($r_{AB} = +1.0$)	σ_p: Case II ($r_{AB} = 0$)	σ_p: Case III ($r_{AB} = -1.0$)
1.00	0.00	5.00%	4.0%	4.0%	4.0%
0.75	0.25	5.75	5.5	3.9	0.5
0.50	0.50	6.50	7.0	5.4	3.0
0.25	0.75	7.25	8.5	7.6	6.5
0.00	1.00	8.00	10.0	10.0	10.0

FIGURE 7-2 Illustrations of Portfolio Returns, Risk, and the Attainable Set of Portfolios

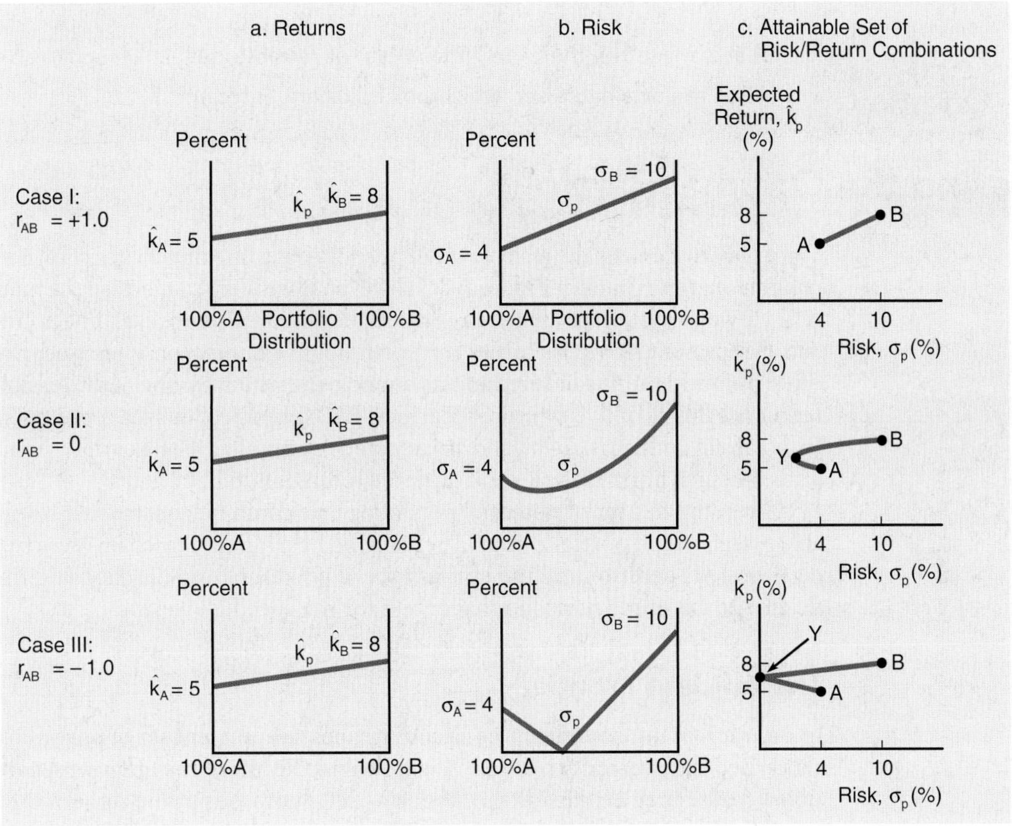

5. Note that in both Cases II and III, but not in Case I, someone holding only Stock A could sell some A, buy some B, and both increase his or her expected return and lower risk.
6. The right column of graphs shows the attainable, or feasible set of portfolios constructed with different mixes of Securities A and B. Unlike the other columns, which plotted return and risk versus the portfolio's composition, each of the three graphs here were plotted from pairs of $\hat{k}_p$ and σ_p as shown in Table 7-2. For example, Point A in the upper right graph is the point $\hat{k}_p = 5\%$, $\sigma_p = 4\%$ from the Case I data. All other points on the curves were plotted similarly. With only two securities in the portfolio, the attainable set is a curve or line, and we can achieve each risk/return combination on the relevant curve by some allocation of our investment funds between Securities A and B.
7. Are all combinations on the attainable set equally good? The answer is no: Only that part of the attainable set from Y to B in Cases II and III is defined to be efficient. The part from A to Y is inefficient because for any degree of risk on the line segment AY, a higher return can be found on segment YB. Thus, no rational investor would hold a portfolio that lay on segment AY. In Case I, however, the entire feasible set is efficient—no combination of the securities can be ruled out.

From these examples we see that in one extreme case (r = −1.0), risk can be completely eliminated, while in the other extreme case (r = +1.0), diversification does no good whatever. In between these extremes, combining two stocks into a portfolio reduces but does not eliminate the risk inherent in the individual stocks.[3]

Self-Test Questions

What is meant by the term "attainable, or feasible, set"?

Within the attainable set, which portfolios are "efficient"?

Choosing the Optimal Portfolio

With only two assets, the feasible set of portfolios is a line or curve as shown in the third column of graphs back in Figure 7-2. However, if we were to increase the number of assets, we would obtain an area such as the shaded area in Figure 7-3. The points A, H, G, and E represent single securities (or portfolios containing only one security). All the other points in the shaded area and its boundaries, which comprise the feasible set, represent portfolios of two or more securities. Each point in this area represents a particular portfolio with a risk of σ_p and an expected return of $\hat{k}_p$. For example, point X represents one such portfolio's risk and expected return, as do B, C, and D.

Given the full set of potential portfolios that could be constructed from the available assets, which portfolio should actually be held? This choice involves two separate decisions: (1) determining the efficient set of portfolios and (2) choosing from the efficient set the single portfolio that is best for the specific investor.

The Efficient Frontier

In Figure 7-3, the boundary line BCDE defines the efficient set of portfolios, which is also called the **efficient frontier.**[4] Portfolios to the left of the efficient set are not possible because they lie outside the attainable set. Portfolios to the right of the boundary line (interior portfolios) are inefficient because some other portfolio would provide either a higher return for the same degree of risk or a lower risk for the same rate of return. For example, Portfolio X is dominated by Portfolios C and D.

Risk/Return Indifference Curves

Given the efficient set of portfolios, which specific portfolio should an investor choose? To determine the optimal portfolio for a particular investor, we must know the investor's attitude toward risk as reflected in his or her risk/return trade-off function, or **indifference curve.**

An investor's risk/return trade-off function is based on the standard economic concepts of utility theory and indifference curves, which are illustrated in Figure 7-4. The curves labeled I_Y and I_Z represent the indifference curves of Individuals Y and Z. Ms.

---

[3]If we differentiate Equation 7-4, set the derivative equal to zero, and then solve for w_A, we obtain the fraction of the portfolio that should be invested in Security A if we wish to form the least-risky portfolio. Here is the equation:

$$\text{Minimum risk portfolio: } w_A = \frac{\sigma_B(\sigma_B - r_{AB}\sigma_A)}{\sigma_A^2 + \sigma_B^2 - 2r_{AB}\sigma_A\sigma_B}.$$

As a rule, we limit w_A to the range 0 to +1.0; that is, if the solution value is $w_A > 1.0$, set $w_A = 1.0$, and if w_A is negative, set $w_A = 0$. A w_A value that is either negative or greater than 1.0 implies short sales. (See Footnote 7 for a definition of a short sale.)

[4]A computational procedure for determining the efficient set of portfolios was developed by Harry Markowitz and first reported in his article "Portfolio Selection," *Journal of Finance*, March 1952. In this article, Markowitz developed the basic concepts of portfolio theory, and he later won the Nobel Prize in economics for his work.

FIGURE 7-3 The Efficient Set of Investments

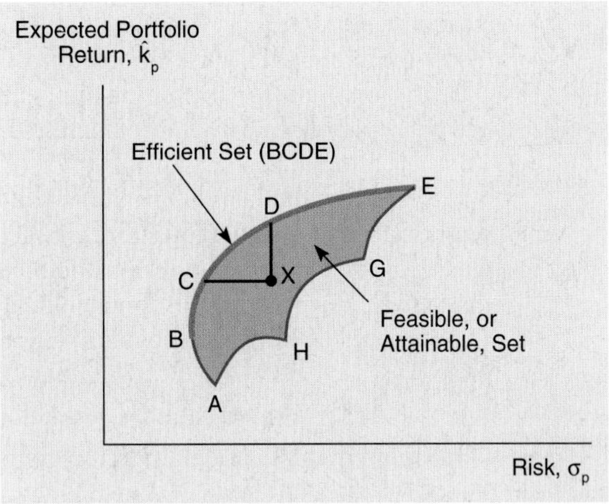

Y is indifferent with regard to the riskless 5 percent portfolio, a portfolio with an expected return of 6 percent but a risk of $\sigma_p = 1.4\%$, and so on. Mr. Z is indifferent between a riskless 5 percent return, an expected 6 percent return with risk of $\sigma_p = 3.3\%$, and so on.

Note that Ms. Y requires a higher expected rate of return to compensate for any given amount of risk; thus, Ms. Y is said to be more **risk averse** than Mr. Z. Her

FIGURE 7-4 Risk/Return Indifference Curves

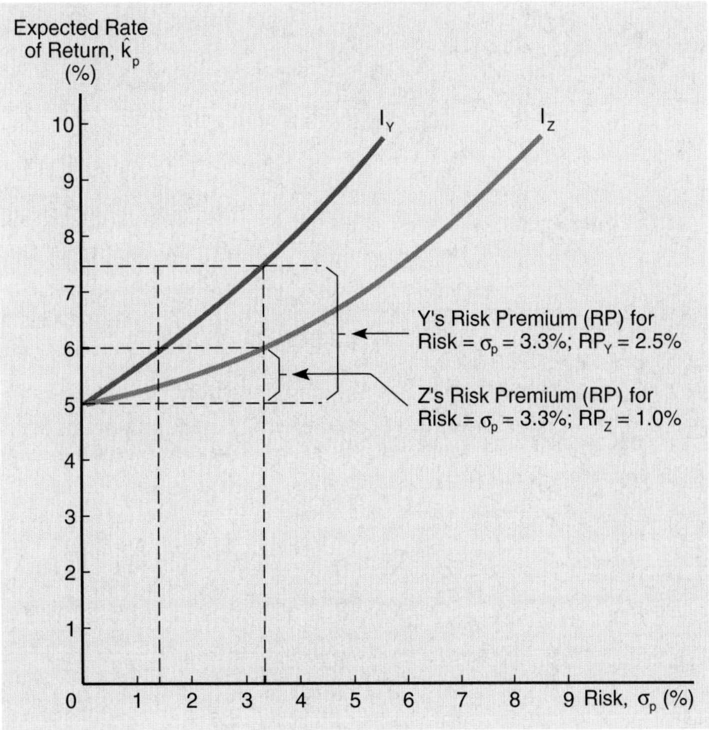

higher risk aversion causes Ms. Y to require a higher **risk premium**—defined here as the difference between the 5 percent riskless return and the expected return required to compensate for any specific amount of risk—than does Mr. Z. Thus, Ms. Y requires a risk premium (RP_Y) of 2.5 percent to compensate for a risk of $\sigma_p = 3.3\%$, while Mr. Z's risk premium for this degree of risk is only $RP_Z = 1.0\%$. *As a generalization, the steeper the slope of an investor's indifference curve, the more risk averse the investor.* Thus, Ms. Y is more risk averse than Mr. Z.

Each individual has a "map" of indifference curves; the indifference maps for Ms. Y and Mr. Z are shown in Figure 7-5. The higher curves denote a greater level of satisfaction (or utility). Thus, I_{Z2} is better than I_{Z1} because, for any level of risk, Mr. Z has a higher expected return, hence greater utility. An infinite number of indifference curves could be drawn in the map for each individual, and each individual has a unique map.

The Optimal Portfolio for an Investor

Figure 7-5 also shows the feasible set of portfolios for the two-asset case, under the assumption that $r_{AB} = 0$, as it was developed in Figure 7-2. The optimal portfolio for each investor is found at the tangency point between the efficient set of portfolios and one of the investor's indifference curves. This tangency point marks the highest level of satisfaction the investor can attain. Ms. Y, who is more risk averse than Mr. Z, chooses a portfolio with a lower expected return (about 6 percent) but a risk of only $\sigma_p = 4.2\%$. Mr. Z picks a portfolio that provides an expected return of about 7.2 percent, but it has a risk of about $\sigma_p = 7.1\%$. Ms. Y's portfolio is more heavily weighted

FIGURE 7-5 Selecting the Optimal Portfolio of Risky Assets

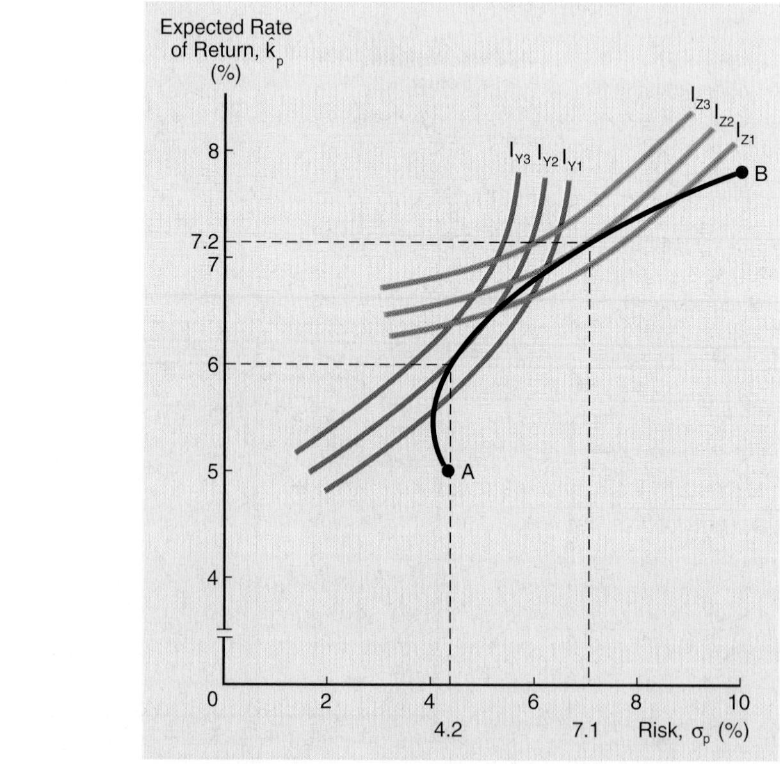

with the less risky security, while Mr. Z's portfolio contains a larger proportion of the more risky security.[5]

Self-Test Questions

What is the efficient frontier?

What are indifference curves?

Conceptually, how does an investor choose his or her optimal portfolio?

The Capital Asset Pricing Model

The **Capital Asset Pricing Model (CAPM),** which was introduced in Chapter 6, specifies the relationship between risk and required rates of return on assets when they are held in well-diversified portfolios. In Chapter 6, we focused on the Security Market Line, because that is the "bottom line" of the CAPM. In this chapter, we expand on that discussion by presenting the assumptions behind the CAPM and by showing how the SML was developed.

Basic Assumptions of the CAPM

As in all financial theories, a number of assumptions were made in the development of the CAPM; they are summarized in the following list:[6]

1. All investors focus on a single holding period, and they seek to maximize the expected utility of their terminal wealth by choosing among alternative portfolios on the basis of each portfolio's expected return and standard deviation.
2. All investors can borrow or lend an unlimited amount at a given risk-free rate of interest, k_{RF}, and there are no restrictions on short sales of any asset.[7]
3. All investors have identical estimates of the expected returns, variances, and covariances among all assets; that is, investors have homogeneous expectations.
4. All assets are perfectly divisible and perfectly liquid (that is, marketable at the going price).
5. There are no transactions costs.
6. There are no taxes.
7. All investors are price takers (that is, all investors assume that their own buying and selling activity will not affect stock prices).
8. The quantities of all assets are given and fixed.

Theoretical extensions in the literature have relaxed some of these assumptions, and in general these extensions have led to conclusions that are reasonably consistent with the basic theory. However, even the extensions contain assumptions which are both

[5]Ms. Y's portfolio would contain 67 percent of Security A and 33 percent of Security B, whereas Mr. Z's portfolio would consist of 27 percent of Security A and 73 percent of Security B. These percentages can be determined with Equation 6-5a by simply seeing what percentage of the two securities is consistent with $\hat{k}_p = 6.0\%$ and 7.2%. For example, $w_A(5\%) + (1 - w_A)(8\%) = 7.2\%$, and solving for w_A, we obtain $w_A = 0.27$ and $(1 - w_A) = 0.73$.

[6]The CAPM was originated by William F. Sharpe in his article "Capital Asset Prices: A Theory of Market Equilibrium under Conditions of Risk," which appeared in the September 1964 issue of the *Journal of Finance.* Note that Professor Sharpe won the Nobel Prize in economics for his capital asset pricing work. The assumptions inherent in Sharpe's model were spelled out by Michael C. Jensen in "Capital Markets: Theory and Evidence," *Bell Journal of Economics and Management Science*, Autumn 1972, 357–398.

[7]In a **short sale,** one borrows a stock and then sells it, expecting to buy it back later (at a lower price) in order to repay the person from whom the stock was borrowed. If you sell short and the stock price rises, you lose, but you win if the price declines.

strong and unrealistic, so the validity of the model can only be established through empirical tests. More will be said later about the empirical validity of the CAPM, but first we must discuss its basic properties and conclusions.

Self-Test Questions

What are the key assumptions of the CAPM?

In what sense are these assumptions unrealistic? Explain.

The Capital Market Line and the Security Market Line

Figure 7-5 showed the set of portfolio opportunities for the two-asset case, and it illustrated how indifference curves can be used to select the optimal portfolio from the feasible set. In Figure 7-6, we show a similar diagram for the many-asset case, but here we also include a risk-free asset with a return k_{RF}. The riskless asset by definition has zero risk, hence $\sigma = 0\%$, so it is plotted on the vertical axis.

The figure shows both the feasible set of portfolios of risky assets (the shaded area) and a set of indifference curves (I_1, I_2, I_3) for a particular investor. Point N, where indifference curve I_1 is tangent to the efficient set, represents a possible portfolio choice; it is the point on the efficient set of risky portfolios where the investor obtains the highest possible return for a given amount of risk and the smallest degree of risk for a given expected return.

However, the investor can do better than Portfolio N—he or she can reach a higher indifference curve. In addition to the feasible set of risky portfolios, we now have a risk-free asset that provides a riskless return, k_{RF}. Given the risk-free asset, investors can create new portfolios that combine the risk-free asset with a portfolio of risky assets. This enables them to achieve any combination of risk and return on the straight line connecting k_{RF} with M, the point of tangency between that straight line and the efficient frontier of risky asset portfolios.[8] Some portfolios on the line $k_{RF}MZ$ will be preferred to most risky portfolios on the efficient frontier BNME, so the points on the line $k_{RF}MZ$ now represent the best attainable combinations of risk and return.

---

[8]The risk/return combinations between a risk-free asset and a risky asset (a single stock or a portfolio of stocks) will always be linear. To see this, consider the following equations, which were developed earlier, for return, $\hat{k}_p$, and risk, σ_p, for any combination w_{RF} and $(1 - w_{RF})$:

$$\hat{k}_p = w_{RF}k_{RF} + (1 - w_{RF})\hat{k}_M, \qquad \textbf{(6-5a)}$$

and

$$\sigma_p = \sqrt{w_{RF}^2\sigma_{RF}^2 + (1 - w_{RF})^2\sigma_M^2 + 2w_{RF}(1 - w_{RF})r_{RF/M}\sigma_{RF}\sigma_M}. \qquad \textbf{(7-4a)}$$

Equation 6-5a is linear. As for Equation 7-4a, we know that k_{RF} is the risk-free asset, so $\sigma_{RF} = 0$; hence, σ^2_{RF} is also zero. Using this information, we can simplify Equation 7-4a as follows:

$$\sigma_p = \sqrt{(1 - w_{RF})^2\sigma_M^2} = (1 - w_{RF})\sigma_M. \qquad \textbf{(7-4b)}$$

Thus, σ_p is also linear when a riskless asset is combined with a portfolio of risky assets.

If expected returns as measured by $\hat{k}_p$ and risk as measured by σ_p are both linear functions of w_{RF}, then the relationship between $\hat{k}_p$ and σ_p, when graphed as in Figure 7-6, must also be linear. For example, if 100 percent of the portfolio is invested in k_{RF} with a return of 8 percent, the portfolio return will be 8 percent and σ_p will be 0. If 100 percent is invested in M, with $k_M = 12\%$ and $\sigma_M = 10\%$, then $\sigma_p = 1.0(10\%) = 10\%$, and $\hat{k}_p = 0(8\%) + 1.0(12\%) = 12\%$. If 50 percent of the portfolio is invested in M and 50 percent in the risk-free asset, then $\sigma_p = 0.5(10\%) = 5\%$, and $\hat{k}_p = 0.5(8\%) + 0.5(12\%) = 10\%$. Plotting these points will reveal the linear relationship given as $k_{RF}MZ$ in Figure 7-6.

FIGURE 7-6 Investor Equilibrium: Combining the Risk-Free Asset with the Market Portfolio

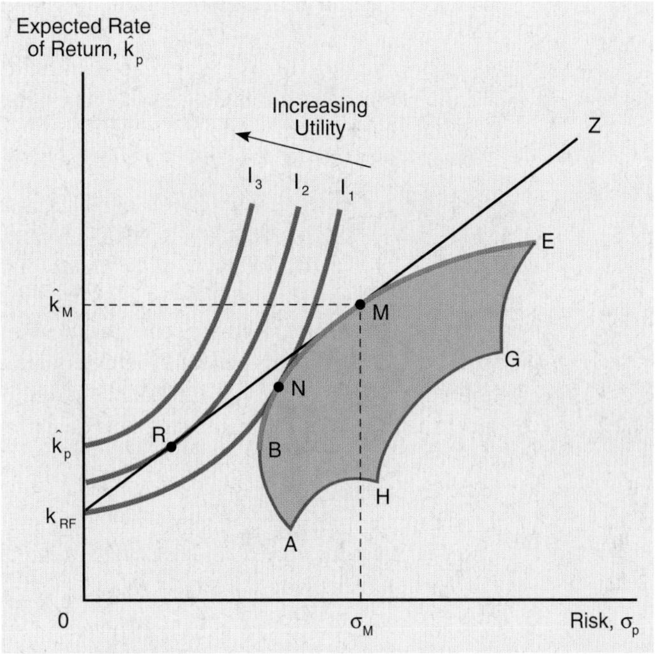

Given the new opportunities along line $k_{RF}MZ$, our investor will move from Point N to Point R, which is on his or her highest attainable risk/return indifference curve. Note that any point on the old efficient frontier BNME (except the point of tangency M) is dominated by some point along the line $k_{RF}MZ$. In general, since investors can include both the risk-free security and a fraction of the risky portfolio, M, in a portfolio, it will be possible to move to a point such as R. In addition, if the investor can borrow as well as lend (lending is equivalent to buying risk-free debt securities) at the riskless rate, k_{RF}, it is possible to move out on the line segment MZ, and one would do so if his or her indifference curve were tangent to $k_{RF}MZ$ to the right of Point M.[9]

All investors should hold portfolios lying on the line $k_{RF}MZ$ under the conditions assumed in the CAPM. This implies that they should hold portfolios that are combinations of the risk-free security and the risky portfolio M. Thus, the addition of the risk-free asset totally changes the efficient set: The efficient set now lies along line $k_{RF}MZ$ rather than along the curve BNME. Also, note that if the capital market is to be in equilibrium, M must be a portfolio that contains every risky asset in exact proportion to that asset's fraction of the total market value of all assets; that is, if Security i is X percent of the total market value of all securities, X percent of the market portfolio M must consist of Security i. (In other words, M is the market-value-weighted

[9]An investor who is highly averse to risk will have a steep indifference curve and will end up holding only the riskless asset, or perhaps at a point such as R, holding some of the risky market portfolio and some of the riskless asset. An investor only slightly averse to risk will have a relatively flat indifference curve, which will cause him or her to move out beyond M toward Z, borrowing to do so. This investor might buy stocks on *margin*, which means borrowing and using the stocks as collateral. If individuals' borrowing rates are higher than k_{RF}, then the line $k_{RF}MZ$ will tilt down (that is, be less steep) beyond M. This condition would invalidate the basic CAPM, or at least require it to be modified. Therefore, the assumption of being able to borrow or lend at the same rate is crucial to CAPM theory.

portfolio of *all* risky assets in the economy.) Thus, all investors should hold portfolios which lie on the line $k_{RF}MZ$, with the particular location of a given individual's portfolio being determined by the point at which his or her indifference curve is tangent to the line.

The line $k_{RF}MZ$ in Figure 7-6 is called the **Capital Market Line (CML).** It has an intercept of k_{RF} and a slope of $(\hat{k}_M - k_{RF})/\sigma_M$.[10] Therefore, the equation for the Capital Market Line may be expressed as follows:

$$\text{CML: } \hat{k}_p = k_{RF} + \left(\frac{\hat{k}_M - k_{RF}}{\sigma_M}\right)\sigma_p. \qquad (7\text{-}5)$$

The expected rate of return *on an efficient portfolio* is equal to the riskless rate plus a risk premium that is equal to $(\hat{k}_M - k_{RF})/\sigma_M$ multiplied by the portfolio's standard deviation, σ_p. Thus, the CML specifies a linear relationship between expected return and risk, with the slope of the CML being equal to the expected return on the market portfolio of risky stocks, $\hat{k}_M$, minus the risk-free rate, k_{RF}, which is called the **market risk premium,** all divided by the standard deviation of returns on the market portfolio, σ_M:

$$\text{Slope of the CML} = (\hat{k}_M - k_{RF})/\sigma_M.$$

For example, suppose $k_{RF} = 10\%$, $\hat{k}_M = 15\%$, and $\sigma_M = 15\%$. Then, the slope of the CML would be $(15\% - 10\%)/15\% = 0.33$, and if a particular portfolio had $\sigma_p = 10\%$, then its $\hat{k}_p$ would be

$$\hat{k}_p = 10\% + 0.33(10\%) = 13.3\%.$$

A riskier portfolio with $\sigma_p = 20\%$ would have $\hat{k}_p = 10\% + 0.33(20\%) = 16.6\%$.

The CML is graphed in Figure 7-7. It is a straight line with an intercept at k_{RF} and a slope equal to the market risk premium $(\hat{k}_M - k_{RF})$ divided by σ_M. The slope of the CML reflects the aggregate attitude of investors toward risk.

Note that an efficient portfolio is one that is well diversified, hence all of its unsystematic risk has been eliminated and its only remaining risk is market risk. Therefore,

[10]Recall that the slope of any line is measured as $\Delta Y/\Delta X$, or the change in height associated with a given change in horizontal distance. k_{RF} is at 0 on the horizontal axis, so $\Delta X = \sigma_M - 0 = \sigma_M$. The vertical axis difference associated with a change from k_{RF} to $\hat{k}_M$ is $\hat{k}_M - k_{RF}$. Therefore, slope $= \Delta Y/\Delta X = (\hat{k}_M - k_{RF})/\sigma_M$.

FIGURE 7-7 The Capital Market Line (CML)

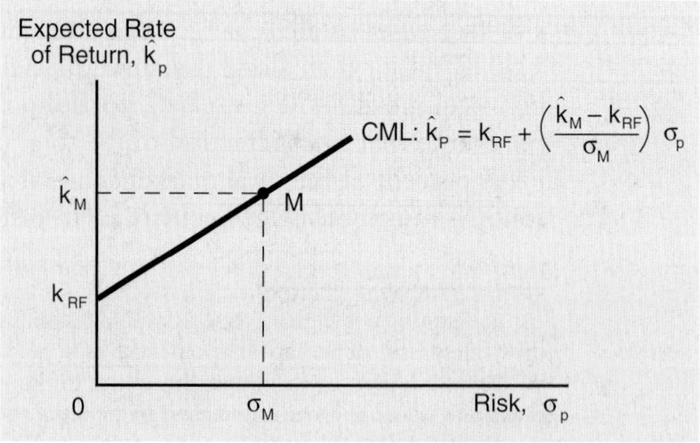

NOTE: We did not draw it in, but you can visualize the shaded space shown in Figure 7-6 in this graph, and the CML as the line formed by connecting k_{RF} with the tangent to the shaded space.

unlike individual stocks, the risk of an efficient portfolio is measured by its standard deviation, σ_p. The CML equation specifies the relationship between risk and return for such efficient portfolios, that is, for portfolios that lie on the CML, and in the CML equation and graph, risk is measured by the portfolio standard deviation.

The CML specifies the relationship between risk and return for an efficient portfolio, but investors and managers are more concerned about the relationship between risk and return for *individual assets*. To develop the risk-return relationship for individual securities, note in Figure 7-6 that all investors are assumed to hold portfolio M, so M must be the market portfolio, that is, the one that contains all stocks. Note also that M is an *efficient* portfolio. Thus, the CML defines the relationship between the market portfolio's expected return and its standard deviation. Equations 6-5a and 7-4 show the formulas for the expected return and standard deviation for a two-asset portfolio, and there exist analogous equations for the expected return and standard deviation of a portfolio that contains many assets, such as the market portfolio.[11] It is possible to take the equations for the expected return and standard deviation of a multi-asset portfolio and show that the required return for each individual stock, i, must conform to the following equation in order for the CML to hold for the market portfolio:

$$
\begin{aligned}
k_i &= k_{RF} + \frac{(k_M - k_{RF})}{\sigma_M}\left(\frac{\mathrm{Cov}(k_i, k_M)}{\sigma_M}\right) \\
&= k_{RF} + (k_M - k_{RF})\left(\frac{\mathrm{Cov}(k_i, k_M)}{\sigma_M^2}\right).
\end{aligned}
\tag{7-6}
$$

The CAPM defines the beta coefficient of company i, b_i, as follows:

$$
\begin{aligned}
b_i &= \frac{\text{Covariance between Stock i and the market}}{\text{Variance of market returns}} = \frac{\mathrm{Cov}(k_i, k_M)}{\sigma_M^2} \\
&= \frac{r_{iM}\sigma_i\sigma_M}{\sigma_M^2} = r_{iM}\left(\frac{\sigma_i}{M}\right).
\end{aligned}
\tag{7-7}
$$

Recall that the risk premium for the market, RP_M, is $k_M - k_{RF}$. Using this definition and substituting Equation 7-7 into Equation 7-6 gives the Security Market Line (SML):

$$
\begin{aligned}
\mathrm{SML} = k_i &= k_{RF} + (k_M - k_{RF})b_i \\
&= k_{RF} + (RP_M)b_i.
\end{aligned}
\tag{7-8}
$$

The SML tells us that an individual stock's required return is equal to the risk-free rate plus a premium for bearing risk. The premium for risk is equal to the risk premium for the market, RP_M, multiplied by the risk of the individual stock, as measured by its beta coefficient. The beta coefficient measures the amount of risk that the stock contributes to the market portfolio.

Unlike the CML for a well-diversified portfolio, the SML tells us that the standard deviation (σ_i) of an individual stock should not be used to measure its risk, because some of the risk as reflected by σ_i can be eliminated by diversification. Therefore, because beta reflects risk after taking diversification benefits into account, beta rather than σ_i is used to measure individual stocks' risk to investors. Be sure to keep in mind the distinction between the SML and the CML, and why that distinction exists.

[11]The percentage of the investment in asset i is w_i, the expected return for asset i is $\hat{k}_i$, the standard deviation of asset i is σ_i, and the correlation between asset i and asset j is r_{ij}. The expected return for a portfolio with N assets is $\hat{k}_p = \sum_{i=1}^{N}(w_i\hat{k}_i)$ and the variance of the portfolio is $\sigma_p^2 = \sum_{i=1}^{N}\sum_{j=1}^{N}(w_iw_j\sigma_i\sigma_jr_{ij})$.

Self-Test Questions

Draw a graph showing the feasible set of risky assets, the efficient frontier, the risk-free asset, and the CML.

Write out the equation for the CML, and explain its meaning.

Write out the equation for the SML, and explain its meaning.

What is the difference between the CML and the SML?

Calculating Beta Coefficients

Equation 7-7 defines beta, but recall from Chapter 6 that this equation for beta also is the formula for the slope coefficient in a regression of the stock return against the market return. Therefore, beta can be calculated by plotting the historical returns of a stock on the y-axis of a graph, the historical returns of the market portfolio on the x-axis, and fitting the regression line. In his 1964 article that set forth the CAPM, Sharpe called this regression line the **characteristic line.** Thus, a stock's beta is the slope of its characteristic line. In Chapter 7 we used this approach to calculate the beta for Wal-Mart Stores. In this chapter, we perform a more detailed analysis of the calculation of beta for Wal-Mart, and we also perform a similar analysis for a portfolio of stocks, Fidelity's Magellan Fund.

Calculating the Beta Coefficient for a Single Stock: Wal-Mart Stores

Table 7-3 shows a portion of the data used in this analysis; the full data set is in the file ***Ch 07 Tool Kit.xls*** on your textbook's CD-ROM. Table 7-3 shows the market returns (defined as the percentage price change of the Wilshire 5000 Index), the stock returns for Wal-Mart, and the returns on the Magellan Fund (which is a well-diversified

TABLE 7-3 Returns Data for Calculating Beta, May 1996–April 2000

Date	Market Return (Wilshire 5000 Index)	Wal-Mart Return	Fidelity Magellan Fund Return	Risk-Free Rate (Monthly Return on 3-Month T-bill)
April 2000	−5.3%	−2.0%	−4.3%	0.47%
March 2000	7.5	16.2	9.1	0.47
February 2000	0.5	−11.0	1.0	0.46
January 2000	−4.2	−20.8	−4.8	0.44
December 1999	5.6	20.1	6.9	0.43
November 1999	5.0	2.3	2.0	0.42
. . .	. . .	. . .	. . .	. . .
. . .	. . .	. . .	. . .	. . .
. . .	. . .	. . .	. . .	. . .
July 1996	−5.5	−5.4	−4.7	0.43
June 1996	−1.0	−1.5	−0.1	0.42
May 1996	2.5	8.4	0.4	0.42
Average return (annual)	19.8%	45.3%	21.5%	4.9%
Standard deviation (annual)	16.6%	32.3%	16.8%	0.1%
Correlation with the market return, r		0.54	0.97	0.15
R^2		0.29	0.94	0.02

portfolio). Table 7-3 also shows the risk-free rate, defined as the rate on a short-term U.S. Treasury bill, which we will use later in this analysis.

As Table 7-3 shows, Wal-Mart had an average annual return of 45.3 percent during this four-year period, while the market had an average annual return of 19.8 percent. As we noted before, it is usually unreasonable to think that the future expected return for a stock will equal the average historical return over a relatively short period, such as four years. However, we might well expect past volatility to be a reasonable estimate of future volatility, at least during the next couple of years. Note that the standard deviation for Wal-Mart's returns during this period was 32.3 percent, and that of the market was 16.6 percent, about half that of Wal-Mart. This is what we would expect, since the market is a well-diversified portfolio from which much risk has been diversified away. The correlation between Wal-Mart's returns and the market's returns is about 0.54, which is close to the correlation for an average stock.

Figure 7-8 shows a plot of Wal-Mart's returns against market returns. As you will notice if you look in the file ***Ch 07 Tool Kit.xls,*** we used the *Excel* Chart feature to add a trend line and to display the equation and R^2 value on the chart itself. We also used the *Excel* regression analysis feature, which provides additional data.

Table 7-4 reports some of the regression results for Wal-Mart. Its estimated beta, which is the slope coefficient, is about 1.05. This means that Wal-Mart's beta is close to the average beta of 1.0. Therefore, Wal-Mart moves up and down, on average, by roughly the same percent as the market. As with all regression results, 1.05 is just an estimate of beta, and not necessarily the true value of beta. Table 7-4 also shows the t statistic and the probability that the true beta is zero. For Wal-Mart, this probability is approximately equal to zero. This means that there is virtually a zero chance that the true beta is equal to zero. Since this probability is less than 5 percent, statisticians

FIGURE 7-8 Calculating a Beta Coefficient for Wal-Mart Stores

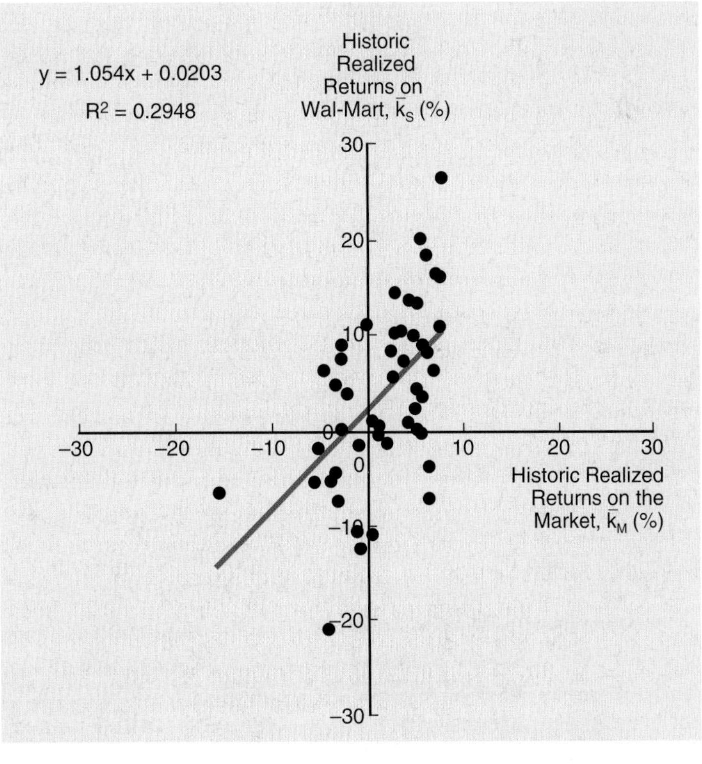

TABLE 7-4 Regression Results for Calculating Beta

	Regression Coefficient	t Statistic	Probability of t Statistic	Lower 95% Confidence Interval	Upper 95% Confidence Interval
Panel a: Wal-Mart (market model)					
Intercept	0.02	1.68	0.10	0.00	0.04
Slope	1.05	4.39	0.00	0.57	1.54
Panel b: Magellan Fund (market model)					
Intercept	0.00	0.96	0.34	0.00	0.01
Slope	0.98	25.67	0.00	0.90	1.05
Panel c: Wal-Mart (CAPM)[a]					
Intercept	0.02	1.74	0.09	0.00	0.04
Slope	1.05	4.39	0.00	0.57	1.54

[a]The market model uses actual historical returns. The CAPM use returns in excess of the risk-free rate.

would say that the slope coefficient, beta, is "statistically significant." The output of the regression analysis also gives us the 95 percent confidence interval for the estimate of beta. For Wal-Mart, the results tell us that we can be 95 percent confident that the true beta is between 0.57 and 1.54. This is an extremely wide range, but it is typical for most individual stocks. Therefore, the regression estimate for the beta of any single company is highly uncertain.

Note also that the points in Figure 7-8 are not clustered very tightly around the regression line. Sometimes Wal-Mart does much better than the market, other times it does much worse. The R^2 value shown in the chart measures the degree of dispersion about the regression line. Statistically speaking, it measures the percent of variance that is explained by the regression equation. An R^2 of 1.0 indicates that all points lie exactly on the line, hence that all of the variance of the y-variable is explained by the x-variable. The R^2 for Wal-Mart is about 0.29, which is typical for most individual stocks. This indicates that about 29 percent of the variance in Wal-Mart's returns is explained by the market return.

Finally, note that the intercept shown in the regression equation displayed on the chart is about 0.02. Since the regression equation is based on monthly data, this means that Wal-Mart had a 2 percent average monthly return that was not explained by the CAPM model. However, the regression results in Table 7-4 also show that the probability of the t statistic is greater than 5 percent, meaning that the "true" intercept might be zero. Therefore, most statisticians would say that this intercept is not statistically significant—the returns of Wal-Mart are so volatile that we cannot be sure that the true intercept is not equal to zero. Translating statistician-talk into English, this means that the part of Wal-Mart's average monthly return that is not explained by the CAPM could very well be zero. Thus, the CAPM might very well explain all of Wal-Mart's average monthly returns.

Calculating the Beta Coefficient for a Portfolio: The Magellan Fund

We repeat the analysis with data for the Magellan Fund, which is a well-diversified portfolio. Figure 7-9 shows the plot of Magellan's monthly returns versus the

FIGURE 7-9 Calculating a Beta Coefficient for Fidelity's Magellan Fund

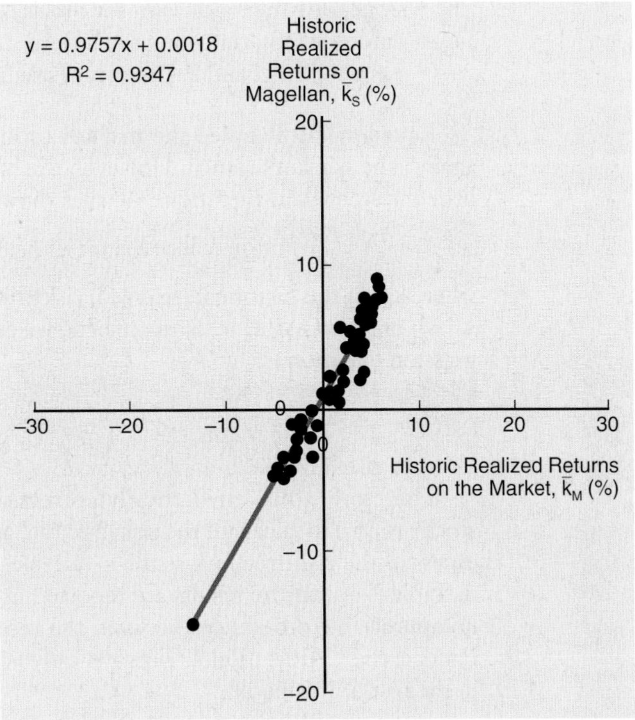

market's monthly returns. Note the differences between this chart and the one for Wal-Mart shown in Figure 7-8. The points for Magellan are tightly clustered around the regression line, indicating that the vast majority of Magellan's volatility is explained by the stock market. The R^2 of 0.94 confirms this visual conclusion. We can also see from Table 7-3 that the Magellan Fund has a standard deviation of 16.8 percent, which is only slightly higher than the 16.6 percent standard deviation of the market.

As Table 7-4 shows, the estimated beta is 0.98, and the 95 percent confidence interval is from 0.90 to 1.05, which is much tighter than the one for Wal-Mart. The intercept is virtually zero, and the probability of the intercept's t statistic is greater than 5 percent. Therefore, the intercept is statistically insignificant, indicating that the CAPM explains the average monthly return of the Magellan Fund. This is good news for CAPM, but neutral for the investors in the Magellan Fund. Their rate of return is exactly what we would expect, given the risk of the Magellan Fund. In other words, the Magellan Fund did not "beat the market," but it did reduce the risk faced by investors vis-à-vis the risk inherent in an individual stock. We will have more to say about this in our discussion of stocks in Chapter 10.

The Market Model versus the CAPM

Note that when we estimated beta, we used the following regression equation:

$$\bar{k}_J = a_J + b_J\bar{k}_M + e_J, \qquad \textbf{(7-9)}$$

where

$\bar{k}_J$ = historical (realized) rate of return on Stock J.
$\bar{k}_M$ = historical (realized) rate of return on the market.

a_J = vertical axis intercept term for Stock J.
b_J = slope, or beta coefficient, for Stock J.
e_J = random error, reflecting the difference between the actual return on Stock J in a given period and the return as predicted by the regression line.

Equation 7-9 is called the **market model,** because it regresses the stock's return against the market's return. However, the SML of the CAPM for realized returns is a little different than Equation 7-9, as is shown below:

$$\text{SML for realized returns: } \bar{k}_J = \bar{k}_{RF} + (\bar{k}_M - \bar{k}_{RF})b_J + e_J, \quad \textbf{(7-8a)}$$

where $\bar{k}_{RF}$ is the historical (realized) risk-free rate.

To use the CAPM to estimate beta, we rearrange Equation 7-8a. The resulting regression equation is:

$$\left(\bar{k}_J - \bar{k}_{RF}\right) = a_J + b_J\left(\bar{k}_M - \bar{k}_{RF}\right) + e_J. \quad \textbf{(7-8b)}$$

Therefore, to be theoretically correct when estimating beta, we should use the stock's return in excess of the risk-free rate as the y-variable and the market's return in excess of the risk-free rate as the x-variable. We did this for Wal-Mart using the data in Table 7-3, and the results are reported in Panel c of Table 7-4. Note that there are no appreciable differences between the results in Panel a, the market model, and in Panel c, the CAPM model. This typically is the case, so we will use the market model in the rest of this book.

Additional Insights into Risk and Return

The CAPM provides some additional insights into the relationship between risk and return. In the following illustrations of these insights, we will use Wal-Mart to represent Stock J:

1. The *predicted future* returns on Stock J are assumed to bear a linear relationship of the following form to those of the market:

$$\text{Predicted future rate of return} = \hat{k}_J = a_J + b_J\hat{k}_M + e_J \quad \textbf{(7-10)}$$
$$= 0.02 + 1.05\hat{k}_M + e_J.$$

   Here we assume that the historical relationship between Stock J and the market as a whole, as given by its characteristic line, will continue into the future.
2. In addition to general market movements, each firm also faces events that are unique to it and thus are independent of the general economic climate. Such events cause the returns on Firm J's stock to move somewhat independently of those for the market as a whole, and these random events are accounted for by the random error term, e_J. Before the fact, the expected value of the error term is zero; after the fact, it is generally either positive or negative. This component of total risk is the stock's **diversifiable,** or **company-specific, risk,** and rational investors will eliminate its effects by holding diversified portfolios of stocks.
3. The regression coefficient, b (the beta coefficient), is a market sensitivity index; it measures the relative volatility of a given stock versus the average stock, or "the market." The tendency of an individual stock to move with the market constitutes a risk, because the market does fluctuate, and these fluctuations cannot be diversified away. This part of total risk is the stock's **market,** or **nondiversifiable, risk.** Even well-diversified portfolios contain some market risk.
4. The relationship between a stock's total risk, market risk, and diversifiable risk can be expressed as follows:

Total risk = Variance = Market risk + Diversifiable risk

$$\sigma_J^2 = b_J^2\sigma_M^2 + \sigma_{e_J}^2.$$

Here σ_J^2 is the variance (or total risk) of Stock J, σ_M^2 is the variance of the market, b_J is Stock J's beta coefficient, and $\sigma_{e_J}^2$ is the variance of Stock J's regression error term.

5. If in Figure 7-8 all the points had plotted exactly on the regression line, then the variance of the error term, $\sigma_{e_J}^2$, would have been zero, and all of the stock's total risk would have been market risk. On the other hand, if the points were widely scattered about the regression line, much of the stock's total risk would be diversifiable. The shares of a large, well-diversified mutual fund would plot very close to the regression line.
6. If the stock market never fluctuated, then stocks would have no market risk. Of course, the market does fluctuate, so market risk is present—even if you hold an extremely well-diversified portfolio, you will still suffer losses if the market falls. In recent years, the standard deviation of annual market returns, σ_M, has been about 20 percent. However, on a single day, October 19, 1987, the market lost about 25 percent of its value.
7. Beta is a measure of relative market risk, but the *actual* market risk of Stock J is $b_J^2\sigma_M^2$. Market risk can also be expressed in standard deviation form, $b_J\sigma_M$, so Stock J's market risk is $b_J\sigma_M = 1.05(16.6\%) = 17.4\%$, while its total risk is $\sigma_J = 32.3\%$. The higher a stock's beta, the higher its market risk. If beta were zero, the stock would have no market risk, while if beta were 1.0, the stock would be exactly as risky as the market—assuming the stock is held in a diversified portfolio—and the stock's market risk would be σ_M.
8. Diversifiable risk can and should be eliminated by diversification, so the *relevant* risk is market risk, not total risk. If Stock J had b = 0.5, then the stock's relevant risk would be $b_J\sigma_M = 0.5(16.6\%) = 8.3\%$. A portfolio of such low-beta stocks would have a standard deviation of expected returns of $\sigma_p = 8.3\%$, or one-half the standard deviation of expected returns on a portfolio of average (b = 1.0) stocks. Had Stock J been a high-beta stock (b = 2.0), then its relevant risk would have been $b_J\sigma_M = 2.0(16.6\%) = 33.2\%$. A portfolio of b = 2.0 stocks would have $\sigma_p = 33.2\%$, so such a portfolio would be twice as risky as a portfolio of average stocks.
9. A stock's risk premium depends only on its market risk, not its total risk: $RP_J = (k_M - k_{RF})b_J$. Mr. S might own only Stock J, and hence be concerned with its total risk and seek a return based on that risk. However, if other investors hold well-diversified portfolios, they would face less risk from Stock J. Therefore, if Stock J offered a return high enough to satisfy Mr. S, it would represent a bargain for other investors, who would then buy it, pushing its price up and its yield down in the process. Since most financial assets are held by diversified investors, and since any given security can have only one price and hence only one rate of return, market action drives each stock's risk premium to the level specified by its relevant, or market, risk.

Advanced Issues in Calculating Beta

Betas are generally estimated from the stock's characteristic line by running a linear regression between past returns on the stock in question and past returns on some market index. We define betas developed in this manner as **historical betas.**

Note, however, that historical betas show how risky a stock was *in the past*, whereas investors are interested in *future* risk. It may be that a given company appeared to be quite safe in the past, but that things have changed, and its future risk is judged to be higher than its past risk, or vice versa. AT&T is a good example. AT&T was among the bluest of the blue chips when it owned the regional telephone companies, but investors now recognize that AT&T as it exists today faces far more intense competition than it faced in the past. Apple, on the other hand, was practically bankrupt a few years ago, but it now appears to be reasonably healthy. Therefore, one would think that Apple's risk had declined while AT&T's had increased.

Now consider the use of beta as a measure of a company's risk. If we use its historical beta in a CAPM framework to measure a firm's cost of equity, we are implicitly assuming that the company's future risk is the same as its past risk. This would be a troublesome assumption for a company such as Apple or AT&T today. But what about most companies in most years? As a general rule, is future risk sufficiently similar to past risk to warrant the use of historical betas in a CAPM analysis? For individual firms, past risk is often *not* a good predictor of future risk, and historical betas of individual firms are often not very stable.

Because historical betas may not be good predictors of future risk, researchers have sought ways to improve them. This has led to the development of two different types of betas: (1) adjusted betas and (2) fundamental betas. **Adjusted betas** grew largely out of the work of Marshall E. Blume, who showed that true betas tend to move toward 1.0 over time.[12] Therefore, one can begin with a firm's pure historical statistical beta, make an adjustment for the expected future movement toward 1.0, and produce an adjusted beta that will, on average, be a better predictor of the future beta than would the unadjusted historical beta. *Value Line* publishes betas based on approximately this formula:

$$\text{Adjusted beta} = 0.33\ (\text{Historical beta}) + 0.67(1.0).$$

Consider American Camping Corporation, a retailer of supplies for outdoor activities. ACC's historical beta is 1.2. Therefore, its adjusted beta is:

$$\text{Adjusted beta} = 0.33(1.2) + 0.67(1.0) = 1.1.$$

Other researchers have extended the adjustment process to include such fundamental risk variables as financial leverage, sales volatility, and the like. The end product here is a **fundamental beta.**[13] These betas are constantly adjusted to reflect changes in a firm's operations and capital structure, whereas with historical betas (including adjusted ones), such changes might not be reflected until several years after the company's "true" beta had changed.

Adjusted betas are obviously heavily dependent on unadjusted historical betas, and so are fundamental betas as they are actually calculated. Therefore, the plain old historical beta, calculated as the slope of the characteristic line, is important even if one goes on to develop a more exotic version. With this in mind, it should be noted that several different sets of data can be used to calculate historical betas, and the different data sets produce different results. Here are some points to note:

1. Betas can be based on historical periods of different lengths. For example, data for the past one, two, three, and so on, years may be used. Most people who calculate betas today use five years of data, but this choice is arbitrary, and different lengths of time usually alter significantly the calculated beta for a given company.[14]

---

[12]See Marshall E. Blume, "Betas and Their Regression Tendencies," *Journal of Finance*, June 1975, 785–796.

[13]See Barr Rosenberg and James Guy, "Beta and Investment Fundamentals," *Financial Analysts Journal*, May–June 1976, 60–72. Rosenberg, a professor at the University of California at Berkeley, later founded a company that calculates fundamental betas by a proprietary procedure and then sells them to institutional investors.

[14]A commercial provider of betas once told the authors that his firm, and others, did not know what the right period was, but they all decided to use five years in order to reduce the apparent differences between various services' betas, because large differences reduced everyone's credibility!

2. Returns may be calculated on holding periods of different lengths—a day, a week, a month, a quarter, a year, and so on. For example, if it has been decided to analyze data on NYSE stocks over a five-year period, then we might obtain 52(5) = 260 weekly returns on each stock and on the market index. We could also use 12(5) = 60 monthly returns, or 1(5) = 5 annual returns. The set of returns on each stock, however large the set turns out to be, would then be regressed on the corresponding market returns to obtain the stock's beta. In statistical analysis, it is generally better to have more rather than fewer observations, because using more observations generally leads to greater statistical confidence. This suggests the use of weekly returns, and, say, five years of data, for a sample size of 260, or even daily returns for a still larger sample size. However, the shorter the holding period, the more likely the data are to exhibit random "noise." Also, the greater the number of years of data, the more likely it is that the company's basic risk position has changed (for example, see the preceding comments on Apple and AT&T). Thus, the choice of both the number of years of data and the length of the holding period for calculating rates of return involves trade-offs between a desire to have many observations versus a desire to rely on recent and consequently more relevant data.
3. The value used to represent "the market" is also an important consideration, as the index used can have a significant effect on the calculated beta. Many analysts today use the New York Stock Exchange Composite Index (based on more than 2,000 common stocks, weighted by the value of each company), but others use the S&P 500 Index or some other group, including one (the Wilshire Index) with more than 5,000 stocks. In theory, the broader the index, the better the beta. Indeed, the index should really include returns on all stocks, bonds, leases, private businesses, real estate, and even "human capital." As a practical matter, however, we cannot get accurate returns data on most other types of assets, so measurement problems largely restrict us to stock indexes.

The bottom line of all this is that one can calculate betas in many different ways and, depending on the method used, different betas, hence different costs of capital, will result. To illustrate this point, consider Table 7-5, which contains the beta coefficients for five well-known companies as reported in 2000 by Yahoo!Finance and *Value Line.* Yahoo!Finance uses the S&P 500 as the market index, while *Value Line* uses the New York Stock Exchange Composite Index. Further, *Value Line* betas are adjusted, while the Yahoo!Finance betas listed in Table 7-5 are pure historical betas. Yahoo!Finance uses five years of monthly returns, or 60 observations; *Value Line* uses 260 weekly observations.

Where does this leave financial managers regarding the proper beta? They must "pay their money and take their choice." Some managers calculate their own betas, using whichever procedure seems most appropriate under the circumstances. Others use betas calculated by organizations such as Yahoo!Finance or *Value Line*, perhaps using one service or perhaps averaging the betas of several services. The choice is a matter of judgment and data availability, for there is no "right" beta. Generally, though, the

TABLE 7-5 Beta Coefficients for Five Companies

	Yahoo!Finance	Value Line
Dell	1.88	1.35
IBM	1.09	1.00
GM	0.93	1.05
Chevron	0.75	0.75
Carolina Power & Light	0.20	0.55

betas derived from different sources will, for a given company, be reasonably close together. If they are not, then our confidence in using the CAPM will be diminished.

Self-Test Questions

Explain the meaning and significance of a stock's beta coefficient. Illustrate your explanation by drawing, on one graph, the characteristic lines for stocks with low, average, and high risk. (Hint: Let your three characteristic lines intersect at $\bar{k}_i = \bar{k}_M = 6\%$, the assumed risk-free rate.)

What is a typical R^2 for the characteristic line of an individual stock? For a portfolio?

What is the market model? How is it different than the SML for the CAPM?

How are stand-alone risk, market risk, and diversifiable risk related?

Empirical Tests of the CAPM

As noted earlier, the CAPM was developed on the basis of a set of assumptions. If those assumptions were all true, then the CAPM would have to be true. However, since the assumptions are clearly not completely correct, the basic SML equation, $k_i = k_{RF} + (k_M - k_{RF})b_i$, might or might not represent an accurate description of how investors behave and of how rates of return are established in the marketplace. For example, if many investors are not fully diversified, hence have not eliminated all diversifiable risk from their portfolios, then (1) beta would not be an adequate measure of risk and (2) the SML would not fully explain how required returns are set. Also, if the interest rate that investors must pay to borrow money is greater than the risk-free rate (that is, if the borrowing rate is greater than the lending rate), then the CML would not continue in a straight line beyond Point M as it does in Figure 7-6, and this too would invalidate the SML. And, of course, taxes and brokerage costs do exist, and their presence could also distort the CAPM relationships.

For all these reasons, it is entirely possible that the CAPM is not completely valid, in which case the SML will not produce accurate estimates of k_i. Therefore, the CAPM must be tested empirically and validated before it can be used with real confidence. The literature dealing with empirical tests of the CAPM is quite extensive, so we can give here only a synopsis of some of the key work.

Tests of the Stability of Beta Coefficients

According to the CAPM, the beta used to estimate a stock's market risk should reflect investors' estimates of the stock's *future* volatility in relation to that of the market. Obviously, we do not know now how a stock will be related to the market in the future, nor do we know how the average investor views this expected future relative volatility. All we have are data on past volatility, which we can use to plot the characteristic line and to calculate *historical betas.* If historical betas have been stable over time, then there would seem to be reason for investors to use past betas as estimators of future volatility. For example, if Stock J's beta had been stable in the past, then its historical b_J would probably be a good proxy for its *ex ante*, or expected, beta. By "stable" we mean that if b_J were calculated with data from the period of say, 1997 to 2001, then this same beta (approximately) should be found from 2002 to 2006.

Robert Levy, Marshall Blume, and others have studied the question of beta stability in depth.[15] Levy calculated betas for individual securities, as well as for

[15]See Robert A. Levy, "On the Short-Term Stationarity of Beta Coefficients," *Financial Analysts Journal,* November–December 1971, 55–62, and Marshall E. Blume, "Betas and Their Regression Tendencies," *Journal of Finance,* June 1975, 785–796.

portfolios of securities, over a range of time intervals. He concluded (1) that the betas of individual stocks are unstable, hence that past betas for *individual securities* are *not* good estimators of their future risk, but (2) that betas of portfolios of ten or more randomly selected stocks are reasonably stable, hence that past *portfolio* betas are good estimators of future portfolio volatility. In effect, the errors in individual securities' betas tend to offset one another in a portfolio. The work of Blume and others supports this position.

The conclusion that follows from the beta stability studies is that the CAPM is a better concept for structuring investment portfolios than it is for estimating the required return for individual securities.

Tests of the CAPM Based on the Slope of the SML

The CAPM states that a linear relationship exists between a security's required rate of return and its beta. Further, when the SML is graphed, the vertical axis intercept should be k_{RF}, and the required rate of return for a stock (or portfolio) with $b = 1.0$ should be k_M, the required rate of return on the market. Various researchers have attempted to test the validity of the CAPM by calculating betas and realized rates of return, plotting these values in graphs such as that in Figure 7-10, and then observing whether or not (1) the intercept is equal to k_{RF}, (2) the regression line is linear, and (3) the line passes through the point $b = 1.0$, k_M. Monthly historical rates of return are generally used for stocks, and both 30-day Treasury bill rates and long-term Treasury bond rates have been used to estimate the value of k_{RF}. Also, most of the studies actually analyzed portfolios rather than individual securities because security betas are so unstable.

Before discussing the results of the tests, it is critical to recognize that although the CAPM is an ex ante, or forward-looking model, the data used to test it are entirely historical. This presents a problem, for there is no reason to believe that *realized* rates of return over past holding periods are necessarily equal to the rates of return people *expect* in the future. Also, historical betas may or may not reflect expected future risk.

FIGURE 7-10 Tests of the CAPM

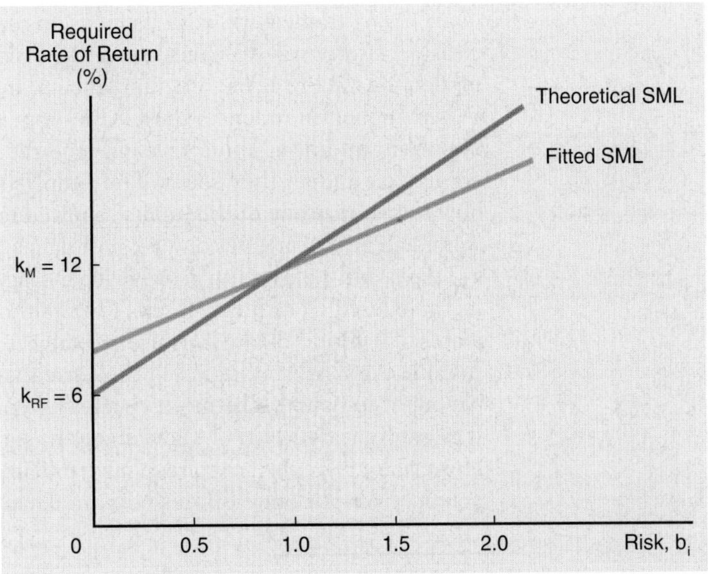

This lack of ex ante data makes it extremely difficult to test the CAPM, but for what it is worth, here is a summary of the key results:

1. The evidence generally shows a significant positive relationship between realized returns and beta. However, the slope of the relationship is usually less than that predicted by the CAPM.
2. The relationship between risk and return appears to be linear. Empirical studies give no evidence of significant curvature in the risk/return relationship.
3. Tests that attempt to assess the relative importance of market and company-specific risk do not yield conclusive results. The CAPM implies that company-specific risk should not be relevant, yet both kinds of risk appear to be positively related to security returns; that is, higher returns seem to be required to compensate for diversifiable as well as market risk. However, it may be that the observed relationships reflect statistical problems rather than the true nature of capital markets.
4. Richard Roll has questioned whether it is even conceptually possible to test the CAPM.[16] Roll showed that the linear relationship which prior researchers had observed in graphs like Figure 7-10 resulted from the mathematical properties of the models being tested, hence that a finding of linearity proved nothing whatsoever about the validity of the CAPM. Roll's work did not disprove the CAPM, but he did show that it is virtually impossible to prove that investors behave in accordance with its predictions.
5. If the CAPM were completely valid, it should apply to all financial assets, including bonds. In fact, when bonds are introduced into the analysis, they *do not* plot on the SML. This is worrisome, to say the least.

Current Status of the CAPM

The CAPM is extremely appealing at an intellectual level: It is logical and rational, and once someone works through and understands the theory, his or her reaction is usually to accept it without question. However, doubts begin to arise when one thinks about the assumptions upon which the model is based, and these doubts are as much reinforced as reduced by the empirical tests. Our own views as to the current status of the CAPM are as follows:

1. The CAPM framework, with its focus on market as opposed to stand-alone risk, is clearly a useful way to think about the riskiness of assets. Thus, as a conceptual model, the CAPM is of truly fundamental importance.
2. When applied in practice, the CAPM appears to provide neat, precise answers to important questions about risk and required rates of return. However, the answers are less clear than they seem. The simple truth is that we do not know precisely how to measure any of the inputs required to implement the CAPM. These inputs should all be ex ante, yet only ex post data are available. Further, historical data on $\bar{k}_M$, k_{RF}, and betas vary greatly depending on the time period studied and the methods used to estimate them. Thus, although the CAPM appears precise, estimates of k_i found through its use are subject to potentially large errors.
3. Because the CAPM is logical in the sense that it represents the way risk-averse people ought to behave, the model is a useful conceptual tool.
4. It is appropriate to think about many financial problems in a CAPM framework. However, it is important to recognize the limitations of the CAPM when using it in practice. We elaborate on this point in Chapters 11, 14, and 15.

---

[16]See Richard Roll, "A Critique of the Asset Pricing Theory's Tests," *Journal of Financial Economics*, March 1977, 129–176.

Self-Test Questions

What are the two major types of tests that have been performed to test the validity of the CAPM? Explain their results. (Hint: Beta stability and slope of the SML.)

Are there any reasons to question the validity of the CAPM? Explain.

Arbitrage Pricing Theory

The CAPM is a single-factor model. That is, it specifies risk as a function of only one factor, the security's beta coefficient. Perhaps the risk/return relationship is more complex, with a stock's required return a function of more than one factor. For example, what if investors, because personal tax rates on capital gains are lower than those on dividends, value capital gains more highly than dividends? Then, if two stocks had the same market risk, the stock paying the higher dividend would have the higher required rate of return. In that case, required returns would be a function of two factors, market risk and dividend policy.

Further, what if many factors are required to specify the equilibrium risk/return relationship rather than just one or two? Stephen Ross has proposed an approach called the **Arbitrage Pricing Theory (APT).**[17] The APT can include any number of risk factors, so the required return could be a function of two, three, four, or more factors. We should note at the outset that the APT is based on complex mathematical and statistical theory that goes far beyond the scope of this text. Also, although the APT model is widely discussed in academic literature, practical usage to date has been limited. However, usage may increase, so students should at least have an intuitive idea of what the APT is all about.

The SML states that each stock's required return is equal to the risk-free rate plus the product of the market risk premium times the stock's beta coefficient:

$$k_i = k_{RF} + (k_M - k_{RF})b_i. \quad \textbf{(7-8)}$$

The historical realized return, $\bar{k}_i$, which will generally be different from the expected return, can be expressed as follows:

$$\bar{k}_i = \hat{k}_i + (\bar{k}_M - \hat{k}_M)b_i + e_i. \quad \textbf{(7-11)}$$

Thus, the realized return, $\bar{k}_i$, will be equal to the expected return, $\hat{k}_i$, plus a positive or negative increment, $(\bar{k}_M - \hat{k}_M)b_i$, which depends jointly on the stock's beta and whether the market did better or worse than was expected, plus a random error term, e_i.

The market's realized return, $\bar{k}_M$, is in turn determined by a number of factors, including domestic economic activity as measured by gross domestic product (GDP), the strength of the world economy, the level of inflation, changes in tax laws, and so forth. Further, different groups of stocks are affected in different ways by these fundamental factors. So, rather than specifying a stock's return as a function of one factor (return on the market), one could specify required and realized returns on individual stocks as a function of various fundamental economic factors. If this were done, we would transform Equation 7-11 into 7-12:

$$\bar{k}_i = \hat{k}_i + (\bar{F}_1 - \hat{F}_1)b_{i1} + \cdots (\bar{F}_j - \hat{F}_j)b_{ij} + e_i. \quad \textbf{(7-12)}$$

Here

$\bar{k}_i$ = realized rate of return on Stock i.
$\hat{k}_i$ = expected rate of return on Stock i.

[17]See Stephen A. Ross, "The Arbitrage Theory of Capital Asset Pricing," *Journal of Economic Theory*, December 1976, 341–360.

$\bar{F}_j$ = realized value of economic Factor j.
$\hat{F}_j$ = expected value of Factor j.
b_{ij} = sensitivity of Stock i to economic Factor j.
e_i = effect of unique events on the realized return of Stock i.

Equation 7-12 shows that the realized return on any stock is equal to (1) the stock's expected return, (2) increases or decreases that depend on unexpected changes in fundamental economic factors times the sensitivity of the stock to these changes, and (3) a random term that reflects changes unique to the firm or industry.

Certain stocks or groups of stocks are most sensitive to Factor 1, others to Factor 2, and so forth, and every portfolio's returns depend on what happened to the different fundamental factors. Theoretically, one could construct a portfolio such that (1) the portfolio was riskless and (2) the net investment in it was zero (some stocks would be sold short, with the proceeds from the short sales being used to buy the stocks held long). Such a zero investment portfolio must have a zero expected return, or else arbitrage operations would occur and cause the prices of the underlying assets to change until the portfolio's expected return was zero. Using some complex mathematics and a set of assumptions including the possibility of short sales, the APT equivalent of the CAPM's Security Market Line can be developed from Equation 7-12:[18]

$$k_i = k_{RF} + (k_1 - k_{RF})b_{i1} + \cdots (k_j - k_{RF})b_{ij}. \qquad \textbf{(7-13)}$$

Here k_j is the required rate of return on a portfolio that is sensitive only to the *j*th economic factor ($b_j = 1.0$) and has zero sensitivity to all other factors. Thus, for example, $(k_2 - k_{RF})$ is the risk premium on a portfolio with $b_2 = 1.0$ and all other $b_j = 0.0$. Note that Equation 7-13 is identical in form to the SML, but it permits a stock's required return to be a function of multiple factors.

To illustrate the APT concept, assume that all stocks' returns depend on only three risk factors: inflation, industrial production, and the aggregate degree of risk aversion (the cost of bearing risk, which we assume is reflected in the spread between the yields on Treasury and low-grade bonds). Further, suppose (1) the risk-free rate is 8.0 percent; (2) the required rate of return is 13 percent on a portfolio with unit sensitivity ($b = 1.0$) to inflation and zero sensitivities ($b = 0.0$) to industrial production and degree of risk aversion; (3) the required return is 10 percent on a portfolio with unit sensitivity to industrial production and zero sensitivities to inflation and degree of risk aversion; and (4) the required return is 6 percent on a portfolio (the risk-bearing portfolio) with unit sensitivity to the degree of risk aversion and zero sensitivities to inflation and industrial production. Finally, assume that Stock i has factor sensitivities (betas) of 0.9 to the inflation portfolio, 1.2 to the industrial production portfolio, and −0.7 to the risk-bearing portfolio. Stock i's required rate of return, according to the APT, would be 16.3 percent:

$$\begin{aligned} k_i &= 8\% + (13\% - 8\%)0.9 + (10\% - 8\%)1.2 + (6\% - 8\%)(-0.7) \\ &= 16.3\%. \end{aligned}$$

Note that if the required rate of return on the market was 15.0 percent and Stock i had a CAPM beta of 1.1, then its required rate of return, according to the SML, would be 15.7 percent:

$$k_i = 8\% + (15\% - 8\%)1.1 = 15.7\%.$$

[18]See Thomas E. Copeland and J. Fred Weston, *Financial Theory and Corporate Policy* (Reading, MA: Addison-Wesley, 1988).

The primary theoretical advantage of the APT is that it permits several economic factors to influence individual stock returns, whereas the CAPM assumes that the effect of all factors, except those unique to the firm, can be captured in a single measure, the volatility of the stock with respect to the market portfolio. Also, the APT requires fewer assumptions than the CAPM and hence is more general. Finally, the APT does not assume that all investors hold the market portfolio, a CAPM requirement that clearly is not met in practice.

However, the APT faces several major hurdles in implementation, the most severe being that the APT does not identify the relevant factors. Thus, APT does not tell us what factors influence returns, nor does it even indicate how many factors should appear in the model. There is some empirical evidence that only three or four factors are relevant: perhaps inflation, industrial production, the spread between low- and high-grade bonds, and the term structure of interest rates, but no one knows for sure.

The APT's proponents argue that it is not actually necessary to identify the relevant factors. Researchers use a complex statistical procedure called **factor analysis** to develop the APT parameters. Basically, they start with hundreds, or even thousands, of stocks and then create several different portfolios, where the returns on each portfolio are not highly correlated with returns on the other portfolios. Thus, each portfolio is apparently more heavily influenced by one of the unknown factors than are the other portfolios. Then, the required rate of return on each portfolio becomes the estimate for that unknown economic factor, shown as k_j in Equation 7-13. The sensitivities of each individual stock's returns to the returns on that portfolio are the factor sensitivities (betas). Unfortunately, the results of factor analysis are not easily interpreted, hence it does not provide significant insights into the underlying economic determinants of risk.

The APT is in an early stage of development, and there are still many unanswered questions. Nevertheless, the basic premise of the APT—that returns can be a function of several factors rather than just one—has considerable intuitive appeal. If the factors can be identified, and if the theory can be satisfactorily explained to practitioners, then the APT someday might replace the CAPM as the primary model describing the relationship between risk and return.

Self-Test Questions

What is the primary difference between the APT and the CAPM?

What are some disadvantages of the APT?

The Fama-French Three-Factor Model

As we mentioned in Chapter 6, the results of two studies by Eugene F. Fama and Kenneth R. French of the University of Chicago seriously challenge the CAPM.[19] In the first of these studies, published in 1992, Fama and French hypothesized that the SML should have three factors. The first is the stock's CAPM beta, which measures the market risk of the stock. The second is the size of the company, measured by the market value of its equity (MVE), because if small companies are riskier than large companies, then we might expect small companies to have higher stock returns than large companies. The third factor is the book value of equity divided by the market value of equity, or the book-to-market ratio (B/M). If the market value is larger than the

[19]See Eugene F. Fama and Kenneth R. French, "The Cross-Section of Expected Stock Returns," *Journal of Finance*, Vol. 47, 1992, 427–465. Also see Eugene F. Fama and Kenneth R. French, "Common Risk Factors in the Returns on Stocks and Bonds," *Journal of Financial Economics*, Vol. 33, 1993, 3–56.

book value, then investors are optimistic about the stock's future. On the other hand, if the book value is larger than the market value, then investors are pessimistic about the stock's future, and it is likely that that a ratio analysis would reveal that the company is experiencing sub-par operating performance and possibly even financial distress. In other words, a stock with a high B/M ratio might be risky, in which case investors would require a higher expected return to induce them to invest in such a stock.

When Fama and French tested their hypotheses, they found that small companies and companies with high B/M ratios had higher rates of return than the average stock, just as they hypothesized. Somewhat surprisingly, however, they found no relation between beta and return. After taking into account the returns due to the company's size and B/M ratio, high beta stocks did not have higher-than-average returns, and low beta stocks did not have lower-than-average returns.

In the second of their two studies, published in 1993, Fama and French developed a 3-factor model based on their previous results. The first factor in the **Fama-French three-factor model** is the market risk premium, which is the market return, $\bar{k}_M$, minus the risk-free rate, $\bar{k}_{RF}$. Thus, their model begins like the CAPM, but they go on to add a second and third factor.[20] To form the second factor, they ranked all actively traded stocks by size and then divided them into two portfolios, consisting of small and big stocks. They calculated the return on each of these two portfolios, and created a third portfolio by subtracting the return from the big portfolio from that of the small one. They called this the SMB portfolio (for small size minus big size). This portfolio is designed to measure the variation in stock returns that is caused by the size effect.

To form the third portfolio, they ranked all stocks according to their book-to-market ratios (B/M). They placed the 30 percent of stocks with the highest ratios into a portfolio that they called the H portfolio (for high B/M ratios). They placed the 30 percent of stocks with the lowest ratios into a portfolio called the L portfolio (for low B/M ratios). They subtracted the return of the L portfolio from the H portfolio, and they called the result the HML portfolio (for high B/M ratio minus low B/M ratio). Their resulting model is shown here):

$$(\bar{k}_i - \bar{k}_{RF}) = a_i + b_i(\bar{k}_M - \bar{k}_{RF}) + c_i(\bar{k}_{SMB}) + d_i(\bar{k}_{HML}) + e_i, \qquad \textbf{(7-14)}$$

where

$\bar{k}_i$	= historical (realized) rate of return on Stock i.
$\bar{k}_{RF}$	= historical (realized) rate of return on the risk free rate.
$\bar{k}_M$	= historical (realized) rate of return on the market.
$\bar{k}_{SMB}$	= historical (realized) rate of return on the small size portfolio minus the big size portfolio.
$\bar{k}_{HML}$	= historical (realized) rate of return on the high B/M portfolio minus the low B/M portfolio.
a_i	= vertical axis intercept term for Stock i.
b_i, c_i and d_i	= slope coefficients for Stock i.
e_i	= random error, reflecting the difference between the actual return on Stock i in a given period and the return as predicted by the regression line.

[20]Although our description captures the essence of their process for forming factors, their actual process is a little more complicated. The interested reader should see their 1993 paper as referenced in Footnote 19.

Here is how you might apply this model. Suppose you ran the regression in Equation 7-14 for a stock, and estimated the following regression coefficients: $a_i = 0.0$, $b_i = 0.9$, $c_i = 0.2$, and $d_i = 0.3$. Assume that the expected market risk premium is 6 percent (that is, $k_M - k_{RF} = 6\%$) and that the risk-free rate is 6.5 percent. Suppose the expected value of k_{SMB} is 3.2 percent and the expected value of k_{HML} is 4.8 percent.[21] Using the CAPM SML, the required return on the stock is:

$$k_i = k_{RF} + a_i + b_i(k_M - k_{RF}) \quad \textbf{(7-8a)}$$

$$= 6.5\% + 0.0\% + 0.9(6\%)$$
$$= 11.9\%.$$

Using the Fama-French three-factor model, the expected return is:

$$k_i = k_{RF} + a_i + b_i(k_M - k_{RF}) + c_i(k_{SMB}) + d_i(k_{HML}) \quad \textbf{(7-15)}$$

$$= 6.5\% + 0.0\% + 0.9(6\%) + 0.2(3.2\%) + 0.3(4.8\%)$$
$$= 13.98\%.$$

To date, the Fama-French three-factor model has been used primarily by academic researchers rather than by managers at actual companies, the majority of whom are using CAPM. One reason for this difference is data availability. Most professors have access to the type of data that is required to calculate the factors, but the data for the size factor and the B/M factor are not readily available to the general public. A second reason is the difficulty in estimating the expected values of the size factor and the B/M factor. Although we know the historical average returns for these factors, we don't know whether the past historical returns are good estimators of the future expected returns. Third, many managers choose to wait and adopt a new theory only after the new theory has been widely accepted by the academic community.

And that isn't the case right now. In fact, there are a number of very recent studies indicating that the Fama-French model is not correct.[22] Several of these studies suggest that the size effect is no longer having an effect on stock returns, that there never was a size effect (the previous results were caused by peculiarities in the data sources), or that the size effect doesn't apply to most companies. Other studies suggest that the book-to-market effect is not as significant as first supposed and that the book-to-market effect is not caused by risk. Another recent study shows that if the composition of a company's assets were changing over time with respect to the mix of physical assets and growth opportunities (such as R&D, patents, etc.), then it would appear as though there were size and book-to-market effects. In other words, even if the returns on the individual assets conform to the CAPM, changes in the mix of assets would cause the firm's beta to change over time in such a way that the firm will appear to have size and book-to-market effects.[23]

---

[21]These are the average returns Fama and French found in their sample period for k_{SMB} and k_{HML}.

[22]See Peter J. Knez and Mark J. Ready, "On the Robustness of Size and Book-to-Market in the Cross-Sectional Regressions," *Journal of Finance*, September 1997, 1355–1382; Dongcheol Kim, "A Reexamination of Firm Size, Book-to-Market, and Earnings Price in the Cross-Section of Expected Stock Returns," *Journal of Financial and Quantitative Analysis*, December 1997, 463–489; Tyler Shumway and Vincent A. Warther, "The Delisting Bias in CRSP's Nasdaq Data and Its Implications for the Size Effect," *Journal of Finance*, December 1999, 2361–2379; Tim Loughran, "Book-to-Market Across Firm Size, Exchange, and Seasonality: Is There an Effect?" *Journal of Financial and Quantitative Analysis*, September 1997, 249–268; and Ilia D. Dichev, "Is the Risk of Bankruptcy a Systematic Risk?" *Journal of Finance*, June 1998, 1131–1147.

[23]See Jonathan B. Berk, Richard C. Green, and Vasant Naik, "Optimal Investment, Growth Options, and Security Returns," *Journal of Finance*, October 1999, 1553–1608,

Self-Test Questions

What are the factors in the Fama-French model?

How can the model be used to estimate the required return on a stock?

Why isn't the model widely used by managers at actual companies?

An Alternative Theory of Risk and Return: Behavioral Finance

In addition to the Arbitrage Pricing Theory and the Fama-French three-factor model, there are several other arguments against the CAPM. First, there is some evidence that stocks may have short-term momentum. Stocks that perform poorly tend to continue performing poorly over the next 3 to 12 months, and stocks that perform well tend to continue performing well in the short-term future. On the other hand, there is some evidence that stocks have long-term reversals. In particular, stocks that have the lowest returns in a five-year period tend to outperform the market during the next five years. The opposite is true for stocks that outperform the market during a five-year period: they tend to have lower than average returns during the next five-year period.[24]

In response to such observations, a number of researchers are blending psychology with finance, creating a new field called **behavioral finance.** There is a large body of evidence in the field of psychology indicating that people don't behave rationally in many areas of their lives, so some argue that we should not expect people to behave rationally with their investments.[25] For example, most people experience "loss aversion," or a strong desire to avoid realizing losses. This leads investors to sell winners much more frequently than losers, even though this is suboptimal for tax purposes.[26] Many psychological tests also show that people are overconfident with respect to their own abilities relative to the abilities of others, which is the basis of Garrison Keillor's joke about a town where all the residents are above average. Humans also tend to have "biased self-attribution," a fancy way of saying that we believe our failures are due to bad luck but that our successes are due to our skill. Some researchers have hypothesized that the combination of overconfidence and biased self-attribution leads to overly volatile stock markets, short-term momentum, and long-term reversals.[27] In other words, stock returns reflect the irrational, but predictable, behavior of humans. We will have much more to say about this when we discuss stock returns in Chapter 10.

Self-Test Questions

What is short-term momentum? What are long-term reversals?

What is behavioral finance?

[24]N. Jegadeesh and S. Titman, "Returns to Buying Winners and Selling Losers: Implications for Stock Market Efficiency," *Journal of Finance*, March 1993, 69–91; and W.F.M. DeBondt and R.H. Thaler, "Does the Stock Market Overreact?" *Journal of Finance*, July 1985, 793–808.

[25]See Brian O'Reilly, "Why Johnny Can't Invest," *Fortune*, November 9, 1998, 173–178.

[26]See Terrance Odean, "Are Investors Reluctant to Realize Their Losses?" *Journal of Finance*, October 1998, 1775–1798.

[27]See Terrance Odean, "Volume, Volatility, Price, and Profit When All Traders Are Above Average," *Journal of Finance*, December 1998, 1887–1934; and Kent Daniel, David Hirshleifer, and Avanidhar Subrahmanyam, "Investor Psychology and Security Market Under- and Overreactions," *Journal of Finance*, December 1998, 1839–1885.

Summary

Chapter 7 completes our discussion of risk and return for traded securities. The primary goal of this chapter was to extend your knowledge of risk and return concepts. The key concepts covered are listed below:

- The **feasible set** of portfolios represents all portfolios that can be constructed from a given set of assets.
- An **efficient portfolio** is one that offers the most return for a given amount of risk, or the least risk for a given amount of return.
- The **optimal portfolio** for an investor is defined by the investor's highest possible **indifference curve** that is tangent to the **efficient set** of portfolios.
- The **Capital Asset Pricing Model (CAPM)** describes the relationship between market risk and required rates of return.
- The **Capital Market Line (CML)** describes the risk/return relationship for efficient portfolios; that is, for portfolios that consist of a mix of the market portfolio and a riskless asset.
- The **Security Market Line (SML)** is an integral part of the CAPM, and it describes the risk/return relationship for individual assets. The required rate of return for any Stock i is equal to the **risk-free rate** plus the **market risk premium** times the stock's **beta coefficient:** $k_i = k_{RF} + (k_M - k_{RF})b_i$.
- Stock i's **beta coefficient, b_i,** is a measure of the stock's **market risk.** Beta measures the **volatility** of returns on a security **relative to returns on the market,** which is the portfolio of all risky assets.
- The beta coefficient is measured by the slope of the stock's **characteristic line,** which is found by regressing historical returns on the stock versus historical returns on the market.
- Although the CAPM provides a convenient framework for thinking about risk and return issues, it *cannot be proven empirically,* and its parameters are very difficult to estimate. Thus, the required rate of return for a stock as estimated by the CAPM may not be exactly equal to the true required rate of return.
- Deficiencies in the CAPM have motivated theorists to seek other risk/return equilibrium models, and the **Arbitrage Pricing Theory (APT)** is one important new model.
- The **Fama-French three-factor model** has one factor for the market return, a second factor for the **size effect,** and a third factor for the **book-to-market** effect.
- **Behavioral finance** assumes that investors don't always behave rationally.

In the next three chapters, we will see how a security's required rate of return affects its value.

Questions

7–1 Define the following terms, using graphs or equations to illustrate your answers wherever feasible:

a. Portfolio
b. Feasible set
c. Efficient portfolio
d. Efficient frontier
e. Indifference curve
f. Optimal portfolio

g. Capital Asset Pricing Model (CAPM)
h. Capital Market Line (CML)
i. Characteristic line
j. Beta coefficient, b; average stock's beta, $b_A = b_M$
k. Arbitrage Pricing Theory (APT)
l. Fama-French three-factor model
m. Behavioral finance

7–2 Security A has an expected rate of return of 6 percent, a standard deviation of expected returns of 30 percent, a correlation coefficient with the market of −0.25, and a beta coefficient of −0.5. Security B has an expected return of 11 percent, a standard deviation of returns of 10 percent, a correlation with the market of 0.75, and a beta coefficient of 0.5. Which security is more risky? Why?

Self-Test Problem (Solution Appears in Appendix A)

ST–1 *RISK AND RETURN* You are planning to invest $200,000. Two securities, A and B, are available, and you can invest in either of them or in a portfolio with some of each. You estimate that the following probability distributions of returns are applicable for A and B:

Security A		Security B	
P_A	k_A	P_B	k_B
0.1	−10%	0.1	−30%
0.2	5	0.2	0
0.4	15	0.4	20
0.2	25	0.2	40
0.1	40	0.1	70
	$\hat{k}_A = ?$		$\hat{k}_B = 20.0\%$
	$\sigma_A = ?$		$\sigma_B = 25.7\%$

a. The expected return for Security B is $\hat{k}_B = 20\%$, and $\sigma_B = 25.7\%$. Find $\hat{k}_A$ and σ_A.
b. Use the equation in Footnote 3 to find the value of w_A that produces the minimum risk portfolio. Assume $r_{AB} = -0.5$ for parts b and c.
c. Construct a table giving $\hat{k}_p$ and σ_p for portfolios with $w_A = 1.00, 0.75, 0.50, 0.25, 0.0$, and the minimum risk value of w_A. (Hint: For $w_A = 0.75$, $\hat{k}_p = 16.25\%$ and $\sigma_p = 8.5\%$; for $w_A = 0.5$, $\hat{k}_p = 17.5\%$ and $\sigma_p = 11.1\%$; for $w_A = 0.25$, $\hat{k}_p = 18.75\%$ and $\sigma_p = 17.9\%$.)
d. Graph the feasible set of portfolios and identify the efficient frontier of the feasible set.
e. Suppose your risk/return trade-off function, or indifference curve, is tangent to the efficient set at the point where $\hat{k}_p = 18\%$. Use this information, plus the graph constructed in part d, to locate (approximately) your optimal portfolio. Draw in a reasonable indifference curve, indicate the percentage of your funds invested in each security, and determine the optimal portfolio's σ_p and $\hat{k}_p$. (Hint: Estimate σ_p and $\hat{k}_p$ graphically, and then use the equation for $\hat{k}_p$ to determine w_A.)
f. Now suppose a riskless asset with a return $k_{RF} = 10\%$ becomes available. How would this change the investment opportunity set? Explain why the efficient frontier becomes linear.
g. Given the indifference curve in part e, would you change your portfolio? If so, how? (Hint: Assume the indifference curves are parallel.)
h. What are the beta coefficients of Stocks A and B? [Hints: (1) Recognize that $k_i = k_{RF} + b_i(k_M - k_{RF})$ and solve for b_i and (2) assume that your preferences match those of most other investors.]

Problems

7–1 CHARACTERISTIC LINE AND SECURITY MARKET LINE

You are given the following set of data:

	Historical Rates of Return	
Year	NYSE	Stock X
1	(26.5%)	(14.0%)
2	37.2	23.0
3	23.8	17.5
4	(7.2)	2.0
5	6.6	8.1
6	20.5	19.4
7	30.6	18.2

a. Use a calculator with a linear regression function (or a spreadsheet) to determine Stock X's beta coefficient, or plot these data points on a scatter diagram, draw in the regression line, and then estimate the value of the beta coefficient.

b. Determine the arithmetic average rates of return for Stock X and the NYSE over the period given. Calculate the standard deviations of returns for both Stock X and the NYSE.

c. Assuming (1) that the situation during Years 1 to 7 is expected to hold true in the future (that is, $\hat{k}_X = \bar{k}_X$; $\hat{k}_M = \bar{k}_M$; and both σ_X and b_X in the future will equal their past values), and (2) that Stock X is in equilibrium (that is, it plots on the Security Market Line), what is the risk-free rate?

d. Plot the Security Market Line.

e. Suppose you hold a large, well-diversified portfolio and are considering adding to the portfolio either Stock X or another stock, Stock Y, that has the same beta as Stock X but a higher standard deviation of returns. Stocks X and Y have the same expected returns; that is, $\hat{k}_X = \hat{k}_Y = 10.6\%$. Which stock should you choose?

7–2 CHARACTERISTIC LINE

You are given the following set of data:

	Historical Rates of Return	
Year	NYSE	Stock Y
1	4.0%	3.0%
2	14.3	18.2
3	19.0	9.1
4	(14.7)	(6.0)
5	(26.5)	(15.3)
6	37.2	33.1
7	23.8	6.1
8	(7.2)	3.2
9	6.6	14.8
10	20.5	24.1
11	30.6	18.0
	Mean = 9.8%	9.8%
	σ = 19.6%	13.8%

a. Construct a scatter diagram showing the relationship between returns on Stock Y and the market, and then draw a freehand approximation of the regression line. What is the approximate value of the beta coefficient? If you have a calculator with a linear regression function or a spreadsheet, check the approximate value of beta obtained from the graph.

b. Give a verbal interpretation of what the regression line and the beta coefficient show about Stock Y's volatility and relative riskiness as compared with those of other stocks.

c. Suppose the scatter of points had been more spread out, but the regression line was exactly where your present graph shows it. How would this affect (1) the firm's risk if the stock is held in a one-asset portfolio and (2) the actual risk premium on the stock if the CAPM holds exactly?

d. Suppose the regression line had been downward sloping and the beta coefficient had been negative. What would this imply about (1) Stock Y's relative riskiness, (2) its correlation with the market, and (3) its probable risk premium?

e. Construct an illustrative probability distribution graph of returns on portfolios consisting of (1) only Stock Y, (2) 1 percent each of 100 stocks with beta coefficients similar to that of Stock Y, and (3) all stocks (that is, the distribution of returns on the market). Use as the expected rate of return the arithmetic mean as given previously for both Stock Y and the market and assume that the distributions are normal. Are the expected returns "reasonable"; that is, is it reasonable that $\hat{k}_Y = \hat{k}_M = 9.8\%$?

7–3
SML AND CML COMPARISON

The beta coefficient of an asset can be expressed as a function of the asset's correlation with the market as follows:

$$b_i = \frac{r_{iM}\sigma_i}{\sigma_M}.$$

a. Substitute this expression for beta into the Security Market Line (SML), Equation 7-8. This results in an alternative form of the SML.

b. Compare your answer to part a with the Capital Market Line (CML), Equation 7-5. What similarities are observed? What conclusions can be drawn?

7–4
CAPM AND THE FAMA-FRENCH THREE-FACTOR MODEL

Suppose you are given the following information. The beta of company i, b_J, is 1.1, the risk-free rate, k_{RF}, is 7 percent, and the expected market premium, $k_M - k_{RF}$, is 6.5 percent. (Assume that $a_i = 0.0$.)

a. Use the Security Market Line (SML) of CAPM to find the required return for this company.

b. Because your company is smaller than average and more successful than average (that is, it has a low book-to-market ratio), you think the Fama-French three-factor model might be more appropriate than the CAPM. You estimate the additional coefficients from the Fama-French three-factor model: The coefficient for the size effect, c_i, is 0.7, and the coefficient for the book-to-market effect, d_i, is -0.3. If the expected value of the size factor is 5 percent and the expected value of the book-to-market factor is 4 percent, what is the required return using the Fama-French three-factor model?

Mini Case

CD

See **Ch 07 Show.ppt** and **Ch 07 Mini Case.xls**.

To begin, briefly review the Chapter 6 Mini Case. Then, extend your knowledge of risk and return by answering the following questions:

a. What is the Capital Asset Pricing Model (CAPM)? What are the assumptions that underlie the model?

b. Construct a reasonable, but hypothetical, graph that shows risk, as measured by portfolio standard deviation, on the X axis and expected rate of return on the Y axis. Now add an illustrative feasible (or attainable) set of portfolios, and show what portion of the feasible set is efficient. What makes a particular portfolio efficient? Don't worry about specific values when constructing the graph—merely illustrate how things look with "reasonable" data.

c. Now add a set of indifference curves to the graph created for part b. What do these curves represent? What is the optimal portfolio for this investor? Finally, add a second set of indifference curves which leads to the selection of a different optimal portfolio. Why do the two investors choose different portfolios?

d. Now add the risk-free asset. What impact does this have on the efficient frontier?
e. Write out the equation for the Capital Market Line (CML) and draw it on the graph. Interpret the CML. Now add a set of indifference curves, and illustrate how an investor's optimal portfolio is some combination of the risky portfolio and the risk-free asset. What is the composition of the risky portfolio?
f. What is a characteristic line? How is this line used to estimate a stock's beta coefficient? Write out and explain the formula that relates total risk, market risk, and diversifiable risk.
g. What are two potential tests that can be conducted to verify the CAPM? What are the results of such tests? What is Roll's critique of CAPM tests?
h. Briefly explain the difference between the CAPM and the Arbitrage Pricing Theory (APT).
i. What is the current status of the APT?
j. Suppose you are given the following information. The beta of company, b_i, is 0.9, the risk-free rate, k_{RF}, is 6.8 percent, and the expected market premium, $k_M - k_{RF}$, is 6.3 percent. Because your company is larger than average and more successful than average (that is, it has a lower book-to-market ratio), you think the Fama-French three-factor model might be more appropriate than the CAPM. You estimate the additional coefficients from the Fama-French three-factor model: The coefficient for the size effect, c_i, is -0.5, and the coefficient for the book-to-market effect, d_i, is -0.3. If the expected value of the size factor is 4 percent and the expected value of the book-to-market factor is 5 percent, what is the required return using the Fama-French three-factor model? (Assume that $a_i = 0.0$.) What is the required return using CAPM?

Selected Additional References and Cases

Probably the best place to find more information on CAPM and APT concepts is one of the investments textbooks. These are some good recent ones:

Francis, Jack C., *Investments: Analysis and Management* (New York: McGraw-Hill, 1991).

Radcliffe, Robert C., *Investment: Concepts, Analysis, and Strategy* (Glenview, IL: Scott, Foresman, 1996).

Reilly, Frank K., and Keith C. Brown, *Investment Analysis and Portfolio Management* (Fort Worth, TX: The Dryden Press, 1997).

Sharpe, William F., *Investments* (Englewood Cliffs, NJ: Prentice-Hall, 1995).

For a thorough discussion of beta stability, see

Kolb, Robert W., and Ricardo J. Rodriguez, "The Regression Tendencies of Betas: A Reappraisal," *The Financial Review*, May 1989, 319–334.

_____ "Is the Distribution of Betas Stationary?" *Journal of Financial Research*, Winter 1990, 279–283.

Those who want to start at the beginning in studying portfolio theory and the CAPM should see

Lintner, John, "Security Prices, Risk, and Maximal Gains from Diversification," *Journal of Finance*, December 1965, 587–616.

Markowitz, Harry M., "Portfolio Selection," *Journal of Finance*, March 1952, 77–91.

Mossin, Jan, "Security Pricing and Investment Criteria in Competitive Markets," *American Economic Review*, December 1969, 749–756.

Sharpe, William F., "Capital Asset Prices: A Theory of Market Equilibrium under Conditions of Risk," *Journal of Finance*, September 1964, 425–442.

_____, "Capital Asset Prices with and without Negative Holdings," *Journal of Finance*, June 1991, 489–509.

Literally thousands of articles providing theoretical extensions and tests of the CAPM theory have appeared in finance journals. Some of the more important earlier papers are contained in a book compiled by Jensen:

Jensen, Michael C., ed., *Studies in the Theory of Capital Markets* (New York: Praeger, 1972).

For one challenge to the CAPM, see

Wallace, Anise, "Is Beta Dead?" *Institutional Investor*, July 1980, 23–30.

For a recent article supporting a positive link between market risk and return, see

Marston, Felicia, and Robert S. Harris, "Risk and Return: A Revisit Using Expected Returns," *Financial Review*, February 1993, 117–137.

For additional discussion of Arbitrage Pricing Theory, see

Bower, Dorothy H., Richard S. Bower, and Dennis E. Logue, "A Primer on Arbitrage Pricing Theory," *Midland Corporate Finance Journal*, Fall 1984, 31–40.

Bubnys, Edward L., "Simulating and Forecasting Utility Stock Returns: Arbitrage Pricing Theory vs. Capital Asset Pricing Model," *The Financial Review*, February 1990, 1–23.

Goldenberg, David H., and Ashok J. Robin, "The Arbitrage Pricing Theory and Cost-of-Capital Estimation: The Case of Electric Utilities," *Journal of Financial Research*, Fall 1991, 181–196.

Robin, Ashok, and Ravi Shukla, "The Magnitude of Pricing Errors in the Arbitrage Pricing Theory," *Journal of Financial Research*, Spring 1991, 65–82.

The following case from the Cases in Financial Management: Dryden Request series covers many of the concepts discussed in this chapter:

Case 2, "Peachtree Securities, Inc. (A)."

8

Time Value of Money[1]

Will you be able to retire? Your reaction to this question is probably, "First things first! I'm worried about getting a job, not retiring!" However, an awareness of the retirement situation could help you land a job because (1) this is an important issue today, (2) employers prefer to hire people who know the issues, and (3) professors often test students on time value of money with problems related to saving for some future purpose, including retirement. So read on.

A recent *Fortune* article began with some interesting facts: (1) The U.S. savings rate is the lowest of any industrial nation. (2) The ratio of U.S. workers to retirees, which was 17 to 1 in 1950, is now down to 3.2 to 1, and it will decline to less than 2 to 1 after 2020. (3) With so few people paying into the Social Security System and so many drawing funds out, Social Security may soon be in serious trouble. The article concluded that even people making $85,000 per year will have trouble maintaining a reasonable standard of living after they retire, and many of today's college students will have to support their parents.

If Ms. Jones, who earns $85,000, retires in 2001, expects to live for another 20 years after retirement, and needs 80 percent of her pre-retirement income, she would require $68,000 during 2001. However, if inflation amounts to 5 percent per year, her income requirement would increase to $110,765 in 10 years and to $180,424 in 20 years. If inflation were 7 percent, her Year 20 requirement would jump to $263,139! How much wealth would Ms. Jones need at retirement to maintain her standard of living, and how much would she have had to save during each working year to accumulate that wealth?

The answer depends on a number of factors, including the rate she could earn on savings, the inflation rate, and when her savings program began. Also, the answer would depend on how much she will get from Social Security and from her corporate retirement plan, if she has one. (She might not get much from Social Security unless she is really down and out.) Note, too, that her plans could be upset if the inflation rate increased, if the return on her savings changed, or if she lived beyond 20 years.

Fortune and other organizations have done studies relating to the retirement issue, using the tools and techniques described in this chapter. The general conclusion is that most Americans have been putting their heads in the sand—many of us have been ignoring what is almost certainly going to be a huge personal and social problem. But if you study this chapter carefully, you can avoid the trap that seems to be catching so many people.

---

[1]This chapter was written on the assumption that most students will have financial calculators. Calculators are relatively inexpensive, and students who cannot use them run the risk of being deemed obsolete and uncompetitive before they even graduate. Therefore, the chapter has been written to include a discussion of financial calculator solutions along with the regular calculator solutions. Those sections that require the use of financial calculators are identified, and instructors may choose to permit students to skip them.

Note also that tutorials on how to use several Hewlett-Packard, Texas Instruments, and Sharp calculators are provided in the *Technology Supplement* to this book, which is available to adopting instructors.

An excellent retirement calculator is available at **http://www.sovereignbank.com/calculate/java_ret.html.** This calculator allows you to input hypothetical retirement savings information, and the program shows graphically if current retirement savings will be sufficient to meet retirement needs.

In Chapter 1, we saw that the primary goal of financial management is to maximize the value of the firm's stock. We also saw that stock values depend in part on the timing of the cash flows investors expect to receive from an investment—a dollar expected soon is worth more than a dollar expected in the distant future. Therefore, it is essential for financial managers to have a clear understanding of the time value of money and its impact on stock prices. These concepts are discussed in this chapter, where we show how the timing of cash flows affects asset values and rates of return.

The principles of time value analysis have many applications, ranging from setting up schedules for paying off loans to decisions about whether to acquire new equipment. *In fact, of all the concepts used in finance, none is more important than the time value of money, which is also called discounted cash flow (DCF) analysis.* Since this concept is used throughout the remainder of the book, it is vital that you understand the material in this chapter before you move on to other topics.

Time Lines

The textbook's CD-ROM contains an *Excel* file that will guide you through the chapter's calculations. The file for this chapter is ***Ch 08 Tool Kit.xls,*** and we encourage you to open the file and follow along as you read the chapter.

One of the most important tools in time value analysis is the **time line,** which is used by analysts to help visualize what is happening in a particular problem and then to help set up the problem for solution. To illustrate the time line concept, consider the following diagram:

Time: 0	1	2	3	4	5

Time 0 is today; Time 1 is one period from today, or the end of Period 1; Time 2 is two periods from today, or the end of Period 2; and so on. Thus, the numbers above the tick marks represent end-of-period values. Often the periods are years, but other time intervals such as semiannual periods, quarters, months, or even days can be used. If each period on the time line represents a year, the interval from the tick mark corresponding to 0 to the tick mark corresponding to 1 would be Year 1, the interval from 1 to 2 would be Year 2, and so on. Note that each tick mark corresponds to the end of one period as well as the beginning of the next period. In other words, the tick mark at Time 1 represents the *end* of Year 1, and it also represents the *beginning* of Year 2 because Year 1 has just passed.

Cash flows are placed directly below the tick marks, and interest rates are shown directly above the time line. Unknown cash flows, which you are trying to find in the analysis, are indicated by question marks. Now consider the following time line:

Time:	0	5%	1	2	3
Cash flows:	−100				?

Here the interest rate for each of the three periods is 5 percent; a single amount (or lump sum) cash **outflow** is made at Time 0; and the Time 3 value is an unknown **inflow.** Since the initial $100 is an outflow (an investment), it has a minus sign. Since the Period 3 amount is an inflow, it does not have a minus sign, which implies a plus sign. Note that no cash flows occur at Times 1 and 2. Note also that we generally do not show dollar signs on time lines to reduce clutter.

Now consider a different situation, where a $100 cash outflow is made today, and we will receive an unknown amount at the end of Time 2:

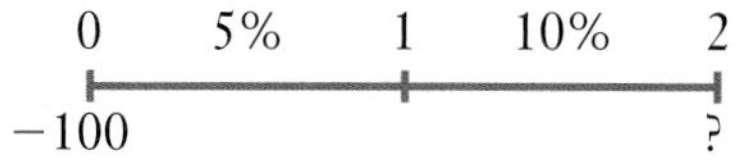

Here the interest rate is 5 percent during the first period, but it rises to 10 percent during the second period. If the interest rate is constant in all periods, we show it only in the first period, but if it changes, we show all the relevant rates on the time line.

Time lines are essential when you are first learning time value concepts, but even experts use time lines to analyze complex problems. We will be using time lines throughout the book, and you should get into the habit of using them when you work problems.

Self-Test Question

Draw a three-year time line to illustrate the following situation: (1) An outflow of $10,000 occurs at Time 0. (2) Inflows of $5,000 then occur at the end of Years 1, 2, and 3. (3) The interest rate during all three years is 10 percent.

Future Value

A dollar in hand today is worth more than a dollar to be received in the future because, if you had it now, you could invest it, earn interest, and end up with more than one dollar in the future. The process of going from today's values, or present values (PVs), to future values (FVs) is called **compounding.** To illustrate, suppose you deposit $100 in a bank that pays 5 percent interest each year. How much would you have at the end of one year? To begin, we define the following terms:

PV = present value, or beginning amount, in your account. Here PV = $100.

i = interest rate the bank pays on the account per year. The interest earned is based on the balance at the beginning of each year, and we assume that it is paid at the end of the year. Here i = 5%, or, expressed as a decimal, i =0.05. Throughout this chapter, we designate the interest rate as i (or I) because that symbol is used on most financial calculators. Note, though, that in later chapters we use the symbol k to denote interest rates because k is used more often in the financial literature.

INT = dollars of interest you earn during the year = Beginning amount × i. Here INT = $100(0.05) = $5.

FV_n = future value, or ending amount, of your account at the end of n years. Whereas PV is the value now, or the *present value*, FV_n is the value n years into the *future*, after the interest earned has been added to the account.

n = number of periods involved in the analysis. Here n = 1.

In our example, n = 1, so FV_n can be calculated as follows:

$$\begin{aligned} FV_n = FV_1 &= PV + INT \\ &= PV + PV(i) \\ &= PV(1 + i) \\ &= \$100(1 + 0.05) = \$100(1.05) = \$105. \end{aligned}$$

Thus, the **future value (FV)** at the end of one year, FV_1, equals the present value multiplied by 1 plus the interest rate, so you will have $105 after one year.

What would you end up with if you left your \$100 in the account for five years? Here is a time line set up to show the amount at the end of each year:

	0 5%	1	2	3	4	5
Initial deposit:	−100	FV_1 = ?	FV_2 = ?	FV_3 = ?	FV_4 = ?	FV_5 = ?
Interest earned:		5.00	5.25	5.51	5.79	6.08
Amount at the end of each period = FV_n:		105.00	110.25	115.76	121.55	**127.63**

Note the following points: (1) You start by depositing \$100 in the account—this is shown as an outflow at t = 0. (2) You earn \$100(0.05) = \$5 of interest during the first year, so the amount at the end of Year 1 (or t = 1) is \$100 + \$5 = \$105. (3) You start the second year with \$105, earn \$5.25 on the now larger amount, and end the second year with \$110.25. Your interest during Year 2, \$5.25, is higher than the first year's interest, \$5, because you earned \$5(0.05) = \$0.25 interest on the first year's interest. (4) This process continues, and because the beginning balance is higher in each succeeding year, the annual interest earned increases. (5) The total interest earned, \$27.63, is reflected in the final balance at t = 5, \$127.63.

Note that the value at the end of Year 2, \$110.25, is equal to

$$\begin{aligned} FV_2 &= FV_1(1 + i) \\ &= PV(1 + i)(1 + i) \\ &= PV(1 + i)^2 \\ &= \$100(1.05)^2 = \$110.25. \end{aligned}$$

Continuing, the balance at the end of Year 3 is

$$\begin{aligned} FV_3 &= FV_2(1 + i) \\ &= PV(1 + i)^3 \\ &= \$100(1.05)^3 = \$115.76, \end{aligned}$$

and

$$FV_5 = \$100(1.05)^5 = \$127.63.$$

In general, the future value of an initial lump sum at the end of n years can be found by applying Equation 8-1:

$$FV_n = PV(1 + i)^n = PV(FVIF_{i,n}). \quad \textbf{(8-1)}$$

The last term in Equation 8-1 defines the **Future Value Interest Factor for i and n, $FVIF_{i,n}$,** as $(1 + i)^n$. This provides a shorthand way to refer to the actual formula in Equation 8-1.

Equation 8-1 and most other time value of money equations can be solved in three ways: numerically with a regular calculator, with a financial calculator, or with a computer spreadsheet program.[2] Most work in financial management will be done with a financial calculator or on a computer, but when learning basic concepts it is best to also work the problem numerically with a regular calculator.

NUMERICAL SOLUTION

One can use a regular calculator and either multiply (1 + i) by itself n − 1 times or else use the exponential function to raise (1 + i) to the *n*th power. With most calculators, you

[2]Prior to the widespread use of financial calculators, a fourth method was used. It is called the "tabular approach," and it is described in the Chapter 8 Web/CD Extension, available on the textbook's CD-ROM and web site.

would enter 1 + i = 1.05 and multiply it by itself four times, or else enter 1.05, then press the y^x (exponential) function key, and then enter 5. In either case, your answer would be 1.2763 (if you set your calculator to display four decimal places), which you would multiply by \$100 to get the final answer, \$127.6282, which would be rounded to \$127.63.

In certain problems, it is extremely difficult to arrive at a solution using a regular calculator. We will tell you this when we have such a problem, and in these cases we will not show a numerical solution. Also, at times we show the numerical solution just below the time line, as a part of the diagram, rather than in a separate section.

FINANCIAL CALCULATOR SOLUTION

A version of Equation 8-1, along with a number of other equations, has been programmed directly into financial calculators, and these calculators can be used to find future values. Note that calculators have five keys that correspond to the five most commonly used time value of money variables:

N I PV PMT FV

Here

N = the number of periods. Some calculators use n rather than N.
I = interest rate per period. Some calculators use i or I/YR rather than I.
PV = present value.
PMT = payment. This key is used only if the cash flows involve a series of equal, or constant, payments (an annuity). If there are no periodic payments in a particular problem, then PMT = 0.
FV = future value.

On some financial calculators, these keys are actually buttons on the face of the calculator, while on others they are shown on a screen after going into the time value of money (TVM) menu.

In this chapter, we deal with equations involving only four of the variables at any one time—three of the variables are known, and the calculator then solves for the fourth (unknown) variable. In the next chapter, when we deal with bonds, we will use all five variables in the bond valuation equation.[3]

To find the future value of \$100 after five years at 5 percent using a financial calculator, note that we must solve Equation 8-1:

$$FV_n = PV(1 + i)^n. \qquad \textbf{(8-1)}$$

The equation has four variables, FV_n, PV, i, and n. If we know any three, we can solve for the fourth. In our example, we enter N = 5, I = 5, PV = 100, and PMT = 0. Then, when we press the FV key, we get the answer, FV = 127.63 (rounded to two decimal places).[4]

---

[3] The equation programmed into the calculators actually has five variables, one for each key. In this chapter, the value of one of the variables is always zero. It is a good idea to get into the habit of inputting a zero for the unused variable (whose value is automatically set equal to zero when you clear the calculator's memory); if you forget to clear your calculator, inputting a zero will help you avoid trouble.

[4] Here we assume that compounding occurs once each year. Most calculators have a setting that can be used to designate the number of compounding periods per year. For example, the HP-10B comes preset with payments at 12 per year. You would need to change it to 1 per year to get FV = 127.63. With the HP-10B, you would do this by typing 1, pressing the gold key, and then pressing the P/YR key.

Many financial calculators require that all cash flows be designated as either inflows or outflows, with outflows being entered as negative numbers. In our illustration, you deposit, or put in, the initial amount (which is an outflow to you) and you take out, or receive, the ending amount (which is an inflow to you). If your calculator requires that you follow this sign convention, the PV would be entered as −100. Enter the −100 by keying in 100 and then pressing the "change sign" or +/− key. (If you entered 100, then the FV would appear as −127.63.) Also, on some calculators you are required to press a "Compute" key before pressing the FV key.

Sometimes the convention of changing signs can be confusing. For example, if you have $100 in the bank now and want to find out how much you will have after five years if your account pays 5 percent interest, the calculator will give you a negative answer, in this case −127.63, because the calculator assumes you are going to withdraw the funds. This sign convention should cause you no problem if you think about what you are doing.

We should also note that financial calculators permit you to specify the number of decimal places that are displayed. Twelve significant digits are actually used in the calculations, but we generally use two places for answers when working with dollars or percentages and four places when working with decimals. The nature of the problem dictates how many decimal places should be displayed.

SPREADSHEET SOLUTION

As noted back in Chapter 2, spreadsheet programs are ideally suited for solving many financial problems, including time value of money problems.[5] With very little effort, the spreadsheet itself becomes a time line. Here is how the problem would look in a spreadsheet:

	A	B	C	D	E	F	G
1	Interest rate	0.05					
2	Time	0	1	2	3	4	5
3	Cash flow	−100					
4	Future value		105.00	110.25	115.76	121.55	**127.63**

Cell B1 shows the interest rate, entered as a decimal number, 0.05. Row 2 shows the periods for the time line. With *Microsoft Excel*, you could enter **0** in Cell B2, then the formula **=B2+1** in Cell C2, and then copy this formula into Cells D2 through G2 to produce the time periods shown on Row 2. Note that if your time line had many years, say, 50, you would simply copy the formula across more columns. Other procedures could also be used to enter the periods.

Row 3 shows the cash flows. In this case, there is only one cash flow, shown in Cell B3. Row 4 shows the future value of this cash flow at the end of each year. Cell C4

[5]In this section, and in other sections and chapters, we discuss spreadsheet solutions to various financial problems. If a reader is not familiar with spreadsheets and has no interest in them, then these sections can be omitted. For those who are interested, ***Ch 8 Tool Kit.xls*** is the file on the CD-ROM for this chapter that does the various calculations using *Excel*. If you have the time, we *highly recommend* that you go through the models. This will give you practice with *Excel*, which will help tremendously in later courses, in the job market, and in the workplace. Also, going through the models will enhance your understanding of financial concepts.

contains the formula for Equation 8-1. The formula could be written as **=−B3*(1+.05)^C2,** but we wrote it as **=−B3*(1+ B1)^C2,** which gives us the flexibility to change the interest rate in Cell B1 to see how the future value changes with changes in interest rates. Note that the formula has a minus sign for the PV (which is in Cell B3) to account for the minus sign of the cash flow. This formula was then copied into Cells D4 through G4. As Cell G4 shows, the value of $100 compounded for five years at 5 percent per year is $127.63.

You could also find the FV by putting the cursor on Cell G4, then clicking the function wizard, then Financial, then scrolling down to FV, and then clicking OK to bring up the FV dialog box. Then enter B1 or .05 for Rate, G2 or 5 for Nper, 0 or leave blank for Pmt because there are no periodic payments, B3 or −100 for PV, and 0 or leave blank for Type to indicate that payments occur at the end of the period. Then, when you click OK, you get the future value, $127.63.

Note that the dialog box prompts you to fill in the arguments in an equation. The equation itself, in *Excel* format, is FV(Rate,Nper,Pmt,PV,Type) = FV(.05,5,0,−100,0). Rather than insert numbers, you could input cell references for Rate, Nper, Pmt, and PV. Either way, when *Excel* sees the equation, it knows to use our Equation 8-1 to fill in the specified arguments, and to deposit the result in the cell where the cursor was located when you began the process. If someone really knows what they are doing and has memorized the formula, they can skip both the time line and the function wizard and just insert data into the formula to get the answer. But until you become an expert, we recommend that you use time lines to visualize the problem and the function wizard to complete the formula.

Comparing the Three Procedures

The first step in solving any time value problem is to understand the verbal description of the problem well enough to diagram it on a time line. Woody Allen said that 90 percent of success is just showing up. With time value problems, 90 percent of success is correctly setting up the time line.

After you diagram the problem on a time line, your next step is to pick an approach to solve the problem. Which of the three approaches should you use—numerical, financial calculator, or spreadsheet? In general, you should use the easiest approach. But which is easiest? The answer depends on the particular situation.

All business students should know Equation 8-1 by heart and should also know how to use a financial calculator. So, for simple problems such as finding the future value of a single payment, it is probably easiest and quickest to use either the numerical approach or a financial calculator.

For problems with more than a couple of cash flows, the numerical approach is usually too time consuming, so here either the calculator or spreadsheet approaches would generally be used. Calculators are portable and quick to set up, but if many calculations of the same type must be done, or if you want to see how changes in an input such as the interest rate affect the future value, the spreadsheet approach is generally more efficient. If the problem has many irregular cash flows, or if you want to analyze many scenarios with different cash flows, then the spreadsheet approach is definitely the most efficient. The important thing is that you understand the various approaches well enough to make a rational choice, given the nature of the problem and the equipment you have available. In any event, you must understand the concepts behind the calculations and know how to set up time lines in order to work complex problems. This is true for stock and bond valuation, capital budgeting, lease analysis, and many other important financial problems.

Problem Format

To help you understand the various types of time value problems, we generally use a standard format. First, we state the problem in words. Next, we diagram the problem on a time line. Then, beneath the time line, we show the equation that must be solved. Finally, we present the three alternative procedures for solving the equation to obtain the answer: (1) use a regular calculator to obtain a numerical solution, (2) use a financial calculator, and (3) use a spreadsheet program. For some very easy problems, we will not show a spreadsheet solution, and for some difficult problems, we will not show numerical solutions because they are too inefficient.

To illustrate the format, consider again our five-year, 5 percent example:

Time Line:

Equation:

$$FV_n = PV(1 + i)^n = \$100(1.05)^5.$$

1. NUMERICAL SOLUTION

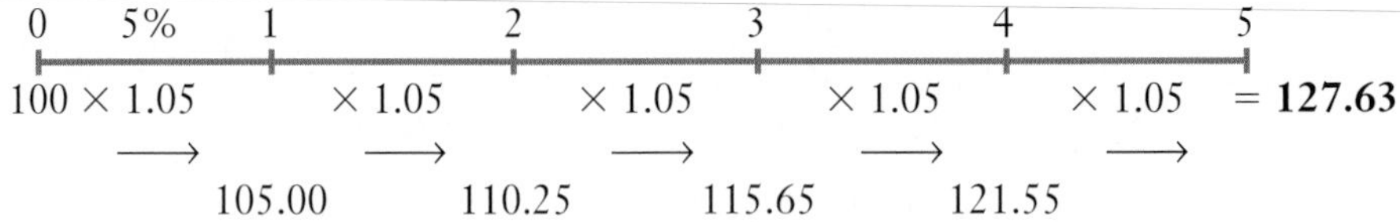

Using a regular calculator, raise 1.05 to the 5th power and multiply by \$100 to get FV_5 = \$127.63.

2. FINANCIAL CALCULATOR SOLUTION

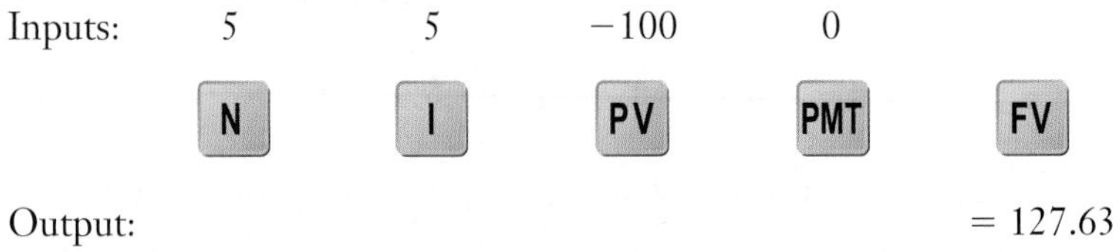

Note that the calculator diagram tells you to input N = 5, I = 5, PV = –100, and PMT = 0, and then to press the FV key to get the answer, 127.63. Interest rates are entered as percentages (5), not decimals (0.05). Also, note that in this particular problem, the PMT key does not come into play, as no constant series of payments is involved.[6] Finally, you should recognize that small rounding differences will often occur among the various solution methods because rounding sometimes is done at intermediate steps in long problems.

[6]We input PMT = 0, but if you cleared the calculator before you started, the PMT register would already have been set to 0.

3. SPREADSHEET SOLUTION

	A	B	C	D	E	F	G
1	Interest rate	0.05					
2	Time	0	1	2	3	4	5
3	Cash flow	−100					
4	Future value		105.00	110.25	115.76	121.55	127.63

Cell G4 contains the formula for Equation 8-1: **=−B3*(1+B1)^G2** or **=−B3*(1+.05)^G2.** You could also use *Excel's* FV function to find the $127.63, following the procedures described in the previous section.

Graphic View of the Compounding Process: Growth

Figure 8-1 shows how $1 (or any other lump sum) grows over time at various interest rates. We generated the data and then made the graph with a spreadsheet model in the file ***Ch 08 Tool Kit.xls***. The higher the rate of interest, the faster the rate of growth. The interest rate is, in fact, a growth rate: If a sum is deposited and earns 5 percent interest, then the funds on deposit will grow at a rate of 5 percent per period. Note also that time value concepts can be applied to anything that is growing—sales, population, earnings per share, your future salary, or whatever.

FIGURE 8-1 Relationships among Future Value, Growth, Interest Rates, and Time

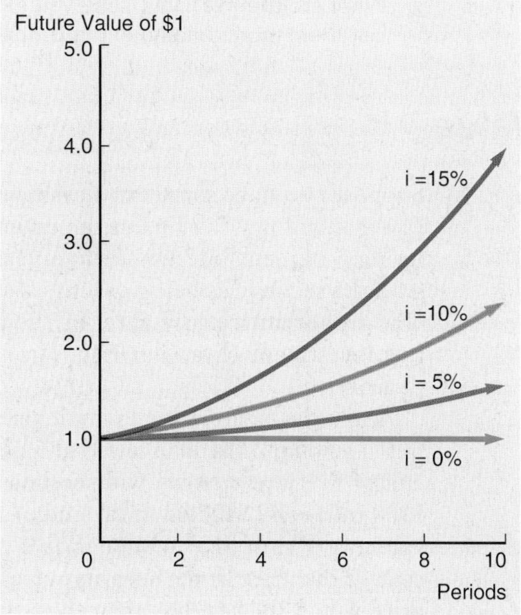

The Power of Compound Interest

Suppose you are 26 years old and just received your MBA. After reading the introduction to this chapter, you decide to start investing in the stock market for your retirement. Your goal is to have $1 million when you retire at age 65. Assuming you earn a 10 percent annual rate on your stock investments, how much must you invest at the end of each year in order to reach your goal?

The answer is $2,490.98, but this amount depends critically on the return earned on your investments. If returns drop to 8 percent, your required annual contributions would rise to $4,185.13, while if returns rise to 12 percent, you would only need to put away $1,641.97 per year.

What if you are like most of us and wait until later to worry about retirement? If you wait until age 40, you will need to save $10,168 per year to reach your $1 million goal, assuming you earn 10 percent, and $13,679 per year if you earn only 8 percent. If you wait until age 50 and then earn 8 percent, the required amount will be $36,830 per year.

While $1 million may seem like a lot of money, it won't be when you get ready to retire. If inflation averages 5 percent a year over the next 39 years, your $1 million nest egg will be worth only $116,861 in today's dollars. At an 8 percent rate of return, and assuming you live for 20 years after retirement, your annual retirement income in today's dollars would be only $11,903 before taxes. So, after celebrating graduation and your new job, start saving!

Self-Test Questions

Explain what is meant by the following statement: "A dollar in hand today is worth more than a dollar to be received next year."

What is compounding? Explain why earning "interest on interest" is called "compound interest."

Explain the following equation: $FV_1 = PV + INT$.

Set up a time line that shows the following situation: (1) Your initial deposit is $100. (2) The account pays 5 percent interest annually. (3) You want to know how much money you will have at the end of three years.

Write out an equation that could be used to solve the preceding problem.

What are the five TVM (time value of money) input keys on a financial calculator? List them (horizontally) in the proper order.

Present Value

Suppose you have some extra cash, and you have a chance to buy a low-risk security that will pay $127.63 at the end of five years. Your local bank is currently offering 5 percent interest on five-year certificates of deposit (CDs), and you regard the security as being exactly as safe as a CD. The 5 percent rate is defined as your **opportunity cost rate,** or the rate of return you could earn on an alternative investment of similar risk. How much should you be willing to pay for the security?

From the future value example presented in the previous section, we saw that an initial amount of $100 invested at 5 percent per year would be worth $127.63 at the end of five years. As we will see in a moment, you should be indifferent between $100 today and $127.63 at the end of five years. The $100 is defined as the **present value,** or **PV,** of $127.63 due in five years when the opportunity cost rate is 5 percent. If the price of the security were less than $100, you should buy it, because its price would then be less than the $100 you would have to spend on a similar-risk alternative to end up with \$127.63 after five years. Conversely, if the security cost more than \$100, you should not buy it, because you would have to invest only \$100 in a similar-risk alternative to end up with \$127.63 after five years. If the price were exactly \$100, then you should be indifferent—you could either buy the security or turn it down. Therefore, \$100 is defined as the security's **fair,** or **equilibrium, value.**

In general, *the present value of a cash flow due n years in the future is the amount which, if it were on hand today, would grow to equal the future amount.* Since \$100 would grow to \$127.63 in five years at a 5 percent interest rate, \$100 is the present value of \$127.63 due in five years when the opportunity cost rate is 5 percent.

Finding present values is called **discounting,** and it is the reverse of compounding—if you know the PV, you can compound to find the FV, while if you know the FV, you can discount to find the PV. When discounting, you would follow these steps:

Time Line:

0	5% 1	2	3	4	5
PV = ?					127.63

Equation:

To develop the discounting equation, we begin with the future value equation, Equation 8-1:

$$FV_n = PV(1 + i)^n = PV(FVIF_{i,n}). \quad \textbf{(8-1)}$$

Next, we solve it for PV in several equivalent forms:

$$PV = \frac{FV_n}{(1 + i)^n} = FV_n\left(\frac{1}{1 + i}\right)^n = FV_n(PVIF_{i,n}). \quad \textbf{(8-2)}$$

The last form of Equation 8-2 recognizes that the **Present Value Interest Factor for i and n, $PVIF_{i,n}$,** is equal to the term in parentheses in the second version of the equation.

1. NUMERICAL SOLUTION

0	5% 1	2	3	4	5
−100 = ←	105.00 ←	110.25 ←	115.76 ←	121.55 ←	127.63
	÷ 1.05	÷ 1.05	÷ 1.05	÷ 1.05	÷ 1.05

Divide \$127.63 by 1.05 five times, or by $(1.05)^5$, to find PV = \$100.

2. FINANCIAL CALCULATOR SOLUTION

Inputs:	5	5		0	127.63
	N	I	PV	PMT	FV
Output:			= −100		

Enter N = 5, I = 5, PMT = 0, and FV = 127.63, and then press PV to get PV = −100.

3. SPREADSHEET SOLUTION

	A	B	C	D	E	F	G
1	Interest rate	0.05					
2	Time	0	1	2	3	4	5
3	Cash flow		0	0	0	0	127.63
4	Present value	100					

You could enter the spreadsheet version of Equation 8-2 in Cell B4, **=127.63/(1+0.05)^5,** but you could also use the built-in spreadsheet PV function. In *Excel,* you would put the cursor on Cell B4, then click the function wizard, indicate that you want a Financial function, scroll down, and double click PV. Then, in the dialog box, enter B1 or 0.05 for Rate, G2 or 5 for Nper, 0 for Pmt (because there are no annual payments), G3 or 127.63 for FV, and 0 (or leave blank) for Type because the cash flow occurs at the end of the year. Then, press OK to get the answer, PV = −$100.00. Note that the PV function returns a negative value, the same as the financial calculator.

Graphic View of the Discounting Process

Figure 8-2 shows how the present value of $1 (or any other sum) to be received in the future diminishes as the years to receipt and the interest rate increase. The graph shows (1) that the present value of a sum to be received at some future date decreases and approaches zero as the payment date is extended further into the future, and (2) that the rate of decrease is greater the higher the interest (discount) rate. At relatively high interest rates, funds due in the future are worth very little today, and even at a

FIGURE 8-2 Relationships among Present Value, Interest Rates, and Time

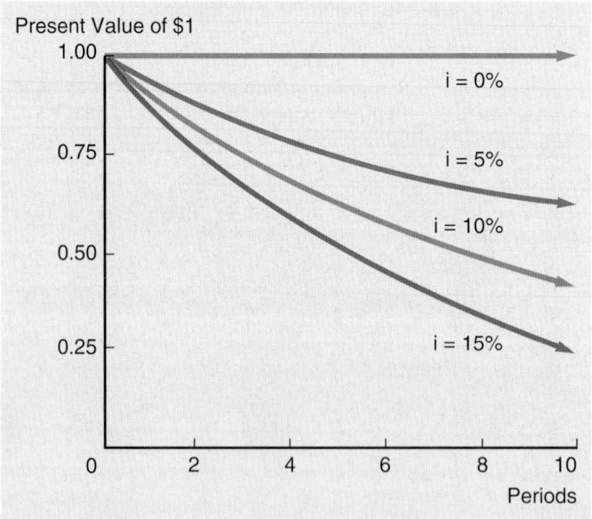

relatively low discount rate, the present value of a sum due in the very distant future is quite small. For example, at a 20 percent discount rate, \$1 million due in 100 years is worth approximately 1 cent today. (However, 1 cent would grow to almost \$1 million in 100 years at 20 percent.)

Self-Test Questions

What is meant by the term "opportunity cost rate"?

What is discounting? How is it related to compounding?

How does the present value of an amount to be received in the future change as the time is extended and the interest rate increased?

Solving for Interest Rate and Time

At this point, you should realize that compounding and discounting are related, and that we have been dealing with one equation that can be solved for either the FV or the PV.

FV Form:

$$FV_n = PV(1 + i)^n. \quad \textbf{(8-1)}$$

PV Form:

$$PV = \frac{FV_n}{(1 + i)^n} = FV_n\left(\frac{1}{1 + i}\right)^n. \quad \textbf{(8-2)}$$

There are four variables in these equations—PV, FV, i, and n—and if you know the values of any three, you can find the value of the fourth. Thus far, we have always given you the interest rate (i) and the number of years (n), plus either the PV or the FV. In many situations, though, you will need to solve for either i or n, as we discuss below.

Solving for i

Suppose you can buy a security at a price of \$78.35, and it will pay you \$100 after five years. Here you know PV, FV, and n, and you want to find i, the interest rate you would earn if you bought the security. Such problems are solved as follows:

Time Line:

0	i = ?	1	2	3	4	5
−78.35						100

Equation:

$$FV_n = PV(1 + i)^n$$
$$\$100 = \$78.35(1 + i)^5. \text{ Solve for i.} \quad \textbf{(8-1)}$$

1. NUMERICAL SOLUTION

Use Equation 8-1 to solve for i:

$$
\begin{aligned}
\$100 &= \$78.35(1 + i)^5 \\
\frac{\$100}{\$78.35} &= (1 + i)^5 \\
(1 + i)^5 &= 1.276 \\
1 + i &= (1.276)^{(1/5)} \\
1 + i &= 1.050 \\
i &= 0.05 = 5\%.
\end{aligned}
$$

Therefore, the interest rate is 5 percent.

2. FINANCIAL CALCULATOR SOLUTION

Inputs:	5		−78.35	0	100
	N	I	PV	PMT	FV
Output:		= 5.0			

Enter N = 5, PV = −78.35, PMT = 0, and FV = 100, and then press I to get I = 5%. This procedure is easy, and it can be used for any interest rate or for any value of n, including fractional values.

3. SPREADSHEET SOLUTION

	A	B	C	D	E	F	G
1	Time	0	1	2	3	4	5
2	Cash flow	−78.35	0	0	0	0	100
3	Interest rate	5%					

Most spreadsheets have a built-in function to find the interest rate. In *Excel*, you would put the cursor on Cell B3, then click the function wizard, indicate that you want a Financial function, scroll down to Rate, and click OK. Then, in the dialog box, enter G1 or 5 for Nper, 0 for Pmt because there are no periodic payments, B2 or −78.35 for PV, G2 or 100 for FV, 0 for type, and leave "Guess" blank to let *Excel* decide where to start its iterations. Then, when you click OK, *Excel* solves for the interest rate, 5.00 percent. *Excel* also has other procedures that could be used to find the 5 percent, but for this problem the Rate function is easiest to apply.

Solving for n

Suppose you know that a security will provide a return of 5 percent per year, that it will cost $78.35, and that you will receive $100 at maturity, but you do not know when the security matures. Thus, you know PV, FV, and i, but you do not know n, the number of periods. Here is the situation:

Time Line:

Equation:

$$FV_n = PV(1 + i)^n$$
$$\$100 = \$78.35(1.05)^n. \text{ Solve for n.} \quad \textbf{(8-1)}$$

1. NUMERICAL SOLUTION

Use Equation 8-1 to solve for n:

$$\$100 = \$78.35\ (1 + 0.05)^n.$$

Transform to:

$$\$100/\$78.35 = 1.276 = (1 + 0.05)^n.$$

Take the natural log of both sides, and then solve for n:

$$n\ LN(1.05) = LN(1.276)$$
$$n = LN(1.276)/LN(1.05)$$

Find the logs with a calculator, and complete the solution:

$$n = 0.2437/0.0488$$
$$= 4.9955 \approx 5.0.$$

Therefore, 5 is the number of years it takes for $78.35 to grow to $100 if the interest rate is 5 percent.

2. FINANCIAL CALCULATOR SOLUTION

	N	I	PV	PMT	FV
Inputs:		5	−78.35	0	100
Output:	= 5.0				

Enter I = 5, PV = −78.35, PMT = 0, and FV = 100, and then press N to get N = 5.

3. SPEADSHEET SOLUTION

	A	B	C	D	E	F	G
1	Time	0	1	2	3	. . .	?
2	Cash flow	−78.35	0	0	0	. . .	100
3	Interest rate	5%					
4	Payment	0					
5	N	5.00					

Most spreadsheets have a built-in function to find the number of periods. In *Excel,* you would put the cursor on Cell B5, then click the function wizard, indicate that you want a Financial function, scroll down to Nper, and click OK. Then, in the dialog box, enter B3 or 5% for Rate, 0 for Pmt because there are no periodic payments, B2 or −78.35 for PV, E2 or 100 for FV, and 0 for Type. When you click OK, *Excel* solves for the number of periods, 5.

Self-Test Questions

Assuming that you are given PV, FV, and the time period, n, write out an equation that can be used to determine the interest rate, i.

Assuming that you are given PV, FV, and the interest rate, i, write out an equation that can be used to determine the time period, n.

Explain how a financial calculator can be used to solve for i and n.

Future Value of an Annuity

An **annuity** is a series of equal payments made at fixed intervals for a specified number of periods. For example, $100 at the end of each of the next three years is a three-year annuity. The payments are given the symbol PMT, and they can occur at either the beginning or the end of each period. If the payments occur at the *end* of each period, as they typically do, the annuity is called an **ordinary,** or **deferred, annuity.** Payments on mortgages, car loans, and student loans are typically set up as ordinary annuities. If payments are made at the *beginning* of each period, the annuity is an **annuity due.** Rental payments for an apartment, life insurance premiums, and lottery payoffs are typically set up as annuities due. Since ordinary annuities are more common in finance, when the term "annuity" is used in this book, you should assume that the payments occur at the end of each period unless otherwise noted.

Ordinary Annuities

An ordinary, or deferred, annuity consists of a series of equal payments made at the *end* of each period. If you deposit $100 at the end of each year for three years in a savings account that pays 5 percent interest per year, how much will you have at the end of three years? To answer this question, we must find the future value of the annuity, $\mathbf{FVA_n}$. Each payment is compounded out to the end of Period n, and the sum of the compounded payments is the future value of the annuity, FVA_n.

Time Line:

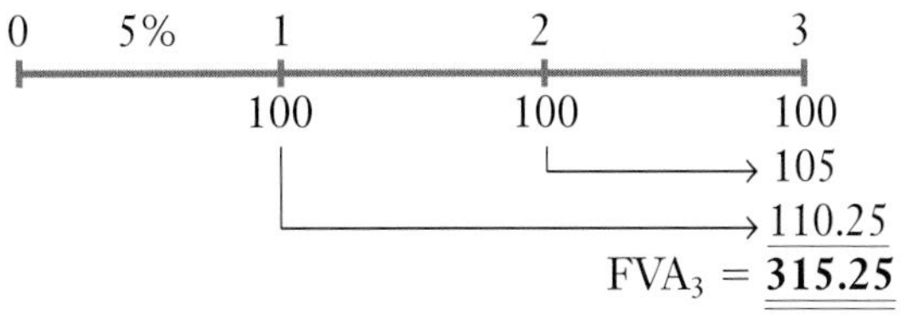

Here we show the regular time line as the top portion of the diagram, but we also show how each cash flow is compounded to produce the value FVA_n in the lower portion of the diagram.

Equation:

$$\begin{aligned} FVA_n &= PMT(1+i)^{n-1} + PMT(1+i)^{n-2} + PMT(1+i)^{n-3} + \cdots + PMT(1+i)^0 \\ &= PMT \sum_{t=1}^{n} (1+i)^{n-t} \\ &= PMT\left(\frac{(1+i)^n - 1}{i}\right) \\ &= PMT(FVIFA_{i,n}). \end{aligned} \tag{8-3}$$

The first line of Equation 8-3 represents the application of Equation 8-1 to each individual payment of the annuity. In other words, each term is the compounded amount of a single payment, with the superscript in each term indicating the number of periods during which the payment earns interest. For example, because the first annuity payment was made at the end of Period 1, interest would be earned in Periods 2 through n only, so compounding would be for n − 1 periods rather than n periods. Compounding for the second payment would be for Period 3 through Period n, or n − 2 periods, and so on. The last payment is made at the end of the annuity's life, so there is no time for interest to be earned.

The second line of Equation 8-3 is just a shorthand version of the first form, but the third line is different—it is found by applying the algebra of geometric progressions. This form of Equation 8-3 is especially useful when no financial calculator is available. Finally, the fourth line shows the payment multiplied by the **Future Value Interest Factor for an Annuity ($FVIFA_{i,n}$)**, which is the shorthand version of the formula.

1. NUMERICAL SOLUTION:

The lower section of the time line shows the numerical solution, which involves using the first line of Equation 8-3. The future value of each cash flow is found, and those FVs are summed to find the FV of the annuity, $315.25. If a long annuity were being evaluated, this process would be quite tedious, and in that case you probably would use the form of Equation 8-3 found on the third line:

$$\begin{aligned} FVA_n &= PMT\left(\frac{(1+i)^n - 1}{i}\right) \\ &= \$100\left(\frac{(1+0.05)^3 - 1}{0.05}\right) = \$100(3.1525) = \$315.25. \end{aligned} \tag{8-3}$$

2. FINANCIAL CALCULATOR SOLUTION

Inputs:	3	5	0	−100	
	N	I	PV	PMT	FV
Output:					= 315.25

Note that in annuity problems, the PMT key is used in conjunction with the N and I keys, plus either the PV or the FV key, depending on whether you are trying to find the PV or the FV of the annuity. In our example, you want the FV, so press the FV key to get the answer, \$315.25. Since there is no initial payment, we input PV = 0.

3. SPREADSHEET SOLUTION

	A	B	C	D	E
1	Interest rate	0.05			
2	Time	0	1	2	3
3	Cash flow		100	100	100
4	Future value				315.25

Most spreadsheets have a built-in function to find the future value of an annuity. In *Excel,* we could put the cursor on Cell E4, then click the function wizard, Financial, FV, and OK to get the FV dialog box. Then, we would enter .05 or B1 for Rate, 3 or E2 for Nper, and −100 for Pmt. (Like the financial calculator approach, the payment is entered as a negative number to show that it is a cash outflow.) We would leave PV blank because there is no initial payment, and we would leave Type blank to signify that payments come at the end of the periods. Then, when we clicked OK, we would get the FV of the annuity, \$315.25. Note that it isn't necessary to show the time line, since the FV function doesn't require you to input a range of cash flows. Still, the time line is useful to help visualize the problem.

Annuities Due

Had the three \$100 payments in the previous example been made at the *beginning* of each year, the annuity would have been an *annuity due.* On the time line, each payment would be shifted to the left one year, so each payment would be compounded for one extra year.

Time Line

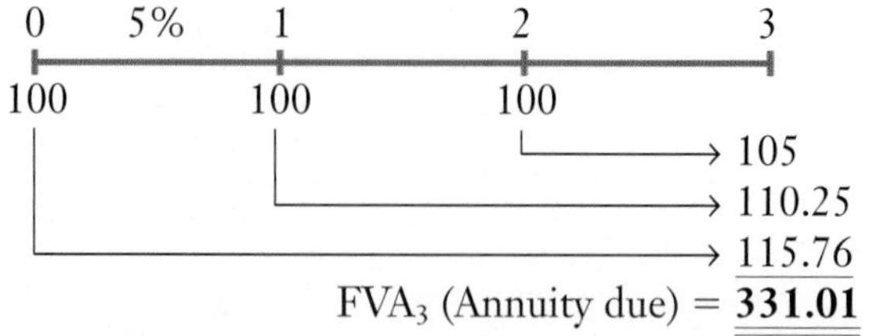

Again, the time line is shown at the top of the diagram, and the values as calculated with a regular calculator are shown under Year 3. The future value of each cash flow is found, and those FVs are summed to find the FV of the annuity due. The payments occur earlier, so more interest is earned. Therefore, the future value of the annuity due is larger—\$331.01 versus \$315.25 for the ordinary annuity.

Equation:

$$\begin{aligned} FVA_n(\text{Due}) &= PMT(1+i)^n + PMT(1+i)^{n-1} + PMT(1+i)^{n-2} + \cdots + PMT(1+i) \\ &= PMT\sum_{t=1}^{n}(1+i)^{n+1-t} \\ &= PMT\left(\frac{(1+i)^n - 1}{i}\right)(1+i) \\ &= PMT(FVIFA_{i,n})(1+i). \end{aligned} \quad \textbf{(8-3a)}$$

The only difference between Equation 8-3a for annuities due and Equation 8-3 for ordinary annuities is that every term in Equation 8-3a is compounded for one extra period, reflecting the fact that each payment for an annuity due occurs one period earlier than for a corresponding ordinary annuity.

1. NUMERICAL SOLUTION:

The lower section of the time line shows the numerical solution using the first line of Equation 8-3a. The future value of each cash flow is found, and those FVs are summed to find the FV of the annuity, \$331.01. Because this process is quite tedious for long annuities, you probably would use the third line of Equation 8-3a:

$$FVA_n(\text{Due}) = PMT\left(\frac{(1+i)^n - 1}{i}\right)(1+i) \quad \textbf{(8-3a)}$$

$$= \$100\left(\frac{(1+0.05)^3 - 1}{0.05}\right)(1+0.05) = \$100(3.1525)(1.05) = \$331.01.$$

2. FINANCIAL CALCULATOR SOLUTION

Most financial calculators have a switch, or key, marked "DUE" or "BEG" that permits you to switch from end-of-period payments (ordinary annuity) to beginning-of-period payments (annuity due). When the beginning mode is activated, the display will normally show the word "BEGIN." Thus, to deal with annuities due, switch your calculator to "BEGIN" and proceed as before:

BEGIN Inputs:	3	5	0	−100	
	N	I	PV	PMT	FV
Output:					= 331.01

Enter N = 3, I = 5, PV = 0, PMT = −100, and then press FV to get the answer, \$331.01. *Since most problems specify end-of-period cash flows, you should always switch your calculator back to "END" mode after you work an annuity due problem.*

3. SPREADSHEET SOLUTION

For the annuity due, proceed just as for the ordinary annuity except enter 1 for Type to indicate that we now have an annuity due. Then, when you click OK, the answer $331.01 will appear.

Self-Test Questions

What is the difference between an ordinary annuity and an annuity due?

How do you modify the equation for determining the value of an ordinary annuity to find the value of an annuity due?

Other things held constant, which annuity has the greater *future* value: an ordinary annuity or an annuity due? Why?

Explain how financial calculators can be used to solve future value of annuity problems.

Present Value of an Annuity

Suppose you were offered the following alternatives: (1) a three-year annuity with payments of $100 or (2) a lump sum payment today. You have no need for the money during the next three years, so if you accept the annuity, you would deposit the payments in a bank account that pays 5 percent interest per year. Similarly, the lump sum payment would be deposited into a bank account. How large must the lump sum payment today be to make it equivalent to the annuity?

Ordinary Annuities

If the payments come at the end of each year, then the annuity is an ordinary annuity, and it would be set up as follows:

Time Line:

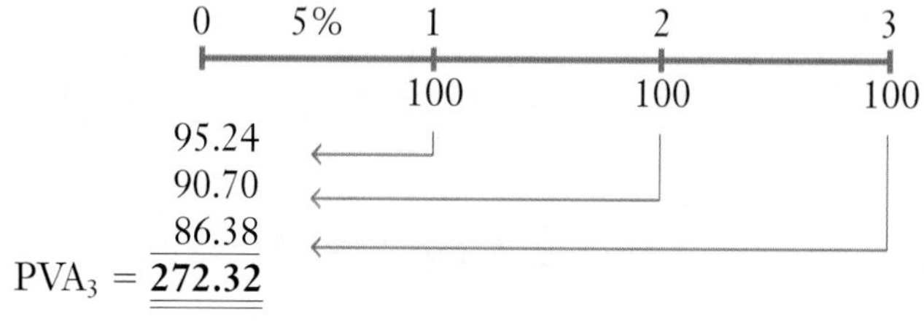

The regular time line is shown at the top of the diagram, and the numerical solution values are shown in the left column. The PV of the annuity, $\mathbf{PVA_n}$, is $272.32.

Equation:

The general equation used to find the PV of an ordinary annuity is shown below:

$$\begin{aligned} PVA_n &= PMT\left(\frac{1}{1+i}\right)^1 + PMT\left(\frac{1}{1+i}\right)^2 + \cdots + PMT\left(\frac{1}{1+i}\right)^n \\ &= PMT\sum_{t=1}^{n}\left(\frac{1}{1+i}\right)^t \\ &= PMT\left(\frac{1-\frac{1}{(1+i)^n}}{i}\right) \\ &= PMT(PVIFA_{i,n}). \end{aligned} \tag{8-4}$$

The **Present Value Interest Factor of an Annuity for i and n, $PVIFA_{i,n}$,** is a shorthand notation for the formula.

1. NUMERICAL SOLUTION:

The lower section of the time line shows the numerical solution, $272.32, calculated by using the first line of Equation 8-4, where the present value of each cash flow is found and then summed to find the PV of the annuity. If the annuity has many payments, it is easier to use the third line of Equation 8-4:

$$PVA_n = PMT\left(\frac{1 - \frac{1}{(1+i)^n}}{i}\right)$$

$$= \$100\left(\frac{1 - \frac{1}{(1+0.05)^3}}{0.05}\right) = \$100(2.7232) = \$272.32.$$

2. FINANCIAL CALCULATOR SOLUTION

Inputs:	3	5		−100	0
	N	I	PV	PMT	FV
Output:			= 272.32		

Enter N = 3, I = 5, PMT = −100, and FV = 0, and then press the PV key to find the PV, $272.32.

3. SPREADSHEET SOLUTION

	A	B	C	D	E
1	Interest rate	0.05			
2	Time	0	1	2	3
3	Cash flow		100	100	100
4	Present value	$272.32			

In *Excel,* put the cursor on Cell B4 and then click the function wizard, Financial, PV, and OK. Then enter B1 or 0.05 for Rate, E2 or 3 for Nper, −100 for Pmt, 0 or leave blank for FV, and 0 or leave blank for Type. Then, when you click OK, you get the answer, $272.32.

One especially important application of the annuity concept relates to loans with constant payments, such as mortgages and auto loans. With such loans, called *amortized loans,* the amount borrowed is the present value of an ordinary annuity, and the payments constitute the annuity stream. We will examine constant payment loans in more depth in a later section of this chapter.

Annuities Due

Had the three \$100 payments in the preceding example been made at the beginning of each year, the annuity would have been an *annuity due*. Each payment would be shifted to the left one year, so each payment would be discounted for one less year. Here is the time line setup:

Time Line:

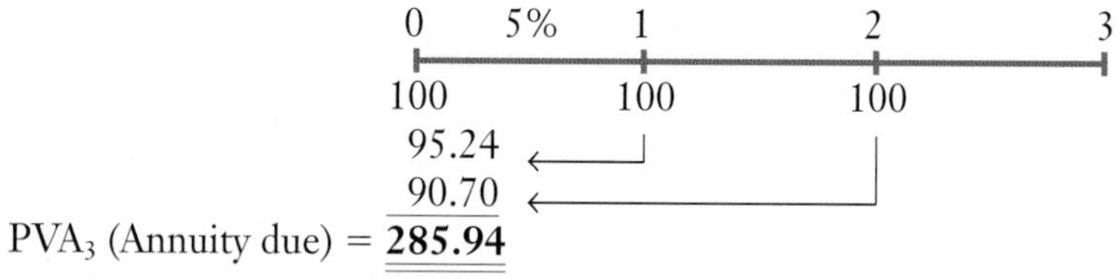

Again, we find the PV of each cash flow and then sum these PVs to find the PV of the annuity due. This procedure is illustrated in the lower section of the time line diagram. Since the cash flows occur sooner, the PV of the annuity due exceeds that of the ordinary annuity, \$285.94 versus \$272.32.

Equation:

$$\begin{aligned} PVA_n(\text{Due}) &= PMT\left(\frac{1}{1+i}\right)^0 + PMT\left(\frac{1}{1+i}\right)^1 + \cdots + PMT\left(\frac{1}{1+i}\right)^{n-1} \\ &= PMT\sum_{t=1}^{n}\left(\frac{1}{1+i}\right)^{t-1} \\ &= PMT\left(\frac{1-\frac{1}{(1+i)^n}}{i}\right)(1+i) \\ &= PMT(PVIFA_{i,n})(1+i). \end{aligned} \qquad \textbf{(8-4a)}$$

1. NUMERICAL SOLUTION:

The lower section of the time line shows the numerical solution, \$285.94, calculated by using the first line of Equation 8-4a, where the present value of each cash flow is found and then summed to find the PV of the annuity due. If the annuity has many payments, it is easier to use the third line of Equation 8-4a:

$$PVA_n(\text{Due}) = PMT\left(\frac{1-\frac{1}{(1+i)^n}}{i}\right)(1+i) \qquad \textbf{(8-4a)}$$

$$\begin{aligned} &= \$100\left(\frac{1-\frac{1}{(1+0.05)^3}}{0.05}\right)(1+0.05) \\ &= \$100(2.7232)(1+0.05) = \$285.94. \end{aligned}$$

2. FINANCIAL CALCULATOR SOLUTION

BEGIN

	N	I	PV	PMT	FV
Inputs:	3	5		−100	0
Output:			= 285.94		

Switch to the beginning-of-period mode, and then enter N = 3, I = 5, PMT = −100, and FV = 0, and then press PV to get the answer, $285.94. *Again, since most problems deal with end-of-period cash flows, don't forget to switch your calculator back to the "END" mode.*

3. SPREADSHEET SOLUTION

For an annuity due, proceed exactly as for a regular annuity except enter 1 rather than 0 for Type to indicate that we now have an annuity due.

Self-Test Questions

Which annuity has the greater present value: an ordinary annuity or an annuity due? Why?

Explain how financial calculators can be used to find the present value of annuities.

Annuities: Solving for Interest Rate, Number of Periods, or Payment

Sometimes it is useful to calculate the interest rate, payment, or number of periods for a given annuity. For example, suppose you can lease a computer from its manufacturer for $78 per month. The lease runs for 36 months, with payments due at the end of the month. As an alternative, you can buy it for $1,988.13. In either case, at the end of the 36 months the computer will be worth zero. You would like to know the "interest rate" the manufacturer has built into the lease; if that rate exceeds your company's cost of money, you should buy the computer rather than lease it.

Or suppose you are thinking ahead to retirement. If you save $4,000 per year at an interest rate of 8 percent, how long will it take for you to accumulate $1 million? Or, viewing the problem another way, if you earn an interest rate of 8 percent, how much must you save for each of the next 20 years to accumulate the $1 million?

To solve problems such as these, we can use an equation that is built into financial calculators and spreadsheets:

$$PV(1+i)^n + PMT\left(\frac{(1+i)^n - 1}{i}\right) + FV = 0. \qquad \textbf{(8-5)}$$

Note that some value must be negative. There are five variables: n, i, PV, PMT, and FV.[7] In each of the three problems above, you know four of the variables. For example, in the computer leasing problem, you know that n = 36, PV = 1,988.12 (this is positive, since you get to keep this amount if you choose to lease rather than purchase), PMT = −78 (this is negative since it is what you must pay each month), and FV = 0. Therefore, the equation is:

$$(1{,}988.12)(1+i)^{36} + (-78)\left(\frac{(1+i)^{36} - 1}{i}\right) + 0 = 0. \qquad \textbf{(8-5a)}$$

Unless you use a financial calculator or a spreadsheet, the only way to solve for i is by trial-and-error. However, with a financial calculator, you simply enter the values for the four known variables (N = 36, PV = 1998.12, PMT = −78, and FV = 0), and then hit the key for the unknown fifth variable, in this case, I = 2. Since this is an

[7]This is the equation for an ordinary annuity. Calculators and spreadsheets have a slightly different equation for an annuity due.

interest rate of 2 percent per month or 12(2%) = 24% per year, you would probably want to buy the computer rather than lease it.

It is worth pointing out that there is no way the left side of the equation can equal zero if you put both the PV and PMT as positive numbers (assuming positive interest rates). If you do this by mistake, most financial calculators will make a rude beeping noise, while spreadsheets will display an error message.

In an *Excel* spreadsheet, you would use the same Rate function that we discussed earlier. In this example, enter 36 for Nper, −78 for Pmt, 1988.12 for PV, 0 for FV, and 0 for type: **= Rate(36,−78,1988.12,0,0).** The result is again 0.02, or 2 percent.

Regarding how long you must save until you accumulate \$1 million, you know i = 8%, PV = 0 (since you don't have any savings when you start), PMT = −4,000 (it is negative since the payment comes out of your pocket), and FV = 1,000,000 (it is positive since you will get the \$1 million). Substituting into Equation 8-5 gives:

$$(0)(1 + 0.08)^n + (-4{,}000)\left(\frac{(1 + 0.08)^n - 1}{0.08}\right) + 1{,}000{,}000 = 0. \quad \textbf{(8-5a)}$$

Using algebra, you could solve for n, but it is easier to find n with a financial calculator. Input I = 8, PV = 0, PMT = −4000, FV = 1000000, and solve for N, which is equal to 39.56. Thus, it will take almost 40 years to accumulate \$1 million if you earn 8 percent interest and only save \$4,000 per year. On a spreadsheet, you could use the same Nper function that we discussed earlier. In this case, enter 8% for Rate, −4000 for Pmt, 0 for PV, 1000000 for FV, and 0 for type: **=Nper(8%,−4000,0,1000000,0).** The result is again 39.56.

If you only plan to save for 20 years, how much must you save each year to accumulate \$1 million? In this case, we know that n = 20, i = 8%, PV = 0, and FV = 1000000. The equation is:

$$(0)(1 + 0.08)^{20} + \text{PMT}\left(\frac{(1 + 0.08)^{20} - 1}{0.08}\right) + 1{,}000{,}000 = 0. \quad \textbf{(8-5a)}$$

You could use algebra to solve for PMT, or you could use a financial calculator and input N = 20, I = 8, PV = 0, and FV = 0. The result is PMT = −21,852.21. On a spreadsheet, you would use the PMT function, inputting 8% for Rate, 20 for Nper, 0 for PV, 1000000 for FV, and 0 for type: **=PMT(8%,20,0,1000000,0).** The result is again −21,852.21.

Self-Test Questions

Write out the equation that is built into a financial calculator.

Explain why a financial calculator cannot find a solution if PV, PMT, and FV all are positive.

Perpetuities

Most annuities call for payments to be made over some finite period of time—for example, \$100 per year for three years. However, some annuities go on indefinitely, or perpetually, and these are called **perpetuities.** The present value of a perpetuity is found by applying Equation 8-6.[8]

$$\text{PV(Perpetuity)} = \frac{\text{Payment}}{\text{Interest rate}} = \frac{\text{PMT}}{\text{i}}. \quad \textbf{(8-6)}$$

[8]The derivation of Equation 8-6 is given in the Web/CD Extension to Chapter 9 of Eugene F. Brigham and Phillip R. Daves, *Intermediate Financial Management*, 7th ed. (Fort Worth, TX: Harcourt College Publishers, 2002).

Perpetuities can be illustrated by some British securities issued after the Napoleonic Wars. In 1815, the British government sold a huge bond issue and used the proceeds to pay off many smaller issues that had been floated in prior years to pay for the wars. Since the purpose of the bonds was to consolidate past debts, the bonds were called **consols.** Suppose each consol promised to pay \$100 per year in perpetuity. (Actually, interest was stated in pounds.) What would each bond be worth if the opportunity cost rate, or discount rate, was 5 percent? The answer is \$2,000:

$$\text{PV(Perpetuity)} = \frac{\$100}{0.05} = \$2{,}000 \text{ if i } = 5\%.$$

Suppose the interest rate rose to 10 percent; what would happen to the consol's value? The value would drop to \$1,000:

$$\text{PV (Perpetuity)} = \frac{\$100}{0.10} = \$1{,}000 \text{ at i } = 10\%.$$

We see that the value of a perpetuity changes dramatically when interest rates change. Perpetuities are discussed further in Chapter 10.

Self-Test Questions

What happens to the value of a perpetuity when interest rates increase?

What happens when interest rates decrease?

Uneven Cash Flow Streams

The definition of an annuity includes the words *constant payment*—in other words, annuities involve payments that are the same in every period. Although many financial decisions do involve constant payments, other important decisions involve uneven, or nonconstant, cash flows. For example, common stocks typically pay an increasing stream of dividends over time, and fixed asset investments such as new equipment normally do not generate constant cash flows. Consequently, it is necessary to extend our time value discussion to include **uneven cash flow streams.**

Throughout the book, we will follow convention and reserve the term **payment (PMT)** for annuity situations where the cash flows are equal amounts, and we will use the term **cash flow (CF)** to denote uneven cash flows. Financial calculators are set up to follow this convention, so if you are dealing with uneven cash flows, you will need to use the "cash flow register."

Present Value of an Uneven Cash Flow Stream

The PV of an uneven cash flow stream is found as the sum of the PVs of the individual cash flows of the stream. For example, suppose we must find the PV of the following cash flow stream, discounted at 6 percent:

0	6% 1	2	3	4	5	6	7
PV = ?	100	200	200	200	200	0	1,000

The PV will be found by applying this general present value equation:

$$\begin{aligned} PV &= CF_1\left(\frac{1}{1+i}\right)^1 + CF_2\left(\frac{1}{1+i}\right)^2 + \cdots + CF_n\left(\frac{1}{1+i}\right)^n \\ &= \sum_{t=1}^{n} CF_t\left(\frac{1}{1+i}\right)^t = \sum_{t=1}^{n} CF_t(PVIF_{i,t}). \end{aligned} \tag{8-7}$$

We could find the PV of each individual cash flow using the numerical, financial calculator, or spreadsheet methods, and then sum these values to find the present value of the stream. Here is what the process would look like:

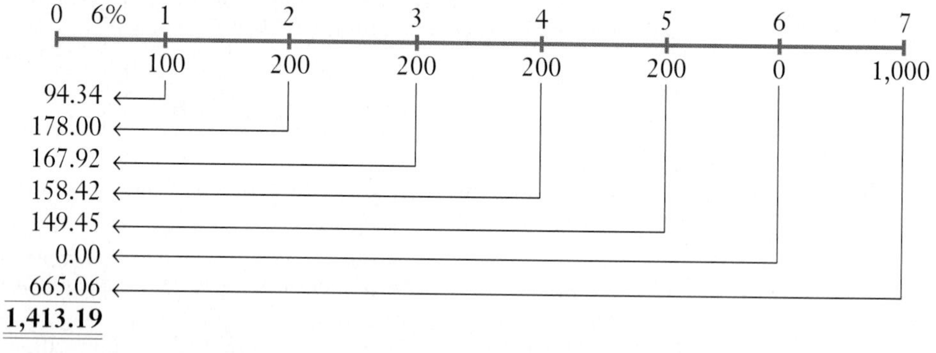

All we did was to apply Equation 8-7, show the individual PVs in the left column of the diagram, and then sum these individual PVs to find the PV of the entire stream.

The present value of a cash flow stream can always be found by summing the present values of the individual cash flows as shown above. However, cash flow regularities within the stream may allow the use of shortcuts. For example, notice that the cash flows in periods 2 through 5 represent an annuity. We can use that fact to solve the problem in a slightly different manner:

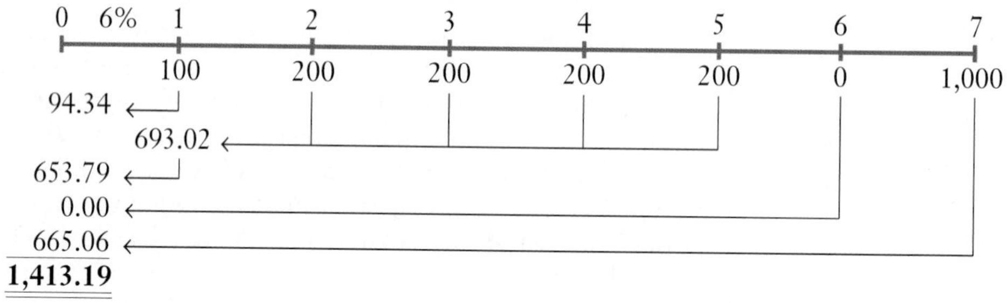

Cash flows during Years 2 to 5 represent an ordinary annuity, and we find its PV at Year 1 (one period before the first payment). This PV ($693.02) must then be discounted back one more period to get its Year 0 value, $653.79.

Problems involving uneven cash flows can be solved in one step with most financial calculators. First, you input the individual cash flows, in chronological order, into the cash flow register. Cash flows are usually designated CF_0, CF_1, CF_2, CF_3, and so on. Next, you enter the interest rate, I. At this point, you have substituted in all the known values of Equation 8-7, so you only need to press the NPV key to find the present value of the stream. The calculator has been programmed to find the PV of each cash flow and then to sum these values to find the PV of the entire stream. To input the cash flows for this problem, enter 0 (because $CF_0 = 0$), 100, 200, 200, 200, 200, 0, 1000 in that order into the cash flow register, enter I = 6, and then press NPV to obtain the answer, $1,413.19.

Two points should be noted. First, when dealing with the cash flow register, the calculator uses the term "NPV" rather than "PV." The N stands for "net," so NPV is the abbreviation for "Net Present Value," which is simply the net present value of a series of positive and negative cash flows. Our example has no negative cash flows, but if it did, we would simply input them with negative signs.[9]

The second point to note is that annuities can be entered into the cash flow register more efficiently by using the N_j key. (On some calculators, you are prompted to enter the number of times the cash flow occurs, and on still other calculators, the procedures for inputting data, as we discuss next, may be different. You should consult your calculator manual or our *Technology Supplement* to determine the appropriate steps for your specific calculator.) In this illustration, you would enter $CF_0 = 0$, $CF_1 = 100$, $CF_2 = 200$, $N_j = 4$ (which tells the calculator that the 200 occurs 4 times), $CF_6 = 0$, and $CF_7 = 1000$. Then enter I = 6 and press the NPV key, and 1,413.19 will appear in the display. Also, note that amounts entered into the cash flow register remain in the register until they are cleared. Thus, if you had previously worked a problem with eight cash flows, and then moved to a problem with only four cash flows, the calculator would simply add the cash flows from the second problem to those of the first problem. Therefore, you must be sure to clear the cash flow register before starting a new problem.

Spreadsheets are especially useful for solving problems with uneven cash flows. Just as with a financial calculator, you must enter the cash flows in the spreadsheet:

	A	B	C	D	E	F	G	H	I
1	Interest rate	0.06							
2	Time	0	1	2	3	4	5	6	7
3	Cash flow		100	200	200	200	200	0	1,000
4	Present value	1,413.19							

To find the PV of these cash flows with *Excel*, put the cursor on Cell B4, click the function wizard, click Financial, scroll down to NPV, and click OK to get the dialog box. Then enter B1 or 0.06 for Rate and the range of cells containing the cash flows, C3:I3, for Value 1. N stands for Net, so the NPV is the net present value of a stream of cash flows, some of which may be negative. Now, when you click OK, you get the PV of the stream, $1,413.19. Note that you use the PV function if the cash flows (or payments) are constant, but the NPV function if they are not constant. Note too that one of the advantages of spreadsheets over financial calculators is that you can see the cash flows, which makes it easy to spot any typing errors.

Future Value of an Uneven Cash Flow Stream

The future value of an uneven cash flow stream (sometimes called the **terminal value**) is found by compounding each payment to the end of the stream and then summing the future values:

$$\begin{aligned} FV_n &= CF_1(1+i)^{n-1} + CF_2(1+i)^{n-2} + \cdots + CF_{n-1}(1+i) + CF_n \\ &= \sum_{t=1}^{n} CF_t(1+i)^{n-t} = \sum_{t=1}^{n} CF_t(FVIF_{i,n-t}). \end{aligned} \quad (8\text{-}8)$$

[9]To input a negative number, type in the positive number, then press the +/− key to change the sign to negative. If you begin by typing the minus sign, you make the mistake of subtracting the negative number from the last number that was entered in the calculator.

The future value of our illustrative uneven cash flow stream is $2,124.92:

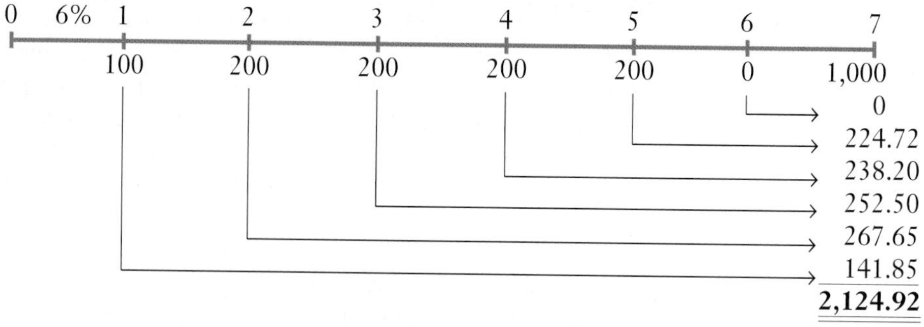

Some financial calculators have a net future value (NFV) key which, after the cash flows and interest rate have been entered, can be used to obtain the future value of an uneven cash flow stream. In any event, it is easy enough to compound the individual cash flows to the terminal year and then sum them to find the FV of the stream. Also, we are generally more interested in the present value of an asset's cash flow stream than in the future value because the present value represents today's value, which is used to find the fair value of the asset. Finally, note that the cash flow stream's net present value can be used to find its net future value: NFV = NPV $(1 + i)^n$. Thus, in our example, you could find the PV of the stream, then find the FV of that PV, compounded for n periods at i percent. In the illustrative problem, find PV = 1,413.19 using the cash flow register and I = 6. Then enter N = 7, I = 6, PV = −1413.19, and PMT = 0, and then press FV to find FV = 2,124.92, which equals the NFV shown on the time line above.

Solving for i with Uneven Cash Flow Streams

It is relatively easy to solve for i numerically when the cash flows are lump sums or annuities. However, it is *extremely difficult* to solve for i if the cash flows are uneven, because then you would have to go through many tedious trial-and-error calculations. With a spreadsheet program or a financial calculator, though, it is easy to find the value of i. Simply input the CF values into the cash flow register and then press the IRR key. IRR stands for "internal rate of return," which is the percentage return on an investment. We will defer further discussion of this calculation for now, but we will take it up later, in our discussion of capital budgeting methods in Chapter 12.[10]

Self-Test Questions

Give two examples of financial decisions that would typically involve uneven cash flows. (Hint: Think about a bond or a stock that you plan to hold for five years.)

What is meant by the term "terminal value"?

Growing Annuities

Normally, an annuity is defined as a series of *constant* payments to be received over a specified number of periods. However, the term **growing annuity** is used to describe a series of payments that is growing at a constant rate for a specified number of

[10] To obtain an IRR solution, at least one of the cash flows must have a negative sign, indicating that it is an investment. Since none of the CFs in our example were negative, the cash flow stream has no IRR. However, had we input a cost for CF_0, say, −$1,000, we could have obtained an IRR, which would be the rate of return earned on the $1,000 investment. Here IRR would be 13.96 percent.

periods. The most common application of growing annuities is in the area of financial planning, where someone wants to maintain a constant *real*, or *inflation-adjusted*, income over some specified number of years. For example, suppose a 65-year-old person is contemplating retirement, expects to live for another 20 years, has $1 million of investment funds, expects to earn 10 percent on the investments, expects inflation to average 5 percent per year, and wants to withdraw a constant *real* amount per year. What is the maximum amount that he or she can withdraw at the end of each year?

We explain in the spreadsheet model for this chapter, ***Ch 08 Tool Kit.xls*** that the problem can be solved in three ways. (1) Use the real rate of return for I in a financial calculator. (2) Use a relatively complicated formula. Or (3) use a spreadsheet model, with *Excel's* Goal Seek feature used to find the maximum withdrawal that will leave a zero balance in the account at the end of 20 years. The financial calculator approach is the easiest to use, but the spreadsheet model provides the clearest picture of what is happening. Also, the spreadsheet approach can be adapted to find other parameters of the general model, such as the maximum number of years a given constant income can be provided by the initial portfolio.

To implement the calculator approach, first calculate the expected real rate of return as follows, where k_r is the real rate and k_{nom} is the nominal rate of return:

$$\text{Real rate} = k_r = [(1 + k_{nom})/(1 + \text{Inflation})] - 1.0$$
$$[1.10/1.05] - 1.0 = 4.761905\%.$$

Now, with a financial calculator, input N = 20, I = 4.761905, PV = −1000000, and FV = 0, and then press PMT to get the answer, $78,630.64. Thus, a portfolio worth $1 million will provide 20 annual payments with a current dollar value of $78,630.64 under the stated assumptions. The actual payments will be growing at 5 percent per year to offset inflation. The (nominal) value of the portfolio will be growing at first and then declining, and it will hit zero at the end of the 20th year. The spreadsheet shows all this in both tabular and graphic form.[11]

Self-Test Questions

Differentiate between a "regular" and a growing annuity.

What three methods can be used to deal with growing annuities?

Semiannual and Other Compounding Periods

In all of our examples thus far, we have assumed that interest is compounded once a year, or annually. This is called **annual compounding.** Suppose, however, that you put $100 into a bank which states that it pays a 6 percent annual interest rate but that interest is credited each six months. This is called **semiannual compounding.** How much would you have accumulated at the end of one year, two years, or some other period under semiannual compounding? Note that virtually all bonds pay interest semiannually, most stocks pay dividends quarterly, and most mortgages, student loans, and auto loans require monthly payments. Therefore, it is essential that you understand how to deal with nonannual compounding.

---

[11]The formula used to find the payment is shown below. Other formulas can be developed to solve for n and other terms, but they are even more complex.

$$\text{PV of Growing Annuity} = \text{PVIFGA} = [1 - [(1 + g)/(1 + i)]^n]/[(i - g)/(1 + g)] = 12.72.$$

$$\text{Payment} = \text{PMT} = \text{PV}/\text{PVIFGA} = \$1{,}000{,}000/12.72 = \$78{,}630.64.$$

Using the Internet for Personal Financial Planning

People continually face important financial decisions that require an understanding of the time value of money. Should we buy or lease a car? How much and how soon do we need to save for our children's education? What size house can we afford? Should we refinance our home mortgage? How much must we save in order to retire comfortably?

The answers to these questions are often complicated, and they depend on a number of factors, such as housing and education costs, interest rates, inflation, expected family income, and stock market returns. Hopefully, after completing this chapter, you will have a better idea of how to answer such questions. Moreover, there are a number of online resources available to help with financial planning.

A good place to start is **http://www.smartmoney.com.** *Smartmoney* is a personal finance magazine produced by the publishers of *The Wall Street Journal.* If you go to *Smartmoney*'s web site you will find a section entitled "Tools." This section has a number of financial calculators, spreadsheets, and descriptive materials that cover a wide range of personal finance issues.

Another good place to look is Quicken's web site, **http://www.quicken.com.** Here you will find several interesting sections that deal with a variety of personal finance issues. Within these sections you will find background articles plus spreadsheets and calculators that you can use to analyze your own situation.

Finally, **http://www.financialengines.com** is a great place to visit if you are focusing specifically on retirement planning. This web site, developed by Nobel Prize–winning financial economist William Sharpe, considers a wide range of alternative scenarios that might occur. This approach, which enables you to see a full range of potential outcomes, is much better than some of the more basic online calculators that give you simple answers to complicated questions.

To illustrate semiannual compounding, assume that \$100 is placed in an account at an interest rate of 6 percent and left there for three years. First, consider again what would happen under *annual* compounding:

0 6% 1 2 3
−100 FV = ?

$$FV_n = PV(1 + i)^n = \$100(1.06)^3$$
$$= \$119.10.$$

We would, of course, get this same answer using a financial calculator or a spreadsheet.

How would things change if interest were paid semiannually rather than annually? First, whenever payments occur more frequently than once a year, or when interest is stated to be compounded more than once a year, then you must (1) convert the stated interest rate to a "periodic rate," and (2) convert the number of years to "number of periods," as follows:

$$\text{Periodic rate} = \text{Stated rate/Number of payments per year.}$$
$$\text{Number of periods} = \text{Number of years} \times \text{Periods per year.}$$

In our example, where we must find the value of \$100 after three years when the stated interest rate is 6 percent, compounded semiannually (or twice a year), you would begin by making the following conversions:

$$\text{Periodic rate} = 6\%/2 = 3\%.$$
$$\text{Periods} = N = 3 \times 2 = 6.$$

In this situation, the investment will earn 3 percent every six months for six periods, not 6 percent per year for three years. As we shall see, there is a significant difference between these two procedures.

You should make the conversions as your first step when working on such a problem *because calculations must be done using the appropriate number of periods and periodic rate, not the number of years and stated rate.* Periodic rates and number of periods, not yearly rates and number of years, should normally be shown on time lines and entered into your calculator whenever you are dealing with nonannual compounding.[12]

With this background, we can now find the value of $100 after three years if it is held in an account that pays a stated rate of 6 percent, but with semiannual compounding. Here is the time line:

Time Line:

0 3%	1	2	3	4	5	6	6-month periods
−100						FV = ?	

1. EQUATION AND NUMERICAL SOLUTION

$$FV_n = PV(1 + i)^n = \$100(1.03)^6$$
$$= \$100(1.1941) = \$119.41.$$

Here i = rate per period = annual rate/compounding periods per year = 6%/2 = 3%, and n = the total number of periods = years × periods per year = 3 × 2 = 6.

2. FINANCIAL CALCULATOR SOLUTION

Inputs:	6	3	−100	0	
	N	I	PV	PMT	FV
Output:					= 119.41

Enter N = years × periods per year = 3 × 2 = 6, I = annual rate/periods per year = 6/2 = 3, PV = −100, and PMT = 0. Then press FV to find the answer, $119.41.

3. SPREADSHEET SOLUTION

The spreadsheet developed to find the future value of a lump sum under semiannual compounding would look like the one for annual compounding, but with two changes: The interest rate would be halved, and the time line would show twice as many periods. The future value under semiannual compounding, $119.41, would be larger than $119.10, the future value under annual compounding, because interest on interest is being earned more frequently.

Throughout the world economy, different compounding periods are used for different types of investments. For example, bank accounts generally pay interest daily; most bonds pay interest semiannually; and stocks generally pay dividends quarterly.[13]

---

[12]With some financial calculators, you can enter the annual (nominal) rate and the number of compounding periods rather than make the conversion we recommend. We prefer making the conversion because it is easier to see the problem setup in a time line, and also because it is easy to forget to readjust your calculator after you change its settings and to then make an error on the next problem because of the incorrect setting.

[13]Some banks and savings and loans even pay interest compounded *continuously*. Continuous compounding is discussed in the Chapter 8 Web/CD Extension found on the textbook's CD-ROM and on the textbook's web page, **http://www.harcourtcollege.com/finance/theory**.

If we are to compare securities with different compounding periods, we need to put them on a common basis. This requires us to distinguish between ***nominal,*** or ***quoted, interest rates*** and ***effective,*** or ***equivalent, annual rates.***[14]

The nominal, or quoted, or stated, interest rate in our example is 6 percent. *The effective (or equivalent) annual rate (EAR, also called EFF%) is defined as the rate that would produce the same ending (future) value if annual compounding had been used.* In our example, the effective annual rate is the once-a-year rate that would produce an FV of \$119.41 at the end of Year 3. Here is a time line of the situation:

Years	0	EAR (or EFF%)	1	2	3
	−100				119.41

Our task now is to find the effective annual rate, EAR or EFF%, that is equivalent to 6 percent with semiannual compounding.

We can determine the effective annual rate, given the nominal rate and the number of compounding periods per year, by solving this equation:

$$\text{Effective annual rate} = \text{EAR (or EFF\%)} = \left(1 + \frac{i_{Nom}}{m}\right)^m - 1.0. \quad \textbf{(8-9)}$$

Here i_{Nom} is the nominal, or quoted, interest rate, and m is the number of compounding periods per year. For example, to find the effective annual rate if the nominal rate is 6 percent and semiannual compounding is used, we have[15]

$$\text{Effective annual rate} = \text{EAR (or EFF\%)} = \left(1 + \frac{0.06}{2}\right)^2 - 1.0$$

$$= (1.03)^2 - 1.0$$

$$= 1.0609 - 1.0 = 0.0609 = 6.09\%.$$

The points made about semiannual compounding can be generalized as follows. When compounding occurs more frequently than once a year, we can use a modified version of Equation 8-1 to find the future value of any lump sum:

$$\text{Annual compounding: } FV_n = PV(1 + i)^n. \quad \textbf{(8-1)}$$

$$\text{More frequent compounding: } FV_n = PV\left(1 + \frac{i_{Nom}}{m}\right)^{mn}. \quad \textbf{(8-10)}$$

Here i_{Nom} is the nominal, or quoted, rate, m is the number of times compounding occurs per year, and n is the number of years. For example, when banks pay daily interest, the value of m is set at 365 and Equation 8-10 is applied.[16]

To illustrate further the effect of compounding monthly rather than annually, consider the interest rate charged on credit cards. Many banks charge 1.5 percent per month, and, in their advertising, they state that the **Annual Percentage Rate**

---

[14]The term *nominal rate* as it is used here has a different meaning than the way it was used in Chapter 5. There, nominal interest rates referred to stated market rates as opposed to real (zero inflation) rates. In this chapter, the term *nominal rate* means the stated, or quoted, annual rate as opposed to the effective annual rate. In both cases, though, *nominal* means *stated,* or *quoted,* as opposed to some adjusted rate.

[15]Most financial calculators are programmed to find the EAR or, given the EAR, to find the nominal rate. This is called "interest rate conversion," and you simply enter the nominal rate and the number of compounding periods per year and then press the EFF% key to find the effective annual rate.

[16]To illustrate, the future value of \$1 invested at 10 percent for 1 year under daily compounding is \$1.1052:

$$FV_n = \$1\left(1 + \frac{0.10}{365}\right)^{365(1)} = \$1(1.105156) = \$1.1052.$$

Note also that banks sometimes use 360 as the number of days per year for this and other calculations.

(APR) is 1.5% × 12 = 18%. However, the "true" rate is the effective annual rate of 19.6 percent:

$$\begin{aligned}\text{Effective annual rate} = \text{EAR (or EFF\%)} &= \left(1 + \frac{0.18}{12}\right)^{12} - 1.0 \\ &= (1.015)^{12} - 1.0 \\ &= 0.196 = 19.6\%.\end{aligned}$$

Semiannual and other compounding periods can also be used for discounting, and for both lump sums and annuities. First, consider the case where we want to find the PV of an ordinary annuity of \$100 per year for three years when the interest rate is 8 percent, *compounded annually:*

Time Line:

0 (8%)	1	2	3
PV = ?	100	100	100

1. NUMERICAL SOLUTION

Find the PV of each cash flow and sum them. The PV of the annuity is \$257.71.

2. FINANCIAL CALCULATOR SOLUTION

	N	I	PV	PMT	FV
Inputs:	3	8		100	0
Output:			= −257.71		

3. SPREADSHEET SOLUTION

A spreadsheet could be developed as we did earlier in the chapter in our discussion of the present value of an annuity. Rows would be set up to show the interest rate (8 percent), time (t = 0 through t = 3), and cash flows (100 at t = 1 through t = 3). Then the present value of the annuity, \$257.71, could be determined using the *Excel* PV function.

Now, let's change the situation to *semiannual compounding*, where the annuity calls for payments of \$50 each six months rather than \$100 per year, and the rate is 8 percent, compounded semiannually. Here is the time line:

Time Line:

0 (4%)	1	2	3	4	5	6 (6-month periods)
PV = ?	50	50	50	50	50	50

1. NUMERICAL SOLUTION

Find the PV of each cash flow by discounting at 4 percent. There are six periods. The PV of the annuity is \$262.11 versus \$257.71 under annual compounding.

2. FINANCIAL CALCULATOR SOLUTION

Inputs:	6	4		50	0
	N	I	PV	PMT	FV
Output:			= −262.11		

3. SPREADSHEET SOLUTION

The spreadsheet developed to find the present value of an annuity under semiannual compounding would look like the one for annual compounding, but the interest rate and annuity payment would be halved, and the time line would have twice as many periods.

The annuity value with semiannual compounding is $262.11, which is greater than the annual annuity value. The reason is that the semiannual payments come in sooner, so the $50 semiannual annuity is more valuable than the $100 annual annuity.

Self-Test Questions

What changes must you make in your calculations to determine the future value of an amount that is being compounded at 8 percent semiannually versus one being compounded annually at 8 percent?

Why is semiannual compounding better than annual compounding from a saver's standpoint? What about a borrower's standpoint?

Define the terms "annual percentage rate," "effective (or equivalent) annual rate," and "nominal interest rate."

How does the term "nominal rate" as used in this chapter differ from the term as it was used in Chapter 5?

Comparison of Different Types of Interest Rates

Finance deals with three types of interest rates: nominal rates, i_{Nom}; periodic rates, i_{PER}; and effective annual rates, EAR or EFF%. It is essential that you understand what each one is and when it should be used.

1. **Nominal, or quoted, rate.** This is the rate that is quoted by banks, brokers, and other financial institutions. So, if you talk with a banker, broker, mortgage lender, auto finance company, or student loan officer about rates, the nominal rate is the one he or she will normally quote you. However, to be meaningful, the quoted nominal rate must also include the number of compounding periods per year. For example, a bank might offer 6 percent, compounded quarterly, on CDs, or a mutual fund might offer 5 percent, compounded monthly, on its money market account.

   The nominal rate on loans to consumers is also called the Annual Percentage Rate (APR). If a credit card issuer quotes an APR of 18 percent, monthly, this means an interest rate of 18%/12 = 1.5 percent per month.

   Nominal rates can be compared with one another, *but only if the instruments being compared use the same number of compounding periods per year.* Thus, you could compare the quoted yields on two bonds if they both pay interest semiannually. However, to compare a 6 percent, annual payment CD with a 5 percent, daily payment money market fund, we would need to put both instruments on an *effective (or equivalent) annual rate (EAR)* basis as discussed later in this section.

Note that the nominal rate is never shown on a time line, and it is never used as an input in a financial calculator (unless compounding occurs only once a year, in which case i_{Nom} = periodic rate = EAR). If more frequent compounding occurs, you should use the periodic rate as discussed below.

2. **Periodic rate, i_{PER}.** This is the rate charged by a lender or paid by a borrower each period. It can be a rate per year, per six-month period, per quarter, per month, per day, or per any other time interval. For example, a bank might charge 1.5 percent per month on its credit card loans, or a finance company might charge 3 percent per quarter on installment loans. We find the periodic rate as follows:

$$\text{Periodic rate, } i_{PER} = i_{Nom}/m, \qquad \textbf{(8-11)}$$

which implies that

$$\text{Nominal annual rate} = i_{Nom} = (\text{Periodic rate})(m). \qquad \textbf{(8-12)}$$

Here i_{Nom} is the nominal annual rate and m is the number of compounding periods per year. To illustrate, consider a finance company loan at 3 percent per quarter:

$$\text{Nominal annual rate} = i_{Nom} = (\text{Periodic rate})(m) = (3\%)(4) = 12\%,$$

or

$$\text{Periodic rate} = i_{Nom}/m = 12\%/4 = 3\% \text{ per quarter.}$$

If there is only one payment per year, or if interest is added only once a year, then m = 1, and the periodic rate is equal to the nominal rate.

The periodic rate is the rate that is generally shown on time lines and used in calculations.[17] To illustrate use of the periodic rate, suppose you make the following eight quarterly payments of $100 each into an account that pays a nominal rate of 12 percent, compounded quarterly. How much would you have after two years?

Time Line and Equation:

0 (3%)	1	2	3	4	5	6	7	8	Quarters
	−100	−100	−100	−100	−100	−100	−100	− 100	
								FV = ?	

$$FVA_n = \sum_{t=1}^{n} PMT(1+i)^{n-t} = \sum_{t=1}^{8} \$100(1.03)^{8-t}.$$

[17]The only exception is in situations where (1) annuities are involved and (2) the payment periods do not correspond to the compounding periods. If an annuity is involved and if its payment periods do not correspond to the compounding periods—for example, if you are making quarterly payments into a bank account to build up a specified future sum, but the bank pays interest on a daily basis—then the calculations are more complicated. For such problems, one can proceed in two alternative ways. (1) Determine the periodic (daily) interest rate by dividing the nominal rate by 360 (or 365 if the bank uses a 365-day year), then compound each payment over the exact number of days from the payment date to the terminal point, and then sum the compounded payments to find the future value of the annuity. This is what would generally be done in the real world, because with a computer, it would be a simple process. (2) Calculate the EAR based on daily compounding, then find the corresponding nominal rate based on quarterly compounding (because the annuity payments are made quarterly), then find the quarterly periodic rate, and then use that rate with standard annuity procedures. The second procedure is faster with a calculator, but hard to explain and generally not used in practice given the ready availability of computers.

1. NUMERICAL SOLUTION

Compound each $100 payment at 12/4 = 3 percent for the appropriate number of periods, and then sum these individual FVs to find the FV of the payment stream, $889.23.

2. FINANCIAL CALCULATOR SOLUTION

Inputs:	8	3	0	−100	
	N	I	PV	PMT	FV
Output:					= 889.23

Input N = 2 × 4 = 8, I = 12/4 = 3, PV = 0, and PMT = −100, and then press the FV key to get FV = $889.23.

3. SPREADSHEET SOLUTION

A spreadsheet could be developed as we did earlier in the chapter in our discussion of the future value of an annuity. Rows would be set up to show the interest rate, time, cash flow, and future value of the annuity. The interest rate used in the spreadsheet would be the periodic interest rate (i_{Nom}/m) and the number of time periods shown would be (m)(n).

3. **Effective (or equivalent) annual rate (EAR).** This is the annual rate that produces the same result as if we had compounded at a given periodic rate m times per year. The EAR is found as follows:

$$\text{EAR (or EFF\%)} = \left(1 + \frac{i_{Nom}}{m}\right)^m - 1.0. \quad \textbf{(8-9)}$$

You could also use the interest conversion feature of a financial calculator.

In the EAR equation, i_{Nom}/m is the periodic rate, and m is the number of periods per year. For example, suppose you could borrow using either a credit card that charges 1 percent per month or a bank loan with a 12 percent quoted nominal interest rate that is compounded quarterly. Which should you choose? To answer this question, the cost rate of each alternative must be expressed as an EAR:

$$\begin{aligned}\text{Credit card loan: EAR} &= (1 + 0.01)^{12} - 1.0 = (1.01)^{12} - 1.0\\ &= 1.126825 - 1.0 = 0.126825 = 12.6825\%.\\ \text{Bank loan: EAR} &= (1 + 0.03)^4 - 1.0 = (1.03)^4 - 1.0\\ &= 1.125509 - 1.0 = 0.125509 = 12.5509\%.\end{aligned}$$

Thus, the credit card loan is slightly more costly than the bank loan. This result should have been intuitive to you—both loans have the same 12 percent nominal rate, yet you would have to make monthly payments on the credit card versus quarterly payments under the bank loan.

The EAR rate is not used in calculations. However, it should be used to compare the effective cost or rate of return on loans or investments when payment periods differ, as in the credit card versus bank loan example.

Self-Test Questions

Define the nominal (or quoted) rate, the periodic rate, and the effective annual rate.

How are the nominal rate, the periodic rate, and the effective annual rate related?

What is the one situation where all three of these rates will be the same?

Which rate should be shown on time lines and used in calculations?

Fractional Time Periods

In all the examples used thus far in the chapter, we have assumed that payments occur at either the beginning or the end of periods, but not at some date *within* a period. However, we often encounter situations that require compounding or discounting over fractional periods. For example, suppose you deposited \$100 in a bank that adds interest to your account daily, that is, uses daily compounding, and pays a nominal rate of 10 percent with a 360-day year. How much will be in your account after nine months? The answer is \$107.79:[18]

$$\begin{aligned} \text{Periodic rate} &= i_{PER} = 0.10/360 = 0.00027778 \text{ per day.} \\ \text{Number of days} &= 0.75(360) = 270. \\ \text{Ending amount} &= \$100(1.00027778)^{270} = \$107.79. \end{aligned}$$

Now suppose you borrow \$100 from a bank that charges 10 percent per year "simple interest," which means annual rather than daily compounding, but you borrow the \$100 for only 270 days. How much interest would you have to pay for the use of \$100 for 270 days? Here we would calculate a daily interest rate, i_{PER}, as above, but multiply by 270 rather than use it as an exponent:

$$\text{Interest owed} = \$100(0.00027778)(270) = \$7.50 \text{ interest charged.}$$

You would owe the bank a total of \$107.50 after 270 days. This is the procedure most banks actually use to calculate interest on loans, except that they generally require you to pay the interest on a monthly basis rather than after 270 days.

Finally, let's consider a somewhat different situation. Say an Internet access firm had 100 customers at the end of 2000, and its customer base is expected to grow steadily at the rate of 10 percent per year. What is the estimated customer base nine months into the new year? This problem would be set up exactly like the bank account with daily compounding, and the estimate would be 107.79 customers, rounded to 108.

The most important thing in problems like these, as in all time value problems, is to be careful! Think about what is involved in a logical, systematic manner, draw a time line if it would help you visualize the situation, and then apply the appropriate equations.

Amortized Loans

One of the most important applications of compound interest involves loans that are paid off in installments over time. Included are automobile loans, home mortgage loans, student loans, and most business loans other than very short-term loans and

[18]Here we assumed a 360-day year, and we also assumed that the nine months all have 30 days. This convention is often used. However, some contracts specify that actual days be used. Computers (and many financial calculators) have a built-in calendar, and if you input the beginning and ending dates, the computer or calculator would tell you the exact number of days, taking account of 30-day months, 31-day months, and 28- or 29-day months.

TABLE 8-1 Loan Amortization Schedule, 6 Percent Interest Rate

Year	Beginning Amount (1)	Payment (2)	Interest[a] (3)	Repayment of Principal[b] (2) − (3) = (4)	Remaining Balance (1) − (4) = (5)
1	$1,000.00	$ 374.11	$ 60.00	$ 314.11	$685.89
2	685.89	374.11	41.15	332.96	352.93
3	352.93	374.11	21.18	352.93	0.00
		$1,122.33	$122.33	$1,000.00	

[a]Interest is calculated by multiplying the loan balance at the beginning of the year by the interest rate. Therefore, interest in Year 1 is $1,000(0.06) = $60; in Year 2 it is $685.89(0.06) = $41.15; and in Year 3 it is $352.93(0.06) = $21.18.

[b]Repayment of principal is equal to the payment of $374.11 minus the interest charge for each year.

long-term bonds. If a loan is to be repaid in equal periodic amounts (monthly, quarterly, or annually), it is said to be an **amortized loan.**[19]

Table 8-1 illustrates the amortization process. A firm borrows $1,000, and the loan is to be repaid in three equal payments at the end of each of the next three years. (In this case, there is only one payment per year, so years = periods and the stated rate = periodic rate.) The lender charges a 6 percent interest rate on the loan balance that is outstanding at the beginning of each year. The first task is to determine the amount the firm must repay each year, or the constant annual payment. To find this amount, recognize that the $1,000 represents the present value of an annuity of PMT dollars per year for three years, discounted at 6 percent:

Time Line:

0	6%	1	2	3
1,000		PMT	PMT	PMT

Equation:

The same general equation used to find the PV of an ordinary annuity is shown below:

$$\begin{aligned} PVA_n &= PMT\left(\frac{1}{1+i}\right)^1 + PMT\left(\frac{1}{1+i}\right)^2 + \cdots + PMT\left(\frac{1}{1+i}\right)^n \\ &= PMT\sum_{t=1}^{n}\left(\frac{1}{1+i}\right)^t \\ &= PMT\left(\frac{1-\dfrac{1}{1+i^n}}{i}\right) \\ &= PMT(PVIFA_{i,n}). \end{aligned} \tag{8-4}$$

1. NUMERICAL SOLUTION

We know the PV, the interest rate, and the number of periods. The only unknown variable is the payment:

[19]The word *amortized* comes from the Latin *mors*, meaning "death," so an amortized loan is one that is "killed off" over time.

$$\$1{,}000 = \text{PMT}\sum_{t=1}^{3}\left(\frac{1}{1+0.06}\right)^t$$

$$= \text{PMT}\left(\frac{1-\frac{1}{(1+0.06)^3}}{0.06}\right). \quad \textbf{(8-4a)}$$

Using Equation 8-4a, we can solve the equation for the payment:

$$\$1{,}000 = \text{PMT}\left(\frac{1-\frac{1}{(1+0.06)^3}}{0.06}\right) = \text{PMT}(2.6730)$$

$$\text{PMT} = \$1{,}000/2.6730 = \$374.11.$$

2. FINANCIAL CALCULATOR SOLUTION

Inputs:	3	6	1000		0
	N	I	PV	PMT	FV
Output:				= −374.11	

Enter N = 3, I = 6, PV = 1000, and FV = 0, and then press the PMT key to find PMT = −\$374.11.

3. SPREADSHEET SOLUTION

See ***Ch 08 Tool Kit.xls*** for details.

The spreadsheet is ideal for developing amortization tables. The setup is similar to Table 8-1, but you would want to include "input" cells for the interest rate, principal value, and the length of the loan. This would make the spreadsheet flexible in the sense that the loan terms could be changed and a new amortization table would be recalculated instantly. Then use the function wizard to find the payment. If you had I = 6% in B1, N = 3 in B2, and PV = 1000 in B3, then the function **= PMT(B1, B2, B3)** would return a result of −\$374.11.

Therefore, the firm must pay the lender \$374.11 at the end of each of the next three years, and the percentage cost to the borrower, which is also the rate of return to the lender, will be 6 percent. Each payment consists partly of interest and partly of repayment of principal. This breakdown is given in the **amortization schedule** shown in Table 8-1. The interest component is largest in the first year, and it declines as the outstanding balance of the loan decreases. For tax purposes, a business borrower or homeowner reports the interest component shown in Column 3 as a deductible cost each year, while the lender reports this same amount as taxable income.

Financial calculators are programmed to calculate amortization tables—you simply enter the input data, and then press one key to get each entry in Table 8-1. If you have a financial calculator, it is worthwhile to read the appropriate section of the calculator manual and learn how to use its amortization feature. As we show in the model for this chapter, with a spreadsheet such as *Excel* it is easy to set up and print out a full amortization schedule.

Self-Test Questions

To construct an amortization schedule, how do you determine the amount of the periodic payments?

How do you determine the amount of each payment that goes to interest and to principal?

Summary

Most financial decisions involve situations in which someone pays money at one point in time and receives money at some later time. Dollars paid or received at two different points in time are different, and this difference is recognized and accounted for by *time value of money (TVM) analysis*. We summarize below the types of TVM analysis and the key concepts covered in this chapter, using the data shown in Figure 8-3 to illustrate the various points. Refer to the figure constantly, and try to find in it an example of the points covered as you go through this summary.

- **Compounding** is the process of determining the **future value (FV)** of a cash flow or a series of cash flows. The compounded amount, or future value, is equal to the beginning amount plus the interest earned.
- Future value: $FV_n = PV(1 + i)^n = PV(FVIF_{i,n})$.
(single payment)

  Example: \$1,000 compounded for 1 year at 4 percent:

$$FV_1 = \$1{,}000(1.04)^1 = \$1{,}040.$$

- **Discounting** is the process of finding the **present value (PV)** of a future cash flow or a series of cash flows; discounting is the reciprocal, or reverse, of compounding.
- Present value: $PV = \dfrac{FV_n}{(1 + i)^n} = FV_n\left(\dfrac{1}{1 + i}\right)^n = FV_n(PVIF_{i,n})$.

  (single payment)

  Example: \$1,000 discounted back for 2 years at 4 percent:

$$PV = \frac{\$1{,}000}{(1.04)^2} = \$1{,}000\left(\frac{1}{1.04}\right)^2 = \$1{,}000(0.9246) = \$924.60.$$

- An **annuity** is defined as a series of equal periodic payments (PMT) for a specified number of periods.
- Future value:
(annuity)

FIGURE 8-3 Illustration for Chapter Summary (i = 4%, Annual Compounding)

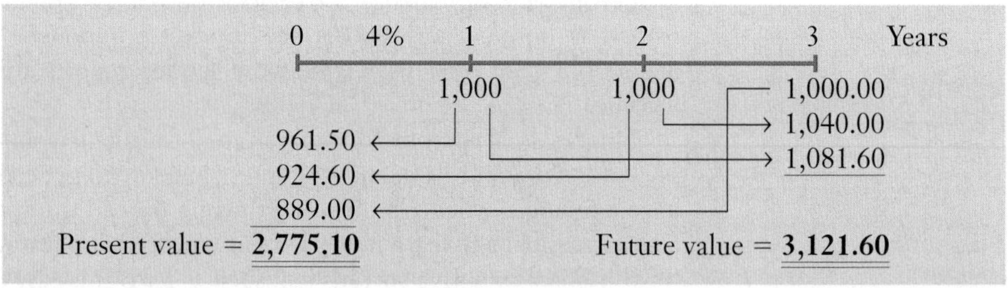

$$FVA_n = PMT(1 + i)^{n-1} + PMT(1 + i)^{n-2} + PMT(1 + i)^{n-3} + \cdots + PMT(1 + i)^0$$
$$= PMT \sum_{t=1}^{n} (1 + i)^{n-t}$$
$$= PMT\left(\frac{(1 + i)^n - 1}{i}\right)$$
$$= PMT(FVIFA_{i,n}).$$

Example: FVA of 3 payments of \$1,000 when i = 4%:

$$FVA_3 = \$1,000(3.1216) = \$3,121.60.$$

- Present value: $PVA_n = \frac{PMT}{(1 + i)^1} + \frac{PMT}{(1 + i)^2} + \cdots + \frac{PMT}{(1 + i)^n}$
(annuity)

$$= PMT \sum_{t=1}^{n} \left[\frac{1}{1 + i}\right]^t$$
$$= PMT\left(\frac{1 - \frac{1}{(1 + i)^n}}{i}\right)$$
$$= PMT(PVIFA_{i,n}).$$

Example: PVA of 3 payments of \$1,000 when i = 4% per period:

$$PVA_3 = \$1,000(2.7751) = \$2,775.10.$$

- An annuity whose payments occur at the *end* of each period is called an **ordinary annuity.** The formulas above are for ordinary annuities.
- If each payment occurs at the beginning of the period rather than at the end, then we have an **annuity due.** In Figure 8-3, the payments would be shown at Years 0, 1, and 2 rather than at Years 1, 2, and 3. The PV of each payment would be larger, because each payment would be discounted back one year less, so the PV of the annuity would also be larger. Similarly, the FV of the annuity due would also be larger because each payment would be compounded for an extra year. The following formulas can be used to convert the PV and FV of an ordinary annuity to an annuity due:

$$\text{PVA (annuity due)} = \text{PVA of an ordinary annuity} \times (1 + i).$$

$$\text{FVA (annuity due)} = \text{FVA of an ordinary annuity} \times (1 + i).$$

Example: PVA of 3 beginning-of-year payments of \$1,000 when i = 4%:

$$\text{PVA (annuity due)} = \$1,000(2.7751)(1.04) = \$2,886.10.$$

Example: FVA of 3 beginning-of-year payments of \$1,000 when i = 4%:

$$\text{FVA (annuity due)} = \$1,000(3.1216)(1.04) = \$3,246.46.$$

- If the time line in Figure 8-3 were extended out forever so that the \$1,000 payments went on forever, we would have a **perpetuity** whose value could be found as follows:

$$\text{Value of perpetuity} = \frac{PMT}{i} = \frac{\$1,000}{0.04} = \$25,000.$$

- If the cash flows in Figure 8-3 were unequal, we could not use the annuity formulas. To find the PV or FV of an uneven series, find the PV or FV of each individual cash flow and then sum them. Note, though, that if some of the cash flows constitute an annuity, then the annuity formula can be used to calculate the present value of that part of the cash flow stream.

- **Financial calculators** have built-in programs that perform all of the operations discussed in this chapter. It would be useful for you to buy such a calculator and to learn how to use it.
- **Spreadsheet programs** are especially useful for problems with many uneven cash flows. They are also very useful if you want to solve a problem repeatedly with different inputs. See ***Ch 08 Tool Kit.xls*** on the CD-ROM that accompanies this text for spreadsheet models of the topics covered in this chapter.
- TVM calculations generally involve equations that have four variables, and if you know three of the values, you (or your calculator) can solve for the fourth.
- If you know the cash flows and the PV (or FV) of a cash flow stream, you can **determine the interest rate.** For example, in the Figure 8-3 illustration, if you were given the information that a loan called for 3 payments of \$1,000 each, and that the loan had a value today of PV = \$2,775.10, then you could find the interest rate that caused the sum of the PVs of the payments to equal \$2,775.10. Since we are dealing with an annuity, you could proceed as follows:

  With a financial calculator, enter N = 3, PV = 2775.10, PMT = −1000, FV = 0, and then press the I key to find I = 4%.
- Thus far in this section we have assumed that payments are made, and interest is earned, annually. However, many contracts call for more frequent payments; for example, mortgage and auto loans call for monthly payments, and most bonds pay interest semiannually. Similarly, most banks compute interest daily. When compounding occurs more frequently than once a year, this fact must be recognized. We can use the Figure 8-3 example to illustrate semiannual compounding. First, recognize that the 4 percent stated rate is a nominal rate that must be converted to a periodic rate, and the number of years must be converted to periods:

  $$i_{PER} = \text{Stated rate/Periods per year} = 4\%/2 = 2\%.$$
  $$\text{Periods} = \text{Years} \times \text{Periods per year} = 3 \times 2 = 6.$$

  The periodic rate and number of periods would be used for calculations and shown on time lines.

  If the \$1,000 per-year payments were actually payable as \$500 each 6 months, you would simply redraw Figure 8-3 to show 6 payments of \$500 each, but you would also use a **periodic interest rate** of 4%/2 = 2% for determining the PV or FV of the payments.
- If we are comparing the costs of loans that require payments more than once a year, or the rates of return on investments that pay interest more frequently, then the comparisons should be based on **equivalent** (or **effective**) rates of return using this formula:

  $$\text{Effective annual rate} = \text{EAR (or EFF\%)} = \left(1 + \frac{i_{Nom}}{m}\right)^m - 1.0.$$

  For semiannual compounding, the effective annual rate is 4.04 percent:

  $$\left(1 + \frac{0.04}{2}\right)^2 - 1.0 = (1.02)^2 - 1.0 = 1.0404 - 1.0 = 0.0404 = 4.04\%.$$
- The general equation for finding the future value for any number of compounding periods per year is:

  $$FV_n = PV\left(1 + \frac{i_{Nom}}{m}\right)^{mn},$$

where

$$i_{Nom} = \text{quoted interest rate.}$$
$$m = \text{number of compounding periods per year.}$$
$$n = \text{number of years.}$$

- An **amortized loan** is one that is paid off in equal payments over a specified period. An **amortization schedule** shows how much of each payment constitutes interest, how much is used to reduce the principal, and the unpaid balance at each point in time.

The concepts covered in this chapter will be used throughout the remainder of the book. For example, in Chapters 9 and 10, we apply present value concepts to find the values of bonds and stocks, and we see that the market prices of securities are established by determining the present values of the cash flows they are expected to provide. In later chapters, the same basic concepts are applied to corporate decisions involving expenditures on capital assets, to the types of capital that should be used to pay for assets, to leasing decisions, and so forth.

Questions

8–1 Define each of the following terms:

a. PV; i; INT; FV_n; PVA_n; FVA_n; PMT; m; i_{Nom}

b. $FVIF_{i,n}$; $PVIF_{i,n}$; $FVIFA_{i,n}$; $PVIFA_{i,n}$

c. Opportunity cost rate

d. Annuity; lump sum payment; cash flow; uneven cash flow stream

e. Ordinary (deferred) annuity; annuity due

f. Perpetuity; consol

g. Outflow; inflow; time line

h. Compounding; discounting

i. Annual, semiannual, quarterly, monthly, and daily compounding

j. Effective annual rate (EAR); nominal (quoted) interest rate; APR; periodic rate

k. Amortization schedule; principal component versus interest component of a payment; amortized loan

l. Terminal value

8–2 What is an *opportunity cost rate?* How is this rate used in discounted cash flow analysis, and where is it shown on a time line? Is the opportunity rate a single number which is used in all situations?

8–3 An *annuity* is defined as a series of payments of a fixed amount for a specific number of periods. Thus, \$100 a year for 10 years is an annuity, but \$100 in Year 1, \$200 in Year 2, and \$400 in Years 3 through 10 does *not* constitute an annuity. However, the second series *contains* an annuity. Is this statement true or false?

8–4 If a firm's earnings per share grew from \$1 to \$2 over a 10-year period, the *total growth* would be 100 percent, but the *annual growth rate* would be *less than* 10 percent. True or false? Explain.

8–5 Would you rather have a savings account that pays 5 percent interest compounded semiannually or one that pays 5 percent interest compounded daily? Explain.

8–6 To find the present value of an uneven series of cash flows, you must find the PVs of the individual cash flows and then sum them. Annuity procedures can never be of use, even if some of the cash flows constitute an annuity (for example, \$100 each for Years 3, 4, 5, and 6), because the entire series is not an annuity. Is this statement true or false? Explain.

8–7 The present value of a perpetuity is equal to the payment on the annuity, PMT, divided by the interest rate, i: PV = PMT/i. What is the *sum*, or future value, of a perpetuity of PMT dollars per year? (Hint: The answer is infinity, but explain why.)

Self-Test Problems (Solutions Appear in Appendix A)

ST–1
FUTURE VALUE

Assume that it is now January 1, 2002. On January 1, 2003, you will deposit $1,000 into a savings account that pays 8 percent.

a. If the bank compounds interest annually, how much will you have in your account on January 1, 2006?
b. What would your January 1, 2006, balance be if the bank used quarterly compounding rather than annual compounding?
c. Suppose you deposited the $1,000 in 4 payments of $250 each on January 1 of 2003, 2004, 2005, and 2006. How much would you have in your account on January 1, 2006, based on 8 percent annual compounding?
d. Suppose you deposited 4 equal payments in your account on January 1 of 2003, 2004, 2005, and 2006. Assuming an 8 percent interest rate, how large would each of your payments have to be for you to obtain the same ending balance as you calculated in part a?

ST–2
TIME VALUE OF MONEY

Assume that it is now January 1, 2002, and you will need $1,000 on January 1, 2006. Your bank compounds interest at an 8 percent annual rate.

a. How much must you deposit on January 1, 2003, to have a balance of $1,000 on January 1, 2006?
b. If you want to make equal payments on each January 1 from 2003 through 2006 to accumulate the $1,000, how large must each of the 4 payments be?
c. If your father were to offer either to make the payments calculated in part b ($221.92) or to give you a lump sum of $750 on January 1, 2003, which would you choose?
d. If you have only $750 on January 1, 2003, what interest rate, compounded annually, would you have to earn to have the necessary $1,000 on January 1, 2006?
e. Suppose you can deposit only $186.29 each January 1 from 2003 through 2006, but you still need $1,000 on January 1, 2006. What interest rate, with annual compounding, must you seek out to achieve your goal?
f. To help you reach your $1,000 goal, your father offers to give you $400 on January 1, 2003. You will get a part-time job and make 6 additional payments of equal amounts each 6 months thereafter. If all of this money is deposited in a bank which pays 8 percent, compounded semiannually, how large must each of the 6 payments be?
g. What is the effective annual rate being paid by the bank in part f?
h. *Reinvestment rate risk* was defined in Chapter 5 as being the risk that maturing securities (and coupon payments on bonds) will have to be reinvested at a lower rate of interest than they were previously earning. Is there a reinvestment rate risk involved in the preceding analysis? If so, how might this risk be eliminated?

ST–3
EFFECTIVE ANNUAL RATES

Bank A pays 8 percent interest, compounded quarterly, on its money market account. The managers of Bank B want its money market account to equal Bank A's effective annual rate, but interest is to be compounded on a monthly basis. What nominal, or quoted, rate must Bank B set?

Problems

8–1
PRESENT AND FUTURE VALUES FOR DIFFERENT PERIODS

Find the following values, *using the equations*, and then work the problems using a financial calculator to check your answers. Disregard rounding differences. (Hint: If you are using a financial calculator, you can enter the known values and then press the appropriate key to find the unknown variable. Then, without clearing the TVM register, you can "override" the variable which changes by simply entering a new value for it and then pressing the key for the unknown variable to obtain the second answer. This procedure can be used in parts b and d, and in many other situations, to see how changes in input variables affect the output variable.)

a. An initial $500 compounded for 1 year at 6 percent.
b. An initial $500 compounded for 2 years at 6 percent.
c. The present value of $500 due in 1 year at a discount rate of 6 percent.
d. The present value of $500 due in 2 years at a discount rate of 6 percent.

8-2 PRESENT AND FUTURE VALUES FOR DIFFERENT INTEREST RATES

Use equations and a financial calculator to find the following values. See the hint for Problem 8-1.

a. An initial $500 compounded for 10 years at 6 percent.
b. An initial $500 compounded for 10 years at 12 percent.
c. The present value of $500 due in 10 years at a 6 percent discount rate.
d. The present value of $1,552.90 due in 10 years at a 12 percent discount rate and at a 6 percent rate. Give a verbal definition of the term *present value,* and illustrate it using a time line with data from this problem. As a part of your answer, explain why present values are dependent upon interest rates.

8-3 TIME FOR A LUMP SUM TO DOUBLE

To the closest year, how long will it take $200 to double if it is deposited and earns the following rates? [Notes: (1) See the hint for Problem 8-1. (2) This problem cannot be solved exactly with some financial calculators. For example, if you enter PV = −200, PMT = 0, FV = 400, and I = 7 in an HP-12C, and then press the N key, you will get 11 years for part a. The correct answer is 10.2448 years, which rounds to 10, but the calculator rounds up. However, the HP-10B and HP-17B give the correct answer.]

a. 7 percent.
b. 10 percent.
c. 18 percent.
d. 100 percent.

8-4 FUTURE VALUE OF AN ANNUITY

Find the *future value* of the following annuities. The first payment in these annuities is made at the *end* of Year 1; that is, they are *ordinary annuities.* (Note: See the hint to Problem 8-1. Also, note that you can leave values in the TVM register, switch to "BEG," press FV, and find the FV of the annuity due.)

a. $400 per year for 10 years at 10 percent.
b. $200 per year for 5 years at 5 percent.
c. $400 per year for 5 years at 0 percent.
d. Now rework parts a, b, and c assuming that payments are made at the *beginning* of each year; that is, they are *annuities due.*

8-5 PRESENT VALUE OF AN ANNUITY

Find the *present value* of the following *ordinary annuities* (see note to Problem 8-4):

a. $400 per year for 10 years at 10 percent.
b. $200 per year for 5 years at 5 percent.
c. $400 per year for 5 years at 0 percent.
d. Now rework parts a, b, and c assuming that payments are made at the *beginning* of each year; that is, they are *annuities due.*

8-6 UNEVEN CASH FLOW STREAM

a. Find the present values of the following cash flow streams. The appropriate interest rate is 8 percent. (Hint: It is fairly easy to work this problem dealing with the individual cash flows. However, if you have a financial calculator, read the section of the manual that describes how to enter cash flows such as the ones in this problem. This will take a little time, but the investment will pay huge dividends throughout the course. Note, if you do work with the cash flow register, then you must enter CF_0 = 0.)

Year	Cash Stream A	Cash Stream B
1	$100	$300
2	400	400
3	400	400
4	400	400
5	300	100

b. What is the value of each cash flow stream at a 0 percent interest rate?

8-7 EFFECTIVE RATE OF INTEREST

Find the interest rates, or rates of return, on each of the following:

a. You *borrow* $700 and promise to pay back $749 at the end of 1 year.
b. You *lend* $700 and receive a promise to be paid $749 at the end of 1 year.
c. You borrow $85,000 and promise to pay back $201,229 at the end of 10 years.
d. You borrow $9,000 and promise to make payments of $2,684.80 per year for 5 years.

8–8
'E FOR VARIOUS ..UNDING PERIODS

Find the amount to which $500 will grow under each of the following conditions:
a. 12 percent compounded annually for 5 years.
b. 12 percent compounded semiannually for 5 years.
c. 12 percent compounded quarterly for 5 years.
d. 12 percent compounded monthly for 5 years.

8–9
PRESENT VALUE FOR VARIOUS COMPOUNDING PERIODS

Find the present value of $500 due in the future under each of the following conditions:
a. 12 percent nominal rate, semiannual compounding, discounted back 5 years.
b. 12 percent nominal rate, quarterly compounding, discounted back 5 years.
c. 12 percent nominal rate, monthly compounding, discounted back 1 year.

8–10
FUTURE VALUE OF AN ANNUITY FOR VARIOUS COMPOUNDING PERIODS

Find the future values of the following ordinary annuities:
a. FV of $400 each 6 months for 5 years at a nominal rate of 12 percent, compounded semiannually.
b. FV of $200 each 3 months for 5 years at a nominal rate of 12 percent, compounded quarterly.
c. The annuities described in parts a and b have the same amount of money paid into them during the 5-year period and both earn interest at the same nominal rate, yet the annuity in part b earns $101.60 more than the one in part a over the 5 years. Why does this occur?

8–11
EFFECTIVE VERSUS NOMINAL INTEREST RATES

Universal Bank pays 7 percent interest, compounded annually, on time deposits. Regional Bank pays 6 percent interest, compounded quarterly.
a. Based on effective interest rates, in which bank would you prefer to deposit your money?
b. Could your choice of banks be influenced by the fact that you might want to withdraw your funds during the year as opposed to at the end of the year? In answering this question, assume that funds must be left on deposit during the entire compounding period in order for you to receive any interest.

8–12
AMORTIZATION SCHEDULE

a. Set up an amortization schedule for a $25,000 loan to be repaid in equal installments at the end of each of the next 5 years. The interest rate is 10 percent.
b. How large must each annual payment be if the loan is for $50,000? Assume that the interest rate remains at 10 percent and that the loan is paid off over 5 years.
c. How large must each payment be if the loan is for $50,000, the interest rate is 10 percent, and the loan is paid off in equal installments at the end of each of the next 10 years? This loan is for the same amount as the loan in part b, but the payments are spread out over twice as many periods. Why are these payments not half as large as the payments on the loan in part b?

8–13
EFFECTIVE RATES OF RETURN

Assume that AT&T's pension fund managers are considering two alternative securities as investments: (1) Security Z (for zero intermediate-year cash flows), which costs $422.41 today, pays nothing during its 10-year life, and then pays $1,000 after 10 years or (2) Security B, which has a cost today of $1,000 and which pays $80 at the end of each of the next 9 years and then $1,080 at the end of Year 10.
a. What is the rate of return on each security?
b. Assume that the interest rate AT&T's pension fund managers can earn on the fund's money falls to 6 percent immediately after the securities are purchased and is expected to remain at that level for the next 10 years. What would the price of each security change to, what would the fund's profit be on each security, and what would be the percentage profit (profit divided by cost) for each security?
c. Assuming that the cash flows for each security had to be reinvested at the new 6 percent market interest rate, (1) what would be the value attributable to each security at the end of 10 years and (2) what "actual, after-the-fact" rate of return would the fund have earned on each security? (Hint: The "actual" rate of return is found as the interest rate that causes the PV of the compounded Year 10 amount to equal the original cost of the security.)
d. Now assume all the facts as given in parts b and c except assume that the interest rate rose to 12 percent rather than fell to 6 percent. What would happen to the profit figures as developed in part b and to the "actual" rates of return as determined in part c? Explain your results.

8–14 REQUIRED ANNUITY PAYMENTS

A father is planning a savings program to put his daughter through college. His daughter is now13 years old. She plans to enroll at the university in 5 years, and it should take her 4 years to complete her education. Currently, the cost per year (for everything—food, clothing, tuition, books, transportation, and so forth) is $12,500, but a 5 percent inflation rate in these costs is forecasted. The daughter recently received $7,500 from her grandfather's estate; this money, which is invested in a bank account paying 8 percent interest, compounded annually, will be used to help meet the costs of the daughter's education. The rest of the costs will be met by money the father will deposit in the savings account. He will make 6 equal deposits to the account—one in each year from now until his daughter starts college. These deposits will begin today and will also earn 8 percent interest.

a. What will be the present value of the cost of 4 years of education at the time the daughter becomes 18? [Hint: Calculate the future value of the cost (at 5%) for each year of her education, then discount three of these costs back (at 8%) to the year in which she turns 18, then sum the four costs.]

b. What will be the value of the $7,500 which the daughter received from her grandfather's estate when she starts college at age 18? (Hint: Compound for 5 years at 8%.)

c. If the father is planning to make the first of 6 deposits today, how large must each deposit be for him to be able to put his daughter through college?

8–15 PRESENT VALUE COMPARISON

Which amount is worth more at 14 percent: $1,000 in hand today or $2,000 due in 6 years?

8–16 GROWTH RATES

Hanebury Corporation's current sales were $12 million. Sales were $6 million 5 years earlier.

a. To the nearest percentage point, at what rate have sales been growing?

b. Suppose someone calculated the sales growth for Hanebury Corporation in part a as follows: "Sales doubled in 5 years. This represents a growth of 100 percent in 5 years, so, dividing 100 percent by 5, we find the growth rate to be 20 percent per year." Explain what is wrong with this calculation.

8–17 EXPECTED RATE OF RETURN

Washington-Pacific invests $4 million to clear a tract of land and to set out some young pine trees. The trees will mature in 10 years, at which time Washington-Pacific plans to sell the forest at an expected price of $8 million. What is Washington-Pacific's expected rate of return?

8–18 EFFECTIVE RATE OF INTEREST

Your broker offers to sell you a note for $13,250 that will pay $2,345.05 per year for 10 years. If you buy the note, what rate of interest (to the closest percent) will you be earning?

8–19 EFFECTIVE RATE OF INTEREST

A mortgage company offers to lend you $85,000; the loan calls for payments of $8,273.59 per year for 30 years. What interest rate is the mortgage company charging you?

8–20 REQUIRED LUMP SUM PAYMENT

To complete your last year in business school and then go through law school, you will need $10,000 per year for 4 years, starting next year (that is, you will need to withdraw the first $10,000 one year from today). Your rich uncle offers to put you through school, and he will deposit in a bank paying 7 percent interest a sum of money that is sufficient to provide the four payments of $10,000 each. His deposit will be made today.

a. How large must the deposit be?

b. How much will be in the account immediately after you make the first withdrawal? After the last withdrawal?

8–21 REPAYING A LOAN

While Mary Corens was a student at the University of Tennessee, she borrowed $12,000 in student loans at an annual interest rate of 9 percent. If Mary repays $1,500 per year, how long, to the nearest year, will it take her to repay the loan?

8–22 REACHING A FINANCIAL GOAL

You need to accumulate $10,000. To do so, you plan to make deposits of $1,250 per year, with the first payment being made a year from today, in a bank account which pays 12 percent annual interest. Your last deposit will be less than $1,250 if less is needed to round out to $10,000. How many years will it take you to reach your $10,000 goal, and how large will the last deposit be?

8–23 PRESENT VALUE OF A PERPETUITY

What is the present value of a perpetuity of $100 per year if the appropriate discount rate is 7 percent? If interest rates in general were to double and the appropriate discount rate rose to 14 percent, what would happen to the present value of the perpetuity?

8–24 *PV AND EFFECTIVE ANNUAL RATE*

Assume that you inherited some money. A friend of yours is working as an unpaid intern at a local brokerage firm, and her boss is selling some securities that call for four payments, $50 at the end of each of the next 3 years, plus a payment of $1,050 at the end of Year 4. Your friend says she can get you some of these securities at a cost of $900 each. Your money is now invested in a bank that pays an 8 percent nominal (quoted) interest rate but with quarterly compounding. You regard the securities as being just as safe, and as liquid, as your bank deposit, so your required effective annual rate of return on the securities is the same as that on your bank deposit. You must calculate the value of the securities to decide whether they are a good investment. What is their present value to you?

8–25 *LOAN AMORTIZATION*

Assume that your aunt sold her house on December 31 and that she took a mortgage in the amount of $10,000 as part of the payment. The mortgage has a quoted (or nominal) interest rate of 10 percent, but it calls for payments every 6 months, beginning on June 30, and the mortgage is to be amortized over 10 years. Now, 1 year later, your aunt must inform the IRS and the person who bought the house of the interest that was included in the two payments made during the year. (This interest will be income to your aunt and a deduction to the buyer of the house.) To the closest dollar, what is the total amount of interest that was paid during the first year?

8–26 *LOAN AMORTIZATION*

Your company is planning to borrow $1,000,000 on a 5-year, 15%, annual payment, fully amortized term loan. What fraction of the payment made at the end of the second year will represent repayment of principal?

8–27 *NONANNUAL COMPOUNDING*

a. It is now January 1, 2002. You plan to make 5 deposits of $100 each, one every 6 months, with the first payment being made *today*. If the bank pays a nominal interest rate of 12 percent but uses semiannual compounding, how much will be in your account after 10 years?

b. You must make a payment of $1,432.02 ten years from today. To prepare for this payment, you will make 5 equal deposits, beginning today and for the next 4 quarters, in a bank that pays a nominal interest rate of 12 percent, quarterly compounding. How large must each of the 5 payments be?

8–28 *NOMINAL RATE OF RETURN*

Anne Lockwood, manager of Oaks Mall Jewelry, wants to sell on credit, giving customers 3 months in which to pay. However, Anne will have to borrow from her bank to carry the accounts payable. The bank will charge a nominal 15 percent, but with monthly compounding. Anne wants to quote a nominal rate to her customers (all of whom are expected to pay on time) which will exactly cover her financing costs. What nominal annual rate should she quote to her credit customers?

8–29 *REQUIRED ANNUITY PAYMENTS*

Assume that your father is now 50 years old, that he plans to retire in 10 years, and that he expects to live for 25 years after he retires, that is, until he is 85. He wants a fixed retirement income that has the same purchasing power at the time he retires as $40,000 has today (he realizes that the real value of his retirement income will decline year by year after he retires). His retirement income will begin the day he retires, 10 years from today, and he will then get 24 additional annual payments. Inflation is expected to be 5 percent per year from today forward; he currently has $100,000 saved up; and he expects to earn a return on his savings of 8 percent per year, annual compounding. To the nearest dollar, how much must he save during each of the next 10 years (with deposits being made at the end of each year) to meet his retirement goal?

Spreadsheet Problems

8–30 *BUILD A MODEL: THE TIME VALUE OF MONEY*

Start with the partial model in the file ***Ch 08-30 Build a Model.xls*** from the textbook's CD-ROM. Answer the following questions, using a spreadsheet model to do the calculations.

a. Find the FV of $1,000 invested to earn 10 percent after 5 years. Answer this question by using a math formula and also by using the *Excel* function wizard.

b. Now create a table that shows the FV at 0 percent, 5 percent, and 20 percent for 0, 1, 2, 3, 4, and 5 years. Then create a graph with years on the horizontal axis and FV on the vertical axis to display your results.

c. Find the PV of $1,000 due in 5 years if the discount rate is 10 percent. Again, work the problem with a formula and also by using the function wizard.

d. A security has a cost of $1,000 and will return $2,000 after 5 years. What rate of return does the security provide?

e. Suppose California's population is 30 million people, and its population is expected to grow by 2 percent per year. How long would it take for the population to double?

f. Find the PV of an annuity that pays $1,000 at the end of each of the next 5 years if the interest rate is 15 percent. Then find the FV of that same annuity.

g. How would the PV and FV of the annuity change if it were an annuity due rather than an ordinary annuity?

h. What would the FV and the PV for parts a and c be if the interest rate were 10 percent with semiannual compounding rather than 10 percent with annual compounding?

i. Find the PV and the FV of an investment that makes the following end-of-year payments. The interest rate is 8 percent.

Year	Payment
1	$100
2	200
3	400

j. Suppose you bought a house and took out a mortgage for $50,000. The interest rate is 8 percent, and you must amortize the loan over 10 years with equal end-of-year payments. Set up an amortization schedule that shows the annual payments and the amount of each payment that goes to pay off the principal and the amount that constitutes interest expense to the borrower and interest income to the lender.

(1) Create a graph that shows how the payments are divided between interest and principal repayment over time.

(2) Suppose the loan called for 10 years of monthly payments, with the same original amount and the same nominal interest rate. What would the amortization schedule show now?

k. Refer to Problem 8-14. Solve this problem using a spreadsheet model.

8–31 *WHAT IF ANALYSIS: LOAN AMORTIZATION*

Start with the model ***Ch 08 What If Analysis.xls*** from the textbook's CD-ROM and answer the questions shown there.

Cyberproblem

The information related to the cyberproblems is likely to change over time, due to the release of new information and the ever-changing nature of the World Wide Web. With these changes in mind, we will periodically update these problems on the textbook's web site.

8–32 *PREPAYMENT VERSUS INVESTMENT ANALYSIS*

In managing one's own finances, as well as those of a business, there are numerous decision situations where applications of Time Value of Money (TVM) concepts and methods help one assess the financial consequences of alternative courses of action. One such situation is the decision to prepay part or all of one's mortgage or loan balance by making extra periodic principal payments. As one makes extra principal payments, the loan balance is reduced faster. This means you pay less interest over the life of the loan and the loan will be repaid earlier (that is, fewer payments). For example, a person might decide to pay $50 per month extra (that is, if their mortgage payment was $900 per month, they might pay $950 each month, $50 extra) on a mortgage loan. The extra payment of $50 would be applied each month to reduce the principal balance. However, there are important factors to consider before making this decision. For example, if the mortgage loan is on the person's primary residence, the interest on the loan may be tax deductible. As you know from previous text chapters, this reduces the net, after-tax cost of the loan.

To consider the financial consequences of this decision, you will visit a web site that offers various web calculators free, including a prepayment versus investment scenario analysis. Before using this web site, you will need to amortize the loan you will use as input data for the analysis.

Suppose you purchase a home for $150,000 and borrow 90 percent of the cost in a mortgage loan, 30-year maturity, at a fixed annual interest rate of 8 percent, with deferred monthly payments. What is the monthly payment for principal and interest (P&I) on this loan?

The loan amount is $150,000 × 0.90 = $135,000. The calculator keystrokes follow. N = 360 (30 years × 12 months per year); I = 8.0/12 = 0.6667; PV = −$135,000; FV = 0 (the loan will be paid off at maturity); solve for PMT = $990.62. (Note: If you enter the interest rate at 0.6667 percent per month you get the payment above. If you carry full precision on your calculator, the PMT = $990.58.)

The data you will need for the prepayment scenario include the following.

Loan balance: $135,000
Current payment: $990.62
Additional payment: $50.00
Loan interest rate: 8.0%
Loan interest deductibility: Yes
Investment rate return: 6.00%*
Tax bracket: 30.00%
Investment type: After-tax

*The investment rate return is your opportunity cost estimate. It is the annual rate you think you can earn on the $50 extra principal payment if you did not make extra principal payments on your mortgage but instead, invested it.

Go to the cyberproblem on the textbook's web site, **http://www.harcourtcollege.com/theory/student/resources/cyberprob/ch08.html,** and answer the questions shown there.

Mini Case

CD

See ***Ch 08 Show.ppt*** and ***Ch 08 Mini Case.xls.***

Assume that you are nearing graduation and that you have applied for a job with a local bank. As part of the bank's evaluation process, you have been asked to take an examination that covers several financial analysis techniques. The first section of the test addresses discounted cash flow analysis. See how you would do by answering the following questions.

a. Draw time lines for (a) a $100 lump sum cash flow at the end of Year 2, (b) an ordinary annuity of $100 per year for 3 years, and (c) an uneven cash flow stream of −$50, $100, $75, and $50 at the end of Years 0 through 3.

b. (1) What is the future value of an initial $100 after 3 years if it is invested in an account paying 10 percent annual interest?

(2) What is the present value of $100 to be received in 3 years if the appropriate interest rate is 10 percent?

c. We sometimes need to find how long it will take a sum of money (or anything else) to grow to some specified amount. For example, if a company's sales are growing at a rate of 20 percent per year, how long will it take sales to double?

d. What is the difference between an ordinary annuity and an annuity due? What type of annuity is shown below? How would you change it to the other type of annuity?

e. (1) What is the future value of a 3-year ordinary annuity of $100 if the appropriate interest rate is 10 percent?

(2) What is the present value of the annuity?

(3) What would the future and present values be if the annuity were an annuity due?

f. What is the present value of the following uneven cash flow stream? The appropriate interest rate is 10 percent, compounded annually.

0	1	2	3	4 Years
0	100	300	300	−50

g. What annual interest rate will cause \$100 to grow to \$125.97 in 3 years?

h. (1) Will the future value be larger or smaller if we compound an initial amount more often than annually, for example, every 6 months, or *semiannually*, holding the stated interest rate constant? Why?

(2) Define (a) the stated, or quoted, or nominal rate (i_{Nom}), (b) the periodic rate (i_{PER}), and (c) the effective annual rate (EAR).

(3) What is the effective annual rate for a nominal rate of 10 percent, compounded semiannually? Compounded quarterly? Compounded daily?

(4) What is the future value of \$100 after 3 years under 10 percent semiannual compounding? Quarterly compounding?

i. Will the effective annual rate ever be equal to the nominal (quoted) rate?

j. (1) What is the value at the end of Year 3 of the following cash flow stream if the quoted interest rate is 10 percent, compounded semiannually?

0		1		2		3 Years
0		100		100		100

(2) What is the PV of the same stream?

(3) Is the stream an annuity?

(4) An important rule is that you should *never* show a nominal rate on a time line or use it in calculations unless what condition holds? (Hint: Think of annual compounding, when $i_{Nom} = EAR = i_{Per}$.) What would be wrong with your answer to Questions j (1) and j (2) if you used the nominal rate (10%) rather than the periodic rate ($i_{Nom}/2 = 10\%/2 = 5\%$)?

k. (1) Construct an amortization schedule for a \$1,000, 10 percent annual rate loan with 3 equal installments.

(2) What is the annual interest expense for the borrower, and the annual interest income for the lender, during Year 2?

l. Suppose on January 1, 2002, you deposit \$100 in an account that pays a nominal, or quoted, interest rate of 11.33463 percent, with interest added (compounded) daily. How much will you have in your account on October 1, or after 9 months?

m. Now suppose you leave your money in the bank for 21 months. Thus, on January 1, 2002, you deposit \$100 in an account that pays a 12 percent effective annual interest rate. How much will be in your account on October 1, 2003?

n. Suppose someone offered to sell you a note calling for the payment of \$1,000 fifteen months from today. They offer to sell it to you for \$850. You have \$850 in a bank time deposit which pays a 6.76649 percent nominal rate with daily compounding, which is a 7 percent effective annual interest rate, and you plan to leave the money in the bank unless you buy the note. The note is not risky—you are sure it will be paid on schedule. Should you buy the note? Check the decision in three ways: (1) by comparing your future value if you buy the note versus leaving your money in the bank, (2) by comparing the PV of the note with your current bank account, and (3) by comparing the EAR on the note versus that of the bank account.

o. Suppose the note discussed in part n had a cost of \$850, but called for 5 quarterly payments of \$190 each, with the first payment due in 3 months rather than \$1,000 at the end of 15 months. Would it be a good investment for you?

Selected Additional References

For a more complete discussion of the mathematics of finance, see

Atkins, Allen B., and Edward A. Dyl, "The Lotto Jackpot: The Lump Sum versus the Annuity," *Financial Practice and Education,* Fall/Winter 1995, 107–111.

Cissell, Robert, Helen Cissell, and David C. Flaspohler, *Mathematics of Finance* (Boston: Houghton Mifflin, 1978).

Lindley, James T., "Compounding Issues Revisited," *Financial Practice and Education,* Fall 1993, 127–129.

To learn more about using financial calculators, see the manual which came with your calculator. For example, see

Hewlett-Packard, *HP-10B Business Calculator Owner's Manual,* June 1990.

White, Mark A., *Financial Analysis with an Electronic Calculator,* 2nd ed. (Chicago: Irwin, 1995).

———, "Financial Problem Solving with an Electronic Calculator: Texas Instruments' BA II Plus," *Financial Practice and Education,* Fall 1993, 123–126.

9

Bonds and Their Valuation

During the summer of 1999 the future course of interest rates was highly uncertain. Continued strength in the economy and growing fears of inflation had led to interest rate increases, and many analysts were concerned that this trend would continue. However, others were forecasting declining rates—they saw no threat from inflation, and they were more concerned about the economy running out of gas. Because of this uncertainty, bond investors tended to wait on the sidelines for some definitive economic news. At the same time, companies were postponing bond issues out of fear that nervous investors would be unwilling to purchase them.

One example of all this was Ford Motor, which in June 1999 decided to put a large bond issue on hold. However, after just three weeks, Ford sensed a shift in the investment climate, and it announced plans to sell $8.6 billion of new bonds. As shown in the table below, the Ford issue set a record, surpassing an $8 billion AT&T issue that had taken place a few months earlier.

Ford's $8.6 billion issue actually consisted of four separate bonds. Ford Credit, a subsidiary that provides customer financing, borrowed $1.0 billion dollars at a 2-year floating rate and another $1.8 billion at a 3-year floating rate. Ford Motor itself borrowed $4 billion as 5-year fixed-rate debt and another $1.8 billion at a 32-year fixed rate.

Most analysts agreed that these bonds had limited default risk. Ford held $24 billion in cash, and it had earned a record $2.5 billion during the second quarter of 1999. However, the auto industry faces some inherent risks. When all the risk factors were balanced, the issues all received a single-A rating. Much to the relief of the jittery bond market, the Ford issue was well received. Dave Cosper, Ford Credit's Treasurer, said "There was a lot of excitement, and demand exceeded our expectations."

The response to the Ford offering revealed that investors had a strong appetite for large bond issues with strong credit ratings. Larger issues are more liquid than smaller ones, and liquidity is particularly important to bond investors when the direction of the overall market is highly uncertain.

Interestingly, large investment-grade issues by well-known companies such as Ford are also helping to fill the vacuum created by the reduction in Treasury debt. The Federal government is forecasting future budget surpluses, and it plans to use a portion of the surplus to reduce its outstanding debt. As this occurs, Treasury bonds outstanding will decrease, forcing many Treasury investors into the corporate bond market, where they will look for investment-grade issues by companies such as Ford.

Already anticipating this demand, Ford is planning to regularly issue large blocks of debt in the global market. Seeing Ford's success, less than one month later Wal-Mart entered the list of top ten U.S. corporate bond financings with a new $5 billion issue. Other large companies have subsequently followed suit.

Source: Gregory Zuckerman, "Ford's Record Issue May Drive Imitators," *The Wall Street Journal*, July 12, 1999, C1.

Top Ten U.S. Corporate Bond Financings as of July 1999

Issuer	Date	Amount (Billions of Dollars)
Ford	July 9, 1999	$8.60
AT&T	March 23, 1999	8.00
RJR Holdings	May 12, 1989	6.11
WorldCom	August 6, 1998	6.10
Sprint	November 10, 1998	5.00
Assoc. Corp. of N. America	October 27, 1998	4.80
Norfolk Southern	May 14, 1997	4.30
US West	January 16, 1997	4.10
Conoco	April 15, 1999	4.00
Charter Communications	March 12, 1999	3.58

Source: Thomson Financial Securities Data, Credit Suisse First Boston as reported in *The Wall Street Journal*, July 12, 1999, C1.

If you skim through *The Wall Street Journal*, you will see references to a wide variety of bonds. This variety may seem confusing, but in actuality just a few characteristics distinguish the various types of bonds.

While bonds are often viewed as relatively safe investments, one can certainly lose money on them. Indeed, "riskless" long-term U.S. Treasury bonds declined by more than 20 percent during 1994, and "safe" Mexican government bonds declined by 25 percent on one day, December 27, 1994. More recently, investors in Russian bonds suffered massive losses when Russia defaulted. In each of these cases, investors who had regarded bonds as being riskless, or at least fairly safe, learned a sad lesson. Note, though, that it is possible to rack up impressive gains in the bond market. High-quality corporate bonds in 1995 provided a total return of nearly 21 percent, and in 1997, U.S. Treasury bonds returned 14.3 percent.

CD

The textbook's CD-ROM contains an *Excel* file that will guide you through the chapter's calculations. The file for this chapter is *Ch 09 Tool Kit.xls,* and we encourage you to open the file and follow along as you read the chapter.

In this chapter, we will discuss the types of bonds companies and government agencies issue, the terms that are contained in bond contracts, the types of risks to which both bond investors and issuers are exposed, and procedures for determining the values of and rates of return on bonds.

Who Issues Bonds?

A **bond** is a long-term contract under which a borrower agrees to make payments of interest and principal, on specific dates, to the holders of the bond. For example, on January 3, 2002, MicroDrive Inc. borrowed $50 million by issuing $50 million of bonds. For convenience, we assume that MicroDrive sold 50,000 individual bonds for $1,000 each. Actually, it could have sold one $50 million bond, 10 bonds with a $5 million face value, or any other combination that totals to $50 million. In any event, MicroDrive received the $50 million, and in exchange it promised to make annual interest payments and to repay the $50 million on a specified maturity date.

Investors have many choices when investing in bonds, but bonds are classified into four main types: Treasury, corporate, municipal, and foreign. Each type differs with respect to expected return and degree of risk.

Treasury bonds, sometimes referred to as government bonds, are issued by the federal government.[1] It is reasonable to assume that the federal government will make good on its promised payments, so these bonds have no default risk. However, Treasury bond prices decline when interest rates rise, so they are not free of all risks.

Corporate bonds, as the name implies, are issued by corporations. Unlike Treasury bonds, corporate bonds are exposed to default risk—if the issuing company gets into trouble, it may be unable to make the promised interest and principal payments. Different corporate bonds have different levels of default risk, depending on the issuing company's characteristics and the terms of the specific bond. Default risk often is referred to as "credit risk," and, as we saw in Chapter 5, the larger the default or credit risk, the higher the interest rate the issuer must pay.

Municipal bonds, or "munis," are issued by state and local governments. Like corporate bonds, munis have default risk. However, munis offer one major advantage over all other bonds: As we discussed in Chapter 2, the interest earned on most municipal bonds is exempt from federal taxes and also from state taxes if the holder is a resident of the issuing state. Consequently, municipal bonds carry interest rates that are considerably lower than those on corporate bonds with the same default risk.

Foreign bonds are issued by foreign governments or foreign corporations. Foreign corporate bonds are, of course, exposed to default risk, and so are some foreign government bonds. An additional risk exists if the bonds are denominated in a currency other than that of the investor's home currency. For example, if a U.S. investor purchases a corporate bond denominated in Japanese yen and the yen subsequently falls relative to the dollar, then the investor will lose money, even if the company does not default on its bonds.

Self-Test Questions

What is a bond?

What are the four main types of bonds?

Why are U.S. Treasury bonds not riskless?

To what types of risk are investors of foreign bonds exposed?

Key Characteristics of Bonds

Although all bonds have some common characteristics, they do not always have the same contractual features. For example, most corporate bonds have provisions for early repayment (call features), but these provisions can be quite different for different bonds. Differences in contractual provisions, and in the underlying strength of the companies backing the bonds, lead to major differences in bonds' risks, prices, and expected returns. To understand bonds, it is important that you understand the following terms.

Par Value

The **par value** is the stated face value of the bond; for illustrative purposes we generally assume a par value of $1,000, although any multiple of $1,000 (for example, $5,000) can be used. The par value generally represents the amount of money the firm borrows and promises to repay on the maturity date.

[1]The U.S. Treasury actually issues three types of securities: "bills," "notes," and "bonds." A bond makes an equal payment every six months until it matures, at which time it makes an additional lump sum payment. If the maturity at the time of issue is less than 10 years, it is called a note rather than a bond. A T-bill has a maturity of 52 weeks or less at the time of issue, and it makes no payments at all until it matures. Thus, bills are sold initially at a discount to their face, or maturity, value.

Coupon Interest Rate

WWW

An excellent site for information on many types of bonds is Bonds Online, which can be found at **http://www.bondsonline.com**. The site has a great deal of information about corporates, municipals, treasuries, and bond funds. It includes free bond searches, through which the user specifies the attributes desired in a bond and then the search returns the publicly traded bonds meeting the criteria. The site also includes a downloadable bond calculator and an excellent glossary of bond terminology.

MicroDrive's bonds require the company to pay a fixed number of dollars of interest each year (or, more typically, each six months). When this **coupon payment,** as it is called, is divided by the par value, the result is the **coupon interest rate.** For example, MicroDrive's bonds have a $1,000 par value, and they pay $100 in interest each year. The bond's coupon interest is $100, so its coupon interest rate is $100/$1,000 = 10 percent. The $100 is the yearly "rent" on the $1,000 loan. This payment, which is fixed at the time the bond is issued, remains in force during the life of the bond.[2] Typically, at the time a bond is issued its coupon payment is set at a level that will enable the bond to be issued at or near its par value.

In some cases, a bond's coupon payment will vary over time. For these **floating rate bonds,** the coupon rate is set for, say, the initial six-month period, after which it is adjusted every six months based on some market rate. Some corporate issues are tied to the Treasury bond rate, while other issues are tied to other rates. Many additional provisions can be included in floating rate issues. For example, some are convertible to fixed rate debt, whereas others have upper and lower limits ("caps" and "floors") on how high or low the rate can go.

Floating rate debt is popular with investors who are worried about the risk of rising interest rates, since the interest paid on such bonds increases whenever market rates rise. This causes the market value of the debt to be stabilized, and it also provides institutional buyers such as banks with income that is better geared to their own obligations. Banks' deposit costs rise with interest rates, so the income on floating rate loans that they have made rises at the same time their deposit costs are rising. The savings and loan industry was virtually destroyed as a result of their practice of making fixed rate mortgage loans but borrowing on floating rate terms. If you are earning 6 percent but paying 10 percent—which they were—you soon go bankrupt—which they did. Moreover, floating rate debt appeals to corporations that want to issue long-term debt without committing themselves to paying a historically high interest rate for the entire life of the loan.

Some bonds pay no coupons at all, but are offered at a substantial discount below their par values and hence provide capital appreciation rather than interest income. These securities are called **zero coupon bonds** *("zeros")*. Other bonds pay some coupon interest, but not enough to be issued at par. In general, any bond originally offered at a price significantly below its par value is called an **original issue discount (OID) bond.** Corporations first used zeros in a major way in 1981. In recent years IBM, Alcoa, JCPenney, ITT, Cities Service, GMAC, Lockheed Martin, and even the U.S. Treasury have used zeros to raise billions of dollars. Some of the details associated with issuing or investing in zero coupon bonds are discussed more fully in Chapter 19.

Maturity Date

Bonds generally have a specified **maturity date** on which the par value must be repaid. MicroDrive's bonds, which were issued on January 3, 2002, will mature on January 2, 2017; thus, they had a 15-year maturity at the time they were issued. Most bonds have **original maturities** (the maturity at the time the bond is issued) ranging from 10 to

[2] At one time, bonds literally had a number of small (1/2- by 2-inch), dated coupons attached to them, and on each interest payment date the owner would clip off the coupon for that date and either cash it at his or her bank or mail it to the company's paying agent, who would then mail back a check for the interest. A 30-year, semiannual bond would start with 60 coupons, whereas a 5-year annual payment bond would start with only 5 coupons. Today, new bonds must be *registered*—no physical coupons are involved, and interest checks are mailed automatically to the registered owners of the bonds. Even so, people continue to use the terms *coupon* and *coupon interest rate* when discussing bonds.

40 years, but any maturity is legally permissible.[3] Of course, the effective maturity of a bond declines each year after it has been issued. Thus, MicroDrive's bonds had a 15-year original maturity, but in 2003, a year later, they will have a 14-year maturity, and so on.

Provisions to Call or Redeem Bonds

Most corporate bonds contain a **call provision,** which gives the issuing corporation the right to call the bonds for redemption.[4] The call provision generally states that the company must pay the bondholders an amount greater than the par value if they are called. The additional sum, which is termed a *call premium,* is often set equal to one year's interest if the bonds are called during the first year, and the premium declines at a constant rate of INT/N each year thereafter, where INT = annual interest and N = original maturity in years. For example, the call premium on a $1,000 par value, 10-year, 10 percent bond would generally be $100 if it were called during the first year, $90 during the second year (calculated by reducing the $100, or 10 percent, premium by one-tenth), and so on. However, bonds are often not callable until several years (generally 5 to 10) after they were issued. This is known as a *deferred call,* and the bonds are said to have *call protection.*

Suppose a company sold bonds when interest rates were relatively high. Provided the issue is callable, the company could sell a new issue of low-yielding securities if and when interest rates drop. It could then use the proceeds of the new issue to retire the high-rate issue and thus reduce its interest expense. This process is called a *refunding operation,* and it is discussed in greater detail in Chapter 19.

A call provision is valuable to the firm but potentially detrimental to investors. If interest rates go up, the company will not call the bond, and the investor will be stuck with the original coupon rate on the bond, even though interest rates in the economy have risen sharply. However, if interest rates fall, the company *will* call the bond and pay off investors, who then must reinvest the proceeds at the current market interest rate, which is lower than the rate they were getting on the original bond. In other words, the investor loses when interest rates go up, but doesn't reap the gains when rates fall. To induce an investor to take this type of risk, a new issue of callable bonds must provide a higher interest rate than an otherwise similar issue of noncallable bonds. For example, on August 30, 1997, Pacific Timber Company issued bonds yielding 9.5 percent; these bonds were callable immediately. On the same day, Northwest Milling Company sold an issue with similar risk and maturity that yielded 9.2 percent, but these bonds were noncallable for ten years. Investors were willing to accept a 0.3 percent lower interest rate on Northwest's bonds for the assurance that the 9.2 percent interest rate would be earned for at least ten years. Pacific, on the other hand, had to incur a 0.3 percent higher annual interest rate to obtain the option of calling the bonds in the event of a subsequent decline in rates.

Bonds that are **redeemable at par** at the holder's option protect investors against a rise in interest rates. If rates rise, the price of fixed-rate bonds declines. However, if holders have the option of turning their bonds in and having them redeemed at par, they are protected against rising rates. Examples of such debt include Transamerica's $50 million issue of 25-year, 8½ percent bonds. The bonds are not callable by the company, but holders can turn them in for redemption at par five years after the date

---

[3]In July 1993, Walt Disney Co., attempting to lock in a low interest rate, issued the first 100-year bonds to be sold by any borrower in modern times. Soon after, Coca-Cola became the second company to stretch the meaning of "long-term bond" by selling $150 million of 100-year bonds.

[4]A majority of municipal bonds also contain call provisions. Although the U.S. Treasury no longer issues callable bonds, some past Treasury issues were callable.

of issue. If interest rates have risen, holders will turn in the bonds and reinvest the proceeds at a higher rate. This feature enabled Transamerica to sell the bonds with an 8½ percent coupon at a time when other similarly rated bonds had yields of 9 percent.

In late 1988, the corporate bond markets were sent into turmoil by the leveraged buyout of RJR Nabisco. RJR's bonds dropped in value by 20 percent within days of the LBO announcement, and the prices of many other corporate bonds also plunged, because investors feared that a boom in LBOs would load up many companies with excessive debt, leading to lower bond ratings and declining bond prices. All this led to a resurgence of concern about *event risk*, which is the risk that some sudden event, such as an LBO, will occur and increase the credit risk of the company, hence lowering the firm's bond rating and the value of its outstanding bonds. Investors' concern over event risk meant that those firms deemed most likely to face events that could harm bondholders had to pay dearly to raise new debt capital, if they could raise it at all. In an attempt to control debt costs, a new type of protective covenant was devised to minimize event risk. This covenant, called a *super poison put*, enables a bondholder to turn in, or "put" a bond back to the issue at par in the event of a takeover, merger, or major recapitalization.

Poison puts had actually been around since 1986, when the leveraged buyout trend took off. However, the earlier puts proved to be almost worthless because they allowed investors to "put" their bonds back to the issue at par value only in the event of an *unfriendly* takeover. But because almost all takeovers are eventually approved by the target firm's board, mergers that started as hostile generally ended as friendly. Also, the earlier poison puts failed to protect investors from voluntary recapitalizations, in which a company sells a big issue of bonds to pay a big, one-time dividend to stockholders or to buy back its own stock. The "super" poison puts that were used following the RJR buyout announcement protected against both of these actions. This is a good illustration of how quickly the financial community reacts to changes in the marketplace.

Sinking Funds

Some bonds also include a **sinking fund provision** that facilitates the orderly retirement of the bond issue. On rare occasions the firm may be required to deposit money with a trustee, which invests the funds and then uses the accumulated sum to retire the bonds when they mature. Usually, though, the sinking fund is used to buy back a certain percentage of the issue each year. A failure to meet the sinking fund requirement causes the bond to be thrown into default, which may force the company into bankruptcy. Obviously, a sinking fund can constitute a significant cash drain on the firm.

In most cases, the firm is given the right to handle the sinking fund in either of two ways:

1. The company can call in for redemption (at par value) a certain percentage of the bonds each year; for example, it might be able to call 5 percent of the total original amount of the issue at a price of $1,000 per bond. The bonds are numbered serially, and those called for redemption are determined by a lottery administered by the trustee.
2. The company may buy the required number of bonds on the open market.

The firm will choose the least-cost method. If interest rates have risen, causing bond prices to fall, it will buy bonds in the open market at a discount; if interest rates have fallen, it will call the bonds. Note that a call for sinking fund purposes is quite different from a refunding call as discussed above. A sinking fund call typically requires no call premium, but only a small percentage of the issue is normally callable in any one year.[5]

---

[5]Some sinking funds require the issuer to pay a call premium.

Although sinking funds are designed to protect bondholders by ensuring that an issue is retired in an orderly fashion, you should recognize that sinking funds can work to the detriment of bondholders. For example, suppose the bond carries a 10 percent interest rate, but yields on similar bonds have fallen to 7.5 percent. A sinking fund call at par would require an investor to give up a bond that pays $100 of interest and then to reinvest in a bond that pays only $75 per year. This obviously harms those bondholders whose bonds are called. On balance, however, bonds that have a sinking fund are regarded as being safer than those without such a provision, so at the time they are issued sinking fund bonds have lower coupon rates than otherwise similar bonds without sinking funds.

Other Features

Several other types of bonds are used sufficiently often to warrant mention. First, **convertible bonds** are bonds that are convertible into shares of common stock, at a fixed price, at the option of the bondholder. Convertibles have a lower coupon rate than nonconvertible debt, but they offer investors a chance for capital gains in exchange for the lower coupon rate. Bonds issued with **warrants** are similar to convertibles. Warrants are options that permit the holder to buy stock for a stated price, thereby providing a capital gain if the price of the stock rises. Bonds that are issued with warrants, like convertibles, carry lower coupon rates than straight bonds. Convertibles and warrants are discussed in detail in Chapter 21.

Another type of bond is an **income bond,** which pays interest only if the interest is earned. These securities cannot bankrupt a company, but from an investor's standpoint they are riskier than "regular" bonds. Yet another bond is the **indexed,** or **purchasing power, bond,** which first became popular in Brazil, Israel, and a few other countries plagued by high inflation rates. The interest rate paid on these bonds is based on an inflation index such as the consumer price index, so the interest paid rises automatically when the inflation rate rises, thus protecting the bondholders against inflation. In January 1997, the U.S. Treasury began issuing indexed bonds, and they currently pay a rate that is roughly 2 to 4 percent plus the rate of inflation during the past year.

Self-Test Questions

Define floating rate bonds and zero coupon bonds.

What problem was solved by the introduction of long-term floating rate debt, and how is the rate on such bonds determined?

Why is a call provision advantageous to a bond issuer? When will the issuer initiate a refunding call? Why?

What are the two ways a sinking fund can be handled? Which method will be chosen by the firm if interest rates have risen? If interest rates have fallen?

Are securities that provide for a sinking fund regarded as being riskier than those without this type of provision? Explain.

What is the difference between a call for sinking fund purposes and a refunding call?

Define convertible bonds, bonds with warrants, income bonds, and indexed bonds.

Why do bonds with warrants and convertible bonds have lower coupons than similarly rated bonds that do not have these features?

Bond Valuation

The value of any financial asset—a stock, a bond, a lease, or even a physical asset such as an apartment building or a piece of machinery—is simply the present value of the cash flows the asset is expected to produce.

The cash flows from a specific bond depend on its contractual features as described above. For a standard coupon-bearing bond such as the one issued by MicroDrive, the cash flows consist of interest payments during the 15-year life of the bond, plus the amount borrowed (generally the $1,000 par value) when the bond matures. In the case of a floating rate bond, the interest payments vary over time. In the case of a zero coupon bond, there are no interest payments, only the face amount when the bond matures. For a "regular" bond with a fixed coupon rate, here is the situation:

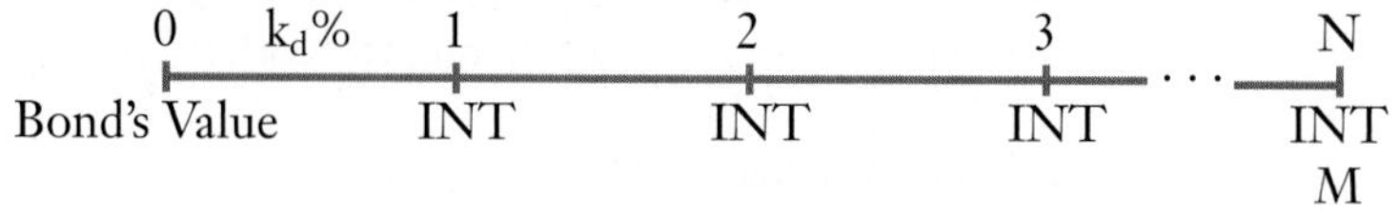

Here

k_d = the bond's market rate of interest = 10%. This is the discount rate that is used to calculate the present value of the bond's cash flows. Note that k_d is *not* the coupon interest rate, and it is equal to the coupon rate only if (as in this case) the bond is selling at par. Generally, most coupon bonds are issued at par, which implies that the coupon rate is set at k_d. Thereafter, interest rates as measured by k_d will fluctuate, but the coupon rate is fixed, so k_d will equal the coupon rate only by chance. We used the term "i" or "I" to designate the interest rate in Chapter 8 because those terms are used on financial calculators, but "k," with the subscript "d" to designate the rate on a debt security, is normally used in finance.[6]

N = the number of years before the bond matures = 15. Note that N declines each year after the bond was issued, so a bond that had a maturity of 15 years when it was issued (original maturity = 15) will have N = 14 after one year, N = 13 after two years, and so on. Note also that at this point we assume that the bond pays interest once a year, or annually, so N is measured in years. Later on, we will deal with semiannual payment bonds, which pay interest each six months.

INT = dollars of interest paid each year = Coupon rate × Par value = 0.10($1,000) = $100. In calculator terminology, INT = PMT = 100. If the bond had been a semiannual payment bond, the payment would have been $50 each six months. The payment would be zero if MicroDrive had issued zero coupon bonds, and it would vary if the bond was a "floater."

M = the par, or maturity, value of the bond = $1,000. This amount must be paid off at maturity.

We can now redraw the time line to show the numerical values for all variables except the bond's value:

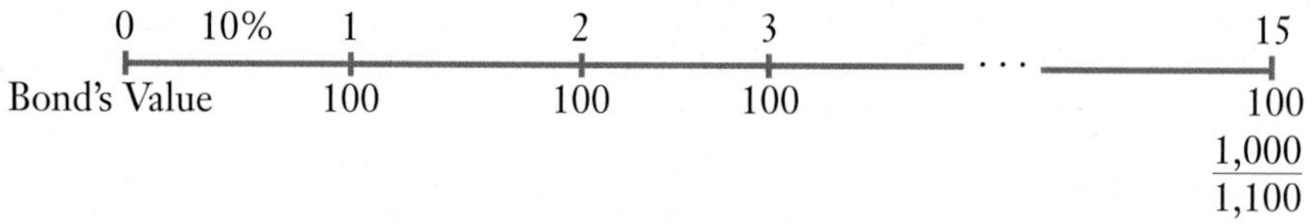

The following general equation, written in several forms, can be solved to find the value of any bond:

[6]The appropriate interest rate on debt securities was discussed in Chapter 5. The bond's risk, liquidity, and years to maturity, as well as supply and demand conditions in the capital markets, all influence the interest rate on bonds.

$$\text{Bond's value} = V_B = \frac{INT}{(1+k_d)^1} + \frac{INT}{(1+k_d)^2} + \cdots + \frac{INT}{(1+k_d)^N} + \frac{M}{(1+k_d)^N}$$
$$= \sum_{t=1}^{N} \frac{INT}{(1+k_d)^t} + \frac{M}{(1+k_d)^N} \qquad \textbf{(9-1)}$$
$$= INT\left(\frac{1 - \frac{1}{(1+k_d)^N}}{k_d}\right) + \frac{M}{(1+k_d)^N}$$
$$= INT(PVIFA_{k_d,N}) + M(PVIF_{k_d,N}).$$

Inserting values for our particular bond, we have

$$V_B = \sum_{t=1}^{15} \frac{\$100}{(1.10)^t} + \frac{\$1{,}000}{(1.10)^{15}}$$
$$= \$100\left(\frac{1 - \frac{1}{(1.1)^{15}}}{0.1}\right) + \frac{\$1{,}000}{(1.1)^{15}}$$
$$= \$100(PVIFA_{10\%,15}) + \$1{,}000(PVIF_{10\%,15}).$$

Note that the cash flows consist of an annuity of N years plus a lump sum payment at the end of Year N, and this fact is reflected in Equation 9-1. Further, Equation 9-1 can be solved by the three procedures discussed in Chapter 8: (1) numerically, (2) with a financial calculator, and (3) with a spreadsheet.

NUMERICAL SOLUTION:

Simply discount each cash flow back to the present and sum these PVs to find the bond's value; see Figure 9-1 for an example. This procedure is not very efficient, especially if the bond has many years to maturity. Alternatively, you could use the formula

FIGURE 9-1 Time Line for MicroDrive Inc.'s Bonds, 10% Interest Rate

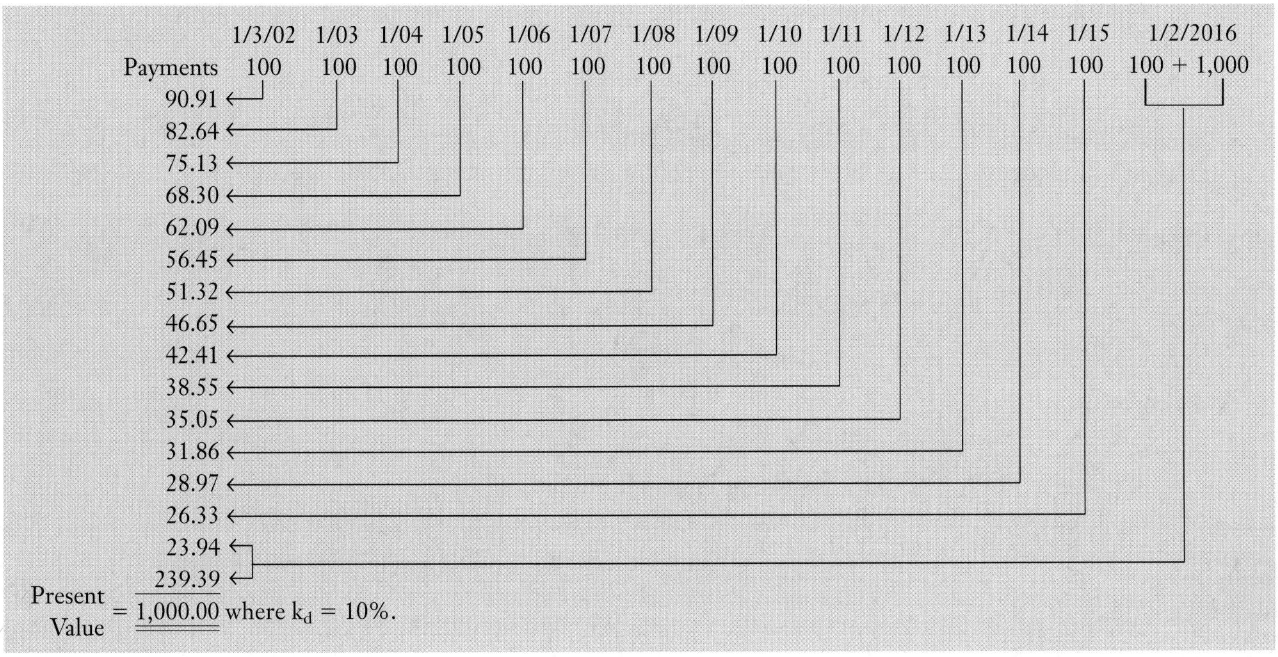

in the third row of Equation 9-1 with a simple or scientific calculator, although this would still be somewhat cumbersome.

FINANCIAL CALCULATOR SOLUTION

In Chapter 8, we worked problems where only four of the five time value of money (TVM) keys were used. However, all five keys are used with bonds. Here is the setup:

Inputs:	15	10		100	1000
	N	I	PV	PMT	FV
Output:			= −1,000		

Simply input N = 15, I = k = 10, INT = PMT = 100, M = FV = 1000, and then press the PV key to find the value of the bond, $1,000. Since the PV is an outflow to the investor, it is shown with a negative sign. The calculator is programmed to solve Equation 9-1: It finds the PV of an annuity of $100 per year for 15 years, discounted at 10 percent, then it finds the PV of the $1,000 maturity payment, and then it adds these two PVs to find the value of the bond.

SPREADSHEET SOLUTION

Here we want to find the PV of the cash flows, so we would use the PV function. Put the cursor on Cell B10, click the function wizard then Financial, PV, and OK. Then fill in the dialog b ox with Rate = 0.1 or F3, Nper = 15 or Q5, Pmt = 100 or C6, FV = 1000 or Q7, and Type = 0 or leave it blank. Then, when you click OK, you will get the value of the bond, −$1,000. Like the financial calculator solution, this is negative because the PMT and FV are positive.

An alternative, and in this case somewhat easier procedure given that the time line has been created, is to use the NPV function. Click the function wizard, then Financial, NPV, and OK. Then input Rate = 0.1 or F3 and Value 1 = C8:Q8. Then click OK to get the answer, $1,000.

	A	B	C	D	E	F	G	H	I	J	K	L	M	N	O	P	Q
1	Spreadsheet for bond value calculation																
2				Going rate,													
3	Coupon rate	10%		or yield		10%											
4																	
5	Time	0	1	2	3	4	5	6	7	8	9	10	11	12	13	14	15
6	Interest Pmt		100	100	100	100	100	100	100	100	100	100	100	100	100	100	100
7	Maturity Pmt																1000
8	Total CF		100	100	100	100	100	100	100	100	100	100	100	100	100	100	1100
9																	
10	PV of CF	1000															

Note that by changing the interest rate in F3, we can instantly find the value of the bond at any other discount rate. Note also that *Excel* and other spreadsheet software packages provide specialized functions for bond prices. For example, in *Excel* you could use the function wizard to enter this formula:

= PRICE(Date(2002,1,3),Date(2017,1,3),10%,10%,100,1,0).

The first two arguments in the function give the current and maturity dates. The next argument is the bond's coupon rate, followed by the current market interest rate, or yield. The fifth argument, 100, is the redemption value of the bond at maturity, expressed as a percent of the face value. The sixth argument is the number of payments per year, and the last argument, 0, tells the program to use the U.S. convention for counting days, which is to assume 30 days per month and 360 days per year. This function produces the value 100, which is the current price expressed as a percent of the bond's par value, which is $1,000. Therefore, you can multiply $1,000 by 100 percent to get the current price, which is $1,000. This function is essential if a bond is being evaluated between coupon payment dates.

Changes in Bond Values over Time

At the time a coupon bond is issued, the coupon is generally set at a level that will cause the market price of the bond to equal its par value. If a lower coupon were set, investors would not be willing to pay $1,000 for the bond, while if a higher coupon were set, investors would clamor for the bond and bid its price up over $1,000. Investment bankers can judge quite precisely the coupon rate that will cause a bond to sell at its $1,000 par value.

A bond that has just been issued is known as a *new issue.* (Investment bankers classify a bond as a new issue for about one month after it has first been issued.) Once the bond has been on the market for a while, it is classified as an *outstanding bond,* also called a *seasoned issue.* Newly issued bonds generally sell very close to par, but the prices of seasoned bonds vary widely from par. Except for floating rate bonds, coupon payments are constant, so when economic conditions change, a bond with a $100 coupon that sold at par when it was issued will sell for more or less than $1,000 thereafter.

MicroDrive's bonds with a 10 percent coupon rate were originally issued at par. If k_d remained constant at 10 percent, what would the value of the bond be one year after it was issued? Now the term to maturity is only 14 years—that is, N = 14. With a financial calculator, just override N = 15 with N = 14, press the PV key, and you find a value of $1,000. If we continued, setting N = 13, N = 12, and so forth, we would see that the value of the bond will remain at $1,000 as long as the going interest rate remains constant at the coupon rate, 10 percent.[7]

---

[7]The bond prices quoted by brokers are calculated as described. However, if you bought a bond between interest payment dates, you would have to pay the basic price plus accrued interest. Thus, if you purchased a MicroDrive bond six months after it was issued, your broker would send you an invoice stating that you must pay $1,000 as the basic price of the bond plus $50 interest, representing one-half the annual interest of $100. The seller of the bond would receive $1,050. If you bought the bond the day before its interest payment date, you would pay $1,000 + (364/365)($100) = $1,099.73. Of course, you would receive an interest payment of $100 at the end of the next day. See Self-Test Problem 1 for a detailed discussion of bond quotations between interest payment dates.

Throughout the chapter, we assume that bonds are being evaluated immediately after an interest payment date. The more expensive financial calculators such as the HP-17B have a built-in calendar that permits the calculation of exact values between interest payment dates, as do spreadsheet programs.

Now suppose interest rates in the economy fell after the MicroDrive bonds were issued, and, as a result, k_d *fell below the coupon rate,* decreasing from 10 to 5 percent. Both the coupon interest payments and the maturity value remain constant, but now 5 percent values for PVIF and PVIFA would have to be used in Equation 9-1. The value of the bond at the end of the first year would be $1,494.96:

$$\begin{aligned} V_B &= \$100(PVIFA_{5\%,14}) + \$1{,}000(PVIF_{5\%,14}) \\ &= \$100(9.8986) + \$1{,}000(0.5051) \\ &= \$989.86 + \$505.10 \\ &= \$1{,}494.96. \end{aligned}$$

With a financial calculator, just change $k_d = I$ from 10 to 5, and then press the PV key to get the answer, $1,494.93. Thus, if k_d fell *below* the coupon rate, the bond would sell above par, or at a *premium.*

The arithmetic of the bond value increase should be clear, but what is the logic behind it? The fact that k_d has fallen to 5 percent means that if you had $1,000 to invest, you could buy new bonds like MicroDrive's (every day some 10 to 12 companies sell new bonds), except that these new bonds would pay $50 of interest each year rather than $100. Naturally, you would prefer $100 to $50, so you would be willing to pay more than $1,000 for a MicroDrive bond to obtain its higher coupons. All investors would react similarly, and as a result, the MicroDrive bonds would be bid up in price to $1,494.93, at which point they would provide the same rate of return to a potential investor as the new bonds, 5 percent.

Assuming that interest rates remain constant at 5 percent for the next 14 years, what would happen to the value of a MicroDrive bond? It would fall gradually from $1,494.93 at present to $1,000 at maturity, when MicroDrive will redeem each bond for $1,000. This point can be illustrated by calculating the value of the bond 1 year later, when it has 13 years remaining to maturity. With a financial calculator, merely input the values for N, I, PMT, and FV, now using N = 13, and press the PV key to find the value of the bond, $1,469.68. Thus, the value of the bond will have fallen from $1,494.93 to $1,469.68, or by $25.25. If you were to calculate the value of the bond at other future dates, the price would continue to fall as the maturity date approached.

Note that if you purchased the bond at a price of $1,494.93 and then sold it one year later with k_d still at 5 percent, you would have a capital loss of $25.25, or a total return of $100.00 − $25.25 = $74.75. Your percentage rate of return would consist of an *interest yield* (also called a *current yield*) plus a *capital gains yield,* calculated as follows:

$$\begin{aligned} \text{Interest, or current, yield} &= \$100/\$1{,}494.93 = 0.0669 = 6.69\% \\ \text{Capital gains yield} &= -\$25.25/\$1{,}494.93 = -0.0169 = -1.69\% \\ \text{Total rate of return, or yield} &= \$74.75/\$1{,}494.93 = 0.0500 = 5.00\% \end{aligned}$$

Had interest rates risen from 10 to 15 percent during the first year after issue rather than fallen from 10 to 5 percent, then you would enter N = 14, I = 15, PMT = 100, and FV = 1000, and then press the PV key to find the value of the bond, $713.78. In this case, the bond would sell at a *discount* of $286.22 below its par value:

$$\begin{aligned} \text{Discount} = \text{Price} - \text{Par value} &= \$713.78 - \$1{,}000.00 \\ &= -\$286.22. \end{aligned}$$

The total expected future return on the bond would again consist of a current yield and a capital gains yield, but now the capital gains yield would be *positive.* The total return would be 15 percent. To see this, calculate the price of the bond with 13 years left to maturity, assuming that interest rates remain at 15 percent. With a calculator, enter N = 13, I = 15, PMT = 100, and FV = 1000, and then press PV to obtain the bond's value, $720.84.

Note that the capital gain for the year is the difference between the bond's value at Year 2 (with 13 years remaining) and the bond's value at Year 1 (with 14 years remaining), or $720.84 − $713.78 = $7.06. The interest yield, capital gains yield, and total yield are calculated as follows:

$$\begin{aligned} \text{Interest, or current, yield} &= \$100/\$713.78 &&= 0.1401 = 14.01\% \\ \text{Capital gains yield} &= \$7.06/\$713.78 &&= 0.0099 = \underline{0.99\%} \\ \text{Total rate of return, or yield} &= \$107.06/\$713.78 &&= 0.1500 = \underline{\underline{15.00\%}} \end{aligned}$$

Figure 9-2 graphs the value of the bond over time, assuming that interest rates in the economy (1) remain constant at 10 percent, (2) fall to 5 percent and then remain constant at that level, or (3) rise to 15 percent and remain constant at that level. Of course, if interest rates do *not* remain constant, then the price of the bond will fluctuate. However, regardless of what future interest rates do, the bond's price will approach $1,000 as it nears the maturity date (barring bankruptcy, in which case the bond's value might fall dramatically).

See ***Ch 09 Tool Kit.xls*** for details.

FIGURE 9-2 Time Path of the Value of a 10% Coupon, $1,000 Par Value Bond When Interest Rates Are 5%, 10%, and 15%

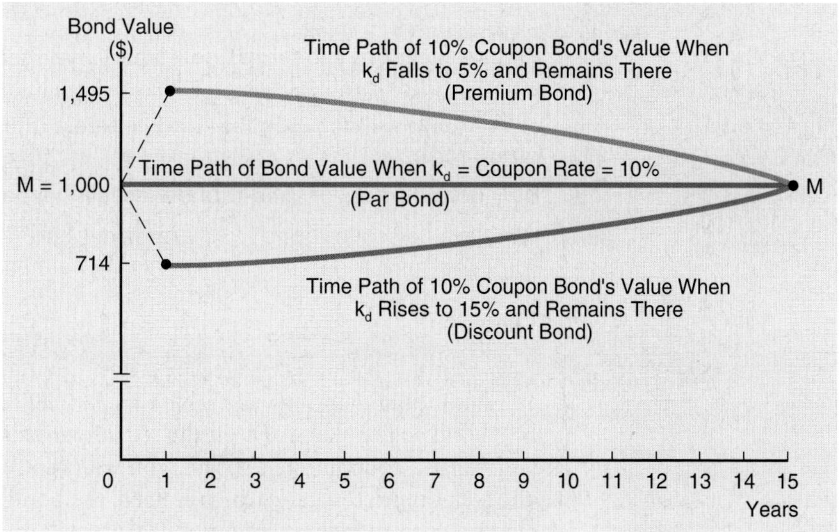

Year	k_d = 5%	k_d = 10%	k_d = 15%
0	—	$1,000	—
1	$1,494.93	1,000	$713.78
.	.	.	.
.	.	.	.
.	.	.	.
15	1,000	1,000	1,000

NOTE: The curves for 5% and 15% have a slight bow.

Figure 9-2 illustrates the following key points:

1. Whenever the going rate of interest, k_d, is equal to the coupon rate, a *fixed-rate* bond will sell at its par value. Normally, the coupon rate is set equal to the going rate when a bond is issued, causing it to sell at par initially.
2. Interest rates do change over time, but the coupon rate remains fixed after the bond has been issued. Whenever the going rate of interest *rises above* the coupon rate, a fixed-rate bond's price will *fall below* its par value. Such a bond is called a **discount bond.**
3. Whenever the going rate of interest *falls below* the coupon rate, a fixed-rate bond's price will *rise above* its par value. Such a bond is called a **premium bond.**
4. Thus, an *increase* in interest rates will cause the prices of outstanding bonds to *fall,* whereas a *decrease* in rates will cause bond prices to *rise.*
5. The market value of a bond will always approach its par value as its maturity date approaches, provided the firm does not go bankrupt.

These points are very important, for they show that bondholders may suffer capital losses or make capital gains, depending on whether interest rates rise or fall after the bond was purchased. And, as we saw in Chapter 5, interest rates do indeed change over time.

Self-Test Questions

Explain, verbally, the following equation:

$$V_B = \sum_{t=1}^{N} \frac{INT}{(1 + k_d)^t} + \frac{M}{(1 + k_d)^N}.$$

What is meant by the terms "new issue" and "seasoned issue"?

Explain what happens to the price of a fixed-rate bond if (1) interest rates rise above the bond's coupon rate or (2) interest rates fall below the bond's coupon rate.

Why do the prices of fixed-rate bonds fall if expectations for inflation rise?

What is a "discount bond"? A "premium bond"?

Bond Yields

If you examine the bond market table of *The Wall Street Journal* or a price sheet put out by a bond dealer, you will typically see information regarding each bond's maturity date, price, and coupon interest rate. You will also see the bond's reported yield. Unlike the coupon interest rate, which is fixed, the bond's yield varies from day to day depending on current market conditions. Moreover, the yield can be calculated in three different ways, and three "answers" can be obtained. These different yields are described in the following sections.

Yield to Maturity

Suppose you were offered a 14-year, 10 percent annual coupon, $1,000 par value bond at a price of $1,494.93. What rate of interest would you earn on your investment if you bought the bond and held it to maturity? This rate is called the bond's **yield to maturity (YTM),** and it is the interest rate generally discussed by investors when they talk about rates of return. The yield to maturity is generally the same as the market rate of interest, k_d, and to find it, all you need to do is solve Equation 9-1 for k_d:

$$V_B = \$1{,}494.93 = \frac{\$100}{(1 + k_d)^1} + \cdots + \frac{\$100}{(1 + k_d)^{14}} + \frac{\$1{,}000}{(1 + k_d)^{14}}.$$

You could substitute values for k_d until you find a value that "works" and forces the sum of the PVs on the right side of the equal sign to equal \$1,494.93. Alternatively, you could substitute values of k_d into the third form of Equation 9-1 until you find a value that works.

Finding k_d = YTM by trial-and-error would be a tedious, time-consuming process, but as you might guess, it is easy with a financial calculator.[8] Here is the setup:

Inputs:	14		−1494.93	100	1000
	N	I	PV	PMT	FV
Output:		= 5			

Simply enter N = 14, PV = −1494.93, PMT = 100, and FV = 1000, and then press the I key. The answer, 5 percent, will then appear.

The yield to maturity is identical to the total rate of return discussed in the preceding section. The yield to maturity can also be viewed as the bond's *promised rate of return*, which is the return that investors will receive if all the promised payments are made. However, the yield to maturity equals the *expected rate of return* only if (1) the probability of default is zero and (2) the bond cannot be called. If there is some default risk, or if the bond may be called, then there is some probability that the promised payments to maturity will not be received, in which case the calculated yield to maturity will differ from the expected return.

The YTM for a bond that sells at par consists entirely of an interest yield, but if the bond sells at a price other than its par value, the YTM will consist of the interest yield plus a positive or negative capital gains yield. Note also that a bond's yield to maturity changes whenever interest rates in the economy change, and this is almost daily. One who purchases a bond and holds it until it matures will receive the YTM that existed on the purchase date, but the bond's calculated YTM will change frequently between the purchase date and the maturity date.

Yield to Call

If you purchased a bond that was callable and the company called it, you would not have the option of holding the bond until it matured. Therefore, the yield to maturity would not be earned. For example, if MicroDrive's 10 percent coupon bonds were callable, and if interest rates fell from 10 percent to 5 percent, then the company could call in the 10 percent bonds, replace them with 5 percent bonds, and save \$100 − \$50 = \$50 interest per bond per year. This would be beneficial to the company, but not to its bondholders.

If current interest rates are well below an outstanding bond's coupon rate, then a callable bond is likely to be called, and investors will estimate its expected rate of return as the **yield to call (YTC)** rather than as the yield to maturity. To calculate the YTC, solve this equation for k_d:

$$\text{Price of bond} = \sum_{t=1}^{N} \frac{\text{INT}}{(1 + k_d)^t} + \frac{\text{Call price}}{(1 + k_d)^N}. \quad \textbf{(9-2)}$$

[8] You could also find the YTM with a spreadsheet. In *Excel*, you would use the Rate function for this bond, inputting Nper = 14, Pmt = 100, PV = −1494.93, FV = 1000, 0 for Type, and leave Guess blank.

Here N is the number of years until the company can call the bond; call price is the price the company must pay in order to call the bond (it is often set equal to the par value plus one year's interest); and k_d is the YTC.

To illustrate, suppose MicroDrive's bonds had a provision that permitted the company, if it desired, to call the bonds 10 years after the issue date at a price of \$1,100. Suppose further that interest rates had fallen, and one year after issuance the going interest rate had declined, causing the price of the bonds to rise to \$1,494.93. Here is the time line and the setup for finding the bond's YTC with a financial calculator:

0	YTC = ?	1	2	...	8	9
−1,494.93		100	100		100	100 1,100

9		−1494.93	100	1100
N	I	PV	PMT	FV
	4.21 = YTC			

The YTC is 4.21 percent—this is the return you would earn if you bought the bond at a price of \$1,494.93 and it was called nine years from today. (The bond could not be called until 10 years after issuance, and one year has gone by, so there are nine years left until the first call date.)

Do you think MicroDrive *will* call the bonds when they become callable? MicroDrive's action would depend on what the going interest rate is when the bonds become callable. If the going rate remains at $k_d = 5\%$, then MicroDrive could save $10\% - 5\% = 5\%$, or \$50 per bond per year, by calling them and replacing the 10 percent bonds with a new 5 percent issue. There would be costs to the company to refund the issue, but the interest savings would probably be worth the cost, so MicroDrive would probably refund the bonds. Therefore, you would probably earn YTC = 4.21% rather than YTM = 5% if you bought the bonds under the indicated conditions.

In the balance of this chapter, we assume that bonds are not callable unless otherwise noted, but some of the end-of-chapter problems deal with yield to call.

Current Yield

If you examine brokerage house reports on bonds, you will often see reference to a bond's **current yield.** The current yield is the annual interest payment divided by the bond's current price. For example, if MicroDrive's bonds with a 10 percent coupon were currently selling at \$985, the bond's current yield would be 10.15 percent (\$100/\$985).

Unlike the yield to maturity, the current yield does not represent the rate of return that investors should expect on the bond. The current yield provides information regarding the amount of cash income that a bond will generate in a given year, but since it does not take account of capital gains or losses that will be realized if the bond is held until maturity (or call), it does not provide an accurate measure of the bond's total expected return.

The fact that the current yield does not provide an accurate measure of a bond's total return can be illustrated with a zero coupon bond. Since zeros pay no annual income, they always have a current yield of zero. This indicates that the bond will not provide any cash interest income, but since the bond will appreciate in value over time, its total rate of return clearly exceeds zero.

Drinking Your Coupons

In 1996 Chateau Teyssier, an English vineyard, was looking for some cash to purchase some additional vines and to modernize its production facilities. Their solution? With the assistance of a leading underwriter, Matrix Securities, the vineyard recently issued 375 bonds, each costing 2,650 British pounds. The issue raised nearly 1 million pounds, which is roughly $1.5 million.

What makes these bonds interesting is that, instead of getting paid with something boring like money, these bonds pay their investors back with wine. Each June until 2002, when the bond matures, investors will receive their "coupons." Between 1997 and 2001, each bond will provide six cases of the vineyard's rose or claret. Starting in 1998 and continuing through maturity in 2002, investors will also receive four cases of its prestigious Saint Emilion Grand Cru. Then, in 2002, they will get their money back.

The bonds are not without risk. The vineyard's owner, Jonathan Malthus, acknowledges that the quality of the wine, "is at the mercy of the gods."

Source: Steven Irvine, "My Wine Is My Bond, and I Drink My Coupons," *Euromoney*, July 1996, 7. Used with permission.

Self-Test Questions

Explain the difference between the yield to maturity and the yield to call.

How does a bond's current yield differ from its total return?

Could the current yield exceed the total return?

Bonds with Semiannual Coupons

Although some bonds pay interest annually, the vast majority actually pay interest semiannually. To evaluate semiannual payment bonds, we must modify the valuation model (Equation 9-1) as follows:

1. Divide the annual coupon interest payment by 2 to determine the dollars of interest paid each six months.
2. Multiply the years to maturity, N, by 2 to determine the number of semiannual periods.
3. Divide the nominal (quoted) interest rate, k_d, by 2 to determine the periodic (semiannual) interest rate.

By making these changes, we obtain the following equation for finding the value of a bond that pays interest semiannually:

$$V_B = \sum_{t=1}^{2N} \frac{INT/2}{(1 + k_d/2)^t} + \frac{M}{(1 + k_d/2)^{2N}} \quad \textbf{(9-1a)}$$

To illustrate, assume now that MicroDrive's bonds pay $50 interest each six months rather than $100 at the end of each year. Thus, each interest payment is only half as large, but there are twice as many of them. The coupon rate is thus "10 percent, semiannual payments." This is the nominal, or quoted, rate.[9]

[9]In this situation, the nominal coupon rate of "10 percent, semiannually," is the rate that bond dealers, corporate treasurers, and investors generally would discuss. Of course, the *effective annual rate* would be higher than 10 percent at the time the bond was issued:

$$EAR = EFF\% = \left(1 + \frac{k_{Nom}}{m}\right)^m - 1 = \left(1 + \frac{0.10}{2}\right)^2 - 1 = (1.05)^2 - 1 = 10.25\%.$$

Note also that 10 percent with annual payments is different than 10 percent with semiannual payments. Thus, we have assumed a change in effective rates in this section from the situation in the preceding section, where we assumed 10 percent with annual payments.

When the going (nominal) rate of interest is 5 percent with semiannual compounding, the value of this 15-year bond is found as follows:

Inputs:	30	2.5		50	1000
	N	I	PV	PMT	FV
Output:			= −1,523.26		

Enter N = 30, k = I = 2.5, PMT = 50, FV = 1000, and then press the PV key to obtain the bond's value, \$1,523.26. The value with semiannual interest payments is slightly larger than \$1,518.98, the value when interest is paid annually. This higher value occurs because interest payments are received somewhat faster under semiannual compounding.

Self-Test Question

Describe how the annual bond valuation formula is changed to evaluate semiannual coupon bonds. Then, write out the revised formula.

Assessing the Risk of a Bond

Interest Rate Risk

As we saw in Chapter 5, interest rates go up and down over time, and an increase in interest rates leads to a decline in the value of outstanding bonds. This risk of a decline in bond values due to rising interest rates is called **interest rate risk.** To illustrate, suppose you bought some 10 percent MicroDrive bonds at a price of \$1,000, and interest rates in the following year rose to 15 percent. As we saw earlier, the price of the bonds would fall to \$713.78, so you would have a loss of \$286.22 per bond.[10] Interest rates can and do rise, and rising rates cause a loss of value for bondholders. Thus, people or firms who invest in bonds are exposed to risk from changing interest rates.

One's exposure to interest rate risk is higher on bonds with long maturities than on those maturing in the near future.[11] This point can be demonstrated by showing how the value of a 1-year bond with a 10 percent annual coupon fluctuates with changes in k_d, and then comparing these changes with those on a 14-year bond as calculated previously. The 1-year bond's values at different interest rates are shown below:

[10]You would have an *accounting* (and tax) loss only if you sold the bond; if you held it to maturity, you would not have such a loss. However, even if you did not sell, you would still have suffered a *real economic loss in an opportunity cost sense* because you would have lost the opportunity to invest at 15 percent and would be stuck with a 10 percent bond in a 15 percent market. In an economic sense, "paper losses" are just as bad as realized accounting losses.

[11]Actually, a bond's maturity and coupon rate both affect interest rate risk. Low coupons mean that most of the bond's return will come from repayment of principal, whereas on a high coupon bond with the same maturity, more of the cash flows will come in during the early years due to the relatively large coupon payments. A measurement called "duration," which finds the average number of years the bond's PV of cash flows remain outstanding, has been developed to combine maturity and coupons. A zero coupon bond, which has no interest payments and whose payments all come at maturity, has a duration equal to the bond's maturity. Coupon bonds all have durations that are shorter than maturity, and the higher the coupon rate, the shorter the duration. Bonds with longer duration are exposed to more interest rate risk. See the Web/CD Extension to Chapter 24 for a more detailed discussion of duration.

Value at $k_d = 5\%$:

Inputs:	1	5		100	1000
	N	I	PV	PMT	FV
Output:		−1,047.62 = 1-year bond's value at $k_d = 5\%$.			

Value at $k_d = 10\%$:

Inputs:	1	10		100	1000
	N	I	PV	PMT	FV
Output:		−1,000.00 = 1-year bond's value at $k_d = 10\%$.			

Value at $k_d = 15\%$:

Inputs:	1	15		100	1000
	N	I	PV	PMT	FV
Output:		−956.52 = 1-year bond's value at $k_d = 15\%$.			

You would obtain the first value with a financial calculator by entering N = 1, I = 5, PMT = 100, and FV = 1000, and then pressing PV to get $1,047.62. With everything still in your calculator, enter I = 10 to override the old I = 5, and press PV to find the bond's value at k_d = I = 10; it is $1,000. Then enter I = 15 and press the PV key to find the last bond value, $956.52.

The values of the 1-year and 14-year bonds at several current market interest rates are summarized and plotted in Figure 9-3. Note how much more sensitive the price of the 14-year bond is to changes in interest rates. At a 10 percent interest rate, both the 14-year and the 1-year bonds are valued at $1,000. When rates rise to 15 percent, the 14-year bond falls to $713.78, but the 1-year bond only falls to $956.52.

For bonds with similar coupons, this differential sensitivity to changes in interest rates always holds true—the longer the maturity of the bond, the more its price changes in response to a given change in interest rates. Thus, even if the risk of default on two bonds is exactly the same, the one with the longer maturity is exposed to more risk from a rise in interest rates.[12]

The logical explanation for this difference in interest rate risk is simple. Suppose you bought a 14-year bond that yielded 10 percent, or $100 a year. Now suppose

---

[12]If a 10-year bond were plotted in Figure 9-3, its curve would lie between those of the 14-year bond and the 1-year bond. The curve of a 1-month bond would be almost horizontal, indicating that its price would change very little in response to an interest rate change, but a 100-year bond (or a perpetuity) would have a very steep slope. Also, zero coupon bond prices are quite sensitive to interest rate changes, and the longer the maturity of the zero, the greater its price sensitivity. Therefore, 30-year zero coupon bonds have a huge amount of interest rate risk.

See ***Ch 09 Tool Kit.xls*** for details.

FIGURE 9-3 Value of Long- and Short-Term 10% Annual Coupon Bonds at Different Market Interest Rates

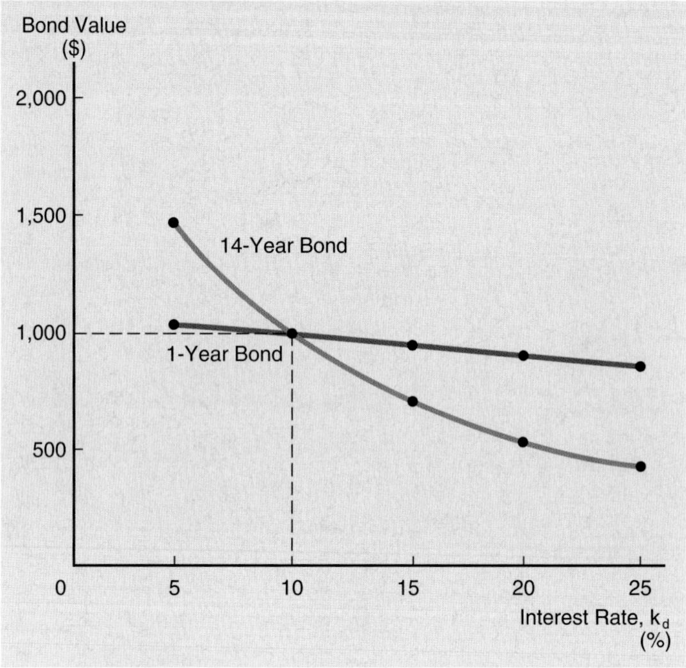

Current Market Interest Rate, k_d	Value of 1-Year Bond	Value of 14-Year Bond
5%	$1,047.62	$1,494.93
10	1,000.00	1,000.00
15	956.52	713.78
20	916.67	538.94
25	880.00	426.39

NOTE: Bond values were calculated using a financial calculator assuming annual, or once-a-year, compounding.

interest rates on comparable-risk bonds rose to 15 percent. You would be stuck with only $100 of interest for the next 14 years. On the other hand, had you bought a 1-year bond, you would have a low return for only 1 year. At the end of the year, you would get your $1,000 back, and you could then reinvest it and receive 15 percent, or $150 per year, for the next 13 years. Thus, interest rate risk reflects the length of time one is committed to a given investment.

As we just saw, the prices of long-term bonds are more sensitive to changes in interest rates than are short-term bonds. To induce an investor to take this extra risk, long-term bonds must have a higher expected rate of return than short-term bonds. This additional return is the maturity risk premium (MRP), which we discussed in Chapter 5. Therefore, one might expect to see higher yields on long-term than on short-term bonds. Does this actually happen? Generally, the answer is yes. Recall from Chapter 5 that the yield curve usually is upward sloping, which is consistent with the idea that longer maturity bonds must have a higher expected rate of return to compensate for their higher risk.

Reinvestment Rate Risk

As we saw in the preceding section, an *increase* in interest rates will hurt bondholders because it will lead to a decline in the value of a bond portfolio. But can a *decrease* in interest rates also hurt bondholders? The answer is yes, because if interest rates fall, a bondholder will probably suffer a reduction in his or her income. For example, consider a retiree who has a portfolio of bonds and lives off the income they produce. The bonds, on average, have a coupon rate of 10 percent. Now suppose interest rates decline to 5 percent. Many of the bonds will be called, and as calls occur, the bondholder will have to replace 10 percent bonds with 5 percent bonds. Even bonds that are not callable will mature, and when they do, they will have to be replaced with lower-yielding bonds. Thus, our retiree will suffer a reduction of income.

The risk of an income decline due to a drop in interest rates is called **reinvestment rate risk,** and its importance has been demonstrated to all bondholders in recent years as a result of the sharp drop in rates since the mid-1980s. Reinvestment rate risk is obviously high on callable bonds. It is also high on short maturity bonds, because the shorter the maturity of a bond, the fewer the years when the relatively high old interest rate will be earned, and the sooner the funds will have to be reinvested at the new low rate. Thus, retirees whose primary holdings are short-term securities, such as bank CDs and short-term bonds, are hurt badly by a decline in rates, but holders of long-term bonds continue to enjoy their old high rates.

Comparing Interest Rate and Reinvestment Rate Risk

Note that interest rate risk relates to the *value* of the bonds in a portfolio, while reinvestment rate risk relates to the *income* the portfolio produces. If you hold long-term bonds, you will face interest rate risk, that is, the value of your bonds will decline if interest rates rise, but you will not face much reinvestment rate risk, so your income will be stable. On the other hand, if you hold short-term bonds, you will not be exposed to much interest rate risk, so the value of your portfolio will be stable, but you will be exposed to reinvestment rate risk, and your income will fluctuate with changes in interest rates.

We see, then, that no fixed-rate bond can be considered totally riskless—even most Treasury bonds are exposed to both interest rate and reinvestment rate risk.[13] One can minimize interest rate risk by holding short-term bonds, or one can minimize reinvestment rate risk by holding long-term bonds, but the actions that lower one type of risk increase the other. Bond portfolio managers try to balance these two risks, but some risk generally remains in any bond.

Self-Test Questions

Differentiate between interest rate risk and reinvestment rate risk.

To which type of risk are holders of long-term bonds more exposed? Short-term bondholders?

Default Risk

Another important risk associated with bonds is default risk. If the issuer defaults, investors receive less than the promised return on the bond. Therefore, investors need to assess a bond's default risk before making a purchase. Recall from Chapter 5 that

[13]Note, though, that indexed Treasury bonds are essentially riskless, but they pay a relatively low real rate. Also, risks have not disappeared—they are simply transferred from bondholders to taxpayers.

the quoted interest rate includes a default risk premium—the greater the default risk, the higher the bond's yield to maturity. The default risk on Treasury securities is zero, but default risk can be substantial for corporate and municipal bonds.

Suppose two bonds have the same promised cash flows, coupon rate, maturity, liquidity, and inflation exposure, but one bond has more default risk than the other. Investors will naturally pay less for the bond with the greater chance of default. As a result, bonds with higher default risk will have higher interest rates: $k_d = k^* + IP + DRP + LP + MRP$.

If its default risk changes, this will affect the price of a bond. For example, if the default risk of the MicroDrive bonds increases, the bonds' price will fall and the yield to maturity ($YTM = k_d$) will increase.

In this section we consider some issues related to default risk. First, we show that corporations can influence the default risk of their bonds by changing the type of bonds they issue. Second we discuss bond ratings, which are used to measure default risk. Third, we describe the "junk bond market," which is the market for bonds with a relatively high probability of default. Finally, we consider bankruptcy and reorganization, which affect how much an investor will recover if a default occurs.

Bond Contract Provisions That Influence Default Risk

Default risk is affected by both the financial strength of the issuer and the terms of the bond contract, especially whether collateral has been pledged to secure the bond. Several types of contract provisions are discussed below.

Bond Indentures An **indenture** is a legal document that spells out the rights of both bondholders and the issuing corporation, and a **trustee** is an official (usually a bank) who represents the bondholders and makes sure the terms of the indenture are carried out. The indenture may be several hundred pages in length, and it will include **restrictive covenants** that cover such points as the conditions under which the issuer can pay off the bonds prior to maturity, the level at which the issuer's times-interest-earned ratio must be maintained if the company is to issue additional debt, and restrictions against the payment of dividends unless earnings meet certain specifications.

The trustee is responsible for monitoring the covenants and for taking appropriate action if a violation does occur. What constitutes "appropriate action" varies with the circumstances. It might be that to insist on immediate compliance would result in bankruptcy and possibly large losses on the bonds. In such a case, the trustee might decide that the bondholders would be better served by giving the company a chance to work out its problems and thus avoid forcing it into bankruptcy.

The Securities and Exchange Commission (1) approves indentures and (2) makes sure that all indenture provisions are met before allowing a company to sell new securities to the public. Also, it should be noted that the indentures of many larger corporations were actually written in the 1930s or 1940s, and that many issues of new bonds sold since then were covered by the same indenture. The interest rates on the bonds, and perhaps also the maturities, varies depending on market conditions at the time of each issue, but bondholders' protection as spelled out in the indenture is the same for all bonds of the same type. A firm will have different indentures for each of the major types of bonds it issues. For example, one indenture will cover its first mortgage bonds, another its debentures, and a third its convertible bonds.

Mortgage Bonds Under a **mortgage bond,** the corporation pledges certain assets as security for the bond. To illustrate, in 2000 Billingham Corporation needed $10 million to build a major regional distribution center. Bonds in the amount of $4 million, secured by a *first mortgage* on the property, were issued. (The remaining $6 million was financed with equity capital.) If Billingham defaults on the bonds, the bondholders can foreclose on the property and sell it to satisfy their claims.

If Billingham chose to, it could issue *second mortgage bonds* secured by the same $10 million of assets. In the event of liquidation, the holders of these second mortgage bonds would have a claim against the property, but only after the first mortgage bondholders had been paid off in full. Thus, second mortgages are sometimes called *junior mortgages*, because they are junior in priority to the claims of *senior mortgages*, or *first mortgage bonds*.

All mortgage bonds are subject to an indenture. The indentures of many major corporations were written 20, 30, 40, or more years ago. These indentures are generally "open ended," meaning that new bonds can be issued from time to time under the same indenture. However, the amount of new bonds that can be issued is virtually always limited to a specified percentage of the firm's total "bondable property," which generally includes all land, plant, and equipment.

For example, in the past Savannah Electric Company had provisions in its bond indenture that allowed it to issue first mortgage bonds totaling up to 60 percent of its fixed assets. If its fixed assets totaled $1 billion, and if it had $500 million of first mortgage bonds outstanding, it could, by the property test, issue another $100 million of bonds (60% of $1 billion = $600 million).

At times, Savannah Electric was unable to issue any new first mortgage bonds because of another indenture provision: its times-interest-earned (TIE) ratio was below 2.5, the minimum coverage that it must have in order to sell new bonds. Thus, although Savannah Electric passed the property test, it failed the coverage test, so it could not issue any more first mortgage bonds. Savannah Electric then had to finance with junior bonds. Because first mortgage bonds carried lower interest rates, this restriction was costly.

Savannah Electric's neighbor, Georgia Power Company, had more flexibility under its indenture—its interest coverage requirement was only 2.0. In hearings before the Georgia Public Service Commission, it was suggested that Savannah Electric should change its indenture coverage to 2.0 so that it could issue more first mortgage bonds. However, this was simply not possible—the holders of the outstanding bonds would have to approve the change, and they would not vote for a change that would seriously weaken their position.

Debentures A **debenture** is an unsecured bond, and as such it provides no lien against specific property as security for the obligation. Debenture holders are, therefore, general creditors whose claims are protected by property not otherwise pledged. In practice, the use of debentures depends both on the nature of the firm's assets and on its general credit strength. Extremely strong companies often use debentures; they simply do not need to put up property as security for their debt. Debentures are also issued by weak companies that have already pledged most of their assets as collateral for mortgage loans. In this latter case, the debentures are quite risky, and they will bear a high interest rate.

Subordinated Debentures The term *subordinate* means "below," or "inferior to," and, in the event of bankruptcy, subordinated debt has claims on assets only after senior debt has been paid off. **Subordinated debentures** may be subordinated either to designated notes payable (usually bank loans) or to all other debt. In the event of liquidation or reorganization, holders of subordinated debentures cannot be paid until all senior debt, as named in the debentures' indenture, has been paid. Precisely how subordination works, and how it strengthens the position of senior debtholders, is explained in detail in Chapter 25.

Development Bonds Some companies may be in a position to benefit from the sale of either **development bonds** or **pollution control bonds**. State and local governments may set up both *industrial development agencies* and *pollution control agencies.* These agencies are allowed, under certain circumstances, to sell **tax-exempt bonds,** then to make the proceeds available to corporations for specific uses deemed (by Congress) to be in the public interest. Thus, an industrial development agency in Florida might sell bonds to provide funds for a paper company to build a plant in the Florida Panhandle, where unemployment is high. Similarly, a Detroit pollution control agency might sell bonds to provide Ford with funds to be used to purchase pollution control equipment. In both cases, the income from the bonds would be tax exempt to the holders, so the bonds would sell at relatively low interest rates. Note, however, that these bonds are guaranteed by the corporation that will use the funds, not by a governmental unit, so their rating reflects the credit strength of the corporation using the funds.

Municipal Bond Insurance Municipalities can have their bonds insured, which means that an insurance company guarantees to pay the coupon and principal payments should the issuer default. This reduces risk to investors, who will thus accept a lower coupon rate for an insured bond vis-à-vis an uninsured one. Even though the municipality must pay a fee to get its bonds insured, its savings due to the lower coupon rate often makes insurance cost-effective. Keep in mind that the insurers are private companies, and the value added by the insurance depends on the creditworthiness of the insurer. However, the larger ones are strong companies, and their own ratings are AAA. Therefore, the bonds they insure are also rated AAA, regardless of the credit strength of the municipal issuer. Bond ratings are discussed in the next section.

Bond Ratings

Since the early 1900s, bonds have been assigned quality ratings that reflect their probability of going into default. The three major rating agencies are Moody's Investors Service (Moody's), Standard & Poor's Corporation (S&P), and Fitch Investors Service. Moody's and S&P's rating designations are shown in Table 9-1.[14] The triple- and double-A bonds are extremely safe. Single-A and triple-B bonds are also strong enough to be called **investment grade bonds,** and they are the lowest-rated bonds that many banks and other institutional investors are permitted by law to hold. Double-B and lower bonds are speculative, or **junk bonds.** These bonds have a

[14]In the discussion to follow, reference to the S&P code is intended to imply the Moody's and Fitch's codes as well. Thus, triple-B bonds mean both BBB and Baa bonds; double-B bonds mean both BB and Ba bonds; and so on.

TABLE 9-1 Moody's and S&P Bond Ratings

	Investment Grade				Junk Bonds			
Moody's	Aaa	Aa	A	Baa	Ba	B	Caa	C
S&P	AAA	AA	A	BBB	BB	B	CCC	D

NOTE: Both Moody's and S&P use "modifiers" for bonds rated below triple-A. S&P uses a plus and minus system; thus, A+ designates the strongest A-rated bonds and A− the weakest. Moody's uses a 1, 2, or 3 designation, with 1 denoting the strongest and 3 the weakest; thus, within the double-A category, Aa1 is the best, Aa2 is average, and Aa3 is the weakest.

significant probability of going into default. A later section discusses junk bonds in more detail.

Bond Rating Criteria Bond ratings are based on both qualitative and quantitative factors, some of which are listed below:

1. Various ratios, including the debt ratio, the times-interest-earned ratio, and the EBITDA coverage ratio. The better the ratios, the higher the rating.
2. Mortgage provisions: Is the bond secured by a mortgage? If it is, and if the property has a high value in relation to the amount of bonded debt, the bond's rating is enhanced.
3. Subordination provisions: Is the bond subordinated to other debt? If so, it will be rated at least one notch below the rating it would have if it were not subordinated. Conversely, a bond with other debt subordinated to it will have a somewhat higher rating.
4. Guarantee provisions: Some bonds are guaranteed by other firms. If a weak company's debt is guaranteed by a strong company (usually the weak company's parent), the bond will be given the strong company's rating.
5. Sinking fund: Does the bond have a sinking fund to ensure systematic repayment? This feature is a plus factor to the rating agencies.
6. Maturity: Other things the same, a bond with a shorter maturity will be judged less risky than a longer-term bond, and this will be reflected in the ratings.
7. Stability: Are the issuer's sales and earnings stable?
8. Regulation: Is the issuer regulated, and could an adverse regulatory climate cause the company's economic position to decline? Regulation is especially important for utilities and telephone companies.
9. Antitrust: Are any antitrust actions pending against the firm that could erode its position?
10. Overseas operations: What percentage of the firm's sales, assets, and profits are from overseas operations, and what is the political climate in the host countries?
11. Environmental factors: Is the firm likely to face heavy expenditures for pollution control equipment?
12. Product liability: Are the firm's products safe? The tobacco companies today are under pressure, and so are their bond ratings.
13. Pension liabilities: Does the firm have unfunded pension liabilities that could pose a future problem?
14. Labor unrest: Are there potential labor problems on the horizon that could weaken the firm's position? As this is written, a number of airlines face this problem, and it has caused their ratings to be lowered.
15. Accounting policies: If a firm uses relatively conservative accounting policies, its reported earnings will be of "higher quality" than if it uses less conservative procedures. Thus, conservative accounting policies are a plus factor in bond ratings.

Representatives of the rating agencies have consistently stated that no precise formula is used to set a firm's rating; all the factors listed, plus others, are taken into account, but not in a mathematically precise manner. Statistical studies have borne out this contention, for researchers who have tried to predict bond ratings on the basis of quantitative data have had only limited success, indicating that the agencies use subjective judgment when establishing a firm's rating.

Nevertheless, as we see in Table 9-2, there is a strong correlation between bond ratings and many of the ratios that we described in Chapter 3. Not surprisingly, companies with lower debt ratios, higher free cash flow to debt, higher returns on invested capital, higher EBITDA coverage ratios, and higher times-interest-earned (TIE) ratios typically have higher bond ratings.

TABLE 9-2 Bond Rating Criteria; Three-Year (1996–1998) Median Financial Ratios for Different Bond Rating Classifications

	AAA	AA	A	BBB	BB	B	CCC
Times-interest-earned (EBIT/Interest)	12.9×	9.2×	7.2×	4.1×	2.5×	1.2×	(0.9)×
EBITDA interest coverage (EBITDA/Interest)	18.7×	14.0×	10.0×	6.3×	3.9×	2.3×	0.2×
Net cash flow/Total debt	89.7%	67.0%	49.5%	32.2%	20.1%	10.5%	7.4%
Free cash flow/Total debt	40.5%	21.6%	17.4%	6.3%	1.0%	(4.0)%	(25.4)%
Return on capital	30.6%	25.1%	19.6%	15.4%	12.6%	9.2%	(8.8)%
Operating income/Sales[a]	30.9%	25.2%	17.9%	15.8%	14.4%	11.2%	5.0%
Long-term debt/Total capital	21.4%	29.3%	33.3%	40.8%	55.3%	68.8%	71.5%
Total debt/Total capital	31.8%	37.0%	39.2%	46.4%	58.5%	71.4%	79.4%

NOTE:
[a]Operating income here is defined as sales minus cost of goods manufactured (before depreciation and amortization), selling, general and administrative, and research and development costs.

Source: "Adjusted Key U.S. Industrial Financial Ratios," *Standard & Poor's CreditWeek*, July 28, 1999, 14–20.

Importance of Bond Ratings Bond ratings are important both to firms and to investors. First, because a bond's rating is an indicator of its default risk, the rating has a direct, measurable influence on the bond's interest rate and the firm's cost of debt. Second, most bonds are purchased by institutional investors rather than individuals, and many institutions are restricted to investment-grade securities. Thus, if a firm's bonds fall below BBB, it will have a difficult time selling new bonds because many potential purchasers will not be allowed to buy them. In addition, the covenants may stipulate that the interest rate is automatically increased if the rating falls below a specified level.

As a result of their higher risk and more restricted market, lower-grade bonds have higher required rates of return, k_d, than high-grade bonds. Figure 9-4 illustrates this point. In each of the years shown on the graph, U.S. government bonds have had the lowest yields, AAAs have been next, and BBB bonds have had the highest yields. The figure also shows that the gaps between yields on the three types of bonds vary over time, indicating that the cost differentials, or risk premiums, fluctuate from year to year. This point is highlighted in Figure 9-5, which gives the yields on the three types of bonds and the risk premiums for AAA and BBB bonds in June 1963 and May 2000.[15] Note first that the risk-free rate, or vertical axis intercept, rose 2.5 percentage points from 1963 to 2000, primarily reflecting the increase in realized and anticipated inflation. Second, the slope of the line has increased since 1963, indicating an increase in investors' risk aversion. Thus, the penalty for having a low credit rating varies over time. Occasionally, as in 1963, the penalty is quite small, but at other times it is large. These slope differences reflect investors' aversion to risk.

[15]The term *risk premium* ought to reflect only the difference in expected (and required) returns between two securities that results from differences in their risk. However, the differences between *yields to maturity* on different types of bonds consist of (1) a true risk premium; (2) a liquidity premium, which reflects the fact that U.S. Treasury bonds are more readily marketable than most corporate bonds; (3) a call premium, because most Treasury bonds are not callable whereas corporate bonds are; and (4) an expected loss differential, which reflects the probability of loss on the corporate bonds. As an example of the last point, suppose the yield to maturity on a BBB bond was 9.0 percent versus 6.5 percent on government bonds, but there was a 5 percent probability of total default loss on the corporate bond. In this case, the expected return on the BBB bond would be 0.95(9.0%) + 0.05(0%) = 8.6%, and the risk premium would be 2.1 percent, not the full 2.5 percentage points difference in "promised" yields to maturity. Because of all these points, the risk premiums given in Figure 9-5 overstate somewhat the true (but unmeasurable) theoretical risk premiums.

FIGURE 9-4 Yields on Selected Long-Term Bonds, 1960–2000

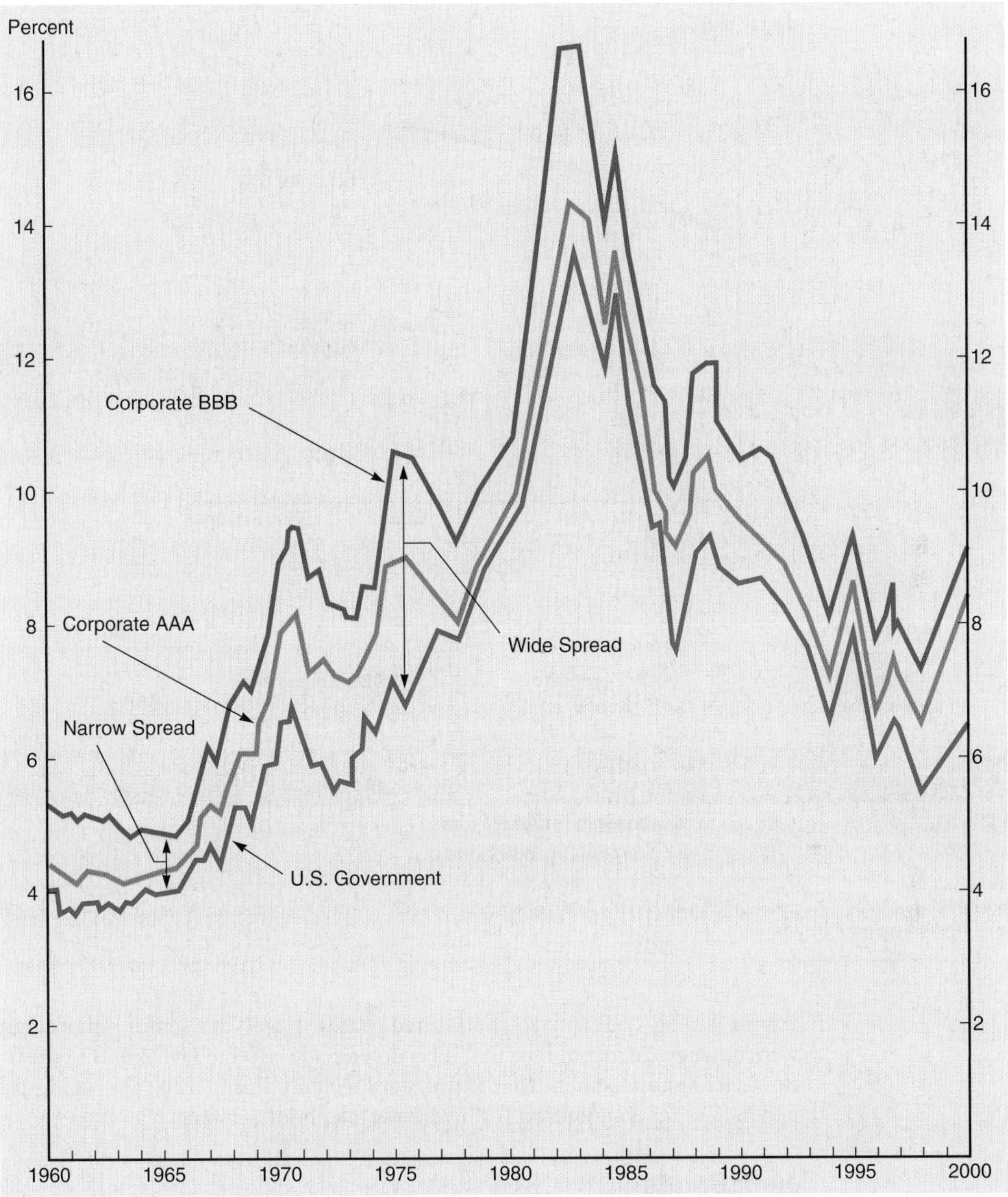

Source: Federal Reserve Board, *Historical Chart Book*, 1983, and *Federal Reserve Bulletin*, various issues.

Changes in Ratings Changes in a firm's bond rating affect both its ability to borrow long-term capital and the cost of that capital. Rating agencies review outstanding bonds on a periodic basis, occasionally upgrading or downgrading a bond as a result of its issuer's changed circumstances. For example, the September 1, 1999, issue of *Standard & Poor's CreditWeek* reported that Apple Computer's senior unsecured debt rating had been upgraded from B+ to BB−. Its rating reflected the competitive environment of the personal computer industry, a weak but improving market share, and an improvement in working capital management that increased operating free cash flow. However, S&P downgraded the securities of Paging Network Inc (PageNet), the

FIGURE 9-5 Relationship between Bond Ratings and Bond Yields, 1963 and 2000

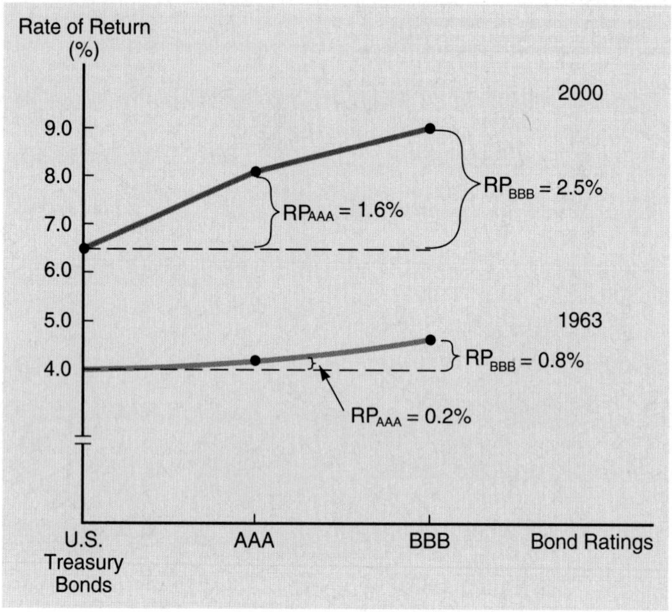

	Long-Term Government Bonds (Default-Free) (1)	AAA Corporate Bonds (2)	BBB Corporate Bonds (3)	Risk Premiums AAA (4) = (2) − (1)	Risk Premiums BBB (5) = (3) − (1)
June 1963	4.0%	4.2%	4.8%	0.2%	0.8%
May 2000	6.5	8.1	9.0	1.6	2.5

RP_{AAA} = risk premium on AAA bonds.
RP_{BBB} = risk premium on BBB bonds.

Source: *Federal Reserve Bulletin*, December 1963, and *Federal Reserve Statistical Release, Selected Interest Rates*, Release date: May 22, 2000 at http://www.federalreserve.gov/releases.

largest paging company in the United States. PageNet's senior subordinated notes were downgraded from B to B−. This downgrade reflected weakness in the firm's cash flows, its announcement that it was unexpectedly losing 120,000 paging customers, and increasing competition from wireless telephone services.

Junk Bonds

Prior to the 1980s, fixed-income investors such as pension funds and insurance companies were generally unwilling to buy risky bonds, so it was almost impossible for risky companies to raise capital in the public bond markets. Then, in the late 1970s, Michael Milken of the investment banking firm Drexel Burnham Lambert, relying on historical studies that showed that risky bonds yielded more than enough to compensate for their risk, began to convince institutional investors of the merits of purchasing risky debt. Thus was born the "junk bond," a high-risk, high-yield bond issued to finance a leveraged buyout, a merger, or a troubled company.[16] For example, Public

[16]Another type of junk bond is one that was highly rated when it was issued but whose rating has fallen because the issuing corporation has fallen on hard times. Such bonds are called "fallen angels."

Santa Fe Bonds Finally Mature after 114 Years

In 1995, Santa Fe Pacific Company made the final payment on some outstanding bonds that were originally issued in 1881! While the bonds were paid off in full, their history has been anything but routine.

Since the bonds were issued in 1881, investors have seen Santa Fe go through two bankruptcy reorganizations, two depressions, several recessions, two world wars, and the collapse of the gold standard. Through it all, the company remained intact, although ironically it did agree to be acquired by Burlington Northern just prior to the bonds' maturity.

When the bonds were issued in 1881, they had a 6 percent coupon. After a promising start, competition in the railroad business, along with the Depression of 1893, dealt a crippling one-two punch to the company's fortunes. After two bankruptcy reorganizations—and two new management teams—the company got back on its feet, and in 1895 it replaced the original bonds with new 100-year bonds. The new bonds, sanctioned by the Bankruptcy Court, matured in 1995 and carried a 4 percent coupon. However, they also had a wrinkle that was in effect until 1900—the company could skip the coupon payment if, in management's opinion, earnings were not sufficiently high to service the debt. After 1900, the company could no longer just ignore the coupon, but it did have the option of deferring the payments if management deemed deferral necessary. In the late 1890s, Santa Fe did skip the interest, and the bonds sold at an all-time low of $285 (28.5% of par) in 1896. The bonds reached a peak in 1946, when they sold for $1,312.50 in the strong, low interest rate economy after World War II.

Interestingly, the bonds' principal payment was originally pegged to the price of gold, meaning that the principal received at maturity would increase if the price of gold increased. This type of contract was declared invalid in 1933 by President Roosevelt and Congress, and the decision was upheld by the Supreme Court in a 5–4 vote. If just one Supreme Court justice had gone the other way, then, due to an increase in the price of gold, the bonds would have been worth $18,626 rather than $1,000 when they matured in 1995!

In many ways, the saga of the Santa Fe bonds is a testament to the stability of the U.S. financial system. On the other hand, it illustrates the many types of risks that investors face when they purchase long-term bonds. Investors in the 100-year bonds issued by Disney and Coca-Cola, among others, should perhaps take note.

Service of New Hampshire financed construction of its troubled Seabrook nuclear plant with junk bonds, and junk bonds were used by Ted Turner to finance the development of CNN and Turner Broadcasting. In junk bond deals, the debt ratio is generally extremely high, so the bondholders must bear as much risk as stockholders normally would. The bonds' yields reflect this fact—a promised return of 25 percent per annum was required to sell some Public Service of New Hampshire bonds.

The emergence of junk bonds as an important type of debt is another example of how the investment banking industry adjusts to and facilitates new developments in capital markets. In the 1980s, mergers and takeovers increased dramatically. People like T. Boone Pickens and Henry Kravis thought that certain old-line, established companies were run inefficiently and were financed too conservatively, and they wanted to take these companies over and restructure them. Michael Milken and his staff at Drexel Burnham Lambert began an active campaign to persuade certain institutions (often S&Ls) to purchase high-yield bonds. Milken developed expertise in putting together deals that were attractive to the institutions yet feasible in the sense that projected cash flows were sufficient to meet the required interest payments. The fact that interest on the bonds was tax deductible, combined with the much higher debt ratios of the restructured firms, also increased after-tax cash flows and helped make the deals feasible.

The development of junk bond financing has done much to reshape the U.S. financial scene. The existence of these securities contributed to the loss of independence of Gulf Oil and hundreds of other companies, and it led to major shake-ups in such companies as CBS, Union Carbide, and USX (formerly U.S. Steel). It also caused

Drexel Burnham Lambert to leap from essentially nowhere in the 1970s to become the most profitable investment banking firm during the 1980s.

The phenomenal growth of the junk bond market was impressive, but controversial. In 1989, Drexel Burnham Lambert was forced into bankruptcy, and "junk bond king" Michael Milken, who had earned $500 million two years earlier, was sent to jail. Those events led to the collapse of the junk bond market in the early 1990s. Since then, however, the junk bond market has rebounded, and junk bonds are here to stay as an important form of corporate financing.

Bankruptcy and Reorganization

During recessions, bankruptcies normally rise, and the most recent recession (in 1991–1992) was no exception. The 1991–1992 casualties included Pan Am, Carter Hawley Hale Stores, Continental Airlines, R. H. Macy & Company, Zale Corporation, and McCrory Corporation. Because of its importance, at least a brief discussion of bankruptcy is warranted within the chapter, and a more detailed discussion is presented in Chapter 25.

When a business becomes *insolvent,* it does not have enough cash to meet its interest and principal payments. A decision must then be made whether to dissolve the firm through *liquidation* or to permit it to *reorganize* and thus stay alive. These issues are addressed in Chapters 7 and 11 of the federal bankruptcy statutes, and the final decision is made by a federal bankruptcy court judge.

The decision to force a firm to liquidate versus permit it to reorganize depends on whether the value of the reorganized firm is likely to be greater than the value of the firm's assets if they are sold off piecemeal. In a reorganization, the firm's creditors negotiate with management on the terms of a potential reorganization. The reorganization plan may call for a *restructuring* of the firm's debt, in which case the interest rate may be reduced, the term to maturity lengthened, or some of the debt may be exchanged for equity. The point of the restructuring is to reduce the financial charges to a level that the firm's cash flows can support. Of course, the common stockholders also have to give up something—they often see their position diluted as a result of additional shares being given to debtholders in exchange for accepting a reduced amount of debt principal and interest. In fact, the original common stockholders often end up with nothing. A trustee may be appointed by the court to oversee the reorganization, but generally the existing management is allowed to retain control.

Liquidation occurs if the company is deemed to be too far gone to be saved—if it is worth more dead than alive. If the bankruptcy court orders a liquidation, assets are sold off and the cash obtained is distributed as specified in Chapter 7 of the Bankruptcy Act. Here is the priority of claims:

1. Secured creditors are entitled to the proceeds from the sale of the specific property that was used to support their loans.
2. The trustee's costs of administering and operating the bankrupt firm are next in line.
3. Expenses incurred after bankruptcy was filed come next.
4. Wages due workers, up to a limit of $2,000 per worker, follow.
5. Claims for unpaid contributions to employee benefit plans are next. This amount, together with wages, cannot exceed $2,000 per worker.
6. Unsecured claims for customer deposits up to $900 per customer are sixth in line.
7. Federal, state, and local taxes due come next.
8. Unfunded pension plan liabilities are next. (Limitations exist as specified in Chapter 26.)
9. General unsecured creditors are ninth on the list.

10. Preferred stockholders come next, up to the par value of their stock.
11. Common stockholders are finally paid, if anything is left, which is rare.

Chapter 25 provides an illustration of how a firm's assets are distributed after it has been liquidated. For now, you should know (1) that the federal bankruptcy statutes govern both reorganization and liquidation, (2) that bankruptcies occur frequently, and (3) that a priority of the specified claims must be followed when distributing the assets of a liquidated firm.

Self-Test Questions

Differentiate between mortgage bonds and debentures.

Name the major rating agencies, and list some factors that affect bond ratings.

Why are bond ratings important both to firms and to investors?

For what purposes have junk bonds typically been used?

Differentiate between a Chapter 7 liquidation and a Chapter 11 reorganization. When would each be used?

List the priority of claims for the distribution of a liquidated firm's assets.

Bond Markets

Corporate bonds are traded primarily in the over-the-counter market. Most bonds are owned by and traded among the large financial institutions (for example, life insurance companies, mutual funds, and pension funds, all of which deal in very large blocks of securities), and it is relatively easy for the over-the-counter bond dealers to arrange the transfer of large blocks of bonds among the relatively few holders of the bonds. It would be much more difficult to conduct similar operations in the stock market, with its literally millions of large and small stockholders, so a higher percentage of stock trades occur on the exchanges.

Information on bond trades in the over-the-counter market is not published, but a representative group of bonds is listed and traded on the bond division of the NYSE. Figure 9-6 gives a section of the bond market page of *The Wall Street Journal* for trading on June 8, 2000. A total of 152 issues were traded on that date, but we show only the bonds of BellSouth Corporation. Note that BellSouth had eight different bonds that were traded on June 8. The company actually had more than 10 bond issues outstanding, but several of them did not trade on that date.

The bonds of BellSouth and other companies can have various denominations, but for convenience we generally think of each bond as having a par value of $1,000—this is how much per bond the company borrowed and how much it must someday repay. However, since other denominations are possible, for trading and reporting purposes bonds are quoted as percentages of par. Looking at the fifth bond listed in the data in Figure 9-6, we see that there is a 7 just after the company's name; this indicates that the bond is of the series that pays 7 percent interest, or 0.07($1,000) = $70.00 of interest per year. The 7 percent is the bond's *coupon rate*. The BellSouth bonds, and all the others listed in the *Journal*, pay interest semiannually, so all rates are nominal, not EAR rates. The 25 which comes next indicates that this bond matures and must be repaid in the year 2025; it is not shown in the figure, but this bond was issued in 1995, so it had a 30-year original maturity. The 7.6 in the second column is the bond's current yield: Current yield = $70.00/$920.00 = 7.61%, rounded to 7.6 percent. The 45 in the third column indicates that 45 of these bonds were traded on this date. Since the price shown in the fourth column is expressed as a percentage of par, the bond closed at 92.00 percent, which translates to $920.00, up 1.375 percent from the previous close.

FIGURE 9-6 NYSE Bond Market Transactions

Corporation Bonds				
Volume $12,336,000				
Bonds	**Cur Yld**	**Vol**	**Close**	**Net Chg.**
BellsoT 6⅜04	6.6	11	96⅞	. . .
BellsoT 7s05	7.0	10	100¼	. . .
BellsoT 6½05	6.7	55	97½	+1
BellsoT 5⅞09	6.5	25	90½	+1½
BellsoT 7s25	7.6	45	92	+1⅜
BellsoT 8¼32	8.3	93	99¾	−¼
BellsoT 7⅞32	8.2	17	95⅞	−⅛
BellsoT 6¾33	8.1	88	83¾	+⅜

Source: *The Wall Street Journal*, June 9, 2000, C20.

Coupon rates are generally set at levels that reflect the "going rate of interest" on the day a bond is issued. If the rates were set lower, investors simply would not buy the bonds at the $1,000 par value, so the company could not borrow the money it needed. Thus, bonds generally sell at their par values on the day they are issued, but their prices fluctuate thereafter as interest rates change.

As shown in Figure 9-7, the BellSouth bonds initially sold at par. The bonds rose above par in 1995 when interest rates dipped below 7 percent, but then fell below par in 1996 when interest rates rose. Over the next three years this pattern was repeated: The price rose above par in 1997 and 1998 when interest rates fell, but the price fell

FIGURE 9-7 BellSouth 7%, 30-Year Bond: Market Value as Interest Rates Change

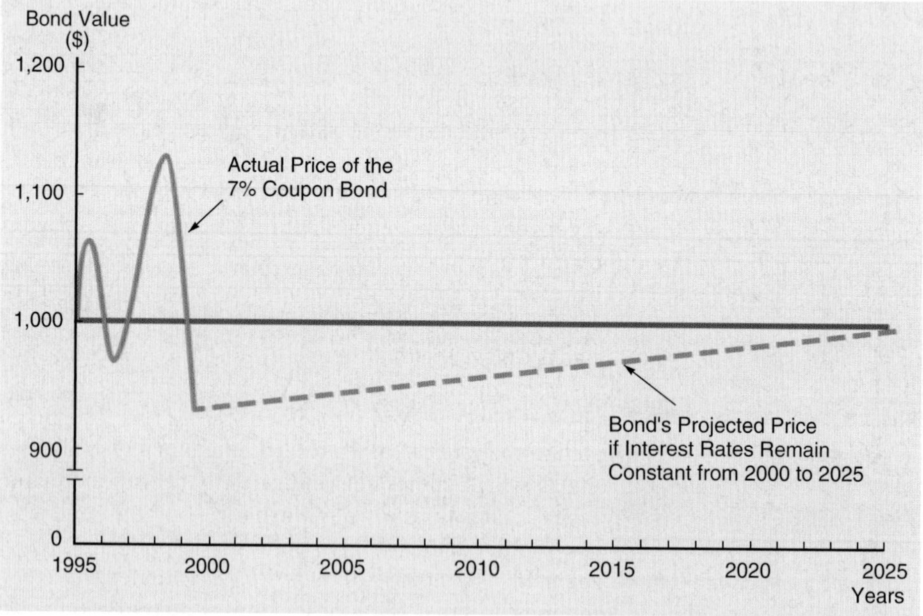

NOTE: The line from 2000 to 2025 appears linear, but it actually has a slight upward curve.

again in 1999 and 2000 after additional increases in interest rates. The dashed line in Figure 9-7 shows the projected price of the bonds, in the unlikely event that interest rates remain constant from 2000 to 2025. Looking at the actual and projected price history of these bonds, we see (1) the inverse relationship between interest rates and bond values and (2) the fact that bond values approach their par values as their maturity date approaches.

Self-Test Questions

Why do most bond trades occur in the over-the-counter market?

If a bond issue is to be sold at par, how will its coupon rate be determined?

Summary

This chapter described the different types of bonds governments and corporations issue, explained how bond prices are established, and discussed how investors estimate the rates of return they can expect to earn. We also discussed the various types of risks that investors face when they buy bonds.

It is important to remember that when an investor purchases a company's bonds, that investor is providing the company with capital. Therefore, when a firm issues bonds, *the return that investors receive represents the cost of debt financing for the issuing company.* This point is emphasized in Chapter 11, where the ideas developed in this chapter are used to help determine a company's overall cost of capital, which is a basic component in the capital budgeting process.

The key concepts covered are summarized below.

- A **bond** is a long-term promissory note issued by a business or governmental unit. The issuer receives money in exchange for promising to make interest payments and to repay the principal on a specified future date.
- Some recent innovations in long-term financing include **zero coupon bonds,** which pay no annual interest but that are issued at a discount; **floating rate debt,** whose interest payments fluctuate with changes in the general level of interest rates; and **junk bonds,** which are high-risk, high-yield instruments issued by firms that use a great deal of financial leverage.
- A **call provision** gives the issuing corporation the right to redeem the bonds prior to maturity under specified terms, usually at a price greater than the maturity value (the difference is a **call premium**). A firm will typically call a bond if interest rates fall substantially below the coupon rate.
- A **redeemable bond** gives the investor the right to sell the bond back to the issuing company at a previously specified price. This is a useful feature (for investors) if interest rates rise or if the company engages in unanticipated risky activities.
- A **sinking fund** is a provision that requires the corporation to retire a portion of the bond issue each year. The purpose of the sinking fund is to provide for the orderly retirement of the issue. A sinking fund typically requires no call premium.
- The **value of a bond** is found as the present value of an **annuity** (the interest payments) plus the present value of a lump sum (the **principal**). The bond is evaluated at the appropriate periodic interest rate over the number of periods for which interest payments are made.
- The equation used to find the value of an annual coupon bond is:

$$V_B = \sum_{t=1}^{N} \frac{INT}{(1 + k_d)^t} + \frac{M}{(1 + k_d)^N}.$$

An adjustment to the formula must be made if the bond pays interest **semiannually:** divide INT and k_d by 2, and multiply N by 2.

- The return earned on a bond held to maturity is defined as the bond's **yield to maturity (YTM)**. If the bond can be redeemed before maturity, it is **callable,** and the return investors receive if it is called is defined as the **yield to call (YTC)**. The YTC is found as the present value of the interest payments received while the bond is outstanding plus the present value of the call price (the par value plus a call premium).
- The longer the maturity of a bond, the more its price will change in response to a given change in interest rates; this is called **interest rate risk**. However, bonds with short maturities expose investors to high **reinvestment rate risk,** which is the risk that income from a bond portfolio will decline because cash flows received from bonds will be rolled over at lower interest rates.
- Corporate and municipal bonds have **default risk**. If an issuer defaults, investors receive less than the promised return on the bond. Therefore, investors should evaluate a bond's default risk before making a purchase.
- There are many different types of bonds with different sets of features. These include **convertible bonds, bonds with warrants, income bonds, purchasing power (indexed) bonds, mortgage bonds, debentures, subordinated debentures, junk bonds, development bonds,** and **insured municipal bonds**. The return required on each type of bond is determined by the bond's riskiness.
- Bonds are assigned **ratings** that reflect the probability of their going into default. The highest rating is AAA, and they go down to D. The higher a bond's rating, the lower its risk and therefore its interest rate.

Questions

9–1 Define each of the following terms:

a. Bond; Treasury bond; corporate bond; municipal bond; foreign bond
b. Par value; maturity date
c. Coupon payment; coupon interest rate
d. Floating rate bond; zero coupon bond; original issue discount bond (OID)
e. Call provision; redeemable bond; sinking fund
f. Convertible bond; warrant; income bond; indexed, or purchasing power, bond
g. Premium bond; discount bond
h. Current yield (on a bond); yield to maturity (YTM); yield to call (YTC)
i. Reinvestment risk; interest rate risk
j. Default risk
k. Indentures; mortgage bond; debenture; subordinated debenture
l. Development bond; municipal bond insurance
m. Junk bond; investment-grade bond

9–2 Is it true that the following equation can be used to find the value of an N-year bond that pays interest once a year?

$$V_B = \sum_{t=1}^{N} \frac{\text{Annual interest}}{(1 + k_d)^t} + \frac{\text{Par value}}{(1 + k_d)^N}.$$

9–3 "The values of outstanding bonds change whenever the going rate of interest changes. In general, short-term interest rates are more volatile than long-term interest rates. Therefore, short-term bond prices are more sensitive to interest rate changes than are long-term bond prices." Is this statement true or false? Explain.

9–4 The rate of return you would get if you bought a bond and held it to its maturity date is called the bond's yield to maturity. If interest rates in the economy rise after a bond has been issued, what will happen to the bond's price and to its YTM? Does the length of time to maturity affect the extent to which a given change in interest rates will affect the bond's price?

9–5 If you buy a *callable* bond and interest rates decline, will the value of your bond rise by as much as it would have risen if the bond had not been callable? Explain.

9–6 A sinking fund can be set up in one of two ways:
(1) The corporation makes annual payments to the trustee, who invests the proceeds in securities (frequently government bonds) and uses the accumulated total to retire the bond issue at maturity.
(2) The trustee uses the annual payments to retire a portion of the issue each year, either calling a given percentage of the issue by a lottery and paying a specified price per bond or buying bonds on the open market, whichever is cheaper.
Discuss the advantages and disadvantages of each procedure from the viewpoint of both the firm and its bondholders.

9–7 Indicate whether each of the following actions will increase or decrease a bond's yield to maturity:
a. A bond's price increases.
b. The company's bonds are downgraded by the rating agencies.
c. A change in the bankruptcy code makes it more difficult for bondholders to receive payments in the event a firm declares bankruptcy.
d. The economy enters a recession.
e. The bonds become subordinated to another debt issue.

Self-Test Problems (Solutions Appear in Appendix A)

ST–1
BOND VALUATION
The Pennington Corporation issued a new series of bonds on January 1, 1978. The bonds were sold at par ($1,000), have a 12 percent coupon, and mature in 30 years, on December 31, 2007. Coupon payments are made semiannually (on June 30 and December 31).
a. What was the YTM of Pennington's bonds on January 1, 1978?
b. What was the price of the bond on January 1, 1983, 5 years later, assuming that the level of interest rates had fallen to 10 percent?
c. Find the current yield and capital gains yield on the bond on January 1, 1983, given the price as determined in part b.
d. On July 1, 2001, Pennington's bonds sold for $916.42. What was the YTM at that date?
e. What were the current yield and capital gains yield on July 1, 2001?
f. Now, assume that you purchased an outstanding Pennington bond on March 1, 2001, when the going rate of interest was 15.5 percent. How large a check must you have written to complete the transaction? This is a hard question! (Hint: $PVIFA_{7.75\%,13} = 8.0136$ and $PVIF_{7.75\%,13} = 0.3789$.)

ST–2
SINKING FUND
The Vancouver Development Company has just sold a $100 million, 10-year, 12 percent bond issue. A sinking fund will retire the issue over its life. Sinking fund payments are of equal amounts and will be made **semiannually,** and the proceeds will be used to retire bonds as the payments are made. Bonds can be called at par for sinking fund purposes, or the funds paid into the sinking fund can be used to buy bonds in the open market.
a. How large must each semiannual sinking fund payment be?
b. What will happen, under the conditions of the problem thus far, to the company's debt service requirements per year for this issue over time?
c. Now suppose Vancouver Development set up its sinking fund so that *equal annual amounts,* payable at the end of each year, are paid into a sinking fund trust held by a bank, with the proceeds being used to buy government bonds that pay 9 percent interest. The payments, plus accumulated interest, must total $100 million at the end of 10 years, and the proceeds will be used to retire the bonds at that time. How large must the annual sinking fund payment be now?
d. What are the annual cash requirements for covering bond service costs under the trusteeship arrangement described in part c? (Note: Interest must be paid on Vancouver's outstanding bonds but not on bonds that have been retired.)
e. What would have to happen to interest rates to cause the company to buy bonds on the open market rather than call them under the original sinking fund plan?

Problems

9–1 BOND VALUATION

Callaghan Motors' bonds have 10 years remaining to maturity. Interest is paid annually, the bonds have a $1,000 par value, and the coupon interest rate is 8 percent. The bonds have a yield to maturity of 9 percent. What is the current market price of these bonds?

9–2 YIELD TO MATURITY; FINANCIAL CALCULATOR NEEDED

Wilson Wonders' bonds have 12 years remaining to maturity. Interest is paid annually, the bonds have a $1,000 par value, and the coupon interest rate is 10 percent. The bonds sell at a price of $850. What is their yield to maturity?

9–3 YIELD TO MATURITY AND CALL; FINANCIAL CALCULATOR NEEDED

Thatcher Corporation's bonds will mature in 10 years. The bonds have a face value of $1,000 and an 8 percent coupon rate, paid semiannually. The price of the bonds is $1,100. The bonds are callable in 5 years at a call price of $1,050. What is the yield to maturity? What is the yield to call?

9–4 CURRENT YIELD

Heath Foods' bonds have 7 years remaining to maturity. The bonds have a face value of $1,000 and a yield to maturity of 8 percent. They pay interest annually and have a 9 percent coupon rate. What is their current yield?

9–5 BOND VALUATION; FINANCIAL CALCULATOR NEEDED

Nungesser Corporation has issued bonds that have a 9 percent coupon rate, payable semiannually. The bonds mature in 8 years, have a face value of $1,000, and a yield to maturity of 8.5 percent. What is the price of the bonds?

9–6 BOND VALUATION

The Garraty Company has two bond issues outstanding. Both bonds pay $100 annual interest plus $1,000 at maturity. Bond L has a maturity of 15 years, and Bond S a maturity of 1 year.

a. What will be the value of each of these bonds when the going rate of interest is (1) 5 percent, (2) 8 percent, and (3) 12 percent? Assume that there is only one more interest payment to be made on Bond S.

b. Why does the longer-term (15-year) bond fluctuate more when interest rates change than does the shorter-term bond (1-year)?

9–7 YIELD TO MATURITY

The Heymann Company's bonds have 4 years remaining to maturity. Interest is paid annually; the bonds have a $1,000 par value; and the coupon interest rate is 9 percent.

a. What is the yield to maturity at a current market price of (1) $829 or (2) $1,104?

b. Would you pay $829 for one of these bonds if you thought that the appropriate rate of interest was 12 percent—that is, if $k_d = 12\%$? Explain your answer.

9–8 YIELD TO CALL

Six years ago, The Singleton Company sold a 20-year bond issue with a 14 percent annual coupon rate and a 9 percent call premium. Today, Singleton called the bonds. The bonds originally were sold at their face value of $1,000. Compute the realized rate of return for investors who purchased the bonds when they were issued and who surrender them today in exchange for the call price.

9–9 BOND YIELDS; FINANCIAL CALCULATOR NEEDED

A 10-year, 12 percent semiannual coupon bond, with a par value of $1,000, may be called in 4 years at a call price of $1,060. The bond sells for $1,100. (Assume that the bond has just been issued.)

a. What is the bond's yield to maturity?

b. What is the bond's current yield?

c. What is the bond's capital gain or loss yield?

d. What is the bond's yield to call?

9–10 YIELD TO MATURITY; FINANCIAL CALCULATOR NEEDED

You just purchased a bond which matures in 5 years. The bond has a face value of $1,000, and has an 8 percent annual coupon. The bond has a current yield of 8.21 percent. What is the bond's yield to maturity?

9–11 CURRENT YIELD; FINANCIAL CALCULATOR NEEDED

A bond which matures in 7 years sells for $1,020. The bond has a face value of $1,000 and a yield to maturity of 10.5883 percent. The bond pays coupons semiannually. What is the bond's current yield?

9–12 NOMINAL INTEREST RATE

Lloyd Corporation's 14 percent coupon rate, semiannual payment, $1,000 par value bonds, which mature in 30 years, are callable 5 years from now at a price of $1,050. The bonds sell at a price of $1,353.54, and the yield curve is flat. Assuming that interest rates in the economy are expected to remain at their current level, what is the best estimate of Lloyd's nominal interest rate on new bonds?

9–13 BOND VALUATION

Suppose Ford Motor Company sold an issue of bonds with a 10-year maturity, a $1,000 par value, a 10 percent coupon rate, and semiannual interest payments.

a. Two years after the bonds were issued, the going rate of interest on bonds such as these fell to 6 percent. At what price would the bonds sell?

b. Suppose that, 2 years after the initial offering, the going interest rate had risen to 12 percent. At what price would the bonds sell?

c. Suppose that the conditions in part a existed—that is, interest rates fell to 6 percent 2 years after the issue date. Suppose further that the interest rate remained at 6 percent for the next 8 years. What would happen to the price of the Ford Motor Company bonds over time?

9–14 BOND REPORTING

Look up the prices of American Telephone & Telegraph's (AT&T) bonds in *The Wall Street Journal* (or some other newspaper that provides this information).

a. If AT&T were to sell a new issue of $1,000 par value long-term bonds, approximately what coupon interest rate would it have to set on the bonds if it wanted to bring them out at par?

b. If you had $10,000 and wanted to invest it in AT&T, what return would you expect to get if you bought AT&T's bonds?

9–15 DISCOUNT BOND VALUATION

Assume that in February 1972 the Los Angeles Airport authority issued a series of 3.4 percent, 30-year bonds. Interest rates rose substantially in the years following the issue, and as they did, the price of the bonds declined. In February 1985, 13 years later, the price of the bonds had dropped from $1,000 to $650. In answering the following questions, assume that the bond requires annual interest payments.

a. Each bond originally sold at its $1,000 par value. What was the yield to maturity of these bonds when they were issued?

b. Calculate the yield to maturity in February 1985.

c. Assume that interest rates stabilized at the 1985 level and stayed there for the remainder of the life of the bonds. What would have been the bonds' price in February 2000, when they had 2 years remaining to maturity?

d. What will the price of the bonds be the day before they mature in 2002? (Disregard the last interest payment.)

e. In 1985, the Los Angeles Airport bonds were classified as "discount bonds." What happens to the price of a discount bond as it approaches maturity? Is there a "built-in capital gain" on such bonds?

f. The coupon interest payment divided by the market price of a bond is called the bond's *current yield.* Using the answers to parts b and c, what would have been the current yield of a Los Angeles Airport bond (1) in February 1985 and (2) in February 2000? What would have been its capital gains yields and total yields (total yield equals yield to maturity) on those same two dates?

9–16 YIELD TO CALL

It is now January 1, 2002, and you are considering the purchase of an outstanding Racette Corporation bond that was issued on January 1, 2000. The Racette bond has a 9.5 percent annual coupon and a 30-year original maturity (it matures on December 31, 2029). There is a 5-year call protection (until December 31, 2004), after which time the bond can be called at 109 (that is, at 109 percent of par, or $1,090). Interest rates have declined since the bond was issued, and the bond is now selling at 116.575 percent of par, or $1,165.75. You want to determine both the yield to maturity and the yield to call for this bond. (Note: The yield to call considers the effect of a call provision on the bond's probable yield. In the calculation, we assume that the bond will be outstanding until the call date, at which time it will be called. Thus, the investor will have received interest payments for the call-protected period and then will receive the call price—in this case, $1,090—on the call date.)

a. What is the yield to maturity in 2002 for the Racette bond? What is its yield to call?

b. If you bought this bond, which return do you think you would actually earn? Explain your reasoning.

c. Suppose the bond had sold at a discount. Would the yield to maturity or the yield to call have been more relevant?

9–17
INTEREST RATE SENSITIVITY; FINANCIAL CALCULATOR NEEDED

A bond trader purchased each of the following bonds at a yield to maturity of 8 percent. Immediately after she purchased the bonds, interest rates fell to 7 percent. What is the percentage change in the price of each bond after the decline in interest rates? Fill in the following table:

	Price @ 8%	Price @ 7%	Percentage Change
10-year, 10% annual coupon	______	______	______
10-year zero	______	______	______
5-year zero	______	______	______
30-year zero	______	______	______
$100 perpetuity	______	______	______

9–18
BOND VALUATION; FINANCIAL CALCULATOR NEEDED

An investor has two bonds in his portfolio. Each bond matures in 4 years, has a face value of $1,000, and has a yield to maturity equal to 9.6 percent. One bond, Bond C, pays an annual coupon of 10 percent, the other bond, Bond Z, is a zero coupon bond.

a. Assuming that the yield to maturity of each bond remains at 9.6 percent over the next 4 years, what will be the price of each of the bonds at the following time periods? Fill in the following table:

t	Price of Bond C	Price of Bond Z
0	______	______
1	______	______
2	______	______
3	______	______
4	______	______

b. Plot the time path of the prices for each of the two bonds.

Spreadsheet Problem

9–19
BUILD A MODEL: BOND VALUATION

Start with the partial model in the file ***Ch 09-19 Build a Model.xls*** from the textbook's CD-ROM. Rework Problem 9-9. After completing parts a through d, answer the following related questions.

e. How would the price of the bond be affected by changing interest rates? (Hint: Conduct a sensitivity analysis of price to changes in the yield to maturity, which is also the going market interest rate for the bond. Assume that the bond will be called if and only if the going rate of interest *falls below* the coupon rate. That is an oversimplification, but assume it anyway for purposes of this problem.)

f. Now assume that the date is 10/25/2001. Assume further that our 12 percent, 10-year bond was issued on 7/1/2001, is callable on 7/1/2005 at $1,060, will mature on 6/30/2011, pays interest semiannually (January 1 and July 1), and sells for $1,100. Use your spreadsheet to find (1) the bond's yield to maturity and (2) its yield to call.

9–20
WHAT IF ANALYSIS: YIELD TO CALL

Start with the model in the file ***Ch 09-20 What If Analysis.xls*** from the textbook's CD-ROM and answer the questions shown there.

Cyberproblem

The information related to the cyberproblems is likely to change over time, due to the release of new information and the ever-changing nature of the World Wide Web. With these changes in mind, we will periodically update these problems on the textbook's web site.

9–21 *BONDS AND THEIR VALUATION*

All bonds have some common characteristics, but they do not always have the same contractual features. Differences in contractual provisions, and in the underlying strength of the companies backing the bonds, lead to major differences in bonds' risks, prices, and expected returns. The risk investors are exposed to in buying a bond is in part gauged by bond rating agencies. The three major bond rating agencies are Moody's, Standard & Poor's, and Fitch's. Bonds are assigned quality ratings that reflect their probability of default. Changes in a firm's bond rating influence its ability to borrow long-term capital and the cost of that capital. Rating agencies review outstanding bonds on a periodic basis, occasionally upgrading or downgrading a bond because of changes in an issuer's circumstances. Go to the cyberproblem on the textbook's web site, **http://www.harcourtcollege.com/theory/student/resources/cyberprob/ch09.html**, and answer the questions shown there.

Mini Case

See **Ch 09 Show.ppt** and **Ch 09 Mini Case.xls.**

Robert Balik and Carol Kiefer are vice-presidents of Mutual of Chicago Insurance Company and codirectors of the company's pension fund management division. A major new client, the California League of Cities, has requested that Mutual of Chicago present an investment seminar to the mayors of the represented cities, and Balik and Kiefer, who will make the actual presentation, have asked you to help them by answering the following questions. Because the Walt Disney Company operates in one of the league's cities, you are to work Disney into the presentation.

a. What are the key features of a bond?

b. What are call provisions and sinking fund provisions? Do these provisions make bonds more or less risky?

c. How is the value of any asset whose value is based on expected future cash flows determined?

d. How is the value of a bond determined? What is the value of a 10-year, $1,000 par value bond with a 10 percent annual coupon if its required rate of return is 10 percent?

e. (1) What would be the value of the bond described in part d if, just after it had been issued, the expected inflation rate rose by 3 percentage points, causing investors to require a 13 percent return? Would we now have a discount or a premium bond? (If you do not have a financial calculator, $PVIF_{13\%,10} = 0.2946$; $PVIFA_{13\%,10} = 5.4262$.)

(2) What would happen to the bond's value if inflation fell, and k_d declined to 7 percent? Would we now have a premium or a discount bond?

(3) What would happen to the value of the 10-year bond over time if the required rate of return remained at 13 percent, or if it remained at 7 percent? (Hint: With a financial calculator, enter PMT, I, FV, and N, and then change (override) N to see what happens to the PV as the bond approaches maturity.)

f. (1) What is the yield to maturity on a 10-year, 9 percent, annual coupon, $1,000 par value bond that sells for $887.00? That sells for $1,134.20? What does the fact that a bond sells at a discount or at a premium tell you about the relationship between k_d and the bond's coupon rate?

(2) What are the total return, the current yield, and the capital gains yield for the discount bond? (Assume the bond is held to maturity and the company does not default on the bond.)

g. What is *interest rate (or price) risk?* Which bond has more interest rate risk, an annual payment 1-year bond or a 10-year bond? Why?

h. What is *reinvestment rate risk?* Which has more reinvestment rate risk, a 1-year bond or a 10-year bond?

i. How does the equation for valuing a bond change if semiannual payments are made? Find the value of a 10-year, semiannual payment, 10 percent coupon bond if nominal $k_d = 13\%$. (Hint: $PVIF_{6.5\%,20} = 0.2838$ and $PVIFA_{6.5\%,20} = 11.0185$.)

j. Suppose you could buy, for $1,000, either a 10 percent, 10-year, annual payment bond or a 10 percent, 10-year, semiannual payment bond. They are equally risky. Which would you prefer? If $1,000 is the proper price for the semiannual bond, what is the equilibrium price for the annual payment bond?

k. Suppose a 10-year, 10 percent, semiannual coupon bond with a par value of $1,000 is currently selling for $1,135.90, producing a nominal yield to maturity of 8 percent. However, the bond can be called after 5 years for a price of $1,050.
   (1) What is the bond's *nominal yield to call (YTC)?*
   (2) If you bought this bond, do you think you would be more likely to earn the YTM or the YTC? Why?

l. Disney's bonds were issued with a yield to maturity of 7.5 percent. Does the yield to maturity represent the promised or expected return on the bond?

m. Disney's bonds were rated AA− by S&P. Would you consider these bonds investment grade or junk bonds?

n. What factors determine a company's bond rating?

o. If this firm were to default on the bonds, would the company be immediately liquidated? Would the bondholders be assured of receiving all of their promised payments?

Selected Additional References and Cases

Many investment textbooks cover bond valuation models in depth and detail. Some of the better ones are listed in the Chapter 6 references.

For some recent works on valuation, see

Bey, Roger P., and J. Markham Collins, "The Relationship between Before- and After-Tax Yields on Financial Assets," *The Financial Review*, August 1988, 313–343.

Taylor, Richard W., "The Valuation of Semiannual Bonds between Interest Payment Dates," *The Financial Review*, August 1988, 365–368.

Tse, K. S. Maurice, and Mark A. White, "The Valuation of Semiannual Bonds between Interest Payment Dates: A Correction," *Financial Review*, November 1990, 659–662.

The following cases in the Cases in Financial Management: Dryden Request *series cover many of the valuation concepts contained in Chapter 9.*

Case 3, "Peachtree Securities, Inc. (B);" Case 43, "Swan Davis;" Case 49, "Beatrice Peabody;" and Case 56, "Laura Henderson."

10

Stocks and Their Valuation

By virtually any measure, the stock market has performed extraordinarily well during the last decade. From slightly less than 4000 in early 1995, the Dow surged to 11723 in early 2000. To put this remarkable 7723-point rise in perspective, consider that the Dow first reached 1000 in 1965, then took another 22 years to hit 2000, then four more years to reach 3000, and another four to get to 4000 (in 1995). Then, in just over five years, it reached 11723. Thus, in those five years investors' have made almost twice as much in the stock market as they made in the previous 70 years!

The bull market has made it possible for many people to take early retirement, buy expensive homes, and afford large expenditures such as college tuition. Encouraged by this performance, more and more investors are flocking to the market, and today more than 79 million Americans own stock. Moreover, a rising stock market makes it easier and cheaper for corporations to raise equity capital, which facilitates continued economic growth.

Some observers are concerned that many investors do not realize just how risky the stock market is. There is no guarantee that the market will continue to rise, and even in bull markets some stocks crash and burn. Indeed, several times during 2000 the market fell to below 10000 and surged above 11000.

Note too that while all boats may rise with the tide, the same does not hold for the stock market—regardless of the trend, some individual stocks make huge gains while others suffer substantial losses. For example, in 2000, Check Point's stock rose from $50 to $133, but during this same period Priceline.com lost nearly 97 percent of its value.

While it is difficult to predict prices, we are not completely in the dark when it comes to valuing stocks. After studying this chapter, you should have a reasonably good understanding of the factors that influence stock prices. With that knowledge—and a little luck—you may be able to find the next Check Point and avoid future Pricelines.

The textbook's CD-ROM contains an *Excel* file that will guide you through the chapter's calculations. The file for this chapter is ***Ch 10 Tool Kit.xls***, and we encourage you to open the file and follow along as you read the chapter.

In Chapter 9 we examined bonds. We now turn to common and preferred stock, beginning with some important background material that helps establish a framework for valuing these securities.

While it is generally easy to predict the cash flows received from bonds, forecasting the cash flows on common stocks is much more difficult. However, two fairly straightforward models can be used to help estimate the "true," or intrinsic, value of a common stock: (1) the dividend growth model, which we describe in this chapter, and (2) the total corporate value model, which we explain in Chapter 12.

The concepts and models developed here will also be used when we estimate the cost of capital in Chapter 11. In subsequent chapters, we demonstrate how the cost of capital is used to help make many important decisions, especially the decision to invest or not invest in new assets. Consequently, it is critically important that you understand the basics of stock valuation.

Legal Rights and Privileges of Common Stockholders

The common stockholders are the *owners* of a corporation, and as such they have certain rights and privileges as discussed in this section.

Control of the Firm

Its common stockholders have the right to elect a firm's directors, who, in turn, elect the officers who manage the business. In a small firm, the largest stockholder typically assumes the positions of president and chairperson of the board of directors. In a large, publicly owned firm, the managers typically have some stock, but their personal holdings are generally insufficient to give them voting control. Thus, the managements of most publicly owned firms can be removed by the stockholders if the management team is not effective.

State and federal laws stipulate how stockholder control is to be exercised. First, corporations must hold an election of directors periodically, usually once a year, with the vote taken at the annual meeting. Frequently, one-third of the directors are elected each year for a three-year term. Each share of stock has one vote; thus, the owner of 1,000 shares has 1,000 votes for each director.[1] Stockholders can appear at the annual meeting and vote in person, but typically they transfer their right to vote to a second party by means of a **proxy.** Management always solicits stockholders' proxies and usually gets them. However, if earnings are poor and stockholders are dissatisfied, an outside group may solicit the proxies in an effort to overthrow management and take control of the business. This is known as a **proxy fight.** Proxy fights are discussed in detail in Chapter 12.

The Preemptive Right

Common stockholders often have the right, called the **preemptive right,** to purchase any additional shares sold by the firm. In some states, the preemptive right is automatically included in every corporate charter; in others, it is necessary to insert it specifically into the charter.

[1]In the situation described, a 1,000-share stockholder could cast 1,000 votes for each of three directors if there were three contested seats on the board. An alternative procedure that may be prescribed in the corporate charter calls for *cumulative voting.* Here the 1,000-share stockholder would get 3,000 votes if there were three vacancies, and he or she could cast all of them for one director. Cumulative voting helps small groups to get representation on the board.

The purpose of the preemptive right is twofold. First, it enables current stockholders to maintain control. If it were not for this safeguard, the management of a corporation could issue a large number of additional shares and purchase these shares itself. Management could thereby seize control of the corporation and steal value from the current stockholders. For example, suppose 1,000 shares of common stock, each with a price of $100, were outstanding, making the total market value of the firm $100,000. If an additional 1,000 shares were sold at $50 a share, or for $50,000, this would raise the total market value to $150,000. When total market value is divided by new total shares outstanding, a value of $75 a share is obtained. The old stockholders thus lose $25 per share, and the new stockholders have an instant profit of $25 per share. Thus, selling common stock at a price below the market value would dilute its price and transfer wealth from the present stockholders to those who were allowed to purchase the new shares. The preemptive right prevents such occurrences.

Self-Test Questions

What is a proxy fight?

What are the two primary reasons for the existence of the preemptive right?

Types of Common Stock

Although most firms have only one type of common stock, in some instances **classified stock** is used to meet the special needs of the company. Generally, when special classifications are used, one type is designated *Class A*, another *Class B*, and so on. Small, new companies seeking funds from outside sources frequently use different types of common stock. For example, when Genetic Concepts went public recently, its Class A stock was sold to the public and paid a dividend, but this stock had no voting rights for five years. Its Class B stock, which was retained by the organizers of the company, had full voting rights for five years, but the legal terms stated that dividends could not be paid on the Class B stock until the company had established its earning power by building up retained earnings to a designated level. The use of classified stock thus enabled the public to take a position in a conservatively financed growth company without sacrificing income, while the founders retained absolute control during the crucial early stages of the firm's development. At the same time, outside investors were protected against excessive withdrawals of funds by the original owners. As is often the case in such situations, the Class B stock was called **founders' shares.**

Note that "Class A," "Class B," and so on, have no standard meanings. Most firms have no classified shares, but a firm that does could designate its Class B shares as founders' shares and its Class A shares as those sold to the public, while another could reverse these designations. Still other firms could use stock classifications for entirely different purposes. For example, when General Motors acquired Hughes Aircraft for $5 billion, it paid in part with a new Class H common, GMH, which had limited voting rights and whose dividends were tied to Hughes's performance as a GM subsidiary. The reasons for the new stock were reported to be (1) that GM wanted to limit voting privileges on the new classified stock because of management's concern about a possible takeover and (2) that Hughes employees wanted to be rewarded more directly on Hughes's own performance than would have been possible through regular GM stock.

GM's deal posed a problem for the NYSE, which had a rule against listing a company's common stock if the company had any nonvoting common stock outstanding. GM made it clear that it was willing to delist if the NYSE did not change its rules. The NYSE concluded that such arrangements as GM had made were logical and were likely to be made by other companies in the future, so it changed its rules to accommodate GM. In reality, though, the NYSE had little choice. In recent years, the

Nasdaq market has proven that it can provide a deep, liquid market for common stocks, and the defection of GM would have hurt the NYSE much more than GM.

As these examples illustrate, the right to vote is often a distinguishing characteristic between different classes of stock. Suppose two classes of stock differ in but one respect: One class has voting rights but the other does not. As you would expect, the stock with voting rights would be more valuable. In the United States, which has a legal system with fairly strong protection for minority stockholders (that is, noncontrolling stockholders), voting stock typically sells at a price 4 to 6 percent above that of otherwise similar nonvoting stock. Thus, if a stock with no voting rights sold for $50, then one with voting rights would probably sell for $52 to $53. In those countries with legal systems that provide less protection for minority stockholders, the right to vote is far more valuable. For example, voting stock on average sells for 45 percent more than nonvoting stock in Israel, and for 82 percent more in Italy.

As we noted above, General Motors created its Class H common stock as a part of its acquisition of Hughes Aircraft. This type of stock, with dividends tied to a particular part of a company, is called **tracking stock.** It also is called **target stock.** Although GM used its tracking stock in an acquisition, other companies are attempting to use such stock to increase shareholder value. For example, in 1995 US West had several business areas with very different growth prospects, ranging from slow-growth local telephone services to high-growth cellular, cable television, and directory services. US West felt that investors were unable to correctly value its high-growth lines of business, since cash flows from slow-growth and high-growth businesses were mingled. To separate the cash flows and to allow separate valuations, the company issued tracking stocks. Other companies in the telephone industry, such as Sprint, have also issued tracking stock. Similarly, Georgia-Pacific Corp. issued tracking stock for its timber business, and USX Corp. has tracking stocks for its oil, natural gas, and steel divisions. Despite this trend, many analysts are skeptical as to whether tracking stock increases a company's total market value. Companies still report consolidated financial statements for the entire company, and they have considerable leeway in allocating costs and reporting the financial results for the various divisions, even those with tracking stock. Thus, a tracking stock is not the same as the stock of an independent, stand-alone company.

Self-Test Question

What are some reasons a company might use classified stock?

The Market for Common Stock

Some companies are so small that their common stocks are not actively traded; they are owned by only a few people, usually the companies' managers. Such firms are said to be *privately owned*, or **closely held, corporations,** and their stock is called *closely held stock*. In contrast, the stocks of most larger companies are owned by a large number of investors, most of whom are not active in management. Such companies are called **publicly owned corporations,** and their stock is called *publicly held stock*.

As we saw in Chapter 5, the stocks of smaller publicly owned firms are not listed on an exchange; they trade in the over-the-counter (OTC) market, and the companies and their stocks are said to be *unlisted*. However, larger publicly owned companies generally apply for listing on a formal exchange, and they and their stocks are said to be *listed*. Many companies are first listed on Nasdaq or on a regional exchange, such as the Pacific Coast or Midwest exchanges. Once they become large enough to be listed on the "Big Board," many, but by no means all, choose to move to the NYSE. The largest company in the world in terms of market value, Microsoft, trades on the Nasdaq market, as do most other high-tech firms.

A recent study found that institutional investors owned more than 60 percent of all publicly held common stocks. Included are pension plans, mutual funds, foreign investors, insurance companies, and brokerage firms. These institutions buy and sell relatively actively, so they account for about 75 percent of all transactions. Thus, institutional investors have a heavy influence on the prices of individual stocks.

Types of Stock Market Transactions

We can classify stock market transactions into three distinct types:

1. *Trading in the outstanding shares of established, publicly owned companies: the secondary market.* MicroDrive Inc., the company we analyzed in earlier chapters, has 50 million shares of stock outstanding. If the owner of 100 shares sells his or her stock, the trade is said to have occurred in the **secondary market.** Thus, the market for outstanding shares, or *used shares*, is the secondary market. The company receives no new money when sales occur in this market.
2. *Additional shares sold by established, publicly owned companies: the primary market.* If MicroDrive decides to sell (or issue) an additional 1 million shares to raise new equity capital, this transaction is said to occur in the **primary market.**[2]
3. *Initial public offerings by privately held firms: the IPO market.* Several years ago, the Coors Brewing Company, which was owned by the Coors family at the time, decided to sell some stock to raise capital needed for a major expansion program.[3] This type of transaction is called **going public**—whenever stock in a closely held corporation is offered to the public for the first time, the company is said to be going public. The market for stock that is just being offered to the public is called the **initial public offering (IPO) market.**

   IPOs have received a lot of attention in recent years, primarily because a number of "hot" issues have realized spectacular gains—often in the first few minutes of trading. Consider the IPO of Boston Rotisserie Chicken, which has since been renamed Boston Market and acquired by McDonald's. The company's underwriter, Merrill Lynch, set an offering price of $20 a share. However, because of intense demand for the issue, the stock's price rose 75 percent within the first two hours of trading. By the end of the first day, the stock price had risen by 143 percent, and the company's end-of-the-day market value was $800 million—which was particularly startling, given that it had recently reported a $5 million loss on only $8.3 million of sales. More recently, shares of the trendy restaurant chain Planet Hollywood rose nearly 50 percent in its first day of trading, and when Netscape first hit the market, its stock's price hit $70 a share versus an offering price of only $28 a share.[4]

   Table 10-1 lists the best performing and the worst performing IPOs of 2000, and it shows how they performed from their offering dates through year-end 2000.

---

[2]MicroDrive has 60 million shares authorized but only 50 million outstanding; thus, it has 10 million authorized but unissued shares. If it had no authorized but unissued shares, management could increase the authorized shares by obtaining stockholders' approval, which would generally be granted without any arguments.

[3]The stock Coors offered to the public was designated Class B, and it was nonvoting. The Coors family retained the founders' shares, called Class A stock, which carried full voting privileges. The company was large enough to obtain an NYSE listing, but at that time the Exchange had a requirement that listed common stocks must have full voting rights, which precluded Coors from obtaining an NYSE listing.

[4]If someone bought Boston Chicken or Planet Hollywood at the initial offering price and sold the shares shortly thereafter, he or she would have done well. A long-term holder would have fared less well—both companies later went bankrupt. Netscape was in serious trouble, but it was sold to AOL in 1998.

Martha Bodyslams WWF

During the week of October 18, 1999, both Martha Stewart Living Omnimedia Inc. and the World Wrestling Federation (WWF) went public in IPOs. This created a lot of public interest, and it led to media reports comparing the two companies. Both deals attracted strong investor demand, and both were well received. In its first day of trading, WWF's stock closed above $25, an increase of nearly 49 percent above its $17 offering price. Martha Stewart did even better—it closed a little above $37, which was 105 percent above its $18 offering price. This performance led CBS MarketWatch reporter Steve Gelsi to write an online report entitled, "Martha Bodyslams the WWF!"

Both stocks generated a lot of interest, but when the hype died down, astute investors recognized that both stocks have risk. Indeed, one month later, WWF had declined to just above $21, while Martha Stewart had fallen to $28 a share. While Martha is still ahead, many analysts believe that over the long term WWF may have both more upside potential and less risk. However, Martha Stewart has a devoted set of investors, so despite all the uncertainty, the one certainty is that this battle is far from over.

Source: Steve Gelsi, "Martha Bodyslams the WWF," **http://cbs.marketwatch.com**, October 19, 1999.

As the table shows, not all IPOs are as well received as were Netscape and Boston Chicken. Moreover, even if you are able to identify a "hot" issue, it is often difficult to purchase shares in the initial offering. These deals are generally *oversubscribed*, which means that the demand for shares at the offering price exceeds the number of shares issued. In such instances, investment bankers favor large institutional investors (who are their best customers), and small investors find it hard, if not impossible, to get in on the ground floor. They can buy the stock in the after-market, but evidence suggests that if you do not get in on the ground floor, the average IPO underperforms the overall market over the longer run.[5]

Before you conclude that it isn't fair to let only the best customers have the stock in an initial offering, think about what it takes to become a best customer. Best customers are usually investors who have done lots of business in the past with the investment banking firm's brokerage department. In other words, they have paid large sums as commissions in the past, and they are expected to continue doing so in the future. As is so often true, there is no free lunch—most of the investors who get in on the ground floor of an IPO have in fact paid for this privilege. See Chapter 19 for a more detailed discussion of investment banking.

Finally, it is important to recognize that firms can go public without raising any additional capital. For example, Ford Motor Company was once owned exclusively by the Ford family. When Henry Ford died, he left a substantial part of his stock to the Ford Foundation. Ford Motor went public when the Foundation later sold some of its stock to the general public, even though the company raised no capital in the transaction.

Self-Test Questions

Differentiate between a closely held corporation and a publicly owned corporation.

Differentiate between a listed stock and an unlisted stock.

Differentiate between primary and secondary markets.

What is an IPO?

[5]See Jay R. Ritter, "The Long-Run Performance of Initial Public Offerings," *Journal of Finance*, March 1991, Vol. 46, No. 1, 3–27.

TABLE 10-1 Initial Public Stock Offerings in 2000

Issuer (Business)	Issue Date	Offer Price	U.S. Proceeds (millions)	% Change from Offer: 1st Day's Trading	% Change from Offer: Year End
The Best Performers					
Embarcadero Technologies	4/20/00	$10.00	$42.0	+60.0%	+350.0%
Krispy Kreme Doughnuts	4/5/00	21.00	63.0	+82.7	+295.2
First Horizon Pharmaceutical	5/31/00	8.00	30.4	+3.1	+284.4
Sonus Networks	5/25/00	7.67	115.0	+119.6	+229.3
Sun Life Fini Svcs of Canada	3/23/00	8.50	305.2	+10.3	+213.2
Stanford Microdevices	5/25/00	12.00	48.0	+28.1	+200.0
Praecis Pharmaceuticals	4/27/00	10.00	80.0	+10.0	+192.5
Ulticom	4/5/00	13.00	55.3	+53.9	+171.2
Community Health Systems	6/9/00	13.00	243.8	+5.3	+169.2
webMethods	2/11/00	35.00	165.0	+507.5	+167.0
The Worst Performers					
Pets.com	2/11/00	$11.00	$66.0	−34.1%	−99.1%
HealthGate Data	1/26/00	11.00	41.3	+6.8	−98.3
VarsityBooks.com	2/15/00	10.00	40.8	−1.3	−98.1
ImproveNet	3/16/00	16.00	44.2	−11.7	−97.7
Asiacontent.com	4/12/00	14.00	70.0	−21.4	−97.3
Uproar	3/17/00	33.88	84.7	−21.0	−97.1
Netpliance	3/17/00	18.00	144.0	+22.6	−97.1
Opus360	4/7/00	10.00	77.0	+25.0	−96.9
Savvis Communications	2/15/00	24.00	408.0	+0.0	−96.4
BusyBox.com	6/28/00	5.00	12.5	+11.3	−96.2

Source: Kara Scannell, "IPO Rocket Lands as Investors Prefer Profits to Pipe Dreams," *The Wall Street Journal,* January 2, 2001, R6.

Common Stock Valuation

Common stock represents an ownership interest in a corporation, but to the typical investor a share of common stock is simply a piece of paper characterized by two features:

1. It entitles its owner to dividends, but only if the company has earnings out of which dividends can be paid, and only if management chooses to pay dividends rather than retaining and reinvesting all the earnings. Whereas a bond contains a *promise* to pay interest, common stock provides no such promise—if you own a stock, you may *expect* a dividend, but your expectations may not in fact be met. To illustrate, Long Island Lighting Company (LILCO) had paid dividends on its common stock for more than 50 years, and people expected those dividends to continue. However, when the company encountered severe problems a few years ago, it stopped paying dividends. Note, though, that LILCO continued to pay interest on its bonds; if it had not, then it would have been declared bankrupt, and the bondholders could potentially have taken over the company.
2. Stock can be sold at some future date, hopefully at a price greater than the purchase price. If the stock is actually sold at a price above its purchase price, the investor

will receive a *capital gain.* Generally, at the time people buy common stocks, they do expect to receive capital gains; otherwise, they would not purchase the stocks. However, after the fact, one can end up with capital losses rather than capital gains. LILCO's stock price dropped from $17.50 to $3.75 in one year, so the *expected* capital gain on that stock turned out to be a huge *actual* capital loss.

Definitions of Terms Used in Stock Valuation Models

Common stocks provide an expected future cash flow stream, and a stock's value is found in the same manner as the values of other financial assets—namely, as the present value of the expected future cash flow stream. The expected cash flows consist of two elements: (1) the dividends expected in each year and (2) the price investors expect to receive when they sell the stock. The expected final stock price includes the return of the original investment plus an expected capital gain.

We saw in Chapter 1 that managers seek to maximize the values of their firms' stocks. A manager's actions affect both the stream of income to investors and the riskiness of that stream. Therefore, managers need to know how alternative actions are likely to affect stock prices. At this point we develop some models to help show how the value of a share of stock is determined. We begin by defining the following terms:

D_t = dividend the stockholder *expects* to receive at the end of Year t. D_0 is the most recent dividend, which has already been paid; D_1 is the first dividend expected, and it will be paid at the end of this year; D_2 is the dividend expected at the end of two years; and so forth. D_1 represents the first cash flow a new purchaser of the stock will receive. Note that D_0, the dividend that has just been paid, is known with certainty. However, all future dividends are expected values, so the estimate of D_t may differ among investors.[6]

P_0 = actual **market price** of the stock today.

$\hat{P}_t$ = expected price of the stock at the end of each Year t (pronounced "P hat t"). $\hat{P}_0$ is the **intrinsic,** or *theoretical,* **value** of the stock today as seen by the particular investor doing the analysis; $\hat{P}_1$ is the price expected at the end of one year; and so on. Note that $\hat{P}_0$ is the intrinsic value of the stock today based on a particular investor's estimate of the stock's expected dividend stream and the riskiness of that stream. Hence, whereas the market price P_0 is fixed and is identical for all investors, $\hat{P}_0$ could differ among investors depending on how optimistic they are regarding the company. The caret, or "hat," is used to indicate that $\hat{P}_t$ is an estimated value. $\hat{P}_0$, the individual investor's estimate of the intrinsic value today, could be above or below P_0, the current stock-price, but an investor would buy the stock only if his or her estimate of $\hat{P}_0$ were equal to or greater than P_0.

[6]Stocks generally pay dividends quarterly, so theoretically we should evaluate them on a quarterly basis. However, in stock valuation, most analysts work on an annual basis because the data generally are not precise enough to warrant refinement to a quarterly model. For additional information on the quarterly model, see Charles M. Linke and J. Kenton Zumwalt, "Estimation Biases in Discounted Cash Flow Analysis of Equity Capital Cost in Rate Regulation," *Financial Management,* Autumn 1984, 15–21.

Since there are many investors in the market, there can be many values for $\hat{P}_0$. However, we can think of a group of "average," or "marginal," investors whose actions actually determine the market price. For these marginal investors, P_0 must equal $\hat{P}_0$; otherwise, a disequilibrium would exist, and buying and selling in the market would change P_0 until $P_0 = \hat{P}_0$ for the marginal investor.

g = expected **growth rate** in dividends as predicted by a marginal investor. If dividends are expected to grow at a constant rate, g is also equal to the expected rate of growth in earnings and in the stock's price. Different investors may use different g's to evaluate a firm's stock, but the market price, P_0, is set on the basis of the g estimated by marginal investors.

k_s = minimum acceptable, or **required, rate of return** on the stock, considering both its riskiness and the returns available on other investments. Again, this term generally relates to marginal investors. The determinants of k_s include the real rate of return, expected inflation, and risk, as discussed in Chapter 6.

$\hat{k}_s$ = **expected rate of return** that an investor who buys the stock expects to receive in the future. $\hat{k}_s$ (pronounced "k hat s") could be above or below k_s, but one would buy the stock only if $\hat{k}_s$ were equal to or greater than k_s.

$\bar{k}_s$ = **actual,** or **realized,** ***after-the-fact*** **rate of return,** pronounced "k bar s." You may *expect* to obtain a return of $\hat{k}_s$ = 15 percent if you buy Exxon Mobil today, but if the market goes down, you may end up next year with an actual realized return that is much lower, perhaps even negative.

D_1/P_0 = expected **dividend yield** during the coming year. If the stock is expected to pay a dividend of D_1 = \$1 during the next 12 months, and if its current price is P_0 = \$10, then the expected dividend yield is \$1/\$10 = 0.10 = 10%.

$\frac{\hat{P}_1 - P_0}{P_0}$ = expected **capital gains yield** during the coming year. If the stock sells for \$10 today, and if it is expected to rise to \$10.50 at the end of one year, then the expected capital gain is $\hat{P}_1 - P_0$ = \$10.50 − \$10.00 = \$0.50, and the expected capital gains yield is \$0.50/\$10 = 0.05 = 5%.

Expected total return = $\hat{k}_s$ = expected dividend yield (D_1/P_0) plus expected capital gains yield [$(\hat{P}_1 - P_0)/P_0$]. In our example, the **expected total return** = $\hat{k}_s$ = 10% + 5% = 15%.

Expected Dividends as the Basis for Stock Values

In our discussion of bonds, we found the value of a bond as the present value of interest payments over the life of the bond plus the present value of the bond's maturity (or par) value:

$$V_B = \frac{INT}{(1 + k_d)^1} + \frac{INT}{(1 + k_d)^2} + \cdots + \frac{INT}{(1 + k_d)^N} + \frac{M}{(1 + k_d)^N}.$$

Stock prices are likewise determined as the present value of a stream of cash flows, and the basic stock valuation equation is similar to the bond valuation equation. What are the cash flows that corporations provide to their stockholders? First, think of yourself as an investor who buys a stock with the intention of holding it (in your family) forever. In this case, all that you (and your heirs) will receive is a stream of dividends, and the value of the stock today is calculated as the present value of an infinite stream of dividends:

$$\text{Value of stock} = \hat{P}_0 = \text{PV of expected future dividends}$$
$$= \frac{D_1}{(1 + k_s)^1} + \frac{D_2}{(1 + k_s)^2} + \cdots + \frac{D_\infty}{(1 + k_s)^\infty} \quad \textbf{(10-1)}$$
$$= \sum_{t=1}^{\infty} \frac{D_t}{(1 + k_s)^t}.$$

What about the more typical case, where you expect to hold the stock for a finite period and then sell it—what will be the value of $\hat{P}_0$ in this case? Unless the company is likely to be liquidated or sold and thus to disappear, *the value of the stock is again determined by Equation 10-1.* To see this, recognize that for any individual investor, the expected cash flows consist of expected dividends plus the expected sale price of the stock. However, the sale price the current investor receives will depend on the dividends some future investor expects. Therefore, for all present and future investors in total, expected cash flows must be based on expected future dividends. Put another way, unless a firm is liquidated or sold to another concern, the cash flows it provides to its stockholders will consist only of a stream of dividends; therefore, the value of a share of its stock must be established as the present value of that expected dividend stream.

The general validity of Equation 10-1 can also be confirmed by asking the following question: Suppose I buy a stock and expect to hold it for one year. I will receive dividends during the year plus the value $\hat{P}_1$ when I sell out at the end of the year. But what will determine the value of $\hat{P}_1$? The answer is that it will be determined as the present value of the dividends expected during Year 2 plus the stock price at the end of that year, which, in turn, will be determined as the present value of another set of future dividends and an even more distant stock price. This process can be continued ad infinitum, and the ultimate result is Equation 10-1.[7]

Self-Test Questions

Explain the following statement: "Whereas a bond contains a promise to pay interest, a share of common stock typically provides an expectation of, but no promise of, dividends plus capital gains."

What are the two parts of most stocks' expected total return?

How does one calculate the capital gains yield and the dividend yield of a stock?

Constant Growth Stocks

Equation 10-1 is a generalized stock valuation model in the sense that the time pattern of D_t can be anything: D_t can be rising, falling, fluctuating randomly, or it can even be zero for several years, and Equation 10-1 will still hold. With a computer spreadsheet

[7]We should note that investors periodically lose sight of the long-run nature of stocks as investments and forget that in order to sell a stock at a profit, one must find a buyer who will pay the higher price. If you analyze a stock's value in accordance with Equation 10-1, conclude that the stock's market price exceeds a reasonable value, and then buy the stock anyway, then you would be following the "bigger fool" theory of investment—you think that you may be a fool to buy the stock at its excessive price, but you also think that when you get ready to sell it, you can find someone who is an even bigger fool. The bigger fool theory was widely followed in the spring of 2000, just before the Nasdaq market lost more than one-third of its value.

we can easily use this equation to find a stock's intrinsic value for any pattern of dividends. In practice, the hard part is getting an accurate forecast of the future dividends. However, in many cases, the stream of dividends is expected to grow at a constant rate. If this is the case, Equation 10-1 may be rewritten as follows:[8]

$$\begin{aligned}\hat{P}_0 &= \frac{D_0(1+g)^1}{(1+k_s)^1} + \frac{D_0(1+g)^2}{(1+k_s)^2} + \cdots + \frac{D_0(1+g)^\infty}{(1+k_s)^\infty}\\ &= D_0 \sum_{t=1}^{\infty} \frac{(1+g)^t}{(1+k_s)^t} \qquad \textbf{(10-2)}\\ &= \frac{D_0(1+g)}{k_s - g} = \frac{D_1}{k_s - g}.\end{aligned}$$

The last term of Equation 10-2 is called the **constant growth model,** or the **Gordon model** after Myron J. Gordon, who did much to develop and popularize it.

Note that a necessary condition for the derivation of Equation 10-2 is that k_s be greater than g. Look back at the second form of Equation 10-2. If g is larger than k_s, then $(1 + g)^t/(1 + k_s)^t$ must always be greater than one. In this case, the second line of Equation 10-2 is the sum of an infinite number of terms, with each term being a number larger than one. Therefore, if the constant g were greater than k_s, the resulting stock price would be infinite! Since no company is worth an infinite price, it is impossible to have a constant growth rate that is greater than k_s. *So, if you try to use the constant growth model in a situation where g is greater than k_s, you will violate laws of economics and mathematics, and your results will be both wrong and meaningless.*

Illustration of a Constant Growth Stock

Assume that MicroDrive just paid a dividend of \$1.15 (that is, D_0 = \$1.15). Its stock has a required rate of return, k_s, of 13.4 percent, and investors expect the dividend to grow at a constant 8 percent rate in the future. The estimated dividend one year hence would be D_1 = \$1.15(1.08) = \$1.24; D_2 would be \$1.34; and the estimated dividend five years hence would be \$1.69:

$$D_t = D_0(1 + g)^t = \$1.15(1.08)^5 = \$1.69.$$

We could use this procedure to estimate each future dividend, and then use Equation 10-1 to determine the current stock value, $\hat{P}_0$. In other words, we could find each expected future dividend, calculate its present value, and then sum all the present values to find the intrinsic value of the stock.

Such a process would be time consuming, but we can take a short cut—just insert the illustrative data into Equation 10-2 to find the stock's intrinsic value, \$23:

$$\hat{P}_0 = \frac{\$1.15(1.08)}{0.134 - 0.08} = \frac{\$1.242}{0.054} = \$23.00.$$

The concept underlying the valuation process for a constant growth stock is graphed in Figure 10-1. Dividends are growing at the rate g = 8%, but because $k_s >$ g, the present value of each future dividend is declining. For example, the dividend in Year 1 is $D_1 = D_0(1 + g)^1$ = \$1.15(1.08) = \$1.242. However, the present value of this dividend, discounted at 13.4 percent, is $PV(D_1)$ = \$1.242/(1.134)^1 = \$1.095.

[8]The last term in Equation 10-2 is derived in the Extensions to Chapter 5 of Eugene F. Brigham and Phillip R. Daves, *Intermediate Financial Management,* 7th ed. (Fort Worth, TX: Harcourt College Publishers, 2002). In essence, Equation 10-2 is the sum of a geometric progression, and the final result is the solution value of the progression.

FIGURE 10-1 Present Values of Dividends of a Constant Growth Stock where D_0 = \$1.15, g = 8%, k_s = 13.4%

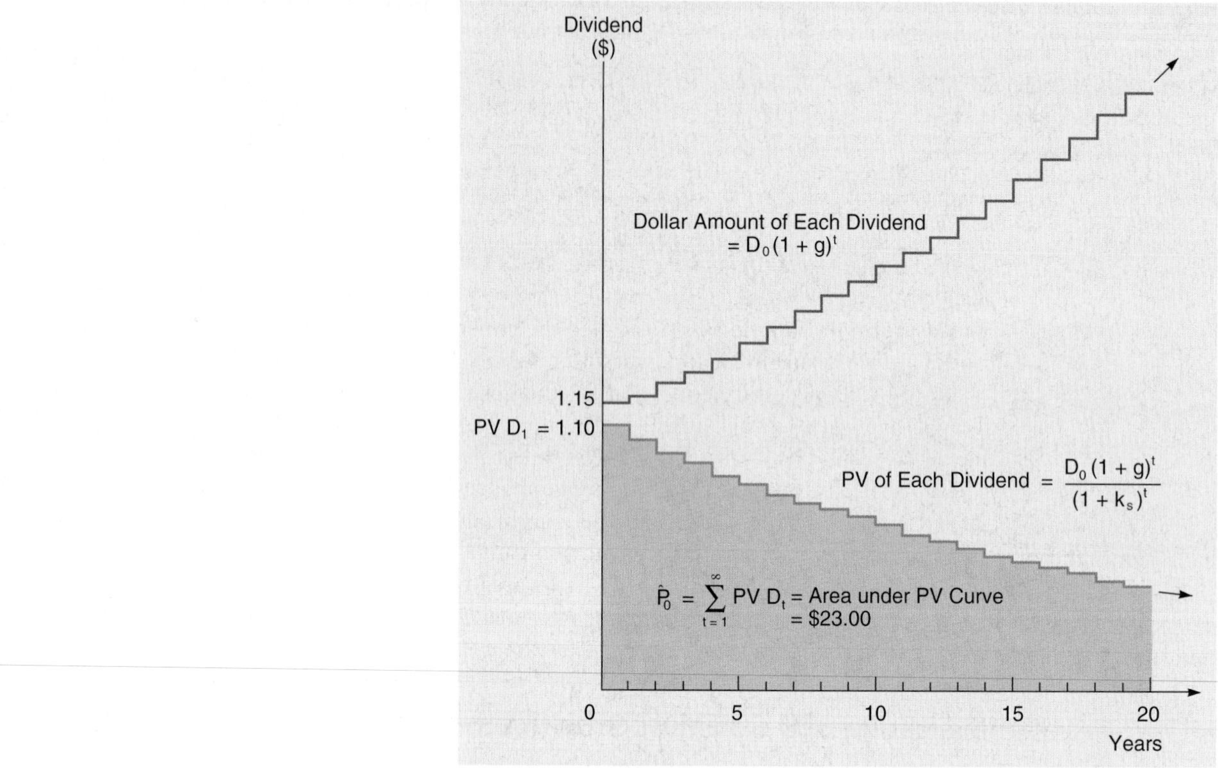

The dividend expected in Year 2 grows to \$1.242(1.08) = \$1.341, but the present value of this dividend falls to \$1.043. Continuing, D_3 = \$1.449 and PV(D_3) = \$0.993, and so on. Thus, the expected dividends are growing, but the present value of each successive dividend is declining, because the dividend growth rate (8%) is less than the rate used for discounting the dividends to the present (13.4%).

If we summed the present values of each future dividend, this summation would be the value of the stock, $\hat{P}_0$. When g is a constant, this summation is equal to $D_1/(k_s - g)$, as shown in Equation 10-2. Therefore, if we extended the lower step function curve in Figure 10-1 on out to infinity and added up the present values of each future dividend, the summation would be identical to the value given by Equation 10-2, \$23.00.

Although Equation 10-2 assumes that dividends grow to infinity, most of the value is based on dividends during a relatively short time period. In our example, 70 percent of the value is attributed to the first 25 years, 91 percent to the first 50 years, and 99.4 percent to the first 100 years. So, companies don't have to live forever for the Gordon growth model to be used.

Dividend and Earnings Growth

Growth in dividends occurs primarily as a result of growth in *earnings per share (EPS)*. Earnings growth, in turn, results from a number of factors, including (1) inflation, (2) the amount of earnings the company retains and reinvests, and (3) the rate of return the company earns on its equity (ROE). Regarding inflation, if output (in units) is stable, but both sales prices and input costs rise at the inflation rate, then EPS will also grow at the inflation rate. Even without inflation, EPS will also grow as a result of the reinvestment, or plowback, of earnings. If the firm's earnings are not all paid out as dividends (that is, if some fraction of earnings is retained), the dollars of investment behind each share will rise over time, which should lead to growth in earnings and dividends.

Even though a stock's value is derived from expected dividends, this does not necessarily mean that corporations can increase their stock prices by simply raising the current dividend. Shareholders care about *all* dividends, both current and those expected in the future. Moreover, there is a trade-off between current dividends and future dividends. Companies that pay high current dividends necessarily retain and reinvest less of their earnings in the business, and that reduces future earnings and dividends. So, the issue is this: Do shareholders prefer higher current dividends at the cost of lower future dividends, the reverse, or are stockholders indifferent? There is no simple answer to this question. Shareholders prefer to have the company retain earnings, hence pay less current dividends, if it has highly profitable investment opportunities, but they want the company to pay earnings out if investment opportunities are poor. Taxes also play a role—since dividends and capital gains are taxed differently, dividend policy affects investors' taxes. We will consider dividend policy in detail in Chapter 18.

Do Stock Prices Reflect Long-Term or Short-Term Events?

Managers often complain that the stock market is shortsighted, and that it cares only about next quarter's performance. Let's use the constant growth model to test this assertion. MicroDrive's most recent dividend was $1.15, and it is expected to grow at a rate of 8 percent per year. Since we know the growth rate, we can forecast the dividends for each of the next five years and then find their present values:

$$\begin{aligned} PV &= \frac{D_0(1+g)^1}{(1+k_s)^1} + \frac{D_0(1+g)^2}{(1+k_s)^2} + \frac{D_0(1+g)^3}{(1+k_s)^3} + \frac{D_0(1+g)^4}{(1+k_s)^4} + \frac{D_0(1+g)^5}{(1+k_s)^5} \\ &= \frac{\$1.15(1.08)^1}{(1.134)^1} + \frac{\$1.15(1.08)^2}{(1.134)^2} + \frac{\$1.15(1.08)^3}{(1.134)^3} + \frac{\$1.15(1.08)^4}{(1.134)^4} + \frac{\$1.15(1.08)^5}{(1.134)^5} \\ &= \frac{\$1.242}{(1.134)^1} + \frac{\$1.341}{(1.134)^2} + \frac{\$1.449}{(1.134)^3} + \frac{\$1.565}{(1.134)^4} + \frac{\$1.690}{(1.134)^5} \\ &= 1.095 + 1.043 + 0.993 + 0.946 + 0.901 \\ &\approx \$5.00. \end{aligned}$$

Recall that MicroDrive's stock price is $23.00. Therefore, only $5.00, or 22 percent, of the $23.00 stock price is attributable to short-term cash flows. This means that MicroDrive's managers will have a bigger effect on the stock price if they work to increase long-term cash flows rather than focus on short-term flows. This situation holds for most companies. Indeed, a number of professors and consulting firms have used actual company data to show that more than 80 percent of a typical company's stock price is due to cash flows expected more than five years in the future.

This brings up an interesting question. If most of a stock's value is due to long-term cash flows, why do managers and analysts pay so much attention to quarterly earnings? Part of the answer lies in the information conveyed by short-term earnings. For example, if actual quarterly earnings are lower than expected, not because of fundamental problems but only because a company has increased its R&D expenditures, studies have shown that the stock price probably won't decline and may actually increase. This makes sense, because R&D should increase future cash flows. On the other hand, if quarterly earnings are lower than expected because customers don't like the company's new products, then this new information will have negative implications for future values of g, the long-term growth rate. As we show later in this chapter, even small changes in g can lead to large changes in stock prices. Therefore, while the quarterly earnings themselves might not be very important, the information they convey about future prospects can be terribly important.

Another reason many managers focus on short-term earnings is that some firms pay managerial bonuses on the basis of current earnings rather than stock prices (which reflect future earnings). For these managers, the concern with quarterly earnings is not due to their effect on stock prices—it's due to their effect on bonuses.[9]

When Can the Constant Growth Model Be Used?

The constant growth model is often appropriate for mature companies with a stable history of growth. Expected growth rates vary somewhat among companies, but dividend growth for most mature firms is generally expected to continue in the future at about the same rate as nominal gross domestic product (real GDP plus inflation). On this basis, one might expect the dividends of an average, or "normal," company to grow at a rate of 5 to 8 percent a year.

Note too that Equation 10-2 is sufficiently general to handle the case of a **zero growth stock,** where the dividend is expected to remain constant over time. If g = 0, Equation 10-2 reduces to Equation 10-3:

$$\hat{P}_0 = \frac{D}{k_s}. \tag{10-3}$$

This is essentially the same equation as the one we developed in Chapter 8 for a perpetuity, and it is simply the dividend divided by the discount rate.

Self-Test Questions

Write out and explain the valuation formula for a constant growth stock.

Explain how the formula for a zero growth stock is related to that for a constant growth stock.

Are stock prices affected more by long-term or short-term events?

Expected Rate of Return on a Constant Growth Stock

We can solve Equation 10-2 for k_s, again using the hat to indicate that we are dealing with an expected rate of return:[10]

$$\begin{array}{ccccc} \text{Expected rate of return} & = & \text{Expected dividend yield} & + & \text{Expected growth rate, or capital gains yield} \\ \hat{k}_s & = & \dfrac{D_1}{P_0} & + & g. \end{array} \tag{10-4}$$

Thus, if you buy a stock for a price P_0 = \$23, and if you expect the stock to pay a dividend D_1 = \$1.242 one year from now and to grow at a constant rate g = 8% in the future, then your expected rate of return will be 13.4 percent:

$$\hat{k}_s = \frac{\$1.242}{\$23} + 8\% = 5.4\% + 8\% = 13.4\%.$$

[9]Many apparent puzzles in finance can be explained either by managerial compensation systems or by peculiar features of the Tax Code. So, if you can't explain a firm's behavior in terms of economic logic, look to bonuses or taxes as possible explanations.

[10]The k_s value in Equation 10-2 is a *required* rate of return, but when we transform to obtain Equation 10-4, we are finding an *expected* rate of return. Obviously, the transformation requires that $k_s = \hat{k}_s$. This equality holds if the stock market is in equilibrium, a condition that will be discussed later in the chapter.

In this form, we see that $\hat{k}_s$ is the *expected total return* and that it consists of an *expected dividend yield*, $D_1/P_0 = 5.4\%$, plus an *expected growth rate or capital gains yield*, $g = 8\%$.

Suppose this analysis had been conducted on January 1, 2002, so $P_0 = \$23$ is the January 1, 2002, stock price, and $D_1 = \$1.242$ is the dividend expected at the end of 2002. What is the expected stock price at the end of 2002? We would again apply Equation 10-2, but this time we would use the year-end dividend, $D_2 = D_1(1 + g) = \$1.242(1.08) = \$1.3414$:

$$\hat{P}_{12/31/02} = \frac{D_{2003}}{k_s - g} = \frac{\$1.3414}{0.134 - 0.08} = \$24.84.$$

Now, note that \$24.84 is 8 percent larger than P_0, the \$23 price on January 1, 2002:

$$\$23(1.08) = \$24.84.$$

Thus, we would expect to make a capital gain of \$24.84 − \$23.00 = \$1.84 during 2002, which would provide a capital gains yield of 8 percent:

$$\text{Capital gains yield}_{2002} = \frac{\text{Capital gain}}{\text{Beginning price}} = \frac{\$1.84}{\$23.00} = 0.08 = 8\%.$$

We could extend the analysis on out, and in each future year the expected capital gains yield would always equal g, the expected dividend growth rate.

Continuing, the dividend yield in 2003 could be estimated as follows:

$$\text{Dividend yield}_{2003} = \frac{D_{2003}}{\hat{P}_{12/31/02}} = \frac{\$1.3414}{\$24.84} = 0.054 = 5.4\%.$$

The dividend yield for 2004 could also be calculated, and again it would be 5.4 percent. Thus, *for a constant growth stock*, the following conditions must hold:

1. The dividend is expected to grow forever at a constant rate, g.
2. The stock price is expected to grow at this same rate.
3. The expected dividend yield is a constant.
4. The expected capital gains yield is also a constant, and it is equal to g.
5. The expected total rate of return, $\hat{k}_s$, is equal to the expected dividend yield plus the expected growth rate: $\hat{k}_s$ = dividend yield + g.

The popular Motley Fool web site **http://www.fool.com/school/introductiontovaluation.htm** provides a good description of some of the benefits and drawbacks of a few of the more commonly used valuation procedures.

The term *expected* should be clarified—it means expected in a probabilistic sense, as the "statistically expected" outcome. Thus, if we say the growth rate is expected to remain constant at 8 percent, we mean that the best prediction for the growth rate in any future year is 8 percent, not that we literally expect the growth rate to be exactly 8 percent in each future year. In this sense, the constant growth assumption is a reasonable one for many large, mature companies.

Self-Test Questions

What conditions must hold if a stock is to be evaluated using the constant growth model?

What does the term "expected" mean when we say expected growth rate?

Valuing Stocks That Have a Nonconstant Growth Rate

For many companies, it is inappropriate to assume that dividends will grow at a constant rate. Firms typically go through *life cycles*. During the early part of their lives, their growth is much faster than that of the economy as a whole; then they match the economy's growth; and finally their growth is slower than that of the economy.[11] Automobile manufacturers in the 1920s, computer software firms such as Microsoft in the 1990s, and Internet firms such as AOL in the 2000s are examples of firms in the early part of the cycle; these firms are called **supernormal,** or **nonconstant, growth** firms. Figure 10-2 illustrates nonconstant growth and also compares it with normal growth, zero growth, and negative growth.[12]

In the figure, the dividends of the supernormal growth firm are expected to grow at a 30 percent rate for three years, after which the growth rate is expected to fall to 8 percent, the assumed average for the economy. The value of this firm, like any other, is the present value of its expected future dividends as determined by Equation 10-1. When D_t is growing at a constant rate, we simplified Equation 10-1 to $\hat{P}_0 = D_1/(k_s - g)$. In the supernormal case, however, the expected growth rate is not a constant—it declines at the end of the period of supernormal growth.

[11]The concept of life cycles could be broadened to *product cycle*, which would include both small startup companies and large companies like Procter & Gamble, which periodically introduce new products that give sales and earnings a boost. We should also mention *business cycles*, which alternately depress and boost sales and profits. The growth rate just after a major new product has been introduced, or just after a firm emerges from the depths of a recession, is likely to be much higher than the "expected long-run average growth rate," which is the proper number for a DCF analysis.

[12]A negative growth rate indicates a declining company. A mining company whose profits are falling because of a declining ore body is an example. Someone buying such a company would expect its earnings, and consequently its dividends and stock price, to decline each year, and this would lead to capital losses rather than capital gains. Obviously, a declining company's stock price will be relatively low, and its dividend yield must be high enough to offset the expected capital loss and still produce a competitive total return. Students sometimes argue that they would never be willing to buy a stock whose price was expected to decline. However, if the annual dividends are large enough to *more than offset* the falling stock price, the stock could still provide a good return.

FIGURE 10-2 Illustrative Dividend Growth Rates

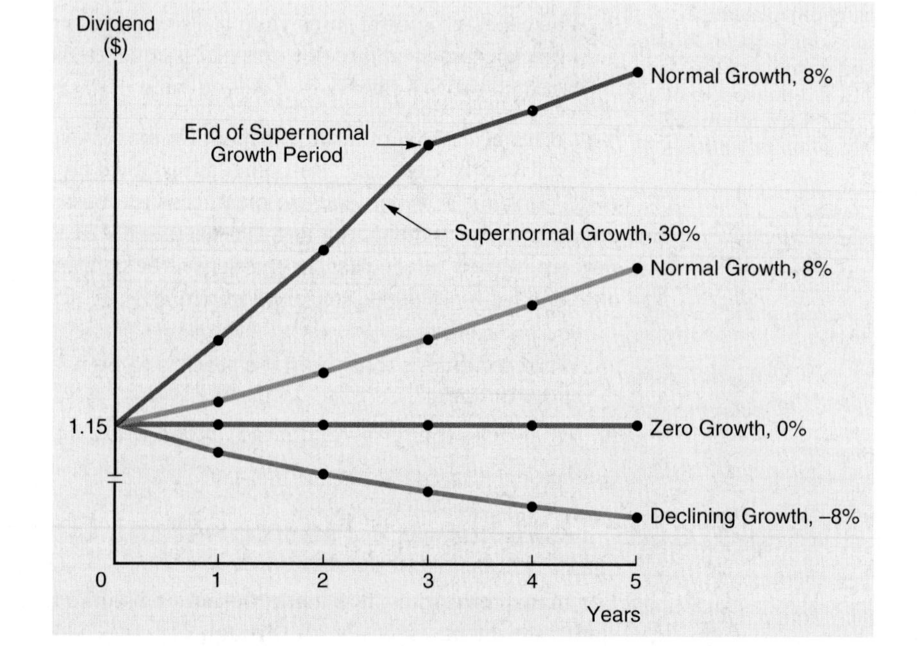

Because Equation 10-2 requires a constant growth rate, we obviously cannot use it to value stocks that have nonconstant growth. However, assuming that a company currently enjoying supernormal growth will eventually slow down and become a constant growth stock, we can combine Equations 10-1 and 10-2 to form a new formula, Equation 10-5, for valuing it. First, we assume that the dividend will grow at a nonconstant rate (generally a relatively high rate) for N periods, after which it will grow at a constant rate, g. N is often called the **terminal date,** or **horizon date.**

We can use the constant growth formula, Equation 10-2, to determine what the stock's **horizon,** or **terminal, value** will be N periods from today:

$$\text{Horizon value} = \hat{P}_N = \frac{D_{N+1}}{k_s - g} = \frac{D_N(1+g)}{k_s - g} \qquad \textbf{(10-2a)}$$

The stock's intrinsic value today, $\hat{P}_0$, is the present value of the dividends during the nonconstant growth period plus the present value of the horizon value:

$$\hat{P}_0 = \underbrace{\frac{D_1}{(1+k_s)^1} + \frac{D_2}{(1+k_s)^2} + \cdots + \frac{D_N}{(1+k_s)^N}}_{\substack{\text{PV of dividends during the}\\ \text{nonconstant growth period}\\ t = 1, \cdots N.}} + \underbrace{\frac{D_{N+1}}{(1+k_s)^{N+1}} + \cdots + \frac{D_\infty}{(1+k_s)^\infty}}_{\substack{\text{PV of dividends during the}\\ \text{constant growth period}\\ t = N+1, \cdots \infty.}}.$$

$$\hat{P}_0 = \underbrace{\frac{D_1}{(1+k_s)^1} + \frac{D_2}{(1+k_s)^2} + \cdots + \frac{D_N}{(1+k_s)^N}}_{\substack{\text{PV of dividends during the}\\ \text{nonconstant growth period}\\ t = 1, \cdots N.}} + \underbrace{\frac{\hat{P}_N}{(1+k_s)^N}}_{\substack{\text{PV of horizon}\\ \text{value, } \hat{P}_N\text{:}\\ \frac{[(D_{N+1})/(k_s - g)]}{(1+k_s)^N}.}}. \qquad \textbf{(10-5)}$$

To implement Equation 10-5, we go through the following three steps:

1. Find the PV of the dividends during the period of nonconstant growth.
2. Find the price of the stock at the end of the nonconstant growth period, at which point it has become a constant growth stock, and discount this price back to the present.
3. Add these two components to find the intrinsic value of the stock, $\hat{P}_0$.

Figure 10-3 can be used to illustrate the process for valuing nonconstant growth stocks. Here we assume the following five facts exist:

k_s = stockholders' required rate of return = 13.4%. This rate is used to discount the cash flows.

N = years of supernormal growth = 3.

g_s = rate of growth in both earnings and dividends during the supernormal growth period = 30%. This rate is shown directly on the time line. Note: The growth rate during the supernormal growth period could vary from year to year. Also, there could be several different supernormal growth periods, e.g., 30% for three years, then 20% for three years, and then a constant 8%.)

g_n = rate of normal, constant growth after the supernormal period = 8%. This rate is also shown on the time line, between Periods 3 and 4.

D_0 = last dividend the company paid = \$1.15.

FIGURE 10-3 Process for Finding the Value of a Supernormal Growth Stock

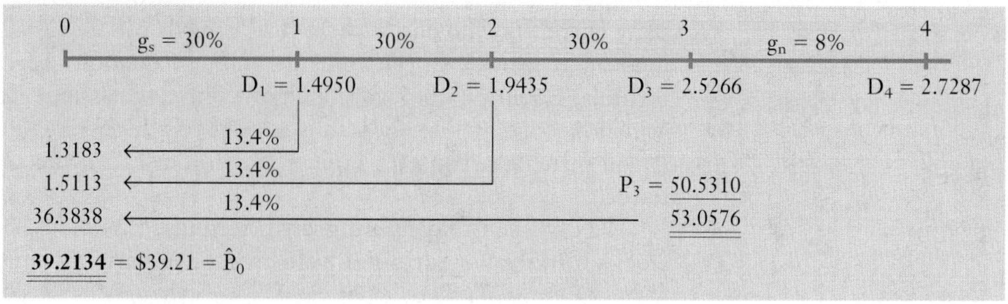

NOTES TO FIGURE 10-3:

Step 1. Calculate the dividends expected at the end of each year during the supernormal growth period. Calculate the first dividend, $D_1 = D_0(1 + g_s) = \$1.15(1.30) = \$1.4950$. Here g_s is the growth rate during the three-year supernormal growth period, 30 percent. Show the $1.4950 on the time line as the cash flow at Time 1. Then, calculate $D_2 = D_1(1 + g_s) = \$1.4950(1.30) = \$1.9435$, and then $D_3 = D_2(1 + g_s) = \$1.9435(1.30) = \$2.5266$. Show these values on the time line as the cash flows at Time 2 and Time 3. Note that D_0 is used only to calculate D_1.

Step 2. The price of the stock is the PV of dividends from Time 1 to infinity, so in theory we could project each future dividend, with the normal growth rate, $g_n = 8\%$, used to calculate D_4 and subsequent dividends. However, we know that after D_3 has been paid, which is at Time 3, the stock becomes a constant growth stock. Therefore, we can use the constant growth formula to find $\hat{P}_3$, which is the PV of the dividends from Time 4 to infinity as evaluated at Time 3.

First, we determine $D_4 = \$2.5266(1.08) = \$2.7287$ for use in the formula, and then we calculate $\hat{P}_3$ as follows:

$$\hat{P}_3 = \frac{D_4}{k_s - g_n} = \frac{\$2.7287}{0.134 - 0.08} = \$50.5310.$$

We show this $50.5310 on the time line as a second cash flow at Time 3. The $50.5310 is a Time 3 cash flow in the sense that the owner of the stock could sell it for $50.5310 at Time 3 and also in the sense that $50.5310 is the present value of the dividend cash flows from Time 4 to infinity. Note that the *total cash flow* at Time 3 consists of the sum of $D_3 + \hat{P}_3 = \$2.5266 + \$50.5310 = \$53.0576$.

Step 3. Now that the cash flows have been placed on the time line, we can discount each cash flow at the required rate of return, $k_s = 13.4\%$. We could discount each flow by dividing by $(1.134)^t$, where $t = 1$ for Time 1, $t = 2$ for Time 2, and $t = 3$ for Time 3. This produces the PVs shown to the left below the time line, and the sum of the PVs is the value of the supernormal growth stock, $39.21.

With a financial calculator, you can find the PV of the cash flows as shown on the time line with the cash flow (CFLO) register of your calculator. Enter 0 for CF_0 because you get no cash flow at Time 0, $CF_1 = 1.495$, $CF_2 = 1.9435$, and $CF_3 = 2.5266 + 50.531 = 53.0576$. Then enter I = 13.4, and press the NPV key to find the value of the stock, $39.21.

The valuation process as diagrammed in Figure 10-3 is explained in the steps set forth below the time line. The value of the supernormal growth stock is calculated to be $39.21.

Self-Test Questions

Explain how one would find the value of a supernormal growth stock.

Explain what is meant by "terminal (horizon) date" and "horizon (terminal) value."

Stock Market Equilibrium

Recall that k_i, the required return on Stock i, can be found using the Security Market Line (SML) equation as it was developed in our discussion of the Capital Asset Pricing Model (CAPM) back in Chapter 6:

$$k_i = k_{RF} + (k_M - k_{RF})b_i.$$

If the risk-free rate of return is 8 percent, the required return on an average stock is 12 percent, and Stock i has a beta of 2, then the marginal investor will require a return of 16 percent on Stock i:

$$k_i = 8\% + (12\% - 8\%)\,2.0$$
$$= 16\%$$

This 16 percent required return is shown as the point on the SML in Figure 10-4 associated with beta = 2.0.

The **marginal investor** will want to buy Stock i if its expected rate of return is more than 16 percent, will want to sell it if the expected rate of return is less than 16 percent, and will be indifferent, hence will hold but not buy or sell, if the expected rate of return is exactly 16 percent. Now suppose the investor's portfolio contains Stock i, and he or she analyzes the stock's prospects and concludes that its earnings, dividends, and price can be expected to grow at a constant rate of 5 percent per year. The last dividend was D_0 = \$2.8571, so the next expected dividend is

$$D_1 = \$2.8571(1.05) = \$3.$$

Our marginal investor observes that the present price of the stock, P_0, is \$30. Should he or she purchase more of Stock i, sell the stock, or maintain the present position?

The investor can calculate Stock i's *expected rate of return* as follows:

$$\hat{k}_i = \frac{D_1}{P_0} + g = \frac{\$3}{\$30} + 5\% = 15\%.$$

This value is plotted on Figure 10-4 as Point i, which is below the SML. Because the expected rate of return is less than the required return, this marginal investor would want to sell the stock, as would most other holders. However, few people would want to buy at the \$30 price, so the present owners would be unable to find buyers unless they cut the price of the stock. Thus, the price would decline, and this decline would continue until the price reached \$27.27, at which point the stock would be in **equilibrium,** defined as the price at which the expected rate of return, 16 percent, is equal to the required rate of return:

$$\hat{k}_i = \frac{\$3}{\$27.27} + 5\% = 11\% + 5\% = 16\% = k_i.$$

Had the stock initially sold for less than \$27.27, say, at \$25, events would have been reversed. Investors would have wanted to buy the stock because its expected rate

FIGURE 10-4 Expected and Required Returns on Stock i

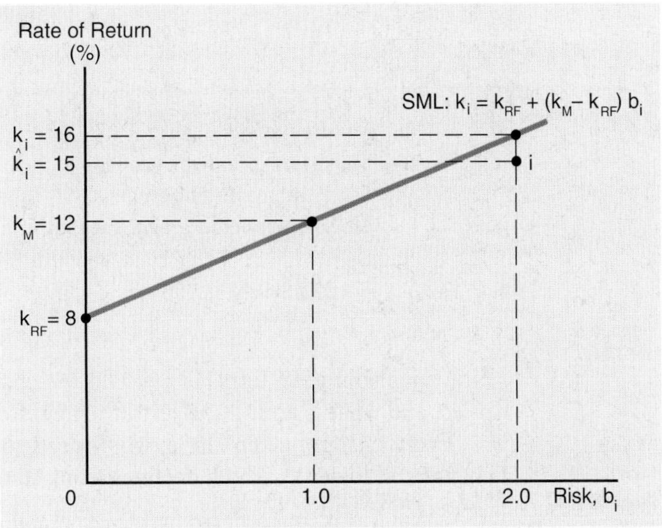

of return would have exceeded its required rate of return, and buy orders would have driven the stock's price up to \$27.27.

To summarize, in equilibrium two related conditions must hold:

1. A stock's expected rate of return as seen by the marginal investor must equal its required rate of return: $\hat{k}_i = k_i$.
2. The actual market price of the stock must equal its intrinsic value as estimated by the marginal investor: $P_0 = \hat{P}_0$.

Of course, some individual investors may believe that $\hat{k}_i > k$ and $\hat{P}_0 > P_0$, hence they would invest most of their funds in the stock, while other investors may have an opposite view and would sell all of their shares. However, it is the marginal investor who establishes the actual market price, and for this investor, we must have $\hat{k}_i = k_i$ and $P_0 = \hat{P}_0$. If these conditions do not hold, trading will occur until they do.

Changes in Equilibrium Stock Prices

Stock prices are not constant—they undergo violent changes at times. For example, on October 19, 1987, the Dow Jones average dropped 508 points, and the average stock lost about 23 percent of its value on that one day. Some individual stocks lost more than 70 percent of their value. Many investors (and companies) were wiped out, and a number of suicides occurred. On a brighter note, the Dow Jones average has increased by more than 300 points on a number of days during the 1990s. But what goes up often comes down. The Dow dropped 554 points on October 27, 1997, wiping out more than \$600 billion of wealth. This was the largest ever single-day point drop, and the 12th worst percentage loss (7.18 percent). On the next day, however, the Dow increased by 337 points, a record single-day increase. At the risk of understatement, the stock market is quite volatile!

To see how such changes can occur, assume that Stock i is in equilibrium, selling at a price of \$27.27. If all expectations were exactly met, during the next year the price would gradually rise to \$28.63, or by 5 percent. However, many different events could occur to cause a change in the equilibrium price. To illustrate, consider again the set of inputs used to develop Stock i's price of \$27.27, along with a new set of assumed input variables:

	Variable Value	
	Original	New
Risk-free rate, k_{RF}	8%	7%
Market risk premium, $k_M - k_{RF}$	4%	3%
Stock i's beta coefficient, b_i	2.0	1.0
Stock i's expected growth rate, g_i	5%	6%
D_0	\$2.8571	\$2.8571
Price of Stock i	\$27.27	?

Now give yourself a test: How would the change in each variable, by itself, affect the price, and what is your guess as to the new stock price?

Every change, taken alone, would lead to an *increase* in the price. The first three changes all lower k_i, which declines from 16 to 10 percent:

$$\text{Original } k_i = 8\% + 4\%(2.0) = 16\%.$$
$$\text{New } k_i = 7\% + 3\%(1.0) = 10\%.$$

Using these values, together with the new g value, we find that $\hat{P}_0$ rises from $27.27 to $75.71.[13]

$$\text{Original } \hat{P}_0 = \frac{\$2.8571(1.05)}{0.16 - 0.05} = \frac{\$3}{0.11} = \$27.27.$$

$$\text{New } \hat{P}_0 = \frac{\$2.8571(1.06)}{0.10 - 0.06} = \frac{\$3.0285}{0.04} = \$75.71.$$

At the new price, the expected and required rates of return are equal:[14]

$$\hat{k}_i = \frac{\$3.0285}{\$75.71} + 6\% = 10\% = k_i.$$

As this example illustrates, even small changes in the size or riskiness of expected future dividends can cause large changes in stock prices. What might cause investors to change their expectations about future dividends? It could be new information about the company, such as preliminary results for an R&D program, initial sales of a new product, or the discovery of harmful side effects from the use of an existing product. Or, new information that will affect many companies could arrive, such as a tightening of interest rates by the Federal Reserve. Given the existence of computers and telecommunications networks, new information hits the market on an almost continuous basis, and it causes frequent and sometimes large changes in stock prices. In other words, *ready availability of information causes stock prices to be volatile!*

If a stock's price is stable, that probably means that little new information is arriving. But if you think it's risky to invest in a volatile stock, imagine how risky it would be to invest in a stock that rarely released new information about its sales or operations. It may be bad to see your stock's price jump around, but it would be a lot worse to see a stable quoted price most of the time but then to see huge moves on the rare days when new information was released. Fortunately, in our economy timely information is readily available, and evidence suggests that stocks, especially those of large companies, adjust rapidly to new information. Consequently, equilibrium ordinarily exists for any given stock, and required and expected returns are generally equal. Stock prices certainly change, sometimes violently and rapidly, but this simply reflects changing conditions and expectations. There are, of course, times when a stock appears to react for several months to favorable or unfavorable developments. However, this does not signify a long adjustment period; rather, it simply indicates that as more new pieces of information about the situation become available, the market adjusts to them. The ability of the market to adjust to new information is discussed in the next section.

The Efficient Markets Hypothesis

A body of theory called the **Efficient Markets Hypothesis (EMH)** holds (1) that stocks are always in equilibrium and (2) that it is impossible for an investor to consistently "beat the market." Essentially, those who believe in the EMH note that there are 100,000 or so full-time, highly trained, professional analysts and traders operating in the market, while there are fewer than 3,000 major stocks. Therefore, if each analyst followed 30 stocks (which is about right, as analysts tend to specialize in the stocks in a

---

[13]A price change of this magnitude is by no means rare. The prices of *many* stocks double or halve during a year. For example, Ciena, a phone equipment maker, fell by 76.1 percent in 1998 but increased by 183 percent in 2000.

[14]It should be obvious by now that *actual realized* rates of return are not necessarily equal to expected and required returns. Thus, an investor might have *expected* to receive a return of 15 percent if he or she had bought Ciena stock, but after the fact, the realized return was far above 15 percent in 2000 and was far below in 1998.

specific industry), there would on average be 1,000 analysts following each stock. Further, these analysts work for organizations such as Citibank, Merrill Lynch, Prudential Insurance, and the like, which have billions of dollars available with which to take advantage of bargains. In addition, as a result of SEC disclosure requirements and electronic information networks, as new information about a stock becomes available, these 1,000 analysts generally receive and evaluate it at about the same time. Therefore, the price of a stock will adjust almost immediately to any new development.

Levels of Market Efficiency

If markets are efficient, stock prices will rapidly reflect all available information. This raises an important question: What types of information are available and, therefore, incorporated into stock prices? Financial theorists have discussed three forms, or levels, of market efficiency.

Weak-Form Efficiency The *weak form* of the EMH states that all information contained in past price movements is fully reflected in current market prices. If this were true, then information about recent trends in stock prices would be of no use in selecting stocks—the fact that a stock has risen for the past three days, for example, would give us no useful clues as to what it will do today or tomorrow. People who believe that weak-form efficiency exists also believe that "tape watchers" and "chartists" are wasting their time.[15]

For example, after studying the past history of the stock market, a chartist might "discover" the following pattern: If a stock falls three consecutive days, its price typically rises 10 percent the following day. The technician would then conclude that investors could make money by purchasing a stock whose price has fallen three consecutive days.

But if this pattern truly existed, wouldn't other investors also discover it, and if so, why would anyone be willing to sell a stock after it had fallen three consecutive days if he or she knows its price is expected to increase by 10 percent the next day? In other words, if a stock is selling at $40 per share after falling three consecutive days, why would investors sell the stock if they expected it to rise to $44 per share one day later? Those who believe in weak-form efficiency argue that if the stock was really likely to rise to $44 tomorrow, its price *today* would actually rise to somewhere near $44 immediately, thereby eliminating the trading opportunity. Consequently, weak-form efficiency implies that any information that comes from past stock prices is rapidly incorporated into the current stock price.

Semistrong-Form Efficiency The *semistrong form* of the EMH states that current market prices reflect all *publicly available* information. Therefore, if semistrong-form efficiency exists, it would do no good to pore over annual reports or other published data because market prices would have adjusted to any good or bad news contained in such reports back when the news came out. With semistrong-form efficiency, investors should expect to earn the returns predicted by the SML, but they should not expect to do any better unless they have either good luck or information that is not publicly available. However, insiders (for example, the presidents of companies) who have information that is not publicly available can earn consistently abnormal returns (returns higher than those predicted by the SML) even under semistrong-form efficiency.

Another implication of semistrong-form efficiency is that whenever information is released to the public, stock prices will respond only if the information is different from

---

[15]Tape watchers are people who watch the NYSE tape, while chartists plot past patterns of stock price movements. Both are called "technical analysts," and both believe that they can tell if something is happening to the stock that will cause its price to move up or down in the near future.

what had been expected. If, for example, a company announces a 30 percent increase in earnings, and if that increase is about what analysts had been expecting, the announcement should have little or no effect on the company's stock price. On the other hand, the stock price would probably fall if analysts had expected earnings to increase by more than 30 percent, but it probably would rise if they had expected a smaller increase.

Strong-Form Efficiency The *strong form* of the EMH states that current market prices reflect all pertinent information, whether publicly available or privately held. If this form holds, even insiders would find it impossible to earn consistently abnormal returns in the stock market.[16]

Implications of Market Efficiency

What bearing does the EMH have on financial decisions? Since stock prices do seem to reflect public information, most stocks appear to be fairly valued. This does not mean that new developments could not cause a stock's price to soar or to plummet, but it does mean that stocks in general are neither overvalued nor undervalued—they are fairly priced and in equilibrium. However, there are certainly cases in which corporate insiders have information not known to outsiders.

If the EMH is correct, it is a waste of time for most of us to analyze stocks by looking for those that are undervalued. If stock prices already reflect all publicly available information, and hence are fairly priced, one can "beat the market" consistently only by luck, and it is difficult, if not impossible, for anyone to consistently outperform the market averages. Empirical tests have shown that the EMH is, in its weak and semi-strong forms, valid. However, people such as corporate officers, who have inside information, can do better than the averages, and individuals and organizations that are especially good at digging out information on small, new companies also seem to do consistently well. Also, some investors may be able to analyze and react more quickly than others to releases of new information, and these investors may have an advantage over others. However, the buy-sell actions of those investors quickly bring market prices into equilibrium. Therefore, it is generally safe to assume that $\hat{k}_i = k$, that $\hat{P}_0 = P_0$, and that stocks plot on the SML.[17]

---

[16]Several cases of illegal insider trading have made the headlines. These cases involved employees of several major investment banking houses and even an employee of the SEC. In the most famous case, Ivan Boesky admitted to making $50 million by purchasing the stock of firms he knew were about to merge. He went to jail, and he had to pay a large fine, but he helped disprove the strong-form EMH.

[17]Market efficiency also has important implications for managerial decisions, especially those pertaining to common stock issues, stock repurchases, and tender offers. Stocks appear to be fairly valued, so decisions based on the premise that a stock is undervalued or overvalued must be approached with caution. However, managers do have better information about their own companies than outsiders, and this information can legally be used to the companies' (but not the managers') advantage.

We should also note that some Wall Street pros have consistently beaten the market over many years, which is inconsistent with the EMH. An interesting article in the April 3, 1995, issue of *Fortune* (Terence P. Paré, "Yes, You Can Beat the Market") argued strongly against the EMH. Paré suggested that each stock has a fundamental value, but when good or bad news about it is announced, most investors fail to interpret that news correctly. As a result, stocks are generally priced above or below their long-term values.

Think of a graph with stock price on the vertical axis and years on the horizontal axis. A stock's fundamental value might be moving up steadily over time as it retains and reinvests earnings. However, its actual price might fluctuate about the intrinsic value line, overreacting to good or bad news and indicating departures from equilibrium. Successful value investors, according to the article, use fundamental analysis to identify stocks' intrinsic values, and then they buy stocks that are undervalued and sell those that are overvalued.

Paré's argument implies that the market is systematically out of equilibrium and that investors can act on this knowledge to beat the market. That position may turn out to be correct, but it may also be that the superior performance Paré noted simply demonstrates that some people are better at obtaining and interpreting information than others, or have just had a run of good luck.

A Nation of Traders

A recent story in *Fortune* profiled the dramatic revolution in the way investors trade stocks. Just a few years ago, the vast majority of investors bought and sold stocks by calling a full-service broker. The typical broker would execute orders, maintain records, assist with stock selection, and provide guidance regarding long-run asset allocations. These services came at a price—when investors bought stocks, the commissions were often well in excess of $100 a trade.

While the full-service broker is far from dead, many are on the ropes. Now large and small investors have online access to the same type of company and market information that brokers provide, and they can trade stocks online at less than $10 a trade.

These technological changes, combined with the euphoria surrounding the long-running bull market, have encouraged more and more investors to become actively involved in managing their own investments. They tune in regularly to CNBC, and they keep their computer screens "at the ready" to trade on any new information that hits the market.

Online trading is by no means relegated to just a few investors—it now represents a significant percentage of all trades that occur. The *Fortune* article pointed out, for example, that in 1989 only 28 percent of households owned stock, while 10 years later this percentage had risen to 48 percent. Moreover, in 1999 there were 150 Internet brokerage firms versus only 5 three years earlier. Virtually nonexistent three years ago, today the percentage of stocks traded online is approximately 12.5 percent, and that number is expected to rise to nearly 30 percent in the next two or three years.

Changing technology is encouraging more and more investors to take control of their own finances. While this trend has lowered traditional brokers' incomes, it has reduced transaction costs, increased information, and empowered investors. Of course, concerns have been raised about whether individual investors fully understand the risks involved, and whether they have sound strategies in place for long-run investing once the current bull market ends.

Good or bad, most observers believe that online trading is here to stay. However, there will surely be a continuing, but changing, need for professional advisors and stockbrokers to work with the many investors who need guidance or who tire of the grind of keeping track of their positions.

Source: Andy Serwer, Christine Y. Chen, and Angela Key, "A Nation of Traders," *Fortune* (Time Inc., 1999), 116–120.

Self-Test Questions

For a stock to be in equilibrium, what two conditions must hold?

What is the Efficient Markets Hypothesis (EMH)?

What are the differences among the three forms of the EMH: (1) weak form, (2) semistrong form, and (3) strong form?

What are the implications of the EMH for financial decisions?

Actual Stock Prices and Returns

Our discussion thus far has focused on *expected* stock prices and *expected* rates of return. Anyone who has ever invested in the stock market knows that there can be, and there generally are, large differences between *expected* and *realized* prices and returns.

Figure 10-5 shows how the market value of a portfolio of stocks has moved in recent years, and Figure 10-6 shows how total realized returns on the portfolio have varied from year to year. The market trend has been strongly up, but it has gone up in some years and down in others, and the stocks of individual companies have likewise gone up and down.[18] We know from theory that expected returns, as estimated by a marginal

[18]If we constructed graphs like Figures 10-5 and 10-6 for individual stocks rather than for a large portfolio, far greater variability would be shown. Also, if we constructed a graph like Figure 10-6 for bonds, it would have the same general shape, but the bars would be smaller, indicating that gains and losses on bonds are generally smaller than those on stocks. Above-average bond returns occur in years when interest rates decline, and losses occur when interest rates rise sharply.

FIGURE 10-5 S&P 500 Index, 1967–2000

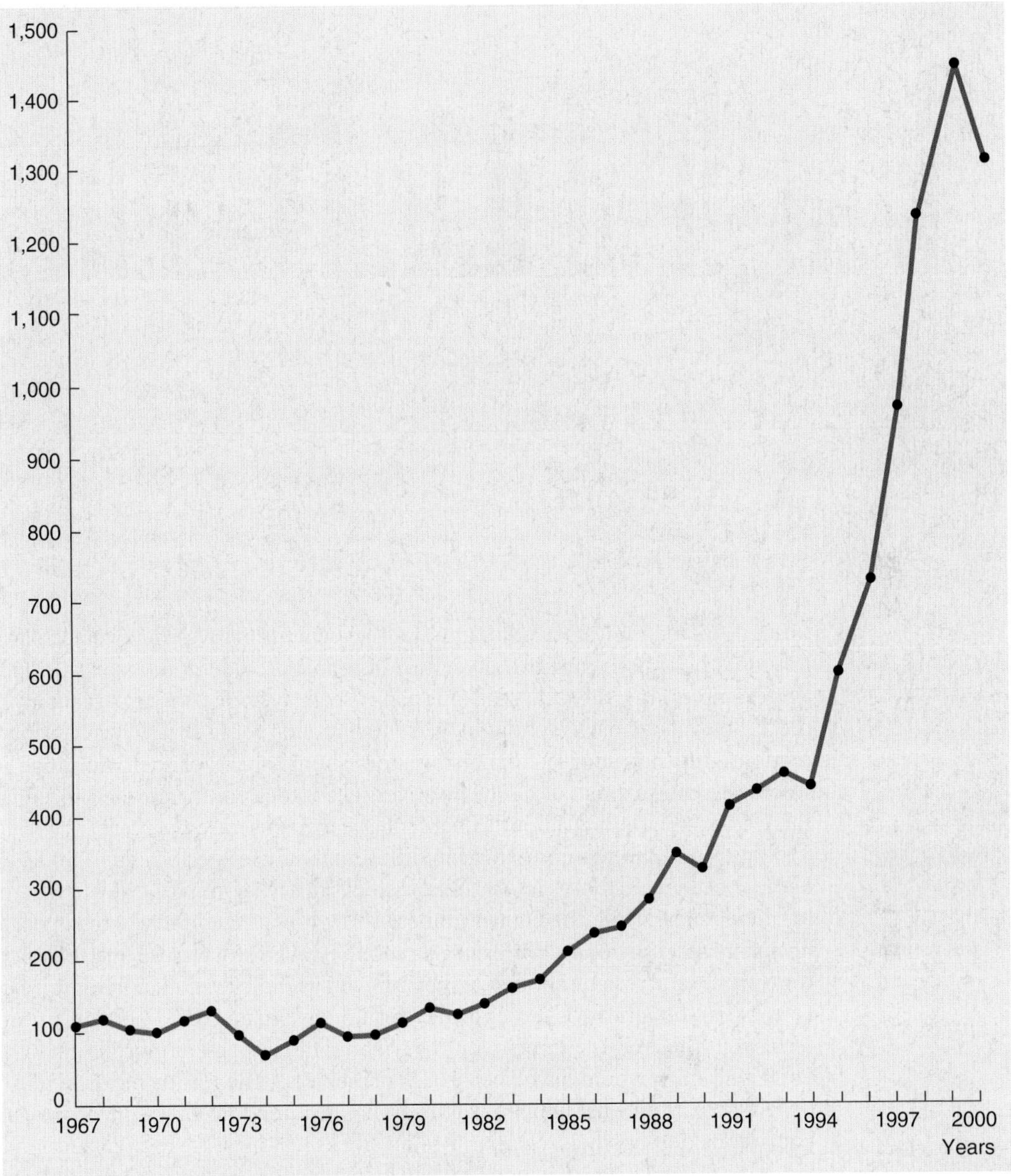

Source: Data taken from various issues of *The Wall Street Journal,* "Stock Market Data Bank" section.

investor, are always positive, but in some years, as Figure 10-6 shows, actual returns are negative. Of course, even in bad years some individual companies do well, so "the name of the game" in security analysis is to pick the winners. Financial managers attempt to take actions that will put their companies into the winners' column, but they don't always succeed. In subsequent chapters, we will examine the actions that managers can take to increase the odds of their firms doing relatively well in the marketplace.

Investing in International Stocks

As noted in Chapter 6, the U.S. stock market amounts to only about 40 percent of the world stock market, and this is prompting many U.S. investors to hold at least some

FIGURE 10-6 S&P 500 Index, Total Returns: Dividend Yield + Capital Gain or Loss, 1967–2000

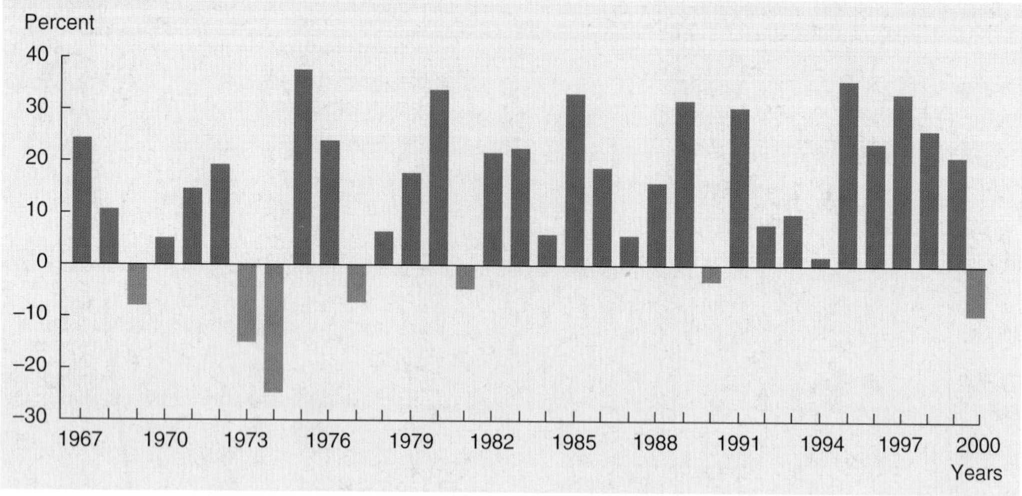

Source: Data taken from various issues of *The Wall Street Journal.*

foreign stocks. Analysts have long touted the benefits of investing overseas, arguing that foreign stocks both improve diversification and provide good growth opportunities. For example, after the U.S. stock market rose an average of 17.5 percent a year during the 1980s, many analysts thought that the U.S. market in the 1990s was due for a correction, and they suggested that investors should increase their holdings of foreign stocks. To the surprise of many, however, U.S. stocks outperformed foreign stocks in the 1990s—they gained about 15 percent a year versus only 3 percent for foreign stocks.

Figure 10-7 shows how stocks in different countries performed in 2000. The number in the left white boxes indicates how stocks in each country performed in terms of its local currency, while the right numbers show how the country's stocks performed in terms of the U.S. dollar. For example, in 2000 Swiss stocks rose by 10.13 percent, but the Swiss Franc rose by about 5.52 percent versus the U.S. dollar. Therefore, if U.S. investors had bought Swiss stocks, they would have made 10.13 percent in Swiss Franc terms, but those Swiss Francs would have bought 5.2 percent more U.S. dollars, so the effective return would have been 16.21 percent. So, the results of foreign investments depend in part on what happens to the exchange rate. Indeed, when you invest overseas, you are making two bets: (1) that foreign stocks will increase in their local markets and (2) that the currencies in which you will be paid will rise relative to the dollar.

Although U.S. stocks have outperformed foreign stocks in recent years, this by no means suggests that investors should avoid foreign stocks. Foreign investments still improve diversification, and it is inevitable that there will be years when foreign stocks outperform domestic stocks. When this occurs, U.S. investors will be glad they put some of their money in overseas markets.

Stock Market Reporting

Figure 10-8, taken from a daily newspaper, is a section of the stock market page for stocks listed on the NYSE. For each stock, the NYSE report provides specific data on the trading that took place the prior day. Similar information is available for stocks listed on the Nasdaq and other exchanges.

Stocks are listed alphabetically, from AAR Industries to Zweig; the data in Figure 10-8 were taken from the top of the listing. We will examine the data for Abbott

FIGURE 10-7 2000 Performance of the Dow Jones Global Stock Indexes

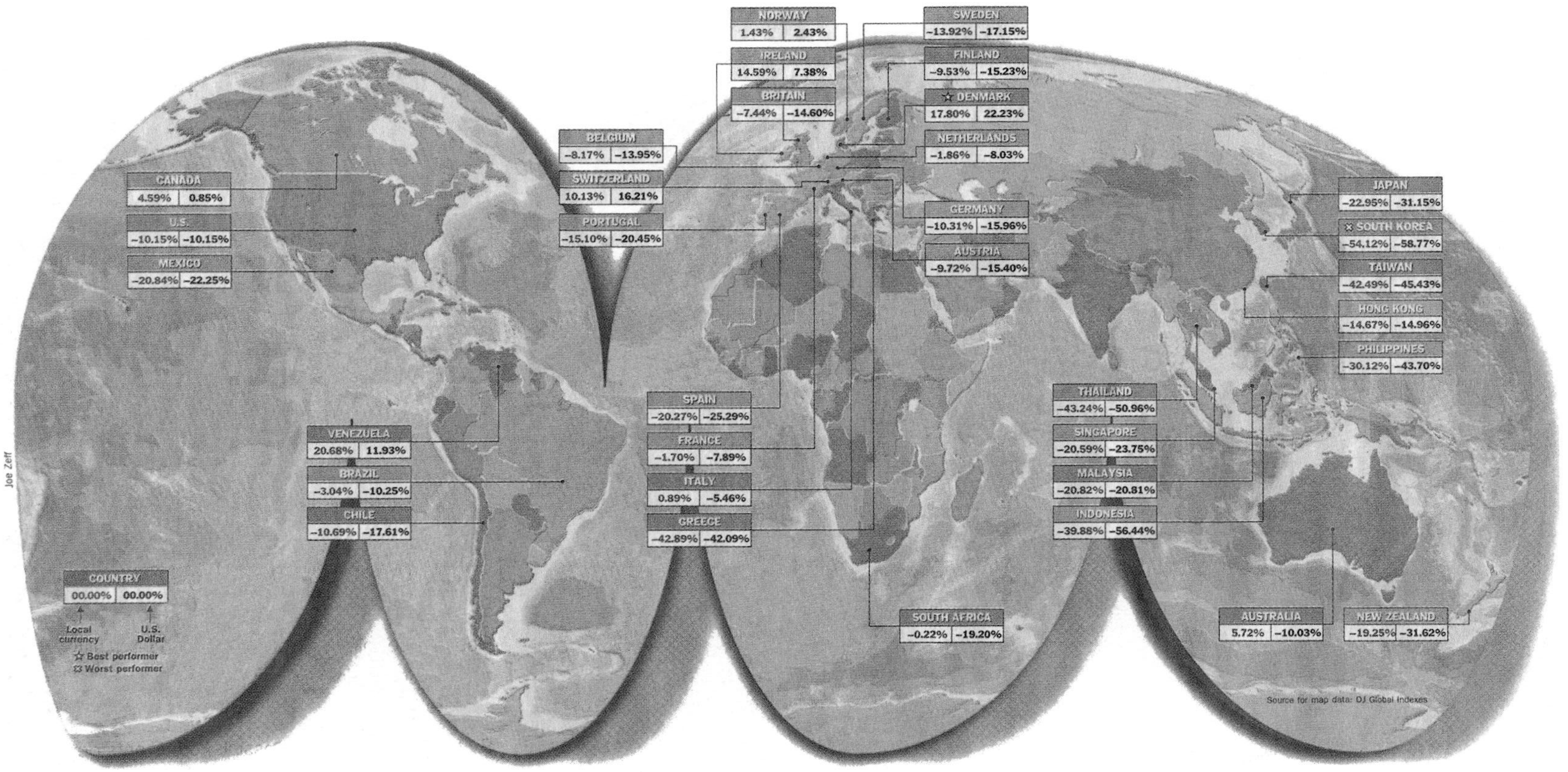

Source: "Indexes Track Web Stocks Off a Cliff," *The Wall Street Journal*, January 2, 2001, R21. ©2000 Dow Jones & Company, Inc. All Rights Reserved Worldwide.

FIGURE 10-8 Stock Market Transactions, June 15, 2000

Quotations as of 4 p.m. Eastern Time
Thursday, June 15, 2000

	52 Weeks Hi	52 Weeks Lo	Stock	Sym	Div	Yld %	PE	Vol 100s	Hi	Lo	Close	Net Chg
			-A-A-A-									
	28½	13⅝	AAR	AIR	.34	2.3	9	541	15 5/16	14 9/16	14⅞	+ ⅛
	30 15/16	19¼	ABM Indus	ABM	.62	2.4	15	545	25 13/16	25	25⅝	+ ⅜
	25 13/16	19⅜	ABN Am ADR	ABN	1.23e	4.9	...	362	25⅜	24⅞	25	...
	25⅛	19 3/16	ABN Am pfA		1.88	8.2	...	304	23¼	22⅜	22 15/16	+ 7/16
	24⅝	18⅞	ABN Am pfB		1.78	8.2	...	415	21¾	21 5/16	21⅝	+ ¼
n	25	20¼	ACE CapTr		1.18e	4.8	...	53	24¾	24¼	24 7/16	− 5/16
	31 7/16	14 1/16	♣ACE Ltd	ACL	.52f	1.8	12	11688	29½	27⅝	28 3/16	− ¾
n	65½	47 11/16	ACE LtdPRIDES		.38p	...	...	3999	63½	61¼	62⅜	− ⅝
	8¾	6 5/16	ACM GvtFd	ACG	.78	10.9	...	1649	7 3/16	7 1/16	7 3/16	+ 1/16
	8	6¼	ACM OppFd	AOF	.72a	10.5	...	226	7 1/16	6⅞	6⅞	− ⅛
	8¼	6 3/16	ACM SecFd	GSF	.78	11.2	...	3286	7	6⅞	6 15/16	+ 1/16
	6	5⅛	ACM SpctmFd	SI	.60	10.4	...	478	5¾	5 11/16	5¾	...
			• • •									
	25 5/16	20 11/16	ANZ pf		2.00	8.7	...	173	23⅛	22 13/16	22 15/16	− 1/16
	25⅜	20⅞	ANZ II pf		2.02	8.7	...	165	23⅜	23	23⅛	− ¼
	9¼	3⅝	APT Satelt	ATS	.35p	...	...	496	5	4 9/16	4⅞	− ⅛
	24	14 15/16	ASA	ASA	.60	3.6	...	328	16 13/16	16 7/16	16 9/16	− ¼
	26	21 11/16	AT&T 8 1/4 PNS		2.06	8.3	...	220	24 15/16	24⅝	24 11/16	− 3/16
	25⅝	21 9/16	AT&T 8 1/8 PNS		2.03	8.3	...	1055	24½	24⅜	24⅜	...
▼	61	33½	AT&T	T	.88	2.6	18	187062	34⅜	33¼	33 15/16	+ 5/16
n	36	24⅜	AT&T Wrls	AWE		...	...	17409	28 1/16	27 9/16	27⅞	− ⅛
s	50	12 3/16	♣AVX Cp	AVX	.14	.5	34	6426	31 11/16	29½	30⅝	− 1 5/16
	81½	53¾	AXA ADS	AXA	2.16e	2.7	...	716	81⅛	78⅝	79⅞	− ⅝
s	44	25½	♣AXA Fnl	AXF	.10	.2	16	12925	41¾	40⅜	40⅞	− 1/16
s	9⅜	13/16	AamesFnl	AAM		...	dd	157	15/16	13/16	15/16	+ 1/16
	22¼	12½	AaronRent	RNT	.04	.3	11	81	14 3/16	13 11/16	13 15/16	− 3/16
	23½	19	AbbeyNtl	SUA	1.75	8.3	...	88	21⅛	21	21	...
n	23 15/16	19½	AbbeyNtl 7 1/4%	SUD	1.81	8.5	...	28	21⅜	21⅛	21⅜	+ 3/16
	25⅝	22⅛	AbbeyNtl pfA		2.19	9.3	...	21	23¾	23 9/16	23⅝	− 7/64
→	45⅞	29⅜	AbbotLab	ABT	.76	1.8	27	24726	43 1/16	41⅞	42⅞	+ ⅞ ←
	49 11/16	8	Abercrombie A	ANF		...	7	6637	10⅛	9⅝	9⅝	− 5/16
	13 13/16	7¾	Abitibi g	ABY	.40g	...	...	1165	10¼	9 13/16	10¼	+ 3/16
	6⅛	4⅜	♣AcadiaRlty	AKR	.48	8.4	18	22	5¾	5⅝	5 11/16	+ 1/16

NOTES: The "pf" following the stock name of the ABN Am listing tells us that this one is a preferred stock rather than a common stock. A "▲" preceding the columns containing a stock's 52-week high and low prices indicates that the price hit a new 52-week high, whereas a "▼" indicates a new 52-week low. An "x" preceding the columns containing the 52-week high and low prices indicates that the stock went ex-dividend that day; this means that someone who buys the stock will not receive the next dividend. An "s" preceding the 52-week high and low prices indicates that the stock was split within the past 52 weeks. (See Chapter 18 for a discussion of stock splits.) AVX Corp. had a stock split during the past 52-week period. An "n" preceding the 52-week high and low prices indicates that the stock is newly issued within the past 52 weeks. An "f" following the dividend column indicates that the annual dividend was increased on the last declaration date. An "e" following the dividend column indicates that a dividend was declared or paid in the preceding 12 months, but there is no regular dividend rate. Other dividend indicators are also occasionally used. Finally, a "club" appearing before the company name indicates that *Journal* readers can obtain a copy of the company's annual report.

Source: *The Wall Street Journal*, June 16, 2000.

Laboratories, AbbotLab, shown toward the bottom of the table. The two columns on the left show the highest and lowest prices at which the stocks have sold during the past year; Abbott Labs has traded in the range from \$29⅜ to \$45⅞ during the preceding 52 weeks. The figure just to the right of the company's ticker symbol is the dividend; Abbott Labs had a current indicated annual dividend rate of \$0.76 per share and a dividend yield (which is the current dividend divided by the closing stock price) of 1.8 percent. Next comes the ratio of the stock's price to its last 12 months' earnings (the P/E ratio), followed by the volume of trading for the day: 2,472,600 shares of

Abbott Labs stock were traded on June 15, 2000. Following the volume come the high and low prices for the day, and then the closing price. On June 15, Abbott Labs traded as high as $43\frac{1}{16}$ and as low as $41\frac{7}{8}$, while the last trade was at $42\frac{7}{8}$. The last column gives the change from the closing price on the previous day. Abbott Labs' closing price was up $\frac{7}{16}$ from the previous day's closing price.

Self-Test Questions

If a stock is *not* in equilibrium, explain how financial markets adjust to bring it into equilibrium.

Explain why expected, required, and realized returns are often different.

What are the key benefits of adding foreign stocks to a portfolio?

When a U.S. investor purchases foreign stocks, what two things is he or she hoping will happen?

Preferred Stock

We discuss preferred stock in more detail in Chapter 21, but for now you should recognize that it is a *hybrid*—it is similar to bonds in some respects and to common stock in others. The hybrid nature of preferred stock becomes apparent when we try to classify it in relation to bonds and common stock. Like bonds, preferred stock has a par value and a fixed amount of dividends that must be paid before dividends can be paid on the common stock. However, if the preferred dividend is not earned, the directors can omit (or "pass") it without throwing the company into bankruptcy. So, although preferred stock has a fixed payment like bonds, a failure to make this payment will not lead to bankruptcy.

As noted above, a preferred stock entitles its owners to regular, fixed dividend payments. If the payments last forever, the issue is a perpetuity whose value, V_p, is found as follows:

$$V_p = \frac{D_p}{k_p}. \tag{10-6}$$

V_p is the value of the preferred stock, D_p is the preferred dividend, and k_p is the required rate of return. MicroDrive has preferred stock outstanding that pays a dividend of $10 per year. If the required rate of return on this preferred stock is 10 percent, then its value is $100, found by solving Equation 10-6 as follows:

$$V_p = \frac{\$10.00}{0.10} = \$100.00.$$

If we know the current price of a preferred stock and its dividend, we can solve for the rate of return as follows:

$$k_p = \frac{D_p}{V_p}. \tag{10-6a}$$

Some preferred stocks have a stated maturity date, say, 50 years. If MicroDrive's preferred matured in 50 years, paid a $10 annual dividend, and had a required return of 8 percent, then we could find its price as follows: Enter N = 50, I = 8, PMT = 10, and FV = 100. Then press PV to find the price, V_p = $124.47. If k = I = 10%, change I = 8 to I = 10, and find P = V_p = PV = $100. If you know the price of a share of preferred stock, you can solve for I to find the expected rate of return, $\hat{k}_p$.

Most preferred stocks pay dividends quarterly. This is true for MicroDrive, so we could find the effective rate of return on its preferred stock (perpetual or maturing) as follows:

$$\text{EFF\%} = \text{EAR}_p = \left(1 + \frac{k_{Nom}}{m}\right)^m - 1 = \left(1 + \frac{0.10}{4}\right)^4 - 1 = 10.38\%.$$

If an investor wanted to compare the returns on MicroDrive's bonds and its preferred stock, it would be best to convert the nominal rates on each security to effective rates and then compare these "equivalent annual rates."

Self-Test Questions

Explain the following statement: "Preferred stock is a hybrid security."

Is the equation used to value preferred stock more like the one used to evaluate a perpetual bond or the one used for common stock?

Summary

Corporate decisions should be analyzed in terms of how alternative courses of action are likely to affect a firm's value. However, it is necessary to know how stock prices are established before attempting to measure how a given decision will affect a specific firm's value. This chapter showed how stock values are determined, and also how investors go about estimating the rates of return they expect to earn. The key concepts covered are listed below.

- A **proxy** is a document that gives one person the power to act for another, typically the power to vote shares of common stock. A **proxy fight** occurs when an outside group solicits stockholders' proxies in an effort to vote a new management team into office.
- A **takeover** occurs when a person or group succeeds in ousting a firm's management and takes control of the company.
- Stockholders often have the right to purchase any additional shares sold by the firm. This right, called the **preemptive right,** protects the control of the present stockholders and prevents dilution of their value.
- Although most firms have only one type of common stock, in some instances **classified stock** is used to meet the special needs of the company. One type is **founders' shares.** This is stock owned by the firm's founders that carries sole voting rights but restricted dividends for a specified number of years.
- A **closely held corporation** is one that is owned by a few individuals who are typically associated with the firm's management.
- A **publicly owned corporation** is one that is owned by a relatively large number of individuals who are not actively involved in its management.
- Whenever stock in a closely held corporation is offered to the public for the first time, the company is said to be **going public.** The market for stock that is just being offered to the public is called the **initial public offering (IPO) market.**
- The **value of a share of stock** is calculated as the **present value of the stream of dividends** the stock is expected to provide in the future.
- The equation used to find the **value of a constant growth stock** is:

$$\hat{P}_0 = \frac{D_1}{k_s - g}.$$

- The **expected total rate of return** from a stock consists of an **expected dividend yield** plus an **expected capital gains yield.** For a constant growth firm, both the expected dividend yield and the expected capital gains yield are constant.

- The equation for $\hat{k}_s$, the **expected rate of return on a constant growth stock,** can be expressed as follows:

$$\hat{k}_s = \frac{D_1}{P_0} + g.$$

- A **zero growth stock** is one whose future dividends are not expected to grow at all, while a **supernormal growth stock** is one whose earnings and dividends are expected to grow much faster than the economy as a whole over some specified time period and then to grow at the "normal" rate.
- To find the **present value of a supernormal growth stock,** (1) find the dividends expected during the supernormal growth period, (2) find the price of the stock at the end of the supernormal growth period, (3) discount the dividends and the projected price back to the present, and (4) sum these PVs to find the current value of the stock, $\hat{P}_0$.
- The **terminal,** or **horizon, date** is the date when individual dividend forecasts are no longer made because the dividend growth rate is assumed to be constant.
- The **terminal,** or **horizon, value** is the value at the horizon date of all future dividends after that date.
- The **marginal investor** is a representative investor whose actions reflect the beliefs of those people who are currently trading a stock. It is the marginal investor who determines a stock's price.
- **Equilibrium** is the condition under which the expected return on a security as seen by the marginal investor is just equal to its required return, $\hat{k} = k$. Also, the stock's intrinsic value must be equal to its market price, $\hat{P}_0 = P_0$, and the market price is stable.
- The **Efficient Markets Hypothesis (EMH)** holds (1) that stocks are always in equilibrium and (2) that it is impossible for an investor who does not have inside information to consistently "beat the market." Therefore, according to the EMH, stocks are always fairly valued ($\hat{P}_0 = P_0$), the required return on a stock is equal to its expected return ($k = \hat{k}$), and all stocks' expected returns plot on the SML.
- Differences can and do exist between expected and realized returns in the stock and bond markets—only for short-term, risk-free assets are expected and actual (or realized) returns equal.
- When U.S. investors purchase foreign stocks, they hope (1) that stock prices will increase in the local market and (2) that the foreign currencies will rise relative to the U.S. dollar.
- **Preferred stock** is a hybrid security having some characteristics of debt and some of equity.
- Most preferred stocks are **perpetuities,** and the value of a share of perpetual preferred stock is found as the dividend divided by the required rate of return:

$$V_p = \frac{D_p}{k_p}.$$

- **Maturing preferred stock** is evaluated with a formula that is identical in form to the bond value formula.

Questions

10–1 Define each of the following terms:
- **a.** Proxy; proxy fight; takeover
- **b.** Preemptive right
- **c.** Classified stock; founders' shares

d. Closely held corporation; publicly owned corporation
e. Over-the-counter (OTC) market; organized security exchange
f. Secondary market; primary market
g. Going public; initial public offering (IPO) market
h. Intrinsic value ($\hat{P}_0$); market price (P_0)
i. Required rate of return, k_s; expected rate of return, $\hat{k}_s$; actual, or realized, rate of return, $\bar{k}_s$
j. Capital gains yield; dividend yield; expected total return
k. Zero growth stock
l. Normal, or constant, growth; supernormal, or nonconstant, growth
m. Equilibrium
n. Efficient Markets Hypothesis (EMH); three forms of EMH
o. Preferred stock

10–2 Two investors are evaluating AT&T's stock for possible purchase. They agree on the expected value of D_1 and also on the expected future dividend growth rate. Further, they agree on the riskiness of the stock. However, one investor normally holds stocks for 2 years, while the other normally holds stocks for 10 years. On the basis of the type of analysis done in this chapter, they should both be willing to pay the same price for AT&T's stock. True or false? Explain.

10–3 A bond that pays interest forever and has no maturity date is a perpetual bond. In what respect is a perpetual bond similar to a no-growth common stock, and to a share of preferred stock?

10–4 If you bought a share of common stock, you would typically expect to receive dividends plus capital gains. Would you expect the distribution between dividend yield and capital gains to be influenced by the firm's decision to pay more dividends rather than to retain and reinvest more of its earnings?

10–5 Is it true that the following expression can be used to find the value of a constant growth stock?

$$\hat{P}_0 = \frac{D_0}{k_s + g}.$$

10–6 It is frequently stated that the primary purpose of the preemptive right is to allow individuals to maintain their proportionate share of the ownership and control of a corporation.
a. How important do you suppose this consideration is for the average stockholder of a firm whose shares are traded on the New York or American Stock Exchanges?
b. Is the preemptive right likely to be of more importance to stockholders of publicly owned or closely held firms? Explain.

Self-Test Problems (Solutions Appear in Appendix A)

ST–1 *STOCK GROWTH RATES AND VALUATION*

You are considering buying the stocks of two companies that operate in the same industry; they have very similar characteristics except for their dividend payout policies. Both companies are expected to earn \$6 per share this year. However, Company D (for "dividend") is expected to pay out all of its earnings as dividends, while Company G (for "growth") is expected to pay out only one-third of its earnings, or \$2 per share. D's stock price is \$40. G and D are equally risky. Which of the following is most likely to be true?
a. Company G will have a faster growth rate than Company D. Therefore, G's stock price should be greater than \$40.
b. Although G's growth rate should exceed D's, D's current dividend exceeds that of G, and this should cause D's price to exceed G's.
c. An investor in Stock D will get his or her money back faster because D pays out more of its earnings as dividends. Thus, in a sense, D is like a short-term bond, and G is like a long-term bond. Therefore, if economic shifts cause k_D and k_S to increase, and if the expected streams of dividends from D and G remain constant, both Stocks D and G will decline, but D's price should decline further.
d. D's expected and required rate of return is $\hat{k}_S = k_S = 15\%$. G's expected return will be higher because of its higher expected growth rate.
e. If we observe that G's price is also \$40, the best estimate of G's growth rate is 10 percent.

ST–2 CONSTANT GROWTH STOCK VALUATION

Ewald Company's current stock price is \$36, and its last dividend was \$2.40. In view of Ewald's strong financial position and its consequent low risk, its required rate of return is only 12 percent. If dividends are expected to grow at a constant rate, g, in the future, and if k_s is expected to remain at 12 percent, what is Ewald's expected stock price 5 years from now?

ST–3 SUPERNORMAL GROWTH STOCK VALUATION

Snyder Computer Chips Inc. is experiencing a period of rapid growth. Earnings and dividends are expected to grow at a rate of 15 percent during the next 2 years, at 13 percent in the third year, and at a constant rate of 6 percent thereafter. Snyder's last dividend was \$1.15, and the required rate of return on the stock is 12 percent.

a. Calculate the value of the stock today.
b. Calculate $\hat{P}_1$ and $\hat{P}_2$.
c. Calculate the dividend yield and capital gains yield for Years 1, 2, and 3.

Problems

10–1 DPS CALCULATION

Warr Corporation just paid a dividend of \$1.50 a share (i.e., D_0 = \$1.50). The dividend is expected to grow 5 percent a year for the next 3 years, and then 10 percent a year thereafter. What is the expected dividend per share for each of the next 5 years?

10–2 CONSTANT GROWTH VALUATION

Thomas Brothers is expected to pay a \$0.50 per share dividend at the end of the year (i.e., D_1 = \$0.50). The dividend is expected to grow at a constant rate of 7 percent a year. The required rate of return on the stock, k_s, is 15 percent. What is the value per share of the company's stock?

10–3 CONSTANT GROWTH VALUATION

Harrison Clothiers' stock currently sells for \$20 a share. The stock just paid a dividend of \$1.00 a share (i.e., D_0 = \$1.00). The dividend is expected to grow at a constant rate of 10 percent a year. What stock price is expected 1 year from now? What is the required rate of return on the company's stock?

10–4 PREFERRED STOCK VALUATION

Fee Founders has preferred stock outstanding which pays a dividend of \$5 at the end of each year. The preferred stock sells for \$60 a share. What is the preferred stock's required rate of return?

10–5 SUPERNORMAL GROWTH VALUATION

A company currently pays a dividend of \$2 per share, $D_0 = 2$. It is estimated that the company's dividend will grow at a rate of 20 percent per year for the next 2 years, then the dividend will grow at a constant rate of 7 percent thereafter. The company's stock has a beta equal to 1.2, the risk-free rate is 7.5 percent, and the market risk premium is 4 percent. What would you estimate is the stock's current price?

10–6 CONSTANT GROWTH RATE, G

A stock is trading at \$80 per share. The stock is expected to have a year-end dividend of \$4 per share ($D_1 = 4$), which is expected to grow at some constant rate g throughout time. The stock's required rate of return is 14 percent. If you are an analyst who believes in efficient markets, what would be your forecast of g?

10–7 CONSTANT GROWTH VALUATION

You are considering an investment in the common stock of Keller Corp. The stock is expected to pay a dividend of \$2 a share at the end of the year (D_1 = \$2.00). The stock has a beta equal to 0.9. The risk-free rate is 5.6 percent, and the market risk premium is 6 percent. The stock's dividend is expected to grow at some constant rate g. The stock currently sells for \$25 a share. Assuming the market is in equilibrium, what does the market believe will be the stock price at the end of 3 years? (That is, what is $\hat{P}_3$?)

10–8 PREFERRED STOCK RATE OF RETURN

What will be the nominal rate of return on a preferred stock with a \$100 par value, a stated dividend of 8 percent of par, and a current market price of (a) \$60, (b) \$80, (c) \$100, and (d) \$140?

10–9 DECLINING GROWTH STOCK VALUATION

Martell Mining Company's ore reserves are being depleted, so its sales are falling. Also, its pit is getting deeper each year, so its costs are rising. As a result, the company's earnings and dividends are declining at the constant rate of 5 percent per year. If D_0 = \$5 and k_s = 15%, what is the value of Martell Mining's stock?

10–10 RATES OF RETURN AND EQUILIBRIUM

The beta coefficient for Stock C is $b_C = 0.4$, whereas that for Stock D is $b_D = -0.5$. (Stock D's beta is negative, indicating that its rate of return rises whenever returns on most other stocks fall. There are very few negative beta stocks, although collection agency stocks are sometimes cited as an example.)

a. If the risk-free rate is 9 percent and the expected rate of return on an average stock is 13 percent, what are the required rates of return on Stocks C and D?

b. For Stock C, suppose the current price, P_0, is \$25; the next expected dividend, D_1, is \$1.50; and the stock's expected constant growth rate is 4 percent. Is the stock in equilibrium? Explain, and describe what will happen if the stock is not in equilibrium.

10–11 *SUPERNORMAL GROWTH STOCK VALUATION*

Assume that the average firm in your company's industry is expected to grow at a constant rate of 6 percent and its dividend yield is 7 percent. Your company is about as risky as the average firm in the industry, but it has just successfully completed some R&D work that leads you to expect that its earnings and dividends will grow at a rate of 50 percent [$D_1 = D_0(1 + g) = D_0(1.50)$] this year and 25 percent the following year, after which growth should match the 6 percent industry average rate. The last dividend paid (D_0) was \$1. What is the value per share of your firm's stock?

10–12 *SUPERNORMAL GROWTH STOCK VALUATION*

Microtech Corporation is expanding rapidly, and it currently needs to retain all of its earnings, hence it does not pay any dividends. However, investors expect Microtech to begin paying dividends, with the first dividend of \$1.00 coming 3 years from today. The dividend should grow rapidly—at a rate of 50 percent per year—during Years 4 and 5. After Year 5, the company should grow at a constant rate of 8 percent per year. If the required return on the stock is 15 percent, what is the value of the stock today?

10–13 *PREFERRED STOCK VALUATION*

Ezzell Corporation issued preferred stock with a stated dividend of 10 percent of par. Preferred stock of this type currently yields 8 percent, and the par value is \$100. Assume dividends are paid annually.

a. What is the value of Ezzell's preferred stock?

b. Suppose interest rate levels rise to the point where the preferred stock now yields 12 percent. What would be the value of Ezzell's preferred stock?

10–14 *CONSTANT GROWTH STOCK VALUATION*

Your broker offers to sell you some shares of Bahnsen & Co. common stock that paid a dividend of \$2 *yesterday*. You expect the dividend to grow at the rate of 5 percent per year for the next 3 years, and, if you buy the stock, you plan to hold it for 3 years and then sell it.

a. Find the expected dividend for each of the next 3 years; that is, calculate D_1, D_2, and D_3. Note that $D_0 = \$2$.

b. Given that the appropriate discount rate is 12 percent and that the first of these dividend payments will occur 1 year from now, find the present value of the dividend stream; that is, calculate the PV of D_1, D_2, and D_3, and then sum these PVs.

c. You expect the price of the stock 3 years from now to be \$34.73; that is, you expect $\hat{P}_3$ to equal \$34.73. Discounted at a 12 percent rate, what is the present value of this expected future stock price? In other words, calculate the PV of \$34.73.

d. If you plan to buy the stock, hold it for 3 years, and then sell it for \$34.73, what is the most you should pay for it?

e. Use Equation 10-2 to calculate the present value of this stock. Assume that $g = 5\%$, and it is constant.

f. Is the value of this stock dependent upon how long you plan to hold it? In other words, if your planned holding period were 2 years or 5 years rather than 3 years, would this affect the value of the stock today, $\hat{P}_0$?

10–15 *RETURN ON COMMON STOCK*

You buy a share of The Ludwig Corporation stock for \$21.40. You expect it to pay dividends of \$1.07, \$1.1449, and \$1.2250 in Years 1, 2, and 3, respectively, and you expect to sell it at a price of \$26.22 at the end of 3 years.

a. Calculate the growth rate in dividends.

b. Calculate the expected dividend yield.

c. Assuming that the calculated growth rate is expected to continue, you can add the dividend yield to the expected growth rate to get the expected total rate of return. What is this stock's expected total rate of return?

10–16 *CONSTANT GROWTH STOCK VALUATION*

Investors require a 15 percent rate of return on Levine Company's stock ($k_s = 15\%$).

a. What will be Levine's stock value if the previous dividend was $D_0 = \$2$ and if investors expect dividends to grow at a constant compound annual rate of (1) −5 percent, (2) 0 percent, (3) 5 percent, and (4) 10 percent?

b. Using data from part a, what is the Gordon (constant growth) model value for Levine's stock if the required rate of return is 15 percent and the expected growth rate is (1) 15 percent or (2) 20 percent? Are these reasonable results? Explain.

c. Is it reasonable to expect that a constant growth stock would have $g > k_s$?

10–17 STOCK REPORTING

Look up the prices of American Telephone & Telegraph's (AT&T) stock in *The Wall Street Journal* (or some other newspaper which provides this information).

a. What was the stock's price range during the last year?

b. What is AT&T's current dividend? What is its dividend yield?

c. What change occurred in AT&T's stock price the day the newspaper was published?

d. If you had \$10,000 and wanted to invest it in AT&T, what return would you expect to get if you bought AT&T's stock? (Hint: Think about capital gains when you answer this question.)

10–18 SUPERNORMAL GROWTH STOCK VALUATION

It is now January 1, 2002. Wayne-Martin Electric Inc. (WME) has just developed a solar panel capable of generating 200 percent more electricity than any solar panel currently on the market. As a result, WME is expected to experience a 15 percent annual growth rate for the next 5 years. By the end of 5 years, other firms will have developed comparable technology, and WME's growth rate will slow to 5 percent per year indefinitely. Stockholders require a return of 12 percent on WME's stock. The most recent annual dividend (D_0), which was paid yesterday, was \$1.75 per share.

a. Calculate WME's expected dividends for 2002, 2003, 2004, 2005, and 2006.

b. Calculate the value of the stock today, $\hat{P}_0$. Proceed by finding the present value of the dividends expected at the end of 2002, 2003, 2004, 2005, and 2006 plus the present value of the stock price which should exist at the end of 2006. The year-end 2006 stock price can be found by using the constant growth equation. Notice that to find the December 31, 2006, price, you use the dividend expected in 2007, which is 5 percent greater than the 2006 dividend.

c. Calculate the expected dividend yield, D_1/P_0, the capital gains yield expected in 2002, and the expected total return (dividend yield plus capital gains yield) for 2002. (Assume that $\hat{P}_0 = P_0$, and recognize that the capital gains yield is equal to the total return minus the dividend yield.) Also calculate these same three yields for 2007.

d. How might an investor's tax situation affect his or her decision to purchase stocks of companies in the early stages of their lives, when they are growing rapidly, versus stocks of older, more mature firms? When does WME's stock become "mature" in this example?

e. Suppose your boss tells you she believes that WME's annual growth rate will be only 12 percent during the next 5 years and that the firm's normal growth rate will be only 4 percent. Without doing any calculations, what general effect would these growth-rate changes have on the price of WME's stock?

f. Suppose your boss also tells you that she regards WME as being quite risky and that she believes the required rate of return should be 14 percent, not 12 percent. Again, without doing any calculations, how would the higher required rate of return affect the price of the stock, its capital gains yield, and its dividend yield?

10–19 SUPERNORMAL GROWTH STOCK VALUATION

Taussig Technologies Corporation (TTC) has been growing at a rate of 20 percent per year in recent years. This same growth rate is expected to last for another 2 years.

a. If D_0 = \$1.60, k = 10%, and g_n = 6%, what is TTC's stock worth today? What are its expected dividend yield and capital gains yield at this time?

b. Now assume that TTC's period of supernormal growth is to last another 5 years rather than 2 years. How would this affect its price, dividend yield, and capital gains yield? Answer in words only.

c. What will be TTC's dividend yield and capital gains yield once its period of supernormal growth ends? (Hint: These values will be the same regardless of whether you examine the case of 2 or 5 years of supernormal growth; the calculations are very easy.)

d. Of what interest to investors is the changing relationship between dividend yield and capital gains yield over time?

10–20 EQUILIBRIUM STOCK PRICE

The risk-free rate of return, k_{RF}, is 11 percent; the required rate of return on the market, k_M, is 14 percent; and Upton Company's stock has a beta coefficient of 1.5.

a. If the dividend expected during the coming year, D_1, is \$2.25, and if g = a constant 5%, at what price should Upton's stock sell?

b. Now, suppose the Federal Reserve Board increases the money supply, causing the risk-free rate to drop to 9 percent and k_M to fall to 12 percent. What would this do to the price of the stock?

c. In addition to the change in part b, suppose investors' risk aversion declines; this fact, combined with the decline in k_{RF}, causes k_M to fall to 11 percent. At what price would Upton's stock sell?

d. Now, suppose Upton has a change in management. The new group institutes policies that increase the expected constant growth rate to 6 percent. Also, the new management stabilizes sales and profits, and thus causes the beta coefficient to decline from 1.5 to 1.3. Assume that k_{RF} and k_M are equal to the values in part c. After all these changes, what is Upton's new equilibrium price? (Note: D_1 goes to \$2.27.)

10–21 *BETA COEFFICIENTS*

Suppose Chance Chemical Company's management conducts a study and concludes that if Chance expanded its consumer products division (which is less risky than its primary business, industrial chemicals), the firm's beta would decline from 1.2 to 0.9. However, consumer products have a somewhat lower profit margin, and this would cause Chance's constant growth rate in earnings and dividends to fall from 7 to 5 percent.

a. Should management make the change? Assume the following: $k_M = 12\%$; $k_{RF} = 9\%$; $D_0 = \$2$.

b. Assume all the facts as given above except the change in the beta coefficient. How low would the beta have to fall to cause the expansion to be a good one? (Hint: Set $\hat{P}_0$ under the new policy equal to $\hat{P}_0$ under the old one, and find the new beta that will produce this equality.)

Spreadsheet Problem

10–22 *BUILD A MODEL: SUPERNORMAL GROWTH AND CORPORATE VALUATION*

Start with the partial model in the file ***Ch10-22 Build a Model.xls*** from the textbook's CD-ROM. Rework Problem 10-19, parts a, b, and c, using a spreadsheet model. For part b, calculate the price, dividend yield, and capital gains yield as called for in the problem.

10–23 *WHAT IF ANALYSIS: SUPERNORMAL GROWTH STOCK VALUATION*

Start with the model ***Ch 10-23 What If Analysis.xls*** from the textbook's CD-ROM and answer the questions shown there.

Cyberproblem

10–24 *STOCK VALUATION*

The information related to this cyberproblem is likely to change over time, due to the release of new information and the ever-changing nature of the World Wide Web. Accordingly, we will periodically update the problem on the textbook's web site.

In this cyberproblem, you will value the stock for Emerson Electric, a scientific and technical instrument company. While stock valuation is obviously important to investors, it is also vital to companies engaging in a merger or acquisition. Here, the process of stock valuation can often be quite subjective. Frequently, the opposing sides of a merger or acquisition will have vastly differing opinions of a firm's value.

For example, in 1994, part of AT&T's purchase of McCaw Cellular called for AT&T to acquire McCaw's 52 percent stake in LIN Broadcasting and purchase the remaining 48 percent at its fair value. LIN's advisors valued the stock at $162 a share, while AT&T estimated its value at $100 a share. The difference resulted in a whopping $1.6 billion. As this example demonstrates, stock valuation seems to be both art and science.

In this cyberproblem, you will use the dividend growth model's constant growth assumptions to value Emerson's stock. In addition, you will apply the concepts of risk and return by estimating the stock's required return from the CAPM model. In order to arrive at a value for Emerson Electric, you will gather and use information from a variety of sources. Go to the cyberproblem on the textbook's web site, **http://www.harcourtcollege.com/theory/student/resources/cyberprob/ch10.html,** and answer the questions shown there.

Mini Case

CD

See ***Ch 10 Show.ppt*** and ***Ch 10 Mini Case.xls.***

Robert Balik and Carol Kiefer are senior vice-presidents of the Mutual of Chicago Insurance Company. They are co-directors of the company's pension fund management division, with Balik having responsibility for fixed income securities (primarily bonds) and Kiefer being responsible for equity investments. A major new client, the California League of Cities, has requested that Mutual of Chicago present an investment seminar to the mayors of the represented cities, and Balik and Kiefer, who will make the actual presentation, have asked you to help them.

To illustrate the common stock valuation process, Balik and Kiefer have asked you to analyze the Bon Temps Company, an employment agency that supplies word processor operators and computer programmers to businesses with temporarily heavy workloads. You are to answer the following questions.

a. Describe briefly the legal rights and privileges of common stockholders.

b. (1) Write out a formula that can be used to value any stock, regardless of its dividend pattern.
   (2) What is a constant growth stock? How are constant growth stocks valued?
   (3) What happens if a company has a constant g which exceeds its k_s? Will many stocks have expected $g > k_s$ in the short run (i.e., for the next few years)? In the long run (i.e., forever)?

c. Assume that Bon Temps has a beta coefficient of 1.2, that the risk-free rate (the yield on T-bonds) is 7 percent, and that the required rate of return on the market is 12 percent. What is the required rate of return on the firm's stock?

d. Assume that Bon Temps is a constant growth company whose last dividend (D_0, which was paid yesterday) was $2.00 and whose dividend is expected to grow indefinitely at a 6 percent rate.
   (1) What is the firm's expected dividend stream over the next 3 years?
   (2) What is the firm's current stock price?
   (3) What is the stock's expected value 1 year from now?
   (4) What are the expected dividend yield, the capital gains yield, and the total return during the first year?

e. Now assume that the stock is currently selling at $30.29. What is the expected rate of return on the stock?

f. What would the stock price be if its dividends were expected to have zero growth?

g. Now assume that Bon Temps is expected to experience supernormal growth of 30 percent for the next 3 years, then to return to its long-run constant growth rate of 6 percent. What is the stock's value under these conditions? What is its expected dividend yield and capital gains yield in Year 1? In Year 4?

h. Is the stock price based more on long-term or short-term expectations? Answer this by finding the percentage of Bon Temps current stock price based on dividends expected more than 3 years in the future.

i. Suppose Bon Temps is expected to experience zero growth during the first 3 years and then to resume its steady-state growth of 6 percent in the fourth year. What is the stock's value now? What is its expected dividend yield and its capital gains yield in Year 1? In Year 4?

j. Finally, assume that Bon Temps' earnings and dividends are expected to decline by a constant 6 percent per year, that is, g = −6%. Why would anyone be willing to buy such a stock, and at what price should it sell? What would be the dividend yield and capital gains yield in each year?
k. What does market equilibrium mean?
l. If equilibrium does not exist, how will it be established?
m. What is the Efficient Markets Hypothesis, what are its three forms, and what are its implications?
n. Phyfe Company recently issued preferred stock. It pays an annual dividend of $5, and the issue price was $50 per share. What is the expected return to an investor on this preferred stock?

Selected Additional References and Cases

Many investment textbooks cover stock valuation models in depth, and some are listed in the Chapter 6 references.

The seminal work on stock valuation models is

Williams, John Burr, *The Theory of Investment Value* (Cambridge, MA: Harvard University Press, 1938).

The following classic articles extend J. B. Williams' works:

Durand, David, "Growth Stocks and the Petersburg Paradox," *Journal of Finance*, September 1957, 348–363.

Gordon, Myron J., and Eli Shapiro, "Capital Equipment Analysis: The Required Rate of Profit," *Management Science*, October 1956, 102–110.

For some recent works on valuation, see

Bey, Roger P., and J. Markham Collins, "The Relationship between Before- and After-Tax Yields on Financial Assets," *The Financial Review*, August 1988, 313–343.

Brooks, Robert, and Billy Helms, "An N-Stage, Fractional Period, Quarterly Dividend Discount Model," *Financial Review*, November 1990, 651–657.

Copeland, Tom, Tim Koller, and Jack Murrin, *Valuation: Measuring and Managing the Value of Companies*, 2nd ed. (New York: John Wiley & Sons, Inc., 1994).

The following cases in the Cases in Financial Management: Dryden Request *series cover many of the valuation concepts contained in Chapter 9.*

Case 3, "Peachtree Securities, Inc. (B);" Case 43, "Swan-Davis;" Case 49, Beatrice Peabody;" and Case 56, "Laura Henderson."

PART FOUR
Corporate Valuation

CHAPTER 11
The Cost of Capital

CHAPTER 12
Putting the Pieces Together: Corporate Valuation and Value-Based Management

11

The Cost of Capital

General Electric has long been recognized as one of the world's best-managed companies, and it has rewarded its shareholders with outstanding returns. During its corporate life, GE has raised a cumulative $65 billion in capital from its investors, but it has turned that $65 billion investment into a company worth more than $350 billion. Its Market Value Added (MVA), the difference between its market value and the capital investors put up, is a whopping $285 billion! Not surprisingly, GE is always at or near the top of all companies in MVA.

When investors provide a corporation with funding, they expect the company to generate an appropriate return on those funds. From the company's perspective, the investors' expected return is a cost of using the funds, and it is called the cost of capital. A variety of factors influence a firm's cost of capital. Some, such as the level of interest rates, state and federal tax policies, and the regulatory environment, are outside the firm's control. However, the degree of risk in the projects it undertakes and the types of funds it raises *are* under the company's control, and both have a profound effect on its cost of capital.

GE's overall cost of capital has been estimated to be about 11.9 percent. Therefore, to satisfy its investors, GE must generate a return on an average project of at least 11.9 percent. Some of GE's projects are "home grown" in the sense that the company has developed a new product or entered a new geographic market. For example, GE's aircraft engine division won more than 50 percent of the world's engine orders for airline passenger jets, and its appliance division recently introduced the Advantium speedcooking oven and the ultra-quiet Triton dishwasher. GE began Lexan® polycarbonate production at a new plastics plant in Cartagena, Spain, and GE Capital expanded in Japan by creating a new life insurance company. Sometimes GE creates completely new lines of business, such as its recent entry into e-commerce. In fact, GE was named "E-Business of the Year" in 2000 by *InternetWeek* magazine. When GE evaluates potential projects such as these, it must determine whether the return on the capital invested in the project exceeds the cost of that capital.

GE also invests by acquiring other companies. In recent years, GE has spent billions annually to acquire hundreds of companies. For example, GE recently acquired Marquette Medical Systems, a gas turbine division, from Stewart & Stevenson and Phoenixcor's commercial equipment leasing portfolio. GE must estimate its expected return on capital, and the cost of capital, for each of these acquisitions, and then make the investment only if the return is greater than the cost.

How has GE done with its investments? It has produced a return on capital of 19.3 percent, well above its 11.9 percent estimated cost of capital. With such a large differential, it is no wonder that GE has created a great deal of value for its investors.

Source: Shawn Tulley, "America's Wealth Creators," *Fortune,* November 22, 1999, 275–284; and the General Electric web site, **http://www.ge.com.**

The textbook's CD-ROM contains an *Excel* file that will guide you through the chapter's calculations. The file for this chapter is ***Ch 11 Tool Kit.xls,*** and we encourage you to open the file and follow along as you read the chapter.

Most important business decisions require capital. For example, when Daimler-Benz decided to develop the Mercedes ML 320 sports utility vehicle and to build a plant in Alabama to produce it, Daimler had to estimate the total investment that would be required and the cost of the required capital. The expected rate of return exceeded the cost of the capital, so Daimler went ahead with the project. Microsoft had to make a similar decision with Windows 2000, Pfizer with Viagra, and Harcourt when it decided to publish this textbook.

Mergers and acquisitions often require enormous amounts of capital. For example, Vodafone Group, a large telecommunications company in the United Kingdom, spent $60 billion to acquire AirTouch Communications, a U.S. telecommunications company, in 1999. The resulting company, Vodafone AirTouch, later made a $124 billion offer for Mannesmann, a German company. In both cases, Vodafone estimated the incremental cash flows that would result from the acquisition, then discounted those cash flows at the estimated cost of capital. The resulting values were greater than the targets' market prices, so Vodafone made the offers.

As these examples illustrate, the cost of capital is a critical element in business decisions. When the decision involves a single project, it is called a "capital budgeting decision." Companies that consistently make wise capital budgeting choices create value for their investors, hence it is important for managers to understand the capital budgeting process. Chapters 13, 14, and 15 describe capital budgeting in detail. The cost of capital is also necessary to estimate the value of an entire company. When evaluating a potential acquisition, it is vital to have a reliable estimate of the company's value, as we discuss in Chapter 26. It is also important for a company to develop a corporate valuation model for itself. Such a model provides insights into the sources of the company's value, and it can be used to guide managers when they evaluate alternative courses of action. Chapter 12 describes the corporate valuation model.

Recent survey evidence indicates that almost half of all large companies use compensation plans based on the concept of Economic Value Added (EVA). Recall from Chapter 2 that EVA is the difference between net operating profit after-taxes (NOPAT) and a charge for capital, where the capital charge is calculated by multiplying the amount of capital by the cost of capital. Thus, the cost of capital is an increasingly important component of compensation plans.

The cost of capital is also a key factor in decisions relating the use of debt versus equity capital. Chapters 16 and 17 describe such capital structure decisions. Finally, the cost of capital is an important factor in the regulation of electric, gas, and telephone companies. These utilities are natural monopolies in the sense that one firm can supply service at a lower cost than could two or more firms. Because it has a monopoly, your electric or telephone company could, if it were unregulated, exploit you. Therefore, regulators (1) determine the cost of the capital investors have provided the utility and (2) then set rates designed to permit the company to earn its cost of capital, no more and no less.

The Weighted Average Cost of Capital

What precisely do the terms "cost of capital" and "weighted average cost of capital" mean? To begin, note that it is possible to finance a firm entirely with common equity. However, most firms employ several types of capital, called **capital components,** with common and preferred stock, along with debt, being the three most frequently used types.[1] All capital components have one feature in common: The investors who provided the funds expect to receive a return on their investment.

If a firm's only investors were common stockholders, then the cost of capital used in capital budgeting would be the required rate of return on equity. However, most firms employ different types of capital, and, due to differences in risk, these different securities have different required rates of return. The required rate of return on each capital component is called its **component cost,** and the cost of capital used to analyze capital budgeting decisions should be a *weighted average* of the various components' costs. We call this weighted average just that, the **weighted average cost of capital,** or **WACC.**

Most firms set target percentages for the different financing sources. For example, National Computer Corporation (NCC) plans to raise 30 percent of its required capital as debt, 10 percent as preferred stock, and 60 percent as common equity. This is its **target capital structure.** We discuss how targets are established in Chapters 16 and 17, but for now simply accept NCC's 30/10/60 debt, preferred, and common percentages as given.

Although NCC and other firms try to stay close to their target capital structures, they frequently deviate in the short run for several reasons. First, market conditions may be more favorable in one market than another at a particular time. For example, if the stock market is extremely strong, a company may decide that now is a good time to issue common stock. The second, and probably more important, reason for deviations relates to flotation costs, which are the costs that a firm must incur to issue securities. Flotation costs are addressed in detail later in the chapter, but note that these costs are to a large extent fixed, so they become prohibitively high if small amounts of capital are raised. Thus, it is inefficient and expensive to issue relatively small amounts of debt, preferred stock, and common stock. Therefore, a company might issue common stock one year, debt in the next couple of years, and preferred the following year, thus fluctuating around its target capital structure rather than staying right on it all the time.

This situation can cause managers to make a serious error in their capital budgeting. To illustrate, assume that NCC is currently at its target capital structure, and it is now considering how to raise capital to finance next year's projects. NCC could raise a combination of debt and equity, but to minimize flotation costs it will raise either debt or equity, but not both. Let's suppose it decides to issue debt, at a cost of 8 percent. The argument is sometimes made that the cost of capital this year is 8 percent, because only debt at 8 percent will be used. However, this is incorrect. If NCC finances this year's projects with debt, it will move away from its target capital structure. Then, as expansion occurs in the future, it will at some point find it necessary to raise additional equity.

Now suppose NCC borrows heavily at 8 percent during 2002, using up its debt capacity in the process, to finance projects that yield 10 percent. In 2003, it has new projects available that yield 13 percent, well above the return on the 2002 projects. However, because it used up its debt capacity in 2002, it must issue equity, which costs 15.3 percent. Therefore, the company might reject these 13 percent projects because they would have to be financed with 15.3 percent money.

---

[1]There may actually be many variations within these three capital components, such as voting and nonvoting common stock, short-term and long-term debt, secured and unsecured debt, and so forth. There are also hybrid securities, such as convertible bonds, bonds with warrants, and lease financing. We discuss all these variations in later chapters.

However, this entire capital budgeting process would be incorrect. Why should a company accept 10 percent projects one year and then reject 13 percent projects the next? Note also that if NCC had reversed the order of its financing, raising equity in 2002 and debt in 2003, it would have reversed its capital budgeting decisions, rejecting all projects in 2002 and accepting them all in 2003. Does it make sense to accept or reject projects just because of the more or less arbitrary sequence in which capital is raised? The answer is no. *To avoid such errors, managers should view companies as ongoing concerns, and calculate their costs of capital as weighted averages of the various types of funds they use, regardless of the specific source of financing employed in a particular year.*

The following sections discuss each of the component costs in more detail, and then we show how to combine them to calculate the weighted average cost of capital.

Self-Test Questions

What are the three major capital components?

What is a component cost?

What is a target capital structure?

Why should the cost of capital used in capital budgeting be calculated as a weighted average of the various types of funds the firm generally uses rather than the cost of the specific financing used to fund a particular project?

Cost of Debt, $k_d(1 - T)$

The first step in estimating the cost of debt is to determine the rate of return debtholders require, or k_d. Although estimating k_d is conceptually straightforward, some problems arise in practice. Companies use both fixed and floating rate debt, straight and convertible debt, and debt with and without sinking funds, and each form has a somewhat different cost.

It is unlikely that the financial manager will know at the start of a planning period the exact types and amounts of debt that will be used during the period: The type or types used will depend on the specific assets to be financed and on capital market conditions as they develop over time. Even so, the financial manager does know what types of debt are typical for his or her firm. For example, NCC typically issues commercial paper to raise short-term money to finance working capital, and it issues 30-year bonds to raise long-term debt used to finance its capital budgeting projects. Since the WACC is used primarily in capital budgeting, NCC's treasurer uses the cost of 30-year bonds in her WACC estimate.

Assume that it is January 2002, and NCC's treasurer is estimating the WACC for the coming year. How should she calculate the component cost of debt? Most financial managers would begin by discussing current and prospective interest rates with their investment bankers. Assume that NCC's bankers state that a new 30-year, noncallable, straight bond issue would require an 11 percent coupon rate with semiannual payments, and that it would be offered to the public at its $1,000 par value. Therefore, k_d is equal to 11 percent.[2]

Note that the 11 percent is the cost of **new,** or **marginal, debt,** and it will probably not be the same as the average rate on NCC's previously issued debt, which is called the **historical,** or **embedded, rate.** The embedded cost is important for some

---

[2]The effective annual rate is $(1 + 0.11/2)^2 - 1 = 11.3\%$, but NCC and most other companies use nominal rates for all component costs.

decisions but not for others. For example, the average cost of all the capital raised in the past and still outstanding is used by regulators when they determine the rate of return a public utility should be allowed to earn. However, in financial management the WACC is used primarily to make investment decisions, and these decisions hinge on projects' returns versus the cost of new, or marginal, capital. *Thus, for our purposes, the relevant cost is the marginal cost of new debt to be raised during the planning period.*

Suppose NCC had issued debt in the past, and its bonds are publicly traded. The financial staff could use the market price of the bonds to find their yield to maturity (or yield to call if the bonds sell at a premium and are likely to be called). The YTM (or YTC) is the rate of return the existing bondholders expect to receive, and it is also a good estimate of k_d, the rate of return that new bondholders would require.

If NCC had no publicly traded debt, its staff could look at yields on publicly traded debt of similar firms. This too should provide a reasonable estimate of k_d.

The required return to debtholders, k_d, is not equal to the company's cost of debt because, since interest payments are deductible, the government in effect pays part of the total cost. As a result, the cost of debt to the firm is less than the rate of return required by debtholders.

The **after-tax cost of debt, $k_d(1 - T)$,** is used to calculate the weighted average cost of capital, and it is the interest rate on debt, k_d, less the tax savings that result because interest is deductible. This is the same as k_d multiplied by $(1 - T)$, where T is the firm's marginal tax rate:[3]

$$\begin{aligned}\text{After-tax component cost of debt} &= \text{Interest rate} - \text{Tax savings}\\ &= k_d - k_dT \qquad \textbf{(11-1)}\\ &= k_d(1 - T).\end{aligned}$$

Therefore, if NCC can borrow at an interest rate of 11 percent, and if it has a marginal federal-plus-state tax rate of 40 percent, then its after-tax cost of debt is 6.6 percent:

$$\begin{aligned}k_d(1 - T) &= 11\%(1.0 - 0.4)\\ &= 11\%(0.6)\\ &= 6.6\%.\end{aligned}$$

Self-Test Questions

Why is the after-tax cost of debt rather than the before-tax cost used to calculate the weighted average cost of capital?

Is the relevant cost of debt the interest rate on already *outstanding* debt or that on *new* debt? Why?

Cost of Preferred Stock, k_{ps}

A number of firms, including NCC, use preferred stock as part of their permanent financing mix. Preferred dividends are not tax deductible. Therefore, the company

[3]The federal tax rate for most corporations is 35 percent. However, most corporations are also subject to state income taxes, so the marginal tax rate on most corporate income is about 40 percent. For illustrative purposes, we assume that the effective federal-plus-state tax rate on marginal income is 40 percent. Also, note that the cost of debt is considered in isolation. The effect of debt on the cost of equity, as well as on future increments of debt, is ignored when the weighted cost of a combination of debt and equity is calculated in this chapter, but it will be treated in Chapters 16 and 17. Finally, the tax rate is *zero* for a firm with losses. Therefore, for a company that does not pay taxes, the cost of debt is not reduced; that is, in Equation 11-1, the tax rate equals zero, so the after-tax cost of debt is equal to the interest rate.

It should also be noted that we have ignored flotation costs (the costs incurred to sell new bonds.) The reason is that the vast majority of debt (more than 99 percent) is privately placed, hence has no flotation cost. Also, the adjustment for flotation costs usually has a very small effect on the cost of debt. Still, flotation costs are addressed in detail later in the chapter.

bears their full cost, and *no tax adjustment is used when calculating the cost of preferred stock*. Note too that while some preferreds are issued without a stated maturity date, today most have a sinking fund that effectively limits their life. Finally, although it is not mandatory that preferred dividends be paid, firms generally have every intention of doing so, because otherwise (1) they cannot pay dividends on their common stock, (2) they will find it difficult to raise additional funds in the capital markets, and (3) in some cases preferred stockholders can take control of the firm.

The **component cost of preferred stock** used to calculate the weighted average cost of capital, $\mathbf{k_{ps}}$, is the preferred dividend, D_{ps}, divided by the net issuing price, P_n, which is the price the firm receives after deducting flotation costs:

$$\text{Component cost of preferred stock} = k_{ps} = \frac{D_{ps}}{P_n}. \quad \textbf{(11-2)}$$

Flotation costs are higher for preferred stock than for debt, hence they are incorporated into the formula for preferred stocks' costs.

To illustrate the calculation, assume that NCC has preferred stock that pays a $10 dividend per share and sells for $100 per share. If NCC issued new shares of preferred, it would incur an underwriting (or flotation) cost of 2.5 percent, or $2.50 per share, so it would net $97.50 per share. Therefore, NCC's cost of preferred stock is 10.3 percent:

$$k_{ps} = \$10/\$97.50 = 10.3\%.$$

Self-Test Questions

Does the component cost of preferred stock include or exclude flotation costs? Explain.

Why is no tax adjustment made to the cost of preferred stock?

Cost of Common Stock, k_s

Companies can raise common equity in two ways: (1) by issuing new shares and (2) by retaining earnings. If new shares are issued, what rate of return must the company earn to satisfy the new stockholders? In Chapter 6, we saw that investors require a return of k_s. However, a company must earn more than k_s on new external equity to provide this rate of return to investors because there are commissions and fees, called *flotation costs*, when a firm issues new equity.

Few mature firms issue new shares of common stock.[4] In fact, less than 2 percent of all new corporate funds come from the external equity market. There are three reasons for this:

1. Flotation costs can be quite high, as we show later in this chapter.
2. Investors perceive issuing equity as a negative signal with respect to the true value of the company's stock. Investors believe that managers have superior knowledge about companies' future prospects, and that managers are most likely to issue new stock when they think the current stock price is higher than the true value. Therefore, if a mature company announces plans to issue additional shares, this typically causes its stock price to decline.

[4]A few companies issue new shares through new-stock dividend reinvestment plans, which we discuss in Chapter 18. Also, quite a few companies sell stock to their employees, and companies occasionally issue stock to finance huge projects or mergers.

3. An increase in the supply of stock will put pressure on the stock's price, forcing the company to sell the new stock at a lower price than existed before the new issue was announced.

There are times when companies should issue stock in spite of these problems, hence we discuss stock issues later in the chapter. However, for the most part we assume that the companies in our examples, like most, do not plan to issue new shares.

Does new equity capital raised by retaining earnings have a cost? The answer is a resounding yes. If some of its earnings are retained, then stockholders will incur an **opportunity cost**—the earnings could have been paid out as dividends (or used to repurchase stock), in which case stockholders could then have reinvested the money in stocks, bonds, real estate, and so on. *Thus, the firm should earn on its reinvested earnings at least as much as its stockholders themselves could earn on alternative investments of equivalent risk.*

What rate of return can stockholders expect to earn on equivalent-risk investments? The answer is k_s, because they expect to earn that return by simply buying the stock of the firm in question or that of a similar firm. *Therefore, k_s is the cost of common equity raised internally by retaining earnings.* If a company cannot earn at least k_s on reinvested earnings, then it should pass those earnings on to its stockholders and let them invest the money themselves in assets that do provide k_s.

Whereas debt and preferred stock are contractual obligations that have easily determined costs, it is more difficult to estimate k_s. However, we can employ the principles described in Chapters 6 and 10 to produce reasonably good cost of equity estimates. Three methods typically are used: (1) the Capital Asset Pricing Model (CAPM), (2) the discounted cash flow (DCF) method, and (3) the bond-yield-plus-risk-premium approach. These methods are not mutually exclusive—no method dominates the others, and all are subject to error when used in practice. Therefore, when faced with the task of estimating a company's cost of equity, we generally use all three methods and then choose among them on the basis of our confidence in the data used for each in the specific case at hand.

Self-Test Questions

What are the two sources of equity capital?

Why do most established firms not issue additional shares of common equity?

Explain why there is a cost to using retained earnings; that is, why aren't retained earnings a free source of capital?

The CAPM Approach

To estimate the cost of common stock using the Capital Asset Pricing Model (CAPM) as discussed in Chapter 6, we proceed as follows:

Step 1. Estimate the risk-free rate, k_{RF}.

Step 2. Estimate the current expected market risk premium, RP_M.[5]

Step 3. Estimate the stock's beta coefficient, b_i, and use it as an index of the stock's risk. The i signifies the *i*th company's beta.

Step 4. Substitute the preceding values into the CAPM equation to estimate the required rate of return on the stock in question:

$$k_s = k_{RF} + (RP_M)b_i. \quad \textbf{(11-3)}$$

[5]Recall from Chapter 6 that the market risk premium is the expected market return minus the risk-free rate.

Equation 11-3 shows that the CAPM estimate of k_s begins with the risk-free rate, k_{RF}, to which is added a risk premium set equal to the risk premium on the market, RP_M, scaled up or down to reflect the particular stock's risk as measured by its beta coefficient. The following sections explain how to implement the four-step process.

Estimating the Risk-Free Rate

The starting point for the CAPM cost of equity estimate is k_{RF}, the risk-free rate. There is really no such thing as a truly riskless asset in the U.S. economy. Treasury securities are essentially free of default risk, but nonindexed long-term T-bonds will suffer capital losses if interest rates rise, and a portfolio of short-term T-bills will provide a volatile earnings stream because the rate earned on T-bills varies over time.

Since we cannot in practice find a truly riskless rate upon which to base the CAPM, what rate should we use? A recent survey of highly regarded companies shows that about two-thirds of the companies use the rate on long-term Treasury bonds.[6] We agree with their choice, and here are our reasons:

1. Common stocks are long-term securities, and although a particular stockholder may not have a long investment horizon, most stockholders do invest on a long-term basis. Therefore, it is reasonable to think that stock returns embody long-term inflation expectations similar to those reflected in bonds rather than the short-term expectations in bills.
2. Treasury bill rates are more volatile than are Treasury bond rates and, most experts agree, more volatile than k_s.
3. In theory, the CAPM is supposed to measure the expected return over a particular holding period. When it is used to estimate the cost of equity for a project, the theoretically correct holding period is the life of the project. Since many projects have long lives, the holding period for the CAPM also should be long. Therefore, the rate on a long-term T-bond is a logical choice for the risk-free rate.

In light of the preceding discussion, we believe that the cost of common equity is more closely related to Treasury bond rates than to T-bill rates. This leads us to favor T-bonds as the base rate, or k_{RF}, in a CAPM cost of equity analysis. T-bond rates can be found in *The Wall Street Journal* or the *Federal Reserve Bulletin.* Generally, we use the yield on a 10-year T-bond as the proxy for the risk-free rate.

Estimating the Market Risk Premium

The market risk premium, RP_M, is the expected market return minus the risk-free rate, $k_M - k_{RF}$. It can be estimated on the basis of (1) historical data or (2) forward-looking data.

Historical Risk Premium A very complete and accurate historical risk premium study, updated annually, is available from Ibbotson Associates, who examine market data over long periods of time to find the average annual rates of return on stocks, T-bills, T-bonds, and a set of high-grade corporate bonds.[7] For example, Table 11-1 summarizes some results from their 2000 study, which covers the period 1926–1999.

---

[6]See Robert F. Bruner, Kenneth M. Eades, Robert S. Harris, and Robert C. Higgins, "Best Practices in Estimating the Cost of Capital: Survey and Synthesis," *Financial Practice and Education*, Spring/Summer 1998, 13–28.

[7]See Stocks, Bonds, Bills and Inflation: 2000 Yearbook (Chicago: Ibbotson Associates, 2000). Also, note that Ibbotson now recommends using the T-bond rate as the proxy for the risk-free rate when using the CAPM. Before 1988, Ibbotson recommended that T-bills be used.

TABLE 11-1 Selected Ibbotson Associates Data, 1926–1999

	Arithmetic Mean[a]	Geometric Mean[a]
Average Rates of Return		
Common stocks	13.3%	11.3%
Long-term corporate bonds	5.9	5.6
Long-term government bonds	5.5	5.1
Treasury bills	3.8	3.8
Inflation rate	3.2	3.1
Implied Risk Premiums		
Common stocks over T-bills	9.5%	7.5%
Common stocks over T-bonds	7.8	6.2

[a]Ibbotson Associates calculates average returns in two ways: (1) by taking each of the annual holding period returns and deriving the arithmetic average of these annual returns and (2) by finding the compound annual rate of return over the whole period, which amounts to a geometric average.

Note that common stocks provided the highest average return over the 74-year period, while Treasury bills gave the lowest. T-bills barely covered inflation, while common stock provided a substantial real return. Table 11-1 also reports the implied risk premiums, or differences, between stocks and Treasury securities. Note that the risk premium of stocks over long-term T-bonds is about 7.8 percent when using the arithmetic average and about 6.2 percent when using the geometric average. This leads to the question of which average to use. Keep in mind that the logic behind using historical risk premiums to estimate the current risk premium is the basic assumption that the future will resemble the past. If this assumption is reasonable, then the annual arithmetic average is the theoretically correct predictor for next year's risk premium. On the other hand, the geometric average is a better predictor of the risk premium over a longer future interval, say, the next 20 years.

However, it is not at all clear that the future will be like the past. For example, the choice of the beginning and ending periods can have a major effect on the calculated risk premiums. Ibbotson Associates used the longest period available to them, but had their data begun some years earlier or later, or ended earlier, their results would have been very different. In fact, using data for the past 30 or 40 years, the arithmetic average market risk premium has ranged from 5 to 6 percent, which is quite different than the 7.8 percent over the last 74 years. Note too that using periods as short as 5 to 10 years can lead to bizarre results. Indeed, over many periods the Ibbotson data would indicate *negative* risk premiums, which would lead to the conclusion that Treasury securities have a higher required return than common stocks. That, of course, is contrary to both financial theory and common sense. All this suggests that historical risk premiums should be approached with caution. As one businessman muttered after listening to a professor give a lecture on the CAPM, "Beware of academicians bearing gifts!"

Forward-Looking Risk Premiums The historical approach to risk premiums used by Ibbotson Associates assumes that investors expect future results, on average, to equal past results. However, as we noted, the estimated risk premium varies greatly depending on the period selected, and, in any event, investors today probably expect results in the future to be different from those achieved during the Great Depression of the 1930s, the World War II years of the 1940s, and the peaceful boom years of the 1950s, all of which are included (and given equal weight with more recent results) in the

Ibbotson data. The questionable assumption that future expectations are equal to past realizations, together with the sometimes nonsensical results obtained in historical risk premium studies, has led to a search for forward-looking, or ex ante, risk premiums.

The most common approach to forward-looking premiums is to use the discounted cash flow (DCF) model to estimate the expected market rate of return, $\hat{k}_M = k_M$, then to calculate RP_M as $k_M - k_{RF}$, and finally to use this estimate of RP_M in the Security Market Line. This procedure recognizes that if markets are in equilibrium, the expected rate of return on the market is also its required rate of return, so when we estimate $\hat{k}_M$, we are also estimating k_M:

$$\text{Expected rate of return} = \hat{k}_M = \frac{D_1}{P_0} + g = k_{RF} + RP_M = k_M = \text{Required rate of return}.$$

Since D_1 for the market as measured by the S&P 500 or some other index can be predicted quite accurately, and since the current market value of the index (used for P_0) is also known, the major task is to estimate g, the average expected long-term growth rate for the market index. Even here, however, the estimation task is simplified because one can reasonably assume a constant long-term growth rate for a portfolio of mature stocks such as those in the S&P 500.

Financial services companies such as *Value Line* publish, on a regular basis, a forecast based on DCF methodology for the expected rate of return on the market, $\hat{k}_M$. One can subtract the current T-bond rate from such a market forecast to obtain an estimate of the current market risk premium, RP_M.

Two potential problems arise when we attempt to use data from organizations such as *Value Line*. First, what we really want is the *marginal investor's* expectations, not those of a security analyst. However, this is probably not a major problem, since several studies have proved beyond much doubt that investors, on average, form their own expectations on the basis of professional analysts' forecasts. The second problem is that there are a number of securities firms besides *Value Line*, and, at any given time, different analysts' forecasts of future market returns are somewhat different. This suggests that it would be most appropriate to obtain a number of forecasts of $\hat{k}_M$ and then to use the average value to estimate RP_M for use in the SML. Several services (including Zacks and Institutional Brokers Estimate System, or IBES) publish data on the forecasts of essentially all widely followed analysts. Therefore, one can use the Zacks or IBES aggregate growth rate forecast, along with an aggregate dividend yield, to develop a consensus RP_M forecast and thus avoid potential bias from the use of only one organization's estimate. However, we have followed the forecasts of several of the larger organizations over a period of several years, and we have rarely found their $\hat{k}_M$ estimates to differ by more than ±0.3 percentage point from one another. Note, though, that ex ante risk premiums are not stable: they vary over time. Therefore, when using the CAPM to estimate the cost of equity, it is best to use a current estimate of the ex ante RP_M. In recent years, the forward-looking risk premium has been in the range of 4.5 to 6.5 percent.

Our View on the Market Risk Premium After reading the previous sections, you might well be confused about the correct market risk premium, since the different approaches give different results. Using the historical Ibbotson data over the last 74 years, it appears that the market risk premium is somewhere between 6.2 and 7.8 percent, depending on whether you use an arithmetic average or a geometric average. However, in the past 30 to 40 years, the historical premium has been in the range of 5 to 6 percent. Using the forward-looking approach, it appears that the market risk premium is somewhere in the area of 4.5 to 5.5 percent. To further muddy the waters, the previously cited survey indicates that 37 percent of responding companies use a market risk premium of 5 to 6 percent, 15 percent use a premium provided by their financial advisors (who typically make a recommendation of about 7 percent), and 11 percent use a premium in the range of 4 to 4.5 percent. Moreover, it has been toward the low end of the range when interest rates were high and toward the high end when rates were low.

Here is our opinion. The risk premium is driven primarily by investors' attitudes toward risk, and there are good reasons to believe that investors are less risk averse today than 50 years ago. The advent of pension plans, Social Security, health insurance, and disability insurance means that people today can take more chances with their investments, which should make them less risk averse. Also, many households have dual incomes, which also allows investors to take more chances. Finally, the historical average return on the market as Ibbotson measures it is probably too high due to a survivorship bias. Putting it all together, we conclude that the true risk premium in 2001 is almost certainly lower than the long-term historical average of more than 7 percent.

But how much lower is the current premium? In our consulting, we typically use a risk premium of 5 percent, but we would have a hard time arguing with someone who used a risk premium in the range of 4.5 to 5.5 percent. The bottom line is that there is no way to prove that a particular risk premium is either right or wrong, although we are extremely doubtful that the premium market is less than 4 percent or greater than 6 percent.

Estimating Beta

Recall from Chapter 6 that beta is usually estimated as the slope coefficient in a regression, with the company's stock returns on the y-axis and market returns on the x-axis. The resulting beta is called the *historical beta,* since it is based on historical data. Although this approach is conceptually straightforward, complications quickly arise in practice. We described these complications in detail in Chapter 7, but it is worthwhile to repeat some of them here.

First, there is no theoretical guidance as to the correct holding period over which to measure returns. The returns for a company can be calculated using daily, weekly, or monthly time periods, and the resulting estimates of beta will differ. Beta is also sensitive to the number of observations used in the regression. With too few observations, the regression loses statistical power, but with too many, the "true" beta may have changed during the sample period. In practice, it is common to use either four to five years of monthly returns or one to two years of weekly returns.

Second, the market return should, theoretically, reflect every asset, even the human capital being built by students. In practice, however, it is common to use only an index of common stocks such as the S&P 500, the NYSE Composite, or the Wilshire 5000. Even though these indexes are highly correlated with one another, using different indexes in the regression will often result in different estimates of beta.

Third, some organizations modify the calculated historical beta in order to produce what they deem to be a more accurate estimate of the "true" beta, where the true beta is the one that reflects the risk perceptions of the marginal investor. One modification, called an *adjusted beta,* attempts to correct a possible statistical bias by adjusting the historical beta to make it closer to the average beta of 1.0. Another modification, called a *fundamental beta,* incorporates information about the company, such as changes in its product lines and capital structure.

Fourth, even the best estimates of beta for an individual company are statistically imprecise. The average company has an estimated beta of 1.0, but the 95 percent confidence interval ranges from about 0.6 to 1.4. For example, if your regression produces an estimated beta of 1.0, then you can be 95 percent sure that the true beta is in the range of 0.6 to 1.4.

So, you should always bear in mind that while the estimated beta is useful when calculating the required return on stock, it is not absolutely correct. Therefore, managers and financial analysts must learn to live with some uncertainty when estimating the cost of capital.

An Illustration of the CAPM Approach

To illustrate the CAPM approach for NCC, assume that $k_{RF} = 8\%$, $RP_M = 6\%$, and $b_i = 1.1$, indicating that NCC is somewhat riskier than average. Therefore, NCC's cost of equity is 14.6 percent:

$$\begin{aligned} k_s &= 8\% + (6\%)(1.1) \\ &= 8\% + 6.6\% \\ &= 14.6\%. \end{aligned} \qquad \textbf{(11-3a)}$$

It should be noted that although the CAPM approach appears to yield an accurate, precise estimate of k_s, there are actually several problems with it. First, if a firm's stockholders are not well diversified, they may be concerned with *stand-alone risk* in addition to market risk. In that case, the firm's true investment risk would not be measured by its beta, and the CAPM procedure would understate the correct value of k_s. Further, even if the CAPM method is valid, it is hard to know the correct estimates of the inputs required to make it operational because (1) it is hard to estimate the beta that investors expect the company to have in the future, and (2) it is difficult to estimate the market risk premium.

Self-Test Questions

What is generally considered to be the most appropriate estimate of the risk-free rate, the yield on a short-term T-bill or the yield on a long-term T-bond?

Explain the two methods for estimating the market risk premium, that is, the historical data approach and the forward-looking approach.

What are some of the problems encountered when estimating beta?

Dividend-Yield-plus-Growth-Rate, or Discounted Cash Flow (DCF), Approach

In Chapter 10, we saw that both the price and the expected rate of return on a share of common stock depends on the dividends expected on the stock:

$$\begin{aligned} P_0 &= \frac{D_1}{(1 + k_s)^1} + \frac{D_2}{(1 + k_s)^2} + \cdots \\ &= \sum_{t=1}^{\infty} \frac{D_t}{(1 + k_s)^t}. \end{aligned} \qquad \textbf{(11-4)}$$

Here P_0 is the current price of the stock; D_t is the dividend expected to be paid at the end of Year t; and k_s is the required rate of return. If dividends are expected to grow at a constant rate, then Equation 11-4 reduces to

$$P_0 = \frac{D_1}{k_s - g}. \qquad \textbf{(11-5)}$$

We can solve for k_s to obtain the required rate of return on common equity, which for the marginal investor is also equal to the expected rate of return:

$$k_s = \hat{k}_s = \frac{D_1}{P_0} + \text{Expected } g. \qquad \textbf{(11-6)}$$

Thus, investors expect to receive a dividend yield, D_1/P_0, plus a capital gain, g, for a total expected return of $\hat{k}_s$. In equilibrium this expected return is also equal to the required return, k_s. This method of estimating the cost of equity is called the **discounted cash flow, or DCF, method.** Henceforth, we will assume that equilibrium exists, hence $k_s = \hat{k}_s$, so we can use the terms k_s and $\hat{k}_s$ interchangeably.

Estimating Inputs for the DCF Approach

Three inputs are required to use the DCF approach: the current stock price, the current dividend, and the expected growth in dividends. Of these inputs, the growth rate is by far the most difficult to estimate. The following sections describe the most commonly used approaches for estimating the growth rate: (1) historical growth rates, (2) the retention growth model, and (3) analysts' forecasts.

Historical Growth Rates First, if earnings and dividend growth rates have been relatively stable in the past, and if investors expect these trends to continue, then the past realized growth rate may be used as an estimate of the expected future growth rate.

We illustrate several different methods for estimating historical growth in the file ***Ch 11 Tool Kit.xls*** on the textbook's CD-ROM. For NCC, these different methods produce estimates of historical growth ranging from 4.6 percent to 11.0 percent, with most estimates fairly close to 7 percent.

As the ***Ch 11 Tool Kit.xls*** shows, one can take a given set of historical data and, depending on the years and the calculation method used, obtain a large number of quite different growth rates. Now recall our purpose in making these calculations: We are seeking the future dividend growth rate that investors expect, and we reasoned that, if past growth rates have been stable, then investors might base future expectations on past trends. This is a reasonable proposition, but, unfortunately, we rarely find much historical stability. Therefore, the use of historical growth rates in a DCF analysis must be applied with judgment, and also be used (if at all) in conjunction with other growth estimation methods as discussed next.

Retention Growth Model Another method for estimating the growth rate is to use the *retention growth model:*

$$g = b(r). \qquad \textbf{(11-7)}$$

Here r is the expected future return on equity (ROE), and b is the fraction of its earnings that a firm is expected to retain (1 − Payout ratio).[8] Equation 11-7 produces a constant growth rate, but when we use it we are, by implication, making four important assumptions: (1) We expect the payout rate, and thus the retention rate, b = 1 − Payout, to remain constant; (2) we expect the return on equity on new investment, r, to equal the firm's current ROE, which implies that we expect the return on equity to remain constant; (3) the firm is not expected to issue new common stock, or, if it does, we expect this new stock to be sold at a price equal to its book value; and (4) future projects are expected to have the same degree of risk as the firm's existing assets.

[8]Since there are more terms for which symbols are needed than there are letters in the alphabet, some letters are used to denote several different things. This is one of those instances, and b is standard notation for both the beta coefficient and the retention rate. Note also that the retention rate is the complement of the payout rate, that is, Retention rate = (1 − Payout rate).

NCC has had an average return on equity of about 14.5 percent over the past 15 years. The ROE has been relatively steady, but even so it has ranged from a low of 11.0 percent to a high of 17.6 percent. In addition, NCC's dividend payout rate has averaged 0.52 over the past 15 years, so its retention rate, b, has averaged 1.0 − 0.52 = 0.48. Using Equation 11-7, we estimate g to be 7 percent:

$$g = 0.48(14.5\%) = 7\%.$$

Analysts' Forecasts A third technique calls for using security analysts' forecasts. Analysts publish growth rate estimates for most of the larger publicly owned companies. For example, *Value Line* provides such forecasts on 1,700 companies, and all of the larger brokerage houses provide similar forecasts. Further, several companies compile analysts' forecasts on a regular basis and provide summary information such as the median and range of forecasts on widely followed companies. These growth rate summaries, such as the one compiled by Zack's or by Lynch, Jones & Ryan in its Institutional Brokers Estimate System (IBES), can be found on the Internet.

However, these forecasts often involve nonconstant growth. For example, some analysts were forecasting that NCC would have a 10.4 percent annual growth rate in earnings and dividends over the next five years, but a growth rate beyond that of 6.5 percent.

This nonconstant growth forecast can be used to develop a proxy constant growth rate. Computer simulations indicate that dividends beyond Year 50 contribute very little to the value of any stock—the present value of dividends beyond Year 50 is virtually zero, so for practical purposes, we can ignore anything beyond 50 years. If we consider only a 50-year horizon, we can develop a weighted average growth rate and use it as a constant growth rate for cost of capital purposes. In the NCC case, we assumed a growth rate of 10.4 percent for 5 years followed by a growth rate of 6.5 percent for 45 years. We weight the short-term growth by 5/50 = 10% and the long-term growth by 45/50 = 90%. This produces an average growth rate of 0.10(10.4%) + 0.90(6.5%) = 6.9%.

Illustration of the Discounted Cash Flow Approach

To illustrate the DCF approach, suppose NCC's stock sells for $32; its next expected dividend is $2.40; and its expected growth rate is 7 percent. NCC's expected and required rate of return, hence its cost of common stock, would then be 14.5 percent:

$$\begin{aligned} \hat{k}_s = k_s &= \frac{\$2.40}{\$32.00} + 7.0\% \\ &= 7.5\% + 7.0\% \\ &= 14.5\%. \end{aligned}$$

Evaluating the Methods for Estimating Growth

Note that the DCF approach expresses the cost of common equity as the dividend yield (the expected dividend divided by the current price) and the growth rate. The dividend yield can be estimated with a high degree of certainty, but the growth estimate causes uncertainty as to the DCF cost estimate. We discussed three methods: (1) historical growth rates, (2) retention growth model, and (3) analysts' forecasts. Of these three methods, studies have shown that analysts' forecasts usually represent the best source of growth rate data for DCF cost of capital estimates.[9]

---

[9]See Robert Harris, "Using Analysts' Growth Rate Forecasts to Estimate Shareholder Required Rates of Return," *Financial Management*, Spring 1986, 58–67. Analysts' forecasts are the best predictors of actual future growth, and also the growth rate investors say they use in valuing stocks.

Using Nonconstant Growth Estimates to Estimate the Cost of Stock

As we noted earlier, analysts often provide nonconstant estimates of future growth. We can use a modified version of the DCF procedure for nonconstant growth from Chapter 10 to estimate the cost of equity. Suppose the current dividend is $2.16 per share and the current actual price is $32 per share. Analysts forecast growth of 11 percent the first year, 10 percent the second year, 9 percent the third year, 8 percent the fourth year, and 7 percent thereafter. Given these estimates of growth, we can construct a time line with expected future dividend payments. For example, the dividend at Year 1 is the current dividend times 1.0 plus the growth rate: $2.16(1 + 0.11) = $2.40. The estimates of growth and expected future dividends for Years 1 through 5 are shown in Table 11-2.

Note that dividends grow at a constant rate after Year 4. Therefore, we can use the constant dividend growth formula to determine the price at Year 4, based on the Year 5 dividend and the long-term constant growth rate:

$$P_4 = \frac{D_5}{(k_s - g)}. \tag{11-8}$$

To find the current price, P_0, we must calculate the present value of the future expected dividend payments for Years 1 through 4, and then add to that the present value of the price at Year 4, P_4. This calculation is shown in Equation 11-9:

$$\begin{aligned} P_0 &= \left[\frac{D_1}{(1+k_s)} + \frac{D_2}{(1+k_s)^2} + \frac{D_3}{(1+k_s)^3} + \frac{D_4}{(1+k_s)^4}\right] + \frac{P_4}{(1+k_s)^4} \\ &= \left[\frac{D_1}{(1+k_s)} + \frac{D_2}{(1+k_s)^2} + \frac{D_3}{(1+k_s)^3} + \frac{D_4}{(1+k_s)^4}\right] + \frac{\left[\frac{D_5}{(k_s - g)}\right]}{(1+k_s)^4}. \end{aligned} \tag{11-9}$$

We know the current price, the expected future dividends, and the long-term constant growth rate. Substituting these known values into Equation 11-9 gives the following equation:

$$\$32.00 = \left[\frac{\$2.40}{(1+k_s)} + \frac{\$2.64}{(1+k_s)^2} + \frac{\$2.87}{(1+k_s)^3} + \frac{\$3.10}{(1+k_s)^4}\right] + \frac{\left[\frac{\$3.32}{(k_s - 0.7)}\right]}{(1+k_s)^4}. \tag{11-9a}$$

We have good news, bad news, and good news. The good news is that k_s is the only unknown variable in Equation 11-9a, so we can solve for it. The bad news is that the only way to solve for k_s is by an iterative process. But the second good news is that the iterative process is very easy to implement with a spreadsheet. Using the Solver feature of *Excel*, we find that k_s = 14.9%. See ***Ch 11 Tool Kit.xls*** for an illustration of this approach.

Self-Test Question

Explain how to estimate the cost of equity when the expected dividend growth rate is not constant.

TABLE 11-2 Expected Future Dividends with Nonconstant Growth

Year	0	1	2	3	4	5
Growth		11%	10%	9%	8%	7%
Dividend	$2.16	$2.40	$2.64	$2.87	$3.10	$3.32

Bond-Yield-plus-Risk-Premium Approach

Some analysts use a subjective, ad hoc procedure to estimate a firm's cost of common equity: they simply add a judgmental risk premium of 3 to 5 percentage points to the interest rate on the firm's own long-term debt. It is logical to think that firms with risky, low-rated, and consequently high-interest-rate debt will also have risky, high-cost equity, and the procedure of basing the cost of equity on a readily observable debt cost utilizes this logic. For example, if an extremely strong firm such as BellSouth had bonds which yielded 8 percent, its cost of equity might be estimated as follows:

$$k_s = \text{Bond yield} + \text{Risk premium} = 8\% + 4\% = 12\%.$$

The bonds of NCC, a riskier company, have a yield of 10.4 percent, making its estimated cost of equity 14.4 percent:

$$k_s = 10.4\% + 4\% = 14.4\%.$$

Because the 4 percent risk premium is a judgmental estimate, the estimated value of k_s is also judgmental. Empirical work in recent years suggests that the risk premium over a firm's own bond yield has generally ranged from 3 to 5 percentage points, so this method is not likely to produce a precise cost of equity. However, it can get us "into the right ballpark."

Self-Test Question

What is the reasoning behind the bond-yield-plus-risk-premium approach?

Comparison of the CAPM, DCF, and Bond-Yield-plus-Risk-Premium Methods

We have discussed three methods for estimating the required return on common stock. For NCC, the CAPM estimate is 14.6 percent, the DCF constant growth estimate is 14.5 percent, and the bond-yield-plus-risk-premium is 14.4 percent. The overall average of these three methods is (14.6% + 14.5% + 14.4%)/3 = 14.5%. These results are unusually consistent, so it would make little difference which one we used. However, if the methods produced widely varied estimates, then a financial analyst would have to use his or her judgment as to the relative merits of each estimate and then choose the estimate that seemed most reasonable under the circumstances.

A 2000 research paper that reported the results of two surveys found that the CAPM approach is by far the most widely used method. Although most firms use more than one method, almost 74 percent of respondents in one survey, and 85 percent in the other, used the CAPM.[10] This is in sharp contrast to a 1982 survey, which found that only 30 percent of respondents used the CAPM.[11] Approximately 16

[10]See John R. Graham and Campbell Harvey, "The Theory and Practice of Corporate Finance: Evidence from the Field," *Journal of Financial Economics*, Vol. 60, no. 1, 2001, and the paper cited in Footnote 6. Interestingly, a growing number of firms (about 34 percent) also are using CAPM-type models with more than one factor, such as the models we describe in Chapter 7. Of these firms, over 40 percent include factors for interest-rate risk, foreign exchange risk, and business cycle risk (proxied by gross domestic product). More than 20 percent of these firms include a factor for inflation, size, and exposure to particular commodity prices. Less than 20 percent of these firms make adjustments due to distress factors, book-to-market ratios, or momentum factors.

[11]See Lawrence J. Gitman and Vincent Mecurio, "Cost of Capital Techniques Used by Major U.S. Firms: Survey Analysis of *Fortune's* 1000, *Financial Management*, Vol. 14, 1982, 21–29.

percent now use the DCF approach, down from 31 percent in 1982. The bond-yield-plus-risk-premium is used primarily by companies that are not publicly traded.

People experienced in estimating equity capital costs recognize that both careful analysis and sound judgment are required. It would be nice to pretend that judgment is unnecessary and to specify an easy, precise way of determining the exact cost of equity capital. Unfortunately, this is not possible—finance is in large part a matter of judgment, and we simply must face that fact.

Self-Test Question

Which approach is used most often by businesses today?

Composite, or Weighted Average, Cost of Capital, WACC

As we shall see in Chapters 16 and 17, each firm has an optimal capital structure, defined as that mix of debt, preferred, and common equity that causes its stock price to be maximized. Therefore, a value-maximizing firm will establish a *target (optimal) capital structure* and then raise new capital in a manner that will keep the actual capital structure on target over time. In this chapter, we assume that the firm has identified its optimal capital structure, that it uses this optimum as the target, and that it finances so as to remain constantly on target. How the target is established will be examined in Chapters 16 and 17.

The target proportions of debt, preferred stock, and common equity, along with the component costs of capital, are used to calculate the firm's WACC. To illustrate, suppose NCC has a target capital structure calling for 30 percent debt, 10 percent preferred stock, and 60 percent common equity. Its before-tax cost of debt, k_d, is 11 percent; its after-tax cost of debt is $k_d(1 - T) = 11\%(0.6) = 6.6\%$; its cost of preferred stock, k_{ps}, is 10.3 percent; its cost of common equity, k_s, is 14.5 percent; its marginal tax rate is 40 percent; and all of its new equity will come from retained earnings. We can calculate NCC's weighted average cost of capital, WACC, as follows:

$$\text{WACC} = w_d k_d(1 - T) + w_{ps}k_{ps} + w_{ce}k_s \tag{11-10}$$

$$= 0.3(11.0\%)(0.6) + 0.1(10.3\%) + 0.6(14.5\%)$$
$$= 11.7\%.$$

Here w_d, w_{ps}, and w_{ce} are the weights used for debt, preferred, and common equity, respectively.

Every dollar of new capital that NCC obtains will on average consist of 30 cents of debt with an after-tax cost of 6.6 percent, 10 cents of preferred stock with a cost of 10.3 percent, and 60 cents of common equity with a cost of 14.5 percent. The average cost of each whole dollar, the WACC, is 11.7 percent.

Two points should be noted. First, the WACC is the weighted average cost of each new, or *marginal*, dollar of capital—it is not the average cost of all dollars raised in the past. We are primarily interested in obtaining a cost of capital for use in capital budgeting, and for this purpose the cost of the new money that will be invested is the relevant cost. On average, each of these new dollars will consist of some debt, some preferred, and some common equity.

Second, the percentages of each capital component, called weights, could be based on (1) accounting values as shown on the balance sheet (book values), (2) current market values of the capital components, or (3) management's target capital structure, which is presumably an estimate of the firm's optimal capital structure. *The correct weights are those based on the firm's target capital structure, since this is the best estimate of how the firm will, on average, raise money in the future.* Recent survey evidence indicates

WACC Estimates for Some Large U.S. Corporations

As noted in Chapter 2, the New York consulting firm of Stern Stewart & Company regularly estimates EVAs and MVAs for large U.S. corporations. To obtain these estimates, Stern Stewart must calculate a WACC for each company. Our table presents some recent WACC estimates as calculated by Stern Stewart for a sample of corporations, along with their long-term debt-to-total-capital ratios.

These estimates suggest that a typical company has a WACC somewhere in the 9 to 15 percent range and that WACCs vary considerably depending on (1) the company's risk and (2) the amount of debt it uses. Companies in riskier businesses, such as Intel, presumably have higher costs of common equity. Moreover, they tend not to use as much debt. These two factors, in combination, result in higher WACCs than those of companies that operate in more stable businesses, such as BellSouth. We will discuss the effects of capital structure on WACC in more detail in Chapters 16 and 17.

Note that riskier companies may also have the potential for producing higher returns, and what really matters to shareholders is whether a company is able to generate returns in excess of its cost of capital, resulting in a positive EVA. Therefore, a high cost of capital is not necessarily bad if it is accompanied by projects with high rates of return.

Source: "America's Wealth Creators," *Fortune*, November 22, 1999, 275-284; and *Value Line Investment Survey*, May 1999.

Company	WACC	Book Value Debt Ratio[a]
Intel	12.9%	2.3%
General Electric	11.9	2.1
Motorola	11.3	13.9
Coca-Cola	11.2	9.9
Walt Disney	10.0	33.0
Wal-Mart	9.8	34.3
AT&T	9.8	23.2
Exxon	8.8	13.9
H.J. Heinz	8.5	55.5
BellSouth	8.2	32.6

[a]Long-term debt only.

that the majority of firms do base their weights on target capital structures, and that the target structures reflect market values.

Self-Test Questions

How does one calculate the weighted average cost of capital? Write out the equation.

On what should the weights be based?

Factors That Affect the Weighted Average Cost of Capital

The cost of capital is affected by a number of factors. Some are beyond the firm's control, but others are influenced by its financing and investment policies.

Factors the Firm Cannot Control

The three most important factors that are beyond a firm's direct control are (1) the level of interest rates, (2) the market risk premium, and (3) tax rates.

The Level of Interest Rates If interest rates in the economy rise, the cost of debt increases because firms will have to pay bondholders a higher interest rate to obtain debt capital. Also, recall from our discussion of the CAPM that higher interest rates also increase the costs of common and preferred equity. During the 1990s, interest rates in the United States declined significantly. This reduced the cost of both debt and equity capital for all firms, which encouraged additional investment. Our lower interest rates also enabled U.S. firms to compete more effectively with German and Japanese firms, which in the past had enjoyed relatively low costs of capital.

Market Risk Premium The perceived risk inherent in stocks, along with investors' aversion to risk, determine the market risk premium. Individual firms have no control over this factor, but it affects the cost of equity and, through a substitution effect, the cost of debt, and thus the WACC.

Tax Rates Tax rates, which are largely beyond the control of an individual firm (although firms do lobby for more favorable tax treatment), have an important effect on the cost of capital. Tax rates are used in the calculation of the cost of debt as used in the WACC, and there are other less obvious ways in which tax policy affects the cost of capital. For example, lowering the capital gains tax rate relative to the rate on ordinary income would make stocks more attractive, which would reduce the cost of equity relative to that of debt. That would, as we will see in Chapters 16 and 17, lead to a change in a firm's optimal capital structure toward less debt and more equity.

Factors the Firm Can Control

A firm can affect its cost of capital through (1) its capital structure policy, (2) its dividend policy, and (3) its investment (capital budgeting) policy.

Capital Structure Policy In this chapter, we assume that a firm has a given target capital structure, and we use weights based on that target structure to calculate the WACC. It is clear, though, that a firm can change its capital structure, and such a change can affect its cost of capital. First, beta is a function of financial leverage, so capital structure affects the cost of equity. Second, the after-tax cost of debt is lower than the cost of equity. Therefore, if the firm decides to use more debt and less common equity, this change in the weights in the WACC equation will tend to lower the WACC. However, an increase in the use of debt will increase the riskiness of both the debt and the equity, and increases in component costs will tend to offset the effects of the change in the weights. In Chapters 16 and 17, we will discuss this in more depth, and we will demonstrate that a firm's optimal capital structure is the one that minimizes its cost of capital.

Dividend Policy As we shall see in Chapter 18, the percentage of earnings paid out in dividends may affect a stock's required rate of return, k_s. Also, if a firm's payout ratio is so high that it must issue new stock to fund its capital budget, this will force it to incur flotation costs, and this too will affect its cost of capital. This second point is discussed in detail later in this chapter and also in Chapter 18.

Investment Policy When we estimate the cost of capital, we use as the starting point the required rates of return on the firm's outstanding stock and bonds. Those rates reflect the riskiness of the firm's existing assets. Therefore, we have implicitly been assuming that new capital will be invested in assets and with the same degree of risk as existing assets. This assumption is generally correct, as most firms do invest in assets similar to those they currently use. However, it would be incorrect if a firm dramatically changed its investment policy. For example, if a firm invests in an entirely new line of business, its marginal cost of capital should reflect the riskiness of that new business. To illustrate, ITT Corporation recently sold its finance company and purchased Caesar's World, a casino gambling firm. This dramatic shift in corporate focus

Global Variations in the Cost of Capital

For U.S. firms to be competitive with foreign companies, they must have a cost of capital no greater than that faced by their international competitors. In the past, many experts argued that U.S. firms were at a disadvantage. In particular, Japanese firms enjoyed a very low cost of capital, which lowered their total costs and thus made it hard for U.S. firms to compete. Recent events, however, have considerably narrowed cost of capital differences between U.S. and Japanese firms. In particular, the U.S. stock market has outperformed the Japanese market in recent years, which has made it easier and cheaper for U.S. firms to raise equity capital.

As capital markets become increasingly integrated, cross-country differences in the cost of capital are disappearing. Today, most large corporations raise capital throughout the world, hence we are moving toward one global capital market rather than distinct capital markets in each country. Although government policies and market conditions can affect the cost of capital within a given country, this primarily affects smaller firms that do not have access to global capital markets, and even these differences are becoming less important as time goes by. What matters most is the risk of the individual firm, not the market in which it raises capital.

almost certainly affected ITT's cost of capital. Likewise, Disney's purchase of the ABC television network changed the nature and risk of its assets in a way that might also influence its cost of capital. The effect of investment policy on capital costs is discussed in detail in the next section and in Chapter 14.

Self-Test Questions

What three factors that affect the cost of capital are generally beyond the firm's control?

What three policies under the firm's control are likely to affect its cost of capital?

Explain how a change in interest rates in the economy would affect each component of the weighted average cost of capital.

Adjusting the Cost of Capital for Risk

As noted earlier, the cost of capital is a key element in the capital budgeting process. As you will see in the next four chapters, a project should be accepted if and only if its estimated return exceeds its cost of capital. For this reason, the cost of capital is sometimes referred to as a "hurdle rate"—project returns must "jump the hurdle" to be accepted.

As we saw in Chapter 6, investors require higher returns for riskier investments. Consequently, a company that invests in risky projects will have a higher cost of capital than a company that invests in safer projects. Figure 11-1 illustrates the trade-off between risk and the cost of capital. Firm L is a low-risk business with a WACC of 8 percent, whereas Firm H is exposed to high risks and has a 12 percent WACC. Thus, Firm L will accept one of its typical projects only if the project's expected return is above 8 percent, while the corresponding hurdle rate for Firm H is 12 percent.

It is important to remember that the cost of capital values presented in Figure 11-1 represent the overall, or composite, WACCs for each firm and, thus, only represent the hurdle rate of a "typical" project for each firm. Different projects generally have different risks. Moreover, the hurdle rate for each project should reflect the risk of the project itself, not necessarily the risk associated with the firm's average project as reflected in its composite WACC. For example, assume that Firms L and H are both considering the same Project A. This project has more risk than a typical Firm L project but less risk than a typical Firm H project. As shown in Figure 11-1, Project A

FIGURE 11-1 Risk and the Cost of Capital

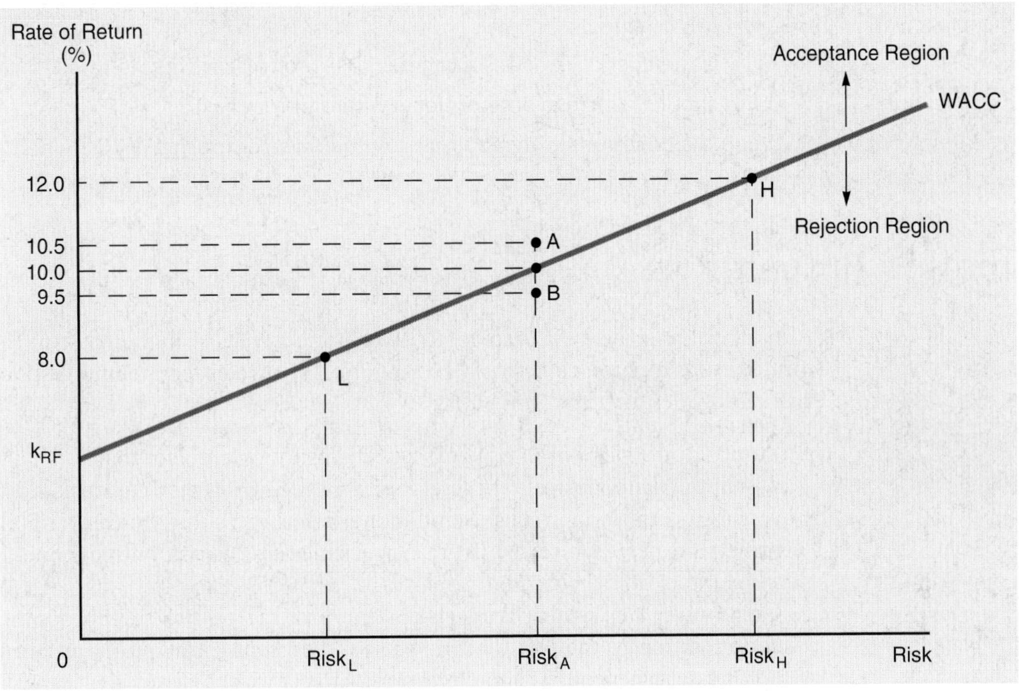

has a 10.5 percent expected return. At first, we might be tempted to conclude that Firm L should accept Project A because its 10.5 percent return is above its 8 percent WACC, while Firm H should turn the project down because its return is less than H's 12 percent WACC. However, this would be wrong. The relevant hurdle rate is the *project's WACC*, which is 10 percent, as read from the WACC line in Figure 11-1. Since the project's return exceeds its 10 percent cost, *both* firms should accept Project A.

Next, consider Project B. It has the same risk as Project A, but its expected return is 9.5 percent versus its 10 percent hurdle rate. Both firms should reject Project B. However, if they based their decisions on their overall WACCs rather than on Project B's own risk-adjusted cost of capital, Firm L would accept Project B because its return is above L's 8 percent WACC. Note, though, that if Firm L's managers accept Project B, they would reduce their shareholders' wealth, because the project's return is not high enough to justify its risk. Applying a specific hurdle rate to each project ensures that every project will be evaluated properly.

Similarly, if a company has different divisional costs of capital, then it would be incorrect to use the company's overall cost of capital to find the NPV of all its projects. For example, consider Starlight Sandwich Shops, a company with two divisions—a bakery operation and a chain of cafes. The bakery division is low risk and has a 10 percent cost of capital. The cafe division is riskier and has a 14 percent cost of capital. Each division is approximately the same size, so Starlight's overall cost of capital is 12 percent. The bakery manager has a project with an 11 percent expected rate of return, and the cafe division manager has a project with a 13 percent expected return. Should these projects be accepted or rejected? Starlight can create value if it accepts the bakery's project, since its rate of return is greater than its cost of capital (11% > 10%), but the cafe project's rate of return is less than its cost of capital (13% < 14%), so it should be rejected. However, if one simply compared the two projects' returns with Starlight's 12 percent overall cost of capital, then the bakery's value-adding project would be rejected while the cafe's value-destroying project would be accepted.

Self-Test Questions

Why is the cost of capital sometimes referred to as a "hurdle rate"?

How should firms evaluate projects with different risks?

Should all divisions within a firm use the firm's composite WACC when considering capital budgeting projects? Explain.

Estimating Project Risk

Although it is intuitively clear that riskier projects have a higher cost of capital, it is difficult to estimate project risk. First, note that three separate and distinct types of risk can be identified:

1. **Stand-alone risk** is the project's risk disregarding the fact that it is but one asset within the firm's portfolio of assets and that the firm is but one stock in a typical investor's portfolio of stocks. Stand-alone risk is measured by the variability of the project's expected returns. It is a correct measure of risk only for one-asset firms whose stockholders own only one stock.
2. **Corporate, or within-firm, risk** is the project's risk to the corporation, giving consideration to the fact that the project represents only one of the firm's portfolio of assets, hence that some of its risk effects will be diversified away. Corporate risk is measured by the project's effect on uncertainty about the firm's future earnings.
3. **Market, or beta, risk** is the riskiness of the project as seen by a well-diversified stockholder who recognizes that the project is only one of the firm's assets and that the firm's stock is but one part of his or her total portfolio. Market risk is measured by the project's effect on the firm's beta coefficient.

Taking on a project with a high degree of either stand-alone or corporate risk will not necessarily affect the firm's beta. However, if the project has highly uncertain returns, and if those returns are highly correlated with returns on the firm's other assets and with most other assets in the economy, then the project will have a high degree of all types of risk. For example, suppose General Motors decides to undertake a major expansion to build electric autos. GM is not sure how its technology will work on a mass production basis, so there is much risk in the venture—its stand-alone risk is high. Management also estimates that the project will do best if the economy is strong, for then people will have more money to spend on the new autos. This means that the project will tend to do well if GM's other divisions are doing well and will tend to do badly if other divisions are doing badly. This being the case, the project will also have high corporate risk. Finally, since GM's profits are highly correlated with those of most other firms, the project's beta will also be high. Thus, this project will be risky under all three definitions of risk.

Of the three measures, market risk is theoretically the most relevant because of its direct effect on stock prices. Unfortunately, the market risk for a project is also the most difficult to estimate. In practice, most decision makers consider all three risk measures in a judgmental manner, and then they group projects into subjective risk categories. Then, using the composite WACC as a starting point, **risk-adjusted costs of capital** are developed for each category. For example, a firm might establish three risk classes—high, average, and low—then assign average-risk projects the average (composite) cost of capital, higher-risk projects an above-average cost, and lower-risk projects a below-average cost. Thus, if a company's composite WACC were 10 percent, its managers might use 10 percent to evaluate average-risk projects, 12 percent for high-risk projects, and 8 percent for low-risk projects. While this approach is better than not risk adjusting at all, these risk adjustments are necessarily subjective and somewhat arbitrary. Unfortunately, given the data, there is no completely satisfactory way to specify exactly how much higher or lower we should go in setting risk-adjusted costs of capital.

Self-Test Questions

What are the three types of project risk?

Which type of risk is theoretically the most relevant? Why?

Describe a procedure firms can use to develop costs of capital for projects with differing degrees of risk.

Using the CAPM to Estimate a Project's Risk-Adjusted Cost of Capital

Many firms use the CAPM to estimate the cost of capital for specific projects or divisions. To begin, recall from Chapter 6 that the Security Market Line equation expresses the risk/return relationship as follows:

$$k_s = k_{RF} + (k_M - k_{RF})b_i.$$

As an example, consider the case of Huron Steel Company, an integrated steel producer operating in the Great Lakes region. For simplicity, assume that Huron uses only equity capital, so its cost of equity is also its corporate cost of capital, or WACC. Huron's beta $= b = 1.1$; $k_{RF} = 7\%$; and $RP_M = 6.5\%$. Thus, Huron's cost of equity is 14.2 percent:

$$\begin{aligned} k_s &= 7\% + (6.5\%)1.1 \\ &= 14.2\%. \end{aligned}$$

This suggests that investors should be willing to give Huron money to invest in average-risk projects if the company expects to earn 14.2 percent or more on this money. Here again, by average risk we mean projects having risk similar to the firm's existing assets. *Therefore, as a first approximation Huron should invest in capital projects if and only if these projects have an expected return of 14.2 percent or more.*[12] Huron should use 14.2 percent as its discount rate to determine the NPV of an average-risk project.

Suppose, however, that taking on a particular project would cause a change in Huron's beta coefficient, which, in turn, would change the company's cost of equity. For example, suppose Huron is considering the construction of a fleet of barges to haul iron ore, and barge operations have betas of 1.5 rather than 1.1. Since the firm itself may be regarded as a "portfolio of assets," and since the beta of any portfolio is a weighted average of the betas of its individual assets, taking on the barge project would cause the overall corporate beta to rise to somewhere between the original beta of 1.1 and the barge project's beta of 1.5. The exact value of the new beta would depend on the relative size of the investment in barge operations versus Huron's other assets. If 80 percent of Huron's total funds ended up in basic steel operations with a beta of 1.1 and 20 percent in barge operations with a beta of 1.5, the new corporate beta would be 1.18:

$$\begin{aligned} \text{New beta} &= 0.8(1.1) + 0.2(1.5) \\ &= 1.18. \end{aligned}$$

[12] To simplify things somewhat, we assume that the firm uses only equity capital. If debt is used, the cost of capital used must be a weighted average of the costs of debt and equity.

This increase in Huron's beta coefficient would cause its stock price to decline *unless the increased beta were offset by a higher expected rate of return.* Specifically, taking on the new project would cause the overall corporate cost of capital to rise from the original 14.2 percent to 14.7 percent:

$$\begin{aligned} k_s &= 7\% + (6.5\%)1.18 \\ &= 14.7\%. \end{aligned}$$

Therefore, to keep the barge investment from lowering the value of the firm, Huron's overall expected rate of return must also rise from 14.2 to 14.7 percent.

If investments in basic steel must earn 14.2 percent, how much must Huron expect to earn on the barge investment to cause the new overall expected rate of return to equal 14.7 percent? We know that if Huron undertakes the barge investment, it will have 80 percent of its assets invested in basic steel projects earning 14.2 percent and 20 percent in barge operations earning X percent, and the average required rate of return will be 14.7 percent. Therefore,

$$\begin{aligned} 0.8(14.2\%) + 0.2X &= 14.7\% \\ 0.2X &= 3.34\% \\ X &= 16.7\%. \end{aligned}$$

Since X = 16.7%, we see that the barge project must have an expected return of at least 16.7 percent if the corporation is to earn its new cost of capital.

In summary, if Huron takes on the barge project, its corporate beta will rise from 1.1 to 1.18, its cost of capital will rise from 14.2 to 14.7 percent, and the barge investment must earn 16.7 percent if the company is to earn its new overall cost of capital.

This line of reasoning leads to the conclusion that if the beta coefficient for each project, b_p, could be determined, then a **project cost of capital, $k_{Project}$,** for each individual project could be found as follows:

$$k_{Project} = k_{RF} + (k_M - k_{RF})b_p.$$

Thus, for basic steel projects with b = 1.1, Huron should use 14.2 percent as the cost of capital. The barge project, with b = 1.5, should be evaluated at a 16.75 percent cost of capital:

$$\begin{aligned} k_{Barge} &= 7\% + (6.5\%)1.5 \\ &= 16.75\%. \end{aligned}$$

Note that this is the same cost of capital as above, except for a rounding difference. On the other hand, a low-risk project, such as a new distribution center with a beta of only 0.5, would have a cost of capital of 10 percent:

$$\begin{aligned} k_{Center} &= 7\% + (6.5\%)0.5 \\ &= 10.3\%. \end{aligned}$$

Figure 11-2 gives a graphic summary of these concepts as applied to Huron Steel. Note the following points:

1. The SML is the same Security Market Line that we discussed in Chapter 6. It shows how investors are willing to make trade-offs between risk as measured by beta and expected returns. The higher the beta risk, the higher the rate of return needed to compensate investors for bearing this risk. The SML specifies the nature of this relationship.
2. Huron Steel initially has a beta of 1.1, so its required rate of return on average-risk investments is 14.2 percent.

FIGURE 11-2 Using the Security Market Line Concept in Capital Budgeting

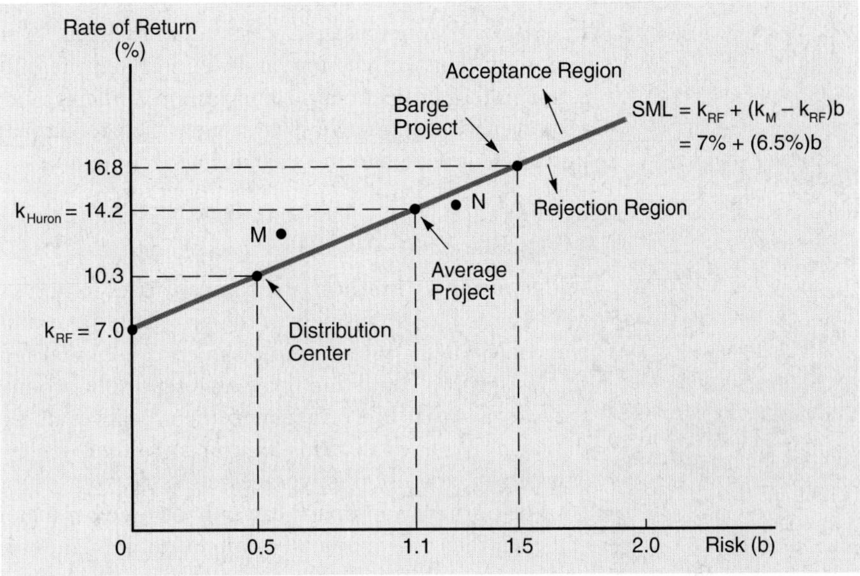

3. High-risk investments such as the barge line require higher rates of return, whereas low-risk investments such as the distribution center require lower rates of return. If Huron concentrates its new investments in either high- or low-risk projects as opposed to average-risk projects, its corporate beta will rise or fall from the current value of 1.1. Consequently, Huron's required rate of return on common stock will change from its current value of 14.2 percent.
4. If the expected rate of return on a given capital project lies *above* the SML, the expected rate of return on the project is more than enough to compensate for its risk, and the project should be accepted. Conversely, if the project's rate of return lies *below* the SML, it should be rejected. Thus, Project M in Figure 11-2 is acceptable, whereas Project N should be rejected. N has a higher expected return than M, but the differential is not enough to offset its much higher risk.
5. For simplicity, the Huron Steel illustration is based on the assumption that the company used no debt financing, which allows us to use the SML to plot the company's cost of capital. The basic concepts presented in the Huron illustration also hold for companies that use debt financing. The discount rate applied in capital budgeting is the firm's weighted average cost of capital. When debt financing is used, the project's cost of equity must be combined with the cost of debt to obtain the project's overall cost of capital.

Self-Test Questions

What is meant by the term "average-risk project"? Based on the CAPM, how would one find the cost of capital for such a project, for a low-risk project, and for a high-risk project?

Complete the following sentence: An increase in a company's beta coefficient would cause its stock price to decline unless its expected rate of return . . .

Explain why you should accept a given capital project if its expected rate of return lies above the SML. What if the expected rate of return lies on the SML? Below the SML?

Techniques for Measuring Beta Risk

In Chapter 6 we discussed the estimation of betas for stocks. In Chapter 7 we provided a more in-depth discussion, and we indicated the difficulties in estimating beta. The estimation of project betas is much more difficult, and more fraught with uncertainty. However, two approaches have been used to estimate individual assets' betas—the pure play method and the accounting beta method.

The Pure Play Method

In the **pure play method,** the company tries to find several single-product companies in the same line of business as the project being evaluated, and it then averages those companies' betas to determine the cost of capital for its own project. For example, suppose Huron could find three existing single-product firms that operate barges, and suppose also that Huron's management believes its barge project would be subject to the same risks as those firms. Huron could then determine the betas of those firms, average them, and use this average beta as a proxy for the barge project's beta.[13]

The pure play approach can only be used for major assets such as whole divisions, and even then it is frequently difficult to implement because it is often impossible to find pure play proxy firms. However, when IBM was considering going into personal computers, it was able to obtain data on Apple Computer and several other essentially pure play personal computer companies. This is often the case when a firm considers a major investment outside its primary field.

The Accounting Beta Method

As noted above, it may be impossible to find single-product, publicly traded firms suitable for the pure play approach. If that is the case, we may be able to use the **accounting beta method.** Betas normally are found by regressing the returns of a particular company's *stock* against returns on a *stock market index*. However, we could run a regression of the company's *accounting return on assets* against the *average return on assets* for a large sample of companies, such as those included in the S&P 500. Betas determined in this way (that is, by using accounting data rather than stock market data) are called **accounting betas.**

Accounting betas for a totally new project can be calculated only after the project has been accepted, placed in operation, and begun to generate output and accounting results—too late for the capital budgeting decision. However, to the extent management thinks a given project is similar to other projects the firm has undertaken in the past, the similar project's accounting beta can be used as a proxy for that of the project in question. In practice, accounting betas are normally calculated for divisions or other large units, not for single assets, and divisional betas are then used for the division's projects.

Self-Test Questions

Describe the pure play and the accounting beta methods for estimating individual projects' betas.

[13]If the pure play firms employ different capital structures than that of Huron, this fact must be dealt with by adjusting the beta coefficients. See Chapter 16 for a discussion of this aspect of the pure play method. For a technique that can be used when pure play firms are not available, see Yatin Bhagwat and Michael Ehrhardt, "A Full Information Approach for Estimating Divisional Betas," *Financial Management*, Summer 1991, 60–69.

Adjusting the Cost of Capital for Flotation Costs

As we noted earlier in the chapter, most debt is privately placed, and most equity is raised internally as retained earnings. In these cases, there are no flotation costs, hence the component costs of debt and equity should be estimated as discussed above. However, if companies issue debt or new stock to the public, then the issue of flotation costs can become important. In the following sections, we explain how to estimate the component costs of publicly issued debt and stock, and we show how these new component costs affect the marginal cost of capital.

Axis Goods Inc., a retailer of trendy sportswear, has a target capital structure of 45 percent debt, 2 percent preferred stock, and 53 percent common stock. Its common stock sells for $23, the next expected dividend is $1.24, and the expected constant growth rate is 8 percent. Based on the constant growth DCF model, Axis' cost of common equity is k_s = 13.4% when the equity is raised as retained earnings. Axis' cost of preferred stock is 10.3 percent, based on the method discussed in the chapter, which incorporates flotation costs. In the following sections, we examine the effects of flotation costs on the component costs of debt and common stock, and on the marginal cost of capital.

Flotation Costs and the Component Cost of Debt

Axis can issue a 30-year, $1,000 par value bond with an interest rate of 10 percent, paid annually. Here T = 40%, so the after-tax component cost of debt is $k_d(1.0 - 0.4)10\% = 6.0\%$. However, if Axis must incur flotation costs, F, of 1 percent of the value of the issue, then this formula must be used to find the after-tax cost of debt:

$$M(1 - F) = \sum_{t=1}^{N} \frac{INT(1 - T)}{(1 + k_d)^t} + \frac{M}{(1 + k_d)^N}.$$

Here M is the bond's par value, F is the flotation percentage, N is the bond's maturity, T is the firm's tax rate, INT is the dollars of interest per period, and k_d is the after-tax cost of debt adjusted for flotation. With a financial calculator, enter N = 30, PV = −990, PMT = 60, and FV = 1000. Solving for I, we find I = $k_d(1 - T)$ = 6.07%, which is the after-tax component cost of debt. Note that the 6.07 percent theoretically correct after-tax cost of debt is quite close to the original 6.00 percent after-tax cost, so in this instance adjusting for flotation doesn't make much difference.

However, the flotation adjustment would be higher if F were larger or if the bond's life were shorter. For example, if F were 10 percent rather than 1 percent, then the flotation-adjusted $k_d(1 - T)$ would have been 6.79 percent. With N at 1 year rather than 30 years, and F still equal to 1 percent, then $k_d(1 - T) = 7.07\%$. Finally, if F = 10% and N = 1, then $k_d(1 - T) = 17.78\%$. In all of these cases the differential would be too high to ignore.

Strictly speaking, the after-tax cost of debt should reflect the *expected* cost of debt. While Axis' bonds have a promised return of 10 percent, there is some chance of default, so its bondholders' expected return (and consequently Axis' cost) is a bit less than 10 percent. However, for a relatively strong company such as Axis, this difference is quite small. Note too that flotation costs raise the true costs of debt, while default possibilities lower the true cost. Because these two factors have opposite effects, ignoring both of them is, to some extent, a situation where "two wrongs make a right." Therefore, if F is relatively low, if N is relatively long, and if the risk of default is not very high (as is typically true when firms issue debt to the public), then the unadjusted $k_d(1 - T)$ is generally a good approximation of the cost of debt. Also, as we shall see in subsequent chapters, the cost of capital is used to discount capital budgeting cash flows, and those cash flows are generally uncertain (hence measured with a large amount of error). It is generally not terribly important to measure one number (the cost of capital) out to four-decimal-place accuracy when some other number in the equation (the cash flows to be discounted) is subject to extremely large errors. For this reason, few people in the real world spend a lot of time worrying about debt flotation adjustments, except when they are obviously high.

Cost of Newly Issued Common Stock, or External Equity, k_e

The **cost of new common equity, k_e,** or external equity, is higher than the cost of equity raised internally by reinvesting earnings, k_s, because of flotation costs involved in issuing new common stock. What rate of return must be earned on funds raised by selling new stock to make issuing stock worthwhile? To put it another way, what is the cost of new common stock?

The answer for a constant growth stock is found by applying this formula:[14]

$$k_e = \frac{D_1}{P_0(1 - F)} + g. \tag{11-11}$$

Here F is the **percentage flotation cost** incurred in selling the new stock, so $P_0(1 - F)$ is the net price per share received by the company.

Assuming that Axis has a flotation cost of 10 percent, its cost of new outside equity is computed as follows:

$$\begin{aligned} k_e &= \frac{\$1.24}{\$23(1 - 0.10)} + 8.0\% \\ &= \frac{\$1.24}{\$20.70} + 8.0\% \\ &= 6.0\% + 8.0\% = 14.0\%. \end{aligned}$$

Investors require a return of $k_s = 13.4\%$ on the stock. However, because of flotation costs the company must earn *more* than 13.4 percent on the net funds obtained by selling stock if investors are to receive a 13.4 percent return on the money they put up. Specifically, if the firm earns 14 percent on funds obtained by issuing new stock, then

---

[14]Equation 11-11 is derived as follows:

Step 1. The old stockholders expect the firm to pay a stream of dividends, D_t, which will be derived from existing assets with a per-share value of P_0. New investors will likewise expect to receive the same stream of dividends, but the funds available to invest in assets will be less than P_0 because of flotation costs. For new investors to receive their expected dividend stream *without impairing the D_t stream of the old investors,* the new funds obtained from the sale of stock must be invested at a return high enough to provide a dividend stream whose present value is equal to the net price the firm will receive:

$$P_n = P_0(1 - F) = \sum_{t=1}^{\infty} \frac{D_t}{(1 + k_e)^t}. \tag{11-12}$$

Here D_t is the dividend stream to new (and old) stockholders, and k_e is the cost of new outside equity.

Step 2. When growth is constant, Equation 11-12 reduces to

$$P_n = P_0(1 - F) = \frac{D_1}{k_e - g}. \tag{11-12a}$$

Step 3. Equation 11-12a can be rearranged to produce Equation 11-11:

$$k_e = \frac{D_1}{P_0(1 - F)} + g.$$

earnings per share will remain at the previously expected level, the firm's expected dividend can be maintained, and, as a result, the price per share will not decline. If the firm earns less than 14 percent, then earnings, dividends, and growth will fall below expectations, causing the stock price to decline. If the firm earns more than 14 percent, the stock price will rise.[15]

The reason for the flotation adjustment can be made clear by a simple example. Suppose Weaver Candy Company has \$100,000 of assets and no debt, it earns a 15 percent return (or \$15,000) on its assets, and it pays all earnings out as dividends, so its growth rate is zero. The company has 1,000 shares of stock outstanding, so EPS = DPS = \$15, and P_0 = \$100. Weaver's cost of equity is thus k_s = \$15/\$100 + 0 = 15%. Now suppose Weaver can get a return of 15 percent on new assets. Should it sell new stock to acquire new assets? If it sold 1,000 new shares of stock to the public for \$100 per share, but incurred a 10 percent flotation cost on the issue, it would net \$100 − 0.10(\$100) = \$90 per share, or \$90,000 in total. It would then invest this \$90,000 and earn 15 percent, or \$13,500. Its new total earnings would be \$15,000 from the old assets plus \$13,500 from the new assets, or \$28,500 in total. However, it would now have 2,000 shares of stock outstanding, so its EPS and DPS would decline from \$15 to \$14.25:

$$\text{New EPS and DPS} = \frac{\$28{,}500}{2{,}000} = \$14.25.$$

Because its EPS and DPS would fall, the stock price also would fall, from P_0 = \$100 to P_1 = \$14.25/0.15 = \$95.00. This result occurs because while investors put up \$100 per share, the company received and invested only \$90 per share. Thus, we see that the \$90 must earn more than 15 percent to provide investors with a 15 percent return on the \$100 they put up. Put another way, dollars raised by selling new stock must "work harder" than dollars raised by retaining earnings.

Now suppose Weaver earned a return of k_e = 16.667% based on Equation 11-11 on the \$90,000 of new assets:

$$\begin{aligned} k_e &= \frac{D_1}{P_0(1 - F)} + g \\ &= \frac{\$15}{\$100(0.90)} + 0 = 16.667\%. \end{aligned}$$

Here is the new situation:

$$\begin{aligned} \text{New total earnings} &= \$15{,}000 + \$90{,}000(0.16667) \\ &= \$15{,}000 + \$15{,}000 \\ &= \$30{,}000. \\ \text{New EPS and DPS} &= \$30{,}000/2{,}000 = \$15. \\ \text{New price} &= \$15/0.15 = \$100 = \text{Original price.} \end{aligned}$$

---

[15]On occasion it is useful to use another equation to calculate the cost of external equity:

$$k_e = \frac{\text{Dividend yield}}{(1 - F)} + g = \frac{D_1/P_0}{(1 - F)} + g. \qquad \textbf{(11-11a)}$$

Equation 11-11a is derived algebraically from Equation 11-11, and it is useful when information on dividend yields, but not on dollar dividends and stock prices, is available.

Thus, if the return on the new assets is equal to k_e as calculated by Equation 11-11, then EPS, DPS, and the stock price will all remain constant. If the return on the new assets exceeds k_e, then EPS, DPS, and P_0 will rise. This confirms the fact that because of flotation costs, the cost of external equity exceeds the cost of equity raised internally from retained earnings.

As we noted earlier, most analysts use the CAPM to estimate the cost of equity. Suppose the CAPM cost of equity for Axis is 13.8 percent. How could the analyst incorporate flotation costs? In the example above, application of the DCF methodology gives a cost of equity of 13.4 percent if flotation costs are ignored and a cost of equity of 14.0 percent if flotation costs are included. Therefore, flotation costs add 0.6 percentage point to the cost of equity (14.0 − 13.4 = 0.6). To incorporate flotation costs into the CAPM estimate, you would add the 0.6 percentage point to the 13.8 percent CAPM estimate, resulting in a 14.4 percent estimated cost of external equity. As an alternative, you could find the average of the CAPM, DCF, and bond-yield-plus-risk-premium costs of equity ignoring flotation costs, and then add to it the 0.6 percentage point due to flotation costs.

How Much Does It Cost to Raise External Capital?

A recent study by four professors provides some insights into how much it costs U.S. corporations to raise external capital. Using information from the Securities Data Company, they found the average flotation cost for debt and equity issued in the 1990s as presented in Table 11-3.

The common stock flotation costs are for non-IPOs. Costs associated with IPOs are even higher—about 17 percent of gross proceeds for common equity if the amount raised is less than $10 million and about 6 percent if more than $500 million is raised. The data include both utility and nonutility companies. If utilities were excluded, flotation costs would be even higher.

Self-Test Questions

What are flotation costs?

Are flotation costs higher for debt or equity?

TABLE 11-3 Average Flotation Costs for Debt and Equity

Amount of Capital Raised (Millions of Dollars)	Average Flotation Cost for Common Stock (% of Total Capital Raised)	Average Flotation Cost for New Debt (% of Total Capital Raised)
2–9.99	13.28	4.39
10–19.99	8.72	2.76
20–39.99	6.93	2.42
40–59.99	5.87	2.32
60–79.99	5.18	2.34
80–99.99	4.73	2.16
100–199.99	4.22	2.31
200–499.99	3.47	2.19
500 and up	3.15	1.64

Source: Inmoo Lee, Scott Lochhead, Jay Ritter, and Quanshui Zhao, "The Costs of Raising Capital," *The Journal of Financial Research,* Vol. XIX, No. 1, Spring 1996, 59–74. Reprinted with permission.

Some Problem Areas in Cost of Capital

A number of difficult issues relating to the cost of capital either have not been mentioned or were glossed over in this chapter. These topics are beyond the scope of this text, but they deserve some mention both to alert you to potential dangers and to provide you with a preview of some of the matters dealt with in advanced courses.

1. **Privately owned firms.** Our discussion of the cost of equity was related primarily to publicly owned corporations, and we concentrated on the rate of return required by public stockholders. However, there is a serious question about how one should measure the cost of equity for a firm whose stock is not traded. Tax issues are also especially important in these cases. As a general rule, the same principles of cost of capital estimation apply to both privately held and publicly owned firms, but the problems of obtaining input data are somewhat different for each.
2. **Small businesses.** Small businesses are generally privately owned, making it difficult to estimate their cost of equity.
3. **Measurement problems.** One cannot overemphasize the practical difficulties encountered when estimating the cost of equity. It is very difficult to obtain good input data for the CAPM, for g in the formula $k_s = D_1/P_0 + g$, and for the risk premium in the formula k_s = Bond yield + Risk premium. As a result, we can never be sure just how accurate our estimated cost of capital is.
4. **Costs of capital for projects of differing riskiness.** As we will see in Chapter 14, it is difficult to measure projects' risks, hence to assign risk-adjusted discount rates to capital budgeting projects of differing degrees of riskiness.
5. **Capital structure weights.** In this chapter, we simply took as given the target capital structure and used this target to obtain the weights used to calculate WACC. As we shall see in Chapters 16 and 17, establishing the target capital structure is a major task in itself.

Although this list of problems may appear formidable, the state of the art in cost of capital estimation is really not in bad shape. The procedures outlined in this chapter can be used to obtain cost of capital estimates that are sufficiently accurate for practical purposes, and the problems listed here merely indicate the desirability of refinements. The refinements are not unimportant, but the problems we have identified do not invalidate the usefulness of the procedures outlined in the chapter.

Self-Test Question

Identify some problem areas in cost of capital analysis. Do these problems invalidate the cost of capital procedures discussed in the chapter?

Four Mistakes to Avoid

We often see managers and students make the following mistakes when estimating the cost of capital. Although we have discussed these errors previously at separate places in the chapter, they are worth repeating here:

1. **Use the current cost of debt.** Don't use the coupon rate on a firm's existing debt as the pre-tax cost of debt. The relevant pre-tax cost of debt is the interest rate the firm would pay if it issued debt today.
2. **When estimating the market risk premium for the CAPM method, never use the historical average return on stocks in conjunction with the current risk-free rate.** The historical average return on common stocks has been about 13

percent, the historical return on long-term Treasury bonds about 5.5 percent, and the difference between them, which is the **historical risk premium,** is 7.5 percent. The **current risk premium** is found as the difference between an estimate of the current expected rate of return on common stocks and the current expected yield on T-bonds. To illustrate, suppose an estimate of the future return on common stock is 11 percent, and the current rate on long-term T-bonds is 6 percent. This implies that you expect to earn 11 percent if you buy stock today and 6 percent if you buy bonds. Therefore, this implies a current market risk premium of 11% − 6% = 5%. A case could be made for using either the historical or the current risk premium, but it would be wrong to take the *historical* rate of return on the market, 13 percent, subtract from it the *current* 6 percent rate on T-bonds, and then use 13% − 6% = 7% as the risk premium.

3. **Use the target capital structure to determine the weights for the WACC.** If you are an outside analyst and do not know the target weights, it is better to estimate weights based on the current market values of the capital components than on their book values. This is especially true for equity. For example, the stock of an average U.S. firm in 2001 had a market value that was about four times its book value, and in general, stocks' market values are rarely close to their book values. If the company's debt is not publicly traded, then it is reasonable to use the book value of debt to estimate the weights, since book and market values of debt, especially short-term debt, are usually close to one another. To summarize, if you don't know the target weights, then use market values rather than book values to obtain the weights used to calculate WACC.
4. **Always remember that capital components are funds that come from investors.** If it's not from an investor, then it's not a capital component. Sometimes the argument is made that accounts payable and accruals are sources of funding and should be included in the calculation of the WACC. However, these accounts are due to operating relationships with suppliers and employees, and they are deducted when determining the investment requirement for a project. Therefore, they should not be included in the WACC. Of course, they are not ignored in either corporate valuation or capital budgeting. As we showed in Chapter 2, current liabilities do affect free cash flow, hence have an effect on corporate valuation. Moreover, in Chapter 14 we show that the same is true for capital budgeting, namely, that current liabilities affect the cash flows of a project, but not its WACC.[16]

Self-Test Question

What are four common mistakes people make when estimating the WACC?

Summary

This chapter showed how the cost of capital is developed for use in capital budgeting. The key concepts covered are listed below.

- The cost of capital used in capital budgeting is a **weighted average** of the types of capital the firm uses, typically debt, preferred stock, and common equity.

[16]The same reasoning could be applied to other items on the balance sheet, such as deferred taxes. The existence of deferred taxes means that the government has collected less in taxes than a company would owe if the same depreciation and amortization rates were used for taxes as for stockholder reporting. In this sense, the government is "making a loan to the company." However, the deferred tax account is not a source of funds from investors, hence it is not considered to be a capital component. Moreover, the cash flows that are used in capital budgeting and in corporate valuation reflect the actual taxes that the company must pay, not the "normalized" taxes it might report on its income statement. In other words, the correct adjustment for the deferred tax account is made in the cash flows, not in the WACC.

- The **component cost of debt** is the **after-tax cost of new debt.** It is found by multiplying the cost of new debt by (1 − T), where T is the firm's marginal tax rate: $k_d(1 - T)$.
- The **component cost of preferred stock** is calculated as the preferred dividend divided by the net issuing price, where the net issuing price is the price the firm receives after deducting flotation costs: $k_{ps} = D_{ps}/P_n$.
- The **cost of common equity,** k_s, is also called the **cost of common stock.** It is the rate of return required by the firm's stockholders, and it can be estimated by three methods: (1) the **CAPM approach,** (2) the **dividend-yield-plus-growth-rate,** or **DCF, approach,** and (3) the **bond-yield-plus-risk-premium approach.**
- To use the **CAPM approach,** one (1) estimates the firm's beta, (2) multiplies this beta by the market risk premium to determine the firm's risk premium, and (3) adds the firm's risk premium to the risk-free rate to obtain the cost of common stock: $k_s = k_{RF} + (k_M - k_{RF})b_i = k_{RF} + (RP_M)b_i$.
- The best proxy for the **risk-free rate** is the yield on long-term T-bonds.
- To use the **dividend-yield-plus-growth-rate approach,** which is also called the **discounted cash flow (DCF) approach,** one adds the firm's expected growth rate to its expected dividend yield: $k_s = D_1/P_0 + g$.
- The growth rate can be estimated from **historical earnings and dividends** or by use of the **retention growth model, g = (1 − Payout)(Return on equity) = br,** or it can be based on **analysts' forecasts.**
- The **bond-yield-plus-risk-premium approach** calls for adding a risk premium of from 3 to 5 percentage points to the firm's interest rate on long-term debt: k_s = Bond yield + RP.
- Each firm has a **target capital structure,** defined as that mix of debt, preferred stock, and common equity that minimizes its **weighted average cost of capital (WACC):**

$$\text{WACC} = w_d k_d (1 - T) + w_{ps} k_{ps} + w_{ce} k_s.$$

- **Various factors affect a firm's cost of capital.** Some of these factors are determined by the financial environment, but the firm influences others through its financing, investment, and dividend policies.
- Ideally, the **cost of capital** for each project should reflect the risk of the project itself, not the risks associated with the firm's average project as reflected in its composite WACC.
- **Failing to adjust for differences in project risk** would lead a firm to accept too many value-destroying risky projects and reject too many value-adding safe ones. Over time, the firm would become more risky, its WACC would increase, and its shareholder value would decline.
- A project's **stand-alone risk** is the risk the project would have if it were the firm's only asset and if stockholders held only that one stock. Stand-alone risk is measured by the variability of the asset's expected returns.
- **Corporate,** or **within-firm, risk** reflects the effects of a project on the firm's risk, and it is measured by the project's effect on the firm's earnings variability.
- **Market,** or **beta, risk** reflects the effects of a project on the riskiness of stockholders, assuming they hold diversified portfolios. Market risk is measured by the project's effect on the firm's beta coefficient.
- Most decision makers consider all three risk measures in a judgmental manner and then classify projects into subjective risk categories. Using the composite WACC as a starting point, risk-adjusted costs of capital are developed for each category. The **risk-adjusted cost of capital** is the cost of capital appropriate for a given project, given the riskiness of that project. The greater the risk, the higher the cost of capital.

- Firms may be able to use the **CAPM** to estimate the cost of capital for specific projects or divisions. However, estimating betas for projects is difficult.
- The **pure play** and **accounting beta methods** can sometimes be used to estimate betas for large projects or for divisions.
- Companies generally hire an investment banker to assist them when they issue common stock, preferred stock, or bonds. In return for a fee, the investment banker helps the company with the terms, price, and sale of the issue. The banker's fees are often referred to as **flotation costs.** The total cost of capital should include not only the required return paid to investors but also the flotation fees paid to the investment banker for marketing the issue.
- When calculating the **cost of new common stock,** the DCF approach can be adapted to account for flotation costs. For a constant growth stock, this cost can be expressed as: $k_e = D_1/[P_0(1 - F)] + g$. Note that flotation costs cause k_e to be greater than k_s.
- **Flotation cost adjustments** can also be made for debt. The bond's issue price is reduced for flotation expenses and then used to solve for the after-tax yield to maturity.
- The three equity cost estimating techniques discussed in this chapter have **serious limitations** when applied to small firms, thus increasing the need for the small-business manager to use judgment.
- Stock offerings of less than $10 million have an average flotation cost of 13 percent, while the average flotation cost on large common stock offerings is about 3 percent. As a result, a small firm would have to earn considerably more on the same project than a large firm. Also, the capital market demands higher returns on stocks of small firms than on otherwise similar stocks of large firms—this is called the **small-firm effect.**

The cost of capital as developed in this chapter is used in the following chapters to determine the value of a corporation and to evaluate capital budgeting projects. In addition, we will extend the concepts developed here in Chapters 16 and 17, where we consider the effect of the capital structure on the cost of capital.

Questions

11–1 Define each of the following terms:

a. Weighted average cost of capital, WACC
b. After-tax cost of debt, $k_d(1 - T)$
c. Cost of preferred stock, k_{ps}
d. Cost of common equity or cost of common stock, k_s
e. Target capital structure
f. Flotation cost, F
g. Cost of new external common equity, k_e

11–2 In what sense is the WACC an average cost? A marginal cost?

11–3 How would each of the following affect a firm's cost of debt, $k_d(1 - T)$; its cost of equity, k_s; and its weighted average cost of capital, WACC? Indicate by a plus (+), a minus (−), or a zero (0) if the factor would raise, lower, or have an indeterminate effect on the item in question. Assume other things are held constant. Be prepared to justify your answer, but recognize that several of the parts probably have no single correct answer; these questions are designed to stimulate thought and discussion.

	Effect on		
	$k_d(1 - T)$	k_s	WACC
a. The corporate tax rate is lowered.	_____	_____	_____
b. The Federal Reserve tightens credit.	_____	_____	_____
c. The firm uses more debt.	_____	_____	_____
d. The dividend payout ratio is increased.	_____	_____	_____
e. The firm doubles the amount of capital it raises during the year.	_____	_____	_____
f. The firm expands into a risky new area.	_____	_____	_____
g. The firm merges with another firm whose earnings are countercyclical to those of the first firm and to the stock market.	_____	_____	_____
h. The stock market falls drastically, and our firm's stock price falls along with the rest.	_____	_____	_____
i. Investors become more risk averse.	_____	_____	_____
j. The firm is an electric utility with a large investment in nuclear plants. Several states propose a ban on nuclear power generation.	_____	_____	_____

11–4 Distinguish between beta (or market) risk, within-firm (or corporate) risk, and stand-alone risk for a potential project. Of the three measures, which is theoretically the most relevant, and why?

11–5 Suppose a firm estimates its cost of capital for the coming year to be 10 percent. What might be reasonable costs of capital for average-risk, high-risk, and low-risk projects?

Self-Test Problem (Solution Appears in Appendix A)

ST–1 *WACC* Longstreet Communications Inc. (LCI) has the following capital structure, which it considers to be optimal:

Debt	25%
Preferred stock	15
Common stock	60
Total capital	100%

LCI's tax rate is 40 percent and investors expect earnings and dividends to grow at a constant rate of 9 percent in the future. LCI paid a dividend of \$3.60 per share last year (D_0), and its stock currently sells at a price of \$60 per share. Treasury bonds yield 11 percent; an average stock has a 14 percent expected rate of return; and LCI's beta is 1.51. These terms would apply to new security offerings:

Preferred: New preferred could be sold to the public at a price of \$100 per share, with a dividend of \$11. Flotation costs of \$5 per share would be incurred.

Debt: Debt could be sold at an interest rate of 12 percent.

a. Find the component costs of debt, preferred stock, and common stock. Assume LCI does not have to issue any additional shares of common stock.
b. What is the WACC?

Problems

11–1 COST OF EQUITY

David Ortiz Motors has a target capital structure of 40 percent debt and 60 percent equity. The yield to maturity on the company's outstanding bonds is 9 percent, and the company's tax rate is 40 percent. Ortiz's CFO has calculated the company's WACC as 9.96 percent. What is the company's cost of equity capital?

11–2 COST OF PREFERRED STOCK

Tunney Industries can issue perpetual preferred stock at a price of $50 a share. The issue is expected to pay a constant annual dividend of $3.80 a share. The flotation cost on the issue is estimated to be 5 percent. What is the company's cost of preferred stock, k_{ps}?

11–3 COST OF EQUITY

Javits & Sons' common stock is currently trading at $30 a share. The stock is expected to pay a dividend of $3.00 a share at the end of the year (D_1 = $3.00), and the dividend is expected to grow at a constant rate of 5 percent a year. What is the cost of common equity?

11–4 AFTER-TAX COST OF DEBT

Calculate the after-tax cost of debt under each of the following conditions:

a. Interest rate, 13 percent; tax rate, 0 percent.
b. Interest rate, 13 percent; tax rate, 20 percent.
c. Interest rate, 13 percent; tax rate, 35 percent.

11–5 AFTER-TAX COST OF DEBT

The Heuser Company's currently outstanding 10 percent coupon bonds have a yield to maturity of 12 percent. Heuser believes it could issue at par new bonds that would provide a similar yield to maturity. If its marginal tax rate is 35 percent, what is Heuser's after-tax cost of debt?

11–6 COST OF PREFERRED STOCK

Trivoli Industries plans to issue some $100 par preferred stock with an 11 percent dividend. The stock is selling on the market for $97.00, and Trivoli must pay flotation costs of 5 percent of the market price. What is the cost of the preferred stock for Trivoli?

11–7 AFTER-TAX COST OF DEBT

A company's 6 percent coupon rate, semiannual payment, $1,000 par value bond which matures in 30 years sells at a price of $515.16. The company's federal-plus-state tax rate is 40 percent. What is the firm's component cost of debt for purposes of calculating the WACC? (Hint: Base your answer on the *nominal* rate.)

11–8 COST OF EQUITY

The earnings, dividends, and stock price of Carpetto Technologies Inc. are expected to grow at 7 percent per year in the future. Carpetto's common stock sells for $23 per share, its last dividend was $2.00, and the company will pay a dividend of $2.14 at the end of the current year.

a. Using the discounted cash flow approach, what is its cost of equity?
b. If the firm's beta is 1.6, the risk-free rate is 9 percent, and the expected return on the market is 13 percent, what will be the firm's cost of equity using the CAPM approach?
c. If the firm's bonds earn a return of 12 percent, what will k_s be using the bond-yield-plus-risk-premium approach? (Hint: Use the midpoint of the risk premium range.)
d. On the basis of the results of parts a through c, what would you estimate Carpetto's cost of equity to be?

11–9 COST OF EQUITY

The Bouchard Company's EPS was $6.50 in 2001 and $4.42 in 1996. The company pays out 40 percent of its earnings as dividends, and the stock sells for $36.

a. Calculate the past growth rate in earnings. (Hint: This is a 5-year growth period.)
b. Calculate the *next* expected dividend per share, D_1. (D_0 = 0.4($6.50) = $2.60.) Assume that the past growth rate will continue.
c. What is the cost of equity, k_s, for the Bouchard Company?

11–10 CALCULATION OF G AND EPS

Sidman Products' stock is currently selling for $60 a share. The firm is expected to earn $5.40 per share this year and to pay a year-end dividend of $3.60.

a. If investors require a 9 percent return, what rate of growth must be expected for Sidman?
b. If Sidman reinvests earnings in projects whose average return is equal to the stock's expected rate of return, what will be next year's EPS? [Hint: g = b(ROE), where b = fraction of earnings reinvested.]

11–11 WACC ESTIMATION

On January 1, the total market value of the Tysseland Company was $60 million. During the year, the company plans to raise and invest $30 million in new projects. The firm's present market value capital structure, shown below, is considered to be optimal. Assume that there is no short-term debt.

Debt	$30,000,000
Common equity	30,000,000
Total capital	$60,000,000

New bonds will have an 8 percent coupon rate, and they will be sold at par. Common stock is currently selling at $30 a share. Stockholders' required rate of return is estimated to be 12 percent, consisting of a dividend yield of 4 percent and an expected constant growth rate of 8 percent. (The next expected dividend is $1.20, so $1.20/$30 = 4%.) The marginal corporate tax rate is 40 percent.

a. To maintain the present capital structure, how much of the new investment must be financed by common equity?

b. Assume that there is sufficient cash flow such that Tysseland can maintain its target capital structure without issuing additional shares of equity. What is the WACC?

c. Suppose now that there is not enough internal cash flow and the firm must issue new shares of stock. Qualitatively speaking, what will happen to the WACC?

11–12 *WACC ESTIMATION*

The following tabulation gives earnings per share figures for Pappas Manufacturing during the preceding 10 years. The firm's common stock, 140,000 shares outstanding, is now selling for $50 a share, and the expected dividend for the coming year (2002) is 50 percent of EPS for the year. Investors expect past trends to continue, so g may be based on the historical earnings growth rate.

Year	EPS
1992	$2.00
1993	2.16
1994	2.33
1995	2.52
1996	2.72
1997	2.94
1998	3.18
1999	3.43
2000	3.70
2001	4.00

The current interest rate on new debt is 8 percent. The firm's marginal federal-plus-state tax rate is 40 percent. The firm's market value capital structure, considered to be optimal, is as follows:

Debt	$ 3,000,000
Common equity	7,000,000
Total capital	$10,000,000

a. Calculate the firm's after-tax cost of new debt and of common equity, assuming new equity comes only from reinvested cash flow. Calculate the cost of equity, assuming constant growth; that is, $\hat{k}_s = D_1/P_0 + g = k_s$.

b. Find the firm's WACC, assuming no new common stock is sold.

11–13 *MARKET VALUE CAPITAL STRUCTURE*

Suppose the Schoof Company has this *book value* balance sheet:

Current assets	$30,000,000	Current liabilities	$10,000,000
Fixed assets	50,000,000	Long-term debt	30,000,000
		Common equity	
		Common stock (1 million shares)	1,000,000
		Retained earnings	39,000,000
Total assets	$80,000,000	Total claims	$80,000,000

The current liabilities consist entirely of notes payable to banks, and the interest rate on this debt is 10 percent, the same as the rate on new bank loans. The long-term debt consists of 30,000 bonds, each of which has a par value of \$1,000, carries an annual coupon interest rate of 6 percent, and matures in 20 years. The going rate of interest on new long-term debt, k_d, is 10 percent, and this is the present yield to maturity on the bonds. The common stock sells at a price of \$60 per share. Calculate the firm's market value capital structure.

11–14 *COST OF EQUITY ESTIMATION METHODS*

You have just estimated the cost of equity for Shrieves Shipping Company using all three estimation techniques. The results are summarized in the following table:

Method	k_s Estimate
CAPM	12.1%
DCF	14.0
Bond-yield-plus-risk-premium	15.4

The inconsistency of the results is worrisome, but you must still develop your equity cost estimate. What factors might you consider as you attempt to place confidence in the above estimates?

11–15 *WACC ESTIMATION*

A summary of the balance sheet of Travellers Inn Inc. (TII), a company which was formed by merging a number of regional motel chains and which hopes to rival Holiday Inn on the national scene, is shown in the table:

Travellers Inn: December 31, 2001 (Millions of Dollars)

Cash	\$ 10	Accounts payable	\$ 10
Accounts receivable	20	Accruals	10
Inventories	20	Short-term debt	5
Current assets	\$ 50	Current liabilities	\$ 25
Net fixed assets	50	Long-term debt	30
		Preferred stock	5
		Common equity	
		Common stock	\$ 10
		Retained earnings	30
		Total common equity	\$ 40
Total assets	\$100	Total liabilities and equity	\$100

These facts are also given for TII:

(1) Short-term debt consists of bank loans that currently cost 10 percent, with interest payable quarterly. These loans are used to finance receivables and inventories on a seasonal basis, so in the off-season, bank loans are zero.

(2) The long-term debt consists of 20-year, semiannual payment mortgage bonds with a coupon rate of 8 percent. Currently, these bonds provide a yield to investors of $k_d = 12\%$. If new bonds were sold, they would yield investors 12 percent.

(3) TII's perpetual preferred stock has a \$100 par value, pays a quarterly dividend of \$2, and has a yield to investors of 11 percent. New perpetual preferred would have to provide the same yield to investors, and the company would incur a 5 percent flotation cost to sell it.

(4) The company has 4 million shares of common stock outstanding. $P_0 = \$20$, but the stock has recently traded in a range of \$17 to \$23. $D_0 = \$1$ and $EPS_0 = \$2$. ROE based on average equity was 24 percent in 2001, but management expects to increase this return on equity to 30 percent; however, security analysts are not aware of management's optimism in this regard.

(5) Betas, as reported by security analysts, range from 1.3 to 1.7; the T-bond rate is 10 percent; and k_M is estimated by various brokerage houses to be in the range of 14.5 to 15.5 percent.

Brokerage house reports forecast growth rates in the range of 10 to 15 percent over the foreseeable future. However, some analysts do not explicitly forecast growth rates, but they indicate to their clients that they expect TII's historical trends as shown in the table below to continue.

(6) At a recent conference, TII's financial vice-president polled some pension fund investment managers on the minimum rate of return they would have to expect on TII's common to make them willing to buy the common rather than TII bonds, when the bonds yielded 12 percent. The responses suggested a risk premium over TII bonds of 4 to 6 percentage points.

(7) TII is in the 40 percent federal-plus-state tax bracket.

(8) TII's principal investment banker, Henry, Kaufman & Company, predicts a decline in interest rates, with k_d falling to 10 percent and the T-bond rate to 8 percent, although Henry, Kaufman & Company acknowledges that an increase in the expected inflation rate could lead to an increase rather than a decrease in rates.

(9) Here is the historical record of EPS and DPS:

Year	EPS[a]	DPS[a]	Year	EPS[a]	DPS[a]
1987	\$0.09	\$0.00	1995	\$0.78	\$0.00
1988	−0.20	0.00	1996	0.80	0.00
1989	0.40	0.00	1997	1.20	0.20
1990	0.52	0.00	1998	0.95	0.40
1991	0.10	0.00	1999	1.30	0.60
1992	0.57	0.00	2000	1.60	0.80
1993	0.61	0.00	2001	2.00	1.00
1994	0.70	0.00			

[a]Adjusted for a 2:1 stock split in 1988, a 3:1 split in 1999, and 10 percent stock dividends in 1988 and 1996.

Assume that you are a recently hired financial analyst, and your boss, the treasurer, has asked you to estimate the company's WACC; assume no new equity will be issued. Your cost of capital should be appropriate for use in evaluating projects which are in the same risk class as the firm's average assets now on books.

11–16 *FLOTATION COSTS AND THE COST OF EQUITY*

Rework Problem 11-3, assuming that new stock will be issued. The stock will be issued for \$30 and the flotation cost is 10 percent of the issue proceeds. The expected dividend and growth remain at \$3.00 per share and 5 percent, respectively.

11–17 *FLOTATION COSTS AND THE COST OF DEBT*

Suppose a company will issue new 20-year debt with a par value of \$1,000 and a coupon rate of 9 percent, paid annually. The tax rate is 40 percent. If the flotation cost is 2 percent of the issue proceeds, what is the after-tax cost of debt?

Spreadsheet Problem

11–18 *BUILD A MODEL: WACC*

Start with the partial model in the file ***Ch 11-18 Build a Model.xls*** from the textbook's CD-ROM. The stock of Gao Computing sells for \$55, and last year's dividend was \$2.10. A flotation cost of 10 percent would be required to issue new common stock. Gao's preferred stock pays a dividend of \$3.30 per share, and new preferred could be sold at a price to net the company \$30 per share. Security analysts are projecting that the common dividend will grow at a rate of 7 percent a year. The firm can also issue additional long-term debt at an interest rate (or before-tax cost) of 10 percent, and it marginal tax rate is 35 percent. The market risk premium is 6 percent, the risk-free rate is 6.5 percent, and Gao's beta is 0.83. In its cost of capital calculations, Gao uses a target capital structure with 45 percent debt, 5 percent preferred stock, and 50 percent common equity.

a. Calculate the cost of each capital component (that is, the after-tax cost of debt), the cost of preferred stock (including flotation costs), and the cost of equity (ignoring flotation costs) with the DCF method and the CAPM method.

b. Calculate the cost of new stock using the DCF model.

c. What is the cost of new common stock, based on the CAPM? (Hint: Find the difference between k_e and k_s as determined by the DCF method and add that differential to the CAPM value for k_s.)

d. Assuming that Gao will not issue new equity and will continue to use the same target capital structure, what is the company's WACC?

e. Suppose Gao is evaluating three projects with the following characteristics:

(1) Each project has a cost of $1 million. They will all be financed using the target mix of long-term debt, preferred stock, and common equity. The cost of the common equity for each project should be based on the beta estimated for the project. All equity will come from retained earnings.

(2) Equity invested in Project A would have a beta of 0.5 and an expected return of 9.0 percent.

(3) Equity invested in Project B would have a beta of 1.0 and an expected return of 10.0 percent.

(4) Equity invested in Project C would have a beta of 2.0 and an expected return of 11.0 percent.

f. Analyze the company's situation and explain why each project should be accepted or rejected.

Cyberproblem

The information in many of the cyberproblems is likely to change over time, due to the release of new information and the ever-changing nature of the World Wide Web. With this in mind, we plan to periodically update these problems on the textbook's web site.

11–19 *THE COST OF CAPITAL*

Capital budgeting involves decisions about whether or not to invest in fixed assets, and it has a major influence on firms' future performance and value. Discounted cash flow analysis is used in capital budgeting, and a key element of this procedure is the discount rate used in the analysis. Capital must be raised to finance fixed assets, and this capital comes from different types of debt, from preferred stock, and from common equity. Each of these capital components has a cost, and these cost rates, along with the target pro-portions of each, are used to calculate the firm's weighted average cost of capital, WACC. In this cyberproblem, you must obtain information from **www.att.com, www.marketguide.com,** and **www.stocktrader.com** to estimate AT&T's WACC. Take a look at the cyberproblem on the textbook's web site **http://www.harcourtcollege.com/finance/theory/student/resources/cyberprob/ch11.html,** and answer the questions shown there.

Mini Case

See ***Ch 11 Show.ppt*** and ***Ch 11 Mini Case.xls.***

During the last few years, Cox Technologies has been too constrained by the high cost of capital to make many capital investments. Recently, though, capital costs have been declining, and the company has decided to look seriously at a major expansion program that had been proposed by the marketing department. Assume that you are an assistant to Jerry Lee, the financial vice-president. Your first task is to estimate Cox's cost of capital. Lee has provided you with the following data, which he believes may be relevant to your task:

(1) The firm's tax rate is 40 percent.

(2) The current price of Cox's 12 percent coupon, semiannual payment, noncallable bonds with 15 years remaining to maturity is $1,153.72. Cox does not use short-term interest-bearing debt on a permanent basis. New bonds would be privately placed with no flotation cost.

(3) The current price of the firm's 10 percent, $100 par value, quarterly dividend, perpetual preferred stock is $113.10. Cox would incur flotation costs of $2.00 per share on a new issue.

(4) Cox's common stock is currently selling at $50 per share. Its last dividend (D_0) was $4.19, and dividends are expected to grow at a constant rate of 5 percent in the foreseeable future. Cox's beta is 1.2, the yield on T-bonds is 7 percent, and the market risk premium is estimated to be 6 percent. For the bond-yield-plus-risk-premium approach, the firm uses a 4 percentage point risk premium.

(5) Cox's target capital structure is 30 percent long-term debt, 10 percent preferred stock, and 60 percent common equity.

To structure the task somewhat, Lee has asked you to answer the following questions.

a. (1) What sources of capital should be included when you estimate Cox's weighted average cost of capital (WACC)?
   (2) Should the component costs be figured on a before-tax or an after-tax basis?
   (3) Should the costs be historical (embedded) costs or new (marginal) costs?

b. What is the market interest rate on Cox's debt and its component cost of debt?

c. (1) What is the firm's cost of preferred stock?
   (2) Cox's preferred stock is riskier to investors than its debt, yet the preferred's yield to investors is lower than the yield to maturity on the debt. Does this suggest that you have made a mistake? (Hint: Think about taxes.)

d. (1) What are the two primary ways companies raise common equity?
   (2) Why is there a cost associated with reinvested earnings?
   (3) Cox doesn't plan to issue new shares of common stock. Using the CAPM approach, what is Cox's estimated cost of equity?

e. (1) What is the estimated cost of equity using the discounted cash flow (DCF) approach?
   (2) Suppose the firm has historically earned 15 percent on equity (ROE) and retained 35 percent of earnings, and investors expect this situation to continue in the future. How could you use this information to estimate the future dividend growth rate, and what growth rate would you get? Is this consistent with the 5 percent growth rate given earlier?
   (3) Could the DCF method be applied if the growth rate was not constant? How?

f. What is the cost of equity based on the bond-yield-plus-risk-premium method?

g. What is your final estimate for the cost of equity, k_s?

h. What is Cox's weighted average cost of capital (WACC)?

i. What factors influence a company's WACC?

j. Should the company use the composite WACC as the hurdle rate for each of its projects?

k. What are three types of project risk? How is each type of risk used?

l. What procedures are used to determine the risk-adjusted cost of capital for a particular project or division? What approaches are used to measure a project's beta?

m. Cox is interested in establishing a new division, which will focus primarily on developing new Internet-based projects. In trying to determine the cost of capital for this new division, you discover that stand-alone firms involved in similar projects have on average the following characteristics:
   - Their capital structure is 10 percent debt and 90 percent common equity.
   - Their cost of debt is typically 12 percent.
   - The beta is 1.7.

   Given this information, what would your estimate be for the division's cost of capital?

n. Explain in words why new common stock that is raised externally has a higher percentage cost than equity that is raised internally by reinvesting earnings.

o. (1) Cox estimates that if it issues new common stock, the flotation cost will be 15 percent. Cox incorporates the flotation costs into the DCF approach. What is the estimated cost of newly issued common stock, taking into account the flotation cost?
   (2) Suppose Cox issues 30-year debt with a par value of $1,000 and a coupon rate of 10 percent, paid annually. If flotation costs are 2 percent, what is the after-tax cost of debt for the new bond issue?

p. What four common mistakes in estimating the WACC should Cox avoid?

Selected Additional References and Cases

For a comprehensive treatment of the cost of capital, see

Ehrhardt, Michael C., *The Search for Value: Measuring the Company's Cost of Capital* (Boston: Harvard Business School Press, 1994).

The following articles provide some valuable insights into the CAPM approach to estimating the cost of equity:

Beaver, William H., Paul Kettler, and Myron Scholes, "The Association between Market Determined and Accounting Determined Risk Measures," *Accounting Review*, October 1970, 654–682.

Bowman, Robert G., "The Theoretical Relationship between Systematic Risk and Financial (Accounting) Variables," *Journal of Finance*, June 1979, 617–630.

Chen, Carl R., "Time-Series Analysis of Beta Stationarity and Its Determinants: A Case of Public Utilities," *Financial Management*, Autumn 1982, 64–70.

Cooley, Philip L., "A Review of the Use of Beta in Regulatory Proceedings," *Financial Management*, Winter 1981, 75–81.

The weighted average cost of capital as described in this chapter is widely used in both industry and academic circles. It has been criticized on several counts, but to date it has withstood the challenges. See the following articles:

Arditti, Fred D., and Haim Levy, "The Weighted Average Cost of Capital as a Cutoff Rate: A Critical Examination of the Classical Textbook Weighted Average," *Financial Management*, Fall 1977, 24–34.

Beranek, William, "The Weighted Average Cost of Capital and Shareholder Wealth Maximization," *Journal of Financial and Quantitative Analysis*, March 1977, 17–32.

Boudreaux, Kenneth J., and Hugh W. Long; John R. Ezzell and R. Burr Porter; Moshe Ben Horim; and Alan C. Shapiro, "The Weighted Average Cost of Capital: A Discussion," *Financial Management*, Summer 1979, 7–23.

Reilly, Raymond R., and William E. Wacker, "On the Weighted Average Cost of Capital," *Journal of Financial and Quantitative Analysis*, January 1973, 123–126.

Some other works that are relevant include the following:

Alberts, W. W., and Stephen H. Archer, "Some Evidence on the Effect of Company Size on the Cost of Equity Capital," *Journal of Financial and Quantitative Analysis*, March 1973, 229–242.

Amihud, Yakov, and Haim Mendelson, "Liquidity and Cost of Capital: Implications for Corporate Management," *Journal of Applied Corporate Finance*, Fall 1989, 65–73.

Brigham, Eugene F., Dilip K. Shome, and Steve R. Vinson, "The Risk Premium Approach to Measuring a Utility's Cost of Equity," *Financial Management*, Spring 1985, 33–45.

Chen, Andrew, "Recent Developments in the Cost of Debt Capital," *Journal of Finance*, June 1978, 863–883.

Harris, Robert S., "Using Analysts' Growth Forecasts to Estimate Shareholder Required Rates of Return," *Financial Management*, Spring 1986, 58–67.

Harris, Robert S., and Felecia C. Marston, "Estimating Shareholder Risk Premia Using Analysts' Growth Forecasts," *Financial Management*, Summer 1992, 63–70.

Myers, Stewart C., "Interactions of Corporate Financing and Investments Decisions—Implications for Capital Budgeting," *Journal of Finance*, March 1974, 1–25.

Nantell, Timothy J., and C. Robert Carlson, "The Cost of Capital as a Weighted Average," *Journal of Finance*, December 1975, 1343–1355.

Siegal, Jeremy J., "The Application of DCF Methodology for Determining the Cost of Equity Capital," *Financial Management*, Spring 1985, 46–53.

Taggart, Robert A., Jr., "Consistent Valuation and Cost of Capital Expressions with Corporate and Personal Taxes," *Financial Management*, Autumn 1991, 8–20.

Timme, Stephen G., and Peter C. Eisemann, "On the Use of Consensus Forecasts of Growth in the Constant Growth Model: The Case of Electric Utilities," *Financial Management*, Winter 1989, 23–35.

For some insights into the cost of capital techniques used by major firms, see

Gitman, Lawrence J., and Vincent A. Mercurio, "Cost of Capital Techniques Used by Major U.S. Firms: Survey and Analysis of Fortune's 1000," *Financial Management*, Winter 1982, 21–29.

The following cases in the Cases in Financial Management: Dryden Request *series cover concepts related to the cost of capital:*

Case 4A, "West Coast Semiconductor;" Case 4B, "Ace Repair;" Case 4C, "Premier Paint & Body;" Case 6, "Randolph Corporation;" and Case 57, "Auto Hut."

12

Putting the Pieces Together: Corporate Valuation and Value-Based Management

If you had invested $1,000 in the NYSE Composite Index at the beginning of the 1990s, by the end of the decade your investment would have grown to $3,426, resulting in a 13 percent annual rate of return. Had you put the $1,000 in Berkshire Hathaway, you would now have $6,868, which is a 21 percent annual return. And if you had been really smart (or lucky) and invested in Dell, you would now have $797,459, which translates into a whopping 95 percent annual return!

Berkshire Hathaway and Dell compete in very different industries and have very different strategies, yet both beat the market by sharing an operating philosophy: They created value for shareholders by focusing on the free cash flows of their underlying businesses. When this focus is applied systematically throughout a company, it is called value-based management, which is the central theme of this chapter.

Berkshire Hathaway's primary strategy has been to grow through acquisitions. Warren Buffett, Berkshire's CEO, wrote in a recent letter to shareholders that he seeks to own "businesses that generate cash and consistently earn above-average returns on their capital." When evaluating a potential acquisition, Buffett says he compares its purchase price with its "intrinsic value," which he defines as "the discounted value of the cash that can be taken out of a business during its remaining life." Thus, Buffet's growth strategy is governed by the principles of value-based management.

Instead of growing primarily through acquisitions, Dell has chosen to grow "organically" by expanding its existing businesses and developing new products and markets. For most companies, rapid growth in sales requires rapid growth in operating capital, which reduces free cash flow. But Dell is relentless in minimizing the amount of operating capital required to support sales. During the last four years, Dell's sales grew by 48 percent per year. However, growth in operating capital was held to only 18 percent, largely because of reductions in inventory as a result of its produce-to-order strategy. Dell also increased its net operating profit after taxes (NOPAT) faster than sales, 55 percent for NOPAT versus 48 percent per year for sales. Thus, Dell has excelled at improving three primary drivers of value-based management: (1) Its sales growth rate was a huge 48 percent. (2) Its profit margin rose from a good NOPAT-to-sales ratio of 5.1 percent to an excellent ratio of 6.1 percent. (3) Its capital requirements were held in check as a result of lowering the capital-to-sales ratio from 29.3 percent to 11.8 percent.

Sources: Various annual reports of Berkshire Hathaway Inc. and Dell Computers.

As we have emphasized throughout the book, maximizing shareholder value should be management's primary goal. However, to maximize value, managers need a tool for estimating the effects of alternative strategies. In this chapter, we develop and illustrate such a tool—the **corporate valuation model,** which is the present value of expected future free cash flows, discounted at the weighted average cost of capital. In a sense, the corporate valuation model is the culmination of all the material covered thus far, because it pulls together financial statements, cash flows, financial projections, time value of money, risk, and the cost of capital. Companies practice **value-based management** by systematically using the corporate valuation model to guide their decisions.

Overview of Corporate Valuation

CD

The textbook's CD-ROM contains an *Excel* file that will guide you through the chapter's calculations. The file for this chapter is ***Ch 12 Tool Kit.xls,*** and we encourage you to open the file and follow along as you read the chapter.

As stated earlier, managers should evaluate the effects of alternative strategies on their firms' values. This really means forecasting financial statements under alternative strategies, finding the present value of each strategy's cash flow stream, and then choosing the strategy that provides the maximum value. The financial statements should be projected using the techniques and procedures discussed in Chapter 4, and the discount rate should be the risk-adjusted cost of capital as discussed in Chapter 11. But what model should managers use to discount the cash flows? One possibility is the dividend growth model from Chapter 10. However, that model is often unsuitable for managerial purposes. For example, suppose a startup company is formed to develop and market a new product. Its managers will focus on product development, marketing, and raising capital. They will probably be thinking about an eventual IPO, or perhaps the sale of the company to a larger firm—Cisco, Microsoft, Intel, IBM, or other industry leaders that buy hundreds of successful new companies each year. For the managers of such a startup, the decision to initiate dividend payments in the foreseeable future will be totally off the radar screen. Thus, the dividend growth model is not useful for valuing most startup companies.

Also, many established firms, including giants such as Microsoft, pay no dividends. Investors may expect them to pay dividends some time in the future, but when, and how much? As long as internal opportunities and acquisitions are so attractive, the initiation of dividends will be postponed, and this makes the dividend growth model of little use.

Finally, the dividend growth model often is of limited use for internal management purposes even for a dividend-paying company. If the firm consisted of just one big asset, and that asset produced all of the cash flows used to pay dividends, then alternative strategies could be judged through the use of the dividend growth model. However, most firms have several different divisions with many assets, so the corporation's value depends on the cash flows from many different assets, and on the actions of many managers. These managers need a way to measure the effects of their decisions on corporate value, but the discounted dividend model isn't very useful because individual divisions don't pay dividends.

Fortunately, the corporate valuation model does not depend on dividends, and it can be applied to divisions and subunits as well as to the entire firm.

Another important aspect of value-based management is the concept of corporate governance. The corporate valuation model shows how corporate decisions affect *stockholders.* However, corporate decisions are made by managers, not stockholders, and maximizing shareholder wealth is not the same as individual managers maximizing their own "satisfaction."[1] Thus, a key aspect of value-based manage-

[1]A distinction is sometimes made between "executives" and "managers," with executives being corporate officers and others members of the top management team. We do not make that distinction in this book—all people with important decision-making powers are designated as "managers."

ment is making sure that managers focus on the goal of stockholder wealth maximization.

The set of rules and procedures used to motivate managers falls under the general heading of **corporate governance.** At the risk of oversimplification, it involves two primary mechanisms: "sticks" and "carrots." The sticks make it easier to replace a poorly performing CEO. They include (1) provisions in the corporate charter that affect the likelihood of a takeover and (2) the composition of the board of directors. The corporate charter may make it relatively easy for a takeover to occur, so that a poorly performing CEO can be replaced; or the charter may make a takeover more difficult, in which case poor managers can continue to perform poorly. The board of directors can consist of strong outsiders, who will likely monitor the CEO's performance closely and replace him or her if things are not going well, or of friends and colleagues of the CEO, who are willing to let things slide. The carrot involves the type of managerial compensation plan the company uses. If managerial compensation is linked to the firm's stock price, then managers are more likely to focus on shareholder wealth maximization than if their compensation is just a fixed salary.

This chapter discusses the corporate valuation model, value-based management, and corporate governance, beginning with the corporate valuation model.

Self-Test Questions

Why is the corporate valuation model applicable in more circumstances than the dividend growth model?

What is value-based management?

What is corporate governance?

The Corporate Valuation Model

Corporate assets are of two types: **operating** and **nonoperating.** Operating assets, in turn, take two forms: **assets-in-place** and **growth options.** Assets-in-place include such tangible assets as land, buildings, machines, and inventory, plus intangible assets such as patents, customer lists, reputation, and general know-how. Growth options are opportunities to expand that arise from the firm's current operating knowledge, experience, and other resources. The assets-in-place provide an expected stream of cash flows, and so do the growth options. To illustrate, Wal-Mart owns stores, inventory, and other tangible assets, it has a well-known name and reputation, and it has a lot of business know-how. These assets produce current sales and cash flows, and they also provide opportunities for new investments that will produce additional cash flows in the future. Similarly, Merck owns manufacturing plants, patents, and other real assets, and it has a knowledge base that facilitates the development of new drugs and thus new cash flow streams.

Most companies also own some nonoperating assets, which come in two forms. The first is a marketable securities portfolio over and above the cash needed to operate the business. For example, Ford Motor Company had about \$18.9 billion in marketable securities as of mid-2000, and it reported that at least \$10 billion of that amount represented "redundant liquidity." Second, Ford also had \$2.7 billion of investments in other businesses, which were reported on the asset side of the balance sheet as "Equity in Net Assets of Affiliated Companies." So, in total Ford had \$18.9 + \$2.7 = \$21.6 billion of nonoperating assets, compared with its \$254.6 billion of operating assets, or 7.8 percent of total assets. For most companies, the percentage is even lower. For example, Wal-Mart's percentage of nonoperating assets was only 1 percent, which is more typical.

We see, then, that for most companies operating assets are far more important than nonoperating assets. Moreover, companies can influence the values of their operating assets, but the values of nonoperating assets are largely out of their direct control. Therefore, value-based management, hence this chapter, focuses on operating assets.

Estimating the Value of Operations

Tables 12-1 and 12-2 contain the actual 2001 and projected 2002 to 2005 financial statements for MagnaVision Inc., which produces optical systems for use in medical photography. (See Chapter 4 for more details on how to project financial statements.) Growth has been rapid in the past, but the market is becoming saturated, so the sales growth rate is expected to decline from 21 percent in 2002 to a sustainable rate of 5 percent in 2005 and beyond. Profit margins are expected to improve as the production process becomes more efficient and because MagnaVision will no longer be incurring marketing costs associated with the introduction of a major product. All items on the financial statements are projected to grow at a 5 percent rate after 2005. Note that the company does not pay a dividend, but it is expected to start paying out about 75 percent of its earnings beginning in 2004. (Chapter 18 explains in more detail how companies decide how much to pay out in dividends.)

Recall that free cash flow (FCF) is the cash from operations that is actually available for distribution to investors, including stockholders, bondholders, and preferred stockholders. The value of operations is the present value of the free cash flows the firm is expected to generate out into the future. Therefore, MagnaVision's value can be calculated as the present value of its expected future free cash flows from operations, discounted at its weighted average cost of capital, WACC, plus the value of its

See **Ch 12 Tool Kit.xls** for details.

TABLE 12-1 MagnaVision Inc.: Income Statements (Millions of Dollars Except for Per Share Data)

	Actual		Projected		
	2001	2002	2003[b]	2004	2005
Net sales	$700.0	$850.0	$1,000.0	$1,100.0	$1,155.0
Costs (except depreciation)	$599.0	$734.0	$ 911.0	$ 935.0	$ 982.0
Depreciation	28.0	31.0	34.0	36.0	38.0
Total operating costs	$627.0	$765.0	$ 945.0	$ 971.0	$1,020.0
Earnings before interest and taxes (EBIT)	$ 73.0	$ 85.0	$ 55.0	$ 129.0	$ 135.0
Less: Net interest[a]	13.0	15.0	16.0	17.0	19.0
Earnings before taxes	$ 60.0	$ 70.0	$ 39.0	$ 112.0	$ 116.0
Taxes (40%)	24.0	28.0	15.6	44.8	46.4
Net income before preferred dividends	$ 36.0	$ 42.0	$ 23.4	$ 67.2	$ 69.6
Preferred dividends	6.0	7.0	7.4	8.0	8.3
Net income available for common dividends	$ 30.0	$ 35.0	$ 16.0	$ 59.2	$ 61.3
Common dividends	—	—	—	$ 44.2	$ 45.3
Addition to retained earnings	$ 30.0	$ 35.0	$ 16.0	$ 15.0	$ 16.0
Number of shares	100	100	100	100	100
Dividends per share	—	—	—	$0.442	$0.453

NOTES:

[a]"Net interest" is interest paid on debt less interest earned on marketable securities. Both items could be shown separately on the income statements, but for this example we combine them and show net interest. MagnaVision pays more interest than it earns, hence its net interest is subtracted.

[b]Net income is projected to decline in 2003. This is due to the projected cost for a one-time marketing program in that year.

TABLE 12-2 MagnaVision Inc.: Balance Sheets (Millions of Dollars)

	Actual	Projected			
	2001	2002	2003	2004	2005
Assets					
Cash	$ 17.0	$ 20.0	$ 22.0	$ 23.0	$ 24.0
Marketable securities[a]	63.0	70.0	80.0	84.0	88.0
Accounts receivable	85.0	100.0	110.0	116.0	121.0
Inventories	170.0	200.0	220.0	231.0	243.0
Total current assets	$ 335.0	$ 390.0	$ 432.0	$ 454.0	$ 476.0
Net plant and equipment	279.0	310.0	341.0	358.0	376.0
Total assets	$ 614.0	$ 700.0	$ 773.0	$ 812.0	$ 852.0
Liabilities and Equity					
Accounts payable	$ 17.0	$ 20.0	$ 22.0	$ 23.0	$ 24.0
Notes payable	123.0	140.0	160.0	168.0	176.0
Accruals	43.0	50.0	55.0	58.0	61.0
Total current liabilities	$ 183.0	$ 210.0	$ 237.0	$ 249.0	$ 261.0
Long-term bonds	$ 124.0	$ 140.0	$ 160.0	$ 168.0	$ 176.0
Preferred stock	62.0	70.0	80.0	84.0	88.0
Common stock[b]	200.0	200.0	200.0	200.0	200.0
Retained earnings	45.0	80.0	96.0	111.0	127.0
Common equity	$ 245.0	$ 280.0	$ 296.0	$ 311.0	$ 327.0
Total liabilities and equity	$ 614.0	$ 700.0	$ 773.0	$ 812.0	$ 852.0

Notes:
[a]All assets except marketable securities are operating assets required to support sales. The marketable securities are financial assets not required in operations.
[b]Par plus paid-in capital.

nonoperating assets. Here is the equation for the value of operations, which is the firm's value as a going concern:

$$\text{Value of operations} = V_{op} = \text{PV of expected future free cash flow}$$
$$= \frac{FCF_1}{(1+WACC)^1} + \frac{FCF_2}{(1+WACC)^2} + \cdots + \frac{FCF_\infty}{(1+WACC)^\infty} \quad \textbf{(12-1)}$$
$$= \sum_{t=1}^{\infty} \frac{FCF_t}{(1+WACC)^t}.$$

MagnaVision's cost of capital is 10.84 percent. To find its value of operations as a going concern, we use an approach similar to the nonconstant dividend growth model, proceeding as follows:

1. Assume that the firm will experience nonconstant growth for N years, after which it will grow at some constant rate.
2. Calculate the expected free cash flow for each of the N nonconstant growth years.
3. Recognize that after Year N growth will be constant, so we can use the constant growth formula to find the firm's value at Year N. This is the sum of the PVs for year N + 1 and all subsequent years, discounted back to Year N.
4. Find the PV of the free cash flows for each of the N nonconstant growth years. Also, find the PV of the firm's value at Year N.

5. Now sum all the PVs, those of the annual free cash flows during the nonconstant period plus the PV of the Year N value, to find the firm's value of operations.

Table 12-3 calculates free cash flow for each year, using procedures discussed in Chapter 2. Line 1, with data for 2001 from the balance sheets in Table 12-2, shows the required net operating working capital, or operating current assets minus operating current liabilities, for 2001:

$$\text{Required net operating working capital} = \left(\begin{array}{c}\text{Cash +}\\ \text{Accounts receivable}\\ \text{+ Inventories}\end{array}\right) - \left(\begin{array}{c}\text{Accounts}\\ \text{payable +}\\ \text{Accruals}\end{array}\right)$$

$$= (\$17.00 + \$85.00 + \$170.00) - (\$17.00 + \$43.00)$$
$$= \$212.00.$$

Line 2 shows required net plant and equipment, and Line 3, which is the sum of Lines 1 and 2, shows the required net operating assets, also called net operating capital. For 2001, net operating capital is \$212 + \$279 = \$491 million.

Line 4 shows the required net annual addition to operating assets, found as the change in net operating assets from the previous year. For 2002, the required net investment in operating assets is \$560 − \$491 = \$69 million.

Line 5 shows NOPAT, or net operating profit after taxes. Note that EBIT is operating earnings *before* taxes, while NOPAT is operating earnings *after* taxes. Therefore, NOPAT = EBIT(1 − T). With 2002 EBIT of \$85 as shown in Table 12-3 and a tax rate of 40 percent, NOPAT as projected for 2002 is \$51 million:

$$\text{NOPAT} = \text{EBIT}(1 - T) = \$85(1.0 - 0.4) = \$51 \text{ million.}$$

Although MagnaVision's operating assets are projected to produce \$51 million of after-tax profits in 2002, the company must invest \$69 million in new assets in 2002 to support its growth plan. Therefore, the free cash flow for 2002, shown on Line 7, is a negative \$18 million:

$$\text{Free cash flow (FCF)} = \$51 - \$69 = -\$18 \text{ million.}$$

TABLE 12-3 Calculating MagnaVision's Expected Free Cash Flow (Millions of Dollars)

	Actual	Projected			
	2001	2002	2003	2004	2005
Calculation of Free Cash Flow					
1. Required net operating working capital	\$212.00	\$250.00	\$275.00	\$289.00	\$303.00
2. Required net plant and equipment	279.00	310.00	341.00	358.00	376.00
3. Required net operating capital	\$491.00	\$560.00	\$616.00	\$647.00	\$679.00
4. Required net new investment in operating capital = change in net operating capital from previous year		69.00	56.00	31.00	32.00
5. NOPAT [Net operating profit after taxes = EBIT × (1 − Tax rate)]		\$ 51.00	\$ 33.00	\$ 77.40	\$ 81.00
6. Less: Required investment in operating capital		69.00	56.00	31.00	32.00
7. Free cash flow		(\$ 18.00)	(\$ 23.00)	\$ 46.40	\$ 49.00

Note: NOPAT declines in 2003 because of a marketing expenditure projected for that year. See Note b in Table 12-1.

This negative free cash flow in the early years is typical for young, high-growth companies. Even though net operating profit after taxes (NOPAT) is positive in all years, free cash flow is negative because of the need to invest in operating assets. The negative free cash flow means the company will have to obtain new funds from investors, and the balance sheets in Table 12-2 show that notes payable, long-term bonds, and preferred stock all increase from 2001 to 2002. Stockholders will also help fund MagnaVision's growth—they will receive no dividends until 2004, so all of the net income from 2002 and 2003 will be reinvested. However, as growth slows, free cash flow will become positive, and MagnaVision plans to use some of its FCF to pay dividends beginning in 2004.[2]

A variant of the constant growth dividend model is shown below as Equation 12-2. This equation can be used to find the value of MagnaVision's operations at time N, when its free cash flows stabilize and begin to grow at a constant rate. This is the value of all FCFs beyond time N, discounted back to time N, which is 2005 for MagnaVision.

$$V_{op(at\ time\ N)} = \sum_{t=N+1}^{\infty} \frac{FCF_t}{(1 + WACC)^{t-N}} = \frac{FCF_N(1 + g)}{WACC - g} = \frac{FCF_{N+1}}{WACC - g}. \tag{12-2}$$

Based on a 10.84 percent cost of capital, $49 million of free cash flow in 2005, and a 5 percent growth rate, the value of MagnaVision's operations as of December 31, 2005, is forecasted to be $880.99 million:

$$V_{op(12/31/05)} = \frac{FCF_{12/31/05}(1 + g)}{WACC - g} = \frac{FCF_{12/31/06}}{WACC - g} \tag{12-2a}$$

$$= \frac{\$49(1 + 0.05)}{0.1084 - 0.05} = \frac{\$51.45}{0.1084 - 0.05} = \$880.99.$$

This $880.99 million figure is called the company's **terminal,** or **horizon, value,** because it is the value at the end of the forecast period. It is also sometimes called a **continuing value.** In any case, it is the amount that MagnaVision could expect to receive if it sold its operating assets on December 31, 2005.

Figure 12-1 shows the free cash flow for each year during the nonconstant growth period, along with the terminal value of operations in 2005. To find the value of operations as of "today," December 31, 2001, we find the PV of each annual cash flow in Figure 12-1, discounting at the 10.84 percent cost of capital. The sum of the PVs is approximately $615 million, and it represents an estimate of the price MagnaVision could expect to receive if it sold its operating assets today, December 31, 2001.

Estimating the Price per Share

The total value of any company is the value of its operations plus the value of its nonoperating assets.[3] As the December 31, 2001, balance sheet in Table 12-2 shows, MagnaVision had $63 million of marketable securities on that date. Unlike operating assets, we do not have to calculate a present value for marketable securities because short-term financial assets as reported on the balance sheet are at, or close to,

---

[2]MagnaVision plans to increase its debt and preferred stock each year so as to maintain a constant capital structure. We discuss capital structure in detail in Chapters 16 and 17.

[3]The total value also includes the value of growth options not associated with assets-in-place, but Magna Vision has none. Chapter 15 describes such growth options in detail.

FIGURE 12-1 Process for Finding the Value of Operations for a Nonconstant Growth Company

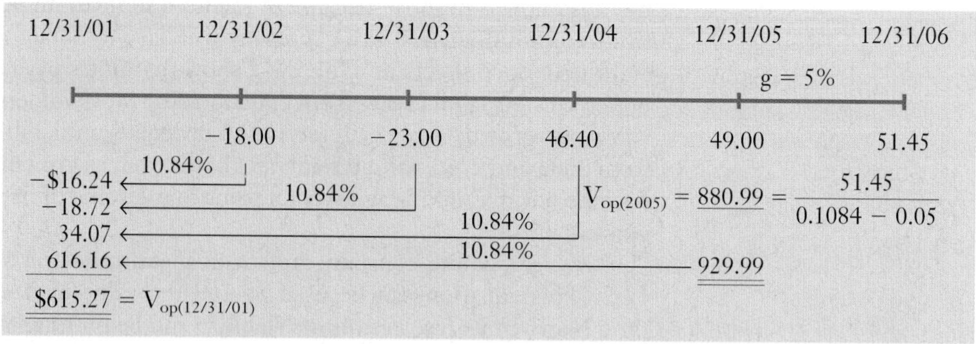

their market value. Therefore, MagnaVision's total value on December 31, 2001, is $615.27 + $63.00 = $678.27 million.

If the company's total value on December 31, 2001, is $678.27 million, what is the value of its common equity? First, the sum of notes payable and long-term debt is $123 + $124 = $247 million, and these securities have the first claim on assets and income. Accounts payable and accruals were netted out earlier when calculating free cash flow, so they have been accounted for. However, the preferred stock has a claim of $62 million, and it also ranks above the common. Therefore, the value left for common stockholders is $678.27 − $247 − $62 = $369.27 million.

Figure 12-2 is a bar chart that provides a breakdown of MagnaVision's value. The left bar shows the company's total value as the sum of its nonoperating assets plus its

FIGURE 12-2 MagnaVision's Value as of December 31, 2001

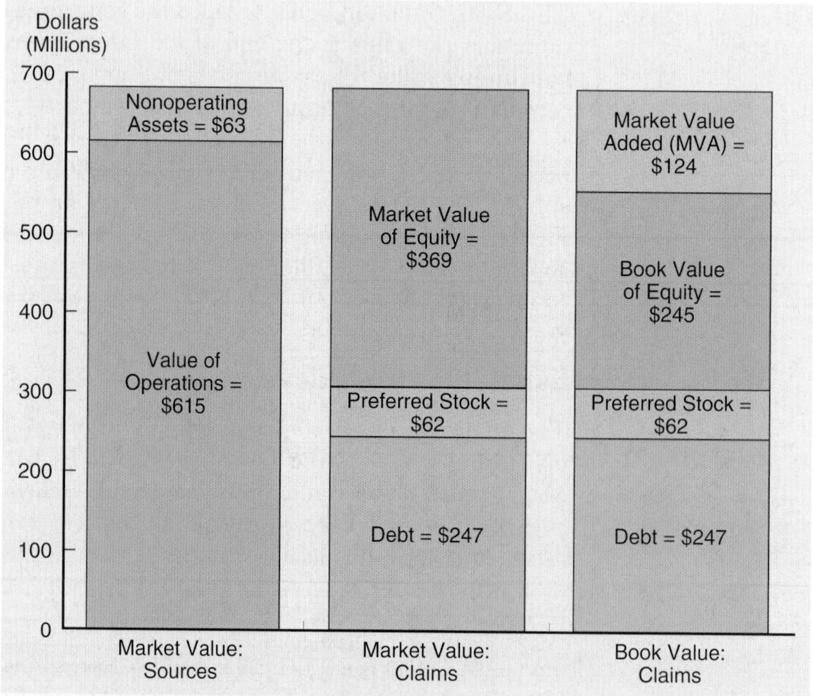

going concern value. Next, the middle bar shows the claim of each class of investors on that total value. Debtholders have the highest priority claim, and MagnaVision owes \$123 million on notes payable and \$124 million on long-term bonds, for a total of \$247 million. The preferred stockholders have the next claim, \$62 million. The remaining value belongs to the common equity, and it amounts to \$678.27 − \$247.00 − \$62.00 = \$369.27 million.[4] Finally, the bar on the right side divides the market value of the equity into the book value, which represents the actual investment stockholders have made, and the additional market value added by management (MVA).

Table 12-4 summarizes the calculations used to find MagnaVision's stock value. There are 100 million shares outstanding, and their total value is \$369.27 million. Therefore, the value of a single share is \$369.27/100 = \$3.69.

The Dividend Growth Model Applied to MagnaVision

MagnaVision has not yet begun to pay dividends. However, as we saw in Table 12-1, a cash dividend of \$0.442 per share is forecasted for 2004. The dividend is expected to grow by about 2.5 percent in 2005, and then at a constant 5 percent rate thereafter. MagnaVision's cost of equity is 14 percent. In this situation, we can apply the nonconstant dividend growth model as developed earlier in Chapter 10. Figure 12-3 shows that the value of MagnaVision's stock, based on this model, is \$3.70 per share, which is the same as the value found using the corporate valuation model except for a rounding difference.

Comparing the Corporate Valuation and Dividend Growth Models

Because the corporate valuation and dividend growth models give the same answer, does it matter which model you choose? In general, it does. For example, if you were a financial analyst estimating the value of a mature company whose dividends are expected to grow steadily in the future, it would probably be more efficient to use the dividend growth model. Here you would only need to estimate the growth rate in dividends, not the entire set of pro forma financial statements.

However, if a company is paying a dividend but is still in the high-growth stage of its life cycle, you would need to project the future financial statements before you

[4]Rather than subtracting the book values of debt and preferred stock, it would be better to subtract their market values. In most cases, including this one, the book values of fixed income securities are close to their market values, and when this is true, one can simply work with book values.

TABLE 12-4 Finding the Value of MagnaVision's Stock (Millions of Dollars Except for Per Share Data)

1. Value of operations (present value of free cash flows)	\$615.27
2. Plus value of nonoperating assets	63.00
3. Total market value of the firm	\$678.27
4. Less: Value of debt	247.00
Value of preferred stock	62.00
5. Value of common equity	\$369.27
6. Divide by number of shares	100.00
7. Value per share	\$3.69

FIGURE 12-3 Using the DCF Dividend Model to Find MagnaVision's Stock Value

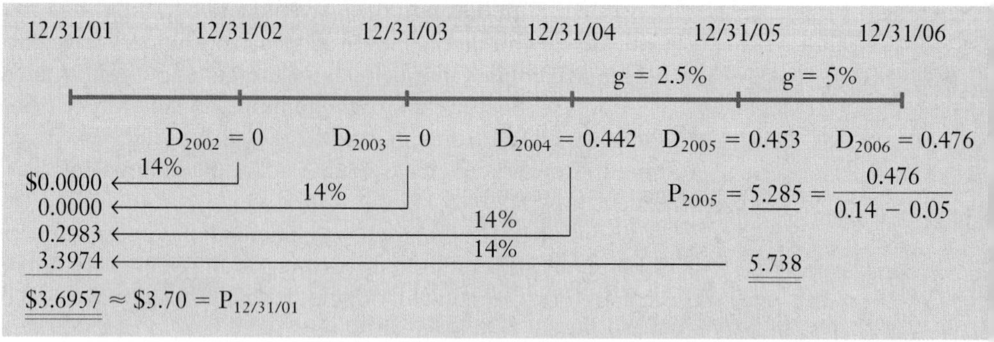

could make a reasonable estimate of future dividends. Then, because you would have already estimated future financial statements, it would be a toss-up as to whether the corporate valuation model or the dividend growth model would be easier to apply. Intel, which pays a dividend of about 8 cents versus earnings of about $2.33, is an example of a company to which you could apply either model.

Now suppose you were trying to estimate the value of a company that has never paid a dividend, such as Microsoft, or a new firm that is about to go public, or a division that GE or some other large company is planning to sell. In all of these situations, you would have no choice: You would have to estimate future financial statements and use the corporate valuation model.

Actually, even if a company is paying steady dividends, much can be learned from the corporate valuation model, hence many analysts today use it for all types of valuations. The process of projecting the future financial statements can reveal quite a bit about the company's operations and financing needs. Also, such an analysis can provide insights into actions that might be taken to increase the company's value. This is value-based management, which we discuss in the next section.

Self-Test Questions

Give some examples of assets-in-place, growth options, and nonoperating assets.

Write out the equation for the value of operations.

What is the terminal, or horizon, value? Why is it also called the continuing value?

Explain how to estimate the price per share using the corporate valuation model.

What conditions are necessary if one is to use the dividend growth model? When is it essential to use the corporate valuation model?

Why might someone use the corporate valuation model even though the dividend model could be used?

Value-Based Management

Bell Electronics Inc. has two divisions, Memory and Instruments, with total sales of $1.5 billion and a book value of assets of $1.07 billion. Based on its current stock and bond prices, the company's total market value is about $1.215 billion, giving it an MVA of $145 million, found as $1.215 − $1.070 = $0.145 billion = $145 million. Because it has a positive MVA, Bell has created value for its investors. Even so,

CD See *Ch 12 Tool Kit.xls* for details.

management is considering several new strategic plans in its efforts to increase the firm's value. All of the assets are used in operations.

The Memory Division produces memory chips for such handheld electronic devices as cellular phones and PDAs (personal digital assistants), while the Instruments Division produces devices for measuring and controlling sewage and water treatment facilities. Table 12-5 shows the latest financial results for the two divisions and for the company as a whole.

As Table 12-5 shows, Bell Memory is the larger of the two divisions, with higher sales and more operating capital. Bell Memory is also more profitable, with a NOPAT/Sales ratio of 7.9 percent versus 7.2 percent for Bell Instruments. This year, as in other recent years, the focus of the initial strategic planning sessions was on the Memory division. Bell Memory has grown rapidly because of the phenomenal growth in consumer electronics, and this division rocketed past Instruments several years ago. Although Memory's growth had tapered off, senior management generally agreed that this division would receive the lion's share of corporate attention and resources because it is larger, more profitable, and, frankly, more exciting. After all, Bell Memory is associated with the glamorous market for telecommunications and personal electronic devices, whereas Bell Instruments is associated with sewage and sludge.

The financial assumptions and projections associated with the preliminary strategic plans for the two divisions are shown in Tables 12-6 and 12-7. Based on the initial strategic plans, each division is projected to have 5 percent annual growth for the next five years and thereafter. The strategic plans also assume that the cost structures of the two divisions will remain unchanged from the current year, 2001. Only partial financial results are shown in Tables 12-6 and 12-7, but when Bell's management decides on a final strategic plan, it will develop complete financial statements for the company as a whole and use them to determine financing requirements, as described in Chapter 4.

To evaluate the plans, Bell's management applied the corporate valuation model to each division, thus valuing them using the free cash flow valuation technique. Each division has a WACC of 10.5 percent, and Table 12-8 shows the results. The three key items are NOPAT, the required investment in operating capital, and the resulting free cash flows for each year. In addition, the table shows each division's horizon value of operations at 2006, which is the end of the five years of explicit forecasts, calculated with Equation 12-2. The value of operations at 2001 is the present value of the free cash flows and the horizon value, discounted at the weighted average cost of capital. As expected, Bell Memory has the greater value of operations, $709.6 million versus $505.5 million for Bell Instruments. However, the managers were surprised to see that Bell Memory's market value added (MVA) is *negative:* $709.6 value of operations − $870.0 required operating capital = −$160.4 million. In contrast, Bell Instruments' MVA is positive: $505.5 value of operations − $200 operating capital = $305 million.

A second strategic planning meeting was called to address this unexpected result. In it, Bell Memory's managers proposed a $20 million marketing campaign to boost

TABLE 12-5 Financial Results for Bell Electronics Inc. (Millions of Dollars)

	Division 1: Bell Memory	Division 2: Bell Instruments	Total Company
Sales	$1,000.0	$500.0	$1,500.0
Operating capital	870.0	200.0	1,070.0
Earnings before interest and taxes (EBIT)	131.0	60.0	191.0
Net operating profit after taxes (NOPAT)	78.6	36.0	114.6
Operating profitability (NOPAT/Sales)	7.9%	7.2%	7.6%

TABLE 12-6 Initial Projections for the Bell Memory Division (Millions of Dollars, Except for Percentages)

	Actual	Projected				
	2001	2002	2003	2004	2005	2006
PANEL A: INPUTS						
Sales growth rate		5%	5%	5%	5%	5%
Costs/sales	81%	81	81	81	81	81
Depreciation/net plant	10	10	10	10	10	10
Cash/sales	1	1	1	1	1	1
Accounts receivable/sales	8	8	8	8	8	8
Inventories/sales	30	30	30	30	30	30
Net plant/sales	59	59	59	59	59	59
Accounts payable/sales	5	5	5	5	5	5
Accruals/sales	6	6	6	6	6	6
Tax rate	40	40	40	40	40	40
PANEL B: PARTIAL INCOME STATEMENT						
Net sales	$1,000.0	$1,050.0	$1,102.5	$1,157.6	$1,215.5	$1,276.3
Costs (except depreciation)	810.0	850.5	893.0	937.7	984.6	1,033.8
Depreciation	59.0	62.0	65.0	68.3	71.7	75.3
Total operating costs	$ 869.0	$ 912.5	$ 958.1	$1,006.0	$1,056.3	$1,109.1
EBIT	$ 131.0	$ 137.6	$ 144.4	$ 151.6	$ 159.2	$ 167.2
PANEL C: PARTIAL BALANCE SHEETS						
Assets						
Cash	$ 10.0	$ 10.5	$ 11.0	$ 11.6	$ 12.2	$ 12.8
Accounts receivable	80.0	84.0	88.2	92.6	97.2	102.1
Inventories	300.0	315.0	330.8	347.3	364.7	382.9
Operating current assets	$390.0	$409.5	$430.0	$451.5	$474.0	$497.7
Net plant and equipment	$590.0	$619.5	$650.5	$683.0	$717.1	$753.0
Liabilities and Equity						
Accounts payable	$ 50.0	$ 52.5	$ 55.1	$ 57.9	$ 60.8	$ 63.8
Accruals	60.0	63.0	66.2	69.5	72.9	76.6
Operating current liabilities	$110.0	$115.5	$121.3	$127.3	$133.7	$140.4

their sales growth rate from 5 to 6 percent. They argued that because Bell Memory is so profitable, its value would be much higher if they could push up sales. Before accepting this proposal, though, the proposed changes were run through the valuation model. The managers changed the Bell Memory division's growth rate from 5 to 6 percent; see the file ***Ch 12 Tool Kit.xls*** on the textbook's CD-ROM for details. To their surprise, the division's value of operations fell to $691.5, and its MVA also declined, from −$160.4 million to −$178.5 million. Although Bell Memory was profitable, increasing its sales growth actually reduced its value!

TABLE 12-7 Initial Projections for the Bell Instruments Division (Millions of Dollars)

	Actual	Projected				
	2001	2002	2003	2004	2005	2006
PANEL A: INPUTS						
Sales growth rate		5%	5%	5%	5%	5%
Costs/sales	85%	85	85	85	85	85
Depreciation/net plant	10	10	10	10	10	10
Cash/sales	1	1	1	1	1	1
Accounts receivable/sales	5	5	5	5	5	5
Inventories/sales	15	15	15	15	15	15
Net plant/sales	30	30	30	30	30	30
Accounts payable/sales	5	5	5	5	5	5
Accruals/sales	6	6	6	6	6	6
Tax rate	40	40	40	40	40	40
PANEL B: PARTIAL INCOME STATEMENT						
Net sales	$500.0	$525.0	$551.3	$578.8	$607.8	$638.1
Costs (except depreciation)	$425.0	$446.3	$468.6	$492.0	$516.6	$542.4
Depreciation	15.0	15.8	16.5	17.4	18.2	19.1
Total operating costs	$440.0	$462.0	$485.1	$509.4	$534.8	$561.6
EBIT	$ 60.0	$ 63.0	$ 66.2	$ 69.5	$ 72.9	$ 76.6
PANEL C: PARTIAL BALANCE SHEETS						
Assets						
Cash	$ 5.0	$ 5.3	$ 5.5	$ 5.8	$ 6.1	$ 6.4
Accounts receivable	25.0	26.3	27.6	28.9	30.4	31.9
Inventories	75.0	78.8	82.7	86.8	91.2	95.7
Operating current assets	$105.0	$110.3	$115.8	$121.6	$127.6	$134.0
Net plant and equipment	$150.0	$157.5	$165.4	$173.6	$182.3	$191.4
Liabilities and Equity						
Accounts payable	$25.0	$26.3	$27.6	$28.9	$30.4	$31.9
Accruals	30.0	31.5	33.1	34.7	36.5	38.3
Operating current liabilities	$55.0	$57.8	$60.6	$63.7	$66.9	$70.2

To better understand these results, we can express the firm's value in terms of four fundamental wealth drivers:

$$\begin{aligned} g &= \text{growth in sales} \\ \text{OP} &= \text{Operating profitability (OP)} = \text{NOPAT/Sales} \\ \text{CR} &= \text{Capital requirements (CR)} = \text{Operating capital/Sales} \\ \text{WACC} &= \text{Weighted average cost of capital} \end{aligned}$$

How do these drivers affect the value of a firm? First, the sales growth rate generally, but not always, has a positive effect on value, provided the company is profitable.

TABLE 12-8 Initial FCF Valuation of Each Division (Millions of Dollars)

PANEL A: FCF VALUATION OF THE BELL MEMORY DIVISION

	Actual	Projected				
	2001	2002	2003	2004	2005	2006
Calculation of FCF						
Net operating working capital	$280.0	$294.0	$308.7	$ 324.1	$ 340.3	$ 357.4
Net plant	590.0	619.5	650.5	683.0	717.1	753.0
Net operating capital	$870.0	$913.5	$959.2	$1,007.1	$1,057.5	$1,110.4
Investment in operating capital		$43.5	$45.7	$48.0	$50.4	$52.9
NOPAT	$78.6	$82.5	$86.7	$91.0	$95.5	$100.3
Free cash flow		$39.0	$41.0	$43.0	$45.2	$47.4
Growth in FCF			5.0%	5.0%	5.0%	5.0%
Value of Operations						
Horizon value						$905.7
Value of operations	$709.6					
Divisional MVA (Value of operations − capital)	($160.4)					

PANEL B: FCF VALUATION OF THE BELL INSTRUMENTS DIVISION

Calculation of FCF						
Net operating working capital	$ 50.0	$ 52.5	$ 55.1	$ 57.9	$ 60.8	$ 63.8
Net plant	150.0	157.5	165.4	173.6	182.3	191.4
Net operating capital	$200.0	$210.0	$220.5	$231.5	$243.1	$255.3
Investment in operating capital		$10.0	$10.5	$11.0	$11.6	$12.2
NOPAT	$36.0	$37.8	$39.7	$41.7	$43.8	$45.9
Free cash flow		$27.8	$29.2	$30.6	$32.2	$33.8
Growth in FCF		5.0%	5.0%	5.0%	5.0%	5.0%
Value of Operations						
Horizon value						$645.1
Value of operations	$505.5					
Divisional MVA (Value of operations − capital)	$305.5					

NOTES: The WACC is 10.5 percent for each division. The horizon value (HV) at 2006 is calculated using Equation 12-2, the constant growth formula for free cash flows: $HV_{2006} = [FCF_{2006} \times (1 + g)]/(WACC - g)$. The value of operations is the present value of the horizon value and the free cash flows discounted at the WACC, calculated in a manner similar to Figure 12-1. See the file ***Ch 12 Tool Kit.xls*** on the textbook's CD-ROM for details.

However, the effect can be negative if growth requires a great deal of capital, and the cost of that capital is high. Second, operating profitability, which measures the after-tax profit per dollar of sales, always has a positive effect—the higher the better. Third, the capital requirements ratio, which measures how much operating capital is needed to generate a dollar of sales, also has a consistent effect—the lower the CR the better, since a low CR means that the company can generate new sales with smaller amounts of new capital. Finally, the fourth factor, the WACC, also has a consistent effect—the lower it is, the higher the firm's value.

Another important metric in the corporate valuation model is the expected return on invested capital (EROIC), defined as the expected NOPAT for the coming year divided by the amount of operating capital the beginning of the year (which is the end of the preceding year). Thus, EROIC represents the expected return on the capital that has already been invested. To illustrate, the EROIC of the Bell Memory division for 2006, the last year in the forecast period, is:

$$\text{EROIC}_{2006} = \frac{\text{NOPAT}_{2007}}{\text{Capital}_{2006}} = \frac{\$100.3(1.05)}{\$1{,}110.4} = 9.5\%.$$

To see exactly how the four value drivers and ROIC determine value, we can start with Equation 12-2,

$$V_{\text{op(at time N)}} = \frac{\text{FCF}_{N+1}}{\text{WACC} - g}, \qquad \textbf{(12-2)}$$

and rewrite it in terms of the value drivers:

$$V_{\text{op(at time N)}} = \text{Capital}_N + \left[\frac{\text{Sales}_N(1+g)}{\text{WACC} - g}\right]\left[\text{OP} - \text{WACC}\left(\frac{\text{CR}}{1+g}\right)\right]. \qquad \textbf{(12-3)}$$

Equation 12-3 shows that the value of operations can be divided into two components: (1) the dollars of operating capital that investors have provided and (2) the additional value that management has added or subtracted, which is equivalent to MVA.

Note that the first bracket of Equation 12-3 shows the present value of growing sales, discounted at the WACC. This would be the MVA of a firm that had no costs and that never needs to invest additional capital. But firms do have costs and capital requirements, and their effect is shown in the second bracket. Here we see that, holding g constant, MVA will improve if operating profitability (OP) increases, capital requirements (CR) decrease, or WACC decreases.

Note that an increase in growth will not necessarily increase value. OP could be positive, but if CR is quite high, meaning that a lot of new capital is needed to support a given increase in sales, then the second bracket can be negative. In this situation, growth causes the term in the first bracket to increase, but it is being multiplied by a negative term in the second bracket, and the net result will be a decrease in MVA.

We can also rewrite Equation 12-2 in terms of EROIC:

$$V_{\text{op(at time N)}} = \text{Capital}_N + \frac{\text{Capital}_N(\text{EROIC}_N - \text{WACC})}{\text{WACC} - g}. \qquad \textbf{(12-4)}$$

Equation 12-4 also breaks value into two components, the value of capital and the MVA, shown in the second term. This term shows that value depends on the spread between the expected return on invested capital, EROIC, and WACC. If EROIC is greater than WACC, then the return on capital is greater than the return investors expect, and management is adding value. In this case, an increase in the growth rate causes value to go up. If EROIC is exactly equal to WACC, then the firm is, in an economic sense, "breaking even." It has positive accounting profits and cash flow, but these cash flows are just sufficient to satisfy investors, causing value to exactly equal the amount of capital that has been provided. If EROIC is less than WACC, the term in brackets is negative, management is destroying value, and growth is harmful. Here the faster the growth rate is, the lower the firm's value.

We should also note that the insights from Equations 12-3 and 12-4 apply to all firms, but the equations themselves can only be applied to relatively stable firms whose growth has leveled out at a constant rate. For example, Home Depot has been growing at more than 20 percent per year, so we cannot apply Equations 12-3 and 12-4 directly (although we can always apply Equation 12-1). Home Depot's

Who Is Creating Wealth?

A recent article in *Fortune* demonstrates the relationship between wealth creation as measured by Market Value Added (MVA) and the spread between the return on invested capital (ROIC) and the cost of capital (WACC). The accompanying table shows that companies such as Microsoft and Coca-Cola have created enormous MVA by having a large spread between ROIC and WACC, even though they employ relatively small amounts of capital. On the other hand, Wal-Mart and Ford have created extraordinary MVA with a relatively small spread between ROIC and WACC because they are earning that spread on a large amount of capital.

The table also shows some companies with negative MVAs. Note that all of them have a negative spread: Their return on capital is less than investors expect. With the possible exception of the two railroad companies, the negative MVAs cannot be attributed to industry conditions. Several pairs of wealth creators and destroyers are in the same industries: Wal-Mart versus Kmart, Philip Morris versus RJR Nabisco, and Ford versus General Motors.

	MVA (billions of dollars)	ROIC	WACC	Capital (billions of dollars)
Wealth Creators				
Microsoft	$328	56.2%	12.6%	$11
General Electric	258	19.3	11.9	65
Intel	167	35.4	12.9	24
Wal-Mart Stores	159	13.2	9.8	36
Coca-Cola	158	31.2	11.2	13
Philip Morris	99	21.2	9.1	47
Ford	39	13.8	9.5	37
Wealth Destroyers				
Kmart	($ 1)	6.4%	8.1%	$15
CSX	(2)	5.5	8.0	21
Union Pacific	(5)	2.4	7.3	30
RJR Nabisco	(12)	3.4	7.5	35
General Motors	(18)	2.0	9.4	85

Source: Shawn Tulley, "America's Wealth Creators," *Fortune*, November 22, 1999, 275–284.

NOPAT/sales ratio is 5.4 percent, which is excellent for its industry, but even though it is profitable, it has negative free cash flows. This is because Home Depot is still in its high-growth phase, which requires enormous investments in operating capital. When we forecast out to the point where Home Depot's sales growth slows due to market saturation, its free cash flows become very large and positive, which explains its high MVA of $81 billion. Note also that Home Depot currently has an expected ROIC of 18.3 percent versus a WACC of only 9.8 percent. This large spread contributes to its $81 billion MVA.

Table 12-9 shows the value drivers for Bell's two divisions, measured at 2006, the end of the forecast period. We report these for the end of the forecast period because ratios can change during the forecast period due to input changes. By the end of the forecast period, however, all inputs and ratios should be stable.

Table 12-9 shows that both divisions have the same growth rate and the same WACC. Bell Memory is more profitable, but it also has much higher capital requirements. The result is that Bell Memory's expected ROIC is only 9.5 percent, well

TABLE 12-9 Bell Electronics' Forecasted Value Drivers for 2006

	Division 1: Bell Memory	Division 2: Bell Instruments
Growth, g	5.0%	5.0%
Profitability		
($NOPAT_{2006}/Sales_{2006}$)	7.9	7.2
Capital requirement		
($Capital_{2006}/Sales_{2006}$)	87.0	40.0
WACC	10.5	10.5
Expected return on invested capital, EROIC		
($NOPAT_{2006}(1 + g)/Capital_{2006}$)	9.5	18.9

below its 10.5 percent WACC. Thus, growth doesn't help Bell Memory—indeed, it lowers the division's value.

Based on this analysis, Bell Memory's managers decided not to request funds for a marketing campaign. Instead, they developed a plan to reduce capital requirements. The new plan called for spending \$50 million on an integrated supply chain information system that would allow them to cut their inventory/sales ratio from 30 percent to 20 percent and also reduce the net plant/sales ratio from 59 percent to 50 percent. Table 12-10 shows operating results based on this new plan. The value of operations increases from \$709.6 million to \$1.1574 billion, or by \$447.4 million. Because this is well over the \$50 million required to implement the plan, top management decided to approve the plan. Note also that MVA becomes positive at \$287.4 million, and the divisional ROIC rises to 13.0 percent, well over the 10.5 percent WACC.

Bell Instruments' managers also used the valuation model to assess changes in plans for their division. Given their high expected ROIC, the Instruments Division proposed (1) an aggressive marketing campaign and (2) an increase in inventory that

TABLE 12-10 Comparison of the Preliminary and Final Plans (Millions of Dollars)

	Bell Memory		Bell Instruments	
	Preliminary	Final	Preliminary	Final
Inputs				
Sales growth rate, g	5%	5%	5%	6%
Inventory/sales	30	20	15	16
Net plant/sales	59	50	30	30
Results				
EROIC (2006)[a]	9.5%	13.0%	18.9%	18.6%
Invested (operating) capital (2006)[a]	\$1,110.4	\$867.9	\$255.3	\$274.3
Current value of operations (2001)[b]	\$709.6	\$1,157.4	\$505.5	\$570.1
Current MVA (2001)[b]	(\$160.4)	\$287.4	\$305.5	\$370.1

Notes:

[a]We report expected EROIC and capital for the end of the forecast period because ratios can change during the forecast period if inputs change during the forecast period. By the end of the forecast period, however, all inputs and ratios should be stable.

[b]We report the value of operations and the MVA as of the current date, 2001, because we want to see the effect that the proposed plans have on the current value of the divisions.

Value-Based Management in Practice

The corporate valuation model, in which free cash flows are discounted at the weighted average cost of capital to determine the value of the company, lies at the heart of value-based management. Therefore, before adopting value-based management, managers would be wise to ask if the corporate valuation model produces results that are consistent with actual market values. The answer, according to a study by Copeland, Koller, and Murrin of the consulting firm McKinsey & Company, is a resounding yes. They applied the model to 35 companies and found a 0.94 correlation between the model's estimated values and the actual market values. Additional evidence of the model's usefulness was provided by McCafferty's recent survey, in which CFOs rated the corporate valuation model as the most important technique for estimating the value of a potential acquisition.

Finally, a recent *Fortune* article described how much corporations are paying consultants to help them implement the model. Marakon Associates, a leading advocate of value-based management, prides itself on having a single-minded view that a company should have one, and only one, goal—to increase shareholder wealth. It often takes Marakon several years to fully implement a value-based management system at a company. One reason for the lengthy implementation period is that Marakon breaks the company into segments to determine where value is currently being created or destroyed. These segments might be divisions, product lines, customers, or even channels of distribution. "Deep drilling," as they call this process, is arduous and time-consuming, and it requires a great deal of data and analysis. Also, and perhaps even more important, full implementation requires both a change in corporate culture and the creation of an "organization's collective ability to out-think its rivals." In other words, the skill-set to use value-based management must permeate the entire company.

Although Marakon is a relatively small firm, with only 275 consultants versus almost 5,000 for McKinsey, it generates about $475,000 in revenue per consultant, which ties them with McKinsey as the most expensive consulting company. Note, though, that its rates seem to be justified. During the last five years, Marakon's client companies have created an additional $68 billion of wealth versus what they would have created had they matched their industry peers' results.

Sources: Thomas A. Stewart, "Marakon Runners," *Fortune*, September 28, 1998, 153–158; Joseph McCafferty, "What Acquiring Minds Want to Know," *CFO*, February, 1999, 14; Tom Copeland, Tim Koller, and Jack Murrin, *Valuation: Measuring and Managing the Value of Companies* (New York: John Wiley & Sons, 1994), 83.

would allow faster delivery and fewer stock-outs. Together, these changes would boost the growth rate from 5 to 6 percent. The direct cost to implement the plan was $20 million, but there was also an indirect cost in that significantly more inventory would have to be carried. Indeed, the ratio of inventory to sales was forecasted to increase from 15 to 16 percent.

Should Instruments' new plan be implemented? Table 12-10 shows the forecasted results. The capital requirements associated with the increased inventory caused the expected ROIC to fall from 18.9 to 18.6 percent, but (1) the 18.6 percent return greatly exceeded the 10.5 percent WACC, and (2) the spread between 18.6 percent and 10.5 percent would be earned on additional capital. This caused the forecasted value of operations to increase from $505.5 to $570.1 million, or by $64.6 million. An 18.6 percent return on $274.3 million of capital is more valuable than an 18.9 percent return on $255.3 million of capital.[5] You, or one of Bell's stockholders, would surely rather have an asset that provides a 50 percent return on an investment of $1,000 than one that provides a 100 percent return on an investment of $1. Therefore, the new plan should be accepted, even though it lowers the Instruments Division's ROIC.

[5]A potential fly in the ointment is the possibility that Bell has a compensation plan based on rates of return and not on changes in wealth. In such a plan, which is fairly typical, the managers might reject the new proposed strategic plan if it lowers ROIC and, hence, their bonuses, even though the plan is good for the company's stockholders. We discuss the effect of compensation plans in more detail later in the chapter.

Sometimes companies focus on their profitability and growth, without giving adequate consideration to their capital requirements. This is a big mistake—all the wealth creation drivers must be taken into account, not just growth. Fortunately for Bell's investors, the revised plan was accepted. However, as this example illustrates, it is easy for a company to mistakenly focus only on profitability and growth. They are important, but so are the other value drivers—capital requirements and the weighted average cost of capital. Value-based management explicitly includes the effects of all the value drivers because it uses the corporate valuation model, and they are all embodied in the model.

Self-Test Questions

What are the four value drivers?

How is it possible that sales growth would decrease the value of a profitable firm?

Corporate Governance and Shareholder Wealth

WWW

See the web pages of CalPERS (the California Public Employees' Retirement System), **http://www.calpers.org,** and TIAA-CREF (Teachers Insurance and Annuity Association-College Retirement Equity Fund), **http://www.tiaa.org,** for excellent discussions of shareholder-friendly corporate governance.

Shareholders want companies to hire managers who are able and willing to take whatever legal and ethical actions they can to maximize stock prices. This obviously requires managers with technical competence, but it also requires managers who are willing to put forth the extra effort necessary to identify and implement value-adding activities. However, managers are people, and people have both personal and corporate goals. Logically, therefore, managers can be expected to act in their own self-interests, and if their self-interests are not aligned with those of stockholders, then corporate value will not be maximized. Managers may spend too much time golfing, lunching, surfing the net, and so forth, rather than focusing on corporate tasks, and they may also use corporate resources on activities that benefit themselves rather than shareholders. So, a key aspect of value-based management is to motivate executives and other managers to actually take the actions required under value-based management.

This section deals with **corporate governance,** which is defined as the set of rules and procedures that ensure that managers do indeed employ the principles of value-based management. The essence of corporate governance is to make sure that the key shareholder objective—wealth maximization—is implemented. Most corporate governance provisions come in two forms, sticks and carrots. The primary stick is the *threat of removal,* either as a decision by the board of directors or as the result of a hostile takeover. If a firm's managers are maximizing the value of the resources entrusted to them, they need not fear the loss of their jobs. On the other hand, if managers are not maximizing value, they may well be removed, either by their own boards of directors by dissident stockholders, or other companies seeking to profit by installing a better management team. The main carrot is *compensation.* If compensation is strictly in the form of salary, then managers will have less incentive to focus on their firms' values than if compensation is somehow linked to firms' performance, especially stock price performance. We discuss different types of motivational devices in the following subsections.

Provisions to Prevent Managerial Entrenchment

Suppose a company has a weak board of directors and strong anti-takeover provisions in its corporate charter, causing senior managers to feel that there is little chance that they will be removed. In this case, management is said to be *entrenched.* Such a company faces a high risk of being poorly run, because entrenched managers are able to act in their own interests rather than in those of shareholders. For example, they can spend company money on such perquisites as lavish offices, memberships at country clubs, and corporate jets. Because these perks are not actually cash payments, they are called **nonpecuniary benefits.**

Also, entrenched managers are often reluctant to reduce fixed costs by closing or selling off redundant plants, laying off employees whose services are no longer needed, and abandoning projects that show little promise of future profits. Managers often hate to admit mistakes, and they are also reluctant to lay off people, especially old friends and colleagues, even when these actions really should be taken. Entrenchment also enables managers to acquire other companies at too high a price, as well as to accept projects that make the company larger but that have negative MVAs. These actions occur because managerial prestige and salary are associated with larger size, and they result in things that are bad for stockholders but good for the senior executives. Note, though, that if a firm has a strong board, dominated by shareholder-oriented people such as Warren Buffet, or if its charter does not make it too difficult for an outside group to seize control and oust a poorly performing management, then such value-destroying actions are minimized.

Barriers to Hostile Takeovers Hostile takeovers usually occur when managers have not been willing or able to maximize the profit potential of the resources under their control. In such a situation, another company can acquire the poorly performing firm, replace its managers, increase free cash flow, and improve MVA. Chapter 26 discusses mergers in detail, but the following paragraphs describe some provisions that can be included in a corporate charter to make it harder for poorly performing managers to remain in control.[6]

A shareholder-friendly charter should ban **targeted share repurchases,** also known as **greenmail.** For example, suppose a company's stock is selling for $20 per share. Now a hostile bidder, who plans to replace management if the takeover is successful, buys 5 percent of the company's stock at the $20 price.[7] The raider then makes an offer to purchase the remainder of the stock for $30 per share. The company might offer to buy back the bidder's stock at a price of say $35 per share. This is called a targeted share repurchase, since the stock will be purchased only from the bidder and not from any other shareholders. Because the bidder paid only $20 per share for the stock, he or she would be making a quick profit of $15 per share, which could easily total several hundred million dollars. As a part of the deal, the raider would sign a document promising not to attempt to take over the company for a specified number of years, hence the buyback also is called greenmail. Greenmail

[6]Some states have laws that go further than others to protect management. This is one reason that many companies are incorporated in Delaware. Some companies have even shifted their state of incorporation to Delaware because their managers felt that a hostile takeover attempt was likely. Note that a "shareholder-friendly charter" could and would waive the company's rights to strong anti-takeover protection, even if the state allows it.

[7]Someone can, under the law, acquire up to five percent of a firm's stock without announcing the acquisition. Once the five-percent limit has been hit, the acquirer must "announce" the acquisition by filing a report with the SEC, and the report must list not only the acquirer's position but also his or her intentions, e.g., a passive investment or a takeover. These reports are monitored closely, so as soon as one is filed, management is alerted to the imminent danger of a takeover.

hurts shareholders in two ways. First, they are left with \$20 stock when they could have received \$30 per share. Second, the company purchased stock from the bidder at \$35 per share, which represents a direct loss by the remaining shareholders of \$15 for each repurchased share.

Managers who buy back stock in targeted repurchases typically argue that their firms are worth more than the raiders offered, and that in time the "true value" will be revealed in the form of a much higher stock price. This situation might be true if a company were in the process of restructuring itself, or if new products with high potential were in the pipeline. But if the old management had been in power for a long time, and if it had a history of making empty promises, then one should question whether the true purpose of the buyback was to protect stockholders or management.

Another aspect of a stockholder-friendly charter is that it does not contain a **shareholder rights provision,** better described as a **poison pill.** These provisions give the shareholders of target firms the right to buy a specified number of shares in the company at a very low price if an outside group or firm acquires a specified percentage of the firm's stock. Therefore, if a potential acquirer tries to take over a company, its other shareholders will be entitled to purchase additional shares of stock at a bargain price, thus seriously diluting the holdings of the raider. For this reason, these clauses are called poison pills, because if they are in the charter, the acquirer will end up swallowing a poison pill if the acquisition is successful. Obviously, the existence of a poison pill makes a takeover more difficult, and this helps to entrench management.

A third management entrenchment tool is a **restricted voting rights** provision, which automatically deprives a shareholder of voting rights if the shareholder owns more than a specified amount of stock. The board can grant voting rights to such a shareholder, but this is unlikely if the shareholder plans to take over the company.

Effective Monitoring by a Strong Board of Directors High compensation and prestige go with a position on the board of a major company, so board seats are prized possessions. Board members typically want to retain their positions, and they are grateful to whoever helped get them on the board. This situation has important implications for corporate governance as it affects stockholders. First, note that 30 years ago a firm's CEO was in all likelihood also the chairman of its board. Moreover, many of the other board members were "insiders," that is, people who held managerial positions within the company, such as the CFO. The CEO, who could remove them from their inside position if they raised objections to his policies, generally nominated them to the board. Even outside board members usually had strong connections with the CEO through personal friendships, consulting or other fee-generating activities, or **interlocking boards of directors,** where Company A's CEO sits on Company B's board and B's CEO sits on A's board. In these situations, even the outside directors are not truly independent and impartial.

Under an "old boy network" board as described above, the CEO had a much more protected position than is typical today. Now most boards are comprised primarily of outsiders who are not beholden to the CEO, which makes it much more likely that an ineffective CEO will be removed. Also, in the earlier period board members were compensated in the form of salary, whereas today directors are generally given stock or options, so an ineffective management team costs the directors money. The changes in director compensation, together with directors' greater independence, have done much to improve the way boards monitor managerial performance and react to poor results.[8]

Why have these changes occurred? The primary reason has to do with a shift in the ownership of common stocks. Prior to the 1960s, most stock was owned by a large number of individual investors, each of whom owned a diversified portfolio of stocks. Because these individuals had just a small amount of any given company's stock, they could do little to influence its operations. Also, with just a small investment, it was not cost effective for them to monitor companies closely. Indeed, if a stockholder was dissatisfied, he or she would typically just "vote with his feet," that is, sell his or her stock. This situation began to change as institutional investors such as pension and mutual funds gained control of a larger and larger share of investment capital, and as they then acquired a larger and larger percentage of all outstanding stock. Given their large holdings, it makes sense for institutional investors to monitor management, and they have the clout to influence the board. In some cases, they have actually elected their own representatives to the board. For example, when TIAA-CREF, a huge private pension fund, became frustrated with the performance and leadership of Furr's/Bishop, a cafeteria chain, the fund led a fight that ousted the entire board and then elected a new board, which consisted only of outsiders.

In general, activist investors with large stakes in companies have been good for all shareholders. They have searched for firms with poor profitability, then replaced management with new teams that are well-versed in value-based management techniques, and thereby improved profitability. Not surprisingly, stock prices usually rise when the news comes out that a well-known activist investor has taken a major position in an underperforming company.

Note that activist investors can improve performance even if they don't go so far as to take over a firm. More often, they get a few people on the board, those people point out the firm's problems, and then the other board members change their attitudes and become less tolerant when they realize that the management team is not following the dictates of value-based management. Moreover, the firm's top managers recognize what will happen if they don't whip the company into shape, and they go about doing just that.

As power has shifted from CEOs to boards as a whole, there has been a tendency to replace insiders with strong, independent outsiders. Today, the typical board has about one-third insiders and two-thirds outsiders, and most outsiders are truly independent. Moreover, they are compensated primarily with stock rather than a straight salary. All of this has clearly decreased the patience of boards with poorly performing CEOs, and within the past several years the CEOs of Proctor & Gamble, Coca-Cola, GM, IBM, Mattel, Campbell Soup, and Xerox, to name just a few, have been removed. This would have been unheard of 30 years ago.

---

[8]Note that boards can be elected by either cumulative or noncumulative voting. Under cumulative voting, each shareholder is given a number of votes equal to his or her shares times the number of board seats up for election. For example, the holder of 100 shares of stock will receive 1,000 votes if 10 seats are to be filled. Then, the shareholder can distribute his or her votes however he or she sees fit. One hundred votes could be cast for each of 10 candidates, or all 1,000 votes could be cast for one candidate. If noncumulative voting is used, our illustrative stockholder cannot concentrate his or her votes—no more than 100 votes can be cast for any one candidate.

With noncumulative voting, if management controls 51 percent of the shares, they can fill every seat on the board—dissident stockholders cannot put a representative on the board. With cumulative voting, however, if 10 seats are to be filled, dissidents can elect a representative, provided they have 10 percent plus one share of the stock.

Note also that bylaws specify whether the entire board is to be elected annually or if directors are to have staggered terms, with, say, one-third of the seats to be filled each year and directors to serve three-year terms. With staggered terms, fewer seats come up each year, making it harder for dissidents to gain representation on the board.

Using Compensation to Align Managerial and Shareholder Interests

In the preceding section we discussed the stick side of corporate governance. Now we turn to the carrot, managerial compensation. The typical CEO today receives a fixed salary plus a bonus that is zero if the firm's performance is poor but that rises as performance becomes better and better. In 1997, salary for an average executive amounted to about 21 percent of total compensation versus bonuses of about 79 percent. So, performance certainly matters![9]

Executive bonuses are based on a number of criteria, some reflecting short-term, or very recent, performance and others reflecting performance over a longer period. Bonuses also reflect internal operating statistics as well as stock prices, which reflect both internal operations and general stock market movements. On average, short-run operating factors such as this year's growth in earnings per share account for about 34 percent of the bonus, 20 percent is based on longer-term operating performance such as earnings growth over the last three years, and the remaining 46 percent is linked to the company's stock price. Bonuses can be paid in cash, in stock, or in options to buy stock. Moreover, they can be paid immediately after the relevant period (immediate vesting) or be awarded in stages over a number of years (deferred vesting). To illustrate deferred vesting, an executive might be awarded 10,000 shares of stock, but at the rate of 2,000 per year for each of the next five years, provided he or she is still with the company on each payment date.

Stock Options The majority of stock-based compensation is in the form of options. Chapter 15 discusses option valuation in detail, but we discuss here how a standard stock option compensation plan works. Suppose IBM decides to grant an option to an employee, allowing him or her to purchase a specified number of IBM shares at a fixed price, called the **exercise price,** regardless of the actual price of the stock. The exercise price is usually set equal to the current stock price at the time the option is granted. Thus, if IBM's current price were $100, then the option would have an exercise price of $100. Options usually cannot be exercised until after some specified period (the **vesting period**), which is usually one to five years. Moreover, they have an **expiration date,** usually 10 years after issue. For our IBM example, assume that the vesting period is 3 years and the expiration date is 10 years. Thus, the employee can exercise the option 3 years after issue or wait as long as 10 years. Of course, the employee would not exercise unless IBM's stock is above the $100 exercise price, and if the price never rose above $100, the option would expire unexercised. However, if the stock price were above $100 on the expiration date, the option would surely be exercised.

Suppose the stock price had grown to $134 after five years, at which point the employee decided to exercise the option. He or she would buy stock from IBM for $100, so IBM would get only $100 for stock worth $134. The employee would (probably) sell the stock the same day he or she exercised the option, hence would receive in cash the $34 difference between the $134 stock price and the $100 exercise price. People often time the exercise of options to the purchase a new home or some other large expenditure.

Let's suppose the employee is actually a senior executive and the grant was for 1 million shares. In this case, the executive would receive $34 for each share, or a total of $34 million. Keep in mind that this is in addition to an annual salary and other bonuses. The logic behind employee options is that they motivate people to work

---

[9]See Thomas A. Stewart, "CEO Pay: Mom Wouldn't Approve," *Fortune*, March 31, 1997, 119–120.

harder and smarter, thus making the company more valuable and benefiting shareholders. But take a closer look at this example. If the risk-free rate is 6.5 percent, the market risk premium is 6 percent, and IBM's beta is 1.09, then the expected return, based on the CAPM, is 13 percent [6.5% + 1.09(6%) = 13%]. IBM's dividend yield is only 0.4 percent, so the expected annual price appreciation must be around 12.6 percent (13% − 0.4% = 12.6%). Now note that if IBM's stock price grew from $100 to $134 over five years, that would translate to an annual growth rate of only 5 percent, not the 12.6 percent shareholders expected. Thus, the executive would receive $34 million for helping run a company that performed below shareholders' expectations. As this example illustrates, standard stock options do not necessarily link executives' wealth with that of shareholders. As a result, companies today are experimenting with different types of compensation plans, with different vesting periods and different measures of performance.[10]

Employee Stock Ownership Plans (ESOPs) Studies show that 90 percent of the employees who receive stock under **option** plans sell the stock as soon as they exercise their options, so the plans motivate employees only for a limited period.[11] Moreover, many companies limit their stock option plans to key managers and executives. To help provide long-term productivity gains, and also to help improve retirement incomes for all employees, Congress authorized the use of **Employee Stock Ownership Plans (ESOPs).** Today about 8,500 privately held companies and 1,500 publicly held firms have ESOPs, and more are being created every day. Typically, the ESOP's major asset is shares of the common stock of the company that created it, and of the 10,000 total ESOPs, about 2,500 of them actually own a majority of their company's stock.[12]

To illustrate how an ESOP works, consider Gallagher & Fowler Inc. (G&A), a Knoxville, Tennessee, construction company. G&A's simplified balance sheet is shown below.

G&A's Balance Sheet Prior to ESOP (millions of dollars)

Assets		Liabilities and Equity	
Cash	$ 10	Debt	$100
Other	190	Equity (1 million shares)	100
Total	$200	**Total**	$200

Now G&A creates an ESOP, which is a new legal entity. The company issues 500,000 shares of new stock at $100 per share, or $50 million in total, which it sells to the ESOP. G&A's employees are the ESOP's stockholders, and each employee receives an

[10]It should be noted that the empirical literature listed in the end-of-chapter references shows that the correlation between executive compensation and corporate performance is mixed. Some studies suggest that the type of compensation plan used affects company performance, while others suggest little if any effect. Note also that just as "all ships rise in a rising tide," so too do most stocks rise in a bull market such as the one we have enjoyed over the past 12 years. In a strong market, even the stocks of companies whose performance ranks in the bottom 10 percent of their peer group can rise and thus trigger handsome executive bonuses. This situation is leading to compensation plans that are based on *relative* as opposed to *absolute* stock price performance. For example, some compensation plans have indexed options, whose exercise prices depend on the performance of the market or of a subset of competitors.

[11]See Gary Laufman, "To Have and Have Not," *CFO*, March 1998, 58–66.

[12]See Eugene Pilotte, "Employee Stock Ownership Plans, Management Motives, and Shareholder Wealth: A Review of the Evidence," *Journal of Financial Education*, Spring 1997, 41–46; and Daniel Eisenberg, "No ESOP Fable," *Time*, May 10, 1999, 95.

International Corporate Governance

Corporate governance includes the following factors: (1) the likelihood that a poorly performing firm can be taken over; (2) whether the board of directors is dominated by insiders or outsiders; (3) the extent to which most of the stock is held by a few large "blockholders" versus many small shareholders; and (4) the size and form of executive compensation. A recent study compared Germany, Japan, and the United States.

First, note from the accompanying table that the threat of a takeover serves as a stick in the United States but not in Japan or Germany. This threat, which reduces management entrenchment, should benefit shareholders in the United States relative to the other two countries. Second, German and Japanese boards are larger than those in the United States, and Japanese boards consist primarily of insiders versus German and American boards, which have similar inside/outside mixes. It should be noted, though, that the boards of most large German corporations include representatives of labor, whereas U.S. boards represent just shareholders. Thus, it would appear that U.S. boards, with a higher percentage of outsiders, would have interests most closely aligned with those of shareholders.

German and Japanese firms are also more likely to be controlled by large blocks of stock than in the United States. Although pension and mutual funds, as well as other institutional investors, are increasingly important in the United States, block ownership is still less than in Germany and Japan. In both Germany and Japan, banks often own large blocks of stock, something that is not permitted by law in the United States, and corporations also own large blocks of stock in other corporations. In Japan, combinations of companies, called **keiretsus,** have cross-ownership of stock among the member companies, and these interlocking blocks distort the definition of an outside board member. For example, when the performance of a company in a keiretsu deteriorates, new directors are often appointed from the staffs of other members of the keiretsu. Such appointees might be classified officially as insiders, but they represent interests other than those of the troubled company's CEO.

In general, large blockholders are better able to monitor management than are small investors, so one might expect the blockholder factor to favor German and Japanese shareholders. However, these blockholders have other relationships with the company that might be detrimental to outside shareholders. For example, if one company buys from another, they might use transfer pricing to shift wealth to a favored company, or a company might be forced to buy from a sister company in spite of the availability of lower-cost resources from outside the group.

Executive compensation packages differ dramatically across the three countries, with U.S. executives receiving by far the highest compensation. However, compensation plans are remarkably similar in terms of how sensitive total compensation is to corporate performance.

Which country's system of corporate governance is best from the standpoint of a shareholder whose goal is stock price maximization? There is no definitive answer. U.S. stocks have had the best performance in recent years. Moreover, German and Japanese companies are slowly moving toward the U.S. system with respect to size of compensation, and compensation plans in all three countries are being linked ever stronger to performance. At the same time, though, U.S. companies are moving toward the others in the sense of having larger ownership blocks, and since those blocks are primarily held by pension and mutual funds rather than banks and related corporations, they better represent the interests of shareholders.

Source: Steven N. Kaplan, "Top Executive Incentives in Germany, Japan, and the USA: A Comparison," in *Executive Compensation and Shareholder Value*, Jennifer Carpenter and David Yermack, eds. (Boston: Kluwer Academic Publishers, 1999), 3–12.

International Characteristics of Corporate Governance

	Germany	Japan	United States
Threat of a takeover	Moderate	Low	High
Board of directors			
Size of board	26	21	14
Percent insiders	27%	91%	33%
Percent outsiders	73%	9%	67%
Are large blocks of stock typically owned by			
A controlling family?	Yes	No	No
Another corporation?	Yes	Yes	No
A bank?	Yes	Yes	No
Executive compensation			
Amount of compensation	Moderate	Low	Large
Sensitivity to performance	Low to moderate	Low to moderate	Low to moderate

ownership interest based on the size of his or her salary and years of service. The ESOP borrows the $50 million to buy the newly issued stock.[13] Financial institutions are willing to lend the ESOP the money because G&A signs a guarantee for the loan. Here is the company's new balance sheet:

G&A's Balance Sheet after the ESOP (millions of dollars)

Assets		Liabilities and Equity	
Cash	$ 60	Debt[a]	$100
Other	190	Equity (1.5 mil. shares)	150
Total	$250	**Total**	$250

[a]The company has guaranteed the ESOP's loan, and it has promised to make payments to the ESOP sufficient to retire the loan, but this does not show up on the balance sheet.

The company now has an additional $50 million of cash and $50 million more of book equity, but it has a de facto liability due to its guarantee of the ESOP's debt. It could use the cash to finance an expansion, but many companies use the cash to repurchase their own common stock, so we assume that G&A will do likewise. The company's new balance sheets, and that of the ESOP, are shown below:

G&A's Balance Sheet after the ESOP and Share Repurchase (millions of dollars)

Assets		Liabilities and Equity	
Cash	$ 10	Debt	$100
Other	$190	Equity (1.5 mil. shares)	150
		Treasury stock	(50)
Total	$200	**Total**	$200

ESOP's Initial Balance Sheet (millions of dollars)

Assets		Liabilities and Equity	
G&A Stock	$50	Debt	$50
		Equity	0
Total	$50	**Total**	$50

Note that while the company's balance sheet looks exactly as it did initially, there is really a huge difference—the footnote that discloses that the company has guaranteed the ESOP's debt, hence that it has an off-balance-sheet liability of $50 million. Moreover, because the ESOP has no equity, the guarantee is very real indeed. Finally, note that operating assets have not been increased at all, but the total debt outstanding and supported by those assets has increased by $50 million.[14]

[13]Our description is somewhat simplified. Technically, the stock would be placed in a suspense account and then be allocated to employees as the debt is repaid.

[14]We assumed that the company used the $50 million paid to it by the ESOP to repurchase common stock and thus to increase its de facto debt. It could have used the $50 million to retire debt, in which case its true debt ratio would remain unchanged, or it could have used the money to support an expansion.

If this were the whole story, there would be no reason to have an ESOP. However, G&A has promised to make payments to the ESOP in sufficient amounts to enable the ESOP to pay interest and principal charges on the debt so as to amortize the debt over 15 years. Thus, after 15 years the debt will be paid off, and the ESOP's equity holders, who are the employees, will have equity with a book value of $50 million and a market value that could be much higher if G&A's stock increases, as it should over time. Then, as employees retire, the ESOP will distribute a pro rata amount of the G&A stock to each employee, who can then use it as a part of his or her retirement plan.

An ESOP is clearly beneficial for employees, but why would a company want to establish one? There are five primary reasons:

1. Congress passed the enabling legislation in hopes of enhancing employees' productivity and thus making the economy more efficient. In theory, if an employee has equity in the enterprise, he or she will work harder and smarter. Note too that if employees are more productive and creative, this will benefit outside shareholders, because productivity enhancements that benefit ESOP shareholders also benefit outside shareholders.
2. The ESOP represents additional compensation to employees, because in our example there is a $50 million (or more) transfer of wealth from existing shareholders to employees over the 15-year period. Presumably, if the ESOP were not created, then some other form of compensation would have been required, and that alternative compensation might not have the secondary benefit of enhancing productivity. Note too that the ESOP's payments to employees (as opposed to the payment by the company) come primarily at retirement, and Congress wanted to boost retirement incomes.
3. Depending on when an employee's rights to the ESOP are vested, the ESOP may help the firm retain employees.
4. There are also strong tax incentives to encourage companies to form ESOPs. First, Congress decreed that in cases where the ESOP owns 50 percent or more of the company's common stock, the financial institutions that lend money to ESOPs can exclude from taxable income 50 percent of the interest they receive on the loan. This improves the financial institutions' after-tax returns, making them willing to lend to ESOPs at below-market rates. Therefore, a company that establishes an ESOP can borrow through the ESOP at a lower rate than would otherwise be available—in our example, the $50 million of debt would be at a reduced rate.

   There is also a second tax advantage. If the company were to borrow directly, it could deduct interest but not principal payments from its taxable income. However, companies typically make the required payments to their ESOPs in the form of cash dividends. Dividends are not normally deductible from taxable income, *but cash dividends paid on ESOP stock are deductible if the dividends are paid to plan participants or are used to repay the loan.* Thus, companies whose ESOPs own 50 percent of their stock can in effect borrow on ESOP loans at subsidized rates and then deduct both the interest and principal payments made on the loans. American Airlines and Publix Supermarkets are two of the many firms that have used ESOPs to obtain this benefit, along with motivating employees by giving them an equity interest in the enterprise.
5. A less desirable use of ESOPs is to help companies avoid being acquired by another company. The company's CEO, or someone appointed by the CEO, typically acts as trustee for its ESOP, and the trustee is supposed to vote the ESOP's shares according to the will of the plan participants. Moreover, the participants, who are the company's employees, usually oppose takeovers because they frequently involve labor cutbacks. Therefore, if an ESOP owns a significant percentage of the company's shares, then management has a powerful tool for warding off takeovers. This is not good for outside stockholders.

Are ESOPs good for a company's shareholders? In theory, ESOPs motivate employees by providing them with an ownership interest. That should increase productivity and thereby enhance stock values. Moreover, tax incentives mitigate the costs associated with some ESOPs. However, an ESOP can be used to help entrench management, and that could hurt stockholders. How do the pros and cons balance out? The empirical evidence is not entirely clear, but certain findings are worth noting. First, if an ESOP is established to help defend against a takeover, then the firm's stock price typically falls when plans for the ESOP are announced. The market does not like the prospect of entrenching management and having to give up the premium normally associated with a takeover. However, if the ESOP is established for tax purposes and/or to motivate employees, the stock price generally goes up at the time of the announcement. In these cases, the company typically has a subsequent improvement in sales per employee and other long-term performance measures, which stimulates the stock price. Indeed, a recent study showed that companies with ESOPs enjoyed a 26 percent average annual stock return versus a return of only 19 percent for peer companies without ESOPs.[15] Therefore, it appears that ESOPs, if used appropriately, can be a powerful tool to help create shareholder value.

Self-Test Questions

What are two primary forms of corporate governance (that is, the carrot and the stick)?

What are three provisions in many corporate charters that deter takeovers?

Describe briefly how a typical stock option plan works.

What are ESOPs? What are some of their advantages and disadvantages?

Summary

- **Corporate assets** consist of operating assets and financial, or nonoperating, assets.
- **Operating assets** take two forms: assets-in-place and growth options.
- **Assets-in-place,** include the land, buildings, machines, and inventory that the firm uses in its operations to produce products and services.
- **Growth options** refer to opportunities the firm has to increase sales. They include opportunities arising from R&D expenditures, customer relationships, and the like.
- **Financial,** or **nonoperating, assets** are distinguished from operating assets and include items such as investments in marketable securities and noncontrolling interests in the stock of other companies.
- The **value of nonoperating assets** is usually close to the figure reported on the balance sheet.
- The **value of operations** is the present value of all the future free cash flows expected from operations when discounted at the weighted average cost of capital:

$$V_{op(at\ time\ 0)} = \sum_{t=1}^{\infty} \frac{FCF_t}{(1 + WACC)^t}.$$

[15]See Daniel Eisenberg, "No ESOP Fable," *Time*, May 10, 1999, 95.

- The **terminal,** or **horizon, value,** is the value of operations at the end of the explicit forecast period. It is also called the **continuing** value, and it is equal to the present value of all free cash flows beyond the forecast period, discounted back to the end of the forecast period at the weighted average cost of capital:

$$\text{Continuing value} = V_{op(\text{at time N})} = \frac{FCF_{N+1}}{WACC - g} = \frac{FCF_N(1 + g)}{WACC - g}.$$

- The **corporate valuation model** can be used to calculate the total value of a company by finding the value of operations plus the value of nonoperating assets.
- The **value of equity** is the total value of the company minus the value of the debt and preferred stock. The **price per share** is the total value of the equity divided by the number of shares.
- **Value-based management** involves the systematic use of the corporate valuation model to evaluate a company's potential decisions.
- The four **value drivers** are (1) the growth rate in sales (g), (2) operating profitability (OP), which is measured by the ratio of NOPAT to sales, (3) capital requirements (CR) as measured by the ratio of operating capital to sales, and (4) the weighted average cost of capital (WACC).
- **Expected return on invested capital (EROIC)** is equal to expected NOPAT divided by the amount of capital that is available at the beginning of the year.
- A company creates value when the spread between expected ROIC and WACC is positive, i.e., when EROIC − WACC > 0.
- **Corporate governance** involves the manner in which shareholders' objectives are implemented, and it is reflected in a company's policies and actions.
- The two primary mechanisms used in corporate governance are: (1) the threat of removal of a poorly performing CEO and (2) the type of plan used to compensate executives and managers.
- Poorly performing managers can be removed either by a takeover or by the company's own board of directors. Provisions in the corporate charter affect the difficulty of a successful takeover, and the composition of the board of directors affects the likelihood of a manager being removed by the board.
- **Managerial entrenchment** is most likely when a company has a weak board of directors coupled with strong anti-takeover provisions in its corporate charter. In this situation, the likelihood that badly performing senior managers will be fired is low.
- **Nonpecuniary benefits** are noncash perks such as lavish offices, memberships at country clubs, corporate jets, foreign junkets, and the like. Some of these expenditures may be cost effective, but others are wasteful and simply reduce profits. Such fat is almost always cut after a hostile takeover.
- **Targeted share repurchases,** also known as **greenmail,** occur when a company buys back stock from a potential acquiror at a higher-than-fair-market price. In return, the potential acquiror agrees not to attempt to take over the company.
- **Shareholder rights provisions,** also known as **poison pills,** allow existing shareholders to purchase additional shares of stock at a lower than market value if a potential acquiror purchases a controlling stake in the company.
- A **restricted voting rights** provision automatically deprives a shareholder of voting rights if the shareholder owns more than a specified amount of stock.
- **Interlocking boards of directors** occur when the CEO of Company A sits on the board of Company B, and B's CEO sits on A's board.
- A **stock option** provides for the purchase of a share of stock at a fixed price, called the **exercise price,** no matter what the actual price of the stock is. Stock options have an **expiration date,** after which they cannot be exercised.
- An **Employee Stock Ownership Plan,** or **ESOP,** is a plan that facilitates employees' ownership of stock in the company for which they work.

Questions

12–1 Define each of the following terms:
a. Assets-in-place; growth options; nonoperating assets
b. Net operating working capital; operating capital; NOPAT; free cash flow
c. Value of operations; horizon value; corporate valuation model
d. Value-based management; value drivers; ROIC
e. Managerial entrenchment; nonpecuniary benefits
f. Greenmail; poison pills; restricted voting rights
g. Stock option; ESOP

12–2 Explain how to use the corporate valuation model to find the price per share of common equity.

12–3 Explain how it is possible for sales growth to decrease the value of a profitable company.

12–4 What are some actions an entrenched management might take that would harm shareholders?

12–5 How is it possible for an employee stock option to be valuable even if the firm's stock price fails to meet shareholders' expectations?

Self-Test Problem (Solutions Appear in Appendix A)

ST–1 *CORPORATE VALUATION*
Watkins Inc. has never paid a dividend, and when it might begin paying dividends is unknown. Its current free cash flow is \$100,000, and this FCF is expected to grow at a constant 7 percent rate. The weighted average cost of capital is WACC = 11%. Watkins currently holds \$325,000 of nonoperating marketable securities. Its long-term debt is \$1,000,000, but it has never issued preferred stock.
a. Calculate Watkins' value of operations.
b. Calculate the company's total value.
c. Calculate the value of its common equity.

Problems

12–1 *FREE CASH FLOW*
Use the following income statements and balance sheets to calculate Garnet Inc.'s free cash flow for 2002.

Garnet Inc.

INCOME STATEMENT	2002	2001
Net sales	\$530.0	\$500.0
Costs (except depreciation)	400.0	380.0
Depreciation	30.0	25.0
Total operating costs	\$430.0	\$405.0
Earnings before interest and taxes (EBIT)	100.0	95.0
Less interest	23.0	21.0
Earnings before taxes	77.0	74.0
Taxes (40%)	30.8	29.6
Net income	\$ 46.2	\$ 44.4

continued

Garnet Inc.—continued

BALANCE SHEET	**2002**	**2001**
Assets		
Cash	$ 28.0	$ 27.0
Marketable securities	69.0	66.0
Accounts receivable	84.0	80.0
Inventories	112.0	106.0
Total current assets	$293.0	$279.0
Net plant and equipment	281.0	265.0
Total assets	$574.0	$544.0
Liabilities and Equity		
Accounts payable	$ 56.0	$ 52.0
Notes payable	138.0	130.0
Accruals	28.0	28.0
Total current liabilities	$222.0	$210.0
Long-term bonds	$173.0	$164.0
Common stock	100.0	100.0
Retained earnings	79.0	70.0
Common equity	$179.0	$170.0
Total liabilities and equity	$574.0	$544.0

12–2 *VALUE OF OPERATIONS* EMC Corporation has never paid a dividend. Its current free cash flow is $400,000 and is expected to grow at a constant rate of 5 percent. The weighted average cost of capital is WACC = 12%. Calculate EMC's value of operations.

12–3 *VALUE OF OPERATIONS* Brooks Enterprises has never paid a dividend. Free cash flow is projected to be $80,000 and $100,000 for the next 2 years, respectively, and after the second year it is expected to grow at a constant rate of 8 percent. The company's weighted average cost of capital is WACC = 12%.

a. What is the terminal, or horizon, value of operations? (Hint: Find the value of all free cash flows beyond Year 2 discounted back to Year 2.)

b. Calculate the value of Brooks' operations.

12–4 *CORPORATE VALUATION* Dozier Corporation is a fast-growing supplier of office products. Analysts project the following free cash flows (FCFs) during the next 3 years, after which FCF is expected to grow at a constant 7 percent rate. Dozier's cost of capital is WACC = 13%.

Time	1	2	3
Free cash flow ($ millions)	−$20	$30	$40

a. What is Dozier's terminal, or horizon, value? (Hint: Find the value of all free cash flows beyond Year 3 discounted back to Year 3.)

b. What is the current value of operations for Dozier?

c. Suppose Dozier has $10 million in marketable securities, $100 million in debt, and 10 million shares of stock. What is the price per share?

12–5 *HORIZON VALUE* Current and projected free cash flows for Radell Global Operations are shown below. Growth is expected to be constant after 2003. The weighted average cost of capital is 11 percent. What is the horizon, or continuing, value?

	Actual	Projected		
	2001	2002	2003	2004
Free cash flow (millions of dollars)	$606.82	$667.50	$707.55	$750.00

12–6 *MVA* A company has capital of $200,000,000. It has an expected ROIC of 9 percent, forecasted constant growth of 5 percent, and a WACC of 10 percent. What is its value of operations? What is its MVA? (Hint: Use Equation 12-4.)

12–7 *HORIZON VALUE* You are given the following forecasted information for the year 2005: Sales = $300,000,000; Operating profitability (OP) = 6%; Capital requirements (CR) = 43%; Growth (g) = 5%; and the weighted average cost of capital (WACC) = 9.8%. If these values remain constant, what is the horizon value (that is, the 2005 value of operations)? (Hint: Use Equation 12-3.)

12–8 *VALUE OF EQUITY* The balance sheets of Hutter Amalgamated are shown below. If the 12/31/2001 value of operations is $756 million, what is the 12/31/2001 value of equity?

Balance Sheets, December 31, 2001 (Millions of Dollars)

Assets		*Liabilities and Equity*	
Cash	$ 20.0	Accounts payable	$ 19.0
Marketable securities	77.0	Notes payable	151.0
Accounts receivable	100.0	Accruals	51.0
Inventories	200.0	Total current liabilities	$221.0
Total current assets	$397.0	Long-term bonds	190.0
Net plant and equipment	279.0	Preferred stock	$ 76.0
		Common stock (par plus PIC)	$100.0
		Retained earnings	89.0
		Common equity	$189.0
Total assets	$676.0	Total liabilities and equity	$676.0

12–9 *PRICE PER SHARE* The balance sheets of Roop Industries are shown below. The 12/31/2001 value of operations is $651 million and there are 10 million shares of common equity. What is the price per share?

Balance Sheets, December 31, 2001 (Millions of Dollars)

Assets		*Liabilities and Equity*	
Cash	$ 20.0	Accounts payable	$ 19.0
Marketable securities	47.0	Notes payable	65.0
Accounts receivable	100.0	Accruals	51.0
Inventories	200.0	Total current liabilities	$135.0
Total current assets	$367.0	Long-term bonds	131.0
Net plant and equipment	279.0	Preferred stock	$ 33.0
		Common stock (par plus PIC)	$160.0
		Retained earnings	187.0
		Common equity	$347.0
Total assets	$646.0	Total liabilities and equity	$646.0

12–10 *CORPORATE VALUATION*

The financial statements of Lioi Steel Fabricators are shown below, with the actual results for 2001 and the projections for 2002. Free cash flow is expected to grow at a 6 percent rate after 2002. The weighted average cost of capital is 11 percent.

a. If operating capital as of 12/31/2001 is $502.2 million, what is the free cash flow for 12/31/2002?
b. What is the horizon value as of 12/31/2002?
c. What is the value of operations as of 12/31/2001?
d. What is the total value of the company as of 12/31/2001?
e. What is the price per share for 12/31/2001?

Income Statement for the Year Ending December 31 (Millions of Dollars)

	Actual 2001	Projected 2002
Net sales	$500.0	$530.0
Costs (except depreciation)	360.0	381.6
Depreciation	37.5	39.8
Total operating costs	$397.5	$421.4
Earnings before interest and tax	$102.5	108.6
Less interest	13.9	16.0
Earnings before taxes	$ 88.6	$ 92.6
Taxes (40%)	35.4	37.0
Net income before preferred dividends	$ 53.2	$ 55.6
Preferred dividends	6.0	7.4
Net income avail. for common dividends	$ 47.2	$ 48.2
Common dividends	$ 40.8	$ 29.7
Addition to retained earnings	$ 6.4	$ 18.5
Number of shares	10	10
Dividends per share	$ 4.08	$ 2.97

Balance Sheets for December 31 (Millions of Dollars)

	Actual 2001	Projected 2002
Assets		
Cash	$ 5.3	$ 5.6
Marketable securities	49.9	51.9
Accounts receivable	53.0	56.2
Inventories	106.0	112.4
Total current assets	$214.2	$226.1
Net plant and equipment	375.0	397.5
Total assets	$589.2	$623.6

	Actual 2001	Projected 2002
Liabilities and Equity		
Accounts payable	$ 9.6	$ 11.2
Notes payable	69.9	74.1
Accruals	27.5	28.1
Total current liabilities	$107.0	$113.4
Long-term bonds	140.8	148.2
Preferred stock	$ 35.0	$ 37.1
Common stock (par plus PIC)	$160.0	$160.0
Retained earnings	146.4	164.9
Common equity	$305.9	$324.9
Total liabilities and equity	$589.4	$623.6

Spreadsheet Problems

12–11 BUILD A MODEL: CORPORATE VALUATION

Start with the partial model in the file ***Ch12-11 Build a Model.xls*** from the textbook's CD-ROM. The Henley Corporation is a privately held company specializing in lawn care products and services. The most recent financial statements are shown below.

CD

Income Statement for the Year Ending December 31 (Millions of Dollars)

	2001
Net sales	$800.0
Costs (except depreciation)	576.0
Depreciation	60.0
Total operating costs	636.0
Earnings before interest and taxes	164.0
Less interest	32.0
Earnings before taxes	132.0
Taxes (40%)	52.8
Net income before preferred dividends	79.2
Preferred dividends	1.4
Net income avail. for common dividends	$ 77.9
Common dividends	$ 31.1
Addition to retained earnings	$ 46.7
Number of shares (in millions)	10
Dividends per share	$ 3.11

Balance Sheets for December 31 (Millions of Dollars)

Assets	2001	*Liabilities and Equity*	2001
Cash	$ 8.0	Accounts payable	$ 16.0
Marketable Securities	20.0	Notes payable	40.0
Accounts receivable	80.0	Accruals	40.0
Inventories	160.0	Total current liabilities	$ 96.0
Total current assets	$268.0	Long-term bonds	300.0
Net plant and equipment	600.0	Preferred stock	$ 15.0
		Common stock (par plus PIC)	$257.0
		Retained earnings	200.0
		Common equity	$457.0
Total assets	$868.0	Total liabilities and equity	$868.0

The ratios and selected information for the current and projected years are shown below.

	Actual	Projected			
	2001	2002	2003	2004	2005
Sales growth rate		15%	10%	6%	6%
Costs/sales	72%	72	72	72	72
Depreciation/net PPE	10	10	10	10	10
Cash/sales	1	1	1	1	1
Accounts receivable/sales	10	10	10	10	10
Inventories/sales	20	20	20	20	20
Net PPE/sales	75	75	75	75	75
Accounts payable/sales	2	2	2	2	2
Accruals/sales	5	5	5	5	5
Tax rate	40	40	40	40	40
Weighted average cost of capital (WACC)	10.5	10.5	10.5	10.5	10.5

a. Forecast the parts of the income statement and balance sheets necessary to calculate free cash flow.

b. Calculate free cash flow for each projected year. Also calculate the growth rates of free cash flow each year to ensure that there is constant growth (that is, the same as the constant growth rate in sales) by the end of the forecast period.

c. Calculate operating profitability (OP = NOPAT/Sales), capital requirements (CR = Operating capital/Sales), and expected return on invested capital (EROIC = Expected NOPAT/Operating capital at beginning of year). Based on the spread between expected ROIC and WACC, do you think that the company will have a positive market value added (MVA = Market value of company − Book value of company = Value of operations − Operating capital)?

d. Calculate the value of operations and MVA. (Hint: First calculate the horizon value at the end of the forecast period, which is equal to the value of operations at the end of the forecast period. Assume that growth beyond the horizon is 6 percent.)

e. Calculate the price per share of common equity as of 12/31/2001.

12–12 *WHAT IF ANALYSIS: VALUE-BASED MANAGEMENT* Start with the model in the file ***Ch12-12 What If Analysis.xls*** from the textbook's CD-ROM and answer the questions shown there.

CD

Cyberproblem

The information related to the cyberproblems is likely to change over time, due to the release of new information and the ever-changing nature of the World Wide Web. With these changes in mind, we will periodically update these problems on the textbook's web site.

12–12
ROIC AND WACC

A key principal in value-based management is that value is created when a company earns more on its capital than its investors require. In other words, value is created when the ROIC is greater than the WACC.

Let's take a look at the ROIC and WACC for some particular companies and see which companies are creating value. Stern Stewart & Co. have the most comprehensive source of data for ROIC and WACC. Go to the textbook's web site, **http://www.harcourtcollege.com/finance/theory/student/resources/cyberprob/ch12.html,** and answer the questions shown there.

Mini Case

See **Ch 12 Show.ppt** and **Ch 12 Mini Case.xls.**

You have been hired as a consultant to Kulpa Fishing Supplies (KFS), a company that is seeking to increase its value. KFS has asked you to estimate the value of two privately held companies that KFS is considering acquiring. But first, the senior management of KFS would like for you to explain how to value companies that don't pay any dividends. You have structured your presentation around the following questions:

a. List the two types of assets that companies own.
b. What are assets-in-place? How can their value be estimated?
c. What are nonoperating assets? How can their value be estimated?
d. What is the total value of a corporation? Who has claims on this value?
e. The first acquisition target is a privately held company in a mature industry. The company currently has free cash flow of \$20 million. Its WACC is 10 percent and it is expected to grow at a constant rate of 5 percent. The company has marketable securities of \$100 million. It is financed with \$200 million of debt, \$50 million of preferred stock, and \$210 million of book equity.
   (1) What is its value of operations?
   (2) What is its total corporate value? What is its value of equity?
   (3) What is its MVA (MVA = Total corporate value − total book value)?
f. The second acquisition target is a privately held company in a growing industry. The target has recently borrowed \$40 million to finance its expansion; it has no other debt or preferred stock. It pays no dividends and currently has no marketable securities. KFS expects the company to produce free cash flows of −\$5 million in 1 year, \$10 million in 2 years, and \$20 million in 3 years. After 3 years, free cash flow will grow at a rate of 6 percent. Its WACC is 10 percent and it currently has 10 million shares of stock.
   (1) What is its horizon value (that is, its value of operations at Year 3)? What is its current value of operations (that is, at time zero)?
   (2) What is its value of equity on a price per share basis?
g. KFS is also interested in applying value-based management to its own divisions. Explain what value-based management is.
h. What are the four value drivers? How does each of them affect value?
i. What is expected return on invested capital (EROIC)? Why is the spread between expected ROIC and WACC so important?
j. KFS has two divisions. Both have current sales of \$1,000, current expected growth of 5 percent, and a WACC of 10 percent. Division A has high profitability (OP = 6%) but high capital requirements (CR = 78%). Division B has low profitability (OP = 4%) but low capital requirements (CR = 27%). What is the MVA of each division, based on the current growth of 5 percent? What is the MVA of each division if growth is 6 percent?
k. What is the expected ROIC of each division for 5 percent growth and for 6 percent growth? How is this related to MVA?

l. The managers at KFS have heard that corporate governance can affect shareholder value. List for them the two primary mechanisms of corporate governance.
m. Why is entrenched management potentially harmful to shareholders?
n. List three provisions in the corporate charter that affect takeovers.
o. Explain the difference between insiders and outsiders on the board of directors. What are interlocking boards?
p. What is a stock option in a compensation plan?

Selected Additional References

For explanations of corporate valuation and value-based management, see

Copeland, Tom, Tim Koller, and Jack Murrin, *Valuation: Measuring and Managing the Value of Companies* (New York: John Wiley & Sons, Inc., 1992).

Martin, John D., and J. William Petty, *Value Based Management: The Corporate Response to the Shareholder Revolution* (Boston: Harvard Business School Press, 2000).

McTaggart, James M., Peter W. Kontes, and Michael C. Mankins, *The Value Imperative* (New York: The Free Press, 1994).

Stewart, G. Bennett, *The Quest for Value* (New York: Harper Collins, 1991).

For additional discussions of corporate governance, see

Carpenter, Jennifer, and David Yermack, Editors, *Executive Compensation and Shareholder Value* (Boston: Kluwer Academic Publishers, 1999).

For more on EVA and performance, see

Peterson, Pamela P., and David R. Peterson, *Company Performance and Measures of Value Added* (The Research Foundation of the Institute of Chartered Financial Analysts, 1996).

13

The Basics of Capital Budgeting: Evaluating Cash Flows

In 1970, the Adolph Coors Company was a small brewer serving a regional market. But due to its quality products and aggressive marketing, by 1990 Coors had risen to the number three brand in the U.S. beer market. During this high-growth phase, the corporate emphasis was on marketing, technology, engineering, and capacity additions. When investing in new equipment or factories, Coors always went "the Cadillac route," with little scrutiny of proposed projects. In effect, their motto was "If you build it, they will come." Indeed, for two decades consumers did switch to Coors.

However, the brewing industry began to experience major problems in the 1990s. Many consumers were drawn to wine, causing growth in beer sales to fall below 1 percent per year. In addition, large numbers of microbreweries opened, providing beer drinkers with an alternative to the national brands. These events proved particularly painful to Coors, whose lack of financial discipline had led to a frivolous use of capital and thus to a high-cost infrastructure.

In February 1995, Coors hired a new CFO, Timothy Wolf, who soon learned that Coors had a low return on invested capital, negative free cash flow, and an unreliable planning/forecasting process. Wolf quickly created an in-house education program to teach managers and engineers how to conduct a rational project analysis. Even more important, he began to shift the corporate culture from a focus on undisciplined growth and high-technology engineering to creating shareholder value. This new focus was put to the test in 1996, when Coors reexamined its plans for a major new bottle-washing facility in Virginia. Using the capital budgeting processes established by Wolf, the project team was able to reduce the cost of the investment by 25 percent. They also implemented design changes that led to lower operating costs.

Under Wolf's guidance, Coors has steadily improved both its return on invested capital and its free cash flow. Financial analysts are impressed with Wolf's efforts. Skip Carpenter of Donaldson, Lufkin & Jenrette says, "From a financial perspective, there's absolutely no question Coors is better positioned to deal with the difficulties of the beer industry."[1] Investors seem to agree, as Coors' stock price has climbed from about $14 per share when Wolf joined to over $63 per share in mid-2000, an annualized average gain of more than 28 percent.

[1]See an article by Stephen Barr, "Coors's New Brew," *CFO*, March 1998, 91–93.

The last chapter showed how to determine the value of an entire company and how different corporate strategies affect value. Now we turn to *capital budgeting,* the process of evaluating specific investment decisions. Here the term *capital* refers to operating assets used in production, while a *budget* is a plan that details projected cash flows during some future period. Thus, the *capital budget* is an outline of planned investments in operating assets, and **capital budgeting** is the whole process of analyzing projects and deciding which ones to include in the capital budget.

The textbook's CD-ROM contains an *Excel* file that will guide you through the chapter's calculations. The file for this chapter is ***Ch 13 Tool Kit.xls,*** and we encourage you to open the file and follow along as you read the chapter.

Our treatment of capital budgeting is divided into three chapters. This chapter provides an overview of the capital budgeting process and explains the basic techniques used to evaluate cash flows. Chapter 14 then explains how to estimate a project's cash flows and risk. Finally, some projects provide managers with opportunities to react to changing market conditions. These opportunities, called "real options," are described in Chapter 15.

As you read this chapter, think about Coors and how it uses capital budgeting to create value for shareholders.

Importance of Capital Budgeting

A number of factors combine to make capital budgeting perhaps the most important task faced by financial managers and their staffs. First, since the results of capital budgeting decisions continue for many years, the firm loses some of its flexibility. For example, the purchase of an asset with an economic life of 10 years "locks in" the firm for a 10-year period. Further, because asset expansion is based on expected future sales, a decision to buy an asset that is expected to last 10 years requires a 10-year sales forecast. Finally, a firm's capital budgeting decisions define its strategic direction, because moves into new products, services, or markets must be preceded by capital expenditures.

An erroneous forecast of asset requirements can have serious consequences. If the firm invests too much, it will incur unnecessarily high depreciation and other expenses. On the other hand, if it does not invest enough, two problems may arise. First, its equipment and computer software may not be sufficiently modern to enable it to produce competitively. Second, if it has inadequate capacity, it may lose market share to rival firms, and regaining lost customers requires heavy selling expenses, price reductions, or product improvements, all of which are costly.

Timing is also important—capital assets must be available when they are needed. Edward Ford, executive vice-president of Western Design, a decorative tile company, gave the authors an illustration of the importance of capital budgeting. His firm tried to operate near capacity most of the time. During a four-year period, Western experienced intermittent spurts in the demand for its products, which forced it to turn away orders. After these sharp increases in demand, Western would add capacity by renting an additional building, then purchasing and installing the appropriate equipment. It would take six to eight months to get the additional capacity ready, but by then demand had dried up—other firms with available capacity had already taken an increased share of the market. Once Western began to properly forecast demand and plan its capacity requirements a year or so in advance, it was able to maintain and even increase its market share.

Effective capital budgeting can improve both the timing and the quality of asset acquisitions. If a firm forecasts its needs for capital assets in advance, it can purchase and install the assets before they are needed. Unfortunately, many firms do not order capital goods until existing assets are approaching full-capacity usage. If sales increase because of an increase in general market demand, all firms in the industry will tend to order capital goods at about the same time. This results in backlogs, long waiting times for machinery, a deterioration in the quality of the capital equipment, and an increase in costs. The firm that foresees its needs and purchases capital assets during slack periods can avoid these problems. Note, though, that if a firm forecasts an increase in demand and then expands to meet the anticipated demand, but sales do not increase, it will be saddled with excess capacity and high costs, which can lead to losses or even bankruptcy. Thus, an accurate sales forecast is critical.

Capital budgeting typically involves substantial expenditures, and before a firm can spend a large amount of money, it must have the funds lined up—large amounts of money are not available automatically. Therefore, a firm contemplating a major capital expenditure program should plan its financing far enough in advance to be sure funds are available.

Self-Test Questions

Why are capital budgeting decisions so important?

Why is the sales forecast a key element in a capital budgeting decision?

Generating Ideas for Capital Projects

The same general concepts that are used in security valuation are also involved in capital budgeting. However, whereas a set of stocks and bonds exists in the securities market, and investors select from this set, *capital budgeting projects are created by the firm*. For example, a sales representative may report that customers are asking for a particular product that the company does not now produce. The sales manager then discusses the idea with the marketing research group to determine the size of the market for the proposed product. If it appears that a significant market does exist, cost accountants and engineers will be asked to estimate production costs. If they conclude that the product can be produced and sold at a sufficient profit, the project will be undertaken.

A firm's growth, and even its ability to remain competitive and to survive, depends on a constant flow of ideas for new products, for ways to make existing products better, and for ways to operate at a lower cost. Accordingly, a well-managed firm will go to great lengths to develop good capital budgeting proposals. For example, the executive vice-president of one very successful corporation indicated that his company takes the following steps to generate projects:

> Our R&D department is constantly searching for new products and for ways to improve existing products. In addition, our executive committee, which consists of senior executives in marketing, production, and finance, identifies the products and markets in which our company should compete, and the committee sets long-run targets for each division. These targets, which are spelled out in the corporation's strategic business plan, provide a general guide to the operating executives who must meet them. The operating executives then seek new products, set expansion plans for existing products, and look for ways to reduce production and distribution costs. Since bonuses and promotions are based on each unit's ability to meet or exceed its targets, these economic incentives encourage our operating executives to seek out profitable investment opportunities.
>
> While our senior executives are judged and rewarded on the basis of how well their units perform, people further down the line are given bonuses and stock options for suggestions that lead to profitable investments. Additionally, a percentage of our corporate profit is set aside for distribution to nonexecutive employees, and we have an Employees' Stock Ownership Plan (ESOP) to provide further incentives. Our objective is to encourage employees at all levels to keep an eye out for good ideas, including those that lead to capital investments.

If a firm has capable and imaginative executives and employees, and if its incentive system is working properly, many ideas for capital investment will be advanced. Some ideas will be good ones, but others will not. Therefore, procedures must be established for screening projects, the primary topic of this chapter.

Self-Test Question

What are some ways firms get ideas for capital projects?

Project Classifications

Analyzing capital expenditure proposals is not a costless operation—benefits can be gained, but analysis does have a cost. For certain types of projects, a relatively detailed analysis may be warranted; for others, simpler procedures should be used. Accordingly, firms generally categorize projects and then analyze those in each category somewhat differently:

1. **Replacement: maintenance of business.** One category consists of expenditures to replace worn-out or damaged equipment used in the production of profitable products. Replacement projects are necessary if the firm is to continue in business. The only issues here are (a) should this operation be continued and (b) should we continue to use the same production processes? The answers are usually yes, so maintenance decisions are normally made without going through an elaborate decision process.
2. **Replacement: cost reduction.** This category includes expenditures to replace serviceable but obsolete equipment. The purpose here is to lower the costs of labor, materials, and other inputs such as electricity. These decisions are discretionary, and a fairly detailed analysis is generally required.
3. **Expansion of existing products or markets.** Expenditures to increase output of existing products, or to expand retail outlets or distribution facilities in markets now being served, are included here. These decisions are more complex because they require an explicit forecast of growth in demand. Mistakes are more likely, so a more detailed analysis is required. Also, the go/no-go decision is generally made at a higher level within the firm.
4. **Expansion into new products or markets.** These are investments to produce a new product or to expand into a geographic area not currently being served. These projects involve strategic decisions that could change the fundamental nature of the business, and they normally require the expenditure of large sums with delayed paybacks. Invariably, a detailed analysis is required, and the final decision is generally made at the very top—by the board of directors as a part of the firm's strategic plan.
5. **Safety and/or environmental projects.** Expenditures necessary to comply with government orders, labor agreements, or insurance policy terms fall into this category. These expenditures are called *mandatory investments*, and they often involve *nonrevenue-producing projects*. How they are handled depends on their size, with small ones being treated much like the Category 1 projects described above.
6. **Research and development.** For many firms, R&D constitutes the largest and most important type of capital expenditure. Although these expenditures can, conceptually, be analyzed in the same way as tangible asset investments, the cash flows they produce are often too uncertain to warrant a standard discounted cash flow (DCF) analysis. What happens, generally, is that managers think in subjective DCF terms about R&D expenditures, then appropriate a certain amount of money to conduct research on a given project or set of projects. Since R&D results are almost always highly uncertain, and since continuing to fund a project will depend

on results at earlier stages, the decision tree analysis and real options approach discussed in Chapter 15 are often used.

7. **Long-term contracts.** Companies often make long-term contractual arrangements to provide products or services to specific customers. For example, IBM has signed agreements to handle computer services for other companies for periods of 5 to 10 years. There may or may not be much up-front investment, but costs and revenues will accrue over multiple years, and a DCF analysis should be performed before the contract is signed.
8. **Other.** This catch-all includes office buildings, parking lots, executive aircraft, and so on. DCF should be used, but how they are actually handled varies among companies.

In general, relatively simple calculations and only a few supporting documents are required for replacement decisions, especially maintenance-type investments in profitable plants. A more detailed analysis is required for cost-reduction replacements, for expansion of existing product lines, and especially for investments in new products or areas. Also, within each category projects are broken down by their dollar costs: Larger investments require increasingly detailed analysis and approval at a higher level within the firm. Thus, whereas a plant manager may be authorized to approve maintenance expenditures up to $10,000 on the basis of a relatively unsophisticated analysis, the full board of directors may have to approve decisions that involve either amounts over $1 million or expansions into new products or markets. Statistical data are generally lacking for new-product decisions, so here judgments, as opposed to detailed cost data, are especially important.

Note that the term "assets" encompasses more than buildings and equipment. Computer software that a firm develops to help it buy supplies and materials more efficiently, or to communicate with customers, is also an asset. So is a customer base like the one AOL developed by sending out millions of free CDs to potential customers, and contracts IBM has executed with its customers. And so is the design of a new computer chip, airplane, or movie. All of these are "intangible" as opposed to "tangible" assets, but decisions to invest in them are analyzed in the same way as decisions related to tangible assets. Keep this in mind as you go through the remainder of the chapter.

Self-Test Question

Identify the major project classification categories, and explain how they are used.

Similarities between Capital Budgeting and Security Valuation

Once a potential capital budgeting project has been identified, its evaluation involves the same steps that security analysts use.

1. First, the cost of the project must be determined. This is similar to finding the price that must be paid for a stock or bond.
2. Next, management estimates the expected cash flows from the project, including the salvage value of the asset at the end of its expected life. This is similar to estimating the future dividend or interest payment stream on a stock or bond, along with the stock's expected sales price or the bond's maturity value.
3. Third, the risk of the projected cash flows must be estimated. This requires information about the probability distribution (risk) of the cash flows.
4. Given the project's risk, management determines the cost of capital at which the cash flows should be discounted.

5. Next, the expected cash flows are put on a present value basis to obtain an estimate of the asset's value. This is equivalent to finding the present value of a stock's expected future dividends.
6. Finally, the present value of the expected cash flows is compared with the required outlay. If the PV of the cash flows exceeds the cost, the project should be accepted. Otherwise, it should be rejected. (Alternatively, if the expected rate of return on the project exceeds its cost of capital, the project is accepted.)

If an individual investor identifies and invests in a stock or bond whose market price is less than its true value, the investor's wealth will increase. Similarly, if a firm identifies (or creates) an investment opportunity with a present value greater than its cost, the value of the firm will increase. Thus, there is a direct link between capital budgeting and stock values: The more effective the firm's capital budgeting procedures, the higher its stock price.

Self-Test Question List the six steps in the capital budgeting process, and compare them with the steps in security valuation.

Capital Budgeting Decision Rules

Six key methods are used to rank projects and to decide whether or not they should be accepted for inclusion in the capital budget: (1) payback, (2) discounted payback, (3) net present value (NPV), (4) internal rate of return (IRR), (5) modified internal rate of return (MIRR), and (6) profitability index (PI). We will explain how each ranking criterion is calculated, and then we will evaluate how well each performs in terms of identifying those projects that will maximize the firm's stock price.

We use the cash flow data shown in Figure 13-1 for Projects S and L to illustrate each method. Also, we assume that the projects are equally risky. Note that the cash flows, CF_t, are expected values, and that they have been adjusted to reflect taxes, depreciation, and salvage values. Further, because many projects require an investment in both fixed assets and working capital, the investment outlays shown as CF_0

FIGURE 13-1 Net Cash Flows for Projects S and L

	Expected After-Tax Net Cash Flows, CF_t	
Year (t)	Project S	Project L
0[a]	($1,000)	($1,000)
1	500	100
2	400	300
3	300	400
4	100	600

	0	1	2	3	4
Project S:	−1,000	500	400	300	100
Project L:	−1,000	100	300	400	600

[a] CF_0 represents the net investment outlay, or initial cost.

include any necessary changes in net operating working capital.[2] Finally, we assume that all cash flows occur at the end of the designated year. Incidentally, the S stands for *short* and the L for *long:* Project S is a short-term project in the sense that its cash inflows come in sooner than L's.

Payback Period

The **payback period,** defined as the expected number of years required to recover the original investment, was the first formal method used to evaluate capital budgeting projects. The payback calculation is diagrammed in Figure 13-2, and it is explained below for Project S.

1. Enter $CF_0 = -1000$ in your calculator. (You do not need to use the cash flow register; just have your display show −1,000.)
2. Now add $CF_1 = 500$ to find the cumulative cash flow at the end of Year 1. The result is −500.
3. Now add $CF_2 = 400$ to find the cumulative cash flow at the end of Year 2. This is −100.
4. Now add $CF_3 = 300$ to find the cumulative cash flow at the end of Year 3. This is +200.
5. We see that by the end of Year 3 the cumulative inflows have more than recovered the initial outflow. Thus, the payback occurred during the third year. If the $300 of inflows comes in evenly during Year 3, then the exact payback period can be found as follows:

$$\text{Payback}_S = \text{Year before full recovery} + \frac{\text{Unrecovered cost at start of year}}{\text{Cash flow during year}}$$

$$= 2 + \frac{\$100}{\$300} = 2.33 \text{ years.}$$

Applying the same procedure to Project L, we find $\text{Payback}_L = 3.33$ years.

The shorter the payback period, the better. Therefore, if the firm required a payback of three years or less, Project S would be accepted but Project L would be rejected. If the projects were **mutually exclusive,** S would be ranked over L because S has the

[2]The most difficult part of the capital budgeting process is estimating the relevant cash flows. For simplicity, the net cash flows are treated as a given in this chapter, which allows us to focus on the capital budgeting decision rules. However, in Chapter 14 we will discuss cash flow estimation in detail. Also, note that *net operating working capital* is current operating assets minus current operating liabilities.

FIGURE 13-2 Payback Period for Projects S and L

Project S:	0	1	2	3	4
Net cash flow	−1,000	500	400	300	100
Cumulative NCF	−1,000	−500	−100	200	300

$\text{Payback}_S = 2.33$ years.

Project L:	0	1	2	3	4
Net cash flow	−1,000	100	300	400	600
Cumulative NCF	−1,000	−900	−600	−200	400

$\text{Payback}_L = 3.33$ years.

shorter payback. *Mutually exclusive* means that if one project is taken on, the other must be rejected. For example, the installation of a conveyor-belt system in a warehouse and the purchase of a fleet of forklifts for the same warehouse would be mutually exclusive projects—accepting one implies rejection of the other. **Independent projects** are projects whose cash flows are independent of one another.

Discounted Payback Period

Some firms use a variant of the regular payback, the **discounted payback period,** which is similar to the regular payback period except that the expected cash flows are discounted by the project's cost of capital. Thus, the discounted payback period is defined as the number of years required to recover the investment from *discounted* net cash flows. Figure 13-3 contains the discounted net cash flows for Projects S and L, assuming both projects have a cost of capital of 10 percent. To construct Figure 13-3, each cash inflow is divided by $(1 + k)^t = (1.10)^t$, where t is the year in which the cash flow occurs and k is the project's cost of capital. After three years, Project S will have generated $1,011 in discounted cash inflows. Because the cost is $1,000, the discounted payback is just under three years, or, to be precise, 2 + ($214/$225) = 2.95 years. Project L's discounted payback is 3.88 years:

$$\text{Discounted payback}_S = 2.0 + \$214/\$225 = 2.95 \text{ years.}$$
$$\text{Discounted payback}_L = 3.0 + \$360/\$410 = 3.88 \text{ years.}$$

For Projects S and L, the rankings are the same regardless of which payback method is used; that is, Project S is preferred to Project L, and Project S would still be selected if the firm were to require a discounted payback of three years or less. Often, however, the regular and the discounted paybacks produce conflicting rankings.

Note that the payback is a type of "breakeven" calculation in the sense that if cash flows come in at the expected rate until the payback year, then the project will break even. However, the regular payback does not consider the cost of capital—no cost for the debt or equity used to undertake the project is reflected in the cash flows or the calculation. The discounted payback does consider capital costs—it shows the breakeven year after covering debt and equity costs.

An important drawback of both the payback and discounted payback methods is that they ignore cash flows that are paid or received after the payback period. For example, consider two projects, X and Y, each of which requires an up-front cash outflow of $3,000, so $CF_0 = -\$3{,}000$. Assume that both projects have a cost of capital of 10

FIGURE 13-3 Projects S and L: Discounted Payback Period

Project S:	0	1	2	3	4
Net cash flow	−1,000	500	400	300	100
Discounted NCF (at 10%)	−1,000	455	331	225	68
Cumulative disounted NCF	−1,000	−545	−214	11	79
Payback_S = 2.95 years.					

Project L:	0	1	2	3	4
Net cash flow	−1,000	100	300	400	600
Discounted NCF (at 10%)	−1,000	91	248	301	410
Cumulative disounted NCF	−1,000	−909	−661	−360	50
Payback_L = 3.88 years.					

percent. Project X is expected to produce cash inflows of \$1,000 each of the next four years, while Project Y will produce no cash flows the first four years but then generate a cash inflow of \$1,000,000 five years from now. Common sense suggests that Project Y creates more value for the firm's shareholders, yet its payback and discounted payback make it look worse than Project X. Consequently, both payback methods have serious deficiencies. Therefore, we will not dwell on the finer points of payback analysis.[3]

Although the payback method has some serious faults as a ranking criterion, it does provide information on how long funds will be tied up in a project. Thus, the shorter the payback period, other things held constant, the greater the project's *liquidity*. Also, since cash flows expected in the distant future are generally riskier than near-term cash flows, the payback is often used as an indicator of a project's *riskiness*.

Net Present Value (NPV)

As the flaws in the payback were recognized, people began to search for ways to improve the effectiveness of project evaluations. One such method is the **net present value (NPV) method,** which relies on **discounted cash flow (DCF) techniques.** To implement this approach, we proceed as follows:

1. Find the present value of each cash flow, including both inflows and outflows, discounted at the project's cost of capital.
2. Sum these discounted cash flows; this sum is defined as the project's NPV.
3. If the NPV is positive, the project should be accepted, while if the NPV is negative, it should be rejected. If two projects with positive NPVs are mutually exclusive, the one with the higher NPV should be chosen.

The equation for the NPV is as follows:

$$\begin{aligned} NPV &= CF_0 + \frac{CF_1}{(1+k)^1} + \frac{CF_2}{(1+k)^2} + \cdots + \frac{CF_n}{(1+k)^n} \\ &= \sum_{t=0}^{n} \frac{CF_t}{(1+k)^t}. \end{aligned} \qquad \textbf{(13-1)}$$

Here CF_t is the expected net cash flow at Period t, k is the project's cost of capital, and n is its life. Cash outflows (expenditures such as the cost of buying equipment or building factories) are treated as *negative* cash flows. In evaluating Projects S and L, only CF_0 is negative, but for many large projects such as the Alaska Pipeline, an electric generating plant, or a new Boeing jet aircraft, outflows occur for several years before operations begin and cash flows turn positive.

At a 10 percent cost of capital, Project S's NPV is \$78.82:

	0 (k = 10%)	1	2	3	4
Cash Flows	−1,000.00	500	400	300	100
	454.55 ←	500			
	330.58 ←		400		
	225.39 ←			300	
	68.30 ←				100
Net Present Value	**78.82**				

[3]Another capital budgeting technique that was once used widely is the *accounting rate of return (ARR)*, which examines a project's contribution to the firm's net income. Although some companies still calculate an ARR, it really has no redeeming features, so we will not discuss it in this text. See Eugene F. Brigham and Phillip R. Daves, *Intermediate Financial Management*, 7th ed. (Fort Worth, TX: Harcourt College Publishers, 2002), Chapter 11.

By a similar process, we find $NPV_L = \$49.18$. On this basis, both projects should be accepted if they are independent, but S should be chosen over L if they are mutually exclusive.

It is not hard to calculate the NPV as was done in the time line by using Equation 13-1 and a regular calculator. However, it is more efficient to use a financial calculator. Different calculators are set up somewhat differently, but they all have a section of memory called the "cash flow register" that is used for uneven cash flows such as those in Projects S and L (as opposed to equal annuity cash flows). A solution process for Equation 13-1 is literally programmed into financial calculators, and all you have to do is enter the cash flows (being sure to observe the signs), along with the value of k = I. At that point, you have (in your calculator) this equation:

$$NPV_S = -1{,}000 + \frac{500}{(1.10)^1} + \frac{400}{(1.10)^2} + \frac{300}{(1.10)^3} + \frac{100}{(1.10)^4}.$$

Note that the equation has one unknown, NPV. Now all you need to do is to ask the calculator to solve the equation for you, which you do by pressing the NPV button (and, on some calculators, the "compute" button). The answer, 78.82, will appear on the screen.[4]

---

[4]The *Technology Supplement* that accompanies this text explains this and other commonly used calculator applications. For those who do not have the *Supplement*, the steps for two popular calculators, the HP-10B and the HP-17B, are shown below. If you have another type of financial calculator, see its manual or the *Supplement*.

HP-10B:

1. Clear the memory.
2. Enter CF_0 as follows: 1000 +/− CFj.
3. Enter CF_1 as follows: 500 CFj.
4. Repeat the process to enter the other cash flows. Note that CF 0, CF 1, and so forth, flash on the screen as you press the CFj button. If you hold the button down, CF 0 and so forth, will remain on the screen until you release it.
5. Once the CFs have been entered, enter k = I = 10%: 10 I/YR.
6. Now that all of the inputs have been entered, you can press NPV to get the answer, NPV = \$78.82.
7. If a cash flow is repeated for several years, you can avoid having to enter the CFs for each year. For example, if the \$500 cash flow for Year 1 had also been the CF for Years 2 through 10, making 10 of these \$500 cash flows, then after entering 500 CFj the first time, you could enter 10 Nj. This would automatically enter 10 CFs of 500.

HP-17B:

1. Go to the cash flow (CFLO) menu, clear if FLOW(0) = ? does not appear on the screen.
2. Enter CF_0 as follows: 1000 +/− INPUT.
3. Enter CF_1 as follows: 500 INPUT.
4. Now, the calculator will ask you if the 500 is for Period 1 only or if it is also used for several following periods. Since it is only used for Period 1, press INPUT to answer "1." Alternatively, you could press EXIT and then #T? to turn off the prompt for the remainder of the problem. For some problems, you will want to use the repeat feature.
5. Enter the remaining CFs, being sure to turn off the prompt or else to specify "1" for each entry.
6. Once the CFs have all been entered, press EXIT and then CALC.
7. Now enter k = I = 10% as follows: 10 I%.
8. Now press NPV to get the answer, NPV = \$78.82.

Most projects last for more than four years, and, as you will see in Chapter 14, we must go through a number of steps to develop the estimated cash flows. Therefore, financial analysts generally use spreadsheets when dealing with capital budgeting projects. For Project S, this spreadsheet could be used (disregard for now the IRR on Row 6; we discuss it in the next section):

	A	B	C	D	E	F	G
1	Project S						
2	k =	**10%**					
3	Time	1	2	3	4	5	
4	Cash flow =	**−1000**	**500**	**400**	**300**	**100**	
5	NPV =	**$78.82**					
6	IRR =	**14.5%**					
7							

See ***Ch 13 Tool Kit.xls.***

In *Excel*, the formula in Cell B5 is: **=B4+NPV(B2,C4:F4),** and it results in a value of $78.82.[5] For a simple problem such as this, setting up a spreadsheet may not seem worth the trouble. However, in real-world problems there will be a number of rows above our cash flow line, starting with expected sales, then deducting various costs and taxes, and ending up with the cash flows shown on Row 4. Moreover, once a spreadsheet has been set up, it is easy to change input values to see what would happen under different conditions. For example, we could see what would happen if lower sales caused all cash flows to decline by $15, or if the cost of capital rose to 10.5 percent. Using *Excel*, it is easy to make such changes and then see the effects on NPV.

Rationale for the NPV Method

The rationale for the NPV method is straightforward. An NPV of zero signifies that the project's cash flows are exactly sufficient to repay the invested capital and to provide the required rate of return on that capital. If a project has a positive NPV, then it is generating more cash than is needed to service the debt and to provide the required return to shareholders, and this excess cash accrues solely to the firm's stockholders. Therefore, if a firm takes on a project with a positive NPV, the position of the stockholders is improved. In our example, shareholders' wealth would increase by $78.82 if the firm takes on Project S, but by only $49.18 if it takes on Project L. Viewed in this manner, it is easy to see why S is preferred to L, and it is also easy to see the logic of the NPV approach.[6]

[5]You could click the function wizard, f_x, then Financial, then NPV, and then OK. Then insert B2 as the rate and C4:F4 as "Value 1," which is the cash flow range. Then click OK, and edit the equation by adding B4. Note that you cannot enter the 2$1,000 cost as part of the NPV range. It occurs at t 5 0, but the Excel NPV function assumes that all cash flows occur at the end of the periods.

[6]This description of the process is somewhat oversimplified. Both analysts and investors anticipate that firms will identify and accept positive NPV projects, and current stock prices reflect these expectations. Thus, stock prices react to announcements of new capital projects only to the extent that such projects were not already expected. In this sense, we may think of a firm's market value as consisting of the value of its existing assets and the value of positive NPV "growth opportunities."

There is also a direct relationship between NPV and EVA (economic value added)—NPV is equal to the present value of the project's future EVAs. Therefore, accepting positive NPV projects should result in a positive EVA and a positive MVA (market value added, or the excess of the firm's market value over its book value). So, a reward system that compensates managers for producing positive EVA will lead to the use of NPV for making capital budgeting decisions.

Internal Rate of Return (IRR)

In Chapter 9 we presented procedures for finding the yield to maturity, or rate of return, on a bond—if you invest in a bond, hold it to maturity, and receive all of the promised cash flows, you will earn the YTM on the money you invested. Exactly the same concepts are employed in capital budgeting when the **internal rate of return (IRR) method** is used. The **IRR** is defined as the discount rate that equates the present value of a project's expected cash inflows to the present value of the project's costs:

$$\text{PV(Inflows)} = \text{PV(Investment costs)},$$

or, equivalently, the IRR rate that forces the NPV to equal zero:

$$CF_0 + \frac{CF_1}{(1+\text{IRR})^1} + \frac{CF_2}{(1+\text{IRR})^2} + \cdots + \frac{CF_n}{(1+\text{IRR})^n} = 0$$

$$\text{NPV} = \sum_{t=0}^{n} \frac{CF_t}{(1+\text{IRR})^t} = 0. \tag{13-2}$$

For our Project S, here is the time line setup:

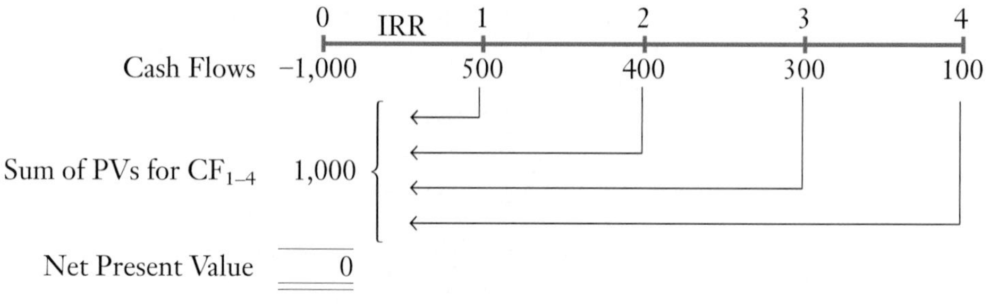

$$-1{,}000 + \frac{500}{(1+\text{IRR})^1} + \frac{400}{(1+\text{IRR})^2} + \frac{300}{(1+\text{IRR})^3} + \frac{100}{(1+\text{IRR})^4} = 0.$$

Thus, we have an equation with one unknown, IRR, and we need to solve for IRR.

Although it is easy to find the NPV without a financial calculator, this is *not* true of the IRR. If the cash flows are constant from year to year, then we have an annuity, and we can use annuity formulas as discussed in Chapter 8 to find the IRR. However, if the cash flows are not constant, as is generally the case in capital budgeting, then it is difficult to find the IRR without a financial calculator. Without a calculator, you must solve Equation 13-2 by trial-and-error—try some discount rate and see if the equation solves to zero, and if it does not, try a different discount rate, and continue until you find the rate that forces the equation to equal zero. The discount rate that causes the equation (and the NPV) to equal zero is defined as the IRR. For a realistic project with a fairly long life, the trial-and-error approach is a tedious, time-consuming task.

Fortunately, it is easy to find IRRs with a financial calculator. You follow procedures almost identical to those used to find the NPV. First, you enter the cash flows as shown on the preceding time line into the calculator's cash flow register. In effect, you have entered the cash flows into the equation shown below the time line. Note that we have one unknown, IRR, which is the discount rate that forces the equation to equal zero. The calculator has been programmed to solve for the IRR, and you activate this program by pressing the button labeled "IRR." Then the calculator solves for IRR and displays it on the screen. Here are the IRRs for Projects S and L as found with a financial calculator:[7]

$$IRR_S = 14.5\%.$$
$$IRR_L = 11.8\%.$$

It is also easy to find the IRR using the same spreadsheet we used for the NPV. With *Excel*, we simply enter this formula in Cell B6: **=IRR(B4:F4).** For Project S, the result is 14.5 percent.[8]

If both projects have a cost of capital, or **hurdle rate,** of 10 percent, then the internal rate of return rule indicates that if the projects are independent, both should be accepted—they are both expected to earn more than the cost of the capital needed to finance them. If they are mutually exclusive, S ranks higher and should be accepted, so L should be rejected. If the cost of capital is above 14.5 percent, both projects should be rejected.

Notice that the internal rate of return formula, Equation 13-2, is simply the NPV formula, Equation 13-1, solved for the particular discount rate that forces the NPV to equal zero. Thus, the same basic equation is used for both methods, but in the NPV method the discount rate, k, is specified and the NPV is found, whereas in the IRR method the NPV is specified to equal zero, and the interest rate that forces this equality (the IRR) is calculated.

Mathematically, the NPV and IRR methods will always lead to the same accept/reject decisions for independent projects. This occurs because if NPV is positive, IRR must exceed k. However, NPV and IRR can give conflicting rankings for mutually exclusive projects. This point will be discussed in more detail in a later section.

Rationale for the IRR Method

Why is the particular discount rate that equates a project's cost with the present value of its receipts (the IRR) so special? The reason is based on this logic: (1) The IRR on a project is its expected rate of return. (2) If the internal rate of return exceeds the cost of the funds used to finance the project, a surplus will remain after paying for the capital, and this surplus will accrue to the firm's stockholders. (3) Therefore, taking on a project whose IRR exceeds its cost of capital increases shareholders' wealth. On the other hand, if the internal rate of return is less than the cost of capital, then taking on the project will impose a cost on current stockholders. It is this "breakeven" characteristic that makes the IRR useful in evaluating capital projects.

---

[7]To find the IRR with an HP-10B or HP-17B, repeat the steps given in Footnote 4. Then, with an HP-10B, press [ ] IRR/YR, and, after a pause, 14.49, Project S's IRR, will appear. With the HP-17B, simply press IRR% to get the IRR. With both calculators, you would generally want to get both the NPV and the IRR after entering the input data, before clearing the cash flow register. The *Technology Supplement* explains how to find IRR with several other calculators.

[8]Note that the full range can be specified with the IRR formula, because *Excel's* IRR function assumes that the first cash flow (the negative \$1,000) occurs at t = 0. Note too that you can use the function wizard to find the IRR. This is convenient if you don't have the formula committed to memory.

Self-Test Questions

What four capital budgeting ranking methods were discussed in this section?

Describe each method, and give the rationale for its use.

What two methods always lead to the same accept/reject decision for independent projects?

What two pieces of information does the payback period convey that are not conveyed by the other methods?

Comparison of the NPV and IRR Methods

In many respects the NPV method is better than IRR, so it is tempting to explain NPV only, to state that it should be used to select projects, and to go on to the next topic. However, the IRR is familiar to many corporate executives, it is widely entrenched in industry, and it does have some virtues. Therefore, it is important for you to understand the IRR method but also to be able to explain why, at times, a project with a lower IRR may be preferable to a mutually exclusive alternative with a higher IRR.

NPV Profiles

A graph that plots a project's NPV against the cost of capital rates is defined as the project's **net present value profile;** profiles for Projects L and S are shown in Figure 13-4. To construct NPV profiles, first note that at a zero cost of capital, the NPV is simply the total of the project's undiscounted cash flows. Thus, at a zero cost of capital NPV_S = \$300, and NPV_L = \$400. These values are plotted as the vertical axis intercepts in Figure 13-4. Next, we calculate the projects' NPVs at three costs of capital, 5, 10, and 15 percent, and plot these values. The four points plotted on our graph for each project are shown at the bottom of the figure.[9]

Recall that the IRR is defined as the discount rate at which a project's NPV equals zero. Therefore, *the point where its net present value profile crosses the horizontal axis indicates a project's internal rate of return.* Since we calculated IRR_S and IRR_L in an earlier section, we can confirm the validity of the graph.

When we connect the data points, we have the net present value profiles.[10] NPV profiles can be very useful in project analysis, and we will use them often in the remainder of the chapter.

NPV Rankings Depend on the Cost of Capital

Figure 13-4 shows that the NPV profiles of both Project L and Project S decline as the cost of capital increases. But notice in the figure that Project L has the higher NPV at a low cost of capital, while Project S has the higher NPV if the cost of capital

[9]To calculate the points with a financial calculator, enter the cash flows in the cash flow register, enter I = 0, and press the NPV button to find the NPV at a zero cost of capital. Then enter I = 5 to override the zero, and press NPV to get the NPV at 5 percent. Repeat these steps for 10 and 15 percent. However, we did the calculations and made the graph with our *Excel* model. See ***Ch 13 Tool Kit.xls***.

[10]Notice that the NPV profiles are curved—they are *not* straight lines. NPV approaches the t = 0 cash flow (the cost of the project) as the cost of capital increases without limit. The reason is that, at an infinitely high cost of capital, the PV of the inflows would be zero, so NPV at ($k = \infty$) is simply CF_0, which in our example is −\$1,000. We should also note that under certain conditions the NPV profiles can cross the horizontal axis several times, or never cross it. This point is discussed later in the chapter.

is greater than the 7.2 percent **crossover rate.** Notice also that Project L's NPV is "more sensitive" to changes in the cost of capital than is NPV_S; that is, Project L's net present value profile has the steeper slope, indicating that a given change in k has a greater effect on NPV_L than on NPV_S.

To see why L has the greater sensitivity, recall first that the cash flows from S are received faster than those from L. In a payback sense, S is a short-term project, while L is a long-term project. Next, recall the equation for the NPV:

$$NPV = \frac{CF_0}{(1+k)^0} + \frac{CF_1}{(1+k)^1} + \ldots + \frac{CF_n}{(1+k)^n}.$$

The impact of an increase in the cost of capital is much greater on distant than on near-term cash flows. To illustrate, consider the following:

$$\text{PV of \$100 due in 1 year @ k = 5\%: } \frac{\$100}{(1.05)^1} = \$95.24.$$

$$\text{PV of \$100 due in 1 year @ k = 10\%: } \frac{\$100}{(1.10)^1} = \$90.91.$$

$$\text{Percentage decline due to higher k} = \frac{\$95.24 - \$90.91}{\$95.24} = 4.5\%.$$

$$\text{PV of \$100 due in 20 years @ k = 5\%: } \frac{\$100}{(1.05)^{20}} = \$37.69.$$

$$\text{PV of \$100 due in 20 years @ k = 10\%: } \frac{\$100}{(1.10)^{20}} = \$14.86.$$

$$\text{Percentage decline due to higher k} = \frac{\$37.69 - \$14.86}{\$37.69} = 60.6\%.$$

Thus, a doubling of the discount rate causes only a 4.5 percent decline in the PV of a Year 1 cash flow, but the same doubling of the discount rate causes the PV of a Year 20 cash flow to fall by more than 60 percent. Therefore, if a project has most of its cash flows coming in the early years, its NPV will not decline very much if the cost of capital increases, but a project whose cash flows come later will be severely penalized by high capital costs. Accordingly, Project L, which has its largest cash flows in the later years, is hurt badly if the cost of capital is high, while Project S, which has relatively rapid cash flows, is affected less by high capital costs. Therefore, Project L's NPV profile has the steeper slope.

Independent Projects

If an *independent* project is being evaluated, then the NPV and IRR criteria always lead to the same accept/reject decision: if NPV says accept, IRR also says accept. To see why this is so, assume that Projects L and S are independent, and then look back at Figure 13-4 and notice (1) that the IRR criterion for acceptance for either project is that the project's cost of capital is less than (or to the left of) the IRR and (2) that whenever a project's cost of capital is less than its IRR, its NPV is positive. Thus, at any cost of capital less than 11.8 percent, Project L will be acceptable by both the NPV and the IRR criteria, while both methods reject the project if the cost of capital is greater than 11.8 percent. Project S—and all other independent projects under consideration—could be analyzed similarly, and it will always turn out that if the IRR method says accept, then so will the NPV method.

FIGURE 13-4 Net Present Value Profiles: NPVs of Projects S and L at Different Costs of Capital

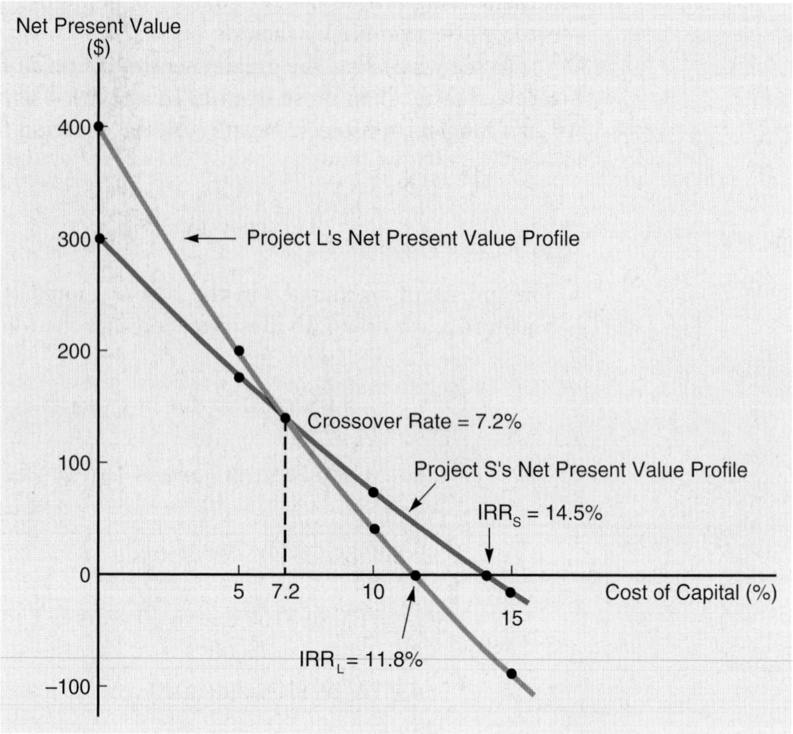

Cost of Capital	NPV_S	NPV_L
0%	$300.00	$400.00
5	180.42	206.50
10	78.82	49.18
15	(8.33)	(80.14)

Mutually Exclusive Projects

Now assume that Projects S and L are *mutually exclusive* rather than independent. That is, we can choose either Project S or Project L, or we can reject both, but we cannot accept both projects. Notice in Figure 13-4 that as long as the cost of capital is *greater than* the crossover rate of 7.2 percent, then (1) NPV_S is larger than NPV_L and (2) IRR_S exceeds IRR_L. Therefore, if k is *greater* than the crossover rate of 7.2 percent, the two methods both lead to the selection of Project S. However, if the cost of capital is *less than* the crossover rate, the NPV method ranks Project L higher, but the IRR method indicates that Project S is better. *Thus, a conflict exists if the cost of capital is less than the crossover rate.*[11] NPV says choose mutually exclusive L, while IRR says take S.

[11]The crossover rate is easy to calculate. Simply go back to Figure 13-1, where we set forth the two projects' cash flows, and calculate the difference in those flows in each year. The differences are $CF_S - CF_L = \$0$, +\$400, +\$100, +\$100, and −\$500, respectively. Enter these values in the cash flow register of a financial calculator, press the IRR button, and the crossover rate, 7.17% ≈ 7.2%, appears. Be sure to enter $CF_0 = 0$ or else you will not get the correct answer.

Which answer is correct? Logic suggests that the NPV method is better, because it selects the project that adds the most to shareholder wealth.

There are two basic conditions that can cause NPV profiles to cross, and thus conflicts to arise between NPV and IRR: (1) when *project size (or scale) differences* exist, meaning that the cost of one project is larger than that of the other, or (2) when *timing differences* exist, meaning that the timing of cash flows from the two projects differs such that most of the cash flows from one project come in the early years while most of the cash flows from the other project come in the later years, as occurred with our Projects L and S.[12]

When either size or timing differences occur, the firm will have different amounts of funds to invest in the various years, depending on which of the two mutually exclusive projects it chooses. For example, if one project costs more than the other, then the firm will have more money at t = 0 to invest elsewhere if it selects the smaller project. Similarly, for projects of equal size, the one with the larger early cash inflows—in our example, Project S—provides more funds for reinvestment in the early years. Given this situation, the rate of return at which differential cash flows can be invested is a critical issue.

The key to resolving conflicts between mutually exclusive projects is this: How useful is it to generate cash flows sooner rather than later? The value of early cash flows depends on the return we can earn on those cash flows, that is, the rate at which we can reinvest them. *The NPV method implicitly assumes that the rate at which cash flows can be reinvested is the cost of capital, whereas the IRR method assumes that the firm can reinvest at the IRR.* These assumptions are inherent in the mathematics of the discounting process. The cash flows may actually be withdrawn as dividends by the stockholders and spent on beer and pizza, but the NPV method still assumes that cash flows can be reinvested at the cost of capital, while the IRR method assumes reinvestment at the project's IRR.

Which is the better assumption—that cash flows can be reinvested at the cost of capital, or that they can be reinvested at the project's IRR? It can be demonstrated that the best assumption is that projects' cash flows are reinvested at the cost of capital.[13] Therefore, we conclude that *the best* **reinvestment rate assumption** *is the cost of capital, which is consistent with the NPV method.* This, in turn, leads us to prefer the NPV method, at least for a firm willing and able to obtain capital at a cost reasonably close to its current cost of capital.

We should reiterate that, when projects are independent, the NPV and IRR methods both lead to exactly the same accept/reject decision. However, *when evaluating mutually exclusive projects, especially those that differ in scale and/or timing, the NPV method should be used.*

Multiple IRRs

There is one other situation in which the IRR approach may not be usable—when projects with nonnormal cash flows are involved. A project has *normal* cash flows if it has one or more cash outflows (costs) followed by a series of cash inflows. If, however, a project calls for a large cash outflow sometime during or at the end of

---

[12]Of course, it is possible for mutually exclusive projects to differ with respect to both scale and timing. Also, if mutually exclusive projects have different lives (as opposed to different cash flow patterns over a common life), this introduces further complications, and for meaningful comparisons, some mutually exclusive projects must be evaluated over a common life. This point will be discussed later in this chapter.

[13]Again, see Brigham and Daves, *Intermediate Financial Management*, 7th ed., Chapter 11, for a discussion of this point.

its life, then the project has *nonnormal* cash flows. Projects with nonnormal cash flows can present unique difficulties when they are evaluated by the IRR method, with the most common problem being the existence of **multiple IRRs.**

When one solves Equation 13-2 to find the IRR for a project with nonnormal cash flows,

$$\sum_{t=0}^{n} \frac{CF_t}{(1 + IRR)^t} = 0, \qquad \textbf{(13-2)}$$

it is possible to obtain more than one solution value for IRR, which means that multiple IRRs occur. Notice that Equation 13-2 is a polynomial of degree n, so it has n different roots, or solutions. All except one of the roots are imaginary numbers when investments have normal cash flows (one or more cash outflows followed by cash inflows), so in the normal case, only one value of IRR appears. However, the possibility of multiple real roots, hence multiple IRRs, arises when the project has nonnormal cash flows (negative net cash flows occur during some year after the project has been placed in operation).

To illustrate, suppose a firm is considering the expenditure of $1.6 million to develop a strip mine (Project M). The mine will produce a cash flow of $10 million at the end of Year 1. Then, at the end of Year 2, $10 million must be expended to restore the land to its original condition. Therefore, the project's expected net cash flows are as follows (in millions of dollars):

Expected Net Cash Flows		
Year 0	End of Year 1	End of Year 2
−$1.6	+$10	−$10

These values can be substituted into Equation 13-2 to derive the IRR for the investment:

$$NPV = \frac{-\$1.6 \text{ million}}{(1 + IRR)^0} + \frac{\$10 \text{ million}}{(1 + IRR)^1} + \frac{-\$10 \text{ million}}{(1 + IRR)^2} = 0.$$

When solved, we find that NPV = 0 when IRR = 25% and also when IRR = 400%.[14] Therefore, the IRR of the investment is both 25 and 400 percent. This relationship is

[14]If you attempted to find the IRR of Project M with many financial calculators, you would get an error message. This same message would be given for all projects with multiple IRRs. However, you can still find Project M's IRRs by first calculating NPVs using several different values for k and then plotting the NPV profile. The intersections with the X-axis give a rough idea of the IRR values. Finally, you can use trial-and-error to find the exact values of k that force NPV = 0.

Note, too, that some calculators, including the HP-10B and 17B, can find the IRR. At the error message, key in a guess, store it, and repress the IRR key. With the HP-10B, type 10 STO IRR, and the answer, 25.00, appears. If you enter as your guess a cost of capital less than the one at which NPV in Figure 13-5 is maximized (about 100%), the lower IRR, 25%, is displayed. If you guess a high rate, say, 150, the higher IRR is shown.

The IRR function in spreadsheets also begins its trial-and-error search for a solution with an initial guess. If you omit the initial guess, the *Excel* default starting point is 10 percent. Now suppose the values −1.6, +10, and −10 were in Cells A1:C1. You could use this *Excel* formula: **=IRR(A1:C1,10%),** where 10 percent is the initial guess, and it would produce a result of 25 percent. If you used a guess of 150 percent, you would have this formula: **=IRR(A1:C1,150%),** and it would produce a result of 400 percent.

FIGURE 13-5 NPV Profile for Project M

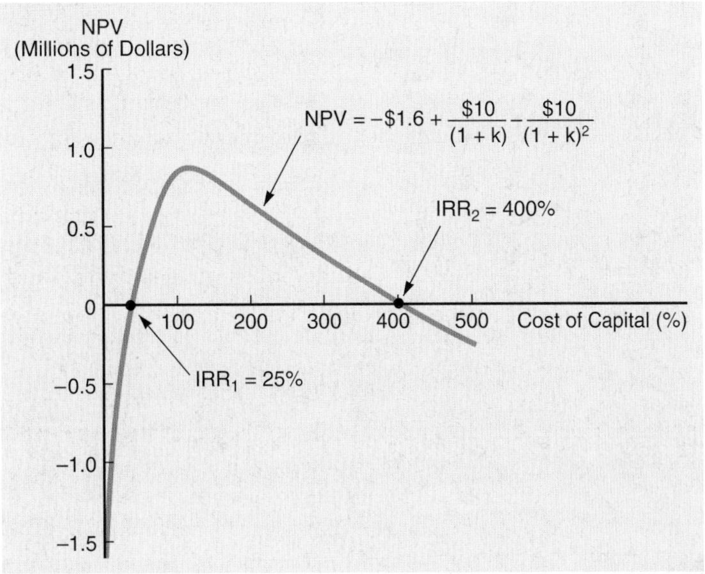

depicted graphically in Figure 13-5.[15] Note that no dilemma would arise if the NPV method were used; we would simply use Equation 13-1, find the NPV, and use this to evaluate the project. If Project M's cost of capital were 10 percent, then its NPV would be −\$0.77 million, and the project should be rejected. If k were between 25 and 400 percent, the NPV would be positive.

One of the authors encountered another example of multiple internal rates of return when a major California bank *borrowed* funds from an insurance company and then used these funds (plus an initial investment of its own) to buy a number of jet engines, which it then leased to a major airline. The bank expected to receive positive net cash flows (lease payments plus tax savings minus interest on the insurance company loan) for a number of years, then several large negative cash flows as it repaid the insurance company loan, and, finally, a large inflow from the sale of the engines when the lease expired.

The bank discovered two IRRs and wondered which was correct. It could not ignore the IRR and use the NPV method since the lease was already on the books, and the bank's senior loan committee, as well as Federal Reserve bank examiners, wanted to know the return on the lease. The bank's solution called for calculating and then using the "modified internal rate of return" as discussed in the next section.

The examples just presented illustrate one problem, multiple IRRs, that can arise when the IRR criterion is used with a project that has nonnormal cash flows. Use of the IRR method on projects having nonnormal cash flows could produce other problems such as no IRR or an IRR that leads to an incorrect accept/reject decision. In all such cases, the NPV criterion could be easily applied, and this method leads to conceptually correct capital budgeting decisions.

---

[15]Does Figure 13-5 suggest that the firm should try to *raise* its cost of capital to about 100 percent in order to maximize the NPV of the project? Certainly not. The firm should seek to *minimize* its cost of capital; this will cause its stock price to be maximized. Actions taken to raise the cost of capital might make this particular project look good, but those actions would be terribly harmful to the firm's more numerous projects with normal cash flows. Only if the firm's cost of capital is high in spite of efforts to keep it down will the illustrative project have a positive NPV.

Self-Test Questions

Describe how NPV profiles are constructed.

What is the crossover rate, and how does it affect the choice between mutually exclusive projects?

What two basic conditions can lead to conflicts between the NPV and IRR methods?

How is the "reinvestment rate" related to conflicts between the NPV and IRR methods?

If a conflict exists, should the capital budgeting decision be made on the basis of the NPV or the IRR ranking? Why?

Explain the difference between normal and nonnormal cash flows.

What is the "multiple IRR problem," and what condition is necessary for it to occur?

Modified Internal Rate of Return (MIRR)

In spite of a strong academic preference for NPV, surveys indicate that many executives prefer IRR over NPV. Apparently, managers find it intuitively more appealing to evaluate investments in terms of percentage rates of return than dollars of NPV. Given this fact, can we devise a percentage evaluator that is better than the regular IRR? The answer is yes—we can modify the IRR and make it a better indicator of relative profitability, hence better for use in capital budgeting. The new measure is called the **modified IRR,** or **MIRR,** and it is defined as follows:

$$\text{PV costs} = \text{PV terminal value}$$

$$\sum_{t=0}^{n} \frac{COF_t}{(1+k)^t} = \frac{\sum_{t=0}^{n} CIF_t(1+k)^{n-t}}{(1+MIRR)^n} \qquad \textbf{(13-2a)}$$

$$\text{PV costs} = \frac{TV}{(1+MIRR)^n}.$$

Here COF refers to cash outflows (negative numbers), or the cost of the project, and CIF refers to cash inflows (positive numbers). The left term is simply the PV of the investment outlays when discounted at the cost of capital, and the numerator of the right term is the compounded value of the inflows, assuming that the cash inflows are reinvested at the cost of capital. The compounded value of the cash inflows is also called the *terminal value,* or *TV.* The discount rate that forces the PV of the TV to equal the PV of the costs is defined as the MIRR.[16]

If the investment costs are all incurred at $t = 0$, and if the first operating inflow occurs at $t = 1$, as is true for the illustrative Projects S and L which we first presented in Figure 13-1, then this equation may be used:

[16]There are several alternative definitions for the MIRR. The differences primarily relate to whether negative cash flows that occur after positive cash flows begin should be compounded and treated as part of the TV or discounted and treated as a cost. A related issue is whether negative and positive flows in a given year should be netted or treated separately. For a complete discussion, see William R. McDaniel, Daniel E. McCarty, and Kenneth A. Jessell, "Discounted Cash Flow with Explicit Reinvestment Rates: Tutorial and Extension," *The Financial Review,* August 1988, 369–385, and David M. Shull, "Interpreting Rates of Return: A Modified Rate of Return Approach," *Financial Practice and Education,* Fall 1993, 67–71

$$\text{Cost} = \frac{TV}{(1 + MIRR)^n} = \frac{\sum_{t=1}^{n} CIF_t(1 + k)^{n-t}}{(1 + MIRR)^n}. \quad \textbf{(13-2b)}$$

We can illustrate the calculation with Project S:

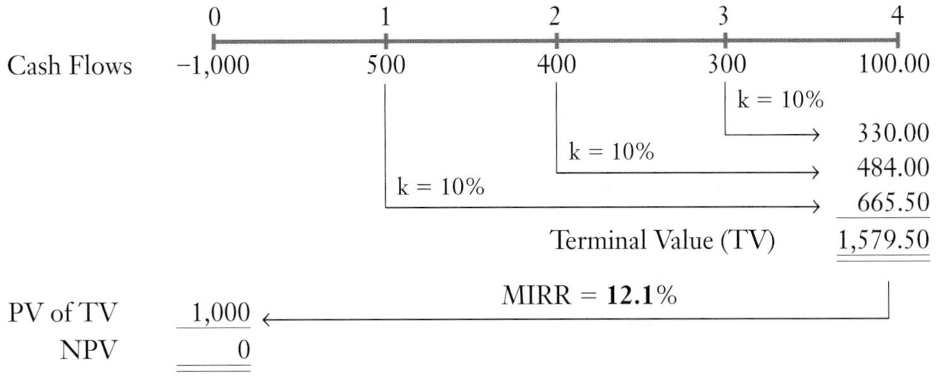

Using the cash flows as set out on the time line, first find the terminal value by compounding each cash inflow at the 10 percent cost of capital. Then enter N = 4, PV = −1000, PMT = 0, FV = 1579.5, and then press the I button to find $MIRR_S = 12.1\%$. Similarly, we find $MIRR_L = 11.3\%$.[17]

The modified IRR has a significant advantage over the regular IRR. MIRR assumes that cash flows from all projects are reinvested at the cost of capital, while the regular IRR assumes that the cash flows from each project are reinvested at the project's own IRR. Since reinvestment at the cost of capital is generally more correct, the modified IRR is a better indicator of a project's true profitability. The MIRR also solves the multiple IRR problem. To illustrate, with k = 10%, Project M (the strip mine project) has MIRR = 5.6% versus its 10 percent cost of capital, so it should be rejected. This is consistent with the decision based on the NPV method, because at k = 10%, NPV = −$0.77 million.

Is MIRR as good as NPV for choosing between mutually exclusive projects? If two projects are of equal size and have the same life, then NPV and MIRR will always lead to the same decision. Thus, for any set of projects like our Projects S and L, if $NPV_S > NPV_L$, then $MIRR_S > MIRR_L$, and the kinds of conflicts we encountered between NPV and the regular IRR will not occur. Also, if the projects are of equal size, but differ in lives, the MIRR will always lead to the same decision as the NPV if the MIRRs are both calculated using as the terminal year the life of the longer project.

[17]With some calculators, including the HP-17B, you could enter the cash inflows in the cash flow register (being sure to enter $CF_0 = 0$), enter I = 10, and then press the NFV key to find $TV_S = 1{,}579.50$. The HP-10B does not have an NFV key, but you can still use the cash flow register to find TV. Enter the cash inflows in the cash flow register (with $CF_0 = 0$), then enter I = 10, then press NPV to find the PV of the inflows, which is 1,078.82. Now, with the regular time value keys, enter N = 4, I = 10, PV = −1078.82, PMT = 0, and press FV to find $TV_S = 1{,}579.50$. Similar procedures can be used with other financial calculators.

Most spreadsheets have a function for finding the MIRR. Refer back to our spreadsheet for Project S, with cash flows of −1,000, 500, 400, 300, and 100 in Cells B4:F4. You could use the *Excel* function wizard to set up the following formula: **=MIRR(B4:F4,10%,10%).** Here the first 10 percent is the cost of capital used for discounting, and the second one is the rate used for compounding, or the reinvestment rate. In our definition of the MIRR, we assume that reinvestment is at the cost of capital, so we enter 10 percent twice. The result is an MIRR of 12.1 percent.

(Just fill in zeros for the shorter project's missing cash flows.) However, if the projects differ in size, then conflicts can still occur. For example, if we were choosing between a large project and a small mutually exclusive one, then we might find $NPV_L > NPV_S$, but $MIRR_S > MIRR_L$.

Our conclusion is that the MIRR is superior to the regular IRR as an indicator of a project's "true" rate of return, or "expected long-term rate of return," but the NPV method is still the best way to choose among competing projects because it provides the best indication of how much each project will add to the value of the firm.

Self-Test Questions

Describe how the modified IRR (MIRR) is calculated.

What is the primary difference between the MIRR and the regular IRR?

What advantages does the MIRR have over the regular IRR for making capital budgeting decisions?

What condition can cause the MIRR and NPV methods to produce conflicting rankings?

Profitability Index

Another method used to evaluate projects is the **profitability index (PI)**:

$$PI = \frac{\text{PV of future cash flows}}{\text{Initial cost}} = \frac{\sum_{t=1}^{n} \frac{CF_t}{(1+k)^t}}{CF_0}. \quad (13\text{-}3)$$

Here CF_t represents the expected future cash flows, and CF_0 represents the initial cost. The PI shows the *relative* profitability of any project, or the present value per dollar of initial cost. The PI for Project S, based on a 10 percent cost of capital, is 1.079:

$$PI_S = \frac{\$1,078.82}{\$1,000} = 1.079.$$

Thus, on a present value basis, Project S is expected to produce \$1.079 for each \$1 of investment. Project L, with a PI of 1.049, should produce \$1.049 for each dollar invested.

A project is acceptable if its PI is greater than 1.0, and the higher the PI, the higher the project's ranking. Therefore, both S and L would be accepted by the PI criterion if they were independent, and S would be ranked ahead of L if they were mutually exclusive.

Mathematically, the NPV, IRR, MIRR, and PI methods will always lead to the same accept/reject decisions for *independent* projects: If a project's NPV is positive, its IRR and MIRR will always exceed k, and its PI will always be greater than 1.0. However, these methods can give conflicting rankings for *mutually exclusive* projects. This point is discussed in more detail in the next section.

Self-Test Question

Explain how the PI is calculated. Why might someone be interested in the PI?

Conclusions on Capital Budgeting Methods

We have discussed six capital budgeting decision methods, comparing the methods with one another, and highlighting their relative strengths and weaknesses. In the process, we probably created the impression that "sophisticated" firms should use only one method in the decision process, NPV. However, virtually all capital budgeting decisions are analyzed by computer, so it is easy to calculate and list all the decision measures: payback and discounted payback, NPV, IRR, modified IRR (MIRR), and profitability index (PI). In making the accept/reject decision, most large, sophisticated firms such as IBM, GE, and Royal Dutch Petroleum calculate and consider all of the measures, because each one provides decision makers with a somewhat different piece of relevant information.

Payback and discounted payback provide an indication of both the *risk* and the *liquidity* of a project—a long payback means (1) that the investment dollars will be locked up for many years, hence the project is relatively illiquid, and (2) that the project's cash flows must be forecasted far out into the future, hence the project is probably quite risky. A good analogy for this is the bond valuation process. An investor should never compare the yields to maturity on two bonds without also considering their terms to maturity, because a bond's riskiness is affected by its maturity.

NPV is important because it gives a direct measure of the dollar benefit of the project to shareholders. Therefore, we regard NPV as the best single measure of *profitability*. IRR also measures profitability, but here it is expressed as a percentage rate of return, which many decision makers prefer. Further, IRR contains information concerning a project's "safety margin." To illustrate, consider the following two projects: Project S (for small) costs $10,000 and is expected to return $16,500 at the end of one year, while Project L (for large) costs $100,000 and has an expected payoff of $115,500 after one year. At a 10 percent cost of capital, both projects have an NPV of $5,000, so by the NPV rule we should be indifferent between them. However, Project S has a much larger margin for error. Even if its realized cash inflow were 39 percent below the $16,500 forecast, the firm would still recover its $10,000 investment. On the other hand, if Project L's inflows fell by only 13 percent from the forecasted $115,500, the firm would not recover its investment. Further, if no inflows were generated at all, the firm would lose only $10,000 with Project S, but $100,000 if it took on Project L.

The NPV provides no information about either of these factors—the "safety margin" inherent in the cash flow forecasts or the amount of capital at risk. However, the IRR does provide "safety margin" information—Project S's IRR is a whopping 65 percent, while Project L's IRR is only 15.5 percent. As a result, the realized return could fall substantially for Project S, and it would still make money. The modified IRR has all the virtues of the IRR, but (1) it incorporates a better reinvestment rate assumption, and (2) it avoids the multiple rate of return problem.

The PI measures profitability relative to the cost of a project—it shows the "bang per buck." Like the IRR, it gives an indication of the project's risk, because a high PI means that cash flows could fall quite a bit and the project would still be profitable.

The different measures provide different types of information to decision makers. Since it is easy to calculate all of them, all should be considered in the decision process. For any specific decision, more weight might be given to one measure than another, but it would be foolish to ignore the information provided by any of the methods.

Just as it would be foolish to ignore these capital budgeting methods, it would also be foolish to make decisions based *solely* on them. One cannot know at Time 0 the exact cost of future capital, or the exact future cash flows. These inputs are simply estimates, and if they turn out to be incorrect, then so will be the calculated NPVs and IRRs. *Thus, quantitative methods provide valuable information, but they should not be used as the sole criteria for accept/reject decisions* in the capital budgeting process. Rather, managers should use quantitative methods in the decision-making process but also consider the likelihood that actual results will differ from the forecasts. Qualitative factors, such as the chances of a tax increase, or a war, or a major product liability suit, should also be considered. *In summary, quantitative methods such as NPV and IRR should be considered as an aid to informed decisions but not as a substitute for sound managerial judgment.*

In this same vein, managers should ask sharp questions about any project that has a large NPV, a high IRR, or a high PI. In a perfectly competitive economy, there would be no positive NPV projects—all companies would have the same opportunities, and competition would quickly eliminate any positive NPV. Therefore, positive NPV projects must be predicated on some imperfection in the marketplace, and the longer the life of the project, the longer that imperfection must last. Therefore, managers should be able to identify the imperfection and explain why it will persist before accepting that a project will really have a positive NPV. Valid explanations might include patents or proprietary technology, which is how pharmaceutical and software firms create positive NPV projects. Hoechst's Allegra® allergy medicine and Microsoft's Windows ME® operating system are examples. Companies can also create positive NPV by being the first entrant into a new market or by creating new products that meet some previously unidentified consumer needs. The Post-it® notes invented by 3M is an example. Similarly, Dell developed procedures for direct sales of microcomputers, and in the process created projects with enormous NPV. Also, companies such as Southwest Airlines have managed to train and motivate their workers better than their competitors, and this has led to positive NPV projects. In all of these cases, the companies developed some source of competitive advantage, and that advantage resulted in positive NPV projects.

This discussion suggests three things: (1) If you can't identify the reason a project has a positive projected NPV, then its actual NPV will probably not be positive. (2) Positive NPV projects don't just happen—they result from hard work to develop some competitive advantage. At the risk of oversimplification, the primary job of a manager is to find and develop areas of competitive advantage. (3) Some competitive advantages last longer than others, with their durability depending on competitors' ability to replicate them. Patents, the control of scarce resources, or large size in an industry where strong economies of scale exist can keep competitors at bay. However, it is relatively easy to replicate nonpatentable features on products. The bottom line is that managers should strive to develop nonreplicatible sources of competitive advantage, and if such an advantage cannot be demonstrated, then you should question projects with high NPV, especially if they have long lives.

Self-Test Questions

Describe the advantages and disadvantages of the six capital budgeting methods discussed in this chapter.

Should capital budgeting decisions be made solely on the basis of a project's NPV?

What are some possible reasons that a project might have a large NPV?

Business Practices

The findings of a 1993 survey of the capital budgeting methods used by the *Fortune* 500 industrial companies are shown below:[18]

[18]Harold Bierman, "Capital Budgeting in 1993: A Survey," *Financial Management*, Autumn 1993, 24.

1. Every responding firm used some type of DCF method. In 1955, a similar study reported that only 4 percent of large companies used a DCF method. Thus, large firms' usage of DCF methodology increased dramatically in the last half of the 20th century.
2. The payback period was used by 84 percent of Bierman's surveyed companies. However, no company used it as the primary method, and most companies gave the greatest weight to a DCF method. In 1955, surveys similar to Bierman's found that payback was the most important method.
3. In 1993, 99 percent of the *Fortune* 500 companies uses IRR, while 85 percent used NPV. Thus, most firms actually used both methods.
4. Ninety-three percent of Bierman's companies calculated a weighted average cost of capital as part of their capital budgeting process. A few companies apparently used the same WACC for all projects, but 73 percent adjusted the corporate WACC to account for project risk, and 23 percent made adjustments to reflect divisional risk.
5. An examination of surveys done by other authors led Bierman to conclude that there has been a strong trend toward the acceptance of academic recommendations, at least by large companies.

A second 1993 study, conducted by Joe Walker, Richard Burns, and Chad Denson (WBD), focused on small companies.[19] WBD began by noting the same trend toward the use of DCF that Bierman cited, but they reported that only 21 percent of small companies used DCF versus 100 percent for Bierman's large companies. WBD also noted that within their sample, the smaller the firm, the smaller the likelihood that DCF would be used. The focal point of the WBD study was *why* small companies use DCF so much less frequently than large firms. The three most frequently cited reasons, according to the survey, were (1) small firms' preoccupation with liquidity, which is best indicated by payback, (2) a lack of familiarity with DCF methods, and (3) a belief that small project sizes make DCF not worth the effort.

The general conclusion one can reach from these studies is that large firms should and do use the procedures we recommend, and that managers of small firms, especially managers with aspirations for future growth, should at least understand DCF procedures well enough to make rational decisions about using or not using them. Moreover, as computer technology makes it easier and less expensive for small firms to use DCF methods, and as more and more of their competitors begin using these methods, survival will necessitate increased DCF usage.

Self-Test Questions

What were Bierman's findings from his survey of capital budgeting methods used by the *Fortune* 500 companies?

How did WBD's findings differ from those of Bierman?

What general considerations can be reached from these studies?

The Post-Audit

An important aspect of the capital budgeting process is the **post-audit,** which involves (1) comparing actual results with those predicted by the project's sponsors and (2) explaining why any differences occurred. For example, many firms require that the operating divisions send a monthly report for the first six months after a project goes into operation, and a quarterly report thereafter, until the project's results are up to

[19] Joe Walker, Richard Burns, and Chad Denson, "Why Small Manufacturing Firms Shun DCF," *Journal of Small Business Finance*, 1993, 233–249.

Techniques Firms Use to Evaluate Corporate Projects

Professors John Graham and Campbell Harvey of Duke University recently surveyed 392 chief financial officers (CFOs) about their companies' corporate practices. Of those firms, 26 percent had sales less than $100 million, 32 percent had sales between $100 million and $1 billion, and 42 percent exceeded $1 billion.

The CFOs were asked to indicate what approaches they used to estimate the cost of equity: 73.5 percent used the Capital Asset Pricing Model (CAPM), 34.3 percent used a multi-beta version of the CAPM, and 15.7 percent used the dividend discount model. The CFOs also used a variety of risk adjustment techniques, but most still choose to used a single hurdle rate to evaluate all corporate projects.

The CFOs were also asked about the capital budgeting techniques they used. Most used NPV (74.9 percent) and IRR (75.7 percent) to evaluate projects, but many (56.7 percent) also used the payback approach. These results confirm that most firms use more than one approach to evaluate projects.

The survey also found important differences between the practices of small firms (less than $1 billion in sales) and large firms (more than $1 billion in sales). Consistent with the earlier studies by Bierman and by Walker, Burns, and Denson (WBD) described in the text, Graham and Harvey found that smaller firms are more likely to rely on the payback approach, while larger firms are more likely to rely on NPV and/or IRR.

Source: John R. Graham and Campbell R. Harvey, "The Theory and Practice of Corporate Finance: Evidence from the Field," *Journal of Financial Economics*, Vol. 60, no. 1.

expectations. From then on, reports on the operation are reviewed on a regular basis like those of other operations.

The post-audit has three main purposes:

1. **Improve forecasts.** When decision makers are forced to compare their projections to actual outcomes, there is a tendency for estimates to improve. Conscious or unconscious biases are observed and eliminated; new forecasting methods are sought as the need for them becomes apparent; and people simply tend to do everything better, including forecasting, if they know that their actions are being monitored.
2. **Improve operations.** Businesses are run by people, and people can perform at higher or lower levels of efficiency. When a divisional team has made a forecast about an investment, its members are, in a sense, putting their reputations on the line. If costs are above predicted levels, sales below expectations, and so on, executives in production, sales, and other areas will strive to improve operations and to bring results into line with forecasts. In a discussion related to this point, one executive made this statement: "You academicians worry only about making good decisions. In business, we also worry about making decisions good."
3. **Identify termination opportunities.** Although the decision to undertake a project may be the correct one based on information at hand, things don't always turn out as expected. If initial operating results indicate that a project is not likely to achieve its expected profitability, it may be best for the firm to terminate rather than continue the project. Furthermore, most projects, at some point in their lives, lose their economic viability and should be terminated. Both the post-audit and a continuing review of ongoing operations help identify the optimal point for the termination of a project.

The post-audit is not a simple process, and a number of factors can cause complications. First, we must recognize that each element of the cash flow forecast is subject to uncertainty, so a percentage of all projects undertaken by any reasonably aggressive firm will necessarily go awry. This fact must be considered when appraising the performances of the operating executives who submit capital expenditure requests. Second, projects sometimes fail to meet expectations for reasons beyond the control of the operating executives and for reasons that no one could realistically be expected to anticipate. For example, the 1999 runup in oil prices adversely affected many projects. Third, it is often difficult to separate the operating results of one investment from those of a larger system. Although some projects stand alone and permit ready identification of costs and revenues, the cost savings that result from a new computer, for example, may be very hard to measure. Fourth, it is often hard to hand out blame or praise because the executives who were responsible for launching a given investment have moved on by the time the results are known.

The results of post-audits often conclude that (1) the actual NPVs of most cost reduction projects exceed their expected NPVs by a slight amount, (2) expansion projects generally fall short of their expected NPVs by a slight amount, and (3) new product and new market projects often fall short by relatively large amounts. Thus, biases seem to exist, and companies that understand them can build in corrections and thus design better capital budgeting programs. Our observations of businesses and governmental units suggest that the best-run and most successful organizations put great emphasis on post-audits. Accordingly, we regard the post-audit as being one of the most important elements in a good capital budgeting system.

Self-Test Questions

What is done in the post-audit?

Identify several purposes of the post-audit.

What are some factors that can cause complications in the post-audit?

Using Capital Budgeting Techniques in Other Contexts

The techniques developed in this chapter can help managers make a number of different types of decisions. One example is the use of these techniques when evaluating corporate mergers. Companies frequently decide to acquire other firms to obtain low-cost production facilities, to increase capacity, or to expand into new markets, and the analysis related to such mergers is conceptually similar to that related to regular capital budgeting. Thus, when AT&T decided to go into the cellular telephone business, it had the choice of building facilities from the ground up or acquiring an existing business. AT&T chose to acquire McCaw Cellular. In the analysis related to the merger, AT&T's managers used the techniques employed in regular capital budgeting analysis.

Managers also use capital budgeting techniques when deciding whether to downsize personnel or to sell off particular assets or divisions. Like capital budgeting, such an analysis requires an assessment of how the action will affect the firm's cash flows. In a downsizing, companies typically spend money (that is, invest) in severance payments to employees who are no longer needed, but the companies then receive benefits in the form of lower future wage costs. When assets are sold, the pattern of cash flows is reversed from those in a typical capital budgeting decision—positive cash flows are realized at the outset, but the firm is sacrificing future cash flows that it would have received if it had continued to use the asset. So, when deciding whether it makes sense to shed assets, managers compare the cash received with the present value of the lost outflows. If the net present value is positive, the asset sale would increase shareholder value.

Most decisions should be based on whether they contribute to shareholder value, and that, in turn, can be determined by estimating the net present value of a set of cash flows. However, as you will see in the next chapter, the hardest part is coming up with reasonable estimates of those cash flows.

Self-Test Question

Give some examples of other decisions that can be analyzed with the capital budgeting techniques developed in this chapter.

Special Applications of Cash Flow Evaluation

As we noted earlier, misapplication of the NPV method can lead to errors when two mutually exclusive projects have unequal lives. There are also situations in which an asset should not be operated for its full life. The following sections explain how to evaluate cash flows in these situations.

Comparing Projects with Unequal Lives

Note that a replacement decision involves comparing two mutually exclusive projects: retaining the old asset versus buying a new one. When choosing between two mutually exclusive alternatives with significantly different lives, an adjustment is necessary. We now discuss two procedures—(1) the replacement chain method and (2) the equivalent annual annuity method—to illustrate the problem and to show how to deal with it.

Suppose a company is planning to modernize its production facilities, and it is considering either a conveyor system (Project C) or some forklift trucks (Project F) for moving materials. Figure 13-6 shows both the expected net cash flows and the NPVs for these two mutually exclusive alternatives. We see that Project C, when discounted at the firm's 11.5 percent cost of capital, has the higher NPV and thus appears to be the better project.

Although the NPV shown in Figure 13-6 suggests that Project C should be selected, this analysis is incomplete, and the decision to choose Project C is actually incorrect. If we choose Project F, we will have an opportunity to make a similar investment in three years, and if cost and revenue conditions continue at the Figure 13-6 levels, this second investment will also be profitable. However, if we choose Project C,

FIGURE 13-6 Expected Net Cash Flows for Projects C and F

Project C:

0 (11.5%)	1	2	3	4	5	6
−40,000	8,000	14,000	13,000	12,000	11,000	10,000

NPV_C at 11.5% = $7,165; IRR = 17.5%.

Project F:

0 (11.5%)	1	2	3
−20,000	7,000	13,000	12,000

NPV_F at 11.5% = $5,391; IRR = 25.2%.

we cannot make this second investment. To make a proper comparison of Projects C and F, we could apply the **replacement chain (common life) approach;** that is, we could find the NPV of Project F over a six-year period, and then compare this extended NPV with the NPV of Project C over the same six years.[20]

The NPV for Project C as calculated in Figure 13-6 is already over the six-year common life. For Project F, however, we must add in a second project to extend the overall life of the combined projects to six years. Here we assume (1) that Project F's cost and annual cash inflows will not change if the project is repeated in three years and (2) that the cost of capital will remain at 11.5 percent:

0 (11.5%)	1	2	3	4	5	6
−20,000	7,000	13,000	12,000	7,000	13,000	12,000
			−20,000			
			−8,000			

NPV at 11.5% = \$9,281; IRR = 25.2%.

The NPV of this extended Project F is \$9,281, and its IRR is 25.2 percent. (The IRR of two Project Fs is the same as the IRR for one Project F.) Since the \$9,281 extended NPV of Project F over the six-year common life is greater than the \$7,165 NPV of Project C, Project F should be selected.[21]

When should we worry about unequal life analysis? The unequal life issue (1) does not arise for independent projects, but (2) it can arise if mutually exclusive projects with significantly different lives are being compared. However, even for mutually exclusive projects, it is not always appropriate to extend the analysis to a common life. This should only be done if there is a high probability that the projects will actually be repeated at the end of their initial lives.

We should note several potentially serious weaknesses inherent in this type of analysis: (1) If inflation is expected, then replacement equipment will have a higher price. Moreover, both sales prices and operating costs will probably change. Thus, the static conditions built into the analysis would be invalid. (2) Replacements that occur down the road would probably employ new technology, which in turn might change the cash flows. (3) It is difficult enough to estimate the lives of most projects, so estimating the lives of a series of projects is often just a speculation.

In view of these problems, no experienced financial analyst would be too concerned about comparing mutually exclusive projects with lives of, say, eight years and ten years. Given all the uncertainties in the estimation process, such projects would, for all practical purposes, be assumed to have the same life. Still, it is important to recognize that a problem exists if mutually exclusive projects have substantially different

[20]The equivalent annual annuity (EAA) approach is an alternative to the replacement chain approach. Given the widespread use of spreadsheets, the EAA approach is used infrequently in practice. However, the file ***Ch 13 Tool Kit.xls*** on the textbook's CD-ROM explains and illustrates the EAA approach.

[21]Alternatively, we could recognize that the value of the cash flow stream of two consecutive Project Fs can be summarized by two NPVs: one at Year 0 representing the value of the initial project, and one at Year 3 representing the value of the replication project:

0 (11.5%)	1	2	3	4	5	6
5,391			5,391			

NPV = \$9,281.

Ignoring rounding differences, the present value of these two cash flows, when discounted at 11.5 percent, is again \$9,281.

lives. When we encounter such problems in practice, we use a computer spreadsheet and build expected inflation and/or possible efficiency gains directly into the cash flow estimates, and then use the replacement chain approach. The cash flow estimation is a bit more complicated, but the concepts involved are exactly the same as in our example.

Economic Life versus Physical Life

Projects are normally analyzed under the assumption that the firm will operate the asset over its full physical life. However, this may not be the best course of action—it may be best to terminate a project before the end of its potential life, and this possibility can materially affect the project's estimated profitability.[22] The situation in Table 13-1 can be used to illustrate this concept and its effects on capital budgeting. The salvage values listed in the third column are after taxes, and they have been estimated for each year of Project A's life.

Using a 10 percent cost of capital, the expected NPV based on three years of operating cash flows and the zero abandonment (salvage) value is −$14.12:

0 (10%)	1	2	3
($4,800)	$2,000	$2,000	$1,750
			0

$$\text{NPV} = -\$4{,}800 + \$2{,}000/(1.10)^1 + \$2{,}000/(1.10)^2 + \$1{,}750/(1.10)^3$$
$$= -\$14.12.$$

Thus, Project A would not be accepted if we assume that it will be operated over its full three-year life. However, what would its NPV be if the project were terminated after two years? In this case, we would receive operating cash flows in Years 1 and 2, plus the salvage value at the end of Year 2, and the project's NPV would be $34.71:

0 (10%)	1	2
($4,800)	$2,000	$2,000
		1,650

$$\text{NPV} = -\$4{,}800 + \$2{,}000/(1.10)^1 + \$2{,}000/(1.10)^2 + \$1{,}650/(1.10)^2$$
$$= \$34.71.$$

Thus, Project A would be profitable if we operate it for two years and then dispose of it. To complete the analysis, note that if the project were terminated after one year, its NPV would be −$254.55. Thus, the optimal life for this project is two years.

[22]The classic work on this subject is Alexander A. Robichek and James C. Van Horne, "Abandonment Value and Capital Budgeting," *Journal of Finance*, December 1967, 577–589.

TABLE 13-1 Project A: Investment, Operating, and Salvage Cash Flows

Year (t)	Initial (Year 0) Investment and After-tax Operating Cash Flows	Net Salvage Value at End of Year t
0	($4,800)	$4,800
1	2,000	3,000
2	2,000	1,650
3	1,750	0

This type of analysis can be used to determine a project's **economic life,** which is the life that maximizes the NPV and thus maximizes shareholder wealth. For Project A, the economic life is two years versus the three-year **physical,** or **engineering, life.** Note that this analysis was based on the expected cash flows and the expected salvage values, and it should always be conducted as a part of the capital budgeting evaluation if salvage values are relatively high.

Self-Test Questions

Briefly describe the replacement chain (common life) approach.

Define the economic life of a project (as opposed to its physical life).

Should projects be viewed as having only one life, or should alternative lives be considered in the capital budgeting process?

The Optimal Capital Budget

The **optimal capital budget** is the set of projects that maximizes the value of the firm. Finance theory states that all projects with positive NPVs should be accepted, and the optimal capital budget consists of these positive NPV projects. However, two complications arise in practice: (1) an increasing marginal cost of capital and (2) capital rationing.

An Increasing Marginal Cost of Capital

The cost of capital may depend on the size of the capital budget. As we discussed in Chapter 11, the flotation costs associated with issuing new equity or public debt can be quite high. This means that the cost of capital jumps upward after a company invests all of its internally generated cash and must sell new common stock. In addition, investors often perceive extremely large capital investments to be riskier, which may also drive up the cost of capital as the size of the capital budget increases. As a result, a project might have a positive NPV if it is part of a "normal size" capital budget, but the same project might have a negative NPV if it is part of an unusually large capital budget. Fortunately, this problem occurs very rarely for most firms, and it is unusual for an established firm to require new outside equity. Still, the Web/CD Extension for Chapter 13 on the textbook's web site and CD-ROM contains a more detailed discussion of this problem and shows how to deal with the existence of an increasing marginal cost of capital.

Capital Rationing

Armbrister Pyrotechnics, a manufacturer of fireworks and lasers for light shows, has identified 40 potential independent projects, with 15 having a positive NPV based on the firm's 12 percent cost of capital. The total cost of implementing these 15 projects is $75 million. Based on finance theory, the optimal capital budget is $75 million, and Armbrister should accept the 15 projects with positive NPVs. However, Armbrister's management has imposed a limit of $50 million for capital expenditures during the upcoming year. Due to this restriction, the company must forego a number of value-adding projects. This is an example of **capital rationing,** defined as a situation in which a firm limits its capital expenditures to less than the amount required to fund the optimal capital budget. Despite being at odds with finance theory, this practice is quite common.

Why would any company forego value-adding projects? Here are some potential explanations, along with some suggestions for better ways to handle these situations:

1. **Reluctance to issue new stock.** Many firms are extremely reluctant to issue new stock, so all of their capital expenditures must be funded out of debt and internally generated cash. Also, most firms try to stay near their target capital structure, and, combined with the limit on equity, this limits the amount of debt that can be added during any one year. The result can be a serious constraint on the amount of funds available for investment in new projects.

   This reluctance to issue new stock could be based on some sound reasons: (a) flotation costs can be very expensive; (b) investors might perceive new stock offerings as a signal that the company's equity is overvalued; and (c) the company might have to reveal sensitive strategic information to investors, thereby reducing some of its competitive advantages. To avoid these costs, many companies simply limit their capital expenditures.

   However, rather than placing a somewhat artificial limit on capital expenditures, a company might be better off explicitly incorporating the costs of raising external capital into its cost of capital. If there still are positive NPV projects even using this higher cost of capital, then the company should go ahead and raise external equity and accept the projects. See the Web/CD Extension for this chapter on the textbook's CD-ROM and web site for more details concerning an increasing marginal cost of capital.
2. **Constraints on nonmonetary resources.** Sometimes a firm simply does not have the necessary managerial, marketing, or engineering talent to immediately accept all positive NPV projects. In other words, the potential projects are not really independent, because the firm cannot accept them all. To avoid potential problems due to spreading existing talent too thinly, many firms simply limit the capital budget to a size that can be accommodated by their current personnel.

   A better solution might be to employ a technique called **linear programming.** Each potential project has an expected NPV, and each potential project requires a certain level of support by different types of employees. A linear program can identify the set of projects that maximizes NPV, subject to the constraint that the total amount of support required for these projects does not exceed the available resources.[23]
3. **Controlling estimation bias.** Many managers become overly optimistic when estimating the cash flows for a project. Some firms try to control this estimation bias by requiring managers to use an unrealistically high cost of capital. Others try to control the bias by limiting the size of the capital budget. Neither solution is generally effective since managers quickly learn the rules of the game and then increase their own estimates of project cash flows, which might have been biased upward to begin with.

   A better solution is to implement a post-audit program and to link the accuracy of forecasts to the compensation of the managers who initiated the projects.

Self-Test Questions

What factors can lead to an increasing marginal cost of capital? How might this affect capital budgeting?

What is capital rationing?

What are three explanations for capital rationing? How might firms handle these situations?

---

[23]For further information on mathematical programming solutions to capital rationing, and for a review and analysis of the literature on this issue, see H. Martin Weingarten, "Capital Rationing: n Authors in Search of a Plot," *Journal of Finance*, December 1977, 1403–1431; and Stephen P. Bradley and Sherwood C. Frey, Jr., "Equivalent Mathematical Programming Models of Pure Capital Rationing," *Journal of Financial and Quantitative Analysis*, June 1978, 345–361.

Summary

This chapter has described six techniques (payback, discounted payback, NPV, IRR, MIRR, and PI) that are used in capital budgeting analysis. Each approach provides a different piece of information, so in this age of computers, managers often look at all of them when evaluating projects. However, NPV is the best single measure, and its use has been increasing over time.

We simplified things in this chapter. You were given a set of cash flows and a cost of capital, and you were then asked to evaluate the projects. The hard part, however, is estimating a project's cash flows and its risk, which affects its cost of capital. We will address these issues in the next chapter. Before proceeding, though, the key concepts covered in this chapter are listed below:

- **Capital budgeting** is the process of analyzing potential fixed asset investments. Capital budgeting decisions are probably the most important ones financial managers must make.
- The **payback period** is defined as the number of years required to recover a project's cost. The regular payback method ignores cash flows beyond the payback period, and it does not consider the time value of money. The payback does, however, provide an indication of a project's risk and liquidity, because it shows how long the invested capital will be "at risk."
- The **discounted payback method** is similar to the regular payback method except that it discounts cash flows at the project's cost of capital. It considers the time value of money, but it ignores cash flows beyond the payback period.
- The **net present value (NPV) method** discounts all cash flows at the project's cost of capital and then sums those cash flows. The project is accepted if the NPV is positive.
- The **internal rate of return (IRR)** is defined as the discount rate that forces a project's NPV to equal zero. The project is accepted if the IRR is greater than the cost of capital.
- The NPV and IRR methods make the same accept/reject decisions for **independent projects,** but if projects are **mutually exclusive,** then ranking conflicts can arise. If conflicts arise, the NPV method should be used. The NPV and IRR methods are both superior to the payback, but NPV is superior to IRR.
- The NPV method assumes that cash flows will be reinvested at the firm's cost of capital, while the IRR method assumes reinvestment at the project's IRR. **Reinvestment at the cost of capital is generally a better assumption** because it is closer to reality.
- The **modified IRR (MIRR) method** corrects some of the problems with the regular IRR. MIRR involves finding the **terminal value (TV)** of the cash inflows, compounded at the firm's cost of capital, and then determining the discount rate that forces the present value of the TV to equal the present value of the outflows.
- The **profitability index (PI)** shows the dollars of present value divided by the initial cost, so it measures relative profitability.
- Sophisticated managers consider all of the project evaluation measures because each measure provides a useful piece of information.
- The **post-audit** is a key element of capital budgeting. By comparing actual results with predicted results and then determining why differences occurred, decision makers can improve both their operations and their forecasts of projects' outcomes.
- Small firms tend to use the payback method rather than a discounted cash flow method. This may be rational, because (1) the **cost** of conducting a DCF analysis

may outweigh the benefits for the project being considered, (2) **the firm's cost of capital cannot be estimated accurately,** or (3) the small-business owner may be considering **nonmonetary goals.**

- If mutually exclusive projects have **unequal lives,** it may be necessary to adjust the analysis to put the projects on an equal life basis. This can be done using the **replacement chain (common life) approach.**
- A project's true value may be greater than the NPV based on its **physical life** if it can be **terminated** at the end of its **economic life.**
- Flotation costs and increased riskiness associated with unusually large expansion programs can cause the **marginal cost of capital** to rise as the size of the capital budget increases.
- **Capital rationing** occurs when management places a constraint on the size of the firm's capital budget during a particular period.

Although this chapter has presented the basic elements of the capital budgeting process, there are many other aspects of this crucial topic. Some of the more important ones are discussed in the following chapter.

Questions

13–1 Define each of the following terms:

a. The capital budget; capital budgeting; strategic business plan
b. Regular payback period; discounted payback period
c. Independent projects; mutually exclusive projects
d. DCF techniques; net present value (NPV) method
e. Internal rate of return (IRR) method
f. Modified internal rate of return (MIRR) method; profitability index
g. NPV profile; crossover rate
h. Nonnormal cash flow projects; normal cash flow projects; multiple IRRs
i. Hurdle rate
j. Reinvestment rate assumption
k. Post-audit
l. Replacement chain
m. Economic life
n. Capital rationing

13–2 How is a project classification scheme (for example, replacement, expansion into new markets, and so forth) used in the capital budgeting process?

13–3 Explain why the NPV of a relatively long-term project, defined as one for which a high percentage of its cash flows are expected in the distant future, is more sensitive to changes in the cost of capital than is the NPV of a short-term project.

13–4 Explain why, if two mutually exclusive projects are being compared, the short-term project might have the higher ranking under the NPV criterion if the cost of capital is high, but the long-term project might be deemed better if the cost of capital is low. Would changes in the cost of capital ever cause a change in the IRR ranking of two such projects?

13–5 In what sense is a reinvestment rate assumption embodied in the NPV, IRR, and MIRR methods? What is the assumed reinvestment rate of each method?

13–6 "If a firm has no mutually exclusive projects, only independent ones, and it also has both a constant cost of capital and projects with normal cash flows in the sense that each project has one or more outflows followed by a stream of inflows, then the NPV and IRR methods will always lead to identical capital budgeting decisions." Discuss this statement. What does it imply about using the IRR method in lieu of the NPV method? If each of the assumptions made in the question were changed (one by one), how would these changes affect your answer?

13–7 Are there conditions under which a firm might be better off if it were to choose a machine with a rapid payback rather than one with a larger NPV?

13–8 A firm has $100 million available for capital expenditures. It is considering investing in one of two projects; each has a cost of $100 million. Project A has an IRR of 20 percent and an NPV of $9 million. It will be terminated at the end of 1 year at a profit of $20 million, resulting in an immediate increase in earnings per share (EPS). Project B, which cannot be postponed, has an IRR of 30 percent and an NPV of $50 million. However, the firm's short-run EPS will be reduced if it accepts Project B, because no revenues will be generated for several years.

a. Should the short-run effects on EPS influence the choice between the two projects?

b. How might situations like the one described here influence a firm's decision to use payback as a part of the capital budgeting process?

13–9 Suppose a firm is considering two mutually exclusive projects. One has a life of 6 years and the other a life of 10 years. Would the failure to employ some type of replacement chain analysis bias an NPV analysis against one of the projects? Explain.

Self-Test Problem (Solution Appears in Appendix A)

ST–1
PROJECT ANALYSIS

You are a financial analyst for the Hittle Company. The director of capital budgeting has asked you to analyze two proposed capital investments, Projects X and Y. Each project has a cost of $10,000, and the cost of capital for each project is 12 percent. The projects' expected net cash flows are as follows:

	Expected Net Cash Flows	
Year	Project X	Project Y
0	($10,000)	($10,000)
1	6,500	3,500
2	3,000	3,500
3	3,000	3,500
4	1,000	3,500

a. Calculate each project's payback period, net present value (NPV), internal rate of return (IRR), and modified internal rate of return (MIRR).

b. Which project or projects should be accepted if they are independent?

c. Which project should be accepted if they are mutually exclusive?

d. How might a change in the cost of capital produce a conflict between the NPV and IRR rankings of these two projects? Would this conflict exist if k were 5%? (Hint: Plot the NPV profiles.)

e. Why does the conflict exist?

Problems

13–1
PAYBACK PERIOD

Project K has a cost of $52,125, its expected net cash inflows are $12,000 per year for 8 years, and its cost of capital is 12 percent. What is the project's payback period (to the closest year)? (Hint: Begin by constructing a time line.)

13–2
NPV

Refer to Problem 13-1. What is the project's NPV?

13–3
IRR

Refer to Problem 13-1. What is the project's IRR?

13–4
DISCOUNTED PAYBACK PERIOD

Refer to Problem 13-1. What is the project's discounted payback period?

13–5
MIRR

Refer to Problem 13-1. What is the project's MIRR?

13–6 *NPV*

Your division is considering two investment projects, each of which requires an up-front expenditure of $15 million. You estimate that the investments will produce the following net cash flows:

Year	Project A	Project B
1	$ 5,000,000	$20,000,000
2	10,000,000	10,000,000
3	20,000,000	6,000,000

What are the two projects' net present values, assuming the cost of capital is 10 percent? 5 percent? 15 percent?

13–7 *NPV; FINANCIAL CALCULATOR REQUIRED*

Northwest Utility Corporation has a cost of capital of 11.5 percent, and it has a project with the following net cash flows:

t	Net Cash Flow
0	−$200
1	235
2	−65
3	300

What is the project's NPV?

13–8 *NPVs, IRRs, AND MIRRs FOR INDEPENDENT PROJECTS*

Edelman Engineering is considering including two pieces of equipment, a truck and an overhead pulley system, in this year's capital budget. The projects are independent. The cash outlay for the truck is $17,100, and that for the pulley system is $22,430. The firm's cost of capital is 14 percent. After-tax cash flows, including depreciation, are as follows:

Year	Truck	Pulley
1	$5,100	$7,500
2	5,100	7,500
3	5,100	7,500
4	5,100	7,500
5	5,100	7,500

Calculate the IRR, the NPV, and the MIRR for each project, and indicate the correct accept/reject decision for each.

13–9 *NPVs AND IRRs FOR MUTUALLY EXCLUSIVE PROJECTS*

B. Davis Industries must choose between a gas-powered and an electric-powered forklift truck for moving materials in its factory. Since both forklifts perform the same function, the firm will choose only one. (They are mutually exclusive investments.) The electric-powered truck will cost more, but it will be less expensive to operate; it will cost $22,000, whereas the gas-powered truck will cost $17,500. The cost of capital that applies to both investments is 12 percent. The life for both types of truck is estimated to be 6 years, during which time the net cash flows for the electric-powered truck will be $6,290 per year and those for the gas-powered truck will be $5,000 per year. Annual net cash flows include depreciation expenses. Calculate the NPV and IRR for each type of truck, and decide which to recommend.

13–10 *CAPITAL BUDGETING METHODS*

Project S has a cost of $10,000 and is expected to produce benefits (cash flows) of $3,000 per year for 5 years. Project L costs $25,000 and is expected to produce cash flows of $7,400 per year for 5 years. Calculate the two projects' NPVs, IRRs, MIRRs, and PIs, assuming a cost of capital of 12 percent. Which project would be selected, assuming they are mutually exclusive, using each ranking method? Which should actually be selected?

13–11 *PRESENT VALUE OF COSTS*

The Costa Rican Coffee Company is evaluating the within-plant distribution system for its new roasting, grinding, and packing plant. The two alternatives are (1) a conveyor system with a high initial cost but low annual operating costs and (2) several forklift trucks, which cost less but have considerably higher operating costs. The decision to construct the plant has already been made, and the choice here will have no effect on the overall revenues of the project. The cost of capital for the plant is 9 percent, and the projects' expected net costs are listed below:

	Expected Net Cash Costs	
Year	Conveyor	Forklift
0	($300,000)	($120,000)
1	(66,000)	(96,000)
2	(66,000)	(96,000)
3	(66,000)	(96,000)
4	(66,000)	(96,000)
5	(66,000)	(96,000)

a. What is the IRR of each alternative?
b. What is the present value of costs of each alternative? Which method should be chosen?

13–12 *MIRR AND NPV* Your company is considering two mutually exclusive projects, X and Y, whose costs and cash flows are shown below:

Year	X	Y
0	($1,000)	($1,000)
1	100	1,000
2	300	100
3	400	50
4	700	50

The projects are equally risky, and their cost of capital is 12 percent. You must make a recommendation, and you must base it on the modified IRR (MIRR). What is the MIRR of the better project?

13–13 *NPV AND IRR* A company is analyzing two mutually exclusive projects, S and L, whose cash flows are shown below:

	0	1	2	3	4
S	−1,000	900	250	10	10
L	−1,000	0	250	400	800

The company's cost of capital is 10 percent, and it can get an unlimited amount of capital at that cost. What is the *regular IRR* (not MIRR) of the *better* project? (Hint: Note that the better project may or may not be the one with the higher IRR.)

13–14 *MIRR* Project X has a cost of $1,000 at t = 0, and it is expected to produce a uniform cash flow stream for 10 years, i.e., the CFs are the same in Years 1 through 10, and it has a regular IRR of 12 percent. The cost of capital for the project is 10 percent. What is the project's modified IRR (MIRR)?

13–15 *NPV AND IRR ANALYSIS* After discovering a new gold vein in the Colorado mountains, CTC Mining Corporation must decide whether to mine the deposit. The most cost-effective method of mining gold is sulfuric acid extraction, a process that results in environmental damage. To go ahead with the extraction, CTC must spend $900,000 for new mining equipment and pay $165,000 for its installation. The gold mined will net the firm an estimated $350,000 each year over the 5-year life of the vein. CTC's cost of capital is 14 percent. For the purposes of this problem, assume that the cash inflows occur at the end of the year.
a. What is the NPV and IRR of this project?
b. Should this project be undertaken, ignoring environmental concerns?

c. How should environmental effects be considered when evaluating this, or any other, project? How might these effects change your decision in Part b?

13–16
NPV AND IRR

John's Publishing Company, a new service that writes term papers for college students, provides 10-page term papers from a list of more than 500 topics. Each paper will cost $7.50 and is written by a graduate in the topic area. John's will pay $20,000 for the rights to all of the manuscripts. In addition, each author will receive $0.50 in royalties for every paper sold. Marketing expenses are estimated to be a total of $20,000 divided equally between Years 1 and 2, and John's cost of capital is 11 percent. Sales are expected as follows:

Year	Volume
1	10,000
2	7,000
3	3,000

a. What is the payback period for this investment? Its NPV? Its IRR?
b. What are the ethical implications of this investment?

13–17
NPV AND IRR ANALYSIS

Sharon Evans, who graduated from the local university 3 years ago with a degree in marketing, is manager of Ann Naylor's store in the Southwest Mall. Sharon's store has 5 years remaining on its lease. Rent is $2,000 per month, 60 payments remain, and the next payment is due in 1 month. The mall's owner plans to sell the property in a year and wants rents at that time to be high so the property will appear more valuable. Therefore, Sharon has been offered a "great deal" (owner's words) on a new 5-year lease. The new lease calls for zero rent for 9 months, then payments of $2,600 per month for the next 51 months. The lease cannot be broken, and Ann Naylor Corporation's cost of capital is 12 percent (or 1 percent per month). Sharon must make a decision. A good one could help her career and move her up in management, but a bad one could hurt her prospects for promotion.

a. Should Sharon accept the new lease? (Hint: Be sure to use 1 percent per month.)
b. Suppose Sharon decided to bargain with the mall's owner over the new lease payment. What new lease payment would make Sharon indifferent between the new and the old leases? (Hint: Find FV of the first 9 payments at $t = 9$, then treat this as the PV of a 51-period annuity whose payments represent the incremental rent during Months 10 to 60.)
c. Sharon is not sure of the 12 percent cost of capital—it could be higher or lower. At what *nominal cost* of capital would Sharon be indifferent between the two leases? (Hint: Calculate the differences between the two payment streams, and find the IRR of this difference stream.)

13–18
NPV AND IRR ANALYSIS

Cummings Products Company is considering two mutually exclusive investments. The projects' expected net cash flows are as follows:

	Expected Net Cash Flows	
Year	Project A	Project B
0	($300)	($405)
1	(387)	134
2	(193)	134
3	(100)	134
4	600	134
5	600	134
6	850	134
7	(180)	0

a. Construct NPV profiles for Projects A and B.
b. What is each project's IRR?
c. If you were told that each project's cost of capital was 10 percent, which project should be selected? If the cost of capital was 17 percent, what would be the proper choice?

d. What is each project's MIRR at a cost of capital of 10 percent? At k = 17%? (Hint: Consider Period 7 as the end of Project B's life.)
e. What is the crossover rate, and what is its significance?

13–19
TIMING DIFFERENCES

The Ewert Exploration Company is considering two mutually exclusive plans for extracting oil on property for which it has mineral rights. Both plans call for the expenditure of $10,000,000 to drill development wells. Under Plan A, all the oil will be extracted in 1 year, producing a cash flow at t = 1 of $12,000,000, while under Plan B, cash flows will be $1,750,000 per year for 20 years.

a. What are the annual incremental cash flows that will be available to Ewert Exploration if it undertakes Plan B rather than Plan A? (Hint: Subtract Plan A's flows from B's.)
b. If the firm accepts Plan A, then invests the extra cash generated at the end of Year 1, what rate of return (reinvestment rate) would cause the cash flows from reinvestment to equal the cash flows from Plan B?
c. Suppose a company has a cost of capital of 10 percent. Is it logical to assume that it would take on all available independent projects (of average risk) with returns greater than 10 percent? Further, if all available projects with returns greater than 10 percent have been taken, would this mean that cash flows from past investments would have an opportunity cost of only 10 percent, because all the firm could do with these cash flows would be to replace money that has a cost of 10 percent? Finally, does this imply that the cost of capital is the correct rate to assume for the reinvestment of a project's cash flows?
d. Construct NPV profiles for Plans A and B, identify each project's IRR, and indicate the crossover rate of return.

13–20
SCALE DIFFERENCES

The Pinkerton Publishing Company is considering two mutually exclusive expansion plans. Plan A calls for the expenditure of $50 million on a large-scale, integrated plant which will provide an expected cash flow stream of $8 million per year for 20 years. Plan B calls for the expenditure of $15 million to build a somewhat less efficient, more labor-intensive plant which has an expected cash flow stream of $3.4 million per year for 20 years. The firm's cost of capital is 10 percent.

a. Calculate each project's NPV and IRR.
b. Set up a Project Δ by showing the cash flows that will exist if the firm goes with the large plant rather than the smaller plant. What are the NPV and the IRR for this Project Δ?
c. Graph the NPV profiles for Plan A, Plan B, and Project Δ.
d. Give a logical explanation, based on reinvestment rates and opportunity costs, as to why the NPV method is better than the IRR method when the firm's cost of capital is constant at some value such as 10 percent.

13–21
MULTIPLE RATES OF RETURN

The Ulmer Uranium Company is deciding whether or not it should open a strip mine, the net cost of which is $4.4 million. Net cash inflows are expected to be $27.7 million, all coming at the end of Year 1. The land must be returned to its natural state at a cost of $25 million, payable at the end of Year 2.

a. Plot the project's NPV profile.
b. Should the project be accepted if k = 8%? If k = 14%? Explain your reasoning.
c. Can you think of some other capital budgeting situations where negative cash flows during or at the end of the project's life might lead to multiple IRRs?
d. What is the project's MIRR at k = 8%? At k = 14%? Does the MIRR method lead to the same accept/reject decision as the NPV method?

13–22
MULTIPLE RATES OF RETURN

The Durst Development Company (DDC) has many excellent investment opportunities, but it has insufficient cash to undertake them all. Now DDC is offered the chance to borrow $2 million from the Rancho Palisades Retirement Fund at 10 percent, and the loan is to be repaid at the end of 1 year. Also, a "consulting fee" of $700,000 will be paid to Rancho Palisades' mayor at the end of 1 year for helping to arrange the credit. Of the $2 million received, $1 million will be used immediately to buy an old city-owned hotel and to convert it into a gambling casino. The other $1 million will be invested in other lucrative DDC projects that otherwise would have to be foregone because of a lack of capital. For 2 years, all cash generated by the casino will be plowed back into the casino project. At the end of the 2 years, the casino will be sold for $2 million.

Assuming that (1) the deal has been worked out in the sunshine and is completely legal and (2) cash from other DDC Company operations will be available to make the required payments at the end of Year 1, under what rate of return conditions should DDC accept the offer? Disregard taxes.

13–23 *PRESENT VALUE OF COSTS*

The Aubey Coffee Company is evaluating the within-plant distribution system for its new roasting, grinding, and packing plant. The two alternatives are (1) a conveyor system with a high initial cost, but low annual operating costs, and (2) several forklift trucks, which cost less, but have considerably higher operating costs. The decision to construct the plant has already been made, and the choice here will have no effect on the overall revenues of the project. The cost of capital for the plant is 8 percent, and the projects' expected net costs are listed in the table:

	Expected Net Cost	
Year	**Conveyor**	**Forklift**
0	($500,000)	($200,000)
1	(120,000)	(160,000)
2	(120,000)	(160,000)
3	(120,000)	(160,000)
4	(120,000)	(160,000)
5	(120,000)	(160,000)

a. What is the IRR of each alternative?
b. What is the present value of costs of each alternative? Which method should be chosen?

13–24 *PAYBACK, NPV, AND MIRR*

Your division is considering two investment projects, each of which requires an up-front expenditure of $25 million. You estimate that the cost of capital is 10 percent and that the investments will produce the following after-tax cash flows (in millions of dollars):

Year	Project A	Project B
1	5	20
2	10	10
3	15	8
4	20	6

a. What is the regular payback period for each of the projects?
b. What is the discounted payback period for each of the projects?
c. If the two projects are independent and the cost of capital is 10 percent, which project or projects should the firm undertake?
d. If the two projects are mutually exclusive and the cost of capital is 5 percent, which project should the firm undertake?
e. If the two projects are mutually exclusive and the cost of capital is 15 percent, which project should the firm undertake?
f. What is the crossover rate?
g. If the cost of capital is 10 percent, what is the modified IRR (MIRR) of each project?

13–25 *UNEQUAL LIVES*

Shao Airlines is considering two alternative planes. Plane A has an expected life of 5 years, will cost $100 million, and will produce net cash flows of $30 million per year. Plane B has a life of 10 years, will cost $132 million, and will produce net cash flows of $25 million per year. Shao plans to serve the route for 10 years. Inflation in operating costs, airplane costs, and fares is expected to be zero, and the company's cost of capital is 12 percent. By how much would the value of the company increase if it accepted the better project (plane)?

13–26 *UNEQUAL LIVES*

The Perez Company has the opportunity to invest in one of two mutually exclusive machines which will produce a product it will need for the foreseeable future. Machine A costs $10 million but realizes after-tax inflows of $4 million per year for 4 years. After 4 years, the machine must be replaced. Machine B costs $15 million and realizes after-tax inflows of $3.5 million per year for 8 years, after which it must be replaced. Assume that machine prices are not expected to rise because inflation will be offset by cheaper components used in the machines. If the cost of capital is 10 percent, which machine should the company use?

13–27 *UNEQUAL LIVES* Filkins Fabric Company is considering the replacement of its old, fully depreciated knitting machine. Two new models are available: Machine 190-3, which has a cost of $190,000, a 3-year expected life, and after-tax cash flows (labor savings and depreciation) of $87,000 per year; and Machine 360-6, which has a cost of $360,000, a 6-year life, and after-tax cash flows of $98,300 per year. Knitting machine prices are not expected to rise, because inflation will be offset by cheaper components (microprocessors) used in the machines. Assume that Filkins' cost of capital is 14 percent. Should the firm replace its old knitting machine, and, if so, which new machine should it use?

13–28 *ECONOMIC LIFE* The Scampini Supplies Company recently purchased a new delivery truck. The new truck cost $22,500, and it is expected to generate net after-tax operating cash flows, including depreciation, of $6,250 per year. The truck has a 5-year expected life. The expected salvage values after tax adjustments for the truck are given below. The company's cost of capital is 10 percent.

Year	Annual Operating Cash Flow	Salvage Value
0	($22,500)	$22,500
1	6,250	17,500
2	6,250	14,000
3	6,250	11,000
4	6,250	5,000
5	6,250	0

a. Should the firm operate the truck until the end of its 5-year physical life, or, if not, what is its optimal economic life?

b. Would the introduction of salvage values, in addition to operating cash flows, ever *reduce* the expected NPV and/or IRR of a project?

Spreadsheet Problems

13–29 *BUILD A MODEL: CAPITAL BUDGETING TOOLS* Start with the partial model in the file ***Ch 13-29 Build a Model.xls*** from the textbook's CD-ROM. Gardial Fisheries is considering two mutually exclusive investments. The projects' expected net cash flows are as follows:

	Expected Net Cash Flows	
Year	Project A	Project B
0	($375)	($405)
1	(387)	134
2	(193)	134
3	(100)	134
4	600	134
5	600	134
6	850	134
7	(180)	0

a. If you were told that each project's cost of capital was 12 percent, which project should be selected? If the cost of capital was 18 percent, what would be the proper choice?

b. Construct NPV profiles for Projects A and B.

c. What is each project's IRR?

d. What is the crossover rate, and what is its significance?

e. What is each project's MIRR at a cost of capital of 12 percent? At k = 18%? (Hint: Consider Period 7 as the end of Project B's life.)
f. What is the regular payback period for these two projects?
g. At a cost of capital of 12 percent, what is the discounted payback period for these two projects?

13–30 WHAT IF ANALYSIS: MUTUALLY EXCLUSIVE PROJECTS

Start with the model ***Ch 13-30 What If Analysis.xls*** from the textbook's CD-ROM and answer the questions shown there.

Cyberproblem

The information related to the cyberproblems is likely to change over time, due to the release of new information and the ever-changing nature of the World Wide Web. With these changes in mind, we will periodically update these problems on the textbook's web site.

13–31 CAPITAL BUDGETING—IBM

Capital budgeting is the process of evaluating potential projects and determining which are likely to be profitable and which are not. A company's capital budget is a function of its corporate strategy, and its effects are felt throughout the organization long after the actual decisions are made. Because of the size and importance of capital investments, companies must ensure that their capital budgeting decisions are based on good information and sound analysis. For a large, multinational corporation such as IBM, there are many challenges in the capital budgeting process. Go to the textbook's web site, **http://www.harcourtcollege.com/finance/theory/student/resources/cyberprob/ch13.html,** and answer the questions shown there.

Mini Case

See **Ch 13 Show.ppt** and **Ch 13 Mini Case.xls**.

Assume that you recently went to work for Axis Components Company, a supplier of auto repair parts used in the after-market with products from Chrysler, Ford, and other auto makers. Your boss, the chief financial officer (CFO), has just handed you the estimated cash flows for two proposed projects. Project L involves adding a new item to the firm's ignition system line; it would take some time to build up the market for this product, so the cash inflows would increase over time. Project S involves an add-on to an existing line, and its cash flows would decrease over time. Both projects have 3-year lives, because Axis is planning to introduce entirely new models after 3 years.

Here are the projects' net cash flows (in thousands of dollars):

	Expected Net Cash Flow	
Year	**Project L**	**Project S**
0	($100)	($100)
1	10	70
2	60	50
3	80	20

Depreciation, salvage values, net working capital requirements, and tax effects are all included in these cash flows.

The CFO also made subjective risk assessments of each project, and he concluded that both projects have risk characteristics which are similar to the firm's average project. Axis's weighted average cost of capital is 10 percent. You must now determine whether one or both of the projects should be accepted.

a. What is capital budgeting? Are there any similarities between a firm's capital budgeting decisions and an individual's investment decisions?

b. What is the difference between independent and mutually exclusive projects? Between projects with normal and nonnormal cash flows?
c. (1) What is the payback period? Find the paybacks for Projects L and S.
   (2) What is the rationale for the payback method? According to the payback criterion, which project or projects should be accepted if the firm's maximum acceptable payback is 2 years, and if Projects L and S are independent? If they are mutually exclusive?
   (3) What is the difference between the regular and discounted payback periods?
   (4) What is the main disadvantage of discounted payback? Is the payback method of any real usefulness in capital budgeting decisions?
d. (1) Define the term *net present value (NPV)*. What is each project's NPV?
   (2) What is the rationale behind the NPV method? According to NPV, which project or projects should be accepted if they are independent? Mutually exclusive?
   (3) Would the NPVs change if the cost of capital changed?
e. (1) Define the term *internal rate of return (IRR)*. What is each project's IRR?
   (2) How is the IRR on a project related to the YTM on a bond?
   (3) What is the logic behind the IRR method? According to IRR, which projects should be accepted if they are independent? Mutually exclusive?
   (4) Would the projects' IRRs change if the cost of capital changed?
f. (1) Draw NPV profiles for Projects L and S. At what discount rate do the profiles cross?
   (2) Look at your NPV profile graph without referring to the actual NPVs and IRRs. Which project or projects should be accepted if they are independent? Mutually exclusive? Explain. Are your answers correct at any cost of capital less than 23.6 percent?
g. (1) What is the underlying cause of ranking conflicts between NPV and IRR?
   (2) What is the "reinvestment rate assumption," and how does it affect the NPV versus IRR conflict?
   (3) Which method is the best? Why?
h. (1) Define the term *modified IRR (MIRR)*. Find the MIRRs for Projects L and S.
   (2) What are the MIRR's advantages and disadvantages vis-à-vis the regular IRR? What are the MIRR's advantages and disadvantages vis-à-vis the NPV?
i. As a separate project (Project P), the firm is considering sponsoring a pavilion at the upcoming World's Fair. The pavilion would cost $800,000, and it is expected to result in $5 million of incremental cash inflows during its 1 year of operation. However, it would then take another year, and $5 million of costs, to demolish the site and return it to its original condition. Thus, Project P's expected net cash flows look like this (in millions of dollars):

Year	Net Cash Flows
0	($0.8)
1	5.0
2	(5.0)

The project is estimated to be of average risk, so its cost of capital is 10 percent.
(1) What is Project P's NPV? What is its IRR? Its MIRR?
(2) Draw Project P's NPV profile. Does Project P have normal or nonnormal cash flows? Should this project be accepted?

j. In an unrelated analysis, Axis must choose between the following two mutually exclusive projects:

	Expected Net Cash Flow	
Year	Project S	Project L
0	($100,000)	($100,000)
1	60,000	33,500
2	60,000	33,500
3	—	33,500
4	—	33,500

The projects provide a necessary service, so whichever one is selected is expected to be repeated into the foreseeable future. Both projects have a 10 percent cost of capital.
(1) What is each project's initial NPV without replication?
(2) Now apply the replacement chain approach to determine the projects' extended NPVs. Which project should be chosen?
(3) Now assume that the cost to replicate Project S in 2 years will increase to $105,000 because of inflationary pressures. How should the analysis be handled now, and which project should be chosen?

k. Axis is also considering another project which has a physical life of 3 years; that is, the machinery will be totally worn out after 3 years. However, if the project were terminated prior to the end of 3 years, the machinery would have a positive salvage value. Here are the project's estimated cash flows:

Year	Initial Investment and Operating Cash Flows	End-of-Year Net Salvage Value
0	($5,000)	$5,000
1	2,100	3,100
2	2,000	2,000
3	1,750	0

Using the 10 percent cost of capital, what is the project's NPV if it is operated for the full 3 years? Would the NPV change if the company planned to terminate the project at the end of Year 2? At the end of Year 1? What is the project's optimal (economic) life?

l. After examining all the potential projects, the CFO discovers that there are many more projects this year with positive NPVs than in a normal year. What two problems might this extra large capital budget cause?

Selected Additional References and Cases

For an in-depth treatment of capital budgeting techniques, see

Bierman, Harold, Jr., and Seymour Smidt, *The Capital Budgeting Decision* (New York: Macmillan, 1993).

Grant, Eugene L., William G. Ireson, and Richard S. Leavenworth, *Principles of Engineering Economy* (New York: John Wiley & Sons, 1990).

Levy, Haim, and Marshall Sarnat, *Capital Investment and Financial Decisions* (Englewood Cliffs, NJ: Prentice-Hall, 1994).

Seitz, Neil E., and Mitch Ellison, *Capital Budgeting and Long-Term Financing Decisions* (Fort Worth, TX: The Dryden Press, 1995).

For a discussion of strategic considerations in capital budgeting, see

Crum, Roy L., and Frans G. J. Derkinderen, eds., *Readings in Strategies for Corporate Investments* (New York: Pitman, 1981).

The following articles present interesting comparisons of four different approaches to finding NPV:

Brick, Ivan E., and Daniel G. Weaver, "A Comparison of Capital Budgeting Techniques in Identifying Profitable Investments," *Financial Management*, Winter 1984, 29–39.

Greenfield, Robert L., Maury R. Randall, and John C. Woods, "Financial Leverage and Use of the Net Present Value Investment Criterion," *Financial Management*, Autumn 1983, 40–44.

Five articles related directly to the topics in this chapter are

Bacon, Peter W., "The Evaluation of Mutually Exclusive Investments," *Financial Management*, Summer 1977, 55–58.

Chaney, Paul K., "Moral Hazard and Capital Budgeting," *Journal of Financial Research*, Summer 1989, 113–128.

Lewellen, Wilbur G., Howard P. Lanser, and John J. McConnell, "Payback Substitutes for Discounted Cash Flow," *Financial Management*, Summer 1973, 17–23.

Miller, Edward M., "Safety Margins and Capital Budgeting Criteria," *Managerial Finance*, Number 2/3, 1988, 1–8.

Woods, John C., and Maury R. Randall, "The Net Present Value of Future Investment Opportunities: Its Impact on Shareholder Wealth and Implications for Capital Budgeting Theory," *Financial Management*, Summer 1989, 85–92.

For some articles that discuss the capital budgeting methods actually used in practice, see

Kim, Suk H., Trevor Crick, and Seung H. Kim, "Do Executives Practice What Academics Preach?" *Management Accounting*, November 1986, 49–52.

Mukherjee, Tarun K., "Capital Budgeting Surveys: The Past and the Future," *Review of Business and Economic Research*, Spring 1987, 37–56.

———, "The Capital Budgeting Process of Large U.S. Firms: An Analysis of Capital Budgeting Manuals," *Managerial Finance*, Number 2/3, 1988, 28–35.

Ross, Marc, "Capital Budgeting Practices of Twelve Large Manufacturers," *Financial Management*, Winter 1986, 15–22.

Runyan, L. R., "Capital Expenditure Decision Making in Small Firms," *Journal of Business Research*, September 1983, 389–397.

Weaver, Samuel C., Donald Peters, Roger Cason, and Joe Daleiden, "Capital Budgeting," *Financial Management*, Spring 1989, 10–17.

Additional capital budgeting references are provided in Chapters 14 and 15.

For a case which focuses on capital budgeting decision methods, see

Case 11, "Chicago Valve Company," in the *Cases in Financial Management: Dryden Request* series.

14

Cash Flow Estimation and Risk Analysis

Home Depot Inc. grew phenomenally during the 1990s, and it shows no sign of slowing down. At the beginning of 1990, it had 118 stores and annual sales of $2.8 billion. By the end of 1999, it had more than 900 stores, and its sales were $37 billion. The company continues to open stores at a rate of about two per week, and it expects to open another 200 stores in fiscal 2001. The stock has more than matched the sales growth—a $10,000 investment in 1990 would now be worth about $250,000!

It costs Home Depot, on average, $16 million to purchase land, construct a new store, and stock it with inventory. (The inventory costs about $5 million, but about $2 million of this is financed through accounts payable.) Each new store thus represents a major capital expenditure, so the company must use capital budgeting techniques to determine if a potential store's expected cash flows are sufficient to cover its costs.

Home Depot uses information from its existing stores to forecast new stores' expected cash flows. Thus far, its forecasts have been outstanding, but there are always risks that must be considered. First, sales might be less than projected if the economy weakens. Second, some of Home Depot's customers might in the future bypass it altogether and buy directly from manufacturers through the Internet. Third, new stores could "cannibalize," that is, take sales away from, existing stores. This last point was made in the July 16, 1999, issue of *Value Line:*

> The retailer has picked the "low-hanging fruit;" it has already entered the most attractive markets. To avoid "cannibalization"—which occurs when duplicative stores are located too closely together—the company is developing complementary formats. For example, Home Depot is beginning to roll out its *Expo Design Center* chain, which offers one-stop sales and service for kitchen and bath and other remodeling and renovation work . . .

The decision to expand requires a detailed assessment of the forecasted cash flows, including the risk that the forecasted level of sales might not be realized. In this chapter, we describe techniques for estimating a project's cash flows and their associated risk. Companies such as Home Depot use these techniques on a regular basis to evaluate capital budgeting decisions.

The basic principles of capital budgeting were covered in Chapter 13. Given a project's expected cash flows, it is easy to calculate its payback, discounted payback, NPV, IRR, MIRR, and PI. Unfortunately, cash flows are rarely just given—rather, managers must estimate them based on information collected from sources both inside and outside the company. Moreover, uncertainty surrounds the cash flow estimates, and some projects are riskier than others. In the first part of the chapter, we develop procedures for estimating the cash flows associated with capital budgeting projects. Then, in the second part, we discuss techniques used to measure and take account of project risk.

Estimating Cash Flows

The textbook's CD-ROM contains an *Excel* file that will guide you through the chapter's calculations. The file for this chapter is ***Ch 14 Tool Kit.xls,*** and we encourage you to open the file and follow along as you read the chapter.

The most important, but also the most difficult, step in capital budgeting is estimating projects' cash flows—the investment outlays and the annual net cash inflows after a project goes into operation. Many variables are involved, and many individuals and departments participate in the process. For example, the forecasts of unit sales and sales prices are normally made by the marketing group, based on their knowledge of price elasticity, advertising effects, the state of the economy, competitors' reactions, and trends in consumers' tastes. Similarly, the capital outlays associated with a new product are generally obtained from the engineering and product development staffs, while operating costs are estimated by cost accountants, production experts, personnel specialists, purchasing agents, and so forth.

It is difficult to forecast the costs and revenues associated with a large, complex project, so forecast errors can be quite large. For example, when several major oil companies decided to build the Alaska Pipeline, the original cost estimates were in the neighborhood of $700 million, but the final cost was closer to $7 billion. Similar (or even worse) miscalculations are common in forecasts of product design costs, such as the costs to develop a new personal computer. Further, as difficult as plant and equipment costs are to estimate, sales revenues and operating costs over the project's life are even more uncertain. For example, several years ago, Federal Express developed an electronic delivery service system (ZapMail). It used the correct capital budgeting technique, NPV, but it incorrectly estimated the project's cash flows: Projected revenues were too high, projected costs were too low, and virtually no one was willing to pay the price required to cover the project's costs. As a result, cash flows failed to meet the forecasted levels, and Federal Express ended up losing about $200 million before it folded the venture. This example demonstrates a basic truth—if cash flow estimates are not reasonably accurate, any analytical technique, no matter how sophisticated, can lead to poor decisions. Because of its financial strength, Federal Express was able to absorb losses on the project, but the ZapMail venture could have forced a weaker firm into bankruptcy.

The financial staff's role in the forecasting process includes (1) obtaining information from various departments such as engineering and marketing, (2) ensuring that everyone involved with the forecast uses a consistent set of economic assumptions, and (3) making sure that no biases are inherent in the forecasts. This last point is extremely important, because some managers become emotionally involved with pet projects, and others seek to build empires. Both problems cause cash flow forecast biases which make bad projects look good—on paper.

It is almost impossible to overstate the problems one can encounter in cash flow forecasts. It is also difficult to overstate the importance of these forecasts. Still, observing the principles discussed in the next several sections will help minimize forecasting errors.

Self-Test Questions

What is the most important step in a capital budgeting analysis?

What departments are involved in estimating a project's cash flows?

What is the financial staff's role in the forecasting process for capital projects?

Identifying the Relevant Cash Flows

The first step in capital budgeting is to identify the **relevant cash flows,** defined as the specific set of cash flows that should be considered in the decision at hand. Analysts often make errors in estimating cash flows, but two cardinal rules can help you minimize mistakes: (1) Capital budgeting decisions must be based on *cash flows*, not accounting income. (2) Only *incremental cash flows* are relevant.

Recall from Chapter 2 that *free cash flow* is the cash flow available for distribution to investors. In a nutshell, the relevant cash flow for a project is the *additional* free cash flow that the company can expect if it implements the project. It is the cash flow above and beyond what the company could expect if it doesn't implement the project. The following sections discuss the relevant cash flows in more detail.

Project Cash Flow versus Accounting Income

Recall that free cash flow is calculated as follows:

$$\text{Free cash flow} = \begin{array}{c}\text{Net operating}\\ \text{profit after taxes}\\ \text{(NOPAT)}\end{array} + \text{Depreciation} - \begin{array}{c}\text{Gross capital}\\ \text{expenditures}\end{array} - \begin{array}{c}\text{Change in net}\\ \text{operating}\\ \text{working capital}\end{array}$$

$$= \text{EBIT}(1-\text{T}) + \text{Depreciation} - \begin{array}{c}\text{Gross capital}\\ \text{expenditures}\end{array} - \begin{bmatrix}\Delta\ \text{Current operating assets} - \\ \Delta\ \text{Current operating liabilities}\end{bmatrix}.$$

Just as a firm's value depends on its free cash flows, so does the value of a project depend on its free cash flow. We illustrate the estimation of project cash flow later in the chapter with a comprehensive example, but it is important for you to understand that project cash flow differs from accounting income.

Costs of Fixed Assets Most projects require assets, and asset purchases represent *negative* cash flows. Even though the acquisition of assets results in a cash outflow, accountants do not show the purchase of fixed assets as a deduction from accounting income. Instead, they deduct a depreciation expense each year throughout the life of the asset.

Note that the full cost of fixed assets includes any shipping and installation costs. When a firm acquires fixed assets, it often must incur substantial costs for shipping and installing the equipment. These charges are added to the price of the equipment when the project's cost is being determined. Then, the full cost of the equipment, including shipping and installation costs, is used as the *depreciable basis* when depreciation charges are being calculated. For example, if a company bought a computer with an invoice price of $100,000 and paid another $10,000 for shipping and installation, then the full cost of the computer (and its depreciable basis) would be $110,000. Note too that fixed assets can often be sold at the end of a project's life. If this is the case, then the after-tax cash proceeds represent a positive cash flow. We will illustrate both depreciation and cash flow from asset sales later in the chapter.

Noncash Charges In calculating net income, accountants usually subtract depreciation from revenues. So, while accountants do not subtract the purchase price of fixed assets when calculating accounting income, they do subtract a charge each year for depreciation. Depreciation shelters income from taxation, and this has an impact on cash flow, but depreciation itself is not a cash flow. Therefore, depreciation must be added to NOPAT when estimating a project's cash flow.

Changes in Net Operating Working Capital Normally, additional inventories are required to support a new operation, and expanded sales tie up additional funds in accounts receivable. However, payables and accruals increase as a result of the expansion, and this reduces the cash needed to finance inventories and receivables. The difference between the required increase in current operating assets and the increase in current operating liabilities is the **change in net operating working capital.** If this change is positive, as it generally is for expansion projects, then additional financing, over and above the cost of the fixed assets, will be needed.

Toward the end of a project's life, inventories will be used but not replaced, and receivables will be collected without corresponding replacements. As these changes occur, the firm will receive cash inflows, and as a result, the investment in net operating working capital will be returned by the end of the project's life.

Interest Expenses Are Not Included in Project Cash Flows Recall from Chapter 13 that we discount a project's cash flows by its cost of capital, and that the cost of capital is a weighted average (WACC) of the costs of debt, preferred stock, and common equity, adjusted for the project's risk. Moreover, the WACC is the rate of return necessary to satisfy all of the firm's investors—debtholders and stockholders. The discounting process *reduces* the cash flows to account for the project's capital costs. If interest charges were first deducted and then the resulting cash flows were discounted at the WACC, this would double count the cost of debt. *Therefore, you should not subtract interest expenses when finding a project's cash flows.*

Note that this differs from the procedures used to calculate accounting income. Accountants measure the profit available for stockholders, so interest expenses are subtracted. However, project cash flow is the cash flow available for all investors, bondholders as well as stockholders, so interest expenses are not subtracted. This is completely analogous to the procedures used in the corporate valuation model of Chapter 12, where the company's free cash flows are discounted at the WACC.[1]

Incremental Cash Flows

In evaluating a project, we focus on those cash flows that occur if and only if we accept the project. These cash flows, called **incremental cash flows,** represent the change in the firm's total cash flow that occurs as a direct result of accepting the project. Three special problems in determining incremental cash flows are discussed next.

Sunk Costs A **sunk cost** is an outlay that has already occurred, hence is not affected by the decision under consideration. Since sunk costs are not incremental costs, they should not be included in the analysis. To illustrate, in 2001, Northeast BankCorp was considering the establishment of a branch office in a newly developed section of Boston. To help with its evaluation, Northeast had, back in 2000, hired a consulting

[1]An alternative approach to capital budgeting is to estimate the cash flows that are available for equity holders. Although this produces the same NPV as our approach, we do not recommend it because to apply it correctly requires that we determine the amount of debt and equity for every year of the project's life.

firm to perform a site analysis; the cost was $100,000, and this amount was expensed for tax purposes in 2000. Is this 2000 expenditure a relevant cost with respect to the 2001 capital budgeting decision? The answer is no—the $100,000 is a *sunk cost,* and it will not affect Northeast's future cash flows regardless of whether or not the new branch is built. It often turns out that a particular project has a negative NPV if all the associated costs, including sunk costs, are considered. However, on an incremental basis, the project may be a good one because the *future incremental cash flows* are large enough to produce a positive NPV on the *incremental investment.*

Opportunity Costs A second potential problem relates to **opportunity costs,** which are cash flows that could be generated from an asset the firm already owns provided it is not used for the project in question. To illustrate, Northeast BankCorp already owns a piece of land that is suitable for the branch location. When evaluating the prospective branch, should the cost of the land be disregarded because no additional cash outlay would be required? The answer is no, because there is an *opportunity cost* inherent in the use of the property. In this case, the land could be sold to yield $150,000 after taxes. Use of the site for the branch would require forgoing this inflow, so the $150,000 must be charged as an opportunity cost against the project. Note that the proper land cost in this example is the $150,000 market-determined value, irrespective of whether Northeast originally paid $50,000 or $500,000 for the property. (What Northeast paid would, of course, have an effect on taxes, hence on the after-tax opportunity cost.)

Effects on Other Parts of the Firm: Externalities The third potential problem involves the effects of a project on other parts of the firm, which economists call **externalities.** For example, some of Northeast's customers who would use the new branch are already banking with Northeast's downtown office. The loans and deposits, hence profits, generated by these customers would not be new to the bank; rather, they would represent a transfer from the main office to the branch. Thus, the net income produced by these customers should not be treated as incremental income in the capital budgeting decision. On the other hand, having a suburban branch would help the bank attract new business to its downtown office, because some people like to be able to bank both close to home and close to work. In this case, the additional income that would actually flow to the downtown office should be attributed to the branch. Although they are often difficult to quantify, *externalities* (which can be either positive or negative) should be considered.

When a new project takes sales from an existing product, this is often called **cannibalization.** Naturally, firms do not like to cannibalize their existing products, but it often turns out that if they do not, someone else will. To illustrate, IBM for years refused to provide full support for its PC division because it did not want to steal sales from its highly profitable mainframe business. That turned out to be a huge strategic error, because it allowed Intel, Microsoft, Compaq, and others to become dominant forces in the computer industry. Therefore, when considering externalities, the full implications of the proposed new project should be taken into account.

A few young firms, including Dell Computer, have been successful selling their products only over the Internet. Many firms, however, had established retail channels long before the Internet became a reality. For these firms, the decision to begin selling directly to consumers over the Internet is not a simple one. For example, Nautica Enterprises Inc. is an international company that designs, sources, markets, and distributes sportswear. Nautica sells its products to traditional retailers such as Saks Fifth Avenue and Parisian, who then sell to consumers. If Nautica opens its own online Internet store, it could potentially increase its profit margin by avoiding the substantial markup added by dealers. However, Internet sales would probably cannibalize sales through its retailer network. Even worse, retailers might react adversely to Nautica's Internet sales by redirecting the marketing effort and display space they now provide Nautica to other brands that do not compete over the Internet. Nautica, and many other producers, must determine whether the new profits from Internet sales will compensate for lost profits from existing channels. Thus far, Nautica has decided to stay with its traditional retailers.

Rather than focusing narrowly on the project at hand, analysts must anticipate the project's impact on the rest of the firm, which requires imagination and creative thinking. As the IBM and Nautica examples illustrate, it is critical to identify and account for all externalities when evaluating a proposed project.

Timing of Cash Flow

We must account properly for the timing of cash flows. Accounting income statements are for periods such as years or months, so they do not reflect exactly when during the period cash revenues or expenses occur. Because of the time value of money, capital budgeting cash flows should in theory be analyzed exactly as they occur. Of course, there must be a compromise between accuracy and feasibility. A time line with daily cash flows would in theory be most accurate, but daily cash flow estimates would be costly to construct, unwieldy to use, and probably no more accurate than annual cash flow estimates because we simply cannot forecast well enough to warrant this degree of detail. Therefore, in most cases, we simply assume that all cash flows occur at the end of every year. However, for some projects, it may be useful to assume that cash flows occur at mid-year, or even quarterly or monthly.

Self-Test Questions

Why should companies use project cash flow rather than accounting income when finding the NPV of a project?

How do shipping and installation costs affect the costs of fixed assets and the depreciable basis?

What is the most common noncash charge that must be added back when finding project cash flows?

What is net operating working capital, and how does it affect a project's costs in capital budgeting?

How does the company get back the dollars it invests in net operating working capital?

Explain the following terms: incremental cash flow, sunk cost, opportunity cost, externality, and cannibalization.

Give an example of a "good" externality, that is, one that makes a project look better.

Tax Effects

Taxes can have a major effect on cash flows, and in many cases tax effects will make or break a project. Therefore, it is critical that taxes be dealt with correctly. Our tax laws are extremely complex, and they are subject to interpretation and to change. The financial staff can get assistance from the firm's accountants and tax lawyers, but even so, it is necessary for financial analysts to have a working knowledge of the current tax laws and their effects on cash flows.

An Overview of Depreciation

Suppose a firm buys a milling machine for $100,000 and uses it for five years, after which it is scrapped. The cost of the goods produced by the machine must include a charge for the machine, and this charge is called **depreciation.** In the following sections, we review some of the depreciation concepts covered in accounting courses.

Companies often calculate depreciation one way when figuring taxes and another way when reporting income to investors: many use the *straight-line* method for stockholder reporting (or "book" purposes), but they use the fastest rate permitted by law for tax purposes. Under the straight-line method used for stockholder reporting, one normally takes the cost of the asset, subtracts its estimated salvage value, and divides the net amount by the asset's useful economic life. For an asset with a 5-year life, which costs \$100,000 and has a \$12,500 salvage value, the annual straight-line depreciation charge is (\$100,000 − \$12,500)/5 = \$17,500. Note, however, as we discuss later, that salvage value is *not* considered for tax depreciation purposes.

For tax purposes, Congress changes the permissible tax depreciation methods from time to time. Prior to 1954, the straight-line method was required for tax purposes, but in 1954 *accelerated* methods (double-declining balance and sum-of-years'-digits) were permitted. Then, in 1981, the old accelerated methods were replaced by a simpler procedure known as the Accelerated Cost Recovery System (ACRS). The ACRS system was changed again in 1986 as a part of the Tax Reform Act, and it is now known as the *Modified Accelerated Cost Recovery System (MACRS)*; a 1993 tax law made further changes in this area.

Note that U.S. tax laws are very complicated, and in this text we can only provide an overview of MACRS designed to give you a basic understanding of the impact of depreciation on capital budgeting decisions. Further, the tax laws change so often that the numbers we present may be outdated before the book is even published. Thus, when dealing with tax depreciation in real-world situations, current Internal Revenue Service (IRS) publications or individuals with expertise in tax matters should be consulted.

Tax Depreciation Life

For tax purposes, the entire cost of an asset is expensed over its **depreciable life.** Historically, an asset's depreciable life was set equal to its estimated useful economic life; it was intended that an asset would be fully depreciated at approximately the same time that it reached the end of its useful economic life. However, MACRS totally abandoned that practice and set simple guidelines that created several classes of assets, each with a more-or-less arbitrarily prescribed life called a *recovery period* or *class life*. The MACRS class lives bear only a rough relationship to assets' expected useful economic lives.

A major effect of the MACRS system has been to shorten the depreciable lives of assets, thus giving businesses larger tax deductions and thereby increasing their cash flows available for investment. Table 14-1 describes the types of property that fit into the different class life groups, and Table 14-2 sets forth the MACRS recovery allowance percentages (depreciation rates) for selected classes of investment property.

Consider Table 14-1, which gives the MACRS class life and the types of assets that fall into each category. Property in the 27.5- and 39-year categories (real estate) must be depreciated by the straight-line method, but 3-, 5-, 7-, and 10-year property (personal property) can be depreciated either by the accelerated method set forth in Table 14-2 or by the straight-line method.[2]

[2]As a benefit to very small companies, the Tax Code also permits companies to *expense*, which is equivalent to depreciating over one year, up to \$20,000 of equipment for 2000 and \$24,000 for 2001. Thus, if a small company bought one asset worth up to \$20,000, it could write the asset off in the year it was acquired. This is called "Section 179 expensing." We shall disregard this provision throughout the book.

TABLE 14-1 Major Classes and Asset Lives for MACRS

Class	Type of Property
3-year	Certain special manufacturing tools
5-year	Automobiles, light-duty trucks, computers, and certain special manufacturing equipment
7-year	Most industrial equipment, office furniture, and fixtures
10-year	Certain longer-lived types of equipment
27.5-year	Residential rental real property such as apartment buildings
39-year	All nonresidential real property, including commercial and industrial buildings

TABLE 14-2 Recovery Allowance Percentage for Personal Property

	Class of Investment			
Ownership Year	3-Year	5-Year	7-Year	10-Year
1	33%	20%	14%	10%
2	45	32	25	18
3	15	19	17	14
4	7	12	13	12
5		11	9	9
6		6	9	7
7			9	7
8			4	7
9				7
10				6
11				3
	100%	100%	100%	100%

Notes:

a. We developed these recovery allowance percentages based on the 200 percent declining balance method prescribed by MACRS, with a switch to straight-line depreciation at some point in the asset's life. For example, consider the 5-year recovery allowance percentages. The straight line percentage would be 20 percent per year, so the 200 percent declining balance multiplier is 2.0(20%) = 40% = 0.4. However, because the half-year convention applies, the MACRS percentage for Year 1 is 20 percent. For Year 2, there is 80 percent of the depreciable basis remaining to be depreciated, so the recovery allowance percentage is 0.40(80%) = 32%. In Year 3, 20% + 32% = 52% of the depreciation has been taken, leaving 48%, so the percentage is 0.4(48%) ≈ 19%. In Year 4, the percentage is 0.4(29%) ≈ 12%. After 4 years, straight-line depreciation exceeds the declining balance depreciation, so a switch is made to straight-line (this is permitted under the law). However, the half-year convention must also be applied at the end of the class life, and the remaining 17 percent of depreciation must be taken (amortized) over 1.5 years. Thus, the percentage in Year 5 is 17%/1.5 ≈ 11%, and in Year 6, 17% − 11% = 6%. Although the tax tables carry the allowance percentages out to two decimal places, we have rounded to the nearest whole number for ease of illustration.

b. Residential rental property (apartments) is depreciated over a 27.5-year life, whereas commercial and industrial structures are depreciated over 39 years. In both cases, straight-line depreciation must be used. The depreciation allowance for the first year is based, pro rata, on the month the asset was placed in service, with the remainder of the first year's depreciation being taken in the 28th or 40th year. A half-month convention is assumed; that is, an asset placed in service in February would receive 10.5 months of depreciation in the first year.

As we saw earlier in the chapter, higher depreciation expenses result in lower taxes, hence higher cash flows. Therefore, since a firm has the choice of using straight-line rates or the accelerated rates shown in Table 14-2, most elect to use the accelerated rates.

The yearly recovery allowance, or depreciation expense, is determined by multiplying each asset's *depreciable basis* by the applicable recovery percentage shown in Table 14-2. Calculations are discussed in the following sections.

Half-Year Convention Under MACRS, the assumption is generally made that property is placed in service in the middle of the first year. Thus, for 3-year class life property, the recovery period begins in the middle of the year the asset is placed in service and ends three years later. The effect of the *half-year convention* is to extend the recovery period out one more year, so 3-year class life property is depreciated over four calendar years, 5-year property is depreciated over six calendar years, and so on. This convention is incorporated into Table 14-2's recovery allowance percentages.[3]

Depreciable Basis The *depreciable basis* is a critical element of MACRS because each year's allowance (depreciation expense) depends jointly on the asset's depreciable basis and its MACRS class life. The depreciable basis under MACRS is equal to the purchase price of the asset plus any shipping and installation costs. The basis is *not* adjusted for *salvage value* (which is the estimated market value of the asset at the end of its useful life) regardless of whether accelerated or straight-line depreciation is taken.

Sale of a Depreciable Asset If a depreciable asset is sold, the sale price (actual salvage value) minus the then-existing undepreciated book value is added to operating income and taxed at the firm's marginal tax rate. For example, suppose a firm buys a 5-year class life asset for \$100,000 and sells it at the end of the fourth year for \$25,000. The asset's book value is equal to \$100,000(0.11 + 0.06) = \$100,000(0.17) = \$17,000. Therefore, \$25,000 − \$17,000 = \$8,000 is added to the firm's operating income and is taxed.

Depreciation Illustration Assume that Stango Food Products buys a \$150,000 machine that falls into the MACRS 5-year class life and places it into service on March 15, 2002. Stango must pay an additional \$30,000 for delivery and installation. Salvage value is not considered, so the machine's depreciable basis is \$180,000. (Delivery and installation charges are included in the depreciable basis rather than expensed in the year incurred.) Each year's recovery allowance (tax depreciation expense) is determined by multiplying the depreciable basis by the applicable recovery allowance percentage. Thus, the depreciation expense for 2002 is 0.20(\$180,000) = \$36,000, and for 2003 it is 0.32(\$180,000) = \$57,600. Similarly, the depreciation expense is \$34,200 for 2004, \$21,600 for 2005, \$19,800 for 2006, and \$10,800 for 2007. The total depreciation expense over the six-year recovery period is \$180,000, which is equal to the depreciable basis of the machine.

---

[3]The half-year convention also applies if the straight-line alternative is used, with half of one year's depreciation taken in the first year, a full year's depreciation taken in each of the remaining years of the asset's class life, and the remaining half-year's depreciation taken in the year following the end of the class life. You should recognize that virtually all companies have computerized depreciation systems. Each asset's depreciation pattern is programmed into the system at the time of its acquisition, and the computer aggregates the depreciation allowances for all assets when the accountants close the books and prepare financial statements and tax returns.

As noted above, most firms use straight-line depreciation for stockholder reporting purposes but MACRS for tax purposes. *In this case, for capital budgeting purposes MACRS should be used.* In capital budgeting, we are concerned with cash flows, not reported income. Since MACRS depreciation is used for taxes, this type of depreciation must be used to determine the taxes that will be assessed against a particular project. Only if the depreciation method used for tax purposes is also used for capital budgeting analysis will we obtain an accurate cash flow estimate.

Self-Test Questions

What do the acronyms ACRS and MACRS stand for?

Briefly describe the tax depreciation system under MACRS.

How does the sale of a depreciable asset affect a firm's cash flows?

Evaluating Capital Budgeting Projects

Up to now, we have discussed several important aspects of cash flow analysis, but we have not seen how they affect capital budgeting decisions. Conceptually, capital budgeting is straightforward: A potential project creates value for the firm's shareholders if and only if the net present value of the incremental cash flows from the project is positive. In practice, however, estimating these cash flows can be difficult.

Incremental cash flows are affected by whether the project is an expansion project or replacement project. A **new expansion project** is defined as one where the firm invests in new assets to increase sales. Here the incremental cash flows are simply the project's cash inflows and outflows. In effect, the company is comparing what its value would be with and without the proposed project. By contrast, a **replacement project** occurs when the firm replaces an existing asset with a new one. In this case, the incremental cash flows are the firm's *additional* inflows and outflows that result from investing in the new project. In a replacement analysis, the company is comparing its value if it takes on the new project to its value if it continues to use the existing asset.[4]

Despite these differences, the basic principles for evaluating expansion and replacement projects are the same. In each case, the cash flows typically include the following items:

1. **Initial investment outlay.** The initial investment includes the up-front cost of fixed assets associated with the project plus any increases in net operating working capital.
2. **Operating cash flows over the project's life.** These are the incremental cash inflows over the project's economic life. Annual operating cash flows equal after-tax operating income plus depreciation. Recall (a) that depreciation is added back because it is a noncash expense and (b) that financing costs (including interest expense) are not included because they are accounted for in the discounting process.
3. **Terminal year cash flows.** At the end of a project's life, some extra cash flows are frequently received. These include the salvage value of the fixed assets, adjusted for taxes if assets are not sold at their book value, plus the return of the net operating working capital.

[4]For more discussion on replacement analysis decisions, refer to the Web/CD Extension for this chapter on the textbook's CD-ROM and web site, **http://www.harcourtcollege.com/finance/theory/**. Also, the file ***Ch 14 Tool Kit.xls***, on the textbook's CD-ROM, provides an example of replacement analysis.

For each year of the project's life, the *net cash flow* is determined as the sum of the cash flows from each of the three categories. These annual net cash flows are then plotted on a time line and used to calculate the project's NPV and IRR.

We will illustrate the principles of capital budgeting analysis by examining a new project being considered by Regency Integrated Chips (RIC), a large Nashville-based technology company. RIC's research and development department has been applying its expertise in microprocessor technology to develop a small computer designed to control home appliances. Once programmed, the computer will automatically control the heating and air-conditioning systems, security system, hot water heater, and even small appliances such as a coffee maker. By increasing a home's energy efficiency, the computer can cut costs enough to pay for itself within a few years. Developments have now reached the stage where a decision must be made about whether or not to go forward with full-scale production.

RIC's marketing vice-president believes that annual sales would be 20,000 units if the units were priced at \$3,000 each, so annual sales are estimated at \$60 million. RIC expects no growth in sales, and it believes that the unit price will rise by 2 percent each year. The engineering department has reported that the project will require additional manufacturing space, and RIC currently has an option to purchase an existing building, at a cost of \$12 million, which would meet this need. The building would be bought and paid for on December 31, 2002, and for depreciation purposes it would fall into the MACRS 39-year class.

The necessary equipment would be purchased and installed in late 2002, and it would also be paid for on December 31, 2002. The equipment would fall into the MACRS 5-year class, and it would cost \$8 million, including transportation and installation.

The project's estimated economic life is four years. At the end of that time, the building is expected to have a market value of \$7.5 million and a book value of \$10.908 million, whereas the equipment would have a market value of \$2 million and a book value of \$1.36 million.

The production department has estimated that variable manufacturing costs would be \$2,100 per unit, and that fixed overhead costs, excluding depreciation, would be \$8 million a year. They expect variable costs to rise by 2 percent per year, and fixed costs to rise by 1 percent per year. Depreciation expenses would be determined in accordance with MACRS rates.

RIC's marginal federal-plus-state tax rate is 40 percent; its cost of capital is 12 percent; and, for capital budgeting purposes, the company's policy is to assume that operating cash flows occur at the end of each year. Because the plant would begin operations on January 1, 2003, the first operating cash flows would occur on December 31, 2003.

Several other points should be noted: (1) RIC is a relatively large corporation, with sales of more than \$4 billion, and it takes on many investments each year. Thus, if the computer control project does not work out, it will not bankrupt the company—management can afford to take a chance on the computer control project. (2) If the project is accepted, the company will be contractually obligated to operate it for its full four-year life. Management must make this commitment to its component suppliers. (3) Returns on this project would be positively correlated with returns on RIC's other projects and also with the stock market—the project should do well if other parts of the firm and the general economy are strong.

Assume that you have been assigned to conduct the capital budgeting analysis. For now, assume that the project has the same risk as an average project, and use the corporate weighted average cost of capital, 12 percent.

Analysis of the Cash Flows

Capital projects can be analyzed using a calculator, paper, and a pencil, or with a spreadsheet program such as *Excel.* Either way, you must set the analysis up as shown in Table 14-3 and go through the steps outlined in Parts 1 through 5 of the table. For exam purposes, you will probably have to work problems with a calculator. However, for reasons that will become obvious as you go through the chapter, in practice spreadsheets are virtually always used. Still, the steps involved in a capital budgeting analysis are the same regardless of whether you use a calculator or a computer to "get the answer."

See ***Ch 14 Tool Kit.xls*** for Table 14-3 details.

Table 14-3, which is a printout from the CD-ROM file ***Ch 14 Tool Kit.xls***, is divided into five parts: (1) Input Data, (2) Depreciation Schedule, (3) Net Salvage Values, (4) Projected Net Cash Flows, and (5) Key Output. There are also two extensions, Parts 6 and 7, that deal with risk analysis and which we will discuss later in the chapter when we cover sensitivity and scenario analyses. Note also that the table shows row and column indicators, so cells in the table have designations such as "Cell D33," which is the location of the cost of the building, found in Part 1, Input Data. If we deleted the row and column indicators, the table would look exactly like the setup for pencil-and-paper calculations.[5] Note also that the first row shown is Row 30; the first 29 rows contain information about the model that we omitted from the text. Finally, the numbers in the printed table are rounded from the actual numbers in the spreadsheet.

Part 1, the Input Data section, provides the basic data used in the analysis. The inputs are really "assumptions"—thus, in the analysis we *assume* that 20,000 units can be sold at a price of $3 per unit.[6] Some of the inputs are known with near certainty—for example, the 40 percent tax rate is not likely to change. Others are more speculative—units sold and the variable cost percentage are in this category. Obviously, if sales or costs are different from the assumed levels, then profits and cash flows, hence NPV and IRR, will differ from their projected levels. Later in the chapter, we discuss how changes in the inputs affect the results.

Part 2, which calculates depreciation over the project's four-year life, is divided into two sections, one for the building and one for the equipment. The first row in each section (Rows 44 and 48) gives the yearly depreciation rates as taken from Table 14-2. The second row in each section (Rows 45 and 49) gives the dollars of depreciation, found as the rate times the asset's depreciable basis, which, in this example, is the initial cost. The third row (Rows 46 and 50) shows the book value at the end of Year 4, found by subtracting the accumulated depreciation from the depreciable basis.

Part 3 estimates the cash flows the firm will realize when it disposes of the assets. Row 57 shows the salvage value, which is the sales price the company expects to receive when it sells the assets four years hence. Row 58 shows the book values at the end of Year 4; these values were calculated in Part 2. Row 59 shows the expected gain or loss, defined as the difference between the sale price and the book value. As explained in notes c and d to Table 14-3, gains and losses are treated as

---

[5]We first set up Table 14-3 as a "regular" table and did all the calculations with a calculator. We then typed all the labels into a spreadsheet and used the spreadsheet to do the calculations. The "answers" derived were identical. We show the spreadsheet version in Table 14-3, but the only visible difference is that it shows row and column indicators. If you have access to a computer, you might want to look at the model, which is on a file named ***Ch 14 Tool kit.xls*** on the CD-ROM that accompanies this book.

[6]Recall that the sales price is actually $3,000, but for convenience we show all dollars in thousands.

TABLE 14-3 Analysis of a New (Expansion) Project
Parts 1 and 2

	A	B	C	D	E	F	G	H	I
30									
31	**Part 1. Input Data (in thousands of dollars)**								
32							**Key Output: NPV**	=	**$5,809**
33	**Building cost (= Depreciable basis)**			**$12,000**					
34	**Equipment cost (= Depreciable basis)**			**$8,000**		**Market value of building in 2006**			**$7,500**
35	**Net Operating WC / Sales**			**10%**		**Market value of equip. in 2006**			**$2,000**
36	**First year sales (in units)**			**20,000**		**Tax rate**			**40%**
37	**Growth rate in units sold**			**0.0%**		**WACC**			**12%**
38	**Sales price per unit**			**$3.00**		**Inflation: growth in sales price**			**2.0%**
39	**Variable cost per unit**			**$2.10**		**Inflation: growth in VC per unit**			**2.0%**
40	**Fixed costs**			**$8,000**		**Inflation: growth in fixed costs**			**1.0%**
41									
42	**Part 2. Depreciation Schedule** [a]				**Years**				**Cumulative**
43					1	2	3	4	**Depr'n**
44	**Building Depr'n Rate**				**1.3%**	**2.6%**	**2.6%**	**2.6%**	
45	**Building Depr'n**				**$156**	**$312**	**$312**	**$312**	**$1,092**
46	**Ending Book Val: Cost - Cum. Depr'n**				**11,844**	**11,532**	**11,220**	**$10,908**	
47									
48	**Equipment Depr'n Rate**				**20.0%**	**32.0%**	**19.0%**	**12.0%**	
49	**Equipment Depr'n**				**$1,600**	**$2,560**	**$1,520**	**$960**	**$6,640**
50	**Ending Book Val: Cost - Cum. Depr'n**				**6,400**	**3,840**	**2,320**	**$1,360**	
51									
52	[a] **The indicated percentages are multiplied by the depreciable basis ($12,000 for the building and $8,000 for the equipment) to determine the depreciation expense for the year. The correct depreciation percentages for the building depend upon the month that the building is put in service. Because this analysis assumes that all cash flows occur at the end of the year, and to prevent unnecessary complexity, we have rounded the depreciation percentages for the building. See the Tab named Depreciation for more**								
53	**details.**								

ordinary income, not capital gains or losses.[7] Therefore, gains result in tax liabilities, and losses produce tax credits, that are equal to the gain or loss times the 40 percent tax rate. Taxes paid and tax credits are shown on Row 60. Row 61 shows the after-tax cash flow the company expects when it disposes of the asset, found as the expected sale price minus the tax liability or plus the credit. Thus, the firm expects to net $8,863 from the sale of the building and $1,744 from the equipment, for a total of $10,607.

Next, in Part 4, we use the information developed in Parts 1, 2, and 3 to find the projected cash flows over the project's life. Five periods are shown, from Year 0 (2002) to Year 4 (2006). The cash outlays required at Year 0 are the negative numbers in

[7]Note again that if an asset is sold for exactly its book value, there will be no gain or loss, hence no tax liability or credit. However, if an asset is sold for other than its book value, a gain or loss will be created. For example, RIC's building will have a book value of $10,908, but the company only expects to realize $7,500 when it is sold. This would result in a loss of $3,408. This indicates that the building should have been depreciated at a faster rate—only if depreciation had been $3,408 larger would the book and market values have been equal. So, the Tax Code stipulates that losses on the sale of operating assets can be used to reduce ordinary income, just as depreciation reduces income. On the other hand, if an asset is sold for more than its book value, as is the case for the equipment, then this signifies that the depreciation rates were too high, so the gain is called "depreciation recapture" by the IRS and is taxed as ordinary income.

TABLE 14-3 Analysis of a New (Expansion) Project
Part 3

	A	B	C	D	E	F	G	H	I
55	**Part 3 of Table 14-3. Net Salvage Values in 2006**								
56					Building	Equipment	Total		
57	Estimated Market Value in 2006				$7,500	$2,000			
58	Book Value in 2006[b]				10,908	1,360			
59	Expected Gain or Loss[c]				-3,408	640			
60	Taxes paid or tax credit				-1,363	256			
61	Net cash flow from salvage[d]				$8,863	$1,744	$10,607		
62									
63	[b] Book value equals depreciable basis (initial cost in this case) minus accumulated MACRS depreciation. For the								
64	building, accumulated depreciation equals $1,092, so book value equals $12,000 - $1,092 = $10,908. For the equipment,								
65	accumulated depreciation equals $6,640, so book value equals $8,000 - $6,640 = $1,360.								
66									
67	[c] Building: $7,500 market value - $10,908 book value = -$3,408, a loss. This represents a shortfall in depreciation								
68	taken versus "true" depreciation, and it is treated as an operating expense for 2006. Equipment: $2,000 market value -								
69	$1,360 book value = $640 profit. Here the depreciation charge exceeds the "true" depreciation, and the difference is called								
70	"depreciation recapture". It is taxed as ordinary income in 2006. The actual book value at the time of disposition depends on the month of disposition. We have simplified the analysis and assumed that there will be a full year of depreciation in 2006.								
71									
72	[d] Net cash flow from salvage equals salvage (market) value minus taxes. For the building, the loss results in a tax credit, so								
73	net salvage value = $7,500 - (-$1,363) = $8,863.								

Column E for 2002, and their sum, −$26,000, is shown at the bottom in cell E105. Then, in the next four columns, we calculate the operating cash flows. We begin with sales revenues, found as the product of units sold and the sales price. Next, we subtract variable costs, which were assumed to be $2.10 per unit. We then deduct fixed operating costs and depreciation to obtain taxable operating income, or EBIT. When taxes (at a 40 percent rate) are subtracted, we are left with net operating profit after taxes, or NOPAT. Note, though, that we are seeking cash flows, not accounting income. Thus, depreciation must be added back.

RIC must purchase raw materials and replenish them each year as they are used. In Part 1 we assume that RIC must have an amount of NOWC on hand equal to 10 percent of the upcoming year's sales. For example, sales in Year 1 are $60,000, so RIC must have $6,000 in NOWC at Year 0, as shown in Cell E97. Because RIC had no NOWC prior to Year 0, it must make a $6,000 investment in NOWC at Year 0, as shown in Cell E98. Sales increase to $61,200 in Year 2, so RIC must have $6,120 of NOWC at Year 1. Because it already had $6,000 in NOWC on hand, its net investment at Year 1 is just $120, shown in Cell F98. Note that RIC will have no sales after Year 4, so it will require no NOWC at Year 4. Thus, it has a positive cash flow of $6,367 at Year 4 as working capital is sold but not replaced.

When the project's life ends, the company will receive the "Salvage Cash Flows" as shown in the column for Year 4 in the lower part of the table. When the company disposes of the building and equipment at the end of Year 4, it will receive cash as estimated back in Part 3 of the table. Thus, the total salvage cash flow amounts to $10,607 as shown on Row 103. When we sum the subtotals in Part 4, we obtain the net cash flows shown on Row 105. Those cash flows constitute a *cash flow time line*, and they are then evaluated in Part 5 of Table 14-3.

TABLE 14-3 Analysis of a New (Expansion) Project
Part 4

	A B C D	E	F	G	H	I
75	**Part 4 of Table 14-3. Projected Net Cash**			Years		
76	**Flows (Time line of annual cash flows)**	0	1	2	3	4
77		2002	2003	2004	2005	2006
78	*Investment Outlays: Long-Term Assets*					
79	Building	($12,000)				
80	Equipment	(8,000)				
81						
82	*Operating Cash Flows over the Project's Life*					
83	Units sold		20,000	20,000	20,000	20,000
84	Sales price		$3.00	$3.06	$3.12	$3.18
85	Sales revenue		$60,000	$61,200	$62,424	$63,672
86	Variable costs		42,000	42,840	43,697	44,571
87	Fixed operating costs		8,000	8,080	8,161	8,242
88	Depreciation (building)		156	312	312	312
89	Depreciation (equipment)		1,600	2,560	1,520	960
90	Oper. income before taxes (EBIT)		8,244	7,408	8,734	9,587
91	Taxes on operating income (40%)		3,298	2,963	3,494	3,835
92	Net Operating Profit After Taxes (NOPAT)		4,946	4,445	5,241	5,752
93	Add back depreciation		1,756	2,872	1,832	1,272
94	Operating cash flow		$6,702	$7,317	$7,073	$7,024
95						
96	*Cash Flows Due to Net Operating Working Capital*					
97	Net Operating Working Capital (based on sales)	$6,000	$6,120	$6,242	$6,367	$0
98	Cash flow due to investment in NOWC	($6,000)	($120)	($122)	($125)	$6,367
99						
100	*Salvage Cash Flows: Long-Term Assets*					
101	Net salvage cash flow: Building					$8,863
102	Net salvage cash flow: Equipment					1,744
103	Total salvage cash flows					$10,607
104						
105	Net Cash Flow (Time line of cash flows)	($26,000)	$6,582	$7,194	$6,948	$23,999
106						

Making the Decision

Part 5 of the table shows the standard evaluation criteria—NPV, IRR, MIRR, and payback—based on the cash flows shown on Row 105. The NPV is positive, the IRR and MIRR both exceed the 12 percent cost of capital, and the payback indicates that the project will return the invested funds in 3.22 years. Therefore, on the basis of the analysis thus far, it appears that the project should be accepted. Note, though, that we have been assuming that the project is about as risky as the company's average project. If the project were judged to be riskier than average, it would be necessary to increase the cost of capital, which might cause the NPV to become negative and the IRR and MIRR to drop below the then-higher WACC. Therefore, we cannot make a final "go, no-go" decision until we evaluate the project's risk, the topic of a later section.

Self-Test Questions

What three types of cash flows must be considered when evaluating a proposed project?

Differentiate between a new expansion project and a replacement project.

TABLE 14-3 Analysis of a New (Expansion) Project
Part 5

	A	B	C	D	E	F	G	H	I
107	**Part 5 of Table 14-3. Key Output and Appraisal of the Proposed Project**								
108									
109	Net Present Value (at 12%)			$5,809					
110	IRR			20.12%					
111	MIRR			17.79%			Years		
112					0	1	2	3	4
113	Cumulative cash flow for payback				(26,000)	(19,418)	(12,223)	(5,275)	18,723
114	Cum. CF > 0, hence Payback Year:				FALSE	FALSE	FALSE	FALSE	3.22
115	Payback found with Excel function =			3.22	See note below for an explanation of the Excel calculation.				
116	Check: Payback = 3 + 5,275/23,999 =			3.22	Manual calculation for the base case.				
117									
118	The Excel payback calculation is based on the logical IF function. Returns FALSE if the cumulative CF is negative or								
119	the actual payback if the cumulative CF is positive. Then, we use the MIN (minimum) function to find first year when								
120	payback is positive. The Min function procedure is necessary for projects with longer lives, because then values, not the								
121	word FALSE, would appear in a number of cells. The Min function picks the smallest number, which is the payback.								

Adjusting for Inflation

Inflation is a fact of life in the United States and most other nations, so it must be considered in any sound capital budgeting analysis.[8]

Inflation-Induced Bias

Note that *in the absence of inflation*, the real rate, k_r, would be equal to the nominal rate, k_n. Moreover, the real and nominal expected net cash flows—RCF_t and NCF_t—would also be equal. Remember that *real* interest rates and cash flows do not include inflation effects, while *nominal* rates and flows do reflect the effects of inflation. In particular, an inflation premium, IP, is built into all nominal market interest rates. In the absence of inflation, NPV can thus be calculated in either of two ways:

$$\text{NPV (no inflation)} = \sum_{t=0}^{n} \frac{RCF_t}{(1 + k_r)^t} = \sum_{t=0}^{n} \frac{NCF_t}{(1 + k_n)^t}. \qquad \textbf{(14-1)}$$

Now suppose the expected rate of inflation is positive, and we expect *all* of the project's cash flows—including those related to depreciation—to rise at the rate i. Further, assume that this same inflation rate, i, is built into the market cost of capital as an inflation premium, IP = i. In this situation, the nominal net cash flow, NCF_t, will increase annually at the rate of i percent, producing this result:

$$NCF_t = RCF_t(1 + i)^t.$$

For example, if we expected a net cash flow of \$100 in Year 5 in the absence of inflation, then with a 5 percent annual rate of inflation, $NCF_5 = \$100(1.05)^5 = \$127.63$.

In general, the cost of capital used as the discount rate in capital budgeting analysis is based on the market-determined costs of debt and equity, so it is a nominal rate.

[8]For some classic articles on this subject, see James C. Van Horne, "A Note on Biases in Capital Budgeting Introduced by Inflation," *Journal of Financial and Quantitative Analysis*, January 1971, 653–658; Philip L. Cooley, Rodney L. Roenfeldt, and It-Keong Chew, "Capital Budgeting Procedures under Inflation," *Financial Management*, Winter 1975, 18–27; and "Cooley, Roenfeldt, and Chew vs. Findlay and Frankle," *Financial Management*, Autumn 1976, 83–90.

To convert a real interest rate to a nominal rate when the inflation rate is i, we use this formula:

$$(1 + k_n) = (1 + k_r)(1 + i).$$

For example, if the real cost of capital is 7 percent and the inflation rate is 5 percent, then $1 + k_n = (1.07)(1.05) = 1.1235$, so $k_n = 12.35\%$.

Now if net cash flows increase at the rate of i percent per year, and if this same inflation premium is built into the firm's cost of capital, then the NPV would be calculated as follows:

$$\text{NPV (with inflation)} = \sum_{t=0}^{n} \frac{NCF_t}{(1 + k_n)^t} = \sum_{t=0}^{n} \frac{RCF_t(1 + i)^t}{(1 + k_r)^t(1 + i)^t}. \qquad \textbf{(14-2)}$$

Since the $(1 + i)^t$ terms in the numerator and denominator cancel, we are left with Equation 14-1:

$$\text{NPV} = \sum_{t=0}^{n} \frac{RCF_t}{(1 + k_r)^t}.$$

Thus, if all costs and also the sales price, hence annual cash flows, are expected to rise at the same inflation rate that investors have built into the cost of capital, then the inflation-adjusted NPV as determined using Equation 14-2 is identical to the real NPV found using Equation 14-1.[9] For example, the PV of a real \$100 at Year 5 at a real rate of 7 percent is \$71.30 = \$100/(1.07)^5. The PV of a nominal \$127.63 at Year 5 at a nominal rate of 12.35 percent is also \$71.30 = \$127.63/(1.1235)^5.

However, firms occasionally use base year, or constant (unadjusted), dollars throughout the analysis—say, 2002 dollars if the analysis is done in 2002—along with a cost of capital as determined in the marketplace as we described in Chapter 11. This is wrong: *If the cost of capital includes an inflation premium, as it typically does, but the cash flows are all stated in constant (unadjusted) dollars, then the calculated NPV will be downward biased.* The denominator will reflect inflation, but the numerator will not, and this will produce a downward-biased NPV.

Making the Inflation Adjustment

There are two ways to adjust for inflation. First, all project cash flows can be expressed as real (unadjusted) flows, with no consideration of inflation, and then the cost of capital can be adjusted to a real rate by removing the inflation premiums from the component costs. This approach is simple in theory, but to produce an unbiased NPV it requires (1) that all project cash flows, including depreciation, be affected identically by inflation, and (2) that this rate of increase equals the inflation rate built into investors' required returns. Since these assumptions do not necessarily hold in practice, this method is not commonly used.

The second method involves leaving the cost of capital in its nominal form, and then adjusting the individual cash flows to reflect expected inflation. This is what we did earlier in our RIC example as summarized in Table 14-3. There we assumed that sales prices and variable costs would increase at a rate of 2 percent per year, fixed costs would increase by 1 percent per year, and that depreciation charges would not be

---

[9]To focus on inflation effects, we have simplified the situation somewhat. The actual project cost of capital is made up of debt and equity components, both of which are affected by inflation, but only the debt component is adjusted for tax effects. Thus, the relationship between nominal and real costs of capital is more complex than indicated in our discussion here.

affected by inflation. One should always build inflation into the cash flow analysis, with the specific adjustment reflecting as accurately as possible the most likely set of circumstances. With a spreadsheet, it is easy to make the adjustments.

Our conclusions about inflation may be summarized as follows. First, inflation is critically important, for it can and does have major effects on businesses. Therefore, it must be recognized and dealt with. Second, the most effective way of dealing with inflation in capital budgeting analyses is to build inflation estimates into each cash flow element, using the best available information on how each element will be affected. Third, since we cannot estimate future inflation rates with precision, errors are bound to be made. Thus, inflation adds to the uncertainty, or riskiness, of capital budgeting as well as to its complexity.

Self-Test Questions

Under what seemingly straightforward method of analysis would inflation cause a bias in a project's estimated NPV? Would the bias be upward or downward?

What is the best way of handling inflation, and how does this procedure eliminate the potential bias?

Introduction to Project Risk Analysis

Up to now we have simply assumed that projects will produce a given set of cash flows, and we then analyzed those cash flows to decide whether to accept or reject the project. Obviously, though, cash flows are not known with certainty. We now turn to risk in capital budgeting, examining the techniques firms use to determine a project's risk and then to decide whether its profit potential is worth the risk.

Recall from Chapter 11 that there are three distinct types of risk: stand-alone risk, corporate risk, and market risk. Given that the firm's primary objective is to maximize stockholder value, what ultimately matters is the risk that a project imposes on stockholders. Because stockholders are generally diversified, market risk is theoretically the most relevant measure of risk. Corporate risk is also important for these three reasons:

1. Undiversified stockholders, including the owners of small businesses, are more concerned about corporate risk than about market risk.
2. Empirical studies of the determinants of required rates of return generally find that both market and corporate risk affect stock prices. This suggests that investors, even those who are well diversified, consider factors other than market risk when they establish required returns.
3. The firm's stability is important to its managers, workers, customers, suppliers, and creditors, as well as to the community in which it operates. Firms that are in serious danger of bankruptcy, or even of suffering low profits and reduced output, have difficulty attracting and retaining good managers and workers. Also, both suppliers and customers are reluctant to depend on weak firms, and such firms have difficulty borrowing money at reasonable interest rates. These factors tend to reduce risky firms' profitability and hence their stock prices, and this makes corporate risk significant.

For these three reasons, corporate risk is important even if a firm's stockholders are well diversified.

Self-Test Questions

What are the three types of project risk?

Why are (1) market and (2) corporate risk both important?

Techniques for Measuring Stand-Alone Risk

Why should a project's stand-alone risk be important to anyone? In theory, this type of risk should be of little or no concern. However, it is actually of great importance for two reasons:

1. It is easier to estimate a project's stand-alone risk than its corporate risk, and it is far easier to measure stand-alone risk than market risk.
2. In the vast majority of cases, all three types of risk are highly correlated—if the general economy does well, so will the firm, and if the firm does well, so will most of its projects. Because of this high correlation, stand-alone risk is generally a good proxy for hard-to-measure corporate and market risk.

The starting point for analyzing a project's stand-alone risk involves determining the uncertainty inherent in its cash flows. To illustrate what is involved, consider again Regency Integrated Chips' appliance control computer project that we discussed above. Many of the key inputs shown in Part 1 of Table 14-3 are subject to uncertainty. For example, sales were projected at 20,000 units to be sold at a net price of $3,000 per unit. However, actual unit sales will almost certainly be somewhat higher or lower than 20,000, and the sales price will probably turn out to be different from the projected $3,000 per unit. *In effect, the sales quantity and price estimates are really expected values based on probability distributions, as are many of the other values that were shown in Part 1 of Table 14-3.* The distributions could be relatively "tight," reflecting small standard deviations and low risk, or they could be "wide," denoting a great deal of uncertainty about the actual value of the variable in question and thus a high degree of stand-alone risk.

The nature of the individual cash flow distributions, and their correlations with one another, determine the nature of the NPV probability distribution and, thus, the project's stand-alone risk. In the following sections, we discuss three techniques for assessing a project's stand-alone risk: (1) sensitivity analysis, (2) scenario analysis, and (3) Monte Carlo simulation.

Sensitivity Analysis

Intuitively, we know that many of the variables that determine a project's cash flows could turn out to be different from the values used in the analysis. We also know that a change in a key input variable, such as units sold, will cause the NPV to change. **Sensitivity analysis** is a technique that indicates how much NPV will change in response to a given change in an input variable, other things held constant.

Sensitivity analysis begins with a *base-case* situation, which is developed using the *expected* values for each input. To illustrate, consider the data given back in Table 14-3, where projected cash flows for RIC's computer project were shown. The values used to develop the table, including unit sales, sales price, fixed costs, and variable costs, are all most likely, or base-case, values, and the resulting $5.809 million NPV shown in Table 14-3 is called the **base-case NPV.** Now we ask a series of "what if" questions: "What if unit sales fall 15 percent below the most likely level?" "What if the sales price per unit falls?" "What if variable costs are $2.50 per unit rather than the expected $2.10?" Sensitivity analysis is designed to provide decision makers with answers to questions such as these.

In a sensitivity analysis, each variable is changed by several percentage points above and below the expected value, holding all other variables constant. Then a new NPV is calculated using each of these values. Finally, the set of NPVs is plotted to show how sensitive NPV is to changes in each variable. Figure 14-1 shows the computer project's sensitivity graphs for six of the input variables. The table below the graph gives the NPVs that were used to construct the graph. The slopes of the lines in the graph show how sensitive NPV is to changes in each of the inputs: *the steeper the slope, the more sensitive the NPV is to a change in the variable.* From the figure and the table, we see that the project's NPV is very sensitive to changes in the sales price and variable costs, fairly sensitive to changes in the growth rate and units sold, and not very sensitive to changes in either fixed costs or the cost of capital.

If we were comparing two projects, the one with the steeper sensitivity lines would be riskier, because for that project a relatively small error in estimating a variable such as unit sales would produce a large error in the project's expected NPV. Thus, sensitivity analysis can provide useful insights into the riskiness of a project.

Before we move on, we should note that spreadsheet computer programs such as *Excel* are ideally suited for sensitivity analysis. We used the model that generated Table

FIGURE 14-1 Evaluating Risk: Sensitivity Analysis (Dollars in Thousands)

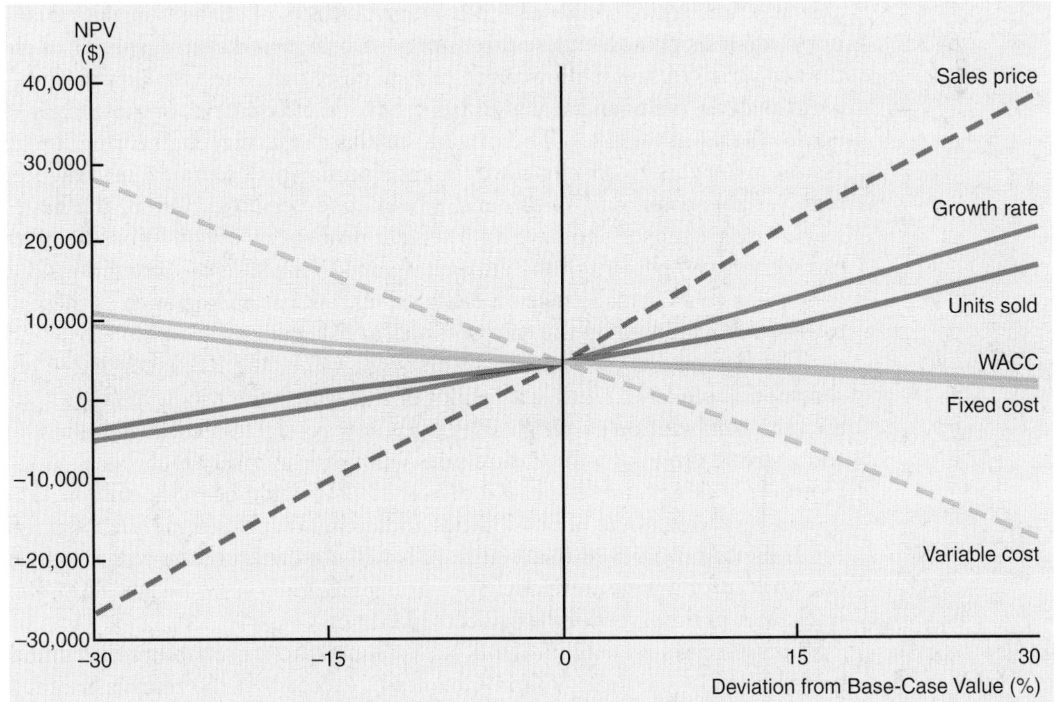

NPV at Different Deviations from Base

Deviation from Base Case	Sales Price	Variable Cost/Unit	Growth Rate	Year 1 Units Sold	Fixed Cost	WACC
−30%	($27,223)	$29,404	($ 4,923)	($ 3,628)	$10,243	$9,030
−15	(10,707)	17,607	(115)	1,091	8,026	7,362
0	5,809	5,809	5,809	5,809	5,809	5,809
15	22,326	(5,988)	12,987	10,528	3,593	4,363
30	38,842	(17,785)	21,556	15,247	1,376	3,014
Range	$66,064	$47,189	$26,479	$18,875	$8,867	$6,016

14-3 for the analyses represented in Figure 14-1; the model generated the NPVs and then drew the graphs. To conduct such an analysis by hand would be extremely time consuming.

Scenario Analysis

Although sensitivity analysis is probably the most widely used risk analysis technique, it does have limitations. For example, we saw earlier that the computer project's NPV is highly sensitive to changes in the sales price and the variable cost per unit. Those sensitivities suggest that the project is risky. Suppose, however, that Home Depot or Circuit City was anxious to get the new computer product and would sign a contract to purchase 20,000 units per year for four years at $3,000 per unit. Moreover, suppose Intel would agree to provide the principal component at a price that would ensure that the variable cost per unit would not exceed $2,200. Under these conditions, there would be a low probability of high or low sales prices and input costs, so the project would not be at all risky in spite of its sensitivity to those variables.

We see, then, that we need to extend sensitivity analysis to deal with the *probability distributions* of the inputs. In addition, it would be useful to vary more than one variable at a time so we could see the combined effects of changes in the variables. **Scenario analysis** provides these extensions—it brings in the probabilities of changes in the key variables, and it allows us to change more than one variable at a time. In a scenario analysis, the financial analyst begins with the **base case,** or most likely set of values for the input variables. Then, he or she asks marketing, engineering, and other operating managers to specify a **worst-case scenario** (low unit sales, low sales price, high variable costs, and so on) and a **best-case scenario.** Often, the best case and worst case are set so as to have a 25 percent probability of conditions being that good or bad, and a 50 percent probability is assigned to the base-case conditions. Obviously, conditions could actually take on other values, but parameters such as these are useful to get people focused on the central issues in risk analysis.

The best-case, base-case, and worst-case values for RIC's computer project are shown in Table 14-4, along with a plot of the data. If the product is highly successful, then the combination of a high sales price, low production costs, high first year sales, and a strong growth rate in future sales will result in a very high NPV, $146 million. However, if things turn out badly, then the NPV would be −$32 million. The graphs show a very wide range of possibilities, indicating that this is indeed a very risky project. If the bad conditions materialize, this will not bankrupt the company—this is just one project for a large company. Still, losing $32 million would certainly not help the stock price or the career of the project's manager.

The scenario probabilities and NPVs constitute a probability distribution of returns like those we dealt with in Chapter 6, except that the returns are measured in dollars instead of percentages (rates of return). The expected NPV (in thousands of dollars) is $31,385:[10]

$$\begin{aligned}\text{Expected NPV} &= \sum_{i=1}^{n} P_i(\text{NPV}_i)\\ &= 0.25(\$146{,}180) + 0.50(\$5{,}809) + 0.25(-\$32{,}257)\\ &= \$31{,}385.\end{aligned}$$

[10]Note that the expected NPV, $31,385, is *not* the same as the base-case NPV, $5,809 (in thousands). This is because the two uncertain variables, sales volume and sales price, are multiplied together to obtain dollar sales, and this process causes the NPV distribution to be skewed to the right. A big number times another big number produces a very big number, which, in turn, causes the average, or expected value, to increase.

TABLE 14-4 Scenario Analysis (Dollars in Thousands)

Scenario	Probability	Sales Price	Unit Sales	Variable Costs	Growth Rate	NPV
Best case	25%	$3.90	26,000	$1.47	30%	$146,180
Base case	50	3.00	20,000	2.10	0	5,809
Worst case	25	2.10	14,000	2.73	−30	(32,257)
		Expected NPV =				$31,385
		Standard deviation =				$68,074
		Coefficient of variation = Standard deviation/Expected NPV				2.17

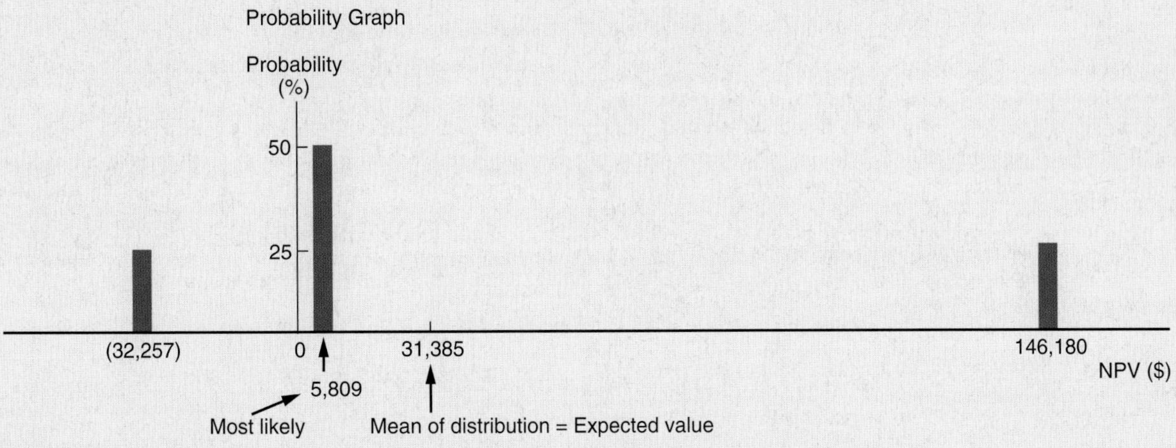

Note: The scenario analysis calculations were performed in the *Excel* model, ***Ch 14 Tool Kit.xls***.

The standard deviation of the NPV is $68,074 (in thousands of dollars):

$$\sigma_{NPV} = \sqrt{\sum_{i=1}^{n} P_i(NPV_i - \text{Expected NPV})^2}$$

$$= \sqrt{\begin{aligned}&0.25(\$146{,}180 - \$31{,}385)^2 + 0.50(\$5{,}809 - \$31{,}385)^2\\ &+ 0.25(-\$32{,}257 - \$31{,}385)^2\end{aligned}}$$

$$= \$68{,}074.$$

Finally, the project's coefficient of variation is 2.17:

$$CV_{NPV} = \frac{\sigma_{NPV}}{E(NPV)} = \frac{\$68{,}074}{\$31{,}385} = 2.17.$$

The project's coefficient of variation can be compared with the coefficient of variation of RIC's "average" project to get an idea of the relative riskiness of the watering system project. RIC's existing projects, on average, have a coefficient of variation of about 1.0, so, on the basis of this stand-alone risk measure, we conclude that the project is much riskier than an "average" project.

Scenario analysis provides useful information about a project's stand-alone risk. However, it is limited in that it considers only a few discrete outcomes (NPVs), even though there are an infinite number of possibilities. We describe a more complete method of assessing a project's stand-alone risk in the next section.

Capital Budgeting Practices in the Asia/Pacific Region

A recent survey of executives in Australia, Hong Kong, Indonesia, Malaysia, the Philippines, and Singapore asked several questions about their companies' capital budgeting practices. The study yielded some interesting results, which are summarized here.

Techniques for Evaluating Corporate Projects

Consistent with evidence on U.S. companies, most companies in this region evaluate projects using IRR, NPV, and payback. IRR use ranged from 86 percent (in Hong Kong) to 96 percent (in Australia). NPV use ranged from 81 percent (in the Philippines) to 96 percent (in Australia). Payback use ranged from 81 percent (in Indonesia) to 100 percent (in Hong Kong and the Philippines).

Techniques for Estimating the Cost of Equity Capital

Recall from Chapter 11 that three basic approaches can be used to estimate the cost of equity: CAPM, dividend yield plus growth rate (DCF), and cost of debt plus a risk premium. The use of these methods varied considerably from country to country (see Table A).

We noted in Chapter 13 that the CAPM is used most often by U.S. firms. (See the box in Chapter 13 entitled, "Techniques Firms Use to Evaluate Corporate Projects".) Except for Australia, this is not the case for Asian/Pacific firms, who instead more often use the other two approaches.

Techniques for Assessing Risk

Finally, firms in these six countries rely heavily on scenario and sensitivity analyses to assess project risk. They also use decision trees (which we discuss in Chapter 15) and Monte Carlo simulation, but less frequently than the other techniques (see Table B).

Source: George W. Kester et al., "Capital Budgeting Practices in the Asia-Pacific Region: Australia, Hong Kong, Indonesia, Malaysia, Philippines, and Singapore," *Financial Practice and Education*, vol. 9, no. 1, Spring/Summer 1999, 25–33.

TABLE A

Method	Australia	Hong Kong	Indonesia	Malaysia	Philippines	Singapore
CAPM	72.7%	26.9%	0.0%	6.2%	24.1%	17.0%
Dividend yield plus growth rate	16.4	53.8	33.3	50.0	34.5	42.6
Cost of debt plus risk premium	10.9	23.1	53.4	37.5	58.6	42.6

TABLE B

Risk Assessment Technique	Australia	Hong Kong	Indonesia	Malaysia	Philippines	Singapore
Scenario analysis	96%	100%	94%	80%	97%	90%
Sensitivity analysis	100	100	88	83	94	79
Decision tree analysis	44	58	50	37	33	46
Monte Carlo simulation	38	35	25	9	24	35

Monte Carlo Simulation

Monte Carlo simulation, so named because this type of analysis grew out of work on the mathematics of casino gambling, ties together sensitivities and probability distributions. While Monte Carlo simulation is considerably more complex than scenario analysis, simulation software packages make this process manageable. Many of these packages are included as add-ons to spreadsheet programs such as *Microsoft Excel.*

High-Tech CFOs

Recent developments in technology have made it easier for corporations to utilize complex risk analysis techniques. New software and higher-powered computers enable financial managers to process large amounts of information, so technically astute finance people can consider a broad range of scenarios using computers to estimate the effects of changes in sales, operating costs, interest rates, the overall economy, and even the weather. Given such analysis, financial managers can make better decisions as to which course of action is most likely to maximize shareholder wealth.

Risk analysis can also take account of the correlation between various types of risk. For example, if interest rates and currencies tend to move together in a particular way, this tendency can be incorporated into the model. This can enable financial managers to make better estimates of the likelihood and effect of "worst-case" outcomes.

While this type of risk analysis is undeniably useful, it is only as good as the information and assumptions used in the models. Also, risk models frequently involve complex calculations, and they generate output that requires financial managers to have a fair amount of mathematical sophistication. However, technology is helping to solve these problems, and new programs have been developed to present risk analysis in an intuitive way. For example, Andrew Lo, an MIT finance professor, has developed a program that summarizes the risk, return, and liquidity profiles of various strategies using a new data visualization process that enables complicated relationships to be plotted along three-dimensional graphs that are easy to interpret. While some old-guard CFOs may bristle at these new approaches, younger and more computer-savvy CFOs are likely to embrace them. As Lo puts it: "The video-game generation just loves these 3-D tools."

Source: Adapted from "The CFO Goes 3-D: Higher Math and Savvy Software Are Crucial," *Business Week*, October 28, 1996, 144, 150.

WWW

There are several Monte Carlo simulation software packages available that work as add-ons to popular PC spreadsheet programs. A demo version of one, called @RISK, can be downloaded from **http://www.palisade.com/html/risk.html**.

In a simulation analysis, the computer begins by picking at random a value for each variable—sales in units, the sales price, the variable cost per unit, and so on. Then those values are combined, and the project's NPV is calculated and stored in the computer's memory. Next, a second set of input values is selected at random, and a second NPV is calculated. This process is repeated perhaps 1,000 times, generating 1,000 NPVs. The mean and standard deviation of the set of NPVs is determined. The mean, or average value, is used as a measure of the project's expected NPV, and the standard deviation (or coefficient of variation) is used as a measure of risk.

Using this procedure, we conducted a simulation analysis of RIC's proposed project. As in our scenario analysis, we simplified the illustration by specifying the distributions for only four key variables: (1) sales price, (2) variable cost, (3) Year 1 units sold, and (4) growth rate.

We assumed that sales price can be represented by a continuous normal distribution with an expected value of $3.00 and a standard deviation of $0.35. Recall from Chapter 6 that there is about a 68 percent chance that the actual price will be within one standard deviation of the expected price, which results in a range of $2.65 to $3.35. Put another way, there is only a 32 percent chance that the price will fall outside the indicated range. Note too that there is less than a 1 percent chance that the actual price will be more than three standard deviations of the expected price, which gives us a range of $1.95 to $4.05. Therefore, the sales price is very unlikely to be less than $1.95 or more than $4.05.

RIC has existing labor contracts and strong relationships with some of its suppliers, which makes the variable cost less uncertain. In the simulation we assumed that the variable cost can be described by a triangular distribution, with a lower bound of $1.40, a most likely value of $2.10, and an upper bound of $2.50. Note that this is not a symmetric distribution. The lower bound is $0.70 less than the most likely value, but the upper bound is only $0.40 higher than the most likely value. This is because RIC has an active risk management program under which it hedges against increases in the prices of the commodities used in its production processes. We discuss risk management in more detail in Chapter 25, but the net effect is that RIC's hedging activities reduce its exposure to price increases but still allow it to take advantage of falling prices.

Based on preliminary purchase agreements with major customers, RIC is certain that sales in the first year will be at least 15,000 units. The marketing department believes the most likely demand will be 20,000 units, but it is possible that demand will be much higher. The plant can produce a maximum of 30,000 units in the first year, although production can be expanded in subsequent years if there is higher than expected demand. Therefore, we represented Year 1 unit sales with a triangular distribution with a lower bound of 15,000 units, a most likely value of 20,000 units, and an upper bound of 30,000 units.

The marketing department anticipates no growth in unit sales after the first year, but it recognizes that actual sales growth could be either positive or negative. Moreover, actual growth is likely to be positively correlated with units sold in the first year, which means that if demand is higher than expected in the first year, then growth will probably be higher than expected in subsequent years. We represented growth with a normal distribution having an expected value of 0 percent and a standard deviation of 15 percent. We also specified the correlation between Year 1 unit sales and growth in sales to be 65 percent.

We used these inputs and the model from ***Ch 14 Tool Kit.xls*** to conduct the simulation analysis. If you want to do the simulation yourself, you should first read the instructions in the file ***Explanation of Simulation.doc***. This explains how to install an Excel add-in, ***Simtools.xla,*** which is necessary to run the simulation. After you have installed ***Simtools.xla,*** you can run the simulation analysis, which is in a separate spreadsheet, ***Ch 14 Simulation.xls.***[11] All three files are included with your textbook's CD-ROM. Using this model, we simulated 1,000 outcomes for the capital budgeting project. Table 14-5 presents selected results from the simulation.

After running the simulation, the first thing to do is to ensure that the results are consistent with our assumptions. The resulting mean and standard deviation of sales price are \$3.01 and \$0.35, respectively, which are virtually identical to our

[11]We are grateful to Professor Roger Myerson of Northwestern University for making ***Simtool.xla*** available to us.

Note too that there are a number of commercially available simulation programs that can be used with *Excel*, including *@Risk* and *Crystal Ball*. Many universities and companies have such a program installed on their networks, and they can also be installed on PCs.

TABLE 14-5 Summary of Simulation Results (Thousands of Dollars)

	Risky Inputs				Output
	Sales Price	Variable Cost	Unit Sales	Growth	NPV
Mean	\$3.01	\$2.00	21,662	−0.4%	\$13,867
Standard deviation	0.35	0.23	3,201	14.8	22,643
Maximum	4.00	2.47	29,741	42.7	124,091
Minimum	1.92	1.40	15,149	−51.5	−49,550
Median					10,607
Probability of NPV > 0					72.8%
Coefficient of variation					1.63

assumptions. Similarly, the resulting mean of −0.4 percent and standard deviation of 14.8 percent for growth are very close to our assumed distribution. The maximum for variable cost is $2.47, which is just under our specified maximum of $2.50, and the minimum is $1.40, which is equal to our specified minimum. Unit sales have a maximum of 29,741 and a minimum of 15,149, both of which are consistent with our assumptions. Finally, the resulting correlation between unit sales and growth is 66.4 percent, which is very close to our assumed correlation of 65 percent. Therefore, the results of the simulation are consistent with our assumptions.

Table 14-5 also reports summary statistics for the project's NPV. The mean is $13,867, which suggests that the project should be accepted. However, the range of outcomes is quite large, from a loss of $49,550 to a gain of $124,091, so the project is clearly risky. The standard deviation of $22,643 indicates that losses could easily occur, and this is consistent with this wide range of possible outcomes.[12] The coefficient of variation is 1.63, which is large compared with most of RIC's other projects. Table 14-5 also reports a median NPV of $10,607, which means

[12]Note that the standard deviation of NPV in the simulation is much smaller than the standard deviation in the scenario analysis. In the scenario analysis, we assumed that all of the poor outcomes would occur together in the worst-case scenario, and all of the positive outcomes would occur together in the best-case scenario. In other words, we implicitly assumed that all of the risky variables were perfectly positively correlated. In the simulation, we assumed that the variables were independent, with the exception of the correlation between unit sales and growth. The independence of variables in the simulation reduces the range of outcomes. For example, in the simulation, sometimes the sales price is high, but the sales growth is low. In the scenario analysis, a high sales price is always coupled with high growth. Because the scenario analysis's assumption of perfect correlation is unlikely, simulation may provide a better estimate of project risk. However, if the standard deviations and correlations used as inputs in the simulation are not estimated accurately, then the simulation output will likewise be inaccurate. Remember the terms GIGO, or "garbage in, garbage out," and SWAG, or "scientific wild a_ _ guess"!

FIGURE 14-2 NPV Probability Distribution

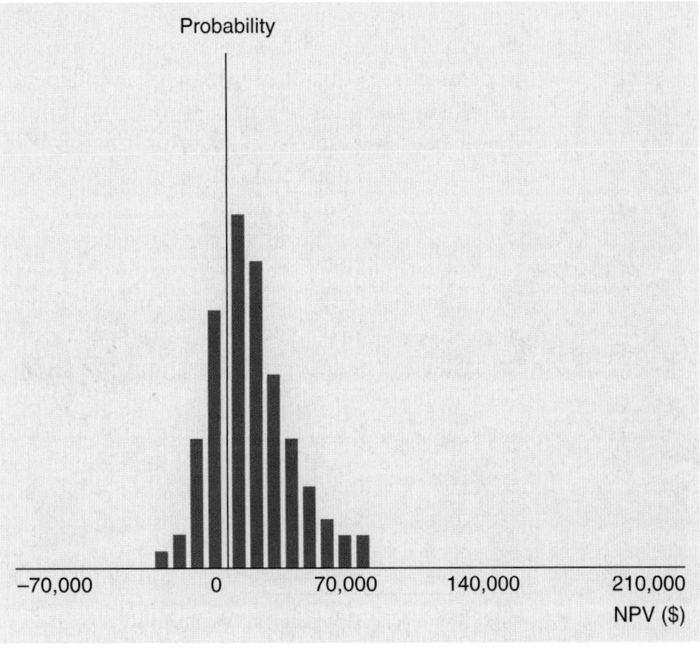

that half the time the project will have an NPV greater than $10,607. The table also reports that 72.8 percent of the time we would expect the project to have a positive NPV.

A picture is worth a thousand words, and Figure 14-2 shows the probability distribution of the outcomes. Note that the distribution of outcomes is skewed to the right. As the figure shows, the potential downside losses are not as large as the potential upside gains. Our conclusion is that this is a very risky project, as indicated by the coefficient of variation, but it does have a positive expected NPV and the potential to be a home run.

Self-Test Questions

List two reasons why, in practice, a project's stand-alone risk is important.

Differentiate between sensitivity and scenario analyses. What advantage does scenario analysis have over sensitivity analysis?

What is Monte Carlo simulation?

Project Risk Conclusions

We have discussed the three types of risk normally considered in capital budgeting analysis—stand-alone risk, within-firm (or corporate) risk, and market risk—and we have discussed ways of assessing each. However, two important questions remain: (1) Should firms be concerned with stand-alone or corporate risk in their capital budgeting decisions, and (2) what do we do when the stand-alone, within-firm, and market risk assessments lead to different conclusions?

These questions do not have easy answers. From a theoretical standpoint, well-diversified investors should be concerned only with market risk, managers should be concerned only with stock price maximization, and this should lead to the conclusion that market (beta) risk ought to be given virtually all the weight in capital budgeting decisions. However, if investors are not well diversified, if the CAPM does not operate exactly as theory says it should, or if measurement problems keep managers from having confidence in the CAPM approach in capital budgeting, it may be appropriate to give stand-alone and corporate risk more weight than financial theory suggests. Note also that the CAPM ignores bankruptcy costs, even though such costs can be substantial, and the probability of bankruptcy depends on a firm's corporate risk, not on its beta risk. Therefore, even well-diversified investors should want a firm's management to give at least some consideration to a project's corporate risk instead of concentrating entirely on market risk.

Although it would be nice to reconcile these problems and to measure project risk on some absolute scale, the best we can do in practice is to estimate project risk in a somewhat nebulous, relative sense. For example, we can generally say with a fair degree of confidence that a particular project has more or less stand-alone risk than the firm's average project. Then, assuming that stand-alone and corporate risk are highly correlated (which is typical), the project's stand-alone risk will be a good measure of its corporate risk. Finally, assuming that market risk and corporate risk are highly correlated (as is true for most companies), a project with more corporate risk than average will also have more market risk, and vice versa for projects with low corporate risk.[13]

[13]For example, see M. Chapman Findlay III, Arthur E. Gooding, and Wallace Q. Weaver, Jr., "On the Relevant Risk for Determining Capital Expenditure Hurdle Rates," *Financial Management*, Winter 1976, 9–16.

Self-Test Questions

In theory, should a firm be concerned with stand-alone and corporate risk? Should the firm be concerned with these risks in practice?

If a project's stand-alone, corporate, and market risk are highly correlated, would this make the task of measuring risk easier or harder? Explain.

Incorporating Project Risk and Capital Structure into Capital Budgeting

Capital budgeting can affect a firm's market risk, its corporate risk, or both, but it is extremely difficult to quantify either type of risk. Although it may be possible to reach the general conclusion that one project is riskier than another, it is difficult to develop a really good *quantitative measure* of project risk. This makes it difficult to incorporate differential risk into capital budgeting decisions.

Two methods are used to incorporate project risk into capital budgeting. One is called the *certainty equivalent* approach. Here every cash inflow that is not known with certainty is scaled down, and the riskier the flow, the lower its certainty equivalent value. Chapter 15 Web/CD Extension explains the certainty equivalent approach in more detail. The other method, and the one we focus on here, is the **risk-adjusted discount rate** approach, under which differential project risk is dealt with by changing the discount rate. Average-risk projects are discounted at the firm's average cost of capital, higher-risk projects are discounted at a higher cost of capital, and lower-risk projects are discounted at a rate below the firm's average cost of capital. Unfortunately, there is no good way of specifying exactly *how much* higher or lower these discount rates should be. Given the present state of the art, risk adjustments are necessarily judgmental and somewhat arbitrary.

As a final consideration, capital structure must also be taken into account if a firm finances different assets in different ways. For example, one division might have a lot of real estate that is well suited as collateral for loans, whereas some other division might have most of its capital tied up in specialized machinery, which is not good collateral. As a result, the division with the real estate might have a higher *debt capacity* than the division with the machinery, hence an optimal capital structure that contains a higher percentage of debt. In this case, the financial staff might calculate the cost of capital differently for the two divisions.[14]

Self-Test Question

How are risk-adjusted discount rates used to incorporate project risk into the capital budget decision process?

Summary

Throughout the book, we have indicated that the value of any asset depends on the amount, timing, and riskiness of the cash flows it produces. In this chapter, we developed a framework for analyzing a project's cash flows and risk. Given a set of inputs, we can use the techniques described back in Chapter 13 to evaluate whether projects should be accepted or rejected. In the next chapter, we discuss some interesting extensions to the basic model. Before proceeding, however, you should review the key concepts listed below:

- The most important (and most difficult) step in analyzing a capital budgeting project is **estimating the incremental after-tax cash flows** the project will produce.

[14]We will say more about the optimal capital structure and debt capacity in Chapter 16.

- **Project cash flow** is different from accounting income. Project cash flow reflects: (1) **cash outlays for fixed assets,** (2) the **tax shield provided by depreciation,** and (3) cash flows due to **changes in net operating working capital.** Project cash flow does not include **interest payments.**
- In determining incremental cash flows, **opportunity costs** (the cash flows forgone by using an asset) must be included, but **sunk costs** (cash outlays that have been made and that cannot be recouped) are not included. Any **externalities** (effects of a project on other parts of the firm) should also be reflected in the analysis.
- **Cannibalization** occurs when a new project leads to a reduction in sales of an existing product.
- **Tax laws** affect cash flow analysis in two ways: (1) They reduce operating cash flows, and (2) they determine the depreciation expense that can be taken in each year.
- Capital projects often require additional investments in **net operating working capital (NOWC).**
- The incremental cash flows from a typical project can be classified into three categories: (1) **initial investment outlay,** (2) **operating cash flows over the project's life,** and (3) **terminal year cash flows.**
- **Inflation effects** must be considered in project analysis. The best procedure is to build expected inflation into the cash flow estimates.
- Since stockholders are generally diversified, **market risk** is theoretically the most relevant measure of risk. Market, or beta, risk is important because beta affects the cost of capital, which, in turn, affects stock prices.
- **Corporate risk** is important because it influences the firm's ability to use low-cost debt, to maintain smooth operations over time, and to avoid crises that might consume management's energy and disrupt its employees, customers, suppliers, and community.
- **Sensitivity analysis** is a technique that shows how much a project's NPV will change in response to a given change in an input variable such as sales, other things held constant.
- **Scenario analysis** is a risk analysis technique in which the best- and worst-case NPVs are compared with the project's expected NPV.
- **Monte Carlo simulation** is a risk analysis technique that uses a computer to simulate future events and thus to estimate the profitability and riskiness of a project.
- The **risk-adjusted discount rate,** or **project cost of capital,** is the rate used to evaluate a particular project. It is based on the corporate WACC, which is increased for projects that are riskier than the firm's average project but decreased for less risky projects.

Questions

14–1 Define each of the following terms:

a. Cash flow; accounting income
b. Incremental cash flow; sunk cost; opportunity cost
c. Net operating working capital changes
d. Salvage value
e. Real rate of return, k_r, versus nominal rate of return, k_n
f. Sensitivity analysis
g. Worst-case scenario; best-case scenario; base case
h. Scenario analysis
i. Monte Carlo simulation analysis
j. Coefficient of variation versus standard deviation
k. Corporate diversification versus stockholder diversification
l. Risk-adjusted discount rate; project cost of capital

14–2 Operating cash flows, rather than accounting profits, are listed in Table 14-3. What is the basis for this emphasis on cash flows as opposed to net income?

14–3 Why is it true, in general, that a failure to adjust expected cash flows for expected inflation biases the calculated NPV downward?

14–4 Explain why sunk costs should not be included in a capital budgeting analysis, but opportunity costs and externalities should be included.

14–5 Explain how net operating working capital is recovered at the end of a project's life, and why it is included in a capital budgeting analysis.

14–6 Define (a) simulation analysis, (b) scenario analysis, and (c) sensitivity analysis. If AT&T were considering two investments, one calling for the expenditure of $200 million to develop a satellite communications system and the other involving the expenditure of $12,000 for a new truck, on which one would the company be more likely to use simulation analysis?

14–7 Distinguish between beta (or market) risk, within-firm (or corporate) risk, and stand-alone risk for a project being considered for inclusion in the capital budget. Which type of risk do you believe should be given the greatest weight in capital budgeting decisions? Explain.

Self-Test Problems (Solutions Appear in Appendix A)

ST–1
NEW PROJECT ANALYSIS

You have been asked by the president of the Farr Construction Company to evaluate the proposed acquisition of a new earth mover. The mover's basic price is $50,000, and it would cost another $10,000 to modify it for special use. Assume that the mover falls into the MACRS 3-year class, it would be sold after 3 years for $20,000, and it would require an increase in net working capital (spare parts inventory) of $2,000. The earth mover would have no effect on revenues, but it is expected to save the firm $20,000 per year in before-tax operating costs, mainly labor. The firm's marginal federal-plus-state tax rate is 40 percent.

a. What is the net cost of the earth mover? (That is, what are the Year 0 cash flows?)
b. What are the operating cash flows in Years 1, 2, and 3?
c. What are the additional (nonoperating) cash flows in Year 3?
d. If the project's cost of capital is 10 percent, should the earth mover be purchased?

ST–2
CORPORATE RISK ANALYSIS

The staff of Porter Manufacturing has estimated the following net cash flows and probabilities for a new manufacturing process:

	Net Cash Flows		
Year	P = 0.2	P = 0.6	P = 0.2
0	($100,000)	($100,000)	($100,000)
1	20,000	30,000	40,000
2	20,000	30,000	40,000
3	20,000	30,000	40,000
4	20,000	30,000	40,000
5	20,000	30,000	40,000
5*	0	20,000	30,000

Line 0 gives the cost of the process, Lines 1 through 5 give operating cash flows, and Line 5* contains the estimated salvage values. Porter's cost of capital for an average-risk project is 10 percent.

a. Assume that the project has average risk. Find the project's expected NPV. (Hint: Use expected values for the net cash flow in each year.)
b. Find the best-case and worst-case NPVs. What is the probability of occurrence of the worst case if the cash flows are perfectly dependent (perfectly positively correlated) over time? If they are independent over time?

c. Assume that all the cash flows are perfectly positively correlated, that is, there are only three possible cash flow streams over time: (1) the worst case, (2) the most likely, or base, case, and (3) the best case, with probabilities of 0.2, 0.6, and 0.2, respectively. These cases are represented by each of the columns in the table. Find the expected NPV, its standard deviation, and its coefficient of variation.

d. The coefficient of variation of Porter's average project is in the range 0.8 to 1.0. If the coefficient of variation of a project being evaluated is greater than 1.0, 2 percentage points are added to the firm's cost of capital. Similarly, if the coefficient of variation is less than 0.8, 1 percentage point is deducted from the cost of capital. What is the project's cost of capital? Should Porter accept or reject the project?

Problems

14–1 *INVESTMENT OUTLAY*

Johnson Industries is considering an expansion project. The necessary equipment could be purchased for $9 million, and the project would also require an initial $3 million investment in net working capital. The company's tax rate is 40 percent. What is the project's initial investment outlay?

14–2 *OPERATING CASH FLOW*

Nixon Communications is trying to estimate the first-year operating cash flow (at t = 1) for a proposed project. The financial staff has collected the following information:

Projected sales	$10 million
Operating costs (not including depreciation)	$7 million
Depreciation	$2 million
Interest expense	$2 million

The company faces a 40 percent tax rate. What is the project's operating cash flow for the first year (t = 1)?

14–3 *NET SALVAGE VALUE*

Carter Air Lines is now in the terminal year of a project. The equipment originally cost $20 million, of which 80 percent has been depreciated. Carter can sell the used equipment today to another airline for $5 million, and its tax rate is 40 percent. What is the equipment's after-tax net salvage value?

14–4 *NEW PROJECT ANALYSIS*

The Campbell Company is evaluating the proposed acquisition of a new milling machine. The machine's base price is $108,000, and it would cost another $12,500 to modify it for special use by your firm. The machine falls into the MACRS 3-year class, and it would be sold after 3 years for $65,000. The machine would require an increase in net working capital (inventory) of $5,500. The milling machine would have no effect on revenues, but it is expected to save the firm $44,000 per year in before-tax operating costs, mainly labor. Campbell's marginal tax rate is 35 percent.

a. What is the net cost of the machine for capital budgeting purposes? (That is, what is the Year 0 net cash flow?)

b. What are the net operating cash flows in Years 1, 2, and 3?

c. What is the terminal year cash flow?

d. If the project's cost of capital is 12 percent, should the machine be purchased?

14–5 *DEPRECIATION EFFECTS*

Susan Fischer, great-granddaughter of the founder of Taussig Tile Products and current president of the company, believes in simple, conservative accounting. In keeping with her philosophy, she has decreed that the company shall use alternative straight line depreciation, based on the MACRS class lives, for all newly acquired assets. Your boss, the financial vice-president and the only nonfamily officer, has asked you to develop an exhibit which shows how much this policy costs the company in terms of market value. Ms. Fischer is interested in increasing the value of the firm's stock because she fears a family stockholder revolt which might remove her from office. For your exhibit, assume that the company spends $50 million each year on new capital projects, that the projects have on average a 10-year class life, that the company has a 10 percent cost of capital, and that its tax rate is 34 percent. (Hint: Show how much the NPV of projects in an average year would increase if Taussig used the standard MACRS recovery allowances. Also, ignore the half-year convention on the straight line calculation.)

14–6 *NEW PROJECT ANALYSIS*

You have been asked by the president of your company to evaluate the proposed acquisition of a new spectrometer for the firm's R&D department. The equipment's basic price is $70,000, and it would cost another $15,000 to modify it for special use by your firm. The spectrometer, which falls into the MACRS 3-year class, would be sold after 3 years for $30,000. Use of the equipment would require an increase in net working capital (spare parts inventory) of $4,000. The spectrometer would have no effect on revenues, but it is expected to save the firm $25,000 per year in before-tax operating costs, mainly labor. The firm's marginal federal-plus-state tax rate is 40 percent.

a. What is the net cost of the spectrometer? (That is, what is the Year 0 net cash flow?)
b. What are the net operating cash flows in Years 1, 2, and 3?
c. What is the additional (nonoperating) cash flow in Year 3?
d. If the project's cost of capital is 10 percent, should the spectrometer be purchased?

14–7 *INFLATION ADJUSTMENTS*

The Rodriguez Company is considering an average-risk investment in a mineral water spring project that has a cost of $150,000. The project will produce 1,000 cases of mineral water per year indefinitely. The current sales price is $138 per case, and the current cost per case (all variable) is $105. The firm is taxed at a rate of 34 percent. Both prices and costs are expected to rise at a rate of 6 percent per year. The firm uses only equity, and it has a cost of capital of 15 percent. Assume that cash flows consist only of after-tax profits, since the spring has an indefinite life and will not be depreciated.

a. Should the firm accept the project? (Hint: The project is a perpetuity, so you must use the formula for a perpetuity to find its NPV.)
b. If total costs consisted of a fixed cost of $10,000 per year and variable costs of $95 per unit, and if only the variable costs were expected to increase with inflation, would this make the project better or worse? Continue with the assumption that the sales price will rise with inflation.

14–8 *CORPORATE RISK ANALYSIS*

Shao Industries is considering a proposed project for its capital budget. The company estimates that the project's NPV is $12 million. This estimate assumes that the economy and market conditions will be average over the next few years. The company's CFO, however, forecasts that there is only a 50 percent chance that the economy will be average. Recognizing this uncertainty, she has also performed the following scenario analysis:

Economic Scenario	Probability of Outcome	NPV
Recession	0.05	($70 million)
Below average	0.20	(25 million)
Average	0.50	12 million
Above average	0.20	20 million
Boom	0.05	30 million

What is the project's expected NPV, its standard deviation, and its coefficient of variation?

14–9 *RISKY CASH FLOWS*

The Bartram-Pulley Company (BPC) must decide between two mutually exclusive investment projects. Each project costs $6,750 and has an expected life of 3 years. Annual net cash flows from each project begin 1 year after the initial investment is made and have the following probability distributions:

Project A		Project B	
Probability	Net Cash Flows	Probability	Net Cash Flows
0.2	$6,000	0.2	$ 0
0.6	6,750	0.6	6,750
0.2	7,500	0.2	18,000

BPC has decided to evaluate the riskier project at a 12 percent rate and the less risky project at a 10 percent rate.

a. What is the expected value of the annual net cash flows from each project? What is the coefficient of variation (CV)? (Hint: $\sigma_B = \$5,798$ and $CV_B = 0.76$.)

b. What is the risk-adjusted NPV of each project?

c. If it were known that Project B was negatively correlated with other cash flows of the firm whereas Project A was positively correlated, how would this knowledge affect the decision? If Project B's cash flows were negatively correlated with gross domestic product (GDP), would that influence your assessment of its risk?

14–10 *SIMULATION* Singleton Supplies Corporation (SSC) manufactures medical products for hospitals, clinics, and nursing homes. SSC may introduce a new type of X-ray scanner designed to identify certain types of cancers in their early stages. There are a number of uncertainties about the proposed project, but the following data are believed to be reasonably accurate.

	Probability	Value	Random Numbers
Developmental costs	0.3	$2,000,000	00–29
	0.4	4,000,000	30–69
	0.3	6,000,000	70–99
Project life	0.2	3 years	00–19
	0.6	8 years	20–79
	0.2	13 years	80–99
Sales in units	0.2	100	00–19
	0.6	200	20–79
	0.2	300	80–99
Sales price	0.1	$13,000	00–09
	0.8	13,500	10–89
	0.1	14,000	90–99
Cost per unit (excluding developmental costs)	0.3	$5,000	00–29
	0.4	6,000	30–69
	0.3	7,000	70–99

SSC uses a cost of capital of 15 percent to analyze average-risk projects, 12 percent for low-risk projects, and 18 percent for high-risk projects. These risk adjustments reflect primarily the uncertainty about each project's NPV and IRR as measured by the coefficients of variation of NPV and IRR. SSC is in the 40 percent federal-plus-state income tax bracket.

a. What is the expected IRR for the X-ray scanner project? Base your answer on the expected values of the variables. Also, assume the after-tax "profits" figure you develop is equal to annual cash flows. All facilities are leased, so depreciation may be disregarded. Can you determine the value of σ_{IRR} short of actual simulation or a fairly complex statistical analysis?

b. Assume that SSC uses a 15 percent cost of capital for this project. What is the project's NPV? Could you estimate σ_{NPV} without either simulation or a complex statistical analysis?

c. Show the process by which a computer would perform a simulation analysis for this project. Use the random numbers 44, 17, 16, 58, 1; 79, 83, 86; and 19, 62, 6 to illustrate the process with the first computer run. Actually calculate the first-run NPV and IRR. Assume that the cash flows for each year are independent of cash flows for other years. Also, assume that the computer operates as follows: (1) A developmental cost and a project life are estimated for the first run. (2) Next, sales volume, sales price, and cost per unit are estimated and used to derive a cash flow for the first year. (3) Then, the next three random numbers are used to estimate sales volume, sales price, and cost per unit for the second year, hence the cash flow for the second year. (4) Cash flows for other years are developed similarly, on out to the first run's estimated life. (5) With the developmental cost and the cash flow stream established, NPV and IRR for the first run are derived and stored in the computer's memory. (6) The process is repeated to generate perhaps 500 other NPVs and IRRs. (7) Frequency distributions for NPV and IRR are plotted by the computer, and the distributions' means and standard deviations are calculated.

d. Does it seem a little strange to conduct a risk analysis such as the one here *after* having already established a cost of capital for use in the analysis? What might be done to improve this situation?

e. In this problem, we assumed that the probability distributions were all independent of one another. It would have been possible to use conditional probabilities where, for example, the probability distribution for cost per unit would vary from trial to trial, depending on the unit sales for the trial. Also, it would be possible to construct a simulation model such that the sales distribution in Year t would depend on the sales level attained in Year t − 1. Had these modifications been made in this problem, do you think the standard deviation of the NPV distribution would have been larger (riskier) or smaller (less risky) than where complete independence is assumed?

f. Name two *major* difficulties not mentioned earlier that occur in the kind of analysis discussed in this problem.

Spreadsheet Problems

14–11
BUILD A MODEL: ISSUES IN CAPITAL BUDGETING

Start with the partial model in the file ***Ch 14-11 Build a Model.xls*** from the textbook's CD-ROM. Webmasters.com has developed a powerful new server that would be used for corporations' Internet activities. It would cost $10 million to buy the equipment necessary to manufacture the server, and $3 million of net operating working capital would be required. The servers would sell for $24,000 per unit, and Webmasters believes that variable costs would amount to $17,500 per unit. The company's fixed costs would also rise by $1 million per year. It would take 1 year to buy the required equipment and set up operations, and the server project would have a life of 4 years. Conditions are expected to remain stable during each year of the operating life; that is, unit sales, sales price, and costs would be unchanged. If the project is undertaken, it must be continued for the entire 4 years. Also, the project's returns are expected to be highly correlated with returns on the firm's other assets. The firm believes it could sell 1,000 units.

The equipment would be depreciated over a 5-year period, using MACRS rates. The estimated market value of the equipment at the end of the project's 4-year life is $500,000. Webmasters' federal-plus-state tax rate is 40 percent. Its cost of capital is 10 percent for average-risk projects, defined as projects with a coefficient of variation of NPV between 0.8 and 1.2. Low-risk projects are evaluated with a WACC of 8 percent, and high-risk projects at 13 percent.

a. Develop a spreadsheet model and use it to find the project's NPV, IRR, and payback.

b. Now conduct a sensitivity analysis to determine the sensitivity of NPV to changes in the sales price, variable costs per unit, and number of units sold. Set these variables' values at 10 percent and 20 percent above and below their base-case values. Include a graph in your analysis.

c. Now conduct a scenario analysis. Assume that there is a 25 percent probability that "best-case" conditions, with each of the variables discussed in part b being 20 percent better than its base-case value, will occur. There is a 25 percent probability of "worst-case" conditions, with the variables 20 percent worse than base, and a 50 percent probability of base-case conditions.

d. If the project appears to be more or less risky than an average project, find its risk-adjusted NPV, IRR, and payback.

e. On the basis of information in the problem, would you recommend that the project be accepted?

14–12
WHAT IF ANALYSIS: NEW PROJECT ANALYSIS

Start with the file ***Ch 14-12 What If Analysis.xls*** from the textbook's CD-ROM and answer the questions shown there.

14–13
WHAT IF ANALYSIS: INFLATION ADJUSTMENTS

Start with the file ***Ch14-13 What If Analysis.xls*** from the textbook's CD-ROM and answer the questions shown there.

14–14
WHAT IF ANALYSIS: SCENARIO AND SENSITIVITY ANALYSIS

Start with the file ***Ch 14-14 What If Analysis.xls*** from the textbook's CD-ROM and answer the questions shown there.

Cyberproblem

The information related to this cyberproblem is likely to change over time, due to the release of new information and the ever-changing nature of the World Wide Web. Accordingly, we will periodically update the problem on the textbook's web site.

14–15
ISSUES IN CAPITAL BUDGETING—COCA-COLA

A company's capital budgeting program evolves from and is a function of its corporate strategy. The firm must evaluate itself and identify its place and direction in the business environment. Issues of liquidity and capital investment become primal necessities as the firm strives to maximize shareholder value by generating free cash flows. Go to the textbook's web site at **http://www.harcourtcollege.com/finance/theory/student/resources/cyberprob/ch14.html** and answer the questions shown there.

Mini Case

CD

See **Ch 14 Show.ppt** and **Ch 14 Mini Case.xls.**

John Crockett Furniture Company is considering adding a new line to its product mix, and the capital budgeting analysis is being conducted by Joan Samuels, a recently graduated finance MBA. The production line would be set up in unused space in Crockett's main plant. The machinery's invoice price would be approximately $200,000; another $10,000 in shipping charges would be required; and it would cost an additional $30,000 to install the equipment. Further, the firm's inventories would have to be increased by $25,000 to handle the new line, but its accounts payable would rise by $5,000. The machinery has an economic life of 4 years, and Crockett has obtained a special tax ruling which places the equipment in the MACRS 3-year class. The machinery is expected to have a salvage value of $25,000 after 4 years of use.

The new line would generate incremental sales of 1,250 units per year for 4 years at an incremental cost of $100 per unit, excluding depreciation. Each unit can be sold for $200. The firm's tax rate is 40 percent, and its weighted average cost of capital is 10 percent.

a. Set up, without numbers, a time line for the project's cash flows.

b. (1) Construct incremental operating cash flow statements for the project's 4 years of operations.

(2) Does your cash flow statement include any financial flows such as interest expense or dividends? Why or why not?

c. (1) Suppose the firm had spent $100,000 last year to rehabilitate the production line site. Should this cost be included in the analysis? Explain.

(2) Now assume that the plant space could be leased out to another firm at $25,000 a year. Should this be included in the analysis? If so, how?

(3) Finally, assume that the new product line is expected to decrease sales of the firm's other lines by $50,000 per year. Should this be considered in the analysis? If so, how?

d. Disregard the assumptions in part c. What is Crockett's net investment outlay on this project? What is the net nonoperating cash flow at the time the project is terminated? Based on these cash flows, what are the project's NPV, IRR, MIRR, and payback? Do these indicators suggest that the project should be undertaken?

e. Assume that inflation is expected to average 5 percent over the next 4 years. Does it appear that Crockett's cash flow estimates are real or nominal? That is, are all the cash flows stated in the Time 0 dollars or have the cash flows been increased to account for expected inflation? Further, would it appear that the 10 percent cost of capital is a nominal or real interest rate? Does it appear that the current NPV is biased because of inflation effects? If so, in what direction, and how could any bias be removed?

f. What does the term "risk" mean in the context of capital budgeting, to what extent can risk be quantified, and when risk is quantified, is the quantification based primarily on statistical analysis of historical data or on subjective, judgmental estimates?

g. (1) What are the three types of risk that are relevant in capital budgeting?
(2) How is each of these risk types measured, and how do they relate to one another?
(3) How is each type of risk used in the capital budgeting process?

h. (1) What is sensitivity analysis?
(2) Perform a sensitivity analysis on the unit sales, salvage value, and cost of capital for the project. Assume that each of these variables can vary from its base case, or expected, value by plus and minus 10, 20, and 30 percent. Include a sensitivity diagram, and discuss the results.
(3) What is the primary weakness of sensitivity analysis? What is its primary usefulness?

i. Assume that Joan Samuels is confident of her estimates of all the variables that affect the project's cash flows except unit sales: If product acceptance is poor, unit sales would be only 900 units a year, while a strong consumer response would produce sales of 1,600 units. In either case, cash costs would still amount to 50 percent of revenues. Joan believes that there is a 25 percent chance of poor acceptance, a 25 percent chance of excellent acceptance, and a 50 percent chance of average acceptance (the base case).
(1) What is scenario analysis?
(2) What is the worst-case NPV? The best-case NPV?
(3) Use the worst-, base-, and best-case NPVs and probabilities of occurrence to find the project's expected NPV, standard deviation, and coefficient of variation.

j. (1) Assume that Crockett's average project has a coefficient of variation in the range of 0.2–0.4. Would the new furniture line be classified as high risk, average risk, or low risk? What type of risk is being measured here?
(2) Based on common sense, how highly correlated do you think that the project would be to the firm's other assets? (Give a correlation coefficient, or range of coefficients, based on your judgment.)
(3) How would this correlation coefficient and the previously calculated σ combine to affect the project's contribution to corporate, or within-firm, risk? Explain.

k. (1) Based on your judgment, what do you think the project's correlation coefficient would be with the general economy and thus with returns on "the market"?
(2) How would this correlation affect the project's market risk?

l. (1) Crockett typically adds or subtracts 3 percentage points to the overall cost of capital to adjust for risk. Should the new furniture line be accepted?
(2) Are there any subjective risk factors that should be considered before the final decision is made?

m. Are the problems with scenario analysis? Define simulation analysis, and discuss its principal advantages and disadvantages.

Selected Additional References and Cases

Several articles have been written regarding the implications of the Accelerated Cost Recovery System (ACRS). Among them are the following:

Angell, Robert J., and Tony R. Wingler, "A Note on Expensing versus Depreciating Under the Accelerated Cost Recovery System," *Financial Management,* Winter 1982, 34–35.

McCarty, Daniel E., and William R. McDaniel, "A Note on Expensing versus Depreciating Under the Accelerated Cost Recovery System: Comment," *Financial Management,* Summer 1983, 37–39.

Three additional papers on the effect of inflation on capital budgeting are the following:

Bailey, Andrew D., and Daniel L. Jensen, "General Price Level Adjustments in the Capital Budgeting Decision," *Financial Management,* Spring 1977, 26–32.

Mehta, Dileep R., Michael D. Curley, and Hung-Gay Fung, "Inflation, Cost of Capital, and Capital Budgeting Procedures," *Financial Management,* Winter 1984, 48–54.

Rappaport, Alfred, and Robert A. Taggart, Jr., "Evaluation of Capital Expenditure Proposals Under Inflation," *Financial Management,* Spring 1982, 5–13.

The following articles pertain to other topics in this chapter:

Kroll, Yoram, "On the Differences between Accrual Accounting Figures and Cash Flows: The Case of Working Capital," *Financial Management*, Spring 1985, 75–82.

Mukherjee, Tarun K., "Reducing the Uncertainty-Induced Bias in Capital Budgeting Decisions—A Hurdle Rate Approach," *Journal of Business Finance & Accounting*, September 1991, 747–753.

The literature on risk analysis in capital budgeting is vast; here is a small but useful selection of additional references that bear directly on the topics covered in this chapter:

Ang, James S., and Wilbur G. Lewellen, "Risk Adjustment in Capital Investment Project Evaluations," *Financial Management*, Summer 1982, 5–14.

Bower, Richard S., and Jeffrey M. Jenks, "Divisional Screening Rates," *Financial Management*, Autumn 1975, 42–49.

Butler, J. S., and Barry Schachter, "The Investment Decision: Estimation Risk and Risk Adjusted Discount Rates," *Financial Management*, Winter 1989, 13–22.

Fama, Eugene F., "Risk-Adjusted Discount Rates and Capital Budgeting under Uncertainty," *Journal of Financial Economics*, August 1977, 3–24.

Findlay, M. Chapman III, Arthur E. Gooding, and Wallace Q. Weaver, Jr., "On the Relevant Risk for Determining Capital Expenditure Hurdle Rates," *Financial Management*, Winter 1976, 9–16.

Gehr, Adam K., Jr., "Risk-Adjusted Capital Budgeting Using Arbitrage," *Financial Management*, Winter 1981, 14–19.

Gup, Benton E., and S. W. Norwood III, "Divisional Cost of Capital: A Practical Approach," *Financial Management*, Spring 1982, 20–24.

Robichek, Alexander A., "Interpreting the Results of Risk Analysis," *Journal of Finance*, December 1975, 1384–1386.

Weaver, Samuel C., Peter J. Clemmens III, Jack A. Gunn, and Bruce D. Danneburg, "Divisional Hurdle Rates and the Cost of Capital," *Financial Management*, Spring 1989, 18–25.

The Cases in Financial Management: Dryden Request *series contains the following cases that focus on capital budgeting under uncertainty:*

Case 12, "Indian River Citrus Company (A)," Case 12A, "Cranfield, Inc. (A)," Case 14, "Robert Montoya, Inc." focus on cash flow estimation. Case 13, "Indian River Citrus (B)," Case 13A, "Cranfield, Inc. (B)," Case 13B, "Tasty Foods (B)," Case 13C, "Heavenly Foods," and Case 15, "Robert Montoya, Inc. (B)," illustrate project risk analysis. Case 58, "Universal Corporation," is a comprehensive case that illustrates Chapters 13 and 14, as do Cases 47 and 48, "The Western Company (A and B)."

15

Option Pricing with Applications to Real Options

Enron Corporation recently began building three new power plants even though they had negative NPVs as calculated using standard capital budgeting procedures. At first glance, the decision seemed irrational, but it was not, because it provided Enron with an opportunity to profit from changing market conditions. Such an opportunity is called a "real option," and it can add considerable value to certain projects.

Enron and other power producers have choices when they design new plants. They can opt to build "base load" plants, which are expensive to build but whose operating costs are low, or "peaking units," which cost less to build but more expensive to run. If Enron knew for certain what demand conditions would exist in the future, it could build the optimal type of plant. However, it takes several years to get the necessary permits and then build a plant, and both the demand patterns and output prices can change while construction is under way.

Enron's management chose an imaginative way to solve this problem. Its engineers designed three plants with very low construction costs but whose operating costs were 70 percent higher than the industry average. Based on the expected demand for electricity, the plants had negative expected NPVs. But Enron doesn't plan to run the plants and incur the high operating costs if expected demand occurs! Instead, it will run the plants only if demand and prices are higher than expected, because only then will prices be high enough to more than compensate for the plants' high operating costs. Thus the plants in effect give Enron an option to supply power when prices, and consequently profits, are high. The value of the option was greater than the cost of building the plants, so Enron undertook the project.

Cadence Design Systems, which develops electronic products and services, provides another illustration of a real option. Rather than create all the necessary software itself, Cadence often contracts with specialized software developers. As a part of the license, Cadence must make a royalty payment to the software developer each time it sells a product that contains the software. Many of the software contracts build in a floor that requires Cadence to make a specified minimum number of royalty payments, even if actual sales are lower than the floor. Because the expected demand for Cadence's products is very uncertain, sales may be less than the floor, causing Cadence to make a large payment without revenue to cover it. Of course, if sales are higher than expected, Cadence must make more royalty payments than expected, but then it would also have high revenues and thus could afford the payments.

In negotiating with its software suppliers, Cadence proposed an arrangement that had a relatively low floor but a higher per-unit royalty. Using a standard NPV analysis, Cadence's proposal produced a negative NPV. However, like the Enron project, option pricing techniques showed that Cadence's proposed royalty arrangement actually added value.

As you read this chapter, think about the ways that option pricing techniques can lead to better decisions.

Sources: Peter Coy, "Exploiting Uncertainty: The 'Real-Option' Revolution in Decision-Making," *Business Week*, June 7, 1999, 118; S. L. Mintz, "Getting Real," *CFO*, November 1999, 52–60.

Traditional discounted cash flow (DCF) analysis—where an asset's cash flows are estimated and then discounted to obtain the asset's NPV—has been the cornerstone for valuing all types of assets since the 1950s. Accordingly, most of our discussion of capital budgeting has focused on DCF valuation techniques. However, in recent years a growing number of academics and practitioners have demonstrated that DCF valuation techniques do not always tell the complete story about a project's value, and that rote use of DCF can, at times, lead to incorrect capital budgeting decisions.[1]

The textbook's CD-ROM contains an *Excel* file that will guide you through the chapter's calculations. The file for this chapter is *Ch 15 Tool Kit.xls,* and we encourage you to open the file and follow along as you read the chapter.

DCF techniques were originally developed to value securities such as stocks and bonds. These securities are passive investments—once they have been purchased, most investors have no influence over the cash flows the assets produce. However, real assets are *not* passive investments—managerial actions can influence their results. Furthermore, investing in a new project often brings with it the potential for increasing the firm's future opportunities. Opportunities are, in effect, *options*—the right but not the obligation to take some action in the future. As we demonstrate in the next section, options are valuable, so any project that expands the firm's set of opportunities has positive **option value.** Similarly, any project that reduces the set of future opportunities has negative option value. A project's impact on the firm's opportunities, or its option value, may not be captured by conventional NPV analysis, so this option value should be considered separately. We begin the chapter with an explanation of financial options, after which we build on this foundation to discuss real options.

Financial Options

An **option** is a contract that gives its holder the right to buy (or sell) an asset at some predetermined price within a specified period of time. All managers should understand option pricing theory, since many projects create opportunities that are in essence options. In addition, financial managers must understand option pricing theory when they use derivative securities for risk management or issue hybrid securities such as convertible bonds. We will discuss risk management in Chapter 24 and hybrid securities in Chapter 21, but for now we focus on option pricing theory and its applications to real options.

Option Types and Markets

There are many types of options and option markets.[2] To illustrate how options work, suppose you owned 100 shares of General Computer Corporation (GCC), which on Friday, January 12, 2001, sold for $53.50 per share. You could sell to someone the right to buy your 100 shares at any time during the next four months at a price of, say, $55 per share. The $55 is called the **strike,** or **exercise, price.** Such options exist, and

[1]For an excellent general discussion of the problems inherent in discounted cash flow valuation techniques as applied to capital budgeting, see Avinash K. Dixit and Robert S. Pindyck, "The Options Approach to Capital Investment," *Harvard Business Review*, May–June 1995, 105–115. For more information on the option value inherent in investment timing decisions, see Stephen A. Ross, "Uses, Abuses, and Alternatives to the Net-Present-Value Rule," *Financial Management*, Autumn 1995, 96–101. Also, the Spring 1987 issue of the *Midland Corporate Finance Journal* contains several interesting articles on the use of option concepts in capital budgeting.

[2]For an in-depth treatment of options, see Don M. Chance, *An Introduction to Derivatives* (Fort Worth, TX: The Dryden Press, 1995).

they are traded on a number of exchanges, with the Chicago Board Options Exchange (CBOE) being the oldest and the largest. This type of option is defined as a **call option,** because the buyer has a "call" on 100 shares of stock. The seller of an option is called the option *writer.* An investor who "writes" call options against stock held in his or her portfolio is said to be selling *covered options.* Options sold without the stock to back them up are called *naked options.* When the exercise price exceeds the current stock price, a call option is said to be *out-of-the-money.* When the exercise price is less than the current price of the stock, the option is *in-the-money.*

You can also buy an option that gives you the right to *sell* a stock at a specified price within some future period—this is called a **put option.** For example, suppose you think GCC's stock price is likely to decline from its current level of $53.50 sometime during the next four months. A put option will give you the right to sell at somewhere close to the current price even after the market price declines. You could then buy at the new low price, sell at the old high price, and earn a profit. Table 15-1 provides data on GCC's options. You could buy the four-month May put option for $218.75 ($2 3/16 × 100). That would give you the right to sell 100 shares (that you would not necessarily own) at a price of $50 per share ($50 is the strike price). Suppose you bought this 100-share contract for $218.75 and then GCC's stock fell to $45. You could buy the stock at $45 and exercise your put option by selling it at $50. Your profit from exercising the option would be ($50 − $45)(100) = $500. After subtracting the $218.75 you paid for the option, your profit (before taxes and commissions) would be $281.25.

Table 15-1 contains an extract from the Listed Options Quotations Table as it would appear the next day in a daily newspaper. Sport World's February $55 call option sold for $0.50. Thus, for $0.50(100) = $50 you could buy options that would give you the right to buy 100 shares of Sport World stock at a price of $55 per share from January until February, or during the next month.[3] If the stock price stayed below $55 during that period, you would lose your $50, but if it rose to $65, your $50 investment would increase in value to ($65 − $55)(100) = $1,000 in less than 30 days. That translates into a very healthy annualized rate of return. Incidentally, if the stock price did go up, you would not actually exercise your options and buy the stock—rather, you would sell the options, which would then have a value of at least $1,000 versus the $50 you paid, to another option buyer or to the original seller.

In addition to options on individual stocks, options are also available on several stock indexes such as the NYSE Index and the S&P 100 Index. Index options permit one to hedge (or bet) on a rise or fall in the general market as well as on individual stocks.

Option trading is one of the hottest financial activities in the United States. The leverage involved makes it possible for speculators with just a few dollars to make a fortune almost overnight. Also, investors with sizable portfolios can sell options against their stocks and earn the value of the option (less brokerage commissions), even if the stock's price remains constant. Most importantly, though, options can be used to create *hedges* that protect the value of an individual stock or portfolio. We will discuss hedging strategies in more detail later in Chapter 24.[4]

---

[3]Actually, the *expiration date,* which is the last date that the option can be exercised, is the Friday before the third Saturday of the exercise month. Also, note that option contracts are generally written in 100-share multiples.

[4]It should be noted that insiders who trade illegally generally buy options rather than stock because the leverage inherent in options increases the profit potential. Note, though, that it is illegal to use insider information for personal gain, and an insider using such information would be taking advantage of the option seller. Insider trading, in addition to being unfair and essentially equivalent to stealing, hurts the economy: Investors lose confidence in the capital markets and raise their required returns because of an increased element of risk, and this raises the cost of capital and thus reduces the level of real investment.

TABLE 15-1 January 12, 2001, Listed Options Quotations

		Calls—Last Quote			Puts—Last Quote		
Closing Price	**Strike Price**	**February**	**March**	**May**	**February**	**March**	**May**
General Computer Corporation (GCC)							
53½	50	4¼	4¾	5½	⅝	1⅜	2 3/16
53½	55	1 5/16	2 1/16	3⅛	2⅝	r	4½
53½	60	5/16	11/16	1½	6⅝	r	8
U.S. Medical							
56⅝	55	4¼	5⅛	7	2¼	3¾	r
Sport World							
53⅛	55	½	1⅛	r	2⅛	r	r

Note: r means not traded on January 12.

The Chicago Board Options Exchange provides 20-minute delayed quotes for equity, index, and LEAP options at **http://www.cboe.com**.

Conventional options are generally written for six months or less, but a new type of option called a **Long-term Equity AnticiPation Security (LEAPS)** has been trading in recent years. Like conventional options, LEAPS are listed on exchanges and are available on both individual stocks and stock indexes. The major difference is that LEAPS are long-term options, having maturities of up to 2½ years. One-year LEAPS cost about twice as much as the matching three-month option, but because of their much longer time to expiration, LEAPS provide buyers with more potential for gains and offer better long-term protection for a portfolio.

Corporations on whose stocks options are written have nothing to do with the option market. Corporations do not raise money in the option market, nor do they have any direct transactions in it. Moreover, option holders do not vote for corporate directors or receive dividends. There have been studies by the SEC and others as to whether option trading stabilizes or destabilizes the stock market, and whether this activity helps or hinders corporations seeking to raise new capital. The studies have not been conclusive, but option trading is here to stay, and many regard it as the most exciting game in town.

Factors That Affect the Value of a Call Option

Table 15-1 can provide some insights into call option valuation. First, we see that at least three factors affect a call option's value:

1. **Market price versus strike price.** The higher the stock's market price in relation to the strike price, the higher will be the call option price. Thus, Sport World's $55 February call option sells for $0.50, whereas U.S. Medical's $55 February option sells for $4.25. This difference arises because U.S. Medical's current stock price is $56⅝ versus only $53⅛ for Sport World.
2. **Level of strike price.** The higher the strike price, the lower the call option price. Thus, all of GCC's call options, regardless of exercise month, decline as the strike price increases.
3. **Length of option.** The longer the option period, the higher the option price. This occurs because the longer the time before expiration, the greater the chance that the stock price will climb substantially above the exercise price. Thus, option prices increase as the expiration date is lengthened.

Other factors that affect option values, especially the volatility of the underlying stock, are discussed in later sections.

Exercise Value versus Option Price

How is the actual price of a call option determined in the market? In a later section, we present a widely used model (the Black-Scholes model) for pricing call options, but first it is useful to establish some basic concepts. To begin, we define a call option's **exercise value** as follows:

Exercise value = Current price of the stock − Strike price.

The exercise value is what the option would be worth if it expired immediately. For example, if a stock sells for $50 and its option has a strike price of $20, then you could buy the stock for $20 by exercising the option. You would own a stock worth $50, but you would only have to pay $20. Therefore, the option would be worth $30 if you had to exercise it immediately. Note that the calculated exercise value of a call option could be negative, but realistically the minimum "true" value of an option is zero, because no one would exercise an out-of-the-money option. Note also that an option's exercise value is only a first approximation value—it merely provides a starting point for finding the actual value of the option.

Now consider Figure 15-1, which presents some data on Space Technology Inc. (STI), a company that recently went public and whose stock price has fluctuated widely during its short history. The third column in the tabular data shows the exercise values for STI's call option when the stock was selling at different prices; the fourth column gives the actual market prices for the option; and the fifth column shows the premium of the actual option price over its exercise value. At any stock price below $20, the exercise value is set at zero, but above $20, each $1 increase in the price of the stock brings with it a $1 increase in the option's exercise value. Note, however, that the actual market price of the option lies above the exercise value at each price of the common stock, although the premium declines as the price of the stock increases. For example, when the stock sold for $20 and the option had a zero exercise value, its actual price, and the premium, was $9. Then, as the price of the stock rose, the *exercise value's increase* matched the stock's increase dollar for dollar, but the *market price* of the option climbed less rapidly, causing the premium to decline. The premium was $9 when the stock sold for $20 a share, but it had declined to $1 by the time the stock price had risen to $73 a share. Beyond that point, the premium virtually disappeared.

Why does this pattern exist? Why should a call option ever sell for more than its exercise value, and why does the premium decline as the price of the stock increases? The answer lies in part in the speculative appeal of options—they enable someone to gain a high degree of personal leverage when buying securities. To illustrate, suppose STI's option sold for exactly its exercise value. Now suppose you were thinking of investing in the company's common stock at a time when it was selling for $21 a share. If you bought a share and the price rose to $42, you would have made a 100 percent capital gain. However, had you bought the option at its exercise value ($1 when the stock was selling for $21), your capital gain would have been $22 − $1 = $21 on a $1 investment, or 2,100 percent! At the same time, your total loss potential with the option would be only $1 versus a potential loss of $21 if you purchased the stock. The huge capital gains potential, combined with the loss limitation, is clearly worth something—the exact amount it is worth to investors is the amount of the premium. Note, however, that buying the option is riskier than buying STI's stock, because there is a higher probability of losing money on the option. If STI's stock price fell from $21 to $20, you would have a 4.76 percent loss if you bought the stock (ignoring transaction costs), but you would have a 100 percent loss on the option investment.

FIGURE 15-1 Space Technology Inc.: Option Price and Exercise Value

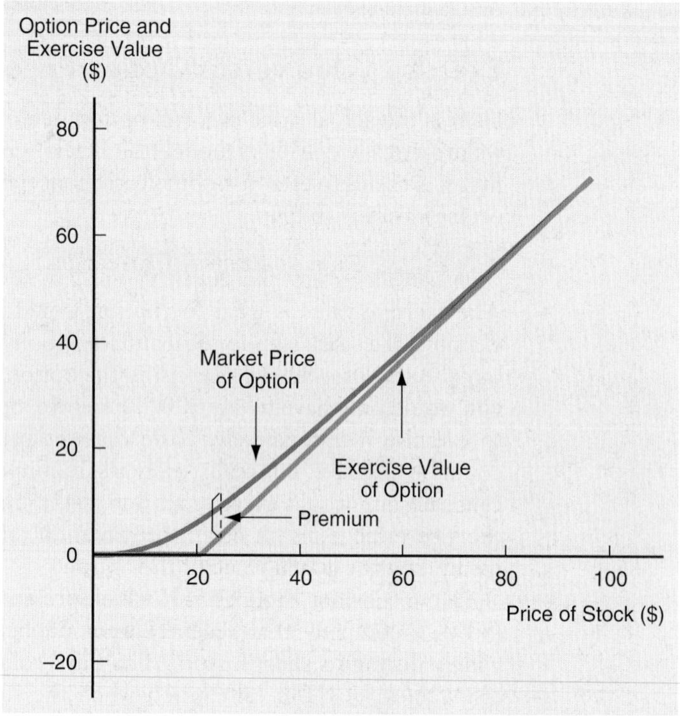

Price of Stock (1)	Strike Price (2)	Exercise Value of Option (1) − (2) = (3)	Market Price of Option (4)	Premium 4) − (3) (= (5)
$20.00	$20.00	$ 0.00	$ 9.00	$9.00
21.00	20.00	1.00	9.75	8.75
22.00	20.00	2.00	10.50	8.50
35.00	20.00	15.00	21.00	6.00
42.00	20.00	22.00	26.00	4.00
50.00	20.00	30.00	32.00	2.00
73.00	20.00	53.00	54.00	1.00
98.00	20.00	78.00	78.50	0.50

Why does the premium decline as the price of the stock rises above the exercise price? The answer is that both the leverage effect and the loss protection feature decline at high stock prices. For example, if you were thinking of buying STI stock when its price was $73 a share, the exercise value of the option would be $53. If the stock price doubled to $146, you would have a 100 percent gain on the stock. Now note that the exercise value of the option would go from $53 to $126, for a percentage gain of 138 percent versus 2,100 percent in the earlier case. Note also that the potential loss per dollar of potential gain on the option is much greater when the option is selling at high prices. These two factors, the declining leverage impact and the increasing danger of larger losses, explain why the premium diminishes as the price of the common stock rises.

In addition to the stock price and the exercise price, the price of an option depends on three other factors: (1) the option's term to maturity, (2) the variability of the stock price, and (3) the risk-free rate. We will explain precisely how these factors affect call option prices later, but for now, note these points:

1. The longer a call option has to run, the greater its value and the larger its premium. If an option expires at 4 P.M. today, there is not much chance that the stock price will go up very much, so the option will sell at close to its exercise value and its premium will be small. On the other hand, if the expiration date is a year away, the stock price could rise sharply, pulling the option's value up with it.
2. An option on an extremely volatile stock is worth more than one on a very stable stock. If the stock price rarely moves, then there is little chance of a large gain on the stock, hence the option will not be worth much. However, if the stock is highly volatile, the option could easily become very valuable. At the same time, losses on options are limited—you can make an unlimited amount, but you can only lose what you paid for the option. Therefore, a large decline in a stock's price does not have a corresponding bad effect on option holders. As a result of the unlimited upside but limited downside potential, the more volatile a stock, the higher the value of its options.
3. Options will be exercised in the future, and part of a call option's value depends on the present value of the cost to exercise it. If interest rates are high, then the present value of the cost to exercise and that is low, which increases the option's value.

Because of Points 1 and 2, a graph such as Figure 15-1 shows that the longer an option's life, the higher its market price line is above the exercise value line. Similarly, the more volatile the price of the underlying stock, the higher is the market price line. We will see precisely how these factors, and also the risk-free rate, affect option values when we discuss the Black-Scholes model.

Self-Test Questions

What is an option? A call option? A put option?

Define a call option's exercise value. Why is the actual market price of a call option usually above its exercise value?

What are some factors that affect a call option's value?

Introduction to Option Pricing Models

In the next section, we discuss a widely used option pricing formula, the Black-Scholes model. First, though, we go through a simple example to illustrate basic principles. To begin, note that all option pricing models are based on the concept of a **riskless hedge.** Here an investor buys some shares and simultaneously sells a call option on the stock. If the stock's price goes up, the investor will earn a profit, but the holder of the option will exercise it, and that will cost the investor money. Conversely, if the stock goes down, the investor will lose on his or her investment in the stock, but gain from the option (which will expire worthless if the stock price declines). As we demonstrate, it is possible to set things up so that the investor will end up with a riskless position—regardless of what the stock does, the value of the portfolio will remain constant. Thus, a riskless investment will have been created.

If an investment is riskless, it must, in equilibrium, yield the riskless rate. If it offered a higher rate of return, arbitrageurs would buy it and in the process push the price up and the rate of return down, and vice versa if it offered less than the riskless rate.

Given the price of the stock, its volatility, the option's exercise price, the life of the option, and the risk-free rate, there is but one price for the option if it is to meet the equilibrium condition, namely, that a portfolio that consists of the stock and the call option will earn the riskless rate. We value a hypothetical option below, and then we use the Black-Scholes model to value options under more realistic conditions.

1. **Assumptions of the example.** The stock of Western Cellular, a manufacturer of cell phones, sells for $40 per share. Options exist that permit the holder to buy one

share of Western at an exercise price of $35. These options will expire at the end of one year, at which time Western's stock will be selling at one of two prices, either $30 or $50. Also, the risk-free rate is 8.0 percent. Based on these assumptions, we must find the value of the options.

2. **Find the range of values at expiration.** When the option expires at the end of the year, Western's stock will sell for either $30 or $50, and here is the situation with regard to the value of the options:

	Ending Stock Price	−	Strike Price Value	=	Ending Option Value
	$50.00	−	$35.00	=	$15.00
	30.00	−	35.00	=	0.00 (The option will be worthless. It cannot have a negative value.)
Range	$20.00				$15.00

3. **Equalize the range of payoffs for the stock and the option.** As shown above, the ranges of payoffs for the stock and the option are $20 and $15. To construct the riskless portfolio, we need to equalize these ranges. We do so by buying 0.75 share and selling one option (or 75 shares and 100 options) to produce the following situation, where the range for both the stock and the option is $15:

	Ending Stock Price	×	0.75	=	Ending Value of Stock	Ending Value of Option
	$50.00	×	0.75	=	$37.50	$15.00
	30.00	×	0.75	=	22.50	0.00
Range	$20.00				$15.00	$15.00

4. **Create a riskless hedged investment.** We can now create a riskless portfolio by buying 0.75 share of the stock and selling one call option. Here is the situation:

Ending Stock Price	×	0.75	=	Ending Value of Stock in the Portfolio	+	Ending Value of Option in the Portfolio	=	Ending Total Value of the Portfolio
$50.00	×	0.75	=	$37.50	+	−$15.00	=	$22.50
30.00	×	0.75	=	22.50	+	0.00	=	22.50

The stock in the portfolio will have a value of either $22.50 or $37.50, depending on what happens to the price of the stock. The call option that was sold will have no effect on the value of the portfolio if Western's price falls to $30, because it will then not be exercised—it will expire worthless. However, if the stock price ends at $50, the holder of the option will exercise it, paying the $35 exercise price for stock that would cost $50 on the open market, so in that case, the option would have a cost of $15 to the holder of the portfolio.

Now note that the value of the portfolio is $22.50 regardless of whether Western's stock goes up or down, so the portfolio is riskless. A hedge has been created that protects against both increases or decreases in the price of the stock.

5. **Pricing the call option.** To this point, we have not mentioned the price of the call option that was sold to create the riskless hedge. How much should it sell for? Obviously, the seller would like to get a high price, but the buyer would want a low price. What is the *fair*, or *equilibrium*, price? To find this price, we proceed as follows:
   a. The value of the portfolio will be \$22.50 at the end of the year, regardless of what happens to the price of the stock. This \$22.50 is riskless.
   b. The risk-free rate is 8 percent, so the present value of the riskless \$22.50 year-end value is

$$PV = \$22.50/(1.08) = \$20.83.$$

   c. Since Western's stock is currently selling for \$40, and since the portfolio contains 0.75 share, the cost of the stock in the portfolio is

$$0.75(\$40) = \$30.00.$$

   d. If one paid \$30 for the stock, and if the present value of the portfolio is \$20.83, the option would have to sell for \$9.17:

$$\text{Price of option} = \text{Cost of stock} - \text{PV of portfolio}$$
$$= \$30 - \$20.83 = \$9.17.$$

If this option sold at a price higher than \$9.17, other investors could create riskless portfolios as described above and earn more than the riskless rate. Investors (especially the large investment banking firms) would create such portfolios—and options—until their price fell to \$9.17, at which point the market would be in equilibrium. Conversely, if the options sold for less than \$9.17, investors would create an "opposite" portfolio by buying a call option and selling short the stock.[5] The resulting supply shortage would drive the price up to \$9.17. Thus, investors (or arbitrageurs) would buy and sell in the market until the options were priced at their equilibrium level.

Clearly, this example is unrealistic—Western's stock price could be almost anything after one year, and you could not purchase 0.75 share of stock (but you could do so in effect by buying 75 shares and selling 100 options). Still, the example does illustrate that investors can, in theory, create riskless portfolios by buying stocks and selling call options against those stocks, and the return on such portfolios should be the risk-free rate. If call options are not priced to reflect this condition, arbitrageurs will actively trade stocks and options until option prices reflect equilibrium conditions. In the next section, we discuss the Black-Scholes Option Pricing Model, which is based on the general premise we developed here—the creation of a riskless portfolio—but which is applicable to "real-world" option pricing because it allows for a complete range of ending stock prices.

Self-Test Questions

Describe how a risk-free portfolio can be created using stocks and options.

How can such a portfolio be used to help estimate a call option's value?

---

[5]Suppose an investor (or speculator) does not now own any IBM stock. If the investor anticipates a rise in the stock price and consequently buys IBM stock, he or she is said to have *gone long* in IBM. On the other hand, if the investor thinks IBM's stock is likely to fall, he or she could *go short*, or *sell IBM short*. Because the short seller has no IBM stock, he or she would have to borrow the shares sold short from a broker. If the stock price falls, the short seller could, later on, buy shares on the open market and pay back the ones borrowed from the broker. The short seller's profit, before commissions and taxes, would be the difference between the price received from the short sale and the price paid later to purchase the replacement stock.

The Black-Scholes Option Pricing Model (OPM)

The **Black-Scholes Option Pricing Model (OPM),** developed in 1973, helped give rise to the rapid growth in options trading.[6] This model, which has even been programmed into the permanent memories of some hand-held calculators, is widely used by option traders.

OPM Assumptions and Equations

In deriving their option pricing model, Fischer Black and Myron Scholes made the following assumptions:

1. The stock underlying the call option provides no dividends or other distributions during the life of the option.
2. There are no transaction costs for buying or selling either the stock or the option.
3. The short-term, risk-free interest rate is known and is constant during the life of the option.
4. Any purchaser of a security may borrow any fraction of the purchase price at the short-term, risk-free interest rate.
5. Short selling is permitted, and the short seller will receive immediately the full cash proceeds of today's price for a security sold short.
6. The call option can be exercised only on its expiration date.
7. Trading in all securities takes place continuously, and the stock price moves randomly.

The derivation of the Black-Scholes model rests on the concept of a riskless hedge such as the one we set up in the last section. By buying shares of a stock and simultaneously selling call options on that stock, an investor can create a risk-free investment position, where gains on the stock will exactly offset losses on the option. This riskless hedged position must earn a rate of return equal to the risk-free rate. Otherwise, an arbitrage opportunity would exist, and people trying to take advantage of this opportunity would drive the price of the option to the equilibrium level as specified by the Black-Scholes model.

The Black-Scholes model consists of the following three equations:

$$V = P[N(d_1)] - Xe^{-k_{RF}t}[N(d_2)]. \tag{15-1}$$

$$d_1 = \frac{\ln(P/X) + [k_{RF} + (\sigma^2/2)]t}{\sigma\sqrt{t}}. \tag{15-2}$$

$$d_2 = d_1 - \sigma\sqrt{t}. \tag{15-3}$$

Here

V = current value of the call option.

P = current price of the underlying stock.

$N(d_i)$ = probability that a deviation less than d_i will occur in a standard normal distribution. Thus, $N(d_1)$ and $N(d_2)$ represent areas under a standard normal distribution function.

X = exercise, or strike, price of the option.

$e \approx 2.7183$.

[6] See Fischer Black and Myron Scholes, "The Pricing of Options and Corporate Liabilities," *Journal of Political Economy*, May/June 1973, 637–659.

k_{RF} = risk-free interest rate.
t = time until the option expires (the option period).
$\ln(P/X)$ = natural logarithm of P/X.
σ^2 = variance of the rate of return on the stock.

Note that the value of the option is a function of the variables we discussed earlier: (1) P, the stock's price; (2) t, the option's time to expiration; (3) X, the strike price; (4) σ^2, the variance of the underlying stock; and (5) k_{RF}, the risk-free rate. We do not derive the Black-Scholes model—the derivation involves some extremely complicated mathematics that go far beyond the scope of this text. However, it is not difficult to use the model. Under the assumptions set forth previously, if the option price is different from the one found by Equation 15-1, this would provide the opportunity for arbitrage profits, which would force the option price back to the value indicated by the model.[7] As we noted earlier, the Black-Scholes model is widely used by traders, so actual option prices conform reasonably well to values derived from the model.

WWW

Robert's Online Option Pricer can be accessed at **http://www.intrepid.com/~robertl/option-pricer.html**. The site is designed to provide a financial service over the Internet to small investors for option pricing, giving anyone a means to price option trades without having to buy expensive software and hardware.

Loosely speaking, the first term of Equation 15-1, $P[N(d_1)]$, can be thought of as the expected present value of the terminal stock price, given that $P > X$ and the option will be exercised. The second term, $Xe^{-k_{RF}t}[N(d_2)]$, can be thought of as the present value of the exercise price, given that the option will be exercised. However, rather than try to figure out exactly what the equations mean, it is more productive to plug in some numbers to see how changes in the inputs affect the value of an option. The following example is also in the file ***Ch 15 Tool Kit.xls,*** on the textbook's CD-ROM.

OPM Illustration

The current stock price, P, the exercise price, X, and the time to maturity, t, can all be obtained from a newspaper such as *The Wall Street Journal.* The risk-free rate, k_{RF}, is the yield on a Treasury bill with a maturity equal to the option expiration date. The annualized variance of stock returns, σ^2, can be estimated by multiplying the variance of the percentage change in daily stock prices for the past year [that is, the variance of $(P_t - P_{t-1})/P_t$] by 365 days.

Assume that the following information has been obtained:

P = \$20.
X = \$20.
t = 3 months or 0.25 year.
$k_{RF} = 12\% = 0.12$.
$\sigma^2 = 0.16$. Note that if $\sigma^2 = 0.16$, then $\sigma = \sqrt{0.16} = 0.4$.

Given this information, we can now use the OPM by solving Equations 15-1, 15-2, and 15-3. Since d_1 and d_2 are required inputs for Equation 15-1, we solve Equations 15-2 and 15-3 first:

$$d_1 = \frac{\ln(\$20/\$20) + [0.12 + (0.16/2)](0.25)}{0.40(0.50)}$$

$$= \frac{0 + 0.05}{0.20} = 0.25.$$

$$d_2 = d_1 - 0.4\sqrt{0.25} = 0.25 - 0.20 = 0.05.$$

[7] *Programmed trading,* in which stocks are bought and options are sold, or vice versa, is an example of arbitrage between stocks and options.

Note that $N(d_1) = N(0.25)$ and $N(d_2) = N(0.05)$ represent areas under a standard normal distribution function. From the Table in Appendix D, or from the *Excel* function NORMSDIST, we see that the value $d_1 = 0.25$ implies a probability of 0.0987 + 0.5000 = 0.5987, so $N(d_1) = 0.5987$. Similarly, $N(d_2) = 0.5199$. We can use those values to solve Equation 15-1:

$$\begin{aligned} V &= \$20[N(d_1)] - \$20e^{-(0.12)(0.25)}[N(d_2)] \\ &= \$20[N(0.25)] - \$20(0.9704)[N(0.05)] \\ &= \$20(0.5987) - \$19.41(0.5199) \\ &= \$11.97 - \$10.09 = \$1.88. \end{aligned}$$

Thus the value of the option, under the assumed conditions, is \$1.88. Suppose the actual option price were \$2.25. Arbitrageurs could simultaneously sell the option, buy the underlying stock, and earn a riskless profit. Such trading would occur until the price of the option was driven down to \$1.88. The reverse would occur if the option sold for less than \$1.88. Thus, investors would be unwilling to pay more than \$1.88 for the option, and they could not buy it for less, so \$1.88 is the *equilibrium value* of the option.

To see how the five OPM factors affect the value of the option, consider Table 15-2. Here the top row shows the base-case input values that were used above to illustrate the OPM and the resulting option value, V = \$1.88. In each of the subsequent rows, the boldfaced factor is increased, while the other four are held constant at their base-case levels. The resulting value of the call option is given in the last column. Now let's consider the effects of the changes:

1. **Current stock price.** If the current stock price, P, increases from \$20 to \$25, the option value increases from \$1.88 to \$5.81. Thus, the value of the option increases as the stock price increases, but by less than the stock price increase, \$3.93 versus \$5.00. Note, though, that the percentage increase in the option value, (\$5.81 − \$1.88)/\$1.88 = 209%, far exceeds the percentage increase in the stock price, (\$25 − \$20)/\$20 = 25%.
2. **Exercise price.** If the exercise price, X, increases from \$20 to \$25, the value of the option declines. Again, the decrease in the option value is less than the exercise price increase, but the percentage change in the option value, (\$0.39 − \$1.88)/\$1.88 = −79%, exceeds the percentage change in the exercise price, (\$25 − \$20)/\$20 = 25%.
3. **Option period.** As the time to expiration increases from t = 3 months (or 0.25 year) to t = 6 months (or 0.50 year), the value of the option increases from \$1.88 to \$2.81. This occurs because the value of the option depends on the chances for an increase in the price of the underlying stock, and the longer the option has to go, the higher the stock price may climb. Thus, a six-month option is worth more than a three-month option.

TABLE 15-2 Effects of OPM Factors on the Value of a Call Option

	Input Factors					Output
Case	P	X	t	k_{RF}	σ^2	V
Base case	\$20	\$20	0.25	12%	0.16	\$1.88
Increase P by \$5	**25**	20	0.25	12	0.16	5.81
Increase X by \$5	20	**25**	0.25	12	0.16	0.39
Increase t to 6 months	20	20	**0.50**	12	0.16	2.81
Increase k_{RF} to 16%	20	20	0.25	**16**	0.16	1.98
Increase σ^2 to 0.25	20	20	0.25	12	**0.25**	2.27

4. **Risk-free rate.** As the risk-free rate increases from 12 to 16 percent, the value of the option increases slightly, from \$1.88 to \$1.98. Equations 15-1, 15-2, and 15-3 suggest that the principal effect of an increase in k_{RF} is to reduce the present value of the exercise price, $Xe^{-k_{RF}t}$, hence to increase the current value of the option.[8] The risk-free rate also plays a role in determining the values of the normal distribution functions $N(d_1)$ and $N(d_2)$, but this effect is of secondary importance. Indeed, option prices in general are not very sensitive to interest rate changes, at least not to changes within the ranges normally encountered.
5. **Variance.** As the variance increases from the base case 0.16 to 0.25, the value of the option increases from \$1.88 to \$2.27. Therefore, the riskier the underlying security, the more valuable the option. This result is logical. First, if you bought an option to buy a stock that sells at its exercise price, and if $\sigma_2 = 0$, then there would be a zero probability of the stock going up, hence a zero probability of making money on the option. On the other hand, if you bought an option on a high-variance stock, there would be a fairly high probability that the stock would go way up, hence that you would make a large profit on the option. Of course, a high-variance stock could go way down, but as an option holder, your losses would be limited to the price paid for the option—only the right-hand side of the stock's probability distribution counts. Put another way, an increase in the price of the stock helps option holders more than a decrease hurts them, so the greater the variance, the greater is the value of the option. This makes options on risky stocks more valuable than those on safer, low-variance stocks.

Myron Scholes and Robert Merton were awarded the 1997 Nobel Prize in Economics, and Fischer Black would have been a co-recipient had he still been living.[9] Their work provided analytical tools and methodologies that are widely used to solve many types of financial problems, not just option pricing. Indeed, the entire field of modern risk management, discussed in Chapter 24, is based primarily on their contributions. The next section discusses the application of option pricing to real options.

Self-Test Questions

What is the purpose of the Black-Scholes Option Pricing Model?

Explain what a "riskless hedge" is and how the riskless hedge concept is used in the Black-Scholes OPM.

Describe the effect of a change in each of the following factors on the value of a call option:

(1) Stock price.

(2) Exercise price.

(3) Option life.

(4) Risk-free rate.

(5) Stock price variance, that is, riskiness of stock.

---

[8]At this point, you may be wondering why the first term in Equation 15-1, $P[N(d_1)]$, is not discounted. In fact, it has been, because the current stock price, P, already represents the present value of the expected stock price at expiration. In other words, P is a discounted value, and the discount rate used in the market to determine today's stock price includes the risk-free rate. Thus, Equation 15-1 can be thought of as the present value of the end-of-option-period spread between the stock price and the strike price, adjusted for the probability that the stock price will be higher than the strike price.

[9]See Robert C. Merton, "Theory of Rational Option Pricing," *Bell Journal of Economics and Management Science*, Vol. 4, 1973, 141–183.

Introduction to Real Options

According to traditional capital budgeting theory, a project's NPV is the present value of its expected future cash flows, discounted at a rate that reflects the riskiness of the expected future cash flows. If the NPV is not positive, then the project should be rejected. Note, however, that traditional capital budgeting theory says nothing about actions that can be taken after the project has been accepted and placed in operation that might cause the cash flows to increase. In other words, traditional capital budgeting theory assumes that a project is like a roulette wheel. A gambler can choose whether or not to spin the wheel, but once the wheel has been spun, there is nothing he or she can do to influence the outcome. Once the game begins, the outcome depends purely on chance, with no skill involved.

Contrast roulette with other games, such as draw poker. Chance plays a role in poker, and it continues to play a role after the initial deal because players receive additional cards throughout the game. However, poker players are able to respond to their opponents' actions, so skillful players usually win.

Capital budgeting decisions have more in common with poker than roulette because (1) chance plays a continuing role throughout the life of the project and (2) managers can respond to changing market conditions and to competitors' actions. Opportunities to respond to changing circumstances are called **managerial options** because they give managers a chance to influence the outcome of a project. They are also called **strategic options** because they are often associated with large, strategic projects rather than routine maintenance projects. Finally, they are called **real options,** and they are differentiated from financial options, because they involve real, rather than financial, assets.

Self-Test Questions

Explain the similarities and differences between capital budgeting projects and such games of chance as roulette and poker.

What are real options?

Types of Real Options

The first step in valuing projects that have embedded options is to identify the options. Even though no two projects are exactly identical, several types of real options are often present, and managers should always look for them. Even more important, managers should try to create options within projects.

Investment Timing Options

Conventional NPV analysis implicitly assumes that projects will either be accepted or rejected, which implies that they will be undertaken now or never. In practice, however, companies sometimes have a third choice—delay the decision until later, when more information is available. Such **investment timing options** can dramatically affect a project's estimated profitability and risk.

For example, suppose Sony plans to introduce an interactive DVD-TV system, and your company has two alternatives: (1) immediately begin full scale production of game software on DVDs for the new system or (2) delay investment in the project until you get a better idea of the size of the market for interactive DVDs. You would probably prefer delaying implementation. Keep in mind, though, that the *option to delay* is valuable only if it more than offsets any harm that might come from delaying. For example, if you delay, some other company might establish a loyal customer base that makes it difficult for your company to later enter the market. The option to delay is usually most valuable to firms with proprietary technology, patents, licenses, or other barriers to entry, because these factors lessen the threat of competition. The option to delay is valuable when market demand is uncertain, but it is also valuable during periods of volatile interest rates, since the ability to wait can allow firms to delay raising capital for projects until interest rates are lower.

Growth Options

A **growth option** allows a company to increase its capacity if market conditions are better than expected. There are several types of growth options. One lets a company *increase the capacity of an existing product line.* Enron's power plant project, as described in the chapter's opening vignette, illustrates this type of growth option, because it permits Enron to produce additional power if demand and therefore prices are high.

The second type of growth option allows a company to *expand into new geographic markets.* Many companies are investing in Eastern Europe, Russia, and China even though standard NPV analysis produces negative NPVs. However, if these developing markets really take off, the option to open more facilities could be quite valuable.

The third type of growth option is the opportunity to *add new products* including complementary products and successive "generations" of the original product. Toshiba probably lost money on its first laptop computers, but the manufacturing skills and consumer recognition it gained helped turn subsequent generations of laptops into money makers. In addition, Toshiba used its experience and name recognition in laptops as a springboard into the desktop computer market.

Abandonment Options

Many projects contain an **abandonment option.** When evaluating a potential project, standard DCF analysis assumes that the assets will be used over a specified economic life. While some projects must be operated over their full economic life, even though market conditions might deteriorate and cause lower than expected cash flows, others can be abandoned. For example, some contracts between automobile manufacturers and their suppliers specify the quantity and price of the parts that must be delivered. If the supplier's labor costs increase, then the supplier might well lose money on each part it ships. Including the option to abandon in such a contract might be quite valuable.

Note too that some projects can be structured so that they provide the option to *reduce capacity or temporarily suspend operations.* Such options are common in the natural resource industry, including mining, oil, and timber, and they should be reflected in the analysis when NPVs are being estimated.

Flexibility Options

Many projects offer **flexibility options** that permit the firm to alter operations depending on how conditions change during the life of the project. Typically, either inputs or outputs (or both) can be changed. BMW's Spartanburg, South Carolina, auto assembly plant provides a good example of output flexibility. BMW needed the plant to produce sports coupes. If it built the plant configured to produce only these vehicles, the construction cost would be minimized. However, the company thought that later on it might want to switch production to some other vehicle type, and that would be difficult if the plant were designed just for coupes. Therefore, BMW decided to spend additional funds to construct a more flexible plant—one that could produce different types of vehicles should demand patterns shift. Sure enough, things did change. Demand for coupes dropped a bit and that for sports utility vehicles soared. But BMW was ready, and the

Spartanburg plant is now spewing out hot-selling 2000 model X5 SUVs at $49,970 each. The plant's cash flows are much higher than they would have been without the flexibility option that BMW "bought" by paying more to build a more flexible plant.

Electric power plants provide an example of input flexibility. Utilities can build plants that generate electricity by burning coal, oil, or natural gas. The prices of those fuels change over time, depending on events in the Middle East, changing environmental policies, and weather conditions. Some years ago, virtually all power plants were designed to burn just one type of fuel, because this resulted in the lowest construction cost. However, as fuel cost volatility increased, power companies began to build higher-cost but more flexible plants, especially ones that could switch from oil to gas and back again, depending on relative fuel prices.

Self-Test Question

Name some different types of real options.

Valuing Real Options

How can we estimate the value of a real option? To begin answering this question, consider a simple project consisting of a single risk-free cash flow due one year from today. The pure DCF value of this project is found as follows:

$$\text{Project DCF value} = \frac{\text{Cash flow}}{(1 + k_{RF})}.$$

The only required inputs are the cash flow, which is known, and the risk-free rate, which can be estimated as the rate on a 52-week Treasury bill. Given these inputs, we can calculate an accurate estimate of the project's DCF value.

In contrast, valuing a real option requires a great deal of judgment, both to formulate the model and to estimate the inputs. This means the "answer" will not be nearly as precise for a real option as for the simple one-period project described above. But does this mean the answer won't be useful? Definitely not. For example, the models used by NASA only approximate the centers of gravity for the moon, the earth, and other heavenly bodies, yet even with these "errors" in their models, NASA was able to put a man on the moon. As one professor said, "All models are wrong, but some are still quite useful." This is especially true for real options. We might not be able to find the exact value of a real option, but the value we find can be helpful in deciding whether or not to accept the project. Equally as important, the process of looking for and then valuing real options often identifies critical issues that might otherwise go unnoticed.

Five possible procedures can be used to deal with real options. Starting with the simplest, these are as follows:

1. Use discounted cash flow (DCF) valuation and ignore any real options by assuming their values are zero.
2. Use DCF valuation and include a qualitative recognition of any real options' value.
3. Use decision tree analysis.
4. Use a standard model for a financial option.
5. Develop a unique, project-specific model using financial engineering techniques.

The following sections illustrate these procedures.

Self-Test Question

List the five possible procedures for dealing with real options.

The Investment Timing Option: An Illustration

All calculations for the analysis of the investment timing option are also shown in ***Ch 15 Tool Kit.xls.***

Murphy Systems is considering a project for a new type of hand-held device that provides wireless Internet connections. The cost of the project is \$50 million, but the future cash flows depend on the demand for wireless Internet connections, which is uncertain. Murphy believes there is a 25 percent chance that demand for the new device will be very high, in which case the project will generate cash flows of \$33 million each year for three years. There is a 50 percent chance of average demand, with cash flows of \$25 million per year, and a 25 percent chance that demand will be low and annual cash flows will be only \$5 million. A preliminary analysis indicates that the project is somewhat riskier than average, so it has been assigned a cost of capital of 14 percent versus 12 percent for an average project. Here is a summary of the project's data:

Demand	Probability	Annual Cash Flow
High	0.25	\$33 million
Average	0.50	25 million
Low	0.25	5 million
Expected annual cash flow		\$22 million
Project's cost of capital		14%
Life of project		3 years
Required investment, or cost of project		\$50 million

Murphy could accept the project and implement it immediately, but since the company has a patent on the device's core modules, it can also choose to delay the decision until next year, when more information about demand for the product will be available. The cost will still be \$50 million if Murphy waits, and the project will still be expected to generate the indicated cash flows, but each flow will be pushed back one year. However, if Murphy waits, it will know which of the demand conditions, hence which set of cash flows, will exist. If it waits, Murphy will of course make the investment only if demand is sufficient to provide a positive NPV.

Note that this real timing option resembles a call option on a stock. A call gives its owner the right to purchase a stock at a fixed exercise price, but only if the stock's price is higher than the exercise price will the owner exercise the option and buy the stock. Similarly, if Murphy defers implementation, then it will have the right to "purchase" the project by making the investment if the NPV as calculated next year, when new information is available, is positive.

Approach 1. DCF Analysis Ignoring the Timing Option

Based on probabilities for the different levels of demand, the expected annual cash flows are \$22 million per year:

$$\text{Expected cash flow per year} = 0.25(\$33) + 0.50(\$25) + 0.25(\$5) = \$22 \text{ million.}$$

Ignoring the investment timing option, the traditional NPV is \$1.08 million, found as follows:

$$\text{NPV} = -\$50 + \frac{\$22}{(1 + 0.14)} + \frac{\$22}{(1 + 0.14)^2} + \frac{\$22}{(1 + 0.14)^3} = \$1.08.$$

Based just on this DCF analysis, Murphy should accept the project. Note, though, that if the expected cash flows had been slightly lower, say, \$21.5 million, the NPV would have been negative and the project would have been rejected. Also, note that the project is risky—there is a 25 percent probability that demand will be weak, in which case the NPV would turn out to be a negative $38.4 million.

Approach 2. DCF with a Qualitative Consideration of the Timing Option

The discounted cash flow analysis suggests that the project should be accepted, but just barely, and it ignores the existence of a possibly valuable real option. If Murphy implements the project now, it gains an expected (but risky) NPV of $1.08 million. However, accepting now means that it is also giving up the option of waiting to learn more about market demand before making the commitment. Thus, the decision is this: Is the option Murphy would be giving up worth more or less than $1.08 million? If the option is worth more than $1.08 million, then Murphy should not give up the option, which means deferring the decision, and vice versa if the option is worth less than $1.08 million.

Based on the discussion of financial options earlier in the chapter, what qualitative assessment can we make regarding the option's value? Put another way, without doing any additional calculations, does it appear that Murphy should go forward now or wait? In thinking about this decision, first note that the value of an option is higher if the current value of the underlying asset is high relative to its exercise price, other things held constant. For example, a call option with an exercise cost of $50 on a stock with a current price of $50 is worth more than if the price were $20. We will calculate the exact value of Murphy's underlying asset later, but the DCF analysis does suggest that the underlying asset's value will be close to the exercise price, so the option should be valuable. We also know that an option's value is higher the longer its time to expiration. Here the option has a one-year life, which is fairly long for an option, and that too suggests that the option is probably valuable. Finally, we know that the value of an option increases with the risk of the underlying asset. The data used in the DCF analysis indicate that the project is quite risky, which again suggests that the option is valuable.

Thus, our qualitative assessment indicates that the option to delay might well be more valuable than the expected NPV of $1.08 if we undertake the project immediately. This is quite subjective, but the qualitative assessment should make Murphy's management pause, and then go on to make a quantitative assessment of the situation.

Approach 3. Decision Tree Analysis of the Timing Option

Part 1 of Figure 15-2 presents a scenario analysis similar to the ones in Chapter 14, except now the cash flows are shown as a **decision tree** diagram. Each possible outcome is shown as a "branch" on the tree. Each branch shows the cash flows and probability of a scenario, laid out as a time line. Thus, the top line, which gives the payoffs of the high-demand scenario, has positive cash flows of $33 million for the next three years, and its NPV is $26.61 million. The average-demand branch in the middle has an NPV of $8.04 million, while the NPV of the low-demand branch is a negative $38.39 million. Since Murphy will suffer a $38.39 million loss if demand is weak, and since there is a 25 percent probability of weak demand, the project is clearly risky.

The expected NPV is the weighted average of the three possible outcomes, with the weight for each outcome being its probability. The sum in the last column in Part 1 shows that the expected NPV is $1.08 million, the same as in the original DCF analysis. Part 1 also shows a standard deviation of $24.02 million for the NPV, and a coefficient of variation, defined as the ratio of standard deviation to the expected NPV, of 22.32, which is quite large. Clearly, the project is quite risky under the analysis thus far.

Part 2 is set up similarly to Part 1 except that it shows what happens if Murphy delays the decision and then implements the project only if demand turns out to be high

FIGURE 15-2 DCF and Decision Tree Analysis for the Investment Timing Option (Millions of Dollars)

PART 1. SCENARIO ANALYSIS: PROCEED WITH PROJECT TODAY

2001		Future Cash Flows 2002	2003	2004	NPV of This Scenario[c]	Probability	Probability × NPV
−$50	High 0.25	$33	$33	$33	$26.61	0.25	$6.65
	Average 0.50	$25	$25	$25	$8.04	0.50	$4.02
	Low 0.25	$5	$5	$5	−$38.39	0.25	−$9.60
						1.00	

Expected value of NPVs = $1.08

Standard deviation[a] = $24.02

Coefficient of variation[b] = 22.32

PART 2. DECISION TREE ANALYSIS: IMPLEMENT NEXT YEAR ONLY IF OPTIMAL

2001		Future Cash Flows 2002	2003	2004	2005	NPV of this Scenario[d]	Probability	Probability × NPV
Wait	High 0.25	−$50	$33	$33	$33	$23.35	0.25	$5.84
	Average 0.50	−$50	$25	$25	$25	$7.05	0.50	$3.53
	Low 0.25	$0	$0	$0	$0	$0.00	0.25	$0.00
							1.00	

Expected value of NPVs = $9.36

Standard deviation[a] = $8.57

Coefficient of variation[b] = 0.92

Notes:
[a]The standard deviation is calculated as explained in Chapter 6.
[b]The coefficient of variation is the standard deviation divided by the expected value.
[c]The WACC is 14 percent.
[d]The NPV in Part 2 is as of 2001. Therefore, each of the project cash flows is discounted back one more year than in Part 1.

or average. No cost is incurred in 2001—here the only action is to wait. Then, if demand is average or high, Murphy will spend $50 million in 2002 and receive either $33 million or $25 million per year for the following three years. If demand is low, as shown on the bottom branch, Murphy will spend nothing in 2002 and will receive no cash flows in subsequent years. The NPV of the high-demand branch is $23.35 million and that of the average-demand branch is $7.05 million. Because all cash flows under the low-demand scenario are zero, the NPV in this case will also be zero. The expected NPV if Murphy delays the decision is \$9.36 million.

This analysis shows that the project's expected NPV will be much higher if Murphy delays than if it invests immediately. Also, since there is no possibility of losing money under the delay option, this decision also lowers the project's risk. This clearly indicates that the option to wait is valuable, hence that Murphy should wait until 2002 before deciding whether to proceed with the investment.

Before we conclude the discussion of decision trees, note that we used the same cost of capital, 14 percent, to discount cash flows in the "proceed immediately" scenario analysis in Part 1 and under the "delay one year" scenario in Part 2. However, for three reasons this is not appropriate. First, since there is no possibility of losing money if Murphy delays, the investment under that plan is clearly less risky than if Murphy charges ahead today. Second, the 14 percent cost of capital might be appropriate for risky cash flows, yet the investment in the project in 2002 in Part 2 is known with certainty. Perhaps, then, we should discount it at the risk-free rate.[10] Third, the project's cash inflows (excluding the initial investment) are different in Part 2 than in Part 1 because the low-demand cash flows are eliminated. This suggests that if 14 percent is the appropriate cost of capital in the "proceed immediately" case, some lower rate would be appropriate in the "delay decision" case.

In Figure 15-3, Part 1, we repeat the "delay decision" analysis, with one exception. We continue to discount the operating cash flows in years 2003, 2004, and 2005 at the 14 percent WACC, but now we discount the project's cost back to 2001 at the risk-free rate, 6 percent. This increases the PV of the cost at 2001, and that lowers the NPV from \$9.36 million to \$6.88 million. Note, though, that we really don't know the precisely appropriate WACC for the project—the 14 percent we used might be too high or too low for the operating cash flows in 2003, 2004, and 2005.[11] Therefore, in Part 2 of Figure 15-3 we show a sensitivity analysis of the NPV where the discount rate used for both the operating cash flows and for the project's cost vary. This sensitivity analysis shows that under all reasonable WACCs, the NPV of delaying is greater than \$1.08 million, the NPV of immediate implementation. This means that the option to wait is more valuable than the \$1.08 million resulting from immediate implementation. Therefore, Murphy should wait rather than implement the project immediately.

Approach 4. Valuing the Timing Option with the Black-Scholes Model[12]

The decision tree approach, coupled with a sensitivity analysis, may provide enough information for a good decision. However, it is often useful to obtain additional insights into the real option's value, which means using the fourth procedure, an option pricing model. To do this, the analyst must find a standard financial option that

[10]See Timothy A. Luehrman, "Investment Opportunities as Real Options: Getting Started on the Numbers," *Harvard Business Review*, July–August 1998, 51–67, for a more detailed explanation of the rationale for using the risk-free rate to discount the project cost. This paper also provides a discussion of real option valuation. Professor Luehrman also has a follow-up paper that provides an excellent discussion of the ways real options affect strategy. See Timothy A. Luehrman, "Strategy as a Portfolio of Real Options," *Harvard Business Review*, September–October 1998, 89–99.

[11]The cash inflows if we delay might be considered more risky if there is a chance that the delay might cause those flows to decline due to the loss of Murphy's "first mover advantage." Put another way, we might gain information by waiting, and that could lower risk, but if a delay would enable others to enter and perhaps preempt the market, this could increase risk. In our example, we assumed that Murphy has a patent on critical components of the device, hence that no one could come in and preempt its position in the market.

[12]This section is relatively technical, but it can be omitted without loss of continuity.

FIGURE 15-3 Decision Tree and Sensitivity Analysis for the Investment Timing Option (Millions of Dollars)

PART 1. DECISION TREE ANALYSIS: IMPLEMENT IN ONE YEAR ONLY IF OPTIMAL (DISCOUNT COST AT THE RISK-FREE RATE AND OPERATING CASH FLOWS AT THE WACC)

2001			Future Cash Flows 2002	2003	2004	2005	NPV of This Scenario[c]	Probability	Probability × NPV
	High	0.25	−$50	$33	$33	$33	$20.04	0.25	$5.01
Wait	Average	0.50	−$50	$25	$25	$25	$3.74	0.50	$1.87
	Low	0.25	$0	$0	$0	$0	$0.00	0.25	$0.00
								1.00	

Expected value of NPVs = $6.88

Standard deviation[a] = $7.75

Coefficient of variation[b] = 1.13

PART 2. SENSITIVITY ANALYSIS OF NPV TO CHANGES IN THE COST OF CAPITAL USED TO DISCOUNT COST AND CASH FLOWS

Cost of Capital Used to Discount the 2003–2005 Operating Cash Flows	Cost of Capital Used to Discount the 2002 Cost: 3.0%	4.0%	5.0%	6.0%	7.0%	8.0%	9.0%
8.0%	$13.11	$13.46	$13.80	$14.14	$14.47	$14.79	$15.11
9.0%	11.78	12.13	12.47	12.81	13.14	13.47	13.78
10.0%	10.50	10.85	11.20	11.53	11.86	12.19	12.51
11.0%	9.27	9.62	9.97	10.30	10.64	10.96	11.28
12.0%	8.09	8.44	8.78	9.12	9.45	9.78	10.09
13.0%	6.95	7.30	7.64	7.98	8.31	8.64	8.95
14.0%	5.85	6.20	6.54	**6.88**	7.21	7.54	7.85
15.0%	4.79	5.14	5.48	5.82	6.15	6.48	6.79
16.0%	3.77	4.12	4.46	4.80	5.13	5.45	5.77
17.0%	2.78	3.13	3.47	3.81	4.14	4.46	4.78
18.0%	1.83	2.18	2.52	2.86	3.19	3.51	3.83

Notes:
[a] The standard deviation is calculated as in Chapter 6.
[b] The coefficient of variation is the standard deviation divided by the expected value.
[c] The operating cash flows in years 2003–2005 are discounted at the WACC of 14 percent. The cost in 2002 is discounted at the risk-free rate of 6 percent.

resembles the project's real option.[13] As noted earlier, Murphy's option to delay the project is similar to a call option on a stock, hence the Black-Scholes option pricing model can be used. This model requires five inputs: (1) the risk-free rate, (2) the time

[13] In theory, financial option pricing models apply only to assets that are continuously traded in a market. Even though real options usually don't meet this criterion, financial option models often provide a reasonably accurate approximation of the real option's value.

until the option expires, (3) the exercise price, (4) the current price of the stock, and (5) the variance of the stock's rate of return. Therefore, we need to estimate values for those five factors.

First, assuming that the rate on a 52-week Treasury bill is 6 percent, this rate can be used as the risk-free rate. Second, Murphy must decide within a year whether or not to implement the project, so there is one year until the option expires. Third, it will cost $50 million to implement the project, so $50 million can be used for the exercise price. Fourth, we need a proxy for the value of the underlying asset, which in Black-Scholes is the current price of the stock. Note that a stock's current price is the present value of its expected future cash flows. For Murphy's real option, the underlying asset is the project itself, and its current "price" is the present value of its expected future cash flows. Therefore, as a proxy for the stock price we can use the present value of the project's future cash flows. And fifth, the variance of the project's expected return can be used to represent the variance of the stock's return in the Black-Scholes model.

Figure 15-4 shows how one can estimate the present value of the project's cash inflows. We need to find the current value of the underlying asset, that is, the project. For a stock, the current price is the present value of all expected future cash flows, including those that are expected even if we do not exercise the call option. Note also that the exercise price for a call option has no effect on the stock's current price.[14] For our real option, the underlying asset is the delayed project, and its current "price" is the present value of all its future expected cash flows. Just as the price of a stock includes all of its future cash flows, the present value of the project should

[14]The company itself is not involved with traded stock options. However, if the option were a warrant issued by the company, then the exercise price would affect the company's cash flows, hence its stock price.

FIGURE 15-4 Estimating the Input for Stock Price in the Option Analysis of the Investment Timing Option (Millions of Dollars)

			Future Cash Flows				
2001	2002		2003	2004	2005	PV of This Scenario[c]	Probability	Probability × PV
	High	0.25 →	$33	$33	$33	$67.21	0.25	$16.80
Wait	Average	0.50 →	$25	$25	$25	$50.91	0.50	$25.46
	Low	0.25 →	$5	$5	$5	$10.18	0.25	$2.55
							1.00	

Expected value of PVs[d] = $44.80

Standard deviation[a] = $21.07

Coefficient of variation[b] = 0.47

Notes:
[a]The standard deviation is calculated as in Chapter 6.
[b]The coefficient of variation is the standard deviation divided by the expected value.
[c]The WACC is 14 percent. All cash flows in this scenario are discounted back to 2001.
[d]Here we find the PV, not the NPV, as the project's cost is ignored.

include all its possible future cash flows. Moreover, since the price of a stock is not affected by the exercise price of a call option, we ignore the project's "exercise price," or cost, when we find its present value. Figure 15-4 shows the expected cash flows if the project is delayed. The PV of these cash flows as of today (2001) is $44.80 million, and this is the input we should use for the current price in the Black-Scholes model.

The last required input is the variance of the project's return. Three different approaches could be used to estimate this input. First, we could use judgment—an educated guess. Here we would begin by recalling that a company is a portfolio of projects (or assets), with each project having its own risk. Since returns on the company's stock reflect the diversification gained by combining many projects, we might expect the variance of the stock's returns to be lower than the variance of one of its average projects. The variance of an average company's stock return is about 12 percent, so we might expect the variance for a typical project to be somewhat higher, say, 15 to 25 percent. Companies in the Internet infrastructure industry are riskier than average, so we might subjectively estimate the variance of Murphy's project to be in the range of 18 percent to 30 percent.

The second approach, called the direct method, is to estimate the rate of return for each possible outcome and then calculate the variance of those returns. First, Part 1 in Figure 15-5 shows the PV for each possible outcome as of 2002, the time when the option expires. Here we simply find the present value of all future operating cash flows discounted back to 2002, using the WACC of 14 percent. The 2002 present value is $76.61 million for high demand, $58.04 million for average demand, and $11.61 million for low demand. Then, in Part 2, we show the percentage return from the current time until the option expires for each scenario, based on the $44.80 million starting "price" of the project in 2001 as calculated in Figure 15.4. If demand is high, we will obtain a return of 71.0 percent: ($76.61 − $44.80)/$44.80 = 0.710 = 71.0 percent). Similar calculations show returns of 29.5 percent for average demand and −74.1 percent for low demand. The expected percentage return is 14 percent, the standard deviation is 53.6 percent, and the variance is 28.7 percent.[15]

The third approach for estimating the variance is also based on the scenario data, but the data are used in a different manner. First, we know that demand is not really limited to three scenarios—rather, a wide range of outcomes is possible. Similarly, the stock price at the time a call option expires could take on one of many values. It is reasonable to assume that the value of the project at the time when we must decide on undertaking it behaves similarly to the price of a stock at the time a call option expires. Under this assumption, we can use the expected value and standard deviation of the project's value to calculate the variance of its rate of return, σ^2, with this formula:[16]

$$\sigma^2 = \frac{\ln(CV^2 + 1)}{t}. \tag{15-4}$$

Here CV is the coefficient of variation of the underlying asset's price at the time the option expires and t is the time until the option expires. Thus, while the three scenarios are simplifications of the true condition, where there are an infinite number of

[15] Two points should be made about the percentage return. First, for use in the Black-Scholes model, we need a percentage return calculated as shown, not an IRR return. The IRR is not used in the option pricing approach. Second, the expected return turns out to be 14 percent, the same as the WACC. This is because the 2001 price and the 2002 PVs were all calculated using the 14 percent WACC, and because we are measuring return over only one year. If we measure the compound return over more than one year, then the average return generally will not equal 14 percent.

[16] See David C. Shimko, *Finance in Continuous Time* (Miami, FL: Kolb Publishing Company, 1992), for a more detailed explanation.

FIGURE 15-5 Estimating the Input for Variance in the Option Analysis of the Investment Timing Option (Millions of Dollars)

PART 1. FIND THE VALUE AND RISK OF FUTURE CASH FLOWS AT THE TIME THE OPTION EXPIRES

2001	2002		Future Cash Flows 2003	2004	2005	PV in 2002 for This Scenario[c]	Probability	Probability × PV_{2002}
Wait	High	0.25	$33	$33	$33	$76.61	0.25	$19.15
	Average	0.50	$25	$25	$25	$58.04	0.50	$29.02
	Low	0.25	$5	$5	$5	$11.61	0.25	$2.90
							1.00	

Expected value of PV_{2002} = $51.08

Standard deviation of PV_{2002}[a] = $24.02

Coefficient of variation of PV_{2002}[b] = 0.47

PART 2. DIRECT METHOD: USE THE SCENARIOS TO DIRECTLY ESTIMATE THE VARIANCE OF THE PROJECT'S RETURN

$Price_{2001}$[d]			PV_{2002}[e]	$Return_{2002}$[f]	Probability	Probability × $Return_{2002}$
$44.80	High	0.25	$76.61	71.0%	0.25	17.8%
	Average	0.50	$58.04	29.5%	0.50	14.8%
	Low	0.25	$11.61	−74.1%	0.25	−18.5%
					1.00	

Expected return = 14.0%

Standard deviation of return[a] = 53.6%

Variance of return[g] = 28.7%

PART 3. INDIRECT METHOD: USE THE SCENARIOS TO INDIRECTLY ESTIMATE THE VARIANCE OF THE PROJECT'S RETURN

Expected "price" at the time the option expires[h] =	$51.08
Standard deviation of expected "price" at the time the option expires[i] =	$24.02
Coefficient of variation (CV) =	0.47
Time (in years) until the option expires (t) =	1
Variance of the project's expected return = $\ln(CV^2 + 1)/t$ =	20.0%

Notes:

[a]The standard deviation is calculated as explained in Chapter 6.

[b]The coefficient of variation is the standard deviation divided by the expected value.

[c]The WACC is 14 percent. The 2003–2005 cash flows are discounted back to 2002.

[d]The 2001 price is the expected PV from Figure 15-4.

[e]The 2002 PVs are from Part 1.

[f]The returns for each scenario are calculated as $(PV_{2002} - Price_{2001})/Price_{2001}$.

[g]The variance of return is the standard deviation squared.

[h]The expected "price" at the time the option expires is taken from Part 1.

[i]The standard deviation of expected "price" at the time the option expires is taken from Part 1.

possible outcomes, we can still use the scenario data to estimate the variance of the project's rate of return if it had an infinite number of possible outcomes.

For Murphy's project, this indirect method produces the following estimate of the variance of the project's return:

$$\sigma^2 = \frac{\ln(0.47^2 + 1)}{1} = 0.20 = 20\%. \qquad \textbf{(15-4a)}$$

Which of the three approaches is best? Obviously, they all involve judgment, so an analyst might want to consider all three. In our example, all three methods produce similar estimates, but for illustrative purposes we will simply use 20 percent as our initial estimate for the variance of the project's rate of return.

Part 1 of Figure 15-6 calculates the value of the option to defer investment in the project based on the Black-Scholes model, and the result is $7.04 million. Since this is significantly higher than the $1.08 million NPV under immediate implementation, and

FIGURE 15-6 Estimating the Value of the Investment Timing Option Using a Standard Financial Option (Millions of Dollars)

PART 1. FIND THE VALUE OF A CALL OPTION USING THE BLACK-SCHOLES MODEL

	Real Option		
k_{RF} =	Risk-free interest rate	=	6%
t =	Time in years until the option expires	=	1
X =	Cost to implement the project	=	$50.00
P =	Current value of the project	=	$44.80[a]
σ^2 =	Variance of the project's rate of return	=	20.0%[b]
d_1 =	$\{\ln(P/X) + [k_{RF} + (\sigma^2/2)]t\}/(\sigma t^{1/2})$	=	0.112
d_2 =	$d_1 - \sigma(t^{1/2})$	=	−0.33
$N(d_1)$ =		=	0.54
$N(d_2)$ =		=	0.37
V =	$P[N(d_1)] - Xe^{-k_{RF}t}[N(d_2)]$	=	**$7.04**

PART 2. SENSITIVITY ANALYSIS OF OPTION VALUE TO CHANGES IN VARIANCE

Variance	Option Value
12.0%	$5.24
14.0	5.74
16.0	6.20
18.0	6.63
20.0	**7.04**
22.0	7.42
24.0	7.79
26.0	8.15
28.0	8.49
30.0	8.81
32.0	9.13

Notes:
[a]The current value of the project is taken from Figure 15-4.
[b]The variance of the project's rate of return is taken from Part 3 of Figure 15-5.

Growth Options at Dot-com Companies

In September 2000, several dot-com companies had recently failed, including DEN (Digital Entertainment Network) and Boo.com, an e-tailer of clothing. Other dot-coms had incredible market valuations, such as Yahoo! ($58.2 billion), Amazon.com ($15.5 billion) and America Online ($126.9 billion).

What explains these wide variations in values? It's certainly not the physical assets the companies own, since Yahoo! has enormous value but virtually no physical assets. Based on the corporate valuation model of Chapter 12, we might be tempted to say the differences are explained by free cash flows. Perhaps dot-coms such as Amazon and Yahoo! have large expected future free cash flows, and their high values reflect this, but we certainly can't base that conclusion on their past results.

This is where real options come into play. Given its name recognition, infrastructure, and customer base, Amazon is in a position to grow into a variety of businesses, some of which might be very profitable. The same is true for Yahoo! and AOL. In other words, they have many growth options with very low exercise prices. We know from our discussion of real options that an option is more valuable if the underlying source of risk is very volatile, and it's hard to imagine anything more volatile than the prospects of profitability in e-commerce. The field of e-commerce may end up being so competitive that there is little profit for the participating companies, or it may replace most existing forms of commerce, with the first-movers having an enormous advantage. This uncertainty means that a growth option in e-commerce is very valuable. Therefore, companies with many growth options should have high valuations.

Note that just being a dot-com company is not enough to create value. DEN and Boo.com had substantial obligations but very few options, which led to their demise. For dot-com companies, the key to high valuations is to create as many growth options as possible.

Source: Adapted from Geoffrey Colvin, "You're Only as Good as Your Choices," *Fortune*, June 12, 2000, 75.

since the option would be forfeited if Murphy goes ahead right now, we conclude that the company should defer the final decision until more information is available.

Note, though, that judgmental estimates were made at many points in the analysis, and it is useful to see how sensitive the final outcome is to certain of the key inputs. Thus, in Part 2 of Figure 15-6 we show the sensitivity of the option's value to different estimates of the variance. It is comforting to see that for all reasonable estimates of variance, the option to delay remains more valuable than immediate implementation.

Approach 5. Financial Engineering

Sometimes an analyst might not be satisfied with the results of a decision tree analysis and cannot find a standard financial option that corresponds to the real option. In such a situation the only alternative is to develop a unique model for the specific real option being analyzed, which is called **financial engineering.** When financial engineering is applied on Wall Street, where it was developed, the result is a newly designed financial product.[17] When it is applied to real options, the result is the value of a project that contains embedded options.

Although financial engineering was originally developed on Wall Street, many financial engineering techniques have been applied to real options during the last ten years. We expect this trend to continue, especially in light of the rapid improvements in computer processing speed and spreadsheet software capabilities. One financial

[17]Financial engineering techniques are widely used for the creation and valuation of derivative securities, which we discuss in Chapter 24.

engineering technique is called **risk-neutral valuation.** This technique uses simulation, and we discuss it in the Chapter 15 Web/CD Extension located on the textbook's CD-ROM and web site. Most other financial engineering techniques are too complicated for an introductory course in financial management, and so we leave a detailed discussion of them to a later course.

For illustrative valuations of growth options and abandonment options, see the Chapter 15 Web/CD Extension. The calculations are also shown in ***Ch 15 Tool Kit.xls***, found on the textbook's CD-ROM.

Self-Test Questions

What is a decision tree?

In a qualitative analysis, what factors affect the value of a real option?

Concluding Thoughts on Real Options

We don't deny that real options can be pretty complicated. Keep in mind, however, that 50 years ago very few companies used NPV because it seemed too complicated. Now NPV is a basic tool used by virtually all companies and taught in all business schools. A similar, but more rapid, pattern of adoption is occurring with real options. Ten years ago very few companies used real options, but a recent survey of CFOs reported that more than 26 percent of companies now use real option techniques when evaluating projects.[18] Just as with NPV, it's only a matter of time before virtually all companies use real option techniques.

We have provided you with some basic tools necessary for evaluating real options, starting with the ability to identify real options and make qualitative assessments regarding a real option's value. Decision trees are another important tool, since they require an explicit identification of the embedded options, which is very important in the decision-making process. However, keep in mind that the decision tree should not use the original project's cost of capital. Although finance theory has not yet provided a way to estimate the appropriate cost of capital for a decision tree, sensitivity analysis can identify the effect that different costs of capital have on the project's value.

Many real options can be analyzed using a standard model for an existing financial option, such as the Black-Scholes model for calls and puts. There are also other financial models for a variety of options. These include the option to exchange one asset for another, the option to purchase the minimum or the maximum of two or more assets, the option on an average of several assets, and even an option on an option.[19] In fact, there are entire textbooks that describe even more options.[20] Given the large number of standard models for existing financial options, it is often possible to find a financial option that resembles the real option being analyzed.

---

[18]See John R. Graham and Cambell R. Harvey, "The Theory and Practice of Corporate Finance: Evidence from the Field," *Journal of Financial Economics*, Vol. 60, no. 1.

[19]See W. Margrabe, "The Value of an Option to Exchange One Asset for Another," *Journal of Finance*, March 1978, 177–186; R. Stulz, "Options on the Minimum or Maximum of Two Risky Assets: Analysis and Applications," *Journal of Financial Economics*, 1982, 161–185; H. Johnson, "Options on the Maximum or Minimum of Several Assets," *Journal of Financial and Quantitative Analysis*, September 1987, 277–283; P. Ritchken, L. Sankarasubramanian, and A. M. Vijh, "Averaging Options for Capping Total Costs," *Financial Management*, Autumn 1990, 35–41; and R. Geske, "The Valuation of Compound Options," *Journal of Financial Economics*, March 1979, 63–81.

[20]See John C. Hull, *Options, Futures, and Other Derivatives*, 3rd ed. (Upper Saddle River, NJ: Prentice Hall, 1997).

Sometimes there are some real options that don't resemble any financial options. But the good news is that many of these options can be valued using techniques from financial engineering. This is frequently the case if there is a traded financial asset that matches the risk of the real option. For example, many oil companies use oil futures contracts to price the real options that are embedded in various exploration and leasing strategies. With the explosion in the markets for derivatives, which we discuss in Chapter 24, there are now financial contracts that span an incredible variety of risks. This means that an ever-increasing number of real options can be valued using these financial instruments. Most financial engineering techniques are beyond the scope of this book, but we list some useful sources in the references at the end of the chapter. In addition, the Chapter 15 Web/CD Extension describes one particularly useful financial engineering technique called risk-neutral valuation.

Self-Test Questions

How widely used is real option analysis?

What techniques can be used to analyze real options?

Summary

The last three chapters focused on capital budgeting. Given a set of cash flows and an estimated cost of capital, we described in Chapter 13 several approaches used to evaluate projects. We demonstrated that net present value (NPV) analysis is conceptually the best approach for evaluating projects. Next, Chapter 14 described techniques for estimating a project's cash flows and risk. Finally, in this chapter we discussed some topics that go beyond the simple capital budgeting framework, including the following:

- Investing in a new project often brings with it a potential increase in the firm's future opportunities. Opportunities are, in effect, **options**—the right but not the obligation to take some future action.
- A project may have an **option value** that is not accounted for in a conventional NPV analysis. Any project that expands the firm's set of opportunities has positive option value.
- **Financial options** are instruments that (1) are created by exchanges rather than firms, (2) are bought and sold primarily by investors, and (3) are of importance to both investors and financial managers.
- The two primary types of financial options are (1) **call options,** which give the holder the right to purchase a specified asset at a given price (the **exercise,** or **strike, price**) for a given period of time, and (2) **put options,** which give the holder the right to sell an asset at a given price for a given period of time.
- A call option's **exercise value** is defined as the current price of the stock less the strike price.
- The **Black-Scholes Option Pricing Model (OPM)** can be used to estimate the value of a call option.
- Opportunities to respond to changing circumstances are called **managerial options** because they give managers the option to influence the outcome of a project. They are also called **strategic options** because they are often associated with large, strategic projects rather than routine maintenance projects. Finally, they are also called **real options** because they involve "real," rather than "financial," assets.
- Many projects include a variety of **embedded options** that can dramatically affect the true NPV. Examples of embedded options include (1) "investment timing options" that allow a firm to delay a project, (2) "growth options" that enable a firm to manage its capacity in response to changing market conditions, (3) "abandonment options," and (4) "flexibility" options that allow a firm to modify its operations over time.

- An **investment timing option** involves not only the decision of *whether* to proceed with a project but also the decision of *when* to proceed with it. This opportunity to affect a project's timing can dramatically change its estimated value.
- A **growth option** occurs if an investment creates the opportunity to make other potentially profitable investments that would not otherwise be possible. These include: (1) options to expand output, (2) options to enter a new geographical market, and (3) options to introduce complementary products or successive generations of products.
- The **abandonment option** is the ability to abandon a project if the operating cash flows and/or abandonment value turn out to be lower than expected. It reduces the riskiness of a project and increases its value. Instead of total abandonment, some options allow a company to reduce capacity or temporarily suspend operations.
- A **flexibility option** is the option to modify operations depending on how conditions develop during a project's life, especially the type of output produced or the inputs used.
- There are five possible procedures for valuing real options: (1) **DCF analysis only, and ignore the real option;** (2) **DCF analysis and a qualitative assessment of the real option's value;** (3) **decision tree analysis;** (4) **analysis with a standard model for an existing financial option;** and (5) **financial engineering techniques.**

Questions

15–1 Define each of the following terms:
a. Option; call option; put option
b. Exercise value; strike price
c. Black-Scholes Option Pricing Model
d. Real options; managerial options; strategic options; embedded option
e. Investment timing option; growth option; abandonment option; flexibility option
f. Decision trees

15–2 Why do options typically sell at prices higher than their exercise values?

15–3 What factors should a company consider when it decides whether to invest in a project today or to wait until more information becomes available?

15–4 In general, do timing options make it more or less likely that a project will be accepted today?

15–5 If a company has an option to abandon a project, would this tend to make the company more or less likely to accept the project today?

Self-Test Problems (Solutions Appear in Appendix A)

ST–1 *OPTIONS*
A call option on the stock of Bedrock Boulders has a market price of $7. The stock sells for $30 a share, and the option has an exercise price of $25 a share.
a. What is the exercise value of the call option?
b. What is the premium on the option?

ST–2 *OPTIONS*
Which of the following events are likely to increase the market value of a call option on a common stock? Explain.
a. An increase in the stock's price.
b. An increase in the volatility of the stock price.
c. An increase in the risk-free rate.
d. A decrease in the time until the option expires.

Problems

15–1
BLACK-SCHOLES MODEL

Assume you have been given the following information on Purcell Industries:

Current stock price = \$15	Exercise price of option = \$15
Time to maturity of option = 6 months	Risk-free rate = 10%
Variance of stock price = 0.12	$d_1 = 0.32660$
$d_2 = 0.08165$	$N(d_1) = 0.62795$
$N(d_2) = 0.53252$	

Using the Black-Scholes Option Pricing Model, what would be the value of the option?

15–2
OPTIONS

The exercise price on one of Flanagan Company's options is \$15, its exercise value is \$22, and its premium is \$5. What are the option's market value and the price of the stock?

15–3
INVESTMENT TIMING OPTION: DECISION TREE ANALYSIS

Kim Hotels is interested in developing a new hotel in Seoul. The company estimates that the hotel would require an initial investment of \$20 million. Kim expects that the hotel will produce positive cash flows of \$3 million a year at the end of each of the next 20 years. The project's cost of capital is 13 percent.

a. What is the project's net present value?

b. While Kim expects the cash flows to be \$3 million a year, it recognizes that the cash flows could, in fact, be much higher or lower, depending on whether the Korean government imposes a large hotel tax. One year from now, Kim will know whether the tax will be imposed. There is a 50 percent chance that the tax will be imposed, in which case the yearly cash flows will be only \$2.2 million. At the same time, there is a 50 percent chance that the tax will not be imposed, in which case the yearly cash flows will be \$3.8 million. Kim is deciding whether to proceed with the hotel today or to wait 1 year to find out whether the tax will be imposed. If Kim waits a year, the initial investment will remain at \$20 million. Assume that all cash flows are discounted at 13 percent. Using decision tree analysis, should Kim proceed with the project today or should it wait a year before deciding?

15–4
INVESTMENT TIMING OPTION: DECISION TREE ANALYSIS

The Karns Oil Company is deciding whether to drill for oil on a tract of land that the company owns. The company estimates that the project would cost \$8 million today. Karns estimates that once drilled, the oil will generate positive net cash flows of \$4 million a year at the end of each of the next 4 years. While the company is fairly confident about its cash flow forecast, it recognizes that if it waits 2 years, it would have more information about the local geology as well as the price of oil. Karns estimates that if it waits 2 years, the project would cost \$9 million. Moreover, if it waits 2 years, there is a 90 percent chance that the net cash flows would be \$4.2 million a year for 4 years, and there is a 10 percent chance that the cash flows will be \$2.2 million a year for 4 years. Assume that all cash flows are discounted at 10 percent.

a. If the company chooses to drill today, what is the project's net present value?

b. Using decision tree analysis, would it make sense to wait 2 years before deciding whether to drill?

15–5
INVESTMENT TIMING OPTION: DECISION TREE ANALYSIS

Hart Lumber is considering the purchase of a paper company. Purchasing the company would require an initial investment of \$300 million. Hart estimates that the paper company would provide net cash flows of \$40 million at the end of each of the next 20 years. The cost of capital for the paper company is 13 percent.

a. Should Hart purchase the paper company?

b. While Hart's best guess is that cash flows will be \$40 million a year, it recognizes that there is a 50 percent chance the cash flows will be \$50 million a year, and a 50 percent chance that the cash flows will be \$30 million a year. One year from now, it will find out whether the cash flows will be \$30 million or \$50 million. In addition, 1 year from now, Hart also recognizes that if it wanted, it could sell the company in 2 years for \$280 million. Given this additional information, does using decision tree analysis indicate that it makes sense to purchase the paper company? Again, assume that all cash flows are discounted at 13 percent.

15–6
REAL OPTIONS: DECISION TREE ANALYSIS

Utah Enterprises is considering buying a vacant lot that sells for \$1.2 million. If the property is purchased, the company's plan is to spend another \$5 million today ($t = 0$) to build a hotel on the property. The after-tax cash flows from the hotel will depend critically on whether the state imposes a tourism tax in this year's legislative session. If the tax is imposed, the hotel is expected to produce after-tax cash inflows of \$600,000 at the end of each of the next 15 years. If the tax is not imposed, the hotel is expected to produce after-tax cash inflows of \$1,200,000 at the end of each of the next 15 years. The project has a 12 percent cost of capital. Assume at the outset that the company does not have the option to delay the project. Use decision tree analysis to answer the following questions.

a. What is the project's expected NPV if the tax is imposed?

b. What is the project's expected NPV if the tax is not imposed?

c. Given that there is a 50 percent chance that the tax will be imposed, what is the project's expected NPV if they proceed with it today?

d. While the company does not have an option to delay construction, it does have the option to abandon the project 1 year from now if the tax is imposed. If it abandons the project, it would sell the complete property 1 year from now at an expected price of \$6 million. Once the project is abandoned the company would no longer receive any cash inflows from it. Assuming that all cash flows are discounted at 12 percent, would the existence of this abandonment option affect the company's decision to proceed with the project today?

e. Finally, assume that there is no option to abandon or delay the project, but that the company has an option to purchase an adjacent property in 1 year at a price of \$1.5 million. If the tourism tax is imposed, the net present value of developing this property (as of $t = 1$) is only \$300,000 (so it wouldn't make sense to purchase the property for \$1.5 million). However, if the tax is not imposed, the net present value of the future opportunities from developing the property would be \$4 million (as of $t = 1$). Thus, under this scenario it would make sense to purchase the property for \$1.5 million. Assume that these cash flows are discounted at 12 percent, and the probability that the tax will be imposed is still 50 percent. How much would the company pay today for the option to purchase this property 1 year from now for \$1.5 million?

15–7 *INVESTMENT TIMING OPTION: OPTION ANALYSIS*

Rework Problem 15-3 using the Black-Scholes model to estimate the value of the option. (Hint: Assume the variance of the projects rate of return is 6.87 percent and the risk-free rate is 8 percent.)

15–8 *INVESTMENT TIMING OPTION: OPTION ANALYSIS*

Rework Problem 15-4 using the Black-Scholes model to estimate the value of the option: The risk-free rate is 6 percent. (Hint: Assume the variance of the project's rate of return is 1.11 percent.)

Spreadsheet Problems

15–9 *BUILD A MODEL: BLACK-SCHOLES MODEL*

Start with the partial model in the file ***Ch 15-9 Build a Model.xls*** from the textbook's CD-ROM. Rework Problem 15-1. Then work the next two parts of this problem given below.

a. Construct data tables for the exercise value and Black-Scholes option value for this option, and graph this relationship. Include possible stock price values ranging up to \$30.00.

b. Suppose this call option is purchased today. Draw the profit diagram of this option position at expiration.

15–10 *BUILD A MODEL: REAL OPTIONS*

Start with the partial model in the file ***Ch 15-10 Build a Model.xls*** from the textbook's CD-ROM. Bradford Services Inc. (BSI) is considering a project that has a cost of \$10 million and an expected life of 3 years. There is a 30 percent probability of good conditions, in which case the project will provide a cash flow of \$9 million at the end of each year for 3 years. There is 40 percent probability of medium conditions, in which case the annual cash flows will be \$4 million, and there is a 30 percent probability of bad conditions and a cash flow of −\$1 million per year. BSI uses a 12 percent cost of capital to evaluate projects like this.

a. Find the project's expected present value, NPV, and the coefficient of variation of the present value.

b. Now suppose that BSI can abandon the project at the end of the first year by selling it for \$6 million. BSI will still receive the Year 1 cash flows, but will receive no cash flows in subsequent years.

c. Now assume that the project cannot be shut down. However, expertise gained by taking it on will lead to an opportunity at the end of Year 3 to undertake a venture that would have the same cost as the original project, and the new project's cash flows would follow whichever branch resulted for the original project. In other words, there would be a second $10 million cost at the end of Year 3, and then cash flows of either $9 million, $4 million, or −$1 million for the following 3 years. Use decision tree analysis to estimate the value of the project, including the opportunity to implement the new project at Year 3. Assume the $10 million cost at Year 3 is known with certainty and should be discounted at the risk-free rate of 6 percent.

d. Now suppose the original (no abandonment and no additional growth) project could be delayed a year. All the cash flows would remain unchanged, but information obtained during that year would tell the company exactly which set of demand conditions existed. Use decision tree analysis to estimate the value of the project if it is delayed by 1 year. (Hint: Discount the $10 million cost at the risk-free rate of 6 percent since it is known with certainty.)

CD

e. Go back to part c. Instead of using decision tree analysis, use the Black-Scholes model to estimate the value of the growth option. The risk-free rate is 6 percent, and the variance of the project's rate of return is 22 percent.

15–11
WHAT IF ANALYSIS: OPTIONS

Start with the file ***Ch 15-11 What If Analysis.xls*** from the textbook's CD-ROM and answer the questions shown there.

Cyberproblem

The information related to this cyberproblem is likely to change over time, due to the release of new information and the ever-changing nature of the World Wide Web. Accordingly, we will periodically update the problem on the textbook's web site.

15–12
A VIRTUAL VISIT THROUGH THE CHICAGO BOARD OPTIONS EXCHANGE

An option is a contract that gives its holder the right to buy (or sell) an asset at some predetermined price within a specified period of time. The major advantage of options is versatility, as they can serve a number of different investor needs. Options can be used to protect stock holdings from a decline in market prices, to increase income against a current stock holding, to position an investor for a big market move, or to benefit from a stock price rise without incurring the cost of buying the stock itself. Ultimately, an option's most powerful tool, if used correctly, is to hedge risk borne by the investor.

This cyberproblem looks at the Chicago Board Options Exchange (CBOE), where options trading occurs. Go to the textbook's web site at **http://www.harcourtcollege.com/finance/theory/student/resources/cyberprob/ch15.html** and answer the questions shown there.

Mini Case

CD

See ***Ch 15 Show.ppt*** and ***Ch 15 Mini Case.xls.***

Assume that you have just been hired as a financial analyst by Tropical Sweets Inc., a mid-sized California company that specializes in creating exotic candies from tropical fruits such as mangoes, papayas, and dates. The firm's CEO, George Yamaguchi, recently returned from an industry corporate executive conference in San Francisco, and one of the sessions he attended was on real options. Because no one at Tropical Sweets is familiar with the basics of either financial or real options, Yamaguchi has asked you to prepare a brief report that the firm's executives could use to gain at least a cursory understanding of the topics.

To begin, you gathered some outside materials on the subject and used these materials to draft a list of pertinent questions that need to be answered. In fact, one possible approach to the paper is to use a question-and-answer format. Now that the questions have been drafted, you have to develop the answers.

a. What is a real option? What is a financial option? What is the single most important characteristic of an option?

b. Options have a unique set of terminology. Define the following terms:
   (1) Call option
   (2) Put option
   (3) Exercise price
   (4) Striking, or strike, price
   (5) Option price

(6) Expiration date
(7) Exercise value
(8) Covered option
(9) Naked option
(10) In-the-money call
(11) Out-of-the-money call
(12) LEAP

c. Consider Tropical Sweets' call option with a $25 strike price. The following table contains historical values for this option at different stock prices:

Stock Price	Call Option Price
$25	$3.00
30	7.50
35	12.00
40	16.50
45	21.00
50	25.50

(1) Create a table which shows (a) stock price, (b) strike price, (c) exercise value, (d) option price, and (e) the premium of option price over exercise value.
(2) What happens to the premium of option price over exercise value as the stock price rises? Why?

d. In 1973, Fischer Black and Myron Scholes developed the Black-Scholes Option Pricing Model (OPM).
(1) What assumptions underlie the OPM?
(2) Write out the three equations that constitute the model.
(3) What is the value of the following call option according to the OPM?

Stock price = $27.00
Exercise price = $25.00
Time to expiration = 6 months
Risk-free rate = 6.0%
Stock return variance = 0.11

e. What impact does each of the following call option parameters have on the value of a call option?
(1) Current stock price
(2) Exercise price
(3) Option's term to maturity
(4) Risk-free rate
(5) Variability of the stock price

f. What are some types of real options?

g. What are five possible procedures for analyzing a real option?

h. Tropical Sweets is considering a project that will cost $70 million and will generate expected cash flows of $30 million per year for 3 years. The cost of capital for this type of project is 10 percent and the risk-free rate is 6 percent. After discussions with the marketing department, you learn that there is a 30 percent chance of high demand, with future cash flows of $45 million per year. There is a 40 percent chance of average demand, with cash flows of $30 million per year. If demand is low (a 30 percent chance), cash flows will be only $15 million per year. What is the expected NPV?

i. Now suppose this project has an investment timing option, since it can be delayed for a year. The cost will still be $70 million at the end of the year, and the cash flows for the scenarios will still last 3 years. However, Tropical Sweets will know the level of demand, and will implement the project only if it adds value to the company. Perform a qualitative assessment of the investment timing option's value.

j. Use decision tree analysis to calculate the NPV of the project with the investment timing option.
k. Use a financial option pricing model to estimate the value of the investment timing option.
l. Now suppose the cost of the project is $75 million and the project cannot be delayed. But if Tropical Sweets implements the project, then Tropical Sweets will have a growth option. It will have the opportunity to replicate the original project at the end of its life. What is the total expected NPV of the two projects if both are implemented?
m. Tropical Sweets will replicate the original project only if demand is high. Using decision tree analysis, estimate the value of the project with the growth option.
n. Use a financial option model to estimate the value of the project with the growth option.
o. What happens to the value of the growth option if the variance of the project's return is 14.2 percent? What if it is 50 percent? How might this explain the high valuations of many dot-com companies?

Selected Additional References

For more information on the derivatives markets, see

Chance, Don M., *An Introduction to Derivatives* (Fort Worth, TX: Dryden Press, 1995).

The original Black-Scholes article tested the OPM to see how well predicted prices conformed to market values. For additional empirical tests, see

Galai, Dan, "Tests of Market Efficiency of the Chicago Board Options Exchange," *Journal of Business*, April 1977, 167–197.

Gultekin, N. Bulent, Richard J. Rogalski, and Seha M. Tinic, "Option Pricing Model Estimates: Some Empirical Results," *Financial Management*, Spring 1982, 58–69.

MacBeth, James D., and Larry J. Merville, "An Empirical Examination of the Black-Scholes Call Option Pricing Model," *Journal of Finance*, December 1979, 1173–1186.

Here are some references on real options:

Amram, Martha, and Nalin Kulatilaka, *Real Options: Managing Strategic Investment in an Uncertain World* (Boston, MA: Harvard Business School Press, 1999).

Trigeorgis, Lenos, *Real Options in Capital Investment: Models, Strategies, and Applications* (Westport, CT: Praeger, 1995).

Trigeorgis, Lenos, *Real Options: Managerial Flexibility and Strategy in Resource Allocation* (Cambridge, MA: The MIT Press, 1996).

Several journals have had special issues with sections devoted to the topic of real options:

Midland Corporate Finance Journal, Spring 1987.

Managerial Finance, Spring 1991.

Financial Management, Autumn 1993.

16

Capital Structure Decisions: The Basics

When a firm expands, it needs capital, and that capital can come from debt or equity. Debt has two important advantages. First, the interest paid is a tax deduction, which lowers debt's effective cost. Second, debtholders get a fixed return, so stockholders do not have to share the profits if the business is extremely successful.

However, debt also has disadvantages. First, the higher the debt ratio, the riskier the company, hence the higher its cost of both debt and equity. Second, if a company falls on hard times and operating income is not sufficient to cover interest charges, its stockholders will have to make up the shortfall, and if they cannot, bankruptcy will result.

Companies whose earnings and operating cash flows are volatile should therefore limit their use of debt. On the other hand, companies with less business risk and more stable operating cash flows can take on more debt. General Mills, a consumer-goods company with such well-known brands as Cheerios, Wheaties, Betty Crocker, and Hamburger Helper, is a good example of a stable company that uses a lot of debt financing. Indeed, General Mills' current capital structure as shown on its balance sheet is 90 percent debt and 10 percent equity.

At first glance, a 90 percent debt ratio seems extraordinarily high. In the past, there have been numerous examples of high debt pushing otherwise well-regarded companies into bankruptcy. For example, a few years ago, two of the nation's largest retailers, Federated Department Stores and R. H. Macy, were forced to declare bankruptcy as a result of their excessive use of debt.

Still, given the stability of its basic business, General Mills' high debt ratio might be appropriate. After all, the consumption of Cheerios and Hamburger Helper has historically remained stable even during economic downturns. Moreover, if we examine General Mills' capital structure in more detail, it soon becomes apparent that there is more here than first meets the eye. According to its year-end 1999 balance sheet, General Mills had roughly $2.5 billion of total debt versus only $164 million of stockholders' equity. However, the market value of General Mills' equity is much higher than its book value. At year-end 1999, the company's market capitalization of the equity (which is simply the stock price times the number of shares outstanding) was approximately $13 billion. From a market value perspective, General Mills' capital structure ($2.5 billion of debt versus $13 billion of equity) is thus quite conservative, and it also helps explain why General Mills has an A-level bond rating.

General Mills and other companies can finance with either debt or equity. Is one better than the other? If so, should firms finance either with all debt or all equity? If the best solution is a mix of debt and equity, what is the optimal mix?[1]

---

[1]Chapter 16 covers the basics of capital structure decisions, while Chapter 17 provides some extensions related primarily to the theory of capital structure. Both chapters are useful, but Chapter 16 does cover all of the concepts (including theory) needed to understand the material presented in succeeding chapters. Therefore, if time pressures preclude coverage of both chapters, Chapter 17 can be omitted.

In Chapter 12 we saw that the value of a firm is the present value of its expected future free cash flows, discounted at its weighted average cost of capital (WACC). Changes in capital structure affect the WACC by changing the percentage, risk, and cost of each type of capital. Capital structure changes can also affect the free cash flows, both by influencing managers in their capital budgeting decisions and also by altering the potential costs associated with bankruptcy and financial distress. Thus, capital structure affects both free cash flows and WACC, and thus stock prices.

Managers do not make the capital structure decision once and then forget about it. Instead, firms regularly raise capital to invest in assets to support growth, and each time they must choose the mix of equity and debt used to obtain these funds. Many firms also pay dividends, which reduces retained earnings and thus increases the amount they must raise externally to support their operating plans. Therefore, the capital structure decision is interrelated with dividend policy. We focus on the choice of capital structure in this chapter, but we show how it is related to dividend policy in Chapter 18.

Many factors influence the capital structure decision, and, as you will see, determining the optimal capital structure is not an exact science. Therefore, even firms in the same industry often have quite different capital structures. In this chapter we first consider the effect of capital structure on risk, after which we use these insights to help determine the optimal mix of debt and equity.

CD

The textbook's CD-ROM contains an *Excel* file that will guide you through the chapter's calculations. The file for this chapter is ***Ch 16 Tool Kit.xls,*** and we encourage you to open the file and follow along as you read the chapter.

The Target Capital Structure

Firms should first analyze a number of factors, then establish a **target capital structure.** This target may change over time as conditions change, but at any given moment, management should have a specific capital structure in mind. If the actual debt ratio is below the target level, expansion capital should generally be raised by issuing debt, whereas if the debt ratio is above the target, equity should generally be issued.

Capital structure policy involves a trade-off between risk and return:

- Using more debt raises the risk borne by stockholders.
- However, using more debt generally leads to a higher expected rate of return on equity, ROE.

Higher risk tends to lower a stock's price, but a higher expected ROE raises it. *Therefore, the optimal capital structure must strike a balance between risk and return so as to maximize the firm's stock price.*

Five primary factors influence capital structure decisions.

1. *Business risk*, or the riskiness inherent in the firm's operations if it used no debt. The greater the firm's business risk, the lower its optimal debt ratio.
2. The firm's *tax position*. A major reason for using debt is that interest is deductible, which lowers the effective cost of debt. However, if most of a firm's income is already sheltered from taxes by depreciation tax shields, by interest on currently outstanding debt, or by tax loss carry-forwards, its tax rate will be low, so additional debt will not be as advantageous as it would be to a firm with a higher effective tax rate.
3. *Financial flexibility*, or the ability to raise capital on reasonable terms under adverse conditions. Corporate treasurers know that a steady supply of capital is necessary for stable operations, which is vital for long-run success. They also know that when money is tight in the economy, or when a firm is experiencing operating difficulties, suppliers of capital prefer to provide funds to companies with strong balance

WWW

Two video clips of Steve Walsh, Assistant Treasurer at JCPenney, talking about capital structure are available at **http:// www.cob.ohio-state.edu/dept/fin/resources_education/clips.htm**. The first clip on capital structure discusses the cost of capital and debt, while the second clip discusses optimal capital structure at JCPenney relative to the capital structure theory of Modigliani/Miller.

sheets. Therefore, both the potential future need for funds and the consequences of a funds shortage influence the target capital structure—the greater the probable future need for capital, and the worse the consequences of a capital shortage, the stronger the balance sheet should be.

4. *Managerial conservatism or aggressiveness.* Some managers are more aggressive than others, hence some firms are more inclined to use debt in an effort to boost profits. This factor does not affect the true optimal, or value-maximizing, capital structure, but it does influence the manager-determined target capital structure.
5. *Growth opportunities.* As discussed in Chapter 12, a firm's operating value is equal to the value of its assets-in-place plus its growth options, and this mix varies considerably across different firms. For example, Duke Power's value consists primarily of assets-in-place, while Amazon.com has a high proportion of growth opportunities. The mix of assets-in-place versus growth opportunities has four implications for capital structure. First, a high assets-in-place firm has better collateral for loans than a high-growth-opportunities firm. Second, bankruptcy costs and the disruption caused by financial distress are much worse for a firm with high growth opportunities. This is partially due to the lack of good collateral, but it also is because growth opportunities are often in the form of intellectual capital. Intellectual capital resides in the brains of the firm's employees, who tend to jump ship when a firm experiences financial distress. Third, managers know more about their company's prospects than do outsiders. This is called **information asymmetry,** and the condition is especially important for firms with many growth opportunities, because managers can't fully disclose their future plans for fear of tipping off the competition. Creditors realize that managers know more than they do about the firm's prospects, and suspect that managers will invest in overly risky projects. Thus, creditors charge higher interest rates to firms with a high proportion of growth opportunities. Fourth, financial flexibility is more important for firms with growth opportunities. Not only is there a greater probability that these firms will discover new projects that need additional funding, but these firms also are the ones that will have the most difficulty convincing investors that the project is acceptable, given their greater problem with information asymmetry. Thus, firms with many growth opportunities need more financial flexibility than assets-in-place firms.

These five points largely determine the optimal target capital structure, but operating conditions can cause the actual capital structure to vary from the target. For example, Illinois Power has a target debt ratio of about 45 percent, but large losses associated with a nuclear plant forced it to write down its common equity, and that raised the debt ratio above the target level. The company then had to get its equity back up to the target level.

Self-Test Questions

What five factors affect the target capital structure?

In what sense does capital structure policy involve a trade-off between risk and return?

Business and Financial Risk

In Chapter 6, when we examined risk from the viewpoint of a stock investor, we distinguished between *market risk*, which is measured by the firm's beta coefficient, and *stand-alone risk*, which includes both market risk and an element of risk that can be eliminated by diversification. Now we introduce two new dimensions of risk: (1) *business risk*, or the riskiness of the firm's stock if it uses no debt, and (2) *financial risk*, which is the additional risk placed on the common stockholders as a result of the firm's decision to use debt.[2]

Conceptually, the firm has a certain amount of risk inherent in its operations: this is its business risk. If it uses debt, then, in effect, it partitions its investors into two groups and concentrates most of its business risk on one class of investors—the common stockholders. However, the common stockholders will demand compensation for assuming more risk and thus require a higher rate of return. In this section, we examine business and financial risk within a stand-alone risk framework, which ignores the benefits of stockholder diversification.

Business Risk

Business risk in a stand-alone sense is a function of the uncertainty inherent in projections of a firm's return on invested capital (ROIC), defined as follows:

$$\text{ROIC} = \frac{\text{NOPAT}}{\text{Capital}} = \frac{\text{EBIT}(1-\text{T})}{\text{Capital}} = \frac{\text{Net income to common stockholders} + \text{After-tax interest payments}}{\text{Capital}}.$$

Here NOPAT is net operating profit after taxes and capital is the sum of the firm's debt and common equity, which is numerically equivalent to our definition of operating capital in Chapter 2. If a firm uses no debt, then its interest payments will be zero, its capital will be all equity, and its ROIC will equal its return on equity, ROE:

$$\text{ROIC (zero debt)} = \text{ROE} = \frac{\text{Net income to common stockholders}}{\text{Common equity}}.$$

Therefore, the business risk of a *leverage-free* firm can be measured by the standard deviation of its ROE, σ_{ROE}.

To illustrate, consider Strasburg Electronics Company, a *debt-free (unlevered)* firm. Figure 16-1 gives some clues about the company's business risk. The top graph shows the trend in ROE from 1991 through 2001; this graph gives both security analysts and Strasburg's management an idea of the degree to which ROE has varied in the past and might vary in the future.

The lower graph shows the beginning-of-year subjectively estimated probability distribution of Strasburg's ROE for 2001, based on the trend line in the top section of Figure 16-1. As both graphs indicate, Strasburg's actual ROE in 2001 was only 8 percent, well below the expected value of 12 percent—2001 was a bad year.

Strasburg's past fluctuations in ROE were caused by many factors—booms and recessions in the national economy, successful new products introduced both by Strasburg and by its competitors, labor strikes, a fire in Strasburg's main plant, and so on. Similar events will doubtless occur in the future, and when they do, the realized ROE will be higher or lower than the projected level. Further, there is always the possibility that a long-term disaster will strike, permanently depressing the company's earning power; for example, a competitor might introduce a new product that would permanently lower Strasburg's earnings. This uncertainty regarding Strasburg's future ROE, *assuming it uses no debt*, is defined as the company's *business risk*. Because Strasburg uses no debt, stockholders bear all of the company's business risk.

Business risk varies not only from industry to industry but also among firms in a given industry. Further, business risk can change over time. For example, the electric

[2]Preferred stock also adds to financial risk. To simplify matters, we concentrate on debt and common equity in this chapter.

FIGURE 16-1 Strasburg Electronics: Trend in ROE, 1991–2001, and Subjective Probability Distribution of ROE, 2001

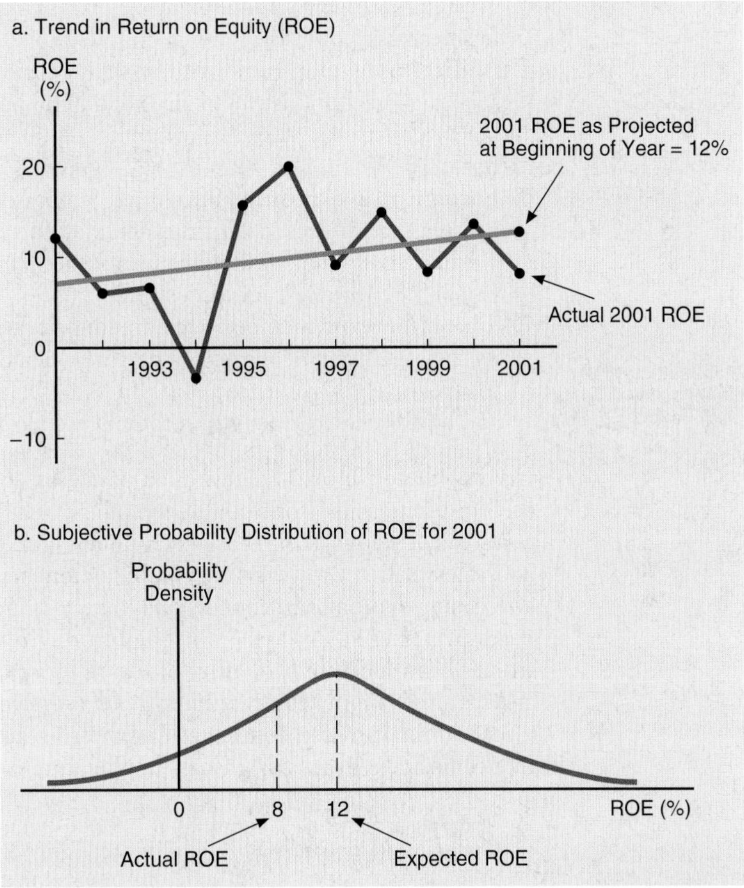

utilities were regarded for years as having little business risk, but a combination of events in recent years altered the utilities' situation, producing sharp declines in their ROEs and greatly increasing the industry's business risk. Now, food processors and grocery retailers frequently are given as examples of industries with low business risk, while cyclical manufacturing industries such as autos and steel, as well as many small startup companies, are regarded as having especially high business risk.[3]

Business risk depends on a number of factors, the more important of which are listed below:

1. **Demand variability.** The more stable the demand for a firm's products, other things held constant, the lower its business risk.
2. **Sales price variability.** Firms whose products are sold in highly volatile markets are exposed to more business risk than similar firms whose output prices are more stable.
3. **Input cost variability.** Firms whose input costs are highly uncertain are exposed to a high degree of business risk.

[3]We have avoided any discussion of market versus company-specific risk in this section. We note now (1) that any action that increases business risk in the stand-alone risk sense will generally also increase a firm's beta coefficient and (2) that a part of business risk as we define it will generally be company-specific, hence subject to elimination by diversification by the firm's stockholders.

4. **Ability to adjust output prices for changes in input costs.** Some firms are better able than others to raise their own output prices when input costs rise. The greater the ability to adjust output prices to reflect cost conditions, the lower the business risk.
5. **Ability to develop new products in a timely, cost-effective manner.** Firms in such high-tech industries as drugs and computers depend on a constant stream of new products. The faster its products become obsolete, the greater a firm's business risk.
6. **Foreign risk exposure.** Firms that generate a high percentage of their earnings overseas are subject to earnings declines due to exchange rate fluctuations. Also, if a firm operates in a politically unstable area, it may be subject to political risks. See Chapter 27 for a further discussion.
7. **The extent to which costs are fixed: operating leverage.** If a high percentage of its costs are fixed, hence do not decline when demand falls, then the firm is exposed to a relatively high degree of business risk. This factor is called *operating leverage,* and it is discussed at length in the next section.

Each of these factors is determined partly by the firm's industry characteristics, but each of them is also controllable to some extent by management. For example, most firms can, through their marketing policies, take actions to stabilize both unit sales and sales prices. However, this stabilization may require spending a great deal on advertising and/or price concessions to get commitments from customers to purchase fixed quantities at fixed prices in the future. Similarly, firms such as Strasburg Electronics can reduce the volatility of future input costs by negotiating long-term labor and materials supply contracts, but they may have to pay prices above the current spot price to obtain these contracts. Many firms are also using hedging techniques to reduce business risk, as we discuss in Chapter 24.

Operating Leverage

As noted above, business risk depends in part on the extent to which a firm builds fixed costs into its operations—if fixed costs are high, even a small decline in sales can lead to a large decline in ROE. So, other things held constant, the higher a firm's fixed costs, the greater its business risk. Higher fixed costs are generally associated with more highly automated, capital intensive firms and industries. However, businesses that employ highly skilled workers who must be retained and paid even during recessions also have relatively high fixed costs, as do firms with high product development costs, because the amortization of development costs is an element of fixed costs.

See ***Ch 16 Tool Kit.xls*** for detailed calculations.

If a high percentage of total costs are fixed, then the firm is said to have a high degree of **operating leverage.** In physics, leverage implies the use of a lever to raise a heavy object with a small force. In politics, if people have leverage, their smallest word or action can accomplish a lot. *In business terminology, a high degree of operating leverage, other factors held constant, implies that a relatively small change in sales results in a large change in earnings and ROE.*

Figure 16-2 illustrates the concept of operating leverage by comparing the results that Strasburg could expect if it used different degrees of operating leverage. Plan A calls for a relatively small amount of fixed costs, \$20,000. Here the firm would not have much automated equipment, so its depreciation, maintenance, property taxes, and so on would be low. However, the total operating costs line has a relatively steep slope, indicating that variable costs per unit are higher than they would be if the firm used more operating leverage. Plan B calls for a higher level of fixed costs, \$60,000. Here the firm uses automated equipment (with which one operator can turn out a few or many units

FIGURE 16-2 Illustration of Operating Leverage

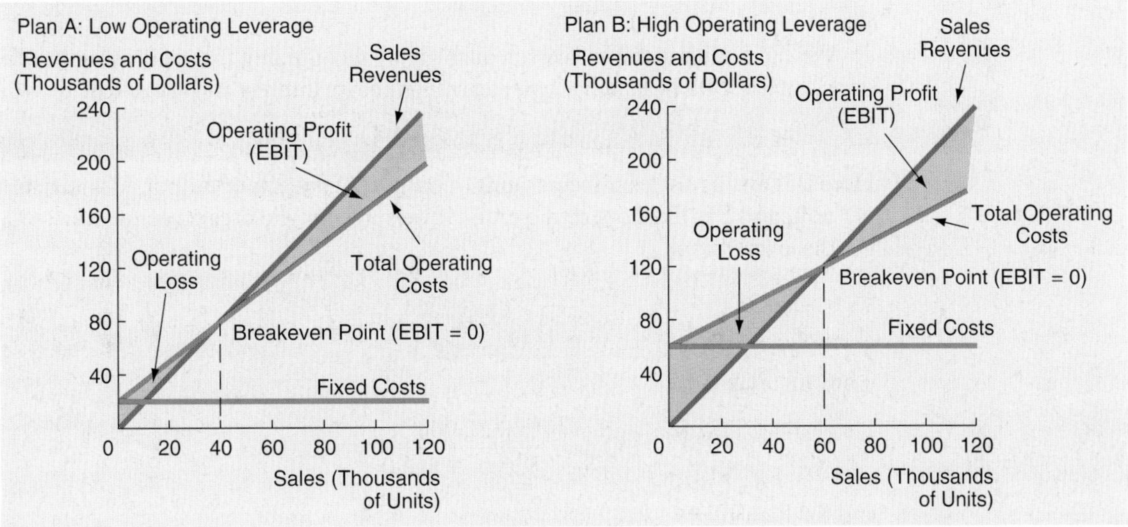

	Plan A	Plan B
Price	$2.00	$2.00
Variable costs	$1.50	$1.00
Fixed costs	$20,000	$60,000
Assets	$200,000	$200,000
Tax rate	40%	40%

				Plan A				Plan B			
Demand	Probability	Units Sold	Dollar Sales	Operating Costs	Operating Profits (EBIT)	Net Income	ROE	Operating Costs	Operating Profits (EBIT)	Net Income	ROE
Terrible	0.05	0	$ 0	$ 20,000	($20,000)	($12,000)	−6.00%	$ 60,000	($ 60,000)	($36,000)	−18.00%
Poor	0.20	40,000	80,000	80,000	0	0	0.00	100,000	(20,000)	(12,000)	−6.00
Normal	0.50	100,000	200,000	170,000	30,000	18,000	9.00	160,000	40,000	24,000	12.00
Good	0.20	160,000	320,000	260,000	60,000	36,000	18.00	220,000	100,000	60,000	30.00
Wonderful	0.05	200,000	400,000	320,000	80,000	48,000	24.00	260,000	140,000	84,000	42.00
Expected value:		100,000	$200,000	$170,000	$30,000	$18,000	9.00%	$160,000	$ 40,000	$24,000	12.00%
Standard deviation:					$24,698		7.41%		$ 49,396		14.82%
Coefficient of variation:					0.82		0.82		1.23		1.23

Notes:

a. Operating costs = Variable costs + Fixed costs.

b. The federal-plus-state tax rate is 40 percent, so NI = EBIT(1 − Tax rate) = EBIT(0.6).

c. ROE = NI/Equity. The firm has no debt, so Assets = Equity = $200,000.

d. The breakeven sales level for Plan B is not shown in the table, but it is 60,000 units or $120,000.

e. The expected values, standard deviations, and coefficients of variation were found using the procedures discussed in Chapter 6.

at the same labor cost) to a much larger extent. The breakeven point is higher under Plan B—breakeven occurs at 60,000 units under Plan B versus only 40,000 units under Plan A.

We can calculate the breakeven quantity by recognizing that **operating breakeven** occurs when ROE = 0, hence when earnings before interest and taxes (EBIT) = 0:[4]

$$\text{EBIT} = \text{PQ} - \text{VQ} - \text{F} = 0. \tag{16-1}$$

Here P is average sales price per unit of output, Q is units of output, V is variable cost per unit, and F is fixed operating costs. If we solve for the breakeven quantity, Q_{BE}, we get this expression:

$$Q_{BE} = \frac{F}{P - V}. \tag{16-1a}$$

Thus for Plan A,

$$Q_{BE} = \frac{\$20{,}000}{\$2.00 - \$1.50} = 40{,}000 \text{ units},$$

and for Plan B,

$$Q_{BE} = \frac{\$60{,}000}{\$2.00 - \$1.00} = 60{,}000 \text{ units}.$$

How does operating leverage affect business risk? *Other things held constant, the higher a firm's operating leverage, the higher its business risk.* This point is demonstrated in Figure 16-3, where we show the probability distributions for ROE under Plans A and B.

Part a of Figure 16-3 graphs the probability distribution of sales that was presented in tabular form in Figure 16-2. The sales probability distribution depends on how demand for the product varies, not on whether the product is manufactured by Plan A or by Plan B. Therefore, the same sales probability distribution applies to both production plans; this distribution has expected sales of \$200,000, and it ranges from zero to about \$400,000, with a standard deviation of $\sigma_{\text{Sales}} = \$98{,}793$.

We use the sales probability distribution, together with the operating costs at each sales level, to develop graphs of the ROE probability distributions under Plans A and B. These are shown in Part b of Figure 16-3. Plan B has a higher expected ROE, but this plan also entails a much higher probability of losses. Clearly, Plan B, the one with more fixed costs and a higher degree of operating leverage, is riskier. *In general, holding other factors constant, the higher the degree of operating leverage, the greater the firm's business risk.* In the discussion that follows, we assume that Strasburg has decided to go ahead with Plan B because they believe that the higher expected return is sufficient to compensate for the higher risk.

To what extent can firms control their operating leverage? To a large extent, operating leverage is determined by technology. Electric utilities, telephone companies, airlines, steel mills, and chemical companies simply *must* have large investments in fixed assets; this results in high fixed costs and operating leverage. Similarly, drug, auto, computer, and other companies must spend heavily to develop new products, and product-development costs increase operating leverage. Grocery stores, on the other hand, generally have significantly lower fixed costs, hence lower operating

[4]This definition of breakeven does not include any fixed financial costs because Strasburg is an unlevered firm. If there were fixed financial costs, the firm would suffer an accounting loss at the operating breakeven point. We will introduce financial costs shortly.

FIGURE 16-3 Analysis of Business Risk

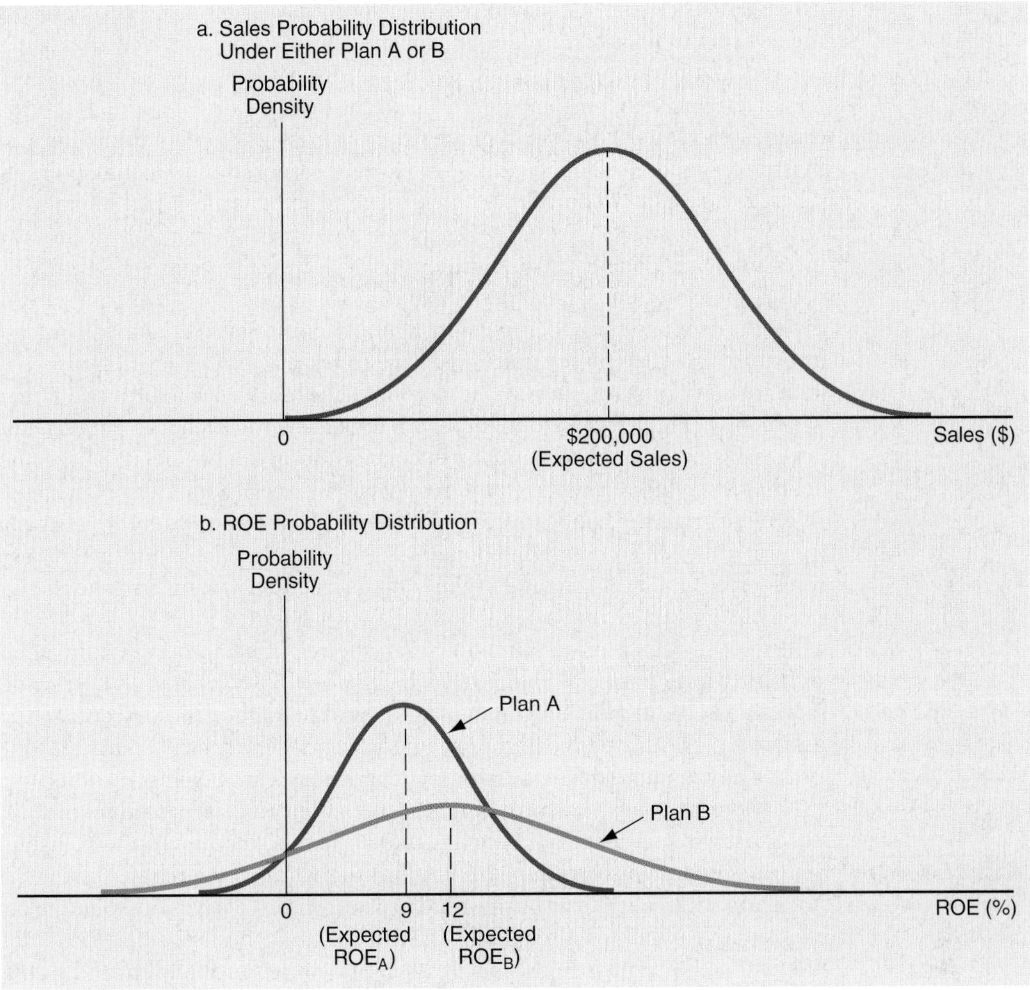

Note: We are using continuous distributions to approximate the discrete distributions contained in Figure 16-2.

leverage. Still, although industry factors do exert a major influence, all firms have some control over their operating leverage. For example, an electric utility can expand its generating capacity by building either a gas-fired or a coal-fired plant. The coal plant would require a larger investment and would have higher fixed costs, but its variable operating costs would be relatively low. The gas-fired plant, on the other hand, would require a smaller investment and would have lower fixed costs, but the variable costs (for gas) would be high. Thus, by its capital budgeting decisions, a utility (or any other company) can influence its operating leverage, hence its business risk.

The concept of operating leverage was originally developed for use in capital budgeting. Mutually exclusive projects that involve alternative methods for producing a given product often have different degrees of operating leverage, hence different breakeven points and different degrees of risk. Strasburg Electronics and many other companies regularly undertake a type of breakeven analysis (the sensitivity analysis discussed in Chapter 14) for each proposed project as a part of their regular capital budgeting process. Still, once a corporation's operating leverage has been established, this factor exerts a major influence on its capital structure decision.

Financial Risk

Financial risk is the additional risk placed on the common stockholders as a result of the decision to finance with debt. Conceptually, stockholders face a certain amount of risk that is inherent in a firm's operations—this is its business risk, which is defined as the uncertainty inherent in projections of future operating income. If a firm uses debt (financial leverage), this concentrates the business risk on common stockholders. To illustrate, suppose ten people decide to form a corporation to manufacture disk drives. There is a certain amount of business risk in the operation. If the firm is capitalized only with common equity, and if each person buys 10 percent of the stock, then each investor shares equally in the business risk. However, suppose the firm is capitalized with 50 percent debt and 50 percent equity, with five of the investors putting up their capital as debt and the other five putting up their money as equity. In this case, the five investors who put up the equity will have to bear all of the business risk, so the common stock will be twice as risky as it would have been had the firm been financed only with equity. Thus, the use of debt, or **financial leverage,** concentrates the firm's business risk on its stockholders. This concentration of business risk occurs because debtholders, who receive fixed interest payments, bear none of the business risk.

To illustrate the concentration of business risk, we can extend the Strasburg Electronics example. To date, the company has never used debt, but the treasurer is now considering a possible change in the capital structure. Changes in the use of debt will cause changes in earnings per share (EPS) as well as changes in risk—both of which will affect the stock price. To understand the relationship between financial leverage and EPS, first consider Table 16-1, which shows how Strasburg's cost of debt would vary if it used different percentages of debt. The higher the percentage of debt, the riskier the debt, hence the higher the interest rate lenders will charge.

For now, assume that only two financing choices are being considered—remaining at 100 percent equity, or shifting to 50 percent debt and 50 percent equity. We also assume that with no debt Strasburg has 10,000 shares of common stock outstanding and, if it changes its capital structure, common stock can be repurchased at the $20 current stock price. In reality, Strasburg would probably have to pay more than the current $20 in a repurchase, as we discuss later in the chapter. Now consider Table 16-2, which shows how the financing choice will affect Strasburg's profitability and risk.

See ***Ch 16 Tool Kit.xls*** for detailed calculations.

First, focus on Section 1 of Table 16-2, which assumes that Strasburg uses no debt. Since debt is zero, interest is also zero, hence pre-tax income is equal to EBIT. Taxes at 40 percent are deducted to obtain net income, which is then divided by the $200,000 of equity to calculate ROE. Note that Strasburg receives a tax credit if the

TABLE 16-1 Interest Rates for Strasburg with Different Debt/Assets Ratios

Amount Borrowed[a]	Debt/Assets Ratio	Interest Rate, k_d, on All Debt
$ 20,000	10%	8.0%
40,000	20	8.3
60,000	30	9.0
80,000	40	10.0
100,000	50	12.0
120,000	60	15.0

[a]We assume that the firm must borrow in increments of $20,000. We also assume that Strasburg is unable to borrow more than $120,000, which is 60 percent of its $200,000 of assets, because of restrictions in its corporate charter.

demand is either terrible or poor (which are the two scenarios where net income is negative). Here we assume that Strasburg's losses can be carried back to offset income earned in the prior year. The ROE at each sales level is then multiplied by the probability of that sales level to calculate the 12 percent expected ROE. Note that this 12 percent is the same as we found in Figure 16-2 for Plan B.

Part a of Table 16-2 also calculates Strasburg's earnings per share (EPS) for each scenario under the assumption that the company continues to use no debt. Net income is divided by the 10,000 common shares outstanding to obtain EPS. If demand is terrible, EPS will be −\$3.60, but if demand is wonderful, EPS will rise to \$8.40. The EPS at each sales level is then multiplied by the probability of that sales level to calculate the expected EPS, which is \$2.40 if Strasburg uses no debt. We also calculate the standard deviation of EPS and the coefficient of variation as indicators of the firm's risk at a zero debt ratio: σ_{EPS} = \$2.96, and CV_{EPS} = 1.23.[5]

Now let's look at the situation if Strasburg decides to use 50 percent debt financing, shown in Section II of Table 16-2, with the debt costing 12 percent. Demand will not be affected, nor will operating costs, hence the EBIT columns are the same for the zero debt and 50 percent debt cases. However, the company will now have \$100,000 of debt with a cost of 12 percent, hence its interest expense will be \$12,000. This interest must be paid regardless of the state of the economy—if it is not paid, the company will be forced into bankruptcy, and stockholders will probably be wiped out. Therefore, we show a \$12,000 cost in Column 4 as a fixed number for all demand conditions. Column 5 shows pre-tax income, Column 6 the applicable taxes, and Column 7 the resulting net income. When the net income figures are divided by the equity investment—which will now be only \$100,000 because \$100,000 of the \$200,000 total requirement was obtained as debt—we find the ROEs under each demand state. If demand is terrible and sales are zero, then a very large loss will be incurred, and the ROE will be −43.2 percent. However, if demand is wonderful, then ROE will be 76.8 percent. The probability-weighted average is the expected ROE, which is 16.8 percent if the company uses 50 percent debt.

Typically, financing with debt increases the expected rate of return for an investment, but debt also increases the riskiness of the investment to the common stockholders. This situation holds with our example—financial leverage raises the expected ROE from 12 percent to 16.8 percent, but it also increases the risk of the investment as measured by the coefficient of variation from 1.23 to 1.76.

Figure 16-4 graphs the data in Table 16-2. It shows in another way that using financial leverage increases the expected ROE, but that leverage also widens the probability distribution and increases the probability of a large loss, thus increasing the risk borne by stockholders.

We can also calculate Strasburg's EPS if it is financed with 50 percent debt. Once again EPS is calculated as net income divided by shares outstanding. With debt = 0, there would be 10,000 shares outstanding. However, if half of the equity were replaced by debt (debt = \$100,000), there would be only 5,000 shares outstanding.[6] With a debt/assets ratio of 50 percent, the EPS figure would be −\$8.64 if sales were terrible;

[5]See Chapter 6 for a review of procedures for calculating the standard deviation and coefficient of variation. Recall that the advantage of the coefficient of variation is that it permits better comparisons when the expected values of EPS vary, as they do here for the two capital structures.

[6]We assume in this example that the firm could change its capital structure by repurchasing common stock at its current market value of \$20 per share. However, the firm may actually have to pay a higher price to repurchase its stock on the open market if it is changing its capital structure. If Strasburg had to pay \$22 per share, then it could repurchase only \$100,000/\$22 = 4,545 shares, and, in this case, expected EPS would be only \$16,800/(10,000 − 4,545) = \$16,800/5,455 = \$3.08 rather than \$3.36. We address this in more detail later in the chapter.

TABLE 16-2 Effects of Financial Leverage: Strasburg Electronics Financed with Zero Debt or with 50 Percent Debt

SECTION I. ZERO DEBT

Debt ratio	0%
Assets	$200,000
Debt	0
Equity	$200,000
Shares outstanding	10,000

Demand for Product (1)	Probability (2)	EBIT (3)	Interest (4)	Pre-Tax Income (5)	Taxes (40%) (6)	Net Income (7)	ROE (8)	EPS[a] (9)
Terrible	0.05	($ 60,000)	$0	($ 60,000)	($24,000)	($36,000)	−18.00%	($3.60)
Poor	0.20	(20,000)	0	(20,000)	(8,000)	(12,000)	−6.00	(1.20)
Normal	0.50	40,000	0	40,000	16,000	24,000	12.00	2.40
Good	0.20	100,000	0	100,000	40,000	60,000	30.00	6.00
Wonderful	0.05	140,000	0	140,000	56,000	84,000	42.00	8.40
Expected value:		$ 40,000	$0	$ 40,000	$16,000	$24,000	12.00%	$2.40
Standard deviation:							14.82%	$2.96
Coefficient of variation:							1.23	1.23

Assumptions: 1. In terms of its operating leverage, Strasburg has chosen Plan B. The probability distribution and EBITs are obtained from Figure 16-2.
2. Sales and operating costs, hence EBIT, are not affected by the financing decision. Therefore, EBIT under both financing plans is identical, and it is taken from the EBIT column for Plan B in Figure 16-2.
3. All losses can be carried back to offset income in the prior year.

[a]The EPS figures can also be obtained using the following formula, in which the numerator amounts to an income statement at a given sales level laid out horizontally:

$$\text{EPS} = \frac{(\text{Sales} - \text{Fixed costs} - \text{Variable costs} - \text{Interest})(1 - \text{Tax rate})}{\text{Shares outstanding}} = \frac{(\text{EBIT} - \text{I})(1 - \text{T})}{\text{Shares outstanding}}.$$

FIGURE 16-4 ROE Probability Distribution for Strasburg Electronics, with and without Leverage

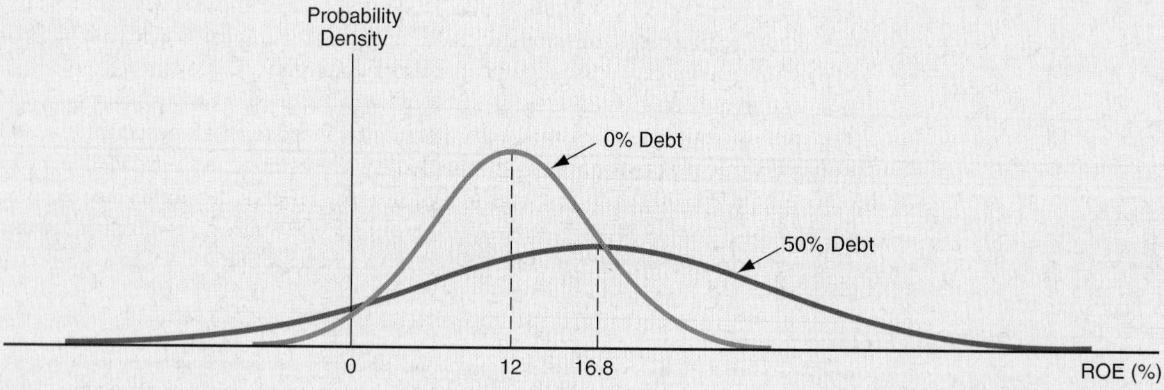

TABLE 16-2 Continued

SECTION II. 50% DEBT

Debt ratio	50%
Assets	$200,000
Debt	$100,000
Interest rate	12%
Equity	$100,000
Shares outstanding	5,000

Demand for Product (1)	Probability (2)	EBIT (3)	Interest (4)	Pre-Tax Income (5)	Taxes (40%) (6)	Net Income (7)	ROE (8)	EPS[a] (9)
Terrible	0.05	($ 60,000)	$12,000	($ 72,000)	($28,800)	($43,200)	−43.20%	($8.64)
Poor	0.20	(20,000)	12,000	(32,000)	(12,800)	(19,200)	−19.20	(3.84)
Normal	0.50	40,000	12,000	28,000	11,200	16,800	16.80	3.36
Good	0.20	100,000	12,000	88,000	35,200	52,800	52.80	10.56
Wonderful	0.05	140,000	12,000	128,000	51,200	76,800	76.80	15.36
Expected values:		$ 40,000	$12,000	$ 28,000	$11,200	$16,800	16.80%	$3.36
Standard deviation:							29.64%	$5.93
Coefficient of variation:							1.76	1.76

[a] For example, with zero debt and Sales = $200,000, EPS is $2.40:

$$EPS_{D/A=0} = \frac{(\$200{,}000 - \$60{,}000 - \$100{,}000 - 0)(0.6)}{10{,}000} = \$2.40.$$

With 50 percent debt and sales = $200,000, EPS is $3.36:

$$EPS_{D/A=0.05} = \frac{(\$200{,}000 - \$60{,}000 - \$100{,}000 - \$12{,}000)(0.6)}{5{,}000} = \$3.36.$$

Refer to the tabular data given in Figure 16-2 to arrive at sales, fixed costs, and variable costs that are used in the equations above.

it would rise to $3.36 if sales were normal; and it would soar to $15.36 if sales were wonderful.

The EPS distributions under the two financial structures are graphed in Figure 16-5, where we use continuous distributions rather than the discrete distributions contained in Table 16-2. Although expected EPS would be much higher if financial leverage were employed, the graph makes it clear that the risk of low, or even negative, EPS would also be higher if debt were used.

Another view of the relationships among expected EPS, risk, and financial leverage is presented in Figure 16-6. The tabular data in the lower section were calculated in the manner set forth in Table 16-2, and the graphs plot these data. Here we see that expected EPS rises until the firm is financed with 50 percent debt. Interest charges rise, but this effect is more than offset by the declining number of shares outstanding as debt is substituted for equity. However, EPS peaks at a debt ratio of 50 percent, beyond which interest rates rise so rapidly that EPS falls in spite of the falling number of shares outstanding.

The right panel of Figure 16-6 shows that risk, as measured by the coefficient of variation of EPS, rises continuously, and at an increasing rate, as debt is substituted for equity.

We see, then, that using leverage has both good and bad effects: higher leverage increases expected earnings per share (in this example, until the D/A ratio equals 50 percent), but it also increases risk. Clearly, Strasburg's debt ratio should not exceed 50

FIGURE 16-5 Probability Distributions of EPS with Different Amounts of Financial Leverage

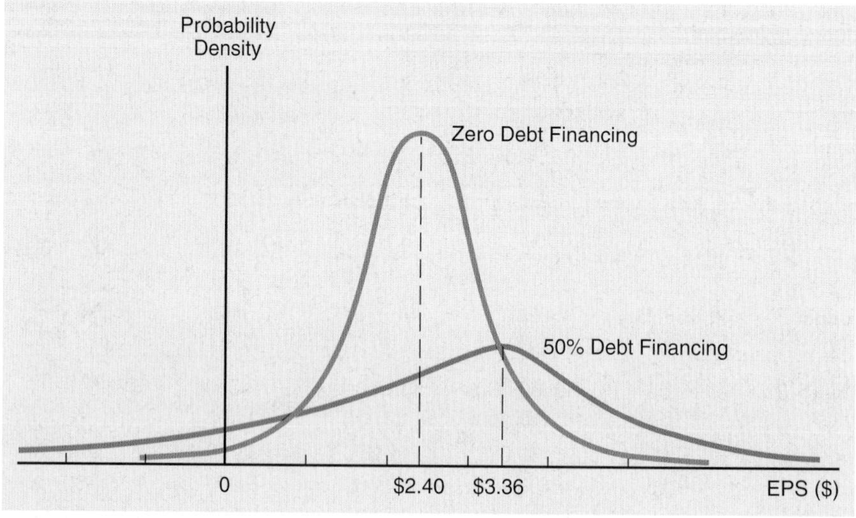

percent, but where, in the range of 0 to 50 percent, should it be set? This issue is discussed in the following sections.

Self-Test Questions

What is business risk, and how can it be measured?

What are some determinants of business risk?

Why does business risk vary from industry to industry?

What is operating leverage?

How does operating leverage affect business risk?

What is financial risk, and how does it arise?

Explain this statement: "Using leverage has both good and bad effects."

Determining the Optimal Capital Structure

As we saw in Figure 16-6, Strasburg's expected EPS is maximized at a debt/assets ratio of 50 percent. Does that mean that Strasburg's optimal capital structure calls for 50 percent debt? The answer is a resounding no—*the optimal capital structure is the one that maximizes the price of the firm's stock, and this generally calls for a debt ratio that is lower than the one that maximizes expected EPS.*

Recall from Chapter 10 that stock prices are positively related to expected dividends but negatively related to the required return on equity. Firms with higher earnings are able to pay higher dividends, so to the extent that higher debt levels raise expected earnings per share, leverage works to increase the stock price. However, higher debt levels also increase the firm's risk, and that raises the cost of equity and works to reduce the stock price. So, even though increasing the debt ratio from 40 to 50 percent raises expected EPS, the higher EPS is more than offset by the corresponding increase in risk.

FIGURE 16-6 Relationships among Expected EPS, Risk, and Financial Leverage

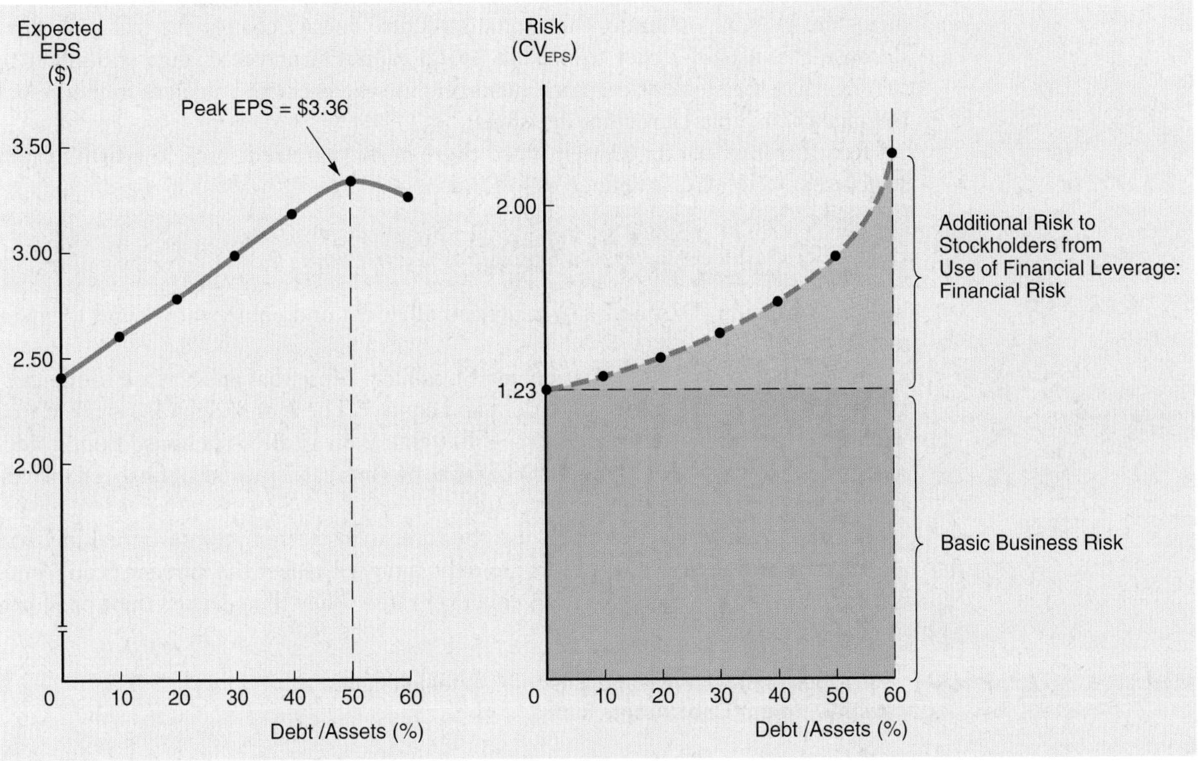

Debt/Assets Ratio	Expected EPS	Standard Deviation of EPS	Coefficient of Variation
0%[a]	$2.40[a]	$2.96[a]	1.23[a]
10	2.56	3.29	1.29
20	2.75	3.70	1.35
30	2.97	4.23	1.43
40	3.20	4.94	1.54
50[a]	3.36[a]	5.93[a]	1.76[a]
60	3.30	7.41	2.25

[a]Values for D/A = 0 and D/A = 50 percent are taken from Table 16-2. Values at other D/A ratios were calculated similarly.

WACC and Capital Structure Changes

Managers should choose the capital structure that maximizes the firm's stock price. However, it is difficult to estimate how a given change in the capital structure will affect the stock price. The corporate valuation model from Chapter 12 shows that the value of operations is equal to the present value of future expected free cash flows, discounted at the WACC:

$$V = \sum_{t=1}^{\infty} \frac{FCF_t}{(1 + WACC)^t}.$$

If a firm has no nonoperating assets, the value of operations is also the total value of the firm. Therefore, the maximum value occurs with the capital structure that minimizes the WACC, assuming the capital structure doesn't change the free cash flows. Because it is usually easier to predict how a capital structure change will affect the WACC than the stock price, many managers use the predicted changes in the WACC to guide their capital structure decisions.

Recall from Chapter 11 that when there is no preferred stock in a firm's capital structure, the WACC is defined as follows:

$$\begin{aligned} \text{WACC} &= w_d(k_d)(1 - T) + w_{ce}(k_s) \\ &= (D/A)(k_d)(1 - T) + (E/A)(k_s). \end{aligned}$$

In this expression, D/A and E/A represent the debt and equity ratios, and they sum to 1.0.

Table 16-3 shows the situation for Strasburg. Note that an increase in the debt/assets ratio raises the costs of both debt and equity. [The cost of debt, k_d, is taken from Table 16-1 and then multiplied by (1 − T) to put it on an after-tax basis.] Bondholders recognize that if a firm has a higher debt ratio, this increases the risk of financial distress, and more risk leads to higher interest rates.

In practice, financial managers use the forecasting techniques described in Chapter 4 to determine how changes in the debt ratio will affect the current ratio, times-interest-earned ratio, and EBITDA coverage ratio. They then discuss their pro forma

TABLE 16-3 Strasburg's Stock Price and Cost of Capital Estimates with Different Debt/Assets Ratios

Debt/ Assets (1)	Debt/ Equity[a] (2)	$(1 - T)k_d$ (3)	Expected EPS (and DPS)[b] (4)	Estimated Beta[c] (5)	$k_s = [k_{RF} + (k_M - k_{RF})b]$[d] (6)	Estimated Price[e] (7)	Resulting P/E Ratio (8)	Weighted Average Cost of Capital, WACC[f] (9)
0%	0.00%	4.8%	$2.40	1.50	12.0%	$20.00	8.33×	12.00%
10	11.11	4.8	2.56	1.60	12.4	20.65	8.06	11.64
20	25.00	5.0	2.75	1.73	12.9	21.33	7.75	11.32
30	42.86	5.4	2.97	1.89	13.5	21.90	7.38	11.10
40	**66.67**	**6.0**	**3.20**	**2.10**	**14.4**	**22.22**	**6.94**	**11.04**
50	100.00	7.2	3.36	2.40	15.6	21.54	6.41	11.40
60	150.00	9.0	3.30	2.85	17.4	18.97	5.75	12.36

[a] $D/E = \frac{D/A}{1 - D/A}$.

[b] Strasburg pays all of its earnings out as dividends, so EPS = DPS.

[c] The firm's unlevered beta, b_U, is 1.5. The remaining betas were calculated using the Hamada equation, given the unlevered beta, tax rate, and D/E ratio as inputs. The Hamada equaton is discussed in Chapter 17 and also in the next section of this chapter.

[d] We assume that $k_{RF} = 6\%$ and $k_M = 10\%$. Therefore, at debt/assets equal to zero, $k_s = 6\% + (10\% - 6\%)1.5 = 6\% + 6\% = 12\%$. Other values of k_s are calculated similarly.

[e] Since all earnings are paid out as dividends, no retained earnings will be plowed back into the business, and growth in EPS and DPS will be zero. Hence, the zero growth stock price model developed in Chapter 10 can be used to estimate the price of Strasburg's stock. For example, at Debt/Assets = 0,

$$P_0 = \frac{DPS}{k_s} = \frac{\$2.40}{0.12} = \$20.$$

Other prices were calculated similarly.

[f] Column 9 is found by use of the weighted average cost of capital (WACC) equation developed in Chapter 11:

$$\begin{aligned} \text{WACC} &= w_d k_d(1 - T) + w_{ce} k_s \\ &= (D/A)(k_d)(1 - T) + (1 - D/A)k_s. \end{aligned}$$

For example, at D/A = 40%,

$$\text{WACC} = 0.4(10\%)(0.6) + 0.6(14.4\%) = 11.04\%.$$

We use book weights here for simplicity. We will incorporate market value weights later in the chapter.

statements with bankers and bond rating agencies, who ask probing questions and may make their own adjustments to the firm's forecasts. The bankers and rating agencies then compare the firm's ratios with those of other firms in its industry, and end up with a rating and corresponding interest rate. Moreover, if the company plans to issue bonds to the public, the SEC requires that it inform investors what the coverages will be after the new bonds have been sold. Recognizing all this, sophisticated financial managers use their forecasted ratios to predict how bankers and other lenders will judge their firms' risks and thus determine their cost of debt. Thus, they can judge quite accurately the effects of capital structure on the cost of debt.

The Hamada Equation

An increase in the debt ratio also increases the risk faced by shareholders, and this has an effect on the cost of equity, k_s. This relationship is harder to quantify, but it can be estimated. Recall from Chapter 6 that a stock's beta is the relevant measure of risk for diversified investors. Moreover, it has been demonstrated, both theoretically and empirically, that beta increases with financial leverage. Indeed, Robert Hamada developed the following equation to specify the effect of financial leverage on beta:[7]

$$b = b_U[1 + (1 - T)(D/E)]. \qquad \textbf{(16-2)}$$

The Hamada equation shows how increases in the debt/equity ratio increase beta. Here b_U is the firm's unlevered beta coefficient, that is, the beta it would have if it has no debt. In that case, beta would depend entirely upon business risk and thus be a measure of the firm's "basic business risk." D/E is the measure of financial leverage used in the Hamada equation.[8]

Note that beta is the only variable that can be influenced by management in the cost of equity equation, $k_s = k_{RF} + (k_M - k_{RF})\,b$. Both k_{RF} and k_M are determined by market forces that are beyond the firm's control. However, b is affected (1) by the firm's operating decisions as discussed earlier in the chapter, which affect b_U, and (2) by its capital structure decisions as reflected in its D/A (or D/E) ratio.

As a starting point, a firm can take its current beta, tax rate, and debt/equity ratio and calculate its **unlevered beta, b_U,** by simply transforming Equation 16-2 as follows:

$$b_U = b/[1 + (1 - T)(D/E)]. \qquad \textbf{(16-2a)}$$

Then, once b_U is determined, the Hamada equation can be used to estimate how changes in the debt/equity ratio would affect the leveraged beta, b, and thus the cost of equity, k_s.

---

[7]See Robert S. Hamada, "Portfolio Analysis, Market Equilibrium, and Corporation Finance," *Journal of Finance*, March 1969, 13–31. Note that Thomas Conine and Maurry Tamarkin extended Hamada's work to include risky debt. See "Divisional Cost of Capital Estimation: Adjusting for Leverage," *Financial Management*, Spring 1985, 54–58. We discuss the Hamada equation in more detail in Chapter 17.

[8]Recall from Chapter 3 that the debt/equity ratio, D/E, is directly related to the D/A ratio:

$$\frac{D}{E} = \frac{D/A}{1 - D/A}$$

For example, if the firm has \$40 of debt and \$60 of equity, then D/A = 0.4, E/A = 0.6, and

$$\frac{D}{E} = \frac{0.4}{1 - 0.4} = 0.4/0.6 = 0.6667.$$

Thus, any D/A ratio can be directly translated into a D/E ratio. Note also that Hamada's equation assumes that assets are reported at market values rather than book values. However, it is a common industry practice to use book values for D/E when calculating b from b_U using Hamada's equation, and we follow that convention here.

We can illustrate the procedure with Strasburg Electronics. First, we assume that the risk-free rate of return, k_{RF}, is 6 percent, and that the required return on an average stock, k_M, is 10 percent. Next, we need the unlevered beta, b_U. Because Strasburg has no debt, its D/E = 0. Therefore, its current beta of 1.5 is also its unlevered beta, hence $b_U = 1.5$. Now, with b_U, k_{RF}, and k_M specified, we can use Equation 16-2 to estimate how much Strasburg's market beta would rise if it began to use financial leverage. Then, we can use the CAPM to estimate the cost of equity at different capital structures. The beta and cost of equity estimates are shown in Column 5 and 6 of Table 16-3.

Currently, based on Plan B and no debt, Strasburg has a beta of b = 1.5. Further, the risk-free rate is $k_{RF} = 6\%$ and the market risk premium is $k_M - k_{RF} = 10\% - 6\% = 4\%$. Therefore, Strasburg's current cost of equity is 12 percent as shown in Column 6:

$$\begin{aligned} k_s &= k_{RF} + \text{Risk premium} \\ &= 6\% + (4\%)(1.5) \\ &= 6\% + 6\% = 12\%. \end{aligned}$$

The first 6 percent is the risk-free rate, the second the risk premium. Because Strasburg currently uses no debt, it has no financial risk. Therefore, the 6 percent risk premium reflects only its business risk.

If Strasburg changes its capital structure by adding debt, this would increase the risk stockholders bear. That, in turn, would result in an additional risk premium. Conceptually, this situation would exist:

$$k_s = k_{RF} + \text{Premium for business risk} + \text{Premium for financial risk.}$$

Figure 16-7 (using data calculated in Column 6 of Table 16-3) graphs Strasburg's required return on equity at different debt ratios. As the figure shows, k_s consists of the 6 percent risk-free rate, a constant 6 percent premium for business risk, and a premium for financial risk that starts at zero but rises at an increasing rate as the debt ratio increases.

The Optimal Capital Structure

Column 9 of Table 16-3 shows Strasburg's weighted average cost of capital, WACC, at different capital structures. Currently, it has no debt, so its capital structure is 100 percent equity, and at this point WACC = k_s = 12%. As Strasburg begins to use lower-cost debt, the WACC declines. However, as the debt ratio increases, the costs of both debt and equity rise, at first slowly but then at a faster and faster rate. Eventually, the increasing costs of the two components offset the fact that more low-cost debt is being used. At 40 percent debt, the WACC hits a minimum of 11.04 percent, and after that it rises with further increases in the debt ratio.

Note too that even though the component cost of equity is always higher than that of debt, using only lower-cost debt would not maximize value because of the feedback effects on the costs of debt and equity. If Strasburg were to issue more than 40 percent debt, it would then be relying more on the cheaper source of capital, but this lower cost would be more than offset by the fact that using more debt would raise the costs of both debt and equity. These thoughts were echoed in a recent Annual Report of the Georgia-Pacific Corporation:

> On a market-value basis, our debt-to-capital ratio was 47 percent. By employing this capital structure, we believe that our weighted average cost of capital is nearly optimized—at approximately 10 percent. Although reducing debt significantly would

FIGURE 16-7 Strasburg's Required Rate of Return on Equity at Different Debt Levels

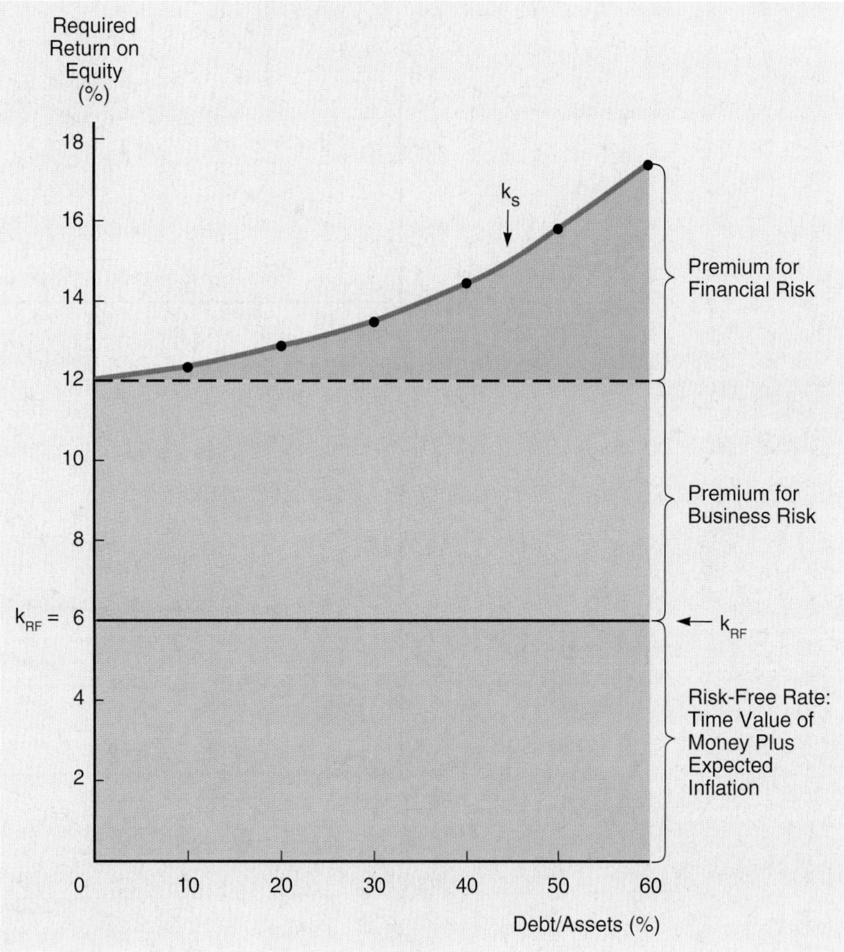

somewhat reduce the marginal cost of debt, significant debt reduction would likely increase our weighted average cost of capital by raising the proportion of higher-cost equity.

Finally, recall that the capital structure that minimizes the WACC is also the structure that maximizes the firm's stock price. In principle, we could use the stock valuation techniques described in Chapter 10 to predict how changes in capital structure would affect the stock price. This exercise is difficult, especially for firms that do not pay a dividend or whose cash flows are not constant over time. However, Strasburg pays out all of its earnings as dividends, so it plows none of its earnings back into the business and its growth in earnings and dividends per share are zero. Thus, in Strasburg's case we can use the zero growth stock price model developed in Chapter 10 to estimate the stock price at each different capital structure. These estimates are shown in Column 7 of Table 16-3. Here we see that the expected price first rises with financial leverage, hits a peak of $22.22 at a debt ratio of 40 percent, and then begins to decline. *Thus, Strasburg's optimal capital structure occurs at a debt ratio of 40 percent, and that debt ratio both maximizes its stock price and minimizes its WACC.*

FIGURE 16-8 Effects of Capital Structure on EPS, Cost of Capital, and Stock Price

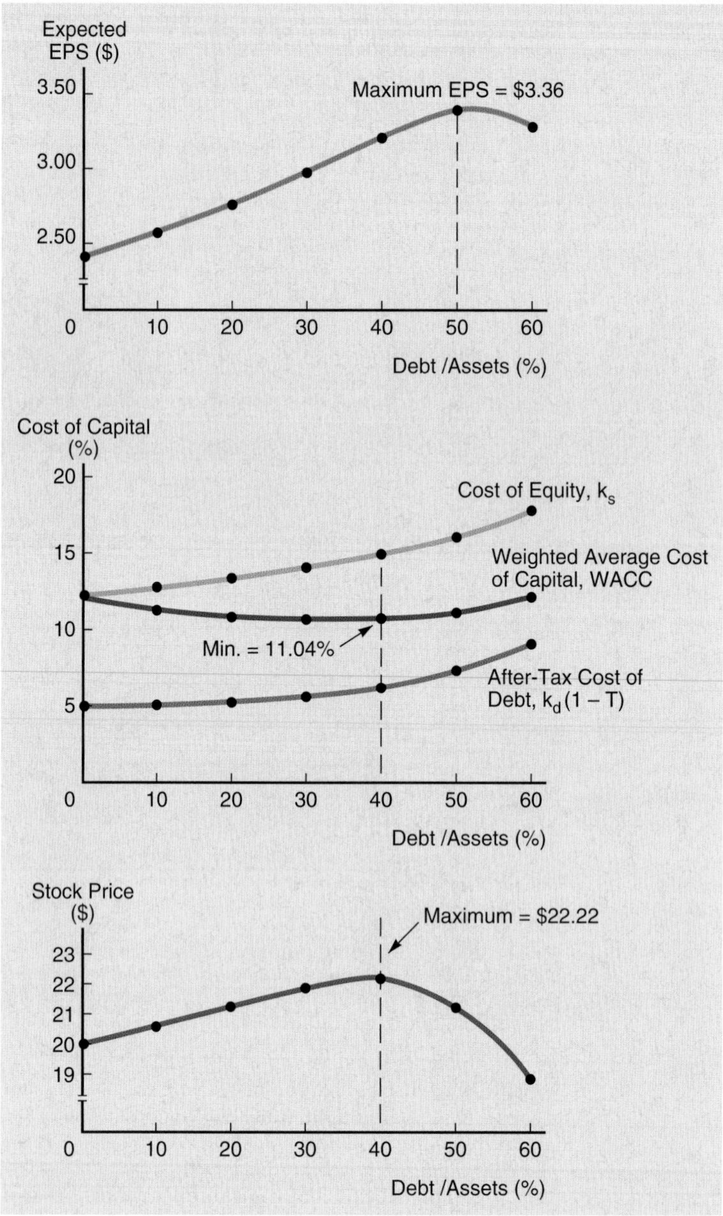

The EPS, cost of capital, and stock price data shown in Table 16-3 are plotted in Figure 16-8. As the graph shows, the debt/assets ratio that maximizes Strasburg's expected EPS is 50 percent. However, the expected stock price is maximized, and the cost of capital is minimized, at a 40 percent debt ratio. *Thus, Strasburg's optimal capital structure calls for 40 percent debt and 60 percent equity.* Management should set its target capital structure at these ratios, and if the existing ratios are off target, it should move toward the target when new security offerings are made.

Self-Test Questions

What happens to the costs of debt and equity when the debt/assets ratio increases? Explain.

Using the Hamada equation, show the effect of financial leverage on beta.

Write out the equation for calculating a firm's unlevered beta.

Using a graph and illustrative data, identify the premiums for financial risk and business risk at different debt levels. Do these premiums vary depending on the debt level? Explain.

Is expected EPS maximized at the optimal capital structure?

Advanced Issues in Determining the Optimal Capital Structure

To more clearly illustrate the basic principles, we made two simplifications in the previous example. First, we used book values for debt and equity instead of market values when calculating the WACC, even though in Chapter 11 we showed that market values should be used for the target weights. Second, we let Strasburg repurchase shares at $20, the price prior to the recapitalization. However, the stock price will increase after the repurchase to reflect the new optimal capital structure. Shareholders will anticipate this, so it's unrealistic to assume that they will sell their shares for $20 when they think the stock will be worth more immediately after the recapitalization. This section extends the analysis to reflect more realistic assumptions.

Using Market Weights

Table 16-4 shows the analysis of the optimal capital structure using market values for equity. Columns 1 through 4 show the dollar value of debt, the cost of debt, the cost of equity, and the total dividend, which are all the same as in the previous analysis

TABLE 16-4 Strasburg's Cost of Capital Based on Market Values

Debt (1)	$(1-T)\ k_d$ (2)	k_s[a] (3)	Earnings = Expected Dividends[b] (4)	MV of Equity[c] (5)	Total Value of Firm[d] (6)	WACC[e] (7)
$ 0	4.8%	12.0%	$24,000	$200,000	$200,000	12.000%
20,000	4.8	12.4	23,040	185,806	205,806	11.661
40,000	5.0	12.9	22,008	170,605	210,605	11.396
60,000	5.4	13.5	20,760	153,291	213,291	11.252
80,000	**6.0**	**14.4**	**19,200**	**133,333**	**213,333**	**11.250**
100,000	7.2	15.6	16,800	107,692	207,692	11.556
120,000	9.0	17.4	13,200	75,862	195,862	12.254

[a] k_d and k_s are taken from Table 16-3.
[b] Expected dividends are equal to earnings = $(EBIT - Dk_d)(1 - T)$ since all earnings are assumed to be paid out. The tax rate is 40 percent.
[c] Market value of equity is calculated as Dividends/k_s.
[d] The total value of the firm is the value of the debt plus the value of the equity.
[e] WACC is calculated using the market values of equity and the book values of debt. Since the debt is newly issued, the market value and book value of debt should be equal.

presented in Table 16-3. Column 5 shows the market value of equity, which is calculated as Dividend/k_s. The market value of the debt is identical to the book amount of debt, since Strasburg issues the debt at the current market interest rate. The total value of the firm, in Column 6, is the market value of the stock plus the market value of debt. Column 7 shows that the minimum WACC is 11.25 percent when based on market values, which is slightly higher than the WACC of 11.04 percent in Table 16-3 based on book values.

If Strasburg borrows \$80,000 and uses the money to repurchase stock, its total value increases from \$200,000 to \$213,333. Because the interest on the debt is deductible, Strasburg pays lower taxes. This means there is more money to pay out to both stockholders and bondholders, so the total value of the firm increases until debt exceeds \$80,000. At higher levels of debt, higher interest costs more than offset the tax benefits, so the total value of the firm begins to decline.

Strasburg's repurchase of stock decreases the amount of equity that shareholders have invested in the company, as shown in Table 16-4. Even though the value of equity decreases, the wealth of the shareholders doesn't necessarily fall. After the recapitalization, shareholder wealth is equal to the cash that is paid to them in the repurchase plus the remaining value of equity. Because Strasburg uses all of the borrowed money to repurchase stock, the shareholders receive a cash payment equal to the amount Strasburg borrows. In other words, the post-recapitalization wealth of the original shareholders is equal to debt plus remaining equity, which is exactly the same as the post-recapitalization value of the firm as shown in Column 6. Therefore, the wealth of the original shareholders increases from \$200,000 to \$213,333 if Strasburg issues \$80,000 in debt. But what happens to the price per share? Is it also maximized with a capital structure containing \$80,000 debt? The next section provides the answer.

Calculating the Equilibrium Share Price in a Recapitalization

A recapitalization occurs when a company issues debt and uses the proceeds to repurchase stock. The previous section analyzed the impact of a recapitalization on Strasburg's risk, value of equity, total value of the firm, and cost of capital. This section explains the effect on price per share.

The price per share is \$20 when Strasburg has no debt. Suppose both investors and management expect the recapitalization to cause the price to rise to \$21.33. In this case, no shareholder would be willing to sell stock back to Strasburg for \$20—the company would have to pay at least \$21.33. On the other hand, if Strasburg offered to buy back shares at \$22, then it would be paying too much. This would be a good deal for the shareholders who sell their stock, but it would harm the remaining shareholders. The **equilibrium recapitalization price** is the price that is expected to prevail after the repurchase, and it is the price that Strasburg should pay for the shares if it is to be fair to all shareholders.

In practice, market forces would cause Strasburg to pay the equilibrium price. First, Strasburg would announce that it intends to issue debt and repurchase a certain number of shares. Second, the stock price would immediately increase to its new fair price based on the repurchase. Third, Strasburg would borrow the money and buy back shares at this new, higher, price.

Of course, the trick is to determine what the prevailing price will be after the repurchase. Recall that before Strasburg announces plans for a recapitalization, its market value is just the value of equity, which is \$200,000. Since it has 10,000 shares, its price per share is \$20. Now suppose Strasburg announces that it will borrow \$20,000 at 8 percent interest and repurchase stock with the proceeds. The first row in Table 16-4 shows that at this level of debt, the total value of the firm will increase to \$205,806. As we showed earlier, the recapitalization will also increase the wealth of shareholders to this level. At the time of the announcement there are 10,000 shares outstanding. Because this increase in value is common knowledge, the share price will increase at the time of the announcement from \$20.00 to \$205,806/10,000 = \$20.58 per share.

Using the \$20,000 in proceeds from the debt issue, Strasburg can repurchase 971.8 shares of stock (\$20,000/\$20.58 = 971.8). What happens to the price per share after the repurchase? The value of equity declines to \$185,806, because shareholders own a smaller part of the firm. Since Strasburg repurchased 971.8 shares of stock, it now has only 9,028.2 shares of stock outstanding (10,000 − 971.8 = 9,028.2). Therefore, its price per share is \$185,806/9,028.2 = \$20.58.

Table 16-5 shows the calculations for the equilibrium repurchase price for each proposed debt level. This price is equal to the stock price that will prevail after the repurchase, and the maximum of \$21.33 occurs with \$80,000 in debt and 3,750 shares repurchased. This is the same debt level that maximized total value in Table 16-4.

Note too that Columns 5 through 8 of Table 16-5 show the calculations for EPS after the repurchase. In our example, expected EPS increases continuously with debt, hitting \$3.41 per share at \$120,000 of debt, which is the most the firm can issue. However, these expected earnings are quite risky, so the stock price is maximized with less debt and a lower, but less risky, expected EPS.

Consistency with Free Cash Flow Valuation

The results in this section are also consistent with the free cash flow (FCF) valuation technique developed in Chapter 12. Before the repurchase Strasburg has no debt, so NOPAT is equal to net income, \$24,000. Growth is zero, so the annual net investment in net operating working capital and fixed assets is zero, so FCF is equal to NOPAT. With no debt, WACC is equal to k_s, which is 12 percent. Therefore, the value of operations is

$$V_{op} = \frac{FCF(1 + g)}{WACC - g} = \frac{\$24{,}000(1 + 0)}{0.12 - 0} = \$200{,}000.$$

Because Strasburg has neither short-term investments nor debt, the total market values of the firm and its equity are equal to the value of operations, \$200,000.

TABLE 16-5 Strasburg's Stock Price using Market Values

Debt (1)	Total Value of Firm (2)	Original Shares Outstanding (3)	Equilibrium Price per Share[a] (4)	Shares Repurchased[b] (5)	Shares after the Repurchase (6)	Earnings = Dividends (7)	Expected EPS (8)
\$ 0.00	\$200,000	10,000	\$20.000	—	10,000.0	\$24,000.0	\$2.40
20,000	205,806	10,000	20.581	971.8	9,028.2	23,040.0	2.55
40,000	210,605	10,000	21.060	1,899.3	8,100.7	22,008.0	2.72
60,000	213,291	10,000	21.329	2,813.1	7,186.9	20,760.0	2.89
80,000	**213,333**	**10,000**	**21.333**	**3,750.0**	**6,250.0**	**19,200.0**	**3.07**
100,000	207,692	10,000	20.769	4,814.8	5,185.2	16,800.0	3.24
120,000	195,862	10,000	19.586	6,126.8	3,873.2	13,200.0	3.41

[a]The equilibrium price per share is calculated as (Market Value of Equity + Debt)/10,000, where 10,000 is the number of shares outstanding before the repurchase.

[b]Shares repurchased are Debt issued/Equilibrium price per share.

If Strasburg recapitalizes and goes to its optimal capital structure, it will issue \$80,000 of debt and repurchase 3,750 shares of stock at \$21.33 per share, as shown in Table 16-5. The recapitalization does not change FCF, but the WACC declines from 12 percent to 11.25 percent. The post-recapitalization value of operations is thus

$$V_{op} = \frac{FCF(1 + g)}{WACC - g} = \frac{\$24{,}000(1 + 0)}{0.1125 - 0} = \$213{,}333.$$

The equity value is the value of operations less debt, which is \$213,333 − 80,000 = \$133,333. Therefore, the value of equity can be calculated as either the value of operations less debt, or as the present value of the cash flows to equity discounted at the cost of equity.

Self-Test Questions

Why is it more appropriate to use market values than book values in cost of capital calculations?

Explain why shares will be repurchased at the equilibrium price rather than the market price that prevailed before the repurchase announcement.

Capital Structure Theory

In the previous section, we showed how a firm might estimate its optimal capital structure. For a number of reasons, we would expect capital structures to vary considerably across industries. For example, pharmaceutical companies generally have very different capital structures than airline companies. Moreover, capital structures vary among firms within a given industry. What factors explain these differences? In an attempt to answer this question, academics and practitioners have developed a number of theories, and the theories have been subjected to many empirical tests.

Modern capital structure theory began in 1958, when Professors Franco Modigliani and Merton Miller (hereafter MM) published what has been called the most influential finance article ever written.[9] MM proved, under a very restrictive set of assumptions, that a firm's value is unaffected by its capital structure. Put another way, MM's results suggest that it does not matter how a firm finances its operations, hence capital structure is irrelevant. However, MM's study was based on some strong assumptions, including the following:

1. There are no brokerage costs.
2. There are no taxes.
3. There are no bankruptcy costs.
4. Investors can borrow at the same rate as corporations.
5. All investors have the same information as management about the firm's future investment opportunities.
6. EBIT is not affected by the use of debt.

Despite the fact that some of these assumptions are obviously unrealistic, MM's irrelevance result is extremely important. By indicating the conditions under which capital structure is irrelevant, MM also provided us with clues about what is required for capital structure to be relevant and hence to affect a firm's value. MM's work marked the beginning of modern capital structure research, and subsequent research has focused on relaxing the MM assumptions in order to develop a more realistic theory of

[9]Franco Modigliani and Merton H. Miller, "The Cost of Capital, Corporation Finance, and the Theory of Investment," *American Economic Review*, June 1958. Modigliani and Miller both won Nobel Prizes for their work.

Yogi Berra on the M&M Proposition

When a waitress asked Yogi Berra (Baseball Hall of Fame catcher for the New York Yankees) whether he wanted his pizza cut into four pieces or eight, Yogi replied: "Better make it four. I don't think I can eat eight."[a]

Yogi's quip helps convey the basic insight of Modigliani and Miller. The firm's choice of leverage "slices" the distribution of future cash flows in a way that is like slicing a pizza. M&M recognized that if you fix a company's investment activities, it's like fixing the size of the pizza; no information costs means that everyone sees the same pizza; no taxes means the IRS gets none of the pie; and no "contracting costs" means nothing sticks to the knife.

So, just as the substance of Yogi's meal is unaffected by whether the pizza is sliced into four pieces or eight, the economic substance of the firm is unaffected by whether the liability side of the balance sheet is sliced to include more or less debt, at least under the M&M assumptions.

[a]Lee Green, *Sportswit* (New York: Fawcett Crest, 1984), 228.

Source: "Yogi Berra on the M&M Proposition," *Journal of Applied Corporate Finance*, Vol. 7, no. 4, Winter 1995, 6. Used by permission.

capital structure. Research in this area is quite extensive, but the highlights are summarized in the following sections.

The Effect of Taxes

MM published a follow-up paper in 1963 in which they relaxed the assumption that there are no corporate taxes.[10] The Tax Code allows corporations to deduct interest payments as an expense, but dividend payments to stockholders are not deductible. This differential treatment encourages corporations to use debt in their capital structures. Indeed, MM demonstrated that if all their other assumptions hold, this differential treatment leads to a situation that calls for 100 percent debt financing.

However, this conclusion was modified several years later by Merton Miller (this time without Modigliani) when he brought in the effects of personal taxes.[11] He noted that all of the income from bonds is generally interest, which is taxed as personal income at rates going up to 39.6 percent, while income from stocks generally comes partly from dividends and partly from capital gains. Further, long-term capital gains are taxed at a rate of 20 percent, and this tax is deferred until the stock is sold and the gain realized. If stock is held until the owner dies, no capital gains tax whatever must be paid. So, on average, returns on stocks are taxed at lower effective rates than returns on debt.

Because of the tax situation, Miller argued that investors are willing to accept relatively low before-tax returns on stock relative to the before-tax returns on bonds. (The situation here is similar to that with tax-exempt municipal bonds as discussed in Chapter 9 and preferred stocks held by corporate investors as discussed in Chapter 10.) For example, an investor might require a return of 10 percent on Strasburg's bonds, and if stock income were taxed at the same rate as bond income, the required rate of return on Strasburg's stock might be 16 percent because of the stock's greater risk. However, in view of the favorable treatment of income on the stock, investors might be willing to accept a before-tax return of only 14 percent on the stock.

[10]Franco Modigliani and Merton H. Miller, "Corporate Income Taxes and the Cost of Capital: A Correction," *American Economic Review* 53, June 1963, 433–443.

[11]Merton H. Miller, "Debt and Taxes," *Journal of Finance* 32, May 1977, 261–275. Miller was president of the American Finance Association, and he delivered the paper as his presidential address.

Thus, as Miller pointed out, (1) the *deductibility of interest* favors the use of debt financing, but (2) the *more favorable tax treatment of income from stock* lowers the required rate of return on stock and thus favors the use of equity financing. It is difficult to say what the net effect of these two factors is. Most observers believe that interest deductibility has the stronger effect, hence that our tax system still favors the corporate use of debt. However, that effect is certainly reduced by the lower long-term capital gains tax rate.

One can observe changes in corporate financing patterns following major changes in tax rates. For example, in 1993 the top personal tax rate on interest and dividends was raised sharply, but the capital gains tax rate was not increased. This could be expected to result in a greater reliance on equity financing, especially through retained earnings, and that has indeed been the case. The lowering of the long-term capital gains tax rate in 1997 continued this trend.

The Effect of Bankruptcy Costs

MM's irrelevance results also depend on the assumption that there are no bankruptcy costs. However, in practice bankruptcy can be quite costly. Firms in bankruptcy have very high legal and accounting expenses, and they also have a hard time retaining customers, suppliers, and employees. Moreover, bankruptcy often forces a firm to liquidate or sell assets for less than they would be worth if the firm were to continue operating. For example, if a steel manufacturer goes out of business, it might be hard to find buyers for the company's blast furnaces, even though they were quite expensive. Assets such as plant and equipment are often illiquid because they are configured to a company's individual needs and also because they are difficult to disassemble and move.

Note, too, that the *threat of bankruptcy*, not just bankruptcy per se, produces these problems. Key employees jump ship, suppliers refuse to grant credit, customers seek more stable suppliers, and lenders demand higher interest rates and impose more restrictive loan covenants if potential bankruptcy looms.

Bankruptcy-related problems are most likely to arise when a firm includes a great deal of debt in its capital structure. Therefore, bankruptcy costs discourage firms from pushing their use of debt to excessive levels.

Bankruptcy-related costs have two components: (1) the probability of their occurrence and (2) the costs that would be incurred given that financial distress has occurred. Firms whose earnings are more volatile, all else equal, face a greater chance of bankruptcy and, therefore, should use less debt than more stable firms. This is consistent with our earlier point that firms with high operating leverage, and thus greater business risk, should limit their use of financial leverage. Likewise, firms that would face high costs in the event of financial distress should rely less heavily on debt. For example, firms whose assets are illiquid and thus would have to be sold at "fire sale" prices should limit their use of debt financing.

Trade-Off Theory

The preceding arguments led to the development of what is called "the trade-off theory of leverage," in which firms trade off the benefits of debt financing (favorable corporate tax treatment) against the higher interest rates and bankruptcy costs. A summary of the trade-off theory is expressed graphically in Figure 16-9. Here are some observations about the figure:

1. The fact that interest is a deductible expense makes debt less expensive than common or preferred stock. In effect, the government pays part of the cost of debt capital, or, to put it another way, debt provides *tax shelter benefits.* As a

FIGURE 16-9 Effect of Leverage on the Value of Strasburg's Stock

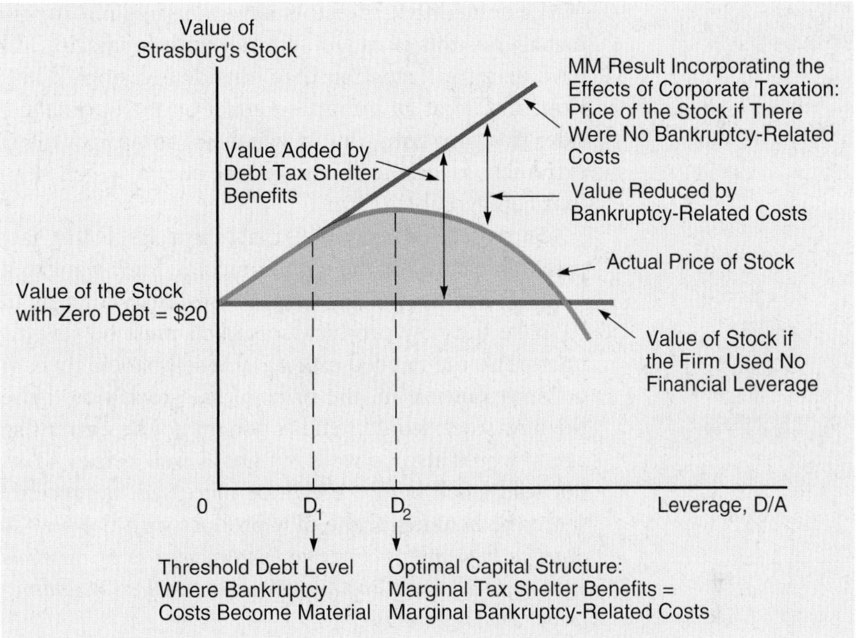

result, using debt causes more of the firm's operating income (EBIT) to flow through to investors. Therefore, the more debt a company uses, the higher its value and stock price. Under the assumptions of the Modigliani-Miller with-taxes paper, a firm's stock price will be maximized if it uses virtually 100 percent debt, and the line labeled "MM Result Incorporating the Effects of Corporate Taxation" in Figure 16-9 expresses the relationship between stock prices and debt under their assumptions.

2. In the real world, firms rarely use 100 percent debt. Trade-off theory advocates argue that firms limit their use of debt to hold down bankruptcy-related costs.
3. There is some threshold level of debt, labeled D_1 in Figure 16-9, below which the probability of bankruptcy is so low as to be immaterial. Beyond D_1, however, bankruptcy-related costs become increasingly important, and they reduce the tax benefits of debt at an increasing rate. In the range from D_1 to D_2, bankruptcy-related costs reduce but do not completely offset the tax benefits of debt, so the stock price rises (but at a decreasing rate) as the debt ratio increases. However, beyond D_2, bankruptcy-related costs exceed the tax benefits, so from this point on increasing the debt ratio lowers the value of the stock. Therefore, D_2 is the optimal capital structure. Of course, D_1 and D_2 vary from firm to firm, depending on their business risks and bankruptcy costs.
4. While theoretical and empirical work supports the general shape of the curves in Figures 16-8 and 16-9, these graphs must be taken as approximations, not as precisely defined functions. The numbers in our examples are shown out to two decimal places, but that is merely for illustrative purposes—the numbers are not nearly that accurate in view of the fact that the data in the examples are judgmental estimates.
5. Another disturbing aspect of capital structure theory as expressed in Figure 16-9 is the fact that many large, successful firms, such as Intel and Microsoft, use far less debt than the theory suggests. This point led to the development of signaling theory, which is discussed below.

Signaling Theory

MM assumed that investors have the same information about a firm's prospects as its managers—this is called **symmetric information.** However, in fact managers often have better information than outside investors. This is called **asymmetric information,** and it has an important effect on the optimal capital structure. To see why, consider two situations, one in which the company's managers know that its prospects are extremely favorable (Firm F) and one in which the managers know that the future looks unfavorable (Firm U).

Suppose, for example, that Firm F's R&D labs have just discovered a non-patentable cure for the common cold. They want to keep the new product a secret as long as possible to delay competitors' entry into the market. New plants must be built to make the new product, so capital must be raised. How should Firm F's management raise the needed capital? If it sells stock, then, when profits from the new product start flowing in, the price of the stock would rise sharply, and the purchasers of the new stock would make a bonanza. The current stockholders (including the managers) would also do well, but not as well as they would have done if the company had not sold stock before the price increased, because then they would not have had to share the benefits of the new product with the new stockholders. *Therefore, one would expect a firm with very favorable prospects to try to avoid selling stock and, rather, to raise any required new capital by other means, including using debt beyond the normal target capital structure.*[12]

Now let's consider Firm U. Suppose its managers have information that new orders are off sharply because a competitor has installed new technology that has improved its products' quality. Firm U must upgrade its own facilities, at a high cost, just to maintain its current sales. As a result, its return on investment will fall (but not by as much as if it took no action, which would lead to a 100 percent loss through bankruptcy). How should Firm U raise the needed capital? Here the situation is just the reverse of that facing Firm F, which did not want to sell stock so as to avoid having to share the benefits of future developments. *A firm with unfavorable prospects would want to sell stock, which would mean bringing in new investors to share the losses!*[13]

The conclusion from all this is that firms with extremely bright prospects prefer not to finance through new stock offerings, whereas firms with poor prospects do like to finance with outside equity. How should you, as an investor, react to this conclusion? You ought to say, "If I see that a company plans to issue new stock, this should worry me because I know that management would not want to issue stock if future prospects looked good. However, management would want to issue stock if things looked bad. Therefore, I should lower my estimate of the firm's value, other things held constant, if it plans to issue new stock."

If you gave the above answer, your views would be consistent with those of sophisticated portfolio managers of institutions such as Morgan Guaranty Trust, Prudential Insurance, and so forth. *In a nutshell, the announcement of a stock offering is generally taken as a* **signal** *that the firm's prospects as seen by its management are not bright.* This, in turn, suggests that when a firm announces a new stock offering, more often than not the price of its stock will decline. Empirical studies have shown that this situation does indeed exist.[14]

---

[12]It would be illegal for Firm F's managers to personally purchase more shares on the basis of their inside knowledge of the new product. They could be sent to jail if they did.

[13]Of course, Firm U would have to make certain disclosures when it offered new shares to the public, but it might be able to meet the legal requirements without fully disclosing management's worst fears.

[14]Paul Asquith and David W. Mullins, Jr., "The Impact of Initiating Dividend Payments on Shareholders' Wealth," *Journal of Business*, January 1983, 77–96.

What are the implications of all this for capital structure decisions? Because issuing stock emits a negative signal and thus tends to depress the stock price, even if the company's prospects are bright, it should, in normal times, maintain a **reserve borrowing capacity** that can be used in the event that some especially good investment opportunity comes along. *This means that firms should, in normal times, use more equity and less debt than is suggested by the tax benefit/bankruptcy cost trade-off model expressed in Figure 16-9.*

Using Debt Financing to Constrain Managers

In Chapter 1 we stated that agency problems may arise if managers and shareholders have different objectives. Such conflicts are particularly likely when the firm's managers have too much cash at their disposal. Managers often use excess cash to finance pet projects or for perquisites such as nicer offices, corporate jets, and sky boxes at sports arenas, all of which may do little to maximize stock prices.[15] By contrast, managers with limited "excess cash flow" are less able to make wasteful expenditures.

Firms can reduce excess cash flow in a variety of ways. One way is to funnel some of it back to shareholders through higher dividends or stock repurchases. Another alternative is to shift the capital structure toward more debt in the hope that higher debt service requirements will force managers to be more disciplined. If debt is not serviced as required, the firm will be forced into bankruptcy, in which case its managers would likely lose their jobs. Therefore, a manager is less likely to buy an expensive new corporate jet if the firm has large debt service requirements that could cost the manager his or her job.

A leveraged buyout (LBO) is one way to reduce excess cash flow. In an LBO debt is used to finance the purchase of a company's shares, after which the firm "goes private." Many leveraged buyouts, which were especially common during the late 1980s, were designed specifically to reduce corporate waste. As noted, high debt payments force managers to conserve cash by eliminating unnecessary expenditures.

Of course, increasing debt and reducing the available cash flow has its downside: It increases the risk of bankruptcy. One professor has argued that adding debt to a firm's capital structure is like putting a dagger into the steering wheel of a car.[16] The dagger—which points toward your stomach—motivates you to drive more carefully, but you may get stabbed if someone runs into you, even if you are being careful. The analogy applies to corporations in the following sense: Higher debt forces managers to be more careful with shareholders' money, but even well-run firms could face bankruptcy (get stabbed) if some event beyond their control such as a war, an earthquake, a strike, or a recession occurs. To complete the analogy, the capital structure decision comes down to deciding how big a dagger stockholders should use to keep managers in line.

Debt and the Investment Opportunity Set

Highly leveraged firms behave differently from low-leverage firms. Bankruptcy and financial distress are costly, and this can discourage highly leveraged firms from undertaking risky new investments. If potential new investments, although risky, have positive net present values, then high levels of debt can be doubly costly—the expected financial distress and bankruptcy costs are high, and the firm loses potential value by not

---

[15]If you don't believe corporate managers can waste money, read Bryan Burrough and John Helyar, *Barbarians at the Gate* (New York: Harper & Row, 1990), the story of the takeover of RJR-Nabisco.

[16]Ben Bernake, "Is There Too Much Corporate Debt?" Federal Reserve Bank of Philadelphia *Business Review*, September/October 1989, 3–13.

making some potentially profitable investments. On the other hand, if a firm has very few profitable investment opportunities, then as we discussed in the previous section, high levels of debt can keep managers from wasting money by investing in poor projects. For such companies, increases in the debt ratio can increase the value of the firm.

Thus, in addition to the tax, signaling, bankruptcy, and managerial constraint effects discussed earlier, the firm's optimal capital structure is related to its set of investment opportunities. Firms with many profitable investments should maintain their ability to invest by using low levels of debt, which is also consistent with maintaining its reserve borrowing capacity. Firms with few profitable investment opportunities should use high levels of debt and thus have substantial interest payments, which means imposing managerial constraint through debt.[17]

If you find our discussion of capital structure theory imprecise and somewhat dissatisfying, you are not alone. In truth, no one knows how to identify precisely a firm's optimal capital structure, or how to measure the effects of capital structure on stock prices and the cost of capital. In practice, capital structure decisions must be made using a combination of judgment and numerical analysis. Still, an understanding of the theoretical issues presented here can help you make better judgments on capital structure issues.[18]

Self-Test Questions

Why does M&M's theory with corporate taxes lead to 100 percent debt?

How would an increase in corporate taxes affect firms' capital structure decisions? What about personal taxes?

Explain how "asymmetric information" and "signals" affect capital structure decisions.

What is meant by *reserve borrowing capacity,* and why is it important to firms?

How can the use of debt serve to discipline managers?

How do the firm's investment opportunities affect its use of debt?

Checklist for Capital Structure Decisions

Firms generally consider the following factors when making capital structure decisions:

1. **Sales stability.** A firm whose sales are relatively stable can safely take on more debt and incur higher fixed charges than a company with unstable sales. Utility companies, because of their stable demand, have historically been able to use more financial leverage than industrial firms.
2. **Asset structure.** Firms whose assets are suitable as security for loans tend to use debt rather heavily. General-purpose assets that can be used by many businesses make good collateral, whereas special-purpose assets do not. Thus, real estate

[17]Michael J. Barclay and Clifford W. Smith, Jr., "The Capital Structure Puzzle: Another Look at the Evidence," *Journal of Applied Corporate Finance,* Vol. 12, no. 1, Spring 1999, 8–20.

[18]One of the authors can report firsthand the usefulness of financial theory in the actual establishment of corporate capital structures. In recent years, he has served as a consultant to several of the regional telephone companies established as a result of the breakup of AT&T, as well as to several large electric utilities. On the basis of finance theory and computer models that simulated results under a range of conditions, the companies were able to specify "optimal capital structure ranges" with at least a reasonable degree of confidence. Without finance theory, setting a target capital structure would have amounted to little more than throwing darts.

companies are usually highly leveraged, whereas companies involved in technological research are not.

3. **Operating leverage.** Other things the same, a firm with less operating leverage is better able to employ financial leverage because it will have less business risk.
4. **Growth rate.** Other things the same, faster-growing firms must rely more heavily on external capital (see Chapter 4). Further, the flotation costs involved in selling common stock exceed those incurred when selling debt, which encourages rapidly growing firms to rely more heavily on debt. At the same time, however, these firms often face greater uncertainty, which tends to reduce their willingness to use debt.
5. **Profitability.** One often observes that firms with very high rates of return on investment use relatively little debt. Although there is no theoretical justification for this fact, one practical explanation is that very profitable firms such as Intel, Microsoft, and Coca-Cola simply do not need to do much debt financing. Their high rates of return enable them to do most of their financing with internally generated funds.
6. **Taxes.** Interest is a deductible expense, and deductions are most valuable to firms with high tax rates. Therefore, the higher a firm's tax rate, the greater the advantage of debt.
7. **Control.** The effect of debt versus stock on a management's control position can influence capital structure. If management currently has voting control (over 50 percent of the stock) but is not in a position to buy any more stock, it may choose debt for new financings. On the other hand, management may decide to use equity if the firm's financial situation is so weak that the use of debt might subject it to serious risk of default, because if the firm goes into default, the managers will almost surely lose their jobs. However, if too little debt is used, management runs the risk of a takeover. Thus, control considerations could lead to the use of *either* debt or equity, because the type of capital that best protects management will vary from situation to situation. In any event, if management is at all insecure, it will consider the control situation.
8. **Management attitudes.** Because no one can prove that one capital structure will lead to higher stock prices than another, management can exercise its own judgment about the proper capital structure. Some managements tend to be more conservative than others, and thus use less debt than the average firm in their industry, whereas aggressive managements use more debt in the quest for higher profits.
9. **Lender and rating agency attitudes.** Regardless of managers' own analyses of the proper leverage factors for their firms, lenders' and rating agencies' attitudes frequently influence financial structure decisions. In the majority of cases, the corporation discusses its capital structure with lenders and rating agencies and gives much weight to their advice. For example, one large utility was recently told by Moody's and Standard & Poor's that its bonds would be downgraded if it issued more debt. This influenced its decision to finance its expansion with common equity.
10. **Market conditions.** Conditions in the stock and bond markets undergo both long- and short-run changes that can have an important bearing on a firm's optimal capital structure. For example, during a recent credit crunch, the junk bond market dried up, and there was simply no market at a "reasonable" interest rate for any new long-term bonds rated below triple B. Therefore, low-rated companies in need of capital were forced to go to the stock market or to the short-term debt market, regardless of their target capital structures. When conditions eased, however, these companies sold bonds to get their capital structures back on target.
11. **The firm's internal condition.** A firm's own internal condition can also have a bearing on its target capital structure. For example, suppose a firm has just successfully completed an R&D program, and it forecasts higher earnings in the

immediate future. However, the new earnings are not yet anticipated by investors, hence are not reflected in the stock price. This company would not want to issue stock—it would prefer to finance with debt until the higher earnings materialize and are reflected in the stock price. Then it could sell an issue of common stock, retire the debt, and return to its target capital structure. This point was discussed earlier in connection with asymmetric information and signaling.

12. **Financial flexibility.** Firms with profitable investment opportunities need to be able to fund them. An astute corporate treasurer made this statement to the authors:

> Our company can earn a lot more money from good capital budgeting and operating decisions than from good financing decisions. Indeed, we are not sure exactly how financing decisions affect our stock price, but we know for sure that having to turn down a promising venture because funds are not available will reduce our long-run profitability. For this reason, my primary goal as treasurer is to always be in a position to raise the capital needed to support operations.
>
> We also know that when times are good, we can raise capital with either stocks or bonds, but when times are bad, suppliers of capital are much more willing to make funds available if we give them a secured position, and this means debt. Further, when we sell a new issue of stock, this sends a negative "signal" to investors, so stock sales by a mature company such as ours are not desirable.

Putting all these thoughts together gives rise to the goal of *maintaining financial flexibility*, which, from an operational viewpoint, means *maintaining adequate reserve borrowing capacity*. Determining an "adequate" reserve borrowing capacity is judgmental, but it clearly depends on the factors discussed in the chapter, including the firm's forecasted need for funds, predicted capital market conditions, management's confidence in its forecasts, and the consequences of a capital shortage.

Self-Test Questions

How does sales stability affect the target capital structure?

How does the type of assets used affect a firm's capital structure?

How do taxes affect the target capital structure?

How do lender and rating agency attitudes affect capital structure?

How does the firm's internal condition affect its actual capital structure?

What is "financial flexibility," and is it increased or decreased by a high debt ratio?

Variations in Capital Structures

As might be expected, wide variations in the use of financial leverage occur both across industries and among the individual firms in each industry. Table 16-6 illustrates differences for selected industries; the ranking is in descending order of the percentage of common equity to total capital, as shown in Column 1.[19]

Pharmaceutical and computer companies do not use much debt (their percentages of common equity are high) because the uncertainties inherent in industries that are cyclical, oriented toward research, or subject to huge product liability suits render the heavy use of debt unwise. The airline and utility companies, on the other hand, use debt relatively heavily. The utilities have traditionally used large amounts of debt,

[19]Information on capital structures and financial strength is available from a multitude of sources. We used the *Dow Jones News Retrieval* system to develop Table 16-6, but published sources include *The Value Line Investment Survey*, *Robert Morris Association Annual Studies*, and *Dun & Bradstreet Key Business Ratios.*

Taking a Look at Global Capital Structures

To what extent does capital structure vary across different countries? The following table, which is taken from a recent study by Raghuram Rajan and Luigi Zingales, both of the University of Chicago, shows the median debt ratios of firms in the largest industrial countries.

Rajan and Zingales also show that there is considerable variation in capital structure among firms within each of the seven countries. However, they also show that capital structures for the firms in each country are generally determined by a similar set of factors: firm size, profitability, market-to-book ratio, and the ratio of fixed assets to total assets. All in all, the Rajan-Zingales study suggests that the points developed in this chapter apply to firms all around the world.

Median Percentage of Debt to Total Assets in Different Countries

Country	Book Value Debt Ratio
Canada	32%
France	18
Germany	11
Italy	21
Japan	21
United Kingdom	10
United States	25

Source: Raghuram G. Rajan and Luigi Zingales, "What Do We Know about Capital Structure? Some Evidence from International Data," *The Journal of Finance*, Vol. 50, no. 5, December 1995, 1421-1460. Used with permission.

particularly long-term debt, because their fixed assets make good security for mortgage bonds, and also because their relatively stable sales make it safe for them to carry more debt than would be true for firms with more business risk.

Particular attention should be given to the times-interest-earned (TIE) ratio because it gives an indication of how safe the debt is and how vulnerable the company is to financial distress. TIE ratios depend on three factors: (1) the percentage of debt, (2) the interest rate on the debt, and (3) the company's profitability. Generally, the least leveraged companies, such as the pharmaceuticals, have the highest coverage ratios, whereas the utilities, which finance heavily with debt, have a low average coverage ratio.

TABLE 16-6 Capital Structure Percentages: Six Industries Ranked by Common Equity Ratios[a]

Industry	Common Equity Percentage[b] (1)	Long-Term Debt Percentage (2)	Times-Interest-Earned Ratio (3)	Return on Equity (4)
Pharmaceuticals	80%	20%	13.3×	31.2%
Computers	72	28	12.0	15.8
Steel	65	35	0.8	−1.8
Aerospace	57	43	4.2	12.3
Gas utilities	52	48	2.9	10.0
Airlines	40	60	3.7	12.1

Notes:
[a]Capital structure ratios are calculated as a percentage of total capital, where total capital is defined as long-term debt plus equity, with both measured at book value.
[b]These ratios are based on accounting (or book) values. Stated on a market-value basis, the equity percentages would rise because most stocks sell at prices that are much higher than their book values.

Source: *Dow Jones News Retrieval*, 2000. Data collected through September 20, 2000.

Wide variations also exist among firms within given industries. For example, although the average ratio of common equity to total capital in the pharmaceutical industry was 80 percent, Eli Lilly & Co. had a ratio of only 63.3 percent. Thus, factors unique to individual firms, including managerial attitudes, play an important role in setting target capital structures.

Self-Test Questions

Why do wide variations in the use of financial leverage occur both across industries and among the individual firms in each industry?

Summary

In Chapter 11, we took the firm's financing choice as given and then calculated the cost of capital based on that capital structure. Then, in Chapters 13 and 14, we described capital budgeting techniques, which use the firm's cost of capital as input. Capital budgeting decisions determine the types of projects that the firm accepts, which affect the nature of the firm's assets and its business risk. In this chapter we reverse the process, taking the firm's assets and business risk as given and then seeking to determine the best way to finance those assets. More specifically, we examined the effects of financial leverage on stock prices, earnings per share, and the cost of capital. The key concepts covered are listed below:

- A firm's **optimal capital structure** is that mix of debt and equity that maximizes the stock price. At any point in time, management has a specific **target capital structure** in mind, presumably the optimal one, although this target may change over time.
- Several factors influence a firm's capital structure. These include its (1) **business risk,** (2) **tax position,** (3) need for **financial flexibility,** (4) **managerial conservatism or aggressiveness,** and **growth opportunities.**
- **Business risk** is the riskiness inherent in the firm's operations if it uses no debt. A firm will have little business risk if the demand for its products is stable, if the prices of its inputs and products remain relatively constant, if it can adjust its prices freely if costs increase, and if a high percentage of its costs are variable and hence will decrease if sales decrease. Other things the same, the lower a firm's business risk, the higher its optimal debt ratio.
- **Financial leverage** is the extent to which fixed-income securities (debt and preferred stock) are used in a firm's capital structure. **Financial risk** is the added risk borne by stockholders as a result of financial leverage.
- **Operating leverage** is the extent to which fixed costs are used in a firm's operations. In business terminology, a high degree of operating leverage, other factors held constant, implies that a relatively small change in sales results in a large change in ROE.
- Robert Hamada used the underlying assumptions of the CAPM, along with the Modigliani and Miller model, to develop the **Hamada equation,** which shows the effect of financial leverage on beta as follows:

  $$b = b_U\,[1 + (1 - T)(D/E)].$$

  Firms can take their current beta, tax rate, and debt/equity ratio to arrive at their **unlevered beta,** b_U, as follows:

  $$b_U = b/[1 + (1 - T)(D/E)].$$

- **Modigliani and Miller** and their followers developed a **trade-off theory of capital structure.** They showed that debt is useful because interest is **tax deductible,** but also that debt brings with it costs associated with actual or potential bankruptcy. The optimal capital structure strikes a balance between the tax benefits of debt and the costs associated with bankruptcy.

- An alternative (or, really, complementary) theory of capital structure relates to the **signals** given to investors by a firm's decision to use debt versus stock to raise new capital. A stock issue sets off a negative signal, while using debt is a positive, or at least a neutral, signal. As a result, companies try to avoid having to issue stock by maintaining a **reserve borrowing capacity**, and this means using less debt in "normal" times than the MM trade-off theory would suggest.
- A firm's owners may decide to use a relatively large amount of debt to constrain the managers. **A high debt ratio raises the threat of bankruptcy**, which carries a cost but which also forces managers to be more careful and less wasteful with shareholders' money. Many of the corporate takeovers and leveraged buyouts in recent years were designed to improve efficiency by reducing the cash flow available to managers.

Although each firm has a theoretically optimal capital structure, as a practical matter we cannot estimate it with precision. Accordingly, financial executives generally treat the optimal capital structure as a range—for example, 40 to 50 percent debt—rather than as a precise point, such as 45 percent. The concepts discussed in this chapter help managers understand the factors they should consider when they set the target capital structure ranges for their firms. In the next chapter, we will examine some additional issues which provide further insights into the capital structure decision.

Questions

16–1 Define each of the following terms:
- **a.** Capital structure
- **b.** Business risk
- **c.** Financial risk
- **d.** Operating leverage
- **e.** Financial leverage
- **f.** Breakeven point
- **g.** Capital structure theory
- **h.** Perpetual cash flow analysis
- **i.** Reserve borrowing capacity

16–2 What term refers to the uncertainty inherent in projections of future ROE?

16–3 Firms with relatively high nonfinancial fixed costs are said to have a high degree of what?

16–4 "One type of leverage affects both EBIT and EPS. The other type affects only EPS." Explain this statement.

16–5 Why is the following statement true? "Other things being the same, firms with relatively stable sales are able to carry relatively high debt ratios."

16–6 Why do public utility companies usually have capital structures that are different from those of retail firms?

16–7 Some economists believe that swings in business cycles will not be as wide in the future as they have been in the past. Assuming that they are correct, what effect might this added stability have on the types of financing used by firms in the United States? Would your answer be true for all firms?

16–8 Why is EBIT generally considered to be independent of financial leverage? Why might EBIT actually be influenced by financial leverage at high debt levels?

16–9 If a firm with no debt could buy back and retire its stock at the pre-announcement price, would its final stock price be higher than that resulting from the procedure outlined in the chapter?

Would it be fair for a firm to buy back its stock without telling stockholders that stock was being repurchased?

16–10 How might increasingly volatile inflation rates, interest rates, and bond prices affect the optimal capital structure for corporations?

16–11 If a firm went from zero debt to successively higher levels of debt, why would you expect its stock price to first rise, then hit a peak, and then begin to decline?

16–12 The stock of Gentech Company is currently selling at its low for the year, but management feels that the stock price is only temporarily depressed because of investor pessimism. The firm's capital budget this year is so large that the use of new outside equity is contemplated. However, management does not want to sell new stock at the current low price and is therefore considering a temporary departure from the firm's "optimal" capital structure by borrowing the funds it would otherwise have raised in the equity markets. Does this seem to be a wise move? Does this action conform to any of the theories presented in the chapter?

16–13 Why is the debt level that maximizes a firm's expected EPS generally higher than the debt level that maximizes its stock price?

Self-Test Problems (Solutions Appear in Appendix A)

ST–1 *OPTIMAL CAPITAL STRUCTURE*

The Rogers Company is currently in this situation: (1) EBIT = \$4 million; (2) tax rate, T = 35%; (3) value of debt, D = \$2 million; (4) k_d = 10%; (5) k_s = 15%; and (6) shares of stock outstanding, n = 600,000. The firm's market is stable, and it expects no growth, so all earnings are paid out as dividends. The debt consists of perpetual bonds.

a. What is the total market value of the firm's stock, S, its price per share, P_0, and the firm's total market value, V?

b. What is the firm's weighted average cost of capital?

c. The firm can increase its debt by \$8 million, to a total of \$10 million, using the new debt to buy back and retire some of its shares. Its interest rate on all debt will be 12 percent (it will have to call and refund the old debt), and its cost of equity will rise from 15 to 17 percent. EBIT will remain constant. Should the firm change its capital structure?

ST–2 *HAMADA EQUATION*

Lighter Industrial Corporation (LIC) is considering a large-scale recapitalization. Currently, LIC is financed with 25 percent debt and 75 percent equity. LIC is considering increasing its level of debt until it is financed with 60 percent debt and 40 percent equity. The beta on its common stock at the current level of debt is 1.5, the risk free rate is 6 percent, the market risk premium is 4 percent, and LIC faces a 40 percent federal-plus-state tax rate.

a. What is LIC's current cost of equity?

b. What is LIC's unlevered beta?

c. What will be the new beta and new cost of equity if LIC recapitalizes?

Problems

16–1 *OPERATING LEVERAGE AND BREAKEVEN*

Schweser Satellites Inc. produces satellite earth stations that sell for \$100,000 each. The firm's fixed costs, F, are \$2 million; 50 earth stations are produced and sold each year; profits total \$500,000; and the firm's assets (all equity financed) are \$5 million. The firm estimates that it can change its production process, adding \$4 million to investment and \$500,000 to fixed operating costs. This change will (1) reduce variable costs per unit by \$10,000 and (2) increase output by 20 units, but (3) the sales price on all units will have to be lowered to \$95,000 to permit sales of the additional output. The firm has tax loss carry-forwards that cause its tax rate to be zero, its cost of equity is 15 percent, and it uses no debt.

a. Should the firm make the change?

b. Would the firm's operating leverage increase or decrease if it made the change? What about its breakeven point?

c. Would the new situation expose the firm to more or less business risk than the old one?

16–2 BUSINESS AND FINANCIAL RISK

Here are the estimated ROE distributions for Firms A, B, and C:

	Probability				
	0.1	0.2	0.4	0.2	0.1
Firm A: ROE_A	0.0%	5.0%	10.0%	15.0%	20.0%
Firm B: ROE_B	(2.0)	5.0	12.0	19.0	26.0
Firm C: ROE_C	(5.0)	5.0	15.0	25.0	35.0

a. Calculate the expected value and standard deviation for Firm C's ROE. $ROE_A = 10.0\%$, $\sigma_A = 5.5\%$; $ROE_B = 12.0\%$, $\sigma_B = 7.7\%$.

b. Discuss the relative riskiness of the three firms' returns. (Assume that these distributions are expected to remain constant over time.)

c. Now suppose all three firms have the same standard deviation of basic earning power (EBIT/Total assets), $\sigma_A = \sigma_B = \sigma_C = 5.5\%$. What can we tell about the financial risk of each firm?

16–3 CAPITAL STRUCTURE ANALYSIS

The following data reflect the current financial conditions of the Levine Corporation:

Value of debt (book = market)	$1,000,000
Market value of equity	$5,257,143
Sales, last 12 months	$12,000,000
Variable operating costs (50% of sales)	$6,000,000
Fixed operating costs	$5,000,000
Tax rate, T (federal-plus-state)	40%

At the current level of debt, the cost of debt, k_d, is 8 percent and the cost of equity, k_s, is 10.5 percent. Management questions whether or not the capital structure is optimal, so the financial vice-president has been asked to consider the possibility of issuing $1 million of additional debt and using the proceeds to repurchase stock. It is estimated that if the leverage were increased by raising the level of debt to $2 million, the interest rate on new debt would rise to 9 percent and k_s would rise to 11.5 percent. The old 8 percent debt is senior to the new debt, and it would remain outstanding, continue to yield 8 percent, and have a market value of $1 million. The firm is a zero-growth firm, with all of its earnings paid out as dividends.

a. Should the firm increase its debt to $2 million?

b. If the firm decided to increase its level of debt to $3 million, its cost of the additional $2 million of debt would be 12 percent and k_s would rise to 15 percent. The original 8 percent of debt would again remain outstanding, and its market value would remain at $1 million. What level of debt should the firm choose: $1 million, $2 million, or $3 million?

c. The market price of the firm's stock was originally $20 per share. Calculate the new equilibrium stock prices at debt levels of $2 million and $3 million.

d. Calculate the firm's earnings per share if it uses debt of $1 million, $2 million, and $3 million. Assume that the firm pays out all of its earnings as dividends. If you find that EPS increases with more debt, does this mean that the firm should choose to increase its debt to $3 million, or possibly higher?

e. What would happen to the value of the old bonds if the firm uses more leverage and the old bonds are not senior to the new bonds?

16–4 CAPITAL STRUCTURE ANALYSIS

The Rivoli Company has no debt outstanding, and its financial position is given by the following data:

Assets (book = market)	$3,000,000
EBIT	$500,000
Cost of equity, k_s	10%
Stock price, P_0	$15
Shares outstanding, n	200,000
Tax rate, T (federal-plus-state)	40%

The firm is considering selling bonds and simultaneously repurchasing some of its stock. If it uses $900,000 of debt, its cost of equity, k_s, will increase to 11 percent to reflect the increased risk. Bonds can be sold at a cost, k_d, of 7 percent. Rivoli is a no-growth firm. Hence, all its earnings are paid out as dividends, and earnings are expectationally constant over time.

a. What effect would this use of leverage have on the value of the firm?

b. What would be the price of Rivoli's stock?

c. What happens to the firm's earnings per share after the recapitalization?

d. The $500,000 EBIT given previously is actually the expected value from the following probability distribution:

Probability	EBIT
0.10	($ 100,000)
0.20	200,000
0.40	500,000
0.20	800,000
0.10	1,100,000

What is the probability distribution of EPS with zero debt and with $900,000 of debt? Which EPS distribution is riskier?

e. Determine the probability distributions of the times-interest-earned ratio for each debt level. What is the probability of not covering the interest payment at the $900,000 debt level?

16–5
CAPITAL STRUCTURE ANALYSIS

Pettit Printing Company has a total market value of $100 million, consisting of 1 million shares selling for $50 per share and $50 million of 10 percent perpetual bonds now selling at par. The company's EBIT is $13.24 million, and its tax rate is 15 percent. Pettit can change its capital structure by either increasing its debt to $70 million or decreasing it to $30 million. If it decides to *increase* its use of leverage, it must call its old bonds and issue new ones with a 12 percent coupon. If it decides to *decrease* its leverage, it will call in its old bonds and replace them with new 8 percent coupon bonds. The company will sell or repurchase stock at the new equilibrium price to complete the capital structure change.

The firm pays out all earnings as dividends; hence, its stock is a zero growth stock. If it increases leverage, k_s will be 16 percent. If it decreases leverage, k_s will be 13 percent.

a. What is the firm's cost of equity at present?

b. Should the firm change its capital structure?

c. Suppose the tax rate is changed to 34 percent. This would lower after-tax income and also cause a decline in the price of the stock and the total value of the equity, other things held constant. Calculate the new stock price (at $50 million of debt).

d. Continue the scenario of part c, but now reexamine the question of the optimal amount of debt. Does the tax rate change affect your decision about the optimal use of financial leverage?

e. Go back to part b; that is, assume T = 15%. How would your analysis of the capital structure change be modified if the firm's presently outstanding debt could not be called, and it did not have to be replaced; that is, if the $50 million of 10 percent debt continued even if the company issued new 12 percent bonds?

f. Suppose these probabilities for EBIT exist: P[EBIT = $5 million] = 0.2; P[EBIT = $15 million] = 0.6; and P[EBIT = $25 million] = 0.2. Under the assumptions of part e, what are (1) expected EPS and σ_{EPS} and (2) expected TIE and σ_{TIE}, assuming an increase in book value of debt to $70 million?

16–6
SUBJECTIVE ANALYSIS

You have been hired as a financial consultant by two firms, Alpha Industries (Firm A) and Zed Corporation (Firm Z). Firm A is in the fast-growing microcomputer retail sales industry, while Firm Z manufactures office equipment such as pencil sharpeners, staplers, and tape dispensers. Your task is to recommend the optimal capital structure for the two firms. Discuss the factors that would influence your decision, and specifically how each of these factors apply to each firm. Here are some additional points about the two firms:

(1) Firm A generally leases its stores, while Firm Z purchases its plants.

(2) Firm A's stock is widely held, while the family of Firm Z's founder holds 40 percent of its stock.

(3) Firm Z has a significant amount of accelerated depreciation expense each year, while Firm A has almost none.

(4) Firm A has demonstrated high growth and profitability over the last few years. On the other hand, Firm Z's growth has averaged a modest 5 percent per year, and its profit margins and ROEs have been unspectacular.

16–7 *OPTIMAL CAPITAL STRUCTURE WITH HAMADA*

Beckman Engineering and Associates (BEA) is considering a change in its capital structure. BEA currently has $20 million in debt carrying a rate of 8 percent, and its stock price is $40 per share with 1 million shares outstanding. BEA's book value of equity is also equal to $40 per share. BEA is a zero growth firm and pays out all of its earnings as dividends. EBIT is $8,333,000, and BEA faces a 40 percent federal-plus-state tax rate. The market risk premium is 4 percent, and the risk free rate is 6 percent. BEA is considering increasing its debt level to a total of either $30 million, $40 million, or $50 million and repurchasing shares with the extra money that it borrows. BEA will have to retire the old debt in order to issue new debt, and the rate on the new debt will be 8.5 percent if the debt is $30 million, 9.5 percent if the debt is $40 million, or 11.2 percent if the debt is $50 million.

a. What is BEA's current cost of equity and its beta?

b. What is BEA's unlevered beta and unlevered cost of equity. Use market value D/E when unlevering.

c. What is BEA's new beta and cost of equity if it has $30 million in debt? $40 million in debt? $50 million in debt? Use book value D/E when re-levering.

d. What is BEA's total value of the firm under each of the three debt scenarios? Which level of debt should BEA have?

16–8 *WACC AND OPTIMAL CAPITAL STRUCTURE*

Elliott Athletics is trying to determine its optimal capital structure, which now consists of only debt and common equity. The firm does not currently use preferred stock in its capital structure, and it does not plan to do so in the future. To estimate how much its debt would cost at different debt levels, the company's treasury staff has consulted with investment bankers and, on the basis of those discussions, has created the following table:

Debt-to-Assets Ratio (w_d)	Equity-to-Assets Ratio (w_c)	Debt-to-Equity Ratio (D/E)	Bond Rating	Before-Tax Cost of Debt (k_d)
0.0	1.0	0.00	A	7.0%
0.2	0.8	0.25	BBB	8.0
0.4	0.6	0.67	BB	10.0
0.6	0.4	1.50	C	12.0
0.8	0.2	4.00	D	15.0

Elliott uses the CAPM to estimate its cost of common equity, k_s. The company estimates that the risk-free rate is 5 percent, the market risk premium is 6 percent, and its tax rate is 40 percent. Elliott estimates that if it had no debt, its "unlevered" beta, b_U, would be 1.2. Based on this information, what is the firm's optimal capital structure, and what would the weighted average cost of capital be at the optimal capital structure?

Spreadsheet Problems

16–9 *BUILD A MODEL: WACC AND OPTIMAL CAPITAL STRUCTURE*

Start with the partial model in the file ***Ch 16-9 Build a Model.xls*** from the textbook's CD-ROM. Rework Problem 16-8 using a spreadsheet model. After completing the problem as it appears, answer the following related questions.

a. Plot a graph of the after-tax cost of debt, the cost of equity, and the WACC versus (1) the debt/assets ratio and (2) the debt/equity ratio.

b. Would the optimal capital structure change if the unlevered beta changed? To answer this question, do a sensitivity analysis of WACC on b_U for different levels of b_U.

16–10
WHAT IF ANALYSIS: CAPITAL STRUCTURE ANALYSIS

Start with the model in the file ***Ch 16-10 What If Analysis.xls*** from the textbook's CD-ROM and answer the questions shown there.

Cyberproblem

The information related to this cyberproblem is likely to change over time, due to the release of new information and the ever-changing nature of the World Wide Web. Accordingly, we will periodically update the problem on the textbook's web site.

16–11
APPLYING THE HAMADA EQUATION

In Chapter 6, we introduced the concept of the Capital Asset Pricing Model (CAPM). The CAPM, as developed by Harry Markowitz and William Sharpe, contends that all stocks have an element of market risk. This market risk is materialized in the form of beta. We arrive at an asset's beta by running a linear regression of an asset's returns against market returns. However, we have never really addressed the matter of what drives beta.

In 1969, Robert Hamada published his paper, "Portfolio Analysis, Market Equilibrium, and Corporation Finance," wherein he combined the traditional CAPM and the Modigliani and Miller capital structure theory to create what is now called the "Hamada equation." The Hamada equation seeks to illustrate how increasing financial leverage increases a firm's risk and, by extension, the firm's beta.

In this cyberproblem, we use the Hamada equation to determine how useful it is when used in practice. Recall from the chapter that the Hamada equation is:

$$b = b_U\,[1 + (1 - T)(D/E)].$$

For this cyberproblem, you will need to access the textbook's web site, **http://www.harcourtcollege.com/finance/theory/student/resources/cyberprob/ch16.html**. Answer the questions given at the cyberproblem.

Mini Case

See ***Ch 16 Show.ppt*** and ***Ch 16 Mini Case.xls.***

Assume you have just been hired as business manager of PizzaPalace, a pizza restaurant located adjacent to campus. The company's EBIT was $500,000 last year, and since the university's enrollment is capped, EBIT is expected to remain constant (in real terms) over time. Since no expansion capital will be required, PizzaPalace plans to pay out all earnings as dividends. The management group owns about 50 percent of the stock, and the stock is traded in the over-the-counter market.

The firm is currently financed with all equity; it has 100,000 shares outstanding; and P_0 = $20 per share. When you took your MBA corporate finance course, your instructor stated that most firms' owners would be financially better off if the firms used some debt. When you suggested this to your new boss, he encouraged you to pursue the idea. As a first step, assume that you obtained from the firm's investment banker the following estimated costs of debt for the firm at different debt levels (in thousands of dollars):

Amount Borrowed	k_d
$ 0	—
250	10.0%
500	11.0
750	13.0
1,000	16.0

If the company were to recapitalize, debt would be issued, and the funds received would be used to repurchase stock. PizzaPalace is in the 40 percent federal-plus-state corporate tax bracket, the risk free rate is 6 percent, and the market risk premiums is 4 percent.

a. Now, to develop an example that can be presented to PizzaPalace's management to illustrate the effects of financial leverage, consider two hypothetical firms: Firm U, which uses no debt financing, and Firm L, which uses $10,000 of 12 percent debt. Both firms have $20,000 in assets, a 40 percent tax rate, and an expected EBIT of $3,000.
   (1) Construct partial income statements, which start with EBIT, for the two firms.
   (2) Now calculate ROE for both firms.
   (3) What does this example illustrate about the impact of financial leverage on ROE?
b. (1) What is business risk? What factors influence a firm's business risk?
   (2) What is operating leverage, and how does it affect a firm's business risk?
c. (1) What is meant by financial leverage and financial risk?
   (2) How does financial risk differ from business risk?
d. Now consider the fact that EBIT is not known with certainty, but rather has the following probability distribution:

Economic State	Probability	EBIT
Bad	0.25	$2,000
Average	0.50	3,000
Good	0.25	4,000

   Redo the part a analysis for Firms U and L, but add basic earning power (BEP), return on investment (ROI) [defined as (Net income + Interest)/(Debt + Equity)], and the times-interest-earned (TIE) ratio to the outcome measures. Find the values for each firm in each state of the economy, and then calculate the expected values. Finally, calculate the standard deviation and coefficient of variation of ROE. What does this example illustrate about the effect of debt financing on risk and return?
e. How are financial and business risk measured in a stand-alone risk framework?
f. What does capital structure theory attempt to do? What lessons can be learned from capital structure theory?
g. With the above points in mind, now consider the optimal capital structure for PizzaPalace.
   (1) What valuation equations can you use in the analysis?
   (2) Could either the MM or the Miller capital structure theories be applied directly in this analysis, and if you presented an analysis based on these theories, how do you think the owners would respond?
h. (1) Describe briefly, without using any numbers, the sequence of events that would take place if PizzaPalace does recapitalize.
   (2) What would be the new stock price if PizzaPalace recapitalized and used these amounts of debt: $250,000; $500,000; $750,000?
   (3) How many shares would remain outstanding after recapitalization under each debt scenario?
   (4) Considering only the levels of debt discussed, what is PizzaPalace's optimal capital structure?
i. It is also useful to determine the effect of any proposed recapitalization on EPS. Calculate the EPS at debt levels of $0, $250,000, $500,000, and $750,000, assuming that the firm begins at zero debt and recapitalizes to each level in a single step. Is EPS maximized at the same level that maximizes stock price?
j. Calculate the firm's WACC at each debt level. What is the relationship between the WACC and the stock price?
k. Suppose you discovered that PizzaPalace had more business risk than you originally estimated. Describe how this would affect the analysis. What if the firm had less business risk than originally estimated?
l. Is it possible to do an analysis similar to the PizzaPalace analysis for most firms? Why or why not? What type of analysis do you think a firm should actually use to help set its optimal, or target, capital structure? What other factors should managers consider when setting the target capital structure?

Selected Additional References and Cases

Chapter 17 provides references that focus on the theory of capital structure; the references listed here are oriented more toward applications than theory.

Donaldson's work on the setting of debt targets is old but still relevant:

Donaldson, Gordon, "New Framework for Corporate Debt Capacity," *Harvard Business Review*, March–April 1962, 117–131.

———, "Strategy for Financial Emergencies," *Harvard Business Review*, November–December 1969, 67–79.

For an article on signaling, see

Baskin, Jonathon, "An Empirical Investigation of the Pecking Order Hypothesis," *Financial Management*, Spring 1989, 26–35.

Definitive references on the empirical relationships between capital structure and (1) the cost of debt, (2) the cost of equity, (3) earnings, and (4) the price of a firm's stock are virtually nonexistent—statistical problems make the precise estimation of these relationships extraordinarily difficult, if not impossible. One good way to get a feel for the issues involved is to obtain a set of the cost of capital testimonies filed in a major utility rate case—such testimony is available from state public utility commissions, the Federal Communications Commission, the Federal Energy Regulatory Commission, and utility companies themselves. For an academic discussion of the issues, see

Caks, John, "Corporate Debt Decisions: A New Analytical Framework," *Journal of Finance*, December 1978, 1297–1315.

Gordon, Myron J., *The Cost of Capital to a Public Utility* (East Lansing, MI: Division of Research, Graduate School of Business Administration, Michigan State University, 1974).

Hamada, Robert S., "The Effect of the Firm's Capital Structure on the Systematic Risk of Common Stocks," *Journal of Finance*, May 1972, 435–452.

Masulis, Ronald W., "The Impact of Capital Structure Change on Firm Value: Some Estimates," *Journal of Finance*, March 1983, 107–126.

Piper, Thomas R., and Wolf A. Weinhold, "How Much Debt Is Right for Your Company?" *Harvard Business Review*, July–August 1982, 106–114.

Shalit, Sol S., "On the Mathematics of Financial Leverage," *Financial Management*, Spring 1975, 57–66.

Shiller, Robert J., and Franco Modigliani, "Coupon and Tax Effects on New and Seasoned Bond Yields and the Measurement of the Cost of Debt Capital," *Journal of Financial Economics*, September 1979, 297–318.

For some insights into how practicing financial managers view the capital structure decision, see

Kamath, Ravindra R., "Long-Term Financing Decisions: Views and Practices of Financial Managers of NYSE Firms," *Financial Review*, May 1997, 331–356.

Norton, Edgar, "Factors Affecting Capital Structure Decisions," *Financial Review*, August 1991, 431–446.

Pinegar, J. Michael, and Lisa Wilbricht, "What Managers Think of Capital Structure Theory: A Survey," *Financial Management*, Winter 1989, 82–91.

Scott, David F., and Dana J. Johnson, "Financing Policies and Practices in Large Corporations," *Financial Management*, Summer 1982, 51–59.

To learn more about the link between market risk and operating and financial leverage, see

Callahan, Carolyn M., and Rosanne M. Mohr, "The Determinants of Systematic Risk: A Synthesis," *The Financial Review*, May 1989, 157–181.

Gahlon, James M., and James A. Gentry, "On the Relationship between Systematic Risk and the Degrees of Operating and Financial Leverage," *Financial Management*, Summer 1982, 15–23.

Prezas, Alexandros P., "Effects of Debt on the Degrees of Operating and Financial Leverage," *Financial Management*, Summer 1987, 39–44.

Here are some additional articles that relate to this chapter:

Easterwood, John C., and Palani-Rajan Kadapakkam, "The Role of Private and Public Debt in Corporate Capital Structures," *Financial Management*, Autumn 1991, 49–57.

Garvey, Gerald T., "Leveraging the Underinvestment Problem: How High Debt and Management Shareholdings Solve the Agency Costs of Free Cash Flow," *Journal of Financial Research*, Summer 1992, 149–166.

Harris, Milton, and Artur Raviv, "Capital Structure and the Informational Role of Debt," *Journal of Finance*, June 1990, 321–349.

Israel, Ronen, "Capital Structure and the Market for Corporate Control: The Defensive Role of Debt Financing," *Journal of Finance*, September 1991, 1391–1409.

See the following three articles for additional insights into the relationship between industry characteristics and financial leverage:

Bowen, Robert M., Lane A. Daley, and Charles C. Huber, Jr., "Evidence on the Existence and Determinants of Inter-Industry Differences in Leverage," *Financial Management*, Winter 1982, 10–20.

Long, Michael, and Ileen Malitz, "The Investment-Financing Nexus: Some Empirical Evidence," *Midland Corporate Finance Journal*, Fall 1985, 53–59.

Scott, David F., Jr., and John D. Martin, "Industry Influence on Financial Structure," *Financial Management*, Spring 1975, 67–73.

For a discussion of the international implications of capital structure, see

Rutterford, Janette, "An International Perspective on the Capital Structure Puzzle," *Midland Corporate Finance Journal*, Fall 1985, 60–72.

The Winter 1995, Winter 1996, and Spring 1997 issues of the Journal of Applied Corporate Finance *all contain featured articles pertaining to the capital structure decision.*

The Dryden Press Cases in Financial Management: Dryden Request *series contains many of the concepts we present in Chapters 16 and 17.*

Case 9, "Home Security Systems, Inc.," Case 10, "Kleen Kar, Inc.," Case 10A, "Mountain Springs, Inc.," and Case 10B, "Greta Cosmetics, Inc.," which present a situation similar to the Strasburg example in the text.

17

Capital Structure Decisions: Extensions[1]

At a recent meeting of the Financial Management Association, a panel session focused on how firms actually set their target capital structures. The participants included financial managers from Hershey Foods, Verizon, EG&G (a high-tech firm), and a number of other firms in various industries. Although there were minor differences in philosophy and procedures among the companies, several themes emerged.

First, in practice it is difficult to specify an optimal capital structure—indeed, managers even feel uncomfortable about specifying an optimal capital structure range. Thus, financial managers worry primarily about whether their firms are using too little or too much debt, not about the precise optimal amount of debt. Second, even if a firm's actual capital structure varies widely from the theoretical optimum, this might not have much effect on its stock price. Thus, financial managers believe that capital structure decisions are secondary in importance to operating decisions, especially those relating to capital budgeting and the strategic direction of the firm.

In general, financial managers focus more on identifying a "prudent" level of debt than on setting a precise optimal level. A prudent level is defined as one that captures most of the benefits of debt yet (1) keeps financial risk at a manageable level, (2) ensures future financing flexibility, and (3) allows the firm to maintain a desirable credit rating. Thus, a prudent level of debt will protect the company against financial distress under all but the worst economic scenarios, and it will ensure access to money and capital markets under most conditions.

As you read this chapter, think about how you would make capital structure decisions if you had that responsibility. At the same time, don't forget the very important message from the FMA panel session: Establishing the right capital structure is an imprecise process at best, and it should be based on both informed judgment and quantitative analyses.

[1]This chapter may be omitted without loss of continuity

Chapter 16 presented some basic material on capital structure, including a brief introduction to capital structure theory. We saw that debt concentrates a firm's business risk on its stockholders, but debt also increases the expected return on equity. We also saw that there is some optimal level of debt that maximizes a company's stock price, and we illustrated this concept with a simple model. Now we go into more detail on capital structure theory. This will give you a deeper understanding of the benefits and costs associated with debt financing.

Capital Structure Theory: The Modigliani-Miller Models

CD

The textbook's CD-ROM contains an *Excel* file that will guide you through the chapter's calculations. The file for this chapter is ***Ch 17 Tool Kit.xls,*** and we encourage you to open the file and follow along as you read the chapter.

Until 1958, capital structure theory consisted of loose assertions about investor behavior rather than carefully constructed models that could be tested by formal statistical analysis. In what has been called the most influential set of financial papers ever published, Franco Modigliani and Merton Miller (MM) addressed capital structure in a rigorous, scientific fashion, and they set off a chain of research that continues to this day.[2]

Assumptions

As we explain in this chapter, MM employed the concept of arbitrage to develop their theory. Arbitrage occurs if two similar assets—in this case, leveraged and unleveraged stocks—sell at different prices. Arbitrageurs will buy the undervalued stock and simultaneously sell the overvalued stock, earning a profit in the process, and this will continue until the prices of the two assets are equal. For arbitrage to work, the assets must be equivalent, or nearly so. MM show that, under their assumptions, leveraged and unleveraged stocks are sufficiently similar for the arbitrage process to operate.

No one, not even MM, believe that their assumptions are sufficiently correct to cause their models to hold exactly in the real world. However, their models do show how money can be made through arbitrage if one can find ways around problems with the assumptions. Here are the initial MM assumptions. Note that some of them were later relaxed:

1. There are no personal or corporate taxes.
2. Business risk can be measured by σ_{EBIT}, and firms with the same degree of business risk are said to be in a **homogeneous risk class.**
3. All present and prospective investors have identical estimates of each firm's future EBIT; that is, investors have **homogeneous expectations** about expected future corporate earnings and the riskiness of those earnings.
4. Stocks and bonds are traded in **perfect capital markets.** This assumption implies, among other things, (a) that there are no brokerage costs and (b) that investors (both individuals and institutions) can borrow at the same rate as corporations.

[2]See Franco Modigliani and Merton H. Miller, "The Cost of Capital, Corporation Finance and the Theory of Investment," *American Economic Review*, June 1958, 261–297; "The Cost of Capital, Corporation Finance and the Theory of Investment: Reply," *American Economic Review*, September 1958, 655–669; "Taxes and the Cost of Capital: A Correction," *American Economic Review*, June 1963, 433–443; and "Reply," *American Economic Review*, June 1965, 524–527. In a survey of Financial Management Association members, the original MM article was judged to have had the greatest impact on the field of finance of any work ever published. See Philip L. Cooley and J. Louis Heck, "Significant Contributions to Finance Literature," *Financial Management*, Tenth Anniversary Issue 1981, 23–33. Note that both Modigliani and Miller won Nobel prizes—Modigliani in 1985 and Miller in 1990.

5. The debt of firms and investors is riskless, so the interest rate on all debt is the risk-free rate. Further, this situation holds regardless of how much debt a firm (or individual) uses.
6. All cash flows are perpetuities; that is, all firms expect zero growth, hence have an "expectationally constant" EBIT, and all bonds are perpetuities. "Expectationally constant" means that the best guess is that EBIT will be constant, but after the fact the realized level could be different from the expected level.

MM without Taxes

MM first analyzed leverage under the assumption that there are no corporate or personal income taxes. On the basis of their assumptions, they stated and algebraically proved two propositions:[3]

Proposition I The value of any firm is established by capitalizing its expected net operating income (EBIT) at a constant rate (k_{sU}) which is based on the firm's risk class:

$$V_L = V_U = \frac{\text{EBIT}}{\text{WACC}} = \frac{\text{EBIT}}{k_{sU}}. \quad \textbf{(17-1)}$$

Here the subscript L designates a levered firm and U designates an unlevered firm. Both firms are assumed to be in the same business risk class, and k_{sU} is the required rate of return for an unlevered, or all-equity, firm. (For our purposes, it is easiest to think in terms of a single firm that has the option of financing either with all equity or with some combination of debt and equity.)

Because V as established by Equation 17-1 is a constant, *then under the MM model, when there are no taxes, the value of the firm is independent of its leverage.* As we shall see, this also implies that

1. The weighted average cost of capital to the firm is completely independent of its capital structure.
2. The WACC for the firm, regardless of the amount of debt it uses, is equal to the cost of equity it would have if it used no debt.

Proposition II The cost of equity to a levered firm, k_{sL}, is equal to (1) the cost of equity to an unlevered firm in the same risk class, k_{sU}, plus (2) a risk premium whose size depends on both the differential between an unlevered firm's costs of debt and equity and the amount of debt used:

$$k_{sL} = k_{sU} + \text{Risk premium} = k_{sU} + (k_{sU} - k_d)(D/S). \quad \textbf{(17-2)}$$

Here D = market value of the firm's debt, S = market value of the firm's equity, and k_d = constant cost of debt. *Equation 17-2 states that as the firm's use of debt increases, its cost of equity also rises, and in a mathematically precise manner.*

Taken together, the two MM propositions imply that the inclusion of more debt in the capital structure will not increase the value of the firm, because the benefits of cheaper debt will be exactly offset by an increase in the riskiness, hence in the cost, of its equity. *Thus, MM argue that in a world without taxes, both the value of a firm and its WACC would be unaffected by its capital structure.*

---

[3]MM actually stated and proved three propositions, but the third one is not material to our discussion here.

MM's Arbitrage Proof

MM used an *arbitrage proof* to support their propositions.[4] They showed that, under their assumptions, if two companies differed only (1) in the way they are financed and (2) in their total market values, then investors would sell shares of the higher-valued firm, buy those of the lower-valued firm, and continue this process until the companies had exactly the same market value. To illustrate, assume that two firms, L and U, are identical in all important respects except that Firm L has \$4,000,000 of 7.5 percent debt while Firm U uses only equity. Both firms have EBIT = \$900,000, and σ_{EBIT} is the same for both firms, so they are in the same business risk class.

MM assumed that all firms are in a zero-growth situation; that is, EBIT is expected to remain constant, and all earnings are paid out as dividends. Under this assumption, the total market value of a firm's common stock, S, is the present value of a perpetuity, which is found as follows:

$$S = \frac{\text{Dividends}}{k_s} = \frac{\text{Net income}}{k_s} = \frac{(\text{EBIT} - k_dD)(1 - T)}{k_s}. \quad \textbf{(17-3)}$$

Equation 17-3 is merely the value of a perpetuity whose numerator is the net income available to common stockholders, which is all paid out as dividends, and whose denominator is the cost of common equity. In MM's zero-tax world, the tax rate, T, is zero, so Equation 17-3 becomes simply $(\text{EBIT} - k_dD)/k_s$.

Assume that initially, *before any arbitrage occurs*, both firms have the same equity capitalization rate: $k_{sU} = k_{sL} = 10\%$. Under this condition, according to Equation 17-3, the following situation would exist:

Firm U:

$$\text{Value of Firm U's stock} = S_U = \frac{\text{EBIT} - k_dD}{k_{sU}} = \frac{\$900{,}000 - \$0}{0.10} = \$9{,}000{,}000.$$

$$\text{Total market value of Firm U} = V_U = D_U + S_U = \$0 + \$9{,}000{,}000 = \$9{,}000{,}000.$$

Firm L:

$$\text{Value of Firm L's stock} = S_L = \frac{\text{EBIT} - k_dD}{k_{sL}}$$

$$= \frac{\$900{,}000 - 0.075(\$4{,}000{,}000)}{0.10} = \frac{\$600{,}000}{0.10} = \$6{,}000{,}000.$$

$$\text{Total market value of Firm L} = V_L = D_L + S_L = \$4{,}000{,}000 + \$6{,}000{,}000 = \$10{,}000{,}000.$$

Thus before arbitrage, and assuming that $k_{sU} = k_{sL}$ (which implies that capital structure has no effect on the cost of equity), the value of the levered Firm L exceeds that of unlevered Firm U.

MM argued that this is a disequilibrium situation that cannot persist. To see why, suppose you owned 10 percent of L's stock, so the market value of your investment was 0.10(\$6,000,000) = \$600,000. According to MM, you could increase your income without increasing your exposure to risk. For example, suppose you (1) sold your stock in L for \$600,000, (2) borrowed an amount equal to 10 percent of L's debt (\$400,000),

[4]By *arbitrage* we mean the simultaneous buying and selling of essentially identical assets that sell at different prices. The buying increases the price of the undervalued asset, and the selling decreases the price of the overvalued asset. Arbitrage operations will continue until prices have been adjusted to the point where the arbitrageur can no longer earn a profit, at which point the markets are in equilibrium. In the absence of transaction costs, equilibrium requires that the prices of the two assets be equal.

and then (3) bought 10 percent of U's stock for $900,000. Note that you would receive $1,000,000 from the sale of your 10 percent of L's stock plus your borrowing, and you would be spending only $900,000 on U's stock, so you would have an extra $100,000, which you could invest in riskless debt to yield 7.5 percent, or $7,500 annually.

Now consider your income positions:

Old Income:	10% of L's $600,000 equity income		$60,000
New Income:	10% of U's $900,000 equity income	$90,000	
	Less 7.5% interest on $400,000 loan	(30,000)	$60,000
	Plus 7.5% interest on extra $100,000		7,500
	Total new income		$67,500

Thus, your net income from common stock would be exactly the same as before, $60,000, but you would have $100,000 left over for investment in riskless debt, which would increase your income by $7,500. Therefore, the total return on your $600,000 net worth would rise to $67,500. Further, your risk, according to MM, would be the same as before, because you would have simply substituted $400,000 of "homemade" leverage for your 10 percent share of Firm L's $4 million of corporate leverage. Thus, neither your "effective" debt nor your risk would have changed. Therefore, you would have increased your income without raising your risk, which is obviously a desirable thing to do.

MM argued that this arbitrage process would actually occur, with sales of L's stock driving its price down, and purchases of U's stock driving its price up, until the market values of the two firms were equal. Until this equality was established, gains could be obtained by switching from one stock to the other, hence the profit motive would force the equality to be reached. When equilibrium is established, the values of Firms L and U, and their weighted average costs of capital, would be equal. Thus, according to Modigliani and Miller, both a firm's value and its WACC must be independent of capital structure.

Note that each of the assumptions listed at the beginning of this section is necessary for the arbitrage proof to work. For example, if the companies do not have identical business risk, or if transactions costs are significant, then the arbitrage process cannot be invoked. We will discuss further implications of the assumptions later in the chapter.

Arbitrage with Short Sales

Even if you did not own any stock in L, you still could reap benefits if U and L do not have the same total market value. Now, your first step would be to sell short $600,000 of stock in L. To do this, your broker would let you borrow stock in L from one of the broker's other clients. Your broker would then sell the stock for you and give you the proceeds, or $600,000 in cash. You would supplement this $600,000 by borrowing $400,000. With the $1 million total, you would buy 10 percent of the stock in U for $900,000, and have $100,000 remaining.

Your position consists of $100,000 in cash and two portfolios. The first portfolio contains $900,000 of stock in U, and it generates $90,000 in income. Because you own the stock, we'll call it the "long" portfolio. The other portfolio consists of $600,000 of stock in L and $400,000 in debt. The value of this portfolio is $1 million, and it generates $60,000 in dividends and $30,000 in interest. However, you do not own this second portfolio—you "owe" it. Since you borrowed the $400,000, you owe the $30,000 in interest. And since you borrowed the stock in L, you "owe the stock" to the broker from whom it was borrowed. Therefore, you must pay your broker the \$60,000 of dividends paid by L, which the broker would then pass on to the client from whom the stock was borrowed. So, your net cash flow from the second portfolio is a negative \$90,000. Because you "owe" this portfolio, we'll call it the "short" portfolio.

Where are you going to get the \$90,000 that you must pay on the short portfolio? The good news is that this is exactly the amount of cash flow generated by the long portfolio that you own. The cash flows generated by each portfolio are the same; in other words, the short portfolio "replicates" the long portfolio.

Here is the bottom line. You started out with no money of your own. By selling L short, borrowing \$400,000, and purchasing stock in U, you ended up with \$100,000 in cash plus the two portfolios. The portfolios mirror one another, so their net cash flow is zero. This is perfect arbitrage: You invest none of your own money, you have no risk, you have no future negative cash flows, but you end up with cash in your pocket.

Not surprising, many traders would want to do this. The selling pressure on L would cause its price to fall, and the buying pressure on U would cause its price to rise, until the two companies' values were equal. To put it another way, *if the long and short replicating portfolios have the same cash flows, then they must have the same value.*

This is one of the most important ideas in modern finance. Not only does it give us insights into capital structure, but it is the fundamental building block underlying the Arbitrage Pricing Theory (APT) of stock returns in Chapter 7, the valuation of financial and real options in Chapter 15, and the valuation of derivatives as discussed in Chapter 24. In fact, without this idea, the options and derivatives markets we have today would not exist.

MM with Corporate Taxes

MM's original work, published in 1958, assumed zero taxes. In 1963, they published a second article that incorporated corporate taxes. With corporate income taxes, they concluded that leverage will increase a firm's value. This occurs because interest is a tax-deductible expense, hence more of a leveraged firm's operating income flows through to investors.

Later in this chapter we present a proof of the propositions when personal taxes as well as corporate taxes are allowed. Here are the MM propositions when corporations are subject to income taxes but there are no personal taxes:

Proposition I The value of a levered firm is equal to the value of an unlevered firm in the same risk class (V_U) *plus* the gain from leverage. The gain from leverage is the value of the tax savings, found as the product of the corporate tax rate (T) times the amount of debt the firm uses (D):

$$V_L = V_U + TD. \tag{17-1a}$$

The important point here is that when corporate taxes are introduced, the value of the levered firm exceeds that of the unlevered firm by the amount TD. Since the gain from leverage increases as debt increases, in theory a firm's value is maximized at 100 percent debt financing.

Because all cash flows are assumed to be perpetuities, the value of the unlevered firm can be found by using Equation 17-4. With zero debt (D = \$0), the value of the firm is its equity value:

$$S = V_U = \frac{EBIT(1 - T)}{k_{sU}}. \tag{17-4}$$

Proposition II The cost of equity to a levered firm is equal to (1) the cost of equity to an unlevered firm in the same risk class plus (2) a risk premium whose size depends on the differential between the costs of equity and debt to an unlevered firm, the amount of financial leverage used, and the corporate tax rate:

$$k_{sL} = k_{sU} + (k_{sU} - k_d)(1 - T)(D/S). \quad \textbf{(17-2a)}$$

Note that Equation 17-2a is identical to the corresponding without-tax equation, 17-2, except for the term (1 − T) in 17-2a. Because (1 − T) is less than 1, corporate taxes cause the cost of equity to rise less rapidly with leverage than it would in the absence of taxes. Proposition II, coupled with the fact that taxes reduce the effective cost of debt, is what produces the Proposition I result, namely, that the firm's value increases as its leverage increases.

Illustration of the MM Models

To illustrate the MM models, assume that the following data and conditions hold for Fredrickson Water Company, an old, established firm that supplies water to residential customers in several no-growth upstate New York communities:

1. Fredrickson currently has no debt; it is an all-equity company.
2. Expected EBIT = \$2,400,000. EBIT is not expected to increase over time, so Fredrickson is in a no-growth situation.
3. Needing no new capital, Fredrickson pays out all of its income as dividends.
4. If Fredrickson begins to use debt, it can borrow at a rate k_d = 8%. This borrowing rate is constant—it does not increase regardless of the amount of debt used. Any money raised by selling debt would be used to repurchase common stock, *so Fredrickson's assets would remain constant.*
5. The business risk inherent in Fredrickson's assets, and thus in its EBIT, is such that its required rate of return, k_{sU}, is 12 percent if no debt is used.

With Zero Taxes To begin, assume that there are no taxes, so T = 0%. At any level of debt, Proposition I (Equation 17-1) can be used to find Fredrickson's value in an MM world, \$20 million:

$$V_L = V_U = \frac{\text{EBIT}}{k_{sU}} = \frac{\$2.4 \text{ million}}{0.12} = \$20.0 \text{ million.}$$

If Fredrickson uses \$10 million of debt, its stock value must be \$10 million:

$$S = V - D = \$20 \text{ million} - \$10 \text{ million} = \$10 \text{ million.}$$

We can also find Fredrickson's cost of equity, k_{sL}, and its WACC at a debt level of \$10 million. First, we use Proposition II (Equation 17-2) to find k_{sL}, Fredrickson's leveraged cost of equity:

$$\begin{aligned} k_{sL} &= k_{sU} + (k_{sU} - k_d)(D/S) \\ &= 12\% + (12\% - 8\%)(\$10 \text{ million}/\$10 \text{ million}) \\ &= 12\% + 4.0\% = 16.0\%. \end{aligned}$$

Now we can find the company's weighted average cost of capital:

$$\begin{aligned} \text{WACC} &= (D/V)(k_d)(1 - T) + (S/V)k_s \\ &= (\$10/\$20)(8\%)(1.0) + (\$10/\$20)(16.0\%) = 12.0\%. \end{aligned}$$

Fredrickson's value and cost of capital based on the MM model without taxes at various debt levels are shown in Panel a on the left side of Figure 17-1. Here we see

FIGURE 17-1 Effects of Leverage: MM Models (Millions of Dollars)

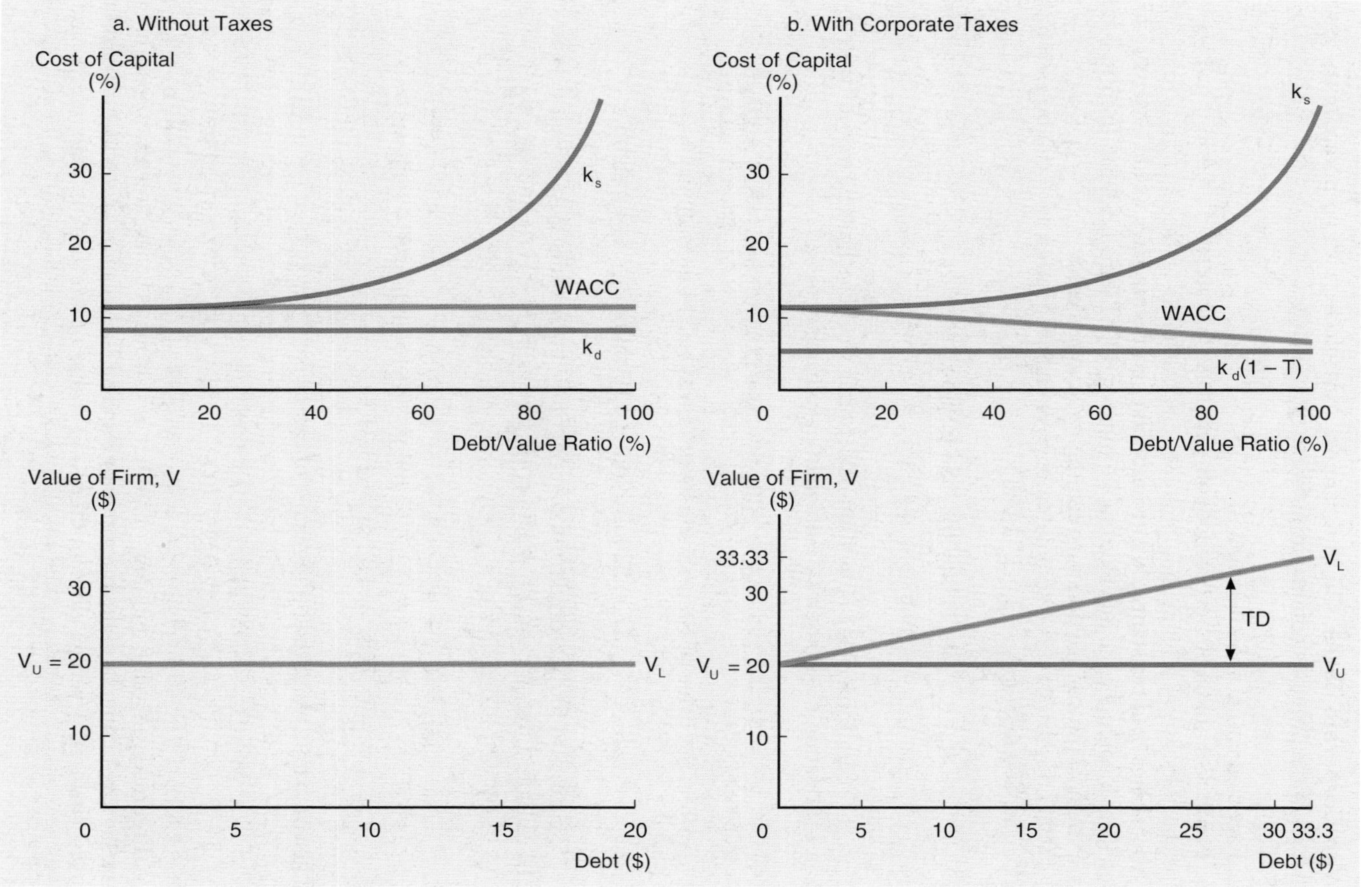

MM without Taxes

D	V	S	D/V	k_d	k_s	WACC
$0	$20.00	$20.00	0.00%	8.0%	12.00%	12.00%
5	20.00	15.00	25.00	8.0	13.33	12.00
10	20.00	10.00	50.00	8.0	16.00	12.00
15	20.00	5.00	75.00	8.0	24.00	12.00
20	20.00	0.00	100.00	12.0	—	12.00

MM with Corporate Taxes

D	V	S	D/V	k_d	k_s	WACC
$ 0	$20.00	$20.00	0.00%	8.0%	12.00%	12.00%
5	22.00	17.00	22.73	8.0	12.71	10.91
10	24.00	14.00	41.67	8.0	13.71	10.00
15	26.00	11.00	57.69	8.0	15.27	9.23
20	28.00	8.00	71.43	8.0	18.00	8.57
25	30.00	5.00	83.33	8.0	24.00	8.00
30	32.00	2.00	93.75	8.0	48.00	7.50
33.33	33.33	0.00	100.00	12.0	—	12.00

that in an MM world without taxes, financial leverage simply does not matter: The value of the firm, and its overall cost of capital, are independent of the amount of debt.

With Corporate Taxes To illustrate the MM model with corporate taxes, assume that all of the previous conditions hold except these two:

1. Expected EBIT = \$4,000,000.[5]
2. Fredrickson has a 40 percent federal-plus-state tax rate, so T = 40%.

Other things held constant, the introduction of corporate taxes would lower Fredrickson's net income, hence its value, so we increased EBIT from \$2.4 million to \$4 million to make the comparison between the two models easier.

When Fredrickson has zero debt but pays taxes, Equation 17-4 can be used to find its value, \$20 million:

$$V_U = \frac{EBIT(1 - T)}{k_{sU}} = \frac{\$4 \text{ million } (0.6)}{0.12} = \$20.0 \text{ million.}$$

Now if Fredrickson uses \$10 million of debt in a world with taxes, we see by Proposition I (Equation 17-1a) that its total market value rises to \$24 million:

$$V_L = V_U + TD = \$20 \text{ million} + 0.4(\$10 \text{ million}) = \$24 \text{ million.}$$

Therefore, the value of Fredrickson's stock must be \$14 million:

$$S = V - D = \$24 \text{ million} - \$10 \text{ million} = \$14 \text{ million.}$$

We can also find Fredrickson's cost of equity, k_{sL}, and its WACC at a debt level of \$10 million. First, we use Proposition II (Equation 17-2a) to find k_{sL}, the leveraged cost of equity:

$$\begin{aligned} k_{sL} &= k_{sU} + (k_{sU} - k_d)(1 - T)(D/S) \\ &= 12\% + (12\% - 8\%)(0.6)(\$10 \text{ million}/\$14 \text{ million}) \\ &= 12\% + 1.71\% = 13.71\%. \end{aligned}$$

The company's weighted average cost of capital is 10 percent:

$$\begin{aligned} WACC &= (D/V)(k_d)(1 - T) + (S/V)k_s \\ &= (\$10/\$24)(8\%)(0.6) + (\$14/\$24)(13.71\%) = 10.0\%. \end{aligned}$$

Fredrickson's value and cost of capital at various debt levels with corporate taxes are shown in Panel b on the right side of Figure 17-1. In an MM world with corporate taxes, financial leverage does matter: The value of the firm is maximized, and its

[5] If we had left Fredrickson's EBIT at \$2.4 million, the introduction of corporate taxes would have reduced the firm's value from \$20 million to \$12 million:

$$V_U = \frac{EBIT(1 - T)}{k_{sU}} = \frac{\$2.4 \text{ million } (0.6)}{0.12} = \$12.0 \text{ million.}$$

Corporate taxes reduce the amount of operating income available to investors in an unlevered firm by the factor (1 − T), so the value of the firm would be reduced by the same amount.

overall cost of capital is minimized, if it uses almost 100 percent debt financing. The increase in value is due solely to the tax deductibility of interest payments, which lowers both the cost of debt and the equity risk premium by (1 − T).[6]

To conclude this section, compare the "Without Taxes" and "With Corporate Taxes" sections of Figure 17-1. Without taxes, both WACC and the firm's value (V) are constant. With corporate taxes, WACC declines and V rises as more and more debt is used, so the optimal capital structure, under MM with corporate taxes, is 100 percent debt.

Self-Test Questions

Is there an optimal capital structure under the MM zero-tax model?

What is the optimal capital structure under the MM model with corporate taxes?

How does the Proposition I equation differ in the two models?

How does the Proposition II equation differ in the two models?

Why do taxes result in a "gain from leverage" in the MM model with corporate taxes?

The Hamada Model: Introducing Market Risk

In our discussion of the optimal capital structure in Chapter 16 we used the Hamada equation to calculate the **market risk** of a levered company. In this section we examine this model in more detail.

Robert Hamada combined the Capital Asset Pricing Model (CAPM) presented in Chapter 6 with the MM after-tax model to obtain this expression for k_{sL}, the cost of equity to a leveraged firm:[7]

$$k_{sL} = \text{Risk-free rate} + \text{Business risk premium} + \text{Financial risk premium} \tag{17-5}$$
$$= k_{RF} + (k_M - k_{RF})b_U + (k_M - k_{RF})b_U(1 - T)(D/S).$$

Here b_U is the beta coefficient the firm would have if it used no financial leverage, and the other terms are as defined previously. In effect, Equation 17-5 partitions

[6]In the limiting case, where the firm used 100 percent debt financing, the bondholders would own the entire company; thus, they would have to bear all the business risk. (Up until this point, MM assume that the stockholders bear all the risk.) If the bondholders bear all the risk, then the capitalization rate on the debt should be equal to the equity capitalization rate at zero debt, $k_d = k_{sU} = 12\%$.

The income stream to the stockholders in the all-equity case was \$4,000,000(1 − T) = \$2,400,000, and the value of the firm was

$$V_U = \frac{\$2{,}400{,}00}{0.12} = \$20{,}000{,}000.$$

With all debt, the entire \$4,000,000 of EBIT would be used to pay interest charges—k_d would be 12 percent, so I = 0.12(Debt) = \$4,000,000. Taxes would be zero, and investors (bondholders) would get the entire \$4,000,000 of operating income; they would not have to share it with the government. Thus, at 100 percent debt, the value of the firm would be

$$V_L = \frac{\$4{,}000{,}000}{0.12} = \$33{,}333{,}333 = D.$$

There is, of course, a transition problem in all this—MM assume that $k_d = 8\%$ regardless of how much debt the firm has until debt reaches 100 percent, at which point k_d jumps to 12 percent, the cost of equity. As we shall see later in the chapter, k_d realistically rises as the use of financial leverage increases.

[7]See Robert S. Hamada, "Portfolio Analysis, Market Equilibrium, and Corporation Finance," *Journal of Finance*, March 1969, 13–31. Note that Thomas Conine and Maurry Tamarkin have extended Hamada's work to include risky debt. See "Divisional Cost of Capital Estimation: Adjusting for Leverage," *Financial Management*, Spring 1985, 54–58.

the required rate of return on a stock into three components: k_{RF}, the risk-free rate, which compensates shareholders for the time value of money; a premium for business risk as reflected by the term $(k_M - k_{RF})b_U$; and a premium for financial risk as reflected by the third term, $(k_M - k_{RF})b_U(1 - T)(D/S)$. If a firm has no financial leverage (D = \$0), then the financial risk premium term would be zero (the third term would drop out) and equity investors would be compensated only for business risk.

Note that Equation 17-5 uses D/S rather than the D/E that was used in Chapter 16. In practice, when calculating the value of a company with various levels of debt as we did in Chapter 16, the market value of the levered company for each level of debt is not known beforehand. That is what we were trying to calculate. So, in order to use Hamada's equation, practitioners frequently use the book value of equity, E, as an approximation to the market value, S. However, Hamada's derivation assumes that assets are reported at their market values rather than their book values, so the market value of the stock will be used in this discussion.

As we will see, the MM model with corporate taxes does not hold exactly, and we also know that the CAPM does not fully describe investor behavior. Therefore, the Hamada model as expressed in Equation 17-5 must be regarded as an approximation. Nevertheless, the Hamada model can provide financial managers with some useful insights. As an illustration, assume that Firm U, an unlevered company with $b_U = 1.5$ and \$100,000 of equity (S = \$100,000), is considering replacing \$20,000 of equity with debt. Assuming also that $k_{RF} = 10\%$, $k_M = 15\%$, and $T = 34\%$, then Firm U's current unlevered required rate of return on equity would be 17.5 percent:

$$\begin{aligned} k_{sU} &= 10\% + (15\% - 10\%)1.5 \\ &= 10\% + 7.5\% = 17.5\%. \end{aligned}$$

This shows that the business risk premium is 7.5 percentage points. If the firm were to add \$20,000 of debt to its capital structure, then its new value, according to MM, would be $V_L = V_U + TD = \$100,000 + 0.34(\$20,000) = \$106,800$, and its k_s, using Equation 17-5, would rise to 18.64 percent:

$$\begin{aligned} k_{sL} &= 10\% + (15\% - 10\%)1.5 + (15\% - 10\%)1.5(1 - 0.34)(\$20,000/\$86,800) \\ &= 10\% + 7.5\% + 1.14\% = 18.64\%. \end{aligned}$$

Thus, adding \$20,000 of debt to the capital structure would result in a financial risk premium on the stock of 1.14 percentage points, which would be added to the business risk premium of 7.5 percentage points.

Hamada also showed that Equation 17-5 can be used to derive another equation that analyzes the effect of financial leverage on beta. We know that the SML can be used to estimate a firm's required rate of return on equity:

$$\text{SML: } k_s = k_{RF} + (k_M - k_{RF})b.$$

Now, by equating the SML equation with Equation 17-5, we obtain:

$$\begin{aligned} k_{RF} + (k_M - k_{RF})b &= k_{RF} + (k_M - k_{RF})b_U + (k_M - k_{RF})b_U(1 - T)(D/S) \\ (k_M - k_{RF})b &= (k_M - k_{RF})b_U + (k_M - k_{RF})b_U(1 - T)(D/S) \qquad \textbf{(17-6)} \\ b &= b_U + b_U(1 - T)(D/S), \end{aligned}$$

or

$$b = b_U[1 + (1 - T)(D/S)]. \qquad \textbf{(17-6a)}$$

Thus, under the MM and CAPM assumptions, the equity beta of any firm is equal to the equity beta the firm would have if it used zero debt, adjusted upward by a factor that depends on (1) the corporate tax rate and (2) the amount of financial leverage employed.[8] Therefore, the stock's market risk, which is measured by b, depends on both the firm's business risk as measured by b_U and its financial risk as measured by $b - b_U = b_U(1 - T)(D/S)$.

To continue our illustration, if Firm U were to replace \$20,000 of equity with debt, its equity beta would increase from 1.5 to 1.728, according to Equation 17-6a:

$$\begin{aligned} b &= b_U[1 + (1 - T)(D/S)] \\ &= 1.5[1 + (1 - 0.34)(20{,}000/\$86{,}800)] \\ &= 1.5(1.152) = 1.728. \end{aligned}$$

We can confirm the Equation 17-5 value of $k_{sL} = 18.64\%$ by using $b = 1.728$ in the SML:

$$\begin{aligned} k_s &= k_{RF} + (k_M - k_{RF})b \\ &= 10\% + (15\% - 10\%)1.728 = 18.64\%. \end{aligned}$$

These relationships can be used to help estimate a company's or a division's cost of equity. In both instances, we proceed by obtaining betas for similar publicly traded firms and then "levering them up or down" to make them consistent with our own firm's (or division's) capital structure and tax rate. The result is an estimate of our firm's (or division's) equity beta, given (1) its business risk as measured by the equity betas of other firms in the same line of business and (2) its financial risk as measured by its own capital structure and tax rate.

Self-Test Questions

According to Hamada, the required rate of return on a stock consists of three elements. What are they?

How is business risk measured within a market risk framework?

How is financial risk measured within a market risk framework?

What is the relationship between levered and unlevered betas according to Hamada?

Capital Structure Theory: The Miller Model

Although MM included **corporate** taxes in the second version of their model, they did not extend the model to include **personal** taxes. However, in his presidential address to the American Finance Association, Merton Miller introduced a model designed to show how leverage affects firms' values when both personal and corporate taxes are taken into account.[9] To explain Miller's model, let us begin by defining T_c as the corporate tax rate, T_s as the personal tax rate on income from stocks, and T_d as the personal tax rate on income from debt. Note that stocks' returns come partly as dividends and partly as capital gains, so T_s is a weighted average of the effective tax rates on dividends and capital gains, while essentially all debt income comes from interest, which is effectively taxed at investors' top rates.

With personal taxes included, *and under the same set of assumptions used in the earlier MM models*, the value of an unlevered firm is found as follows:

$$V_U = \frac{EBIT(1 - T_c)(1 - T_s)}{k_{sU}}. \qquad \textbf{(17-7)}$$

[8]If a firm uses preferred stock, then Equation 17-6 becomes $b = b_U + b_U(P/S) + b_U(1 - T)(D/S)$, where P = market value of preferred stock. Here the unlevered beta is adjusted upward by the preferred stock as well as the debt.

[9]See Merton H. Miller, "Debt and Taxes," *Journal of Finance*, May 1977, 261–275.

The $(1 - T_s)$ term takes account of personal taxes. Therefore, the numerator shows how much of the firm's operating income is left after the unlevered firm pays corporate income taxes and its stockholders subsequently pay personal taxes on their equity income. Because the introduction of personal taxes lowers the income available to investors, personal taxes reduce the value of the unlevered firm, other things held constant.

Miller's results can be supported by an arbitrage proof similar to the one we presented earlier. However, the alternative proof shown below is easier to follow. To begin, we partition the levered firm's annual cash flows, CF_L, into those going to the stockholders and those going to the bondholders, after both corporate and personal taxes:

$$\begin{aligned} CF_L &= \text{Net CF to stockholders} + \text{Net CF to bondholders} \\ &= (EBIT - I)(1 - T_c)(1 - T_s) + I(1 - T_d). \end{aligned} \quad \textbf{(17-8)}$$

Here I is the annual interest payment. Equation 17-8 can be rearranged as follows:

$$CF_L = [EBIT(1 - T_c)(1 - T_s)] - [I(1 - T_c)(1 - T_s)] + [I(1 - T_d)]. \quad \textbf{(17-8a)}$$

The first term in Equation 17-8a is identical to the after-tax cash flow of an unlevered firm as shown in Equation 17-7, and its present value is found by discounting the perpetual cash flow by k_{sU}. The second and third terms, which reflect leverage, result from the cash flows associated with debt financing, which under the MM assumptions is assumed to be riskless. Their present values are obtained by discounting at the cost of debt, k_d. (Remember, these are all perpetual cash flows, so the basic perpetuity valuation model, $V = CF/k$, applies.) Combining the present values of the three terms, we obtain this value for the levered firm:

$$V_L = \frac{EBIT(1 - T_c)(1 - T_s)}{k_{sU}} - \frac{I(1 - T_c)(1 - T_s)}{k_d} + \frac{I(1 - T_d)}{k_d}. \quad \textbf{(17-9)}$$

The first term in Equation 17-9 is identical to V_U in Equation 17-7. Recognizing this, and when we consolidate the second two terms, we obtain this equation:

$$V_L = V_U + \frac{I(1 - T_d)}{k_d}\left[1 - \frac{(1 - T_c(1 - T_s)}{(1 - T_d)}\right]. \quad \textbf{(17-9a)}$$

Now recognize that the after-tax perpetual interest payment divided by the required rate of return on debt, $I(1\text{-}T_d)/k_d$, equals the market value of the debt, D. Substituting D into the preceding equation and rearranging, we obtain this expression, called the **Miller model:**

$$\text{Miller model: } V_L = V_U + \left[1 - \frac{(1 - T_c)(1 - T_s)}{(1 - T_d)}\right]D. \quad \textbf{(17-10)}$$

The Miller model provides an estimate of the value of a levered firm in a world with both corporate and personal taxes.

The Miller model has several important implications:

1. The term in brackets,

$$\left[1 - \frac{(1 - T_c)(1 - T_s)}{(1 - T_d)}\right],$$

when multiplied by D, represents the gain from leverage. The bracketed term thus replaces the corporate tax rate, T in the earlier MM model with corporate taxes, $V_L = V_U + TD$.

2. If we ignore all taxes, that is, if $T_c = T_s = T_d = 0$, then the bracketed term is zero, so in that case Equation 17-10 is the same as the original MM model without taxes.

3. If we ignore personal taxes, that is, if $T_s = T_d = 0$, then the bracketed term reduces to $[1 - (1 - T_c)] = T_c$, so Equation 17-10 is the same as the MM model with corporate taxes.
4. If the effective personal tax rates on stock and bond incomes were equal, that is, if $T_s = T_d$, then $(1 - T_s)$ and $(1 - T_d)$ would cancel, and the bracketed term would again reduce to T_c.
5. If $(1 - T_c)(1 - T_s) = (1 - T_d)$, then the bracketed term would go to zero, and the value of using leverage would also be zero. This implies that the tax advantage of debt to the firm would be exactly offset by the personal tax advantage of equity. Under this condition, capital structure would have no effect on a firm's value or its cost of capital, so we would be back to MM's original zero-tax theory.
6. Because taxes on capital gains are lower than on ordinary income and can be deferred, the effective tax rate on stock income is normally less than that on bond income. This being the case, what would the Miller model predict as the gain from leverage? To answer this question, assume that the tax rate on corporate income is $T_c = 34\%$, the effective rate on bond income is $T_d = 28\%$, and the effective rate on stock income is $T_s = 15\%$.[10] Using these values in the Miller model, we find that a levered firm's value exceeds that of an unlevered firm by 22 percent of the market value of corporate debt:

$$\begin{aligned}\text{Gain from leverage} &= \left[1 - \frac{(1 - T_c)(1 - T_s)}{(1 - T_d)}\right]D \\ &= \left[1 - \frac{(1 - 0.34)(1 - 0.15)}{(1 - 0.28)}\right]D \\ &= [1 - 0.78]D = 0.22D.\end{aligned}$$

Note that the MM model with corporate taxes would indicate a gain from leverage of $T_c(D) = 0.34D$, or 34 percent of the amount of corporate debt. Thus, with these assumed tax rates, adding personal taxes to the model lowers but does not eliminate the benefit from corporate debt. In general, whenever the effective tax rate on income from stock is less than the effective rate on income from bonds, the Miller model produces a lower gain from leverage than is produced by the MM with-tax model.

In his paper, Miller argued that firms in the aggregate would issue a mix of debt and equity securities such that the before-tax yields on corporate securities and the personal tax rates of the investors who bought these securities would adjust until an equilibrium was reached. At equilibrium, $(1 - T_d)$ would equal $(1 - T_c)(1 - T_s)$, so, as we noted earlier in Point 5, the tax advantage of debt to the firm would be exactly offset by personal taxation, and capital structure would have no effect on a firm's value or its cost of capital. Thus, according to Miller, the conclusions derived from the original Modigliani-Miller zero-tax model are correct!

Others have extended and tested Miller's analysis. Generally, these extensions question Miller's conclusion that there is no advantage to the use of corporate debt. In the United States, the effective tax rate on income from stock is less than on income from bonds. Thus, it appears that $(1 - T_c)(1 - T_s)$ is less than $(1 - T_d)$, hence there is an advantage to the use of corporate debt. Still, Miller's work does show that

[10]In a 1978 article, Miller and Scholes described how investors could, theoretically, shelter or delay income from stock to the point where the effective personal tax rate on such income is essentially zero. See Merton H. Miller and Myron S. Scholes, "Dividends and Taxes," *Journal of Financial Economics*, December 1978, 333–364. However, the 1986 changes in the tax law eliminated most of the shelters Miller and Scholes discussed.

personal taxes offset some of the benefits of corporate debt, so the tax advantages of corporate debt are less than were implied by the earlier MM model, where only corporate taxes were considered.

As we note in the next section, there are a number of problems with both the MM and the Miller models, so one should regard our examples as indicating the general effects of leverage on firms' value, not a precise relationship.

Self-Test Questions

How does the Miller model differ from the MM model with corporate taxes?

What are the implications of the Miller model if $T_c = T_s = T_d = 0$?

What are the implications if $T_s = T_d = 0$?

Considering the current tax structure in the United States, what is the primary implication of the Miller model?

Criticisms of the MM and Miller Models

The conclusions of the MM and Miller models follow logically from their initial assumptions. However, both academicians and financial executives have voiced concerns over the validity of the MM and Miller models, and virtually no one believes they hold precisely. The MM zero-tax model leads to the conclusion that capital structure doesn't matter, yet we observe systematic capital structure patterns within industries. Further, when used with "reasonable" tax rates, both the MM model with corporate taxes and the Miller model lead to the conclusion that firms should use 100 percent debt financing, but virtually no firms deliberately go to that extreme.

People who disagree with the MM and Miller theories generally attack them on the grounds that their assumptions are not correct. Here are the main objections:

1. Both MM and Miller assume that personal and corporate leverage are perfect substitutes. However, an individual investing in a levered firm has less loss exposure as a result of corporate *limited liability* than if he or she used "homemade" leverage. For example, in our earlier illustration of the MM arbitrage argument, it should be noted that only the \$600,000 our investor had in Firm L would be lost if that firm went bankrupt. However, if the investor engaged in arbitrage transactions and employed "homemade" leverage to invest in Firm U, then he or she could lose \$900,000—the original \$600,000 investment plus the \$400,000 loan less the \$100,000 investment in riskless bonds. This increased personal risk exposure would tend to restrain investors from engaging in arbitrage, and that could cause the equilibrium values of V_L, V_U, k_{sL}, and k_{sU} to be different from those specified by MM. Restrictions on institutional investors, who dominate capital markets today, may also retard the arbitrage process, because many institutional investors cannot legally borrow to buy stocks, hence are prohibited from engaging in homemade leverage.

   Note, though, that while limited liability may present a problem to individuals, it *does not* present a problem to corporations set up to undertake **leveraged buyouts, or LBOs.** Thus, after MM's work became widely known, literally hundreds of LBO firms were established, and their founders made billions recapitalizing underleveraged firms. "Junk bonds" were created to aid in the process, and the managers of underleveraged firms that did not want their firms to be taken over increased debt usage on their own. Thus, MM's work raised the level of debt in corporate America, and it probably raised the level of economic efficiency.

2. If a leveraged firm's operating income declined, it would sell assets and take other measures to raise the cash necessary to meet its interest obligations and thus avoid bankruptcy. If the unleveraged firm experienced the same decline in operating income, it would probably take the less drastic measure of cutting dividends rather than selling assets. If dividends were cut, the investor who employed homemade leverage would not receive cash to pay the interest on his or her debt. Thus, homemade leverage puts stockholders in greater danger of bankruptcy than does corporate leverage.
3. Brokerage costs were assumed away by MM and Miller, making the switch from L to U costless. However, brokerage and other transaction costs do exist, and they too impede the arbitrage process.
4. MM initially assumed that corporations and investors can borrow at the risk-free rate. Although risky debt has been introduced into the analysis by others, to reach the MM and Miller conclusions it is still necessary to assume that both corporations and investors can borrow at the same rate. While major institutional investors probably can borrow at the corporate rate, many institutions are not allowed to borrow to buy securities. Further, most individual investors must borrow at higher rates than those paid by large corporations.
5. In his article, Miller concluded that an equilibrium would be reached, but to reach his equilibrium the tax benefit from corporate debt must be the same for all firms, and it must be constant for an individual firm regardless of the amount of leverage used. However, we know that tax benefits vary from firm to firm: Highly profitable companies gain the maximum tax benefit from leverage, while the benefits to firms that are struggling are much smaller. Further, some firms have other tax shields such as high depreciation, pension plan contributions, and operating loss carry-forwards, and these shields reduce the tax savings from interest payments.[11] It also appears simplistic to assume that the expected tax shield is unaffected by the amount of debt used. Higher leverage increases the probability that the firm will not be able to use the full tax shield in the future, because higher leverage increases the probability of future unprofitability and consequently lower tax rates. All things considered, it appears likely that the interest tax shield from corporate debt is more valuable to some firms than to others. Note, though, that large, diversified corporations can use losses in one division to offset profits in another. Thus, the tax shelter benefit is more certain in large, diversified firms than in smaller, single product companies. Firms recognize this, and this factor has contributed to an increase in firm size.
6. MM and Miller assume that there are no costs associated with financial distress, and they ignore agency costs. Further, they assume that all market participants have identical information about firms' prospects, which is also incorrect. These topics are discussed in the next section.

Self-Test Questions

Should we accept that one of the models presented thus far (MM with zero taxes, MM with corporate taxes, or Miller) is correct? Why or why not?

Are any of the assumptions used in the models worrisome to you, and what does "worrisome" mean in this context?

---

[11]For a discussion of the impact of tax shields other than debt financing, see Harry DeAngelo and Ronald W. Masulis, "Optimal Capital Structure under Corporate and Personal Taxation," *Journal of Financial Economics*, March 1980, 3–30.

Capital Structure Theory: The Trade-Off Models

Some of the assumptions inherent in the MM and Miller models can be relaxed without changing the basic MM/Miller conclusions.[12] However, introducing financial distress and agency costs alters the MM and Miller results significantly.

Costs of Financial Distress

Financial distress includes, but is not restricted to, bankruptcy, and when financial distress occurs, several things can happen:

1. Arguments between claimants often delay the liquidation of assets. Bankruptcy cases can take many years to settle, and during this time machinery rusts, buildings are vandalized, inventories become obsolete, and the like.
2. Lawyers' fees, court costs, and administrative expenses can absorb a large part of the firm's value. Together, the costs of physical deterioration plus legal fees and administrative expenses are called the *direct costs* of financial distress.
3. Managers and other employees generally lose their jobs when a firm fails. Knowing this, the management of a firm in financial distress may take actions that keep it alive in the short run but that also dilute long-run value. For example, the firm may defer maintenance of machinery, sell off valuable assets at bargain prices to raise cash, or cut costs so much that the quality of its products or services is impaired and the firm's long-run market position is eroded.
4. Both customers and suppliers are aware of the problems that can arise, and they often take "evasive action" that further damages the troubled firm. For example, Eastern Airlines, as it struggled to deal with its unions and to avoid liquidation, had trouble selling tickets because potential customers were worried about buying a seat for a future flight and then having the company shut down before they could take the trip. Some potential customers were also worried that the company might cut back on maintenance, and Eastern's suppliers were reluctant to grant normal credit terms or to gear up to supply parts and other materials on a long-term basis. Finally, Eastern had trouble attracting and retaining the highest-quality workers, as most workers with a choice preferred employment with a more stable airline to one that might go out of business at any time.
5. Nonoptimal managerial actions associated with financial distress, as well as the costs imposed by customers, suppliers, and capital providers, are called the *indirect costs* of financial distress. Of course, these costs may be incurred by a firm in financial distress even if it does not go into bankruptcy: Bankruptcy is just one point on the continuum of financial distress.

All things considered, the direct and indirect costs associated with financial distress are high.[13] Further, financial distress typically occurs only if a firm has debts—debt-free firms usually do not experience financial distress. *Therefore, the greater the use of debt financing, and the larger the fixed interest charges, the greater the probability that a*

[12]For example, see Robert A. Haugen and James L. Pappas, "Equilibrium in the Pricing of Capital Assets, Risk-Bearing Debt Instruments, and the Question of Optimal Capital Structure," *Journal of Financial and Quantitative Analysis*, June 1971, 943–954; Joseph Stiglitz, "A Re-Examination of the Modigliani-Miller Theorem," *American Economic Review*, December 1969, 784–793; and Mark E. Rubenstein, "A Mean-Variance Synthesis of Corporate Financial Theory," *Journal of Finance*, March 1973, 167–181.

[13]See Edward I. Altman, "A Further Empirical Investigation of the Bankruptcy Cost Question," *Journal of Finance*, September 1984, 1067–1089. On the basis of a sample of 26 bankrupt companies, Altman found that bankruptcy costs exceed 20 percent of firm value.

decline in earnings will lead to financial distress, hence the higher the probability that costs associated with financial distress will be incurred.

An increase in the probability of future financial distress lowers the current value of a firm and raises its cost of capital. To see why, suppose we estimate that Fredrickson Water will incur costs of \$7 million if it fails at some future date, and that the *present value* of this possible future cost is \$5 million. Further, the probability of financial distress increases with leverage, causing the expected present value of the cost of financial distress to rise from zero at zero debt to \$4.75 million at \$30 million of debt as shown in Table 17-1.

These expected costs must be subtracted from the values we previously calculated in Panel b of Figure 17-1 to find the firm's value at various amounts of leverage: They would reduce the values of V and S and, as a result, would raise k_s and the WACC. For example, at \$20 million of debt, we would obtain the values in Table 17-2.[14] These changes would, of course, then have carry-through effects on the graphs in Panel b of Figure 17-1. Most important, they would (1) reduce the decline of the WACC line and (2) reduce the slope of the V_L line.

The effects of financial distress are also felt by a firm's bondholders. Firms experiencing financial distress have a higher probability of defaulting on debt payments, so the higher the probability of financial distress, the higher the required return on debt. Thus, as a firm uses more and more debt, hence increasing the probability of distress, the value of k_d also increases, causing several elements in Panel b of Figure 17-1 to change.

Agency Costs

We introduced the concept of agency costs in Chapter 1. One agency relationship is between a firm's stockholders and its bondholders. In the absence of any restrictions, management would be tempted to take actions that would benefit stockholders at the expense of bondholders. For example, if Fredrickson Water were to issue only a small amount of debt, then this debt would have relatively little risk, a high bond rating, and a low interest rate. After it issued the low-risk debt, Fredrickson might issue more debt secured by the same assets as the original debt. This would raise the risks faced by *all bondholders*, cause k_d to rise, and consequently cause the original bondholders to

[14]To find k_s and the WACC in Table 17-2, simply transpose Equation 17-3 and then apply the definition for the WACC:

$$k_s = \frac{(\text{EBIT} - k_dD)(1 - T)}{S} = \frac{[\$4 - 0.08(\$20)](1 - 0.4)}{\$5.5} = 26.18\%.$$

$$\begin{aligned}\text{WACC} &= (D/V)(k_d)(1 - T) + (S/V)(k_s)\\ &= (\$20/\$25.5)(8\%)(0.6) + (\$5.5/\$25.5)(26.18\%)\\ &= 3.76\% + 5.65\% = 9.41\%.\end{aligned}$$

TABLE 17-1 Fredrickson Water Company: Expected Costs of Financial Distress

	Amount of Debt				
	\$0	**\$5 Million**	**\$10 Million**	**\$20 Million**	**\$30 Million**
Probability of financial distress	0.0	0.05	0.15	0.50	0.95
PV of expected costs of financial distress[a]	\$0	\$250,000	\$750,000	\$2,500,000	\$4,750,000

[a]\$5 million times the indicated probability.

TABLE 17-2 Fredrickson Water Company: Effects of Financial Distress (Millions of Dollars)

	Values at D = \$20 Million with Financial Distress Effects Ignored: Pure MM	Values at D = \$20 Million with Financial Distress Effects Considered: Modified MM
V	\$28.00	\$28.00 − \$2.5 = \$25.5
S	\$8.00	\$8.00 − \$2.5 = \$5.5
k_s	18.00%	26.18%
WACC	8.57%	9.41%

suffer capital losses. Similarly, after issuing debt Fredrickson might decide to restructure its assets, selling off those with low business risk and acquiring assets that were more risky but that also had higher expected rates of return. If things worked out well, the stockholders would get all of the benefit, but if things went sour, much of the loss would fall on the bondholders. So, stockholders would be playing a game of "heads, I win; tails, you lose" with bondholders.

Because stockholders might try to exploit bondholders in these and other ways, bonds are protected by restrictive covenants. These covenants hamper the corporation's legitimate operations to some extent. Further, the company must be monitored to ensure that the covenants are being obeyed, and the costs of monitoring are passed on to the stockholders in the form of higher interest rates. The lost efficiency plus monitoring costs are *agency costs* that increase the cost of debt and thus reduce its advantage.[15]

Value and Cost of Capital with Financial Distress and Agency Costs Considered

If the MM model with corporate taxes were correct, a firm's value would rise continuously as it moved from zero debt toward 100 percent debt: The equation $V_L = V_U + TD$ shows that TD, hence V_L, is maximized if D is at a maximum. Recall that the increasing component of value, TD, is a direct result of the tax shelter provided by interest on the debt. However, as noted above, financial distress and agency costs could cause V_L to decline as the level of debt rises. Therefore, the relationship between a firm's value and its use of leverage has two negative components, so the true equation should look like this:

$$V_L = V_U + TD - \begin{pmatrix} \text{PV of} \\ \text{expected} \\ \text{costs of} \\ \text{financial} \\ \text{distress} \end{pmatrix} - \begin{pmatrix} \text{PV of} \\ \text{agency} \\ \text{costs} \end{pmatrix}. \qquad \textbf{(17-11)}$$

The relationship expressed in Equation 17-11 is graphed in Figure 17-2. The tax shelter effects totally dominate until the amount of debt reaches Point A. After Point A, financial distress and agency costs become increasingly important, offsetting some of

[15]Michael C. Jensen and William H. Meckling point out that there are also agency costs between outside stockholders and management. See "Theory of the Firm: Managerial Behavior, Agency Costs, and Ownership Structure," *Journal of Financial Economics*, October 1976, 305–360. Their study further suggests that (1) bondholder agency costs increase as the debt ratio increases, but (2) outside stockholder agency costs move in reverse fashion, falling with increased use of debt.

FIGURE 17-2 Net Effects of Leverage on the Value of the Firm

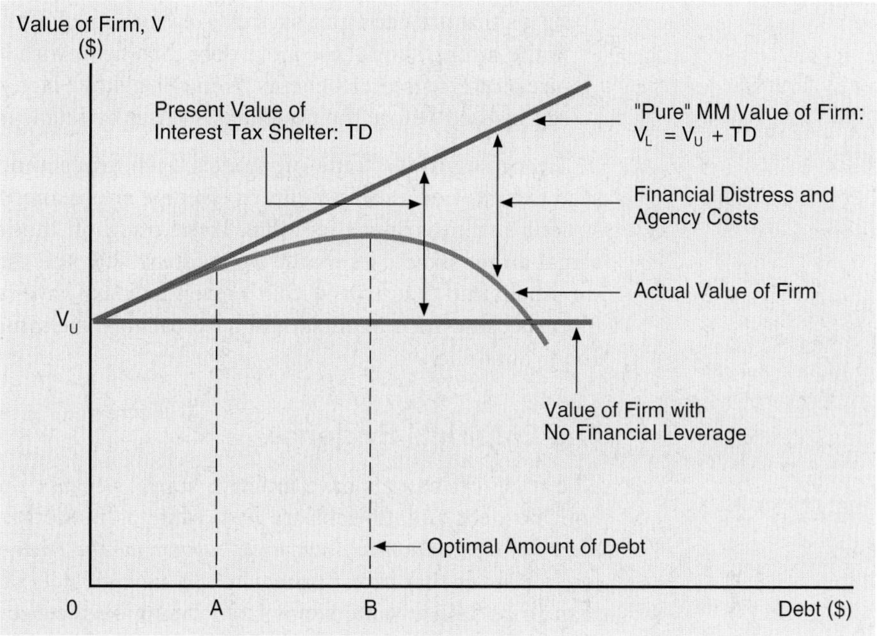

the tax advantages. At Point B, the marginal tax shelter benefit of additional debt is exactly offset by the disadvantages of debt, and beyond Point B, the disadvantages outweigh the tax benefit.

Equation 17-10, the Miller model, can also be modified to reflect financial distress and agency costs. The equation would be identical to Equation 17-11, except that the gain from leverage term, TD, would reflect the addition of personal taxes. In either the MM or Miller models, the gain from leverage can at least be roughly estimated, but the value reduction resulting from potential financial distress and agency costs is almost entirely subjective. We know that these costs must increase as leverage rises, but we do not know the specific functional relationships.

The addition of financial distress and agency costs to either the MM tax model or the Miller model results in a **trade-off model** of capital structure. In such a model, the optimal capital structure can be visualized as a trade-off between the benefit of debt (the interest tax shelter) and the costs of debt (financial distress and agency costs).

Implications of the Trade-Off Models

The trade-off models cannot be used to specify a precise optimal capital structure, but they do enable us to make three statements about leverage:

1. Firms with more business risk ought to use less debt than lower-risk firms, other things being equal, because the greater the business risk, the greater the probability of financial distress at any level of debt, hence the greater the expected costs of distress. Thus, firms with lower business risk can borrow more before the expected costs of distress offset the tax advantages of borrowing (Point B in Figure 17-2).
2. Firms that have tangible, readily marketable assets such as real estate can use more debt than firms whose value is derived primarily from intangible assets such as patents and goodwill. The costs of financial distress depend not only on the probability of incurring distress but also on what happens if distress occurs. Specialized

assets and intangible assets are more likely to lose value if financial distress occurs than are standardized, tangible assets.

3. Firms that are currently paying taxes at the highest rate, and that are likely to do so in the future, should use more debt than firms with lower tax rates. High corporate taxes lead to greater benefits from debt, other factors held constant, so more debt can be used before the tax shield is offset by financial distress and agency costs.

According to the trade-off models, each firm should set its target capital structure such that the costs and benefits of leverage are balanced at the margin, because such a structure will maximize its value. If the trade-off models are correct, we should find actual target structures that are consistent with the three points just noted. Further, we should find that firms within a given industry have reasonably similar capital structures, because such firms should have roughly the same types of assets, business risk, and profitability.

The Empirical Evidence

The trade-off models have intuitive appeal because they lead to the conclusion that both no-debt and all-debt are bad, while a "moderate" debt level is good. *However, there has been only mixed empirical support for the trade-off models.*[16] In support of the models, firms that invest primarily in tangible assets do tend to borrow more heavily than firms whose value stems from intangibles, especially growth options. There is also evidence that firms with higher tax rates have higher debt ratios. Finally, many CFOs have stated that they try to maintain a target capital structure.[17]

However, several empirical studies call the trade-off models into question. First, researchers have examined models of financing behavior to see if firms' financing decisions are consistent with a target capital structure. Although one survey found that many managers apparently try to maintain a target capital structure, the explanatory power of the models testing for evidence of this behavior is low. This suggests that trade-off models account for only a part of actual behavior. Second, actual debt ratios tend to vary widely across apparently similar firms within given industries, whereas the trade-off theory suggests that similar firms should have similar debt ratios.

All in all, the empirical support for the trade-off models is rather weak, which suggests that factors not incorporated into these models are also at work. Thus, the trade-off models do not tell the whole story.

Self-Test Questions

List some examples of financial distress and agency costs.

How are these costs related to the use of financial leverage?

How are the basic MM with corporate taxes and Miller models affected by the inclusion of financial distress and agency costs?

What is a trade-off model of capital structure?

What implications does the trade-off model have regarding capital structure?

Does the empirical evidence support the trade-off model?

---

[16]For examples of the empirical research in this area, see Robert A. Taggart, Jr., "A Model of Corporate Financing Decisions," *Journal of Finance*, December 1977, 1467–1484; Paul Marsh, "The Choice between Equity and Debt: An Empirical Study," *Journal of Finance*, March 1982, 121–144; John R. Graham, "Debt and the Marginal Tax Rate," *Journal of Financial Economics*, vol. 41, 1996, 41–73; and John R. Graham, Michael L. Lemmon, and James S. Schallenheim, "Debt, Leases, Taxes, and the Endogeneity of Corporate Tax Status," *Journal of Finance*, February 1998, 131–162.

[17]See Ravindra R. Kamath, "Long-Term Financing Decisions: Views and Practices of Financial Managers of NYSE Firms," *The Financial Review*, May 1997, 350–356.

Capital Structure Theory: The Signaling Model

Some years ago, Professor Gordon Donaldson of Harvard conducted an extensive study of how corporations actually establish their capital structures.[18] Here is a summary of his findings:

1. Firms prefer to finance with internally generated funds, that is, with retained earnings and depreciation cash flow.
2. Firms set target dividend payout ratios based on expected future investment opportunities and expected future cash flows. The target payout ratio is set at a level that causes retained earnings plus depreciation to cover capital expenditures under normal conditions.
3. Dividends are "sticky" in the short run—firms are reluctant to raise dividends unless they are confident that the higher dividend can be maintained, and they are especially reluctant to cut the dividend. Indeed, they generally do not reduce the dividend unless things are so bad that they simply have to.
4. If a firm has more internal cash flow than is needed to cover its capital expenditures, then it will invest in marketable securities, or use the funds to retire debt, or increase dividends, or repurchase stock, or acquire other firms. On the other hand, if it has insufficient internal cash flow to finance nonpostponable new projects, it will first draw down its marketable securities portfolio and then go to the external capital markets. If it has to go to the external markets, it will first issue debt, then convertible bonds, and then common stock only as a last resort. *Thus, Donaldson observed that there is a "pecking order" of financing, not a balanced approach as would result if the trade-off models accurately described real-world behavior.*

Professor Stewart Myers noted the inconsistency between Donaldson's findings and the trade-off models, and that inconsistency led Myers to propose a new theory.[19] First, Myers noted that Donaldson's pecking-order findings led away from, rather than toward, a well-defined capital structure. Equity is raised in two forms—retained earnings and new stock. Retained earnings are at the top of the pecking order, while new common stock is at the bottom. Therefore, if retained earnings are high relative to investment requirements, the equity ratio will increase, while if retained earnings are insufficient, the firm will borrow rather than issue stock, causing the debt ratio to increase. The trade-off models, on the other hand, assume that equity from the sale of stock is equivalent to that from retained earnings, and they suggest that the debt/equity ratio should remain constant over time.

Next, Myers noted that a critical assumption in the trade-off models is that all market participants have homogeneous expectations, which implies (1) that all participants have the same information and (2) that any changes in operating income are purely random as opposed to being anticipated by some but not all parties. Myers had the insight to see that if expectations are not homogeneous, meaning that different groups of market participants have asymmetric (or different) information, then Donaldson's results can be explained in a logical manner. Myers' work resulted in what is now called the **signaling,** or **asymmetric information, theory** of capital structure.

---

[18]Gordon Donaldson, *Corporate Debt Capacity: A Study of Corporate Debt Policy and the Determination of Corporate Debt Capacity* (Boston: Harvard Graduate School of Business Administration, 1961).

[19]Stewart C. Myers, "The Capital Structure Puzzle," *Journal of Finance,* July 1984, 575–592. It is interesting to note that, like the Miller model, Myers' paper was first presented as a presidential address to the American Finance Association.

To illustrate, assume that a firm has 10,000 common shares outstanding. They sell at a price of \$19 per share, so the market value of its equity is \$190,000. However, its managers have better information regarding the firm's future than stockholders, and the managers believe that the actual value per share based on existing assets is \$21, giving the equity a total "intrinsic" value of \$210,000. Such an information asymmetry (or difference) could easily exist, for managers often know more about their firms' prospects than do current and potential investors.[20]

Suppose further that management now identifies a new project that would require \$100,000 of external financing and which has an estimated NPV of \$5,000. [Remember that a project's NPV represents economic value added (EVA), and that it accrues to the shareholders.] This project is unanticipated by the firm's investors, so the \$5,000 NPV has not been incorporated into the \$190,000 equity market value. Should the firm accept the project? To begin, suppose the firm issues new stock to raise the \$100,000 to finance the project. Several possibilities exist:

1. **Symmetric information.** First, as a point of departure, consider the situation in which management can convey all the information to the public, hence all investors have the same information as management regarding existing asset values. Under these conditions, the stock would immediately rise to its \$21 intrinsic value. Then, when the new project comes along and is financed, the firm would have to sell \$100,000/\$21 = 4,762 new shares. Acceptance of the project would then increase the stock price from \$21 to \$21.34:

$$\text{New stock price} = \frac{\text{Original market value} + \text{New money raised} + \text{NPV}}{\text{Original shares} + \text{New shares}}$$
$$= \frac{\$210{,}000 + \$100{,}000 + \$5{,}000}{10{,}000 + 4{,}762} = \frac{\$315{,}000}{14{,}762} = \$21.34.$$

   Both old and new shareholders would benefit if the project were accepted; each group would gain \$21.34 − \$21.00 = \$0.34 per share as a result of the new project.

2. **Asymmetric information prior to stock issue.** Now suppose management is unable to inform investors about the stock's intrinsic value. Perhaps it is necessary to hold back such information to maintain a competitive edge, or perhaps SEC regulations cause management to refrain from "touting" the stock prior to the new issue (if things did not work out as expected, new shareholders might sue the managers who had provided the rosy forecast). In this situation, new stock would fetch the current price, \$19 per share, so the company would have to sell \$100,000/\$19 = 5,263 shares in order to raise the required \$100,000. If this were done, this new price would result after the project was accepted and the information asymmetry was removed:

$$\text{New stock price} = \frac{\text{New market value} + \text{New money raised} + \text{NPV}}{\text{Original shares} + \text{New shares}}$$
$$= \frac{\$210{,}000 + \$100{,}000 + \$5{,}000}{10{,}000 + 5{,}263} = \frac{\$315{,}000}{15{,}263} = \$20.64.$$

   Under this condition, the project should not be undertaken. If the project were not accepted, so no new shares were sold, then the price of the stock would rise to its \$21 intrinsic value when the information asymmetry was eventually removed.

[20]This assumption is contrary to the strong-form efficient markets hypothesis (EMH) presented in Chapter 10, but as we note there, few observers—including people who strongly support weak-form and semistrong-form efficiency—are willing to accept strong-form efficiency.

The sale of new stock at \$19 per share would lead to a \$0.36 per share loss to the firm's existing shareholders. There would be a \$1.64 gain to the new shareholders, but management wants to maximize the value of *current* stockholders, not new ones.

3. **A more profitable project.** Now suppose the project had an NPV of \$20,000 rather than \$5,000, the stock sold for \$19, and other conditions in Scenario 2 were unchanged. Now the firm's stock price would rise to \$21.62 if it undertook the project:

$$\text{New stock price} = \frac{\$210{,}000 + \$100{,}000 + \$20{,}000}{10{,}000 + 5{,}263} = \frac{\$330{,}000}{15{,}263} = \$21.62.$$

   Under these conditions, the firm should take on the project. Note, though, that most of the positive NPV would go to the new stockholders, who would pay \$19 per share and thus enjoy a capital gain of \$2.62 versus a gain of only \$0.62 for the original stockholders.

4. **Dark clouds on the horizon.** Now suppose an entirely different—and bad—situation faced the firm. Stockholders think the firm is worth \$19 per share, but managers know (a) that outside investors are entirely too optimistic about growth opportunities, (b) that investors have not factored in proposed legislation that will require large, nonearning investments in pollution control equipment, and (c) that the current stock price does not reflect the need for new R&D expenditures that will be required to keep the firm's products competitive. If all of these bad events materialize, profit margins will be under pressure, cash flows will fall, and the company will have difficulty servicing its debt.

   Faced with these conditions, management might well conclude that the stock's intrinsic value is only \$17 per share, and then decide to sell a new issue of 10,000 shares at the current price of \$19, raising \$190,000 and using the funds to retire debt or to support this year's capital budget. This action would increase the intrinsic value of the stock from \$17 to \$18:

$$\begin{aligned}\text{New intrinsic value} &= \frac{\text{Old intrinsic market value} + \text{New money}}{\text{Original shares} + \text{New shares}} \\ &= \frac{\$170{,}000 + \$190{,}000}{10{,}000 + 10{,}000} = \frac{\$360{,}000}{20{,}000} = \$18.00.\end{aligned}$$

   Current stockholders will, if management's expectations come true, suffer a loss when the bad news becomes known, but the sale of new stock would reduce that loss. (Note: Management would have to word the prospectus for the new issue carefully, pointing out the potential problems. However, virtually all prospectuses are filled with cautionary language, so investors have difficulty telling from them what management really expects.)

5. **Finance the original \$5,000 NPV project with debt.** If the firm used debt to finance the original \$100,000 project (Scenario 2), *and then the information asymmetry were removed*, the new stock price would be \$21.50 versus the \$20.64 we found under Scenario 2:

$$\begin{aligned}\text{New stock price} &= \frac{\text{New market value} + \text{NPV}}{\text{Original shares}} \\ &= \frac{\$210{,}000 + \$5{,}000}{10{,}000} = \frac{\$215{,}000}{10{,}000} = \$21.50.\end{aligned}$$

   Thus, if debt were used, all of the intrinsic value of the firm's existing assets, plus the NPV of the new project, would accrue to the original shareholders. If stock were used, we saw earlier that the value of the original stock would end up at \$20.64 rather than \$21, the intrinsic value without the new investment.[21]

What does all this suggest about corporate financial policy? First, in a world where asymmetric information exists, corporations should issue new shares only in the unlikely event (1) that they have extraordinarily profitable investments that cannot be either postponed, signaled to investors, or financed by debt, or (2) in situations where management thinks the shares are overvalued. Second, investors recognize all this, so selling pressure drives down a company's share price when it announces plans to issue new shares. Third, the pecking order that Donaldson observed is rational when asymmetric information exists—it pays to retain a large fraction of earnings, and also to keep the equity ratio up and the debt ratio down, so as to maintain a **reserve borrowing capacity** that can be used to support the capital budget if and when an unusually large number of positive NPV projects come along, or if problems arise which require outside capital.[22]

Note that the use of signaling, and its effect on investors' perceptions, differs substantially across firms. To illustrate, asymmetry is typically much greater in the drug and semiconductor industries than in the retailing and utility industries, because success in the drug and semiconductor industries depends on secretive proprietary research and development. Thus, managers in these industries have significantly more information about their firms' prospects than do outside investors. Also, emerging firms with limited capital but good growth opportunities are recognized as having to use external financing, so the announcement of a new stock offering by a new company is not viewed with as much concern by investors as are offerings by mature firms with limited growth opportunities. Thus, although signaling affects all firms, its impact varies from firm to firm.

Self-Test Questions

Briefly explain the asymmetric information (signaling) theory.

What does this theory suggest about capital structure decisions?

Is the signaling theory equally applicable to all firms?

Capital Structure Theory: Our View

The great contribution of the trade-off models developed by MM, Miller, and their followers is that these models identified the specific benefits and costs of using debt—the tax benefits, financial distress costs, and so on. Prior to MM, no capital structure theory existed, so we had no systematic way of analyzing the effects of debt financing.

The trade-off models are summarized graphically in Figure 17-3. The top graph shows the relationships between the debt ratio and the cost of debt, the cost of equity, and the WACC. Both k_s and $k_d(1 - T_c)$ rise steadily with increases in leverage, but the rate of increase accelerates at higher debt levels, reflecting agency costs and the increased probability of financial distress. The WACC first declines, then hits a

[21]If the additional debt were not proportionally matched with retained earnings, issuing new debt would increase the firm's risk and consequently its required rate of return on equity. Similarly, the issuance of new equity in the previous scenarios might reduce risk and thus lower the cost of equity. We abstract from these effects because (1) they are of second order importance and (2) incorporating them into the analysis would unnecessarily complicate the examples.

[22]Flotation costs also play a role in capital structure theory. In general, flotation costs are smaller on debt than on equity issues, and this provides an additional rationale for using debt rather than outside equity. We will discuss this issue in more detail in Chapter 19.

FIGURE 17-3 Effects of Leverage: The Trade-Off Models

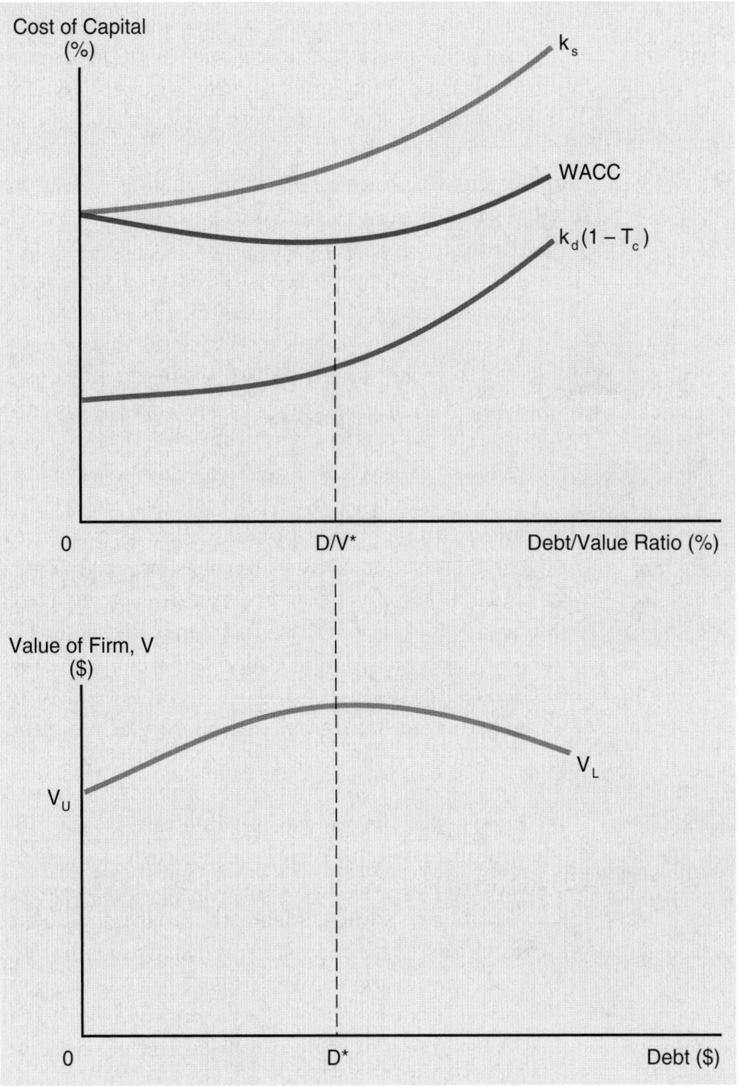

minimum at D/V*, and then begins to rise. Note that the value of D in D/V* in the upper graph is D*, the level of debt in the lower graph that maximizes the firm's value. Thus, a firm's WACC is minimized and its value is maximized at the same capital structure. Note also that the general shapes of the curves apply regardless of whether we are using the modified MM with corporate taxes model, the Miller model, or a variant of these models.

Unfortunately, it is impossible to quantify accurately the costs and benefits of debt financing, so it is impossible to pinpoint D/V*, the capital structure that maximizes a firm's value. Most experts believe such a structure exists for every firm, but that it changes over time as firms' operations and investors' preferences change. Most experts also believe that, as shown in Figure 17-3, the relationship between value and leverage is relatively flat over a fairly broad range, so large deviations from the optimal capital structure can occur without materially affecting the stock price.

Now consider the signaling theory. Because of asymmetric information, investors know less about a firm's prospects than its managers know. Further, managers try to maximize value for *current* stockholders, not new ones. Therefore, if the firm has excellent prospects, management will not want to issue new shares, but if things look bleak, then a new stock offering would benefit current stockholders. Consequently, investors take a stock offering to be a signal of bad news, so stock prices tend to decline when new issues are announced. As a result, new equity financings are relatively expensive. The net effect of signaling is to motivate firms to maintain a reserve borrowing capacity designed to permit future investment opportunities to be financed by debt if internal funds are not available.

By combining the trade-off and asymmetric information theories, we obtain this explanation for firms' behavior: (1) Debt financing provides benefits because of the tax deductibility of interest, so firms should have some debt in their capital structures. (2) However, financial distress and agency costs place limits on debt usage—beyond some point, these costs offset the tax advantage of debt. The costs of financial distress are especially harmful to firms whose values consist primarily of intangible growth options, such as R&D. Such firms should have lower levels of debt than firms whose asset bases consist mostly of tangible assets. (3) Because of problems due to asymmetric information and flotation costs, low-growth firms should follow a pecking order, with capital raised first from internal sources, then by borrowing, and finally by issuing new stock. In fact, such low-growth firms rarely need to issue external equity. High-growth firms whose growth occurs primarily through increases in tangible assets should follow the same pecking order, but usually they will need to issue new stock as well as debt. High-growth firms whose values consist primarily of intangible growth options may run out of internally generated cash, but they should emphasize stock rather than debt due to the severe problems that financial distress imposes on such firms. (4) Finally, because of asymmetric information, firms should maintain a reserve of borrowing capacity in order to be able to take advantage of good investment opportunities without having to issue stock at low prices, and this reserve will cause the actual debt ratio to be lower than that suggested by the trade-off models.

There is some evidence that managers do attempt to behave in ways that are consistent with this view of capital structure. In the survey of CFOs mentioned earlier in this chapter, about two-thirds of the CFOs said that they follow a "hierarchy in which the most advantageous sources of funds are exhausted before other sources are used." The hierarchy usually followed the pecking order of first internally generated cash flow, then debt, and finally external equity, which is consistent with the predicted behavior of most low growth firms. But there were occasions in which external equity was the first source of financing, which would be consistent with the theory for either high growth firms or firms whose agency and financial distress costs have exceeded the benefit of the tax savings.

Self-Test Questions

Summarize the trade-off and signaling theories of capital structure.

Are the trade-off and signaling theories mutually exclusive; that is, might both be correct?

Does capital structure theory provide managers with a model that can be used to set a precise optimal capital structure?

Book Weights versus Market Weights

In Chapter 11, we calculated the weighted average cost of capital with market value rather than book value weights. Further, in our discussions of capital structure thus far in Chapters 16 and 17, we have focused primarily on market values, not book values. However, survey data indicate that financial managers generally focus on book value structures. Thus, there seems to be a conflict between academic theory and business practice. Here are some thoughts on this issue:

1. If stocks and bonds do not sell exactly at book value—and they almost never do—then it would be impossible for a growing firm to establish and maintain at constant levels both a target book value and a target market value capital structure. The firm could finance so as to stay on its book value target or on its market value target, but not on both. To illustrate, assume that a company has, at book value, \$50 million of debt and \$50 million of equity, for a total book value of \$100 million. However, its stock sells at two times book, so the market value of its equity is \$100. Here is the capital structure situation, with dollars in millions:

	Book Value		Market Value	
Debt	\$ 50	50%	\$ 50	33%
Equity	50	50	100	67
Total	\$100	100%	\$150	100%

   Now suppose the company needs to raise an additional \$100 million. If it sells \$50 million of debt and \$50 million of common stock, it will add these amounts to its balance sheet, so its book value capital structure will remain constant. However, adding \$50 million to both debt and equity will cause its market value capital structure to change. On the other hand, if it raises \$33 million as debt and \$67 million as equity, its market value capital structure will remain constant, but its book value structure will change. Thus, it can maintain either its book value or its market value capital structure, but not both.
2. Book values as reported on balance sheets reflect the historical costs of assets. However, historical costs often have little to do with the actual value of assets or with their ability to produce cash flows. Market values would almost always better reflect cash generation and debt service ability.
3. As we have repeatedly noted throughout this chapter and the last one, the point of capital structure analysis is to find the capital structure that maximizes the firm's market value, hence its stock price. Since this optimum is defined in terms of stock prices, it can only be determined by an analysis of market values.
4. Now suppose a firm found its optimal market value structure, but then financed so as to maintain a constant book value structure. This would lead to a departure from value maximization. Therefore, if a firm is growing, it should finance so as to hold constant its market value structure. That will, as we saw above, normally lead to changes in the book value structure.
5. Because the firm should, to keep its value at a maximum, finance so as to hold its market value structure constant, the weighted average cost of capital, WACC, should be found using market value weights.
6. Business executives prefer stability and predictability to volatility and uncertainty. Book values are far more predictable than market values. Further, a financial manager can set a target book value capital structure and then attain it, right on the money. It would be virtually impossible to stay at a target market value structure because of bond and stock price fluctuations. This is one reason executives focus on book value structures rather than on the more logical market value structures. Also, many financial executives have accounting backgrounds, and accountants focus on

accounting numbers. However, as financial executives gain a knowledge of financial (as opposed to accounting) theory, the focus is shifting more toward market values.

7. For purposes of developing the weighted average cost of capital, we strongly recommend the use of market value weights. However, if a company focuses on a book value capital structure, seeks to maintain that structure, and finances in accordance with book value weights, then its weighted average cost of capital should be based on book weights.
8. Some executives have argued against the use of market value weights on the grounds that as stock prices change, so would capital structure weights, with the result being a volatile cost of capital. This argument is incorrect. The cost of capital should be based on *target* weights, not on the actual capital structure, and there is no reason to think that a target market value structure would be any less stable than a target book value structure. In fact, as we discuss in Point 9 below, target market value weights are probably more stable than target book weights.
9. The appropriate target level of the book value debt ratio may change over time even if there is no growth or change in the firm's business risk. For example, consider a firm whose unit sales are constant and that currently has a 50/50 book value debt ratio, which it considers to be optimal. The firm is not acquiring new assets, but it still has to replace its old assets as they wear out, and it finances these replacement assets with a targeted 50/50 (book value) mix of debt and equity. If there is any inflation in the economy (as there generally is), then over time profits will increase even though unit sales are constant, and this increase in reported profits will cause ROE to increase. The higher ROE increases the amount of debt the company can carry, which in turn causes management to continually revise upwards its target book value debt ratio. However, a target market value debt ratio would be unaffected, because as the market value of the stock increases over time with inflation. Therefore, constant target market value debt ratio will automatically lead to an increase in the level of debt.

What can we conclude from all this? We are absolutely convinced that firms should focus on market value capital structures and base their cost of capital calculations on target market value weights. Because market values do change, it would be impossible to keep the actual capital structure on target at all times, but this fact in no way detracts from the validity of market value targets.

Self-Test Questions

Should the target capital structure be expressed in book value or market value weights?

Why do many financial managers prefer to work with book weights?

Summary

In this chapter, we discussed a variety of topics related to capital structure decisions. The key concepts covered are listed below:

- In 1958, **Franco Modigliani and Merton Miller (MM)** proved, under a restrictive set of assumptions including zero taxes, that capital structure is irrelevant; that is, according to the original MM article, a firm's value is not affected by its financing mix.
- MM later added **corporate taxes** to their model and reached the conclusion that capital structure does matter. Indeed, their model led to the conclusion that firms should use 100 percent debt financing.

- MM's model with corporate taxes demonstrated that the primary benefit of debt stems from the **tax deductibility of interest payments.**
- Later, Miller extended the theory to include **personal taxes.** The introduction of personal taxes reduces, but does not eliminate, the benefits of debt financing. Thus, the **Miller model** also leads to 100 percent debt financing.
- The addition of financial distress and agency costs to either the MM corporate tax model or the Miller model results in a **trade-off model.** Here the marginal costs and benefits of debt are balanced against one another, and the result is an optimal capital structure that falls somewhere between zero and 100 percent debt.
- The **Hamada equation** combines the CAPM and the MM with corporate taxes model:

  $$k_{sL} = k_{RF} + (k_M - k_{RF})b_U + (k_M - k_{RF})b_U(1 - T)(D/S).$$

  This equation shows that the required rate of return on a levered company's stock is equal to the risk-free rate, which compensates investors for the time value of money, plus premiums for business risk and financial risk.
- Within a **market risk framework,** business risk can be measured by b_U, market risk by b, and financial risk by $b - b_U = b_U(1 - T)(D/S)$.
- The **asymmetric information,** or **signaling, theory,** which recognizes that managers have better information than most investors, postulates that there is a preferred "pecking order" of financing: first retained earnings (and depreciation), then debt, and then, as a last resort only, new common stock.
- The signaling theory leads to the conclusion that firms should maintain a **reserve borrowing capacity** so that they can always issue debt on reasonable terms rather than have to issue new equity at the wrong time.
- There are clearly benefits to debt financing, but firms should use different amounts of debt depending on their tax rates, asset structures, and business risks.
- Wide variations in capital structure exist, both across industries and among individual firms within industries. The variations across industries can be explained to a large extent by the economic fundamentals of the industry. Variations within industries may also reflect operating differences, but they also reflect differences in managers' attitudes toward debt.
- The optimal capital structure should be thought of in market value rather than book value terms, even though managers often focus on book values.

Questions

17–1 Define each of the following terms.

a. MM Proposition I without taxes; with corporate taxes
b. MM Proposition II without taxes; with corporate taxes
c. Miller model
d. Financial distress costs
e. Agency costs
f. Trade-off model
g. Asymmetric information, or signaling, theory
h. Hamada equation
i. Reserve borrowing capacity

17–2 Explain why agency costs would probably be more of a problem for a large, publicly owned firm that uses both debt and equity capital than for a small, unleveraged, owner-managed firm.

17–3 Explain, verbally, how MM use the arbitrage process to prove the validity of Proposition I. Also, list the major MM assumptions and explain why each of these assumptions is necessary in the arbitrage proof.

17–4 A utility company is supposed to be allowed to charge prices high enough to cover all costs, including its cost of capital. Public service commissions are supposed to take actions to stimulate companies to operate as efficiently as possible in order to keep costs, hence prices, as low as possible. Some time ago, AT&T's debt ratio was about 33 percent. Some people (Myron J. Gordon in particular) argued that a higher debt ratio would lower AT&T's cost of capital and permit it to charge lower rates for telephone service. Gordon thought an optimal debt ratio for AT&T was about 50 percent. Do the theories presented in the chapter support or refute Gordon's position?

Self-Test Problem (Solution Appears in Appendix A)

ST–1 *MM WITH FINANCIAL DISTRESS COSTS*

B. Gibbs Inc. is an unleveraged firm, and it has constant expected operating earnings (EBIT) of \$2 million per year. The firm's tax rate is 40 percent, and its market value is V = S = \$12 million. Management is considering the use of some debt financing. (Debt would be issued and used to buy back stock, so the size of the firm would remain constant.) Because interest expense is tax deductible, the value of the firm would tend to increase as debt is added to the capital structure, but there would be an offset in the form of a rising risk of financial distress. The firm's analysts have estimated, as an approximation, that the present value of any future financial distress costs is \$8 million, and that the probability of distress would increase with leverage according to the following schedule:

Value of Debt	Probability of Financial Distress
\$ 2,500,000	0.00%
5,000,000	1.25
7,500,000	2.50
10,000,000	6.25
12,500,000	12.50
15,000,000	31.25
20,000,000	75.00

a. What is the firm's cost of equity and weighted average cost of capital at this time?
b. According to the "pure" MM with-tax model, what is the optimal level of debt?
c. What is the optimal capital structure when financial distress costs are included?
d. Plot the value of the firm, with and without distress costs, as a function of the level of debt.

Problems

17–1 *BUSINESS AND FINANCIAL RISK*

Air Tampa has just been incorporated, and its board of directors is currently grappling with the question of optimal capital structure. The company plans to offer commuter air services between Tampa and smaller surrounding cities. Jaxair has been around for a few years, and it has about the same basic business risk as Air Tampa would have. Jaxair's market-determined beta is 1.8, and it has a current market value debt ratio (total debt/total assets) of 50 percent and a federal-plus-state tax rate of 40 percent. Air Tampa expects only to be marginally profitable at startup, hence its tax rate would only be 25 percent. Air Tampa's owners expect that the total book and market value of the firm's stock, if it uses zero debt, would be \$10 million.

a. Estimate the beta of an unleveraged firm in the commuter airline business based on Jaxair's market-determined beta. (Hint: Jaxair's market-determined beta is a leveraged beta. Use Equation 17-6a and solve for b_U.)
b. Now assume that k_{RF} = 10% and k_M = 15%. Find the required rate of return on equity for an unleveraged commuter airline. What is the business risk premium for this industry?
c. Air Tampa is considering three capital structures: (1) \$2 million debt, (2) \$4 million debt, and (3) \$6 million debt. Estimate Air Tampa's k_s for these debt levels. What is the financial risk premium at each level?

d. Calculate Air Tampa's k_s and financial risk premium at \$6 million debt assuming its federal-plus-state tax rate is now 40 percent. Compare this with your corresponding answer to part c. (Hint: The increase in the tax rate causes V_U to drop to \$8 million.)

17–2 MM WITHOUT TAXES

Companies U and L are identical in every respect except that U is unleveraged while L has \$10 million of 5 percent bonds outstanding. Assume (1) that all of the MM assumptions are met, (2) that there are no corporate or personal taxes, (3) that EBIT is \$2 million, and (4) that the cost of equity to Company U is 10 percent.

a. What value would MM estimate for each firm?
b. What is k_s for Firm U? For Firm L?
c. Find S_L, and then show that $S_L + D = V_L = \$20$ million.
d. What is the WACC for Firm U? For Firm L?
e. Suppose $V_U = \$20$ million and $V_L = \$22$ million. According to MM, do these values represent an equilibrium? If not, explain the process by which equilibrium would be restored.

17–3 MM WITH CORPORATE TAXES

Refer to Problem 17-2. Assume that all the facts hold, except that both firms are subject to a 40 percent federal-plus-state corporate tax rate.

a. What value would MM now estimate for each firm? (Use Proposition I.)
b. What is k_s for Firm U? Firm L?
c. Find S_L, and then show that $S_L + D = V_L$ results in the same value as obtained in part a.
d. What is the WACC for Firm U? For Firm L?

17–4 MILLER MODEL

Refer to Problems 17-2 and 17-3. Assume that all facts hold, except that both corporate and personal taxes apply. Assume that both firms must pay a federal-plus-state corporate tax rate of T_c = 40%, and that investors in both firms face a tax rate of T_d = 28% on debt income and T_s = 20%, on average, on stock income.

a. What is the value of the unleveraged firm, V_U? (Note that V_U is now reduced by the personal tax on stock income, hence $V_U = \$12$ million as in Problem 17-3.)
b. What is the value of V_L?
c. What is the gain from leverage in this situation? Compare this with the gain from leverage in Problem 17-3.
d. Set $T_c = T_s = T_d = 0$. What is the value of the leveraged firm? The gain from leverage?
e. Now suppose $T_s = T_d = 0$. What are the value of the leveraged firm and the gain from leverage?
f. Assume that T_d = 28%, T_s = 28%, and T_c = 40%. Now what are the value of the leveraged firm and the gain from leverage?

17–5 MM WITH AND WITHOUT TAXES

International Associates (IA) is just about to commence operations as an international trading company. The firm will have book assets of \$10 million, and it expects to earn a 16 percent return on these assets before taxes. However, because of certain tax arrangements with foreign governments, IA will not pay any taxes; that is, its tax rate will be zero. Management is trying to decide how to raise the required \$10 million. It is known that the capitalization rate for an all-equity firm in this business is 11 percent, that is, k_{sU} = 11%. Further, IA can borrow at a rate k_d = 6%. Assume that the MM assumptions apply.

a. According to MM, what will be the value of IA if it uses no debt? If it uses \$6 million of 6 percent debt?
b. What are the values of the WACC and k_s at debt levels of D = \$0, D = \$6 million, and D = \$10 million? What effect does leverage have on firm value? Why?
c. Assume the initial facts of the problem (k_d = 6%, EBIT = \$1.6 million, k_{sU} = 11%), but now assume that a 40 percent federal-plus-state corporate tax rate exists. Find the new market values for IA with zero debt and with \$6 million of debt, using the MM formulas.
d. What are the values of the WACC and k_s at debt levels of D = \$0, D = \$6 million, and D = \$10 million, assuming a 40 percent corporate tax rate? Plot the relationships between the value of the firm and the debt ratio, and between capital costs and the debt ratio.
e. What is the maximum dollar amount of debt financing that can be used? What is the value of the firm at this debt level? What is the cost of this debt?
f. How would each of the following factors tend to change the values you plotted in your graph?
   (1) The interest rate on debt increases as the debt ratio rises.
   (2) At higher levels of debt, the probability of financial distress rises.

17–6 *AGENCY COSTS* Until recently, the Prestopino Company carried a triple-A bond rating and was strong in every respect. However, a series of problems has afflicted the firm: It is currently in severe financial distress, and its ability to make future payments on outstanding debt is questionable. If the firm were forced into bankruptcy at this time, the common stockholders would almost certainly be wiped out. Although the firm has limited financial resources, its cash flows (primarily from depreciation) are sufficient to support one of two mutually exclusive investments, each costing $150 million and having a 10-year expected life. These projects have the same market risk, but different total risk as measured by the variance of returns. Each project has the following after-tax cash inflows for 10 years:

	Annual Cash Inflows	
Probability	**Project A**	**Project B**
0.5	$30,000,000	$10,000,000
0.5	35,000,000	50,000,000

Assume that both projects have the same market risk as the firm's "average" project. The firm's weighted average cost of capital is 15 percent.

a. What is the expected annual cash inflow from each project?
b. Which project has the greater total risk?
c. Which project would you choose if you were a stockholder? Why?
d. Which project would the bondholders prefer to see management select? Why?
e. If the choices conflict, what "protection" do the bondholders have against the firm's making a decision that is contrary to their interests?
f. Who bears the cost of this "protection"? How is this cost related to leverage and the optimal capital structure?

17–7 *MM WITH FINANCIAL DISTRESS COSTS* The Boisjoly Company currently has no debt. An in-house research group has just been assigned the job of determining whether the firm should change its capital structure. Because of the importance of the decision, management has also hired the investment banking firm of Stanley Morgan & Company to conduct a parallel analysis of the situation. Mr. Harris, the in-house analyst, who is well versed in modern finance theory, has decided to carry out the analysis using the MM framework. Ms. Broske, the Stanley Morgan consultant, who has a good knowledge of capital market conditions and is confident of her ability to predict the firm's debt and equity costs at various levels of debt, has decided to estimate the optimal capital structure as that structure which minimizes the firm's weighted average cost of capital. The following data are relevant to both analyses:

EBIT = $4 million per year, in perpetuity.
Federal-plus-state tax rate = 40%.
Dividend payout ratio = 100%.
Current required rate of return on equity = 12%.

The cost of capital schedule predicted by Mr. Harris follows:

	At a Debt Level of (Millions of Dollars)							
	$0	**$2**	**$4**	**$6**	**$8**	**$10**	**$12**	**$14**
Interest rate (%)	—	8.0	8.3	9.0	10.0	11.0	13.0	16.0
Cost of equity (%)	12.0	12.25	12.75	13.0	13.15	13.4	14.65	17.0

Ms. Broske estimated the present value of financial distress costs at $8 million. Additionally, she estimated the following probabilities of financial distress:

	At a Debt Level of (Millions of Dollars)							
	$0	**$2**	**$4**	**$6**	**$8**	**$10**	**$12**	**$14**
Probability of financial distress	0	0	0.05	0.07	0.10	0.17	0.47	0.90

a. What level of debt would Mr. Harris and Ms. Broske recommend as optimal?
b. Comment on the similarities and differences in their recommendations.

Spreadsheet Problem

17–8 *WHAT IF ANALYSIS: MM WITH FINANCIAL DISTRESS COSTS*

Start with the model in the file ***Ch 17-8 What If Analysis.xls*** from the textbook's CD-ROM. The Brandt Corporation is an unleveraged firm, and it has constant expected operating earnings (EBIT) of $2 million per year. Brandt's federal-plus-state tax rate is 40 percent, its cost of equity is 10 percent, and its market value is V = S = $12 million. Management is considering the use of debt that would cost the firm 8 percent regardless of the amount used. (Debt would be issued and used to buy back stock, so the size of the firm would remain constant.) Since interest expense is tax deductible, the value of the firm would tend to increase as debt is added to the capital structure, but there would be an offset in the form of rising risk of financial distress. The firm's analysts have estimated, as an approximation, that the present value of any future financial distress costs is $8 million, and that the probability of distress would increase with leverage according to the following schedule:

Value of Debt	Probability of Distress
$ 0	0.0%
2,500,000	2.5
5,000,000	5.0
7,500,000	10.0
10,000,000	25.0
12,500,000	50.0
15,000,000	75.0

a. According to the "pure" MM with corporate taxes model, what is the optimal level of debt? (Consider only those debt values listed in the table.)
b. What is the optimal capital structure when financial distress costs are included?
c. Plot the value of the firm, with and without financial distress costs, as a function of the level of debt.
d. Assume that the firm's unleveraged cost of equity is 8 percent. What is the firm's optimal capital structure now? (From this point on, include financial distress costs in all your analyses.)
e. Return to the base-case k_{sU} of 10 percent. Now assume that the firm's tax rate increases to 60 percent. What effect does this change have on the firm's optimal capital structure?
f. Return to the base-case tax rate of 40 percent. Assume that the estimated present value of financial distress costs is only $5 million. Now what is the firm's optimal capital structure?

Mini Case

See ***Ch 17 Show.ppt*** and ***Ch 17 Mini Case.xls***.

Donald Cheney, the CEO of Cheney Electronics, is concerned about his firm's level of debt financing. The company uses short-term debt to finance its temporary working capital needs, but it does not use any permanent (long-term) debt. Other electronics companies average about 30 percent debt, and Mr. Cheney wonders why the difference occurs, and what its effects are on stock prices. To gain some insights into the matter, he poses the following questions to you, his recently hired assistant:

a. *Business Week* recently ran an article on companies' debt policies, and the names Modigliani and Miller (MM) were mentioned several times as leading researchers on the theory of capital structure. Briefly, who are MM, and what assumptions are embedded in the MM and Miller models?
b. Assume that Firms U and L are in the same risk class, and that both have EBIT = $500,000. Firm U uses no debt financing, and its cost of equity is k_{sU} = 14%. Firm L has $1 million of debt outstanding at a cost of k_d = 8%. There are no taxes. Assume that the MM assumptions hold, and then:
(1) Find V, S, k_s, and WACC for Firms U and L.
(2) Graph (a) the relationships between capital costs and leverage as measured by D/V, and (b) the relationship between value and D.

c. Using the data given in part b, but now assuming that firms L and U are both subject to a 40 percent corporate tax rate, repeat the analysis called for in b(1) and b(2) under the MM with-tax model.
d. Now suppose investors are subject to the following tax rates: $T_d = 30\%$ and $T_s = 12\%$.
   (1) What is the gain from leverage according to the Miller model?
   (2) How does this gain compare to the gain in the MM model with corporate taxes?
   (3) What does the Miller model imply about the effect of corporate debt on the value of the firm, that is, how do personal taxes affect the situation?
e. What capital structure policy recommendations do the three theories (MM without taxes, MM with corporate taxes, and Miller) suggest to financial managers? Empirically, do firms appear to follow any one of these guidelines?
f. What are financial distress and agency costs? How does the addition of these costs change the MM and Miller models? (Express your answer in words, in equation form, and in graphical form.)
g. How are financial and business risk measured in a market risk framework?
h. What is the asymmetric information, or signaling, theory of capital structure?
i. What is the "pecking order" theory of capital structure?

Selected Additional References and Cases

The body of literature on capital structure—and the number of potential references—is huge. Therefore, only a sampling can be given here. For an extensive review of the recent literature, as well as a detailed bibliography, see

Beranek, William, "Research Directions in Finance," *Quarterly Review of Business and Economics*, Spring 1981, 6–24.

The major theoretical works on capital structure theory are discussed in an integrated framework in

Copeland, Thomas E., and J. Fred Weston, *Financial Theory and Corporate Policy* (Reading, MA: Addison-Wesley, 1988).

Harris, Milton, and Artur Raviv, "The Theory of Capital Structure," *Journal of Finance*, March 1991, 297–355.

The Fall 1988 issue of The Journal of Economic Perspectives *and the Summer 1989 issue of* Financial Management *each contain several interesting and very readable articles that review the MM propositions after 30 years of debate and testing.*

In addition to Miller's work, the effect of personal taxes on capital structure decisions has been addressed by

Gordon, Myron J., and Lawrence I. Gould, "The Cost of Equity Capital with Personal Income Taxes and Flotation Costs," *Journal of Finance*, September 1978, 1201–1212.

Some other references of relevance include the following:

Ben-Horim, Moshe, Shalom Hochman, and Oded Palmon, "The Impact of the 1986 Tax Reform Act on Corporate Financial Policy," *Financial Management*, Autumn 1987, 29–35.

Bradley, Michael, Gregg A. Jarrell, and E. Han Kim, "On the Existence of an Optimal Capital Structure: Theory and Evidence," *Journal of Finance*, July 1984, 857–878.

Conine, Thomas E., Jr., "Debt Capacity and the Capital Budgeting Decision: Comment," *Financial Management*, Spring 1980, 20–22.

Crutchley, Claire E., and Robert S. Hansen, "A Test of the Agency Theory of Managerial Ownership, Corporate Leverage, and Corporate Dividends," *Financial Management*, Winter 1989, 36–46.

Dugan, Michael T., and Keith A. Shriver, "An Empirical Comparison of Alternative Methods for Estimating the Degree of Operating Leverage," *Financial Review*, May 1992, 309–321.

Ferri, Michael, and Wesley H. Jones, "Determinants of Financial Structure: A New Methodological Approach," *Journal of Finance*, June 1979, 631–644.

Flath, David, and Charles R. Knoeber, "Taxes, Failure Costs, and Optimal Industry Capital Structure," *Journal of Finance*, March 1980, 89–117.

Ghosh, Dilip K., "Optimum Capital Structure Redefined," *Financial Review*, August 1992, 411–429.

Kelly, William A., Jr., and James A. Miles, "Capital Structure Theory and the Fisher Effect," *The Financial Review*, February 1989, 53–73.

Lee, Wayne Y., and Henry H. Barker, "Bankruptcy Costs and the Firm's Optimal Debt Capacity: A Positive Theory of Capital Structure," *Southern Economic Journal*, April 1977, 1453–1465.

Mackie-Mason, Jeffrey K., "Do Taxes Affect Corporate Financing Decisions," *Journal of Finance*, December 1990, 1471–1493.

Martin, John D., and David F. Scott, "Debt Capacity and the Capital Budgeting Decision: A Revisitation," *Financial Management*, Spring 1980, 23–26.

Miller, Merton H., "The Modigliani-Miller Propositions after Thirty Years," *Journal of Applied Corporate Finance*, Spring 1989, 6–18.

———, "Leverage," *Journal of Finance*, June 1991, 479–488.

Pinegar, J. Michael, and Lisa Wilbricht, "What Managers Think of Capital Structure Theory: A Survey," *Financial Management*, Winter 1989, 82–91.

Scherr, Frederick C., "A Multiperiod Mean-Variance Model of Optimal Capital Structure," *The Financial Review*, February 1987, 1–31.

Schneller, Meir I., "Taxes and the Optimal Capital Structure of the Firm," *Journal of Finance*, March 1980, 119–127.

Taggart, Robert A., Jr., "Taxes and Corporate Capital Structure in an Incomplete Market," *Journal of Finance*, June 1980, 645–659.

Thakor, Anjan V., "Strategic Issues in Financial Contracting: An Overview," *Financial Management*, Summer 1989, 39–58.

There has been considerable discussion in the literature concerning a financial leverage clientele effect. Many theorists postulate that firms with low leverage are favored by high-tax-bracket investors and vice versa. Two articles on this subject are

Harris, John M., Jr., Rodney L. Roenfeldt, and Philip L. Cooley, "Evidence of Financial Leverage Clienteles," *Journal of Finance*, September 1983, 1125–1132.

Kim, E. Han, "Miller's Equilibrium, Shareholder Leverage Clienteles, and Optimal Capital Leverage," *Journal of Finance*, May 1982, 301–319.

For a very readable discussion of the many issues involved in capital structure theory, see

"A Discussion of Corporate Capital Structure," *Midland Corporate Finance Journal*, Fall 1985, 19–48.

The Dryden Press Cases in Financial Management: Dryden Request *series has the following cases that apply to this chapter:*

Case 7, "Seattle Steel Products," Case 9, "Kleen Kar, Inc.," Case 10, "Aspeon Sparkling Water," Case 10A, "Mountain Springs," Case 10B, "Greta Cosmetics," and Case 45, "The Western Company," focus on capital structure theory.

Case 8, "Johnson Window Company," and Case 8A, "Isle Marine Boat Company," cover operating and financial leverage.

18

Distributions to Shareholders: Dividends and Repurchases

A profitable company regularly faces three important questions. (1) How much of its free cash flow should it pass on to shareholders? (2) Should it provide this cash to stockholders by raising the dividend or by repurchasing stock? (3) Should it maintain a stable, consistent payment policy, or should it let the payments vary as conditions change?

In this chapter we will discuss the issues that affect a firm's cash distribution policy. As we will see, most firms establish a policy that considers their forecasted cash flows and forecasted capital expenditures, and then try to stick to it. The policy can be changed, but this can cause problems because such changes inconvenience the firm's stockholders and send unintended signals, both of which have negative implications for stock prices. Still, economic circumstances do change, and occasionally such changes require firms to change their dividend policies.

One of the most striking examples of a dividend policy change occurred in May 1994, when FPL Group, a utility holding company whose primary subsidiary is Florida Power & Light, announced a cut in its quarterly dividend from $0.62 per share to $0.42. At the same time, FPL stated that it would buy back 10 million of its common shares over the next three years to bolster its stock price.[1]

Security analysts called the FPL decision a watershed event for the electric utility industry. FPL saw that its circumstances were changing—its core electric business was moving from a regulated monopoly environment to one of increasing competition, and the new environment required a stronger balance sheet and more financial flexibility than was consistent with a 90 percent payout policy.

What did the market think about FPL's dividend policy change? The company's stock price fell by 14 percent the day the announcement was made. In the past, hundreds of dividend cuts followed by sharply lower earnings had conditioned investors to expect the worst when a company reduces its dividend—this is the signaling effect, which is discussed later in the chapter. However, over the next few months, as they understood FPL's actions better, analysts began to praise the decision and to recommend the stock. As a result, FPL's stock has outperformed the average utility and soon exceeded the preannouncement price.

[1]For a complete discussion of the FPL decision, see Dennis Soter, Eugene Brigham, and Paul Evanson, "The Dividend Cut Heard 'Round the World: The Case of FPL," *Journal of Applied Corporate Finance*, Spring 1996, 4–15. Also, note that stock repurchases are discussed in a later section of this chapter.

The textbook's CD-ROM contains an *Excel* file that will guide you through the chapter's calculations. The file for this chapter is ***Ch 18 Tool Kit.xls,*** and we encourage you to open the file and follow along as you read the chapter.

Successful companies earn income. That income can then be reinvested in operating assets, used to acquire securities, used to retire debt, or distributed to stockholders. If the decision is made to distribute income to stockholders, three key issues arise: (1) How much should be distributed? (2) Should the distribution be as cash dividends, or should the cash be passed on to shareholders by buying back some of the stock they hold? (3) How stable should the distribution be; that is, should the funds paid out from year to year be stable and dependable, which stockholders would probably prefer, or be allowed to vary with the firms' cash flows and investment requirements, which would probably be better from the firms' standpoint? These three issues are the primary focus of this chapter, but we also consider two related issues, stock dividends and stock splits.

Dividends versus Capital Gains: What Do Investors Prefer?

An excellent source of recent dividend new releases for major corporations is available at the web site of Corporate Financials Online at **http://www.cfonews.com/scs.** By clicking the down arrow of the "News Category" box to the left of the screen, students may select "Dividends" to receive a list of companies with dividend news. Click on any company, and you will see its latest dividend news.

When deciding how much cash to distribute to stockholders, financial managers must keep in mind that the firm's objective is to maximize shareholder value. Consequently, the **target payout ratio**—defined as the percentage of net income to be paid out as cash dividends—should be based in large part on investors' preferences for dividends versus capital gains: do investors prefer (1) to have the firm distribute income as cash dividends or (2) to have it either repurchase stock or else plow the earnings back into the business, both of which should result in capital gains? This preference can be considered in terms of the constant growth stock valuation model:

$$\hat{P}_0 = \frac{D_1}{k_s - g}.$$

If the company increases the payout ratio, this raises D_1. This increase in the numerator, taken alone, would cause the stock price to rise. However, if D_1 is raised, then less money will be available for reinvestment, that will cause the expected growth rate to decline, and that will tend to lower the stock's price. Thus, any change in payout policy will have two opposing effects. Therefore, the firm's **optimal dividend policy** must strike a balance between current dividends and future growth so as to maximize the stock price.

In this section we examine three theories of investor preference: (1) the dividend irrelevance theory, (2) the "bird-in-the-hand" theory, and (3) the tax preference theory.

Dividend Irrelevance Theory

It has been argued that dividend policy has no effect on either the price of a firm's stock or its cost of capital. If dividend policy has no significant effects, then it would be *irrelevant*. The principal proponents of the **dividend irrelevance theory** are Merton Miller and Franco Modigliani (MM).[2] They argued that the firm's value is determined only by its basic earning power and its business risk. In other words, MM argued that the value of the firm depends only on the income produced by its assets, not on how this income is split between dividends and retained earnings.

To understand MM's argument that dividend policy is irrelevant, recognize that any shareholder can in theory construct his or her own dividend policy. For example, if a firm does not pay dividends, a shareholder who wants a 5 percent dividend can

---

[2]Merton H. Miller and Franco Modigliani, "Dividend Policy, Growth, and the Valuation of Shares," *Journal of Business*, October 1961, 411–433.

"create" it by selling 5 percent of his or her stock. Conversely, if a company pays a higher dividend than an investor desires, the investor can use the unwanted dividends to buy additional shares of the company's stock. If investors could buy and sell shares and thus create their own dividend policy without incurring costs, then the firm's dividend policy would truly be irrelevant. Note, though, that investors who want additional dividends must incur brokerage costs to sell shares, and investors who do not want dividends must first pay taxes on the unwanted dividends and then incur brokerage costs to purchase shares with the after-tax dividends. Because taxes and brokerage costs certainly exist, dividend policy may well be relevant.

In developing their dividend theory, MM made a number of assumptions, especially the absence of taxes and brokerage costs. Obviously, taxes and brokerage costs do exist, so the MM irrelevance theory may not be true. However, MM argued (correctly) that all economic theories are based on simplifying assumptions, and that the validity of a theory must be judged by empirical tests, not by the realism of its assumptions. We will discuss empirical tests of MM's dividend irrelevance theory shortly.

Bird-in-the-Hand Theory: Dividends Are Safer

The principal conclusion of MM's dividend irrelevance theory is that dividend policy does not affect the required rate of return on equity, k_s. This conclusion has been hotly debated in academic circles. In particular, Myron Gordon and John Lintner argued that k_s *decreases* as the dividend payout is increased because investors are less certain of receiving the capital gains which are supposed to result from retaining earnings than they are of receiving dividend payments.[3] Gordon and Lintner said, in effect, that investors value a dollar of expected dividends more highly than a dollar of expected capital gains because the dividend yield component, D_1/P_0, is less risky than the g component in the total expected return equation, $k_s = D_1/P_0 + g$.

MM disagreed. They argued that k_s is independent of dividend policy, which implies that investors are indifferent between D_1/P_0 and g and, hence, between dividends and capital gains. MM called the Gordon-Lintner argument the **bird-in-the-hand** fallacy because, in MM's view, most investors plan to reinvest their dividends in the stock of the same or similar firms, and, in any event, the riskiness of the firm's cash flows to investors in the long run is determined by the riskiness of operating cash flows, not by dividend payout policy.

Tax Preference Theory

There are three tax-related reasons for thinking that investors might prefer a low dividend payout to a high payout: (1) Recall from Chapter 2 that long-term capital gains are taxed at a maximum rate of 20 percent, whereas dividends are taxed at effective rates that go up to 39.6 percent. Therefore, wealthy investors (who own most of the stock and receive most of the dividends) might prefer to have companies retain and plow earnings back into the business. Earnings growth would presumably lead to stock price increases, and thus lower-taxed capital gains would be substituted for higher-taxed dividends. (2) Taxes are not paid on the gain until a stock is sold. Due to time value effects, a dollar of taxes paid in the future has a lower effective cost than a dollar paid today. (3) If a stock is held by someone until he or she dies, no capital gains

[3]Myron J. Gordon, "Optimal Investment and Financing Policy," *Journal of Finance*, May 1963, 264–272, and John Lintner, "Dividends, Earnings, Leverage, Stock Prices, and the Supply of Capital to Corporations," *Review of Economics and Statistics*, August 1962, 243–269.

tax is due at all—the beneficiaries who receive the stock can use the stock's value on the death day as their cost basis and thus completely escape the capital gains tax.

Because of these tax advantages, investors may prefer to have companies retain most of their earnings. If so, investors would be willing to pay more for low-payout companies than for otherwise similar high-payout companies.

Illustration of the Three Dividend Policy Theories

Figure 18-1 illustrates the three alternative dividend policy theories: (1) Miller and Modigliani's dividend irrelevance theory, (2) Gordon and Lintner's "dividends are safer" theory that MM called the bird-in-the-hand fallacy, and (3) the tax preference theory. To understand the three theories, consider the case of Hardin Electronics, which has from its inception plowed all earnings back into the business and thus has never paid a dividend. Hardin's management is now reconsidering its dividend policy, and it wants to adopt the policy that will maximize its stock price.

Consider first the data presented below the graph. Columns 1 through 4 show three alternative payout policies: (1) Retain all earnings and pay out nothing, which is the present policy, (2) pay out 50 percent of earnings, and (3) pay out 100 percent of earnings. In the example, we assume that the company will have a 15 percent ROE regardless of which payout policy it follows, so with a book value per share of \$30, EPS will be 0.15(\$30) = \$4.50 under all payout policies.[4] Given an EPS of \$4.50, dividends per share are shown in Column 3 under each payout policy.

Under the assumption of a constant ROE, the growth rate shown in Column 4 will be g = (% Retained)(ROE), and it will vary from 15 percent at a zero payout to zero at a 100 percent payout. For example, if Hardin pays out 50 percent of its earnings, then its dividend growth rate will be g = 0.5(15%) = 7.5%.

Columns 5, 6, and 7 show how the situation would look if MM's irrelevance theory were correct. Under this theory, neither the stock price nor the cost of equity would be affected by the payout policy—the stock price would remain constant at \$30, and k_s would be stable at 15 percent. Note that k_s is found as the sum of the growth rate in Column 4 plus the dividend yield in Column 6.

Columns 8, 9, and 10 show the situation if the bird-in-the-hand theory were true. Under this theory, investors prefer dividends, and the more of its earnings the company pays out, the higher its stock price and the lower its cost of equity. In our example, the bird-in-the-hand theory indicates that adopting a 100 percent payout policy would cause the stock price to rise from \$30 to \$40, and the cost of equity would decline from 15 percent to 11.25 percent.

Finally, Columns 11, 12, and 13 show the situation if the tax preference theory were correct. Under this theory, investors prefer companies that retain earnings and thus provide returns in the form of lower-taxed capital gains rather than higher-taxed dividends. If the tax preference theory were correct, then an increase in the dividend payout ratio from its current zero level would cause the stock price to decline and the cost of equity to rise.

The data in the table are plotted to produce the two graphs shown in Figure 18-1. The upper graph shows how the stock price would react to dividend policy under each of the theories, and the lower graph shows how the cost of equity would be affected.

[4]When the three theories were developed, it was assumed that a company's investment opportunities would be held constant and that if the company increased its dividends, its capital budget could be funded by selling common stock. Conversely, if a high-payout company lowered its payout to the point where earnings exceeded good investment opportunities, it was assumed that the company would repurchase shares. Transactions costs were assumed to be immaterial. We maintain those assumptions in our example.

FIGURE 18-1 Dividend Irrelevance, Bird-in-the-Hand, and Tax Preference Dividend Theories

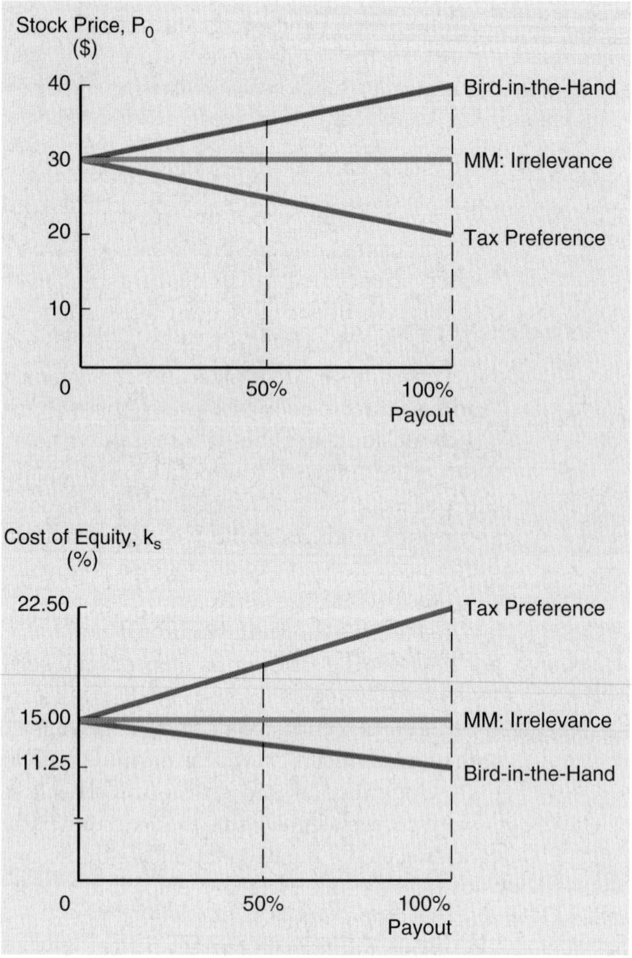

Alternative Payout Policies				Possible Situations (Only One Can Be True)								
				MM: Irrelevance			Bird-in-the-Hand			Tax Preference		
Percent Payout (1)	Percent Retained (2)	DPS (3)	g (4)	P_0 (5)	D/P_0 (6)	k_s (7)	P_0 (8)	D/P_0 (9)	k_s (10)	P_0 (11)	D/P_0 (12)	k_s (13)
0%	100%	$0.00	15.0%	$30	0.0%	15.0%	$30	0.00%	15.00%	$30	0.0%	15.0%
50	50	2.25	7.5	30	7.5	15.0	35	6.43	13.93	25	9.0	16.5
100	0	4.50	0.0	30	15.0	15.0	40	11.25	11.25	20	22.5	22.5

Notes:

1. Book value = Initial market value = $30 per share.
2. ROE = 15%.
3. EPS = $30(0.15) = $4.50.
4. g = (% retained)(ROE) = (% retained)(15%). Example: At payout = 50%, g = 0.5(15%) = 7.5%. If payout = 100%, g = 0.0%.
5. k_s = Dividend yield + Growth rate.

Using Empirical Evidence to Decide Which Theory Is Best

These three theories offer contradictory advice to corporate managers, so which, if any, should we believe? The most logical way to proceed is to test the theories empirically. Many such tests have been conducted, but their results have been unclear. There are two reasons for this: (1) For a valid statistical test, things other than dividend policy must be held constant; that is, the sample companies must differ only in their dividend policies, and (2) we must be able to measure with a high degree of accuracy each firm's cost of equity. Neither of these two conditions holds: We cannot find a set of publicly owned firms that differ only in their dividend policies, nor can we obtain precise estimates of the cost of equity.

Therefore, no one can establish a clear relationship between dividend policy and the cost of equity. Investors in the aggregate cannot be shown to uniformly prefer either higher or lower dividends. Nevertheless, *individual* investors do have strong preferences. Some prefer high dividends, while others prefer all capital gains. These differences among individuals help explain why it is difficult to reach any definitive conclusions regarding the optimal dividend payout. Even so, both evidence and logic suggest that investors prefer firms that follow a *stable, predictable* dividend policy (regardless of the payout level). We will consider the issue of dividend stability later in the chapter.

Self-Test Questions

Explain the dividend irrelevance theory, the bird-in-the-hand theory, and the tax preference theory. Use a graph such as Figure 18-1 to illustrate your answer.

What did Modigliani and Miller assume about taxes and brokerage costs when they developed their dividend irrelevance theory?

How did the bird-in-the-hand theory get its name?

In what sense does MM's theory represent a middle-ground position between the other two theories?

What have been the results of empirical tests of the dividend theories?

Other Dividend Policy Issues

Before we discuss how dividend policy is set in practice, we must examine two other theoretical issues that could affect dividend policy: (1) the *information content*, or *signaling, hypothesis* and (2) the *clientele effect.*

Information Content, or Signaling, Hypothesis

When MM set forth their dividend irrelevance theory, they assumed that everyone—investors and managers alike—has identical information regarding the firm's future earnings and dividends. In reality, however, different investors have different views on both the level of future dividend payments and the uncertainty inherent in those payments, and managers have better information about future prospects than public stockholders.

It has been observed that an increase in the dividend is often accompanied by an increase in the price of a stock, while a dividend cut generally leads to a stock price decline. Some have argued that this indicates that investors prefer dividends to capital gains. However, MM argued differently. They noted the well-established fact that corporations are reluctant to cut dividends, hence do not raise dividends unless they anticipate higher earnings in the future. Thus, MM argued that a higher-than-expected dividend increase is a "signal" to investors that the firm's management

Dividend Yields Around the World

Dividend yields vary considerably in different stock markets throughout the world. In 1999 in the United States, dividend yields averaged 1.6 percent for the large blue chip stocks in the Dow Jones Industrials, 1.2 percent for a broader sample of stocks in the S&P 500, and 0.3 percent for stocks in the high-tech-dominated Nasdaq. Outside the United States, average dividend yields ranged from 5.7 percent in New Zealand to 0.7 percent in Taiwan. The accompanying table summarizes the dividend picture in 1999.

World Stock Market (Index)	Dividend Yield
New Zealand	5.7%
Australia	3.1
Britain FTSE 100	2.4
Hong Kong	2.4
France	2.1
Germany	2.1
Belgium	2.0
Singapore	1.7
United States (Dow Jones Industrials)	1.6
Canada (TSE 300)	1.5
United States (S&P 500)	1.2
Mexico	1.1
Japan Nikkei	0.7
Taiwan	0.7
United States (Nasdaq)	0.3

Source: Alexandra Eadie, "On the Grid Looking for Dividend Yield Around the World," *The Globe and Mail,* June 23, 1999, B16. Eadie's source was Bloomberg Financial Services.

forecasts good future earnings.[5] Conversely, a dividend reduction, or a smaller-than-expected increase, is a signal that management is forecasting poor earnings in the future. Thus, MM argued that investors' reactions to changes in dividend policy do not necessarily show that investors prefer dividends to retained earnings. Rather, they argue that price changes following dividend actions simply indicate that there is an important **information, or signaling, content** in dividend announcements.

Like most other aspects of dividend policy, empirical studies of signaling have had mixed results. There is clearly some information content in dividend announcements. However, it is difficult to tell whether the stock price changes that follow increases or

[5]Stephen Ross has suggested that managers can use capital structure as well as dividends to give signals concerning firms' future prospects. For example, a firm with good earnings prospects can carry more debt than a similar firm with poor earnings prospects. This theory, called *incentive signaling,* rests on the premise that signals with cash-based variables (either debt interest or dividends) cannot be mimicked by unsuccessful firms because such firms do not have the future cash-generating power to maintain the announced interest or dividend payment. Thus, investors are more likely to believe a glowing verbal report when it is accompanied by a dividend increase or a debt-financed expansion program. See Stephen A. Ross, "The Determination of Financial Structure: The Incentive-Signaling Approach," *The Bell Journal of Economics,* Spring 1977, 23–40.

decreases in dividends reflect only signaling effects or both signaling and dividend preference. Still, signaling effects should definitely be considered when a firm is contemplating a change in dividend policy.

Clientele Effect

As we indicated earlier, different groups, or *clienteles*, of stockholders prefer different dividend payout policies. For example, retired individuals, pension funds, and university endowment funds generally prefer cash income, so they may want the firm to pay out a high percentage of its earnings. Such investors are often in low or even zero tax brackets, so taxes are of no concern. On the other hand, stockholders in their peak earning years might prefer reinvestment, because they have less need for current investment income and would simply reinvest dividends received, after first paying income taxes on those dividends.

If a firm retains and reinvests income rather than paying dividends, those stockholders who need current income would be disadvantaged. The value of their stock might increase, but they would be forced to go to the trouble and expense of selling off some of their shares to obtain cash. Also, some institutional investors (or trustees for individuals) would be legally precluded from selling stock and then "spending capital." On the other hand, stockholders who are saving rather than spending dividends might favor the low dividend policy, for the less the firm pays out in dividends, the less these stockholders will have to pay in current taxes, and the less trouble and expense they will have to go through to reinvest their after-tax dividends. Therefore, investors who want current investment income should own shares in high dividend payout firms, while investors with no need for current investment income should own shares in low dividend payout firms. For example, investors seeking high cash income might invest in electric utilities, which averaged a 73 percent payout from 1996 through 2000, while those favoring growth could invest in the semiconductor industry, which paid out only 7 percent during the same time period.

To the extent that stockholders can switch firms, a firm can change from one dividend payout policy to another and then let stockholders who do not like the new policy sell to other investors who do. However, frequent switching would be inefficient because of (1) brokerage costs, (2) the likelihood that stockholders who are selling will have to pay capital gains taxes, and (3) a possible shortage of investors who like the firm's newly adopted dividend policy. Thus, management should be hesitant to change its dividend policy, because a change might cause current shareholders to sell their stock, forcing the stock price down. Such a price decline might be temporary, but it might also be permanent—if few new investors are attracted by the new dividend policy, then the stock price would remain depressed. Of course, the new policy might attract an even larger clientele than the firm had before, in which case the stock price would rise.

Evidence from several studies suggests that there is in fact a **clientele effect.**[6] MM and others have argued that one clientele is as good as another, so the existence of a clientele effect does not necessarily imply that one dividend policy is better than any other. MM may be wrong, though, and neither they nor anyone else can prove that the aggregate makeup of investors permits firms to disregard clientele effects. This issue, like most others in the dividend arena, is still up in the air.

---

[6]For example, see R. Richardson Pettit, "Taxes, Transactions Costs and the Clientele Effect of Dividends," *The Journal of Financial Economics*, December 1977, 419–436.

Self-Test Question

Define (1) information content and (2) the clientele effect, and explain how they affect dividend policy.

Dividend Stability

As we noted at the beginning of the chapter, the stability of dividends is also important. Profits and cash flows vary over time, as do investment opportunities. Taken alone, this suggests that corporations should vary their dividends over time, increasing them when cash flows are large and the need for funds is low and lowering them when cash is in short supply relative to investment opportunities. However, many stockholders rely on dividends to meet expenses, and they would be seriously inconvenienced if the dividend stream were unstable. Further, reducing dividends to make funds available for capital investment could send incorrect signals to investors, who might push down the stock price because they interpreted the dividend cut to mean that the company's future earnings prospects have been diminished. Thus, maximizing its stock price requires a firm to balance its internal needs for funds against the needs and desires of its stockholders.

How should this balance be struck; that is, how stable and dependable should a firm attempt to make its dividends? It is impossible to give a definitive answer to this question, but the following points are relevant:

1. Virtually every publicly owned company makes a five- to ten-year financial forecast of earnings and dividends. Such forecasts are never made public—they are used for internal planning purposes only. However, security analysts construct similar forecasts and do make them available to investors; see *Value Line* for an example. Further, virtually every internal five- to ten-year corporate forecast we have seen for a "normal" company projects a trend of higher earnings and dividends. Both managers and investors know that economic conditions may cause actual results to differ from forecasted results, but "normal" companies expect to grow.
2. Years ago, when inflation was not persistent, the term "stable dividend policy" meant a policy of paying the same dollar dividend year after year. AT&T was a prime example of a company with a stable dividend policy—it paid $9 per year ($2.25 per quarter) for 25 straight years. Today, though, most companies and stockholders expect earnings to grow over time as a result of retained earnings and inflation. Further, dividends are normally expected to grow more or less in line with earnings. Thus, today a "stable dividend policy" generally means increasing the dividend at a reasonably steady rate. For example, Rubbermaid made this statement in its annual report:

> Dividends per share were increased . . . for the 34th consecutive year. . . . Our goal is to increase sales, earnings, and earnings per share by 15% per year, while achieving a 21% return on beginning shareholders' equity. It is also the Company's objective to pay approximately 30% of current year's earnings as dividends, which will permit us to retain sufficient capital to provide for future growth.

Rubbermaid used the word "approximately" in discussing its payout ratio, because even if earnings vary a bit from the target level, the company still planned to increase the dividend by the target growth rate. Even though Rubbermaid did not mention the dividend growth rate in the statement, analysts can calculate the growth rate and see that it is the same 15 percent as indicated for sales and earnings:

$$
\begin{aligned}
g &= \text{(Retention rate)(ROE)} \\
&= (1 - \text{Payout rate})\text{(ROE)} \\
&= 0.7(21\%) \approx 15\%.
\end{aligned}
$$

Companies with volatile earnings and cash flows would be reluctant to make a commitment to increase the dividend each year, so they would not make such a detailed statement. Even so, most companies would like to be able to exhibit the kind of stability Rubbermaid had shown, and they try to come as close to it as they can.[7]

Dividend stability has two components: (1) How dependable is the growth rate, and (2) can we count on at least receiving the current dividend in the future? The most stable policy, from an investor's standpoint, is that of a firm whose dividend growth rate is predictable—such a company's total return (dividend yield plus capital gains yield) would be relatively stable over the long run, and its stock would be a good hedge against inflation. The second most stable policy is where stockholders can be reasonably sure that the current dividend will not be reduced—it may not grow at a steady rate, but management will probably be able to avoid cutting the dividend. The least stable situation is where earnings and cash flows are so volatile that investors cannot count on the current dividend in the future.

3. Most observers believe that dividend stability is desirable and that investors prefer stocks that pay more predictable dividends to stocks that pay the same average amount of dividends but in a more erratic manner. This means that the cost of equity will be minimized, and the stock price maximized, if a firm stabilizes its dividends as much as possible.

Self-Test Questions

What does the term "stable dividend policy" mean?

What are the two components of dividend stability?

Establishing the Dividend Policy in Practice

In the preceding sections we saw that investors may or may not prefer dividends to capital gains, but that they do prefer predictable dividends. Given this situation, how should firms set their basic dividend policies? For example, how should a company like Rubbermaid establish the specific percentage of earnings it will pay out? Rubbermaid's target was stated to be 30 percent, but why not 40 percent, 50 percent, or some other percentage? In this section, we describe how most firms establish their target payout ratios.

Setting the Target Payout Ratio: The Residual Dividend Model[8]

When deciding how much cash to distribute to stockholders, two points should be kept in mind: (1) The overriding objective is to maximize shareholder value, and (2) the firm's

---

[7]Rubbermaid was unable to remain on target. A new CEO was appointed in the early 1990s. He tried to accelerate growth by changing strategic policies but was unable to execute the new plans. Sales, profits, and cash flows plummeted. The company tried to maintain the dividend, using up cash. Finally, in 1998, after things had deteriorated to the point where survival was questionable, Rubbermaid was acquired by Newall Corp., which was renamed Newall Rubbermaid.

[8]The term "payout ratio" can be interpreted in two ways: (1) the conventional way, where the payout ratio means the percentage of net income paid out as cash dividends, or (2) the percentage of net income distributed to stockholders both through dividends and through share repurchases. In this section, we assume that no repurchases occur. Increasingly, though, firms are using the residual model to determine "distributions to shareholders" and then making a separate decision as to the form of that distribution. Further, an increasing percentage of the distribution is in the form of share repurchases.

cash flows really belong to its shareholders, so management should refrain from retaining income unless they can reinvest it to produce returns higher than shareholders could themselves earn by investing the cash in investments of equal risk. On the other hand, recall from Chapter 11 that internal equity (retained earnings) is cheaper than external equity (new common stock). This encourages firms to retain earnings so as to avoid having to issue new stock.

When establishing a dividend policy, one size does not fit all. Some firms produce a lot of cash but have limited investment opportunities—this is true for firms in profitable but mature industries where few opportunities for growth exist. Such firms typically distribute a large percentage of their cash to shareholders, thereby attracting investment clienteles that prefer high dividends. Other firms generate little or no excess cash but have many good investment opportunities. Such firms generally distribute little or no cash but enjoy rising earnings and stock prices, thereby attracting investors who prefer capital gains.

As Table 18-1 suggests, dividend payouts and dividend yields for large corporations vary considerably. Generally, firms in stable, cash-producing industries such as utilities, financial services, and tobacco pay relatively high dividends, whereas companies in rapidly growing industries such as computer software tend to pay lower dividends.

For a given firm, the optimal payout ratio is a function of four factors: (1) investor's preferences for dividends versus capital gains, (2) the firm's investment opportunities, (3) its target capital structure, and (4) the availability and cost of external capital. The last three elements are combined in what we call the **residual dividend model.** Under this model a firm follows these four steps when establishing its target payout ratio: (1) It determines the optimal capital budget; (2) it determines the amount of equity needed to finance that budget, given its target capital structure; (3) it uses retained earnings to meet equity requirements to the extent possible; and (4) it pays dividends only if more earnings are available than are needed to support the optimal capital

TABLE 18-1 Dividend Payouts

Company	Industry	Dividend Payout	Dividend Yield
I. Companies that Pay High Dividends			
WD-40 Company	Household products	96.3%	6.1%
Kansas City Power and Light	Utility	89.6	6.7
Louisiana-Pacific Corp.	Forest products	80.1	6.6
R. J. Reynolds Tobacco	Tobacco products	77.4	8.9
Union Planters Corp.	Regional banks	68.4	5.8
Ingles Markets Inc.	Retail (grocery)	67.0	6.6
II. Companies that Pay Little or No Dividends			
Tiffany and Company	Specialty retail	13.8%	0.4%
Harley-Davidson Inc.	Recreational products	9.4	0.2
Aaron Rents Inc.	Rental and leasing	2.9	0.3
Delta Air Lines Inc.	Airline	1.1	0.2
Papa John's Intl. Inc.	Restaurants	0.0	0.0
Microsoft Corp.	Software and programming	0.0	0.0

Source: www.marketguide.com, November 2000.

budget. The word *residual* implies "leftover," and the residual policy implies that dividends are paid out of "leftover" earnings.

If a firm rigidly follows the residual dividend policy, then dividends paid in any given year can be expressed as follows:

$$\begin{aligned}\text{Dividends} &= \text{Net income} - \text{Retained earnings needed to finance new investments}\\ &= \text{Net income} - [(\text{Target equity ratio})(\text{Total capital budget})].\end{aligned}$$

For example, suppose the target equity ratio is 60 percent and the firm plans to spend \$50 million on capital projects. In that case, it would need \$50(0.6) = \$30 million of common equity. Then, if its net income were \$100 million, its dividends would be \$100 − \$30 = \$70 million. So, if the company had \$100 million of earnings and a capital budget of \$50 million, it would use \$30 million of the retained earnings plus \$50 − \$30 = \$20 million of new debt to finance the capital budget, and this would keep its capital structure on target. Note that the amount of equity needed to finance new investments might exceed the net income; in our example, this would happen if the capital budget were \$200 million. In that case, no dividends would be paid, and the company would have to issue new common stock in order to maintain its target capital structure.

Most firms have a target capital structure that calls for at least some debt, so new financing is done partly with debt and partly with equity. As long as the firm finances with the optimal mix of debt and equity, and provided it uses only internally generated equity (retained earnings), then the marginal cost of each new dollar of capital will be minimized. Internally generated equity is available for financing a certain amount of new investment, but beyond that amount, the firm must turn to more expensive new common stock. At the point where new stock must be sold, the cost of equity, and consequently the marginal cost of capital, rises.

To illustrate these points, consider the case of Texas and Western (T&W) Transport Company. T&W's overall composite cost of capital is 10 percent. However, this cost assumes that all new equity comes from retained earnings. If the company must issue new stock, its cost of capital will be higher. T&W has \$60 million in net income and a target capital structure of 60 percent equity and 40 percent debt. Provided that it does not pay any cash dividends, T&W could make net investments (investments in addition to asset replacements from depreciation) of \$100 million, consisting of \$60 million from retained earnings plus \$40 million of new debt supported by the retained earnings, at a 10 percent marginal cost of capital. If the capital budget exceeded \$100 million, the required equity component would exceed net income, which is of course the maximum amount of retained earnings. In this case, T&W would have to issue new common stock, thereby pushing its cost of capital above 10 percent.[9]

At the beginning of its planning period, T&W's financial staff considers all proposed projects for the upcoming period. Independent projects are accepted if their estimated returns exceed the risk-adjusted cost of capital. In choosing among mutually exclusive projects, T&W chooses the project with the highest positive NPV. The capital budget represents the amount of capital that is required to finance all accepted projects. If T&W follows a strict residual dividend policy, we can see from Table 18-2 that the estimated capital budget will cause larger changes in the dividend payout ratio.

[9]If T&W does not retain all of its earnings, its cost of capital will rise above 10 percent before its capital budget reaches \$100 million. For example, if T&W chose to retain \$36 million, its cost of capital would increase once the capital budget exceeded \$36/0.6 = \$60 million.

TABLE 18-2 T&W's Dividend Payout Ratio with $60 Million of Net Income When Faced with Different Investment Opportunities (Dollars in Millions)

	Investment Opportunities		
	Poor	Average	Good
Capital budget	$40	$70	$150
Net income	$60	$60	$ 60
Required equity (0.6 × Capital budget)	24	42	90
Dividends paid (NI − Required equity)	$36	$18	−$ 30[a]
Dividend payout ratio (Dividend/NI)	60%	30%	0%

[a]With a $150 million capital budget, T&W would retain all of its earnings and also issue $30 million of new stock.

If T&W forecasts poor investment opportunities, its estimated capital budget will be only $40 million. To maintain the target capital structure, 40 percent of this capital ($16 million) must be raised as debt, and 60 percent ($24 million) must be equity. If it followed a strict residual policy, T&W would retain $24 million of its $60 million earnings to help finance new investments, then pay out the remaining $36 million as dividends. Under this scenario, the company's dividend payout ratio would be $36 million/$60 million = 0.6 = 60%.

By contrast, if the company's investment opportunities were average, its optimal capital budget would rise to $70 million. Here it would require $42 million of retained earnings, so dividends would be $60 − $42 = $18 million, for a payout of $18/$60 = 30%. Finally, if investment opportunities are good, the capital budget would be $150 million, which would require 0.6($150) = $90 million of equity. T&W would retain all of its net income ($60 million), thus pay no dividends. Moreover, since the required equity exceeds the retained earnings, the company would have to issue some new common stock to maintain the target capital structure.

Since both investment opportunities and earnings will surely vary from year to year, strict adherence to the residual dividend policy would result in unstable dividends. One year the firm might pay zero dividends because it needed the money to finance good investment opportunities, but the next year it might pay a large dividend because investment opportunities were poor and it therefore did not need to retain much. Similarly, fluctuating earnings could also lead to variable dividends, even if investment opportunities were stable. Therefore, following the residual dividend policy rigidly would lead to fluctuating, unstable dividends. Since investors desire stable, dependable dividends, k_s would be high, and the stock price low, if the firm followed the residual model in a strict sense rather than attempting to stabilize its dividends over time. Therefore, firms should

1. Estimate earnings and investment opportunities, on average, over the next five or so years.
2. Use this forecasted information to find the average residual model payout ratio and dollars of dividends during the planning period.
3. Then set a *target payout ratio* based on the average projected data.

Thus, firms should use the residual policy to help set their long-run target payout ratios, but not as a guide to the payout in any one year.

Companies use the residual dividend model as discussed above to help understand the determinants of an optimal dividend policy, along with computerized financial forecasting models. Most larger corporations forecast their financial statements over the next five to ten years. Information on projected capital expenditures and working capital requirements is entered into the model, along with sales forecasts, profit margins, depreciation, and the other elements required to forecast cash flows. The target capital structure is also specified, and the model shows the amount of debt and equity that will be required to meet the capital budgeting requirements while maintaining the target capital structure. Then, dividend payments are introduced. Naturally, the higher the payout ratio, the greater the required external equity. Most companies use the model to find a dividend pattern over the forecast period (generally five years) that will provide sufficient equity to support the capital budget without forcing it to sell new common stock or move the capital structure ratios outside the optimal range. The end result might include a memo from the CFO to the CEO such as the following:

> We forecasted the total market demand for our products, what our share of the market is likely to be, and our required investments in capital assets and working capital. Using this information, we developed projected balance sheets and income statements for the period 2002–2006.
>
> Our 2001 dividends totaled $50 million, or $2 per share. On the basis of projected earnings, cash flows, and capital requirements, we can increase the dividend by 8 percent per year. This is consistent with a payout ratio of 42 percent, on average, over the forecast period. Any faster dividend growth rate (or higher payout) would require us to sell common stock, cut the capital budget, or raise the debt ratio. Any slower growth rate would lead to increases in the common equity ratio. Therefore, I recommend that the Board increase the dividend for 2002 by 8 percent, to $2.16, and that it plan for similar increases in the future.
>
> Events over the next five years will undoubtedly lead to differences between our forecasts and actual results. If and when such events occur, we will want to reexamine our position. However, I am confident that we can meet any random cash shortfalls by increasing our borrowings—we have unused debt capacity that gives us flexibility in this regard.
>
> We ran the corporate model under several recession scenarios. If the economy really crashes, our earnings will not cover the dividend. However, in all "reasonable" scenarios our cash flows do cover the dividend. I know the Board does not want to push the dividend up to a level where we would have to cut it under bad economic conditions. Our model runs indicate, though, that the $2.16 dividend can be maintained under any reasonable set of forecasts. Only if we increased the dividend to over $3 would we be seriously exposed to the danger of having to cut the dividend.
>
> I might also note that *Value Line* and most other analysts' reports are forecasting that our dividends will grow in the 6 percent to 8 percent range. Thus, if we go to $2.16, we will be at the high end of the range, which should give our stock a boost. With takeover rumors so widespread, getting the stock up a bit would make us all breathe a little easier.
>
> Finally, we considered distributing cash to shareholders through a stock repurchase program. Here we would reduce the dividend payout ratio and use the funds so generated to buy our stock on the open market. Such a program has several advantages, but it would also have drawbacks. I do not recommend that we institute a stock repurchase program at this time. However, if our free cash flows exceed our forecasts, I would recommend that we use these surpluses to buy back stock. Also, I plan to continue looking into a regular repurchase program, and I may recommend such a program in the future.

This company has very stable operations, so it can plan its dividends with a fairly high degree of confidence. Other companies, especially those in cyclical industries, have difficulty maintaining in bad times a dividend that is too low in good times. Such companies can set a very low "regular" dividend and then supplement it with an "extra" dividend when times are good. General motors, Ford, and other auto companies have followed the **low-regular-dividend-plus-extras** policy in the past. Each company announced a low regular dividend that it was sure could be maintained "through hell or high water," and stockholders could count on receiving that dividend under all conditions. Then, when times were good and profits and cash flows were high, the companies paid a clearly designated extra dividend. Investors recognized that the extras might not be maintained in the future, so they did not interpret them as a signal that the companies' earnings were going up permanently, nor did they take the elimination of the extra as a negative signal. In recent years, however, the auto companies and many other companies have replaced the "extras" in their low-regular-dividend-plus-extras policy with stock repurchases.

At times, however, companies must make substantial cuts in dividends in order to conserve cash. In October 2000, facing increasing competition, technology changes, a decline in its bond rating, and a cutoff from the commercial paper market, Xerox Corporation rolled back its quarterly dividend from $0.20 per share to $0.05 per share. This was a dividend rate not seen by Xerox shareholders since 1966. In the week prior to the dividend cut, the share price had declined significantly in response to an announcement that there would be a loss for the quarter rather than a modest profit, and a warning that a dividend cut was being considered. Xerox took a substantial stock price hit when it conceded that cash flows would not be sufficient to cover the old dividend—the price declined from about $15 to about $8. However, some analysts viewed the cut as a positive action that would preserve cash and maintain Xerox's ability to service its debt.

Earnings, Cash Flows, and Dividends

We normally think of earnings as being the primary determinant of dividends, but in reality cash flows are more important. This situation is revealed in Figure 18-2, which gives data for Chevron Corporation from 1981 through 2000. After 1981, oil prices declined sharply, pulling earnings down. Cash flows, though, remained well above the dividend requirement.

Chevron acquired Gulf Oil in 1984, and it issued more than $10 billion of debt to finance the acquisition. Interest on the debt hurt earnings immediately after the merger, as did certain write-offs connected with the merger. Further, Chevron's management wanted to pay off the new debt as fast as possible. All of this influenced the company's decision to hold the dividend constant from 1982 through 1987. Earnings improved dramatically in 1988, and the dividend has increased more or less steadily since then. Note that the dividend was increased in 1991 in spite of the weak earnings and cash flow resulting from the Persian Gulf War. Cash flows and earnings fell sharply in 1998, but they subsequently rebounded.

Now look at Columns 4 and 6, which show payout ratios based on earnings and on cash flows. The earnings payout is quite volatile—dividends ranged from 32 percent to 120 percent of earnings. The cash flow payout, on the other hand, is much more stable—it ranged from 19 percent to 44 percent. Further, the correlation between dividends and cash flows was 0.72 versus only 0.30 between dividends and earnings. Thus, dividends clearly depend more on cash flows, which reflect the company's *ability* to pay dividends, than on current earnings, which are heavily influenced

FIGURE 18-2 Chevron: Earnings, Cash Flows, and Dividends, 1981–2000

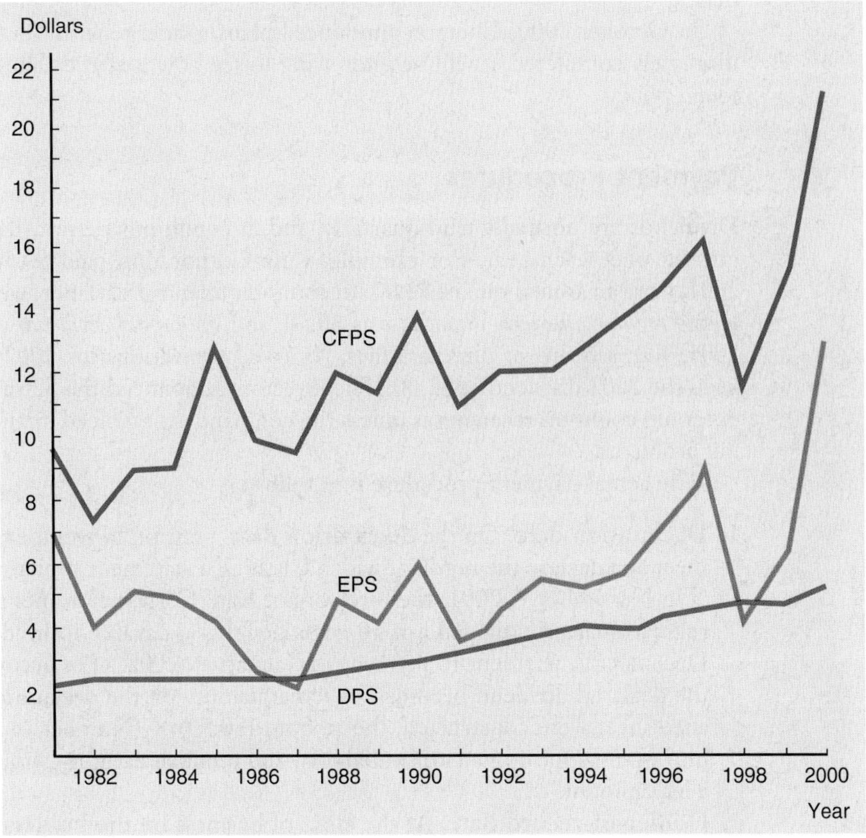

Year (1)	Dividends per Share (2)	Earnings per Share (3)	Earnings Payout (4)	Cash Flow per Share (5)	Cash Flow Payout (6)
1981	$2.20	$6.96	32%	$9.61	23%
1982	2.40	4.03	60	7.35	33
1983	2.40	5.15	47	8.93	27
1984	2.40	4.94	49	9.00	27
1985	2.40	4.19	57	12.76	19
1986	2.40	2.63	91	9.86	24
1987	2.40	2.13	113	9.47	25
1988	2.55	4.86	52	11.97	21
1989	2.80	4.16	67	11.33	25
1990	2.95	6.02	49	13.75	21
1991	3.25	3.69	88	11.14	29
1992	3.30	4.70	70	12.88	26
1993	3.50	5.60	63	13.12	27
1994	3.70	5.20	71	12.66	29
1995	3.85	6.02	64	13.36	29
1996	4.16	8.12	51	14.90	28
1997	4.56	9.90	47	16.70	27
1998	4.88	4.08	120	11.20	44
1999	4.96	6.28	79	15.04	33
2000	5.20	13.10	40	21.10	25

Note: For consistency, data have not been adjusted for a two-for-one split in 1994.

Source: *Value Line Investment Survey*, various issues.

by accounting practices and which do not necessarily reflect the ability to pay dividends.

In October 2000, Chevron announced plans to merge with Texaco. If the deal is ultimately completed, it will be interesting to see how it affects Chevron's future dividend policy.

Payment Procedures

Dividends are normally paid quarterly, and, if conditions permit, the dividend is increased once each year. For example, Katz Corporation paid \$0.50 per quarter in 2001, or at an annual rate of \$2.00. In common financial parlance, we say that in 2001 Katz's *regular quarterly dividend* was \$0.50, and its *annual dividend* was \$2.00. In late 2001, Katz's board of directors met, reviewed projections for 2002, and decided to keep the 2002 dividend at \$2.00. The directors announced the \$2 rate, so stockholders could count on receiving it unless the company experienced unanticipated operating problems.

The actual payment procedure is as follows:

1. **Declaration date.** On the **declaration date**—say, on November 9—the directors meet and declare the regular dividend, issuing a statement similar to the following: "On November 9, 2001, the directors of Katz Corporation met and declared the regular quarterly dividend of 50 cents per share, payable to holders of record on December 7, payment to be made on January 4, 2002." For accounting purposes, the declared dividend becomes an actual liability on the declaration date. If a balance sheet were constructed, the amount (\$0.50) × (Number of shares outstanding) would appear as a current liability, and retained earnings would be reduced by a like amount.
2. **Holder-of-record date.** At the close of business on the **holder-of-record date,** December 7, the company closes its stock transfer books and makes up a list of shareholders as of that date. If Katz Corporation is notified of the sales before 5 P.M. on December 7, then the new owner receives the dividend. However, if notification is received on or after December 8, the previous owner gets the dividend check.
3. **Ex-dividend date.** Suppose Jean Buyer buys 100 shares of stock from John Seller on December 4. Will the company be notified of the transfer in time to list Buyer as the new owner and thus pay the dividend to her? To avoid conflict, the securities industry has set up a convention under which the right to the dividend remains with the stock until two business days prior to the holder-of-record date; on the second day before that date, the right to the dividend no longer goes with the shares. The date when the right to the dividend leaves the stock is called the **ex-dividend date.** In this case, the ex-dividend date is two days prior to December 7, or December 5:

Dividend goes with stock:	December 4
Ex-dividend date:	December 5
	December 6
Holder-of-record date:	December 7

Therefore, if Buyer is to receive the dividend, she must buy the stock on or before December 4. If she buys it on December 5 or later, Seller will receive the dividend because he will be the official holder of record.

Katz's dividend amounts to \$0.50, so the ex-dividend date is important. Barring fluctuations in the stock market, one would normally expect the price of a stock to drop by approximately the amount of the dividend on the ex-dividend date. Thus, if Katz closed at \$30½ on December 4, it would probably open at about \$30 on December 5.[10]

4. **Payment date.** The company actually mails the checks to the holders of record on January 4, the **payment date.**

Self-Test Questions

Explain the logic of the residual dividend model, the steps a firm would take to implement it, and why it is more likely to be used to establish a long-run payout target than to set the actual year-by-year payout ratio.

How do firms use planning models to help set dividend policy?

Which are more critical to the dividend decision, earnings or cash flow? Explain.

Explain the procedures used to actually pay the dividend.

Why is the ex-dividend date important to investors?

Dividend Reinvestment Plans

During the 1970s, most large companies instituted **dividend reinvestment plans (DRIPs),** under which stockholders can automatically reinvest their dividends in the stock of the paying corporation.[11] Today most larger companies offer DRIPs, and although participation rates vary considerably, about 25 percent of the average firm's shareholders are enrolled. There are two types of DRIPs: (1) plans that involve only "old stock" that is already outstanding and (2) plans that involve newly issued stock. In either case, the stockholder must pay taxes on the amount of the dividends, even though stock rather than cash is received.

Under both types of DRIPs, stockholders choose between continuing to receive dividend checks or having the company use the dividends to buy more stock in the corporation. Under the "old stock" type of plan, if a stockholder elects reinvestment, a bank, acting as trustee, takes the total funds available for reinvestment, purchases the corporation's stock on the open market, and allocates the shares purchased to the participating stockholders' accounts on a pro rata basis. The transactions costs of buying shares (brokerage costs) are low because of volume purchases, so these plans benefit small stockholders who do not need cash dividends for current consumption.

The "new stock" type of DRIP uses the reinvested funds to buy newly issued stock, hence these plans raise new capital for the firm. AT&T, Union Carbide, and many

---

[10] Tax effects cause the price decline on average to be less than the full amount of the dividend. Suppose you were an investor in the 40 percent federal-plus-state tax bracket. If you bought Katz's stock on December 4, you would receive the dividend, but you would almost immediately pay 40 percent of it out in taxes. Thus, you would want to wait until December 5 to buy the stock if you thought you could get it for \$0.50 less per share. Your reaction, and that of others, would influence stock prices around dividend payment dates. Here is what would happen:

1. Other things held constant, a stock's price should rise during the quarter, with the daily price increase (for Katz) equal to \$0.50/90 = \$0.005556. Therefore, if the price started at \$30 just after its last ex-dividend date, it would rise to \$30.50 on December 4.
2. In the absence of taxes, the stock's price would fall to \$30 on December 5 and then start up as the next dividend accrual period began. Thus, over time, if everything else were held constant, the stock's price would follow a sawtooth pattern if it were plotted on a graph.
3. Because of taxes, the stock's price would neither rise by the full amount of the dividend nor fall by the full dividend amount when it goes ex-dividend.
4. The amount of the rise and subsequent fall would depend on the average investor's marginal tax rate.

See Edwin J. Elton and Martin J. Gruber, "Marginal Stockholder Tax Rates and the Clientele Effect," *Review of Economics and Statistics*, February 1970, 68–74, for an interesting discussion of all this.

[11] See Richard H. Pettway and R. Phil Malone, "Automatic Dividend Reinvestment Plans," *Financial Management*, Winter 1973, 11–18, for an old but still excellent discussion of the subject.

other companies have had new stock plans in effect in recent years, using them to raise substantial amounts of new equity capital. No fees are charged to stockholders, and many companies offer stock at a discount of 3 percent to 5 percent below the actual market price. The companies offer discounts as a trade-off against flotation costs that would have been incurred if new stock had been issued through investment bankers rather than through the dividend reinvestment plans.

One interesting aspect of DRIPs is that they are forcing corporations to reexamine their basic dividend policies. A high participation rate in a DRIP suggests that stockholders might be better off if the firm simply reduced cash dividends, which would save stockholders some personal income taxes. Quite a few firms are surveying their stockholders to learn more about their preferences and to find out how they would react to a change in dividend policy. A more rational approach to basic dividend policy decisions may emerge from this research.

Note that companies start or stop using new stock DRIPs depending on their need for equity capital. Thus, both Union Carbide and AT&T recently stopped offering new stock DRIPs with a 5 percent discount because their needs for equity capital declined.

Some companies have expanded their DRIPs by moving to "open enrollment," whereby anyone can purchase the firm's stock directly and thus bypass brokers' commissions. Exxon Mobil not only allows investors to buy their initial shares at no fee but also lets them pick up additional shares through automatic bank account withdrawals. Several plans, including Exxon Mobil's, offer dividend reinvestment for individual retirement accounts, and some, such as U.S. West, allow participants to invest weekly or monthly rather than on the quarterly dividend schedule. In all of these plans, and many others, stockholders can invest more than the dividends they are foregoing—they simply send a check to the company and buy shares without a brokerage commission. According to First Chicago Trust, which handles the paperwork for 13 million shareholder DRIP accounts, at least half of all DRIPs will offer open enrollment, extra purchases, and other expanded services within the next few years.

Self-Test Questions

What are dividend reinvestment plans?

What are their advantages and disadvantages from both the stockholders' and the firm's perspectives?

Summary of Factors Influencing Dividend Policy

In earlier sections, we described both the major theories of investor preference and some issues concerning the effects of dividend policy on the value of a firm. We also discussed the residual dividend model for setting a firm's long-run target payout ratio. In this section, we discuss several other factors that affect the dividend decision. These factors may be grouped into four broad categories: (1) constraints on dividend payments, (2) investment opportunities, (3) availability and cost of alternative sources of capital, and (4) effects of dividend policy on k_s. Each of these categories has several subparts, which we discuss in the following paragraphs.

Constraints

1. **Bond indentures.** Debt contracts often limit dividend payments to earnings generated after the loan was granted. Also, debt contracts often stipulate that no dividends can be paid unless the current ratio, times-interest-earned ratio, and other safety ratios exceed stated minimums.
2. **Preferred stock restrictions.** Typically, common dividends cannot be paid if the company has omitted its preferred dividend. The preferred arrearages must be satisfied before common dividends can be resumed.

3. **Impairment of capital rule.** Dividend payments cannot exceed the balance sheet item "retained earnings." This legal restriction, known as the *impairment of capital rule*, is designed to protect creditors. Without the rule, a company that is in trouble might distribute most of its assets to stockholders and leave its debtholders out in the cold. (*Liquidating dividends* can be paid out of capital, but they must be indicated as such, and they must not reduce capital below the limits stated in debt contracts.)
4. **Availability of cash.** Cash dividends can be paid only with cash, so a shortage of cash in the bank can restrict dividend payments. However, the ability to borrow can offset this factor.
5. **Penalty tax on improperly accumulated earnings.** To prevent wealthy individuals from using corporations to avoid personal taxes, the Tax Code provides for a special surtax on improperly accumulated income. Thus, if the IRS can demonstrate that a firm's dividend payout ratio is being deliberately held down to help its stockholders avoid personal taxes, the firm is subject to heavy penalties. This factor is generally relevant only to privately owned firms.

Investment Opportunities

1. **Number of profitable investment opportunities.** If a firm expects a large number of profitable investment opportunities, this will lower the target payout ratio, and vice versa if there are few profitable investment opportunities.
2. **Possibility of accelerating or delaying projects.** The ability to accelerate or postpone projects will permit a firm to adhere more closely to a stable dividend policy.

Alternative Sources of Capital

1. **Cost of selling new stock.** If a firm needs to finance a given level of investment, it can obtain equity by retaining earnings or by issuing new common stock. If flotation costs (including any negative signaling effects of a stock offering) are high, k_e will be well above k_s, making it better to set a low payout ratio and to finance through retention rather than through sale of new common stock. On the other hand, a high dividend payout ratio is more feasible for a firm whose flotation costs are low. Flotation costs differ among firms—for example, the flotation percentage is generally higher for small firms, so they tend to set low payout ratios.
2. **Ability to substitute debt for equity.** A firm can finance a given level of investment with either debt or equity. As noted above, low stock flotation costs permit a more flexible dividend policy because equity can be raised either by retaining earnings or by selling new stock. A similar situation holds for debt policy: If the firm can adjust its debt ratio without raising costs sharply, it can pay the expected dividend, even if earnings fluctuate, by increasing its debt ratio.
3. **Control.** If management is concerned about maintaining control, it may be reluctant to sell new stock, hence the company may retain more earnings than it otherwise would. However, if stockholders want higher dividends and a proxy fight looms, then the dividend will be increased.

Effects of Dividend Policy on ks

The effects of dividend policy on k_s may be considered in terms of four factors: (1) stockholders' desire for current versus future income, (2) perceived riskiness of dividends versus capital gains, (3) the tax advantage of capital gains over dividends, and (4) the information content of dividends (signaling). Since we discussed each of these factors in detail earlier, we need only note here that the importance of each factor in terms of its effect on k_s varies from firm to firm depending on the makeup of its current and possible future stockholders.

It should be apparent that dividend policy decisions are truly exercises in informed judgment, not decisions that can be quantified precisely. Even so, to make rational dividend decisions, financial managers must take account of all the points discussed in the preceding sections.

Self-Test Questions

Identify the four broad sets of factors that affect dividend policy.

What constraints affect dividend policy?

How do investment opportunities affect dividend policy?

How does the availability and cost of outside capital affect dividend policy?

Overview of the Dividend Policy Decision

In many ways, our discussion of dividend policy parallels our discussion of capital structure: We presented the relevant theories and issues, and we listed some additional factors that influence dividend policy, but we did not come up with any hard-and-fast guidelines that managers can follow. You should recognize that dividend policy decisions are exercises in informed judgment, not decisions that can be based on a precise mathematical model.

In practice, dividend policy is not an independent decision—the dividend decision is made jointly with capital structure and capital budgeting decisions. The underlying reason for joining these decisions is asymmetric information, which influences managerial actions in two ways:

1. In general, managers do not want to issue new common stock. First, new common stock involves issuance costs—commissions, fees, and so on—and those costs can be avoided by using retained earnings to finance equity needs. Second, as we discussed in Chapter 16, asymmetric information causes investors to view new common stock issues as negative signals and thus lowers expectations regarding the firm's future prospects. The end result is that the announcement of a new stock issue usually leads to a decrease in the stock price. Considering the total costs involved, including both issuance and asymmetric information costs, managers prefer to use retained earnings as the primary source of new equity.
2. Dividend changes provide signals about managers' beliefs as to their firms' future prospects. Thus, dividend reductions generally have a significant negative effect on a firm's stock price. Since managers recognize this, they try to set dollar dividends low enough so that there is only a remote chance that the dividend will have to be reduced in the future.

The effects of asymmetric information suggest that, to the extent possible, managers should avoid both new common stock sales and dividend cuts, because both actions tend to lower stock prices. Thus, in setting dividend policy, managers should begin by considering the firm's future investment opportunities relative to its projected internal sources of funds. The target capital structure also plays a part, but because the optimal capital structure is a *range*, firms can vary their actual capital structures somewhat from year to year. Since it is best to avoid issuing new common stock, the target long-term payout ratio should be designed to permit the firm to meet all of its equity capital requirements with retained earnings. *In effect, managers should use the residual dividend model to set dividends, but in a long-term framework.* Finally, the current dollar dividend should be set so that there is an extremely low probability that the dividend, once set, will ever have to be lowered or omitted.

Of course, the dividend decision is made during the planning process, so there is uncertainty about future investment opportunities and operating cash flows. Thus, the actual payout ratio in any year will probably be above or below the firm's long-range target. However, the dollar dividend should be maintained, or increased as planned, unless the firm's financial condition deteriorates to the point where the planned policy simply cannot be maintained. A steady or increasing stream of dividends over the long run signals that the firm's financial condition is under control. Further, investor uncertainty is decreased by stable dividends, so a steady dividend stream reduces the negative effect of a new stock issue, should one become absolutely necessary.

In general, firms with superior investment opportunities should set lower payouts, hence retain more earnings, than firms with poor investment opportunities. The degree of uncertainty also influences the decision. If there is a great deal of uncertainty regarding the forecasts of free cash flows, which are defined here as the firm's operating cash flows minus mandatory equity investments, then it is best to be conservative and to set a lower current dollar dividend. Also, firms with postponable investment opportunities can afford to set a higher dollar dividend, because in times of stress investments can be postponed for a year or two, thus increasing the cash available for dividends. Finally, firms whose cost of capital is largely unaffected by changes in the debt ratio can also afford to set a higher payout ratio, because they can, in times of stress, more easily issue additional debt to maintain the capital budgeting program without having to cut dividends or issue stock.

Firms have only one opportunity to set the dividend payment from scratch. Therefore, today's dividend decisions are constrained by policies that were set in the past, hence setting a policy for the next five years necessarily begins with a review of the current situation.

Although we have outlined a rational process for managers to use when considering their firms' dividend policies, dividend policy still remains one of the most judgmental decisions managers must make. For this reason, dividend policy is always set by the board of directors—the financial staff analyzes the situation and makes a recommendation, but the board makes the final decision.

Self-Test Question

Describe the dividend policy decision process. Be sure to discuss all the factors that influence the decision.

Stock Dividends and Stock Splits

Stock dividends and stock splits are related to the firm's cash dividend policy. The rationale for stock dividends and splits can best be explained through an example. We will use Porter Electronic Controls Inc., a $700 million electronic components manufacturer, for this purpose. Since its inception, Porter's markets have been expanding, and the company has enjoyed growth in sales and earnings. Some of its earnings have been paid out in dividends, but some are also retained each year, causing its earnings per share and stock price to grow. The company began its life with only a few thousand shares outstanding, and, after some years of growth, each of Porter's shares had a very high EPS and DPS. When a "normal" P/E ratio was applied, the derived market price was so high that few people could afford to buy a "round lot" of 100 shares. This limited the demand for the stock and thus kept the total market value of the firm below what it would have been if more shares, at a lower price, had been outstanding. To correct this situation, Porter "split its stock," as described in the next section.

Stock Splits

Although there is little empirical evidence to support the contention, there is nevertheless a widespread belief in financial circles that an *optimal price range* exists for stocks. "Optimal" means that if the price is within this range, the price/earnings ratio, hence the firm's value, will be maximized. Many observers, including Porter's management, believe that the best range for most stocks is from $20 to $80 per share. Accordingly, if the price of Porter's stock rose to $80, management would probably declare a two-for-one **stock split,** thus doubling the number of shares outstanding, halving the earnings and dividends per share, and thereby lowering the stock price. Each stockholder would have more shares, but each share would be worth less. If the post-split price were $40, Porter's stockholders would be exactly as well off as were before the split. However, if the stock price were to stabilize above $40, stockholders would be better off. Stock splits can be of any size—for example, the stock could be split two-for-one, three-for-one, one-and-a-half-for-one, or in any other way.[12]

Stock Dividends

Stock dividends are similar to stock splits in that they "divide the pie into smaller slices" without affecting the fundamental position of the current stockholders. On a 5 percent stock dividend, the holder of 100 shares would receive an additional 5 shares (without cost); on a 20 percent stock dividend, the same holder would receive 20 new shares; and so on. Again, the total number of shares is increased, so earnings, dividends, and price per share all decline.

If a firm wants to reduce the price of its stock, should it use a stock split or a stock dividend? Stock splits are generally used after a sharp price run-up to produce a large price reduction. Stock dividends used on a regular annual basis will keep the stock price more or less constrained. For example, if a firm's earnings and dividends were growing at about 10 percent per year, its stock price would tend to go up at about that same rate, and it would soon be outside the desired trading range. A 10 percent annual stock dividend would maintain the stock price within the optimal trading range. Note, though, that small stock dividends create bookkeeping problems and unnecessary expenses, so firms today use stock splits far more often than stock dividends.[13]

Effect on Stock Prices

If a company splits its stock or declares a stock dividend, will this increase the market value of its stock? Several empirical studies have sought to answer this question. Here is a summary of their findings.[14]

---

[12] *Reverse splits,* which reduce the shares outstanding, can even be used. For example, a company whose stock sells for $5 might employ a one-for-five reverse split, exchanging one new share for five old ones and raising the value of the shares to about $25, which is within the optimal price range. LTV Corporation did this after several years of losses had driven its stock price below the optimal range.

[13] Accountants treat stock splits and stock dividends somewhat differently. For example, in a two-for-one stock split, the number of shares outstanding is doubled and the par value is halved, and that is about all there is to it. With a stock dividend, a bookkeeping entry is made transferring "retained earnings" to "common stock." For example, if a firm had 1,000,000 shares outstanding, if the stock price was $10, and if it wanted to pay a 10 percent stock dividend, then (1) each stockholder would be given one new share of stock for each ten shares held, and (2) the accounting entries would involve showing 100,000 more shares outstanding and transferring 100,000($10) = $1,000,000 from "retained earnings" to "common stock." The retained earnings transfer limits the size of stock dividends, but that is not important because companies can always split their stock in any way they choose.

[14] See Eugene F. Fama, Lawrence Fisher, Michael C. Jensen, and Richard Roll, "The Adjustment of Stock Prices to New Information," *International Economic Review,* February 1969, 1–21; Mark S. Grinblatt, Ronald M. Masulis, and Sheridan Titman, "The Valuation Effects of Stock Splits and Stock Dividends," *Journal of Financial Economics,* December 1984, 461–490; C. Austin Barker, "Evaluation of Stock Dividends," *Harvard Business Review,* July–August 1958, 99–114; and Thomas E. Copeland, "Liquidity Changes Following Stock Splits," *Journal of Finance,* March 1979, 115–141.

1. On average, the price of a company's stock rises shortly after it announces a stock split or dividend.
2. However, these price increases are more the result of the fact that investors take stock splits/dividends as signals of higher future earnings and dividends than of a desire for stock dividends/splits per se. Because only companies whose managements think things look good tend to split their stocks, the announcement of a stock split is taken as a signal that earnings and cash dividends are likely to rise. Thus, the price increases associated with stock splits/dividends are probably the result of signals of favorable prospects for earnings and dividends, not a desire for stock splits/dividends per se.
3. If a company announces a stock split or dividend, its price will tend to rise. However, if during the next few months it does not announce an increase in earnings and dividends, then its stock price will drop back to the earlier level.
4. As we noted earlier, brokerage commissions are generally higher in percentage terms on lower-priced stocks. This means that it is more expensive to trade low-priced than high-priced stocks, and this, in turn, means that stock splits may reduce the liquidity of a company's shares. This particular piece of evidence suggests that stock splits/dividends might actually be harmful, although a lower price does mean that more investors can afford to trade in round lots (100 shares), which carry lower commissions than do odd lots (less than 100 shares).

What do we conclude from all this? From a purely economic standpoint, stock dividends and splits are just additional pieces of paper. However, they provide management with a relatively low-cost way of signaling that the firm's prospects look good. Further, we should note that since few large, publicly owned stocks sell at prices above several hundred dollars, we simply do not know what the effect would be if Microsoft, Xerox, Hewlett-Packard, and other highly successful firms had never split their stocks, and consequently sold at prices in the thousands or even tens of thousands of dollars. All in all, it probably makes sense to employ stock dividends/splits when a firm's prospects are favorable, especially if the price of its stock has gone beyond the normal trading range.[15]

Self-Test Questions

What are stock dividends and stock splits?

How do stock dividends and splits affect stock prices?

In what situations should managers consider the use of stock dividends?

In what situations should they consider the use of stock splits?

Stock Repurchases

Several years ago, a *Fortune* article entitled "Beating the Market by Buying Back Stock" discussed the fact that during a one-year period, more than 600 major corporations repurchased significant amounts of their own stock. It also gave illustrations of some specific companies' repurchase programs and the effects of these programs on stock prices. The article's conclusion was that "buybacks have made a mint for shareholders who stay with the companies carrying them out."

---

[15]It is interesting to note that Berkshire Hathaway, which is controlled by billionaire Warren Buffett, one of the most successful financiers of the twentieth century, has never had a stock split, and its stock sold on the NYSE for $65,600 per share in November 2000. But, in response to investment trusts that were being formed to sell fractional units of the stock, and thus, in effect, split it, Buffett himself created a new class of Berkshire Hathaway stock (Class B) worth about 1/30 of a Class A (regular) share.

In addition, we noted earlier that FPL cut its dividends several years ago but simultaneously instituted a program to repurchase shares of its stock. Thus it substituted share repurchases for cash dividends as a way to distribute funds to stockholders. FPL is not alone—in recent years Philip Morris, GE, Disney, Citicorp, Merck, and more than 800 other companies took similar actions, and the dollars used to repurchase shares approximately matched the amount paid out as dividends.

Why are stock repurchase programs becoming so popular? The short answer is that they enhance shareholder value. A more complete answer is given in the remainder of this section, where we explain what a **stock repurchase** is, how it is carried out, and how the financial manager should analyze a possible repurchase program.

There are three principal types of repurchases: (1) situations where the firm has cash available for distribution to its stockholders, and it distributes this cash by repurchasing shares rather than by paying cash dividends; (2) situations where the firm concludes that its capital structure is too heavily weighted with equity, and then it sells debt and uses the proceeds to buy back its stock; and (3) situations where a firm has issued options to employees and then uses open market repurchases to obtain stock for use when the options are exercised.

Stock that has been repurchased by a firm is called *treasury stock.* If some of the outstanding shares are repurchased, fewer will remain outstanding. Assuming that the repurchase does not adversely affect the firm's future earnings, the earnings per share on the remaining shares will increase, resulting in a higher share price. As a result, capital gains will have been substituted for dividends.

The Effects of Stock Repurchases

Many companies have been repurchasing their stock in recent years. Until the 1980s, most repurchases amounted to a few million dollars, but in 1985, Phillips Petroleum announced plans for the largest repurchase on record—81 million of its shares with a market value of $4.1 billion. Other large repurchases have been made by Texaco, IBM, CBS, Coca-Cola, Teledyne, Atlantic Richfield, Goodyear, and Xerox. Indeed, since 1985 large companies have repurchased more shares than they have issued.

The effects of a repurchase can be illustrated with data on American Development Corporation (ADC). The company expects to earn $4.4 million in 2002, and 50 percent of this amount, or $2.2 million, has been allocated for distribution to common shareholders. There are 1.1 million shares outstanding, and the market price is $20 a share. ADC believes that it can either use the $2.2 million to repurchase 100,000 of its shares through a tender offer at $22 a share or else pay a cash dividend of $2 a share.[16]

The effect of the repurchase on the EPS and market price per share of the remaining stock can be analyzed in the following way:

---

[16]Stock repurchases are generally made in one of three ways: (1) A publicly owned firm can simply buy its own stock through a broker on the open market. (2) It can make a *tender offer,* under which it permits stockholders to send in (that is, "tender") their shares to the firm in exchange for a specified price per share. In this case, it generally indicates that it will buy up to a specified number of shares within a particular time period (usually about two weeks); if more shares are tendered than the company wishes to purchase, purchases are made on a pro rata basis. (3) The firm can purchase a block of shares from one large holder on a negotiated basis. If a negotiated purchase is employed, care must be taken to ensure that this one stockholder does not receive preferential treatment over other stockholders or that any preference given can be justified by "sound business reasons." Texaco's management was sued by stockholders who were unhappy over the company's repurchase of about $600 million of stock from the Bass Brothers' interests at a substantial premium over the market price. The suit charged that Texaco's management, afraid the Bass Brothers would attempt a takeover, used the buy-back to get them off its back. Such payments have been dubbed "greenmail."

1. $\text{Current EPS} = \frac{\text{Total earnings}}{\text{Number of shares}} = \frac{\$4.4 \text{ million}}{1.1 \text{ million}} = \$4 \text{ per share.}$
2. $\text{P/E ratio} = \frac{\$20}{\$4} = 5\times.$
3. $\text{EPS after repurchasing 100,000 shares} = \frac{4.4 \text{ million}}{1 \text{ million}} = \$4.40 \text{ per share.}$
4. $\text{Expected market price after repurchase} = (\text{P/E})(\text{EPS}) = (5)(\$4.40) = \$22 \text{ per share.}$

It should be noted from this example that investors would receive before-tax benefits of $2 per share in any case, either in the form of a $2 cash dividend or a $2 increase in the stock price. This result would occur because we assumed, first, that shares could be repurchased at exactly $22 a share and, second, that the P/E ratio would remain constant. If shares could be bought for less than $22, the operation would be even better for *remaining* stockholders, but the reverse would hold if ADC had to pay more than $22 a share. Furthermore, the P/E ratio might change as a result of the repurchase operation, rising if investors viewed it favorably and falling if they viewed it unfavorably. Some factors that might affect P/E ratios are considered next.

Advantages of Repurchases

The advantages of repurchases are as follows:

1. Repurchase announcements are viewed as positive signals by investors because the repurchase is often motivated by management's belief that the firm's shares are undervalued.
2. The stockholders have a choice when the firm distributes cash by repurchasing stock—they can sell or not sell. With a cash dividend, on the other hand, stockholders must accept a dividend payment and pay the tax. Thus, those stockholders who need cash can sell back some of their shares, while those who do not want additional cash can simply retain their stock. From a tax standpoint, a repurchase permits both types of stockholders to get what they want.
3. A third advantage is that a repurchase can remove a large block of stock that is "overhanging" the market and keeping the price per share down.
4. Dividends are "sticky" in the short run because managements are reluctant to raise the dividend if the increase cannot be maintained in the future—managements dislike cutting cash dividends because of the negative signal a cut gives. Hence, if the excess cash flow is thought to be only temporary, management may prefer to make the distribution in the form of a share repurchase rather than to declare an increased cash dividend that cannot be maintained.
5. Companies can use the residual model to set a *target cash distribution* level, then divide the distribution into a *dividend component* and a *repurchase component.* The dividend payout ratio will be relatively low, but the dividend itself will be relatively secure, and it will grow as a result of the declining number of shares outstanding. The company has more flexibility in adjusting the total distribution than it would if the entire distribution were in the form of cash dividends, because repurchases can be varied from year to year without giving off adverse signals. This procedure, which is what FPL employed, has much to recommend it, and it is one reason for the dramatic increase in the volume of share repurchases.
6. Repurchases can be used to produce large-scale changes in capital structures. For example, several years ago Consolidated Edison decided to borrow $400 million

Buybacks Have Lowered Dividend Yields

Dividend payouts and yields have fallen sharply over the past two decades. In 1980, the average large company paid out 55 percent of its earnings as dividends, and its dividend yield exceeded 5 percent. Today, the average payout is less than 40 percent, and the yield has dipped below 1.5 percent.

A number of theories have been offered to explain these results. First, declining dividend yields imply that stock prices have increased faster than dividends paid. Some analysts point to the low yields as evidence that the stock market is overvalued. Second, lower interest rates led to a decline in required stock returns. This increased stock prices, which, in turn, resulted in lower dividend yields. Third, over the past two decades the composition of the stock market has changed dramatically. In 1980, the market was dominated by oil, industrial, utility, and retail companies that paid high dividends. Today the market includes many high-tech companies that pay little or no dividends.

In addition, dividend yields have fallen because more and more companies now recognize the tax and other advantages of stock repurchases over dividends as a way of distributing cash to shareholders. Indeed, stock repurchases have tripled in recent years, and in each year since 1997 stock repurchases have exceeded cash dividends paid.

The popularity of stock repurchases led Federal Reserve Board economists Nellie Liang and Steve Sharpe to redefine a stock's "total yield." First, they developed a "net repurchases yield," calculated as the dollars per share spent on repurchases minus the cost of shares used to cover the exercise of stock options, divided by the stock price. Then, the stock's "total yield" is found as the sum of the traditional dividend yield plus the net repurchases yield.

Liang and Sharpe's estimated yields for the largest 144 companies in the S&P 500 during 1994–1998 are reported in the accompanying table. These data confirm the declining importance of dividends and the increasing importance of stock repurchases. They also indicate that total yields have been trending downward. It is not shown in our table, but even after including stock repurchases, total yields are still only half of what the dividend yield alone was in 1980. Thus, no matter how you slice it, payouts to shareholders have declined. This is, of course, consistent with lower interest rates and a declining cost of equity capital.

Source: Gene Epstein, "Soaring Buybacks Make Dividend Yield a Misleading Measure of a Stock's Value," *Barron's Online*, November 1, 1999.

Yields	1994	1995	1996	1997	1998
Dividend yield	2.76%	2.41%	2.06%	1.73%	1.41%
Net repurchase yield	1.19	1.34	1.56	1.98	1.49
Total yield	3.95%	3.75%	3.62%	3.71%	2.90%
Percent from repurchases	30%	36%	43%	53%	51%

and use the funds to repurchase some of its common stock. Thus, Con Ed was able to quickly change its capital structure.

7. Companies that use stock options as an important component of employee compensation can repurchase shares and then use those shares when employees exercise their options. This avoids having to issue new shares and thus diluting earnings. Microsoft and other high-tech companies have used this procedure in recent years.

Disadvantages of Repurchases

Disadvantages of repurchases include the following:

1. Stockholders may not be indifferent between dividends and capital gains, and the price of the stock might benefit more from cash dividends than from repurchases. Cash dividends are generally dependable, but repurchases are not.
2. The *selling* stockholders may not be fully aware of all the implications of a repurchase, or they may not have all the pertinent information about the corporation's

Stock Repurchases: An Easy Way to Boost Stock Prices?

Looking for a way to boost your company's stock price? Why not buy back some of your company's shares? That reflects the thinking of an increasing number of financial managers.

The buyback rage is in some ways surprising. Given the recent performance of the stock market, it has become quite expensive to buy back shares. Nevertheless, the market's response to a buyback announcement is usually positive. For example, in mid-1996 Reebok announced that it would buy back one-third of its outstanding shares, and on the announcement day, the stock price rose 10 percent. Reebok's experience is not unique. A recent study found (1) that the average company's stock rose 3.5 percent the day a buyback was announced and (2) that companies that repurchase shares outperform the market over a four-year period following the announcement.[a]

Why are buybacks so popular with investors? The general view is that financial managers are signaling to the investment community a belief that the stock is undervalued, hence that the company thinks its own stock is an attractive investment. In this respect, stock repurchases have the opposite effect of stock issuances, which are thought to signal that the firm's stock is overvalued. Buybacks also help assure investors that the company is not wasting its shareholders' money by investing in sub-par investments. Michael O'Neill, the CFO of BankAmerica, puts it this way: "We look very hard internally, but if we don't have a profitable use for capital, we think we should return it to shareholders."

Despite all the recent hoopla surrounding buybacks, many analysts stress that in some instances repurchases have a downside: If a firm's stock is actually overvalued, buying back shares at the inflated price will harm the remaining stockholders. In this regard, buybacks should not be viewed as a gimmick to boost stock prices in the short run, but should be used only if they are part of a well-thought-out strategy for investment and for distributing cash to stockholders. Indeed, buybacks do not always succeed—Disney, for example, announced a buyback in April 1996, and its stock price fell more than 10 percent in the next six months.

[a]David Ikenberry, Josef Lakonishok, and Theo Vermaelen, "Market Under-Reaction to Open Market Share Repurchases," *Journal of Financial Economics*, 1995, Vol. 39, 181–208.

Source: Adapted from "Buybacks Make News, But Do They Make Sense?" *BusinessWeek*, August 12, 1996, 76.

present and future activities. However, firms generally announce repurchase programs before embarking on them to avoid potential stockholder suits.

3. The corporation may pay too much for the repurchased stock, to the disadvantage of remaining stockholders. If the firm seeks to acquire a relatively large amount of its stock, then the price may be bid above its equilibrium level and then fall after the firm ceases its repurchase operations.

Conclusions on Stock Repurchases

When all the pros and cons on stock repurchases have been totaled, where do we stand? Our conclusions may be summarized as follows:

1. Because of the lower capital gains tax rate and the deferred tax on capital gains, repurchases have a significant tax advantage over dividends as a way to distribute income to stockholders. This advantage is reinforced by the fact that repurchases provide cash to stockholders who want cash while allowing those who do not need current cash to delay its receipt. On the other hand, dividends are more dependable and are thus better suited for those who need a steady source of income.
2. Because of signaling effects, companies should not vary their dividends—that would lower investors' confidence in the company and adversely affect its cost of equity and its stock price. However, cash flows vary over time, as do investment opportunities, so the "proper" dividend in the residual model sense varies. To get around this problem, a company can set its dividend low enough to keep dividend payments from constraining operations and then use repurchases on a more or less

regular basis to distribute excess cash. Such a procedure would provide regular, dependable dividends plus additional cash flow to those stockholders who want it.

3. Repurchases are also useful when a firm wants to make a large shift in its capital structure, wants to distribute cash from a one-time event such as the sale of a division, or wants to obtain shares for use in an employee stock option plan.

In an earlier edition of this book, we stated that companies ought to be doing more repurchasing and paying out less cash as dividends than they were. Events in recent years indicate that companies have reached this same conclusion.

Self-Test Questions

Explain how repurchases can (1) help stockholders hold down taxes and (2) help firms change their capital structures.

What is treasury stock?

What are three procedures a firm can use to repurchase its stock?

What are some advantages and disadvantages of stock repurchases?

How can stock repurchases help a company operate in accordance with the residual dividend model?

Summary

Once a company becomes profitable, it must decide what to do with the cash it generates. It may choose to retain cash and use it either to purchase additional assets or to reduce outstanding debt. Alternatively, it may choose to return the cash to shareholders. Keep in mind that every dollar that management chooses to retain is a dollar that shareholders could have received and invested elsewhere. Therefore, managers should retain earnings if and only if they can invest the money within the firm and earn more than stockholders could earn outside the firm. Consequently, high-growth companies with many good projects will tend to retain a high percentage of earnings, whereas mature companies with lots of cash but limited investment opportunities will have generous cash distributions.

This basic tendency has a major influence on firms' long-run distribution policies. However, as we saw in this chapter, in any given year several important situations could complicate the long-run policy. Companies with excess cash have to decide whether to pay dividends or repurchase stock. In addition, due to the importance of signaling and the clientele effect, companies generally find it desirable to maintain a stable, consistent dividend policy over time. The key concepts covered in this chapter are listed below:

- **Dividend policy** involves three issues: (1) What fraction of earnings should be distributed? (2) Should the distribution be in the form of cash dividends or stock repurchases? (3) Should the firm maintain a steady, stable dividend growth rate?
- The **optimal dividend policy** strikes a balance between current dividends and future growth so as to maximize the firm's stock price.
- Miller and Modigliani developed the **dividend irrelevance theory,** which holds that a firm's dividend policy has no effect on either the value of its stock or its cost of capital.
- The **bird-in-the-hand theory** holds that the firm's value will be maximized by a high dividend payout ratio, because investors regard cash dividends as being less risky than potential capital gains.
- The **tax preference theory** states that because long-term capital gains are subject to less onerous taxes than dividends, investors prefer to have companies retain earnings rather than pay them out as dividends.

- **Empirical tests** of the three theories **have been inconclusive.** Therefore, academicians cannot tell corporate managers how a given change in dividend policy will affect stock prices and capital costs.
- Dividend policy should take account of the **information content of dividends (signaling)** and the **clientele effect.** The information content, or signaling, effect relates to the fact that investors regard an unexpected dividend change as a signal of management's forecast of future earnings. The clientele effect suggests that a firm will attract investors who like the firm's dividend payout policy. Both factors should be considered by firms that are considering a change in dividend policy.
- In practice, most firms try to follow a policy of paying a **steadily increasing dividend.** This policy provides investors with stable, dependable income, and departures from it give investors signals about management's expectations for future earnings.
- Most firms use the **residual dividend model** to set the long-run target payout ratio at a level that will permit the firm to meet its equity requirements with retained earnings.
- A **dividend reinvestment plan (DRIP)** allows stockholders to have the company automatically use dividends to purchase additional shares. DRIPs are popular because they allow stockholders to acquire additional shares without brokerage fees.
- **Legal constraints, investment opportunities, availability and cost of funds from other sources,** and **taxes** are also considered when firms establish dividend policies.
- A **stock split** increases the number of shares outstanding. Normally, splits reduce the price per share in proportion to the increase in shares because splits merely "divide the pie into smaller slices." However, firms generally split their stocks only if (1) the price is quite high and (2) management thinks the future is bright. Therefore, stock splits are often taken as positive signals and thus boost stock prices.
- A **stock dividend** is a dividend paid in additional shares rather than in cash. Both stock dividends and splits are used to keep stock prices within an "optimal" trading range.
- Under a **stock repurchase plan,** a firm buys back some of its outstanding stock, thereby decreasing the number of shares, which should increase both EPS and the stock price. Repurchases substitute low-taxed capital gains for high-taxed dividends.

Questions

18–1 Define each of the following terms:
a. Optimal dividend policy
b. Dividend irrelevance theory; bird-in-the-hand theory; tax preference theory
c. Information content, or signaling, hypothesis; clientele effect
d. Residual dividend model
e. Extra dividend
f. Declaration date; holder-of-record date; ex-dividend date; payment date
g. Dividend reinvestment plan (DRIP)
h. Stock split; stock dividend
i. Stock repurchase

18–2 How would each of the following changes tend to affect aggregate (that is, the average for all corporations) payout ratios, other things held constant? Explain your answers.
a. An increase in the personal income tax rate.
b. A liberalization of depreciation for federal income tax purposes—that is, faster tax write-offs.

c. A rise in interest rates.
d. An increase in corporate profits.
e. A decline in investment opportunities.
f. Permission for corporations to deduct dividends for tax purposes as they now do interest charges.
g. A change in the Tax Code so that both realized and unrealized capital gains in any year were taxed at the same rate as dividends.

18–3 Discuss the pros and cons of having the directors formally announce what a firm's dividend policy will be in the future.

18–4 Most firms would like to have their stock selling at a high P/E ratio, and they would also like to have extensive public ownership (many different shareholders). Explain how stock dividends or stock splits may help achieve these goals.

18–5 What is the difference between a stock dividend and a stock split? As a stockholder, would you prefer to see your company declare a 100 percent stock dividend or a two-for-one split? Assume that either action is feasible.

18–6 "The cost of retained earnings is less than the cost of new outside equity capital. Consequently, it is totally irrational for a firm to sell a new issue of stock and to pay dividends during the same year." Discuss this statement.

18–7 Would it ever be rational for a firm to borrow money in order to pay dividends? Explain.

18–8 "Executive salaries have been shown to be more closely correlated to the size of the firm than to its profitability. If a firm's board of directors is controlled by management instead of by outside directors, this might result in the firm's retaining more earnings than can be justified from the stockholders' point of view." Discuss the statement, being sure (a) to discuss the interrelationships among cost of capital, investment opportunities, and new investment and (b) to explain the implied relationship between dividend policy and stock prices.

18–9 Modigliani and Miller (MM) on the one hand and Gordon and Lintner (GL) on the other have expressed strong views regarding the effect of dividend policy on a firm's cost of capital and value.
a. In essence, what are the MM and GL views regarding the effect of dividend policy on the cost of capital and stock prices?
b. How does the tax preference theory differ from the views of MM and GL?
c. According to the text, which of the theories, if any, has received statistical confirmation from empirical tests?
d. How could MM use the *information content*, or *signaling, hypothesis* to counter their opponents' arguments? If you were debating MM, how would you counter them?
e. How could MM use the *clientele effect* concept to counter their opponents' arguments? If you were debating MM, how would you counter them?

18–10 More NYSE companies had stock dividends and stock splits during 1983 and 1984 than ever before. What events in these years could have made stock splits and stock dividends so popular? Explain the rationale that a financial vice-president might give his or her board of directors to support a stock split/dividend recommendation.

18–11 One position expressed in the financial literature is that firms set their dividends as a residual after using income to support new investment.
a. Explain what a residual dividend policy implies, illustrating your answer with a table showing how different investment opportunities could lead to different dividend payout ratios.
b. Think back to Chapter 16, where we considered the relationship between capital structure and the cost of capital. If the WACC-versus-debt-ratio plot was shaped like a sharp V, would this have a different implication for the importance of setting dividends according to the residual policy than if the plot was shaped like a shallow bowl (or a flattened U)?

18–12 Indicate whether the following statements are true or false. If the statement is false, explain why.
a. If a firm repurchases its stock in the open market, the shareholders who tender the stock are subject to capital gains taxes.
b. If you own 100 shares in a company's stock and the company's stock splits 2 for 1, you will own 200 shares in the company following the split.

c. Some dividend reinvestment plans increase the amount of equity capital available to the firm.
d. The Tax Code encourages companies to pay a large percentage of their net income in the form of dividends.
e. If your company has established a clientele of investors who prefer large dividends, the company is unlikely to adopt a residual dividend policy.
f. If a firm follows a residual dividend policy, holding all else constant, its dividend payout will tend to rise whenever the firm's investment opportunities improve.

Self-Test Problem (Solution Appears in Appendix A)

ST–1 *ALTERNATIVE DIVIDEND POLICIES*

Components Manufacturing Corporation (CMC) has an all-common-equity capital structure. It has 200,000 shares of \$2 par value common stock outstanding. When CMC's founder, who was also its research director and most successful inventor, retired unexpectedly to the South Pacific in late 2001, CMC was left suddenly and permanently with materially lower growth expectations and relatively few attractive new investment opportunities. Unfortunately, there was no way to replace the founder's contributions to the firm. Previously, CMC found it necessary to plow back most of its earnings to finance growth, which averaged 12 percent per year. Future growth at a 5 percent rate is considered realistic, but that level would call for an increase in the dividend payout. Further, it now appears that new investment projects with at least the 14 percent rate of return required by CMC's stockholders (k_s = 14%) would amount to only \$800,000 for 2002 in comparison to a projected \$2,000,000 of net income. If the existing 20 percent dividend payout were continued, retained earnings would be \$1.6 million in 2002, but, as noted, investments that yield the 14 percent cost of capital would amount to only \$800,000.

The one encouraging thing is that the high earnings from existing assets are expected to continue, and net income of \$2 million is still expected for 2002. Given the dramatically changed circumstances, CMC's management is reviewing the firm's dividend policy.

a. Assuming that the acceptable 2002 investment projects would be financed entirely by earnings retained during the year, calculate DPS in 2002, assuming that CMC uses the residual dividend model.
b. What payout ratio does your answer to part a imply for 2002?
c. If a 60 percent payout ratio is maintained for the foreseeable future, what is your estimate of the present market price of the common stock? How does this compare with the market price that should have prevailed under the assumptions existing just before the news about the founder's retirement? If the two values of P_0 are different, comment on why.
d. What would happen to the price of the stock if the old 20 percent payout were continued? Assume that if this payout is maintained, the average rate of return on the retained earnings will fall to 7.5 percent and the new growth rate will be

$$\begin{aligned} g &= (1.0 - \text{Payment ratio})(\text{ROE}) \\ &= (1.0 - 0.2)(7.5\%) \\ &= (0.8)(7.5\%) = 6.0\%. \end{aligned}$$

Problems

18–1 *RESIDUAL DIVIDEND MODEL*

Axel Telecommunications has a target capital structure that consists of 70 percent debt and 30 percent equity. The company anticipates that its capital budget for the upcoming year will be \$3,000,000. If Axel reports net income of \$2,000,000 and it follows a residual dividend payout policy, what will be its dividend payout ratio?

18–2 *STOCK SPLIT*

Gamma Medical's stock trades at \$90 a share. The company is contemplating a 3-for-2 stock split. Assuming that the stock split will have no effect on the total market value of its equity, what will be the company's stock price following the stock split?

18–3 *STOCK REPURCHASES*

Beta Industries has net income of \$2,000,000 and it has 1,000,000 shares of common stock outstanding. The company's stock currently trades at \$32 a share. Beta is considering a plan where it will use available cash to repurchase 20 percent of its shares in the open market. The repurchase is expected to have no effect on either net income or the company's P/E ratio. What will be its stock price following the stock repurchase?

18–4 EXTERNAL EQUITY FINANCING

Northern Pacific Heating and Cooling Inc. has a 6-month backlog of orders for its patented solar heating system. To meet this demand, management plans to expand production capacity by 40 percent with a $10 million investment in plant and machinery. The firm wants to maintain a 40 percent debt-to-total-assets ratio in its capital structure; it also wants to maintain its past dividend policy of distributing 45 percent of last year's net income. In 2001, net income was $5 million. How much external equity must Northern Pacific seek at the beginning of 2002 to expand capacity as desired?

18–5 RESIDUAL DIVIDEND POLICY

Petersen Company has a capital budget of $1.2 million. The company wants to maintain a target capital structure which is 60 percent debt and 40 percent equity. The company forecasts that its net income this year will be $600,000. If the company follows a residual dividend policy, what will be its payout ratio?

18–6 DIVIDEND PAYOUT

The Wei Corporation expects next year's net income to be $15 million. The firm's debt ratio is currently 40 percent. Wei has $12 million of profitable investment opportunities, and it wishes to maintain its existing debt ratio. According to the residual dividend model, how large should Wei's dividend payout ratio be next year?

18–7 STOCK SPLIT

After a 5-for-1 stock split, the Strasburg Company paid a dividend of $0.75 per new share, which represents a 9 percent increase over last year's pre-split dividend. What was last year's dividend per share?

18–8 DIVIDEND RESIDUAL POLICY

The Welch Company is considering three independent projects, each of which requires a $5 million investment. The estimated internal rate of return (IRR) and cost of capital for these projects are presented below:

Project H (high risk):	Cost of capital = 16%; IRR = 20%
Project M (medium risk):	Cost of capital = 12%; IRR = 10%
Project L (low risk):	Cost of capital = 8%; IRR = 9%

Note that the projects' cost of capital varies because the projects have different levels of risk. The company's optimal capital structure calls for 50 percent debt and 50 percent common equity. Welch expects to have net income of $7,287,500. If Welch bases its dividends on the residual model, what will its payout ratio be?

18–9 ALTERNATIVE DIVIDEND POLICIES

In 2001 the Keenan Company paid dividends totaling $3,600,000 on net income of $10.8 million. 2001 was a normal year, and for the past 10 years, earnings have grown at a constant rate of 10 percent. However, in 2002, earnings are expected to jump to $14.4 million, and the firm expects to have profitable investment opportunities of $8.4 million. It is predicted that Keenan will not be able to maintain the 2002 level of earnings growth—the high 2002 earnings level is attributable to an exceptionally profitable new product line introduced that year—and the company will return to its previous 10 percent growth rate. Keenan's target debt ratio is 40 percent.

a. Calculate Keenan's total dividends for 2002 if it follows each of the following policies:
 (1) Its 2002 dividend payment is set to force dividends to grow at the long-run growth rate in earnings.
 (2) It continues the 2001 dividend payout ratio.
 (3) It uses a pure residual dividend policy (40 percent of the $8.4 million investment is financed with debt).
 (4) It employs a regular-dividend-plus-extras policy, with the regular dividend being based on the long-run growth rate and the extra dividend being set according to the residual policy.

b. Which of the preceding policies would you recommend? Restrict your choices to the ones listed, but justify your answer.

c. Assume that investors expect Keenan to pay total dividends of $9,000,000 in 2002 and to have the dividend grow at 10 percent after 2002. The stock's total market value is $180 million. What is the company's cost of equity?

d. What is Keenan's long-run average return on equity? [Hint: g = (Retention rate)(ROE) = (1.0 − Payout rate)(ROE).]

e. Does a 2002 dividend of $9,000,000 seem reasonable in view of your answers to parts c and d? If not, should the dividend be higher or lower?

18–10 ALTERNATIVE DIVIDEND POLICIES

Buena Terra Corporation is reviewing its capital budget for the upcoming year. It has paid a $3.00 dividend per share (DPS) for the past several years, and its shareholders expect the dividend to remain constant for the next several years. The company's target capital structure is 60 percent equity and 40 percent debt; it has 1,000,000 shares of common equity outstanding; and its net income is $8 million. The company forecasts that it would require $10 million to fund all of its profitable (that is, positive NPV) projects for the upcoming year.

a. If Buena Terra follows the residual dividend model, how much retained earnings will it need to fund its capital budget?

b. If Buena Terra follows the residual dividend model, what will be the company's dividend per share and payout ratio for the upcoming year?

c. If Buena Terra maintains its current $3.00 DPS for next year, how much retained earnings will be available for the firm's capital budget?

d. Can the company maintain its current capital structure, maintain the $3.00 DPS, and maintain a $10 million capital budget without having to raise new common stock?

e. Suppose that Buena Terra's management is firmly opposed to cutting the dividend; that is, it wishes to maintain the $3.00 dividend for the next year. Also assume that the company was committed to funding all profitable projects, and was willing to issue more debt (along with the available retained earnings) to help finance the company's capital budget. Assume that the resulting change in capital structure has a minimal impact on the company's composite cost of capital, so that the capital budget remains at $10 million. What portion of this year's capital budget would have to be financed with debt?

f. Suppose once again that Buena Terra's management wants to maintain the $3.00 DPS. In addition, the company wants to maintain its target capital structure (60 percent equity, 40 percent debt), and maintain its $10 million capital budget. What is the minimum dollar amount of new common stock that the company would have to issue in order to meet each of its objectives?

g. Now consider the case where Buena Terra's management wants to maintain the $3.00 DPS and its target capital structure, but it wants to avoid issuing new common stock. The company is willing to cut its capital budget in order to meet its other objectives. Assuming that the company's projects are divisible, what will be the company's capital budget for the next year?

h. What actions can a firm that follows the residual dividend policy take when its forecasted retained earnings are less than the retained earnings required to fund its capital budget?

Spreadsheet Problem

18–11 BUILD A MODEL: RESIDUAL DIVIDEND MODEL

Start with the partial model in the file ***Ch 18-11 Build a Model.xls*** from the textbook's CD-ROM. Rework Problem 18-10, parts a through g, using a spreadsheet model.

Cyberproblem

The information related to this cyberproblem is likely to change over time, due to the release of new information and the ever-changing nature of the World Wide Web. Accordingly, we will periodically update the problem on the textbook's web site.

18–12 DIVIDEND REINVESTMENT PLANS

Dividend reinvestment plans (DRIPs) enable stockholders to automatically reinvest dividends received back into the stock of the paying firm. In addition, many DRIPs allow their shareholders the option to buy more shares directly from the company by just writing a check. The major advantage is that investors are able to avoid brokerage commissions. Although some plans require small service fees, these service fees usually pale in comparison to brokerage fees; however, the specific details of DRIPs will vary from plan to plan.

To learn about dividend reinvestment plans, you need to get back to basics. Let's find out what fools think about them, specifically the Motley Fool. For this cyberproblem, you will be going back to school with "Motley Fool's School." Go to the cyberproblem on the textbook's website, **http://www.harcourtcollege.com/student/resources/cyberprob/Ch18.html**, and answer the questions shown there.

Mini Case

CD

See ***Ch 18 Show.ppt*** and ***Ch 18 Mini Case.xls.***

Southeastern Steel Company (SSC) was formed 5 years ago to exploit a new continuous-casting process. SSC's founders, Donald Brown and Margo Valencia, had been employed in the research department of a major integrated-steel company, but when that company decided against using the new process (which Brown and Valencia had developed), they decided to strike out on their own. One advantage of the new process was that it required relatively little capital in comparison with the typical steel company, so Brown and Valencia have been able to avoid issuing new stock, and thus they own all of the shares. However, SSC has now reached the stage where outside equity capital is necessary if the firm is to achieve its growth targets yet still maintain its target capital structure of 60 percent equity and 40 percent debt. Therefore, Brown and Valencia have decided to take the company public. Until now, Brown and Valencia have paid themselves reasonable salaries but routinely reinvested all after-tax earnings in the firm, so dividend policy has not been an issue. However, before talking with potential outside investors, they must decide on a dividend policy.

Assume that you were recently hired by Arthur Adamson & Company (AA), a national consulting firm, which has been asked to help SSC prepare for its public offering. Martha Millon, the senior AA consultant in your group, has asked you to make a presentation to Brown and Valencia in which you review the theory of dividend policy and discuss the following questions.

a. (1) What is meant by the term "dividend policy"?
   (2) The terms "irrelevance," "bird-in-the-hand," and "tax preference" have been used to describe three major theories regarding the way dividend policy affects a firm's value. Explain what these terms mean, and briefly describe each theory.
   (3) What do the three theories indicate regarding the actions management should take with respect to dividend policy?
   (4) Explain the relationships between dividend policy, stock price, and the cost of equity under each dividend policy theory by constructing two graphs such as those shown in Figure 18-1. Dividend payout should be placed on the X axis.
   (5) What results have empirical studies of the dividend theories produced? How does all this affect what we can tell managers about dividend policy?

b. Discuss (1) the information content, or signaling, hypothesis, (2) the clientele effect, and (3) their effects on dividend policy.

c. (1) Assume that SSC has an \$800,000 capital budget planned for the coming year. You have determined that its present capital structure (60 percent equity and 40 percent debt) is optimal, and its net income is forecasted at \$600,000. Use the residual dividend model approach to determine SSC's total dollar dividend and payout ratio. In the process, explain what the residual dividend model is. Then, explain what would happen if net income were forecasted at \$400,000, or at \$800,000.
   (2) In general terms, how would a change in investment opportunities affect the payout ratio under the residual payment policy?
   (3) What are the advantages and disadvantages of the residual policy? (Hint: Don't neglect signaling and clientele effects.)

d. What is a dividend reinvestment plan (DRIP), and how does it work?

e. Describe the series of steps that most firms take in setting dividend policy in practice.

f. What are stock repurchases? Discuss the advantages and disadvantages of a firm's repurchasing its own shares.

g. What are stock dividends and stock splits? What are the advantages and disadvantages of stock dividends and stock splits?

Selected Additional References and Cases

Dividend policy has been studied extensively by academicians. The first major academic work, and still a classic that we recommend highly, is Lintner's analysis of the way corporations actually set their dividend payment policies.

Lintner, John, "Distribution of Incomes of Corporations among Dividends, Retained Earnings, and Taxes," *American Economic Review*, May 1956, 97–113.

The effects of dividend policy on stock prices and capital costs have been examined by many researchers. The classic theoretical argument that dividend policy is important, and that stockholders like dividends, was set forth by Gordon, while Miller and Modigliani (MM) developed the notion that dividend policy is not important. Many researchers have extended both Gordon's and MM's theoretical arguments, and have attempted to test the effects of dividend policy in a variety of ways. Although statistical problems have precluded definitive conclusions, the following articles, among others, have helped to clarify the issues:

Brennan, Michael, "Taxes, Market Valuation, and Corporate Financial Policy," *National Tax Journal*, Spring 1975, 417–427.

Hayes, Linda S., "Fresh Evidence That Dividends Don't Matter," *Fortune*, May 4, 1981, 351–354.

Lewellen, Wilbur G., Kenneth L. Stanley, Ronald C. Lease, and Gary G. Schlarbaum, "Some Direct Evidence on the Dividend Clientele Phenomenon," *Journal of Finance*, December 1978, 1385–1399.

Mukherjee, Tarun, and Larry M. Austin, "An Empirical Investigation of Small Bank Stock Valuation and Dividend Policy," *Financial Management*, Spring 1980, 27–31.

On stock dividends and stock splits, see

Baker, H. Kent, and Patricia L. Gallagher, "Management's View of Stock Splits," *Financial Management*, Summer 1980, 73–77.

Baker, H. Kent, Aaron L. Phillips, and Gary E. Powell, "The Stock Distribution Puzzle: A Synthesis of the Literature on Stock Splits and Stock Dividends," *Financial Practice and Education*, Spring/Summer 1995, 24–37.

Copeland, Thomas E., "Liquidity Changes Following Stock Splits," *Journal of Finance*, March 1979, 115–141.

McNichols, Maureen, and Ajay Dravid, "Stock Dividends, Stock Splits, and Signaling," *Journal of Finance*, July 1990, 857–879.

On repurchases, see

Denis, David J., "Defensive Changes in Corporate Payout Policy: Share Repurchases and Special Dividends," *Journal of Finance*, December 1990, 1433–1456.

Finnerty, Joseph E., "Corporate Stock Issue and Repurchase, *Financial Management*, Autumn 1975, 62–71.

Gay, Gerald D., Jayant R. Kale, and Thomas H. Noe, "Share Repurchase Mechanisms: A Comparative Analysis of Efficacy, Shareholder Wealth and Corporate Control Effects," *Financial Management*, Spring 1991, 44–59.

Klein, April, and James Rosenfeld, "The Impact of Targeted Share Repurchases on the Wealth of Non-Participating Shareholders," *Journal of Financial Research*, Summer 1988, 89–97.

Netter, Jeffry M., and Mark L. Mitchell, "Stock-Repurchase Announcements and Insider Transactions after the October 1987 Stock Market Crash," *Financial Management*, Autumn 1989, 84–96.

Pugh, William, and John S. Jahera, Jr., "Stock Repurchases and Excess Returns: An Empirical Examination," *The Financial Review*, February 1990, 127–142.

Stewart, Samuel S., Jr., "Should a Corporation Repurchase Its Own Stock?" *Journal of Finance*, June 1976, 911–921.

Wansley, James W., William R. Lane, and Salil Sarkar, "Managements' View on Share Repurchase and Tender Offer Premiums," *Financial Management*, Autumn 1989, 97–110.

Woolridge, J. Randall, and Donald R. Chambers, "Reverse Splits and Shareholder Wealth," *Financial Management*, Autumn 1983, 5–15.

For surveys of managers' views on dividend policy, see

Baker, H. Kent, Gail E. Farrelly, and Richard B. Edelman, "A Survey of Management Views on Dividend Policy," *Financial Management*, Autumn 1985, 78–84.

Pruitt, Stephen W., and Lawrence J. Gitman, "The Interactions between the Investment, Financing, and Dividend Decisions of Major U.S. Firms," *Financial Review*, August 1991, 409–430.

Other pertinent articles include

Asquith, Paul, and David W. Mullins, Jr., "Signalling with Dividends, Stock Repurchases, and Equity Issues," *Financial Management*, Autumn 1986, 27–44.

Born, Jeffrey A., "Insider Ownership and Signals—Evidence from Dividend Initiation Announcement Effects," *Financial Management*, Spring 1988, 38–45.

Brealey, Richard A., "Does Dividend Policy Matter?" *Midland Corporate Finance Journal*, Spring 1983, 17–25.

Brennan, Michael J., and Anjan V. Thakor, "Shareholder Preferences and Dividend Policy," *Journal of Finance*, September 1990, 993–1018.

Chang, Rosita P., and S. Ghon Rhee, "The Impact of Personal Taxes on Corporate Dividend Policy and Capital Structure Decisions," *Financial Management*, Summer 1990, 21–31.

DeAngelo, Harry, and Linda DeAngelo, "Dividend Policy and Financial Distress: An Empirical Investigation of Troubled NYSE Firms," *Journal of Finance*, December 1990, 1415–1432.

DeAngelo, Harry, Linda DeAngelo, and Douglas J. Skinner, "Dividends and Losses," *Journal of Finance*, December 1992, 1837–1863.

Dempsey, Stephen J., and Gene Laber, "Effects of Agency and Transactions Costs on Dividend Payout Ratios: Further Evidence of the Agency-Transaction Cost Hypothesis," *Journal of Financial Research*, Winter 1992, 317–321.

Fehrs, Donald H., Gary A. Benesh, and David R. Peterson, "Evidence of a Relation between Stock Price Reactions Around Cash Dividend Changes and Yields," *Journal of Financial Research*, Summer 1988, 111–123.

Ghosh, Chinmoy, and J. Randall Woolridge, "An Analysis of Shareholder Reaction to Dividend Cuts and Omissions," *Journal of Financial Research*, Winter 1988, 281–294.

Healy, Paul M., and Krishna G. Palepu, "How Investors Interpret Changes in Corporate Financial Policy," *Journal of Applied Corporate Finance*, Fall 1989, 59–64.

Impson, C. Michael, and Imre Karafiath, "A Note on the Stock Market Reaction to Dividend Announcements," *The Financial Review*, May 1992, 259–271.

Kale, Jayant R., and Thomas H. Noe, "Dividends, Uncertainty, and Underwriting Costs Under Asymmetric Information," *Journal of Financial Research*, Winter 1990, 265–277.

Manakyan, Herman, and Carolyn Carroll, "An Empirical Examination of the Existence of a Signaling Value Function for Dividends," *Journal of Financial Research*, Fall 1990, 201–210.

Miller, Merton H., "Behavioral Rationality in Finance: The Case of Dividends," *Midland Corporate Finance Journal*, Winter 1987, 6–15.

Peterson, David R., and Pamela P. Peterson, "A Further Understanding of Stock Distributions: The Case of Reverse Stock Splits," *Journal of Financial Research*, Fall 1992, 189–205.

Peterson, Pamela P., David R. Peterson, and Norman H. Moore, "The Adoption of New-Issue Dividend Reinvestment Plans and Shareholder Wealth," *Financial Review*, May 1987, 221–232.

Talmor, Eli, and Sheridan Titman, "Taxes and Dividend Policy," *Financial Management*, Summer 1990, 32–35.

Wansley, James W., C. F. Sirmans, James D. Shilling, and Young-jin Lee, "Dividend Change Announcement Effects and Earnings Volatility and Timing," *Journal of Financial Research*, Spring 1991, 37–49.

Woolridge, J. Randall, and Chinmoy Ghosh, "Dividend Cuts: Do They Always Signal Bad News?" *Midland Corporate Finance Journal*, Summer 1985, 20–32.

The following cases in the Cases in Financial Management: Dryden Request series focus on the issues contained in this chapter:

Case 19, "Georgia Atlantic Company," Case 19A, "Floral Fragrance, Inc.," Case 19B, "Cook Transportation, Inc.," and Case 20, "Bessemer Steel Products, Inc.," which illustrate the dividend policy decision. Case 60, "Consolidated Electric," is a longer and more comprehensive case on dividend policy.

PART SEVEN
Tactical Financing Decisions

19

Initial Public Offerings, Investment Banking, and Financial Restructuring

On any given day, thousands of businesses go to the market to raise capital. For example, the following are some of the securities sold during September 2000:

1. Durect Corp sold 7 million shares of common stock in an initial public offering. The company develops and produces equipment that controls the rate at which drugs are delivered into patients' bloodstreams. It plans to use the proceeds for research, development, and general corporate purposes. Morgan Stanley Dean Witter & Co., the lead underwriter, had anticipated that the stock could be sold in the range of $10 to $12. The actual offering price was $12, and the stock rose to $18.50 during its first day of trading on Nasdaq, but it closed that day at $14.41. Although the initial investors paid $12 per share, Durect received only $11.16—the difference went to the underwriters as a fee for bringing the issue to market. Thus, out of the $84 million paid by investors, Durect received $78.12 million, and the underwriters and their sales forces received $5.88 million. Because the stock ended the day $2.41 higher than the offering price, Durect left an additional $16.87 million "on the table."
2. Informatica Corp., already a publicly traded company, sold an additional 2.5 million shares of common stock at $85 per share. Of the total, 2.0 million shares were newly issued, and 500,000 were already outstanding shares owned by some of the company's founders and early investors. Of the $170 million paid for the 2.0 million new shares, Informatica received about $161 million, with the remainder going to underwriters, including Morgan Stanley Dean Witter, Credit Suisse First Boston, Robertson Stephens, Thomas Weisel Partners LLC, and FAC/Equities. The proceeds from the 500,000 "old shares" were similarly divided between the investment bankers and the selling stockholders.
3. M&T Bank Corp. sold $500 million of senior subordinated, noncallable notes. The coupon rate was 8.0 percent, and the maturity was 10 years. Lehman Brothers and Salomon Smith Barney were the lead underwriters. The notes are rated A3 by Moody's and BBB+ by Standard & Poor's. At the time of issue, the notes had a yield that was 2.2 percentage points above that on a U.S. 10-year Treasury bond.

Although these three issues represent just a tiny fraction of the securities issued that month, they do illustrate an initial public offering, a subsequent stock offering, and a debt offering. After reading this chapter, you should have a better understanding of the procedures firms use when they issue securities.

The previous three chapters described how a company makes capital structure and dividend policy decisions. Those decisions affect the firm's need for new capital, and the forms in which capital is raised. This chapter explains the actual process of raising capital. Throughout the chapter we discuss the roles played by investment bankers and regulatory agencies.

The Financial Life Cycle of a Startup Company

CD

The textbook's CD-ROM contains an *Excel* file that will guide you through the chapter's calculations. The file for this chapter is ***Ch 19 Tool Kit.xls,*** and we encourage you to open the file and follow along as you read the chapter.

Most businesses begin life as proprietorships or partnerships, and then, as the more successful ones grow, at some point they find it desirable to become corporations. Initially, most corporate stock is owned by the firms' founding managers and key employees. Even startup firms that are ultimately successful usually begin with negative free cash flows due to their high growth rates and product development costs; hence, they must raise capital during these high-growth years. If the founding owners-managers have invested all of their own financial resources in the company, they must turn to outside sources of capital. Startup firms generally have high growth opportunities relative to assets-in-place, and they suffer from especially large problems with asymmetric information. Therefore, as we discussed in Chapter 16, they must raise external capital primarily as equity rather than debt.

To protect investors from fraudulent stock issues, in 1933 Congress enacted the Securities Act, which created the **Securities and Exchange Commission (SEC)** to regulate the financial markets.[1] The Securities Act regulates interstate public offerings, which we explain later in this section, but it also provides several exemptions that allow companies to issue securities through **private placements** that are not registered with the SEC. The rules governing these exemptions are quite complex, but in general they restrict the number and type of investors who may participate in an issue. **Accredited investors** include the officers and directors of the company, high-wealth individuals, and institutional investors. In a nonregistered private placement, the company may issue securities to an unlimited number of accredited investors, but to only 35 nonaccredited investors. In addition, none of the investors can sell their securities in the secondary market to the general public.

For most startups, the first round of external financing comes through a private placement of equity to one or two individual investors, called **angels.** In return for a typical investment in the range of $50,000 to $400,000, the angels receive stock and perhaps also a seat on the board of directors. Because angels can influence the strategic direction of the company, it is best that they bring experience and industry contacts to the table, not just cash.

As the company grows, its financing requirements may exceed the resources of individual investors, in which case it is likely to turn to a **venture capital fund.** A venture capital fund is a private limited partnership, which typically raises $30 million to $80 million dollars from a relatively small group of primarily institutional investors, including pension funds, college endowments, and corporations.[2] The managers of a venture

[1] In addition to federal statutes, which affect transactions that cross state borders, states have "Blue Sky" laws that regulate securities sold just within the one state. These laws prevent unscrupulous dealers from selling something of little worth, such as blue sky, to naïve investors.

[2] The typical venture capital fund is a private limited partnership, with limited partners and a general partner. The limited partners contribute cash but are prohibited from being involved in the partnership's decision making. Because of their limited participation, they are not held liable for any of the partnership's liabilities, except to the extent of their original investment. The general partner usually contributes a relatively modest amount of cash, but acts as the partnership's manager. In return, the general partner normally receives annual compensation equal to 1 to 2 percent of the fund's assets plus a 20 percent share of the funds' eventual profits.

capital fund, called **venture capitalists,** or **VCs,** are usually very knowledgeable and experienced in a particular industry, such as health care. They screen hundreds of companies, and ultimately fund around a dozen, called **portfolio companies.** The venture fund buys shares of the portfolio companies, and the VCs sit on the companies' boards of directors. The venture capital fund usually has a prespecified life of seven to ten years, after which it is dissolved, either by selling the portfolio companies' stock and distributing the proceeds to the funds' investors or by directly distributing the stock to the investors.

Self-Test Questions

What is a private placement?

What is an angel?

What is a venture capital fund? A VC?

The Decision to Go Public: Initial Public Offerings

Going public means selling some of a company's stock to outside investors and then letting the stock trade in public markets. For example, Centra Software, John Hancock Financial Services, Krispy Kreme Doughnuts, and hundreds of other companies took this step in 2000. The advantages and disadvantages of public stock ownership are discussed next.

Advantages of Going Public

1. **Permits founders to diversify.** As a company grows and becomes more valuable, its founders often have most of their wealth tied up in the company. By selling some of their stock in a public offering, they can diversify their holdings, thereby reducing the riskiness of their personal portfolios.
2. **Increases liquidity.** The stock of a private, or closely held, corporation is illiquid: It has no ready market. If one of the owners wants to sell some shares to raise cash, it is hard to find a ready buyer, and even if a buyer is located, there is no established price on which to base the transaction. These problems do not exist with publicly owned firms.
3. **Facilitates raising new corporate cash.** If a privately held company wants to raise cash by selling new stock, it must either go to its existing owners, who may not have any money or may not want to put more eggs in this particular basket, or else shop around for wealthy investors. However, it is usually quite difficult to get outsiders to put money into a closely held company, because if the outsiders do not have voting control (more than 50 percent of the stock), the inside stockholders/managers can run roughshod over them. The insiders can pay or not pay dividends, pay themselves exorbitant salaries, have private deals with the company, and so on. For example, the president might buy a warehouse and lease it to the company at a high rate, get the use of a Rolls Royce, and enjoy frequent "all-the-frills" travel to conventions. The insiders can even keep the outsiders from knowing the company's actual earnings, or its real worth. There are few positions more vulnerable than that of an outside stockholder in a closely held company, and for this reason, it is hard for closely held companies to raise new equity capital. Going public, which brings with it both public disclosure of information and regulation by the SEC, greatly reduces these problems, makes people more willing to invest in the company, and thus makes it easier for the firm to raise capital.
4. **Establishes a value for the firm.** For a number of reasons, it is often useful to establish a firm's value in the marketplace. For one thing, when the owner of a privately owned business dies, state and federal tax appraisers must set a value on the company

for estate tax purposes. Often, these appraisers set too high a value, which creates an obvious problem. However, a company that is publicly owned has an established value. Similarly, if a company wants to give incentive stock options to key employees, it is useful to know the exact value of those options, and employees much prefer to own stock, or options on stock, that is publicly traded and therefore liquid.

5. **Sets up merger negotiations.** If there is an established market price, this helps when a company is either being acquired or seeking to acquire another company where it will pay for the acquisition with stock.
6. **Increases potential markets.** Many companies report that it is easier to sell their products and services to potential customers after they become a publicly traded company.

Disadvantages of Going Public

1. **Cost of reporting.** A publicly owned company must file quarterly and annual reports with the SEC and/or various state agencies. These reports can be a costly burden, especially for small firms.
2. **Disclosure.** Management may not like the idea of reporting operating data, because these data will then be available to competitors. Similarly, the owners of the company may not want people to know their net worth, and since a publicly owned company must disclose the number of shares owned by its officers, directors, and major stockholders, it is easy enough for anyone to multiply shares held by price per share to estimate the net worth of the insiders.
3. **Self-dealings.** The owners-managers of closely held companies have many opportunities for various types of questionable but legal self-dealings, including the payment of high salaries, nepotism, personal transactions with the business (such as a leasing arrangement), and not-truly-necessary fringe benefits. Such self-dealings, which are often designed to minimize their personal tax liabilities, are much harder to arrange if a company is publicly owned.
4. **Inactive market/low price.** If the firm is very small, and if its shares are not traded frequently, its stock will not really be liquid, and the market price may not represent the stock's true value. Security analysts and stockbrokers simply will not follow the stock, because there will not be sufficient trading activity to generate enough brokerage commissions to cover the costs of following the stock.
5. **Control.** Because of possible tender offers and proxy fights, the managers of publicly owned firms who do not have voting control must be concerned about maintaining control. Further, there is pressure on such managers to produce annual earnings gains, even when it might be in the shareholders' best long-term interests to adopt a strategy that reduces short-term earnings but raises them in future years. These factors have led a number of public companies to "go private" in "leveraged buyout" deals where the managers borrow the money to buy out the nonmanagement stockholders. We discuss the decision to go private in a later section.
6. **Investor relations.** Public companies must keep investors abreast of current developments. Many CFOs of newly public firms report that they spend two full days a week talking with investors and analysts.

Conclusions on Going Public

There are no hard-and-fast rules regarding if or when a company should go public. This is an individual decision that should be made on the basis of the company's and stockholders' own unique circumstances. If a company does decide to go public, either by selling newly issued stock to raise new capital or by the sale of stock by the current owners, the key issue is setting the price at which shares will be offered to the public.

The company and its current owners should want to set the price as high as possible—the higher the offering price, the smaller the fraction of the company the current owners will have to give up to obtain any specified amount of money. On the other hand, potential buyers want the price set as low as possible. We will return to the establishment of the offering price later in the chapter, after we have described some other aspects of common stock financing.

Self-Test Questions

What are the major advantages of going public?

What are the major disadvantages?

The Process of Going Public

As the following sections show, the process of going public is a lot more complicated, expensive, and time consuming than simply making the decision to go public.

Selecting an Investment Banker

After a company decides to go public, it faces the problem of how to sell its stock to a large number of investors. While most companies know how to sell their products, few have experience in selling securities. To help in this process, the company will interview a number of different **investment banks,** also called **underwriters,** and then select one to be the lead underwriter. To understand the factors that affect this choice, it helps to understand exactly what investment bankers do.

First, the investment bank helps the firm determine the preliminary offering price, or price range, for the stock and the number of shares to be sold. The investment bank's reputation and experience in the company's industry are very important in convincing potential investors to purchase the stock at the offering price. In effect, the investment banker certifies that the stock is not overpriced, which obviously comforts investors. Second, the investment bank actually sells the shares to its existing clients, which includes a mix of institutional investors and retail (that is, individual) customers. Third, the investment bank, through its associated brokerage house, will have an analyst "cover" the stock after it is issued. This analyst will regularly distribute reports to investors describing the stock's prospects, which will help to maintain an interest in the stock. Well-respected analysts increase the likelihood that there will be a liquid secondary market for the stock and that its price will reflect the company's true value.

Table 19-1 shows the leading investment bankers for initial public offerings in 2000. If a bank shows a high return, this improves its reputation with investors and helps it sell future issues. However, as we discuss in a later section, what's good for investors is not necessarily good for the issuing company. Also, note that 2000 was the worst year in history for high-tech stocks, so the returns shown are not typical. For this reason, it is useful to examine underwriters' records over several years.

The Underwriting Syndicate

The firm and its investment banker must next decide whether the banker will work on a **best efforts** basis or will **underwrite** the issue. In a best efforts sale, the banker does not guarantee that the securities will be sold or that the company will get the cash it needs, only that it will put forth its "best efforts" to sell the issue. On an underwritten issue, the company does get a guarantee, because the banker agrees to buy the entire issue and then resell the stock to its customers. Therefore, the banker bears significant risks in underwritten offerings. For example, on one IBM bond issue, interest rates rose sharply, and bond prices fell, after the deal had been set but before the investment

TABLE 19-1 Leading Underwriters for Initial Public Offerings in 1999

Rank	Underwriter	Number of IPOs	Value of Deals ($ Billions)	Average Return During Year
1	Goldman, Sachs & Co.	60	$40.1	−13.91%
2	Morgan Stanley Dean Witter	52	27.5	−21.76
3	Merrill Lynch & Co.	40	25.4	1.15
4	Salomon Smith Barney	33	22.1	−12.70
5	Credit Suisse First Boston	65	14.5	−13.59
6	Deutsche Banc Alex. Brown	32	8.5	0.99
7	China International Capital Corp.	3	8.4	−44.65
8	ABN AMRO Rothschild	3	4.7	13.46
9	Donaldson, Lufkin & Jenrette	23	4.2	−7.12
10	Lehman Brothers	33	4.0	−20.79

Note: Excludes units, closed-end funds, and deals priced below $5.

Source: **http://www.ipo.com.**

bankers could sell the bonds to the ultimate purchasers. The bankers lost somewhere between $10 million and $20 million. Had the offering been on a best efforts basis, IBM would have been the loser.

Except for extremely small issues, virtually all IPOs are underwritten. Investors are required to pay for securities within ten days, and the investment banker must pay the issuing firm within four days of the official commencement of the offering. Typically, the banker sells the stock within a day or two after the offering begins, but on occasion, the banker miscalculates, sets the offering price too high, and thus is unable to move the issue. At other times, the market declines during the offering period, forcing the banker to reduce the price of the stock or bonds. In either instance, on an underwritten offering the firm receives the price that was agreed upon, so the banker must absorb any losses that are incurred.

Because they are exposed to large potential losses, investment bankers typically do not handle the purchase and distribution of issues single-handedly unless the issue is a very small one. If the sum of money involved is large, investment bankers form **underwriting syndicates** in an effort to minimize the risk each banker faces. The banking house that sets up the deal is called the **lead,** or **managing, underwriter.** Syndicated offerings are usually covered by more analysts, which contributes to greater liquidity in the post-IPO secondary market. Thus, syndication provides benefits to both underwriters and issuers.

In addition to the underwriting syndicate, on larger offerings still more investment bankers are included in a **selling group,** which handles the distribution of securities to individual investors. The selling group includes all members of the underwriting syndicate plus additional dealers who take relatively small percentages of the total issue from the members of the underwriting syndicate. Thus, the underwriters act as wholesalers, while members of the selling group act as retailers. The number of houses in a selling group depends partly upon the size of the issue, but is normally in the range of 10 to 15.

A new selling procedure has recently emerged that takes advantage of the trend toward institutional ownership of stock. In this type of sale, called an **unsyndicated stock offering,** the managing underwriter, acting alone, sells the issue entirely to a group of institutional investors, thus bypassing both retail stockbrokers and individual investors. In recent years, about 50 percent of all stock sold has been by unsyndicated offerings. Behind this phenomenon is a simple motivating force: money. The fees that issuers pay on a syndicated offering, which includes commissions paid to retail brokers, can run a full percentage point higher than those on unsyndicated offerings. Further, although total fees are lower in unsyndicated offerings, managing underwriters usually come out ahead because they do not have to share the fees with an underwriting syndicate. Recent issuers of unsyndicated stock include Transamerica Corporation and Public Service Company of New Mexico. However, some types of stock do not appeal to institutional investors, so not all firms can use unsyndicated offers.

Regulation of Securities Sales

Sales of new securities, and also sales in the secondary markets, are regulated by the Securities and Exchange Commission and, to a lesser extent, by each of the 50 states. Here are the primary elements of SEC regulation:

1. The SEC has jurisdiction over all **interstate public offerings** in amounts of $1.5 million or more.
2. Newly issued securities (stocks and bonds) must be registered with the SEC at least 20 days before they are publicly offered. The **registration statement,** called Form S-1, provides financial, legal, and technical information about the company to the SEC. A **prospectus,** which is embedded in the S-1, summarizes this information for investors. The SEC's lawyers and accountants analyze both the registration statement and the prospectus; if the information is inadequate or misleading, the SEC will delay or stop the public offering.[3]
3. After the SEC declares the registration to be effective, new securities may be advertised, but all sales solicitations must be accompanied by the prospectus. Preliminary, or **"red herring," prospectuses** may be distributed to potential buyers during the 20-day waiting period after the registration is effective, but no sales may be finalized during this time. The "red herring" prospectus contains all the key information that will appear in the final prospectus except the final price, which is generally set after the market closes the day before the new securities are actually offered to the public.
4. If the registration statement or prospectus contains **misrepresentations or omissions** of material facts, any purchaser who suffers a loss may sue for damages. Severe penalties may be imposed on the issuer or its officers, directors, accountants, engineers, appraisers, underwriters, and all others who participated in the preparation of the registration statement or prospectus.

WWW

The primary registration statement for an IPO is the S-1 statement. These can be downloaded from the SEC's Edgar web site, **http://www.sec.gov/edaux/formlynx.htm**.

The Roadshow and Book-Building

After the registration statement has been filed, the senior management team, the investment bankers, and the company's lawyers go on a **roadshow.** The management team will make three to seven presentations each day to potential institutional investors, who are typically existing clients of the underwriters. The institutional investors ask questions during the presentation, but the management team may not give any information that is not in the registration statement due to the SEC mandated

[3]Now that the Internet is with us, it is extremely easy to obtain the S-1 form, which typically has 50 to 100 pages of financial statements, a detailed discussion of the firm's business, the risks and opportunities the firm faces, details on its principal stockholders and managers, what will be done with the funds raised, and the like. This statement is filed with the SEC and is immediately available, through the Internet, to investors. The SEC staff reviews the filed S-1, and amendments may be issued, labeled S-1A, S-1B, etc. Most importantly, the likely range for the offering price will be reported, for example, $13 to $15 per share. If the market strengthens or weakens while the stock is undergoing SEC review, the price may be increased or decreased, right up to the last day. The SEC web site is **http://www.sec.gov/edaux/formlynx.htm.**

quiet period. This quiet period begins when the registration statement is made effective and lasts for 25 days after the stock begins trading. Its purpose is to create a level playing field for all investors, by ensuring that they all have access to the same information. It is not uncommon for the SEC to delay an IPO if managers violate the quiet period rules. The typical roadshow may last 10 to 14 days, with stops in 10 to 20 different cities. In many ways it resembles a coming out party for the company, but it is much more grueling and has much higher stakes.

After a presentation, the investment bankers ask the investor for an indication of interest, based on the offering price range shown in the registration statement. For example, the price range for Durect Corp., the company in the opening vignette, was \$10 to \$12. The investment banker records the number of shares that each investor is willing to buy, which is called **book-building.** As the roadshow progresses, the investment banker's "book" shows how demand for the offering is building. Many IPOs are **oversubscribed,** with investors wishing to purchase more shares than are available. In such a case the investment banker will allocate shares to the investors.[4] If demand is high enough, then sometimes they will increase the offering price. If demand is low, then they will either reduce the offering price or withdraw the IPO. Sometimes low demand is specifically due to concern over the company's future prospects, but sometimes low demand is caused by a fall in the general stock market. Thus, the timing of the roadshow and offering date are very important. As the old saying goes, sometimes it is better to be lucky than good.

If all goes well with the roadshow, the investment banker will finalize the offering price on the evening before the actual offering date. For Durect, the offering price was set at \$12, which was at the high end of the preliminary range, indicating strong but not overwhelming demand.

For useful and interesting information on IPOs, see **http://www.ipo.com, http://www.ipocentral.com,** and **http://www.ipomaven.com.** Professor Jay Ritter also has a great site for IPOs at **http://bear.cba.ufl.edu/ritter.**

The First Day of Trading

The first day of trading for many IPOs is wild and exciting. Table 19-2 shows the largest first-day returns for IPOs in 2000. Some stocks end the day with phenomenal returns, such as the 508 percent price increase of webMethods, as shown in Table 19-2. Others have a sharp run-up and then fall back by the end of the day. For example, Durect's stock increased from its offering price of \$12 to \$18.50, but fell back to \$14.41 by the day's close. A few IPOs actually end their first day with a loss.

According to a study by Professors Tim Loughran and Jay Ritter, about 27.3 percent of IPOs have an offer price that is lower than the low range in their initial registration filing, and these stocks have an average first-day return of 4.0 percent.[5] Even though the average return is positive, 47 percent of these stocks actually end the day with a loss or no gain. About 48.4 percent of IPOs have an offering price that is within the range of their initial filing, such as Durect, which had a filing range reported in the S-1 of \$10 to \$12 and an offering price of \$12. For such companies, the average first-day return was 10.8 percent. Due to indications of high demand during the roadshow, 24.3 percent of IPOs had a final offer price that was higher than their original range. These stocks had an average first-day return of 31.9 percent. Overall, the average first-day return was 14.1 percent during 1990–1998, with 75 percent of all IPOs having a positive return. During 1999, the first-day return was an astronomical 70 percent!

---

[4]Most underwriting agreements contain an "overallotment option" that permits the underwriter to purchase additional shares up to 15 percent of the issue size to cover promises made to potential buyers. This is called a "green shoe" agreement because it was first used in the 1963 underwriting of a company named Green Shoe.

[5]See Tim Loughran and Jay R. Ritter, "Why Don't Issuers Get Upset about Leaving Money on the Table in IPOs?" *Review of Financial Studies,* forthcoming.

TABLE 19-2 Highest First-Day IPO Returns in 2000

Rank	Company (Symbol)	Offer Date	Shares (in million)	Offering Price	First Day Closing Price	Gain/ Loss	12/29/ 2000 Close
1	webMethods (WEBM)	2/10/00	4.10	$35.00	$212.63	507.51%	$88.94
2	Crayfish (CRFH)	3/6/00	4.35	24.50	126.00	414.28	8.75
3	Avanex Corporation (AVNX)	2/3/00	6.00	36.00	172.00	377.77	59.56
4	Selectica (SLTC)	3/9/00	4.00	30.00	141.23	370.76	24.19
5	FirePond (FIRE)	2/3/00	5.00	22.00	100.25	355.68	9.44
6	Asia Info Holdings (ASIA)	3/2/00	5.00	24.00	99.56	314.83	9.38
7	Neoforma.com (NEOF)	1/24/00	7.00	13.00	52.38	302.92	0.81
8	Versata (VATA)	3/2/00	3.85	24.00	92.75	286.45	8.94
9	UTStarcom (UTSI)	3/2/00	10.00	18.00	68.88	282.66	15.50
10	Marvell Technology Group (MRVL)	6/26/00	6.00	15.00	56.63	277.53	21.94

Note:
Offer price is adjusted to reflect stock splits.

Source: http://www.ipo.com

You're probably asking yourself two questions: (1) How can you get in on these deals, and (2) why is the offering price so low? First, you probably can't get the chance to buy an IPO at its offering price, especially not a "hot" one. Virtually all sales go to institutional investors and preferred retail customers. There are a few web-based investment bankers who are trying to change this, such as the OpenIPO of W. R. Hambrecht & Co., but right now it is difficult for small investors to get in on the better first-day IPOs.

Various theories have been put forth to explain IPO underpricing. As long as issuing companies don't complain, investment bankers have strong incentives to underprice the issue. First, underpricing increases the likelihood of oversubscription, which reduces the risk to the underwriter. Second, most investors who get to purchase the IPO at its offering price are preferred customers of the investment bank, and they became preferred customers because they generated lots of commissions in the investment bank's sister brokerage company. Therefore, the IPO is an easy way for the underwriter to reward customers for past and future commissions. Third, the underwriter needs an honest indication of interest when building the book prior to the offering, and underpricing is a possible way to secure this information from the institutional investors.

But why don't issuing companies object to underpricing? Some do, and are seeking alternative ways to issue securities, such as OpenIPO. However, most seem content to leave some money on the table. The best explanation seems to be that (1) the company wants to create excitement, and a price run-up on the first day does that; (2) only a small percentage of the company's stock is generally offered to the public, so current stockholders give away less due to underpricing than appears at first glance; and (3) IPO companies generally plan to have further offerings in the future, and the best way to ensure future success is to have a successful IPO, which underpricing guarantees.

Although IPOs on average provide large first-day returns, their long-term returns over the following three years are below average. For example, if you could not get in at the IPO price but purchased a portfolio of IPO stocks on their second day of trading, your three-year return would have been lower than the return on a portfolio of similar but seasoned stocks. In summary, the offering price appears to be too low, but the first-day run-up is generally too high.

The Costs of Going Public

During recent years, virtually all investment banks have charged a 7 percent **spread** between the price they pay the issuing company and the price at which they sell shares to the public. Thus, they keep 7 percent of the offering price as their compensation. For Durect, the offer price was $12 per share and the underwriters' direct compensation was $0.84 per share. With 7 million shares issued, these direct underwriting costs totaled about $5.88 million.

But Durect also had other direct costs, such as lawyer's fees, accountant's costs, printing, engraving, and so on. These fees can easily amount to several hundred thousand dollars, which can be a large percentage of a small IPO.

Last, but not least, are the indirect costs. The money left on the table, which is equal to the number of shares multiplied by the difference in the closing price and the offering price, can be quite large. For Durect, it was 7,000,000($14.41 − $12.00) = $15.47 million. In addition, senior managers spend an enormous amount of time working on the IPO rather than managing the business, which certainly carries a high cost, even if it cannot be easily measured.

Thus, as we listed in the opening vignette, Durect received proceeds of $78.12 million, the underwriters and their sales forces received $5.88 million, and Durect left $15.47 million on the table. Durect undoubtedly had other direct costs of several hundred thousand dollars, and indirect costs due to the diversion of its management team. As you can see, an IPO is quite expensive.

The Importance of the Secondary Market

An active secondary market after the IPO provides the pre-IPO shareholders with a chance to convert some of their wealth into cash, makes it easier for the company to raise additional capital later, makes employee stock options more attractive, and makes it easier for the company to use their stock to acquire other companies. Without an active secondary market, there would be little reason to have an IPO. Thus, companies should try to ensure that their stock will trade in an active secondary market before they incur the high costs of an IPO.

As described in Chapter 5, there are several types of secondary markets: physical stock exchanges, dealer markets, and bulletin boards. We discuss each of these below.

The physical exchanges, such as the NYSE and AMEX, conduct their trading in an actual location. In general, the NYSE and AMEX provide excellent liquidity. In order to have its stock listed, a company must apply to an exchange, pay a relatively small fee, and meet the exchange's minimum requirements. These requirements relate to the size of the company's net income, its market value, and its "float," which is the number of shares outstanding and in the hands of outsiders (as opposed to the number held by insiders, who generally do not actively trade their stock). Also, the company must agree to disclose certain information to the exchange and to help the exchange track trading patterns and thus ensure that no one is attempting to manipulate the stock's price. The size qualifications increase as a company moves from the AMEX to the NYSE.

Assuming a company qualifies, many believe that listing is beneficial to the company and to its stockholders. Listed companies receive a certain amount of free advertising and publicity, and their status as a listed company may enhance their prestige and reputation, which often leads to higher sales. Investors respond favorably to increased information, increased liquidity, and the confidence that the quoted price is not being manipulated. Listing provides investors with these benefits, which may help managers lower their firms' cost of equity and increase the value of their stock.

The advantages of physical exchanges have been eroded—some would say eliminated—by computers and the Internet, which have benefited the dealer markets. The primary dealer markets are administered by Nasdaq, and they include the Nasdaq National Market and the Nasdaq SmallCap Market. Almost 85 percent of new IPO stocks trade in these markets. Unlike the physical exchanges, these consist of a network of dealers, with each dealer making a market in one or more stocks. A dealer makes a market in a company's stock by holding an inventory of the shares and then making offers to buy or sell the stock. Many stocks have excellent liquidity in these markets, and remain there even though they easily meet the requirements for listing on the NYSE. Examples include Microsoft, Intel, Apple, and Cisco Systems.

Investment banks generally agree to make a market in a company's stock as part of their IPO duties. The diligence with which they carry out this task can have a huge effect on the stock's liquidity in the secondary market, and, thus, the success of the IPO.

Although the requirements for listing on the Nasdaq National Market or SmallCap Market are not as stringent as for the NYSE, some companies fail to maintain them and hence are "delisted." For these companies, offers to buy or sell the stock may be posted on the OTC Bulletin Board, an electronic bulletin board administered by Nasdaq. However, there is very little liquidity in these stocks, and an IPO would be considered a failure if the company's stock ended up on the OTC Bulletin Board.

Regulating the Secondary Market

As we stated earlier, a liquid and crime-free secondary market is critical to the success of an IPO or any other publicly traded security. So, in addition to regulating the process for issuing securities, the Securities Exchange Commission also has responsibilities in the secondary markets. The primary elements of SEC regulation are set forth below.

1. The SEC **regulates all national stock exchanges,** and companies whose securities are listed on an exchange must file annual reports similar to the registration statement with both the SEC and the exchange.
2. The SEC has control over trading by corporate **insiders.** Officers, directors, and major stockholders must file monthly reports of changes in their holdings of the stock of the corporation. Any short-term profits from such transactions must be turned over to the corporation.
3. The SEC has the power to **prohibit manipulation** by such devices as pools (large amounts of money used to buy or sell stocks to artificially affect prices) or wash sales (sales between members of the same group to record artificial transaction prices).
4. The SEC has **control over the proxy statement** and the way the company uses it to solicit votes.

Control over credit used to buy securities is exercised by the Federal Reserve Board through **margin requirements,** which specify the maximum percentage of the purchase price someone can borrow. If a great deal of margin borrowing has been going on, then a decline in stock prices can result in inadequate coverages. This could force stockbrokers to issue **margin calls,** which require investors either to put up more money or have their margined stock sold to pay off their loans. Such forced sales further depress the stock market and thus can set off a downward spiral. The margin at the time a stock is purchased has been 50 percent since 1974 (subsequent "maintenance margins" are lower and are generally set by individual lenders).

The securities industry itself realizes the importance of stable markets, sound brokerage firms, and the absence of stock manipulation.[6] Therefore, the various exchanges work closely with the SEC to police transactions and to maintain the integrity and credibility of the system. Similarly, the **National Association of Securities Dealers (NASD)** cooperates with the SEC to police trading in its dealer and OTC markets. These industry groups also cooperate with regulatory authorities to set net worth and other standards for securities firms, to develop insurance programs to protect the customers of failed brokerage houses, and the like.

In general, government regulation of securities trading, as well as industry self-regulation, is designed to ensure (1) that investors receive information that is as accurate as possible, (2) that no one artificially manipulates the market price of a given stock, and (3) that corporate insiders do not take advantage of their position to profit in their companies' stocks at the expense of other stockholders. Neither the SEC, the state regulators, nor the industry itself can prevent investors from making foolish decisions or from having "bad luck," but they can and do help investors obtain the best data possible for making sound investment decisions.

Self-Test Questions

What is the difference between "best efforts" and "underwriting"?

What are some SEC regulations regarding sales of new securities?

What is a roadshow? What is book-building?

What is underpricing? Leaving money on the table?

What are some of the costs of going public?

Equity Carve-Outs: A Special Type of IPO

A few years ago, Condec Corporation sold to the public about 20 percent of the equity in its wholly owned subsidiary, Unimation Inc. In this transaction, the subsidiary, like the parent, became publicly owned, but the parent retained full control of the subsidiary by retaining about 80 percent of the subsidiary's common stock. (Parent companies typically retain at least 80 percent of the subsidiary's common stock to preserve their ability to file a consolidated tax return.) This type of transaction is called an **equity carve-out** (or **partial public offering,** or **spin-out**). The market's response to Condec's carve-out announcement was very positive—the stock price rose 19 percent after correcting for the overall movement in the market.[7] Equity carve-outs raise an interesting question: Why do carve-out announcements typically result in stock price increases while the announcements of new stock issues by parent corporations generally decrease stock prices?

One possible answer is that carve-outs facilitate the evaluation of corporate growth opportunities on a line-of-business basis. Thus, Condec, a conglomerate operating mostly in the defense industry, enabled investors to separately value its Unimation

[6]It is illegal for anyone to attempt to manipulate the price of a stock. During the 1920s, and earlier, syndicates would buy and sell stocks back and forth at rigged prices so the public would believe that a particular stock was worth more or less than its true value. The exchanges, with the encouragement and support of the SEC, utilize sophisticated computer programs to help spot any irregularities that suggest manipulation, and they require disclosures to help identify manipulators. This same system helps to identify illegal insider trading. It is now illegal to manipulate a stock's price by spreading false news on the Internet.

[7]For more information on equity carve-outs, see Katherine Schipper and Abbie Smith, "Equity Carve-Outs," *Midland Corporate Finance Journal,* Spring 1986, 23–32; David M. Glassman, "Spin-Offs and Spin-Outs: Using 'Securitization' to Beat the Bureaucracy," *Journal of Applied Corporate Finance,* Fall 1988, 82–89; and Anand Vijh, "Long-Term Returns from Equity Carveouts," *Journal of Financial Economics,* Vol. 51, 1999, 273–308.

subsidiary, which manufactures industrial robots, by offering its stock to the public. Also, by creating a separate public market for Unimation's common stock, Condec offered investors a "pure play" in robotics, a relatively scarce commodity.

Another advantage to carve-outs is that they improve the ability of the parent to offer incentives to a subsidiary's managers. For example, McKesson Corporation, a $6 billion firm in the drug and health care industry, recently sold 17 percent of its Armor All subsidiary to the public. At the time, Neil Harlan, McKesson's chairman, said that Armor All is "different than most of our operations. It is heavily marketing-driven and entrepreneurial in nature." Creation of a public market for the shares of Armor All provided the opportunity for McKesson to offer incentive shares in the subsidiary to Armor All's top managers. Such shares, which hinge directly on the market value of Armor All, are clearly a better inducement to superior performance than a compensation plan tied to the parent corporation's stock price, since Armor All accounted for only 2 percent of McKesson's total sales.

Another potential advantage of carve-outs is that they can increase the effectiveness of capital allocation. Internally, the competition for capital is often waged on political rather than economic grounds, and thus the use, and hence value, of new capital is very uncertain. After a carve-out, it is easier to measure the cost of capital for the different business units, and this can improve the capital budgeting process. Also, by selling an ownership interest in a narrowly focused line of business rather than offering a stake in the conglomerate parent, management can reduce the uncertainty faced by investors. This can lower the cost of capital for the various units, and thus increase the aggregate value of the consolidated enterprise.

Equity carve-outs do have some associated costs. First, the underwriting commission involved in a carve-out is larger than for an equity offering by the parent. Second, because an equity carve-out is a type of initial public offering, there is a potential for underpricing the new offering. Third, key managers of the subsidiary must spend a significant amount of time marketing the new stock. Fourth, there are costs associated with the minority interest that is created in the carve-out. For example, the subsidiary's new board of directors must monitor all transactions between the subsidiary and the parent to ensure that the minority investors are not being exploited. Finally, there are additional costs including annual reports, SEC filings, analyst presentations, and so on, that must now be borne by both the parent and the subsidiary.

In summary, there are costs to equity carve-outs, but there are also benefits, and the benefits may make the carve-out an attractive option in many situations. In essence, a carve-out is a form of corporate **securitization,** which is the issuance of public securities backed by assets that have been segregated from the remaining assets of the company. By creating such securities, and a liquid market for trading them, a corporation can potentially reduce investor risk and increase the value of the firm as a whole. We will cover securitization in more depth later in the chapter.

Self-Test Questions

Explain what is meant by an equity carve-out.

On average, equity carve-outs have increased shareholder wealth. What are some potential explanations for this observed phenomenon?

Non-IPO Investment Banking Activities

In addition to helping with IPOs, investment banks also help public companies raise additional debt and equity capital. As shown in Table 19-3, investment banks helped firms raise just over $3 trillion during 2000. In this section we describe some of the ways that investment banks and public companies work together to raise capital.

TABLE 19-3 Top Ten Underwriters of Debt and Equity in 2000

Manager	Proceeds (in billions)	Issues	Market Share
Merrill Lynch	$380.4	3,148	12.5%
Salomon Smith Barney	328.9	1,893	10.8
Morgan Stanley Dean Witter	280.5	2,581	9.2
Credit Suisse First Boston	280.4	1,872	9.2
J. P. Morgan	271.4	1,592	8.9
Goldman Sachs	252.0	1,145	8.3
Deutsche Bank	185.4	879	6.1
Lehman Brothers	170.3	985	5.6
UBS Warburg	136.1	890	4.5
Banc of America Securities	104.0	813	3.4
Top 10 Totals	$2,389.4	15,798	78.5%
Industry Totals	$3,042.2	20,427	100.0%

Source: *The Wall Street Journal*, January 3, 2001, p. R19. Reprinted by permission of *The Wall Street Journal*,

Preliminary Decisions

Before raising capital, the firm makes some initial, preliminary decisions, including the following:

1. **Dollars to be raised.** How much new capital is needed?
2. **Type of securities used.** Should common, preferred, bonds, hybrid securities, or a combination, be used? Further, if common stock is to be issued, should it be done as a rights offering or by a direct sale to the general public?
3. **Competitive bid versus a negotiated deal.** Should the company simply offer a block of its securities for sale to the highest bidder, or should it negotiate a deal with an investment banker? These two procedures are called **competitive bids** and **negotiated deals,** respectively. Only about 100 of the largest firms listed on the NYSE, whose securities are already well known to the investment banking community, are in a position to use the competitive bidding process. The investment banks must do a great deal of investigative work ("due diligence") to bid on an issue unless they are already quite familiar with the firm, and such costs would be too high to make it worthwhile unless the bank was sure of getting the deal. Therefore, except for the largest firms, offerings of stock and bonds are generally on a negotiated basis.
4. **Selection of an investment banker.** Most deals are negotiated, so the firm must select an investment banker. This can be an important decision for a firm that is going public. On the other hand, an older firm that has already "been to market" will have an established relationship with an investment banker. However, it is easy to change bankers if the firm is dissatisfied. Different investment banking houses are better suited for different companies. For example, Goldman Sachs and Morgan Stanley Dean Witter are the leading tech-IPO underwriters. Investment banking houses sell new issues largely to their own regular brokerage customers, so the nature of these customers has a major effect on the ability of the house to do a good job for corporate issuers. Finally, a major factor in choosing an underwriter is the reputation of the analyst who will cover the stock in the secondary market, since a strong buy recommendation from a well-respected analyst can trigger a sharp price run-up.

Private Placements

In a **private placement,** securities are sold to one or a few investors, generally institutional investors. Private placements are most common with bonds, but they also occur with stocks. The primary advantages of private placements are (1) lower flotation costs and (2) greater speed, since the shares do not have to go through the SEC registration process.

The most common type of private placement occurs when a company places securities directly with a financial institution, often an insurance company or a pension fund. In fact, Prudential Insurance Company has begun sending salespeople to call on businesses—not to sell them policies, but to sell them on raising funds privately from Prudential. To illustrate a private placement, AT&T sold 6.3 million shares of common stock worth about $650 million to Capital Group Inc., a Los Angeles institutional investor that manages both mutual and pension funds. The transaction was a blow to three Wall Street firms, Morgan Stanley Dean Witter, Dillon Reed, and Goldman Sachs, which wanted to sell the stock in a conventional public offering. AT&T's treasurer said selling the stock in a private placement saved about 2.5 percent, or $16.3 million, in underwriting expenses.

One type of private placement that is occurring with increasing frequency is where a large company makes an equity investment in a smaller supplier. For example, Compaq Computer and AMP Corporation each recently invested several million in Intellon Corporation, a telecommunications equipment manufacturer. Intellon needed capital for expansion, and Compaq and AMP were both engaged in joint development ventures with Intellon and wanted it to be financially strong. Similar arrangements are quite common, and some of them go back many years. For example, Sears, Roebuck has for many years supplied equity capital to some of its major suppliers, including Johnson Controls, which furnished Sears with "Die-Hard" batteries, and DeSoto Chemical, which supplied most of the paints that Sears sells.

The primary disadvantage of a private placement is that the securities generally do not go through the SEC registration process, so under SEC rules they cannot be sold except to another large, "sophisticated" purchaser in the event the original buyer wants to sell them. However, SEC rules permit any institution with $100 million or more to buy and sell private placement securities. Since many institutions exceed that limit, private placements are becoming increasingly popular, and today they constitute almost 40 percent of all nonbank debt financing.

Shelf Registrations

The selling procedures described previously, including the 20-day waiting period after registration with the SEC, apply to most security sales. However, under the SEC's Rule 415, large, well-known public companies that issue securities frequently may file a master registration statement with the SEC and then update it with a short-form statement just prior to each individual offering. Under this procedure, a company can decide at 10 A.M. to sell securities and have the sale completed before noon. This procedure is known as **shelf registration** because, in effect, the company puts its new securities "on the shelf" and then sells them to investors when it feels the market is "right." Firms with less than $150 million in stock held by outside investors cannot use shelf registrations. The rationale for this distinction is to protect investors who may not be able to get adequate financial data about a little-known company in the short time between announcement of a shelf issue and its sale. Shelf registrations have two advantages over standard registrations: (1) lower flotation costs and (2) more control over the timing of the issue.

Seasoned Equity Offerings

When a company with publicly traded stock issues additional shares, this is called a **seasoned equity offering**, also known as a follow-on offering. Because the stock is already publicly traded, the offering price will be based upon the existing market price of the stock. Typically, the investment banker buys the securities at a prescribed number of points below the closing price on the last day of registration. For example, suppose that in August 2001, the stock of Microwave Telecommunications Inc. (MTI) had a price of \$28.60 per share, and the stock had traded between \$25 and \$30 per share during the previous three months. Suppose further that MTI and its underwriter agreed that the investment banker would buy 10 million new shares at \$1 per share below the closing price on the last day of registration. If the stock closed at \$25 on the day the SEC released the issue, MTI would receive \$24 per share. Typically, such agreements have an escape clause that provides for the contract to be voided if the price of the securities drops below some predetermined figure. In the illustrative case, this "upset" price might be set at \$24 per share. Thus, if the closing price of the shares on the last day of registration had been \$23.50, MTI would have had the option of withdrawing from the agreement.

The investment banker will have an easier job if the issue is priced relatively low. However, the issuer naturally wants as high a price as possible. A conflict of interest on price therefore arises between the investment banker and the issuer. If the issuer is financially sophisticated and makes comparisons with similar security issues, the investment banker will be forced to price close to the market.

As we discussed in Chapters 16 and 17, the announcement of a new stock offering by a mature firm is often taken as a negative signal—if the firm's prospects were good, management would not want to issue new stock and thus share the rosy future with new stockholders. Therefore, the announcement of a new offering is taken as bad news. Consequently, the price will probably fall when the announcement is made, so the offering price will probably have to be set at a price substantially below the preannouncement market price. Consider Figure 19-1, in which d_0 is the estimated market demand curve for MTI's stock and S_0 is the number of shares currently outstanding. Initially, there are 50 million shares outstanding, and the equilibrium price is \$28.60 per share, determined as follows:

$$\hat{P}_0 = \frac{D_1}{k_s - g} = \frac{\$2.00}{0.12 - 0.05} \approx \$28.60.$$

The values shown for D_1, k_s, and g are the *estimates of a marginal investor.* Investors who do not now own MTI's stock probably, on average, regard the stock as being riskier and thus assign it a higher k_s, or perhaps they estimate the company's growth rate as being lower than do people who now own the stock. In any event, people who do not now own the stock think it is worth less than \$28.60.

When MTI announces that it plans to sell another 10 million shares, this is taken as a negative signal. Consequently, the demand curve for the stock drops from d_0 to d_1, and the price falls. The new equilibrium price, if 50 million shares were outstanding and if the marginal investor now expects MTI's growth rate to be 4.2 percent, would be about \$25.60:

$$\hat{P}_0 = \frac{\$2.00}{0.12 - 0.042} \approx \$25.60.$$

However, if MTI is to sell another 10 million shares of stock, it will either have to attract investors who would not be willing to own the stock at the \$25.60 per share price or else induce present stockholders to buy additional shares. There are two ways this can be accomplished: (1) by reducing the offering price of the stock or (2) by "promoting" or "advertising" the company and thus shifting the demand curve for its stock back to the

FIGURE 19-1 Microwave Telecommunications Inc.: Estimated Common Stock Demand Curves

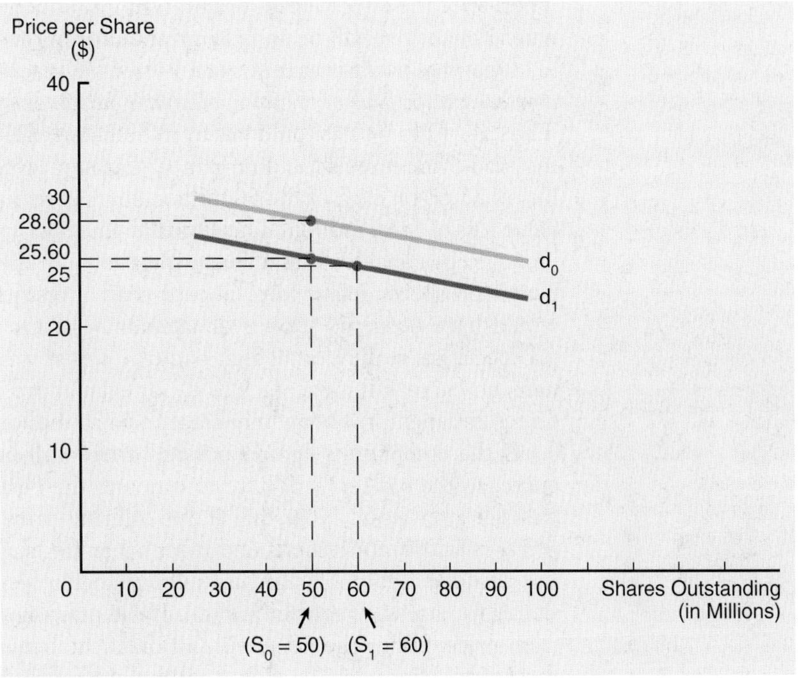

right.[8] If the demand curve does not shift at all from d_1, we see from Figure 19-1 that the only way the 10 million additional shares could be sold would be by setting the offering price at about \$25 per share. However, if the investment banker could promote the stock sufficiently to shift the demand curve back up to d_0, then the offering price could be set much closer to the pre-announcement equilibrium price of \$28.60 per share.[9]

The extent to which the demand curve can be shifted depends primarily on two factors: (1) what investors think the company can do with the money brought in by the stock sale and (2) how effectively the brokers promote the issue. If investors can be convinced that the new money will be invested in highly profitable projects that will raise earnings and the earnings growth rate, then the demand curve shift will occur, and the stock price might actually go above \$28.60. Even if investors do not radically change their expectations about the company's fundamental factors, the fact that MTI's stock is brought to the attention of new investors may shift the demand curve.

[8]It should be noted that investors can buy newly issued stock without paying normal brokerage commissions, and brokers are quick to point this out to potential purchasers. Thus, if an investor were to buy MTI's stock at \$28 per share in the regular market, the commission would be about 1 percent, or 28 cents per share. If the stock were purchased in an underwriting, this commission would be avoided.

It should also be noted that for years many academicians argued that the demand curve for a firm's stock is either horizontal or has an extremely slight downward slope, and that signaling effects are minimal. Most corporate treasurers, on the other hand, have long felt that both effects exist for mature companies, and empirical studies confirm the treasurers' position. For example, see Andrei Shleifer, "Do Demand Curves for Stocks Slope Down?" *Journal of Finance*, July 1986, 579–590; or Anthony Lynch and Richard Mendenhall, "New Evidence on Stock Price Effects Associated with Changes in the S&P 500 Index," *Journal of Business*, July 1997, 351–383.

[9]Note that the supply curve is a vertical line, first at 50 million and then, after the new issue, at 60 million.

The extent to which this promotion campaign is successful in shifting the demand curve depends, of course, upon the effectiveness of the investment banking firm. Therefore, the effectiveness of different investment bankers, as perceived by MTI's financial manager, will be an important factor in the choice of an underwriter.

One final point is that *if pressure from the new shares and/or negative signaling effects drives down the price of the stock, all shares outstanding, not just the new shares, are affected.* Thus, if MTI's stock should fall from $28.60 to $25 per share as a result of the financing, and if the price should remain at that new level, then the company would incur a loss of $3.60 on each of the 50 million shares previously outstanding, or a total market value loss of $180 million. This loss, like underwriting expenses, is a flotation cost, and it should be considered as a cost associated with the stock issue. However, if the company's prospects really were poorer than investors thought, then the price decline would have occurred sooner or later anyway. On the other hand, if the company's prospects are really not all that bad (the signal was incorrect), then over time MTI's demand curve will move back to d_0, or even above d_0, so the company would not suffer a permanent loss anywhere close to $180 million.

If the company is "going public," there will be no established price or demand curve, so the bankers will have to estimate the **equilibrium price** at which the stock will sell after issue. Note that if the offering price is set below the true equilibrium price, as with webMethods and most other IPOs, the stock will rise sharply after the issue, and the company and its selling stockholders will have given away too many shares to raise the required capital. If the offering price is set above the true equilibrium price, either the issue will fail or, if the bankers succeed in selling the stock to their retail clients, these clients will be unhappy when the stock subsequently falls to its equilibrium level. Therefore, it is important that the equilibrium price be closely approximated, although it is hard to estimate this price.

Rights Offerings

As we discussed in Chapter 10, common stockholders often have the right, called the **preemptive right,** to purchase any additional shares sold by the firm. The preemptive right may or may not be included in the corporate charter; this is a decision of the incorporators, but it can be changed by a later vote of stockholders. The purpose of the preemptive right is twofold. First, it protects the control position of present stockholders. Second, and by far the more important reason for publicly owned companies, it protects stockholders against dilution of value. These points will become clear shortly.

If the preemptive right is contained in a particular firm's charter, the company must offer any newly issued common stock to existing stockholders. If the charter does not prescribe a preemptive right, the firm can choose to sell to its existing stockholders or to the public at large. If it sells to the existing stockholders, the issue is called a **rights offering.** Each stockholder is issued an option to buy a certain number of new shares, and the terms of the option are listed on a certificate called a **stock purchase right,** or simply a **right.** Each stockholder receives one right for each share of stock held. If a stockholder does not wish to purchase any additional shares, then he or she can sell the rights to some other person who does want to buy the stock.

Several issues confront a financial manager who is setting the terms of a rights offering. The various considerations can be illustrated with data from Southeast Airlines, whose partial balance sheet and income statement are given in Table 19-4. Southeast earns $8 million after taxes, and it has 1 million shares outstanding, so earnings per share are $8. The stock sells at 12.5 times earnings, or for $100 a share. The company announces plans to raise $10 million of new equity capital through a rights offering, and it decides to sell the new stock to shareholders for $80 a share. The questions facing the financial manager are these:

TABLE 19-4 Southeast Airlines: Financial Statements before Rights Offering

See ***Ch 19 Tool Kit.xls*** for detailed calculations.

Partial Balance Sheet

		Total debt	$ 40,000,000
		Common stock	10,000,000
		Retained earnings	50,000,000
Total assets	$100,000,000	Total claims	$100,000,000

Partial Income Statement

Earnings before interest and taxes	$16,121,212
Interest on debt	4,000,000
Income before taxes	$12,121,212
Taxes (34%)	4,121,212
Net income	$ 8,000,000
Earnings per share (1,000,000 shares)	$8
Market price of stock (price/earnings ratio of 12.5)	$100

1. How many rights will be required to purchase a share of the newly issued stock?
2. What is the value of each right?
3. What effect will the rights offering have on the price of the existing stock?

We will now analyze each of these questions.

Number of Rights Needed to Purchase One New Share Southeast plans to raise $10 million in new equity and to sell the new stock at a price of $80 a share. Dividing the total funds to be raised by the subscription price gives the number of shares to be issued:

$$\text{Number of new shares} = \frac{\text{Funds to be raised}}{\text{Subscription price}} = \frac{\$10{,}000{,}000}{\$80} = 125{,}000 \text{ shares.}$$

The next step is to divide the number of previously outstanding shares by the number of new shares to get the number of rights required to subscribe to one share of the new stock. Note that stockholders always get one right for each share of stock they own, so

$$\begin{array}{c}\text{Number of rights needed to}\\ \text{buy a share of the stock}\end{array} = \frac{\text{Old shares}}{\text{New shares}} = \frac{1{,}000{,}000}{125{,}000} = 8 \text{ rights.}$$

Therefore, a stockholder will have to surrender 8 rights plus $80 to receive one of the newly issued shares. Had the subscription price been set at $95 a share, 9.5 rights would have been required to subscribe to each new share; at $10 a share, only one right would have been needed to buy a new share.

Value of a Right It is clearly worth something to be able to buy for $80 a share of stock selling for $100. The right provides this privilege, so the right must have value. To see how the theoretical value of a right is established, we continue with the example of Southeast Airlines, assuming that it will raise $10 million by selling 125,000 new shares at $80 a share.

First, notice that the **total market value** of the old stock was $100 million: $100 a share times 1 million shares. (The book value is irrelevant.) When the firm sells the new stock, it brings in an additional $10 million. As a first approximation, we assume that the total market value of the common stock increases by exactly this $10 million, to $110 million. Actually, the market value of all the common stock will go up by more than $10 million if investors think the company will be able to invest these funds at a return in excess of the cost of equity capital, that is, the funds will be invested in positive NPV projects. However, it will go up by less than \$10 million if investors are doubtful of the company's ability to put the new funds to work profitably in the near future.

Under the assumption that the change in market value equals the new funds brought in, the total market value of the common stock after the new issue will be \$110 million. Dividing this new value by the new total number of shares outstanding, 1.125 million, we obtain a new market value of \$97.78 a share:

$$\text{New market value} = \frac{\$100{,}000{,}000 + \$10{,}000{,}000}{1{,}000{,}000 + 125{,}000} = \$97.78.$$

Because the rights give stockholders the privilege of buying for only \$80 a share of stock that will end up being worth \$97.78, thus saving \$17.78, is \$17.78 the value of each right? The answer is no, because eight rights are required to buy one new share. We must divide \$17.78 by 8 to get the value of each right, so each right is worth \$2.22.

Ex Rights Southeast Airline's rights have a very definite value, which accrues to the holders of the common stock. What will the price of the stock be if it is traded during the offering period? This depends on who will receive the rights, the old owners or the new. As we described in Chapter 18 for dividends, the standard procedure calls for the company to set a "holder-of-record date," then for the stock to go **ex rights** two trading days prior to the holder-of-record date. If the stock is sold prior to the ex-rights date, it is sold **rights on;** that is, the new owner will receive the rights. If the stock is sold on or after the ex-rights date, the old owner will receive them. The exact time at which the stock goes ex rights is at the close of business (say, 5 P.M.) on the third trading day before the holder-of-record date, so the ex-rights day is the second trading day before the record date. The following illustration indicates what is involved (assume that November 10 is a Friday and the 13th is a Monday):

	Date	Price
Rights on:	November 7	\$100.00
	November 8	100.00
Ex-rights date:	November 9	97.78
	November 10	97.78
Holder-of-record date:	November 13	97.78

On October 24, Southeast Airlines announced the terms of the new financing, stating that rights would be mailed out on December 1 to stockholders of record as of the close of business on November 13. Anyone who buys the old stock on or before November 8 will receive the rights; anyone who buys the stock on or after November 9 will not receive the rights. In the case of Southeast Airlines, the rights-on price is \$100, whereas the ex-rights price is \$97.78.

Formula Value of a Right before the Ex-Rights Date To simplify the procedures described previously, equations have been developed to determine the value of rights. While the stock is still selling rights on, the value at which the rights will sell when they are issued can be found by use of the following formula:

$$\text{Value of one right} = \frac{\text{Market value of stock, rights on} - \text{Subscription price}}{\text{Number of rights required to purchase one share} + 1}.$$

$$R = \frac{M_o - S}{N + 1}. \tag{19-1}$$

Here

R = value of one right.
M_o = rights-on market price of the stock.
S = subscription price.
N = number of rights required to purchase one new share of stock.

Substituting in the appropriate values for Southeast Airlines, we obtain

$$R = \frac{\$100 - \$80}{8 + 1} = \frac{\$20}{9} = \$2.22.$$

This agrees with the value of the rights we found by the long procedure.

Formula Value of a Right on or after the Ex-Rights Date Suppose you are a stockholder in Southeast Airlines. When you return to the United States from a trip to Europe, you read about the rights offering in the newspaper. The stock is now selling ex rights for $97.78 a share. How can you calculate the theoretical value of a right? Simply use the following formula, which follows the logic described in preceding sections:[10]

$$\text{Value of one right} = \frac{\text{Market value of stock, ex rights} - \text{Subscription price}}{\text{Number of rights required to purchase one share}}.$$

$$R = \frac{M_e - S}{N}. \qquad \textbf{(19-2)}$$

$$= \frac{\$97.78 - \$80}{8} = \frac{\$17.78}{8} = \$2.22.$$

Here M_e is the ex-rights market price of the stock.

---

[10]We developed Equation 19-2 directly from the verbal explanation given in the section "Value of a Right." Equation 19-1 can then be derived from Equation 19-2 as follows:

1. Note that

$$M_e = M_o - R. \qquad \textbf{(19-3)}$$

2. Substitute Equation 19-3 into Equation 19-2, obtaining

$$R = \frac{M_o - R - S}{N}. \qquad \textbf{(19-4)}$$

3. Simplify Equation 19-4 as follows, ending with Equation 19-1:

$$R = \frac{M_o - S}{N} - \frac{R}{N}$$

$$R + \frac{R}{N} = \frac{M_o - S}{N}$$

$$R\left(\frac{N + 1}{N}\right) = \frac{M_o - S}{N}$$

$$R = \frac{M_o - S}{N}\left(\frac{N}{N + 1}\right)$$

$$R = \frac{M_o - S}{N + 1}. \qquad \textbf{(19-1)}$$

This completes the derivation.

Effects on Position on Stockholders Stockholders have the choice of exercising their rights or selling them. Those who have sufficient funds and a desire to own more shares of the company's stock will exercise their rights. Other investors can sell theirs. In either case, provided the formula value of the right holds true, the stockholders will neither benefit nor lose by the rights offering. This statement can be illustrated by the position of an individual stockholder in Southeast Airlines.

Assume the stockholder has eight shares of stock before the rights offering. Each share has a market value of $100 a share, so the stockholder has a total market value of $800 in the company's stock. If the rights are exercised, one additional share can be purchased at $80 a share, a new investment of $80. The total investment is now $880, and the investor owns nine shares of the company's stock, which has a value of $97.78 a share after the rights offering. The value of the stock is 9($97.78) = $880, exactly what is invested in it.

Alternatively, if the eight rights are sold at their value of $2.22 a right, the investor will receive $17.78, ending up with the original eight shares of stock plus $17.78 in cash. The original eight shares of stock now have a market price of $97.78 a share, or 8($97.78) = $782.24. This new $782.24 market value of the stock, plus the $17.78 in cash, is the same as the original $800 market value of the stock except for a rounding error. From a theoretical standpoint, stockholders neither gain nor lose from the sale of additional shares of stock through rights, irrespective of whether they exercise or sell their rights. Of course, if they forget to exercise or to sell the rights, or if the brokerage costs of selling the rights are excessive, then stockholders can suffer losses. However, the issuing firm generally makes special efforts to minimize brokerage costs and to allow enough time for stockholders to take action, so such losses are minimal.

Note that the price of the company's stock will be lower after a rights offering than prior to an offering. Stockholders have not suffered a loss, however, because they receive the value of the rights. Thus, the stock price decline is similar in nature to a stock split. The larger the underpricing in the rights offering, the greater the stock split effect, and the lower the final stock price. If a company wants to lower the price of its stock by a substantial amount, it will set the subscription price well below the current market price. If it does not want to lower the price very much, it will set the subscription price just far enough below the current price to ensure that the market price will remain above the subscription price during the offering period, assuring that the new shares will be purchased and the new funds will come into the corporation.

For example, Time Warner issued 34.5 million new shares worth $2.76 billion using a rights offering. Holders of each share outstanding were entitled to buy 0.6 shares at a price of $80 per share. At the time the offering was announced, the company's stock was selling at $120 per share. At expiration of the rights offering, Time Warner's stock was trading at $85 a share.

Self-Test Questions

What is the difference between a competitive bid and a negotiated deal?

What is a private placement?

What is shelf registration?

What is a rights offering?

The Decision to Go Private

In a **going private** transaction, the entire equity of a publicly held firm is purchased by a small group of investors that usually includes the firm's current senior management.[11] In some of these transactions, the current management group acquires all of the equity of the company. In others, current management participates in the ownership with a small group of outside investors who typically place directors on the now-private firm's board and arrange for the financing needed to purchase the publicly held stock. Such deals almost always involve substantial borrowing, often up to 90 percent, and thus are commonly known as **leveraged buyouts (LBOs).**

Regardless of the structure of the deal, going private initially affects the right-hand side of the balance sheet, the liabilities and capital, and not the assets—going private simply rearranges the ownership structure. Thus, going private involves no obvious operating economies, yet the new owners are generally willing to pay a large premium over the stock's current price in order to take the firm private. For example, prior to its acquisition by Columbia, the managers of Hospital Corporation of America (HCA) paid $51 a share to outside (public) shareholders although the stock was selling for only about $31 before the LBO offer was made. It is hard to believe that the managers of a company, who have the best information about the firm's potential profitability, would knowingly pay too much for the firm. Thus, HCA's managers must have regarded the firm as being grossly undervalued or else thought that they could significantly boost the firm's value under private ownership. This suggests that going private can increase the value of some firms sufficiently to enrich both managers and public stockholders. The primary advantages to going private are (1) administrative cost savings, (2) increased managerial incentives, (3) increased managerial flexibility, (4) increased shareholder participation, and (5) increased use of financial leverage, which of course reduces taxes. We will discuss each of these advantages in more detail in the following paragraphs.

1. **Administrative cost savings.** Because going private takes the stock of a firm out of public hands, it saves on costs associated with securities registration, annual reports, SEC and exchange reporting, responding to stockholder inquiries, and so on. More important, the top managers of private firms are free from meetings with security analysts, government bodies, and other outside parties. Byron C. Radaker, CEO of Congoleum Corporation, a company that went private in the early 1980s, estimated the cost savings to his company from going private at between $6 million and $8 million per year.
2. **Increased managerial incentives.** An even larger potential gain comes from the improvement in incentives for high-level managerial performance. Their increased ownership means that the firm's managers will benefit more directly from their own efforts, hence managerial efficiency tends to increase after going private. If the firm is highly successful, its managers can easily see their personal net worth increase 10- to 20-fold, while if the firm fails, its managers will end up with nothing. Further, a highly leveraged position will tend to drive the firm toward the extremes—large losses or large profits. The managers of companies that have gone through an LBO tell us that heavy interest payments, combined with a knowledge that success will bring great wealth, does a lot to cut fat and improve decisions.
3. **Increased managerial flexibility.** Another source of value stems from the increased flexibility available to managers of private firms. These managers do not have to worry about what a drop in next quarter's earnings will do to the firm's stock price, hence they can focus on long-term, strategic actions that ultimately

[11]See Harry DeAngelo, Linda DeAngelo, and Edward M. Rice, "Going Private: The Effects of a Change in Corporate Ownership," *Midland Corporate Finance Journal*, Summer 1984, 35–43, for a more complete discussion of going private. The discussion in this section draws heavily from their work.

will have the greatest positive impact on the firm's value. Managerial flexibility concerning asset sales is also greater in a private firm, since such sales do not have to be justified to a large number of shareholders with potentially diverse interests.

4. **Increased shareholder participation.** Going private typically results in replacing a dispersed, largely passive group of public shareholders with a small group of investors who take a much more active role in managing the firm. These new equity investors have a substantial position in the private firm, hence they have a greater motivation to monitor management and to provide incentives to management than do the typical stockholders of a public corporation. Further, the new nonmanagement equity investors, such as Kohlberg Kravis Roberts & Company (KKR), are typically represented on the board, and they bring both sophisticated financial expertise and hard-nosed attitudes to the new firm. These outsiders don't have good friends running money-losing divisions, so they are more willing to force major operating changes than are entrenched managers. For example, within a few weeks after KKR won the battle for RJR Nabisco, the much touted but unprofitable Premier "smokeless" cigarette project was abandoned.
5. **Increased financial leverage.** Going private usually entails a drastic increase in the firm's use of debt financing, which has two effects. First, the firm's taxes are reduced because of the increase in deductible interest payments, so more of the operating income flows through to investors. Second, the increased debt servicing requirements force managers to hold costs down to ensure that the firm has sufficient cash flow to meet its obligations—a highly leveraged firm simply cannot afford any fat.

One might ask why all firms are not privately held. The answer is that, while there are real benefits to private ownership, there are also benefits to being publicly owned. Most notably, public corporations have access to large amounts of equity capital on advantageous terms, and for most companies, the advantage of access to public capital markets dominates the advantages of going private. Also, note that most companies that go private end up going public again after several years of operation as private firms. For example, HCA, which went private in 1987, again went public in 1992. During the private phase, management shed inefficient businesses, cut costs throughout the corporation, and, generally, rationalized operations. These actions increased the value of the firm to investors. Once the company had been "straightened up," going public allowed the private equity holders to recover their investment, take their profit, and move on to new ventures.

Note too that the examples set by LBO companies are not lost on companies that maintain their publicly owned status. Thus, companies such as Phillips Petroleum and Union Carbide have changed their operations to the point where they resemble LBO companies. This has increased their value and thus made them less attractive to KKR and other LBO specialists, and this benefited both managers and shareholders.

Self-Test Questions

What is meant by the term "going private"?

What are the main benefits of going private?

Why don't all firms go private to capture these benefits?

Managing the Maturity Structure of Debt

Chapters 16 and 17 described the capital structure decision. But after a firm chooses the total amount of debt in its capital structure, it must still choose the maturities of the various securities that make up its debt. The following sections explain the factors associated with the choice of maturity structure.

Maturity Matching

Assume that Consolidated Tools, a Cincinnati machine tool manufacturer, made the decision to float a $25 million nonconvertible bond issue to help finance its 2002 capital budget. It must choose a maturity for the issue, taking into consideration the shape of the yield curve, management's own expectations about future interest rates, and the maturity of the assets being financed. To illustrate how asset maturities affect the choice of debt maturities, suppose Consolidated's capital projects consist primarily of new milling machinery. This machinery has an expected economic life of 10 years (even though it falls into the MACRS 5-year class life). Should Consolidated use debt with a 5-year, 10-year, 20-year, or 30-year, or some other, maturity?

Note that some of the new capital will come from common equity, which is permanent capital. On the other hand, debt maturities can be specified at the time of issue. If Consolidated financed its capital budget with 10-year sinking fund bonds, it would be matching asset and liability maturities. The cash flows resulting from the new machinery could be used to make the interest and sinking fund payments on the issue, so the bonds would be retired as the machinery wore out. If Consolidated used 1-year debt, it would have to pay off this debt with cash flows derived from assets other than the machinery in question. Conversely, if it used 20-year or 30-year debt, it would have to service the debt long after the assets that were purchased with the funds had been scrapped and had ceased providing cash flows. This would worry lenders.

Of course, the 1-year debt could probably be rolled over year after year, out to the 10-year asset maturity. However, if interest rates rose, Consolidated would have to pay a higher rate when it rolled over its debt, and if the company experienced difficulties, it might not be able to refund the debt at any reasonable rate.

For all these reasons, the best all-around financing strategy is to match debt maturities with asset maturities. In recognition of this fact, firms generally place great emphasis on maturity matching, and this factor often dominates the debt maturity decision.

Effects of Interest Rate Levels and Forecasts

Financial managers also consider interest rate levels and forecasts, both absolute and relative, when making financing decisions. For example, if long-term interest rates are high by historical standards and are expected to fall, managers will be reluctant to issue long-term debt and thus lock in those costs for long periods. We already know that one solution to this problem is for firms to use a call provision—callability permits refunding should interest rates drop. However, there is a cost, because of the call premium and also because the firm must set a higher coupon on callable debt. Floating rate debt could be used, but another alternative would be to finance with short-term debt whenever long-term rates were historically high, and then, assuming that interest rates subsequently fall, sell a long-term issue to replace the short-term debt. Of course, this strategy has its risks: If interest rates move even higher, the firm will be forced to renew its short-term debt at higher and higher rates, or to replace the short-term debt with a long-term bond that costs even more than it would have when the original decision was made.

One could argue that capital markets are efficient, hence that it is impossible to predict what future interest rates will be because these rates will be determined by information which is not now known. Thus, under the efficient markets hypothesis, it would be unproductive for firms to try to "beat the market" by forecasting future capital costs and then acting on these forecasts. According to this view, financial managers ought to arrange their capital structures in such a manner that they can ride out almost any economic storm, and this generally calls for (1) using some "reasonable" mix of debt and equity and (2) using debt with maturities which more or less match the maturities of the assets being financed.

Although the efficient markets hypothesis has merit, there is no question that many managers disagree. They are influenced by current cost levels and forecasts, and they act accordingly. One manifestation of this behavior is the heavy use of shelf registrations. Some firms use shelf registrations because managers believe that financing "windows" exist. In the volatile interest rate environment that has characterized recent years, a company might decide to issue bonds when the rate is 8 percent but then find, six weeks later when it has SEC approval to go ahead with the issue, that rates are up to 9 percent. If it had "bonds on the shelf," it could have gone ahead and sold the issue while the low-cost window was open. (Another way to protect against rising rates is to hedge against this possibility with interest rate futures. We discuss futures markets and the use of futures for hedging in Chapter 24.)

Some years ago, the interest rate on AAA corporate bonds was about 12.5 percent. Exxon's investment bankers advised the company to tap the Eurobond market for relatively cheap fixed-rate financing.[12] At the time, Exxon could issue its bonds in London at 0.4 percentage point *below* comparable maturity U.S. Treasury bonds. However, one of Exxon's officers was quoted as saying, "I say so what. The absolute level of rates is too high. Our people would rather wait." The managers of Exxon, as well as many other companies, were betting that the next move in interest rates would be down. Since interest rates are now much lower, it turned out that Exxon was right.

These attitudes confirm that many firms base their financing decisions on expectations about future interest rates. It is easy to be right on one interest rate call—if you predict a decline in interest rates, you have a 50-50 chance of being correct. However, the success of a strategy based on forecasting rates requires that those forecasts be right more often than they are wrong, and it is very difficult to find someone with a long-term track record that is better than 50-50. Finance would be easy if we could accurately predict future interest rates. Unfortunately, predicting future interest rates with consistent accuracy is somewhere between difficult and impossible—people who make a living selling interest rate forecasts say it is difficult; many others say it is impossible.

Information Asymmetries

In Chapter 9, we discussed bond ratings and the effects of changes in ratings on the cost and availability of capital. If a firm's current financial condition is poor, its managers may be reluctant to issue new long-term debt because (1) a new debt issue would probably trigger a review by the rating agencies, and (2) debt issued when a firm is in poor financial shape would probably cost more and be subject to more severe restrictive covenants than debt issued from strength. Further, in Chapters 16 and 17 we pointed out that firms are reluctant to use new common stock financing, especially when this might be taken as a negative signal. Thus, a firm that is in a weakened condition, but whose internal forecasts indicate greater financial strength in the future, would be inclined to delay long-term financing of any type until things improved. Such a firm would be motivated to use short-term debt even to finance long-term assets, with the expectation of replacing the short-term debt in the future with cheaper, higher-rated long-term debt.

Conversely, a firm that is strong now but that forecasts a potentially bad time in the period just ahead would be motivated to finance long term now rather than to wait. Each of these scenarios implies either that the capital markets are inefficient or

---

[12] See Chapter 27 for a discussion of Eurobonds.

that investors do not have the same information regarding the firm's future as does its financial manager. The second situation is undoubtedly true at times, and the first one possibly is true at times.

The firm's earnings outlook, and the extent to which forecasted higher earnings per share are reflected in stock prices, also has an effect on the choice of securities. If a successful R&D program has just been concluded, and as a result management forecasts higher earnings than do most investors, then the firm would not want to issue common stock. It would use debt and then, once earnings rise and push up the stock price, sell common to restore the capital structure to its target level.

Amount of Financing Required

Obviously, the amount of financing required will influence the financing decision. This is mainly due to flotation costs. A $5 million debt financing, which is small in Wall Street terms, would most likely be done with a term loan or a privately placed bond issue, while a firm seeking $2 billion of new debt would most likely use a public offering of long-term bonds.

Availability of Collateral

Generally, secured debt is less costly than unsecured debt. Thus, firms with large amounts of marketable fixed assets are likely to use a relatively large amount of long-term debt, especially mortgage bonds. Additionally, each year's financing decision would be influenced by the amount of qualified assets available as security for new bonds.

Self-Test Questions

What are some factors that financial managers consider when choosing the maturity structure of their debt?

How do information asymmetries affect financing decisions?

Zero (or Very Low) Coupon Bonds

Some bonds pay no interest but are offered at a substantial discount below their par values and hence provide capital appreciation rather than interest income. These securities are called **zero coupon bonds ("zeros")**, or **original issue discount bonds (OIDs).** Some corporations use these bonds to manage their maturity structure. In addition, these bonds provide some desirable tax features for corporations, as we discuss later in this section.

Corporations first used zeros in a major way in 1981. In recent years IBM, Alcoa, JCPenney, ITT, Cities Service, GMAC, Martin-Marietta, and many other companies have used them to raise billions of dollars. Municipal governments also sell "zero munis." Shortly after corporations began to issue zeros, investment bankers figured out a way to create zeros from U.S. Treasury bonds, which were issued only in coupon form. In 1983 Salomon Brothers bought $1 billion of 7 percent, 30-year Treasuries. Each bond had 60 coupons worth $35 each, which represented the interest payments due every six months. Salomon then in effect clipped the coupons and placed them in 60 piles; the last pile also contained the now "stripped" bond itself, which represented a promise of $1,000 in the year 2013. These 60 piles of U.S. Treasury promises were then placed with the trust department of a bank and used as collateral for "zero coupon U.S. Treasury Trust Certificates," which are, in essence, zero coupon Treasury bonds. A pension fund that, in 1983, expected to need money in 2004 could have bought 21-year certificates backed by the interest the Treasury will pay in 2004.

In 1985 the Treasury Department began allowing investors to strip long-term U.S. Treasury bonds and directly register the newly created zero coupon bonds, called STRIPs, with the Treasury Department. This bypasses the role formerly played by investment banks. Now virtually all U.S. Treasury zeros are held in the form of STRIPs. These STRIPs are, of course, safer than corporate zeros, so they are very popular with pension fund managers.

To understand how zeros are used and analyzed, consider the zeros of Vandenberg Corporation, a shopping center developer. Vandenberg is developing a new shopping center in Orange County, California, and it needs \$50 million. The company does not anticipate major cash flows from the project for about five years. However, Pieter Vandenberg, the president, plans to sell the center once it is fully developed and rented, which should take about five years. Therefore, Vandenberg wants to use a financing vehicle that will not require cash outflows for five years. He has decided on a five-year zero coupon bond, with a maturity value of \$1,000.

Vandenberg Corporation is an A-rated company, and A-rated zeros with five-year maturities yield 9 percent at this time (five-year coupon bonds also yield 9 percent). The company is in the 40 percent federal-plus-state tax bracket. Pieter Vandenberg wants to know the firm's after-tax cost of capital if it uses 9 percent, five-year maturity zeros, and he also wants to know what the bond's cash flows will be. Table 19-5 provides an analysis of the situation, and the following numbered paragraphs explain the table itself.

1. The information in the "Basic Data" section, except the issue price, was given in the preceding paragraph, and the information in the "Analysis" section was calculated using the known data. The maturity value of the bond is always set at \$1,000 or some multiple thereof.
2. The issue price is the PV of \$1,000, discounted back five years at the rate $k_d = 9\%$. Using a financial calculator, we input N = 5, I = 9, and FV = 1000, then press the PV key to find PV = \$649.93. Note that \$649.93, compounded annually for five years at 9 percent, will grow to \$1,000 as shown on the time line in Table 19-5.
3. The accrued values as shown on Line 1 in the analysis section represent the compounded value of the bond at the end of each year. The accrued value for Year 0 is the issue price; the accrued value for Year 1 is found as $\$649.93(1.09)^1 = \$708.42$; the accrued value at the end of Year 2 is $\$649.93(1.09)^2 = \$772.18$; and, in general, the value at the end of any Year n is

$$\text{Accrued value at the end of Year n} = \text{Issue price} \times (1 + k_d)^n.$$

4. The interest deduction as shown on Line 2 represents the increase in accrued value during the year. Thus, interest in Year 1 = \$708.42 − \$649.93 = \$58.49. In general,

$$\text{Interest in Year n} = \text{Accrued value}_n - \text{Accrued value}_{n-1}.$$

This method of calculating taxable interest is specified in the Tax Code.

5. The company can take a tax deduction for interest each year, even though the payment is not made in cash. This deduction lowers the taxes that would otherwise be paid, producing the following savings:

$$\begin{aligned}\text{Tax savings} &= \text{(Interest deduction)(T)}\\ &= \$58.49(0.4)\\ &= \$23.40 \text{ in Year 1.}\end{aligned}$$

6. Line 4 represents a cash flow time line; it shows the cash flow at the end of Years 0 through 5. At Year 0, the company receives the \$649.93 issue price. The company then has positive cash inflows equal to the tax savings during Years 1 through 4. Finally, in

TABLE 19-5 Analysis of a Zero Coupon Bond

Basic Data

Maturity value	\$1,000
k_d	9.00%
Maturity	5 years
Corporate tax rate	40.00%
Issue price	\$649.93

Analysis

	Years					
	0	1	2	3	4	5
(1) Year-end accrued value	649.93	708.42	772.18	841.68	917.43	1000.00
(2) Interest deduction		58.49	63.76	69.50	75.75	82.57
(3) Tax savings (40%)		23.40	25.50	27.80	30.30	33.03
(4) Cash flow to Vandenburg	+649.93	+23.40	+25.50	+27.80	+30.30	−966.97

After-tax cost of debt = 5.40%.

Number of \$1,000 zeros the company must issue to raise \$50 million = Amount needed/Price per bond
= \$50,000,000/\$649.93
= 76,931 bonds.

Face amount of bonds: (76,931)(\$1,000) = \$76,931,000.

See ***Ch 19 Tool Kit.xls*** for detailed calculations.

Year 5, it must pay the \$1,000 maturity value, but it gets one more interest tax saving for that year. Therefore, the net cash flow in Year 5 is −\$1,000 + \$33.03 = −\$966.97.

7. We can find the IRR of the cash flows shown on Line 4 using the IRR function of a financial calculator by simply inputting the annual cash flows in the cash flow register. The IRR is 5.4 percent, and it is the after-tax cost of zero coupon debt to the company. Conceptually, here is the situation:

$$\sum_{t=0}^{n} \frac{CF_n}{(1 + k_{d(AT)})^n} = 0$$

$$\frac{\$649.93}{(1 + k_{d(AT)})^0} + \frac{\$23.40}{(1 + k_{d(AT)})^1} + \frac{\$25.50}{(1 + k_{d(AT)})^2} + \frac{\$27.80}{(1 + k_{d(AT)})^3} + \frac{\$30.30}{(1 + k_{d(AT)})^4} + \frac{-\$966.97}{(1 + k_{d(AT)})^5} = 0.$$

The value $k_{d(AT)} = 0.054 = 5.4\%$, found with a financial calculator, produces the equality, and it is the after-tax cost of the zero coupon bond.

8. Note that $k_d(1 - T) = 9\%(0.6) = 5.4\%$. As we saw in Chapter 11, the cost of capital for regular coupon debt is found using the formula $k_d(1 = T)$. Thus, there is symmetrical treatment for tax purposes for zero coupon and regular coupon debt, so both have the same tax implications. This was Congress's intent, and it is why the Tax Code specifies the treatment set forth in Table 19-5.[13]

[13]The purchaser of a zero coupon bond must calculate interest income on the bond in the same manner as the issuer calculates the interest deduction. Thus, in Year 1, a buyer of a bond would report interest income of \$58.49 and would pay taxes in the amount of T(Interest income), even though no cash was received. T, of course, would be the bondholder's personal tax rate. Because of the tax situation, most zero coupon bonds are bought by pension funds and other tax-exempt entities. Individuals do, however, buy taxable zeros for their Individual Retirement Accounts (IRAs). Also, state and local governments issue "tax-exempt muni zeros," which are purchased by individuals in high tax brackets.

Note too that we have analyzed the bond as if the cash flows accrued annually. Generally, to facilitate comparisons with semiannual payment coupon bonds, the analysis is conducted on a semiannual basis.

Not all original issue discount bonds (OIDs) have zero coupons. For example, Vandenberg might have sold an issue of five-year bonds with a 5 percent coupon at a time when other bonds with similar ratings and maturities were yielding 9 percent. Such a bond would have had a value of \$844.41:

$$\text{Bond value} = \sum_{t=1}^{5} \frac{\$50}{(1.09)^t} + \frac{\$1{,}000}{(1.09)^5} = \$844.41.$$

If an investor had purchased these bonds at a price of \$844.41, the yield to maturity would have been 9 percent. The discount of \$1,000 − \$844.41 = \$155.59 would have been amortized over the bond's five-year life, and it would have been handled by both Vandenberg and the bondholders exactly as the discount on the zeros was handled.

Thus, zero coupon bonds are just one type of original issue discount bond. Any nonconvertible bond whose coupon rate is set below the going market rate at the time of its issue will sell at a discount, and it will be classified (for tax and other purposes) as an OID bond.

Corporate (and municipal) zeros are generally callable at the option of the issuer, just like coupon bonds, after some stated call protection period. The call price is set at a premium over the accrued value at the time of the call. Stripped U.S. Treasury bonds (Treasury zeros) are not callable. Thus, Treasury zeros are completely protected against reinvestment risk (the risk of having to invest cash flows from a bond at a lower rate because of a decline in interest rates).

Self-Test Questions

What are zero coupon bonds? OID bonds?

What are their advantages and disadvantages for issuers and purchasers?

Refunding Operations

A great deal of corporate debt was sold during the late 1980s at interest rates in the 9 to 12 percent range. Because the call protection on much of this debt has ended or is about to end, and because interest rates have fallen since the debt was issued, many companies are analyzing the pros and cons of bond refundings. Refunding decisions actually involve two separate questions: (1) Is it profitable to call an outstanding issue in the current period and replace it with a new issue; and (2) even if refunding is currently profitable, would the firm's expected value be increased even more if the refunding were postponed to a later date? We consider both questions in this section.

Note that the decision to refund a security is analyzed in much the same way as a capital budgeting expenditure. The costs of refunding (the investment outlays) include (1) the call premium paid for the privilege of calling the old issue, (2) the costs of selling the new issue, (3) the tax savings from writing off the unexpensed flotation costs on the old issue, and (4) the net interest that must be paid while both issues are outstanding (the new issue is often sold prior to the refunding to ensure that the funds will be available). The annual cash flows, in a capital budgeting sense, are the interest payments that are saved each year plus the net tax savings that the firm receives for amortizing the flotation expenses. For example, if the interest expense on the old issue is \$1,000,000, whereas that on the new issue is \$700,000, the \$300,000 reduction in interest savings constitutes an annual benefit.[14]

The net present value method is used to analyze the advantages of refunding: the future cash flows are discounted back to the present, and then this discounted value is compared with the cash outlays associated with the refunding. The firm should refund the bond only if the present value of the savings exceeds the cost—that is, if the NPV of the refunding operation is positive.

In the discounting process, the after-tax cost of the new debt, k_d, *should be used as the discount rate.* The reason is that there is relatively little risk to the savings—cash flows in a refunding decision are known with relative certainty, which is quite unlike the situation with cash flows in most capital budgeting decisions.

The easiest way to examine the refunding decision is through an example. Microchip Computer Company has a \$60 million bond issue outstanding that has a 12 percent annual coupon interest rate and 20 years remaining to maturity. This issue, which was sold five years ago, had flotation costs of \$3 million that the firm has been amortizing on a straight-line basis over the 25-year original life of the issue. The bond has a call provision that makes it possible for the company to retire the issue at this time by calling the bonds in at a 10 percent call premium. Investment bankers have assured the company that it could sell an additional \$60 million to \$70 million worth of new 20-year bonds at an interest rate of 9 percent. To ensure that the funds required to pay off the old debt will be available, the new bonds will be sold one month before the old issue is called, so for one month, interest will have to be paid on two issues. Current short-term interest rates are 6 percent. Predictions are that long-term interest rates are unlikely to fall below 9 percent.[15] Flotation costs on a new refunding issue will amount to \$2,650,000, and the firm's marginal federal-plus-state tax rate is 40 percent. Should the company refund the \$60 million of 12 percent bonds?

The following steps outline the decision process; they are summarized in the spreadsheet in Table 19-6. This spreadsheet is part of the spreadsheet model, ***Ch 19 Tool Kit.xls*** developed for this chapter. Click on the "Bond Refunding" tab at the bottom of the chapter model to view the bond refunding model. The range of cells from A15 through H21 shows input data needed for the analysis, which were just discussed.

Step 1: Determine the Investment Outlay Required to Refund the Issue

Row 26. Call premium on old issue:

$$\text{Before tax: } 0.10(\$60{,}000{,}000) = \$6{,}000{,}000.$$
$$\text{After tax: } \$6{,}000{,}000(1 - T) = \$6{,}000{,}000(0.6)$$
$$= \$3{,}600{,}000.$$

Although Microchip must spend \$6 million on the call premium, this is a deductible expense in the year the call is made. Because the company is in

[14] During the early 1980s, there was a flurry of work on the pros and cons of refunding bond issues that had fallen to deep discounts as a result of rising interest rates. At such times, the company could go into the market, buy its debt at a low price, and retire it. The difference between the bonds' par value and the price the company paid would be reported as income, and taxes would have to be paid on it. The results of the research on the refunding of discount issues suggest that bonds should not, in general, be refunded after a rise in rates. See Andrew J. Kalotay, "On the Structure and Valuation of Debt Refundings," *Financial Management*, Spring 1982, 41–42; and Robert S. Harris, "The Refunding of Discounted Debt: An Adjusted Present Value Analysis," *Financial Management*, Winter 1980, 7–12.

[15] The firm's management has estimated that interest rates will probably remain at their present level of 9 percent or else rise; there is only a 25 percent probability that they will fall further.

TABLE 19-6 Spreadsheet for the Bond Refunding Decision **(Ch 19 Tool Kit.xls)**

	A	B	C	D	E	F	G	H	I
13	Input Data (in thousands of dollars)								
14									
15	Existing bond issue			$60,000		New bond issue		$60,000	
16	Original flotation cost			$3,000		New flotation cost		$2,650	
17	Maturity of original debt			25		New bond maturity		20	
18	Years since old debt issue			5		New cost of debt		9%	
19	Call premium (%)			10%					
20	Original coupon rate			12%		Tax rate		40%	
21	After-tax cost of new debt			5.4%		Short-term interest rat		6%	
22									
23	Schedule of cash flows								
24						Before-tax	After-tax		
25	*Investment Outlay*								
26	Call premium on the old bond					($6,000)	($3,600)		
27	Flotation costs on new issue					(2,650)	(2,650)		
28	Immediate tax savings on old flotation cost expense					2,400	960		
29	Extra interest paid on old issue					(600)	(360)		
30	Interest earned on short-term investment					300	180		
31	Total after-tax investment						($5,470)		
32									
33	*Annual Flotation Cost Tax Effects: t=1 to 20*								
34	Annual tax savings from new issue flotation costs					$133	$53		
35	Annual lost tax savings from old issue flotation costs					(120)	(48)		
36	Net flotation cost tax savings					$13	$5		
37									
38	*Annual Interest Savings Due to Refunding: t=1 to 20*								
39	Interest on old bond					$7,200	$4,320		
40	Interest on new bond					(5,400)	(3,240)		
41	Net interest savings					$1,800	$1,080		
42									
43	Since the annual flotation cost tax effects and interest savings occur for the next 20 years, they represent								
44	annuities. To evaluate this project, we must find the present values of these savings. Using the function								
45	wizard and solving for present value, we find that the present values of these annuities are:								
46									
47	Calculating the annual flotation cost tax effects and the annual interest savings								
48									
49	Annual flotation Cost Tax Effects					Annual Interest Savings			
50	Maturity of the new bond (Nper)			20		Maturity of the new bond (Nper)			20
51	After-tax cost of new debt (Rate)			5.4%		After-tax cost of new debt (Rate)			5.4%
52	Annual flotation cost tax savings (Pmt)			$5		Annual interest savings (Pmt)			$1,080
53									
54	NPV of annual flotation cost savings			$60		NPV of annual interest savings			$13,014
55									
56	Hence, the net present value of this bond refunding project will be the sum of the initial outlay and the present								
57	values of the annual flotation cost tax effects and interest savings.								
58									
59	Bond Refunding NPV =		Initial Outlay	+	PV of flotation costs	+	PV of interest savings		
60	Bond Refunding NPV =		($5,470)	+	$60	+	$13,014		
61									
62	Bond Refund NPV =		$7,604						

the 40 percent tax bracket, it saves \$2.4 million in taxes; therefore, the after tax cost of the call is only \$3.6 million. This amount is shown on Row 26 of Table 19-6.

Row 27. Flotation costs on new issue: Flotation costs on the new issue will be \$2,650,000. This amount cannot be expensed for tax purposes, so it provides no immediate tax benefit.

Row 28. Flotation costs on old issue: The old issue has an unamortized flotation cost of (20/25) (\$3,000,000) = \$2,400,000 at this time. If the issue is retired, the unamortized flotation cost may be recognized immediately as an expense, thus creating an after-tax savings of \$2,400,000(T) = \$960,000. Because this is a cash inflow, it is shown as a positive number on Row 28.

Rows 29 and 30. Additional interest: One month's "extra" interest on the old issue, after taxes, costs \$360,000:

$$(\text{Dollar amount})(1/12 \text{ of } 12\%)(1 - T) = \text{Interest cost}$$
$$(\$60{,}000{,}000)(0.01)(0.6) = \$360{,}000.$$

However, the proceeds from the new issue can be invested in short-term securities for one month. Thus, \$60 million invested at a rate of 6 percent will return \$180,000 in after-tax interest:

$$(\$60{,}000{,}000)(1/12 \text{ of } 6\%)(1 - T) = \text{Interest earned}$$
$$(\$60{,}000{,}000)(0.005)(0.6) = \$180{,}000.$$

The net after-tax additional interest cost is thus \$180,000:

Interest paid on old issue	(\$360,000)
Interest earned on short-term securities	180,000
Net additional interest	(\$180,000)

These figures are reflected on Rows 29 and 30 of Table 19-6.

Row 31. Total after-tax investment: The total investment outlay required to refund the bond issue, which will be financed by debt, is thus \$5,470,000:[16]

Call premium	(\$3,600,000)
Flotation costs, new	(2,650,000)
Flotation costs, old, tax savings	960,000
Net additional interest	(180,000)
Total investment	(\$5,470,000)

This total is shown on Row 31 of Table 19-6.

Step 2: Calculate the Annual Flotation Cost Tax Effects

Row 34. Tax savings on flotation costs on the new issue: For tax purposes, flotation costs must be amortized over the life of the new bond, or for 20 years. Therefore, the annual tax deduction is

$$\frac{\$2{,}650{,}000}{20} = \$132{,}500.$$

Since our spreadsheet shows dollars in thousands, this number appears as 133 on the spreadsheet. Because the firm is in the 40 percent tax bracket, it has a tax savings of \$132,500(0.4) = \$53,000 a year for 20 years. This is an annuity of \$53,000 for 20 years, and it is shown on Row 34.

Row 35. Tax benefits lost on flotation costs on the old issue: The firm, however, will no longer receive a tax deduction of \$120,000 a year for 20 years, so it loses an after-tax benefit of \$48,000 a year. This is shown on Row 35.

[16]The investment outlay (in this case, \$5,470,000) is usually obtained by increasing the amount of the new bond issue. In the example given, the new issue would be \$65,470,000. However, the interest on the additional debt *should not* be deducted at Step 3 because the \$5,470,000 itself will be deducted at Step 4. If additional interest on the \$5,470,000 were deducted at Step 3, interest would, in effect, be deducted twice. The situation here is exactly like that in regular capital budgeting decisions. Even though some debt may be used to finance a project, interest on that debt is not subtracted when developing the annual cash flows. Rather, the annual cash flows are *discounted* at the project's cost of capital.

Row 36. Net amortization tax effect: The after-tax difference between the amortization tax effects of flotation on the new and old issues is $5,000 a year for 20 years. This is shown on Row 36.

Step 3: Calculate the Annual Interest Savings

Row 39. Interest on old bond, after tax: The annual after-tax interest on the old issue is $4.32 million:

$$(\$60{,}000{,}000)(0.12)(0.6) = \$4{,}320{,}000.$$

This is shown on Row 39 of Table 19-6.

Row 40. Interest on new bond, after tax: The new issue has an annual after-tax cost of $3,240,000:

$$(\$60{,}000{,}000)(0.09)(0.6) = \$3{,}240{,}000.$$

This is shown on Row 40.

Row 41. Net annual interest savings: Thus, the net annual interest savings is $1,080,000:

Interest on old bonds, after tax	$4,320,000
Interest on new bonds, after tax	(3,240,000)
Annual interest savings, after tax	$1,080,000

This is shown on Row 41.

Step 4: Determine the NPV of the Refunding

Row 54. PV of the benefits: The PV of the annual after-tax flotation cost benefit of $5,000 a year for 20 years is $60,251, and the PV of the $1,080,000 annual after-tax interest savings for 20 years is $13,014,216:[17]

$$\begin{aligned} PV &= \$5{,}000(PVIFA_{5.4\%,20}) \\ &= \$5{,}000(12.0502) \\ &= \$60{,}251. \\ PV &= \$1{,}080{,}000(PVIFA_{5.4\%,20}) \\ &= \$1{,}080{,}000(12.0502) \\ &= \$13{,}014{,}216. \end{aligned}$$

These values are used on Row 60 when finding the NPV of the refunding operation:

Amortization tax effects	$ 60,251
Interest savings	13,014,216
Net investment outlay	(5,470,000)
NPV from refunding	$ 7,604,467

Because the net present value of the refunding is positive, it would be profitable to refund the old bond issue.

[17]The PVIFA for 5.4 percent over 20 years is 12.0502, found with a financial calculator. Note that the spreadsheet uses *Excel's* PV function to solve for the present values of the annual flotation cost and interest savings.

We can summarize the data shown in Table 19-6 using a time line (amounts in thousands) as shown below:

Time Period	0	5.4% 1	2	. . .	20
After-tax investment	−5,470				
Flotation cost tax effects		5	5	. . .	5
Interest savings		1,080	1,080	. . .	1,080
Net cash flows	−5,470	1,085	1,085	. . .	1,085

$NPV_{5.4\%} = \$7{,}604.$

Several other points should be made. First, because the cash flows are based on differences between contractual obligations, their risk is the same as that of the underlying obligations. Therefore, the present values of the cash flows should be found by discounting at the firm's least risky rate—its after-tax cost of marginal debt. Second, since the refunding operation is advantageous to the firm, it must be disadvantageous to bondholders; they must give up their 12 percent bonds and reinvest in new ones yielding 9 percent. This points out the danger of the call provision to bondholders, and it also explains why noncallable bonds command higher prices than callable bonds. Third, although it is not emphasized in the example, we assumed that the firm raises the investment required to undertake the refunding operation (the $5,470,000 shown on Row 31 of Table 19-6) as debt. This should be feasible because the refunding operation will improve the interest coverage ratio, even though a larger amount of debt is outstanding.[18] Fourth, we set up our example in such a way that the new issue had the same maturity as the remaining life of the old one. Often, the old bonds have a relatively short time to maturity (say, 5 to 10 years), whereas the new bonds have a much longer maturity (say, 25 to 30 years). In such a situation, the analysis should be set up similarly to a replacement chain analysis in capital budgeting, which was discussed in Chapter 13. Fifth, refunding decisions are well suited for analysis with a computer spreadsheet program. Spreadsheets such as the one shown in Table 19-6 are easy to set up, and once the model has been constructed, it is easy to vary the assumptions (especially the assumption about the interest rate on the refunding issue), and to see how such changes affect the NPV.

One final point should be addressed: Although our analysis shows that the refunding would increase the firm's value, would refunding *at this time* truly maximize the firm's expected value? If interest rates continue to fall, the company might be better off waiting, for this would increase the NPV of the refunding operation even more. The mechanics of calculating the NPV in a refunding are easy, but the decision of *when* to refund is not simple at all because it requires a forecast of future interest rates. Thus, the final decision on refunding now versus waiting for a possibly more favorable time is a judgmental decision.

To illustrate the timing decision, assume that Microchip's managers forecast that long-term interest rates have a 50 percent probability of remaining at their present level of 9 percent over the next year. However, there is a 25 percent probability that

[18]See Ahron R. Ofer and Robert A. Taggart, Jr., "Bond Refunding: A Clarifying Analysis," *Journal of Finance*, March 1977, 21–30, for a discussion of how the method of financing the refunding affects the analysis. Ofer and Taggart prove that if the refunding investment outlay is to be raised as common equity, the before-tax cost of debt is the proper discount rate, whereas if these funds are to be raised as debt, the after-tax cost of debt is the proper discount rate. Since a profitable refunding will virtually always raise the firm's debt-carrying capacity (because total interest charges after the refunding will be lower than before it), it is more logical to use debt than either equity or a combination of debt and equity to finance the operation. Therefore, firms generally do use additional debt to finance refunding operations.

TVA Ratchets Down Its Interest Expenses

In 1998, TVA raised $575 million in 30-year debt. If it had issued fixed-rate debt, it would be stuck with high coupon payments if interest rates in the market fall. If it had issued floating-rate debt, it would be stuck with high coupon payments if interest rates rise. If it had issued callable debt, then it could refinance if interest rates fall. But the costs of refunding are high, and TVA would have to agonize over the decision of whether to refund or wait in the hopes that rates will fall. None of these three choices seemed desirable, so TVA issued a new type of security that finesses these problems.

The new bonds are officially called Putable Automatic Rate Reset Securities (PARRs), but they are commonly known as ratchet bonds. After 2003, these bonds have a feature that resets the coupon rate each year to 94 basis points over the rate on the prevailing 30-year Treasury bond, if the new coupon would be lower than the ratchet bond's current coupon. In other words, the coupon on the bond will fall if interest rates fall, but will never increase from year to year, letting TVA lock in the lowest interest rates that prevail during the bond's life. In essence, TVA gets to refund its debt in any year when rates fall, thus the term "ratchet."

The 94-basis-point spread is higher than the spread over Treasuries that normally exist on TVA's noncallable bonds, given its bond rating. However, if the bond rating deteriorates, then investors can "put" the bond by selling it back to TVA. The net effect is that investors are exposed to interest rate risk but not to credit risk, and they are compensated for interest rate risk by the relatively high spread.

Source: Andrew Kalotay and Leslie Abreo, "Ratchet Bonds: Maximum Refunding Efficiency at Minimum Transaction Cost," *Journal of Applied Corporate Finance*, Vol. 41, no. 1, Spring 1999, 40–47.

rates could fall to 7 percent, and a 25 percent probability that they could rise to 11 percent. Further, assume that short-term rates are expected to remain three percentage points below long-term rates, and that the call premium would be reduced by one-twentieth if the call were delayed for one year.

The refunding analysis could then be repeated, as previously, but assuming it would take place one year from now. Thus, the old bonds would have only 19 years remaining to maturity. We performed the analysis and found the NPV distribution of refunding one year from now:

Probability	Long-Term Interest Rate	NPV of Refunding One Year from Now
25%	7%	$17,947,071
50	9	7,390,083
25	11	(1,359,939)

At first blush, it would seem reasonable to calculate the expected NPV of refunding next year in terms of the probability distribution. However, that would not be correct. If interest rates did rise to 11 percent, Microchip would not refund the issue; therefore, the actual NPV if rates rise to 11 percent would be zero. The expected NPV from refunding one year hence is, therefore, 0.25($17,947,071) + 0.50($7,390,083) + 0.25($0) = $8,181,809 versus $7,604,425 if refunding occurred today.

Even though the expected NPV of refunding in one year is higher, Microchip's managers would probably decide to refund today. The $7,604,425 represents a sure increase in firm value, whereas the $8,181,809 is only an expected increase. Also, proper comparison requires that the $8,181,809 be discounted back one year to today. Microchip's managers should opt to delay refunding only if the expected NPV from later refunding is sufficiently above today's sure NPV to compensate for the risk and time value involved.

Clearly, the decision to refund now versus refund later is complicated by the fact that there would be numerous opportunities to refund in the future rather than just a single opportunity one year from now. Furthermore, the decision must be based on a large set of interest rate forecasts, a daunting task in itself. Fortunately, financial managers making bond refunding decisions can now use the values of derivative securities to estimate the value of the bond issue's embedded call option. If the call option is worth more than the NPV of refunding today, the issue should not be immediately refunded. Rather, the issuer should either delay the refunding to take advantage of the information obtained from the derivative market or actually create a derivative transaction to lock in the value of the call option.[19]

Self-Test Question

How is bond refunding like a capital budgeting project?

Managing the Risk Structure of Debt

There are several techniques that firms use to manage the risk of their debt, including project financing and securitization.

Project Financing

In recent years, many large projects such as the Alaska pipeline have been financed by what is called **project financing.**[20] We can only present an overview of the concept, for in practice it involves very complicated provisions and can take many forms.

Project financing has been used to finance energy explorations, oil tankers, refineries, and electric generating plants. Generally, one or more firms will sponsor the project, putting up the required equity capital, while the remainder of the financing is furnished by lenders or lessors.[21] Most often, a separate legal entity is formed to operate the project. Normally, the project's creditors do not have full recourse against the sponsors. In other words, the lenders and lessors must be paid from the project's cash flows, plus the sponsors' equity in the project, because the creditors have no claims against the sponsors' other assets or cash flows. Often the sponsors write "comfort" letters, giving general assurances that they will strive diligently to make the project successful. However, these letters are not legally binding, so in project financing the lenders and lessors must focus their analysis on the inherent merits of the project plus the equity cushion provided by the sponsors.[22]

---

[19]For more information on derivatives in general, see Chapter 25. For more information on the use of derivatives to help make call decisions, see Andrew J. Kalotay and George O. Williams, "How to Succeed in Derivatives without Really Buying," *Journal of Applied Corporate Finance,* Fall 1993, 100–103.

[20]For an excellent discussion of project financing, see John W. Kensinger and John D. Martin, "Project Finance: Raising Money the Old-Fashioned Way," *Journal of Applied Corporate Finance,* Fall 1988, 69–81; and Benjamin C. Esty, "Petrozuata: A Case Study on the Effective Use of Project Finance," *Journal of Applied Corporate Finance,* Fall 1999, 26–42.

[21]A lessor is an individual or firm that owns buildings and equipment and then leases them to another firm. Leasing is discussed in Chapter 20.

[22]In another type of project financing, each sponsor guarantees its share of the project's debt obligations. Here the creditors would also consider the creditworthiness of the sponsors in addition to the project's own prospects. It should be noted that project financing with multiple sponsors in the electric utility industry has led to problems when one or more of the sponsors has gotten into financial trouble. For example, Long Island Lighting, one of the sponsors in the Nine Mile Point nuclear project, became unable to meet its commitments to the project, which forced other sponsors to shoulder an additional burden or else see the project cancelled and lose all their investment up to that point. Utility executives have stated that this default, and others, will make companies reluctant to enter into similar projects in the future.

Project financing is not a new development. Indeed, back in 1299, the English Crown negotiated a loan with Florentine merchant bankers that was to be repaid with one year's output from the Devon silver mines. Essentially, the Italians were allowed to operate the mines for one year, paying all the operating costs and mining as much ore as they could. The Crown made no guarantees as to how much ore could be mined, or the value of the refined silver. A more current example involved GE Capital, the credit arm of General Electric, which recently financed a $72 million project to build an aluminum can plant. The plant is owned by several beverage makers, but it is operated independently, and GE Capital must depend on the cash flows from the plant to repay the loan. About half of all project financings in recent years have been for electric generating plants, including both plants owned by electric utilities and cogeneration plants operated by industrial companies. Project financings are generally characterized by large size and a high degree of complexity. However, because project financing is tied to a specific project, it can be tailored to meet the specific needs of both the creditors and the sponsors. In particular, the financing can be structured so that both the funds provided during the construction phase and the subsequent repayments match the timing of the project's projected cash outflows and inflows.

Project financing offers several potential benefits over conventional debt financing. For one, project financing usually restricts the usage of the project's cash flows, which means that the lenders, rather than the managers, can decide whether to reinvest excess cash flows or to use them to reduce the loan balance by more than the minimum required. Conferring this power on the lenders reduces their risks. Project financings also have advantages for borrowers. First, because risks to the lenders are reduced, the interest rate built into a project financing deal may be relatively low. Second, since suppliers of project financing capital have no recourse against the sponsoring firms' other assets and cash flows, project financings insulate the firms' other assets from risks associated with the project being financed. Managers may be more willing to take on a very large, risky project if they know that the company's existence would not be threatened if it fails.

Project financings increase the number and type of investment opportunities, hence they make capital markets "more complete." At the same time, project financings reduce the costs to investors of obtaining information and monitoring the borrower's operations. To illustrate, consider an oil and gas exploration project that is funded using project financing. If the project were financed as an integral part of the firm's normal operations, investors in all the firm's outstanding securities would need information on the project. By isolating the project, the need for information is confined to the investors in the project financing, and they need to monitor only the project's operations, and not those of the entire firm.

Project financings also permit firms whose earnings are below the minimum requirements specified in their existing bond indentures to obtain additional debt financing. In such situations, lenders look only at the merits of the new project, and its cash flows may support additional debt even though the firm's overall situation does not. Project financings also permit managers to reveal proprietary information to a smaller group of investors, hence project financings increase the ability of a firm to maintain confidentiality. Finally, project financings can improve incentives for key managers by enabling them to take direct ownership stakes in the operations under their control. By establishing separate projects, companies can provide incentives that are much more directly based upon individual performance than is typically possible within a large corporation.

Securitization

As the term is generally used, a **security** refers to a publicly traded financial instrument, as opposed to a privately placed instrument. Thus, securities have greater liquidity than otherwise similar instruments that are not traded in an open market. In recent years, procedures have been developed to **securitize** various types of debt instruments, thus increasing their liquidity, lowering the cost of capital to borrowers, and generally increasing the efficiency of the financial markets.[23]

Securitization has occurred in two major ways. First, some debt instruments that were formerly rarely traded are now actively traded, with the change being due to decisions by certain financial institutions to "make a market," which means to stand willing to buy or sell the security, and to hold an inventory of the security in order to balance buy and sell orders. This occurred many years ago in the case of common stocks and investment-grade bonds. More recently, it occurred in the commercial paper market, in which large, financially strong firms issue short-term, unsecured debt in lieu of obtaining bank loans. The commercial paper market has grown from about $50 billion outstanding in the mid-1970s to over $350 billion today, and this market permits large, strong firms to finance their working capital needs at lower cost than with bank loans.

Another example of securitization is the junk bond market. Before this market developed, firms with poor credit were forced to obtain debt financing on a private placement basis, typically from the firm's bank. It was difficult for firms to shop around for the best rate, because lenders who were not familiar with them were unwilling to spend the time and money necessary to determine the feasibility of the loan. Moreover, lenders were concerned about (and hence charged a higher rate for) the illiquidity of privately placed debt. Then, Michael Milken developed procedures for analyzing the repayment feasibility of junk bonds, and Drexel Burnham Lambert put its reputation and credibility behind these issues and made a market for them in case a purchaser needed to cash out. Subsequently, Morgan Stanley Dean Witter, Merrill Lynch, Salomon Smith Barney, and the other major investment banks entered the junk bond market, and today they have "securitized" much of the old private placement market for below-investment-grade debt.

The second major development in securitization involves the pledging of specific assets, **asset securitization,** or the creation of **asset-backed securities.** The oldest type of asset securitization is the mortgage-backed bond. Here, individual home mortgages are combined into pools, and then bonds are created that use the pool of mortgages as collateral. The financial institution that originated the mortgage generally continues to act as the servicing agent, but the mortgage itself is sold to other investors. The securitization of mortgages has created a national mortgage market with many players, and this has benefited borrowers. The development has also benefited lenders, for the original lending institution no longer owns the relatively long-term mortgage, hence it is better able to match the maturity of its assets (loans) with its liabilities (deposit accounts). Today, many different types of assets are being used as collateral, including auto loans, credit card balances, and even the royalties from David Bowie's music!

The asset securitization process involves the pooling and repackaging of loans secured by relatively homogeneous, small-dollar assets into liquid securities. In the past, such financing was provided by a single lending institution, which would write the loan, structure the terms, absorb the credit and interest rate risk, provide the capital, and service the collections. Under securitization, several different institutions are involved, with each playing a different functional role. A savings and loan might originate the loan, an investment banker might pool the loans and structure the security, a federal agency might insure against credit risk, a second investment banker might sell the securities, and a pension fund might supply the final capital.

[23]The Fall 1988 issue of the *Journal of Applied Corporate Finance* is devoted to securitization.

Bowie Bonds Ch-Ch-Change Asset Securitization

Asset securitization was already booming, with bonds being backed by mortgages, car loans, credit cards, and student loans. But David Bowie juiced it up even more by issuing Bowie Bonds, which are backed by future royalties on more than 250 of his older songs. These bonds have a 10-year maturity and pay an interest rate of 7.9 percent. With a total issue size of $55 million, that amounts to a whopping $4.345 million in interest payments each year. Moody's Investor Service must be bullish on Bowie, since they gave his issue a rating of A3, high enough that the bonds were issued with an interest rate only 1.53 percentage points higher than 10-year Treasury bonds.

Source: "Bowie Ch-Ch-Changes the Market," *CFO*, April 1997, 20.

The process of securitization has, in general, lowered costs and increased the availability of funds to borrowers, decreased risks to lenders, and created new investment opportunities for many investors. With these potential benefits, we predict that securitization will continue to expand in the future.

Self-Test Questions

What is project financing? What are its advantages and disadvantages?

What is securitization? What are its advantages to borrowers? What are its advantages to lenders?

Summary

- The **Securities and Exchange Commission (SEC)** regulates securities markets.
- **Private placements** are securities offerings to a limited number of investors who are exempt from registration with the SEC.
- **Accredited investors** include the officers and directors of a company, high-wealth individuals, and institutional investors. These investors are eligible to buy securities in private placements.
- An **angel** is a wealthy individual who makes an equity investment in a startup company.
- The managers of a **venture capital fund** are called **venture capitalists**, or **VCs.** They raise money from investors and make equity investments in startup companies, called **portfolio companies.**
- **Going public** in an **initial public offering (IPO)** facilitates stockholder diversification, increases liquidity of the firm's stock, makes it easier for the firm to raise capital, establishes a value for the firm, and makes it easier for a firm to sell its products. However, reporting costs are high, operating data must be disclosed, management self-dealings are harder to arrange, the price may sink to a low level if the stock is not traded actively, and public ownership may make it harder for management to maintain control.
- **Investment bankers** assist in issuing securities by helping the firm determine the size of the issue and the type of securities to be used, establishing the selling price, selling the issue, and, in some cases, maintaining an after-market for the stock.
- An investment banker may sell a security issue on a **best efforts** basis, or may guarantee the sale by **underwriting** the issue.
- Before an IPO, the investment banker and management team go on a **roadshow** and make presentations to potential institutional investors.

- An IPO is **oversubscribed** if investors are willing to purchase more shares than are being offered at the IPO price.
- The **spread** is the difference between the price at which an underwriter sells a security and the proceeds that the underwriter gives to the issuing company. In recent years the spread for almost all IPOs has been 7 percent.
- An **equity carve-out** (also called a **partial public offering** or **spin-out**) is a special IPO in which a publicly traded company converts a subsidiary into a separately traded public company by selling shares of stock in the subsidiary. The parent typically retains a controlling interest.
- SEC Rule 415, also known as **shelf registration,** allows a company to register an issue and then sell the issue in pieces over time rather than all at once.
- A **seasoned equity offering** occurs when a public company issues additional shares of stock.
- In a **rights offering,** current shareholders are given the right to buy additional shares of stock. They may exercise the right or sell it to someone else.
- A company **goes private** when a small group of investors, including the firm's senior management, purchases all of the equity in the company. Such deals usually involve high levels of debt, and are commonly called **leveraged buyouts (LBOs).**
- **Zero coupon bonds** pay no interest but are issued at a discount.
- If a bond has a call provision, the issuer may **refund (call)** the bond prior to maturity and pay for it with a new debt issue at a lower interest rate.
- In **project financing,** the payments on debt are secured by the cash flows of a particular project.
- **Asset securitization** occurs when assets such as mortgages or credit card receivables are bundled together into a pool. Then bonds are created which use the payments into the pool to make interest and principle payments on the bonds.

Questions

19–1 Define each of the following terms:

a. Going public; new issue market; initial public offering (IPO)
b. Rights offering
c. Public offering; private placement
d. Venture capitalists; roadshow; spread
e. Securities and Exchange Commission (SEC); registration statement; shelf registration; margin requirement; insiders
f. Prospectus; "red herring" prospectus
g. National Association of Securities Dealers (NASD)
h. Best efforts arrangement; underwritten arrangement
i. Zero coupon bond; original issue discount bond (OID)
j. Refunding
k. Project financing
l. Securitization
m. Maturity matching

19–2 Is it true that the "flatter," or more nearly horizontal, the demand curve for a particular firm's stock, and the less important investors regard the signaling effect of the offering, the more important the role of investment bankers when the company sells a new issue of stock?

19–3 The SEC attempts to protect investors who are purchasing newly issued securities by making sure that the information put out by a company and its investment bankers is correct and is not misleading. However, the SEC does not provide an opinion about the real value of the securities; hence, an investor might pay too much for some new stock and consequently lose heavily. Do you think the SEC should, as a part of every new stock or bond offering, render an opinion to investors on the proper value of the securities being offered? Explain.

19–4 How do you think each of the following items would affect a company's ability to attract new capital and the flotation costs involved in doing so?
a. A decision of a privately held company to go public.
b. The increasing institutionalization of the "buy side" of the stock and bond markets.
c. The trend toward "financial conglomerates" as opposed to stand-alone investment banking houses.
d. Elimination of the preemptive right.
e. The introduction of "shelf registrations" in 1981.

19–5 Before entering a formal agreement, investment bankers carefully investigate the companies whose securities they underwrite; this is especially true of the issues of firms going public for the first time. Since the bankers do not themselves plan to hold the securities but intend to sell them to others as soon as possible, why are they so concerned about making careful investigations?

19–6 It is frequently stated that the primary purpose of the preemptive right is to allow individuals to maintain their proportionate share of the ownership and control of a corporation.
a. How important do you suppose this consideration is for the average stockholder of a firm whose shares are traded on the New York or American Stock Exchanges?
b. Is the preemptive right likely to be of more importance to stockholders of publicly owned or closely held firms? Explain.
c. Is a firm likely to get a wider distribution of shares if it sells new stock through a preemptive rights offering to existing stockholders or directly to underwriters?
d. Why would management be interested in getting a wider distribution of its shares?

Problems

19–1 *PROFIT OR LOSS ON NEW STOCK ISSUE*

Security Brokers Inc. specializes in underwriting new issues by small firms. On a recent offering of Beedles Inc., the terms were as follows:

Price to public:	$5 per share
Number of shares:	3 million
Proceeds to Beedles:	$14,000,000

The out-of-pocket expenses incurred by Security Brokers in the design and distribution of the issue were $300,000. What profit or loss would Security Brokers incur if the issue were sold to the public at an average price of
a. $5 per share?
b. $6 per share?
c. $4 per share?

19–2 *UNDERWRITING AND FLOTATION EXPENSES*

The Beranek Company, whose stock price is now $25, needs to raise $20 million in common stock. Underwriters have informed the firm's management that they must price the new issue to the public at $22 per share because of a downward-sloping demand curve. The underwriters' compensation will be 5 percent of the issue price, so Beranek will net $20.90 per share. The firm will also incur expenses in the amount of $150,000.

How many shares must the firm sell to net $20 million after underwriting and flotation expenses?

19–3 *NEW STOCK ISSUE*

The Edelman Gem Company, a small jewelry manufacturer, has been successful and has enjoyed a good growth trend. Now Edelman is planning to go public with an issue of common stock, and it faces the problem of setting an appropriate price on the stock. The company and its investment bankers believe that the proper procedure is to select several similar firms with publicly traded common stock and to make relevant comparisons.

Several jewelry manufacturers are reasonably similar to Edelman with respect to product mix, asset composition, and debt/equity proportions. Of these companies, Kennedy Jewelers and Strasburg Fashions are most similar. When analyzing the following data, assume that 1996 and 2001 were reasonably "normal" years for all three companies—that is, these years were neither especially good nor especially bad in terms of sales, earnings, and dividends. At the time of the analysis, k_{RF} was 8 percent and k_M was 12 percent. Kennedy is listed on the AMEX and Strasburg on the NYSE, while Edelman will be traded in the Nasdaq market.

	Kennedy	Strasburg	Edelman (Totals)
Earnings per share			
2001	\$ 4.50	\$ 7.50	\$1,200,000
1996	3.00	5.50	816,000
Price per share			
2001	\$36.00	\$65.00	—
Dividends per share			
2001	\$ 2.25	\$ 3.75	\$ 600,000
1996	1.50	2.75	420,000
Book value per share, 2001	\$30.00	\$55.00	\$ 9 million
Market/book ratio, 2001	120%	118%	—
Total assets, 2001	\$28 million	\$ 82 million	\$20 million
Total debt, 2001	\$12 million	\$ 30 million	\$11 million
Sales, 2001	\$41 million	\$140 million	\$37 million

a. Assume that Edelman has 100 shares of stock outstanding. Use this information to calculate earnings per share (EPS), dividends per share (DPS), and book value per share for Edelman. (Hint: Edelman's 2001 EPS = \$12,000.)

b. Calculate earnings and dividend growth rates for the three companies. (Hint: Edelman's EPS growth rate is 8 percent.)

c. On the basis of your answer to part a, do you think Edelman's stock would sell at a price in the same "ballpark" as that of Kennedy and Strasburg, that is, in the range of \$25 to \$100 per share?

d. Assuming that Edelman's management can split the stock so that the 100 shares could be changed to 1,000 shares, 100,000 shares, or any other number, would such an action make sense in this case? Why?

e. Now assume that Edelman did split its stock and has 400,000 shares. Calculate new values for EPS, DPS, and book value per share. (Hint: Edelman's new 2001 EPS is \$3.00.)

f. Return on equity (ROE) can be measured as EPS/book value per share or as total earnings/total equity. Calculate ROEs for the three companies for 2001. (Hint: Edelman's 2001 ROE = 13.3%.)

g. Calculate dividend payout ratios for the three companies for both years. (Hint: Edelman's 2001 payout ratio is 50%.)

h. Calculate debt/total assets ratios for the three companies for 2001. (Hint: Edelman's 2001 debt ratio is 55%.)

i. Calculate the P/E ratios for Kennedy and Strasburg for 2001. Are these P/Es reasonable in view of relative growth, payout, and ROE data? If not, what other factors might explain them? (Hint: Kennedy's P/E = 8×).

j. Now determine a range of values for Edelman's stock price, with 400,000 shares outstanding, by applying Kennedy's and Strasburg's P/E ratios, price/dividends ratios, and price/book value ratios to your data for Edelman. For example, one possible price for Edelman's stock is (P/E Kennedy)(EPS Edelman) = 8(\$3) = \$24 per share. Similar calculations would produce a range of prices based on both Kennedy's and Strasburg's data. (Hint: Our range was \$24 to \$27.)

k. Using the equation $k_s = D_1/P_0 + g$, find approximate k_s values for Kennedy and Strasburg. Then use these values in the constant growth stock price model to find a price for Edelman's stock. (Hint: We averaged the EPS and DPS g's for Edelman.)

l. At what price do you think Edelman's shares should be offered to the public? You will want to select a price that will be low enough to induce investors to buy the stock but not so low that it will rise sharply immediately after it is issued. Think about relative growth rates, ROEs, dividend yields, and total returns ($k_s = D_1/P_0 + g$).

19–4 *REFUNDING ANALYSIS* Jan Volk, financial manager of Green Sea Transport (GST), has been asked by her boss to review GST's outstanding debt issues for possible bond refunding. Five years ago, GST issued \$40,000,000 of 11 percent, 25-year debt. The issue, with semiannual coupons, is currently callable at a premium of 11 percent, or \$110 for each \$1,000 par value bond. Flotation costs on this issue were 6 percent, or \$2,400,000.

Volk believes that GST could issue 20-year debt today with a coupon rate of 8 percent. The firm has placed many issues in the capital markets during the last 10 years, and its debt flotation costs are currently estimated to be 4 percent of the issue's value. GST's federal-plus-state tax rate is 40 percent.

Help Volk conduct the refunding analysis by answering the following questions:

a. What is the total dollar call premium required to call the old issue? Is it tax deductible? What is the net after-tax cost of the call?

b. What is the dollar flotation cost on the new issue? Is it immediately tax deductible? What is the after-tax flotation cost?

c. What amount of old issue flotation costs have not been expensed? Can these deferred costs be expensed immediately if the old issue is refunded? What is the value of the tax savings?

d. What is the net after-tax cash outlay required to refund the old issue?

e. What is the semiannual tax savings that arises from amortizing the flotation costs on the new issue? What is the foregone semiannual tax savings on the old issue flotation costs?

f. What is the semiannual after-tax interest savings that would result from the refunding?

g. Thus far, Volk has identified two future cash flows: (1) the net of new issue flotation cost tax savings and old issue flotation cost tax savings that are lost if refunding occurs and (2) after-tax interest savings. What is the sum of these two semiannual cash flows? What is the appropriate discount rate to apply to these future cash flows? What is the present value of these cash flows? (Hint: The $PVIFA_{2.4\%,40} = 25.5309$.)

h. What is the NPV of refunding? Should GST refund now or wait until later?

19–5 *REFUNDING ANALYSIS* Mullet Technologies is considering whether or not to refund a \$75 million, 12 percent coupon, 30-year bond issue that was sold 5 years ago. It is amortizing \$5 million of flotation costs on the 12 percent bonds over the issue's 30-year life. Mullet's investment bankers have indicated that the company could sell a new 25-year issue at an interest rate of 10 percent in today's market. Neither they nor Mullet's management anticipate that interest rates will fall below 10 percent any time soon, but there is a chance that rates will increase.

A call premium of 12 percent would be required to retire the old bonds, and flotation costs on the new issue would amount to \$5 million. Mullet's marginal federal-plus-state tax rate is 40 percent. The new bonds would be issued 1 month before the old bonds are called, with the proceeds being invested in short-term government securities returning 6 percent annually during the interim period.

a. Perform a complete bond refunding analysis. What is the bond refunding's NPV?

b. What factors would influence Mullet's decision to refund now rather than later?

Spreadsheet Problem

19–6 *WHAT IF ANALYSIS: ZERO COUPON BONDS* Start with the file ***Ch 19-6 What If Analysis.xls*** from the textbook's CD-ROM. Suppose Southern States Insurance Company needs to raise \$400 million, and its investment bankers have indicated that 10-year zero coupon bonds could be sold at a YTM of 12 percent while a 14 percent yield would be required on *annual* payment coupon bonds sold at par. Southern State's tax rate is 34 percent. (Assume that the discount can be amortized by the issuer using the straight line method. This cannot be done under current tax laws, but assume it anyway.)

a. How many \$1,000 par value bonds would Southern States have to sell under each plan?

b. What would be the after-tax YTM on each type of bond (1) to a holder who is tax exempt and (2) to a taxpayer in the 50 percent federal-plus-state bracket?

c. What would be the after-tax cost of each type of bond to Southern States?

d. Why would investors be willing to buy the zero coupon bonds?

e. Why might Southern States turn down the offer to issue zero coupon bonds?

f. Recalculate parts a, b, and c assuming that the YTM on zero coupon bonds falls to 10 percent and that on annual coupon bonds falls to 12 percent. As in the previous analysis, the after-tax yield to investors on the annual coupon bond exceeds that of the zero coupon bond. Has the differential between the annual and zero coupon bond yields changed? Would investors be more willing to purchase the zero coupon bond under the original assumptions or under the new assumptions? If the before-tax YTM were 10 percent on each type of bond, what would the after-tax YTMs be to zero and to 50 percent taxpayers, what would the after-tax cost be to the company, and what type of investors would be likely to hold the zeros and what type the regular coupon bonds?

Cyberproblem

19–7
INITIAL PUBLIC OFFERING

Each year the IPO market takes many companies on a wild ride. In this cyberproblem you will identify the biggest IPOs, the biggest winners, and the biggest losers during the past year. Go to the textbook's web site, **http://www.harcourtcollege.com/theory/student/resources/cyberprob/Ch19.html**, and answer the questions shown there.

Mini Case

CD

See ***Ch 19 Show.ppt*** and ***Ch 19 Mini Case.xls***.

Randy's, a family-owned restaurant chain operating in Alabama, has grown to the point where expansion throughout the entire Southeast is feasible. The proposed expansion would require the firm to raise about $15 million in new capital. Because Randy's currently has a debt ratio of 50 percent, and also because the family members already have all their personal wealth invested in the company, the family would like to sell common stock to the public to raise the $15 million. However, the family does want to retain voting control. You have been asked to brief the family members on the issues involved by answering the following questions:

a. What agencies regulate securities markets?
b. How are startup firms usually financed?
c. Differentiate between a private placement and a public offering.
d. Why would a company consider going public? What are some advantages and disadvantages?
e. What are the steps of an initial public offering?
f. What criteria are important in choosing an investment banker?
g. Would companies going public use a negotiated deal or a competitive bid?
h. Would the sale be on an underwritten or best efforts basis?
i. Without actually doing any calculations, describe how the preliminary offering range for the price of an IPO would be determined.
j. What is a roadshow? What is book-building?
k. Describe the typical first-day return of an IPO and the long-term returns to IPO investors.
l. What are the direct and indirect costs of an IPO?
m. What are equity carve-outs?
n. In what other ways are investment banks involved in issuing securities?
o. What is a rights offering?
p. What is meant by going private? What are some advantages and disadvantages?
q. How do companies manage the maturity structure of their debt?
r. What are zero coupon bonds? Briefly describe their tax treatment.
s. Under what conditions would a firm exercise a bond call provision?
t. Explain how firms manage the risk structure of their debt with
   (1) Project financing.
   (2) Securitization.

Selected Additional References and Cases

For a wealth of facts and figures on a major segment of the stock market, see New York Stock Exchange, Fact Book (New York: published annually).

For a discussion of investment banking see

Auerbach, Joseph, and Samuel L. Hayes III, *Investment Banking and Diligence: What Price Deregulation* (Boston: HBS Press, 1986).

Eccles, Robert G., and Dwight B. Crane, *Doing Deals: Investment Bankers at Work* (Boston: HBS Press, 1988).

Hayes, S. L., "The Transformation of Investment Banking," *Harvard Business Review*, January–February 1979, 153–170.

Rogowski, Robert, and Eric Sorensen, "The New Competitive Environment of Investment Banking: Transactional Finance and Concession Pricing of New Issues," *Midland Corporate Finance Journal*, Spring 1986, 64–71.

For additional insights on the benefits of listing, see

Baker, H. Kent, and Richard B. Edelman, "AMEX-to-NYSE Transfers, Market Microstructure, and Shareholder Wealth," *Financial Management*, Winter 1992, 60–72.

Edelman, Richard B., and H. Kent Baker, "Liquidity and Stock Exchange Listing," *The Financial Review*, May 1990, 231–249.

Other good references on specific aspects of equity financing include the following:

Aggarwal, Reena, and Pietra Rivoli, "Fads in the Initial Public Offering Market?" *Financial Management*, Winter 1990, 45–57.

Block, Stanley, and Marjorie Stanley, "The Financial Characteristics and Price Movement Patterns of Companies Approaching the Unseasoned Securities Market in the Late 1970s," *Financial Management*, Winter 1980, 30–36.

Bowyer, John W., and Jess B. Yawitz, "Effect of New Equity Issues on Utility Stock Prices," *Public Utilities Fortnightly*, May 22, 1980, 25–28.

Brickley, James A., and Kathleen T. Hevert, "Direct Employee Stock Ownership: An Empirical Investigation," *Financial Management*, Summer 1991, 70–84.

Carter, Richard, and Steven Manaster, "Initial Public Offerings and Underwriter Reputation," *Journal of Finance*, September 1990, 1045–1067.

Denis, David J., "The Costs of Equity Issues Since Rule 415: A Closer Look," *Journal of Financial Research*, Spring 1993, 77–88.

Fabozzi, Frank J., "Does Listing on the AMEX Increase the Value of Equity?" *Financial Management*, Spring 1981, 43–50.

Hansen, Robert S., and John M. Pinkerton, "Direct Equity Financing: A Resolution to a Paradox," *Journal of Finance*, June 1982, 651–665.

Ibbotson, Roger G., Jody L. Sindelar, and Jay R. Ritter, "Initial Public Offerings," *Journal of Applied Corporate Finance*, Summer 1988, 37–45.

———, "The Market's Problems with the Pricing of Initial Public Offerings," *Journal of Applied Corporate Finance*, Spring 1994, 66–74.

Jurin, Bruce, "Raising Equity in an Efficient Market," *Midland Corporate Finance Journal*, Winter 1988, 53–60.

Loderer, Claudio, John W. Cooney, and Leonard D. Van Drunen, "The Price Elasticity of Demand for Common Stock," *Journal of Finance*, June 1991, 621–651.

Logue, Dennis, and Robert A. Jarrow, "Negotiation versus Competitive Bidding in the Sale of Securities by Public Utilities," *Financial Management*, Autumn 1978, 31–39.

Lucas, Deborah J., and Robert L. McDonald, "Equity Issues and Stock Price Dynamics," *Journal of Finance*, September 1990, 1019–1043.

Michaely, Roni, and Wayne H. Shaw, "The Choice of Going Public: Spin-offs vs. Carve-outs," *Financial Management*, Autumn 1995, 5–21.

Muscarella, Chris J., and Michael R. Vetsuypens, "The Underpricing of 'Second' Initial Public Offerings," *Journal of Financial Research*, Fall 1989, 183–192.

Ritter, Jay R., "The Long-Run Performance of Initial Public Offerings," *Journal of Finance*, March 1991, 3–27.

For more information on shelf registration, see

Bhagat, Sanjai, "The Evidence on Shelf Registration," *Midland Corporate Finance Journal*, Spring 1984, 6–12.

For excellent discussions of the various procedures used to raise capital, see

Ritter, Jay R., "Initial Public Offerings," "*Contemporary Finance Digest*, Spring 1998, 5–30.

———, "Investment Banking and Securities Issuance," forthcoming in *North-Holland Handbook of the Economics of Finance*, edited by George Constantinides, Milton Harris, and René Stolz.

Smith, Clifford W., Jr., "Raising Capital: Theory and Evidence," *Midland Corporate Finance Journal*, Spring 1986, 6–22. Also, pages 72–76 of the Spring 1986 issue of the *Midland Corporate Finance Journal* contain a bibliography of recent articles pertaining to investment banking and capital acquisition.

The Spring 1993 issue of Financial Management *contains several articles on IPOs and LBOs.*

The Winter 1993 issue of the Journal of Applied Corporate Finance *is devoted to the SEC and securities regulation.*

References on bond refunding include the following:

Ang, James S., "The Two Faces of Bond Refunding," *Journal of Finance*, June 1975, 869–874.

———, "The Two Faces of Bond Refunding: Reply," *Journal of Finance*, March 1978, 354–356.

Chiang, Raymond C., and M. P. Narayanan, "Bond Refunding in Efficient Markets: A Dynamic Analysis with Tax Effects," *Journal of Financial Research*, Winter 1991, 287–302.

Dyl, Edward A. and Michael D. Joehnk, "Refunding Tax Exempt Bonds," *Financial Management*, Summer 1976, 59–66.

Emery, Douglas R., "Overlapping Interest in Bond Refunding: A Reconsideration," *Financial Management*, Summer 1978, 19-20.

Finnerty, John D., "Refunding High-Coupon Debt," *Midland Corporate Finance Journal*, Winter 1986, 59–74.

Harris, Robert S., "The Refunding of Discounted Debt: An Adjusted Present Value Analysis," *Financial Management*, Winter 1980, 7–12.

Kalotay, Andrew J., "On the Advanced Refunding of Discounted Debt," *Financial Management*, Summer 1978, 14–18.

———, "On the Structure and Valuation of Debt Refundings," *Financial Management*, Spring 1982, 41–42.

Kraus, Alan, "An Analysis of Call Provisions and the Corporate Refunding Decision," *Midland Corporate Finance Journal*, Spring 1983, 46–60.

Laber, Gene, "The Effect of Bond Refunding of Discounted Debt," *Financial Management*, June 1979, 795–799.

———, "Implications of Discount Rates and Financing Assumptions for Bond Refunding Decisions," *Financial Management*, Spring 1979, 7–12.

———, "Repurchases of Bonds through Tender Offers: Implications for Shareholder Wealth," *Financial Management*, Summer 1978, 7–13.

Livingston, Miles, "The Effect of Bond Refunding on Shareholder Wealth: Comment," *Journal of Finance*, June 1979, 801–804.

———, "Bond Refunding Reconsidered: Comment," *Journal of Finance*, March 1980, 191–196.

Mauer, David C., "Optimal Bond Call Policies under Transactions Costs," *Journal of Financial Research*, Spring 1993, 23–37.

Mayor, Thomas H., and Kenneth G. McCoin, "Bond Refunding: One or Two Faces?" *Journal of Finance*, March 1978, 349–353.

Ofer, Aharon R., and Robert A. Taggart, Jr., "Bond Refunding: Reconsidered: Reply," *Journal of Finance*, March 1980, 197–200.

Riener, Kenneth D., "Financial Structure Effects of Bond Refunding," *Financial Management*, Summer 1980, 18–23.

Thatcher, Janet S., and John G. Thatcher, "An Empirical Test of the Timing of Bond-Refunding Decisions," *Journal of Financial Research*, Fall 1992, 219–230.

Yawitz, Jess B., and James A. Anderson, "The Effect of Bond Refunding on Shareholder Wealth," *Journal of Finance*, December 1977, 1738–1746.

———, "The Effect of Bond Refunding on Shareholder Wealth: Reply," *Journal of Finance*, June 1979, 805–809.

Zeise, Charles H., and Roger K. Taylor, "Advance Refunding: A Practitioner's Perspective," *Financial Management*, Summer 1977, 73–76.

The following cases from the Cases in Financial Management: Dryden Request *series focus on the issues contained in this chapter:*

Case 21, "Sun Coast Savings Bank," which illustrates the decision to go public.

Case 22, "Precision Tool Company," which emphasizes the investment banking process.

Case 23, "Art Deco Reproductions, Inc.," which focuses on the analysis of a rights offering.

Case 24, "Bay Area Telephone Company," Case 24A, "Shenandoah Power Company," and Case 24B, "Tucson Entertainment, Inc.," which illustrate the bond refunding decision.

20

Lease Financing

Some of the biggest players in the airline business have never issued a ticket, lost a passenger's luggage, or landed a plane in bad weather. They are the aircraft leasing companies—the merchant bankers of aviation—and their role is to help finance aircraft and to help airlines respond more quickly and efficiently to market changes. Among the major players in aircraft leasing are GPA Group, a closely held company based in Shannon, Ireland, and International Lease Finance of Beverly Hills.

Aircraft leasing companies purchase airplanes from manufacturers such as Boeing and Airbus and then lease them, often on a relatively short-term basis, to carriers such as American, British Airways, Delta, Lufthansa, and United. Leasing separates the risks and rewards of owning aircraft from those of operating them. Currently, leasing companies buy about 50 percent of all new commercial aircraft.

The airline industry is undergoing major changes due to global deregulation. The highly competitive nature of the industry has forced both TWA and Continental to seek bankruptcy protection twice, and it has caused many airlines to fail, including Braniff, Eastern, Midway, and Pan Am. In the days of regulation, airlines knew precisely the routes they would serve, and they could raise prices to cover any cost increases. Thus, airlines could buy planes confident that route structures would be relatively stable and that revenues would cover financing costs. Now, however, airlines constantly drop and add routes in response to changing competitive conditions. Because different types of aircraft are better suited for some routes than others, for optimal operations airlines must frequently restructure their fleets. If an airline had purchased all of its aircraft, it could not respond quickly to changing conditions. The leasing companies, on the other hand, lease all types of aircraft to all types of airlines, and there is usually some airline somewhere interested in a given aircraft when its lease is dropped by another airline. Therefore, leasing improves airlines' flexibility.

Global deregulation also has spawned a host of startup airlines, both in the United States and in Europe. Such airlines find it difficult to raise the capital needed to purchase aircraft, but leasing helps them get started. Startup airlines typically are in a precarious financial condition, and leasing companies often are more willing than lenders to take the financing risk because lessors are in a more favorable legal position should the airline actually go bankrupt. Thus, it is easier for a leasing company to repossess and redeploy an aircraft than it would be for a lender.

Interestingly, Airbus Industrie, the European aircraft consortium, has adopted short-term leases as a sales tool. In recent years, Delta and United "bought" aircraft from Airbus on "walkaway" leases under which the aircraft could be returned to the manufacturer in less than a year. U.S. manufacturers complained that Airbus can offer such terms only because it is subsidized by the four European countries that back the consortium. The Clinton administration reportedly lobbied to force Airbus to discontinue its short-term lease program, which would help Boeing but potentially hurt U.S. airlines.

As you read this chapter, think about the airline industry and why leasing can be more attractive than buying. Also, think about why leasing companies and manufacturers are able to offer such attractive lease rates. When you finish the chapter, you should understand both how leases are analyzed, and also the conditions under which leasing is likely to be attractive.

Firms generally own fixed assets and report them on their balance sheets, but it is the *use* of assets that is important, not their ownership per se. One way to obtain the use of facilities and equipment is to buy them, but an alternative is to lease them. Prior to the 1950s, leasing was generally associated with real estate—land and buildings. Today, however, it is possible to lease virtually any kind of fixed asset, and currently over 30 percent of all new capital equipment is financed through lease arrangements.[1]

The Two Parties to Leasing

Lease transactions involve two parties: the **lessor,** who owns the property, and the **lessee,** who obtains use of the property in exchange for one or more **lease,** or **rental, payments.** (Note that the term *lessee* is pronounced "less-ee," not "lease-ee," and *lessor* is pronounced "less-or.") Because both parties must agree before a lease transaction can be completed, this chapter discusses leasing from the perspectives of both the lessor and the lessee.

Self-Test Question

Who are the two parties to a lease transaction?

Types of Leases

CD

The textbook's CD-ROM contains an *Excel* file that will guide you through the chapter's calculations. The file for this chapter is ***Ch 20 Tool Kit.xls,*** and we encourage you to open the file and follow along as you read the chapter.

Leasing takes several different forms, the four most important being (1) operating leases, (2) financial, or capital, leases, (3) sale-and-leaseback arrangements, and (4) combination leases.

Operating Leases

Operating leases generally provide for both *financing* and *maintenance.* IBM was one of the pioneers of the operating lease contract, and computers and office copying machines, together with automobiles, trucks, and aircraft, are the primary types of equipment involved in operating leases. Ordinarily, operating leases require the lessor to maintain and service the leased equipment, and the cost of the maintenance is built into the lease payments.

Another important characteristic of operating leases is the fact that they are *not fully amortized.* In other words, the rental payments required under the lease contract are not sufficient for the lessor to recover the full cost of the asset. However, the lease contract is written for a period considerably shorter than the expected economic life of the asset, so the lessor can expect to recover all costs either by subsequent renewal payments, by re-leasing the asset to another lessee, or by selling the asset.

A final feature of operating leases is that they often contain a *cancellation clause* that gives the lessee the right to cancel the lease and return the asset before the expiration of the basic lease agreement. This is an important consideration to the lessee, for it means that the asset can be returned if it is rendered obsolete by technological developments or is no longer needed because of a change in the lessee's business.

---

[1]For a detailed treatment of leasing, see James S. Schallheim, *Lease or Buy? Principles for Sound Decision Making* (Boston: Harvard Business School Press, 1994).

Financial, or Capital, Leases

Financial leases, sometimes called **capital leases,** are differentiated from operating leases in that they (1) *do not* provide for maintenance service, (2) *are not* cancellable, and (3) *are* fully amortized (that is, the lessor receives rental payments equal to the full price of the leased equipment plus a return on invested capital). In a typical arrangement, the firm that will use the equipment (the lessee) selects the specific items it requires and negotiates the price with the manufacturer. The user firm then arranges to have a leasing company (the lessor) buy the equipment from the manufacturer and simultaneously executes a lease contract. The terms of the lease generally call for full amortization of the lessor's investment, plus a rate of return on the unamortized balance that is close to the percentage rate the lessee would have paid on a secured loan. For example, if the lessee would have to pay 10 percent for a loan, then a rate of about 10 percent would be built into the lease contract.

The lessee is generally given an option to renew the lease at a reduced rate upon expiration of the basic lease. However, the basic lease usually cannot be cancelled unless the lessor is paid in full. Also, the lessee generally pays the property taxes and insurance on the leased property. Since the lessor receives a return *after*, or *net of*, these payments, this type of lease is often called a "net, net" lease.

Sale-and-Leaseback Arrangements

Under a **sale-and-leaseback arrangement,** a firm that owns land, buildings, or equipment sells the property to another firm and simultaneously executes an agreement to lease the property back for a stated period under specific terms. The capital supplier could be an insurance company, a commercial bank, a specialized leasing company, the finance arm of an industrial firm, a limited partnership, or an individual investor. The sale-and-leaseback plan is an alternative to a mortgage.

Note that the seller immediately receives the purchase price put up by the buyer. At the same time, the seller-lessee retains the use of the property. The parallel to borrowing is carried over to the lease payment schedule. Under a mortgage loan arrangement, the lender would normally receive a series of equal payments just sufficient to amortize the loan and to provide a specified rate of return on the outstanding loan balance. Under a sale-and-leaseback arrangement, the lease payments are set up exactly the same way—the payments are just sufficient to return the full purchase price to the investor, plus a stated return on the lessor's investment.

Sale-and-leaseback arrangements are almost the same as financial leases, the major difference being that the leased equipment is used, not new, and the lessor buys it from the user-lessee instead of a manufacturer or a distributor. A sale and leaseback is thus a special type of financial lease.

Combination Leases

Many lessors now offer leases under a wide variety of terms. Therefore, in practice leases often do not fit exactly into the operating lease or financial lease category but combine some features of each. Such leases are called **combination leases.** To illustrate, cancellation clauses are normally associated with operating leases, but many of today's financial leases also contain cancellation clauses. However, in financial leases these clauses generally include prepayment provisions whereby the lessee must make penalty payments sufficient to enable the lessor to recover the unamortized cost of the leased property.

Self-Test Questions

What is the difference between an operating lease and a financial, or capital, lease?

What is a sale-and-leaseback transaction?

What is a combination lease?

Tax Effects

The full amount of the lease payments is a tax-deductible expense for the lessee *provided the Internal Revenue Service agrees that a particular contract is a genuine lease and not simply a loan called a lease.* This makes it important that a lease contract be written in a form acceptable to the IRS. A lease that complies with all IRS requirements is called a **guideline,** or **tax-oriented, lease,** and the tax benefits of ownership (depreciation and any investment tax credits) belong to the lessor. The main provisions of the tax guidelines are as follows:[2]

1. The lease term (including any extensions or renewals at a fixed rental rate) must not exceed 80 percent of the estimated useful life of the equipment at the commencement of the lease transaction. Thus, an asset with a 10-year life can be leased for no more than eight years. Further, the remaining useful life must not be less than one year. Note that an asset's expected useful life is normally much longer than its MACRS depreciation class life.
2. The equipment's estimated residual value (in constant dollars without adjustment for inflation) at the expiration of the lease must be at least 20 percent of its value at the start of the lease. This requirement can have the effect of limiting the maximum lease term.
3. Neither the lessee nor any related party can have the right to purchase the property at a predetermined fixed price. However, the lessee can be given an option to buy the asset at its fair market value.
4. Neither the lessee nor any related party can pay or guarantee payment of any part of the price of the leased equipment. Simply put, the lessee cannot make any investment in the equipment, other than through the lease payments.
5. The leased equipment must not be "limited use" property, defined as equipment that can only be used by the lessee or a related party at the end of the lease.

The reason for the IRS's concern about lease terms is that, without restrictions, a company could set up a "lease" transaction calling for very rapid payments, which would be tax deductions. The effect would be to depreciate the equipment over a much shorter period than its MACRS class life. For example, suppose a firm planned to acquire a $2,000,000 computer that had a three-year MACRS class life. The annual depreciation allowances would be $660,000 in Year 1, $900,000 in Year 2, $300,000 in Year 3, and $140,000 in Year 4. If the firm were in the 40 percent federal-plus-state tax bracket, the depreciation would provide a tax saving of $264,000 in Year 1, $360,000 in Year 2, $120,000 in Year 3, and $56,000 in Year 4, for a total savings of $800,000. At a 6 percent discount rate, the present value of these tax savings would be $714,567.

Now suppose the firm could acquire the computer through a one-year lease arrangement with a leasing company for a payment of $2 million, with a $1 purchase option. If the $2,000,000 payment were treated as a lease payment, it would be fully deductible, so it would provide a tax savings of 0.4($2,000,000) = $800,000 versus a present value of only $714,567 for the depreciation shelters. Thus, the lease payment and the depreciation would both provide the same total amount of tax savings (40% of $2,000,000, or $800,000), but the savings would come in faster, hence have a higher present value, with the one-year lease. Therefore, if just any type of contract could be called a lease and given tax treatment as a lease, then the timing of the tax shelters could be speeded up as compared with ownership depreciation tax shelters. This speedup would benefit companies, but it would be costly to the government. For this

[2]See Schallheim, *op. cit.*, Chapter 3, for more on taxes and leasing.

reason, the IRS has established the rules described above for defining a lease for tax purposes.

Even though leasing can be used only within limits to speed up the effective depreciation schedule, there are still times when very substantial tax benefits can be derived from a leasing arrangement. For example, if a firm has incurred losses and hence has no current tax liabilities, then its depreciation shelters are not very useful. In this case, a leasing company set up by profitable companies such as GE or Philip Morris can buy the equipment, receive the depreciation shelters, and then share these benefits with the lessee by charging lower lease payments. This point will be discussed in detail later in the chapter, but the point now is that if firms are to obtain tax benefits from leasing, the lease contract must be written in a manner that will qualify it as a true lease under IRS guidelines. If there is any question about the legal status of the contract, the financial manager must be sure to have the firm's lawyers and accountants check the latest IRS regulations.[3]

Note that a lease that does not meet the tax guidelines is called a **non-tax-oriented lease.** For this type of lease, the lessee (1) is the effective owner of the leased property, (2) can depreciate it for tax purposes, and (3) can deduct only the interest portion of each lease payment.

Self-Test Questions

What is the difference between a tax-oriented lease and a non-tax-oriented lease?

What are some lease provisions that would cause a lease to be classified as a non-tax-oriented lease?

Why does the IRS place limits on lease provisions?

Financial Statement Effects[4]

Under certain conditions, neither the leased assets nor the liabilities under the lease contract appear directly on the firm's balance sheet. For this reason, leasing is often called *off-balance sheet* financing. This point is illustrated in Table 20-1 by the balance sheets of two hypothetical firms, B (for "borrow") and L (for "lease"). Initially, the balance sheets of both firms are identical, and they both have debt ratios of 50 percent. Next, each firm decides to acquire a fixed asset costing $100. Firm B borrows $100 and buys the asset, so both an asset and a liability go on its balance sheet, and its debt ratio rises from 50 to 75 percent. Firm L leases the equipment. The lease may call for fixed charges as high or even higher than the loan, and the obligations assumed under the lease may be equally or more dangerous from the standpoint of potential bankruptcy, but the firm's debt ratio remains at only 50 percent.

To correct this problem, the Financial Accounting Standards Board issued FASB Statement 13, which requires that, for an unqualified audit report, firms that enter

[3]In 1981, Congress relaxed the normal IRS rules to permit *safe harbor leases,* which had virtually no IRS restrictions and which were explicitly designed to permit the transfer of tax benefits from unprofitable companies that could not use them to high-profit companies that could. The point of safe harbor leases was to provide incentives for capital investment to companies that had little or no tax liability—under safe harbor leasing, companies with no tax liability could sell the benefit to companies in a high marginal tax bracket. In 1981 and 1982, literally billions of dollars were paid by such profitable firms as IBM and Philip Morris for the tax shelters of such unprofitable ones as Ford and Eastern Airlines. However, in 1983, Congress curtailed the use of safe harbor leases.

[4]FASB Statement 13, "Accounting for Leases," spells out in detail both the conditions under which the lease must be capitalized and the procedures for capitalizing it. Also, see Schallheim, *op. cit.,* Chapter 4, for more on the accounting treatment of leases.

TABLE 20-1 Balance Sheet Effects of Leasing

Before Asset Increase				After Asset Increase							
Firms B and L				Firm B, which Borrows and Buys				Firm L, which Leases			
Current assets	$ 50	Debt	$ 50	Current assets	$ 50	Debt	$150	Current assets	$ 50	Debt	$ 50
Fixed assets	50	Equity	50	Fixed assets	150	Equity	50	Fixed assets	50	Equity	50
	$100		$100		$200		$200		$100		$100
Debt/assets ratio:			50%				75%				50%

into financial (or capital) leases must restate their balance sheets and report the leased asset as a fixed asset and the present value of the future lease payments as a liability. This process is called **capitalizing the lease,** and its net effect is to cause Firms B and L to have similar balance sheets, both of which will, in essence, resemble the one shown for Firm B.

The logic behind Statement 13 is as follows. If a firm signs a financial lease contract, its obligation to make lease payments is just as binding as if it had signed a loan agreement—the failure to make lease payments can bankrupt a firm just as fast as the failure to make principal and interest payments on a loan. Therefore, for all intents and purposes, a financial lease is identical to a loan.[5] This being the case, if a firm signs a financial lease agreement, this has the effect of raising its true debt ratio, and thus its true capital structure is changed. Therefore, if the firm had previously established a target capital structure, and if there is no reason to think that the optimal capital structure has changed, then lease financing requires additional equity support exactly like debt financing.

If disclosure of the lease in our Table 20-1 example were not made, then Firm L's investors could be deceived into thinking that its financial position is stronger than it really is. Thus, even before FASB Statement 13 was issued, firms were required to disclose the existence of long-term leases in footnotes to their financial statements. At that time, it was debated as to whether or not investors recognized fully the impact of leases and, in effect, would see that Firms B and L were in essentially the same financial position. Some people argued that leases were not fully recognized, even by sophisticated investors. If this were the case, then leasing could alter the capital structure decision in a significant manner—a firm could increase its true leverage through a lease arrangement, and this procedure would have a smaller effect on its cost of conventional debt, k_d, and on its cost of equity, k_s, than if it had borrowed directly and reflected this fact on its balance sheet. These benefits of leasing would accrue to existing investors at the expense of new investors who would, in effect, be deceived by the fact that the firm's balance sheet did not reflect its true financial leverage.

[5]There are, however, certain legal differences between loans and leases. In the event of liquidation in bankruptcy, a lessor is entitled to take possession of the leased asset, and if the value of the asset is less than the required payments under the lease, the lessor can enter a claim (as a general creditor) for one year's lease payments. Also, after bankruptcy has been declared but before the case has been resolved, lease payments may be continued, whereas all payments on debts are generally stopped. In a reorganization, the lessor receives the asset plus three years' lease payments if needed to cover the value of the lease. The lender under a secured loan arrangement has a security interest in the asset, meaning that if it is sold, the lender will be given the proceeds, and the full unsatisfied portion of the lender's claim will be treated as a general creditor obligation. It is not possible to state, as a general rule, whether a supplier of capital is in a stronger position as a secured creditor or as a lessor. However, in certain situations, lessors may bear less risk than secured lenders if financial distress occurs.

The question of whether investors were truly deceived was debated but never resolved. Those who believed strongly in efficient markets thought that investors were not deceived and that footnotes were sufficient, while those who questioned market efficiency thought that all leases should be capitalized. Statement 13 represents a compromise between these two positions, though one that is tilted heavily toward those who favor capitalization.

A lease is classified as a capital lease, hence must be capitalized and shown directly on the balance sheet, if one or more of the following conditions exist:

1. Under the terms of the lease, ownership of the property is effectively transferred from the lessor to the lessee.
2. The lessee can purchase the property at less than its true market value when the lease expires.
3. The lease runs for a period equal to or greater than 75 percent of the asset's life. Thus, if an asset has a 10-year life and the lease is written for eight years, the lease must be capitalized.
4. The present value of the lease payments is equal to or greater than 90 percent of the initial value of the asset.[6]

These rules, together with strong footnote disclosure rules for operating leases, are sufficient to ensure that no one will be fooled by lease financing. Thus, leases are regarded as debt for capital structure purposes, and they have the same effects as debt on k_d and k_s. Therefore, leasing is not likely to permit a firm to use more financial leverage than could be obtained with conventional debt.[7]

Self-Test Questions

Why is lease financing sometimes referred to as off-balance sheet financing?

What is the intent of FASB Statement 13?

What is the difference in the balance sheet treatment of a lease that is capitalized versus one that is not?

Evaluation by the Lessee

Leases are evaluated by both the lessee and the lessor. The lessee must determine whether leasing an asset is less costly than buying it, and the lessor must decide whether the lease payments provide a satisfactory return on the capital invested in the leased asset. This section focuses on the lessee's analysis.

In the typical case, the events leading to a lease arrangement follow the sequence described below. We should note that a degree of uncertainty exists regarding the theoretically correct way to evaluate lease-versus-purchase decisions, and some very complex decision models have been developed to aid in the analysis. However, the simple analysis given here leads to the correct decision in all the cases we have ever encountered.

1. The firm decides to acquire a particular building or piece of equipment; this decision is based on regular capital budgeting procedures. Whether or not to acquire

[6]The discount rate used to calculate the present value of the lease payments must be the lower of (1) the rate used by the lessor to establish the lease payments (this rate is discussed later in the chapter) or (2) the rate of interest that the lessee would have to pay for new debt with a maturity equal to that of the lease. Also, note that any maintenance payments embedded in the lease payment must be stripped out prior to checking this condition.

[7]Schallheim, *op. cit.*, in Chapter 5, argues that leases and debt may not be perfect substitutes, but the evidence on this point is not conclusive. Still, our lease analysis models are based on the assumption that leasing is a substitute for borrowing, and that assumption is probably valid in most situations.

the asset is *not* part of the typical lease analysis—in a lease analysis, we are concerned simply with whether to obtain the use of the machine by lease or by purchase. Thus, for the lessee, the lease decision is typically just a financing decision. However, if the effective cost of capital obtained by leasing is substantially lower than the cost of debt, then the cost of capital used in the capital budgeting decision would have to be recalculated, and perhaps projects formerly deemed unacceptable might become acceptable. See the Web/CD Extension for this chapter for more information on feedback effects.

2. Once the firm has decided to acquire the asset, the next question is how to finance it. Well-run businesses do not have excess cash lying around, so capital to finance new assets must be obtained from some source.
3. Funds to purchase the asset could be obtained from internally generated cash flows, by borrowing, or by selling new equity. Alternatively, the asset could be leased. Because of the capitalization/disclosure provision for leases, leasing normally has the same capital structure effect as borrowing.
4. As indicated earlier, a lease is comparable to a loan in the sense that the firm is required to make a specified series of payments, and a failure to meet these payments could result in bankruptcy. If a company has a target capital structure, then $1 of lease financing displaces $1 of debt financing. Thus, the most appropriate comparison is lease financing versus debt financing. Note that the analysis should compare the cost of leasing with the cost of debt financing *regardless* of how the asset purchase is actually financed. The asset may be purchased with available cash or cash rasied by issuing stock, but since leasing is a substitute for debt financing, and has the same capital structure effect, the appropriate comparison would still be with debt financing.

To illustrate the basic elements of lease analysis, consider this simplified example (the file ***Ch 20 Tool Kit.xls*** shows this analysis). The Thompson-Grammatikos Company (TGC) needs a two-year asset that costs $100, and the company must choose between leasing and buying the asset. TGC's tax rate is 40 percent. If the asset is purchased, the bank would lend TGC the $100 at a rate of 10 percent on a two-year, simple interest loan. Thus, the firm would have to pay the bank $10 in interest at the end of each year, plus return the $100 of principal at the end of Year 2. For simplicity, assume (1) that TGC could depreciate the asset over two years for tax purposes by the straight line method if it is purchased, resulting in tax depreciation of $50 and tax savings of T(Depreciation) = 0.4($50) = $20 in each year, and (2) that the asset's value at the end of two years will be $0.

Alternatively, TGC could lease the asset under a guideline lease for two years for a payment of $55 at the end of each year. The analysis for the lease-versus-borrow decision consists of (1) estimating the cash flows associated with borrowing and buying the asset, that is, the flows associated with debt financing, (2) estimating the cash flows associated with leasing the asset, and (3) comparing the two financing methods to determine which has the lower present value costs. Here are the borrow-and-buy flows, set up to produce a cash flow time line:

Cash Flows if TGC Buys	Year 0	Year 1	Year 2
Equipment cost	($100)		
Inflow from loan	100		
Interest expense		($10)	($ 10)
Tax savings from interest		4	4
Principal repayment			(100)
Tax savings from depreciation		20	20
Net cash flow (time line)	$ 0	$14	($ 86)

The net cash flow is zero in Year 0, positive in Year 1, and negative in Year 2. The operating cash flows are not shown, but they must, of course, have a PV greater than the PV of the financing costs or else TGC would not want to acquire the asset. Because the operating cash flows will be the same regardless of whether the asset is leased or purchased, they can be ignored.

Here are the cash flows associated with the lease:

Cash Flows if TGC Leases	Year 0	Year 1	Year 2
Lease payment		($55)	($55)
Tax savings from payment		22	22
Net cash flow (time line)	$0	($33)	($33)

Note that the two sets of cash flows reflect the tax deductibility of interest and depreciation if the asset is purchased, and the deductibility of lease payments if it is leased. Thus, the net cash flows include the tax savings from these items.[8]

To compare the cost streams of buying versus leasing, we must put them on a present value basis. As we explain later, the correct discount rate is the after-tax cost of debt, which for TGC is 10%(1 − 0.4) = 6.0%. Applying this rate, we find the present value cost of buying to be $63.33 versus a present value cost of leasing of $60.50. Since leasing has the lower present value of costs, the company should lease this particular asset.

Now we examine a more realistic example, one from the Anderson Company, which is conducting a lease analysis on some assembly line equipment that it will procure during the coming year (the file ***Ch 20 Tool Kit.xls*** shows this analysis). The following data have been developed:

1. Anderson plans to acquire automated assembly line equipment with a 10-year life at a cost of $10 million, delivered and installed. However, Anderson plans to use the equipment for only 5 years, and then discontinue the product line.
2. Anderson can borrow the required $10 million at a before-tax cost of 10 percent.
3. The equipment's estimated scrap value is $50,000 after 10 years of use, but its estimated salvage value after only 5 years of use is $1,000,000. Thus, if Anderson buys the equipment, it would expect to receive $1,000,000 before taxes when the equipment is sold in 5 years. Note that in leasing, the asset's value at the end of the lease is called its **residual value.**
4. Anderson can lease the equipment for 5 years at a rental charge of $2,750,000, payable at the beginning of each year, but the lessor will own the equipment upon the expiration of the lease. (The lease payment schedule is established by the potential lessor, as described in the next major section, and Anderson can accept it, reject it, or negotiate.)
5. The lease contract stipulates that the lessor will maintain the equipment at no additional charge to Anderson. However, if Anderson borrows and buys, it will have to bear the cost of maintenance, which will be done by the equipment manufacturer at a fixed contract rate of $500,000 per year, payable at the beginning of each year.
6. The equipment falls in the MACRS 5-year class life, Anderson's marginal tax rate is 40 percent, and the lease qualifies as a guideline lease.

[8]If the lease had not met IRS guidelines, then ownership would effectively reside with the lessee, and TGC would depreciate the asset for tax purposes whether it was leased or purchased. However, only the implied interest portion of the lease payment would be tax deductible. Thus, the analysis for a nonguideline lease would consist of simply comparing the after-tax financing flows on the loan with the after-tax lease payment stream.

Table 20-2 shows the steps involved in the analysis. Part I of the table is devoted to the costs of borrowing and buying. The company borrows \$10 million and uses it to pay for the equipment, so these two items net out to zero and thus are not shown in Table 20-2. Then, the company makes the *after-tax* payments shown on Line 1. In Year 1, the after-tax interest charge is 0.10(\$10 million)(0.6) = \$600,000, and other payments are calculated similarly. The \$10 million loan is repaid at the end of Year 5. Line 2 shows the maintenance cost. Line 3 gives the maintenance tax savings. Line 4 contains the depreciation tax savings, which is the depreciation expense times the tax rate. The notes to Table 20-2 explain the depreciation calculation. Lines 5 and 6 contain the residual (or salvage) value cash flows. The tax is on the excess of the residual value over the asset's book value, not on the full residual value. Line 7 contains the net cash flows, and Line 8 shows the net present value of these flows, discounted at 6 percent.

Part II of Table 20-2 analyzes the lease. The lease payments, shown on Line 9, are \$2,750,000 per year; this rate, which includes maintenance, was established by the prospective lessor and offered to Anderson Equipment. If Anderson accepts the lease, the full amount will be a deductible expense, so the tax savings, shown on Line 10, is 0.40(Lease payment) = 0.40(\$2,750,000) = \$1,100,000. Thus, the after-tax cost of the lease payment is Lease payment − Tax savings = \$2,750,000 − \$1,100,000 = \$1,650,000. This amount is shown on Line 11, Years 0 through 4.

TABLE 20-2 Anderson Company: Dollar Cost Analysis (Thousands of Dollars)

	Year 0	Year 1	Year 2	Year 3	Year 4	Year 5
I. Cost of Owning (Borrowing and Buying)						
1. After-tax loan payments		(\$ 600)	(\$ 600)	(\$ 600)	(\$ 600)	(\$10,600)
2. Maintenance cost	(\$ 500)	(500)	(500)	(500)	(500)	
3. Maintenance tax savings	200	200	200	200	200	
4. Depreciation tax savings		800	1,280	760	480	\$ 440
5. Residual value						1,000
6. Tax on residual value						(160)
7. Net cash flow (time line)	(\$ 300)	(\$ 100)	\$ 380	(\$ 140)	(\$ 420)	(\$ 9,320)
8. PV cost of owning =	\$7,471					
II. Cost of Leasing						
9. Lease payment	(\$2,750)	(\$2,750)	(\$2,750)	(\$2,750)	(\$2,750)	
10. Payment tax savings	1,100	1,100	1,100	1,100	1,100	
11. Net cash flow (time line)	(\$1,650)	(\$1,650)	(\$1,650)	(\$1,650)	(\$1,650)	\$0
12. PV cost of leasing =	\$7,367					

III. Cost Comparison

13. Net advantage to leasing (NAL) = PV cost of owning − PV cost of leasing = \$7,471 − \$7,367 = \$104.

Notes:
a. The after-tax loan payments consist of after-tax interest for Years 1–4 and after-tax interest plus the principal amount in Year 5.
b. The net cash flows shown in Lines 7 and 11 are discounted at the lessee's after-tax cost of debt, 6.0 percent.
c. The MACRS depreciation allowances are 0.20, 0.32, 0.19, and 0.11 in Years 1 through 5, respectively. Thus, the depreciation expense is 0.20(\$10,000) = \$2,000 in Year 1, and so on. The depreciation tax savings in each year is 0.4(Depreciation).
d. The residual value is \$1,000 while the book value is \$600. Thus, Anderson would have to pay 0.4(\$1,000 − \$600) = \$160 in taxes, producing a net after-tax residual value of \$1,000 − \$160 = \$840. These amounts are shown in Lines 5 and 6 in the cost of owning analysis.
e. In practice, a lease analysis such as this would be done using a spreadsheet model.
f. In the NAL equation on Line 13, the PV costs are stated as positive values. If the PV costs are treated as negative values, or outflows, the NAL must be redefined as follows: NAL = PV cost of leasing − PV cost of owning = −\$7,367 − (−\$7,471) = \$104.

Leasing Comes to the Internet

You've probably heard of Internet banking, but how about Internet leasing? Chase Manhattan Corp. recently created a web site for small businesses that are purchasing equipment. In a matter of minutes, an equipment purchaser can log onto **www.smallbizleasing.com,** apply for a lease, and receive notification of the lessor's decision. Lease financing through this program ranges from $3,000 for an office copier to $250,000 for medical, light manufacturing, and construction equipment.

The program is useful for many small businesses because it provides a quick source of financing. It's also good for vendors, who can incorporate this financing arrangement into their sales presentations. And it's good for Chase, since it gives them an efficient way to tap into the small business market. All in all, Internet leasing is often a win-win-win situation.

Source: Scott Leibs, "New Life on Leases," *CFO,* May 2000, 16.

The next step is to compare the net cost of owning with the net cost of leasing. However, we must first put the annual cash flows of leasing and borrowing on a common basis. This requires converting them to present values, which brings up the question of the proper rate at which to discount the costs. Because leasing is a substitute for debt, most analysts recommend that the company's cost of debt be used, and this rate seems reasonable in our example. Further, since the cash flows are after taxes, *the* **after-tax cost of debt,** *which is 10%(1 − T) = 10%(0.6) = 6%, should be used.* Accordingly, we discount the net cash flows on Lines 7 and 11 using a rate of 6.0 percent. The resulting present values are $7,471,000 for the cost of owning and $7,367,000 for the cost of leasing, as shown on Lines 8 and 12. The financing method that produces the smaller present value of costs is the one that should be selected. We define the **net advantage to leasing (NAL)** as follows (see Note e to Table 20-2):

$$\begin{aligned} \text{NAL} &= \text{PV cost of owning} - \text{PV cost of leasing} \\ &= \$7{,}471{,}000 - \$7{,}367{,}000 \\ &= \$104{,}000. \end{aligned}$$

The PV cost of owning exceeds the PV cost of leasing, so the NAL is positive. Therefore, Anderson should lease the equipment.[9]

In this section, we focused on the dollar cost of leasing versus borrowing and buying, which is analogous to the NPV method used in capital budgeting. A second

[9]The more complicated methods that exist for analyzing leasing generally focus on the issue of the discount rate that should be used to discount the cash flows. Conceptually, we could assign a separate discount rate to each individual cash flow component, then find the present values of each of the cash flow components, and finally sum these present values to determine the net advantage or disadvantage to leasing. This approach has been taken by Stewart C. Myers, David A. Dill, and Alberto J. Bautista (MDB) in "Valuation of Financial Lease Contracts," *Journal of Finance,* June 1976, 799–819, among others. MDB correctly note that the use of a single discount rate is valid only if (1) leases and loans are viewed by investors as being equivalent and (2) all cash flows are equally risky, hence appropriately discounted at the same rate. The first assumption is probably valid for most financial leases, and even where it is not, no one knows how to adjust properly for any capital structure effects that leases might have. Regarding the second assumption, advocates of multiple discount rates often point out that the residual value is less certain than are the other cash flows and thus recommend discounting it at a higher rate. However, there is no way of knowing precisely how much to increase the after-tax cost of debt to account for the increased riskiness of the residual value cash flow. Further, in a market risk sense, all cash flows could be equally risky even though individual items such as the residual value might have more or less total variability than others. To complicate matters even more, the market risk of the residual value will usually be different than the firm's market risk. For more on residual value risk, see Schallheim, *op. cit.,* Chapter 8.

method that lessees can use to evaluate leases focuses on the percentage cost of leasing and is analogous to the IRR method used in capital budgeting. The percentage approach is discussed in the Web/CD Extension to this chapter.

Self-Test Questions

Explain how the cash flows are structured in order to estimate the net advantage to leasing.

What discount rate should be used to evaluate a lease? Why?

Define the term "net advantage to leasing, NAL."

Evaluation by the Lessor

Thus far we have considered leasing only from the lessee's viewpoint. It is also useful to analyze the transaction as the lessor sees it: Is the lease a good investment for the party who must put up the money? The lessor will generally be a specialized leasing company, a bank or bank affiliate, an individual or group of individuals organized as a limited partnership or limited liability corporation, or a manufacturer such as IBM or GM that uses leasing as a sales tool. The specialized leasing companies are often owned by profitable companies such as General Electric, which owns General Electric Capital, the largest leasing company in the world. Investment banking houses such as Merrill Lynch also set up and/or work with specialized leasing companies, where brokerage clients' money is made available to leasing customers in deals which permit the investors to share in tax shelters provided by leases.

Any potential lessor needs to know the rate of return on the capital invested in the lease, and this information is also useful to the prospective lessee: Lease terms on large leases are generally negotiated, so the lessee should know what return the lessor is earning. The lessor's analysis involves (1) determining the net cash outlay, which is usually the invoice price of the leased equipment less any lease payments made in advance; (2) determining the periodic cash inflows, which consist of the lease payments minus both income taxes and any maintenance expense the lessor must bear; (3) estimating the after-tax residual value of the property when the lease expires; and (4) determining whether the rate of return on the lease exceeds the lessor's opportunity cost of capital or, equivalently, whether the NPV of the lease exceeds zero.

Analysis by the Lessor

See *Ch 20 Tool Kit.xls*.

To illustrate the lessor's analysis, we assume the same facts as for the Anderson Equipment Company lease, plus the following: (1) The potential lessor is a wealthy individual whose current income is in the form of interest, and whose marginal federal-plus-state income tax rate, T, is 40 percent. (2) The investor can buy 5-year bonds that have a 9 percent yield to maturity, providing an after-tax yield of (9%)(1 − T) = (9%)(0.6) = 5.4%. This is the after-tax return that the investor can obtain on alternative investments of similar risk. (3) The before-tax residual value is \$1,000,000. Because the asset will be depreciated to a book value of \$600,000 at the end of the 5-year lease, \$400,000 of this \$1 million will be taxable at the 40 percent rate because of the recapture of depreciation rule, so the lessor can expect to receive \$1,000,000 − 0.4(\$400,000) = \$840,000 after taxes from the sale of the equipment after the lease expires.

The lessor's cash flows are developed in Table 20-3. Here we see that the lease as an investment has a net present value of \$26,000. On a present value basis, the investor who invests in the lease rather than in the 9 percent bonds (5.4 percent after taxes) is better off by \$26,000, indicating that he or she should be willing to write the lease. As we saw earlier, the lease is also advantageous to Anderson Equipment Company, so the transaction should be completed.

TABLE 20-3 Lease Analysis from the Lessor's Viewpoint (Thousands of Dollars)

	Year 0	Year 1	Year 2	Year 3	Year 4	Year 5
1. Net purchase price	($10,000)					
2. Maintenance cost	(500)	($ 500)	($ 500)	($ 500)	($ 500)	
3. Maintenance tax savings	200	200	200	200	200	
4. Depreciation tax savings[a]		800	1,280	760	480	$ 440
5. Lease payment	2,750	2,750	2,750	2,750	2,750	
6. Tax on lease payment	(1,100)	(1,100)	(1,100)	(1,100)	(1,100)	
7. Residual value						1,000
8. Tax on residual value[b]						(160)
9. Net cash flow	($ 8,650)	$2,150	$2,630	$2,110	$1,830	$1,280

$$\text{NPV} = \sum_{t=0}^{5} \frac{\text{NCF}_t}{(1 + k)^t} = \$26 \text{ when } k = 5.4\%.$$

$$\text{IRR: NPV} = 0 = \sum_{t=0}^{5} \frac{\text{NCF}_t}{(1 + \text{IRR})^t}; \text{ IRR} = 5.5\%.$$

Notes:
[a]Depreciation times the lessor's tax rate.
[b](Residual value − Book value)T.
See the file ***Ch 20 Tool Kit.xls*** on the textbook's CD-ROM for details.

The investor can also calculate the lease investment's IRR based on the net cash flows shown on Line 9 of Table 20-3. The IRR of the lease, which is that discount rate that forces the NPV of the lease to zero, is 5.5 percent. Thus, the lease provides a 5.5 percent after-tax return to this 40 percent tax rate investor. This exceeds the 5.4 percent after-tax return on 9 percent bonds. So, using either the IRR or the NPV method, the lease would appear to be a satisfactory investment.[10]

Setting the Lease Payment

In the preceding sections we evaluated the lease assuming that the lease payments had already been specified. However, in large leases the parties generally sit down and work out an agreement on the size of the lease payments, with these payments being set so as to provide the lessor with some specific rate of return. In situations where the lease terms are not negotiated, which is often the case for small leases, the lessor must still go through the same type of analysis, setting terms that provide a target rate of return, and then offering these terms to the potential lessee on a take-it-or-leave-it basis.

To illustrate all this, suppose the potential lessor described earlier, after examining other alternative investment opportunities, decides that the 5.4 percent after-tax bond return is too low to use to evaluate the lease, and that the required after-tax return on the lease is 6.0 percent. What lease payment schedule would provide this return?

CD

To answer this question, note again that Table 20-3 contains the lessor's cash flow analysis. If the basic analysis is computerized, it is easy to first change the discount rate to 6 percent, and then change the lease payment—either by trial-and-error or by using the goal-seeking function—until the lease's NPV = $0 or, equivalently, its IRR = 6.0 percent. When we did this using ***Ch 20 Tool Kit.xls***, we found that the lessor must

[10]Note that the lease investment is actually slightly more risky than the alternative bond investment because the residual value cash flow is less certain than a principal repayment. Thus, the lessor might require an expected return somewhat above the 5.4 percent promised on a bond investment.

set the lease payment at $2,788,591.44 to obtain an after-tax rate of return of 6.0 percent. If this lease payment is not acceptable to the lessee, Anderson Company, then it may not be possible to strike a deal. Naturally, competition among leasing companies forces lessors to build market-related returns into their lease payment schedules.

Note that a lease payment of $2,788,591.44 would drive Anderson's NAL down to exactly zero. Thus, both the lessee and the lessor would have NAL = NPV = $0. Leasing is not always a zero sum game, but if the inputs to the lessee and the lessor are identical, as in this revised case, then a positive NAL to the lessee implies an equal but negative NPV to the lessor. *However, conditions are often such that leasing can provide net benefits to both parties. This situation arises because of differentials in taxes, in estimated residual values, or in the ability to bear the residual value risk.* We will explore these issues in detail in a later section.

Note that the lessor can, under certain conditions, increase the return on the lease by borrowing some of the funds used to purchase the leased asset. Such a lease is called a **leveraged lease.** Whether or not a lease is leveraged has no effect on the lessee's analysis, but it can have a significant effect on the cash flows to the lessor, hence on the lessor's expected rate of return. We discuss leveraged leases in more detail in the Web/CD Extension to this chapter.

Self-Test Questions

What discount rate is used in a lessor's NPV analysis?

What is the relationship between the lessor's IRR and the size of the lease payments?

Other Issues in Lease Analysis

The basic methods of analysis used by lessees and lessors were presented in the previous sections. However, some other issues warrant discussion.

Estimated Residual Value

It is important to note that the lessor owns the property upon expiration of a lease, hence the lessor has claim to the asset's residual value. Superficially, it would appear that if residual values are expected to be large, owning would have an advantage over leasing. However, this apparent advantage does not hold up. If expected residual values are large—as they may be under inflation for certain types of equipment and also if real estate is involved—competition between leasing companies and other financing sources, as well as competition among leasing companies themselves, will force leasing rates down to the point where potential residual values are fully recognized in the lease contract. Thus, the existence of large residual values is not likely to result in materially higher costs for leasing.

Increased Credit Availability

As noted earlier, leasing is sometimes said to have an advantage for firms that are seeking the maximum degree of financial leverage. First, it is sometimes argued that firms can obtain more money, and for longer terms, under a lease arrangement than under a loan secured by a specific piece of equipment. Second, since some leases do not appear on the balance sheet, lease financing has been said to give the firm a stronger appearance in a *superficial* credit analysis and thus to permit the firm to use more leverage than would be possible if it did not lease.

There may be some truth to these claims for smaller firms, but since firms are required to capitalize financial leases and to report them on their balance sheets, this point is of questionable validity for any firm large enough to have audited financial statements. However, leasing can be a way to circumvent existing loan covenants. If restrictive covenants prohibit a firm from issuing more debt but fail to restrict lease payments, then the firm could effectively increase its leverage by leasing additional assets. Also, firms that are in very poor financial condition and facing possible bankruptcy may be able to obtain lease financing at a lower cost than comparable debt financing because (1) lessors often have a more favorable position than lenders should the lessee actually go bankrupt and (2) lessors that specialize in certain types of equipment may be in a better position to dispose of repossessed equipment than banks or other lenders.

Real Estate Leases

Most of our examples have focused on equipment leasing. However, leasing originated with real estate, and such leases still constitute a huge segment of total lease financing. (We distinguish between housing rentals and long-term business leases; our concern is with business leases.) Retailers lease many of their stores. In some situations, retailers have no choice but to lease—this is true of locations in malls and certain office buildings. In other situations, they have a choice of building and owning versus leasing. Law firms and accounting firms, for example, can choose between buying their own facilities or leasing on a long-term basis (up to 20 or more years).

The type of lease-versus-purchase analysis we discussed in this chapter is just as applicable for real estate as for equipment—conceptually, there is no difference. Of course, such things as maintenance, who the other tenants will be, what alterations can be made, who will pay for alterations, and the like, become especially important with real property, but the analytical procedures upon which the lease-versus-buy decision is based are no different from any other lease analysis.

Vehicle Leases

Vehicle leasing is very popular today, both for large corporations and for individuals, especially professionals such as MBAs, doctors, lawyers, and accountants. For corporations, the key factor is often maintenance and disposal of used vehicles—the leasing companies are specialists here, and many businesses prefer to "outsource" services related to autos and tracks. For individuals, leasing is often more convenient, and it may be easier to justify tax deductions on leased than owned vehicles. Also, most auto leasing to individuals is through dealers. These dealers (and manufacturers) use leasing as a sales tool, and they often make the terms quite attractive, especially when it comes to the down payment, which may be nonexistent in the case of a lease.

Auto leasing also permits many individuals to drive more expensive cars than would otherwise be possible. For example, the monthly payment on a new BMW might be $1,000 when financed with a three-year loan, but the same car, if leased for three years, might cost only $499 a month. At first glance, it appears that leasing is less expensive than owning because the monthly payment is so much lower. However, such a simplistic analysis ignores the fact that payments end after the loan is paid off but continue indefinitely under leasing. By using the techniques described in this chapter, individuals can assess the true costs associated with auto leases and then rationally judge the merits of each type of auto financing.

Leasing and Tax Laws[11]

The ability to structure leases that are advantageous to both lessor and lessee depends in large part on tax laws. The four major tax factors that influence leasing are

[11]See Schallheim, *op. cit.*, Chapters 3 and 6, for an in-depth discussion of tax effects on leasing.

Lease Securitization

Compared with many markets, the leasing market is fragmented and inefficient. There are millions of potential lessees, including all equipment users. Some are in high tax brackets, some in low brackets. Some are financially sophisticated, some are not. Some have excellent credit ratings, some have poor credit. On the other side of the market are millions of potential lessors, including equipment manufacturers, banks, and individual investors, with different tax brackets and risk tolerances. If each lessee had to negotiate a separate deal for each lease, information and search costs would be so high that few leases would be written.

Tax laws complicate the picture. For example, the alternative minimum tax often has the effect of limiting the amount of depreciation a firm can utilize. In addition, a firm can't take a full half-year's depreciation on purchases in the fourth quarter if those purchases comprise more than 40 percent of total annual purchases. Instead, it can only take a half-quarter's depreciation, which is the equivalent of one-eighth of a year's depreciation.

Lease brokers have for many years served as facilitators in this complicated and inefficient market. Working with many different equipment manufacturers and lenders, brokers are in a position to match lessees with appropriate lessors in such a way that the full benefit of tax laws can be utilized.

Lease securitization, a new procedure, is the ultimate method of matching lessees with appropriate lessors. The first step is to create a portfolio consisting of numerous leases. The second step is to divide the leasing cash flows into different streams of income, called *tranches*. For example, one tranche might contain only lease payments, which would appeal to an investor in a low tax bracket. A second tranche might consist of depreciation, which a high tax bracket investor could use to shelter income from other sources. A third might contain the residual cash flows, which will occur in the future when the leases end. This tranche would appeal to a high tax bracket investor who can take some risk. Tranches can also be allocated according to the credit rating of the lessees, allowing investors with different risk tolerances to take on their desired level of risk.

In addition, a company might obtain a lease in its fourth quarter, but if this is the third quarter of the lessor's fiscal year, the lessor can take a full half-year's depreciation.

Sound complicated? It is, but it's an efficient answer to an inefficient market.

Source: SMG Fairfax, Knoxville, Tennessee.

(1) investment tax credits, (2) depreciation rules, (3) tax rates, and (4) the alternative minimum tax. In this section, we briefly discuss each of these factors and how they influence leasing decisions.

The investment tax credit (ITC), when it is allowed, is a direct reduction of taxes that occurs when a firm purchases new capital equipment. Prior to 1987, firms could immediately deduct up to 10 percent of the cost of new capital investments from their corporate tax bills. Thus, a company that bought a $1,000,000 mainframe computer system would get a $100,000 reduction in current-year taxes. Because the ITC goes to the owner of the capital asset, low-tax-bracket companies that could not otherwise use the ITC could use leasing as a vehicle to pass immediate tax savings to high-tax-bracket lessors. The ITC is not currently in effect, but it could be reinstated in the future. If the ITC is put back into law, leasing would become especially attractive to low-tax-bracket firms.

Owners recover their investments in capital assets through depreciation, which is a tax-deductible expense. Because of the time value of money, the faster an asset can be depreciated, the greater the tax advantages of ownership. Recent tax law changes have tended to slow depreciation write-offs, thus reducing the value of ownership. This has also reduced the advantage to leasing by low-tax-bracket lessees from high-tax-bracket lessors. Any move to liberalize depreciation rules would tend to make leasing more desirable in many situations. The value of depreciation also depends on the firm's tax rate, because the depreciation tax saving equals the amount of depreciation multiplied by the tax rate. Thus, higher corporate tax rates mean greater ownership tax savings, hence more incentive for tax-driven leases.

Finally, the alternative minimum tax (AMT) also affects leasing activity. Corporations are permitted to use accelerated depreciation and other tax shelters on their tax books but then use straight-line depreciation for reporting results to shareholders. Thus, some firms report to the IRS that they are doing poorly and hence pay little or no taxes, but report high earnings to shareholders. The corporate AMT, which is roughly computed by applying a 20 percent tax rate to the profits reported to shareholders, is designed to force highly profitable companies to pay at least some taxes even if they have tax shelters that push their taxable income to zero. In effect, all firms (and individuals) must compute the "regular" tax and the AMT tax, and then pay the higher of the two.

Companies with large AMT liabilities look for ways to reduce their tax bills by lowering reported income. Leasing can be beneficial here—a relatively short-term lease with high annual payments will increase reported expenses and thus lower reported profits. Note that the lease does not have to qualify as a guideline lease and be deducted for regular tax purposes—all that is needed is to lower reported income as shown on the income statement.

We see that tax laws and differential tax rates between lessors and lessees can be a motivating force for leasing. However, as we discuss in the next section, there are some sound nontax economic reasons why firms lease plant and equipment.

Self-Test Questions

Does leasing lead to increased credit availability?

How do tax laws affect leasing?

Other Reasons for Leasing

Up to this point, we have noted that tax rate or other differentials are generally necessary to make leasing attractive to both the lessee and lessor. If the lessee and lessor are facing different tax situations, including the alternative minimum tax, then it is often possible to structure a lease that is beneficial to both parties. However, there are other reasons firms might want to lease an asset rather than buy it.

As discussed in the opening section, more than half of all commercial aircraft are leased, and smaller airlines, especially in developing nations, lease an especially high percentage of their planes. One of the reasons for this lease usage is that airlines can reduce their risks by leasing. If an airline purchases all its aircraft, it would be hampered in its ability to respond to changing market conditions. Because they have become specialists at matching airlines with available aircraft, the aircraft lessors (which are multi-billion-dollar concerns) are quite good at managing the changing demand for different types of aircraft. This permits them to offer attractive lease terms. In this situation, **leasing provides operating flexibility.** Leasing is not necessarily less expensive than buying, but the operating flexibility is quite valuable.

Leasing is also an attractive alternative for many high-technology items that are subject to rapid and unpredictable technological obsolescence. Say a small rural hospital wants to buy a magnetic resonance imaging (MRI) device. If it buys the MRI equipment, it is exposed to the risk of technological obsolescence. In a short time some new technology might lower the value of the current system and thus render the project unprofitable. Since it does not use much equipment of this nature, the hospital would bear a great deal of risk if it bought the MRI device. However, a lessor that specializes in state-of-the-art medical equipment would be exposed to significantly less risk. By purchasing and then leasing many different items, the lessor benefits from diversification. Of course, over time some items will probably lose more value than the lessor expected, but this will be offset by other items that retained more value than was expected. Also, because such a leasing company will be especially familiar with the market for used medical equipment, it can refurbish the equipment and then get a better price in the resale market than could a remote rural hospital. For these reasons, leasing can reduce the risk of technological obsolescence.

Leasing can also be attractive when a firm is uncertain about the demand for its products or services, and thus about how long the equipment will be needed. Again, consider the hospital industry. Hospitals often offer services that are dependent on a single staff member—for example, a physician who does liver transplants. To support the physician's practice, the hospital might have to invest millions in equipment that can be used only for this particular procedure. The hospital will charge for the use of the equipment, and if things go as expected, the investment will be profitable. However, if the physician leaves the hospital, and if no replacement can be recruited, then the project is dead, and the equipment becomes useless to the hospital. In this case, a lease with a cancellation clause would permit the hospital to simply return the equipment. The lessor would charge something for the cancellation clause, and this would lower the expected profitability of the project, but it would provide the hospital with an option to abandon the equipment, and the value of the option could easily exceed the incremental cost of the cancellation clause. The leasing company would be willing to write this option because it is in a better position to remarket the equipment, either by writing another lease or by selling it outright.

The leasing industry recently introduced a type of lease that even transfers some of a project's operating risk from the lessee to the lessor, and also motivates the lessor to maintain the leased equipment in good working order. Instead of making a fixed rental payment, the lessee pays a fee each time the leased equipment is used. This type of lease originated with copy machines, where the lessee pays so much per month plus an additional amount per copy made. If the machine breaks down, no copies are made, and the lessor's rental income declines. This motivates the lessor to repair the machine quickly.

This type of lease is also used in the health care industry, where it is called a "per-procedure lease." For example, a hospital might lease an X-ray machine for a fixed fee per X-ray, say, $5. If demand for the machine's X rays is less than expected by the hospital, revenues will be lower than expected, but so will the machine's capital costs. Conversely, high demand would lead to higher-than-expected lease costs, but these would be offset by higher-than-expected revenues. By using a per-procedure lease, the hospital is converting a fixed cost for the equipment into a variable cost, hence reducing the machine's operating leverage and breakeven point. The net effect is to reduce the project's risk. Of course, the expected cost of a per-procedure lease might be more than the cost of a conventional lease, but the risk reduction benefit could be worth the cost. Note too that if the lessor writes a large number of per-procedure leases, much of the riskiness inherent in such leases could be eliminated by diversification, so the risk premiums that lessors build into per-procedure lease payments could be low enough to attract potential lessees.

Some companies also find leasing attractive because the lessor is able to provide servicing on favorable terms. For example, Virco Manufacturing, a company that makes school desks and other furniture, recently leased 25 truck tractors and 140 trailers that it uses to ship furniture from its plant. The lease agreement, with a large leasing company that specializes in purchasing, maintaining, and then reselling trucks, permitted the replacement of an aging fleet that Virco had built up over the years. "We are pretty good at manufacturing furniture, but we aren't very good at maintaining a truck fleet," said Virco's CFO.

There are other reasons that might cause a firm to lease an asset rather than buy it. Often, these reasons are difficult to quantify, hence they cannot be easily incorporated into an NPV or IRR analysis. Nevertheless, a sound lease decision must begin with a quantitative analysis, and then qualitative factors can be considered before making the final lease-or-buy decision.

Self-Test Question

Describe some economic factors which might provide an advantage to leasing.

Summary

In the United States, more than 30 percent of all equipment is leased, as is a great deal of real estate. Consequently, leasing is an important financing vehicle. In this chapter, we discussed the leasing decision from the standpoints of both the lessee and lessor. The key concepts covered are listed below:

- The four most important types of lease agreement are (1) **operating lease,** (2) **financial,** or **capital, lease,** (3) **sale and leaseback,** and (4) **combination lease.**
- The IRS has specific guidelines that apply to lease arrangements. A lease that meets these guidelines is called a **guideline,** or **tax-oriented, lease,** because the IRS permits the lessor to deduct the asset's depreciation and allows the lessee to deduct the lease payments. A lease that does not meet the IRS guidelines is called a **non-tax-oriented lease,** in which case ownership for tax purposes resides with the lessee rather than the lessor.
- **FASB Statement 13** spells out the conditions under which a lease must be **capitalized** (shown directly on the balance sheet) as opposed to shown only in the notes to the financial statements. Generally, leases that run for a period equal to or greater than 75 percent of the asset's life must be capitalized.
- The lessee's analysis consists basically of a comparison of the PV of costs associated with leasing versus the PV of costs associated with owning. The difference in these costs is called the **net advantage to leasing (NAL).**
- One of the key issues in the lessee's analysis is the appropriate discount rate. Because a lease is a substitute for debt, because the cash flows in a lease analysis are stated on an after-tax basis, and because they are known with relative certainty, the appropriate discount rate is the **lessee's after-tax cost of debt.** A higher discount rate may be used on the **residual value** if it is substantially riskier than the other flows.
- The lessor evaluates the lease as an **investment.** If the lease's NPV is greater than zero, or if its IRR is greater than the lessor's opportunity cost, then the lease should be written.
- Leasing is motivated by various differences between lessees and lessors. Three of the most important reasons for leasing are (1) **tax rate differentials,** (2) leases in which the lessor is better able to bear the **residual value risk** than the lessee, and (3) situations where the lessor can maintain the leased equipment more efficiently than the lessee.

The Web/CD Extension to this chapter provide some additional information on leasing.

Questions

20–1 Define each of the following terms:

a. Lessee; lessor

b. Operating lease; financial lease; sale and leaseback; combination lease; leveraged lease

c. "Off-balance sheet" financing; capitalizing
d. FASB Statement 13
e. Guideline lease
f. Residual value
g. Lessee's analysis; lessor's analysis
h. Net advantage to leasing (NAL)
i. Alternative minimum tax (AMT)

20–2 Distinguish between operating leases and financial leases. Would you be more likely to find an operating lease employed for a fleet of trucks or for a manufacturing plant?

20–3 Would you be more likely to find that lessees are in high or low income tax brackets as compared with lessors?

20–4 Commercial banks moved heavily into equipment leasing during the early 1970s, acting as lessors. One major reason for this invasion of the leasing industry was to gain the benefits of accelerated depreciation and the investment tax credit on leased equipment. During this same period, commercial banks were investing heavily in municipal securities, and they were also making loans to real estate investment trusts (REITs). In the mid-1970s, these REITs got into such serious difficulty that many banks suffered large losses on their REIT loans. Explain how its investments in municipal bonds and REITs could reduce a bank's willingness to act as a lessor.

20–5 One alleged advantage of leasing voiced in the past is that it kept liabilities off the balance sheet, thus making it possible for a firm to obtain more leverage than it otherwise could have. This raised the question of whether or not both the lease obligation and the asset involved should be capitalized and shown on the balance sheet. Discuss the pros and cons of capitalizing leases and related assets.

20–6 Suppose there were no IRS restrictions on what constituted a valid lease. Explain, in a manner that a legislator might understand, why some restrictions should be imposed. Illustrate your answer with numbers.

20–7 Suppose Congress enacted new tax law changes that would (1) permit equipment to be depreciated over a shorter period, (2) lower corporate tax rates, and (3) reinstate the investment tax credit. Discuss how each of these potential changes would affect the relative volume of leasing versus conventional debt in the U.S. economy.

20–8 In our Anderson Equipment Company example, we assumed that the lease could not be cancelled. What effect would a cancellation clause have on the lessee's analysis? On the lessor's analysis?

Self-Test Problem (Solution Appears in Appendix A)

ST–1 *LEASE VERSUS BUY* The Randolph Teweles Company (RTC) has decided to acquire a new truck. One alternative is to lease the truck on a 4-year guideline contract for a lease payment of $10,000 per year, with payments to be made at the *beginning* of each year. The lease would include maintenance. Alternatively, RTC could purchase the truck outright for $40,000, financing the purchase by a bank loan for the net purchase price and amortizing the loan over a 4-year period at an interest rate of 10 percent per year. Under the borrow-to-purchase arrangement, RTC would have to maintain the truck at a cost of $1,000 per year, payable at year end. The truck falls into the MACRS 3-year class. It has a residual value of $10,000, which is the expected market value after 4 years, when RTC plans to replace the truck irrespective of whether it leases or buys. RTC has a marginal federal-plus-state tax rate of 40 percent.

a. What is RTC's PV cost of leasing?
b. What is RTC's PV cost of owning? Should the truck be leased or purchased?
c. The appropriate discount rate for use in the analysis is the firm's after-tax cost of debt. Why?
d. The residual value is the least certain cash flow in the analysis. How might RTC incorporate differential riskiness of this cash flow into the analysis?

Problems

20–1 BALANCE SHEET EFFECTS

Reynolds Construction needs a piece of equipment that costs $200. Reynolds either can lease the equipment or borrow $200 from a local bank and buy the equipment. If the equipment is leased, the lease would *not* have to be capitalized. Reynolds' balance sheet prior to the acquisition of the equipment is as follows:

Current assets	$300	Debt	$400
Net fixed assets	500	Equity	400
Total assets	$800	Total claims	$800

a. (1) What is Reynolds' current debt ratio?
(2) What would be the company's debt ratio if it purchased the equipment?
(3) What would be the debt ratio if the equipment were leased?

b. Would the company's financial risk be different under the leasing and purchasing alternatives?

20–2 LEASE VERSUS BUY

Assume that Reynolds' tax rate is 40 percent and the equipment's depreciation would be $100 per year. If the company leased the asset on a 2-year lease, the payment would be $110 at the beginning of each year. If Reynolds borrowed and bought, the bank would charge 10 percent interest on the loan. Should Reynolds lease or buy the equipment?

20–3 LEASE VERSUS BUY

Big Sky Mining Company must install $1.5 million of new machinery in its Nevada mine. It can obtain a bank loan for 100 percent of the purchase price, or it can lease the machinery. Assume that the following facts apply:

(1) The machinery falls into the MACRS 3-year class.
(2) Estimated maintenance expenses are $75,000 per year, payable at the beginning of each year.
(3) The firm's tax rate is 40 percent.
(4) The loan would have an interest rate of 15 percent.
(5) The lease terms call for $400,000 payments at the end of each of the next 4 years.
(6) Under either the lease or the purchase, Big Sky must pay for insurance, property taxes, and maintenance.
(7) Assume that Big Sky Mining will continue to use the machine beyond the expiration of the lease and must purchase it at an estimated residual value of $250,000 at the end of the 4th year.

What is the NAL of the lease?

20–4 BALANCE SHEET EFFECTS

Two companies, Energen and Hastings Corporation, began operations with identical balance sheets. A year later, both required additional manufacturing capacity at a cost of $50,000. Energen obtained a 5-year, $50,000 loan at an 8 percent interest rate from its bank. Hastings, on the other hand, decided to lease the required $50,000 capacity for 5 years, and an 8 percent return was built into the lease. The balance sheet for each company, before the asset increases, follows:

		Debt	$50,000
		Equity	100,000
Total assets	$150,000	Total claims	$150,000

a. Show the balance sheets for both firms after the asset increases and calculate each firm's new debt ratio. (Assume that the lease is not capitalized.)

b. Show how Hastings's balance sheet would look immediately after the financing if it capitalized the lease.

c. Would the rate of return (1) on assets and (2) on equity be affected by the choice of financing? How?

20–5
LEASE VERSUS BUY

A. Sadik Industries must install $1 million of new machinery in its Texas plant. It can obtain a bank loan for 100 percent of the required amount. Alternatively, a Texas investment banking firm which represents a group of investors believes that it can arrange for a lease financing plan. Assume that these facts apply:

(1) The equipment falls in the MACRS 3-year class.
(2) Estimated maintenance expenses are $50,000 per year.
(3) The firm's tax rate is 34 percent.
(4) If the money is borrowed, the bank loan will be at a rate of 14 percent, amortized in 3 equal installments at the end of each year.
(5) The tentative lease terms call for payments of $320,000 at the end of each year for 3 years. The lease is a guideline lease.
(6) Under the proposed lease terms, the lessee must pay for insurance, property taxes, and maintenance.
(7) Sadik must use the equipment if it is to continue in business, so it will almost certainly want to acquire the property at the end of the lease. If it does, then under the lease terms it can purchase the machinery at its fair market value at that time. The best estimate of this market value is $200,000, but it could be much higher or lower under certain circumstances.

To assist management in making the proper lease-versus-buy decision, you are asked to answer the following questions:

a. Assuming that the lease can be arranged, should the firm lease or borrow and buy the equipment? Explain. (Hint: In this situation, the firm plans to use the asset beyond the term of the lease. Thus, the residual value becomes a *cost* to leasing in Year 3. Also, there is no Year 3 residual value tax consequence, as the firm cannot immediately deduct the Year 3 purchase price from taxable income.)

b. Consider the $200,000 estimated residual value. Is it appropriate to discount it at the same rate as the other cash flows? What about the other cash flows—are they all equally risky? (Hint: Riskier cash flows are normally discounted at higher rates, but when the cash flows are *costs* rather than *inflows*, the normal procedure must be reversed.)

Spreadsheet Problems

20–6
BUILD A MODEL: LESSEE'S ANALYSIS

Start with the partial model in the file ***Ch 20-6 Build a Model.xls*** from the textbook's CD-ROM. As part of its overall plant modernization and cost reduction program, Western Fabrics' management has decided to install a new automated weaving loom. In the capital budgeting analysis of this equipment, the IRR of the project was found to be 20 percent versus a project required return of 12 percent.

The loom has an invoice price of $250,000, including delivery and installation charges. The funds needed could be borrowed from the bank through a 4-year amortized loan at a 10 percent interest rate, with payments to be made at the end of each year. In the event the loom is purchased, the manufacturer will contract to maintain and service it for a fee of $20,000 per year paid at the end of each year. The loom falls in the MACRS 5-year class, and Western's marginal federal-plus-state tax rate is 40 percent.

Aubey Automation Inc., maker of the loom, has offered to lease the loom to Western for $70,000 upon delivery and installation (at $t = 0$) plus 4 additional annual lease payments of $70,000 to be made at the end of Years 1 to 4. (Note that there are 5 lease payments in total.) The lease agreement includes maintenance and servicing. Actually, the loom has an expected life of 8 years, at which time its expected salvage value is zero; however, after 4 years, its market value is expected to equal its book value of $42,500. Western plans to build an entirely new plant in 4 years, so it has no interest in either leasing or owning the proposed loom for more than that period.

a. Should the loom be leased or purchased?

b. The salvage value is clearly the most uncertain cash flow in the analysis. What effect would a salvage value risk adjustment have on the analysis? (Assume that the appropriate salvage value pre-tax discount rate is 15 percent.)

c. Assuming that the after-tax cost of debt should be used to discount all anticipated cash flows, at what lease payment would the firm be indifferent to either leasing or buying?

20–7 *WHAT IF ANALYSIS: LESSOR'S ANALYSIS* Start with the file ***Ch 20-7 What If Analysis.xls*** from the textbook's CD-ROM and answer the questions shown there.

Cyberproblem

The information related to this cyberproblem is likely to change over time, due to the release of new information and the ever-changing nature of the World Wide Web. Accordingly, we will periodically update the problem on the textbook's web site.

20–8 *LEASE ANALYSIS* This chapter has introduced leasing as a type of financing that companies may use to avoid heavy capital investment in property and equipment. While Chapter 20 examines the prospect of leasing from a corporate standpoint, it is important to realize that leasing can have a rather profound effect upon personal financial decisions.

Imagine that you have decided to get a new automobile. Even as recently as 20 or 30 years ago, your only option was to purchase the vehicle. However, in recent years, the practice of auto leasing has skyrocketed. The determination of a car lease can be very complicated and warrants serious consideration. Suppose you are considering leasing a car. The dealer has given you the following parameters for your lease:

Car price (capitalized cost)	$22,000
Value of trade-in (for your car)	$0
Down payment	$0
Length of the lease	24 months
Residual value of car	$15,000
Sales tax rate	7%
Interest rate	8%

Go to the textbook's web site at **http://www.harcourtcollege.com/finance/theory/student/resources/cyberprob/ch20.html** and answer the questions shown there.

Mini Case

See **Ch 20 Show.ppt** and ***Ch 20 Mini Case.xls***.

Lewis Securities Inc. has decided to acquire a new market data and quotation system for its Richmond home office. The system receives current market prices and other information from several online data services, then either displays the information on a screen or stores it for later retrieval by the firm's brokers. The system also permits customers to call up current quotes on terminals in the lobby.

The equipment costs $1,000,000, and, if it were purchased, Lewis could obtain a term loan for the full purchase price at a 10 percent interest rate. The equipment is classified as a special-purpose computer, so it falls into the MACRS 3-year class. If the system were purchased, a 4-year maintenance contract could be obtained at a cost of $20,000 per year, payable at the *beginning* of each year. The equipment would be sold after 4 years, and the best estimate of its residual value at that time is $100,000. However, since real-time display system technology is changing rapidly, the actual residual value is uncertain.

As an alternative to the borrow-and-buy plan, the equipment manufacturer informed Lewis that Consolidated Leasing would be willing to write a 4-year guideline lease on the equipment, including maintenance, for payments of $280,000 at the *beginning* of each year. Lewis's marginal federal-plus-state tax rate is 40 percent. You have been asked to analyze the lease-versus-purchase decision, and in the process to answer the following questions:

a. (1) Who are the two parties to a lease transaction?
   (2) What are the four primary types of leases, and what are their characteristics?
   (3) How are leases classified for tax purposes?
   (4) What effect does leasing have on a firm's balance sheet?
   (5) What effect does leasing have on a firm's capital structure?

b. (1) What is the present value cost of owning the equipment? (Hint: Set up a time line that shows the net cash flows over the period t = 0 to t = 4, and then find the PV of these net cash flows, or the PV cost of owning.)
   (2) Explain the rationale for the discount rate you used to find the PV.

c. What is Lewis's present value cost of leasing the equipment? (Hint: Again, construct a time line.)

d. What is the net advantage to leasing (NAL)? Does your analysis indicate that Lewis should buy or lease the equipment? Explain.

e. Now assume that the equipment's residual value could be as low as $0 or as high as $200,000, but that $100,000 is the expected value. Since the residual value is riskier than the other cash flows in the analysis, this differential risk should be incorporated into the analysis. Describe how this could be accomplished. (No calculations are necessary, but explain how you would modify the analysis if calculations were required.) What effect would increased uncertainty about the residual value have on Lewis's lease-versus-purchase decision?

f. The lessee compares the cost of owning the equipment with the cost of leasing it. Now put yourself in the lessor's shoes. In a few sentences, how should you analyze the decision to write or not write the lease?

g. (1) Assume that the lease payments were actually $300,000 per year, that Consolidated Leasing is also in the 40 percent tax bracket, and that it also forecasts a $100,000 residual value. Also, to furnish the maintenance support, Consolidated would have to purchase a maintenance contract from the manufacturer at the same $20,000 annual cost, again paid in advance. Consolidated Leasing can obtain an expected 10 percent pre-tax return on investments of similar risk. What would Consolidated's NPV and IRR of leasing be under these conditions?
   (2) What do you think the lessor's NPV would be if the lease payment were set at $280,000 per year? (Hint: The lessor's cash flows would be a "mirror image" of the lessee's cash flows.)

h. Lewis's management has been considering moving to a new downtown location, and they are concerned that these plans may come to fruition prior to the expiration of the lease. If the move occurs, Lewis would buy or lease an entirely new set of equipment, and hence management would like to include a cancellation clause in the lease contract. What effect would such a clause have on the riskiness of the lease from Lewis's standpoint? From the lessor's standpoint? If you were the lessor, would you insist on changing any of the lease terms if a cancellation clause were added? Should the cancellation clause contain any restrictive covenants and/or penalties of the type contained in bond indentures or provisions similar to call premiums?

Selected Additional References and Cases

For information on the percentage cost of leasing, leasing's effects on capital budgeting, and leveraged leases, see the Web/CD Extension to this chapter.

For a description of lease analysis in practice, as well as a comprehensive bibliography of the leasing literature, see

Mukherjee, Tarun K., "A Survey of Corporate Leasing Analysis," *Financial Management*, Autumn 1991, 96–107.

O'Brien, Thomas J., and Bennie H. Nunnally, Jr., "A 1982 Survey of Corporate Leasing Analysis," *Financial Management*, Summer 1983, 30–36.

Many of the theoretical issues surrounding lease analysis are discussed in the following articles:

Finucane, Thomas J., "Some Empirical Evidence on the Use of Financial Leases," *The Journal of Financial Research*, Fall 1988, 321–333.

Hochman, Shalom, and Ramon Rabinovitch, "Financial Leasing under Inflation," *Financial Management*, Spring 1984, 17–26.

Levy, Haim, and Marshall Sarnat, "Leasing, Borrowing, and Financial Risk," *Financial Management*, Winter 1979, 47–54.

Lewellen, Wilbur G., Michael S. Long, and John J. McConnell, "Asset Leasing in Competitive Capital Markets," *Journal of Finance*, June 1976, 787–798.

Miller, Merton H., and Charles W. Upton, "Leasing, Buying, and the Cost of Capital Services," *Journal of Finance*, June 1976, 761–786.

Schall, Lawrence D., "The Evaluation of Lease Financing Opportunities," *Midland Corporate Finance Journal*, Spring 1985, 48–65.

Leveraged lease analysis is discussed in these articles:

Athanasopoulos, Peter J., and Peter W. Bacon, "The Evaluation of Leveraged Leases," *Financial Management*, Spring 1980, 76–80.

Dyl, Edward A., and Stanley A. Martin, Jr., "Setting Terms for Leveraged Leases," *Financial Management*, Winter 1977, 20–27.

Grimlund, Richard A., and Robert Capettini, "A Note on the Evaluation of Leveraged Leases and Other Investments," *Financial Management*, Summer 1982, 68–72.

Perg, Wayne F., "Leveraged Leasing: The Problem of Changing Leverage," *Financial Management*, Autumn 1978, 47–51.

For a discussion of realized returns on lease contracts, see

Lease, Ronald C., John J. McConnell, and James S. Schallheim, "Realized Returns and the Default and Prepayment Experience of Financial Leasing Contracts," *Financial Management*, Summer 1990, 11–20.

The Summer 1987 issue of Financial Management *contains articles by H. Martin Weingartner, Roger L. Cason, and Lawrence D. Schall that focus on the impact of asset life uncertainty on lease analysis.*

The Option Pricing Model (OPM) has been used in lease analysis by

Copeland, Thomas E., and J. Fred Weston, "A Note on the Evaluation of Cancellable Operating Leases," *Financial Management*, Summer 1982, 60–67.

Lee, Wayne Y., John D. Martin, and Andrew J. Senchack, "The Case for Using Options to Evaluate Salvage Values in Financial Leases," *Financial Management*, Autumn 1982, 33–41.

For a discussion of the impact of the AMT on lease decisions, see

"The Effect of the Corporate Alternative Minimum Tax: Amount, Duration, and Effect on the Lease versus Buy Decision," *The Journal of Equipment Lease Financing*, Spring 1989, 7–26.

The Cases in Financial Management: Dryden Request *series contains the following cases that deal with lease analysis:*

Case 25, "Environmental Sciences, Inc.," Case 25A, "Agro Chemical Corporation," and Case 25B, "Friendly Food Stores, Inc.," Case 26, "Prudent Solutions, Inc.," and Case 61, "AgroGrow, Inc.," all of which examine the lease decision from the perspectives of both the lessee and the lessor.

21

Hybrid Financing: Preferred Stock, Warrants, and Convertibles

The use of convertible securities—generally bonds or preferred stocks that can be exchanged for common stock of the issuing corporation—has soared during the last decade. Why do companies use convertibles so heavily? To answer this question, first recognize that convertibles virtually always have coupon rates that are lower than would be required on straight, nonconvertible bonds or preferred stocks. Therefore, if a company raises $100 million by issuing convertible bonds, its interest expense is lower than if it financed with nonconvertible debt. But why would investors be willing to buy convertibles, given their lower cash payments? The answer lies in the conversion feature—if the price of the issuer's stock rises, the convertible bondholder can exchange it for stock and realize a capital gain.

A convertible bond's value is based partly on interest rates in the economy and partly on the price of the stock into which it is convertible, whereas a nonconvertible bond's price is based entirely on interest rates. Therefore, convertibles' prices go up and down much more than regular bonds' prices, which makes convertibles relatively risky. A recent article in *Forbes* reported that if a company's common stock increases in value, the returns on its convertibles also rise, but by only 70 percent of the stock's percentage increase. However, if the stock declines, the convertible will decline by only 50 percent of the stock's decline. Thus, while convertibles are more risky than straight bonds, they are less risky than stock.

To illustrate all this, consider the case of Amazon.com, which in January 1999 issued $1.25 billion of convertible bonds, the largest such offering in history. Amazon's bonds had a par value of $1,000 and a 4.75 percent coupon rate. Because they can be converted to Amazon common stock, changes in the stock price have had a profound effect on the convertibles' value.

During 1999 Amazon's convertibles took their holders on a wild ride. During the first four months Amazon's stock rose about 70 percent, causing its convertibles to rise by 50 percent, to $1,500. During the next four months, the stock lost more than 60 percent of its value, to a level 30 percent below where it was trading when the convertibles were issued. This caused the convertibles' price to drop to $750. Three months later Amazon's stock had rebounded, and its convertibles were once again trading above $1,500, only to decline sharply one month later. By year-end 1999, the convertibles were back to their $1,000 issue price. Thus, someone holding the bond for the entire year would have ended up close to where he or she had started, with a total return just shy of the 4.75 percent coupon rate.

When you finish this chapter, you should have a good understanding of what convertibles are, how they are valued, and why a firm might choose to issue a convertible bond rather than either straight debt or common stock.

Source: John Gorham, "Chicken Little Stocks," *Forbes*, December 27, 1999, 200.

In previous chapters we examined common stocks and the various types of long-term debt. In this chapter, we examine three other types of long-term capital: (1) *preferred stock*, which is a hybrid security that represents a cross between debt and common equity; (2) *warrants*, which are derivative securities issued by firms to facilitate the issuance of some other type of security; and (3) *convertibles*, which combine the features of debt (or preferred stock) and warrants.

Preferred Stock

The textbook's CD-ROM contains an *Excel* file that will guide you through the chapter's calculations. The file for this chapter is ***Ch 21 Tool Kit.xls***, and we encourage you to open the file and follow along as you read the chapter.

Preferred stock is a hybrid—it is similar to bonds in some respects and to common stock in other ways. Accountants classify preferred stock as equity, hence show it on the balance sheet as an equity account. However, from a finance perspective preferred stock lies somewhere between debt and common equity—it imposes a fixed charge and thus increases the firm's financial leverage, yet omitting the preferred dividend does not force a company into bankruptcy. Also, unlike interest on debt, preferred dividends are not deductible by the issuing corporation, so preferred stock has a higher cost of capital than debt. We first describe the basic features of preferred, after which we discuss other types of preferred stock, and the advantages and disadvantages of preferred stock.

Basic Features

Preferred stock has a par (or liquidating) value, often either \$25 or \$100. The dividend is stated as either a percentage of par, as so many dollars per share, or both ways. For example, several years ago Klondike Paper Company sold 150,000 shares of \$100 par value perpetual preferred stock for a total of \$15 million. This preferred had a stated annual dividend of \$12 per share, so the preferred dividend yield was \$12/\$100 = 0.12, or 12 percent, at the time of issue. The dividend was set when the stock was issued; it will not be changed in the future. Therefore, if the required rate of return on preferred, k_p, changes from 12 percent after the issue date—as it did—then the market price of the preferred stock will go up or down. Currently, k_p for Klondike Paper's preferred is 9 percent, and the price of the preferred has risen from \$100 to \$12/0.09 = \$133.33.

If the preferred dividend is not earned, the company does not have to pay it. However, most preferred issues are **cumulative,** meaning that the cumulative total of unpaid preferred dividends must be paid before dividends can be paid on the common stock. Unpaid preferred dividends are called **arrearages.** Dividends in arrears do not earn interest; thus, arrearages do not grow in a compound interest sense—they only grow from additional nonpayments of the preferred dividend. Also, many preferred stocks accrue arrearages for only a limited number of years, say, three years, meaning that the cumulative feature ceases after three years. However, the dividends in arrears continue in force until they are paid.

Preferred stock normally has no voting rights. However, most preferred issues stipulate that the preferred stockholders can elect a minority of the directors—say, three out of ten—if the preferred dividend is passed (omitted). Some preferreds even entitle their holders to elect a majority of the board.

Although nonpayment of preferred dividends will not bankrupt a company, corporations issue preferred with every intention of paying the dividend. Even if passing the dividend does not give the preferred stockholders control of the company, failure to pay a preferred dividend precludes payment of common dividends. In addition, passing the dividend makes it difficult to raise capital by selling bonds, and virtually impossible to sell more preferred or common stock except at rock bottom prices.

However, having preferred stock outstanding does give a firm the chance to overcome its difficulties—if bonds had been used instead of preferred stock, a company could be forced into bankruptcy before it could straighten out its problems. *Thus, from the viewpoint of the issuing corporation, preferred stock is less risky than bonds.*

However, for an investor preferred stock is riskier than bonds: (1) Preferred stockholders' claims are subordinated to those of bondholders in the event of liquidation, and (2) bondholders are more likely to continue receiving income during hard times than are preferred stockholders. Accordingly, investors require a higher after-tax rate of return on a given firm's preferred stock than on its bonds. However, since 70 percent of preferred dividends is exempt from corporate taxes, preferred stock is attractive to corporate investors. Indeed, high-grade preferred stock, on average, sells on a lower pre-tax yield basis than high-grade bonds. As an example, Du Pont's preferred stock recently had a market yield of about 7.0 percent, whereas its bonds provided a yield of 8.3 percent, or 1.3 percentage points *more* than its preferred. The tax treatment accounted for this differential; the *after-tax yield* to corporate investors was greater on the preferred stock than on the bonds.[1]

About half of all preferred stock issued in recent years has been convertible into common stock. For example, Enron Corporation issued preferred stock that stipulated that one share of preferred could be converted into three shares of common, at the option of the preferred stockholder. Convertibles are discussed at length in a later section.

Some preferred stocks are similar to perpetual bonds in that they have no maturity date, but most new issues now have specified maturities. For example, many preferred shares have a sinking fund provision that calls for the retirement of 2 percent of the issue each year, meaning that the issue will "mature" in a maximum of 50 years. Also, many preferred issues are callable by the issuing corporation, which can also limit the life of the preferred.[2]

Nonconvertible preferred stock is virtually all owned by corporations, which can take advantage of the 70 percent dividend exclusion to obtain a higher after-tax yield on preferred stock than on bonds. Individuals should not own preferred stocks (except convertible preferreds)—they can get higher yields on safer bonds, so it is not logical for them to hold preferreds.[3] As a result of this ownership pattern, the volume of preferred stock financing is geared to the supply of money in the hands of corporate investors. When the supply of such money is plentiful, the prices of preferred stocks are bid up, their yields fall, and investment bankers suggest that companies that need financing consider issuing preferred stock.

For issuers, preferred stock has a tax *disadvantage* relative to debt—interest expense is deductible, but preferred dividends are not. Still, firms with low tax rates may have

---

[1]The after-tax yield on an 8.3 percent bond to a corporate investor in the 34 percent marginal tax rate bracket is $8.3\%(1 - T) = 8.3\%(0.66) = 5.48\%$. The after-tax yield on a 7.0 percent preferred stock is $7.0\%(1 - \text{Effective T}) = 7.0\%[1 - (0.30)(0.34)] = 7.0\%(0.898) = 6.29\%$. Also, note that tax law prohibits firms from issuing debt and then using the proceeds to purchase another firm's preferred stock. If debt is used for stock purchases, then the 70 percent dividend exclusion is voided. This provision is designed to prevent a firm from engaging in "tax arbitrage," using tax-deductible debt to purchase largely tax-exempt preferred stock.

[2]Prior to the late 1970s, virtually all preferred stock was perpetual, and almost no issues had sinking funds or call provisions. Then, insurance company regulators, worried about the unrealized losses the companies had been incurring on preferred holdings as a result of rising interest rates, put into effect some regulatory changes that essentially mandated that insurance companies buy only limited life preferreds. From that time on, virtually no new preferred has been perpetual. This example illustrates the way securities change as a result of changes in the economic environment.

[3]Some new preferreds are attractive to individual investors. See the box, "A Rose by Any Other Name: MIPS, QUIPS, TOPrS, and QUIDS."

Where's the Dividend?

Suppose your company needs cash to finance a sure-winner expansion. However, its bond covenants forbid any additional borrowing, and these covenants also prohibit the payment of cash dividends, which rules out conventional preferred stock. To make matters worse, the company's stock price is trading near its 52-week low, so you don't want to issue new common stock. Is there any way you can raise the needed funds?

Two companies recently came up with innovative answers. Intermedia Communications Corp. issued \$300 million of exchangeable preferred stock with a payment-in-kind (PIK) dividend. The 13.5 percent dividend is payable in additional shares of the preferred stock rather than in cash. Therefore, this instrument provided Intermedia with the cash it needed yet still complied with the bond covenants. In addition, the exchange feature allows Intermedia to convert the preferred stock into debt when its financial situation improves to the point where the debt covenants are no longer binding.

Similarly, Nextel Communications issued \$150 million of another first-time-ever security, zero coupon convertible preferred stock. The issue price was \$26 per share, and the maturity value was \$98 per share in 15 years, which resulted in a yield of 9.25 percent. Because it isn't debt and it doesn't pay coupons, the security avoided the restrictions in Nextel's debt covenants. The preferred stock can also be converted into common stock, and the preferred stockholders will exercise this option if Nextel's stock enjoys a sharp increase.

Sources: Ian Springsteel, "Take Your PIK," *CFO*, December 1997, 30; Joseph McCafferty, "Less or More than Zero," *CFO*, March 1999, 20.

an incentive to issue preferred stock that can be bought by corporate investors with high tax rates, who can take advantage of the 70 percent dividend exclusion. If a firm has a lower tax rate than potential corporate buyers, the firm might be better off issuing preferred stock than debt. The key here is that the tax advantage to a high-tax-rate corporation is greater than the tax disadvantage to a low-tax-rate issuer. To illustrate, assume that risk differentials between debt and preferred would require an issuer to set the interest rate on new debt at 10 percent and the dividend yield on new preferred at 12 percent in a no-tax world. However, when taxes are considered, a corporate buyer with a high tax rate, say, 40 percent, might be willing to buy the preferred stock if it has an 8 percent before-tax yield. This would produce an $8\%(1 - \text{Effective T}) = 8\%[1 - 0.30(0.40)] = 7.04\%$ after-tax return on the preferred versus $10\%(1 - 0.40) = 6.0\%$ on the debt. If the issuer has a low tax rate, say, 10 percent, its after-tax costs would be $10\%(1 - T) = 10\%(0.90) = 9\%$ on the bonds and 8 percent on the preferred. Thus, the security with lower risk to the issuer, preferred stock, also has a lower cost. Such situations can make preferred stock a logical financing choice.[4]

Other Types of Preferred Stock

In addition to the "plain vanilla" variety of preferred stocks, several variations are also used. Two of these, floating rate and market auction preferred, are discussed in the following sections.

Adjustable Rate Preferred Stock Instead of paying fixed dividends, **adjustable rate preferred stocks (ARPs)** have their dividends tied to the rate on Treasury securities. The ARPs, which are issued mainly by utilities and large commercial banks,

[4]For a more rigorous treatment of the tax hypothesis of preferred stock, see Iraj Fooladi and Gordon S. Roberts, "On Preferred Stock," *Journal of Financial Research*, Winter 1986, 319–324. For an example of an empirical test of the hypothesis, see Arthur L. Houston, Jr., and Carol Olson Houston, "Financing with Preferred Stock," *Financial Management*, Autumn 1990, 42–54.

A Rose by Any Other Name: MIPS, QUIPS, TOPrS, and QUIDS

Wall Street's "financial engineers" are constantly trying to develop new securities that appeal to issuers and investors. One such new security is a special type of preferred stock created by Goldman Sachs in the mid-1990s. These securities trade under a variety of colorful names, including MIPS (Modified Income Preferred Securities), QUIPS (Quarterly Income Preferred Securities), TOPrS (Trust Originated Preferred Stock), and QUIDS (Quarterly Income Debt Securities). The corporation that wants to raise capital (the "parent") establishes a trust, which issues fixed-dividend preferred stock. The parent then issues bonds (or debt of some type) to the trust, and the trust pays for the bonds with the cash raised from the sale of preferred. At that point, the parent has the cash it needs, the trust holds debt issued by the parent, and the investing public holds preferred stock issued by the trust. The parent then makes interest payments to the trust, and the trust uses that income to make the preferred dividend payments. Because the parent company has issued debt, its interest payments are tax deductible.

If the dividends could be excluded from taxable income by corporate investors, this preferred would really be a great deal—the issuer could deduct the interest, corporate investors could exclude most of the dividends, and the IRS would be the loser. The corporate parent does get to deduct the interest paid to the trust, but IRS regulations do not allow the dividends on these securities to be excluded.

Because there is only one deduction, why are these new securities attractive? The answer is as follows: (1) Because the parent company gets to take the deduction, its cost of funds from the preferred is $k_p(1 - T)$, just as it would be if it used debt. (2) The parent generates tax savings, and it can thus afford to pay a relatively high rate on trust-related preferred; that is, it can pass on some of its tax savings to investors to induce them to buy the new securities. (3) The primary purchasers of the preferred are low-tax-bracket individuals and tax-exempt institutions such as pension funds. For such purchasers, not being able to exclude the dividend from taxable income is not important. (4) Due to the differential tax rates, the arrangement results in net tax savings. Competition in capital markets results in a sharing of the savings between investors and corporations.

A recent *SmartMoney Online* article argued that these hybrid securities are a good deal for low-bracket individual investors for the reason set forth above and also because they are sold in small increments—often as small as \$25. However, these securities are relatively complex, which increases their risk and makes them hard to value. There is also risk to the issuing corporations. The IRS has expressed concerns about these securities, and if at some point the IRS decides to disallow interest paid to the trusts, that will have a profound negative effect on the corporations that have issued them.

Sources: Kerry Capell, "High Yields, Low Cost, Funny Names," *Business Week*, September 9, 1996, 122; Leslie Haggin, "SmartMoney Online: MIPS, QUIDS, and QUIPS," *SmartMoney Interactive*, April 6, 1999.

were touted as nearly perfect short-term corporate investments since (1) only 30 percent of the dividends are taxable to corporations, and (2) the floating rate feature was supposed to keep the issue trading at near par. The new security proved to be so popular as a short-term investment for firms with idle cash that mutual funds designed just to invest in them sprouted like weeds (shares of the funds, in turn, were purchased by corporations). However, the ARPs still had some price volatility due (1) to changes in the riskiness of the issues (some big banks that had issued ARPs, such as Continental Illinois, ran into serious loan default problems) and (2) to the fact that Treasury yields fluctuated between dividend rate adjustments dates. Thus, the ARPs had too much price instability to be held in the liquid asset portfolios of many corporate investors.

Market Auction Preferred Stock In 1984, investment bankers introduced **money market,** or **market auction, preferred.** Here the underwriter conducts an auction on the issue every seven weeks (to get the 70 percent exclusion from taxable income, buyers must hold the stock at least 46 days). Holders who want to sell their shares can put them up for auction at par value. Buyers then submit bids in the form of the yields they are willing to accept over the next seven-week period. The yield set on the issue for the coming period is the lowest yield sufficient to sell all the shares being offered at that auction. The buyers pay the sellers the par value; hence, holders are virtually assured that their shares can be sold at par. The issuer then must pay a dividend rate over the next seven-week period as determined by the auction. From the holder's standpoint, market auction preferred is a low-risk, largely tax-exempt, seven-week maturity security that can be sold between auction dates at close to par. However, if there are not enough buyers to match the sellers (in spite of the high yield), then the auction can fail, which has occurred on occasion.

Advantages and Disadvantages of Preferred Stock

There are both advantages and disadvantages to financing with preferred stock. Here are the major advantages from the issuers' standpoint:

1. In contrast to bonds, the obligation to pay preferred dividends is not firm, and passing a preferred dividend cannot force a firm into bankruptcy.
2. By issuing preferred stock, the firm avoids the dilution of common equity that occurs when common stock is sold.
3. Since preferred stock sometimes has no maturity, and since preferred sinking fund payments, if present, are typically spread over a long period, preferred issues reduce the cash flow drain from repayment of principal that occurs with debt issues.

There are two major disadvantages:

1. Preferred stock dividends are not normally deductible to the issuer, hence the after-tax cost of preferred is typically higher than the after-tax cost of debt. However, the tax advantage of preferreds to corporate purchasers lowers its pre-tax cost and thus its effective cost.
2. Although preferred dividends can be passed, investors expect them to be paid, and firms intend to pay the dividends if conditions permit. Thus, preferred dividends are considered to be a fixed cost. Therefore, their use, like that of debt, increases financial risk and thus the cost of common equity.

Self-Test Questions

Should preferred stock be considered as equity or debt? Explain.

Who are the major purchasers of nonconvertible preferred stock? Why?

Briefly explain the mechanics of adjustable rate and market auction preferred stock.

What are the advantages and disadvantages of preferred stock to the issuer?

Warrants

A **warrant** is a certificate issued by a company that gives the holder the right to buy a stated number of shares of the company's stock at a specified price for some specified length of time. Generally, warrants are issued along with debt, and they are used to induce investors to buy long-term debt with a lower coupon rate than would otherwise be required. For example, when Infomatics Corporation, a rapidly growing high-tech company, wanted to sell $50 million of 20-year bonds in 2001, the company's investment bankers informed the financial vice-president that the bonds would be difficult to sell, and that a coupon rate of 10 percent would be required. However, as an alternative the bankers suggested that investors might be willing to buy the bonds with a coupon rate of only 8 percent if the company would offer 20 warrants with each $1,000 bond, each warrant entitling the holder to buy one share of common stock at an *exercise price* of $22 per share. The stock was selling for $20 per share at the time, and the warrants would expire in the year 2011 if they had not been exercised previously.

Why would investors be willing to buy Infomatics' bonds at a yield of only 8 percent in a 10 percent market just because warrants were also offered as part of the package? It is because the warrants are long-term *call options* that have value because holders can buy the firm's common stock at the exercise price regardless of how high the market price climbs. This option offsets the low interest rate on the bonds and makes the package of low-yield bonds plus warrants attractive to investors. (See Chapter 15 for a discussion of options.)

Initial Market Price of a Bond with Warrants

The Infomatics bonds, if they had been issued as straight debt, would have carried a 10 percent interest rate. However, with warrants attached, the bonds were sold to yield 8 percent. Someone buying the bonds at their $1,000 initial offering price would thus be receiving a package consisting of an 8 percent, 20-year bond plus 20 warrants. Because the going interest rate on bonds as risky as those of Infomatics was 10 percent, we can find the straight-debt value of the bonds, assuming an annual coupon for ease of illustration, as follows:

0	1	2	3	. . .	20
PV	80	80	80		80
					1,000

Using a financial calculator, input N = 20, I = 10, PMT = 80, and FV = 1000. Then, press the PV key to obtain the bond's value, $829.73, or approximately $830. Thus, a person buying the bonds in the initial underwriting would pay $1,000 and receive in exchange a straight bond worth about $830 plus 20 warrants presumably worth about $1,000 − $830 = $170:

$$\begin{array}{ccccc} \text{Price paid for bond with warrants} & = & \text{Straight-debt value of bond} & + & \text{Value of warrants} \\ \$1{,}000 & = & \$830 & + & \$170. \end{array} \qquad (21\text{-}1)$$

Because investors receive 20 warrants with each bond, each warrant has an implied value of $170/20 = $8.50.

The key issue in setting the terms of a bond-with-warrants deal is valuing the warrants. The straight-debt value can be estimated quite accurately, as was done above. However, it is more difficult to estimate the value of the warrants. The Black-Scholes Option Pricing Model (OPM), which we discussed in Chapter 15, can be used to find the value of a call option. There is a temptation to use this model to find the value of a warrant, since call options are similar to warrants in many respects: Both give the investor the right to buy a share of stock at a fixed exercise price on or before the expiration date. However, there are major differences between call options and warrants. When call options are exercised, the stock provided to the optionholder comes from the secondary market, but when warrants are exercised, the stock provided to the warrant holders are newly issued shares. This means that the exercise of warrants dilutes the value of the original equity, which could cause the value of the original warrant to differ from the value of a similar call option. Also, call options typically have a life of just a few months, while warrents often have lives of 10 years or more. Finally, the Black-Scholes model assumes that the underlying stock pays no dividend, which is not unreasonable over a short period but is unreasonable for 5 or 10 years. Therefore, investment bankers cannot use the Black-Scholes model to determine the value of warrants.

Even though the Black-Scholes model and other models cannot be used to determine a precise value for a warrent, investment bankers can still price issues reasonably well. The bankers simply contact portfolio managers of mutual funds, pension funds, and other organizations that would be interested in buying the securities and get an indication of how many they would buy at different prices. In effect, the bankers hold a presale auction and determine the set of terms that will just clear the market. If they do this job properly, they will, in effect, be letting the market determine the value of the warrants.

Use of Warrants in Financing

Warrants generally are used by small, rapidly growing firms as "sweeteners" when they sell debt or preferred stock. Such firms frequently are regarded by investors as being highly risky, so their bonds can be sold only at extremely high coupon rates and with very restrictive indenture provisions. To avoid this, firms such as Infomatics often offer warrants along with the bonds. However, some years ago, AT&T raised $1.57 billion by selling bonds with warrants. This was the largest financing of any type ever undertaken by a business firm, and it marked the first use ever of warrants by a large, strong corporation.[5]

Getting warrants along with bonds enables investors to share in the company's growth, assuming it does in fact grow and prosper. Therefore, investors are willing to accept a lower interest rate and less restrictive indenture provisions. A bond with warrants has some characteristics of debt and some characteristics of equity. It is a hybrid security that provides the financial manager with an opportunity to expand the firm's mix of securities and thus to appeal to a broader group of investors.

Virtually all warrants issued today are **detachable.** Thus, after a bond with attached warrants is sold, the warrants can be detached and traded separately from the bond. Further, even after the warrants have been exercised, the bond (with its low coupon rate) remains outstanding.

The exercise price on warrants is generally set some 20 to 30 percent above the market price of the stock on the date the bond is issued. If the firm grows and prospers, causing its stock price to rise above the exercise price at which shares may be purchased, warrant holders could exercise their warrants and buy stock at the stated price. However, without some incentive, warrants would never be exercised prior to maturity—their value in the open market would be greater than their value if exercised, so holders would sell warrants rather than exercise them. There are three conditions that cause holders to exercise their warrants: (1) Warrant holders will surely exercise and buy stock if the warrants are about to expire and the market price of the stock is above the exercise price. (2) Warrant holders will exercise voluntarily if the company raises the dividend on the common stock by a sufficient amount. No dividend is earned on the warrant, so it provides no current income. However, if the common stock pays a high dividend, it provides an attractive dividend yield but limits price growth. This induces warrant holders to exercise their option to buy the stock.

---

[5]It is interesting to note that before the AT&T issue, the New York Stock Exchange's stated policy was that warrants could not be listed because they were "speculative" instruments rather than "investment" securities. When AT&T issued warrants, however, the Exchange changed its policy, agreeing to list warrants that met certain requirements. Many other warrants have since been listed.

It is also interesting to note that, prior to the sale, AT&T's treasury staff, working with Morgan Stanley analysts, estimated the value of the warrants as a part of the underwriting decision. The package was supposed to sell for a total price in the neighborhood of $1,000. The bond value could be determined accurately, so the trick was to estimate the equilibrium value of the warrant under different possible exercise prices and years to expiration, and then to use an exercise price and life that would cause Bond value + Warrant value ≈ $1,000. Using a warrant pricing model, the AT&T/Morgan Stanley analysts set terms that caused the warrant to sell on the open market at a price that was only 35¢ off from the estimated price.

(3) Warrants sometimes have **stepped-up exercise prices,** which prod owners into exercising them. For example, Williamson Scientific Company has warrants outstanding with an exercise price of \$25 until December 31, 2005, at which time the exercise price rises to \$30. If the price of the common stock is over \$25 just before December 31, 2005, many warrant holders will exercise their options before the stepped-up price takes effect and the value of the warrants falls.

Another desirable feature of warrants is that they generally bring in funds only if funds are needed. If the company grows, it will probably need new equity capital. At the same time, growth will cause the price of the stock to rise and the warrants to be exercised, hence the firm will obtain the cash it needs. If the company is not successful, and it cannot profitably employ additional money, the price of its stock will probably not rise enough to induce exercise of the warrants.

Wealth Effects and Dilution Due to Warrants

See ***Ch 21 Tool Kit.xls.***

Assume that the value of Infomatics' operations and investments, which is \$250 million immediately after issuing the bonds with warrants, is expected to grow, and does grow, at 9 percent per year. When the warrants are due to expire in 10 years, the total value of Infomatics will be $\$250(1.09)^{10} = \$591.841$ million. How is this value allocated among the original stockholders, the bondholders, and the warrant holders?

The bonds will have ten years remaining until maturity, with a fixed coupon payment of \$80. If the expected market interest rate is still 10 percent, then:

0	10%	1	2	3	. . .	10
PV		80	80	80		80
						1,000

Using a financial calculator, input N = 10, I = 10, PMT = 80, and FV = 1000. Press the PV key to obtain the bond's value, \$877.11. The total value of all of the bonds is 50,000(\$877.11) = \$43.856 million.

The value remaining for the original stockholders and the warrant holders is equal to the remaining value of the firm, after deducting the amount owed to the bondholders. This remaining value is \$591.841 − \$43.856 = \$547.985 million. If there had been no warrants, then the original stockholders would have been entitled to all of this remaining value. Recall that there are 10 million shares of stock, so the price per share would be \$547.895/10 = \$54.80. Suppose the company has a basic earning power of 13.5 percent (recall that BEP = EBIT/Total Assets) and total assets of \$591.841 million.[6] This means that EBIT is 0.135(\$591.841) = \$79.899 million; interest payments are \$4 million (\$80 coupon payment per bond × 50,000 bonds); and earnings before taxes are \$79.899 − \$4 = \$75.899 million. With a tax rate of 40 percent, after-tax earnings are equal to \$75.899(1 − 0.4) = \$45.539 million, and earnings per share are \$45.539/10 = \$4.55. To summarize, if Infomatics had no warrants, the stock price would be \$54.80 per share, and the earnings per share would be \$4.55.

But Infomatics *does* have warrants, and with the stock price over \$50 the warrant holders will exercise their warrants. Infomatics will receive \$22 million when the 1 million warrants are exercised at a price of \$22 per warrant. This will make the total value of Infomatics equal to \$613.841 million (the \$591.841 million existing value plus

[6]In this case, the total market value equals the book value of assets, but the same calculations would follow even if market and book values were not equal.

the \$22 million raised by the exercise of the warrants). The total value remaining for stockholders is now \$569.985 million (\$613.841 million less the \$43.856 million allocated to bondholders). There are now 11 million shares of stock (the original 10 million plus the new 1 million due to the exercise of the warrants), so the stock price will be \$569.985/11 = \$51.82 per share. Note that this is lower than the \$54.80 price per share that Infomatics would have had if there had been no warrants. Thus, the warrants dilute the value of the stock.

A similar dilution occurs with earnings per share. After exercise, the asset base would increase from \$591.841 million to \$613.841 million, with the additional \$22 million coming from the sale of 1 million shares of stock at \$22 per share. If the new funds have the same basic earning power as the existing funds, then the new EBIT would be 0.135(\$613.841) = \$82.869 million. Interest payments would still be \$4 million, so earnings before taxes would be \$82.869 − \$4 = \$78.869 million, and after-tax earnings would be \$78.869(1 − 0.4) = \$47.321 million. With 10 + 1 = 11 million shares now outstanding, EPS would be \$47.321/11 = \$4.30, down from \$4.55. Therefore, exercising the warrants would dilute EPS.

Has this wealth transfer harmed the original shareholders? The answer is yes and no. Yes, because the original shareholders clearly are worse off than they would have been if there had been no warrants. However, if there had been no warrants attached to the bonds, then the bonds would have had a 10 percent coupon rate instead of the 8 percent coupon rate. Also, if the value of the company had not increased as expected, then it might not have been profitable for the warrant holders to exercise their warrants. In other words, the original shareholders were willing to trade off the potential dilution for the lower coupon rate. In this example, the original stockholders and the investors in the bonds with warrants would be getting what they expected. Therefore, the answer is no, the wealth transfer at the time of exercise did not harm the original shareholders, because they expected an eventual transfer and were fairly compensated by the lower interest payments.

Note too that investors would recognize the situation, so the actual wealth transfer would occur gradually over time, not in one fell swoop when the warrants were exercised. First, EPS would have been reported on a diluted basis over the years, and on that basis, there would be no decline whatever in EPS. (We discuss this in a later section of this chapter.) Also, investors would know what was happening, so the stock price, over time, would reflect the likely future dilution. Therefore, it too would be stable when the warrants were exercised. Thus, the effects of the warrants would be reflected in EPS and on the stock price on a gradual basis over time.

The Component Cost of Bonds with Warrants

When Infomatics issued its bond with warrants, the firm received \$1,000 for each bond. Simultaneously, the company assumed an obligation to pay \$80 interest for 20 years plus \$1,000 at the end of 20 years. The pre-tax cost of the money would have been 10 percent if no warrants had been attached, but each Infomatics bond had 20 warrants, each of which entitles its holder to buy one share of stock for \$22. What is the percentage cost of the debt? As we shall see, the cost is well above the 8 percent coupon rate on the bonds.

As we demonstrated earlier, when the warrants expire ten years from now, the expected stock price is \$51.82. The company would then have to issue one share of stock worth \$51.82 for each warrant exercised and, in return, Infomatics would receive the exercise price, \$22. Thus, a purchaser of the bonds, if he or she holds the complete package, would realize a profit in Year 10 of \$51.82 − \$22 = \$29.82 for each common share issued. Since each bond has 20 warrants attached, and each warrant entitles the holder to buy one share of common stock, investors would have a gain of

20($29.82) = $596.40 per bond at the end of Year 10. Here is a time line of the cash flow stream to an investor:

0	1	. . .	9	10	11	. . .	20
−$1,000	+$80		+$80	+$ 80.00	+$80		+$ 80
				+ 596.40			+ 1,000
				+$676.40			+ $1,080

The IRR of this stream is 10.7 percent, which is the investor's overall pre-tax rate of return on the issue. This return is 70 basis points higher than the 10 percent return on straight debt. The higher return reflects the fact that the issue is riskier to investors than a straight-debt issue because much of the return is expected to come in the form of stock price appreciation, and that part of the return is more risky than interest income.

The expected rate of return to investors is the same as the before-tax cost to the company—this was true of common stocks, straight bonds, and preferred stocks, and it is also true of bonds sold with warrants.

Self-Test Questions

What is a warrant?

Describe how a new bond issue with warrants is valued.

How are warrants used in corporate financing?

The use of warrants lowers the coupon rate on the corresponding debt issue. Does this mean that the component cost of a debt-plus-warrants package is less than the cost of straight debt? Explain.

Convertibles

Convertible securities are bonds or preferred stocks that, under specified terms and conditions, can be exchanged for (that is, converted into) common stock at the option of the holder. Unlike the exercise of warrants, which brings in additional funds to the firm, conversion does not provide new capital: debt (or preferred stock) is simply replaced on the balance sheet by common stock. Of course, reducing the debt or preferred stock will improve the firm's financial strength and make it easier to raise additional capital, but that requires a separate action.

Conversion Ratio and Conversion Price

CD

See *Ch 21 Tool Kit.xls.*

One of the most important provisions of a convertible security is the **conversion ratio, CR,** defined as the number of shares of stock a bondholder will receive upon conversion. Related to the conversion ratio is the **conversion price, P_c,** which is the effective price investors pay for the common stock when conversion occurs. The relationship between the conversion ratio and the conversion price can be illustrated by Silicon Valley Software Company's convertible debentures issued at their $1,000 par value in July of 2001. At any time prior to maturity on July 15, 2021, a debenture holder can exchange a bond for 20 shares of common stock. Therefore, the conversion ratio, CR, is 20. The bond cost a purchaser $1,000, the par value, when it was issued. Dividing the $1,000 par value by the 20 shares received gives a conversion price of $50 a share:

$$\text{Conversion price} = P_c = \frac{\text{Par value of bond given up}}{\text{Shares received}} \qquad (21\text{-}2)$$

$$= \frac{\$1{,}000}{\text{CR}} = \frac{\$1{,}000}{20} = \$50.$$

Conversely, by solving for CR, we obtain the conversion ratio:

$$\text{Conversion ratio} = \text{CR} = \frac{\$1{,}000}{P_c} \quad \textbf{(21-3)}$$

$$= \frac{\$1{,}000}{\$50} = 20 \text{ shares.}$$

Once CR is set, the value of P_c is established, and vice versa.

Like a warrant's exercise price, the conversion price is typically set some 20 to 30 percent above the prevailing market price of the common stock on the issue date. Generally, the conversion price and conversion ratio are fixed for the life of the bond, although sometimes a stepped-up conversion price is used. For example, the 2001 convertible debentures for Breedon Industries are convertible into 12.5 shares until 2011; into 11.76 shares from 2011 until 2021; and into 11.11 shares from 2021 until maturity in 2031. The conversion price thus starts at $80, rises to $85, and then goes to $90. Breedon's convertibles, like most, have a ten-year call-protection period.

Another factor that may cause a change in the conversion price and ratio is a standard feature of almost all convertibles—the clause protecting the convertible against dilution from stock splits, stock dividends, and the sale of common stock at prices below the conversion price. The typical provision states that if common stock is sold at a price below the conversion price, then the conversion price must be lowered (and the conversion ratio raised) to the price at which the new stock was issued. Also, if the stock is split, or if a stock dividend is declared, the conversion price must be lowered by the percentage amount of the stock dividend or split. For example, if Breedon Industries were to have a two-for-one stock split during the first 10 years of its convertible's life, the conversion ratio would automatically be adjusted from 12.5 to 25, and the conversion price lowered from $80 to $40. If this protection were not contained in the contract, a company could completely thwart conversion by the use of stock splits and stock dividends. Warrants are similarly protected against dilution.

The standard protection against dilution from selling new stock at prices below the conversion price can, however, get a company into trouble. For example, assume that Breedon's stock was selling for $65 per share at the time the convertible was issued. Further, suppose the market went sour, and Breedon's stock price dropped to $30 per share. If Breedon needed new equity to support operations, a new common stock sale would require the company to lower the conversion price on the convertible debentures from $80 to $300. That would raise the value of the convertibles and, in effect, transfer wealth from current shareholders to the convertible holders. This transfer would, de facto, amount to an additional flotation cost on the new common stock. Potential problems such as this must be kept in mind by firms considering the use of convertibles or bonds with warrants.

The Component Cost of Convertibles

In the spring of 2000, Silicon Valley Software was evaluating the use of the convertible bond issue described earlier. The issue would consist of 20-year convertible bonds that would sell at a price of $1,000 per bond; this $1,000 would also be the bond's par (and maturity) value. The bonds would pay a 10 percent annual coupon interest rate, or $100 per year. Each bond would be convertible into 20 shares of stock, so the conversion price would be $1,000/20 = $50. The stock was expected to pay a dividend of $2.80 during the coming year, and it sold at $35 per share. Further, the stock price was expected to grow at a constant rate of 8 percent per year. Therefore, $k_s = \hat{k}_s = D_1/P_0 + g = \$2.80/\$35 + 8\% = 8\% + 8\% = 16\%$. If the bonds were not made convertible, they would have to provide a yield of 13 percent, given their riskiness and the

See *Ch 21 Tool Kit.xls.*

general level of interest rates. The convertible bonds would not be callable for 10 years, after which they could be called at a price of \$1,050, with this price declining by \$5 per year thereafter. If, after 10 years, the conversion value exceeds the call price by at least 20 percent, management would probably call the bonds.

Figure 21-1 shows the expectations of both an average investor and the company.[7]

1. The horizontal line at M = \$1,000 represents the par (and maturity) value. Also, \$1,000 is the price at which the bond is initially offered to the public.
2. The bond is protected against a call for 10 years. It is initially callable at a price of \$1,050, and the call price declines thereafter by \$5 per year. Thus, the call price is represented by the solid section of the line V_0M''.
3. Since the convertible has a 10 percent coupon rate, and since the yield on a non-convertible bond of similar risk is 13 percent, the expected "straight-bond" value of the convertible, B_t, must be less than par. At the time of issue, assuming an annual coupon, B_0 is \$789:

$$\text{Pure-debt value at time of issue} = B_0 = \sum_{t=1}^{N} \frac{\text{Coupon interest}}{(1 + k_d)^t} + \frac{\text{Maturity value}}{(1 + k_d)^N} \quad \textbf{(21-4)}$$

$$= \sum_{t=1}^{20} \frac{\$100}{(1.13)^t} + \frac{\$1{,}000}{(1.13)^{20}} = \$789.$$

Note, however, that the bond's straight-debt value must be \$1,000 at maturity, so the straight-debt value rises over time. B_t follows the line B_0M'' in the graph.

4. The bond's initial **conversion value, C_t,** or the value of the stock an investor would receive if the bonds were converted at t = 0, is P_0(CR) = \$35(20 shares) = \$700. Since the stock price is expected to grow at an 8 percent rate, the conversion value should rise over time. For example, in Year 5 it should be P_5(CR) = $\$35(1.08)^5(20) = \$1{,}029$. The expected conversion value over time is given by the line C_t in Figure 21-1.
5. The actual market price of the bond can never fall below the higher of its straight-debt value or its conversion value. If the market price dropped below the straight-bond value, those who wanted bonds would recognize the bargain and buy the convertible as a bond. Similarly, if the market price dropped below the conversion value, people would buy the convertibles, exercise them to get stock, and then sell the stock at a profit. Therefore, the higher of the bond value and conversion value curves in the graph represents a *floor price* for the bond. In Figure 21-1, the floor price is represented by the thicker shaded line B_0XC_t.
6. The bond's market value will typically exceed its floor value. It will exceed the straight-bond value because the option to convert is worth something—a 10 percent bond with conversion possibilities is worth more than a 10 percent bond without this option. The convertible's price will also exceed its conversion value because holding the convertible is equivalent to holding a call option, and, prior to expiration, the option's true value is higher than its expiration (or conversion) value. We cannot say exactly where the market value line will lie, but as a rule it will be at or above the floor set by the straight-bond and conversion value lines.
7. At some point, the market value line will converge with the conversion value line. This convergence will occur for two reasons. First, the stock should pay higher and higher dividends as the years go by, but the interest payments on the convertible are fixed. For example, Silicon's convertibles would pay \$100 in interest

[7]For a more complete discussion of how the terms of a convertible offering are determined, see M. Wayne Marr and G. Rodney Thompson, "The Pricing of New Convertible Bond Issues," *Financial Management*, Summer 1984, 31–37.

FIGURE 21-1 Silicon Valley Software: Convertible Bond Model

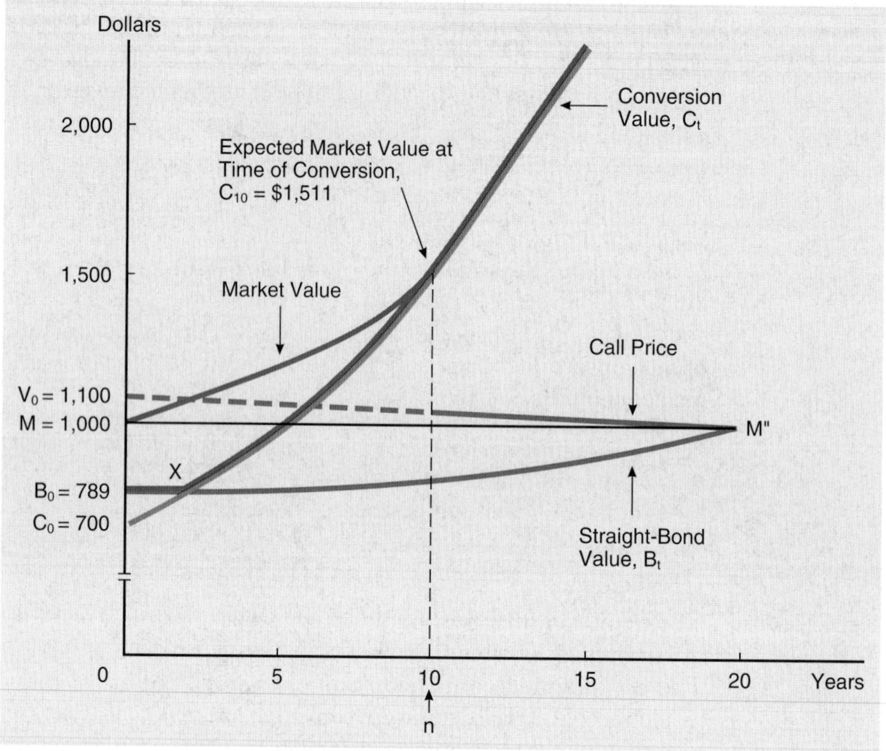

Year	Pure-Bond Value, B_t	Conversion Value, C_t	Maturity Value, M	Market Value	Floor Value	Premium
0	$ 789	$ 700	$1,000	$1,000	$ 789	$211
1	792	756	$1,000	1,023	792	231
2	795	816	$1,000	1,071	816	255
3	798	882	$1,000	1,147	882	265
4	802	952	$1,000	1,192	952	240
5	806	1,029	$1,000	1,241	1,029	212
6	811	1,111	$1,000	1,293	1,111	182
7	816	1,200	$1,000	1,344	1,200	144
8	822	1,296	$1,000	1,398	1,296	102
9	829	1,399	$1,000	1,453	1,399	54
10	837	1,511	$1,000	1,511	1,511	0
11	846	1,632	$1,000	1,632	1,632	0
.	.	.	.	.	.	.
.	.	.	.	.	.	.
.	.	.	.	.	.	.
20	1,000	3,263	$1,000	3,263	3,263	0

annually, while the dividends on the 20 shares received upon conversion would initially be 20($2.80) = $56. However, at an 8 percent growth rate, the dividends after 10 years would be up to $120.90, but the interest would still be $100. Thus, rising dividends will push against the fixed interest payments, causing the premium to disappear and investors to convert voluntarily. Second, once the bond becomes callable, its market value cannot exceed the higher of the conversion value and the call price without exposing investors to the danger of a call. For example, suppose that 10 years after issue (when the bonds become callable), the market value of the bond is \$1,600, the conversion value is \$1,500, and the call price is \$1,050. If the company called the bonds the day after you bought 10 bonds for \$16,000, you would be forced to convert into stock worth only \$15,000, so you would suffer a loss of \$100 per bond, or \$1,000, in one day. Recognizing this danger, you and other investors would simply not pay a premium over the higher of the call price or the conversion value once the bond becomes callable. Therefore, in Figure 21-1, we assume that the market value line hits the conversion value line in Year 10, when the bond becomes callable.

8. Let n represent the year when investors expect conversion to occur, either voluntarily because of rising dividends or because the company calls the convertibles to strengthen its balance sheet by substituting equity for debt. In our example, we assume that n = 10, the first call date.
9. Since n = 10, the expected market value at Year 10 is $\$35(1.08)^{10}(20) = \$1,511$. An investor can find the expected rate of return on the convertible bond, k_c, by finding the IRR of the following cash flow stream:

0	1	. . .	9	10
−\$1,000	+\$100		+\$100	+\$ 100
				+ 1,511
				+ \$1,611

The solution is k_c = IRR = 12.8 percent.

10. The return on a convertible is expected to come partly from interest income and partly from capital gains; in this case, the total expected return is 12.8 percent, with 10 percent representing interest income and 2.8 percent representing the expected capital gain. The interest component is relatively assured, while the capital gain component is more risky. Therefore, a convertible's expected return is more risky than that of a straight bond. This leads us to conclude that k_c should be larger than the cost of straight debt, k_d. Thus, it would seem that the expected rate of return on Silicon's convertibles, k_c, should lie between its cost of straight debt, $k_d = 13\%$, and its cost of common stock, $k_s = 16\%$.
11. Investment bankers use the type of model described here, plus a knowledge of the market, to set the terms on convertibles (the conversion ratio, coupon interest rate, and years of call protection) such that the security will just "clear the market" at its \$1,000 offering price. In our example, the required conditions do not hold—the calculated rate of return on the convertible is only 12.8 percent, which is less than the 13 percent cost of straight debt. Therefore, the terms on the bond would have to be made more attractive to investors. Silicon Valley Software would have to increase the coupon interest rate on the convertible above 10 percent, raise the conversion ratio above 20 (and thereby lower the conversion price from \$50 to a level closer to the current \$35 market price of the stock), lengthen the call-protected period, or use a combination of these changes such that the expected rate of return on the convertible ends up between 13 and 16 percent.[8]

[8]In this discussion, we ignore the tax advantages to investors associated with capital gains. In some situations, tax effects could result in k_c being less than k_d.

Use of Convertibles in Financing

Convertibles have two important advantages from the issuer's standpoint: (1) Convertibles, like bonds with warrants, offer a company the chance to sell debt with a low interest rate in exchange for giving bondholders a chance to participate in the company's success if it does well. (2) In a sense, convertibles provide a way to sell common stock at prices higher than those currently prevailing. Some companies actually want to sell common stock, not debt, but feel that the price of their stock is temporarily depressed. Management may know, for example, that earnings are depressed because of startup costs associated with a new project, but they expect earnings to rise sharply during the next year or so, pulling the price of the stock up with them. Thus, if the company sold stock now, it would be giving up more shares than necessary to raise a given amount of capital. However, if it set the conversion price 20 to 30 percent above the present market price of the stock, then 20 to 30 percent fewer shares would be given up when the bonds were converted than if stock were sold directly at the current time. Note, however, that management is counting on the stock's price to rise above the conversion price to make the bonds attractive in conversion. If earnings do not rise and pull the stock price up, hence conversion does not occur, then the company will be saddled with debt in the face of low earnings, which could be disastrous.

How can the company be sure that conversion will occur if the price of the stock rises above the conversion price? Typically, convertibles contain a call provision that enables the issuing firm to force holders to convert. Suppose the conversion price is $50, the conversion ratio is 20, the market price of the common stock has risen to $60, and the call price on a convertible bond is $1,050. If the company calls the bond, bondholders can either convert into common stock with a market value of 20($60) = $1,200 or allow the company to redeem the bond for $1,050. Naturally, bondholders prefer $1,200 to $1,050, so conversion would occur. The call provision thus gives the company a way to force conversion, provided the market price of the stock is greater than the conversion price. Note, however, that most convertibles have a fairly long period of call protection—10 years is typical. Therefore, if the company wants to be able to force conversion fairly early, then it will have to set a short call-protection period. This will, in turn, require that it set a higher coupon rate or a lower conversion price.

From the standpoint of the issuer, convertibles have three important disadvantages: (1) Although the use of a convertible bond may give the company the opportunity to sell stock at a price higher than the price at which it could be sold currently, if the stock greatly increases in price, the firm would have been better off if it had used straight debt in spite of its higher cost and then later sold common stock and refunded the debt. (2) Convertibles typically have a low coupon interest rate, and the advantage of this low-cost debt will be lost when conversion occurs. (3) If the company truly wants to raise equity capital, and if the price of the stock does not rise sufficiently after the bond is issued, then the company will be stuck with debt.

Convertibles and Agency Costs

A potential agency conflict between bondholders and stockholders is asset substitution, also known as "bait-and-switch." Suppose a company has been investing in low-risk projects, and because its risk is low, bondholders charge a low interest rate. What happens if the company is considering a very risky but highly profitable venture, but potential lenders don't know about it? The company might decide to raise low-interest rate debt without spelling out that the funds will be invested in the risky project. After the funds have been raised and the investment is made, the value of the debt should fall because its interest rate will be too low to compensate debtholders for the high risk they bear. This is a "heads I win, tails you lose" situation, and it results in a wealth transfer from bondholders to stockholders.

Let's use some numbers to illustrate this. The value of a company, based on the present value of its future free cash flows, is $800 million. It has $300 million of debt, based on market value. Therefore, its equity is worth $800 − $300 = $500 million. The company now undertakes some very risky projects, with high but risky expected returns, and its expected NPV remains unchanged. In other words, the actual NPV will probably end up much higher or much lower than under the old situation, but the firm still has the same expected value. Even though its total value is still $800 million, the value of the debt falls because its risk has increased. Note that the debtholders don't benefit if the venture's value is higher than expected, because the most they can receive is the contracted coupon and the principal repayment. However, they will suffer if the value of the projects turns out to be lower than expected, since they might not receive the full value of their contracted payments. In other words, risk doesn't give them any upside potential, but it does expose them to downside losses, so the bondholders' expected value must decline.

With a constant total firm value, if the value of the debt falls from $300 to $200 million, then the value of equity must increase from $500 to $800 − $200 = $600 million. Thus, the bait-and-switch tactic causes a wealth transfer of $100 million from debtholders to stockholders.

If debtholders think that a company might employ the to bait-and-switch tactic, they will they charge a higher interest rate, and this higher interest rate is an agency cost. Debtholders will charge this higher rate even if the company has no intention of engaging in bait-and-switch behavior, since they don't know the company's true intentions. Therefore, they assume the worst and charge a higher interest rate.

Convertible securities are one way to mitigate this type of agency cost. Suppose the debt is convertible and the company does take on the high-risk project. If the value of the company turns out to be higher than expected, then bondholders can convert their debt to equity and benefit from the successful investment. Therefore, bondholders are willing to charge a lower interest rate on convertibles, which serves to minimize the agency costs.

Note that if a company does not engage in bait-and-switch behavior by swapping low-risk projects for high-risk projects, the chance of hitting a home run is reduced. Because there is less chance of a home run, the convertible bond is less likely to be converted. In this situation the convertible bonds are actually similar to nonconvertible debt, except that they carry a lower interest rate.

Now consider a different agency cost, one due to asymmetric information between the managers and potential new stockholders. Suppose its managers know that a company's future prospects are not as good as the market believes, which means that the current stock price is too high. Acting in the interests of existing stockholders, managers can issue stock at the current high price. When the poor future prospects are eventually revealed, the stock price will fall, causing a transfer of wealth from the new shareholders to old shareholders.

To illustrate this, suppose the market estimates an $800 million present value of future free cash flows. For simplicity, assume that the firm has no nonoperating assets and no debt, so the total value of both the firm and the equity is $800 million. However, its managers know that the market has overestimated the future free cash flows, and the true value is only $700 million. When investors eventually discover this, the value of the company will drop to $700 million. But before this happens, suppose the company raises $200 million of new equity. The company uses this new cash to invest in projects with a present value of $200 million, which shouldn't be too hard, since these are projects with a zero NPV. Right after the new stock is sold, the company will have a market value of $800 + $200 = $1,000 million, based on the market's overly optimistic estimate of the company's future prospects. Note that the new shareholders own 20 percent of the company ($200/$1,000 = 0.20), and the original shareholders own 80 percent.

As time passes, the market will realize that the previously estimated value of $800 million for the company's original set of projects was too high, and that these projects are worth only $700 million. The new projects are still worth $200 million, so the total value of the company will fall to $700 + $200 = $900 million. The original shareholders' value is now 80 percent of $900 million, which is $720 million. Note that this is $20 million higher than it would have been if the company had issued no new stock. The new shareholders' value is now 0.20($900) = $180 million, which is $20 million less than their original investment. The net effect is a $20 million wealth transfer from the new shareholders to the original shareholders.

Because potential shareholders know this might occur, they interpret an issue of new stock as a signal of poor future prospects, which causes the stock price to fall. Note also that this will occur even for companies whose future prospects are actually quite good, because the market has no way of distinguishing between companies with good versus poor prospects.

A company with good future prospects might want to issue equity, but it knows the market will interpret this as a negative signal. One way to obtain equity and yet avoid this signaling effect is to issue convertible bonds. Because the company knows its true future prospects are better than the market anticipates, it knows that the bonds will likely end up being converted to equity. Thus, a company in this situation is issuing equity through the back door when it issues convertible debt.

In summary, convertibles are logical securities to use in at least two situations. First, if a company would like to finance with straight debt, but lenders are afraid the funds will be invested in a manner that increases the firm's risk profile, then convertibles are a good choice. Second, if a company wants to issue stock but thinks such a move would cause investors to interpret a stock offering as a signal of tough times ahead, then again convertibles would be a good choice.[9]

Self-Test Questions

What is a conversion ratio? A conversion price? A straight-bond value?

What is meant by a convertible's floor value?

What are the advantages and disadvantages of convertibles to issuers? To investors?

How do convertibles reduce agency costs?

A Final Comparison of Warrants and Convertibles

Convertible debt can be thought of as straight debt with nondetachable warrants. Thus, at first blush, it might appear that debt with warrants and convertible debt are more or less interchangeable. However, a closer look reveals one major and several minor differences between these two securities.[10] First, as we discussed previously, the exercise of warrants brings in new equity capital, while the conversion of convertibles results only in an accounting transfer.

A second difference involves flexibility. Most convertibles contain a call provision that allows the issuer either to refund the debt or to force conversion, depending on the relationship between the conversion value and call price. However, most warrants are not callable, so firms must wait until maturity for the warrants to generate new

[9]See Craig M. Lewis, Richard J. Rogalski, and James K. Seward, "Understanding the Design of Convertible Debt," *Journal of Applied Corporate Finance*, vol. 11, no. 1, Spring 1998, 45–53.

[10]For a more detailed comparison of warrants and convertibles, see Michael S. Long and Stephen F. Sefcik, "Participation Financing: A Comparison of the Characteristics of Convertible Debt and Straight Bonds Issued in Conjunction with Warrants," *Financial Management*, Autumn 1990, 23–34.

equity capital. Generally, maturities also differ between warrants and convertibles. Warrants typically have much shorter maturities than convertibles, and warrants typically expire before their accompanying debt matures. Further, warrants provide for fewer future common shares than do convertibles, because with convertibles all of the debt is converted to common whereas debt remains outstanding when warrants are exercised. Together, these facts suggest that debt-plus-warrant issuers are actually more interested in selling debt than in selling equity.

In general, firms that issue debt with warrants are smaller and riskier than those that issue convertibles. One possible rationale for the use of option securities, especially the use of debt with warrants by small firms, is the difficulty investors have in assessing the risk of small companies. If a startup with a new, untested product seeks debt financing, it is very difficult for potential lenders to judge the riskiness of the venture, hence it is difficult to set a fair interest rate. Under these circumstances, many potential investors will be reluctant to invest, making it necessary to set a very high interest rate to attract debt capital. By issuing debt with warrants, investors obtain a package that offers upside potential to offset the risks of loss.

Finally, there is a significant difference in issuance costs between debt with warrants and convertible debt. Bonds with warrants typically require issuance costs that are about 1.2 percentage points more than the flotation costs for convertibles. In general, bond-with-warrant financings have underwriting fees that approximate the weighted average of the fees associated with debt and equity issues, while underwriting costs for convertibles are more like those associated with straight debt.

Self-Test Questions

What are some differences between debt-with-warrant financing and convertible debt?

Explain how bonds with warrants might help small, risky firms sell debt securities.

Reporting Earnings When Warrants or Convertibles Are Outstanding

If warrants or convertibles are outstanding, a firm could theoretically report earnings per share in one of three ways:

1. *Basic EPS*, calculated as earnings available to common stockholders divided by the average number of shares actually outstanding during the period.
2. *Primary EPS*, calculated as earnings available divided by the average number of shares that would have been outstanding if warrants and convertibles "likely to be converted in the near future" had actually been exercised or converted. In calculating primary EPS, earnings are first adjusted by "backing out" the interest on the convertibles, after which the adjusted earnings are divided by the adjusted number of shares. Accountants have a formula that basically compares the conversion or exercise price with the actual market value of the stock to determine the likelihood of conversion when deciding on the need to use this adjustment procedure.
3. *Diluted EPS*, which is similar to primary EPS except that *all* warrants and convertibles are assumed to be exercised or converted, regardless of the likelihood of exercise or conversion.

Under SEC rules, firms are required to report both basic and diluted EPS. For firms with large amounts of option securities outstanding, there can be a substantial difference between the basic and diluted EPS figures. For financial statement purposes, firms reported diluted EPS until 1997, when the Financial Accounting Standards Board

(FASB) changed to basic EPS. According to FASB, the change was made to give investors a simpler picture of a company's underlying performance. Also, the change makes it easier for investors to compare the performance of U.S. firms with their foreign counterparts, which tend to use basic EPS.

Self-Test Questions

What are the three possible methods for reporting EPS when warrants and convertibles are outstanding?

Which methods are most used in practice?

Why should investors be concerned about a firm's outstanding warrants and convertibles?

Summary

While common stock and long-term debt provide most of the capital used by corporations, companies also use several forms of "hybrid securities." The hybrids include preferred stock, convertibles, and warrants, and they generally have some characteristics of debt and some of equity. We discussed the pros and cons of the hybrids from the standpoints of both issuers and investors, how to determine when to use them, and the factors that affect their values. The basic rationale for these securities, and the procedures used to evaluate them, are based on concepts developed in earlier chapters. The key concepts covered are listed below:

- **Preferred** stock is a hybrid—it is similar to bonds in some respects and to common stock in other ways.
- **Adjustable rate preferred stocks (ARPs)** are those whose dividends are tied to the rate on Treasury securities. **Market auction (money market) preferred** is a low-risk, largely tax-exempt, seven-week maturity security that can be sold between auction dates at close to par.
- A **warrant** is a long-term call option issued along with a bond. Warrants are generally detachable from the bond, and they trade separately in the market. When warrants are exercised, the firm receives additional equity capital, and the original bonds remain outstanding.
- A **convertible** security is a bond or preferred stock that can be exchanged for common stock at the option of the holder. When a security is converted, debt or preferred stock is replaced with common stock, and no money changes hands.
- Warrant and convertible issues are generally structured so that the **exercise** or **conversion price** is 20 to 30 percent above the stock's price at time of issue.
- Although both warrants and convertibles are option securities, there are several differences between the two, including **separability, impact when exercised, callability, maturity,** and **flotation costs.**
- Warrants and convertibles are **"sweeteners"** used to make the underlying debt or preferred stock issue more attractive to investors. Although the coupon rate or dividend yield is lower when options are part of the issue, the overall cost of the issue is higher than the cost of straight debt or preferred, because option-related securities are riskier.

Questions

21–1 Define each of the following terms:
a. Preferred stock
b. Cumulative dividends; arrearages

c. Warrant; detachable warrant
d. Stepped-up price
e. Convertible security
f. Conversion ratio; conversion price; conversion value
g. "Sweetener"

21–2 Is preferred stock more like bonds or common stock? Explain.

21–3 What effect does the trend in stock prices (subsequent to issue) have on a firm's ability to raise funds through (a) convertibles and (b) warrants?

21–4 If a firm expects to have additional financial requirements in the future, would you recommend that it use convertibles or bonds with warrants? What factors would influence your decision?

21–5 How does a firm's dividend policy affect each of the following?
a. The value of its long-term warrants.
b. The likelihood that its convertible bonds will be converted.
c. The likelihood that its warrants will be exercised.

21–6 Evaluate the following statement: "Issuing convertible securities represents a means by which a firm can sell common stock at a price above the existing market."

21–7 Why do corporations often sell convertibles on a rights basis?

21–8 Suppose a company simultaneously issues $50 million of convertible bonds with a coupon rate of 10 percent and $50 million of straight bonds with a coupon rate of 14 percent. Both bonds have the same maturity. Does the fact that the convertible issue has the lower coupon rate suggest that it is less risky than the straight bond? Is the cost of capital lower on the convertible than on the straight bond? Explain.

Problems

21–1 WARRANTS Gregg Company recently issued two types of bonds. The first issue consisted of 20-year straight debt with an 8 percent annual coupon. The second issue consisted of 20-year bonds with a 6 percent annual coupon and attached warrants. Both issues sold at their $1,000 par values. What is the implied value of the warrants attached to each bond?

21–2 CONVERTIBLES Peterson Securities recently issued convertible bonds with a $1,000 par value. The bonds have a conversion price of $40 a share. What is the convertible issue's conversion ratio?

21–3 WARRANTS Maese Industries Inc. has warrants outstanding that permit the holders to purchase 1 share of stock per warrant at a price of $25.

a. Calculate the exercise value of the firm's warrants if the common sells at each of the following prices: (1) $20, (2) $25, (3) $30, (4) $100. (Hint: A warrant's exercise value is the difference between the stock price and the purchase price specified by the warrant if the warrant were to be exercised.)
b. At what approximate price do you think the warrants would actually sell under each condition indicated above? What premium above exercise value is implied in your price? Your answer is a guess, but your prices and premiums should bear reasonable relationships to one another.
c. How would each of the following factors affect your estimates of the warrants' prices and premiums in part b?
   (1) The life of the warrant.
   (2) Expected variability (σ_p) in the stock's price.
   (3) The expected growth rate in the stock's EPS.
   (4) The company announces a change in dividend policy: whereas it formerly paid no dividends, henceforth it will pay out *all* earnings as dividends.
d. Assume the firm's stock now sells for $20 per share. The company wants to sell some 20-year, annual interest, $1,000 par value bonds. Each bond will have attached 50 warrants, each exercisable into 1 share of stock at an exercise price of $25. The firm's straight bonds yield 12 percent. Regardless of your answer to part b, assume that each warrant will have a market

value of $3 when the stock sells at $20. What coupon interest rate, and dollar coupon, must the company set on the bonds with warrants if they are to clear the market?

21–4 *CONVERTIBLE PREMIUMS*

The Tsetsekos Company was planning to finance an expansion in the summer of 2001. The principal executives of the company all agreed that an industrial company such as theirs should finance growth by means of common stock rather than by debt. However, they felt that the price of the company's common stock did not reflect its true worth, so they decided to sell a convertible security. They considered a convertible debenture but feared the burden of fixed interest charges if the common stock did not rise in price to make conversion attractive. They decided on an issue of convertible preferred stock, which would pay a dividend of $2.10 per share.

The common stock was selling for $42 a share at the time. Management projected earnings for 2001 at $3 a share and expected a future growth rate of 10 percent a year in 2002 and beyond. It was agreed by the investment bankers and the management that the common stock would sell at 14 times earnings, the current price/earnings ratio.

a. What conversion price should be set by the issuer? The conversion ratio will be 1.0; that is, each share of convertible preferred can be converted into 1 share of common. Therefore, the convertible's par value (and also the issue price) will be equal to the conversion price, which, in turn, will be determined as a percentage over the current market price of the common. Your answer will be a guess, but make it a reasonable one.

b. Should the preferred stock include a call provision? Why?

21–5 *CONVERTIBLE BOND ANALYSIS*

In 1976, Roop Industries sold $400 million of convertible bonds. The bonds had a 40-year maturity, a 5¾ percent coupon rate, and were sold at their $1,000 par value. The conversion price was set at $62.75 against a current price of $55 per share of common. The bonds were subordinated debentures, and they were given an A rating; straight nonconvertible debentures of the same quality yielded about 8¾ percent at the time.

a. Calculate the premium on the bonds, that is, the percentage excess of the conversion price over the current stock price.

b. What is Roop's annual interest savings on the convertible issue versus a straight-debt issue?

c. Suppose the current price of Roop's common stock fell from $55 on the day the bonds were issued to $32.75 at present. Assume interest rates remained constant. Do you think it is likely that the bonds would have been converted? (Calculate the value of the stock you would receive by converting the bond.)

d. The bonds originally sold for $1,000. If interest rates on A-rated bonds had remained constant at 8¾ percent, what do you think would have happened to the price of the convertible bonds?

e. Now suppose the price of Roop's common stock had fallen from $55 on the day the bonds were issued to $32.75 at present. Suppose also that the rate of interest had fallen from 8¾ to 5¾ percent. Under these conditions, what do you think would have happened to the price of the bonds?

f. Set up a graphic model to illustrate how investors valued the Roop convertibles in 1976. How well were these expectations realized?

21–6 *WARRANT/CONVERTIBLE DECISIONS*

The Howland Carpet Company has grown rapidly during the past 5 years. Recently, its commercial bank urged the company to consider increasing its permanent financing. Its bank loan under a line of credit has risen to $250,000, carrying an 8 percent interest rate. Howland has been 30 to 60 days late in paying trade creditors.

Discussions with an investment banker have resulted in the decision to raise $500,000 at this time. Investment bankers have assured the firm that the following alternatives are feasible (flotation costs will be ignored):

- ***Alternative 1:*** Sell common stock at $8.
- ***Alternative 2:*** Sell convertible bonds at an 8 percent coupon, convertible into 100 shares of common stock for each $1,000 bond (that is, the conversion price is $10 per share).
- ***Alternative 3:*** Sell debentures at an 8 percent coupon, each $1,000 bond carrying 100 warrants to buy common stock at $10.

John L. Howland, the president, owns 80 percent of the common stock and wishes to maintain control of the company. One hundred thousand shares are outstanding. The following are extracts of Howland's latest financial statements:

BALANCE SHEET

		Current liabilities	$400,000
		Common stock, par $1	100,000
		Retained earnings	50,000
Total assets	$550,000	Total claims	$550,000

INCOME STATEMENT

Sales	$1,100,000
All costs except interest	990,000
EBIT	$ 110,000
Interest	20,000
EBT	$ 90,000
Taxes (40%)	36,000
Net income	$ 54,000
Shares outstanding	100,000
Earnings per share	$0.54
Price/earnings ratio	15.83×
Market price of stock	$8.55

a. Show the new balance sheet under each alternative. For Alternatives 2 and 3, show the balance sheet after conversion of the bonds or exercise of the warrants. Assume that half of the funds raised will be used to pay off the bank loan and half to increase total assets.

b. Show Mr. Howland's control position under each alternative, assuming that he does not purchase additional shares.

c. What is the effect on earnings per share of each alternative, if it is assumed that profits before interest and taxes will be 20 percent of total assets?

d. What will be the debt ratio under each alternative?

e. Which of the three alternatives would you recommend to Howland, and why?

21-7 *CONVERTIBLE BOND ANALYSIS*

Niendorf Incorporated needs to raise $25 million to construct production facilities for a new type of diskette drive. The firm's straight nonconvertible debentures currently yield 14 percent. Its stock sells for $30 per share; the last dividend was $2; and the expected growth rate is a constant 9 percent. Investment bankers have tentatively proposed that the firm raise the $25 million by issuing convertible debentures. These convertibles would have a $1,000 par value, carry a coupon rate of 10 percent, have a 20-year maturity, and be convertible into 20 shares of stock. The bonds would be noncallable for 5 years, after which they would be callable at a price of $1,075; this call price would decline by $5 per year in Year 6 and each year thereafter. Management has called convertibles in the past (and presumably it will call them again in the future), once they were eligible for call, when the bonds' conversion value was about 20 percent above the bonds' par value (not their call price).

a. Draw an accurate graph similar to Figure 21-1 representing the expectations set forth above. (Assume an annual coupon.)

b. What is the expected rate of return on the proposed convertible issue?

c. Do you think that these bonds could be successfully offered to the public at par? That is, does $1,000 seem to be an equilibrium price in view of the stated terms? If not, suggest the type of change that would have to be made to cause the bonds to trade at $1,000 in the secondary market, assuming no change in capital market conditions.

d. Suppose the projects outlined here work out on schedule for 2 years, but then the firm begins to experience extremely strong competition from Japanese firms. As a result, Niendorf's expected growth rate drops from 9 percent to zero. Assume that the dividend at the time of the drop is $2.38. The company's credit strength is not impaired, and its value of k_s is also unchanged. What would happen (1) to the stock price, and (2) to the convertible bond's price? Be as precise as you can.

Mini Case

CD

See **Ch 21 Show.ppt** and **Ch 21 Mini Case.xls.**

Paul Duncan, financial manager of EduSoft Inc., is facing a dilemma. The firm was founded 5 years ago to provide educational software for the rapidly expanding primary and secondary school markets. Although EduSoft has done well, the firm's founder believes that an industry shakeout is imminent. To survive, EduSoft must grab market share now, and this will require a large infusion of new capital.

Because he expects earnings to continue rising sharply and looks for the stock price to follow suit, Mr. Duncan does not think it would be wise to issue new common stock at this time. On the other hand, interest rates are currently high by historical standards, and with the firm's B rating, the interest payments on a new debt issue would be prohibitive. Thus, he has narrowed his choice of financing alternatives to two securities: (1) bonds with warrants or (2) convertible bonds. As Duncan's assistant, you have been asked to help in the decision process by answering the following questions:

a. How does preferred stock differ from both common equity and debt? Is preferred stock more risky than common stock? What is floating rate preferred stock?

b. How can a knowledge of call options help a financial manager to better understand warrants and convertibles?

c. One of the firm's alternatives is to issue a bond with warrants attached. EduSoft's current stock price is $20, and its investment banker estimates that the cost of a 20-year, annual coupon bond without warrants would be 12 percent. The bankers suggest attaching 50 warrants, each with an exercise price of $25, to each $1,000 bond. It is estimated that each warrant, when detached and traded separately, would have a value of $3.

(1) What coupon rate should be set on the bond with warrants if the total package is to sell for $1,000?

(2) Suppose the bonds were issued and the warrants immediately traded on the open market for $5 each. What would this imply about the terms of the issue? Did the company "win" or "lose"?

(3) When would you expect the warrants to be exercised? Assume they have a 10-year life; that is, they expire 10 years after issue.

(4) Will the warrants bring in additional capital when exercised? If so, how much, and what type of capital?

(5) Because warrants lower the cost of the accompanying debt issue, shouldn't all debt be issued with warrants? What is the expected return to the holders of the bond with warrants (or the expected cost to the company) if the warrants are expected to be exercised in 5 years, when EduSoft's stock price is expected to be $36.75? How would you expect the cost of the bond with warrants to compare with the cost of straight debt? With the cost of common stock?

d. As an alternative to the bond with warrants, Mr. Duncan is considering convertible bonds. The firm's investment bankers estimate that EduSoft could sell a 20-year, 10.5 percent annual coupon, callable convertible bond for its $1,000 par value, whereas a straight-debt issue would require a 12 percent coupon. The convertibles would be call protected for 5 years, the call price would be $1,100, and the company would probably call the bonds as soon as possible after their conversion value exceeds $1,200. Note, though, that the call must occur on an issue date anniversary. EduSoft's current stock price is $20, its last dividend was $1.48, and the dividend is expected to grow at a constant 8 percent rate. The convertible could be converted into 40 shares of EduSoft stock at the owner's option.

(1) What conversion price is built into the bond?

(2) What is the convertible's straight-debt value? What is the implied value of the convertibility feature?

(3) What is the formula for the bond's expected conversion value in any year? What is its conversion value at Year 0? At Year 10?
(4) What is meant by the "floor value" of a convertible? What is the convertible's expected floor value at Year 0? At Year 10?
(5) Assume that EduSoft intends to force conversion by calling the bond as soon as possible after its conversion value exceeds 20 percent above its par value, or 1.2($1,000) = $1,200. When is the issue expected to be called? (Hint: Recall that the call must be made on an anniversary date of the issue.)
(6) What is the expected cost of capital for the convertible to EduSoft? Does this cost appear to be consistent with the riskiness of the issue?

e. EduSoft's market value capital structure is as follows (in millions of dollars):

Debt	$50
Equity	50
	$100

If the company raises $20 million in additional capital by selling (1) convertibles or (2) bonds with warrants, what would its WACC be, and how would those figures compare with its current WACC? EduSoft's tax rate is 40 percent.

f. Mr. Duncan believes that the costs of both the bond with warrants and the convertible bond are close enough to one another to call them even, and also consistent with the risks involved. Thus, he will make his decision based on other factors. What are some of the factors which he should consider?

g. How do convertible bonds help reduce agency costs?

Selected Additional References and Cases

For additional discussions on preferred stock, see

Alderson, Michael J., and Donald R. Fraser, "Financial Innovations and Excesses Revisited: The Case of Auction Rate Preferred Stock," *Financial Management*, Summer 1993, 61–75.

Alderson, Michael J., Keith C. Brown, and Scott L. Lummer, "Dutch Auction Rate Preferred Stock," *Financial Management*, Summer 1987, 68–73.

Fooladi, Iraj, and Gordon S. Roberts, "On Preferred Stock," *Journal of Financial Research*, Winter 1986, 319–324.

Wansley, James W., Fayez A. Elayan, and Brian A. Maris, "Preferred Stock Returns, CreditWatch, and Preferred Stock Rating Changes," *The Financial Review*, May 1990, 265–285.

Winger, Bernard J., et al., "Adjustable Rate Preferred Stock," *Financial Management*, Spring 1986, 48–57.

Quite a bit of work has been done on warrant pricing. Some of the articles include

Ehrhardt, Michael C., and Ronald E. Shrieves, "The Impact of Warrants and Convertible Securities on the Systematic Risk of Common Equity," *Financial Review*, November 1995, 843–856.

Galai, Dan, and Mier I. Schneller, "The Pricing of Warrants and the Value of the Firm," *Journal of Finance*, December 1978, 1333–1342.

Lauterbach, Beni, and Paul Schultz, "Pricing Warrants: An Empirical Study of the Black-Scholes Model and Its Alternatives," *Journal of Finance*, September 1990, 1181–1209.

Leonard, David C., and Michael E. Solt, "On Using the Black-Scholes Model to Value Warrants," *Journal of Financial Research*, Summer 1990, 81–92.

Phelps, Katherine L., William T. Moore, and Rodney L. Roenfeldt, "Equity Valuation Effects of Warrant-Debt Financing," *Journal of Financial Research*, Summer 1991, 93–103.

Schwartz, Eduardo S., "The Valuation of Warrants: Implementing a New Approach," *Journal of Financial Economics*, January 1977, 79–93.

For more insights into convertible pricing and use, see the Web/CD Extension for this chapter and the following:

Alexander, Gordon J., and Roger D. Stover, "Pricing in the New Issue Convertible Debt Market," *Financial Management*, Fall 1977, 35–39.

Alexander, Gordon J., Roger D. Stover, and D. B. Kuhnau, "Market Timing Strategies in Convertible Debt Financing," *Journal of Finance*, March 1979, 143–155.

Asquith, Paul, and David W. Mullins, Jr., "Convertible Debt: Corporate Call Policy and Voluntary Conversion," *Journal of Finance*, September 1991, 1273–1289.

Billingsley, Randall S., and David M. Smith, "Why Do Firms Issue Convertible Debt?" *Financial Management*, Summer 1996, 93–99.

Brennan, Michael, "The Case for Convertibles," *Issues in Corporate Finance* (New York: Stern Stewart Putnam & Macklis, 1983), 102–111.

Emery, Douglas R., Mai E. Iskandor-Datta, and Jong-Chul Rhim, "Capital Structure Management as a Motivation for Calling Convertible Debt," *Journal of Financial Research*, Spring 1994, 91–104.

Harikumar, T., P. Kadapakkam, and Ronald F. Singer, "Convertible Debt and Investment Incentives," *Journal of Financial Research*, Spring 1994, 15–29.

Ingersoll, Jonathan E., "A Contingent Claims Valuation of Convertible Securities," *Journal of Financial Economics*, May 1977, 289–322.

Janjigian, Vahan, "The Leverage Changing Consequences of Convertible Debt Financing," *Financial Management*, Autumn 1987, 15–21.

Krishnan, V. Sivarama, and Ramesh P. Rao, "Financial Distress Costs and Delayed Calls of Convertible Bonds," *Financial Review*, November 1996, 913–925.

The following case from the Cases in Financial Management: Dryden Request *series covers many of the issues presented in this chapter:*

Case 27, "Virginia May Chocolate Company," which illustrates convertible bond valuation.

PART EIGHT
Working Capital Management

22

Current Asset Management

In Chapter 3 we noted Dell Computer Corporation's phenomenal performance over the past decade, when its stock increased a staggering 72,000 percent. Dramatic improvements in computer technology, along with growth in the Internet, help explain Dell's superb results. However, not all computer companies have prospered, and Dell is clearly "the best of the bunch." How has Dell bested its competitors? Perhaps the number one reason is its working capital management, which is the focus of this chapter.

The key to Dell's success is its ability to build and deliver customized computers very quickly. Traditionally, manufacturers of custom-design products had two choices. They could keep a large supply of inventory on hand to meet customer needs, or they could make their customers wait for weeks while the customized product was being built. Dell changed all that. First, it uses information technology to better coordinate with its suppliers. If a supplier wants to do business with Dell, it must be able to provide the necessary components quickly and cheaply. Suppliers that adapt and meet Dell's demands are rewarded with increased business, and those that don't lose their Dell business.

Second, Dell uses information technology to collect data that enable it to better customize products for its customers. For example, a recent *Fortune* article described how Dell captured most of Ford's PC business:

> Look at what the company does for one big customer, Ford Motor. Dell creates a bunch of different configurations designed for Ford employees in different departments. When Dell receives an order via the Ford Intranet, it knows immediately what type of worker is ordering and what kind of computer he or she needs. The company assembles the proper hardware and even installs the right software, some of which consists of Ford-specific code that's stored at Dell. Since Dell's logistics software is so sophisticated, it can do the customization quickly and inexpensively.

Sound working capital management is necessary if a company wants to compete in the information age, and the lessons taught by Dell extend to other industries. Indeed, Michael Dell, founder and CEO of Dell Computer, recently discussed in an interview with *The Wall Street Journal* how traditional manufacturers, such as the automobile companies, can use the experience of Dell to improve their operations. The article included Michael Dell's five points on how to build a better car:

1. Use the Internet to lower the costs of linking manufacturers with their suppliers and dealers.
2. Turn over to an outside specialist any operation that isn't central to the business.
3. Accelerate the pace of change, and get employees conditioned to accept change.
4. Experiment with Internet businesses. Set up trials to see what happens when customers can access information more easily, and in ways they never could before.
5. Think about what could be done with the capital that would be freed up by shedding excessive inventory and other redundant assets.

Sources: J. William Gurley and Jane Hodges, "A Dell for Every Industry," *Fortune*, October 12, 1998, 167–172; Gary McWilliams and Joseph B. White, "Dell to Detroit: Get into Gear Online!" *The Wall Street Journal*, December 1, 1999, B1.

About 60 percent of a typical financial manager's time is devoted to working capital management, and many students' first jobs will involve working capital. This is particularly true in smaller businesses, where most new jobs are being created.

Working capital policy involves two basic questions: (1) What is the appropriate amount of current assets for the firm to carry, both in total and for each specific account, and (2) how should current assets be financed? This chapter addresses current asset holdings and Chapter 23 addresses their financing. In earlier editions we included a third chapter that contained some specialized topics in working capital management. That material is included on the textbook's Web site and CD-ROM.

The textbook's CD-ROM contains an *Excel* file that will guide you through the chapter's calculations. The file for this chapter is ***Ch 22 Tool Kit.xls,*** and we encourage you to open the file and follow along as you read the chapter.

As you will see, sound working capital management goes beyond finance. Indeed, most of the ideas for improving working capital management often stem from other disciplines. For example, experts in business logistics, operations management, and information technology often work with the marketing group to develop a better way to deliver the firm's products. Where finance comes into play is in evaluating the profitability of alternative systems, which are generally costly to install. For example, let's say that a firm's information technology and marketing groups decide that they want to (1) develop new software and (2) purchase computer terminals that will be installed in their customers' premises. Customers will then keep track of their own inventories and automatically order new supplies when inventory levels hit specified targets. The system will improve inventory management for both the manufacturer and its customers and also help "lock in" good customers.

Significant costs will be incurred to develop and install the new system, but if it is adopted, the company can meet its customers' needs better, and with smaller inventory, and also increase sales. In many respects, this scenario looks like a typical capital budgeting project—it has an up-front cost followed by a series of positive cash flows. The finance group can use the capital budgeting techniques described in Chapters 13, 14, and 15 to evaluate whether the new system is worth the cost and also whether it should be developed in-house or purchased from an outside source.

Working Capital Terminology

We begin our discussion of working capital policy by reviewing some basic definitions and concepts:

1. **Working capital,** sometimes called *gross working capital,* simply refers to current assets used in operations.
2. **Net working capital** is defined as current assets minus current liabilities.
3. **Net operating working capital** (NOWC) is defined as operating current assets minus operating current liabilities. Generally, NOWC is equal to cash, accounts receivable, and inventories less accounts payable and accruals.
4. The **current ratio,** which was discussed in Chapter 3, is calculated by dividing current assets by current liabilities, and it is intended to measure liquidity. However, a high current ratio does not ensure that a firm will have the cash required to meet its needs. If inventories cannot be sold, or if receivables cannot be collected in a timely manner, then the apparent safety reflected in a high current ratio could be illusory.
5. The **quick ratio,** or **acid test,** also attempts to measure liquidity, and it is found by subtracting inventories from current assets and then dividing by current liabilities. The quick ratio removes inventories from current assets because they are the least liquid current asset. Therefore, the quick ratio is an "acid test" of a company's ability to meet its current obligations.
6. The best and most comprehensive picture of a firm's liquidity position is shown by its **cash budget.** This statement, which forecasts cash inflows and outflows, focuses on what really counts, namely, the firm's ability to generate sufficient cash inflows

to meet its required cash outflows. We will discuss cash budgeting in detail later in the chapter.

7. **Working capital policy** refers to the firm's policies regarding (1) target levels for each category of current assets and (2) how current assets will be financed.
8. **Working capital management** involves both setting working capital policy and carrying out that policy in day-to-day operations.

The term *working capital* originated with the old Yankee peddler, who would load up his wagon and then go off to peddle his wares. The merchandise was called working capital because it was what he actually sold, or "turned over," to produce his profits. The wagon and horse were his fixed assets. He generally owned the horse and wagon, so they were financed with "equity" capital, but he borrowed the funds to buy the merchandise. These borrowings were called *working capital loans*, and they had to be repaid after each trip to demonstrate to the bank that the credit was sound. If the peddler was able to repay the loan, then the bank would make another loan, and banks that followed this procedure were said to be employing "sound banking practices."

Self-Test Questions

Why is the quick ratio also called an acid test?

How did the term "working capital" originate?

Alternative Current Asset Investment Policies

Figure 22-1 shows three alternative policies regarding the total amount of current assets carried. Essentially, these policies differ with regard to the amount of current assets carried to support any given level of sales, hence in the turnover of those assets. The line with the steepest slope represents a **relaxed current asset investment** (or "fat cat") **policy,** where relatively large amounts of cash, marketable securities, and inventories are carried, and where sales are stimulated by the use of a credit policy that provides liberal financing to customers and a corresponding high level of receivables. Conversely, with the **restricted current asset investment** (or "lean and mean") **policy,** the holdings of cash, securities, inventories, and receivables are minimized. Under the restricted policy, current assets are turned over more frequently, so each dollar of current assets is forced to "work harder." The **moderate current asset investment policy** is between the two extremes.

Under conditions of certainty—where sales, costs, lead times, payment periods, and so on, are known for sure—all firms would hold only minimal levels of current assets. Any larger amounts would increase the need for external funding without a corresponding increase in profits, while any smaller holdings would involve late payments to suppliers along with lost sales due to inventory shortages and an overly restrictive credit policy.

However, the picture changes when uncertainty is introduced. Here the firm requires some minimum amount of cash and inventories based on expected payments, expected sales, expected order lead times, and so on, plus additional holdings, or *safety stocks*, which enable it to deal with departures from the expected values. Similarly, accounts receivable levels are determined by credit terms, and the tougher the credit terms, the lower the receivables for any given level of sales. With a restricted current asset investment policy, the firm would hold minimal safety stocks of cash and inventories, and it would have a tight credit policy even though this meant running the risk of losing sales. A restricted, lean-and-mean current asset investment policy often provides the highest expected return on this investment, but it entails the greatest risk, while the reverse is true under a relaxed policy. The moderate policy falls in between the two extremes in terms of expected return and risk.

FIGURE 22-1 Alternative Current Asset Investment Policies (Millions of Dollars)

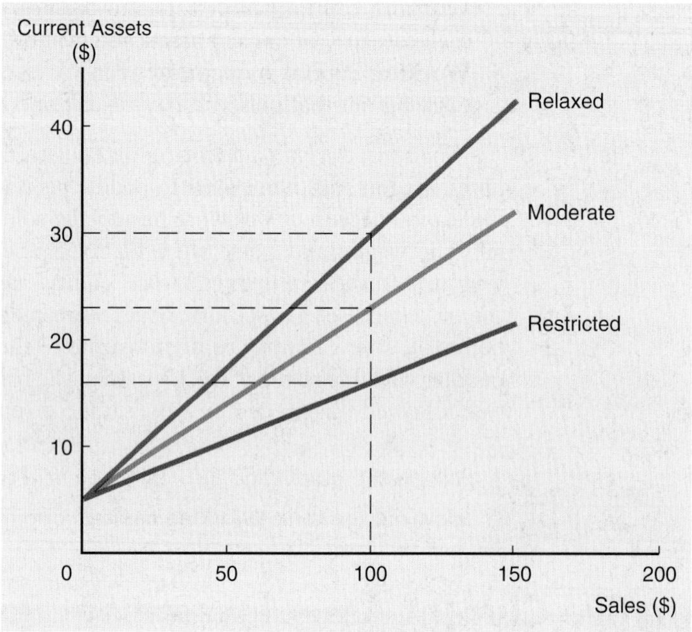

Policy	Current Assets to Support Sales of $100	Turnover of Current Assets
Relaxed (fat cat)	$30	3.3×
Moderate	23	4.3×
Restricted (lean and mean)	16	6.3×

Note: The sales/current assets relationship is shown here as being linear, but the relationship is often curvilinear.

Changing technology can lead to dramatic changes in the optimal current asset investment policy. For example, if new technology makes it possible for a manufacturer to speed up the production of a given product from 10 days to 5 days, then its work-in-progress inventory can be cut in half. Similarly, retailers such as Wal-Mart or Home Depot have installed systems under which bar codes on all merchandise are read at the cash register. The information on the sale is electronically transmitted to a computer that maintains a record of the inventory of each item, and the computer automatically transmits orders to suppliers' computers when stocks fall to prescribed levels. With such a system, inventories will be held at optimal levels; orders will reflect exactly what styles, colors, and sizes consumers are buying; and the firm's profits will be maximized.

Managing the Components of Working Capital

Working capital consists of four main components: cash, marketable securities, inventories, and accounts receivable. The remainder of this chapter focuses on the issues involved with managing each of these components. As you will see, a common thread underlies all current asset management. For each type of asset, firms face a fundamental trade-off: current assets (that is, working capital) are necessary to conduct business, and the greater the holdings of current assets, the smaller the danger of running out, hence the lower the firm's operating risk. However, holding working capital is

Free Cash Flow, EVA, and Working Capital

Recall from Chapter 12 that a company's value depends on its free cash flow (FCF), defined as follows:

$$\begin{aligned} \text{FCF} &= \text{Net operating profit after taxes} - \text{Net investment in operating capital} \\ &= \text{NOPAT} - \text{Net investment in operating capital} \\ &= [\text{EBIT} \times (1 - \text{T})] - (\text{Capital this year} - \text{Capital last year}). \end{aligned}$$

If a company can reduce its inventories, its cash holdings, or its receivables, then its net investment in operating capital will go down. If these actions don't harm operating profit, then FCF will increase, which will lead to a higher stock price.

Economic Value Added (EVA) provides another useful way of thinking about working capital, particularly if a manager's compensation is linked to EVA. Recall from Chapter 2 that EVA is defined as follows:

$$\text{EVA} = \text{NOPAT} - (\text{WACC} \times \text{Total operating capital}).$$

A reduction in working capital decreases total operating capital, which increases EVA. Many firms report that when division managers and other operating people begin to think in these terms, they often find ways to reduce working capital, especially if their compensation depends on their divisions' EVAs.

We can also think of working capital management in terms of ROE and the Du Pont equation:

$$\begin{aligned} \text{ROE} &= \begin{matrix}\text{Profit}\\ \text{margin}\end{matrix} \times \begin{matrix}\text{Total}\\ \text{assets}\\ \text{turnover}\end{matrix} \times \begin{matrix}\text{Leverage}\\ \text{factor}\end{matrix} \\ &= \begin{matrix}\text{Net}\\ \text{income/}\\ \text{Sales}\end{matrix} \times \begin{matrix}\text{Sales/}\\ \text{Total}\\ \text{assets}\end{matrix} \times \begin{matrix}\text{Assets/}\\ \text{Equity}\end{matrix}. \end{aligned}$$

If working capital and hence total assets can be reduced without seriously affecting the profit margin, this will increase the total assets turnover and, consequently, ROE.

costly—if inventories are too large, then the firm will have assets that earn a zero or even negative return if storage and spoilage costs are high. And, of course, firms must acquire capital to buy assets such as inventory. Since this capital has a cost, it increases the downward drag from excessive inventories (or receivables or even cash). So, there is pressure to hold the amount of working capital to the minimum consistent with running the business without interruption.

Self-Test Questions

Identify and explain three alternative current asset investment policies.

What are the principal components of working capital?

What are the reasons for not wanting to hold too little working capital? For not wanting to hold too much?

What is the fundamental trade-off that managers face when managing working capital?

The Cash Conversion Cycle

Firms typically follow a cycle in which they purchase inventory, sell goods on credit, and then collect accounts receivable. This cycle is referred to as the *cash conversion cycle*, and it is discussed in detail in this section. Sound working capital policy is designed to minimize the time between cash expenditures on materials and the collection of cash on sales.

An Illustration

We can illustrate the process with data from Real Time Computer Corporation (RTC), which in early 2001 introduced a new minicomputer that can perform 1 billion instructions per second and that will sell for $250,000. RTC expects to sell 40 computers in its first year of production. The effects of this new product on RTC's working capital position were analyzed in terms of the following five steps:

1. RTC will order and then receive the materials it needs to produce the computers. Because RTC and most other firms purchase materials on credit, this transaction will create an account payable. However, the purchase will have no immediate cash flow effect.
2. Labor will be used to convert the materials into finished computers. However, wages will not be fully paid at the time the work is done, so, like accounts payable, accrued wages will also build up.
3. The finished computers will be sold, but on credit. Therefore, sales will create receivables, not immediate cash inflows.
4. At some point before cash comes in, RTC and most other firms must pay off their accounts payable and accrued wages. This outflow must be financed.
5. The cycle will be completed when RTC's receivables have been collected. At that time, the company can pay off the credit that was used to finance production, and it can then repeat the cycle.

The **cash conversion cycle model,** which focuses on the length of time between when the company makes payments and when it receives cash inflows, formalizes the steps outlined above.[1] The following terms are used in the model:

1. **Inventory conversion period,** which is the average time required to convert materials into finished goods and then to sell those goods. Note that the inventory conversion period is calculated by dividing inventory by sales per day. For example, if average inventories are $2 million and sales are $10 million, then the inventory conversion period is 72 days:

$$\text{Inventory conversion period} = \frac{\text{Inventory}}{\text{Sales per day}} \tag{22-1}$$

$$= \frac{\$2{,}000{,}000}{\$10{,}000{,}000/360}$$

$$= 72 \text{ days.}$$

Thus, it takes an average of 72 days to convert materials into finished goods and then to sell those goods.[2]

2. **Receivables collection period,** which is the average length of time required to convert the firm's receivables into cash, that is, to collect cash following a sale. The receivables collection period is also called the *days sales outstanding (DSO)*, and it is calculated by dividing accounts receivable by the average credit sales per day. If receivables are $666,667 and sales are $10 million, the receivables collection period is

$$\begin{array}{c}\text{Receivables}\\ \text{collection period}\end{array} = \text{DSO} = \frac{\text{Receivables}}{\text{Sales/360}} \tag{22-2}$$

$$= \frac{\$666{,}667}{\$10{,}000{,}000/360} = 24 \text{ days.}$$

Thus, it takes 24 days after a sale to convert the receivables into cash.

[1]See Verlyn D. Richards and Eugene J. Laughlin, "A Cash Conversion Cycle Approach to Liquidity Analysis," *Financial Management*, Spring 1980, 32–38.

[2]Some analysts define the inventory conversion period as inventory divided by daily cost of goods sold (COGS). However, most published sources use the formula we show in Equation 22-1.

3. **Payables deferral period,** which is the average length of time between the purchase of materials and labor and the payment of cash for them. For example, if the firm on average has 30 days to pay for labor and materials, if its cost of goods sold are \$8 million per year, and if its accounts payable average \$666,667, then its payables deferral period can be calculated as follows:

$$\begin{aligned}\text{Payables deferral period} &= \frac{\text{Payables}}{\text{Purchases per day}} \\ &= \frac{\text{Payables}}{\text{Cost of goods sold}/360} \qquad \textbf{(22-3)}\end{aligned}$$

$$\begin{aligned}&= \frac{\$666{,}667}{\$8{,}000{,}000/360} \\ &= 30 \text{ days.}\end{aligned}$$

This calculated figure is consistent with the stated 30-day payment period.[3]

4. **Cash conversion cycle,** which nets out the three periods just defined and which therefore equals the length of time between the firm's actual cash expenditures and its own cash receipts. The cash conversion cycle thus equals the average length of time a dollar is tied up in current assets.

We can use these definitions to set up an equation for the cash conversion cycle. First, the concept is diagrammed in Figure 22-2. Each component is given a number, and then the cash conversion cycle can be expressed by this equation:

$$\underset{\text{Inventory conversion period}}{(1)} + \underset{\text{Receivables collection period}}{(2)} - \underset{\text{Payables deferral period}}{(3)} = \underset{\text{Cash conversion cycle}}{(4)}. \qquad \textbf{(22-4)}$$

To illustrate, suppose it takes RTC an average of 72 days to convert raw materials to computers and then to sell them, and another 24 days to collect its receivables. However, 30 days normally elapse between receipt of raw materials and payment for them. In this case, the cash conversion cycle would be 66 days:

$$\text{Days in cash conversion cycle} = 72 \text{ days} + 24 \text{ days} - 30 \text{ days} = 66 \text{ days.}$$

To look at it another way,

$$\begin{aligned}\text{Cash inflow delay} &- \text{Payment delay} = \text{Net delay} \\ (72 \text{ days} + 24 \text{ days}) &- 30 \text{ days} = 66 \text{ days.}\end{aligned}$$

Shortening the Cash Conversion Cycle

Given these data, RTC knows when it starts producing a computer that it will have to finance the manufacturing costs for 66 days. The firm's goal should be to shorten its cash conversion cycle as much as possible without hurting operations. This would improve profits, because the longer the cash conversion cycle, the greater the need for external financing, and that financing has a cost that lowers EVA.

The cash conversion cycle can be shortened (1) by reducing the inventory conversion period by processing and selling goods more quickly, (2) by reducing the

[3]Some sources define the payables deferral period as payables divided by daily sales.

The Best at Managing Working Capital

What do Boeing, Guess, PepsiCo, Vulcan Materials, Cisco Systems, Johnson Controls, McDonald's, Nucor, Eastman Kodak, and Burlington Northern Santa Fe have in common? Each of these companies leads its industry in *CFO* magazine's annual survey of working capital management, which covers 1,000 firms with sales greater than $500 million. Each company is rated on the number of days in its cash conversion cycle and on its cash conversion efficiency (CCE), defined as cash flow from operations divided by sales.

According to this survey, the median number of days in the cash conversion cycle is about 57.3, which is 6.3 days better than five years ago. Burlington Northern Santa Fe (BNSF) leads the pack, with a cash conversion cycle of −57.2 days, versus an industry average of 24! BNSF achieved this by reengineering its accounts receivable process, starting with the number of days it takes to submit a bill to customers. In 1997 it had about 50,000 bills on hand each day that had not yet been priced and rendered to customers. By working on its information systems, BFNS was able to automate much of the process, and it reduced unprocessed bills to about 15,000. BFNS then turned its attention to the number of days it takes a customer to pay. They found that their large customers would receive a batch of bills, but not pay any of them if the customer disputed any single bill in the batch. Working closely with marketing and sales, BFNS was able to greatly reduce the number of disputed bills. The net result of these efforts was a decrease in the days sales outstanding from 50 to 29. When coupled with very little inventory and its own ability to delay payments to its suppliers, BFNS's cash conversion cycle came in at −57.2 days. This increased its free cash flow to such an extent that BFNS was able to implement a large stock repurchase program.

Source: Randy Myers, "Cash Crop: The 2000 Working Capital Survey," *CFO*, August 2000, 58–82.

receivables collection period by speeding up collections, or (3) by lengthening the payables deferral period by slowing down the firm's own payments. To the extent that these actions can be taken *without increasing costs or depressing sales*, they should be carried out.

Benefits

We can illustrate the benefits of shortening the cash conversion cycle by looking again at Real Time Computer Corporation. Suppose RTC must spend $200,000 on materials and labor to produce one computer, and it takes three days to produce a computer. Thus, it must invest $200,000/3 = $66,667 for each day's output. This investment

FIGURE 22-2 The Cash Conversion Cycle Model

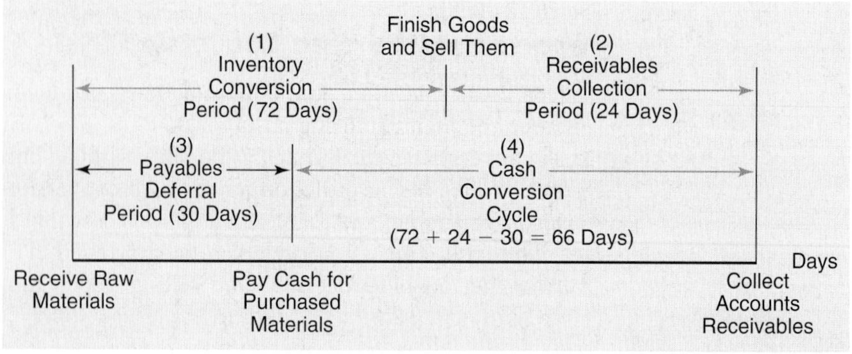

must be financed for 66 days—the length of the cash conversion cycle—so the company's working capital financing needs will be 66 × \$66,667 = \$4.4 million. If RTC could reduce the cash conversion cycle to 56 days, say, by deferring payment of its accounts payable an additional 10 days, or by speeding up either the production process or the collection of its receivables, it could reduce its working capital financing requirements by \$666,667.

Recall that free cash flow (FCF) is equal to NOPAT minus net investments in operating capital. Therefore, if working capital decreases, FCF increases by that same amount. RTC's 10-day reduction in its cash conversion cycle would lead to an increase in FCF of \$666,667. Note also that reducing the cash conversion cycle reduces the ratio of net operating working capital to sales (NOWC/Sales). If sales stay at the same level, then the reduction in working capital is simply a one-time cash inflow. However, if sales are expected to grow, and if the NOWC/Sales ratio remains at its new level, then less working capital will be required to support the additional sales, leading to an increase in projected FCF for each future year.

The combination of the one-time cash inflow and the long-term improvement in working capital can add substantial value to companies. Two professors, Hyun-Han Shin and Luc Soenen, studied more than 2,900 companies during a recent 20-year period, and they found a strong relationship between a company's cash conversion cycle and its performance.[4] In particular, their results showed that for the average company a 10-day improvement in the cash conversion cycle was associated with an increase in pre-tax operating profit from 12.76 to 13.02 percent. They also showed that companies with a cash conversion cycle 10 days shorter than average also had an annual stock return that was 1.7 percentage points higher than that of an average company, even after adjusting for differences in risk. Given results like these, it's no wonder firms now place so much emphasis on working capital management!

Self-Test Questions

Define the following terms: inventory conversion period, receivables collection period, and payables deferral period. Give the equation for each term.

What is the cash conversion cycle? What is its equation?

What should a firm's goal be regarding the cash conversion cycle? Explain your answer.

What are some actions a firm can take to shorten its cash conversion cycle?

The Concept of Zero Working Capital

At first glance, it might seem that working capital management is not as important as capital budgeting, dividend policy, and other decisions that determine a firm's long-term direction. However, in today's world of intense global competition, working capital management is receiving increasing attention from managers striving for peak efficiency. In fact, the goal of many leading companies today—including American Standard, Campbell Soup, General Electric, Quaker Oats, and Whirlpool—is *zero working capital.* Proponents of the zero working capital concept claim that a movement toward this goal not only generates cash but also speeds up production and helps businesses make more timely deliveries and operate more efficiently. The concept has its own definition of working capital: Inventories + Receivables − Payables. The rationale here is (1) that inventories and receivables are the keys to making sales, but (2) that inventories can be financed by suppliers through accounts payable.

[4]See Hyun-Han Shin and Luc Soenen, "Efficiency of Working Capital Management and Corporate Profitability," *Financial Practice and Education,* Fall/Winter 1998, 37–45.

On average, companies use about 20 cents of working capital for each dollar of sales. So, on average, working capital is turned over five times per year. Reducing working capital and thus increasing turnover has two major financial benefits. First, every dollar freed up by reducing inventories or receivables, or by increasing payables, results in a one-time contribution to cash flow. Second, a movement toward zero working capital permanently raises a company's earnings. Like all capital, funds invested in working capital cost money, so reducing those funds yields permanent savings in capital costs. In addition to the financial benefits, reducing working capital forces a company to produce and deliver faster than its competitors, which helps it gain new business and charge premium prices for providing good service. As inventories disappear, warehouses can be sold off, both labor and handling equipment needs are reduced, and obsolete and/or out-of-style goods are minimized.

To illustrate the benefits of striving for zero working capital, in just one year Campbell Soup pared its working capital by $80 million. It used the cash to develop new products and to buy companies in Britain, Australia, and other countries. Equally important, the company expects to increase annual profits by $50 million over the next few years by lowering overtime labor and storage costs.

WWW

American Standard provides a detailed discussion of how they are applying demand flow production concepts to reengineered manufacturing and office processes in an attempt to achieve zero working capital. The site can be accessed at **http://www.teamflow.com** by clicking on American Standard under user profiles.

The most important factor in moving toward zero working capital is increased speed. If the production process is fast enough, companies can produce items as they are ordered rather than having to forecast demand and build up large inventories that are managed by bureaucracies. The best companies are able to start production after an order is received yet still meet customer delivery requirements. This system is known as *demand flow*, or *demand-based management*, and it builds on the just-in-time method of inventory control that we will discuss later in this chapter. However, demand flow management is broader than just-in-time, because it requires that all elements of a production system operate quickly and efficiently.

Achieving zero working capital requires that every order and part move at maximum speed, which generally means replacing paper with electronic data. Then, orders streak from the processing department to the plant, flexible production lines produce each product every day, and finished goods flow directly from the production line onto waiting trucks or rail cars. Instead of cluttering plants or warehouses with inventories, products move directly into the pipeline. As efficiency rises, working capital dwindles.

Clearly, it is not possible for most firms to achieve zero working capital and infinitely efficient production. Still, a focus on minimizing receivables and inventories while maximizing payables will help a firm lower its investment in working capital and achieve financial and production economies.

Self-Test Question

What is the basic idea of zero working capital, and how is working capital defined for this purpose?

Cash Management

Approximately 1.5 percent of the average industrial firm's assets are held in the form of cash, which is defined as demand deposits plus currency. Cash is often called a "nonearning asset." It is needed to pay for labor and raw materials, to buy fixed assets, to pay taxes, to service debt, to pay dividends, and so on. However, cash itself (and also most commercial checking accounts) earns no interest. Thus, the goal of the cash manager is to minimize the amount of cash the firm must hold for use in conducting its normal business activities, yet, at the same time, to have sufficient cash (1) to take trade discounts, (2) to maintain its credit rating, and (3) to meet unexpected cash needs. We begin our analysis with a discussion of the reasons for holding cash.

Reasons for Holding Cash

Firms hold cash for two primary reasons:

1. *Transactions.* Cash balances are necessary in business operations. Payments must be made in cash, and receipts are deposited in the cash account. Cash balances associated with routine payments and collections are known as **transactions balances.**
2. *Compensation to banks for providing loans and services.* A bank makes money by lending out funds that have been deposited with it, so the larger its deposits, the better the bank's profit position. If a bank is providing services to a customer, it may require the customer to leave a minimum balance on deposit to help offset the costs of providing the services. Also, banks may require borrowers to hold deposits at the bank. Both types of deposits are defined as **compensating balances.** In a 1979 survey, 84.7 percent of responding companies reported that they were required to maintain compensating balances to help pay for bank services.[5] Only 13.3 percent reported paying direct fees for banking services. By 1996 those findings were reversed: only 28 percent paid for bank services with compensating balances, while 83 percent paid direct fees.[6] So, while the use of compensating balances to pay for services has declined, it is still a reason some companies hold so much cash.

Two other reasons for holding cash have been noted in the finance and economics literature: for *precaution* and for *speculation.* Cash inflows and outflows are unpredictable, with the degree of predictability varying among firms and industries. Therefore, firms need to hold some cash in reserve for random, unforeseen fluctuations in inflows and outflows. These "safety stocks" are called **precautionary balances,** and the less predictable the firm's cash flows, the larger such balances should be. However, if the firm has easy access to borrowed funds—that is, if it can borrow on short notice—its need for precautionary balances is reduced. Also, as we note later in this chapter, firms that would otherwise need large precautionary balances tend to hold highly liquid marketable securities rather than cash per se. Marketable securities serve many of the purposes of cash, but they provide greater interest income than bank deposits.

Some cash balances may be held to enable the firm to take advantage of bargain purchases that might arise; these funds are called **speculative balances.** However, firms today generally rely on reserve borrowing capacity and/or marketable securities portfolios rather than on cash per se for speculative purposes.

The cash accounts of most firms can be thought of as consisting of transactions, compensating, precautionary, and speculative balances. However, we cannot calculate the amount needed for each purpose, sum them, and produce a total desired cash balance, because the same money often serves more than one purpose. For instance, precautionary and speculative balances can also be used to satisfy compensating balance requirements. Firms do, however, consider all four factors when establishing their target cash positions.

[5]See Lawrence J. Gitman, E. A. Moses, and I. T. White, "An Assessment of Corporate Cash Management Practices," *Financial Management,* Vol. 14, no. 1, Spring 1979, 32–41.

[6]See Charles E. Maxwell, Lawrence J. Gitman, and Stephanie A. M. Smith, "Working Capital Management and Financial-Service Consumption Preferences of US and Foreign Firms: A Comparison of 1979 and 1996 Preferences," *Financial Practice and Education,* Fall/Winter 1998, 46–52.

Advantages of Holding Adequate Cash and Near-Cash Assets

In addition to the four motives just discussed, sound working capital management requires that an ample supply of cash and near-cash assets be maintained for several specific reasons:

1. It is essential that the firm have sufficient cash and near-cash assets to take **trade discounts.** Suppliers frequently offer customers discounts for early payment of bills. As we will see in the next chapter, the cost of not taking discounts is very high, so firms should have enough cash to be able to pay bills in time to take discounts.
2. Adequate holdings of cash and near-cash assets can help the firm maintain its credit rating by keeping its current and acid test ratios in line with those of other firms in its industry. A strong credit rating enables the firm both to purchase goods from suppliers on favorable terms and to maintain an ample line of low-cost credit with its bank.
3. Cash and near-cash are useful for taking advantage of favorable business opportunities, such as special offers from suppliers or the chance to acquire another firm.
4. The firm should have sufficient cash and near-cash to meet such emergencies as strikes, fires, or competitors' marketing campaigns, and to weather seasonal and cyclical downturns.

Self-Test Questions

Why is cash management important?

What are the two primary motives for holding cash?

What are the two secondary motives for holding cash as noted in the finance and economics literature?

The Cash Budget[7]

Firms estimate their needs for cash as a part of their general budgeting, or forecasting, process. First, they forecast sales, fixed asset and inventory requirements, and the times when payments must be made. This information is combined with projections about when accounts receivable will be collected, tax payment dates, dividend and interest payment dates, and so on. All of this information is summarized in the **cash budget,** which shows the firm's projected cash inflows and outflows over some specified period. Generally, firms use a monthly cash budget forecasted over the next year, plus a more detailed daily or weekly cash budget for the coming month. The monthly cash budgets are used for planning purposes, and the daily or weekly budgets for actual cash control.

The cash budget provides more detailed information concerning a firm's future cash flows than do the forecasted financial statements. In Chapter 4, we developed MicroDrive Inc.'s 2002 forecasted financial statements. Projected 2002 sales were \$3,300 million, resulting in a net cash flow from operations of \$162 million. When all expenditures and financing flows are considered, MicroDrive's cash account was projected to increase by \$1 million in 2002. Does this mean that MicroDrive will not have to worry about cash shortages during 2002? Perhaps, but to really answer this question, we must construct a cash budget.

To simplify the example, we will only consider MicroDrive's cash budget for the last half of 2002. Further, we will not list every cash flow but rather focus on the

[7]We used an *Excel* spreadsheet to generate the cash budget shown in Table 22-1. It would be worthwhile to go through the model, ***Ch 22 Tool Kit.xls,*** which is on the CD-ROM that accompanies this text. This will give you a good example of how spreadsheets can be applied to solve practical problems.

operating cash flows. MicroDrive's sales peak is in September. All sales are made on terms of 2/10, net 40, meaning that a 2 percent discount is allowed if payment is made within 10 days, and, if the discount is not taken, the full amount is due in 40 days. However, like most companies, MicroDrive finds that some of its customers delay payment up to 90 days. Experience has shown that payment on 20 percent of the dollar sales is made during the month in which the sale is made—these are the discount sales. On 70 percent of sales, payment is made during the month immediately following the month of sale, and on 10 percent payment is made in the second month following the month of sale.

The costs to MicroDrive of component parts and packaging materials average 70 percent of the sales prices of the finished products. These purchases are generally made one month before the firm expects to sell the finished products, but MicroDrive's purchase terms with its suppliers allow it to delay payments for 30 days. Accordingly, if July sales are forecasted at \$300 million, then purchases during June will amount to \$210 million, and this amount will actually be paid in July.

Such other cash expenditures as wages and lease payments are also built into the cash budget, and MicroDrive must make estimated tax payments of \$30 million on September 15 and \$20 million on December 15. Also, a \$100 million payment for a new plant must be made in October. Assuming that the **target cash balance** is \$10 million, and that \$15 million will be on hand on July 1, 2002, what will the monthly cash surpluses or shortfalls be for the period from July to December?

The file ***Ch 22 Tool Kit.xls*** on your textbook's CD-ROM shows how the calculations are made.

The monthly cash flows are shown in Table 22-1. Section I calculates both collections on sales and payments on purchases. Line 1 gives the sales forecast for the period from May through December. (May and June sales are necessary to determine collections for July and August.) Next, Lines 2 through 5 show cash collections. Line 2 shows that 20 percent of the sales during any given month are collected during that month. Customers who pay in the first month, however, take the discount, so the cash collected in the month of sale is reduced by 2 percent; for example, collections during July for the \$300 million of sales in that month will be 20 percent times sales times 1.0 minus the 2 percent discount $= (0.20)(\$300)(0.98) \approx \$59$ million. Line 3 shows the collections on the previous month's sales, or 70 percent of sales in the preceding month; for example, in July, 70 percent of the \$250 million June sales, or \$175 million, will be collected. Line 4 gives collections from sales two months earlier, which amounts to 10 percent of sales in that month; for example, the July collections for May sales are $(0.10)(\$200) = \$20$ million. The collections during each month are summed and shown on Line 5; thus, the July collections represent 20 percent of July sales (minus the discount) plus 70 percent of June sales plus 10 percent of May sales, or \$254 million in total.

Next, payments for purchases of raw materials are shown. July sales are forecasted at \$300 million, so MicroDrive will purchase \$210 million of materials in June (Line 6) and pay for these purchases in July (Line 7). Similarly, MicroDrive will purchase \$280 million of materials in July to meet August's forecasted sales of \$400 million.

With Section I completed, Section II can be constructed. Cash from collections is shown on Line 8. Lines 9 through 14 list payments made during each month, and these payments are summed on Line 15. The difference between cash receipts and cash payments (Line 8 minus Line 15) is the net cash gain or loss during the month. For July there is a net cash loss of \$11 million, as shown on Line 16.

In Section III, we first determine the cash balance MicroDrive would have at the start of each month if no borrowing were done. This is shown on Line 17. MicroDrive will have \$15 million on hand on July 1. The beginning cash balance (Line 17) is then added to the net cash gain or loss during the month (Line 16) to obtain the cumulative cash that would be on hand if no financing were done (Line 18). At the end of July, MicroDrive forecasts a cumulative cash balance of \$4 million in the absence of borrowing.

TABLE 22-1 MicroDrive Inc.: Cash Budget (Millions of Dollars)

	May	Jun	Jul	Aug	Sep	Oct	Nov	Dec
I. COLLECTIONS AND PURCHASES WORKSHEET								
(1) Sales (gross)[a]	$200	$250	$300	$400	$500	$350	$250	$200
Collections								
(2) During month of sale: (0.2)(0.98)(month's sales)			59	78	98	69	49	39
(3) During first month after sale: 0.7(previous month's sales)			175	210	280	350	245	175
(4) During second month after sale: 0.1(sales 2 months ago)			20	25	30	40	50	35
(5) Total collections (2 + 3 + 4)			$254	$313	$408	$459	$344	$249
Purchases								
(6) 0.7(next month's sales)		$210	$280	$350	$245	$175	$140	
(7) Payments (prior month's purchases)			$210	$280	$350	$245	$175	$140
II. CASH GAIN OR LOSS FOR MONTH								
(8) Collections (from Section I)			$254	$313	$408	$459	$344	$249
(9) Payments for purchases (from Section I)			$210	$280	$350	$245	$175	$140
(10) Wages and salaries			30	40	50	40	30	30
(11) Lease payments			15	15	15	15	15	15
(12) Other expenses			10	15	20	15	10	10
(13) Taxes					30			20
(14) Payment for plant construction						100		
(15) Total payments			$265	$350	$465	$415	$230	$215
(16) Net cash gain (loss) during month (Line 8 − Line 15)			($ 11)	($ 37)	($ 57)	$ 44	$114	$ 34
III. LOAN REQUIREMENT OR CASH SURPLUS								
(17) Cash at start of month if no borrowing is done[b]			$ 15	$ 4	($ 33)	($ 90)	($ 46)	$ 68
(18) Cumulative cash: cash at start if no borrowing +gain or −loss (Line 16 + Line 17)			$ 4	($ 33)	($ 90)	($ 46)	$ 68	$102
(19) Target cash balance			10	10	10	10	10	10
(20) Cumulative surplus cash to invest or loans outstanding to maintain $10 target cash balance (Line 18 − Line 19)[c]			($ 6)	($ 43)	($100)	($ 56)	$ 58	$ 92

[a]Although the budget period is July through December, sales and purchases data for May and June are needed to determine collections and payments during July and August.

[b]The amount shown on Line 17 for July, the $15 balance (in millions), is on hand initially. The values shown for each of the following months on Line 17 are equal to the cumulative cash as shown on Line 18 for the preceding month; for example, the $4 shown on Line 17 for August is taken from Line 18 in the July column.

[c]When the target cash balance of $10 (Line 19) is deducted from the cumulative cash balance (Line 18), a resulting negative figure on Line 20 (shown in parentheses) represents a required loan, whereas a positive figure represents surplus cash. Loans are required from July through October, and surpluses are expected during November and December. Note also that firms can borrow or pay off loans on a daily basis, so the $6 borrowed during July would be done on a daily basis, as needed, and during October the $100 loan that existed at the beginning of the month would be reduced daily to the $56 ending balance, which, in turn, would be completely paid off during November.

The target cash balance, $10 million, is then subtracted from the cumulative cash balance to determine the firm's borrowing requirements, shown in parentheses, or its surplus cash. Because MicroDrive expects to have cumulative cash, as shown on Line 18, of only $4 million in July, it will have to borrow $6 million to bring the cash account up to the target balance of $10 million. Assuming that this amount is indeed borrowed, loans outstanding will total $6 million at the end of July. (MicroDrive did not have any loans outstanding on July 1.) The cash surplus or required loan balance is given on Line 20; a positive value indicates a cash surplus, whereas a negative value indicates a loan requirement. Note that the surplus cash or loan requirement shown on Line 20 is a *cumulative amount.* MicroDrive must borrow $6 million in July. Then it has an additional cash shortfall during August of $37 million as reported on Line 16, so its total loan requirement at the end of August is $6 + $37 = $43 million, as reported on Line 20. MicroDrive's arrangement with the bank permits it to increase its outstanding loans on a daily basis, up to a prearranged maximum, just as you could increase the amount you owe on a credit card. MicroDrive will use any surplus funds it generates to pay off its loans, and because the loan can be paid down at any time, on a daily basis, it will never have both a cash surplus and an outstanding loan balance.

This same procedure is used in the following months. Sales will peak in September, accompanied by increased payments for purchases, wages, and other items. Receipts from sales will also go up, but the firm will still be left with a $57 million net cash outflow during the month. The total loan requirement at the end of September will hit a peak of $100 million, the cumulative cash plus the target cash balance. The $100 million can also be found as the $43 million needed at the end of August plus the $57 million cash deficit for September.

Sales, purchases, and payments for past purchases will fall sharply in October, but collections will be the highest of any month because they will reflect the high September sales. As a result, MicroDrive will enjoy a healthy $44 million net cash gain during October. This cash can be used to pay off borrowings, so loans outstanding will decline by $44 million, to $56 million.

MicroDrive will have an even larger cash surplus in November, which will permit it to pay off all of its loans. In fact, the company is expected to have $58 million in surplus cash by the month's end, and another cash surplus in December will swell the excess cash to $92 million. With such a large amount of unneeded funds, MicroDrive's treasurer will need to invest in interest-bearing securities or to put the funds to use in some other way.

Here are some additional points about cash budgets:

1. For simplicity, our illustrative budget for MicroDrive omitted many important cash flows that are anticipated for 2002, such as dividends and proceeds from stock and bond sales. Such items could easily be added to the table.
2. Our cash budget does not reflect interest on loans or income from investing surplus cash. This refinement could also easily be added.
3. If cash inflows and outflows are not uniform during the month, we could seriously understate the firm's peak financing requirements. The data in Table 22-1 show the situation expected on the last day of each month, but on any given day during the month, it could be quite different. For example, if all payments had to be made on the fifth of each month, but collections came in uniformly throughout the month, the firm would need to borrow much larger amounts than those shown in Table 22-1. In that situation, we would prepare a cash budget that determined requirements on a daily basis.
4. Since depreciation is a noncash charge, it does not appear on the cash budget other than through its effect on taxable income, hence on taxes paid.

5. Because the cash budget represents a forecast, all the values in the table are *expected* values. If actual sales, purchases, and so on, are different from the forecasted levels, then the projected cash deficits and surpluses will not be correct. Thus, MicroDrive might end up needing to borrow more than is indicated on Line 20. For example, if MicroDrive's monthly sales turn out to be only 80 percent of their forecasted levels, its maximum cumulative borrowing requirement will turn out to be \$126 million rather than \$100 million, a 26 percent increase from the expected figure. To guard against being caught short, MicroDrive should arrange a line of credit in excess of that amount.
6. Spreadsheet programs are particularly well suited for constructing and analyzing cash budgets, especially with respect to the sensitivity of cash flows to changes in sales levels, collection periods, and the like. We could change any assumption, say, the projected monthly sales or the lag before customers pay, and the cash budget would automatically and instantly be recalculated. This would show us exactly how the firm's borrowing requirements would change if conditions changed. Also, with a spreadsheet model, it is easy to add features like interest paid on loans, interest earned on marketable securities, and so on. See ***Ch 22 Tool Kit.xls*** for the spreadsheet model we used to generate the cash budget for this chapter.
7. Finally, we should note that the target cash balance probably will be adjusted over time, rising and falling with seasonal patterns and with long-term changes in the scale of the firm's operations. Thus, MicroDrive will probably plan to maintain larger cash balances during August and September than at other times, and as the company grows, so will its required cash balance. Also, the firm might even set the target cash balance at zero—this could be done if it carried a portfolio of marketable securities that could be sold to replenish the cash account, or if it had an arrangement with its bank that permitted it to borrow any funds needed on a daily basis. In that event, the cash budget would simply stop with Line 18, and the amounts on that line would represent projected loans outstanding or surplus cash. Note, though, that most firms would find it difficult to operate with a zero-balance bank account, just as you would, and the costs of such an operation would in most instances more than offset the costs associated with maintaining a positive cash balance. Therefore, most firms do set a positive target cash balance.

Self-Test Questions

What is the purpose of a cash budget?

What are the three major sections of a cash budget?

Suppose a firm's cash flows do not occur uniformly throughout the month. What effect would that have on the accuracy of the forecasted borrowing requirements?

How could uncertainty be handled in a cash budget?

Does depreciation appear in a cash budget? Explain.

Cash Management Techniques

Cash management has changed significantly over the last 20 years for two reasons. First, from the early 1970s to the mid-1980s there was an upward trend in interest rates that increased the opportunity cost of holding cash. This encouraged financial managers to search for more efficient ways of managing cash. Second, technological developments, particularly computerized electronic funds transfer mechanisms, changed the way cash is managed.

Most cash management activities are performed jointly by the firm and its banks. Effective cash management encompasses proper management of cash inflows and outflows, which entails (1) synchronizing cash flows, (2) using float, (3) accelerating collections, (4) getting available funds to where they are needed, and (5) controlling disbursements. Most business is conducted by large firms, many of which operate regionally, nationally, or even globally. They collect cash from many sources and make payments from a number of different cities or even countries. For example, companies such as IBM, General Motors, and Hewlett-Packard have manufacturing plants all around the world, even more sales offices, and bank accounts in virtually every city where they do business. Their collection points follow sales patterns. Some disbursements are made from local offices, but most are made in the cities where manufacturing occurs, or else from the home office. Thus, a major corporation might have hundreds or even thousands of bank accounts, and since there is no reason to think that inflows and outflows will balance in each account, a system must be in place to transfer funds from where they come in to where they are needed, to arrange loans to cover net corporate shortfalls, and to invest net corporate surpluses without delay. We discuss the most commonly used techniques for accomplishing these tasks in the following sections.

Cash Flow Synchronization

If you as an individual were to receive income once a year, you would probably put it in the bank, draw down your account periodically, and have an average balance during the year equal to about half your annual income. If you received income monthly instead of once a year, you would operate similarly, but now your average balance would be much smaller. If you could arrange to receive income daily and to pay rent, tuition, and other charges on a daily basis, and if you were confident of your forecasted inflows and outflows, then you could hold a tiny average cash balance.

Exactly the same situation holds for businesses—by improving their forecasts and by arranging things so that cash receipts coincide with cash requirements, firms can hold their transactions balances to a minimum. Recognizing all this, utility companies, oil companies, credit card companies, and so on, arrange to bill customers, and to pay their own bills, on regular "billing cycles" throughout the month. This **synchronization of cash flows** provides cash when it is needed and thus enables firms to reduce cash balances, decrease bank loans, lower interest expenses, and boost profits.

Speed Up the Check-Clearing Process

When a customer writes and mails a check, this *does not* mean that the funds are immediately available to the receiving firm. Most of us have been told by someone that "the check is in the mail," and we have also deposited a check in our account and then been told that we cannot write our own checks against this deposit until the **check-clearing** process has been completed. Our bank must first make sure that the check we deposited is good and the funds are available before it will give us cash.

In practice, it may take a long time for a firm to process incoming checks and obtain the use of the money. A check must first be delivered through the mail and then be cleared through the banking system before the money can be put to use. Checks received from customers in distant cities are especially subject to delays because of mail delays and also because more banks are involved. For example, assume that we receive a check and deposit it in our bank. Our bank must send the check to the bank on which it was drawn. Only when this latter bank transfers funds to our bank are the funds available for us to use. Checks are generally cleared through the Federal Reserve System or through a clearinghouse set up by the banks in a particular city. Of course, if the check is deposited in the same bank on which it was drawn, that bank merely transfers funds by bookkeeping entries from one depositor to another. The length of time required for checks to clear is thus a function of the distance between the payer's and the payee's banks. In the case of private clearinghouses, clearing can range from one to three days. Checks are generally cleared through the Federal Reserve System in about two days, but mail delays can slow down things on each end of the Fed's involvement in the process.

Using Float

Float is defined as the difference between the balance shown in a firm's (or individual's) checkbook and the balance on the bank's records. Suppose a firm writes, on average, checks in the amount of $5,000 each day, and it takes six days for these checks to clear and be deducted from the firm's bank account. This will cause the firm's own checkbook to show a balance $30,000 smaller than the balance on the bank's records; this difference is called **disbursement float.** Now suppose the firm also receives checks in the amount of $5,000 daily, but it loses four days while they are being deposited and cleared. This will result in $20,000 of **collections float.** In total, the firm's **net float**—the difference between the $30,000 positive disbursement float and the $20,000 negative collections float—will be $10,000.

If the firm's own collection and clearing process is more efficient than that of the recipients of its checks—which is generally true of larger, more efficient firms—then the firm could actually show a *negative* balance on its own books but have a *positive* balance on its bank records. Some firms indicate that they *never* have positive book cash balances. One large manufacturer of construction equipment stated that while its account, according to its bank's records, shows an average cash balance of about $20 million, its *book* cash balance is *minus* $20 million—it has $40 million of net float. Obviously, the firm must be able to forecast its disbursements and collections accurately in order to make such heavy use of float.

Delays that cause float arise because it takes time for checks (1) to travel through the mail (mail float), (2) to be processed by the receiving firm (processing float), and (3) to clear through the banking system (clearing, or availability, float). Basically, the size of a firm's net float is a function of its ability to speed up collections on checks it receives and to slow down collections on checks it writes. Efficient firms go to great lengths to speed up the processing of incoming checks, thus putting the funds to work faster, and they try to stretch their own payments out as long as possible.

Speeding up Receipts

Financial managers have searched for ways to collect receivables faster since credit transactions began. Several techniques are now used both to speed collections and to get funds where they are needed. Included are (1) lockbox plans established close to customers and (2) requiring large customers to pay by wire or automatic debit.

Lockboxes A **lockbox plan** is one of the oldest cash management tools. In a lockbox system, incoming checks are sent to post office boxes rather than to corporate headquarters. For example, a firm headquartered in New York City might have its West Coast customers send their payments to a box in San Francisco, its customers in the Southwest send their checks to Dallas, and so on, rather than having all checks sent to New York City. Several times a day a local bank will collect the contents of the lockbox and deposit the checks into the company's local account. The bank then provides the firm with a daily record of the receipts collected, usually via an electronic data transmission system in a format that permits on-line updating of the firm's accounts receivable records.

A lockbox system reduces the time required for a firm to receive incoming checks, to deposit them, and to get them cleared through the banking system so the funds are

The Great Debate: How Much Cash Is Enough?

"I hate cash on hand," says Fred Salerno, Bell Atlantic's CFO. According to a recent survey, Salerno has backed up his talk with actions. When rated on the number of days of operating expenses held in cash (DOEHIC), Bell Atlantic leads its industry, with a DOEHIC of 6 days versus an industry average of 27. Put another way, Bell Atlantic has cash holdings equal to only 0.90 percent of sales as compared with an industry median cash-to-sales ratio of 5.20 percent.

A great relationship with its banks is a key to keeping low levels of cash. Jim Hopwood, treasurer of Wickes, says, "We have a credit revolver if we ever need it." The same is true at Haverty Furniture, where CFO Dennis Fink says, "You don't have to worry about predicting short-term fluctuations in cash flow" if you have solid bank commitments.

Treasurer Wayne Smith of Avery Dennison says that their low cash holdings have reduced their net operating working capital to such an extent that their return on invested capital (ROIC) is 3 percentage points higher than it would be if their cash holdings were at the industry average. He added that this adds a lot of economic value to their company.

Despite these and other comments about the advantages of low cash holdings, many companies still hold extremely large amounts of cash and marketable securities, including Procter & Gamble ($2.6 billion, 32 days DOEHIC, 7.1 percent cash/sales) and Ford Motor Company ($24 billion, 76 DOEHIC). When asked about the appropriate level of cash holdings, Ford CFO Henry Wallace refused to be pinned down, saying, "There is no answer for a company this size." However, it is interesting to note that Ford recently completed a huge stock repurchase, reducing its cash by about $10 billion.

Source: S. L. Mintz, "Lean Green Machine," *CFO*, July 2000, 76–94.

available for use. Lockbox services can accelerate the availability of funds by two to five days over the "regular" system.

Payment by Wire or Automatic Debit Firms are increasingly demanding payments of larger bills by wire, or even by automatic electronic debits. Under an electronic debit system, funds are automatically deducted from one account and added to another. This is, of course, the ultimate in a speeded-up collection process, and computer technology is making such a process increasingly feasible and efficient.

Self-Test Questions

What is float? How do firms use float to increase cash management efficiency?

What are some methods firms can use to accelerate receipts?

Marketable Securities

Realistically, the management of cash and marketable securities cannot be separated—management of one implies management of the other. In the first part of the chapter, we focused on cash management. Now we turn to **marketable securities.**

Marketable securities typically provide much lower yields than operating assets. For example, DaimlerChrysler recently held approximately $8 billion of short-term marketable securities that provided a much lower yield than its operating assets. Why would such a company have such large holdings of low-yielding assets?

In many cases, companies hold marketable securities for the same reasons they hold cash. Although these securities are not the same as cash, in most cases they can be converted to cash in just a few minutes with a single telephone call. Moreover, while cash and most commercial checking accounts yield nothing, marketable securities provide at least a modest return. For this reason, many firms hold at least some marketable securities in lieu of larger cash balances, liquidating part of the portfolio to increase the cash account when cash outflows exceed inflows. In such situations, the marketable securities can be used as a substitute for transactions balances, for precautionary balances, for speculative balances, or for all three. In most cases, the securities are held primarily for precautionary purposes—most firms prefer to rely on bank credit to make temporary transactions or to meet speculative needs, but they may still hold some liquid assets to guard against a possible shortage of bank credit.

A few years ago, before its merger with Daimler-Benz, Chrysler had essentially no cash—it was incurring huge losses, and those losses had drained its cash account. Then a new management team took over, improved operations, and began generating positive cash flows. By 1999, DaimlerChrysler's cash (and marketable securities) was up to about $8 billion, and analysts were forecasting a further buildup over the next year or so to more than $10 billion. Management indicated, in various statements, that the cash hoard was necessary to enable the company to weather the next downturn in auto sales.

Although setting the target cash balance is, to a large extent, judgmental, analytical rules can be applied to help formulate better judgments. For example, a half century ago William Baumol recognized that the trade-off between cash and marketable securities is similar to the one firms face when setting the optimal level of inventory.[8] Baumol applied the EOQ inventory model to determine the optimal level of cash balances.[9] He suggested that cash holdings should be higher if costs are high and the time to liquidate marketable securities is long, but that those cash holdings should be lower if interest rates are high. His logic was that if it is expensive and time consuming to convert securities to cash, and if securities do not earn much because interest rates are low, then it does not pay to hold securities as opposed to cash. It does pay to hold securities if interest rates are high and the securities can be converted to cash quickly and cheaply.

To summarize, there are both benefits and costs associated with holding cash and marketable securities. The benefits are twofold: (1) The firm reduces transactions costs because it won't have to issue securities or borrow as frequently to raise cash, and (2) it will have ready cash to take advantage of bargain purchases or growth opportunities. The primary disadvantage is that the after-tax return on cash and short-term securities is very low. Thus, firms face a trade-off between benefits and costs.

Recent research supports this trade-off hypothesis as an explanation for firms' cash holdings.[10] Firms with high-growth opportunities suffer the most if they don't have ready cash to quickly take advantage of an opportunity, and the data show that these firms do hold relatively high levels of cash and marketable securities. Firms with volatile cash flows are the ones most likely to run low on cash, so they are the ones that hold the highest levels of cash. In contrast, cash holdings are less important to large firms with high credit ratings, because they have quick and inexpensive access to capital markets. As expected, such firms hold relatively less cash. Of course, there will always be outliers such as Ford, which is large, strong, and cash-rich, but volatile. Firms with good growth opportunities are still the ones with the highest cash balances, in general.

---

[8]William J. Baumol, "The Transactions Demand for Cash: An Inventory Theoretic Approach," *Quarterly Journal of Economics*, November 1952, 545–556.

[9]A more complete description of the Economic Ordering Quantity (EOQ) model can be found in the Web chapter on Working Capital Management on the textbook's Web site.

[10]See Tim Opler, Lee Pinkowitz, René Stulz, and Rohan Williamson, "The Determinants and Implications of Corporate Cash Holdings," *Journal of Financial Economics*, Vol. 52, 1999, 3–46.

Self-Test Questions

Why might a company hold low-yielding marketable securities when it could earn a much higher return on operating assets?

Why would a low interest rate environment lead to larger cash balances?

How might improvements in telecommunications technology affect the level of corporations' cash balances?

Inventory

Inventories, which may be classified as (1) *supplies*, (2) *raw materials*, (3) *work-in-process*, and (4) *finished goods*, are an essential part of virtually all business operations. As is the case with accounts receivable, inventory levels depend heavily upon sales. However, whereas receivables build up *after* sales have been made, inventory must be acquired *ahead* of sales. This is a critical difference, and the necessity of forecasting sales before establishing target inventory levels makes inventory management a difficult task. Also, since errors in the establishment of inventory levels quickly lead either to lost sales or to excessive carrying costs, inventory management is as important as it is difficult.

Inventory management techniques are covered in depth in production management courses. Still, because financial managers have a responsibility both for raising the capital needed to carry inventory and for the firm's overall profitability, we need to cover the financial aspects of inventory management here. Two examples will make clear the types of issues involved in inventory management, and the financial problems poor inventory control can cause.

Retail Clothing Store

Chicago Discount Clothing (CDC) must order swimsuits for summer sales in January, and it must take delivery by April to be sure of having enough suits to meet the heavy May–June demand. Bathing suits come in many styles, colors, and sizes, and if CDC stocks incorrectly, either in total or in terms of the style-color-size distribution, then the store will have trouble. It will lose potential sales if it stocks too few suits, and it will be forced to lower prices and take losses if it stocks too many or the wrong types.

The effects of inventory changes on the balance sheet are important. For simplicity, assume that CDC has a $10,000 base stock of inventory which is financed by common stock. Its balance sheet is as follows:

Inventory (base stock)	$10,000	Common stock	$10,000
Total assets	$10,000	Total claims	$10,000

Now it anticipates that it will sell $5,000 of swimsuits (at cost) this summer. Dollar sales will actually be greater than $5,000, since CDC makes about $200 in profits for every $1,000 of inventory sold. CDC finances its seasonal inventory with bank loans, so its pre-summer balance sheet would look like this:

Inventory (seasonal)	$ 5,000	Notes payable to bank	$ 5,000
Inventory (base stock)	10,000	Common stock	10,000
Total assets	$15,000	Total claims	$15,000

If everything works out as planned, sales will be made, inventory will be converted to cash, the bank loan will be retired, and the company will earn a profit. The balance sheet, after a successful season, might look like this:

Cash	$ 1,000	Notes payable to bank	$ 0
Inventory (seasonal)	0	Common stock	10,000
Inventory (base stock)	10,000	Retained earnings	1,000
Total assets	$11,000	Total claims	$11,000

The company is now in a highly liquid position and is ready to begin a new season.

But suppose the season had not gone well, and CDC had only sold $1,000 of its inventory. As fall approached, the balance sheet would look like this:

Cash	$ 200	Notes payable to bank	$ 4,000
Inventory (seasonal)	4,000	Common stock	10,000
Inventory (base stock)	10,000	Retained earnings	200
Total assets	$14,200	Total claims	$14,200

Now suppose the bank insists on repayment of the $4,000 outstanding on the loan, and it wants cash, not swimsuits. But if the swimsuits did not sell well in the summer, how will out-of-style suits sell in the fall? Assume that CDC is forced to mark the suits down to half their cost (not half the selling price) in order to sell them to raise cash to repay the bank loan. Here is the result:

Cash	$ 2,200	Notes payable to bank	$ 4,000
Inventory (base stock)	10,000	Common stock	10,000
		Retained earnings	(1,800)
Total assets	$12,200	Total claims	$12,200

At this point, CDC is in serious trouble. It does not have the cash to pay off the loan, and the firm's shareholders have lost $1,800 of their equity. If the bank will not extend the loan, and if other sources of cash are not available, CDC will have to mark down its base inventory prices in an effort to stimulate sales, and if this does not work, CDC could be forced into bankruptcy. Clearly, poor inventory decisions can spell trouble.

Appliance Manufacturer

Now consider a different situation, that of Housepro Corporation, an appliance manufacturer. Here is its inventory position, in millions of dollars:

Raw materials	$ 200
Work-in-process	200
Finished goods	600
Total inventory	$1,000

Suppose Housepro anticipates that the economy is about to get much stronger and that the demand for appliances will rise sharply. If it is to share in the expected boom, Housepro will have to increase production. This means it will have to increase inventory, and, since the inventory buildup must precede sales, additional financing will be required—some liability account, perhaps notes payable, will have to be increased in order to finance the inventory buildup.

Proper inventory management requires close coordination among the sales, purchasing, production, and finance departments. The sales/marketing department is generally the first to spot changes in demand. These changes must be worked into the company's purchasing and manufacturing schedules, and the financial manager must arrange any financing needed to support the inventory buildup. Lack of coordination among departments, poor sales forecasts, or both, can lead to disaster.

Self-Test Questions

Why is good inventory management essential to a firm's success?

What departments should be involved in inventory decisions?

Inventory Costs

The twin goals of inventory management are (1) to ensure that the inventories needed to sustain operations are available, but (2) to hold the costs of ordering and carrying inventories to the lowest practical level. Table 22-2 gives a listing of the typical costs associated with inventory, divided into three categories: carrying costs, ordering and receiving costs, and the costs that are incurred if the firm runs short of inventory.

Inventory is costly to store; therefore, there is always pressure to reduce it to lower costs. An article in *Fortune* highlights the fact that an increasing number of corporations are taking drastic steps to control inventory costs.[11] For example, Trane Corporation, which makes air conditioners, recently adopted the type of just-in-time inventory procedures described in the next section.

In the past, Trane produced parts on a steady basis, stored them as inventory, and had them ready whenever the company received an order for a batch of air conditioners. However, the company reached the point where its inventory covered an area equal to three football fields, and it still sometimes took as long as 15 days to fill an order. To make matters worse, occasionally some of the necessary components simply could not be located, while in other instances the components were located but found to have been damaged from long storage.

Then Trane adopted a new inventory policy—it began producing components only after an order is received, and then sending the parts directly from the machines that make them to the final assembly line. The net effect: Inventories fell nearly 40 percent even as sales increased by 30 percent.

However, as Table 22-2 indicates, there are costs associated with holding too little inventory, and these costs can be severe. Generally, if a business carries small inventories, it must reorder frequently. This increases ordering costs. Even more important, firms can miss out on profitable sales, and also suffer a loss of goodwill that can lead to lower future sales. So, it is important to have enough inventory on hand to meet customer demands.

Suppose IBM has developed a new line of notebook computers. How many of them should it produce and have on hand when its marketing campaign is launched?

---

[11]Shawn Tully, "Raiding a Company's Hidden Cash," *Fortune*, August 22, 1994, 82–87.

TABLE 22-2 Costs Associated with Inventory

	Approximate Annual Cost as a Percentage of Inventory Value
I. CARRYING COSTS	
Cost of capital tied up	12.0%
Storage and handling costs	0.5
Insurance	0.5
Property taxes	1.0
Depreciation and obsolescence	12.0
Total	26.0%
II. ORDERING, SHIPPING, AND RECEIVING COSTS	
Cost of placing orders, including production and set-up costs	Varies
Shipping and handling costs	2.5%
III. COSTS OF RUNNING SHORT	
Loss of sales	Varies
Loss of customer goodwill	Varies
Disruption of production schedules	Varies

Note: These costs vary from firm to firm, from item to item, and also over time. The figures shown are U.S. Department of Commerce estimates for an average manufacturing firm. Where costs vary so widely that no meaningful numbers can be assigned, the term "Varies" is reported.

If it fails to produce enough inventory, retailers and customers will be frustrated because they cannot immediately purchase the highly advertised product. Rather than wait, many customers will purchase a similar product elsewhere. On the other hand, if IBM has too much inventory, it will incur unnecessarily high carrying costs. In addition, computers become obsolete quickly, so if sales don't meet expectations, the company may have to discount the notebooks to sell them at a loss. Apart from reducing the profit margin on this line of computers, these discounts may push down computer prices in general, thereby reducing profit margins on the company's other products as well.

Self-Test Questions

What are the three categories of inventory costs?

What are some components of inventory carrying costs?

What are some components of inventory ordering costs?

Inventory Control Systems

Inventory management requires the establishment of an *inventory control system.* Inventory control systems run the gamut from very simple to extremely complex, depending on the size of the firm and the nature of its inventory. For example, one simple control procedure is the **red-line method**—inventory items are stocked in a bin, a red line is drawn around the inside of the bin at the level of the reorder point, and the inventory clerk places an order when the red line shows. The **two-bin method** has inventory items stocked in two bins. When the working bin is empty, an order is placed and inventory is drawn from the second bin. These procedures work well for parts such as bolts in a manufacturing process, or for many items in retail businesses.

Computerized Systems

Most companies today employ **computerized inventory control systems.** The computer starts with an inventory count in memory. As withdrawals are made, they are recorded by the computer, and the inventory balance is revised. When the reorder point is reached, the computer automatically places an order, and when the order is received, the recorded balance is increased. As we noted earlier, retailers such as Wal-Mart have carried this system quite far—each item has a bar code, and, as an item is checked out, the code is read, a signal is sent to the computer, and the inventory balance is adjusted at the same time the price is fed into the cash register tape. When the balance drops to the reorder point, an order is placed. In Wal-Mart's case, the order goes directly from its computers to those of its suppliers.

A good inventory control system is dynamic, not static. A company such as Wal-Mart or General Motors stocks hundreds of thousands of different items. The sales (or use) of individual items can rise or fall quite separately from rising or falling overall corporate sales. As the usage rate for an individual item begins to rise or fall, the inventory manager must adjust its balance to avoid running short or ending up with obsolete items. If the change in the usage rate appears to be permanent, the safety stock level should be reconsidered, and the computer model used in the control process should be reprogrammed.

Just-in-Time Systems

An approach to inventory control called the **just-in-time (JIT) system** was developed by Japanese firms but is now used throughout the world. Toyota provides a good example of the just-in-time system. Eight of Toyota's ten factories, along with most of Toyota's suppliers, dot the countryside around Toyota City. Delivery of components is tied to the speed of the assembly line, and parts are generally delivered no more than a few hours before they are used. The just-in-time system reduces the need for Toyota and other manufacturers to carry large inventories, but it requires a great deal of coordination between the manufacturer and its suppliers, both in the timing of deliveries and the quality of the parts. It also requires that component parts be perfect; otherwise, a few bad parts could stop the entire production line. Therefore, JIT inventory management has been developed in conjunction with total quality management (TQM).

Not surprisingly, U.S. automobile manufacturers were among the first domestic firms to move toward just-in-time systems. Ford has restructured its production system with a goal of increasing its inventory turnover from 20 times a year to 30 or 40 times. Of course, just-in-time systems place considerable pressure on suppliers. GM formerly kept a 10-day supply of seats and other parts made by Lear Siegler; now GM sends in orders at four- to eight-hour intervals and expects immediate shipment. A Lear Siegler spokesman stated, "We can't afford to keep things sitting around either," so Lear Siegler has had to be tough on its own suppliers.

Just-in-time systems are also being adopted by smaller firms. In fact, some production experts say that small companies are better positioned than large ones to use just-in-time methods, because it is easier to redefine job functions and to educate people in small firms. One small-firm example is Fireplace Manufacturers Inc., a manufacturer of prefabricated fireplaces. The company was having cash flow problems, and it was carrying \$1.1 million in inventory to support annual sales of about \$8 million. The company went to a just-in-time system, trimmed its raw material and work-in-process inventory to $750,000, and freed up $350,000 of cash, even as sales doubled.

The close coordination required between the parties using JIT procedures has led to an overall reduction of inventory throughout the production-distribution system, and to a general improvement in economic efficiency. This point is borne out by economic statistics, which show that inventory as a percentage of sales has been declining since the use of just-in-time procedures began. Also, with smaller inventories in the system, economic recessions have become shorter and less severe.

Out-Sourcing

Another important development related to inventory is **out-sourcing,** which is the practice of purchasing components rather than making them in-house. Thus, GM has been moving toward buying radiators, axles, and other parts from suppliers rather than making them itself, so it has been increasing its use of out-sourcing. Out-sourcing is often combined with just-in-time systems to reduce inventory levels. However, perhaps the major reason for out-sourcing has nothing to do with inventory policy—a bureaucratic, unionized company like GM can often buy parts from a smaller, nonunionized supplier at a lower cost than it can make them itself.

The Relationship between Production Scheduling and Inventory Levels

A final point relating to inventory levels is *the relationship between production scheduling and inventory levels.* For example, a greeting card manufacturer has highly seasonal sales. Such a firm could produce on a steady, year-round basis, or it could let production rise and fall with sales. If it established a level production schedule, its inventory would rise sharply during periods when sales were low and then decline during peak sales periods, but its average inventory would be substantially higher than if production rose and fell with sales.

Our discussions of just-in-time systems, out-sourcing, and production scheduling all point out the necessity of coordinating inventory policy with manufacturing/procurement policies. Companies try to minimize *total production and distribution costs,* and inventory costs are just one part of total costs. Still, they are an important cost, and financial managers should be aware of the determinants of inventory costs and how they can be minimized.

Self-Test Questions

Describe some inventory control systems that are used in practice.

What are just-in-time systems? What are their advantages? Why is quality especially important if a JIT system is used?

What is out-sourcing?

Describe the relationship between production scheduling and inventory levels.

Receivables Management

Firms would, in general, rather sell for cash than on credit, but competitive pressures force most firms to offer credit. Thus, goods are shipped, inventories are reduced, and an **account receivable** is created.[12] Eventually, the customer will pay the account, at which time (1) the firm will receive cash and (2) its receivables will decline. Carrying receivables has both direct and indirect costs, but it also has an important benefit—increased sales.

Receivables management begins with the decision of whether or not to grant credit. In this section, we discuss the manner in which receivables build up, and we also discuss several alternative ways to monitor receivables. A monitoring system is important, because without it receivables will build up to excessive levels, cash flows will decline, and bad debts will offset the profits on sales. Corrective action is often needed, and the only way to know whether the situation is getting out of hand is with a good receivables control system.

The Accumulation of Receivables

The total amount of accounts receivable outstanding at any given time is determined by two factors: (1) the volume of credit sales and (2) the average length of time between sales and collections. For example, suppose Boston Lumber Company (BLC), a wholesale distributor of lumber products, opens a warehouse on January 1 and, starting the first day, makes sales of $1,000 each day. For simplicity, we assume that all sales are on credit, and customers are given 10 days to pay. At the end of the first day, accounts receivable will be $1,000; they will rise to $2,000 by the end of the second day; and by January 10, they will have risen to 10($1,000) = $10,000. On January 11, another $1,000 will be added to receivables, but payments for sales made on January 1 will reduce receivables by $1,000, so total accounts receivable will remain constant at $10,000. In general, once the firm's operations have stabilized, this situation will exist:

$$\text{Accounts receivable} = \text{Credit sales per day} \times \text{Length of collection period} \quad (22\text{-}5)$$

$$= \$1,000 \times 10 \text{ days} = \$10,000.$$

If either credit sales or the collection period changes, such changes will be reflected in accounts receivable.

Note that the $10,000 investment in receivables must be financed. To illustrate, suppose that when the warehouse opened on January 1, BLC's shareholders had put up $800 as common stock and used this money to buy the goods sold the first day. The $800 of inventory will be sold for $1,000, so BLC's gross profit on the $800 investment is $200, or 25 percent. In this situation, the beginning balance sheet would be as follows:[13]

Inventories	$800	Common stock	$800
Total assets	$800	Total liabilities and equity	$800

[12]Whenever goods are sold on credit, two accounts are created—an asset item entitled *accounts receivable* appears on the books of the selling firm, and a liability item called *accounts payable* appears on the books of the purchaser. At this point, we are analyzing the transaction from the viewpoint of the seller, so we are concentrating on the variables under its control, in this case, the receivables. We will examine the transaction from the viewpoint of the purchaser in Chapter 23, where we discuss accounts payable as a source of funds and consider their cost relative to the cost of funds obtained from other sources.

[13]Note that the firm would need other assets such as cash, fixed assets, and a permanent stock of inventory. Also, overhead costs and taxes would have to be deducted, so retained earnings would be less than the figures shown here. We abstract from these details here so that we may focus on receivables.

At the end of the day, the balance sheet would look like this:

Accounts receivable	$1,000	Common stock	$ 800
Inventories	0	Retained earnings	200
Total assets	$1,000	Total liabilities and equity	$1,000

To remain in business, BLC must replenish inventories. To do so requires that $800 of goods be purchased, and this requires $800 in cash. Assuming that BLC borrows the $800 from the bank, the balance sheet at the start of the second day will be as follows:

Accounts receivable	$1,000	Notes payable to bank	$ 800
Inventories	800	Common stock	800
		Retained earnings	200
Total assets	$1,800	Total liabilities and equity	$1,800

At the end of the second day, the inventories will have been converted to receivables, and the firm will have to borrow another $800 to restock for the third day.

This process will continue, provided the bank is willing to lend the necessary funds, until the beginning of the 11th day, when the balance sheet read as follows:

Accounts receivable	$10,000	Notes payable to bank	$ 8,000
Inventories	800	Common stock	800
		Retained earnings	2,000
Total assets	$10,800	Total liabilities and equity	$10,800

From this point on, $1,000 of receivables will be collected every day, and $800 of these funds can be used to purchase new inventories.

This example makes it clear (1) that accounts receivable depend jointly on the level of credit sales and the collection period, (2) that any increase in receivables must be financed in some manner, but (3) that the entire amount of receivables does not have to be financed because the profit portion ($200 of each $1,000 of sales) does not represent a cash outflow. In our example, we assumed bank financing, but, as we demonstrate in Chapter 23, there are many alternative ways to finance current assets.

Monitoring the Receivables Position

Investors—both stockholders and bank loan officers—should pay close attention to accounts receivable management, for, as we shall see, one can be misled by reported financial statements and later suffer serious losses on an investment.

When a credit sale is made, the following events occur: (1) Inventories are reduced by the cost of goods sold, (2) accounts receivable are increased by the sales price, and (3) the difference is profit, which is added to retained earnings. If the sale is for cash, then the cash from the sale has actually been received by the firm, but if the sale is on credit, the firm will not receive the cash from the sale unless and until the account is collected. Firms have been known to encourage "sales" to very weak customers in order to report high profits. This could boost the firm's stock price, at least until credit losses begin to lower earnings, at which time the stock price will fall. Analyses along the lines suggested in the following sections will detect any such questionable practice, as well as any unconscious deterioration in the quality of accounts receivable. Such early detection could help both investors and bankers avoid losses.[14]

Days Sales Outstanding (DSO) Suppose Super Sets Inc., a television manufacturer, sells 200,000 television sets a year at a price of \$198 each. Further, assume that all sales are on credit with the following terms: if payment is made within 10 days, customers will receive a 2 percent discount; otherwise the full amount is due within 30 days. Finally, assume that 70 percent of the customers take discounts and pay on Day 10, while the other 30 percent pay on Day 30.

Super Sets's **days sales outstanding (DSO),** sometimes called the *average collection period (ACP)*, is approximately 16 days:[15]

$$\text{DSO} = \text{ACP} = 0.7(10\text{ days}) + 0.3(30\text{ days}) = 16\text{ days}.$$

Super Sets's *average daily sales (ADS)*, assuming a 360-day year, is \$110,000:

$$\text{ADS} = \frac{\text{Annual sales}}{360} = \frac{\text{(Units sold)(Sales price)}}{360} \quad \textbf{(22-6)}$$

$$= \frac{200{,}000(\$198)}{360} = \frac{\$39{,}600{,}000}{360} = \$110{,}000.$$

Super Sets's accounts receivable, assuming a constant, uniform rate of sales throughout the year, will at any point in time be \$1,760,000:

$$\text{Receivables} = \text{(ADS)(DSO)} \quad \textbf{(22-7)}$$

$$= (\$110{,}000)(16) = \$1{,}760{,}000.$$

Note also that its DSO, or average collection period, is a measure of the average length of time it takes Super Sets's customers to pay off their credit purchases, and the DSO is often compared with an industry average DSO. For example, if all television manufacturers sell on the same credit terms, and if the industry average DSO is 25 days versus Super Sets's 16 days, then Super Sets either has a higher percentage of discount customers or else its credit department is exceptionally good at ensuring prompt payment.

Finally, note that if you know both the annual sales and the receivables balance, you can calculate DSO as follows:

$$\text{DSO} = \frac{\text{Receivables}}{\text{Sales per day}} = \frac{\$1{,}760{,}000}{\$110{,}000} = 16\text{ days}.$$

The DSO can also be compared with the firm's own credit terms. For example, suppose Super Sets's DSO had been averaging 35 days. With a 35-day DSO, some customers would obviously be taking more than 30 days to pay their bills. In fact, if many customers were paying within 10 days to take advantage of the discount, the

[14]Accountants are increasingly interested in these matters. Investors have sued several of the major accounting firms for substantial damages when (1) profits were overstated and (2) it could be shown that the auditors should have conducted an analysis along the lines described here and then reported the results to stockholders in their audit opinion.

[15]The DSO as calculated in this section is an approximation because the discount has not been taken out to produce a net sales figure.

others must, on average, be taking much longer than 35 days. One way to check this possibility is to use an aging schedule as described in the next section.

Aging Schedules An **aging schedule** breaks down a firm's receivables by age of account. Table 22-3 contains the December 31, 2001, aging schedules of two television manufacturers, Super Sets and Wonder Vision. Both firms offer the same credit terms, and both show the same total receivables. However, Super Sets's aging schedule indicates that all of its customers pay on time—70 percent pay on Day 10 while 30 percent pay on Day 30. Wonder Vision's schedule, which is more typical, shows that many of its customers are not abiding by its credit terms—some 27 percent of its receivables are more than 30 days past due, even though Wonder Vision's credit terms call for full payment by Day 30.

Aging schedules cannot be constructed from the type of summary data reported in financial statements; they must be developed from the firm's accounts receivable ledger. However, well-run firms have computerized their accounts receivable records, so it is easy to determine the age of each invoice, to sort electronically by age categories, and thus to generate an aging schedule.

Management should constantly monitor both the DSO and the aging schedule to detect trends, to see how the firm's collection experience compares with its credit terms, and to see how effectively the credit department is operating in comparison with other firms in the industry. If the DSO starts to lengthen, or if the aging schedule begins to show an increasing percentage of past-due accounts, then the firm's credit policy may need to be tightened.

Although a change in the DSO or the aging schedule should signal the firm to investigate its credit policy, a deterioration in either of these measures does not necessarily indicate that the firm's credit policy has weakened. In fact, if a firm experiences sharp seasonal variations, or if it is growing rapidly, then both the aging schedule and the DSO may be distorted. To see this point, note that the DSO is calculated as follows:

$$\text{DSO} = \frac{\text{Accounts receivable}}{\text{Sales/360}}.$$

Since receivables at a given point in time reflect sales in the last month or so, but sales as shown in the denominator of the equation are for the last 12 months, a seasonal increase in sales will increase the numerator more than the denominator, hence will raise the DSO. This will occur even if customers are still paying exactly as before. Similar problems arise with the aging schedule if sales fluctuate widely. Therefore, a change in either the DSO or the aging schedule should be taken as a signal to investigate further, but not necessarily as a sign that the firm's credit policy has weakened.

TABLE 22-3 Aging Schedules

	Super Sets		Wonder Vision	
Age of Account (Days)	Value of Account	Percentage of Total Value	Value of Account	Percentage of Total Value
0–10	$1,232,000	70%	$ 825,000	47%
11–30	528,000	30	460,000	26
31–45	0	0	265,000	15
46–60	0	0	179,000	10
Over 60	0	0	31,000	2
Total receivables	$1,760,000	100%	$1,760,000	100%

Still, days sales outstanding and the aging schedule are useful tools for reviewing the credit department's performance.[16]

Self-Test Questions

Explain how a new firm's receivables balance is built up over time.

Define days sales outstanding (DSO). What can be learned from it? How is it affected by sales fluctuations?

What is an aging schedule? What can be learned from it? How is it affected by sales fluctuations?

Credit Policy

The success or failure of a business depends primarily on the demand for its products—as a rule, the higher its sales, the larger its profits and the higher its stock price. Sales, in turn, depend on a number of factors, some exogenous but others under the firm's control. The major controllable determinants of demand are sales prices, product quality, advertising, and the firm's **credit policy.** Credit policy, in turn, consists of these four variables:

1. *Credit period,* which is the length of time buyers are given to pay for their purchases.
2. *Discounts* given for early payment, including the discount percentage and how rapidly payment must be made to qualify for the discount.
3. *Credit standards,* which refer to the required financial strength of acceptable credit customers.
4. *Collection policy,* which is measured by the firm's toughness or laxity in attempting to collect on slow-paying accounts.

The credit manager is responsible for administering the firm's credit policy. However, because of the pervasive importance of credit, the credit policy itself is normally established by the executive committee, which usually consists of the president plus the vice-presidents of finance, marketing, and production.

Self-Test Question

What are the four credit policy variables?

Setting the Credit Period and Standards

A firm's regular **credit terms,** which include the **credit period** and **discount,** might call for sales on a 2/10, net 30 basis to all "acceptable" customers. Here customers who pay within 10 days would be given a 2 percent discount, and others would be required to pay within 30 days. Its **credit standards** would be applied to determine which customers qualify for the regular credit terms, and the amount of credit available to each customer.

Credit Standards

Credit standards refer to the financial strength and creditworthiness a customer must exhibit in order to qualify for credit. If a customer does not qualify for the

[16]See Web/CD Chapter 28, "Working Capital Management: Extensions," for a more complete discussion of the problems with the DSO and aging schedule and ways to correct for them.

regular credit terms, it can still purchase from the firm, but under more restrictive terms. For example, a firm's "regular" credit terms might call for payment after 30 days, and these terms might be offered to all qualified customers. The firm's credit standards would be applied to determine which customers qualified for the regular credit terms, and how much credit each should receive. The major factors considered when setting credit standards relate to the likelihood that a given customer will pay slowly or perhaps end up as a bad debt loss.

Setting credit standards requires a measurement of *credit quality*, which is defined in terms of the probability of a customer's default. The probability estimate for a given customer is, for the most part, a subjective judgment. Nevertheless, credit evaluation is a well-established practice, and a good credit manager can make reasonably accurate judgments of the probability of default by different classes of customers.

Managing a credit department requires fast, accurate, and up-to-date information. To help get such information, the National Association of Credit Management (a group with 43,000 member firms) persuaded TRW, a large credit-reporting agency, to develop a computer-based telecommunications network for the collection, storage, retrieval, and distribution of credit information. A typical business credit report would include the following pieces of information:

1. A summary balance sheet and income statement.
2. A number of key ratios, with trend information.
3. Information obtained from the firm's suppliers telling whether it pays promptly or slowly, and whether it has recently failed to make any payments.
4. A verbal description of the physical condition of the firm's operations.
5. A verbal description of the backgrounds of the firm's owners, including any previous bankruptcies, lawsuits, divorce settlement problems, and the like.
6. A summary rating, ranging from A for the best credit risks down to F for those that are deemed likely to default.

Consumer credit is appraised similarly, using income, years of employment, ownership of home, and past credit history (pays on time or has defaulted) as criteria.

Although a great deal of credit information is available, it must still be processed in a judgmental manner. Computerized information systems can assist in making better credit decisions, but, in the final analysis, most credit decisions are really exercises in informed judgment.[17]

Self-Test Questions

What are credit terms?

What is credit quality, and how is it assessed?

[17]Credit analysts use procedures ranging from highly sophisticated, computerized "credit-scoring" systems, which actually calculate the statistical probability that a given customer will default, to informal procedures, which involve going through a checklist of factors that should be considered when processing a credit application. The credit-scoring systems use various financial ratios such as the current ratio and the debt ratio (for businesses) and income, years with the same employer, and the like (for individuals) to determine the statistical probability of default. Credit is then granted to those with low default probabilities. The informal procedures often involve examining the "5 C's of Credit": character, capacity, capital, collateral, and conditions. Character is obvious; capacity is a subjective estimate of ability to repay; capital means how much net worth the borrower has; collateral means assets pledged to secure the loan; and conditions refers to business conditions, which affect ability to repay.

Setting the Collection Policy

Collection policy refers to the procedures the firm follows to collect past-due accounts. For example, a letter might be sent to customers when a bill is 10 days past due; a more severe letter, followed by a telephone call, would be sent if payment is not received within 30 days; and the account would be turned over to a collection agency after 90 days.

The collection process can be expensive in terms of both out-of-pocket expenditures and lost goodwill—customers dislike being turned over to a collection agency. However, at least some firmness is needed to prevent an undue lengthening of the collection period and to minimize outright losses. A balance must be struck between the costs and benefits of different collection policies.

Changes in collection policy influence sales, the collection period, and the bad debt loss percentage. All of this should be taken into account when setting the credit policy.

Self-Test Question

How does collection policy influence sales, the collection period, and the bad debt loss percentage?

Cash Discounts

The last element in the credit policy decision, the use of **cash discounts** for early payment, is analyzed by balancing the costs and benefits of different cash discounts. For example, a firm might decide to change its credit terms from "net 30," which means that customers must pay within 30 days, to "2/10, net 30," where a 2 percent discount is given if payment is made in ten days. This change should produce two benefits: (1) It should attract new customers who consider the discount to be a price reduction, and (2) the discount should lead to a reduction in the days sales outstanding, because some existing customers will pay more promptly in order to get the discount. Offsetting these benefits is the dollar cost of the discounts. The optimal discount percentage is established at the point where the marginal costs and benefits are exactly offsetting.

If sales are seasonal, a firm may use **seasonal dating** on discounts. For example, Slimware Inc., a swimsuit manufacturer, sells on terms of 2/10, net 30, May 1 dating. This means that the effective invoice date is May 1, even if the sale was made back in January. The discount may be taken up to May 10; otherwise, the full amount must be paid on May 30. Slimware produces throughout the year, but retail sales of bathing suits are concentrated in the spring and early summer. By offering seasonal dating, the company induces some of its customers to stock up early, saving Slimware some storage costs and also "nailing down sales."

Self-Test Questions

How can cash discounts be used to influence sales volume and the DSO?

What is seasonal dating?

Other Factors Influencing Credit Policy

In addition to the factors discussed in previous sections, two other points should be made regarding credit policy.

Profit Potential

We have emphasized the costs of granting credit. *However, if it is possible to sell on credit and also to impose a carrying charge on the receivables that are outstanding, then credit sales can actually be more profitable than cash sales.* This is especially true for consumer durables (autos, appliances, and so on), but it is also true for certain types of industrial equipment. Thus, GM's General Motors Acceptance Corporation (GMAC) unit, which finances automobiles, is highly profitable, as is Sears' credit subsidiary.[18] Some encyclopedia companies even lose money on cash sales but more than make up these losses from the carrying charges on their credit sales. Obviously, such companies would rather sell on credit than for cash!

The carrying charges on outstanding credit are generally about 18 percent on a nominal basis: 1.5 percent per month, so $1.5\% \times 12 = 18\%$. This is equivalent to an effective annual rate of $(1.015)^{12} - 1.0 = 19.6\%$. Having receivables outstanding that earn more than 18 percent is highly profitable unless there are too many bad debt losses.

Legal Considerations

It is illegal, under the Robinson-Patman Act, for a firm to charge prices that discriminate between customers unless these differential prices are cost-justified. The same holds true for credit—it is illegal to offer more favorable credit terms to one customer or class of customers than to another, unless the differences are cost-justified.

Self-Test Question

How do profit potential and legal considerations affect a firm's credit policy?

Summary

This chapter discussed the management of current assets, particularly cash, marketable securities, inventory, and receivables. While there are unique factors relating to each component of working capital, two important themes run through the chapter. First, current assets are necessary, but there are costs associated with holding them. Therefore, if a company can manage its current assets more efficiently and thereby operate with a smaller investment in working capital, this will increase its profitability. At the same time, though, a company will have problems if it reduces its cash, inventory, and receivables too much. Thus, the optimal current asset management policy is one that carefully trades off the costs and benefits of holding working capital.

Second, changing technology has enabled companies to streamline their working capital, which has improved their cash flow and profitability. Indeed, companies today that fail to manage their working capital efficiently are finding themselves at a greater and greater competitive disadvantage. The key concepts in this chapter are listed below:

- **Working capital** refers to current assets, and **net working capital** is defined as current assets minus current liabilities. **Net operating working capital (NOWC)** is operating current assets minus operating current liabilities, which is normally cash,

[18]Companies that do a large volume of sales financing typically set up subsidiary companies called *captive finance companies* to do the actual financing. Thus, General Motors, DaimlerChrysler, and Ford all have captive finance companies, as do Sears, IBM, and General Electric.

inventory, and accounts receivable minus payables and accruals. **Working capital policy** refers to decisions relating to current assets and their financing.

- Under a **relaxed current asset policy,** a firm would hold relatively large amounts of each type of current asset. Under a **restricted current asset policy,** the firm would hold minimal amounts of these items.
- The **cash conversion cycle model** focuses on the length of time between when the company makes payments and when it receives cash inflows.
- The **inventory conversion period** is the average time required to convert materials into finished goods and then to sell those goods.

$$\text{Inventory conversion period} = \text{Inventory/Sales per day.}$$

- The **receivables collection period** is the average length of time required to convert the firm's receivables into cash, that is, to collect cash following a sale.

$$\text{Receivables collection period} = \text{DSO} = \text{Receivables/(Sales/360).}$$

- The **payables deferral period** is the average length of time between the purchase of materials and labor and the payment of cash for them.

$$\text{Payables deferral period} = \text{Payables/Purchases per day.}$$

- The **cash conversion cycle** equals the length of time between the firm's actual cash expenditures to pay for productive resources (materials and labor) and its own cash receipts from the sale of products (that is, the length of time between paying for labor and materials and collecting on receivables).

$$\begin{matrix}\text{Cash} \\ \text{conversion} \\ \text{cycle}\end{matrix} = \begin{matrix}\text{Inventory} \\ \text{conversion} \\ \text{period}\end{matrix} + \begin{matrix}\text{Receivables} \\ \text{collection} \\ \text{period}\end{matrix} - \begin{matrix}\text{Payables} \\ \text{deferral} \\ \text{period}\end{matrix}.$$

- A policy that strives for **zero working capital** not only generates cash but also speeds up production and helps businesses operate more efficiently. This concept has its own definition of working capital: Inventories + Receivables − Payables. The rationale is that inventories and receivables are the keys to making sales, and that inventories can be financed by suppliers through accounts payable.
- The **primary goal of cash management** is to reduce the amount of cash held to the minimum necessary to conduct business.
- The **transactions balance** is the cash necessary to conduct day-to-day business, whereas the **precautionary balance** is a cash reserve held to meet random, unforeseen needs. A **compensating balance** is a minimum checking account balance that a bank requires as compensation either for services provided or as part of a loan agreement. Firms also hold **speculative balances,** which allow them to take advantage of bargain purchases. Note, though, that borrowing capacity and marketable security holdings both reduce the need for precautionary and speculative balances.
- A **cash budget** is a schedule showing projected cash inflows and outflows over some period. The cash budget is used to predict cash surpluses and deficits, and it is the primary cash management planning tool.
- **Cash management techniques** generally fall into five categories: (1) synchronizing cash flows, (2) using float, (3) accelerating collections, (4) determining where and when funds will be needed, and (5) controlling disbursements.
- **Disbursement float** is the amount of funds associated with checks written by a firm that are still in process and hence have not yet been deducted from the firm's bank account.
- **Collections float** is the amount of funds associated with checks written to a firm that have not been cleared, hence are not yet available for the firm's use.

- **Net float** is the difference between disbursement float and collections float, and it also is equal to the difference between the balance in the firm's own checkbook and the balance on the bank's records. The larger the net float, the smaller the cash balance the firm must maintain, so net float is good.
- Two techniques that can be used to speed up collections are (1) **lockboxes** and (2) **wire transfers.**
- Firms can reduce their cash balances by holding **marketable securities,** which can be sold on short notice at close to their quoted prices. Marketable securities serve both as a substitute for cash and as a temporary investment for funds that will be needed in the near future. Safety is the primary consideration when selecting marketable securities.
- **Inventory** can be grouped into four categories: (1) supplies, (2) raw materials, (3) work-in-process, and (4) finished goods.
- The twin goals of **inventory management** are (1) to ensure that the inventories needed to sustain operations are available, but (2) to hold the costs of ordering and carrying inventories to the lowest possible level.
- **Inventory costs** can be divided into three types: carrying costs, ordering costs, and stock-out costs. In general, carrying costs increase as the level of inventory rises, but ordering costs and stock-out costs decline with larger inventory holdings.
- Firms use inventory control systems such as the **red-line method** and the **two-bin method,** as well as **computerized inventory control systems,** to help them keep track of actual inventory levels and to ensure that inventory levels are adjusted as sales change. **Just-in-time (JIT) systems** are used to hold down inventory costs and, simultaneously, to improve the production process. **Out-sourcing** is the practice of purchasing components rather than making them in-house.
- When a firm sells goods to a customer on credit, an **account receivable** is created.
- A firm can use an **aging schedule** and the **days sales outstanding (DSO)** to help keep track of its receivables position and to help avoid an increase in bad debts.
- A firm's **credit policy** consists of four elements: (1) credit period, (2) discounts given for early payment, (3) credit standards, and (4) collection policy. The first two, when combined, are called the **credit terms.**
- Additional factors that influence a firm's overall credit policy are (1) **profit potential** and (2) **legal considerations.**
- The basic objective of the credit manager is to increase profitable sales by extending credit to worthy customers and therefore adding value to the firm.

Working capital policy involves two basic issues. The first, determining the appropriate level for each type of current asset, was addressed in this chapter. The second, how current assets should be financed, is addressed in Chapter 23.

Questions

22–1 Define each of the following terms:

a. Working capital; net working capital; working capital policy

b. Relaxed current asset investment policy; restricted current asset investment policy; moderate current asset investment policy

c. Cash conversion cycle; inventory conversion period; receivables collection period; payables deferral period

d. Transactions balance; compensating balance; precautionary balance; speculative balance

e. Cash budget; target cash balance

f. Trade discounts

g. Synchronized cash flows

h. Check clearing; net float; disbursement float; collections float
i. Lockbox plan
j. Marketable securities
k. Red-line method; two-bin method; computerized inventory control system
l. Just-in-time system; out-sourcing
m. Account receivable; days sales outstanding
n. Aging schedule
o. Credit policy; credit period; credit standards; collection policy; credit terms
p. Cash discounts
q. Seasonal dating

22–2 Assuming the firm's sales volume remained constant, would you expect it to have a higher cash balance during a tight-money period or during an easy-money period? Why?

22–3 What are the two principal reasons for holding cash? Can a firm estimate its target cash balance by summing the cash held to satisfy each of the two?

22–4 Explain how each of the following factors would probably affect a firm's target cash balance if all other factors were held constant.

a. The firm institutes a new billing procedure that better synchronizes its cash inflows and outflows.
b. The firm develops a new sales forecasting technique that improves its forecasts.
c. The firm reduces its portfolio of U.S. Treasury bills.
d. The firm arranges to use an overdraft system for its checking account.
e. The firm borrows a large amount of money from its bank and also begins to write far more checks than it did in the past.
f. Interest rates on Treasury bills rise from 5 percent to 10 percent.

22–5 Why would a lockbox plan make more sense for a firm that makes sales all over the United States than for a firm with the same volume of business but concentrated in its home city?

22–6 Is it true that when one firm sells to another on credit, the seller records the transaction as an account receivable while the buyer records it as an account payable and that, disregarding discounts, the receivable typically exceeds the payable by the amount of profit on the sale?

22–7 What are the four elements of a firm's credit policy? To what extent can firms set their own credit policies as opposed to having to accept policies that are dictated by "the competition"?

22–8 Suppose that a firm makes a purchase and receives the shipment on February 1. The terms of trade as stated on the invoice read "2/10, net 40, May 1 dating." What is the latest date on which payment can be made and the discount still be taken? What is the date on which payment must be made if the discount is not taken?

22–9 a. What is the days sales outstanding (DSO) for a firm whose sales are $2,880,000 per year and whose accounts receivable are $312,000? (Use 360 days per year.)

b. Is it true that if this firm sells on terms of 3/10, net 40, its customers probably all pay on time?

22–10 Is it true that if a firm calculates its days sales outstanding, it has no need for an aging schedule?

22–11 Firm A had no credit losses last year, but 1 percent of Firm B's accounts receivable proved to be uncollectible and resulted in losses. Should Firm B fire its credit manager and hire A's?

22–12 Indicate by a (+), (−), or (0) whether each of the following events would probably cause accounts receivable (A/R), sales, and profits to increase, decrease, or be affected in an indeterminant manner:

	A/R	Sales	Profits
The firm tightens its credit standards.	________	________	________
The terms of trade are changed from 2/10, net 30, to 3/10, net 30.	________	________	________
The terms are changed from 2/10, net 30, to 3/10, net 40.	________	________	________
The credit manager gets tough with past-due accounts.	________	________	________

22–13 A firm can reduce its investment in inventory by having its suppliers hold raw materials inventory and its customers hold finished goods inventory. Explain actions a firm can take that would result in larger inventory for its suppliers and customers and smaller inventory for itself. What are the limitations of such actions?

Self-Test Problems (Solutions Appear in Appendix A)

ST–1 *WORKING CAPITAL POLICY* The Calgary Company is attempting to establish a current assets policy. Fixed assets are \$600,000, and the firm plans to maintain a 50 percent debt-to-assets ratio. The interest rate is 10 percent on all debt. Three alternative current asset policies are under consideration: 40, 50, and 60 percent of projected sales. The company expects to earn 15 percent before interest and taxes on sales of \$3 million. Calgary's effective federal-plus-state tax rate is 40 percent. What is the expected return on equity under each alternative?

ST–2 *FLOAT* The Upton Company is setting up a new checking account with Howe National Bank. Upton plans to issue checks in the amount of \$1 million each day and to deduct them from its own records at the close of business on the day they are written. On average, the bank will receive and clear the checks at 5 P.M. the third day after they are written; for example, a check written on Monday will be cleared on Thursday afternoon. The firm's agreement with the bank requires it to maintain a \$500,000 average compensating balance; this is \$250,000 greater than the cash balance the firm would otherwise have on deposit. It makes a \$500,000 deposit at the time it opens the account.

a. Assuming that the firm makes deposits at 4 P.M. each day (and the bank includes them in that day's transactions), how much must it deposit daily in order to maintain a sufficient balance once it reaches a steady state? Indicate the required deposit on Day 1, Day 2, Day 3, if any, and each day thereafter, assuming that the company will write checks for \$1 million on Day 1 and each day thereafter.

b. How many days of float does Upton have?

c. What ending daily balance should the firm try to maintain (1) on the bank's records and (2) on its own records?

Problems

22–1 *CASH CONVERSION CYCLE* The Boudreaux Corporation has an inventory conversion period of 75 days, a receivables collection period of 38 days, and a payables deferral period of 30 days.

a. What is the length of the firm's cash conversion cycle?

b. If Boudreaux's annual sales are \$3,375,000 and all sales are on credit, what is the firm's investment in accounts receivable?

c. How many times per year does Boudreaux turn over its inventory?

22–2 *NET FLOAT* On a typical day, Troan Corporation writes \$10,000 in checks. It generally takes 4 days for those checks to clear. Each day the firm typically receives \$10,000 in checks that take 3 days to clear. What is the firm's average net float?

22–3 *CASH MANAGEMENT* Williams & Sons last year reported sales of \$10 million and an inventory turnover ratio of 2. The company is now adopting a just-in-time inventory system. If the new system is able to reduce the firm's inventory level and increase the firm's inventory turnover ratio to 5, while maintaining the same level of sales, how much cash will be freed up?

22–4 *RECEIVABLES INVESTMENT* Medwig Corporation has a DSO of 17 days. The company averages \$3,500 in credit sales each day. What is the company's average accounts receivable?

22–5 *LOCKBOX SYSTEM* I. Malitz and Associates Inc. operates a mail-order firm doing business on the West Coast. Malitz receives an average of \$325,000 in payments per day. On average, it takes 4 days from the time customers mail checks until Malitz receives and processes them. Malitz is considering the use of a lockbox system to reduce collection and processing float. The system will cost $6,500 per month and will consist of 10 local depository banks and a concentration bank located in San Francisco. Under this system, customers' checks should be received at the lockbox locations 1 day after they are mailed, and daily totals will be transferred to San Francisco using wire transfers costing $9.75 each. Assume that Malitz has an opportunity cost of 10 percent and that there are $52 \times 5 = 260$ working days, hence 260 transfers from each lockbox location, in a year.

a. What is the total annual cost of operating the lockbox system?
b. What is the benefit of the lockbox system to Malitz?
c. Should Malitz initiate the system?

22–6
RECEIVABLES INVESTMENT

McDowell Industries sells on terms of 3/10, net 30. Total sales for the year are $900,000. Forty percent of the customers pay on the 10th day and take discounts; the other 60 percent pay, on average, 40 days after their purchases.

a. What is the days sales outstanding?
b. What is the average amount of receivables?
c. What would happen to average receivables if McDowell toughened up on its collection policy with the result that all nondiscount customers paid on the 30th day?

22–7
WORKING CAPITAL POLICY

The Rentz Corporation is attempting to determine the optimal level of current assets for the coming year. Management expects sales to increase to approximately $2 million as a result of an asset expansion presently being undertaken. Fixed assets total $1 million, and the firm wishes to maintain a 60 percent debt ratio. Rentz's interest cost is currently 8 percent on both short-term and longer-term debt (which the firm uses in its permanent structure). Three alternatives regarding the projected current asset level are available to the firm: (1) a tight policy requiring current assets of only 45 percent of projected sales, (2) a moderate policy of 50 percent of sales in current assets, and (3) a relaxed policy requiring current assets of 60 percent of sales. The firm expects to generate earnings before interest and taxes at a rate of 12 percent on total sales.

a. What is the expected return on equity under each current asset level? (Assume a 40 percent effective federal-plus-state tax rate.)
b. In this problem, we have assumed that the level of expected sales is independent of current asset policy. Is this a valid assumption?
c. How would the overall riskiness of the firm vary under each policy?

22–8
NET FLOAT

The Stendardi-Stephens Company (SSC) is setting up a new checking account with National Bank. SSC plans to issue checks in the amount of $1.6 million each day and to deduct them from its own records at the close of business on the day they are written. On average, the bank will receive and clear (that is, deduct from the firm's bank balance) the checks at 5 P.M. the 4th day after they are written; for example, a check written on Monday will be cleared on Friday afternoon. The firm's agreement with the bank requires it to maintain a $1.2 million average compensating balance; this is $400,000 greater than the cash balance the firm would otherwise have on deposit. It makes a $1.2 million deposit at the time it opens the account.

a. Assuming that the firm makes deposits at 4 P.M. each day (and the bank includes them in that day's transactions), how much must it deposit daily in order to maintain a sufficient balance once it reaches a steady state? Indicate the required deposit on Day 1, Day 2, Day 3, Day 4, if any, and each day thereafter, assuming that the company will write checks for $1.6 million on Day 1 and each day thereafter.
b How many days of float does SSC carry?
c. What ending daily balance should the firm try to maintain (1) on the bank's records and (2) on its own records?
d. Explain how net float can help increase the value of the firm's common stock.

22–9
LOCKBOX SYSTEM

The Hardin-Gehr Corporation (HGC) began operations 5 years ago as a small firm serving customers in the Detroit area. However, its reputation and market area grew quickly, so that today HGC has customers throughout the entire United States. Despite its broad customer base, HGC has maintained its headquarters in Detroit and keeps its central billing system there. HGC's management is considering an alternative collection procedure to reduce its mail time and processing float. On average, it takes 5 days from the time customers mail payments until HGC is able to receive, process, and deposit them. HGC would like to set up a lockbox collection system, which it estimates would reduce the time lag from customer mailing to deposit by 3 days—bringing it down to 2 days. HGC receives an average of $1,400,000 in payments per day.

a. How many days of collection float now exist (HGC's customers' disbursement float) and what would it be under the lockbox system? What reduction in cash balances could HGC achieve by initiating the lockbox system?

b. If HGC has an opportunity cost of 10 percent, how much is the lockbox system worth on an annual basis?

c. What is the maximum monthly charge HGC should pay for the lockbox system?

22–10 *CASH BUDGETING* Dorothy Koehl recently leased space in the Southside Mall and opened a new business, Koehl's Doll Shop. Business has been good, but Koehl has frequently run out of cash. This has necessitated late payment on certain orders, which, in turn, is beginning to cause a problem with suppliers. Koehl plans to borrow from the bank to have cash ready as needed, but first she needs a forecast of just how much she must borrow. Accordingly, she has asked you to prepare a cash budget for the critical period around Christmas, when needs will be especially high.

Sales are made on a cash basis only. Koehl's purchases must be paid for during the following month. Koehl pays herself a salary of $4,800 per month, and the rent is $2,000 per month. In addition, she must make a tax payment of $12,000 in December. The current cash on hand (on December 1) is $400, but Koehl has agreed to maintain an average bank balance of $6,000—this is her target cash balance. (Disregard till cash, which is insignificant because Koehl keeps only a small amount on hand in order to lessen the chances of robbery.)

The estimated sales and purchases for December, January, and February are shown below. Purchases during November amounted to $140,000.

	Sales	Purchases
December	$160,000	$40,000
January	40,000	40,000
February	60,000	40,000

a. Prepare a cash budget for December, January, and February.

b. Now, suppose Koehl were to start selling on a credit basis on December 1, giving customers 30 days to pay. All customers accept these terms, and all other facts in the problem are unchanged. What would the company's loan requirements be at the end of December in this case? (Hint: The calculations required to answer this question are minimal.)

22–11 *CASH BUDGETING* Helen Bowers, owner of Helen's Fashion Designs, is planning to request a line of credit from her bank. She has estimated the following sales forecasts for the firm for parts of 2002 and 2003:

May 2002	$180,000
June	180,000
July	360,000
August	540,000
September	720,000
October	360,000
November	360,000
December	90,000
January 2003	180,000

Collection estimates obtained from the credit and collection department are as follows: collections within the month of sale, 10 percent; collections the month following the sale, 75 percent; collections the second month following the sale, 15 percent. Payments for labor and raw materials are typically made during the month following the one in which these costs have been incurred. Total labor and raw materials costs are estimated for each month as follows:

May 2002	$ 90,000
June	90,000
July	126,000
August	882,000
September	306,000
October	234,000
November	162,000
December	90,000

General and administrative salaries will amount to approximately $27,000 a month; lease payments under long-term lease contracts will be $9,000 a month; depreciation charges will be $36,000 a month; miscellaneous expenses will be $2,700 a month; income tax payments of $63,000 will be due in both September and December; and a progress payment of $180,000 on a new design studio must be paid in October. Cash on hand on July 1 will amount to $132,000, and a minimum cash balance of $90,000 will be maintained throughout the cash budget period.

a. Prepare a monthly cash budget for the last 6 months of 2002.

b. Prepare an estimate of the required financing (or excess funds)—that is, the amount of money Bowers will need to borrow (or will have available to invest)—for each month during that period.

c. Assume that receipts from sales come in uniformly during the month (that is, cash receipts come in at the rate of 1/30 each day), but all outflows are paid on the 5th of the month. Will this have an effect on the cash budget—in other words, would the cash budget you have prepared be valid under these assumptions? If not, what can be done to make a valid estimate of peak financing requirements? No calculations are required, although calculations can be used to illustrate the effects.

d. Bowers produces on a seasonal basis, just ahead of sales. Without making any calculations, discuss how the company's current ratio and debt ratio would vary during the year assuming all financial requirements were met by short-term bank loans. Could changes in these ratios affect the firm's ability to obtain bank credit?

Spreadsheet Problem

22–12 *BUILD A MODEL: CASH BUDGETING*

Start with the partial model in the file ***Ch 22-12 Build a Model.xls*** from the textbook's CD-ROM. Rework Problem 22-11. After completing parts a through d, answer the following related question.

e. If its customers began to pay late, this would slow down collections and thus increase the required load amount. Also, if sales dropped off, this would have an effect on the required loan. Do a sensitivity analysis that shows the effects of these two factors on the maximum loan requirement.

Cyberproblem

The information related to this cyberproblem is likely to change over time, due to the release of new information and the ever-changing nature of the World Wide Web. Accordingly, we will periodically update the problem on the textbook's web site.

22–13 *THE CASH CONVERSION CYCLE IN PRACTICE*

The text identifies three principal components that jointly comprise the cash conversion cycle. The cash conversion cycle is defined as the average length of time a dollar is tied up in current assets, and it is determined by the interaction between the inventory conversion period, receivables collection period, and the payables deferral period. Ideally, a company wants to minimize the cash conversion cycle as much as possible. In some circumstances, a firm has a comparative advantage in working capital management because of the nature of its business. This cyberproblem looks at two competing booksellers. Barnes and Noble Inc. is a hybrid between the traditional brick and mortar retailer and the Internet retailer. However, approximately 85 percent of its revenues are generated in the traditional retail setting, which will lead us to consider it a traditional retail firm. Amazon.com, on the other hand, represents the new wave of Internet retailing. The success of Amazon.com has spawned the flood of specialty retailing into the Internet marketplace. We will look at the cash conversion cycles of these companies and their implications. Go to the cyberproblem on the textbook's web site, **http:// www.harcourtcollege.com/theory/student/resources/cyberprob/ch22.html,** and answer the questions shown there.

Mini Case

See ***Ch 22 Show.ppt*** and ***Ch 22 Mini Case.xls.***

Dan Barnes, financial manager of Ski Equipment Inc. (SKI), is excited, but apprehensive. The company's founder recently sold his 51 percent controlling block of stock to Kent Koren, who is a big fan of EVA (Economic Value Added). EVA is found by taking the after-tax operating profit and then subtracting the dollar cost of all the capital the firm uses:

$$\begin{aligned} \text{EVA} &= \text{NOPAT} - \text{Capital costs} \\ &= \text{EBIT}(1 - T) - \text{WACC (Operating capital)}. \end{aligned}$$

If EVA is positive, then the firm is creating value. On the other hand, if EVA is negative, the firm is not covering its cost of capital, and stockholders' value is being eroded. Koren rewards managers handsomely if they create value, but those whose operations produce negative EVAs are soon looking for work. Koren frequently points out that if a company can generate its current level of sales with less assets, it would need less capital. That would, other things held constant, lower capital costs and increase its EVA.

Shortly after he took control of SKI, Kent Koren met with SKI's senior executives to tell them of his plans for the company. First, he presented some EVA data that convinced everyone that SKI had not been creating value in recent years. He then stated, in no uncertain terms, that this situation must change. He noted that SKI's designs of skis, boots, and clothing are acclaimed throughout the industry, but something is seriously amiss elsewhere in the company. Costs are too high, prices are too low, or the company employs too much capital, and he wants SKI's managers to correct the problem or else.

Barnes has long felt that SKI's working capital situation should be studied—the company may have the optimal amounts of cash, securities, receivables, and inventories, but it may also have too much or too little of these items. In the past, the production manager resisted Dan's efforts to question his holdings of raw materials inventories, the marketing manager resisted questions about finished goods, the sales staff resisted questions about credit policy (which affects accounts receivable), and the treasurer did not want to talk about her cash and securities balances. Koren's speech made it clear that such resistance would no longer be tolerated.

Dan also knows that decisions about working capital cannot be made in a vacuum. For example, if inventories could be lowered without adversely affecting operations, then less capital would be required, the dollar cost of capital would decline, and EVA would increase. However, lower raw materials inventories might lead to production slowdowns and higher costs, while lower finished goods inventories might lead to the loss of profitable sales. So, before inventories are changed, it will be necessary to study operating as well as financial effects. The situation is the same with regard to cash and receivables. Following are some ratios for SKI:

	SKI	Industry
Current	1.75	2.25
Quick	0.83	1.20
Debt/assets	58.76%	50.00%
Turnover of cash and securities	16.67	22.22
Days sales outstanding	45.00	32.00
Inventory turnover	4.82	7.00
Fixed assets turnover	11.35	12.00
Total assets turnover	2.08	3.00
Profit margin on sales	2.07%	3.50%
Return on equity (ROE)	10.45%	21.00%
Payables deferral period	30.00	33.00

a. Dan plans to use the preceding ratios as the starting point for discussions with SKI's operating executives. He wants everyone to think about the pros and cons of changing each type of current asset and how changes would interact to affect profits and EVA. Based on the data in the table, does SKI seem to be following a relaxed, moderate, or restricted working capital policy?
b. How can one distinguish between a relaxed but rational working capital policy and a situation where a firm simply has a lot of current assets because it is inefficient? Does SKI's working capital policy seem appropriate?
c. Calculate SKI's cash conversion cycle, assuming all calculations use a 360-day year.
d. What might SKI do to reduce its cash and securities without harming operations?
e. What is "float," and how is it affected by the firm's cash manager (treasurer)?

In an attempt to better understand SKI's cash position, Dan developed a cash budget. Data for the first 2 months of the year are shown at the end of this Mini Case. (Note that Dan's preliminary cash budget does not account for interest income or interest expense.) He has the figures for the other months, but they are not shown in this Mini Case.

f. Should depreciation expense be explicitly included in the cash budget? Why or why not?
g. In his preliminary cash budget, Dan has assumed that all sales are collected and, thus, that SKI has no bad debts. Is this realistic? If not, how would bad debts be dealt with in a cash budgeting sense? (Hint: Bad debts will affect collections but not purchases.)
h. Dan's cash budget for the entire year, although not given here, is based heavily on his forecast for monthly sales. Sales are expected to be extremely low between May and September but then increase dramatically in the fall and winter. November is typically the firm's best month, when SKI ships equipment to retailers for the holiday season. Interestingly, Dan's forecasted cash budget indicates that the company's cash holdings will exceed the targeted cash balance every month except for October and November, when shipments will be high but collections will not be coming in until later. Based on the ratios in the first table, does it appear that SKI's target cash balance is appropriate? In addition to possibly lowering the target cash balance, what actions might SKI take to better improve its cash management policies, and how might that affect its EVA?
i. What reasons might SKI have for maintaining a relatively high amount of cash?
j. What are the three categories of inventory costs? If the company takes steps to reduce its inventory, what effect would this have on the various costs of holding inventory?
k. Is there any reason to think that SKI may be holding too much inventory? If so, how would that affect EVA and ROE?
l. If the company reduces its inventory without adversely affecting sales, what effect should this have on the company's cash position (1) in the short run and (2) in the long run? Explain in terms of the cash budget and the balance sheet.

m. Dan knows that SKI sells on the same credit terms as other firms in its industry. Use the ratios presented in the first table to explain whether SKI's customers pay more or less promptly than those of its competitors. If there are differences, does that suggest that SKI should tighten or loosen its credit policy? What four variables make up a firm's credit policy, and in what direction should each be changed by SKI?
n. Does SKI face any risks if it tightens its credit policy?
o. If the company reduces its DSO without seriously affecting sales, what effect would this have on its cash position (1) in the short run and (2) in the long run? Answer in terms of the cash budget and the balance sheet. What effect should this have on EVA in the long run?

	Nov	Dec	Jan	Feb	Mar	Apr
I. COLLECTIONS AND PURCHASES WORKSHEET						
(1) Sales (gross)	$71,218	$68,212	$65,213	$52,475	$42,909	$30,524
Collections						
(2) During month of sale (0.2) (0.98) (month's sales)			12,781.75	10,285.10		
(3) During first month after sale (0.7) (previous month's sales)			47,748.40	45,649.10		
(4) During second month after sale (0.1) (sales 2 months ago)			7,121.80	6,821.20		
(5) Total collections (Lines 2 + 3 + 4)			$67,651.95	$62,755.40		
Purchases						
(6) (0.85) (forecasted sales 2 months from now)		$44,603.75	$36,472.65	$25,945.40		
(7) Payments (1-month lag)			44,603.75	36,472.65		
II. CASH GAIN OR LOSS FOR MONTH						
(8) Collections (from Section I)			$67,651.95	$62,755.40		
(9) Payments for purchases (from Section I)			44,603.75	36,472.65		
(10) Wages and salaries			6,690.56	5,470.90		
(11) Rent			2,500.00	2,500.00		
(12) Taxes						
(13) Total payments			$53,794.31	$44,443.55		
(14) Net cash gain (loss) during month (Line 8 − Line 13)			$13,857.64	$18,311.85		
III. CASH SURPLUS OR LOAN REQUIREMENT						
(15) Cash at beginning of month if no borrowing is done			$ 3,000.00	$16,857.64		
(16) Cumulative cash (cash at start + gain or − loss = Line 14 + Line 15)			16,857.64	35,169.49		
(17) Target cash balance			1,500.00	1,500.00		
(18) Cumulative surplus cash or loans outstanding to maintain $1,500 target cash balance (Line 16 − Line 17)			$15,357.64	$33,669.49		

Selected Additional References and Cases

Some of the more technical issues involved in inventory and receivables management are addressed in the "Working Capital Mangement: Extensions" chapter on the textbook's web site. The following books focus on short-term financial management:

Gallinger, George W., and P. Basil Healy, *Liquidity Analysis and Management* (Reading, MA: Addison-Wesley, 1991).

Hill, Ned C., and William L. Sartoris, *Short-Term Financial Management* (New York: Prentice-Hall, 1995).

Maness, Terry S., and John T. Zietlow, *Short-Term Financial Management: Text, Cases, and Readings* (Minneapolis/St. Paul: West, 1993).

The following articles provide more information on short-term financial management:

Gentry, James A., "State of the Art of Short-Run Financial Management," *Financial Management*, Summer 1988, 41–57.

Gentry, James A., and Jesus M. De La Garza, "Monitoring Accounts Payables," *Financial Review*, November 1990, 559–576.

Gentry, James A., R. Vaidyanathan, and Hei Wai Lee, "A Weighted Cash Conversion Cycle," *Financial Management*, Spring 1990, 90–99.

Lambrix, R. J., and S. S. Singhvi, "Managing the Working Capital Cycle," *Financial Executive*, June 1979, 32–41.

Maier, Steven F., and James H. Vander Weide, "A Practical Approach to Short-Run Financial Planning," *Financial Management*, Winter 1978, 10–16.

Merville, Larry J., and Lee A. Tavis, "Optimal Working Capital Policies: A Chance-Constrained Programming Approach," *Journal of Financial and Quantitative Analysis*, January 1973, 47–60.

Mitchell, Karlyn, "The Debt Maturity Choice: An Empirical Investigation," *Journal of Financial Research*, Winter 1993, 309–320.

Yardini, Edward E., "A Portfolio-Balance Model of Corporate Working Capital," *Journal of Finance*, May 1979, 535–552.

Perhaps the best way to get a good feel for the current state of the art in cash management is to look through recent issues of The Journal of Cash Management, *a publication aimed at professionals in the field.*

For more information on transfer systems, see

Summers, Bruce J., "Clearing and Payment Systems: The Role of the Central Bank," *Federal Reserve Bulletin*, February 1991, 81–91.

Wood, John C., and Dolores D. Smith, "Electronic Transfer of Government Benefits," *Federal Reserve Bulletin*, April 1991, 204–207.

For more information on float management, see

Batlin, C. A., and Susan Hinko, "Lockbox Management and Value Maximization," *Financial Management*, Winter 1981, 39–44.

Gitman, Lawrence J., D. Keith Forrester, and John R. Forrester, Jr., "Maximizing Cash Disbursement Float," *Financial Management*, Summer 1976, 32–41.

Nauss, Robert M., and Robert E. Markland, "Solving Lockbox Location Problems," *Financial Management*, Spring 1979, 21–31.

The following articles provide more information on cash concentration systems:

Stone, Bernell K., and Ned C. Hill, "Cash Transfer Scheduling for Efficient Cash Concentration," *Financial Management*, Autumn 1980, 35–43.

————, "The Design of a Cash Concentration System," *Journal of Financial and Quantitative Analysis*, September 1981, 301–322.

Stone, Bernell K., and Tom W. Miller, "Daily Cash Forecasting with Multiplicative Models of Cash Flow Patterns," *Financial Management*, Winter 1987, 45–54.

For greater insights into compensating balance requirements, see

Campbell, Tim S., and Leland Brendsel, "The Impact of Compensating Balance Requirements on the Cash Balances of Manufacturing Corporations," *Journal of Finance*, March 1977, 31–40.

Frost, Peter A., "Banking Services, Minimum Cash Balances, and the Firm's Demand for Money," *Journal of Finance*, December 1970, 1029–1039.

For more information on marketable securities, see

Brown, Keith C., and Scott L. Lummer, "A Reexamination of the Covered Call Option Strategy for Corporate Cash Management," *Financial Management*, Summer 1986, 13–17.

Kamath, Ravindra R., et al., "Management of Excess Cash: Practices and Developments," *Financial Management*, Autumn 1985, 70–77.

Stigum, M., *The Money Market: Myth, Reality, and Practice* (Homewood, IL: Dow Jones-Irwin, 1978).

Van Horne, J. C., *Financial Market Rates and Flows*, 3rd ed. (Englewood Cliffs, NJ: Prentice-Hall, 1990).

Zivney, Terry L., and Michael J. Alderson, "Hedged Dividend Capture with Stock Index Options," *Financial Management*, Summer 1986, 5–12.

The following articles and books provide additional insights into the problems of inventory management:

Arvan, L., and L. N. Moses, "Inventory Management and the Theory of the Firm," *American Economic Review*, March 1982, 186–193.

Bierman, H., Jr., C. P. Bonini, and W. H. Hausman, *Quantitative Analysis for Business Decisions* (Homewood, IL: Irwin, 1977).

Brooks, L. D., "Risk-Return Criteria and Optimal Inventory Stocks," *Engineering Economist*, Summer 1980, 275–299.

Followill, Richard A., Michael Schellenger, and Patrick H. Marchand, "Economic Order Quantities, Volume Discounts, and Wealth Maximization," *The Financial Review*, February 1990, 143–152.

Kallberg, Jarl G., and Kenneth L. Parkinson, *Current Asset Management: Cash, Credit, and Inventory* (New York: Wiley, 1984).

Magee, John F., "Guides to Inventory Policy, I," *Harvard Business Review*, January–February 1956, 49–60.

———, "Guides to Inventory Policy, II," *Harvard Business Review*, March–April 1956, 103–116.

———, "Guides to Inventory Policy, III," *Harvard Business Review*, May–June 1956, 57–70.

Mehta, Dileep R., *Working Capital Management* (Englewood Cliffs, NJ: Prentice-Hall, 1974).

Shapiro, A., "Optimal Inventory and Credit Granting Strategies under Inflation and Devaluation," *Journal of Financial and Quantitative Analysis*, January 1973, 37–46.

Smith, Keith V., *Guide to Working Capital Management* (New York: McGraw-Hill, 1979).

Hill, Ned C., and Kenneth D. Riener, "Determining the Cash Discount in the Firm's Credit Policy," *Financial Management*, Spring 1979, 68–73.

Kim, Yong H., and Joseph C. Atkins, "Evaluating Investments in Accounts Receivable: A Wealth Maximizing Framework," *Journal of Finance*, May 1978, 403–412.

Mian, Shehzad L., and Clifford W. Smith, "Extending Trade Credit and Financing Receivables," *Journal of Applied Corporate Finance*, Spring 1994, 75–84.

Oh, John S., "Opportunity Cost in the Evaluation of Investment in Accounts Receivables," *Financial Management*, Summer 1976, 32–36.

Roberts, Gordon S., and Jeremy A. Viscione, "Captive Finance Subsidiaries: The Manager's View," *Financial Management*, Spring 1981, 36–42.

Sachdeva, Kanwal S., and Lawrence J. Gitman, "Accounts Receivable Decisions in a Capital Budgeting Framework," *Financial Management*, Winter 1981, 45–49.

Walia, Tinlochan S., "Explicit and Implicit Cost of Changes in the Level of Accounts Receivable and the Credit Policy Decision of the Firm," *Financial Management*, Winter 1977, 75–78.

Weston, J. Fred, and Pham D. Tuan, "Comment on Analysis of Credit Policy Changes," *Financial Management*, Winter 1980, 59–63.

Articles that address credit policy and receivables management include the following:

Atkins, Joseph C., and Yong H. Kim, "Comment and Correction: Opportunity Cost in the Evaluation of Investment in Accounts Receivable," *Financial Management*, Winter 1977, 71–74.

Ben-Horim, Moshe, and Haim Levy, "Management of Accounts Receivable under Inflation," *Financial Management*, Spring 1983, 42–48.

Dyl, Edward A., "Another Look at the Evaluation of Interest in Accounts Receivable," *Financial Management*, Winter 1977, 67–70.

Gallinger, George W., and A. James Ifflander, "Monitoring Accounts Receivable Using Variance Analysis," *Financial Management*, Winter 1986, 69–76.

Gentry, James A., and Jesus M. De La Garza, "A Generalized Model for Monitoring Accounts Receivable," *Financial Management*, Winter 1985, 28–38.

The following cases from the Cases in Financial Management: Dryden Request *casebook focus on the credit policy decision:*

Case 29, "Office Mates, Inc.," which illustrates how changes in current asset policy affect expected profitability and risk.

Case 32, "Alpine Wear, Inc.," which illustrates the mechanics of the cash budget and the rationale behind its use.

Two new cash budgeting cases, Case 32A, "Toy World, Inc.," and Case 32B, "Sorenson Stove Company," have been added to the Dryden case set.

Case 33, "Upscale Toddlers, Inc.," which deals with credit policy changes.

Case 34, "Texas Rose Company," which focuses on receivables management.

Case 62, "Western Supply Company," which illustrates the effects of a change in credit policy on corporate profitability and cash flow.

23

Short-Term Financing

The last chapter discussed steps firms can take to improve their working capital management, thus reducing current assets as a percentage of sales through the use of new technology and improved management techniques. Still, most companies must hold large amounts of current assets, and this investment must be financed in some manner. This involves "working capital financing policy," the focus of the current chapter.

Most firms use several types of short-term debt to finance their working capital requirements. Included are bank loans, trade credit, commercial paper, and accruals. However, the optimal structure of its current liabilities depends on the nature of a firm's business. For example, the sales of Toys Я Us are seasonal—nearly half of all sales occur in the final three months of the year. To meet holiday demands, Toys Я Us must dramatically increase its inventories during the summer and early fall. This inventory buildup must be financed until after Christmas, when collections bring in cash and debts can be reduced. The company finances the buildup with trade credit, loans from U.S. and foreign banks, commercial paper, and the sale of marketable securities built up during the slack season.

Short-term credit is generally cheaper than long-term capital, but it is a riskier, less dependable source of financing. Interest rates can increase dramatically, and changes in a company's financial position can affect both the cost and availability of short-term credit.

After you have completed this chapter, you will have a better understanding of the ways corporations finance their current assets, and of the costs associated with each type of financing.

In the last chapter, we discussed one element of working capital management—determining the optimal level for each type of current asset. Now we turn to the second element—financing those assets. We begin with a discussion of alternative financing policies. Some companies use current liabilities as a major source of financing for current assets, while others rely more heavily on long-term debt and equity. In this chapter we consider the advantages and disadvantages of each policy. In addition, we describe the various sources of short-term financing—accruals, accounts payable, bank loans, and commercial paper. We also show how to estimate the cost of each source, and we discuss how companies choose their banking relationships.

Alternative Current Asset Financing Policies

CD

The textbook's CD-ROM contains an *Excel* file that will guide you through the chapter's calculations. The file for this chapter is ***Ch 23 Tool Kit.xls,*** and we encourage you to open the file and follow along as you read the chapter.

Most businesses experience seasonal and/or cyclical fluctuations. For example, construction firms have peaks in the spring and summer, retailers peak around Christmas, and the manufacturers who supply both construction companies and retailers follow similar patterns. Similarly, virtually all businesses must build up current assets when the economy is strong, but then sell off inventories and reduce receivables when the economy slacks off. Still, current assets rarely drop to zero—companies have some **permanent current assets,** which are the current assets on hand at the low point of the cycle. Then, as sales increase during the upswing, current assets must be increased, and these additional current assets are defined as **temporary current assets.** The manner in which the permanent and temporary current assets are financed is called the firm's *current asset financing policy.*

Maturity Matching, or "Self-Liquidating," Approach

The **maturity matching,** or **"self-liquidating," approach** calls for matching asset and liability maturities as shown in Panel a of Figure 23-1. This strategy minimizes the risk that the firm will be unable to pay off its maturing obligations. To illustrate, suppose a company borrows on a one-year basis and uses the funds obtained to build and equip a plant. Cash flows from the plant (profits plus depreciation) would not be sufficient to pay off the loan at the end of only one year, so the loan would have to be renewed. If for some reason the lender refused to renew the loan, then the company would have problems. Had the plant been financed with long-term debt, however, the required loan payments would have been better matched with cash flows from profits and depreciation, and the problem of renewal would not have arisen.

At the limit, a firm could attempt to match exactly the maturity structure of its assets and liabilities. Inventory expected to be sold in 30 days could be financed with a 30-day bank loan; a machine expected to last for 5 years could be financed with a 5-year loan; a 20-year building could be financed with a 20-year mortgage bond; and so forth. Actually, of course, two factors prevent this exact maturity matching: (1) there is uncertainty about the lives of assets, and (2) some common equity must be used, and common equity has no maturity. To illustrate the uncertainty factor, a firm might finance inventories with a 30-day loan, expecting to sell the inventories and then use the cash to retire the loan. But if sales were slow, the cash would not be forthcoming, and the use of short-term credit could end up causing a problem. Still, if a firm makes an attempt to match asset and liability maturities, we would define this as a moderate current asset financing policy.

In practice, firms don't finance each specific asset with a type of capital that has a maturity equal to the asset's life. However, academic studies do show that most firms

FIGURE 23-1 Alternative Current Asset Financing Policies

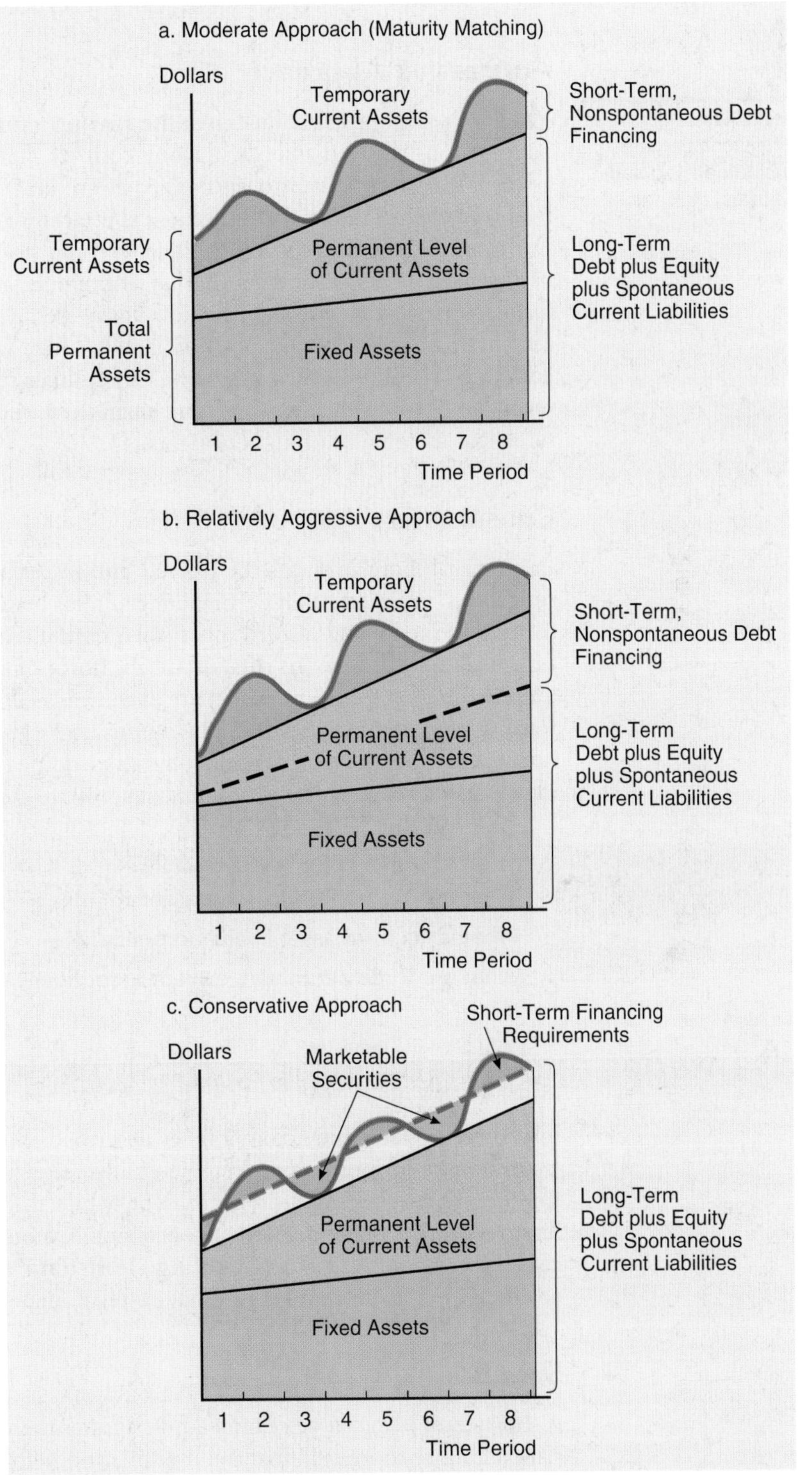

tend to finance short-term assets from short-term sources and long-term assets from long-term sources.[1]

WWW

Students can access various types of historical interest rates, including fixed and variable rates, at the St. Louis Federal Reserve's FRED site. The address is **http://www.stls.frb.org/fred/**.

Aggressive Approach

Panel b of Figure 23-1 illustrates the situation for a relatively aggressive firm. It finances all of its fixed assets with long-term capital but part of its permanent current assets with short-term, nonspontaneous credit. Note that we used the term "relatively" in the title for Panel b because there can be different *degrees* of aggressiveness. For example, the dashed line in Panel b could have been drawn *below* the line designating fixed assets, indicating that all of the permanent current assets and part of the fixed assets were financed with short-term credit; this would be a highly aggressive, extremely nonconservative position, and the firm would be very much subject to dangers from rising interest rates as well as to loan renewal problems. However, short-term debt is often cheaper than long-term debt, and some firms are willing to sacrifice safety for the chance of higher profits.

Conservative Approach

Panel c of Figure 23-1 has the dashed line *above* the line designating permanent current assets, indicating that permanent capital is being used to finance all permanent asset requirements and also to meet some of the seasonal needs. In this situation, the firm uses a small amount of short-term, nonspontaneous credit to meet its peak requirements, but it also meets a part of its seasonal needs by "storing liquidity" in the form of marketable securities. The humps above the dashed line represent short-term financing, while the troughs below the dashed line represent short-term security holdings. Panel c represents a very safe, conservative current asset financing policy.

Self-Test Questions

What are "permanent current assets"?

What are "temporary current assets"?

What is "current asset financing policy"?

What are three alternative current asset financing policies? Is one best?

Advantages and Disadvantages of Short-Term Financing

The three possible financing policies described above were distinguished by the relative amounts of short-term debt used under each policy. The aggressive policy called for the greatest use of short-term debt, while the conservative policy called for the least. Maturity matching fell in between. Although short-term credit is generally riskier than long-term credit, using short-term funds does have some significant advantages. The pros and cons of short-term financing are considered in this section.

Speed

A short-term loan can be obtained much faster than long-term credit. Lenders will insist on a more thorough financial examination before extending long-term credit, and the loan agreement will have to be spelled out in considerable detail because a lot can

[1]For example, see William Beranek, Christopher Cornwell, and Sunho Choi, "External Financing, Liquidity, and Capital Expenditures," *Journal of Financial Research*, Summer 1995, 207–222.

happen during the life of a 10- to 20-year loan. Therefore, if funds are needed in a hurry, the firm should look to the short-term markets.

Flexibility

If its needs for funds are seasonal or cyclical, a firm may not want to commit itself to long-term debt for three reasons: (1) Flotation costs are higher for long-term debt than for short-term credit. (2) Although long-term debt can be repaid early, provided the loan agreement includes a prepayment provision, prepayment penalties can be expensive. Accordingly, if a firm thinks its need for funds will diminish in the near future, it should choose short-term debt. (3) Long-term loan agreements always contain provisions, or covenants, which constrain the firm's future actions. Short-term credit agreements are generally less restrictive.

Cost of Long-Term versus Short-Term Debt

The yield curve is normally upward sloping, indicating that interest rates are generally lower on short-term debt. Thus, under normal conditions, interest costs at the time the funds are obtained will be lower if the firm borrows on a short-term rather than a long-term basis.

Risks of Long-Term versus Short-Term Debt

Even though short-term rates are often lower than long-term rates, short-term credit is riskier for two reasons: (1) If a firm borrows on a long-term basis, its interest costs will be relatively stable over time, but if it uses short-term credit, its interest expense will fluctuate widely, at times going quite high. For example, the rate banks charge large corporations for short-term debt more than tripled over a two-year period in the 1980s, rising from 6.25 to 21 percent. Many firms that had borrowed heavily on a short-term basis simply could not meet their rising interest costs, and as a result, bankruptcies hit record levels during that period. (2) If a firm borrows heavily on a short-term basis, a temporary recession may render it unable to repay this debt. If the borrower is in a weak financial position, the lender may not extend the loan, which could force the firm into bankruptcy. Braniff Airlines, which failed during a credit crunch in the 1980s, is an example.

Another good example of the riskiness of short-term debt is provided by Transamerica Corporation, a major financial services company. Transamerica's former chairman, John R. Beckett, described how his company was moving to reduce its dependency on short-term loans whose costs vary with short-term interest rates. According to Beckett, Transamerica had reduced its variable-rate (short-term) loans by about $450 million over a two-year period. "We aren't going to go through the enormous increase in debt expense again that had such a serious impact on earnings," he said. The company's earnings fell sharply because money rates rose to record highs. "We were almost entirely in variable-rate debt," he said, but currently "about 65 percent is fixed rate and 35 percent variable. We've come a long way, and we'll keep plugging away at it." Transamerica's earnings were badly depressed by the increase in short-term rates, but other companies were even less fortunate—they simply could not pay the rising interest charges, and this forced them into bankruptcy.

Self-Test Question

What are the advantages and disadvantages of short-term debt over long-term debt?

Sources of Short-Term Financing

Statements about the flexibility, cost, and riskiness of short-term versus long-term debt depend, to a large extent, on the type of short-term credit that is actually used. There are numerous sources of short-term funds, and in the following sections we describe four major types: (1) accruals, (2) accounts payable (trade credit), (3) bank loans, and (4) commercial paper.

Accruals

Firms generally pay employees on a weekly, biweekly, or monthly basis, so the balance sheet will typically show some accrued wages. Similarly, the firm's own estimated income taxes, Social Security and income taxes withheld from employee payrolls, and sales taxes collected are generally paid on a weekly, monthly, or quarterly basis. Therefore, the balance sheet will typically show some accrued taxes along with accrued wages.

These **accruals** increase automatically, or spontaneously, as a firm's operations expand. Further, this type of debt is "free" in the sense that no explicit interest is paid on funds raised through accruals. However, a firm cannot ordinarily control its accruals: The timing of wage payments is set by economic forces and industry custom, while tax payment dates are established by law. Thus, firms use all the accruals they can, but they have little control over the levels of these accounts.

Self-Test Questions

What types of short-term credit are classified as accruals?

What is the cost of accruals?

How much control do financial managers have over the dollar amount of accruals?

Accounts Payable (Trade Credit)

Firms generally make purchases from other firms on credit, recording the debt as an *account payable.* Accounts payable, or **trade credit,** is the largest single category of short-term financing, representing about 40 percent of the current liabilities of the average nonfinancial corporation. The percentage is somewhat larger for smaller firms: Because small companies often do not qualify for financing from other sources, they rely especially heavily on trade credit.[2]

Trade credit is a "spontaneous" source of financing in the sense that it arises from ordinary business transactions. For example, suppose a firm makes average purchases of $2,000 a day on terms of net 30, meaning that it must pay for goods 30 days after the invoice date. On average, it will owe 30 times $2,000, or $60,000, to its suppliers. If its sales, and consequently its purchases, were to double, then its accounts payable would also double, to $120,000. So, simply by growing, the firm would spontaneously generate an additional $60,000 of financing. Similarly, if the terms under which it

[2]In a credit sale, the seller records the transaction as a receivable, the buyer as a payable. We examined accounts receivable as an asset in Chapter 22. Our focus in this chapter is on accounts payable, a liability item. We might also note that if a firm's accounts payable exceed its receivables, it is said to be *receiving net trade credit,* whereas if its receivables exceed its payables, it is *extending net trade credit.* Smaller firms frequently receive net credit; larger firms generally extend it.

bought were extended from 30 to 40 days, its accounts payable would expand from \$60,000 to \$80,000. Thus, lengthening the credit period, as well as expanding sales and purchases, generates additional financing.

The Cost of Trade Credit

Firms that sell on credit have a *credit policy* that includes its *terms of credit*. For example, Microchip Electronics sells on terms of 2/10, net 30, meaning that it gives its customers a 2 percent discount if they pay within 10 days of the invoice date, but the full invoice amount is due and payable within 30 days if the discount is not taken.

Note that the true price of Microchip's products is the net price, or 0.98 times the list price, because any customer can purchase an item at that price as long as the customer pays within 10 days. Now consider Personal Computer Company (PCC), which buys its memory chips from Microchip. One commonly used memory chip is listed at \$100, so the "true" price to PCC is \$98. Now if PCC wants an additional 20 days of credit beyond the 10-day discount period, it must incur a finance charge of \$2 per chip for that credit. Thus, the \$100 list price consists of two components:

$$\text{List price} = \$98 \text{ true price} + \$2 \text{ finance charge.}$$

The question PCC must ask before it turns down the discount to obtain the additional 20 days of credit from Microchip is this: Could we obtain credit under better terms from some other lender, say, a bank? In other words, could 20 days of credit be obtained for less than \$2 per chip?

PCC buys an average of \$11,760,000 of memory chips from Microchip each year at the net, or true, price. This amounts to \$11,760,000/360 = \$32,666.67 per day. For simplicity, assume that Microchip is PCC's only supplier. If PCC decides not to take the additional trade credit—that is, if it pays on the 10th day and takes the discount—its payables will average 10(\$32,666.67) = \$326,667. Thus, PCC will be receiving \$326,667 of credit from Microchip.

Now suppose PCC decides to take the additional 20 days credit and thus must pay the finance charge. Since PCC will now pay on the 30th day, its accounts payable will increase to 30(\$32,666.67) = \$980,000.[3] Microchip will now be supplying PCC with an additional \$980,000 − \$326,667 = \$653,333 of credit, which PCC could use to build up its cash account, to pay off debt, to expand inventories, or even to extend credit to its own customers, hence increasing its own accounts receivable.

The additional trade credit offered by Microchip has a cost—PCC must pay a finance charge equal to the 2 percent discount it is foregoing. PCC buys \$11,760,000 of chips at the true price, and the added finance charges increase the total cost to \$11,760,000/0.98 = \$12 million. Therefore, the annual financing cost is \$12,000,000 − \$11,760,000 = \$240,000. Dividing the \$240,000 financing cost by the \$653,333 of additional credit, we find the nominal annual cost rate of the additional trade credit to be 36.7 percent:

$$\text{Nominal annual cost} = \frac{\$240{,}000}{\$653{,}333} = 36.7\%.$$

[3]A question arises here: Should accounts payable reflect gross purchases or purchases net of discounts? Generally accepted accounting principles permit either treatment if the difference is not material, but if the discount is material, then the transaction must be recorded net of discounts, or at "true" prices. Then, the higher payment that results from not taking discounts is reported as an additional expense called "discounts lost." *Thus, we show accounts payable net of discounts even if the company does not expect to take discounts.*

If PCC can borrow from its bank (or from some other source) at an interest rate less than 36.7 percent, it should take discounts and forgo the additional trade credit.

The following equation can be used to calculate the nominal cost, on an annual basis, of not taking discounts, illustrated with terms of 2/10, net 30:

$$\text{Nominal annual cost} = \frac{\text{Discount percent}}{100 - \text{Discount percent}} \times \frac{360 \text{ days}}{\text{Days credit is outstanding} - \text{Discount period}} \qquad (23\text{-}1)$$

$$= \frac{2}{98} \times \frac{360}{20} = 2.04\% \times 18 = 36.7\%.$$

The numerator of the first term, Discount percent, is the cost per dollar of credit, while the denominator in this term, 100 − Discount percent, represents the funds made available by not taking the discount. Thus, the first term, 2.04%, is the cost per period for the trade credit. The denominator of the second term is the number of days of extra credit obtained by not taking the discount, so the entire second term shows how many times each year the cost is incurred, 18 times in this example.

The nominal annual cost formula does not take account of compounding, and in effective annual interest terms, the cost of trade credit is even higher. The discount amounts to interest, and with terms of 2/10, net 30, the firm gains use of the funds for 30 − 10 = 20 days, so there are 360/20 = 18 "interest periods" per year. Remember that the first term in Equation 23-1, (Discount percent)/(100 − Discount percent) = 0.02/0.98 = 0.0204, is the periodic interest rate. This rate is paid 18 times each year, so the effective annual cost of trade credit is

$$\text{Effective annual rate} = (1.0204)^{18} - 1.0 = 1.439 - 1.0 = 43.9\%.$$

Thus, the 36.7 percent nominal cost calculated with Equation 23-1 understates the true cost.

Note, however, that the cost of trade credit can be reduced by paying late. Thus, if PCC could get away with paying in 60 days rather than in the specified 30 days, then the effective credit period would become 60 − 10 = 50 days, the number of times the discount would be lost would fall to 360/50 = 7.2, and the nominal cost would drop from 36.7 percent to 2.04% × 7.2 = 14.7%. The effective annual rate would drop from 43.9 to 15.7 percent:

$$\text{Effective annual rate} = (1.0204)^{7.2} - 1.0 = 1.157 - 1.0 = 15.7\%.$$

In periods of excess capacity, firms may be able to get away with deliberately paying late, or **stretching accounts payable.** However, they will also suffer a variety of problems associated with being branded a "slow payer." These problems are discussed later in the chapter.

The costs of the additional trade credit from forgoing discounts under some other purchase terms are shown below:

	Cost of Additional Credit if the Cash Discount is Not Taken	
Credit Terms	**Nominal Cost**	**Effective Cost**
1/10, net 20	36.4%	43.6%
1/10, net 30	18.2	19.8
2/10, net 20	73.5	106.9
3/15, net 45	37.1	44.1

As these figures show, the cost of not taking discounts can be substantial. Incidentally, throughout the chapter, we assume that payments are made either on the *last day* for taking discounts or on the *last day* of the credit period, unless otherwise noted. It would be foolish to pay, say, on the 5th day or on the 20th day if the credit terms were 2/10, net 30.[4]

Effects of Trade Credit on the Financial Statements

A firm's policy with regard to taking or not taking discounts can have a significant effect on its financial statements. To illustrate, assume that PCC is just beginning its operations. On the first day, it makes net purchases of \$32,666.67. This amount is recorded on its balance sheet under accounts payable.[5] The second day it buys another \$32,666.67. The first day's purchases are not yet paid for, so at the end of the second day, accounts payable total \$65,333.34. Accounts payable increase by another \$32,666.67 on the third day, for a total of \$98,000, and after 10 days, accounts payable are up to \$326,667.

If PCC takes discounts, then on the 11th day it will have to pay for the \$32,666.67 of purchases made on the first day, which will reduce accounts payable. However, it will buy another \$32,666.67, which will increase payables. Thus, after the 10th day of operations, PCC's balance sheet will level off, showing a balance of \$326,667 in accounts payable, assuming the company pays on the 10th day and takes discounts.

Now suppose PCC decides not to take discounts. In this case, on the 11th day it will add another \$32,666.67 to payables, but it will not pay for the purchases made on the 1st day. Thus, the balance sheet figure for accounts payable will rise to 11(\$32,666.67) = \$359,333.37. This buildup will continue through the 30th day, at which point payables will total 30(\$32,666.67) = \$980,000. On the 31st day, PCC will buy another \$32,666.67 of goods, which will increase accounts payable, but it will also pay for the purchases made the 1st day, which will reduce payables. Thus, its accounts payable will stabilize at \$980,000 after 30 days if it does not take discounts.

The top section of Table 23-1 shows PCC's balance sheet, after it reaches a steady state, under the two trade credit policies. Total assets are unchanged by this policy decision, and we also assume that the accruals and common equity accounts are unchanged. The differences show up in accounts payable and notes payable; when PCC elects to take discounts and thus gives up some of the trade credit it otherwise could have obtained, it will have to raise \$653,333 from some other source. It could have sold more common stock, or it could have used long-term bonds, but it chose to use bank credit, which has a 10 percent cost and is reflected in the notes payable account.

The bottom section of Table 23-1 shows PCC's income statement under the two policies. If the company does not take discounts, then its interest expense will be zero, but it will have a \$240,000 expense for discounts lost. On the other hand, if it does

---

[4]A financial calculator can also be used to determine the cost of trade credit. If the terms of credit are 2/10, net 30, this implies that for every \$100 of goods purchased at the full list price, the customer has the choice of paying the full amount in 30 days or else paying \$98 in 10 days. If a customer decides not to take the discount, then it is in effect borrowing \$98, the amount it would otherwise have to pay, from Day 11 to Day 30, or for 20 days. It will then have to pay \$100, which is the \$98 loan plus a \$2 financing charge, at the end of the 20-day loan period. To calculate the interest rate, enter N = 1, PV = 98, PMT = 0, FV = −100, and then press I to obtain 2.04 percent. This is the rate for 20 days. To calculate the effective annual interest rate on a 360-day basis, enter N = 20/360 = 0.05556, PV = 98, PMT = 0, FV = −100, and then press I to obtain 43.86 percent. The 20/360 = 0.05556 is the fraction of a year the "loan" is outstanding, and the 43.86 percent is the annualized cost of not taking discounts.

[5]Inventories also increase by \$32,666.67, but we are not now concerned with inventories. Again, note that both inventories and payables are recorded net of discounts regardless of whether discounts are taken.

TABLE 23-1 PCC's Financial Statements with Different Trade Credit Policies

	Take Discounts; Borrow from Bank (1)	Do Not Take Discounts; Use Maximum Trade Credit (2)	Difference (1) − (2)
I. BALANCE SHEETS			
Cash	$ 500,000	$ 500,000	$ 0
Receivables	1,000,000	1,000,000	0
Inventories	2,000,000	2,000,000	0
Fixed assets	2,980,000	2,980,000	0
Total assets	$ 6,480,000	$ 6,480,000	$ 0
Accounts payable	$ 326,667	$ 980,000	$−653,333
Notes payable (10%)	653,333	0	+653,333
Accruals	500,000	500,000	0
Common equity	5,000,000	5,000,000	0
Total claims	$ 6,480,000	$ 6,480,000	$ 0
II. INCOME STATEMENTS			
Sales	$15,000,000	$15,000,000	$ 0
Less: Purchases	11,760,000	11,760,000	0
Labor	2,000,000	2,000,000	0
Interest	65,333	0	+65,333
Discounts lost	0	240,000	−240,000
Earnings before taxes (EBT)	$1,174,667	$ 1,000,000	$+174,667
Taxes (40%)	469,867	400,000	−69,867
Net income	$ 704,800	$ 600,000	$+104,800

take discounts, it will incur an interest expense of $65,333, but it will avoid the cost of discounts lost. Since discounts lost exceed the interest expense, the take-discounts policy results in a higher net income and, thus, in a higher stock price.

Components of Trade Credit: Free versus Costly

Trade credit can be divided into two components: (1) **free trade credit,** which involves credit received during the discount period and which for PCC amounts to 10 days' net purchases, or $326,667, and (2) **costly trade credit,** which involves credit in excess of the free trade credit and whose cost is based on the forgone discounts.[6] PCC could obtain $653,333, or 20 days' net purchases, of nonfree trade credit at a nominal cost of 37 percent. *Firms should always use the free component, but they should use the costly component only after analyzing the cost of this capital to make sure that it is less than the cost of funds that could be obtained from other sources.* Under the terms of trade found in most industries, the costly component is relatively expensive, so stronger firms avoid using it.

We noted earlier that firms sometimes can and do deviate from the stated credit terms, thus altering the percentage cost figures cited earlier. For example, a California

[6]There is some question as to whether any credit is really "free," because the supplier will have a cost of carrying receivables that must be passed on to the customer in the form of higher prices. Still, if suppliers sell on standard terms such as 2/10, net 30, and if the base price cannot be negotiated downward for early payment, then for all intents and purposes, the 10 days of trade credit is indeed "free."

The Internet Threatens to Transform the Banking Industry

Everywhere you turn you see stories about how the Internet has changed business. Increasingly, businesses and individuals are using the Internet to research and then buy a wide variety of products and services. We discussed in earlier chapters how the Internet has dramatically transformed the brokerage industry. For example, Merrill Lynch, which was slow to respond to the Internet phenomenon, recently became much more aggressive. It just rolled out a new site for online trading, developed a procedure through which companies can issue securities online, and entered several partnerships with Internet-oriented businesses.

The same forces that led to Internet trading are also affecting other parts of the financial services industry. Commercial bankers recognize that while the Internet provides them with a whole host of new opportunities, it will also subject them to increased competition from nontraditional sources. For example, Internet upstart E-LOAN, whose products include mortgages, consumer loans, and small business loans, is currently the nation's leading online lender. While E-LOAN's volume is still relatively small, it represents the tip of the iceberg, because down the road technology companies such as Microsoft will probably enter the industry.

Despite these concerns, there are reasons to believe that the Internet's effect on traditional banking may be smaller and slower than its effect on the brokerage industry. Banking relationships often require close personal contact between the bank and its customers. Corporate borrowers may not want to use the Internet to completely replace the personal relationships they have established with their lenders. Likewise, a large number of customers still prefer to walk into a local branch to do their banking. At a minimum, however, the Internet will be used to supplement these personal relationships.

The traditional banks are not sitting on their hands. Mostly conservative by nature, commercial bankers have slowly begun to embrace the opportunities, and confront the threats, that arise from changing technology. Virtually every leading bank now has an Internet presence. In most cases, customers can see their balances, transfer money, and research the bank's various products. Several banking giants, including Chase, Citigroup, Wells Fargo, and Bank of America, are taking things a step further and spending a lot of money to develop a wider range of online banking products. These banks are hoping to use their size, brand name, and experience to become major players in online financial services. Another leading bank, Bank One, has followed a different strategy. It set up a completely separate bank with a distinct operation and brand name, Wingspan.com. Bank One hopes that its separate identity will enable Wingspan to develop a more entrepreneurial, web-savvy culture. While it is too early to tell which strategies will be most successful, it is clear that the financial services industry will be very different 10 years from now.

manufacturing firm that buys on terms of 2/10, net 30, makes a practice of paying in 15 days (rather than 10), but it still takes discounts. Its treasurer simply waits until 15 days after receipt of the goods to pay, then writes a check for the invoiced amount less the 2 percent discount. The company's suppliers want its business, so they tolerate this practice. Similarly, a Wisconsin firm that also buys on terms of 2/10, net 30, does not take discounts, but it pays in 60 rather than in 30 days, thus "stretching" its trade credit. As we saw earlier, both practices reduce the calculated cost of trade credit. Neither of these firms is "loved" by its suppliers, and neither could continue these practices in times when suppliers were operating at full capacity and had order backlogs, but these practices can and do reduce the costs of trade credit during times when suppliers have excess capacity.

Self-Test Questions

What is trade credit?

What is the difference between free trade credit and costly trade credit?

What is the formula for finding the nominal annual cost of trade credit? What is the formula for the effective annual cost of trade credit?

How does the cost of costly trade credit generally compare with the cost of short-term bank loans?

Short-Term Bank Loans

Commercial banks, whose loans generally appear on balance sheets as notes payable, are second in importance to trade credit as a source of short-term financing for nonfinancial corporations.[7] The banks' influence is actually greater than it appears from the dollar amounts because banks provide *nonspontaneous* funds. As a firm's financing needs increase, it requests additional funds from its bank. If the request is denied, the firm may be forced to abandon attractive growth opportunities. The key features of bank loans are discussed in the following paragraphs.

Maturity

Although banks do make longer-term loans, *the bulk of their lending is on a short-term basis*—about two-thirds of all bank loans mature in a year or less. Bank loans to businesses are frequently written as 90-day notes, so the loan must be repaid or renewed at the end of 90 days. Of course, if a borrower's financial position has deteriorated, the bank may refuse to renew the loan. This can mean serious trouble for the borrower.

Promissory Note

When a bank loan is approved, the agreement is executed by signing a **promissory note.** The note specifies (1) the amount borrowed; (2) the interest rate; (3) the repayment schedule, which can call for either a lump sum or a series of installments; (4) any collateral that might have to be put up as security for the loan; and (5) any other terms and conditions to which the bank and the borrower have agreed. When the note is signed, the bank credits the borrower's checking account with the funds, so on the borrower's balance sheet both cash and notes payable increase.

Compensating Balances

Banks sometimes require borrowers to maintain an average demand deposit (checking account) balance equal to from 10 to 20 percent of the face amount of the loan. This is called a **compensating balance,** and such balances raise the effective interest rate on the loans. For example, if a firm needs $80,000 to pay off outstanding obligations, but if it must maintain a 20 percent compensating balance, then it must borrow $100,000 to obtain a usable $80,000. If the stated annual interest rate is 8 percent, the effective cost is actually 10 percent: $8,000 interest divided by $80,000 of usable funds equals 10 percent.[8]

As we noted in Chapter 22, recent surveys indicate that compensating balances are much less common now than 20 years ago. In a 1979 survey, 84.7 percent of responding companies reported that they were required to maintain compensating balances to pay for bank services.[9] By 1996, only 28 percent reported paying for bank services

[7]Although commercial banks remain the primary source of short-term loans, other sources are available. For example, GE Capital Corporation (GECC) had several billion dollars in commercial loans outstanding. Firms such as GECC, which was initially established to finance consumers' purchases of GE's durable goods, often find business loans to be more profitable than consumer loans.

[8]Note, however, that the compensating balance may be set as a minimum monthly *average*, and if the firm would maintain this average anyway, the compensating balance requirement would not raise the effective interest rate. Also, note that these *loan* compensating balances are added to any compensating balances that the firm's bank may require for *services performed*, such as clearing checks.

[9]See Lawrence J. Gitman, E. A. Moses, and I. T. White, "An Assessment of Corporate Cash Management Practices," *Financial Management*, Vol. 14, no. 1, Spring 1979, 32–41.

with compensating balances.[10] In fact, compensating balances are now illegal in many states. Despite this trend, some small banks in states where compensating balances are legal still require their customers to maintain compensating balances.

Informal Line of Credit

A **line of credit** is an informal agreement between a bank and a borrower indicating the maximum credit the bank will extend to the borrower. For example, on December 31, a bank loan officer might indicate to a financial manager that the bank regards the firm as being "good" for up to $80,000 during the forthcoming year, provided the borrower's financial condition does not deteriorate. If on January 10 the financial manager signs a promissory note for $15,000 for 90 days, this would be called "taking down" $15,000 of the total line of credit. This amount would be credited to the firm's checking account at the bank, and before repayment of the $15,000, the firm could borrow additional amounts up to a total of $80,000 outstanding at any one time.

Revolving Credit Agreement

A **revolving credit agreement** is a formal line of credit. To illustrate, in 2000 Texas Petroleum Company negotiated a revolving credit agreement for $100 million with a group of banks. The banks were formally committed for four years to lend the firm up to $100 million if the funds were needed. Texas Petroleum, in turn, paid an annual commitment fee of 1/4 of 1 percent on the unused balance of the commitment to compensate the banks for making the commitment. Thus, if Texas Petroleum did not take down any of the $100 million commitment during a year, it would still be required to pay a $250,000 annual fee, normally in monthly installments of $20,833.33. If it borrowed $50 million on the first day of the agreement, the unused portion of the line of credit would fall to $50 million, and the annual fee would fall to $125,000. Of course, interest would also have to be paid on the money Texas Petroleum actually borrowed. As a general rule, the interest rate on "revolvers" is pegged to the prime rate, the T-bill rate, or some other market rate, so the cost of the loan varies over time as interest rates change.[11] Texas Petroleum's rate was set at prime plus 0.5 percentage point.

Note that a revolving credit agreement is very similar to an informal line of credit, but with an important difference: The bank has a *legal obligation* to honor a revolving credit agreement, and it receives a commitment fee. Neither the legal obligation nor the fee exists under the informal line of credit.

Often a line of credit will have a **clean-up clause** that requires the borrower to reduce the loan balance to zero at least once a year. Keep in mind that a line of credit typically is designed to help finance negative operating cash flows that are incurred as a natural part of a company's business cycle, not as a source of permanent capital. For example, the *total annual* operating cash flow of Toys Я Us is normally positive, even

[10]See Charles E. Maxwell, Lawrence J. Gitman, and Stephanie A. M. Smith, "Working Capital Management and Financial-Service Consumption Preferences of U.S. and Foreign Firms: A Comparison of 1979 and 1996 Preferences," *Financial Practice and Education*, Fall/Winter 1998, 46–52.

[11]Each bank sets its own prime rate, but, because of competitive forces, most banks' prime rates are identical. Further, most banks follow the rate set by the large New York City banks.

In recent years many banks have been lending to the very strongest companies at rates below the prime rate. As we discuss later in this chapter, larger firms have ready access to the commercial paper market, and if banks want to do business with these larger companies, they must match, or at least come close to, the commercial paper rate.

though its operating cash flow is negative during the fall as it builds up inventory for the Christmas season. However, Toys Я Us has large positive cash flows in December through February, as it collects on Christmas sales. Their bankers would expect Toys Я Us to use those positive cash flows to pay off balances that had been drawn against their credit lines. Otherwise, Toys Я Us would be using its credit lines as a permanent source of financing.

Self-Test Question

Explain how a firm that expects to need funds during the coming year might make sure the needed funds will be available.

The Cost of Bank Loans

The cost of bank loans varies for different types of borrowers at any given point in time and for all borrowers over time. Interest rates are higher for riskier borrowers, and rates are also higher on smaller loans because of the fixed costs involved in making and servicing loans. If a firm can qualify as a "prime credit" because of its size and financial strength, it can borrow at the **prime rate,** which at one time was the lowest rate banks charged. Rates on other loans are generally scaled up from the prime rate, but loans to very strong customers are made at rates below prime. Thus, loans to smaller, riskier borrowers are generally stated to carry an interest rate of "prime *plus* some number of percentage points," but loans to larger, less risky borrowers may have a rate stated as "prime *minus* some percentage points."

Bank rates vary widely over time depending on economic conditions and Federal Reserve policy. When the economy is weak, then (1) loan demand is usually slack, (2) inflation is low, and (3) the Fed also makes plenty of money available to the system. As a result, rates on all types of loans are relatively low. Conversely, when the economy is booming, loan demand is typically strong, the Fed restricts the money supply, and the result is high interest rates. As an indication of the kinds of fluctuations that can occur, the prime rate during 1980 rose from 11 percent to 21 percent in just four months, and it rose from 6 to 9 percent during 1994. The prime rate is currently (January 2001) 9.0 percent. Interest rates on other bank loans also vary, generally moving with the prime rate.

The terms on a short-term bank loan to a business are spelled out in the promissory note. Here are the key elements contained in most promissory notes:

1. **Interest only versus amortized.** Loans are either *interest-only*, meaning that only interest is paid during the life of the loan, and the principal is repaid when the loan matures, or *amortized*, meaning that some of the principal is repaid on each payment date. Amortized loans are called *installment loans.* Note too that loans can be fully or partially amortized. For example, a loan may mature after 10 years, but payments may be based on 20 years, so an unpaid balance will still exist at the end of the 10th year. Such a loan is called a "balloon" loan.
2. **Collateral.** If a short-term loan is secured by some specific collateral, generally accounts receivable or inventories, this fact is indicated in the note. If the collateral is to be kept on the premises of the borrower, then a form called a *UCC-1* (Uniform Commercial Code-1) is filed with the secretary of the state in which the collateral resides, along with a *Security Agreement* (also part of the Uniform Commercial Code) that describes the nature of the agreement. These filings prevent the borrower from using the same collateral to secure loans from different lenders, and they spell out conditions under which the lender can seize the collateral.

3. **Loan guarantees.** If the borrower is a small corporation, its bank will probably insist that the larger stockholders *personally guarantee* the loan. Banks have often seen a troubled company's owner divert assets from the company to some other entity he or she owned, so banks protect themselves by insisting on personal guarantees. However, stockholder guarantees are virtually impossible to get in the case of larger corporations that have many stockholders. Also, guarantees are unnecessary for proprietorships or partnerships because here the owners are already personally liable for the business's debts.
4. **Nominal, or stated, interest rate.** The interest rate can be either *fixed* or *floating*. If it floats, it is generally indexed to the bank's prime rate, to the T-bill rate, or to the London Inter-Bank Offer Rate (LIBOR). Most loans of any size ($25,000 and up) have floating rates if their maturities are greater than 90 days. The note will also indicate whether the bank uses a *360- or 365-day year* for purposes of calculating interest; most banks use a 360-day year.
5. **Frequency of interest payments.** If the note is on an interest-only basis, it will indicate *how frequently interest must be paid.* Interest is typically calculated on a daily basis but paid monthly.
6. **Maturity.** Long-term loans always have specific maturity dates. A short-term loan may or may not have a specified maturity. For example, a loan may mature in 30 days, 90 days, 6 months, or 1 year, or it may call for "payment on demand," in which case the loan can remain outstanding as long as the borrower wants to continue using the funds and the bank agrees. Banks virtually never call demand notes unless the borrower's creditworthiness deteriorates, so some "short-term loans" remain outstanding for years, with the interest rate floating with rates in the economy.
7. **Discount interest.** Most loans call for interest to be paid after it has been earned, but *discount loans* require that interest be paid in advance. If the loan is on a discount basis, the borrower actually receives less than the face amount of the loan, and this increases the loan's effective cost. We discuss discount loans in a later section.
8. **Add-on basis installment loans.** Auto loans and other types of consumer installment loans are generally set up on an "add-on basis," which means that interest over the life of the loan is calculated and then added to the face amount of the loan. Thus, the borrower signs a note for the funds received plus the interest. The add-on feature also raises the effective cost of a loan, as we demonstrate in a later section.
9. **Other cost elements.** As noted above, some loans require compensating balances, and revolving credit agreements often require commitment fees. Both of these conditions will be spelled out in the loan agreement, and both raise the effective cost of a loan above its stated nominal rate.
10. **Key-person insurance.** Often the success of a small company is linked to its owner or to a few important managers. It's a sad fact, but many small companies fail when one of these key individuals dies. Therefore, banks often require small companies to take out *key-person insurance* on their most important managers as part of the loan agreement. Usually the loan becomes due and payable should there be an untimely demise, with the insurance benefits being used to repay the loan. This makes the best of a bad situation—the bank gets its money, and the company reduces its debt burden without having to use any of its operating cash.

Regular, or Simple, Interest

In this and the following sections, we explain how to calculate the effective cost of different bank loans. For illustrative purposes, we assume a loan of $10,000 at a nominal interest rate of 12 percent, with a 365-day year.

For short-term business loans, the most common procedure is called **regular,** or **simple, interest,** based on an interest-only loan. We begin by dividing the nominal interest rate, 12 percent in this case, by 365 (or 360 in some cases) to get the rate per day:

$$\text{Interest rate per day} = \frac{\text{Nominal rate}}{\text{Days in year}} \quad \textbf{(23-2)}$$

$$= 0.12/365 = 0.00032876712.$$

This rate is then multiplied by the number of days during the specific payment period, and then by the amount of the loan. For example, if the loan is interest-only, with monthly payments, then the interest payment for January would be \$101.92:

$$\text{Interest charge for period} = (\text{Days in period})(\text{Rate per day})(\text{Amount of loan}) \quad \textbf{(23-3)}$$

$$= (31\text{ days})(0.00032876712)(\$10{,}000) = \$101.92.$$

If interest were payable quarterly, and if there were 91 days in the particular quarter, then the interest payment would be \$299.18. The annual interest would be 365 × 0.00032876712 × \$10,000 = \$1,200.00. Note that if the bank had based the interest calculation on a 360-day year, as most banks do, the interest charges would have been slightly higher, and the annual charge would have been \$1,216.67. Obviously, banks use a 360-day year to boost their earnings.

The effective interest rate on a loan depends on how frequently interest must be paid—the more frequently, the higher the effective rate. We demonstrate this point with two time lines, one for interest paid once a year and one for quarterly payments:

Interest Paid Annually:

0	0.25	0.5	0.75	1.0
10,000	0	0	0	−1,200.00
				−10,000.00
				−11,200.00

The borrower gets \$10,000 at t = 0 and pays \$11,200 at t = 1. With a financial calculator, enter N = 1, PV = 10000, PMT = 0, and FV = −11200, and then press I to get the effective cost of the loan, 12 percent.

Interest Paid Quarterly:

0	0.25	0.5	0.75	1.0
10,000	−299.18	−299.18	−302.47	−299.18
				−10,000.00
				−10,299.18

Note that the third quarter has 92 days. We enter the data in the cash flow register of a financial calculator (being sure to use the +/− key to enter −299.18), and we find the periodic rate to be 2.9999 percent. The effective annual rate is 12.55 percent:

$$\text{Effective annual rate, quarterly} = (1 + 0.029999)^4 - 1 = 12.55\%.$$

Had the loan called for interest to be paid monthly, the effective rate would have been 12.68 percent, and if interest had been paid daily, the rate would have been 12.75 percent. These rates would be higher if the bank used a 360-day year.

In these examples, we assumed that the loan matured in one year but that interest was paid at various times during the year. The rates we calculated would have been exactly the same as the ones above even if the loan had matured on each interest payment date. In other words, the effective rate on a monthly payment loan would be 12.68 percent regardless of whether it matured after one month, six months, one year, or 10 years, providing the stated rate remains at 12 percent.

Discount Interest

In a **discount interest** loan, the bank deducts the interest in advance (*discounts* the loan). Thus, the borrower receives less than the face value of the loan. On a one-year, \$10,000 loan with a 12 percent (nominal) rate, discount basis, the interest is \$10,000(0.12) = \$1,200. Therefore, the borrower obtains the use of only \$10,000 − \$1,200 = \$8,800. If the loan were for less than a year, the interest charge (the discount) would be lower; in our example, it would be \$600 if the loan were for six months, hence the amount received would be \$9,400.

The effective rate on a discount loan is always higher than the rate on an otherwise similar simple interest loan. To illustrate, consider the situation for a discounted 12 percent loan for one year:

Discount Interest, Paid Annually:

0	0.25	0.5	0.75	1.0
10,000	0	0	0	−10,000.00
−1,200				
8,800				

With a financial calculator, enter N = 1, PV = 8800, PMT = 0, and FV = −10000, and then press I to get the effective cost of the loan, 13.64 percent.[12]

If a discount loan matures in less than a year, say, after one quarter, we have this situation:

Discount Interest, One Quarter:

0	0.25	0.5	0.75	1.0
10,000	−10,000	0	0	0
−300				
9,700				

[12]Note that the firm actually receives less than the face amount of the loan:

$$\text{Funds received} = \text{Face amount of loan } (1.0 - \text{Nominal interest rate}).$$

We can solve for the face amount as follows:

$$\text{Face amount of loan} = \frac{\text{Funds received}}{1.0 - \text{Nominal rate (decimal)}}.$$

Therefore, if the borrowing firm actually requires \$10,000 of cash, it must borrow \$11,363.64:

$$\text{Face value} = \frac{\$10{,}000}{1.0 - 0.12} = \frac{\$10{,}000}{0.88} = \$11{,}363.64.$$

Now, the borrower will receive \$11,363.64 − 0.12(\$11,363.64) = \$10,000. Increasing the face value of the loan does not change the effective rate of 13.64 percent on the \$10,000 of usable funds.

Enter N = 1, PV = 9700, PMT = 0, and FV = −10000, and then press I to find the periodic rate, 3.092784 percent per quarter, which corresponds to an effective annual rate of 12.96 percent. Thus, shortening the period of a discount loan lowers the effective rate of interest.

Effects of Compensating Balances

If the bank requires a compensating balance, and if the amount of the required balance exceeds the amount the firm would normally hold on deposit, then the excess must be deducted at t = 0 and then added back when the loan matures. This has the effect of raising the effective rate on the loan. To illustrate, here is the setup for a one-year discount loan, with a 20 percent compensating balance that the firm would not otherwise hold on deposit:

Discount Interest, Paid Annually, With 20 percent compensating balance:

0	0.25	0.5	0.75	1.0
10,000	0	0	0	−10,000
−1,200				2,000
−2,000				
6,800				−8,000

Note that the bank initially gives, and the borrower gets, $10,000 at time 0. However, the bank takes out the $1,200 of interest in advance, and the company must leave $2,000 in the bank as a compensating balance, hence the borrower's effective net cash flow at t = 0 is $6,800. At t = 1, the borrower must repay the $10,000, but $2,000 is already in the bank (the compensating balance), so the company must repay a net amount of $8,000.

With a financial calculator, enter N = 1, PV = 6800, PMT = 0, and FV = −8000, and then press I to get the effective cost of the discount loan with a compensating balance, 17.65 percent.

Installment Loans: Add-On Interest

Lenders typically charge **add-on interest** on automobile and other types of installment loans. The term "add-on" means that the interest is calculated and then added to the amount received to determine the loan's face value. To illustrate, suppose you borrow $10,000 on an add-on basis at a nominal rate of 12 percent to buy a car, with the loan to be repaid in 12 monthly installments. At a 12 percent add-on rate, you will pay a total interest charge of $10,000(0.12) = $1,200. However, since the loan is paid off in monthly installments, you have the use of the full $10,000 for only the first month, and the outstanding balance declines until, during the last month, only 1⁄12 of the original loan will still be outstanding. Thus, you are paying $1,200 for the use of only about half the loan's face amount, as the average usable funds is only about $5,000. Therefore, we can calculate the approximate annual rate as follows:

$$\text{Approximate annual rate}_{\text{Add-on}} = \frac{\text{Interest paid}}{(\text{Amount received})/2} \tag{23-4}$$

$$= \frac{\$1{,}200}{\$10{,}000/2} = 24.0\%.$$

To determine the effective rate of an add-on loan, we proceed as follows:

1. The total amount to be repaid is \$10,000 of principal, plus \$1,200 of interest, or \$11,200.
2. The monthly payment is \$11,200/12 = \$933.33.
3. You are, in effect, paying off a 12-period annuity of \$933.33 in order to receive \$10,000 today, so \$10,000 is the present value of the annuity. Here is the time line:

0	i = ?	1	2	. . .	11	12 Months
10,000		−933.33	−933.33		−933.33	−933.33

4. With a financial calculator, enter N = 12, PV = 10000, PMT = −933.33, FV = 0, and then press I to obtain 1.7880 percent. However, this is a monthly rate.
5. The effective annual rate is found as follows:[13]

$$\text{Effective annual rate}_{\text{Add-on}} = (1 + k_d)^n - 1.0$$
$$= (1.01788)^{12} - 1.0$$
$$= 1.2370 - 1.0 = 23.7\%.$$

The **annual percentage rate (APR),** which by law the bank is required to state in bold print on all "consumer loan" agreements, would be 21.46 percent:

$$\text{APR rate} = (\text{Periods per year})(\text{Rate per period})$$
$$= 12(1.7880\%) = 21.46\%.$$

Prior to the passage of the truth in lending laws in the 1970s, most banks would have called this a 12 percent loan, period. The truth in lending laws apply primarily to consumer as opposed to business loans.

Self-Test Questions

Name four different ways banks can calculate interest on loans.

What is a compensating balance? What effect does a compensating balance requirement have on the effective interest rate on a loan?

Choosing a Bank

Individuals whose only contact with their bank is through the use of its checking services generally choose a bank for the convenience of its location and the competitive cost of its services. However, a business that borrows from banks must look at other criteria and recognize that important differences exist among banks. Some of these differences are considered next.

Willingness to Assume Risks

Banks have different basic policies toward risk. Some follow relatively conservative lending practices, while others engage in what are properly termed "creative banking practices." These policies reflect partly the personalities of bank officers and partly the characteristics of the bank's deposit liabilities. Thus, a bank with fluctuating deposit liabilities in a static community will tend to be a conservative lender, while a bank

[13]Note that if an installment loan is paid off ahead of schedule, additional complications arise. For the classic discussion of this point, see Dick Bonker, "The Rule of 78," *Journal of Finance*, June 1976, 877–888.

whose deposits are growing with little interruption may follow more liberal credit policies. Similarly, a large bank with broad diversification over geographic regions and across industries can obtain the benefit of combining and averaging risks. Thus, marginal credit risks that might be unacceptable to a small or specialized bank can be pooled by a branch banking system to reduce the overall risk of a group of marginal accounts.[14]

Advice and Counsel

Some bank loan officers are active in providing counsel and in granting loans to firms in their early and formative years. Certain banks have specialized departments that make loans to firms expected to grow and thus to become more important customers. The personnel of these departments can provide valuable counseling to customers: The bankers' experience with other firms in growth situations may enable them to spot, and then to warn their customers about, developing problems.

Loyalty to Customers

Banks differ in their support of borrowers in bad times. This characteristic is referred to as the degree of *loyalty* of the bank. Some banks may put great pressure on a business to liquidate its loans when the firm's outlook becomes clouded, whereas others will stand by the firm and work diligently to help it get back on its feet. An especially dramatic illustration of this point was Bank of America's bailout of Memorex Corporation. The bank could have forced Memorex into bankruptcy, but instead it loaned the company additional capital and helped it survive a bad period. Memorex's stock price subsequently rose from $1.50 to $68, so Bank of America's help was indeed beneficial.

Specialization

Banks differ greatly in their degrees of loan specialization. Larger banks have separate departments that specialize in different kinds of loans—for example, real estate loans, farm loans, and commercial loans. Within these broad categories, there may be a specialization by line of business, such as steel, machinery, cattle, or textiles. The strengths of banks are also likely to reflect the nature of the businesses and the economic environment in the areas in which they operate. For example, some California banks have become specialists in lending to electronics companies, while many Midwestern banks are agricultural specialists. A sound firm can obtain more creative cooperation and more active support by going to a bank that has experience and familiarity with its particular type of business. Therefore, a bank that is excellent for one firm may be unsatisfactory for another.

---

[14]Bank deposits are insured by a federal agency, and banks are required to pay premiums to cover the cost of this insurance. Logically, riskier banks should pay higher premiums, but to date political forces have limited the use of risk-based insurance premiums. As an alternative, banks with riskier loan portfolios are required to have more equity capital per dollar of deposits than less risky banks. The savings and loan industry, until the 1980s, had federal insurance, no differential capital requirements, and lax regulations. As a result, some S&L operators wrote very high interest rate, but very risky, loans using low-cost, insured deposits. If the loans paid off, the S&L owners would get rich. If they went into default, the taxpayers would have to pay off the deposits. Those government policies ended up costing taxpayers more than $100 billion.

Maximum Loan Size

The size of a bank can be an important factor. Since the maximum loan a bank can make to any one customer is limited to 15 percent of the bank's capital accounts (capital stock plus retained earnings), it is generally not appropriate for large firms to develop borrowing relationships with small banks.

Merchant Banking

The term "merchant bank" was originally applied to banks that not only made loans but also provided customers with equity capital and financial advice. Prior to 1933, U.S. commercial banks performed all types of merchant banking functions. However, about one-third of the U.S. banks failed during the Great Depression, in part because of these activities, so in 1933 the Glass-Steagall Act was passed in an effort to reduce banks' exposure to risk. In recent years, commercial banks have been attempting to get back into merchant banking, in part because their foreign competitors offer such services, and U.S. banks compete with foreign banks for multinational corporations' business. Currently, the larger banks, often through subsidiaries that engage in investment banking activities, are being permitted to get back into merchant banking, at least to a limited extent. This trend will probably continue, and if it does, corporations will need to consider a bank's ability to provide a full range of commercial and merchant banking services when choosing a bank.

Other Services

Banks also provide cash management services, assist with electronic funds transfers, help firms obtain foreign exchange, and the like, and the availability of such services should be taken into account when selecting a bank. Also, if the firm is a small business whose manager owns most of its stock, the bank's willingness and ability to provide trust and estate services should be considered.

Self-Test Question

What are some factors that should be considered when choosing a bank?

Commercial Paper

Commercial paper is a type of unsecured promissory note issued by large, strong firms and sold primarily to other business firms, to insurance companies, to pension funds, to money market mutual funds, and to banks. At the end of September 2000, there was approximately $1,558 billion of commercial paper outstanding (much of it issued by financial institutions), versus about $1,081 billion of regular bank loans.

Maturity and Cost

Maturities of commercial paper generally vary from one day to nine months, with an average of about five months.[15] The interest rate on commercial paper fluctuates with supply and demand conditions—it is determined in the marketplace, varying daily as

[15]The maximum maturity without SEC registration is 270 days. Also, commercial paper can only be sold to "sophisticated" investors; otherwise, SEC registration would be required even for maturities of 270 days or less.

conditions change. Recently, commercial paper rates have ranged from 1½ to 3 percentage points below the stated prime rate, and about ⅛ to ½ of a percentage point above the T-bill rate. For example, on January 22, 2001, the average rate on three-month commercial paper was 5.43 percent, the stated prime rate was 9.00 percent, and the three-month T-bill rate was 5.23 percent.

Use of Commercial Paper

The use of commercial paper is restricted to a comparatively small number of very large concerns that are exceptionally good credit risks. Dealers prefer to handle the paper of firms whose net worth is $100 million or more and whose annual borrowing exceeds $10 million. One potential problem with commercial paper is that a debtor who is in temporary financial difficulty may receive little help because commercial paper dealings are generally less personal than are bank relationships. Thus, banks are generally more willing to help a good customer weather a temporary storm than is a commercial paper dealer. On the other hand, using commercial paper permits a corporation to tap a wide range of credit sources, including financial institutions outside its own area and industrial corporations across the country, and this can reduce interest costs.

Self-Test Questions

What is commercial paper?

What types of companies can use commercial paper to meet their short-term financing needs?

How does the cost of commercial paper compare with the cost of short-term bank loans? With the cost of Treasury bills?

Use of Security in Short-Term Financing

Thus far, we have not addressed the question of whether or not short-term loans should be secured. Commercial paper is never secured, but other types of loans can be secured if this is deemed necessary or desirable. Other things held constant, it is better to borrow on an unsecured basis, since the bookkeeping costs of **secured loans** are often high. However, a firm may find that it can borrow only if it puts up some type of collateral to protect the lender, or that by using security it can borrow at a much lower rate.

Several different kinds of collateral can be employed, including marketable stocks or bonds, land or buildings, equipment, inventory, and accounts receivable. Marketable securities make excellent collateral, but few firms that need loans also hold portfolios of stocks and bonds. Similarly, real property (land and buildings) and equipment are good forms of collateral, but they are generally used as security for long-term loans rather than for working capital loans. Therefore, most secured short-term business borrowing involves the use of accounts receivable and inventories as collateral.

To understand the use of security, consider the case of a Chicago hardware dealer who wanted to modernize and expand his store. He requested a $200,000 bank loan. After examining his business's financial statements, the bank indicated that it would lend him a maximum of $100,000 and that the interest rate would be 10 percent, discount interest, for an effective rate of 11.1 percent. The owner had a substantial personal portfolio of stocks, and he offered to put up $300,000 of high-quality stocks to support the $200,000 loan. The bank then granted the full $200,000 loan, and at the prime rate of 8.50 percent, simple interest. The store owner might also have used his inventories or receivables as security for the loan, but processing costs would have been high.[16]

Self-Test Questions

What is a secured loan?

What are some types of current assets that are pledged as security for short-term loans?

Summary

This chapter examined different policies for financing current assets. In particular, we looked at (1) the factors that affect the use of current liabilities versus long-term capital and (2) the specific types of current liabilities. Some companies have very few current liabilities, while others rely heavily on short-term credit to finance current assets. In some cases, companies even use short-term debt to finance a portion of their long-term assets.

In addition to examining various financing policies, we also considered the costs and features of the different types of short-term credit. The key concepts covered are listed below:

- **Permanent current assets** are those current assets that the firm holds even during slack times, whereas **temporary current assets** are the additional current assets that are needed during seasonal or cyclical peaks. The types of capital used to finance permanent and temporary current assets define the firm's **current asset financing policy.**
- A **moderate** approach to current asset financing involves matching, to the extent possible, the maturities of assets and liabilities, so that temporary current assets are financed with short-term nonspontaneous debt, and permanent current assets and fixed assets are financed with long-term debt or equity, plus spontaneous debt. Under an **aggressive** approach, some permanent current assets, and perhaps even some fixed assets, are financed with short-term debt. A **conservative** approach would be to use long-term capital to finance all permanent assets and some of the temporary current assets.
- The advantages of short-term credit are (1) the **speed** with which short-term loans can be arranged, (2) increased **flexibility,** and (3) the fact that short-term **interest rates** are generally **lower** than long-term rates. The principal disadvantage of short-term credit is the **extra risk** the borrower must bear because (1) the lender can demand payment on short notice and (2) the cost of the loan will increase if interest rates rise.
- **Short-term credit** is defined as any liability originally scheduled for payment within one year. The four major sources of short-term credit are (1) accruals, (2) accounts payable, (3) loans from commercial banks and finance companies, and (4) commercial paper.
- **Accruals,** which are continually recurring short-term liabilities, represent free, spontaneous credit.
- **Accounts payable,** or **trade credit,** is the largest category of short-term financing. Trade credit arises spontaneously as a result of credit purchases. Firms should

[16]See the Web/CD Extension for this chapter for a further discussion of secured short-term financing. Also, note that the term "asset-based financing" is often used as a synonym for "secured financing." In recent years, accounts receivable have been used as security for long-term bonds, and this permits corporations to borrow from lenders such as pension funds rather than being restricted to banks and other traditional short-term lenders.

use all the **free trade credit** they can obtain, but they should use **costly trade credit** only if it is less expensive than other forms of short-term debt. Suppliers often offer discounts to customers who pay within a stated discount period. The following equation may be used to calculate the nominal cost, on an annual basis, of not taking discounts:

$$\text{Nominal cost} = \frac{\text{Discount percent}}{100 - \text{Discount percent}} \times \frac{360}{\text{Days credit is outstanding} - \text{Discount period}}.$$

- **Bank loans** are an important source of short-term credit. Interest on bank loans may be quoted as **simple interest, discount interest,** or **add-on interest.** The effective rate on a bank loan always exceeds the quoted nominal rate except for a simple interest loan where the interest is paid once a year.
- When a bank loan is approved, a **promissory note** is signed. It specifies: (1) the amount borrowed, (2) the percentage interest rate, (3) the repayment schedule, (4) the collateral, and (5) any other conditions to which the parties have agreed.
- Banks sometimes require borrowers to maintain **compensating balances,** which are deposit requirements set at between 10 and 20 percent of the loan amount. Compensating balances raise the effective interest rate on bank loans.
- A **line of credit** is an informal agreement between the bank and the borrower indicating the maximum amount of credit the bank will extend to the borrower.
- A **revolving credit agreement** is a formal line of credit often used by large firms; it involves a **commitment fee.**
- With a **regular,** or **simple, interest loan** interest is not compounded; that is, interest is not earned on interest.
- In a **discount interest** loan, the bank deducts the interest in advance. Interest is calculated on the face amount of the loan but it is paid in advance.
- Installment loans are typically **add-on interest** loans. Interest is calculated and added to the funds received to determine the face amount of the loan.
- The **annual percentage rate (APR)** is a rate reported by banks and other lenders on loans when the effective periodic rate exceeds the nominal periodic rate of interest.
- **Commercial paper** is unsecured short-term debt issued by large, financially strong corporations. Although the cost of commercial paper is lower than the cost of bank loans, it can be used only by large firms with exceptionally strong credit ratings.
- Sometimes a borrower will find that it is necessary to borrow on a **secured basis,** in which case the borrower pledges assets such as real estate, securities, equipment, inventories, or accounts receivable as collateral for the loan.

Questions

23–1 Define each of the following terms:

a. Permanent current assets; temporary current assets
b. Moderate current asset financing policy; aggressive current asset financing policy; conservative current asset financing policy
c. Maturity matching, or "self-liquidating," approach
d. Accruals
e. Trade credit; stretching accounts payable; free trade credit; costly trade credit
f. Promissory note; line of credit; revolving credit agreement
g. Prime rate

h. Simple interest; discount interest; add-on interest
i. Compensating balance (CB)
j. Commercial paper
k. Secured loan

23–2 How does the seasonal nature of a firm's sales influence its decision regarding the amount of short-term credit to use in its financial structure?

23–3 What are the advantages of matching the maturities of assets and liabilities? What are the disadvantages?

23–4 From the standpoint of the borrower, is long-term or short-term credit riskier? Explain. Would it ever make sense to borrow on a short-term basis if short-term rates were above long-term rates?

23–5 If long-term credit exposes a borrower to less risk, why would people or firms ever borrow on a short-term basis?

23–6 "Firms can control their accruals within fairly wide limits; depending on the cost of accruals, financing from this source will be increased or decreased." Discuss.

23–7 Is it true that both trade credit and accruals represent a spontaneous source of capital for financing growth? Explain.

23–8 Is it true that most firms are able to obtain some free trade credit and that additional trade credit is often available, but at a cost? Explain.

23–9 The availability of bank credit is often more important to a small firm than to a large one. Why?

23–10 What kinds of firms use commercial paper? Could Mama and Papa Gus's Corner Grocery borrow using this form of credit?

23–11 Given that commercial paper interest rates are generally lower than bank loan rates to a given borrower, why might firms which are capable of selling commercial paper also use bank credit?

23–12 Suppose a firm can obtain funds by borrowing at the prime rate or by selling commercial paper.
a. If the prime rate is 8.25 percent, what is a reasonable estimate for the cost of commercial paper?
b. If a substantial cost differential exists, why might a firm like this one actually borrow some of its funds in each market?

Self-Test Problem (Solution Appears in Appendix A)

ST–1 *CURRENT ASSET FINANCING* Vanderheiden Press Inc. and the Herrenhouse Publishing Company had the following balance sheets as of December 31, 2001 (thousands of dollars):

	Vanderheiden Press	Herrenhouse Publishing
Current assets	$100,000	$ 80,000
Fixed assets (net)	100,000	120,000
Total assets	$200,000	$200,000
Current liabilities	$ 20,000	$ 80,000
Long-term debt	80,000	20,000
Common stock	50,000	50,000
Retained earnings	50,000	50,000
Total liabilities and equity	$200,000	$200,000

Earnings before interest and taxes for both firms are $30 million, and the effective federal-plus-state tax rate is 40 percent.
a. What is the return on equity for each firm if the interest rate on current liabilities is 10 percent and the rate on long-term debt is 13 percent?

b. Assume that the short-term rate rises to 20 percent. While the rate on new long-term debt rises to 16 percent, the rate on existing long-term debt remains unchanged. What would be the return on equity for Vanderheiden Press and Herrenhouse Publishing under these conditions?
c. Which company is in a riskier position? Why?

Problems

23–1 COST OF TRADE CREDIT

What is the nominal and effective cost of trade credit (on a 360-day basis) under the credit terms of 3/15, net 30?

23–2 COST OF TRADE CREDIT

A large retailer obtains merchandise under the credit terms of 1/15, net 45, but routinely takes 60 days to pay its bills. Given that the retailer is an important customer, suppliers allow the firm to stretch its credit terms. What is the retailer's effective cost of trade credit (on a 360-day basis)?

23–3 ACCOUNTS PAYABLE

A chain of appliance stores, APP Corporation, purchases inventory with a net price of $500,000 each day. The company purchases the inventory under the credit terms of 2/15, net 40. APP always takes the discount, but takes the full 15 days to pay its bills. What is the average accounts payable for APP?

23–4 COST OF BANK LOAN

On March 1, Minnerly Motors obtained a business loan from a local bank. The loan is a $25,000 interest-only loan with a nominal rate of 11 percent. Interest is calculated on a simple interest basis with a 365-day year. What is Minnerly's interest charge for the first month (assuming 31 days in the month)?

23–5 COST OF BANK LOAN

Mary Jones recently obtained an automobile loan from a local bank. The loan is for $15,000 with a nominal interest rate of 11 percent. However, this is an installment loan, so the bank also charges add-on interest. Mary must make monthly payments on the loan, and the loan is to be repaid in 1 year. What is the effective annual rate on the loan (assuming a 365-day year)?

23–6 COST OF TRADE CREDIT

Calculate the nominal annual cost of nonfree trade credit under each of the following terms. Assume payment is made either on the due date or on the discount date.
a. 1/15, net 20.
b. 2/10, net 60.
c. 3/10, net 45.
d. 2/10, net 45.
e. 2/15, net 40.

23–7 COST OF TRADE CREDIT

a. If a firm buys under terms of 3/15, net 45, but actually pays on the 20th day and *still takes the discount*, what is the nominal cost of its nonfree trade credit?
b. Does it receive more or less credit than it would if it paid within 15 days?

23–8 COST OF BANK LOANS

Del Hawley, owner of Hawley's Hardware, is negotiating with First City Bank for a $50,000, 1-year loan. First City has offered Hawley the following alternatives. Calculate the effective annual interest rate for each alternative. Which alternative has the lowest effective annual interest rate?
a. A 12 percent annual rate on a simple interest loan, with no compensating balance required and interest due at the end of the year.
b. A 9 percent annual rate on a simple interest loan, with a 20 percent compensating balance required and interest again due at the end of the year.
c. An 8.75 percent annual rate on a discounted loan, with a 15 percent compensating balance.
d. Interest is figured as 8 percent of the $50,000 amount, *payable at the end of the year*, but the $50,000 is repayable in monthly installments during the year.

23–9 COST OF TRADE CREDIT

Grunewald Industries sells on terms of 2/10, net 40. Gross sales last year were $4.5 million, and accounts receivable averaged $437,500. Half of Grunewald's customers paid on the 10th day and took discounts. What are the nominal and effective costs of trade credit to Grunewald's nondiscount customers? (Hint: Calculate sales/day based on a 360-day year; then get average receivables of discount customers; then find the DSO for the nondiscount customers.)

23–10 EFFECTIVE COST OF SHORT-TERM CREDIT

The D. J. Masson Corporation needs to raise $500,000 for 1 year to supply working capital to a new store. Masson buys from its suppliers on terms of 3/10, net 90, and it currently pays on the 10th day and takes discounts, but it could forego discounts, pay on the 90th day, and get the needed $500,000 in the form of costly trade credit. Alternatively, Masson could borrow from its bank on a 12 percent discount interest rate basis. What is the effective annual interest rate of the lower-cost source?

23–11 EFFECTIVE COST OF SHORT-TERM CREDIT

Yonge Corporation must arrange financing for its working capital requirements for the coming year. Yonge can (a) borrow from its bank on a simple interest basis (interest payable at the end of the loan) for 1 year at a 12 percent nominal rate; (b) borrow on a 3-month, but renewable, loan at an 11.5 percent nominal rate; (c) borrow on an installment loan basis at a 6 percent add-on rate with 12 end-of-month payments; or (d) obtain the needed funds by no longer taking discounts and thus increasing its accounts payable. Yonge buys on terms of 1/15, net 60. What is the effective annual cost (*not* the nominal cost) of the *least expensive* type of credit, assuming 360 days per year?

23–12 CASH DISCOUNTS

Suppose a firm makes purchases of $3.6 million per year under terms of 2/10, net 30, and takes discounts.

a. What is the average amount of accounts payable net of discounts? (Assume that the $3.6 million of purchases is net of discounts—that is, gross purchases are $3,673,469, discounts are $73,469, and net purchases are $3.6 million. Also, use 360 days in a year.)
b. Is there a cost of the trade credit the firm uses?
c. If the firm did not take discounts but it did pay on the due date, what would be its average payables and the cost of this nonfree trade credit?
d. What would its cost of not taking discounts be if it could stretch its payments to 40 days?

23–13 TRADE CREDIT VERSUS BANK CREDIT

The Thompson Corporation projects an increase in sales from $1.5 million to $2 million, but it needs an additional $300,000 of current assets to support this expansion. The money can be obtained from the bank at an interest rate of 13 percent, discount interest; no compensating balance is required. Alternatively, Thompson can finance the expansion by no longer taking discounts, thus increasing accounts payable. Thompson purchases under terms of 2/10, net 30, but it can delay payment for an additional 35 days—paying in 65 days and thus becoming 35 days past due—without a penalty because of its suppliers' current excess capacity problems.

a. Based strictly on effective, or equivalent, annual interest rate comparisons, how should Thompson finance its expansion?
b. What additional qualitative factors should Thompson consider before reaching a decision?

23–14 BANK FINANCING

The Raattama Corporation had sales of $3.5 million last year, and it earned a 5 percent return, after taxes, on sales. Recently, the company has fallen behind in its accounts payable. Although its terms of purchase are net 30 days, its accounts payable represent 60 days' purchases. The company's treasurer is seeking to increase bank borrowings in order to become current in meeting its trade obligations (that is, to have 30 days' payables outstanding). The company's balance sheet is as follows (thousands of dollars):

Cash	$ 100	Accounts payable	$ 600
Accounts receivable	300	Bank loans	700
Inventory	1,400	Accruals	200
Current assets	$1,800	Current liabilities	$1,500
Land and buildings	600	Mortgage on real estate	700
Equipment	600	Common stock, $0.10 par	300
		Retained earnings	500
Total assets	$3,000	Total liabilities and equity	$3,000

a. How much bank financing is needed to eliminate the past-due accounts payable?
b. Would you as a bank loan officer make the loan? Why?

23–15 COST OF BANK LOANS

Gifts Galore Inc. borrowed $1.5 million from National City Bank. The loan was made at a simple annual interest rate of 9 percent a year for 3 months. A 20 percent compensating balance requirement raised the effective interest rate.

a. The nominal annual rate on the loan was 11.25 percent. What is the true effective rate?
b. What would be the effective cost of the loan if the note required discount interest?
c. What would be the nominal annual interest rate on the loan if the bank did not require a compensating balance but required repayment in 3 equal monthly installments?

23–16 *SHORT-TERM FINANCING ANALYSIS*

Malone Feed and Supply Company buys on terms of 1/10, net 30, but it has not been taking discounts and has actually been paying in 60 rather than 30 days. Assume that the accounts payable are recorded at full cost, not net of discounts. Malone's balance sheet follows (thousands of dollars):

Cash	$ 50	Accounts payable	$ 500
Accounts receivable	450	Notes payable	50
Inventory	750	Accruals	50
Current assets	$1,250	Current liabilities	$ 600
		Long-term debt	150
Fixed assets	750	Common equity	1,250
Total assets	$2,000	Total liabilities and equity	$2,000

Now, Malone's suppliers are threatening to stop shipments unless the company begins making prompt payments (that is, paying in 30 days or less). The firm can borrow on a 1-year note (call this a current liability) from its bank at a rate of 15 percent, discount interest, with a 20 percent compensating balance required. (Malone's $50,000 of cash is needed for transactions; it cannot be used as part of the compensating balance.)

a. How large would the accounts payable balance be if Malone takes discounts? If it does not take discounts and pays in 30 days?
b. How large must the bank loan be if Malone takes discounts? If Malone doesn't take discounts?
c. What are the nominal and effective costs of nonfree trade credit? What is the effective cost of the bank loan? Based on these costs, what should Malone do?
d. Assume that Malone forgoes the discount and borrows the amount needed to become current on its payables. Construct a pro forma balance sheet based on this decision. (Hint: You will need to include an account called "prepaid interest" under current assets.)
e. Now assume that the $500,000 shown on the balance sheets is recorded net of discounts. How much would Malone have to pay its suppliers to reduce its accounts payables to $250,000? If Malone's tax rate is 40 percent, what is the effect on its net income due to the lost discount when it reduces its accounts payable to $250,000? How much would Malone have to borrow? (Hint: Malone will receive a tax deduction due to the lost discount, which will affect the amount it must borrow). If Malone's tax rate is 40 percent, what is the effect on its net income due to the lost discount when it reduces its accounts payable to $250,000? Construct a pro forma balance sheet based on this scenario. (Hint: You will need to include an account called "prepaid interest" under current assets and adjust retained earnings by the after-tax amount of the lost discount.)

23–17 *ALTERNATIVE FINANCING ARRANGEMENTS*

Suncoast Boats Inc. estimates that because of the seasonal nature of its business, it will require an additional $2 million of cash for the month of July. Suncoast Boats has the following 4 options available for raising the needed funds:

(1) Establish a 1-year line of credit for $2 million with a commercial bank. The commitment fee will be 0.5 percent per year on the unused portion, and the interest charge on the used funds will be 11 percent per annum. Assume that the funds are needed only in July, and that there are 30 days in July and 360 days in the year.
(2) Forgo the trade discount of 2/10, net 40, on $2 million of purchases during July.
(3) Issue $2 million of 30-day commercial paper at a 9.5 percent per annum interest rate. The total transactions fee, including the cost of a backup credit line, on using commercial paper is 0.5 percent of the amount of the issue.
(4) Issue $2 million of 60-day commercial paper at a 9 percent per annum interest rate, plus a transactions fee of 0.5 percent. Since the funds are required for only 30 days, the excess funds ($2 million) can be invested in 9.4 percent per annum marketable securities for the

month of August. The total transactions cost of purchasing and selling the marketable securities is 0.4 percent of the amount of the issue.

a. What is the dollar cost of each financing arrangement?
b. Is the source with the lowest expected cost necessarily the one to select? Why or why not?

Spreadsheet Problems

23–18 BUILD A MODEL: SHORT-TERM FINANCING ANALYSIS

Start with the partial model in the file ***Ch 23-18 Build a Model.xls*** from the textbook's CD-ROM. Rework parts a through d of Problem 23-16 using a spreadsheet model. Then answer the following related question.

e. Do a sensitivity analysis that shows how the size of the bank loan would vary with changes in the interest rate and the compensating balance percentage, using interest rates in the range of 5 to 25 percent and compensating balances in the range of 0 to 30 percent.

23–19 WHAT IF ANALYSIS: WORKING CAPITAL FINANCING

Start with the file ***Ch 23-19 What If Analysis.xls*** from the textbook's CD-ROM and answer the questions shown there.

Cyberproblem

The information related to this cyberproblem is likely to change over time, due to the release of new information and the ever-changing nature of the World Wide Web. Accordingly, we will periodically update the problem on the textbook's web site.

23–20 COMMERCIAL PAPER

At first, commercial paper might seem more like a first wedding anniversary gift than a money market instrument. However, commercial paper has steadily grown to be a major method of corporate short-term borrowing. Commercial paper is defined as a type of unsecured promissory note issued by large, stable, and financially strong firms to mostly institutional investors. Commercial paper rates typically range from 1½ to 3 percentage points below that of the stated prime rate, and about ⅛ to ½ percentage point above the T-bill rate. Because of their unsecured nature, commercial paper is typically only used by a small number of large firms with very high credit ratings.

For this cyberproblem, you will be visiting the Federal Reserve Bank of St. Louis web site. Go to the textbook's web site at **http://www.harcourtcollege.com/finance/theory/student/resources/cyberprob/ch23.html,** and answer the questions shown there.

Mini Case

See ***Ch 23 Show.ppt*** and ***Ch 23 Mini Case.xls.***

Bats and Balls (B&B) Inc., a baseball equipment manufacturer, is a small company with seasonal sales. Each year before the baseball season, B&B purchases inventory that is financed through a combination of trade credit and short-term bank loans. At the end of the season, B&B uses sales revenues to repay its short-term obligations. The company is always looking for ways to become more profitable, and senior management has asked one of its employees, Ann Taylor, to review the company's current asset financing policies. Putting together her report, Ann is trying to answer each of the following questions:

a. B&B tries to match the maturity of its assets and liabilities. Describe how B&B could adopt either a more aggressive or more conservative financing policy.
b. What are the advantages and disadvantages of using short-term credit as a source of financing?
c. Is it likely that B&B could make significantly greater use of accruals?
d. Assume that B&B buys on terms of 1/10, net 30, but that it can get away with paying on the 40th day if it chooses not to take discounts. Also, assume that it purchases $3 million of components per year, net of discounts. How much free trade credit can the company get, how

much costly trade credit can it get, and what is the percentage cost of the costly credit? Should B&B take discounts?

e. What is commercial paper, and would it be feasible for B&B to finance with commercial paper?
f. Suppose B&B decided to raise an additional $100,000 as a 1-year loan from its bank, for which it was quoted a rate of 8 percent. What is the effective annual cost rate assuming (1) simple interest, (2) discount interest, (3) discount interest with a 10 percent compensating balance, and (4) add-on interest on a 12-month installment loan? For the first three of these assumptions, would it matter if the loan were for 90 days, but renewable, rather than for a year?
g. How large would the loan actually be in each of the cases in part f?
h. What are the pros and cons of borrowing on a secured versus an unsecured basis?

Selected Additional References

For more on trade credit, see

Adams, Paul D., Steve R. Wyatt, and Yong H. Kim, "A Contingent Claims Analysis of Trade Credit," *Financial Management*, Autumn 1992, 104–112.

Brosky, John J., *The Implicit Cost of Trade Credit and Theory of Optimal Terms of Sale* (New York: Credit Research Foundation, 1969).

Schwartz, Robert A., "An Economic Analysis of Trade," *Journal of Financial and Quantitative Analysis*, September 1974, 643–658.

For more on bank lending and commercial credit in general, see

Campbell, Tim S., "A Model of the Market for Lines of Credit," *Journal of Finance*, March 1978, 231–243.

Stone, Bernell K., "Allocating Credit Lines, Planned Borrowing, and Tangible Services over a Company's Banking System," *Financial Management*, Summer 1975, 65–78.

For a discussion of effective yields, see

Finnerty, John D., "Bank Discount, Coupon Equivalent, and Compound Yields: Comment," *Financial Management*, Summer 1983, 40–44.

Glasgo, Philip W., William J. Landes, and A. Frank Thompson, "Bank Discount, Coupon Equivalent, and Compound Yields," *Financial Management*, Autumn 1982, 82–84.

24

Derivatives and Risk Management

Bombardier Inc., a manufacturer of snowmobiles in Montreal, has always tried to control risks. However, snowmobile profits depend on a risk that is notoriously hard to control: the weather. Early signs of a cold, snowy winter lead to a brisk sellout, whereas warmer temperatures force Bombardier to cut prices to shed excess inventory.

Bombardier can't change the weather, it has done its best to manage its weather-related risks. For example, the company recently offered to pay a $1,000 rebate to snowmobile buyers in 16 Midwestern cities if the area snowfall that winter turned out to be less than one-half the average snowfall over the previous three years. The rebate offer had a strong, positive effect on sales—in those 16 cities, Bombardier saw a 38 percent increase in its Ski-Doo* Snowmobile sales over the previous year.

In addition, Bombardier took another important step to limit its risks—it bought "snowfall options" from Enron Corporation, a major natural gas supplier. For each snowmobile sold, Bombardier Recreational Products paid Enron between $45 and $400, depending on the city in which the snowmobile was purchased. In return, Enron fully reimbursed Bombardier Recreational Products every time it had to pay a customer the $1,000 rebate.

These snowfall options are just one example of "weather derivatives," a small but rapidly growing market that Enron has helped develop. Until recently, weather derivatives were exclusively traded in the over-the-counter market, and the participants were primarily electric and gas utilities whose earnings would suffer if there were a milder than expected summer or winter. Just recently, though, the Chicago Mercantile Exchange (CME) established the first weather-based futures contracts. These contracts were based on the average monthly temperature in four U.S. cities: Atlanta, Chicago, Cincinnati, and New York.

Like all futures contracts, each weather contract has a buyer and a seller. One side bets that monthly temperatures will be higher than expected, while the other side bets the weather will be relatively cold. For example, an Atlanta-based ice cream maker might purchase a weather derivative contract that pays off if summer temperatures in Atlanta are lower than expected. By doing so, the profits from its weather derivative position serve to offset the decline in ice cream sales due to cooler temperatures.

The initial response to the CME contract has been lukewarm. However, CME executives, who estimate that 20 percent of the U.S. economy is sensitive to the weather, expect trading in these contracts to increase over time as businesses learn more about them.

Weather derivatives represent just one of many approaches companies can use to control risk. As you read this chapter, try to answer these questions: Why should a company try to manage its risks? What financial techniques can be used to manage risk? Can programs designed to limit risks actually increase them, and if so, what safeguards should companies put in place to prevent this unintended consequence?

Source: Mark Golden and Ed Silliere, "Weather Derivatives Are Becoming a Popular Hedge," *The Wall Street Journal,* February 2, 1999, B9A.

*Trademark of Bombardier Inc. and/or its subsidiaries.

The textbook's CD-ROM contains an *Excel* file that will guide you through the chapter's calculations. The file for this chapter is ***Ch 24 Tool Kit.xls,*** and we encourage you to open the file and follow along as you read the chapter.

In this chapter, we discuss risk management, a topic of increasing importance to financial managers. The term risk management can mean many things, but in business it involves identifying events that could have adverse financial consequences and then taking actions to prevent and/or minimize the damage caused by these events. Years ago, corporate risk managers dealt primarily with insurance—they made sure the firm was adequately insured against fire, theft, and other casualties, and that it had adequate liability coverage. More recently, the scope of risk management has been broadened to include such things as controlling the costs of key inputs like petroleum by purchasing oil futures, or protecting against changes in interest rates or exchange rates through transactions in the interest rate or foreign exchange markets. In addition, risk managers try to ensure that actions intended to hedge against risk are not actually increasing risks.

Reasons to Manage Risk

We know that investors dislike risk. We also know that most investors hold well-diversified portfolios, so at least in theory the only "relevant risk" is systematic risk. Therefore, if you asked corporate executives what type of risk they were concerned about, you might expect the answer to be, "beta." However, this is almost certainly not the answer you would get. The most likely answer, if you asked a CEO to define risk, is something like this: "Risk is the possibility that our future earnings and free cash flows will be significantly lower than we expect." For example, consider Plastics Inc., which manufactures dashboards, interior door panels, and other plastic components used by auto companies. Petroleum is the key feedstock for plastic and thus makes up a large percentage of its costs. Plastics has a three-year contract with an auto company to deliver 500,000 door panels each year, at a price of $20 each. When the company signed this contract, oil sold for $19 per barrel, and oil was expected to stay at that level for the next three years. If oil prices fell, Plastics would have higher than expected profits and free cash flows, but if oil prices rose, profits would fall. Since Plastics' value depends on its profits and free cash flows, a change in the price of oil would cause stockholders to earn either more or less than they anticipated.

Now suppose Plastics announces that it plans to lock in a three-year supply of oil at a guaranteed price of $19 per barrel, and the cost of getting the guarantee is zero. Would that cause its stock price to rise? At first glance, it seems that the answer should be yes, but maybe that's not correct. Recall that the value of a stock depends on the present value of its expected future free cash flows, discounted at the weighted average cost of capital (WACC). Locking in the cost of oil will cause an increase in Plastics' stock price if and only if (1) it causes the expected future free cash flows to increase or (2) it causes the WACC to decline.

Consider first the free cash flows. Before the announcement of guaranteed oil costs, investors had formed an estimate of the expected future free cash flows, based on an expected oil price of $19 per barrel. Therefore, while locking in the cost of oil at $19 per barrel will lower the riskiness of the expected future free cash flows, it might not change the *size* of these cash flows, because investors already expected a price of $19 per barrel. Note, though, that declining cash flows can disrupt a firm's operation, and that disruption can adversely affect cash flows.

Now what about the WACC? It will change only if locking in the cost of oil causes a change in the cost of debt or equity, or the target capital structure. Assuming the foreseeable increases in the price of oil were not enough to raise the threat of bankruptcy, Plastics' cost of debt should not change, and neither should its target capital structure. Regarding the cost of equity, recall from Chapter 6 that most investors hold well-diversified portfolios, which means that the cost of equity should depend only on systematic risk. Moreover, even though an increase in oil prices would have a negative effect on Plastics' stock price, it would not have a negative effect on all stocks. Indeed, oil producers should have higher than expected returns and stock prices. Assuming that Plastics' investors hold well-diversified portfolios, including stocks of oil-producing companies, there would not appear to be much reason to expect its cost of equity to decrease. The bottom line is this: If Plastics' expected future cash flows and WACC will not change significantly due to an elimination of the risk of oil price increases, then neither should the value of its stock.

We discuss futures contracts and hedging in detail in the next section, but for now let's assume that Plastics has *not* locked in oil prices. Therefore, if oil prices increase, its stock price will fall. However, if its stockholders know this, they can build portfolios that contain oil futures whose values will rise or fall with oil prices and thus offset changes in the price of Plastics' stock. By choosing the correct amount of futures contracts, investors can thus "hedge" their portfolios and completely eliminate the risk due to changes in oil prices. There will be a cost to hedging, but that cost to large, sophisticated investors should be about the same as the cost to Plastics. Since stockholders can hedge away oil price risk themselves, why should they pay a higher price for Plastics' stock just because the company itself hedged away the risk?

The points raised above not withstanding, companies clearly believe that active risk management is important. A 1998 survey reported that 83 percent of firms with market values greater than $1.2 billion engage in risk management, and that percentage is surely much higher today.[1] Here are several reasons companies manage risks:

1. **Debt capacity.** Risk management can reduce the volatility of cash flows, and this decreases the probability of bankruptcy. As we discussed in Chapter 16, firms with lower operating risks can use more debt, and this can lead to higher stock prices due to the interest tax savings.
2. **Maintaining the optimal capital budget over time.** Recall from Chapter 16 that firms are reluctant to raise external equity due to high flotation costs and market pressure. This means that the capital budget must generally be financed with debt plus internally generated funds, mainly retained earnings and depreciation. In bad years, internal cash flows may be too low to support the optimal capital budget, causing firms to either slow investment below the optimal rate or else incur the high costs associated with external equity. By smoothing out the cash flows, risk management can alleviate this problem. This issue is most relevant for firms with large growth opportunities. A recent study by Professors Gerald Gay and Jouahn Nam found that such firms do in fact use derivatives more than low-growth firms.[2] Thus, maintaining an optimal capital budget is an important determinant of firms' risk management practices.
3. **Financial distress.** Financial distress—which can range from simply worrying stockholders, to higher interest rates on debt, to customer defections, to bankruptcy—is associated with having cash flows fall below expected levels. Risk management can reduce the likelihood of low cash flows, hence of financial distress.
4. **Comparative advantages in hedging.** Most investors cannot hedge as efficiently as a company. First, firms generally have lower transactions costs due to a larger volume of hedging activities. Second, there is the problem of asymmetric information—managers know more about the firm's risk exposure than outside investors, hence managers can create more effective hedges. And third, effective risk

---

[1] See Gordon M. Bodnar, Gregory S. Hayt, and Richard C. Marston, "1998 Wharton Survey of Financial Risk Management by U.S. Non-Financial Firms," *Financial Management*, Winter 1998, 70–91.

[2] See Gerald D. Gay and Jouahn Nam, "The Underinvestment Problem and Corporate Derivatives Use," *Financial Management*, Vol. 27, no. 4, Winter 1998, 53–69.

management requires specialized skills and knowledge that firms are more likely to have.

5. **Borrowing costs.** As discussed later in the chapter, firms can sometimes reduce input costs, especially the interest rate on debt, through the use of derivative instruments called "swaps." Any such cost reduction adds value to the firm.
6. **Tax effects.** Companies with volatile earnings pay more taxes than stable companies due to the treatment of tax credits and the rules governing corporate loss carry-forwards and carry-backs. Moreover, if volatile earnings lead to bankruptcy, then tax loss carry-forwards are generally lost. Therefore, our tax system encourages risk management to stabilize earnings.[3]
7. **Compensation systems.** Many compensation systems establish "floors" and "ceilings" on bonuses, and also reward managers for meeting targets. To illustrate, suppose a firm's compensation system calls for a manager to receive no bonus if net income is below $1 million, a bonus of $10,000 if income is between $1 million and $2 million, and one of $20,000 if income is $2 million or more. Moreover, the manager will receive an additional $10,000 if actual income is at least 90 percent of the forecasted level, which is $1 million. Now consider the following two situations. First, if income is stable at $2 million each year, the manager gets a $30,000 bonus each year, for a two-year total of $60,000. However, if income is zero the first year and $4 million the second, the manager gets no bonus the first year and $30,000 the second, for a two-year total of $30,000. So, even though the company has the same total income ($4 million) over the two years, the manager's bonus is higher if earnings are stable. So, even if hedging does not add much value for stockholders, it may still benefit managers.

Since perhaps the most important aspect of risk management involves derivative securities, the next section explains **derivatives,** which are securities whose values are determined by the market price of some other asset. Derivatives include *options,* whose values depend on the price of some underlying asset; *interest rate and exchange rate futures and swaps,* whose values depend on interest rate and exchange rate levels; and *commodity futures,* whose values depend on commodity prices.

Self-Test Questions

Explain why finance theory, combined with well-diversified investors and "homemade hedging," might suggest that risk management should not add much value to a company.

List and explain some reasons why companies might actually employ risk management techniques.

Background on Derivatives

WWW

The Chicago Board of Trade has an excellent web site at **http://www.cbot.com.** Make sure to check out the wealth of information on the history and operation of the exchange.

An historical perspective is useful when studying derivatives. One of the first formal markets for derivatives was the futures market for wheat. Farmers were concerned about the price they would receive for their wheat when they sold it in the fall, and millers were concerned about the price they would have to pay. The risks faced by both parties could be reduced if they could establish a price earlier in the year. Accordingly, mill agents would go out to the wheat belt and with contracts that called for the farmers to deliver grain at a predetermined price. Both parties benefited from the transaction in the sense that their risks were reduced. The farmers could concentrate

[3]See Clifford W. Smith and René Stulz, "The Determinants of Firms' Hedging Policies," *The Journal of Financial and Quantitative Analysis,* December 1985, 395–406.

on growing their crop without worrying about the price of grain, and the millers could concentrate on their milling operations. Thus, *hedging with futures* lowered aggregate risk in the economy.

These early futures dealings were between two parties who arranged transactions between themselves. Soon, though, middlemen came into the picture, and *trading* in futures was established. The Chicago Board of Trade was an early marketplace for this dealing, and *futures dealers* helped make a market in futures contracts. Thus, farmers could sell futures on the exchange, and millers could buy them there. This improved the efficiency and lowered the cost of hedging operations.

A third group—*speculators*—soon entered the scene. As we will see in the next section, most derivatives, including futures, are highly leveraged, meaning that a small change in the value of the underlying asset will produce a large change in the price of the derivative. This leverage appealed to speculators. At first blush, one might think that the appearance of speculators would increase risk, but this is not true. Speculators add capital and players to the market, and this tends to stabilize the market. Of course, derivatives markets are inherently volatile due to the leverage involved, hence risk to the speculators themselves is high. Still, the speculators bear much of the risk, which makes the derivatives markets more stable for hedgers.

Natural hedges, defined as situations in which aggregate risk can be reduced by derivatives transactions between two parties (called *counterparties*), exist for many commodities, for foreign currencies, for interest rates on securities with different maturities, and even for common stocks where investors want to "hedge their bets." Natural hedges occur when futures are traded between cotton farmers and cotton mills, copper mines and copper fabricators, importers and foreign manufacturers for currency exchange rates, electric utilities and coal mines, and oil producers and oil users. In all such situations, hedging reduces aggregate risk and thus benefits the economy.

Hedging can also be done in situations where no natural hedge exists. Here one party wants to reduce some type of risk, and another party agrees to write a contract that protects the first party from that specific event or situation. Insurance is an obvious example of this type of hedge. Note, though, that with nonsymmetric hedges, risks are generally *transferred* rather than *eliminated.* Even here, though, insurance companies can reduce certain types of risk through diversification.

The derivatives markets have grown more rapidly than any other major market in recent years, for a number of reasons. First, analytical techniques such as the Black-Scholes Option Pricing Model, which was discussed in Chapter 15, have been developed to help establish "fair" prices, and having a good, transparent basis for pricing hedges makes the counterparties more comfortable with deals. Second, computers and electronic communications make it much easier for counterparties to deal with one another. Third, globalization has greatly increased the importance of currency markets and the need for reducing the exchange rate risks brought on by global trade. Recent trends and developments are sure to continue if not accelerate, so the use of derivatives for risk management is bound to grow.

Note, though, that derivatives do have a potential downside. These instruments are highly leveraged, so small miscalculations can lead to huge losses. Also, they are complicated, hence not well understood by most people. This makes mistakes more likely than with less complex instruments, and it makes it harder for a firm's top management to exercise proper control over derivatives transactions. One 28-year-old, relatively low-level employee, operating in the Far East, entered into transactions that led to the bankruptcy of Britain's oldest bank (Barings Bank), the institution that held the accounts of the Queen of England. (See the box entitled, "Barings and Sumitomo Suffer Large Losses in the Derivatives Market.") Just prior to the problems at Barings, Orange County, California, went bankrupt due to its treasurer's speculation in

Barings and Sumitomo Suffer Large Losses in the Derivatives Market

Barings, a conservative English Bank with a long, impressive history dating back to its financing of the Louisiana Purchase in the 19th century, collapsed in 1995 when one of its traders lost $1.4 billion in his derivatives trades. Nicholas Leeson, a 28-year-old trader in Barings' Singapore office, had speculated in Japanese stock index and interest rate futures without his superiors' knowledge. A lack of internal controls at the bank allowed him to accumulate large losses without being detected. Leeson's losses caught many by surprise, and they provided ammunition to those who argue that trading in derivatives should be more highly regulated if not sharply curtailed.

Most knowledgable observers argue that the blame went beyond Leeson—that both the bank and the exchanges were at fault for failing to provide sufficient oversight. For misreporting his trades, Leeson was sentenced to a 6½-year term in a Singapore prison. What remained of Barings was ultimately sold to a Dutch banking concern.

Many analysts, including those who argued that the Barings episode was just an unsettling but isolated incident, were startled by a similar case a year and a half after the Barings debacle. In June 1996, Japan's Sumitomo Corporation disclosed that its well-respected chief copper trader, Yasuo Hamanaka, had been conducting unauthorized speculative trades for more than a decade. The cumulative losses on these trades was $2.6 billion.

These two events illustrate both the dangers of derivatives and the importance of internal controls. While it is unsettling to learn that the actions of a single, relatively low-level employee can suddenly cripple a giant corporation, these losses should be placed in perspective. The overwhelming majority of firms that use derivatives have been successful in enhancing performance and/or reducing risk. For this reason, most analysts argue that it would be a huge mistake to use the rare instances where fraud occurred to limit a market that has, for the most part, been a resounding success. However, given the volume of business in this market, we can in the future expect to see other problems similar to those encountered by Barings and Sumitomo.

derivatives, and Procter & Gamble got into a nasty fight with Bankers Trust over derivative-related losses. More recently, the high-profile hedge fund, Long Term Capital Management LP, nearly collapsed because of bad bets made in the derivatives market.

The P&G, Orange County, Barings Bank, and Long Term Capital Management affairs make the headlines, causing some people to argue that derivatives should be regulated out of existence to "protect the public." However, derivatives are used far more often to hedge risks than in harmful speculations, but these beneficial transactions never make the headlines. So, while the horror stories point out the need for top managers to exercise control over the personnel who deal with derivatives, they certainly do not justify the elimination of derivatives.

In the balance of this chapter, we discuss how firms can manage risks, and how derivatives are used in risk management.

Self-Test Questions

What is a "natural hedge"? Give some examples of natural hedges.

List three reasons the derivatives markets have grown more rapidly than any other major market in recent years.

Types of Derivatives

We discussed put and call options in Chapter 15. They represent an important class of derivative securities, but there are many other types of derivatives, including forward contracts, futures, swaps, structured notes, inverse floaters, and a host of other "exotic" contracts.

Forward Contracts versus Futures Contracts

Forward contracts are agreements where one party agrees to buy a commodity at a specific price on a specific future date and the other party agrees to sell the product. *Goods are actually delivered under forward contracts.* Unless both parties are morally and financially strong, there is a danger that one party will default on the contract, especially if the price of the commodity changes markedly after the agreement is reached.

A **futures contract** is similar to a forward contract, but with three key differences: (1) Futures contracts are "marked to market" on a daily basis, meaning that gains and losses are noted and money must be put up to cover losses. This greatly reduces the risk of default that exists with forward contracts. (2) With futures, physical delivery of the underlying asset is virtually never taken—the two parties simply settle up with cash for the difference between the contracted price and the actual price on the expiration date. (3) Futures contracts are generally standardized instruments that are traded on exchanges, whereas forward contracts are generally tailor-made, are negotiated between two parties, and are not traded after they have been signed.

Futures and forward contracts were originally used for commodities such as wheat, where farmers would sell forward contracts to millers, enabling both parties to lock in prices and thus reduce their risk exposure. Commodities contracts are still important, but today more trading is done in foreign exchange and interest rate futures. To illustrate how foreign exchange contracts are used, suppose GE arranges to buy electric motors from a German manufacturer on terms that call for GE to pay 1 million marks in 180 days. GE would not want to give up the free trade credit, but if the mark appreciated against the dollar during the next six months, the dollar cost of the million marks would rise. GE could hedge the transaction by buying a forward contract under which it agreed to buy the million marks in 180 days at a fixed dollar price. This would lock in the dollar cost of the motors. This transaction would probably be conducted through a money center bank, which would try to find a German company (a "counterparty") that needed dollars in six months. Alternatively, GE could buy a futures contract on an exchange.

Interest rate futures represent another huge and growing market. For example, suppose Simonset Corporation decides to build a new plant at a cost of $20 million. It plans to finance the project with 20-year bonds that would carry an 8 percent interest rate if they were issued today. However, the company will not need the money for about six months. Simonset could go ahead and sell 20-year bonds now, locking in the 8 percent rate, but it would have the money before it was needed, so it would have to invest in short-term securities that would yield less than 8 percent. However, if Simonset waits six months to sell the bond issue, interest rates might be higher than they are today, in which case the value of the plant would be reduced, perhaps to the point of making it unprofitable.

One solution to Simonset's dilemma involves *interest rate futures*, which are based on a hypothetical 20-year Treasury bond with a 6 percent semiannual coupon. If interest rates in the economy go up, the value of the hypothetical T-bond will go down, and vice versa. In our example, Simonset is worried about an increase in interest rates. Should rates rise, the hypothetical Treasury bond's value would decline. Therefore, Simonset could sell T-bond futures for delivery in six months to hedge its position. If interest rates rise, Simonset will have to pay more when it issues its own bonds. However, it will make a profit on its futures position because it will have presold the bonds at a higher price than it will have to pay to cover (repurchase) them. Of course, if interest rates decline, Simonset will lose on its futures position, but this will be offset by the fact that it will get to pay a lower interest rate when it issues its bonds.

Our examples show that forward contracts and futures can be used to hedge, or reduce, risks. It has been estimated that more than 95 percent of all such transactions are indeed designed as hedges, with banks and futures dealers serving as middlemen between hedging counterparties. Interest rate and exchange rate futures can, of course, be used for speculative as well as hedging purposes. One can buy a T-bond contract on \$100,000 of bonds with only \$1,735 down, in which case a small change in interest rates will result in a very large gain or loss. Still, the primary motivation behind the vast majority of these transactions is to hedge risks, not to create them.

Swaps

A **swap** is just what the name implies—two parties agree to swap something, generally obligations to make specified payment streams. Most swaps today involve either interest payments or currencies. To illustrate an interest rate swap, suppose Company S has a 20-year, \$100 million floating-rate bond outstanding, while Company F has a \$100 million, 20-year, fixed-rate issue outstanding. Thus, each company has an obligation to make a stream of interest payments, but one payment stream is fixed while the other will vary as interest rates change in the future. This situation is shown in the top part of Figure 24-1.

Now suppose Company S has stable cash flows, and it wants to lock in its cost of debt. Company F has cash flows that fluctuate with the economy, rising when the economy is strong and falling when it is weak. Recognizing that interest rates also move up and down with the economy, Company F has concluded that it would be better off with variable-rate debt. If the companies swapped their payment obligations, an *interest rate swap* would occur. The bottom half of Figure 24-1 shows that the net cash flows for Company S are at a fixed rate, and those for Company F are based on a floating rate. Company S would now have to make fixed payments, which are consistent with its stable cash inflows, and Company F would have a floating obligation, which for it is less risky.

Our example illustrates how swaps can reduce risks by allowing each company to match the variability of its interest payments with that of its cash flows. However, there are also situations where swaps can reduce both the riskiness and the effective cost of debt. For example, Antron Corporation, which has a high credit rating, can issue either floating rate debt at LIBOR + 1 percent or fixed-rate debt at 10 percent.[4] Bosworth Industries is less creditworthy, so its cost for floating-rate debt would be LIBOR + 1.5 percent, and its fixed-rate cost would be 10.4 percent. Due to the nature of its operations, Antron's CFO has decided that it would be better off with fixed-rate debt, while Bosworth's CFO would prefer floating-rate debt. Paradoxically, both firms can benefit by issuing the type of debt they do not want, but then swapping their payment obligations.

First, each company would issue an identical amount of debt, which is called the **notional principal.** Even though Antron wants fixed-rate debt, it issues floating-rate debt at LIBOR + 1 percent, and Bosworth issues fixed-rate debt at 10.4 percent. Next, the two companies enter into an interest rate swap.[5] Assume that the debt maturities are five years, hence the length of this swap will also be five years. By convention, the floating-rate payments of most swaps are based on LIBOR, with the fixed rate adjusted upward or downward to reflect credit risk and the term structure. The

---

[4]LIBOR stands for the London Interbank Offer Rate, the rate charged on interbank dollar loans in the Eurodollar market.

[5]Actually, such transactions are generally arranged by large money center banks, and payments are made to the bank, which in turn pays the interest on the original loans. The bank assumes the credit risk and guarantees the payments should one of the parties default. For its services, the bank receives a percentage of the payments as its fee.

FIGURE 24-1 Cash Flows under a Swap

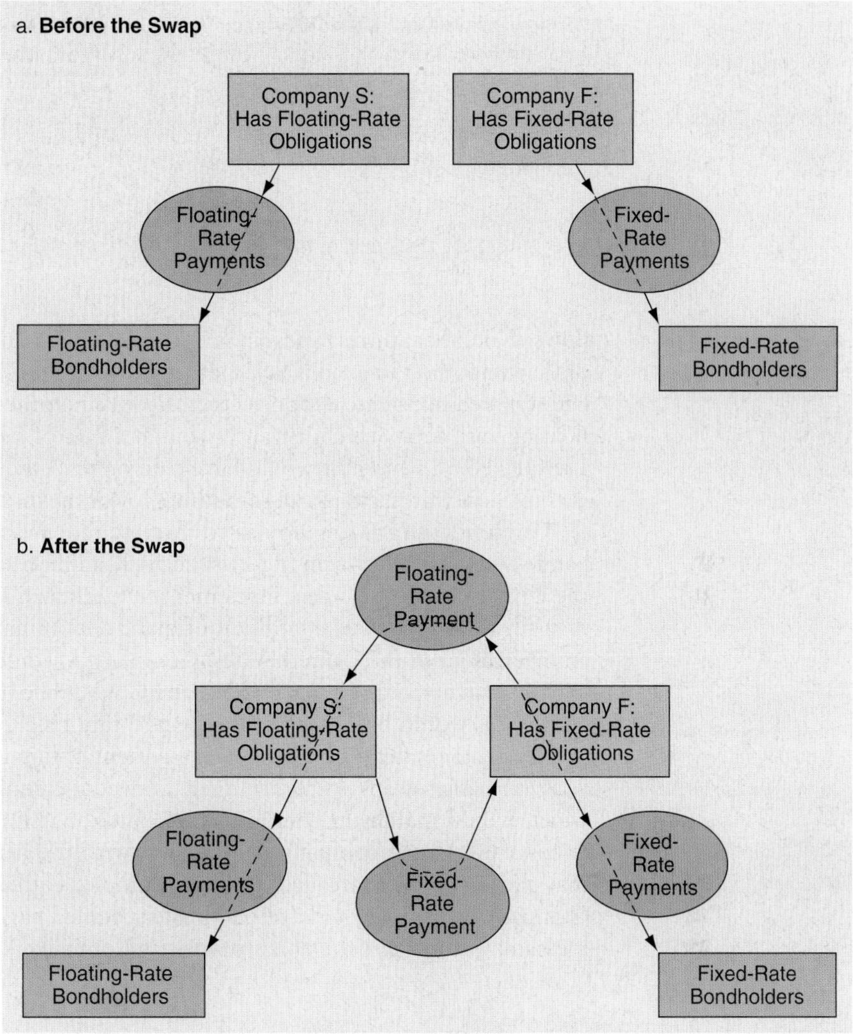

Note: In Panel a, Company S must make floating-rate payments out of its own internal cash flows, but in Panel b, it uses the floating payments from Company F to pay its bondholders. Company F has a reversed position. After the swap, S has de facto fixed payments, which are consistent with its stable internal flows, and F has floating payments, which are consistent with its fluctuating flows.

riskier the company that will receive the floating-rate payments, the higher the fixed-rate payment it must make. In our example, Antron will be receiving floating-rate payments from Bosworth, and those payments will be set at LIBOR times the notional principal. Then, payments will be adjusted every six months to reflect changes in the LIBOR rate.

The fixed payment that Antron must make to Bosworth is set (that is, "fixed") for the duration of the swap at the time the contract is signed, and it depends primarily on two factors: (1) the level of fixed interest rates at the time of the agreement and (2) the relative creditworthiness of the two companies.

In our example, assume that interest rates and creditworthiness are such that 8.95 percent is the appropriate fixed swap rate for Antron, so it will make 8.95 percent fixed-rate payments to Bosworth. Bosworth, in turn, will pay the LIBOR rate to Antron. Table 24-1 shows the net rates paid by each participant, and Figure 24-2 graphs the

TABLE 24-1 Anatomy of an Interest Rate Swap

ANTRON'S PAYMENTS: BORROWS FIXED, SWAPS FOR FLOATING		BOSWORTH'S PAYMENTS: BORROWS FLOATING, SWAPS FOR FIXED	
Payment to lender	−(LIBOR + 1%)	Payment to lender	−10.40% fixed
Payment from Bosworth	+(LIBOR)	Payment from Antron	+8.95% fixed
Payment to Bosworth	−8.95% fixed	Payment to Antron	−(LIBOR)
Net payment by Antron	−9.95% fixed	Net payment by Bosworth	−(LIBOR + 1.45%)

flows. Note that Antron ends up making fixed payments, which it desires, but because of the swap, the rate paid is 9.95 percent versus the 10 percent rate it would have paid had it issued fixed-rate debt directly. At the same time, the swap leaves Bosworth with floating-rate debt, which it wanted, but at a rate of LIBOR +1.45 percent versus the LIBOR +1.50 percent it would have paid on directly issued floating-rate debt. As the example illustrates, swaps can sometimes lower the interest rate paid by each party.

Currency swaps are similar to interest rate swaps. To illustrate, suppose Company A, an American firm, had issued $100 million of dollar-denominated bonds in the United States to fund an investment in Germany. Meanwhile, Company G, a German firm, had issued $100 million of mark-denominated bonds in Germany to make an investment in the United States. Company A would earn marks but be required to make payments in dollars, and Company G would be in a reverse situation. Thus, both companies would be exposed to exchange rate risk. However, both companies' risks would be eliminated if they swapped payment obligations.

Originally, swaps were arranged between companies by money center banks, which would match up counterparties. Such matching still occurs, but today most swaps are between companies and banks, with the banks then taking steps to ensure that their own risks are hedged. For example, Citibank might arrange a swap with Company A, which would agree to make specified payments in marks to the bank, and the bank would make the dollar payments Company A would otherwise owe. Citibank

FIGURE 24-2 The Antron/Bosworth Swap

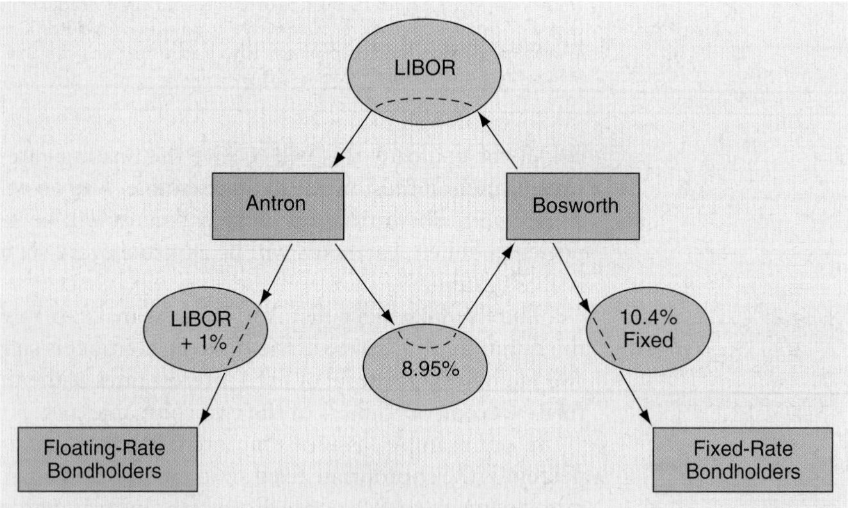

would charge a fee for setting up the swap, and these charges would reflect the creditworthiness of Company A. To protect itself against exchange rate movements, the bank would hedge its position, either by lining up a German company that needed to make dollar payments or else by using currency futures.

Structured Notes

The term **structured note** often means a debt obligation that is derived from some other debt obligation. For example, in the early 1980s, investment bankers began buying large blocks of 30-year, noncallable Treasury bonds and then *stripping* them to create a series of zero coupon bonds. The zero with the shortest maturity was backed by the first interest payment on the T-bond issue, the second shortest zero was backed by the next interest payment, and so forth, on out to a 30-year zero backed by the last interest payment plus the maturity value of the T-bond. Zeros formed by stripping T-bonds were one of the first types of structured notes.

Another important type of structured note is backed by the interest and principal payments on mortgages. In the 1970s, Wall Street firms began to buy large packages of mortgages backed by federal agencies, and then they place these packages, or "pools," with a trustee. Then bonds called *Collateralized Mortgage Obligations (CMOs)*, backed by the mortgage pool held in trust, were sold to pension funds, individuals for their IRA accounts, and other investors who were willing to invest in CMOs but who would not have purchased individual mortgages. This *securitization* of mortgages made billions of dollars of new capital available to home buyers.

CMOs are more difficult to evaluate than straight bonds for several reasons. First, the underlying mortgages can be prepaid at any time, and when this occurs the prepayment proceeds are used to retire part of the CMO debt itself. Therefore, the holder of a CMO is never sure when his or her bond will be called. This situation is further complicated by the fact that when interest rates decline, this normally causes bond prices to rise. However, declining rates also lead to mortgage prepayments, which cause the CMOs to be called especially rapidly, and it is not good to have bonds called and have to reinvest funds at a lower rate. These opposing forces make it difficult to value CMOs.

It should also be noted that a variety of structured notes can be created, ranging from notes whose cash flows can be predicted with virtual certainty to other notes whose payment streams are highly uncertain. For example, investment bankers can (and do) create notes called *IOs* (for *Interest Only*), which provide cash flows from the interest component of the mortgage amortization payments, and *POs* (for *Principal Only*), which are paid from the principal repayment stream. In each case, the value of the note is found as the PV of an expected payment stream, but the length and size of the stream are uncertain. Suppose, for example, that you are offered an IO that you expect to provide payments of $100 for 10 years (you expect the mortgages to be refinanced after 10 years, at which time your payments will cease). Suppose further that you discount the expected payment stream at a rate of 10 percent and determine that the value is $614.46. You have $614.46 to invest, so you buy the IO, expecting to earn 10 percent on your money.

Now suppose interest rates decline. If rates fall, the discount rate would drop, and that would normally imply an increase in the IO's value. However, if rates decline sharply, this would lead to a rash of mortgage refinancings, in which case your payments, which come from interest only, would cease (or be greatly reduced), and the value of your IO would fall sharply. On the other hand, a sharp increase in interest rates would reduce refinancing, lengthen your expected payment stream, and probably increase the value of your IO.

Investment bankers can slice and dice a pool of mortgages into a bewildering array of structured notes, ranging from "plain vanilla" ones with highly predictable cash flows to "exotic" ones (sometimes called "toxic waste") whose risks are almost incalculable but are surely large.

Securitizing mortgages through CMOs serves a useful economic function—it provides an investment outlet for pension funds and others with money to invest, and it makes more money available to homeowners at a reasonable cost. Also, some investors want relatively safe investments, while others are willing to buy more speculative securities for the higher expected returns they provide. Structured notes permit a partitioning of risks to give investors what they want. There are dangers, though. In some cases the "toxic waste" is bought by naive officials managing money for local governments like Orange County, California, when they really ought to be holding only safe securities.

Inverse Floaters

A floating rate note has an interest rate that rises and falls with some interest rate index. For example, the interest rate on a $100,000 note at prime plus 1 percent would be 9.5 percent when the prime rate is 8.5 percent, and the note's rate would move up and down with the prime rate. Because both the cash flows associated with the note and the discount rate used to value it rise and fall together, the market value of the note would be relatively stable.

With an **inverse floater,** the rate paid on the note moves counter to market rates. Thus, if interest rates in the economy rise, the interest rate paid on an inverse floater will fall, lowering its cash interest payments. At the same time, the discount rate used to value the inverse floater's cash flows will rise along with other rates. The combined effect of lower cash flows and a higher discount rate lead to a very large decline in the value of the inverse floater. Thus, inverse floaters are exceptionally vulnerable to increases in interest rates. Of course, if interest rates fall, the value of an inverse floater will soar.

Could an inverse floater be used for hedging purposes? The answer is "yes, perhaps quite effectively." These securities have a magnified effect, so not many are required to hedge a given position. However, because they are so volatile, they could make what is supposed to be a hedged position actually quite risky.

We have discussed the most important types of derivative securities, but certainly not all types. This discussion should, though, give you a good idea of how and why derivatives are created, and how they can be used and misused.

Self-Test Questions

Briefly describe the following types of derivative securities:

(1) Futures and forward contracts.

(2) Swaps.

(3) Structured notes and CMOs.

(4) Inverse floaters.

Risk Management

As businesses become increasingly complex, it is becoming more and more difficult for CEOs and directors to know what problems might lie in wait. Therefore, companies need to have someone systematically look for potential problems and design safeguards to minimize potential damage. With this in mind, most larger firms have a designated "risk manager" who reports to the chief financial officer, while the CFOs of smaller firms personally assume risk management responsibilities. In any event, **risk management** is becoming increasingly important, and it is something finance students should understand. Therefore, in the remainder of this chapter we discuss the basics of risk management, with particular emphasis on how derivatives can be used to hedge financial risks.

Fundamentals of Risk Management

It is useful to begin our discussion of risk management by defining some commonly used terms that describe different risks. Some of these risks can be mitigated, or managed, and that is what risk management is all about.

1. *Pure risks* are risks that offer only the prospect of a loss. Examples include the risk that a plant will be destroyed by fire or that a product liability suit will result in a large judgment against the firm.
2. *Speculative risks* are situations that offer the chance of a gain but might result in a loss. Investments in new projects and marketable securities involve speculative risks.
3. *Demand risks* are associated with the demand for a firm's products or services. Because sales are essential to all businesses, demand risk is one of the most significant risks that firms face.
4. *Input risks* are risks associated with input costs, including both labor and materials. Thus, a company that uses copper as a raw material in its manufacturing process faces the risk that the cost of copper will increase and that it will not be able to pass this increase on to its customers.
5. *Financial risks* are risks that result from financial transactions. As we have seen, if a firm plans to issue new bonds, it faces the risk that interest rates will rise before the bonds can be brought to market. Similarly, if the firm enters into contracts with foreign customers or suppliers, it faces the risk that fluctuations in exchange rates will result in unanticipated losses.
6. *Property risks* are associated with destruction of productive assets. Thus, the threat of fire, floods, and riots imposes property risks on a firm.
7. *Personnel risks* are risks that result from employees' actions. Examples include the risks associated with employee fraud or embezzlement, or suits based on charges of age or sex discrimination.
8. *Environmental risks* include risks associated with polluting the environment. Public awareness in recent years, coupled with the huge costs of environmental cleanup, has increased the importance of this risk.
9. *Liability risks* are associated with product, service, or employee actions. Examples include the very large judgments assessed against asbestos manufacturers and some health care providers, as well as costs incurred as a result of improper actions of employees, such as driving corporate vehicles in a reckless manner.
10. *Insurable risks* are risks that can be covered by insurance. In general, property, personnel, environmental, and liability risks can be transferred to insurance companies. Note, though, that the *ability* to insure a risk does not necessarily mean that the risk *should be* insured. Indeed, a major function of risk management involves evaluating all alternatives for managing a particular risk, including self-insurance, and then choosing the optimal alternative.

Note that the risk classifications we used are somewhat arbitrary, and different classifications are commonly used in different industries. However, the list does give an idea of the wide variety of risks to which a firm can be exposed.

Microsoft's Goal: Manage Every Risk!

Twenty years ago, risk management meant buying insurance against fire, theft, and liability losses. Today, though, due to globalization, volatile markets, and a host of lawyers looking for someone to sue, a multitude of risks can adversely affect companies. Microsoft addressed these risks by creating a virtual consulting practice, called Microsoft Risk Co., to help manage the risks faced by its sales, operations, and product groups.

In a recent article in *CFO*, Scott Lange, head of Microsoft Risk, identified these 12 major sources of risk:

1. *Business partners* (interdependency, confidentiality, cultural conflict, contractual risks)
2. *Competition* (market share, price wars, industrial espionage, antitrust allegations, etc.).
3. *Customers* (product liability, credit risk, poor market timing, inadequate customer support).
4. *Distribution systems* (transportation, service availability, cost, dependence on distributors).
5. *Financial* (foreign exchange, portfolio, cash, interest rate, stock market).
6. *Operations* (facilities, contractual risks, natural hazards, internal processes and control).
7. *People* (employees, independent contractors, training, staffing inadequacy).
8. *Political* (civil unrest, war, terrorism, enforcement of intellectual property rights, change in leadership, revised economic policies).
9. *Regulatory and legislative* (antitrust, export licensing, jurisdiction, reporting and compliance, environmental).
10. *Reputations* (corporate image, brands, reputations of key employees).
11. *Strategic* (mergers and acquisitions, joint ventures and alliances, resource allocation and planning, organizational agility).
12. *Technological* (complexity, obsolescence, the year 2000 problem, virus attacks, workforce skill-sets).

According to Lange, it is important to resist the idea that risk should be categorized by how the insurance industry views it. Insurance coverage lines are a tiny subset of the risks a modern enterprise faces in the pursuit of its business objectives. He also defined the role of finance in risk management: The role of finance is to put on paper all the risks that can be identified and to try to quantify them. When possible, use a number—one number, perhaps, or a probability distribution. For example, what is the probability of losing $1 million on a product, or $10 million? At Microsoft, the finance department works with the product groups to determine the exposure. "We try to use common sense," Lange says.

In many ways risk management mirrors the quality movement of the 1980s and 1990s. The goal of the quality movement was to take the responsibility for quality out of a separate Quality Control Department and to make all managers and employees responsible for quality. Lange has a similar goal for Microsoft—to have risk management permeate the thinking of all Microsoft managers and employees.

Source: Edward Teach, "Microsoft's Universe of Risk," *CFO*, March 1997, 69–72.

An Approach to Risk Management

Firms often use the following process for managing risks.

1. **Identify the risks faced by the firm.** Here the risk manager identifies the potential risks faced by his or her firm. (See the box entitled, "Microsoft's Goal: Manage Every Risk!")
2. **Measure the potential effect of each risk.** Some risks are so small as to be immaterial, whereas others have the potential for dooming the company. It is useful to segregate risks by potential effect and then to focus on the most serious threats.
3. **Decide how each relevant risk should be handled.** In most situations, risk exposure can be reduced through one of the following techniques:
    a. **Transfer the risk to an insurance company.** Often, it is advantageous to insure against, hence transfer, a risk. However, insurability does not necessarily mean that a risk should be covered by insurance. In many instances, it might be better for the company to *self-insure*, which means bearing the risk directly rather than paying another party to bear it.
    b. **Transfer the function that produces the risk to a third party.** For example, suppose a furniture manufacturer is concerned about potential liabilities arising

from its ownership of a fleet of trucks used to transfer products from its manufacturing plant to various points across the country. One way to eliminate this risk would be to contract with a trucking company to do the shipping, thus passing the risks to a third party.

c. **Purchase derivative contracts to reduce risk.** As we indicated earlier, firms use derivatives to hedge risks. Commodity derivatives can be used to reduce input risks. For example, a cereal company may use corn or wheat futures to hedge against increases in grain prices. Similarly, financial derivatives can be used to reduce risks that arise from changes in interest rates and exchange rates.
d. **Reduce the probability of occurrence of an adverse event.** The expected loss arising from any risk is a function of both the probability of occurrence and the dollar loss if the adverse event occurs. In some instances, it is possible to reduce the probability that an adverse event will occur. For example, the probability that a fire will occur can be reduced by instituting a fire prevention program, by replacing old electrical wiring, and by using fire-resistant materials in areas with the greatest fire potential.
e. **Reduce the magnitude of the loss associated with an adverse event.** Continuing with the fire risk example, the dollar cost associated with a fire can be reduced by such actions as installing sprinkler systems, designing facilities with self-contained fire zones, and locating facilities close to a fire station.
f. **Totally avoid the activity that gives rise to the risk.** For example, a company might discontinue a product or service line because the risks outweigh the rewards, as with the recent decision by Dow-Corning to discontinue its manufacture of silicon breast implants.

Note that risk management decisions, like all corporate decisions, should be based on a cost/benefit analysis for each feasible alternative. For example, suppose it would cost $50,000 per year to conduct a comprehensive fire safety training program for all personnel in a high-risk plant. Presumably, this program would reduce the expected value of future fire losses. An alternative to the training program would be to place $50,000 annually in a reserve fund set aside to cover future fire losses. Both alternatives involve expected cash flows, and from an economic standpoint the choice should be made on the basis of the lowest present value of future costs. Thus, the same financial management techniques applied to other corporate decisions can also be applied to risk management decisions. Note, though, that if a fire occurs and a life is lost, the trade-off between fire prevention and expected losses may not sit well with a jury. The same thing holds true for product liability, as Firestone, Ford, GM, and others have learned.

Self-Test Questions

Define the following terms:

(1) Pure risks.
(2) Speculative risks.
(3) Demand risks.
(4) Input risks.
(5) Financial risks.
(6) Property risks.
(7) Personnel risks.
(8) Environmental risks.
(9) Liability risks.
(10) Insurable risks.
(11) Self-insurance.

Should a firm insure itself against all of the insurable risks it faces? Explain.

Using Derivatives to Reduce Risks

Firms are subject to numerous risks related to interest rate, stock price, and exchange rate fluctuations in the financial markets. For an investor, one of the most obvious ways to reduce financial risks is to hold a broadly diversified portfolio of stocks and debt securities, including international securities and debt of varying maturities. However, derivatives can also be used to reduce the risks associated with financial and commodity markets.[6]

WWW

Information from the CBOT on the financial market futures they trade is available at **http://www.cbot.com**. The site provides some general information on the various types of financial market instruments that are available and provides information on how to order specific literature or the CBOT's publications catalog.

Hedging with Futures

One of the most useful tools for reducing interest rate, exchange rate, and commodity risk is to hedge in the futures markets. Most financial and real asset transactions occur in what is known as the *spot*, or *cash, market*, where the asset is delivered immediately (or within a few days). *Futures*, or *futures contracts*, on the other hand, call for the purchase or sale of an asset at some future date, but at a price which is fixed today.

In 2001, futures contracts were available on more than 30 real and financial assets traded on 14 U.S. exchanges, the largest of which are the Chicago Board of Trade (CBOT) and the Chicago Mercantile Exchange (CME). Futures contracts are divided into two classes, **commodity futures** and **financial futures.** Commodity futures, which cover oil, various grains, oilseeds, livestock, meats, fibers, metals, and wood, were first traded in the United States in the mid-1800s. Financial futures, which were first traded in 1975, include Treasury bills, notes, bonds, certificates of deposit, Eurodollar deposits, foreign currencies, and stock indexes.

WWW

You can obtain daily closing prices on Treasury bond futures and other types of futures contracts from the web site of Ira Epstein & Company at **http://www.iepstein.com/frprod.html**.

To illustrate how futures contracts work, consider the CBOT's contract on Treasury bonds. The basic contract is for $100,000 of a hypothetical 6 percent coupon, semiannual payment Treasury bond with 20 years to maturity.[7] Table 24-2 shows an extract from the Treasury bond futures table that appeared in the September 16, 2000, issue of *The Wall Street Journal.*

The first column gives the delivery month, and the next three columns give the opening, high, and low prices for that contract on that day. The opening price for the September future, 100-12, means 100 plus 12/32, or 100.375 percent of par. Column 5 gives the settlement price, which is typically the price at the close of trading. Column

[6]In Chapter 27, we discuss both the risks involved with holding foreign currencies and procedures for reducing such risks.

[7]The coupon rate on the hypothetical bond was changed to 6 percent from 8 percent in March 2000.

TABLE 24-2 Futures Prices

	Treasury Bonds (CBT)—$100,000; Pts. 32nds of 100%							
						Lifetime		
Delivery Month (1)	Open (2)	High (3)	Low (4)	Settle (5)	Change (6)	High (7)	Low (8)	Open Interest (9)
Sept	100-12	100-20	100-04	100-18	0	101-00	88-19	113,402
Dec	100-15	100-22	100-05	100-20	+1	101-02	88-31	331,435
Mar 01	100-22	100-23	100-18	100-22	+1	100-30	88-06	1,195

Source: *The Wall Street Journal,* September 16, 2000, C22.

6 reports the change in the settlement price from the preceding day—the September contract was unchanged. Columns 7 and 8 give the life-of-contract highs and lows. Finally, Column 9 shows the "open interest," which is the number of contracts outstanding.

To illustrate, we focus on the Treasury bonds for March delivery. The settlement price was 100-22, or 100 plus 22⁄32 percent of the $100,000 contract value. Thus, the price at which one could buy $100,000 face value of 6 percent, 20-year Treasury bonds to be delivered in March was 100.6875 percent of par, or 100.6875($100,000) = $100,687.50. The contract price increased by 1⁄32 of 1 percent of $100,000, or by $31.25, from the previous day, so if you had bought the contract yesterday, you would have made $31.25. Over its life, the contract's price has ranged from 88.1875 to 100.9375 percent of par, and there were 1,195 contracts outstanding, representing a total value of about $120 million.

Note that the contract increased by 1⁄32 of a percent on this particular day. Why would the value of the bond futures contract increase? Bond prices increase when interest rates fall, so interest rates must have fallen on that day. Moreover, we can calculate the implied rates inherent in the futures contracts. (*The Wall Street Journal* formerly provided the implied rates, but now we must calculate them.) Recall that the contract relates to a hypothetical 20-year, semiannual payment, 6 percent coupon bond. The closing price (settlement price) was 100 and 22⁄32 , or 100.6875 percent of par. Using a financial calculator, we can solve for k_d in the following equation:

$$\$1,006.875 = \sum_{t=1}^{40} \frac{\$30}{(1 + k_d/2)^t} + \frac{\$1,000}{(1 + k_d/2)^{40}}.$$

The solution value for the six-month rate is 2.9704, which is equivalent to a nominal annual rate of 5.9408 percent, or approximately 5.94 percent. Since the price of the bond rose by 1⁄32 that day, we could find the previous day's closing (settlement) price and its implied interest rate, which would turn out to be 5.9435 percent. Therefore, interest rates fell by less than 1 basis point, but that was enough to increase the value of the contract by $32.50.

Thus, the futures contract for March delivery of this hypothetical bond sold for $100,687.50 for 100 bonds with a par value of $100,000, which translates to a yield to maturity of about 5.94 percent. This yield reflects investors' beliefs about what the interest rate level will be in March. The spot yield on T-bonds was about 5.91 percent at the time, so the marginal trader in the futures market was predicting a 3-basis-point increase in yields over the next eight months. That prediction could, of course, turn out to be incorrect.

Now suppose that three months later interest rates in the futures market had fallen from the earlier levels, say, from 5.94 to 5.5 percent. Falling interest rates mean rising bond prices, and we could calculate that the March contract would then be worth about $106,020. Thus, the contract's value would have increased by $106,020 − $100,688 = $5,332.

When futures contracts are purchased, the purchaser does not have to put up the full amount of the purchase price; rather, the purchaser is required to post an initial *margin*, which for CBT Treasury bond contracts is $1,735 per $100,000 contract. However, investors are required to maintain a certain value in the margin account, called a *maintenance margin*. If the value of the contract declines, then the owner may be required to add additional funds to the margin account, and the more the contract value falls, the more money must be added. The value of the contract is checked at the end of every working day, and margin account adjustments are made at that time. This is called "marking to market." If an investor purchased our illustrative contract and then sold it later for $106,020, he or she would have made a profit of $5,332 on a

$1,735 investment, or a return of more than 200 percent in only three months. It is clear, therefore, that futures contracts offer a considerable amount of leverage. Of course, if interest rates had risen, then the value of the contract would have declined, and the investor could easily have lost his or her $3,000, or more. Futures contracts are rarely settled by delivery of the securities involved. Rather, the transaction is completed by reversing the trade, which amounts to selling the contract back to the original seller.[8] The actual gains and losses on the contract are realized when the futures contract is closed.

Futures contracts and options are similar to one another—so similar that people often confuse the two. Therefore, it is useful to compare the two instruments. A *futures contract* is a definite agreement on the part of one party to buy something on a specific date and at a specific price, and the other party agrees to sell on the same terms. No matter how low or how high the price goes, the two parties must settle the contract at the agreed-upon price. An *option*, on the other hand, gives someone the right to buy (call) or sell (put) an asset, but the holder of the option does not have to complete the transaction. Note also that options exist both for individual stocks and for "bundles" of stocks such as those in the S&P and *Value Line* indexes, but generally not for commodities. Futures, on the other hand, are used for commodities, debt securities, and stock indexes. The two types of instruments can be used for the same purposes. One is not necessarily better or worse than another—they are simply different.

Security Price Exposure

All investors are exposed to losses due to changes in security prices when securities are held in investment portfolios, and firms are also exposed during times when securities are being issued. In addition, firms are exposed to risk if they use floating-rate debt to finance an investment that produces a fixed income stream. Risks such as these can often be mitigated by using derivatives. As we discussed earlier, derivatives are securities whose value stems, or is derived, from the values of other assets. Thus, options and futures contracts are derivatives, because their values depend on the prices of some underlying asset. Now we will explore further the use of two types of derivatives, futures and swaps, to help manage certain types of risk.

Futures Futures are used for both speculation and hedging. **Speculation** involves betting on future price movements, and futures are used because of the leverage inherent in the contract. **Hedging,** on the other hand, is done by a firm or individual to protect against a price change that would otherwise negatively affect profits. For example, rising interest rates and commodity (raw material) prices can hurt profits, as can adverse currency fluctuations. If two parties have mirror-image risks, then they can enter into a transaction that eliminates, as opposed to transfers, risks. This is a "natural hedge." Of course, one party to a futures contract could be a speculator, the other a hedger. Thus, to the extent that speculators broaden the market and make hedging possible, they help decrease risk to those who seek to avoid it.

There are two basic types of hedges: (1) **long hedges,** in which futures contracts are *bought* in anticipation of (or to guard against) price increases, and (2) **short hedges,** where a firm or individual *sells* futures contracts to guard against price

[8]The buyers and sellers of most financial futures contracts do not actually trade with one another—each trader's contractual obligation is with a futures exchange. This feature helps to guarantee the fiscal integrity of the trade. Incidentally, commodities futures traded on the exchanges are settled in the same way as financial futures, but in the case of commodities much of the contracting is done off the exchange, between farmers and processors, as *forward contracts,* in which case actual deliveries occur.

Risk Management in the Cyber Economy

In the old bricks-and-mortar economy, most of a company's value was due to its tangible assets. Not so in the cyber economy, where value is due to intellectual property and networks that manage knowledge bases. Insurance companies are rapidly developing new types of insurance policies to protect these valuable cyber assets.

Intellectual property (IP) insurance now covers "all intellectual property—patents, trademarks, trade secrets, copyright—and includes defense, as well as enforcement, of intellectual property rights," according to Judith Pearson, director of Aon Corp.'s financial services group. These policies can cover losses in excess of $200 million, with premiums ranging from 1 to 5 percent of the coverage.

Insurers also provide coverage for breaches in network security. For example, companies can buy insurance to cover cases of cyberextortion, such as the recent demand for $100,000 by the hacker "Maxus" in exchange for not publicly releasing 300,000 credit card numbers stolen from CD Universe. Other policies cover content defamation, copyright and trademark infringement, denial-of-service attacks, viruses, theft of information, and destruction or alteration of data. Costs of insurance have fallen to between 1 and 3 percent of the policy's coverage, but most insurers subject applicants to a thorough review of their current security measures before granting coverage.

One thing is certain. As the cyber economy matures, look for even more sophisticated risk management techniques.

Sources: John P. Mello, Jr., "Blanketing Intellectual Risk," *CFO*, May 2000, 16; Russ Banham, "Hacking It," *CFO*, August 2000, 115–118.

declines. Recall that rising interest rates lower bond prices and thus decrease the value of bond futures contracts. Therefore, if a firm or individual needs to guard against an *increase* in interest rates, a futures contract that makes money if rates rise should be used. That means selling, or going short, on a futures contract. To illustrate, assume that in September Carson Foods is considering a plan to issue $10,000,000 of 20-year bonds in March to finance a capital expenditure program. The interest rate would be 9 percent if the bonds were issued today, and at that rate the project would have a positive NPV. However, interest rates may rise over the next six months, and when the issue is actually sold, the interest rate might be substantially above 9 percent, which would make the project a bad investment. Carson can protect itself against a rise in rates by hedging in the futures market.

In this situation, Carson would be hurt by an increase in interest rates, so it would use a short hedge. It would choose a futures contract on that security most similar to the one it plans to issue, long-term bonds. In this case, Carson would probably hedge with Treasury bond futures. Because it plans to issue $10,000,000 of bonds, it would sell $10,000,000/$100,000 = 100 Treasury bond contracts for delivery in March. Carson would have to put up 100($1,735) = $173,500 in margin money and also pay brokerage commissions. For illustrative purposes we use the numbers in Table 24-2. We can see from Table 24-2 that each March contract has a value of 100 plus 22/32 percent, so the total value of the 100 contracts is 100.6875($100,000)(100) = $10,068,750. Now suppose renewed fears of inflation push the interest rate on Carson's debt up by 100 basis points, to 10 percent, over the next eight months. If Carson issued 9 percent coupon bonds, they would bring only $914.20 per bond, because investors now require a 10 percent return. Thus, Carson would lose $85.80 per bond times 10,000 bonds, or $858,000, as a result of delaying the financing. However, the increase in interest rates would also bring about a change in the value of Carson's short position in the futures market. Since interest rates have increased, the value of the futures contract would fall, and if the interest rate on the futures contract also increased by the same full percentage point, from 5.94 to 6.94 percent, the contract value would fall to $8,990,830. Carson would then close its position in the futures market by repurchasing for $8,990,830 the contracts which it earlier sold short for $10,068,750, giving it a profit of $1,077,920, less commissions.

Thus, Carson would, if we ignore commissions and the opportunity cost of the margin money, offset the loss on the bond issue. In fact, in our example Carson more than offsets the loss, pocketing an additional $219,920. Of course, if interest rates had fallen, Carson would have lost on its futures position, but this loss would have been offset by the fact that Carson could now sell its bonds with a lower coupon.

If futures contracts existed on Carson's own debt, and interest rates moved identically in the spot and futures markets, then the firm could construct a **perfect hedge,** in which gains on the futures contract would exactly offset losses on the bonds. In reality, it is virtually impossible to construct perfect hedges, because in most cases the underlying asset is not identical to the futures asset, and even when they are, prices (and interest rates) may not move exactly together in the spot and futures markets.

Note too that if Carson had been planning an equity offering, and if its stock tended to move fairly closely with one of the stock indexes, the company could have hedged against falling stock prices by selling short the index future. Even better, if options on Carson's stock were traded in the option market, then it could use options rather than futures to hedge against falling stock prices.

The futures and options markets permit flexibility in the timing of financial transactions, because the firm can be protected, at least partially, against changes that occur between the time a decision is reached and the time when the transaction will be completed. However, this protection has a cost—the firm must pay commissions. Whether or not the protection is worth the cost is a matter of judgment. The decision to hedge also depends on management's risk aversion as well as the company's strength and ability to assume the risk in question. In theory, the reduction in risk resulting from a hedge transaction should have a value exactly equal to the cost of the hedge. Thus, a firm should be indifferent to hedging. However, many firms believe that hedging is worthwhile. Trammell Crow, a large Texas real estate developer, recently used T-bill futures to lock in interest costs on floating rate construction loans, while Dart & Kraft used Eurodollar futures to protect its marketable securities portfolio. Merrill Lynch, Salomon Smith Barney, and the other investment banking houses hedge in the futures and options markets to protect themselves when they are engaged in major underwritings.

Swaps A *swap* is another method for reducing financial risks. As we noted earlier, a swap is an exchange of cash payment obligations in which each party prefers the payment type or pattern of the other party.[9] Generally, one party has a fixed-rate obligation and the other a floating-rate obligation, or one has an obligation denominated in one currency and the other in another currency.

Major changes have occurred over time in the swaps market. First, standardized contracts have been developed for the most common types of swaps, and this has had two effects: (1) Standardized contracts lower the time and effort involved in arranging swaps, and this lowers transactions costs. (2) The development of standardized contracts has led to a secondary market for swaps, which has increased the liquidity and efficiency of the swaps market. A number of international banks now make markets in swaps and offer quotes on several standard types. Also, as noted above, the banks now take counterparty positions in swaps, so it is not necessary to find another firm with mirror-image needs before a swap transaction can be completed. The bank would

[9]For more information on swaps, see Clifford W. Smith, Jr., Charles W. Smithson, and Lee Macdonald Wakeman, "The Evolving Market for Swaps," *Midland Corporate Finance Journal,* Winter 1986, 20–32; and Mary E. Ruth and Steve R. Vinson, "Managing Interest Rate Uncertainty Amidst Change," *Public Utilities Fortnightly,* December 22, 1988, 28–31.

generally find a final counterparty for the swap at a later date, so its positioning helps make the swap market more operationally efficient.[10]

To further illustrate a swap transaction, consider the following situation. An electric utility recently issued a five-year floating-rate note tied to the prime rate. The prime rate could rise significantly over the period, so the note carries a high degree of interest rate risk. The utility could, however, enter into a swap with a counterparty, say, Citibank, wherein the utility would pay Citibank a fixed series of interest payments over the five-year period, and Citibank would make the company's required floating-rate payments. As a result, the utility would have converted a floating-rate loan to a fixed-rate loan, and the risk of rising interest rates would have been passed from the utility to Citibank. Such a transaction can lower both parties' risks—because banks' revenues rise as interest rates rise, Citibank's risk would actually be lower if it had floating-rate obligations.

Longer-term swaps can also be made. Recently, Citibank entered into a 17-year swap in an electricity cogeneration project financing deal. The project's sponsors were unable to obtain fixed-rate financing on reasonable terms, and they were afraid that interest rates would increase and make the project unprofitable. The project's sponsors were, however, able to borrow from local banks on a floating-rate basis and then arrange a simultaneous swap with Citibank for a fixed-rate obligation.

Commodity Price Exposure

As we noted earlier, futures markets were established for many commodities long before they began to be used for financial instruments. We can use Porter Electronics, which uses large quantities of copper as well as several precious metals, to illustrate inventory hedging. Suppose that in May 2001, Porter foresaw a need for 100,000 pounds of copper in March 2002 for use in fulfilling a fixed price contract to supply solar power cells to the U.S. government. Porter's managers are concerned that a strike by Chilean copper miners will occur, which could raise the price of copper in world markets and possibly turn the expected profit into a loss.

Porter could, of course, go ahead and buy the copper that it will need to fulfill the contract, but if it does it will incur substantial carrying costs. As an alternative, the company could hedge against increasing copper prices in the futures market. The New York Commodity Exchange trades standard copper futures contracts of 25,000 pounds each. Thus, Porter could buy four contracts (go long) for delivery in March 2002. Assume that these contracts were trading in May for about $1.00 per pound, and that the spot price at that date was about $1.02 per pound. If copper prices do rise appreciably over the next ten months, the value of Porter's long position in copper futures would increase, thus offsetting some of the price increase in the commodity itself. Of course, if copper prices fall, Porter would lose money on its futures contract, but the company would be buying the copper on the spot market at a cheaper price, so it would make a higher-than-anticipated profit on its sale of solar cells. Thus, hedging in the copper futures market locks in the cost of raw materials and removes some risk to which the firm would otherwise be exposed.

Eastman Kodak uses silver futures to hedge against short-term increases in the price of silver, which is the primary ingredient in black-and-white film. Many other

---

[10]The role of banks in the global swap market is worrisome to the Federal Reserve and other central banks. When banks take positions in swaps, they are themselves exposed to various risks, and if the counterparties cannot meet their obligations, a bank could suddenly become liable for making two sets of payments. Further, swaps are "off balance sheet" transactions, so it is currently impossible to tell just how large the swap market is or who has what obligation. The fear is that if one large multinational bank gets into trouble, the entire worldwide swap market could collapse like a house of cards. See "Swap Fever: Big Money, Big Risks," *Fortune*, June 1, 1992.

manufacturers, such as Alcoa with aluminum and Archer Daniels Midland with grains, routinely use the futures markets to reduce the risks associated with price volatility.

The Use and Misuse of Derivatives

Most of the news stories about derivatives are related to financial disasters. Much less is heard about the benefits of derivatives. However, because of these benefits, more than 83 percent of large U.S. companies use derivatives on a regular basis. In today's market, sophisticated investors and analysts are demanding that firms use derivatives to hedge certain risks. For example, Compaq Computer was recently sued by a shareholder group for failing to properly hedge its foreign exchange exposure. The shareholders lost the suit, but Compaq got the message and now uses currency futures to hedge its international operations. In another example, Prudential Securities reduced its earnings estimate for Cone Mills, a North Carolina textile company, because Cone did not sufficiently hedge its exposure to changing cotton prices. These examples lead to one conclusion: if a company can safely and inexpensively hedge its risks, it should do so.

There can, however, be a downside to the use of derivatives. Hedging is invariably cited by authorities as a "good" use of derivatives, whereas speculating with derivatives is often cited as a "bad" use. Some people and organizations can afford to bear the risks involved in speculating with derivatives, but others are either not sufficiently knowledgeable about the risks or else should not be taking those risks in the first place. Most would agree that the typical corporation should use derivatives only to hedge risks, not to speculate in an effort to increase profits. Hedging allows a manager to concentrate on running his or her core business without having to worry about interest rate, currency, and commodity price variability. However, big problems can arise if hedges are improperly constructed or if a corporate treasurer, eager to report relatively high returns, uses derivatives for speculative purposes.

One interesting example of a derivatives debacle involved Kashima Oil, a Japanese firm that imports oil. It pays with U.S. dollars but then sells oil in the Japanese market for yen. Kashima began by using currency futures to hedge, but it later started to speculate on dollar-yen price movements, hoping to increase profits. When the currency markets moved against Kashima's speculative position, lax accounting rules permitted it to avoid reporting the losses by simply rolling over the contract. By the time Kashima bit the bullet and closed its position, it had lost $1.5 billion. Other companies have experienced similar problems.

Our position is that derivatives can and should be used to hedge against certain risks, but that the leverage inherent in derivatives contracts makes them potentially dangerous. Also, CFOs, CEOs, and board members should be reasonably knowledgeable about the derivatives their firms use, should establish policies regarding when they can and cannot be used, and should establish audit procedures to ensure that the policies are carried out. Moreover, a firm's derivatives position should be reported to stockholders, because stockholders have a right to know when situations such as that involving Kashima might arise.

Self-Test Questions

What is a futures contract?

Explain how a company can use the futures market to hedge against rising interest rates.

What is a swap? Describe the mechanics of a fixed rate to floating rate swap.

Explain how a company can use the futures market to hedge against rising raw materials prices.

How should derivatives be used in risk management? What problems can occur?

Summary

Companies every day face a variety of risks, for it is hard to operate a successful business without taking some chances. Back in Chapter 6, we discussed the trade-off between risk and return. If some action can lower risk without lowering returns too much, then the action can enhance value. With this in mind, we described in this chapter the various types of risks that companies face, and we discussed the basic principles of corporate risk management. One important tool for managing risk is the derivatives market. Consequently, this chapter has also provided an introduction to derivative securities. The key concepts covered are listed below:

- There are several reasons **risk management** might increase the value of a firm. Risk management allows corporations (1) to increase their **use of debt,** (2) to maintain their **capital budget** over time, (3) to avoid costs associated with **financial distress,** (4) to utilize their **comparative advantages in hedging** relative to the hedging ability of individual investors, (5) to reduce both the risks and costs of borrowing by using **swaps,** and (6) to reduce the **higher taxes** that result from fluctuating earnings. Managers may also want to stabilize earnings in order to boost their own compensation.
- **A derivative** is a security whose value is determined by the market price or interest rate of some other security.
- A **hedge** is a transaction that lowers risk. A **natural hedge** is a transaction between two **counterparties** where the parties' risks are mirror images.
- A **futures contract** is a standardized contract that is traded on an exchange and is "marked to market" daily, but where physical delivery of the underlying asset usually does not occur.
- Under a **forward contract,** one party agrees to buy a commodity at a specific price and a specific future date and the other party agrees to make the sale. Delivery does occur.
- A **structured note** is a debt obligation derived from another debt obligation.
- A **swap** is an exchange of cash payment obligations. Swaps occur because the parties involved prefer the other's payment stream.
- In general, **risk management** involves the management of unpredictable events that have adverse consequences for the firm.
- The three key steps in risk management are as follows: (1) **identify** the risks faced by the company, (2) **measure** the potential impacts of these risks, and (3) **decide** how each relevant risk should be dealt with.
- In most situations, risk exposure can be dealt with by one or more of the following techniques: (1) **transfer the risk** to an insurance company, (2) **transfer the function** that produces the risk to a third party, (3) **purchase a derivative contract,** (4) **reduce the probability** of occurrence of an adverse event, (5) **reduce the magnitude** of the loss associated with an adverse event, and (6) totally **avoid** the activity that gives rise to the risk.
- **Financial futures** permit firms to create hedge positions to protect themselves against fluctuating interest rates, stock prices, and exchange rates.
- **Commodity futures** can be used to hedge against input price increases.
- **Long hedges** involve buying futures contracts to guard against price increases.
- **Short hedges** involve selling futures contracts to guard against price declines.
- A **perfect hedge** occurs when the gain or loss on the hedged transaction exactly offsets the loss or gain on the unhedged position.

Questions

24–1 Define each of the following terms:
- **a.** Derivative
- **b.** Corporate risk management
- **c.** Financial futures; forward contract
- **d.** Hedging; natural hedge; long hedges; short hedges; perfect hedge
- **e.** Swap; structured note
- **f.** Commodity futures

24–2 Give two reasons stockholders might be indifferent between owning the stock of a firm with volatile cash flows and that of a firm with stable cash flows.

24–3 List six reasons risk management might increase the value of a firm.

24–4 Discuss some of the techniques available to reduce risk exposures.

24–5 Explain how the futures markets can be used to reduce interest rate and input price risk.

24–6 How can swaps be used to reduce the risks associated with debt contracts?

Self-Test Problem (Solution Appears in Appendix A)

ST–1 *HEDGING* It is now March, and the current cost of debt for Wansley Construction is 12 percent. Wansley plans to issue $5 million in 30-year bonds in September, but is afraid that rates will climb even higher before then. The following data are available:

Future Prices: Treasury Bonds—$100,000; Pts. 32nds of 100%

Delivery Month (1)	Open (2)	High (3)	Low (4)	Settle (5)	Change (6)
Mar	96-28	97-13	97-22	98-05	+7
June	98-03	98-03	97-13	97-25	+8
Sept	97-03	97-17	97-03	97-17	+8

- **a.** What is the implied interest rate on the September contract?
- **b.** Construct a hedge for Wansley.
- **c.** Assume all interest rates rise by 1 percentage point. What is the dollar value of Wansley's increased cost of issuing debt? What is Wansley's gain from the future's contract?

Problems

24–1 *FUTURES* What is the implied interest rate on a Treasury bond ($100,000) futures contract that settled at 100-16? If interest rates increased by 1 percent, what would be the contract's new value?

24–2 *HEDGING* The Zinn Company plans to issue $10,000,000 of 10-year bonds in June to help finance a new research and development laboratory. It is now November, and the current cost of debt to the high-risk biotech company is 11 percent. However, the firm's financial manager is concerned that interest rates will climb even higher in coming months. The following data are available:

Futures Prices: Treasury Bonds—$100,000; Pts. 32nds of 100%

						Lifetime		
Delivery Month (1)	Open (2)	High (3)	Low (4)	Settle (5)	Change (6)	High (7)	Low (8)	Open Interest (9)
Dec	94-28	95-13	94-22	95-05	+7	103-02	93-08	591,944
Mar	96-03	96-03	95-13	95-25	+8	102-24	94-21	120,353
June	95-03	95-17	95-03	95-17	+8	101-02	95-02	13,597

a. Use the given data to create a hedge against rising interest rates.
b. Assume that interest rates in general increase by 200 basis points. How well did your hedge perform?
c. What is a perfect hedge? Are most real-world hedges perfect? Explain.

24–3 *SWAPS* Carter Enterprises can issue floating-rate debt at LIBOR +2 percent or fixed-rate debt at 10.00 percent. Brence Manufacturing can issue floating-rate debt at LIBOR +3.1 percent or fixed-rate debt at 11 percent. Suppose Carter issues floating-rate debt and Brence issues fixed-rate debt. They are considering a swap in which Carter will make a fixed-rate payment of 7.95 percent to Brence, and Brence will make a payment of LIBOR to Carter. What are the net payments of Carter and Brence if they engage in the swap? Will Carter be better off to issue fixed-rate debt or to issue floating-rate debt and engage in the swap? Will Brence be better off to issue floating-rate debt or to issue fixed-rate debt and engage in the swap?

Spreadsheet Problem

24–4 *BUILD A MODEL: HEDGING* Start with the partial model in the file ***Ch 24-4 Build a Model.xls.*** Use the information and data from Problem 24-2.

a. Create a hedge with the futures contract for Zinn Company's planned June debt offering of $10 million. What is the implied yield on the bond underlying the future's contract?
b. Suppose interest rates fall by 300 basis points. What are the dollar savings from issuing the debt at the new interest rate? What is the dollar change in value of the futures position? What is the total dollar value change of the hedged position?
c. Create a graph showing the effectiveness of the hedge if the change in interest rates, in basis points, is: −300, −200, −100, 0, 100, 200, or 300. Show the dollar cost (or savings) from issuing the debt at the new interest rates, the dollar change in value of the futures position, and the total dollar value change.

Mini Case

CD

See ***Ch 24 Show.ppt*** and ***Ch 24 Mini Case.xls.***

Assume that you have just been hired as a financial analyst by Tennessee Sunshine Inc., a mid-sized Tennessee company that specializes in creating exotic sauces from imported fruits and vegetables. The firm's CEO, Bill Stooksbury, recently returned from an industry corporate executive conference in San Francisco, and one of the sessions he attended was on the pressing need for smaller companies to institute corporate risk management programs. Since no one at Tennessee Sunshine is familiar with the basics of derivatives and corporate risk management, Stooksbury has asked you to prepare a brief report that the firm's executives could use to gain at least a cursory understanding of the topics.

To begin, you gathered some outside materials on derivatives and corporate risk management and used these materials to draft a list of pertinent questions that need to be answered. In fact, one possible approach to the paper is to use a question-and-answer format. Now that the questions have been drafted, you have to develop the answers.

a. Why might stockholders be indifferent whether or not a firm reduces the volatility of its cash flows?

b. What are six reasons risk management might increase the value of a corporation?
c. What is corporate risk management? Why is it important to all firms?
d. Risks that firms face can be categorized in many ways. Define the following types of risk:
   (1) Speculative risks
   (2) Pure risks
   (3) Demand risks
   (4) Input risks
   (5) Financial risks
   (6) Property risks
   (7) Personnel risks
   (8) Environmental risks
   (9) Liability risks
   (10) Insurable risks
e. What are the three steps of corporate risk management?
f. What are some actions that companies can take to minimize or reduce risk exposures?
g. What is financial risk exposure? Describe the following concepts and techniques that can be used to reduce financial risks:
   (1) Derivatives
   (2) Futures markets
   (3) Hedging
   (4) Swaps
h. Describe how commodity futures markets can be used to reduce input price risk.

Selected Additional References

For an excellent overview of risk management, see

Froot, Kenneth A., David S. Scharfstein, and Jeremy Stein, "A Framework for Risk Management," *Journal of Applied Corporate Finance*, 1994, Vol. 7, No. 3, 22–32.

For additional insights into the use of financial futures for hedging, see the following publications:

Blake, Marshall, and Nelda Mahady, "How Mid-Sized Companies Manage Risk," *Journal of Applied Corporate Finance*, Spring 1991, 59–65.

Block, Stanley B., and Timothy J. Gallagher, "The Use of Interest Rate Futures and Options by Corporate Managers," *Financial Management*, Autumn 1986, 73–78.

Castelino, Mark G., Jack C. Francis, and Avner Wolf, "Cross-Hedging: Basis Risk and Choice of the Optimal Hedging Vehicle," *Financial Review*, May 1991, 179–210.

McCabe, George M., and Charles T. Franckle, "The Effectiveness of Rolling the Hedge Forward in the Treasury Bill Futures Market," *Financial Management*, Summer 1983, 21–29.

Siegel, Daniel R., and Diane F. Siegel, *Futures Markets* (Hinsdale, IL: Dryden Press, 1990).

For information on hedging, see

Dolde, Walter, "The Trajectory of Corporate Financial Risk Management," *Journal of Applied Corporate Finance*, Fall 1993, 33–41.

Marshall, John F., Vipul K. Bansal, Anthony F. Herbst, and Alan L. Tucker, "Hedging Business Cycle Risk with Macro Swaps and Options," *Journal of Applied Corporate Finance*, Winter 1992, 103–108.

For more information on swaps, see

Brown, Keith C., and Donald J. Smith, "Default Risk and Innovations in the Design of Interest Rate Swaps," *Financial Management*, Summer 1993, 94–105.

Einzig, Robert, and Bruce Lange, "Swaps at Transamerica: Applications and Analysis," *Journal of Applied Corporate Finance*, Winter 1990, 48–58.

Goodman, Laurie S., "The Uses of Interest Rate Swaps in Managing Corporate Liabilities," *Journal of Applied Corporate Finance*, Winter 1990, 35–47.

Much of the Fall 1993 issue of the Journal of Applied Corporate Finance *is devoted to risk management issues.*

For more information on the derivatives markets, see

Chance, Don M., *An Introduction to Derivatives* (Fort Worth, TX: Dryden Press, 1995).

Chapman, Alger B. "Duke," "Future of the Derivatives Markets: Products, Technology, and Participants," *Financial Practice and Education*, Fall/Winter 1994, 124–128.

25

Bankruptcy, Reorganization, and Liquidation

In June 1993, Continental Airlines performed, for the second time, a feat few companies accomplish even once—it emerged from bankruptcy. (TWA managed to duplicate Continental's feat, while Braniff Airlines went into bankruptcy twice but only came out once.) When Continental Airlines Holdings Inc., along with 53 subsidiaries, filed for bankruptcy court protection in December 1990, it owed $3.96 billion. When it emerged from bankruptcy in 1993, the firm had only four subsidiaries, it had shaved its debt to $1.8 billion, and it had $635 million in cash. However, with equity of only $600 million, the company still had an equity ratio of only 25 percent.

While under court protection—which means that the Bankruptcy Court prevented Continental's creditors from seizing the assets securing their debt, or even collecting interest due on those debts—the company was able to take actions unavailable to its nonbankrupt competitors. In particular, it was able to abrogate its labor contracts and lower its wages. This action, along with not having to pay interest on its debt, permitted it to offer very low fares and still generate positive cash flows.

However, the operating and financing advantages provided by the bankruptcy were costly to some participants. The company's reorganization plan, which provided the road map out of bankruptcy, called for paying creditors only a fraction of what they were owed. For example, unsecured creditors received from 5 cents to 40 cents per dollar of claims, depending on the exact type of debt. Creditors were also required to take some stock in the "new" Continental. In addition, 55 percent of the equity went to Air Canada and to Air Partners, a Fort Worth investor group, which, between them, poured $450 million of new cash into the airline. In fact, all of the equity went to creditors and new investors—the firm's original stockholders were totally wiped out.

After emerging from bankruptcy, Continental instituted a new strategy that focused on transoceanic service to Europe and Asia while cutting back on short-haul flights. Continental, along with the rest of the industry, also enjoyed a period of stable fuel and labor costs, and rapid passenger growth. Combined, these factors resulted in Continental reporting positive earnings in both 1995 and 1996, the first time in many years. By the end of 1999, Continental served more than 200 domestic and international airports, had revenues exceeding $8.4 billion, and had net income of more than $450 million.

Continental is one of the success stories of bankruptcy—the corporation itself has survived, its customers are receiving good service, its employees have jobs, its creditors got more than they would have in a liquidation, and its new equity investors have made money. As we discuss in the chapter, though, other bankrupt firms have not fared so well. The decisions that firms' managers, creditors, and other stakeholders make before and during bankruptcy proceedings determine the final results.

As you go through the chapter, think about the decisions that Continental's managers and creditors had to make regarding bankruptcy and reorganization, and the effects the firm's bankruptcy has had on all of its stakeholders as well as on competing airlines.

The Textbook's CD-ROM contains an *Excel* file that will guide you through the chapter's calculations. The file for this chapter is ***Ch 25 Tool Kit.xls,*** and we encourage you to open the file and follow along as you read the chapter.

Thus far, we have dealt with issues faced by growing, successful enterprises. However, many firms encounter financial difficulties, and some, including such big names as Pan American Airlines and Texaco, are forced into bankruptcy. When a firm encounters financial distress, its managers must try to ward off the firm's total collapse and thereby minimize losses. The ability of a firm to hang on during rough times often means the difference between forced liquidation versus rehabilitation and eventual success. An understanding of bankruptcy is also critical to the executives of healthy firms, because they must know the best way to handle things when their customers or suppliers face the threat of bankruptcy.

Financial Distress and Its Consequences

We begin with some background on financial distress and its consequences.[1]

Causes of Business Failure

A recent Dun & Bradstreet compilation assigned percentage values to business failure causes, as shown in Table 25-1. Economic factors include industry weakness and poor location. Financial factors include too much debt and insufficient capital. The importance of the different factors varies over time, depending on such things as the state of the economy and the level of interest rates. Also, most business failures occur because a number of factors combine to make the business unsustainable. Further, case studies show that financial difficulties are usually the result of a series of errors, misjudgments, and interrelated weaknesses that can be attributed directly or indirectly to management. As you might guess, signs of potential financial distress are generally evident in a ratio analysis long before the firm actually fails, and researchers use ratio analysis to predict the probability that a given firm will go bankrupt.

The Business Failure Record

How widespread is business failure in the United States? In Table 25-2, we see that a fairly large number of businesses fail each year, although the failures in any one year are not a large percentage of the total business population. It is interesting to note that whereas the failure rate per 10,000 businesses fluctuates with the state of the economy, the average liability per failure has tended to increase over time, at least into the early 1990s. This is due primarily to inflation, but it also reflects the fact that some very large firms have failed in recent years.

Although bankruptcy is more frequent among smaller firms, it is clear from Table 25-3 that large firms are not immune. However, some firms might be too big or too important to be allowed to fail, and mergers or governmental intervention are often used as an alternative to outright failure and liquidation. The decision to give federal aid to Chrysler (now a part of DaimlerChrysler AG) in the 1980s is an excellent illustration. Also, in recent years federal regulators have arranged the absorption of many "problem" financial institutions by financially sound institutions. In addition, several U.S. government agencies, principally the Defense Department, were able to

[1]Much of the current academic work in the area of financial distress and bankruptcy is based on writings by Edward I. Altman. For a summary of his work and that of others, see Edward I. Altman, *Bankruptcy and Distressed Restructuring* (Homewood, IL: Irwin, 1992).

TABLE 25-1 Causes of Business Failure

Cause of Failure	Percentage of Total
Economic factors	37.1%
Financial factors	47.3
Neglect, disaster, and fraud	14.0
Other factors	1.6
	100.0%

Source: Dun & Bradstreet Inc., *Business Failure Record* (New York, updated annually).

bail out Lockheed when it otherwise would have failed, and the "shotgun marriage" of Douglas Aircraft and McDonnell was designed to prevent Douglas's failure. Another example of intervention is that of Merrill Lynch taking over the brokerage firm Goodbody & Company, which would otherwise have gone bankrupt and would have frozen the accounts of its 225,000 customers while a bankruptcy settlement was being worked out. Goodbody's failure would have panicked investors across the country, so New York Stock Exchange member firms put up $30 million as an inducement to get Merrill Lynch to keep Goodbody from folding. Similar instances in other industries could also be cited.

Why do government and industry seek to avoid failure among larger firms? There are many reasons. In the case of banks, the main reason is to prevent an erosion of confidence and a consequent run on the banks. With Lockheed and Douglas, the Defense Department wanted not only to maintain viable suppliers but also to avoid disrupting local communities. With Chrysler, the government wanted to preserve jobs as well as a competitor in the U.S. auto industry. Even when the public interest is not at stake, the fact that bankruptcy is a very expensive process gives private industry strong incentives to avoid outright bankruptcy. The costs and complexities of a formal

TABLE 25-2 Historical Failure Rate of U.S. Businesses

Years	Average Number of Failures per Year	Average Failure Rate per 10,000 Businesses	Average Liability per Failure
1950–1959	11,119	42	$ 41,082
1960–1969	13,110	52	92,271
1970–1979	9,311	36	296,497
1980	11,742	42	394,744
1985	57,253	115	645,160
1990	60,747	74	923,996
1991	88,140	107	1,098,539
1992	97,069	110	971,653
1993	86,133	109	554,438
1994	71,558	86	404,955
1995	71,128	86	524,175
1996	71,931	80	411,071
1997	83,384	88	448,970

Note: Due to statistical revision, data prior to 1984 are not directly comparable to data in 1984 and thereafter.

Source: Dun & Bradstreet, Inc., *Business Failure Record* (New York, updated annually).

TABLE 25-3 Some Recent Large Bankruptcies (Billions of Dollars)

Company	Business	Assets	Date
Integrated Health Services	Health care	$5.4	February 2, 2000
Montgomery Ward Holding	Retail department stores	4.9	July 7, 1997
Loewen Group International	Funeral services	4.7	June 1, 1999
Safety-Kleen	Chemical waste	4.4	June 9, 2000
Dow Corning Corporation	Silicon	4.1	May 15, 1995
Iridium LLC/Capital Corporation	Wireless communications	3.7	August 13, 1999
CHS Electronics	Computer products	3.6	April 4, 2000
Mariner Post-Acute	Health care	3.0	January 18, 2000
Harnischfeger Industries, Inc.	Surface mining equipment	2.9	June 7, 1999
ICO Global Communications	Wireless communications	2.6	August 27, 1999

Source: Bankruptcy.com, a division of New Generation Research.

bankruptcy are discussed in subsequent sections of this chapter, after we examine some less formal and less expensive procedures.

Self-Test Questions

What are the major causes of business failure?

Do business failures occur evenly over time?

Which size of firm, large or small, is most prone to business failure? Why?

Issues Facing a Firm in Financial Distress

Financial distress begins when a firm is unable to meet scheduled payments or when cash flow projections indicate that it will soon be unable to do so. As the situation develops, these central issues arise:

1. Is the firm's inability to meet scheduled debt payments a temporary cash flow problem, or is it a permanent problem caused by asset values having fallen below debt obligations?
2. If the problem is a temporary one, then an agreement with creditors that gives the firm time to recover and to satisfy everyone may be worked out. However, if basic long-run asset values have truly declined, then economic losses have occurred. In this event, who should bear the losses, and who should get whatever value remains?
3. Is the company "worth more dead than alive"? That is, would the business be more valuable if it were maintained and continued in operation or if it were liquidated and sold off in pieces?
4. Should the firm file for protection under Chapter 11 of the Bankruptcy Act, or should it try to use informal procedures? (Both reorganization and liquidation can be accomplished either informally or under the direction of a bankruptcy court.)
5. Who should control the firm while it is being liquidated or rehabilitated? Should the existing management be left in charge, or should a trustee be placed in charge of operations?

In the remainder of the chapter, we discuss these questions.

Self-Test Question

What five major issues must be addressed when a firm faces financial distress?

Settlements without Going through Formal Bankruptcy

When a firm experiences financial distress, its managers and creditors must decide whether the problem is temporary, and the firm is really financially viable, or whether a permanent problem exists that endangers the firm's life. Then, the parties must decide whether to try to solve the problem informally or under the direction of a bankruptcy court. Because of costs associated with formal bankruptcy, including the disruptions that occur when a firm's customers, suppliers, and employees learn that it has filed under the Bankruptcy Act, it is desirable if possible to reorganize (or liquidate) outside of formal bankruptcy. We first discuss informal settlement procedures, then procedures under a formal bankruptcy.

Informal Reorganization

In the case of an economically sound company whose financial difficulties appear to be temporary, creditors are generally willing to work with the company to help it recover and reestablish itself on a sound financial basis. Such voluntary plans, commonly called **workouts,** usually require a **restructuring** of the firm's debt, because current cash flows are insufficient to service the existing debt. Restructuring typically involves extension and/or composition. In an **extension,** creditors postpone the dates of required interest or principal payments, or both. In a **composition,** creditors voluntarily reduce their fixed claims on the debtor by accepting a lower principal amount, by reducing the interest rate on the debt, by taking equity for debt, or by some combination of these changes.

A debt restructuring begins with a meeting between the failing firm's managers and creditors. The creditors appoint a committee consisting of four or five of the largest creditors, plus one or two of the smaller ones. This meeting is often arranged and conducted by an **adjustment bureau** associated with and run by a local credit managers' association.[2] The first step is for management to draw up a list of creditors, with amounts of debt owed. There are typically different classes of debt, ranging from first-mortgage holders to unsecured creditors. Next, the company develops information showing the value of the firm under different scenarios. Typically, one scenario is going out of business, selling off the assets, and then distributing the proceeds to the various creditors in accordance with the priority of their claims, with any surplus going to the common stockholders. The company may hire an appraiser to get an appraisal of the value of the firm's property to use as a basis for this scenario. Other scenarios include continued operations, frequently with some improvements in capital equipment, marketing, and perhaps some management changes.

This information is then shared with the firm's bankers and other creditors. Frequently, it can be demonstrated that the firm's debts exceed its liquidating value, and it can also be shown that legal fees and other costs associated with a formal liquidation under federal bankruptcy procedures would materially lower the net proceeds available to creditors. Further, it generally takes at least a year, and often several years, to resolve matters in a formal proceeding, so the present value of the eventual proceeds will be lower still. This information, when presented in a credible manner, often convinces creditors that they would be better off accepting something less than the full

[2]There is a nationwide group called the National Association of Credit Management, which consists of bankers and industrial companies' credit managers. This group sponsors research on credit policy and problems, conducts seminars on credit management, and operates local chapters in cities throughout the nation. These local chapters frequently operate adjustment bureaus.

amount of their claims rather than holding out for the full face amount. If management and the major creditors agree that the problems can probably be resolved, then a more formal plan is drafted and presented to all the creditors, along with the reasons creditors should be willing to compromise on their claims.

In developing the reorganization plan, creditors prefer an extension because it promises eventual payment in full. In some cases, creditors may agree not only to postpone the date of payment but also to subordinate existing claims to vendors who are willing to extend new credit during the workout period. Similarly, creditors may agree to accept a lower interest rate on loans during the extension, perhaps in exchange for a pledge of collateral. Because of the sacrifices involved, the creditors must have faith that the debtor firm will be able to solve its problems.

In a composition, creditors agree to reduce their claims. Typically, creditors receive cash and/or new securities that have a combined market value that is less than the amounts owed them. The cash and securities, which might have a value of only 10 percent of the original claim, are taken as full settlement of the original debt. Bargaining will take place between the debtor and the creditors over the savings that result from avoiding the costs of legal bankruptcy: administrative costs, legal fees, investigative costs, and so on. In addition to escaping such costs, the debtor gains in that the stigma of bankruptcy may be avoided. As a result, the debtor may be induced to part with most of the savings from avoiding formal bankruptcy.

Often, the bargaining process will result in a restructuring that involves both extension and composition. For example, the settlement may provide for a cash payment of 25 percent of the debt immediately, plus a new note promising six future installments of 10 percent each, for a total payment of 85 percent.

Voluntary settlements are both informal and simple, and also relatively inexpensive because legal and administrative expenses are held to a minimum. Thus, voluntary procedures generally result in the largest return to creditors. Although creditors do not obtain immediate payment and may even have to accept less than is owed them, they generally recover more money, and sooner, than if the firm were to file for bankruptcy.

In recent years, one factor that has motivated some creditors, especially banks and insurance companies, to agree to voluntary restructurings is the fact that restructurings can sometimes help creditors avoid showing a loss. Thus, a bank that is "in trouble" with its regulators over weak capital ratios may agree to extend further loans that are used to pay the interest on earlier loans in order to keep the bank from having to write down the value of its earlier loans. This particular type of restructuring depends on (1) the willingness of the regulators to go along with the process, and (2) whether the bank is likely to recover more in the end by restructuring the debt than by forcing the borrower into bankruptcy immediately.

We should point out that informal voluntary settlements are not reserved for small firms. International Harvester (now Navistar International) avoided formal bankruptcy proceedings by getting its creditors to agree to restructure more than $3.5 billion of debt. Likewise, Chrysler's creditors accepted both an extension and a composition to help it through its bad years. The biggest problem with informal reorganizations is getting all the parties to agree to the voluntary plan. This problem, called the **holdout problem,** is discussed in a later section.

Informal Liquidation

When it is obvious that a firm is more valuable dead than alive, informal procedures can also be used to **liquidate** the firm. **Assignment** is an informal procedure for liquidating a firm, and it usually yields creditors a larger amount than they would get in a formal bankruptcy liquidation. However, assignments are feasible only if the firm is small and its affairs are not too complex. An assignment calls for title to the debtor's assets to be transferred to a third party, known as an **assignee** or **trustee.** The assignee is instructed to liquidate the assets through a private sale or public auction and then to distribute the proceeds among the creditors on a pro rata basis. The assignment does not automatically discharge the debtor's obligations. However, the debtor may have the assignee write on the check to each creditor the requisite legal language to make endorsement of the check acknowledgment of full settlement of the claim.

Assignment has some advantages over liquidation in federal bankruptcy courts in terms of time, legal formality, and expense. The assignee has more flexibility in disposing of property than does a federal bankruptcy trustee, so action can be taken sooner, before inventory becomes obsolete or machinery rusts. Also, because the assignee is often familiar with the debtor's business, better results may be achieved. However, an assignment does not automatically result in a full and legal discharge of all the debtor's liabilities, nor does it protect the creditors against fraud. Both of these problems can be reduced by formal liquidation in bankruptcy, which we discuss in a later section.

Self-Test Questions

Define the following terms:

(1) Restructuring

(2) Extension

(3) Composition

(4) Assignment

(5) Assignee (trustee)

What are the advantages of liquidation by assignment versus a formal bankruptcy liquidation?

Federal Bankruptcy Law

U.S. bankruptcy laws were first enacted in 1898. They were modified substantially in 1938, then they were changed substantially again in 1978, and some fine-tuning was done in 1986. The primary purpose of the bankruptcy law is to avoid having firms that are worth more as ongoing concerns be put out of business by individual creditors who could force liquidation without regard to the effects on other parties.

Currently, our bankruptcy law consists of eight odd-numbered chapters, plus one even-numbered chapter. (The old even-numbered chapters were deleted when the act was revised in 1978.) Chapters 1, 3, and 5 contain general provisions applicable to the other chapters. Chapter 11, which deals with business reorganization, is the most important section from a financial management viewpoint. Chapter 7 details the procedures to be followed when liquidating a firm; generally, Chapter 7 does not come into play unless it has been determined that reorganization under Chapter 11 is not feasible. Chapter 9 deals with financially distressed municipalities; Chapter 12 covers special procedures for family-owned farms; Chapter 13 covers the adjustment of debts for "individuals with regular income"; and Chapter 15 sets up a system of trustees who help administer proceedings under the act.

A firm is officially bankrupt when it files for bankruptcy with a federal court. When you read that a company such as Southland (the owner of the 7-Eleven convenience store chain) has "filed for court protection under Chapter 11," this means that the company is attempting to reorganize under the supervision of a bankruptcy court. Formal bankruptcy proceedings are designed to protect both the firm and its creditors. On the one hand, if the problem is temporary insolvency, then the firm may use bankruptcy proceedings to gain time to solve its cash flow problems without asset seizure by its creditors. On the other hand, if the firm is truly bankrupt in the sense that liabilities exceed assets, the creditors can use bankruptcy procedures to stop the firm's managers from continuing to operate, lose more money, and thus deplete assets which should go to creditors.

Bankruptcy law is flexible in that it provides scope for negotiations between a company, its creditors, and its stockholders. A case is opened by filing a petition with one of the 291 bankruptcy courts serving 90 judicial districts. The petition may be either **voluntary** or **involuntary;** that is, it may be filed either by the firm's management or by its creditors. After a filing, a committee of unsecured creditors is then appointed by the Office of the U.S. Trustee to negotiate with management for a reorganization, which may include the restructuring of debt. Under Chapter 11, a **trustee** will be appointed to take over the company if the court deems current management incompetent or if fraud is suspected. Normally, though, the existing management retains control. If no fair and feasible reorganization can be worked out, the bankruptcy judge will order that the firm be liquidated under procedures spelled out in Chapter 7 of the Bankruptcy Act, in which case a trustee will always be appointed.

Self-Test Questions

Define the following terms:

(1) Bankruptcy law

(2) Chapter 11

(3) Chapter 7

(4) Trustee

(5) Voluntary bankruptcy

(6) Involuntary bankruptcy

How does a firm formally declare bankruptcy?

Reorganization in Bankruptcy

It might appear that most reorganizations should be handled informally because informal reorganizations are faster and less costly than formal bankruptcy. However, two problems often arise to stymie informal reorganizations and thus force debtors into Chapter 11 bankruptcy—the common pool problem and the holdout problem.[3]

To illustrate these problems, consider a firm that is having financial difficulties. It is worth \$9 million as a going concern (this is the present value of its expected future free cash flows) but only \$7 million if it is liquidated. The firm's debt totals \$10 million at face value—ten creditors with equal priority each have a \$1 million claim. Now suppose the firm's liquidity deteriorates to the point where it defaults on one of its loans. The holder of that loan has the contractual right to *accelerate* the claim, which means the creditor can *foreclose* on the loan and demand payment of the entire balance. Further, since most debt agreements have *cross-default provisions*, defaulting on one loan effectively places all loans in default.

The firm's market value is less than the \$10 million face value of debt, regardless of whether it remains in business or liquidates. Therefore, it would be impossible to pay off all of the creditors in full. However, the creditors in total would be better off if the firm is not shut down, because they can recover \$9 million if the firm remains in

[3]The issues discussed in this section are covered in more detail in Thomas H. Jackson, *The Logic and Limits of Bankruptcy Law* (Cambridge, MA: Harvard University Press, 1986).

business but only $7 million if it is liquidated. The problem here, which is called the **common pool problem,** is that, in the absence of protection under the Bankruptcy Act, individual creditors would have an incentive to foreclose on the firm even though it is worth more as an ongoing concern.

An individual creditor would have the incentive to foreclose because it could then force the firm to liquidate a portion of its assets to pay off that particular creditor's $1 million claim in full. The payment to that creditor would probably require the liquidation of vital assets, which might cause a shutdown of the firm and thus lead to a liquidation. Therefore, the value of the remaining creditors' claims would decline. Of course, all the creditors would recognize the gains to be had from this strategy, so they would storm the debtor with foreclosure notices. Even those creditors who understand the merits of keeping the firm alive would be forced to foreclose, because the foreclosures of the other creditors would reduce the payoff to those who do not. In our hypothetical example, if seven creditors foreclosed and forced liquidation, they would be paid in full, and the remaining three creditors would receive nothing.

With many creditors, as soon as a firm defaults on one loan, there is the potential for a disruptive flood of foreclosures that would make the creditors collectively worse off. In our example, the creditors would lose $9 − $7 = $2 million in value if a flood of foreclosures were to force the firm to liquidate. If the firm had only one creditor, say, a single bank loan, the common pool problem would not exist. If a bank had loaned the company $10 million, it would not force liquidation to get $7 million when it could keep the firm alive and eventually realize $9 million.

Chapter 11 of the Bankruptcy Act provides a solution to the common pool problem through its **automatic stay** provision. *An automatic stay, which is forced on all creditors in a bankruptcy, limits the ability of creditors to foreclose to collect their individual claims.* However, the creditors can collectively foreclose on the debtor and force liquidation.

While bankruptcy gives the firm a chance to work out its problems without the threat of creditor foreclosure, management does not have a completely free reign over the firm's assets. First, bankruptcy law requires the debtor firm to request permission from the court to take many actions, and the law also gives creditors the right to petition the bankruptcy court to block almost any action the firm might take while in bankruptcy. Second, **fraudulent conveyance** statutes, which are part of debtor-creditor law, protect creditors from unjustified transfers of property by a firm in financial distress.

To illustrate fraudulent conveyance, suppose a holding company is contemplating bankruptcy protection for one of its subsidiaries. The holding company might be tempted to sell some or all of the subsidiary's assets to itself (the parent company) for less than the true market value. This transaction would reduce the value of the subsidiary by the difference between the true market value of its assets and the amount paid, and the loss would be borne primarily by the subsidiary's creditors. Such a transaction would be voided by the courts as a fraudulent conveyance. Note also that transactions that favor one creditor at the expense of another can be voided under the same law. For example, a transaction in which an asset is sold and the proceeds are used to pay one creditor in full at the expense of other creditors could be voided. Thus, fraudulent conveyance laws also protect creditors from each other.[4]

The second problem that the bankruptcy law mitigates is the **holdout problem.** To illustrate this problem, consider again our example with ten creditors owed $1 million each but with assets worth only $9 million. The goal of the firm is to avoid

---

[4]The bankruptcy code requires that all transactions undertaken by the firm in the six months prior to a bankruptcy filing be reviewed by the court for fraudulent conveyance, and the review can go back as long as three years.

liquidation by remedying the default. In an informal workout, this would require a reorganization plan that is agreed to by each of the ten creditors. Suppose the firm offers each creditor new debt with a face value of $850,000 in exchange for the old $1,000,000 face value debt. If each of the creditors accepted the offer, the firm could be successfully reorganized. The reorganization would leave the equity holders with some value—the market value of the equity would be $9,000,000 − 10($850,000) = $500,000. Further, the creditors would have claims worth $8.5 million, much more than the $7 million value of their claims in liquidation.

Although such an exchange offer seems to benefit all parties, it might well not be accepted by the creditors. Here's why: Suppose seven of the ten creditors tender their bonds; thus, seven creditors each now have claims with a face value of $850,000 each, or $5,950,000 in total, while the three creditors that did not tender their bonds each still have a claim with a face value of $1 million. The total face value of the debt at this point is $8,950,000, which is less than the $9 million value of the firm. In this situation, the three holdout creditors would receive the full face value of their debt. However, this probably would not happen, because (1) all of the creditors would be sophisticated enough to realize this could happen, and (2) each creditor would want to be one of the three holdouts that gets paid in full. Thus, it is likely that none of the creditors would accept the offer. Thus, the holdout problem makes it difficult to restructure the firm's debts. Again, if the firm had a single creditor, there would be no holdout problem.

The holdout problem is mitigated in bankruptcy proceedings by the bankruptcy court's ability to lump creditors into classes. Each class is considered to have accepted a reorganization plan if two-thirds of the amount of debt and one-half the number of claimants vote for the plan, and the plan will be approved by the court if it is deemed to be "fair and equitable" to the dissenting parties. This procedure, in which the court mandates a reorganization plan in spite of dissent, is called a **cramdown,** because the court crams the plan down the throats of the dissenters. The ability of the court to force acceptance of a reorganization plan greatly reduces the incentive for creditors to hold out. Thus, in our example, if the reorganization plan offered each creditor a new claim worth $850,000 in face value, along with information that each creditor would probably receive only $700,000 under the liquidation alternative, it would have a good chance of success.

It is easier for a firm with few creditors to informally reorganize than it is for a firm with many creditors. A study examined 169 publicly traded firms that experienced severe financial distress from 1978 to 1987.[5] About half of the firms reorganized without filing for bankruptcy, while the other half were forced to reorganize in bankruptcy. The firms that reorganized without filing for bankruptcy owed most of their debt to a few banks, and they had fewer creditors. Generally, bank debt can be reorganized outside of bankruptcy, but a publicly traded bond issue held by thousands of individual bondholders makes reorganization difficult.

Filing for bankruptcy under Chapter 11 has several other features that help the bankrupt firm:

1. Interest and principal payments, including interest on delayed payments, may be delayed without penalty until a reorganization plan is approved, and the plan itself may call for even further delays. This permits cash generated from operations to be used to sustain operations rather than be paid to creditors.
2. The firm is permitted to issue **debtor-in-possession (DIP) financing.** DIP financing enhances the ability of the firm to borrow funds for short-term liquidity

[5] See Stuart Gilson, Kose John, and Larry Lang, "Troubled Debt Restructurings: An Empirical Study of Private Reorganization of Firms in Default," *Journal of Financial Economics*, October 1990, 315–354.

purposes, because such loans are, under the law, senior to all previous unsecured debt.

3. The debtor firm's managers are given the exclusive right for 120 days after filing for bankruptcy protection to submit a reorganization plan, plus another 60 days to obtain agreement on the plan from the affected parties. The court may also extend these dates. After management's first right to submit a plan has expired, any party to the proceedings may propose its own reorganization plan.

Under the early bankruptcy laws, most formal reorganization plans were guided by the **absolute priority doctrine.** This doctrine holds that creditors should be compensated for their claims in a rigid hierarchical order, and that senior claims must be paid in full before junior claims can receive even a dime. If there was any chance that a delay would lead to losses by senior creditors, then the firm would be shut down and liquidated. However, an alternative position, the **relative priority doctrine,** holds that more flexibility should be allowed in a reorganization, and that a balanced consideration should be given to all claimants. The current law represents a movement away from absolute priority toward relative priority.

The primary role of the bankruptcy court in a reorganization is to determine the **fairness** and the **feasibility** of the proposed plan of reorganization. The basic doctrine of fairness states that claims must be recognized in the order of their legal and contractual priority. Feasibility means that there is a reasonable chance that the reorganized company will be viable. Carrying out the concepts of fairness and feasibility in a reorganization involves the following steps:

1. Future sales must be estimated.
2. Operating conditions must be analyzed so that future earnings and cash flows can be predicted.
3. The appropriate capitalization rate must be determined.
4. This capitalization rate must then be applied to the estimated cash flows to obtain an estimate of the company's value.[6]
5. An appropriate capital structure for the company after it emerges from Chapter 11 must be determined.
6. The reorganized firm's securities must be allocated to the various claimants in a fair and equitable manner.

The primary test of feasibility in a reorganization is whether the fixed charges after reorganization will be adequately covered by earnings. Adequate coverage generally requires an improvement in earnings, a reduction of fixed charges, or both. Among the actions that must generally be taken are the following:

1. Debt maturities are usually lengthened, interest rates may be lowered, and some debt is usually converted into equity.
2. When the quality of management has been substandard, a new team must be given control of the company.
3. If inventories have become obsolete or depleted, they must be replaced.
4. Sometimes the plant and equipment must be modernized before the firm can operate and compete successfully.
5. Reorganization may also require an improvement in production, marketing, advertising, and other functions.

---

[6]Several different approaches can be used to estimate a company's value. Market-determined multiples such as the price/earnings ratio, which are obtained from an analysis of comparable firms, can be applied to some measure of the company's earnings or cash flow. Alternatively, discounted cash flow techniques may be used. The key point here is that fairness requires that the value of a company facing reorganization be estimated so that potential offers can be evaluated rationally by the bankruptcy court.

6. It is sometimes necessary to develop new products or markets to enable the firm to move from areas where economic trends are poor into areas with more potential for growth.

These actions usually require at least some new money, so most reorganization plans include new investors who are willing to put up new capital.

It might appear that stockholders have very little to say in a bankruptcy situation where the firm's assets are worth less than the face value of its debt. Under the absolute priority rule, stockholders in such a situation should get nothing of value under a reorganization plan. In fact, however, stockholders may be able to extract some of the firm's value. This occurs because (1) stockholders generally continue to control the firm during the bankruptcy proceedings, (2) stockholders have the first right to file a reorganization plan, and (3) for the creditors, developing a plan and taking it through the courts would be expensive and time consuming. Given this situation, creditors may support a plan under which they are not paid off in full and where the old stockholders will control the reorganized company just because the creditors want to get the problem behind them and to get some money in the near future.

Illustration of a Reorganization

Reorganization procedures may be illustrated with an example involving the Columbia Software Company, a regional firm that specializes in selling, installing, and servicing accounting software for small businesses.[7] Table 25-4 gives Columbia's balance sheet as of March 31, 2001. The company had been suffering losses running to $2.5

[7]This example is based on an actual reorganization, although the company name has been changed and the numbers have been changed slightly to simplify the analysis.

TABLE 25-4 Columbia Software Company: Balance Sheet as of March 31, 2001 (Millions of Dollars)

ASSETS	
Current assets	$ 3.50
Net fixed assets	12.50
Other assets	0.70
Total assets	$16.70
LIABILITIES AND EQUITY	
Accounts payable	$ 1.00
Accrued taxes	0.25
Notes payable	0.25
Other current liabilities	1.75
7½% first mortgage bonds, due 2006	6.00
9% subordinated debentures, due 2001[a]	7.00
Total liabilities	$16.25
Common stock ($1 par)	1.00
Paid-in capital	3.45
Retained earnings	4.00
Total liabilities and equity	$16.70

[a]The debentures are subordinated to the notes payable.

million a year, and, as will be made clear in the following discussion, the asset values in the balance sheet are overstated relative to their market values. The firm was **insolvent,** which means that the book values of its liabilities were greater than the market values of its assets, so it filed a petition with a federal court for reorganization under Chapter 11. Management filed a plan of reorganization with the court on June 13, 2001. The plan was subsequently submitted for review by the SEC.[8]

The plan concluded that the company could not be internally reorganized and that the only feasible solution would be to combine Columbia with a larger, nationwide software company. Accordingly, management solicited the interest of a number of software companies. Late in July 2001, Moreland Software showed an interest in Columbia. On August 3, 2001, Moreland made a formal proposal to take over Columbia's $6 million of 7½ percent first-mortgage bonds, to pay the $250,000 in taxes owed by Columbia, and to provide 40,000 shares of Moreland common stock to satisfy the remaining creditor claims. Since the Moreland stock had a market price of $75 per share, the value of the stock was $3 million. Thus, Moreland was offering $3 million of stock plus assuming $6 million of loans and $250,000 of taxes—a total of $9.25 million for assets that had a book value of $16.7 million.

Moreland's plan is shown in Table 25-5. As in most Chapter 11 plans, the secured creditors' claims are paid in full (in this case, the mortgage bonds are taken over by Moreland Software). However, the total remaining unsecured claims equal $10 million against only $3 million of Moreland stock. Thus, each unsecured creditor would be entitled to receive 30 percent before the adjustment for subordination. Before this adjustment, holders of the notes payable would receive 30 percent of their $250,000 claim, or $75,000 in stock. However, the debentures are subordinated to the notes payable, so an additional $175,000 must be allocated to notes payable. (See footnote a

[8]Reorganization plans must be submitted to the Securities and Exchange Commission (SEC) if (1) the securities of the debtor are publicly held and (2) total indebtedness exceeds $3 million. However, in recent years the only bankruptcy cases that the SEC has become involved in are those that are either precedent setting or that involve issues of national interest.

TABLE 25-5 Columbia Software Company: Reorganization Plan

Senior Claims

Taxes	$ 250,000	Paid off by Moreland
Mortgage bonds	$6,000,000	Assumed by Moreland

The reorganization plan for the remaining $10 million of liabilities, based on 40,000 shares at a price of $75 for a total market value of $3 million, or 30 percent of the remaining liabilities, is as follows:

Junior Claims (1)	Original Amount (2)	30% of Claim Amount (3)	Claim after Subordination (4)	Number of Shares of Common Stock (5)	Percentage of Original Claim Received (6)
Notes payable	$ 250,000	$ 75,000	$ 250,000[a]	3,333	100%
Unsecured creditors	2,750,000	825,000	825,000	11,000	30
Subordinated debentures	7,000,000	2,100,000	$1,925,000[a]	25,667	28
	$10,000,000	$3,000,000	$3,000,000	40,000	30%

[a]Because the debentures are subordinated to the notes payable, $250,000 − $75,000 = $175,000 must be redistributed from the debentures to the notes payable.

in Table 25-5.) In Column 5, the dollar claims of each class of debt are restated in terms of the number of shares of Moreland common stock received by each class of unsecured creditors. Finally, Column 6 shows the percentage of the original claim each group received. Of course, both the taxes and the secured creditors were paid off in full, while the stockholders received nothing.[9]

The bankruptcy court first evaluated the proposal from the standpoint of fairness. The court began by considering the value of Columbia Software as estimated by the unsecured creditors' committee and by a subgroup of debenture holders. After discussions with various experts, one group had arrived at estimated post-reorganization sales of $25 million per year. It further estimated that the profit margin on sales would equal 6 percent, thus producing estimated future annual earnings of $1.5 million.

This subgroup analyzed price/earnings ratios for comparable companies and arrived at 8 times future earnings for a capitalization factor. Multiplying 8 by $1.5 million gave an indicated equity value of the company of $12 million. This value was four times that of the 40,000 shares of Moreland stock offered for the remainder of the company. Thus, the subgroup concluded that the plan for reorganization did not meet the test of fairness. Note that under both Moreland's plan and the subgroup's plan, the holders of common stock were to receive nothing, which is one of the risks of ownership, while the holders of the first-mortgage bonds were to be assumed by Moreland, which amounts to being paid in full.

The bankruptcy judge examined management's plan for feasibility, observing that in the reorganization Moreland Software would take over Columbia's properties. The court judged that the direction and aid of Moreland would remedy the deficiencies that had troubled Columbia. Whereas the debt/assets ratio of Columbia Software had become unbalanced, Moreland has only a moderate amount of debt. After consolidation, Moreland would still have a relatively low 27 percent debt ratio.

Moreland's net income before interest and taxes had been running at a level of approximately $15 million. The interest on its long-term debt after the merger would be $1.5 million and, taking short-term borrowings into account, would total a maximum of $2 million per year. The $15 million in earnings before interest and taxes would therefore provide an interest charge coverage of 7.5 times, exceeding the norm of 5 times for the industry.

Note that the question of feasibility would have been irrelevant had Moreland offered $3 million in cash rather than in stock, and had it offered to pay off the bonds rather than take them over. It is the court's responsibility to protect the interests of Columbia's creditors. Because the creditors are being forced to take common stock or bonds guaranteed by another firm, the law requires the court to look into the feasibility of the transaction. If Moreland had made a cash offer, however, the feasibility of its own operation after the transaction was completed would not have been a concern.

Moreland Software was told of the subgroup's analysis and concern over the fairness of the plan. Further, Moreland was asked to increase the number of shares it offered. Moreland refused, and no other company offered to acquire Columbia. Because no better offer could be obtained, and since the only alternative to the plan was liquidation (with an even lower realized value), Moreland's proposal was ultimately accepted by the creditors despite some disagreement with the valuation.

One interesting aspect of this case had to do with an agency conflict between Columbia's old stockholders and its management. Columbia's management knew, when it

---

[9]We do not show it, but $365,000 of fees for Columbia's attorneys and $123,000 of fees for the creditors' committee lawyers were also deducted. The current assets shown in Table 25-4 were net of these fees. Creditors joke (often bitterly) about the "lawyers first" rule in payouts in bankruptcy cases. It is often said, with much truth, that the only winners in bankruptcy cases are the attorneys.

filed for bankruptcy, that the company was probably worth less than the amount of its debt, hence that stockholders would probably receive nothing. Indeed, that situation did materialize. If management has a primary responsibility to the stockholders, why would it file for bankruptcy knowing that the stockholders would receive nothing? First, management thought, but did not know for sure, that stockholders would receive nothing. What they were sure of was that if they did not file for bankruptcy protection, creditors would foreclose on the company's property and shut the company down, which would surely lead to liquidation and a total loss to stockholders. Also, if the company were liquidated, both management and the work force would lose their jobs, and the managers would get a very black mark on their records. Finally, Columbia's managers thought (correctly) that there was nothing they could do to protect the stockholders, so they might as well do what was best for the work force, the creditors, and themselves, and that meant realizing the most value possible for the company's assets.

Some of the stockholders felt betrayed by management—they thought management should have taken more heroic steps to protect them, regardless of the cost to other parties. One stockholder suggested that management should have sold off assets, taken the cash to Las Vegas, rolled the dice, and then, if they won, paid off the debt and had something left for stockholders, but leave the debtholders holding the bag if they lost. Actually, management had done something a bit like this in the year preceding the bankruptcy. Management realized that the company was floundering and was likely to sink under its current operating plan, and that only a "big winner" project would save the company. Therefore, they took on several very risky "bet the company" projects that had negative expected NPVs but at least some chance for high profits. Unfortunately, those projects did not work out.

Prepackaged Bankruptcies

In recent years, a new type of reorganization that combines the advantages of both the informal workout and formal Chapter 11 reorganization has become popular. This new hybrid is called a **prepackaged bankruptcy,** or **pre-pack.**[10]

In an informal workout, a debtor negotiates a restructuring with its creditors. Even though complex workouts typically involve corporate officers, lenders, lawyers, and investment bankers, workouts are still less expensive and less damaging to reputations than are Chapter 11 reorganizations. In a prepackaged bankruptcy, the debtor firm gets all, or most of, the creditors to agree to the reorganization plan *prior* to filing for bankruptcy. Then, a reorganization plan is filed along with, or shortly after, the bankruptcy petition. If enough creditors have signed on before the filing, a cramdown can be used to bring reluctant creditors along.

A logical question arises: Why would a firm that can arrange an informal reorganization want to file for bankruptcy? The three primary advantages of a prepackaged bankruptcy are (1) reduction of the holdout problem, (2) preserving creditors' claims, and (3) taxes. Perhaps the biggest benefit of a prepackaged bankruptcy is the reduction of the holdout problem—a bankruptcy filing permits a cramdown that would otherwise be impossible. By eliminating holdouts, bankruptcy forces all creditors in each class to participate on a pro rata basis, which preserves the relative value of all claimants. Also, filing for formal bankruptcy can at times have positive tax implications. First, in an informal reorganization in which the debtholders trade debt for equity, if the original equity holders end up with less than 50 percent ownership, the company loses its accumulated tax losses. In formal bankruptcy, the firm may get to keep its loss carry-

[10]For more information on prepackaged bankruptcies, see John J. McConnell and Henri Servaes, "The Economics of Pre-Packaged Bankruptcy," *Journal of Applied Corporate Finance*, Summer 1991, 93–97.

forwards. Second, in a workout, when debt worth, say, $1,000, is exchanged for debt worth, say, $500, the reduction in debt of $500 is considered to be taxable income to the corporation. However, if this same situation occurs in a Chapter 11 reorganization, the difference is not treated as taxable income.[11]

All in all, prepackaged bankruptcies make sense in many situations. If sufficient agreement can be reached among creditors through informal negotiations, a subsequent filing can solve the holdout problem and result in favorable tax treatment. For these reasons, the number of prepackaged bankruptcies has grown dramatically in recent years.

Reorganization Time and Expense

The time, expense, and headaches involved in a reorganization are almost beyond comprehension. Even in $2 to $3 million bankruptcies, many people and groups are involved: lawyers representing the company, the U.S. Bankruptcy Trustee, each class of secured creditor, the general creditors as a group, tax authorities, and the stockholders if they are upset with management. There are time limits within which things are supposed to be done, but the process generally takes at least a year and probably much longer. The company must be given time to file its plan, and creditor groups must be given time to study and seek clarifications to it and then file counterplans to which the company must respond. Also, different creditor classes often disagree among themselves as to how much each class should receive, and hearings must be held to resolve such conflicts.

Management will want to remain in business, while some well-secured creditors may want the company liquidated as quickly as possible. Often, some party's plan will involve selling the business to another concern, as was the case with Columbia Software in our earlier example. Obviously, it can take months to seek out and negotiate with potential merger candidates.

The typical bankruptcy case takes about two years from the time the company files for protection under Chapter 11 until the final reorganization plan is approved or rejected. While all of this is going on, the company's business suffers. Sales certainly won't be helped, key employees may leave, and the remaining employees will be worrying about their jobs rather than concentrating on their work. Further, management will be spending much of its time on the bankruptcy rather than running the business, and it won't be able to take any significant action without court approval, which requires filing a formal petition with the court and giving all parties involved a chance to respond.

Even if its operations do not suffer, the company's assets will surely be reduced by its own legal fees and the required court and trustee costs. Good bankruptcy lawyers charge from $200 to $400 per hour, depending on the location, so those costs are not trivial. The creditors will also be incurring legal costs. Indeed, the sound of all of those meters ticking at $200 or so an hour in a slow-moving hearing can be deafening.

Note that creditors also lose the time value of their money. A creditor with a $100,000 claim and a 10 percent opportunity cost who ends up getting $50,000 after two years would have been better off settling for $41,500 initially. When the creditor's legal fees, executive time, and general aggravation are taken into account, it might make sense to settle for $20,000 or $25,000.

Both the troubled company and its creditors know the drawbacks of formal bankruptcy, or their lawyers will inform them. Armed with a knowledge of how bankruptcy

[11]Note that in both tax situations—loss carryforwards and debt value reductions—favorable tax treatment can be available in workouts if the firm is deemed to be legally insolvent, that is, if the market value of its assets is demonstrated to be less than the face value of its liabilities.

works, management may be in a strong position to persuade creditors to accept a workout which on the surface appears to be unfair and unreasonable. Or, if a Chapter 11 case has already begun, creditors may at some point agree to settle just to stop the bleeding.

One final point should be made before closing this section. In most reorganization plans, creditors with claims of less than $1,000 are paid off in full. Paying off these "nuisance claims" does not cost much money, and it saves time and gets votes to support the plan.

Self-Test Questions

Define the following terms:

(1) Common pool problem
(2) Holdout problem
(3) Automatic stay
(4) Cramdown
(5) Fraudulent conveyance
(6) Absolute priority doctrine
(7) Relative priority doctrine
(8) Fairness
(9) Feasibility
(10) Debtor-in-possession financing
(11) Prepackaged bankruptcy

What are the advantages of a formal reorganization under Chapter 11?

What has been the recent trend regarding absolute versus relative priority doctrines?

How do courts assess the fairness of proposed reorganization plans?

How do courts assess the feasibility of proposed reorganization plans?

Why have prepackaged bankruptcies become so popular in recent years?

Liquidation in Bankruptcy

If a company is "too far gone" to be reorganized, then it must be liquidated. Liquidation should occur when the business is worth more dead than alive, or when the possibility of restoring it to financial health is remote and the creditors are exposed to a high risk of greater loss if operations are continued. Earlier we discussed assignment, which is an informal liquidation procedure. Now we consider **liquidation in bankruptcy,** which is carried out under the jurisdiction of a federal bankruptcy court.

Chapter 7 of the Federal Bankruptcy Reform Act deals with liquidation. It (1) provides safeguards against fraud by the debtor, (2) provides for an equitable distribution of the debtor's assets among the creditors, and (3) allows insolvent debtors to discharge all their obligations and thus be able to start new businesses unhampered by the burdens of prior debt. However, formal liquidation is time consuming and costly, and it extinguishes the business.

The distribution of assets in a liquidation under Chapter 7 is governed by the following priority of claims:

1. **Past-due property taxes.**
2. **Secured creditors, who are entitled to the proceeds of the sale of specific property pledged for a lien or a mortgage.** If the proceeds from the sale of the

pledged property do not fully satisfy a secured creditor's claim, the remaining balance is treated as a general creditor claim (see Item 10 below).[12]

3. **Legal fees and other expenses to administer and operate the bankrupt firm.** These costs include legal fees incurred in trying to reorganize.
4. **Expenses incurred after an involuntary case has begun but before a trustee is appointed.**
5. **Wages due workers if earned within three months prior to the filing of the petition in bankruptcy.** The amount of wages is limited to $2,000 per employee.
6. **Claims for unpaid contributions to employee pension plans that should have been paid within six months prior to filing.** These claims, plus wages in Item 5, may not exceed the $2,000-per-wage-earner limit.
7. **Unsecured claims for customer deposits.** These claims are limited to a maximum of $900 per individual.
8. **Taxes due to federal, state, county, and other government agencies.**
9. **Unfunded pension plan liabilities.** These liabilities have a claim above that of the general creditors for an amount up to 30 percent of the common and preferred equity, and any remaining unfunded pension claims rank with the general creditors.[13]
10. **General, or unsecured, creditors.** Holders of trade credit, unsecured loans, the unsatisfied portion of secured loans, and debenture bonds are classified as general creditors. Holders of subordinated debt also fall into this category, but they must turn over required amounts to the senior debt.
11. **Preferred stockholders.** These stockholders can receive an amount up to the par value of their stock.
12. **Common stockholders.** These stockholders receive any remaining funds.[14]

To illustrate how this priority system works, consider the balance sheet of Whitman Inc., shown in Table 25-6. Assets have a book value of $90 million. The claims are shown on the right-hand side of the balance sheet. Note that the debentures are subordinated to the notes payable to banks. Whitman filed for bankruptcy under Chapter

---

[12]When a firm or individual who goes bankrupt has a bank loan, the bank will attach any deposit balances. The loan agreement may stipulate that the bank has a first-priority claim on any deposits. If this is the case, the deposits are used to offset all or part of the bank loan; this is called, in legal terms, "the right of offset." In this case, the bank will not have to share the deposits with other creditors. Loan contracts often designate compensating balances as security against a loan. Even if the bank has no explicit claim against deposits, the bank will attach the deposits and hold them for the general body of creditors, including the bank itself. Without an explicit statement in the loan agreement, the bank does not receive preferential treatment with regard to attached deposits.

[13]Pension plan liabilities have a significant bearing on bankruptcy settlements. As we discuss in the Web/CD Chapter 29, pension plans may be funded or unfunded. Under a funded plan, the firm makes cash payments to an insurance company or to a trustee (generally a bank), which then uses these funds (and interest earned on them) to pay retirees' pensions. Under an unfunded plan, the firm is obligated to make payments to retirees, but it does not provide cash in advance. Many plans are actually partially funded—some money has been paid in advance, but not enough to provide full pension benefits to all employees.

If a firm goes bankrupt, the funded part of the pension plan remains intact and is available for retirees. Prior to 1974, employees had no explicit claims for unfunded pension liabilities, but under the Employees' Retirement Income Security Act of 1974 (ERISA), an amount up to 30 percent of the equity (common and preferred) is earmarked for employees' pension plans and has a priority over the general creditors, with any remaining pension claims having status equal to that of the general creditors. This means, in effect, that the funded portion of a bankrupt firm's pension plan is completely secured, but that the unfunded portion ranks somewhat above the general creditors. Obviously, unfunded pension fund liabilities should be of great concern to a firm's unsecured creditors.

[14]Note that if different classes of common stock have been issued, differential priorities may exist in stockholder claims.

TABLE 25-6 Whitman Inc.: Balance Sheet at Liquidation (Millions of Dollars)

Current assets	$80.0	Accounts payable	$20.0
Net fixed assets	10.0	Notes payable (to banks)	10.0
		Accrued wages (1,400 @ $500)	0.7
		Federal taxes	1.0
		State and local taxes	0.3
		Current liabilities	$32.0
		First mortgage	$ 6.0
		Second mortgage	1.0
		Subordinated debentures[a]	8.0
		Total long-term debt	$15.0
		Preferred stock	$ 2.0
		Common stock	26.0
		Paid-in capital	4.0
		Retained earnings	11.0
		Total equity	$43.0
Total assets	$90.0	Total liabilities and equity	$90.0

[a]The debentures are subordinated to the notes payable.

11, but since no fair and feasible reorganization could be arranged, the trustee is liquidating the firm under Chapter 7.

The assets as reported in the balance sheet are greatly overstated; they are, in fact, worth less than half the $90 million at which they are carried. The following amounts are realized on liquidation:

From sale of current assets	$28,000,000
From sale of fixed assets	5,000,000
Total receipts	$33,000,000

The distribution of proceeds from the liquidation is shown in Table 25-7. The first-mortgage holders receive the $5 million in net proceeds from the sale of fixed property, leaving $28 million available to the remaining creditors, including a $1 million unsatisfied claim of the first-mortgage holders. Next are the fees and expenses of administering the bankruptcy, which are typically about 20 percent of gross proceeds (including the bankrupt firm's own legal fees); in this example, they are assumed to be $6 million. Next in priority are wages due workers, which total $700,000, and taxes due, which amount to $1.3 million. Thus far, the total amount of claims paid from the $33 million received from the asset sale is $13 million, leaving $20 million for the general creditors. In this example, we assume that there are no claims for unpaid benefit plans or unfunded pension liabilities.

The claims of the general creditors total $40 million. Since $20 million is available, claimants will initially be allocated 50 percent of their claims, as shown in Column 3. However, the subordination adjustment requires that the subordinated debentures turn over to the notes payable all amounts received until the notes are satisfied. In this situation, the claim of the notes payable is $10 million, but only $5 million is available; the deficiency is therefore $5 million. After transfer of $4 million from the subordinated debentures, there remains a deficiency of $1 million on the notes; this amount will remain unsatisfied.

TABLE 25-7 Whitman Inc.: Distribution of Liquidation Proceeds (Millions of Dollars)

DISTRIBUTION TO PRIORITY CLAIMANTS

Proceeds from the sale of assets	$33.0
Less:	
1. First mortgage (paid from the sale of fixed assets)	5.0
2. Fees and expenses of bankruptcy	6.0
3. Wages due to workers within three months of bankruptcy	0.7
4. Taxes due to federal, state, and local governments	1.3
Funds available for distribution to general creditors	$20.0

DISTRIBUTION TO GENERAL CREDITORS

General Creditors' Claims (1)	Amount of Claim[a] (2)	Pro Rata Distribution[b] (3)	Distribution after Subordination Adjustment[c] (4)	Percentage of Original Claim Received[d] (5)
Unsatisfied portion of first mortgage	$ 1.0	$ 0.5	$ 0.5	92%
Second mortgage	1.0	0.5	0.5	50
Notes payable (to banks)	10.0	5.0	9.0	90
Accounts payable	20.0	10.0	10.0	50
Subordinated debentures	8.0	4.0	0.0	0
Total	$40.0	$20.0	$20.0	

[a]Column 2 is the claim of each class of general creditor. Total claims equal $40.0 million.

[b]From the top section of the table, we see that $20 million is available for distribution to general creditors. Since there are $40 million of general creditor claims, the pro rata distribution will be $20/$40 = 0.50, or 50 cents on the dollar.

[c]The debentures are subordinate to the notes payable, so up to $5 million could be reallocated from debentures to notes payable. However, only $4 million is available to the debentures, so this entire amount is reallocated.

[d]Column 5 shows the results of dividing the Column 4 final allocation by the original claim shown in Column 2, except for the first mortgage, where the $5 million received from the sale of fixed assets is included in the calculation.

Note that 90 percent of the bank claim is satisfied, whereas a maximum of 50 percent of other unsecured claims will be satisfied. These figures illustrate the usefulness of the subordination provision to the security to which the subordination is made.

Because no other funds remain, the claims of the holders of preferred and common stocks, as well as the subordinated debentures, are completely wiped out. Studies of the proceeds in bankruptcy liquidations reveal that unsecured creditors receive, on the average, about 15 cents on the dollar, while common stockholders generally receive nothing.

Self-Test Questions

Describe briefly the priority of claims in a formal liquidation.

What is the impact of subordination on the final allocation of proceeds from liquidation?

In general, how much do unsecured creditors receive from a liquidation? How much do stockholders receive?

Other Motivations for Bankruptcy

Normally, bankruptcy proceedings do not commence until a company has become so financially weak that it cannot meet its current obligations. However, bankruptcy law also permits a company to file for bankruptcy if its financial forecasts indicate that a continuation of current conditions would lead to insolvency. This provision was used by Continental Airlines in 1983 to break its union contract and hence lower its labor costs. Continental demonstrated to a bankruptcy court that operations under the then-current union contract would lead to insolvency in a matter of months. The company then filed a reorganization plan that included major changes in all its contracts, including its union contract. The court sided with Continental and allowed the company to abrogate its contract. Continental then reorganized as a nonunion carrier, and that reorganization turned the company from a money loser into a money maker.[15] Congress changed the law after the Continental affair to make it more difficult for companies to use bankruptcy to break union contracts, but this case did set the precedent for using bankruptcy to help head off financial problems as well as to help solve existing ones.

Bankruptcy law has also been used to hasten settlements in major product liability suits. The Manville asbestos and A. H. Robins Dalkon Shield cases are examples. In both situations, the companies were being bombarded by thousands of lawsuits, and the very existence of such huge contingent liabilities made normal operations impossible. Further, in both cases it was relatively easy to prove (1) that if the plaintiffs won, the companies would be unable to pay the full amount of the claims, (2) that a larger amount of funds would be available to the claimants if the companies continued to operate rather than liquidate, (3) that continued operations were possible only if the suits were brought to a conclusion, and (4) that a timely resolution of all the suits was impossible because of their vast number and variety. The bankruptcy statutes were used to consolidate all the suits and to reach settlements under which the plaintiffs obtained more money than they otherwise would have received, and the companies were able to stay in business. The stockholders did poorly under these plans, because most of the companies' future cash flows were assigned to the plaintiffs, but even so, the stockholders probably fared better than they would have if the suits had been concluded through the jury system.

Self-Test Question

What are some situations other than immediate financial distress that lead firms to file for bankruptcy?

Some Criticisms of Bankruptcy Laws

Although bankruptcy laws, for the most part, exist to protect creditors, many critics claim that current laws are not doing what they were intended to do. Before 1978, most bankruptcies ended quickly in liquidation. Then Congress rewrote the laws, giving companies more opportunity to stay alive, on the grounds that this was best for managers, employees, creditors, and stockholders. Before the reform, 90 percent of Chapter 11 filers were liquidated, but now that percentage is less than 80 percent, and the average time between filing and liquidation has almost doubled. Indeed, large public corporations with the ability to hire high-priced legal help can avoid, or at least delay, liquidation, often at the expense of creditors and shareholders.

Critics believe that bankruptcy is great for businesses these days—especially for consultants, lawyers, and investment bankers, who reap hefty fees during bankruptcy proceedings, and for managers, who continue to collect their salaries and bonuses as long as the business is kept alive. The problem, according to critics, is that bankruptcy courts allow cases to drag on too long, depleting assets that could be sold to pay off creditors and shareholders. Too often, quick resolution is impossible because bankruptcy judges are required to deal with issues such as labor disputes, pension plan

[15]Continental's fortunes declined again in 1990 when it was unable to successfully integrate several acquisitions, including Eastern, and the company filed for bankruptcy a second time. It emerged successfully, and in 2001 it was doing well.

funding, and environmental liability—social questions that could be solved by legislative action rather than by bankruptcy courts.

For example, LTV Corporation was in bankruptcy from 1986 to 1993, mainly because of pension disputes between the company, its workers, retirees, and the federal government. During this time, the Dallas-based conglomerate spent $162 million in legal and consulting fees, but, under the final reorganization plan, creditors got only 4 to 53 cents on the dollar, and stockholders got nothing.

Critics contend that bankruptcy judges ought to realize that some sick companies should be allowed to die—and die quickly. Maintaining companies on life support does not serve the interests of the parties the bankruptcy laws were meant to protect. One proposal for overhauling the system calls for limiting the time that companies have to file a reorganization plan. A debtor is supposed to have only 120 days, but the deadline is almost never enforced. It might make more sense to set a deadline of six months or a year and then stick to it. "Bankruptcy is like open-heart surgery—the longer you stay under the knife, the lower the chance of success," says James E. Spiotto, a creditor's lawyer with Chapman & Cutler in Chicago. "We should be seeking a quick, efficient way to give companies a fresh start."

Other critics think the entire bankruptcy system of judicial protection and supervision needs to be scrapped. Some even have proposed a kind of auction procedure, where shareholders and creditors would have the opportunity to gain control of a bankrupt company by raising the cash needed to pay the bills. The rationale here is that the market is a better judge than a bankruptcy court as to whether a company is worth more dead or alive.

Finally, note that companies operating under the protection of Chapter 11 can damage and perhaps even bankrupt their otherwise healthy competitors. To illustrate, Eastern Airlines' cash costs were low during its bankruptcy because it did not have to service its debt, and it was also generating cash by selling off assets. Eastern used its cash to advertise heavily and to cut fares, both of which siphoned off traffic from other airlines. Obviously, this hurt the other airlines and indeed led to other airline bankruptcies. Had Eastern been put down in a timely fashion, the airline industry would be a lot healthier today.

Self-Test Question

According to critics, what are some problems with the bankruptcy system?

Other Topics in Bankruptcy

Some additional insights into the reorganization and liquidation process can be gained by reviewing case histories of bankruptcies. Therefore, in the Web/CD Extension of this chapter, we discuss the Eastern Airlines and Revco bankruptcies. Also, financial analysts are constantly seeking ways to assess a firm's likelihood of going bankrupt. We discuss one method, Multiple Discriminant Analysis (MDA), in the Web/CD Extension.

Summary

This chapter discussed the main issues involved in bankruptcy and financial distress in general. The key concepts are listed below:

- The proportion of businesses that fail fluctuates with the economy, but the average liability per failure has tended to increase over time due to inflation and to an increase in the number of billion-dollar bankruptcies in recent years.

- The fundamental issue that must be addressed when a company encounters financial distress is whether it is "worth more dead than alive"; that is, would the business be more valuable if it continued in operation or if it were liquidated and sold off in pieces?
- In the case of a fundamentally sound company whose financial difficulties appear to be temporary, creditors will frequently work directly with the company, helping it to recover and reestablish itself on a sound financial basis. Such voluntary reorganization plans are called **workouts.**
- Reorganization plans usually require some type of **restructuring** of the firm's debts, involving either an **extension,** which postpones the date of required payment of past-due obligations, or a **composition,** by which the creditors voluntarily reduce their claims on the debtor or the interest rate on their claims.
- When it is obvious that a firm is worth more dead than alive, informal procedures can sometimes be used to **liquidate** the firm. **Assignment** is an informal procedure for liquidating a firm, and it usually yields creditors a larger amount than they would receive in a formal bankruptcy liquidation. However, assignments are feasible only if the firm is small and its affairs are not too complex.
- Current **bankruptcy law** consists of nine chapters, designated by Arabic numbers. For businesses, the most important chapters are **Chapter 7,** which details the procedures to be followed when liquidating a firm, and **Chapter 11,** which contains procedures for formal reorganizations.
- Since the first bankruptcy laws, most formal reorganization plans have been guided by the **absolute priority doctrine.** This doctrine holds that creditors should be compensated for their claims in a rigid hierarchical order, and that senior claims must be paid in full before junior claims can receive even a dime.
- Another position, the **relative priority doctrine,** holds that more flexibility should be allowed in a reorganization, and that a balanced consideration should be given to all claimants. In recent years, there has been a shift away from absolute priority toward relative priority. The primary effect of this shift has been to delay liquidations so as to give managements more time to rehabilitate companies in an effort to provide value to junior claimants.
- The primary role of the bankruptcy court in a reorganization is to determine the **fairness** and the **feasibility** of proposed plans of reorganization.
- Even if some creditors or stockholders dissent and do not accept a reorganization plan, the plan may still be approved by the court if the plan is deemed to be "fair and equitable" to all parties. This procedure, in which the court mandates a reorganization plan in spite of dissent, is called a **cramdown.**
- In the last few years, a new type of reorganization that combines the advantages of both the informal workout and formal Chapter 11 reorganization has become popular. This new hybrid is called a **prepackaged bankruptcy.**
- The distribution of assets in a **liquidation** under Chapter 7 of the Bankruptcy Act is governed by a specific priority of claims.

Questions

25–1 Define each of the following terms:

a. Informal restructuring; reorganization in bankruptcy
b. Assignment; liquidation in bankruptcy
c. Fairness; feasibility
d. Absolute priority doctrine; relative priority doctrine
e. Bankruptcy Reform Act of 1978; Chapter 11; Chapter 7
f. Priority of claims in liquidation

g. Extension; composition
h. Workout; cramdown
i. Prepackaged bankruptcy
j. Holdout

25–2 "A certain number of business failures is a healthy sign. If there are no failures, this is an indication (a) that entrepreneurs are overly cautious, and hence not as inventive and as willing to take risks as a healthy, growing economy requires; (b) that competition is not functioning to weed out inefficient producers; or (c) that both situations exist." Discuss this statement.

25–3 Why do creditors usually accept a plan for financial rehabilitation rather than demand liquidation of the business?

25–4 Would it be possible to form a profitable company by merging two companies, both of which are business failures? Explain.

25–5 Would it be a sound rule to liquidate whenever the liquidation value is above the value of the corporation as a going concern? Discuss.

25–6 Why do liquidations usually result in losses for the creditors or the owners, or both? Would partial liquidation or liquidation over a period limit their losses? Explain.

25–7 Are liquidations likely to be more common for public utility, railroad, or industrial corporations? Why?

Problems

25–1 *REORGANIZATION* The Verbrugge Publishing Company's 2001 balance sheet and income statement are as follows (in millions of dollars). Verbrugge and its creditors have agreed upon a voluntary reorganization plan. In this plan, each share of the $6 preferred will be exchanged for one share of $2.40 preferred with a par value of $37.50 plus one 8 percent subordinated income debenture with a par value of $75. The $10.50 preferred issue will be retired with cash.

BALANCE SHEET

Current assets	$168	Current liabilities	$ 42
Net fixed assets	153	Advance payments	78
Goodwill	15	Reserves	6
		$6 preferred stock, $112.50 par value (1,200,000 shares)	135
		$10.50 preferred stock, no par, callable at $150 (60,000 shares)	9
		Common stock, $1.50 par value (6,000,000 shares)	9
		Retained earnings	57
Total assets	$336	Total claims	$336

INCOME STATEMENT

Net sales	$540.0
Operating expense	516.0
Net operating income	$ 24.0
Other income	3.0
EBT	$ 27.0
Taxes (50%)	13.5
Net income	$ 13.5
Dividends on $6 preferred	7.2
Dividends on $10.50 preferred	0.6
Income available to common stockholders	$ 5.7

a. Construct the pro forma balance sheet assuming that reorganization takes place. Show the new preferred at its par value.
b. Construct the pro forma income statement. How much does the proposed recapitalization increase income available to common shareholders?
c. *Required earnings* is defined as the amount that is just enough to meet fixed charges (debenture interest and/or preferred dividends). What are the required pre-tax earnings before and after the recapitalization?
d. How is the debt ratio affected by the reorganization? If you were a holder of Verbrugge's common stock, would you vote in favor of the reorganization?

25–2 LIQUIDATION At the time it defaulted on its interest payments and filed for bankruptcy, the McDaniel Mining Company had the following balance sheet (in thousands of dollars). The court, after trying unsuccessfully to reorganize the firm, decided that the only recourse was liquidation under Chapter 7. Sale of the fixed assets, which were pledged as collateral to the mortgage bondholders, brought in $400,000, while the current assets were sold for another $200,000. Thus, the total proceeds from the liquidation sale were $600,000. Trustee's costs amounted to $50,000; no single worker was due more than $2,000 in wages; and there were no unfunded pension plan liabilities.

Current assets	$ 400	Accounts payable	$ 50
Net fixed assets	600	Accrued taxes	40
		Accrued wages	30
		Notes payable	180
		Total current liabilities	$ 300
		First-mortgage bonds[a]	300
		Second-mortgage bonds[a]	200
		Debentures	200
		Subordinated debentures[b]	100
		Common stock	50
		Retained earnings	(150)
Total assets	$1,000	Total claims	$1,000

[a]All fixed assets are pledged as collateral to the mortgage bonds.
[b]Subordinated to notes payable only.

a. How much will McDaniel's shareholders receive from the liquidation?
b. How much will the mortgage bondholders receive?
c. Who are the other priority claimants in addition to the mortgage bondholders? How much will they receive from the liquidation?
d. Who are the remaining general creditors? How much will each receive from the distribution before subordination adjustment? What is the effect of adjusting for subordination?

25–3 LIQUIDATION The following balance sheet represents Boles Electronics Corporation's position at the time it filed for bankruptcy (in thousands of dollars):

Cash	$ 10	Accounts payable	$ 1,600
Receivables	100	Notes payable	500
Inventories	890	Wages payable	150
		Taxes payable	50
Total current assets	$ 1,000	Total current liabilities	$ 2,300
Net plant	4,000	Mortgage bonds	2,000
Net equipment	5,000	Subordinated debentures	2,500
		Preferred stock	1,500
		Common stock	1,700
Total assets	$10,000	Total claims	$10,000

The mortgage bonds are secured by the plant, but not by the equipment. The subordinated debentures are subordinated to notes payable. The firm was unable to reorganize under Chapter 11; therefore, it was liquidated under Chapter 7. The trustee, whose legal and administrative fees amounted to $200,000, sold off the assets and received the following proceeds (in thousands of dollars):

Asset	Proceeds
Plant	$1,600
Equipment	1,300
Receivables	50
Inventories	240
Total	$3,190

In addition, the firm had $10,000 in cash available for distribution. No single wage earner had over $2,000 in claims, and there were no unfunded pension plan liabilities.

a. What is the total amount available for distribution to all claimants? What is the total of creditor and trustee claims? Will the preferred and common stockholders receive any distributions?

b. Determine the dollar distribution to each creditor and to the trustee. What percentage of each claim is satisfied?

Mini Case

See **Ch 25 Show.ppt** and **Ch 25 Mini Case.xls**.

Kimberly MacKenzie, president of Kim's Clothes Inc., a medium-sized manufacturer of women's casual clothing, is worried. Her firm has been selling clothes to Russ Brothers Department Store for more than 10 years, and she has never experienced any problems in collecting payment for the merchandise sold. Currently, Russ Brothers owes Kim's Clothes $65,000 for spring sportswear that was delivered to the store just 2 weeks ago. Kim's concern was brought about by an article that appeared in yesterday's *Wall Street Journal* that indicated that Russ Brothers was having serious financial problems. Further, the article stated that Russ Brothers' management was considering filing for reorganization, or even liquidation, with a federal bankruptcy court.

Kim's immediate concern was whether or not her firm would collect its receivables if Russ Brothers went bankrupt. In pondering the situation, Kim also realized that she knew nothing about the process that firms go through when they encounter severe financial distress. To learn more about bankruptcy, reorganization, and liquidation, Kim asked Ron Mitchell, the firm's chief financial officer, to prepare a briefing on the subject for the entire board of directors. In turn, Ron asked you, a newly hired financial analyst, to do the groundwork for the briefing by answering the following questions.

a. (1) What are the major causes of business failure?
   (2) Do business failures occur evenly over time?
   (3) Which size of firm, large or small, is more prone to business failure? Why?

b. What key issues must managers face in the financial distress process?

c. What informal remedies are available to firms in financial distress? In answering this question, define the following terms:
   (1) Workout
   (2) Restructuring
   (3) Extension
   (4) Composition
   (5) Assignment
   (6) Assignee (trustee)

d. Briefly describe U.S. bankruptcy law, including the following terms:
   (1) Chapter 11
   (2) Chapter 7
   (3) Trustee

(4) Voluntary bankruptcy
(5) Involuntary bankruptcy

e. What are the major differences between an informal reorganization and reorganization in bankruptcy? In answering this question, be sure to discuss the following items:
(1) Common pool problem
(2) Holdout problem
(3) Automatic stay
(4) Cramdown
(5) Fraudulent conveyance

f. What is a prepackaged bankruptcy? Why have prepackaged bankruptcies become more popular in recent years?

g. Briefly describe the priority of claims in a Chapter 7 liquidation.

h. Assume that Russ Brothers did indeed fail, and that it had the following balance sheet when it was liquidated (in millions of dollars):

Current assets	$40.0	Accounts payable	$10.0
Net fixed assets	5.0	Notes payable (to banks)	5.0
		Accrued wages	0.3
		Federal taxes	0.5
		State and local taxes	0.2
		Current liabilities	$16.0
		First mortgage	$ 3.0
		Second mortgage	0.5
		Subordinated debentures[a]	4.0
		Total long-term debt	$ 7.5
		Preferred stock	$ 1.0
		Common stock	13.0
		Paid-in capital	2.0
		Retained earnings	5.5
		Total equity	$21.5
Total assets	$45.0	Total claims	$45.0

[a]The debentures are subordinated to the notes payable.

The liquidation sale resulted in the following proceeds:

From sale of current assets	$14,000,000
From sale of fixed assets	2,500,000
Total receipts	$16,500,000

For simplicity, assume that there were no trustee's fees or any other claims against the liquidation proceeds. Also, assume that the mortgage bonds are secured by the entire amount of fixed assets. What would each claimant receive from the liquidation distribution?

Selected Additional References and Cases

For more information on bankruptcy costs, see

Altman, Edward I., "A Further Empirical Investigation of the Bankruptcy Cost Question," *Journal of Finance*, September 1984, 1067–1089.

Guffey, Daryl M., and William T. Moore, "Direct Bankruptcy Costs: Evidence from the Trucking Industry," *Financial Review*, May 1991, 223–235.

Warner, Jerold B., "Bankruptcy Costs: Some Evidence," *Journal of Finance*, May 1977, 337–347.

In addition to those articles cited in the chapter, the Summer 1991 issue of the Journal of Applied Corporate Finance contains the following relevant works:

Fitts, Peter, et al., "Bankruptcies, Workouts, and Turnarounds: A Roundtable Discussion," 34–61.

Gilson, Stuart C., "Managing Default: Some Evidence on How Firms Choose between Workouts and Chapter 11," 62–70.

Weiss, Lawrence A., "The Bankruptcy Code and Violations of Absolute Priority," 71–78.

The following articles and publications provide insights into various aspects of bankruptcy:

Beranek, William, Robert Boehmer, and Brooke Smith, "Much Ado about Nothing: Absolute Priority Deviations in Chapter 11," *Financial Management*, Autumn 1996, 102–109.

Betker, Brian L., "An Empirical Examination of Prepackaged Bankruptcy," *Financial Management*, Spring 1995, 3–18.

Brown, David T., "Claimholder Incentive Conflicts in Reorganization: The Role of Bankruptcy Law," *Review of Financial Studies*, 1989, 109–123.

Business Failure Record (New York: Dun & Bradstreet, Inc., updated annually).

Chatterjee, Sris, Upinder S. Dhillon, and Gabriel G. Ramirez, "Resolution of Financial Distress: Debt Restructurings via Chapter 11, Prepackaged Bankruptcies, and Workouts," *Financial Management*, Spring 1996, 5–18.

Chen, Yehning, J. Fred Weston, and Edward I. Altman, "Financial Distress and Restructuring Models," *Financial Management*, Summer 1995, 57–75.

Eberhart, Allan C., William T. Moore, and Rodney Roenfeldt, "Security Pricing and Deviations from the Absolute Priority Rule in Bankruptcy Proceedings," *Journal of Finance*, December 1990, 1457–1469.

Franks, Julian R., and Walter N. Torous, "An Empirical Investigation of U.S. Firms in Reorganization," *Journal of Finance*, July 1989, 747–769.

Harris, Richard, "The Consequences of Costly Default," *Economic Inquiry*, October 1978, 477–496.

Kaiser, Kevin M. J., "European Bankruptcy Laws: Implications for Corporations Facing Financial Distress," *Financial Management*, Autumn 1996, 67–85.

McConnell, John J., Ronald C. Lease, and Elizabeth Tashjian, "Prepacks as a Mechanism for Resolving Financial Distress," *Journal of Applied Corporate Finance*, Winter 1996, 99–106.

The following bankruptcy case can be found in the Cases in Financial Management: Dryden Request *series:*

Case 65, "Bubbling Springs Water Company," which examines both liquidation and restructuring alternatives for a firm in financial distress.

26

Mergers, LBOs, Divestitures, and Holding Companies

Early January 10, 2000, the wire services reported the proposed blockbuster merger between America Online (AOL) and Time Warner. The announcement stunned the financial markets, and it sent shockwaves throughout the investment community.

When it was announced, the deal represented the largest proposed merger ever. While described as a "merger of equals," in fact AOL acquired Time Warner. Time Warner's shareholders exchanged each of their shares for 1.5 shares of the new company, and AOL's shareholders received 55 percent of the new company's shares.

Before the announcement, AOL's equity had a market value of $160 billion versus $90 billion for Time Warner. Based on these premerger valuations, AOL's value was 64 percent of the combined companies' $250 billion value—considerably higher than the 55 percent that AOL's shareholders ended up with. This led some to conclude that AOL was paying too much for Time Warner. Indeed, in the days immediately following the announcement, Time Warner's stock rose 35 percent while AOL's fell more than 10 percent. However, others argued that AOL's stock had been overvalued prior to the merger and that its managers skillfully used their overvalued stock to buy a blue chip company with real assets, earnings, and cash flow.

The difference in the two companies' valuations was startling when you consider that Time Warner's revenues were $26.8 billion versus AOL's $4.8 billion. Clearly, AOL's 78 percent higher market value reflected the market's belief that its growth prospects were considerably greater than Time Warner's. The announced merger dramatically underscored the phenomenal growth of the Internet in recent years, and it capped a remarkable turnaround for AOL and its often underestimated CEO Stephen Case. Just five years prior to the deal, AOL's equity market value was less than $2 billion, while Time Warner's value was more than $20 billion. At that time, many thought that AOL would have a hard time surviving, and that its best prospects lay in being acquired.

Regardless of who got the best deal, the new company brings together some interesting elements. AOL, with more than 20 million subscribers, is currently the dominant Internet service provider. More than half of all U.S. customers use it to access the Internet. Combining AOL's subscriber base with Time Warner's cable franchise, AOL/Time Warner has the potential to bring high-speed broadband Internet access to many millions of households. If you add Time Warner's impressive content (which includes valuable assets such as Warner Brothers Studios, Warner Music, CNN, HBO, *Time, People, Sports Illustrated,* and *Fortune*), the merger provides an opportunity to bring together the best elements of the new and old media.

Despite the deal's remarkable upside, the combined company will still face a number of potential pitfalls. Deals that look good on paper sometimes fail miserably because of the difficulties of combining two very different cultures. AOL/Time Warner brings together an impressive management team including AOL's CEO Stephen Case and president Robert Pittman, and Time Warner's chairman Gerald Levin and vice-chairman Ted Turner. However, history has proven that talented people often have a hard time working together and managing their egos. Over time, the financial markets will determine how well this deal succeeds.

The textbook's CD-ROM contains an *Excel* file that will guide you through the chapter's calculations. The file for this chapter is ***Ch 26 Tool Kit.xls***, and we encourage you to open the file and follow along as you read the chapter.

Most corporate growth occurs by *internal expansion*, which takes place when a firm's existing divisions grow through normal capital budgeting activities. However, the most dramatic examples of growth, and often the largest increases in firms' stock prices, result from *mergers*, the first topic covered in this chapter. *Leveraged buyouts*, or *LBOs*, occur when a firm's stock is acquired by a small group of investors rather than by another operating company. Because LBOs are similar to mergers in many respects, they are also covered in this chapter. Conditions change over time, causing firms to sell off, or *divest*, major divisions to other firms that can better utilize the divested assets. Divestitures are also discussed in the chapter. Finally, we discuss the *holding company* form of organization, wherein one corporation owns the stock of one or more other companies.

Rationale for Mergers

Many reasons have been proposed by financial managers and theorists to account for the high level of U.S. merger activity. The primary motives behind corporate **mergers** are presented in this section.[1]

Synergy

The primary motivation for most mergers is to increase the value of the combined enterprise. If Companies A and B merge to form Company C, and if C's value exceeds that of A and B taken separately, then **synergy** is said to exist. Such a merger should be beneficial to both A's and B's stockholders.[2] Synergistic effects can arise from five sources: (1) *operating economies*, which result from economies of scale in management, marketing, production, or distribution; (2) *financial economies*, including lower transaction costs and better coverage by security analysts; (3) *tax effects*, where the combined enterprise pays less in taxes than the separate firms would pay; (4) *differential efficiency*, which implies that the management of one firm is more efficient and that the weaker firm's assets will be more productive after the merger; and (5) *increased market power* due to reduced competition. Operating and financial economies are socially desirable, as are mergers that increase managerial efficiency, but mergers that reduce competition are socially undesirable and illegal.[3]

AOL's merger with Time Warner was motivated by perceived synergies between the two companies. The hope is that the deal will successfully unite Time Warner's extensive content and cable distribution system with AOL's massive Internet subscriber base. One analyst has recently estimated these potential synergies to be worth about \$1 billion per year. The combination of Morgan Stanley and Dean Witter is another synergistic merger. This deal "unites Wall Street with Main Street." Morgan Stanley, an elite investment bank that specializes in underwriting securities for the world's

---

[1]As we use the term, *merger* means any combination that forms one economic unit from two or more previous ones. For legal purposes, there are distinctions among the various ways these combinations can occur, but our focus is on the fundamental economic and financial aspects of mergers.

[2]If synergy exists, then the whole is greater than the sum of the parts. Synergy is also called the "2 plus 2 equals 5 effect." The distribution of the synergistic gain between A's and B's stockholders is determined by negotiation. This point is discussed later in the chapter.

[3]In the 1880s and 1890s, many mergers occurred in the United States, and some of them were obviously directed toward gaining market power rather than increasing efficiency. As a result, Congress passed a series of acts designed to ensure that mergers are not used as a method of reducing competition. The principal acts include the Sherman Act (1890), the Clayton Act (1914), and the Celler Act (1950). These acts make it illegal for firms to combine if the combination tends to lessen competition. The acts are enforced by the antitrust division of the Justice Department and by the Federal Trade Commission.

leading corporations, joined forces with Dean Witter, which has thousands of sales representatives and 40 million retail customers. Dean Witter's brokers now distribute securities brought in by Morgan Stanley's investment bankers, and this helps both organizations in the increasingly competitive securities markets. The NationsBank/BankAmerica merger provides almost nationwide banking, and the Citicorp/Travelers merger provides one-stop shopping for financial services.

Tax Considerations

Tax considerations have stimulated a number of mergers. For example, a profitable firm in the highest tax bracket could acquire a firm with large accumulated tax losses. These losses could then be turned into immediate tax savings rather than carried forward and used in the future.[4]

Also, mergers can serve as a way of minimizing taxes when disposing of excess cash. For example, if a firm has a shortage of internal investment opportunities compared with its free cash flow, it could (1) pay an extra dividend, (2) invest in marketable securities, (3) repurchase its own stock, or (4) purchase another firm. If it pays an extra dividend, its stockholders would have to pay immediate taxes on the distribution. Marketable securities often provide a good temporary parking place for money, but they generally earn a rate of return less than that required by stockholders. A stock repurchase might result in a capital gain for the remaining stockholders. However, using surplus cash to acquire another firm would avoid all these problems, and this has motivated a number of mergers. Still, as we discuss later, the tax savings are often less than the premium paid in the acquisition. Thus, mergers motivated only by tax considerations often reduce the acquiring shareholders' wealth.

Purchase of Assets below Their Replacement Cost

Sometimes a firm will be touted as an acquisition candidate because the cost of replacing its assets is considerably higher than its market value. For example, in the early 1980s oil companies could acquire reserves cheaper by buying other oil companies than by doing exploratory drilling. Thus, Chevron acquired Gulf Oil to augment its reserves. Similarly, in the 1980s several steel company executives stated that it was cheaper to buy an existing steel company than to construct a new mill. For example, LTV (the fourth largest steel company) acquired Republic Steel (the sixth largest) to create the second largest firm in the industry.

Diversification

Managers often cite diversification as a reason for mergers. They contend that diversification helps stabilize a firm's earnings and thus benefits its owners. Stabilization of earnings is certainly beneficial to employees, suppliers, and customers, but its value to stockholders is less certain. Why should Firm A acquire Firm B to stabilize earnings when stockholders can simply buy the stocks of both firms? Indeed, research suggests that in most cases diversification does not increase the firm's value. To the contrary, many studies find that diversified firms are worth significantly less than the sum of their individual parts.[5]

---

[4]Mergers undertaken only to use accumulated tax losses would probably be challenged by the IRS. In recent years Congress has made it increasingly difficult for firms to pass along tax savings after mergers.

[5]See, for example, Philip Berger and Eli Ofek, "Diversification's Effect on Firm Value," *Journal of Financial Economics*, Vol. 37, 1995, 37–65; and Larry Lang and René Stulz, "Tobin's Q, Corporate Diversification, and Firm Performance," *Journal of Political Economy*, Vol. 102, 1994, 1248–1280.

Of course, if you were the owner-manager of a closely held firm, it might be nearly impossible to sell part of your stock to diversify. Also, selling your stock would probably lead to a large capital gains tax. So, a diversification merger might be the best way to achieve personal diversification for a privately held firm.

Managers' Personal Incentives

Financial economists like to think that business decisions are based only on economic considerations, especially maximization of firms' values. However, many business decisions are based more on managers' personal motivations than on economic analyses. Business leaders like power, and more power is attached to running a larger corporation than a smaller one. Obviously, no executive would admit that his or her ego was the primary reason behind a merger, but egos do play a prominent role in many mergers.

It has also been observed that executive salaries are highly correlated with company size—the bigger the company, the higher the salaries of its top officers. This too could cause unnecessary acquisitions.

Personal considerations deter as well as motivate mergers. After most takeovers, some managers of the acquired companies lose their jobs, or at least their autonomy. Therefore, managers who own less than 51 percent of their firms' stock look to devices that will lessen the chances of a takeover. Mergers can serve as such a device. For example, a few years ago Paramount made a bid to acquire Time Inc. Time's managers received a lot of criticism when they rejected Paramount's bid and chose instead to enter into a heavily debt-financed merger with Warner Brothers that enabled them to retain power. Such **defensive mergers** are hard to defend on economic grounds. The managers involved invariably argue that synergy, not a desire to protect their own jobs, motivated the acquisition, but observers suspect that many mergers were designed more to benefit managers than stockholders.

Breakup Value

Firms can be valued by book value, economic value, or replacement value. Takeover specialists also recognize **breakup value** as another basis for valuation. Analysts estimate a company's breakup value, which is the value of the individual parts of the firm if they were sold off separately. If this value is higher than the firm's current market value, then a takeover specialist could acquire the firm at or even above its current market value, sell it off in pieces, and earn a profit.

Self-Test Questions

Define synergy. Is synergy a valid rationale for mergers? Describe several situations that might produce synergistic gains.

Suppose your firm could purchase another firm for only half of its replacement value. Would that be a sufficient justification for the acquisition?

Discuss the pros and cons of diversification as a rationale for mergers.

What is breakup value?

Types of Mergers

Economists classify mergers into four types: (1) horizontal, (2) vertical, (3) congeneric, and (4) conglomerate. A **horizontal merger** occurs when one firm combines with another in its same line of business—the DaimlerChrysler merger is an example. An example of a **vertical merger** would be a steel producer's acquisition of one of its own suppliers, such as an iron or coal mining firm, or an oil producer's acquisition of a petrochemical firm that uses oil as a raw material. *Congeneric* means "allied in nature or action," hence a **congeneric merger** involves related enterprises but not producers of the same product (horizontal) or firms in a producer-supplier relationship (vertical). The AOL/Time Warner merger is an example. A **conglomerate merger** occurs when unrelated enterprises combine, as illustrated by Mobil Oil's acquisition of Montgomery Ward.

Operating economies (and also anticompetitive effects) are at least partially dependent on the type of merger involved. Vertical and horizontal mergers generally provide the greatest synergistic operating benefits, but they are also the ones most likely to be attacked by the Department of Justice as anticompetitive. In any event, it is useful to think of these economic classifications when analyzing prospective mergers.

Self-Test Question

What are the four economic types of mergers?

Level of Merger Activity

Five major "merger waves" have occurred in the United States. The first was in the late 1800s, when consolidations occurred in the oil, steel, tobacco, and other basic industries. The second was in the 1920s, when the stock market boom helped financial promoters consolidate firms in a number of industries, including utilities, communications, and autos. The third was in the 1960s, when conglomerate mergers were the rage. The fourth occurred in the 1980s, when LBO firms and others began using junk bonds to finance all manner of acquisitions. The fifth, which involves strategic alliances designed to enable firms to compete better in the global economy, is in progress today.

As can be seen from Table 26-1, some huge mergers have occurred in recent years.[6] In general, recent mergers have been significantly different from those of the 1980s and 1990s. Most earlier mergers were financial transactions in which buyers sought companies that were selling at less than their true values as a result of incompetent or sluggish management. If a target company could be managed better, if redundant assets could be sold, and if operating and administrative costs could be cut, profits and stock prices would rise. In contrast, most recent mergers have been strategic in nature—companies are merging to gain economies of scale or scope and thus be better able to compete in the world economy. Indeed, many recent mergers have involved companies in the financial, defense, media, computer, telecommunications, and health care industries, all of which are experiencing structural changes and intense competition.

Recent deals also differ in the way they are financed and how the target firms' stockholders are compensated. In the 1980s, cash was the preferred method of

[6] For detailed reviews of the 1980s merger wave, see Andrei Shleifer and Robert W. Vishny, "The Takeover Wave of the 1980s," *Journal of Applied Corporate Finance*, Fall 1991, 49–56; Edmund Faltermayer, "The Deal Decade: Verdict on the '80s," *Fortune*, August 26, 1991, 58–70; and "The Best and Worst Deals of the '80s: What We Learned from All Those Mergers, Acquisitions, and Takeovers," *Business Week*, January 15, 1990, 52–57.

TABLE 26-1 The Ten Largest Completed Mergers Worldwide through January 10, 2001

Buyer	Target	Completion Date	Value (Billions, U.S.$)
Vodafone AirTouch	Mannesmann	April 12, 2000	$161
Pfizer	Warner-Lambert	June 19, 2000	116
America Online	Time Warner	January 11, 2001	106
Exxon	Mobil	November 30, 1999	81
Glaxo Wellcome	SmithKline Beecham	December 27, 2000	74
SBC Communications	Ameritech	October 8, 1999	72
VodafoneGroup	Airtouch	June 30, 1999	69
Bell Atlantic	GTE	May 30, 2000	60
Total Fina	Elf Aquitaine	February 9, 2000	54
Viacom	CBS	May 4, 2000	50

Source: "A Look at the Top 10 Global Mergers," *Associated Press Newswires*. January 11, 2001.

payment, because large cash payments could convince even the most reluctant shareholder to approve the deal. Moreover, the cash was generally obtained by borrowing, leaving the consolidated company with a heavy debt burden, which often led to difficulties. In recent years, stock has replaced borrowed cash as the merger currency for two reasons: (1) Many of the 1980s mergers were financed with junk bonds that later went into default. These defaults, along with the demise of Drexel Burnham, the leading junk bond dealer, have made it difficult to arrange debt-financed mergers. (2) Most recent mergers have been strategic—as between MCI WorldCom and Sprint, AT&T and MediaOne Group, and AOL and Time Warner—where the companies' managers realized that they needed one another. Most of these mergers have been friendly, and stock swaps are easier to arrange in friendly mergers than in hostile ones. Also, both sets of managers have been concerned about the postmerger financial strength of the consolidated company, and the surviving company will obviously be stronger if the deal is financed with stock rather than debt.

Although most recent large mergers have generally been stock-for-stock, many of the smaller mergers have been for cash. Even here, though, things have been different. In the 1980s, companies typically borrowed to get the money to finance cash acquisitions. In recent years, corporate cash flows have been very high, so companies have been able to pay for their smaller acquisitions out of cash flow.

There has also been an increase in cross-border mergers. Many of these mergers have been motivated by large shifts in the value of the world's leading currencies. For example, in the early 1990s, the dollar was weak relative to the yen and the mark. The decline in the dollar made it easier for Japanese and German acquirers to buy U.S. corporations. For example, Daimler-Benz acquired Chrysler and Deutschebank has made an offer for J. P. Morgan.

Self-Test Questions

What five major "merger waves" have occurred in the United States?
What are some reasons for the current wave?

Hostile versus Friendly Takeovers

In the vast majority of merger situations, one firm (generally the larger of the two) simply decides to buy another company, negotiates a price with the management of the target firm, and then acquires the target company. Occasionally, the acquired firm will initiate the action, but it is much more common for a firm to seek acquisitions than to seek to be acquired.[7] Following convention, we call a company that seeks to acquire another firm the **acquiring company** and the one that it seeks to acquire the **target company.**

Once an acquiring company has identified a possible target, it must (1) establish a suitable price, or range of prices, and (2) decide on the terms of payment—will it offer cash, its own common stock, bonds, or some combination? Next, the acquiring firm's managers must decide how to approach the target company's managers. If the acquiring firm has reason to believe that the target's management will approve the merger, then one CEO will call the other, propose a merger, and then try to work out suitable terms. If an agreement is reached, the two management groups will issue statements to their stockholders indicating that they approve the merger, and the target firm's management will recommend to its stockholders that they agree to the merger. Generally, the stockholders are asked to *tender* (or send in) their shares to a designated financial institution, along with a signed power of attorney that transfers ownership of the shares to the acquiring firm. The target firm's stockholders then receive the specified payment, either common stock of the acquiring company (in which case the target company's stockholders become stockholders of the acquiring company), cash, bonds, or some mix of cash and securities. This is a **friendly merger.**

The acquisition of Celebrity Cruise Lines by Royal Caribbean International typifies a friendly merger. After secret negotiations between the two boards, an agreement was announced at a joint press conference. The acquisition was fought briefly by Carnival Corporation, which made its own offer for Celebrity, but Royal Caribbean increased its offer by $15 million, and the deal was sealed. The merger was approved by the shareholders of both companies, and no antitrust issues were raised. Therefore, the merger was completed just a few months after the initial announcement. Royal Caribbean paid $515 million in cash and common stock for Celebrity, and it also assumed $800 million of Celebrity's debt.

The acquisition gives Royal Caribbean, which operated Celebrity as a separate brand, instant access to the upscale cruise market. Furthermore, Celebrity now has economies of scale that it could not have achieved operating independently. Mergers in the highly competitive cruise industry have been commonplace in recent years, and many observers predict that only a handful of companies will survive. Royal Caribbean is expected to have about 30,000 berths, but Carnival, the world's largest cruise line, will still dominate the industry with about 50,000.

Often, however, the target company's management resists the merger. Perhaps they feel that the price offered is too low, or perhaps they simply want to keep their jobs. In either case, the acquiring firm's offer is said to be **hostile** rather than friendly, and the acquiring firm must make a direct appeal to the target firm's stockholders. In a hostile merger, the acquiring company will again make a **tender offer,** and again it will ask the stockholders of the target firm to tender their shares in exchange for the offered price. This time, though, the target firm's managers will urge stockholders not to tender their shares, generally stating that the price offered (cash, bonds, or stocks in the acquiring firm) is too low.

While most mergers are friendly, recently there have been a number of interesting cases in which high-profile firms have attempted hostile takeovers. For example,

[7]However, if a firm is in financial difficulty, if its managers are elderly and do not think that suitable replacements are on hand, or if it needs the support (often the capital) of a larger company, then it may seek to be acquired. Thus, when a number of Texas, Ohio, and Maryland financial institutions were in trouble in the 1980s, they lobbied to get their state legislatures to pass laws that would make it easier for them to be acquired. Out-of-state banks then moved in to help salvage the situation and minimize depositor losses.

Warner-Lambert tried to fight off a hostile bid by Pfizer, but was unsuccessful. Looking overseas, Olivetti successfully conducted a hostile takeover of Telecom Italia, and in another telecommunications merger Britain's Vodafone AirTouch made a hostile bid and acquired its German rival, Mannesmann AG.

Perhaps not surprisingly, hostile bids often fail. The battle between Shamrock Holdings and Polaroid illustrates a failed hostile merger attempt. It began when Polaroid's stock was trading in the low \$30s. At the time, many analysts had declared that Polaroid was a likely takeover candidate because of its sluggish performance but strong brand name. Also, Polaroid was expected to receive a substantial settlement from its successful suit against Eastman Kodak, which had been found guilty of violating Polaroid's instant camera patents.

Shamrock Holdings, the investment vehicle of the Roy E. Disney family, proposed a friendly takeover, was rebuffed, and then made a \$45-per-share hostile tender offer. Polaroid responded to the unwanted offer (1) by selling a block of its stock to a newly established employee stock ownership plan (ESOP), (2) by selling another block to a friendly investor (a *white squire*), and (3) by buying back 22 percent of its outstanding shares at \$50 a share. To finance all of this, Polaroid borrowed \$536 million from banks. Additionally, Polaroid announced that it was restructuring its operations by cutting its work force by 15 percent, and that this move would boost profits. Shamrock responded to these actions (1) by initiating a **proxy fight** to elect a new slate of officers at Polaroid and (2) by filing a court suit challenging the legitimacy of Polaroid's defensive maneuvers.

After nine months of heated exchange, an accord was reached. Polaroid agreed to pay Shamrock \$20 million in compensation for expenses incurred in the battle, and Shamrock signed an agreement promising not to seek control of Polaroid for 10 years. Also, Polaroid agreed to spend \$5 million advertising on Shamrock's radio and television stations and to distribute to shareholders much of its pending award from Kodak. Although defeated, Shamrock ended up making about \$35 million before taxes, considering both the cash settlement and the price increase on the Polaroid shares it owned. Polaroid ended up with more debt and less cash. Polaroid's president and CEO said, "The fundamental changes and initiatives put in place during this period made us stronger, despite the pressure." (Note: In the fall of 2000, Polaroid's stock was selling for \$8, substantially below the \$45 offered several years earlier. Meanwhile, the market as measured by the Dow Jones industrials had more than doubled. Were Polaroid's shareholders well served by its managers' resistance to the Shamrock takeover?)

The battle of Ingersoll-Rand for Clark Equipment illustrates a hostile takeover that succeeded. The battle began when Ingersoll-Rand, an industrial machinery maker, approached Clark, a construction equipment manufacturer, with a proposal to negotiate a friendly acquisition. After Clark's management rebuffed the proposal, Ingersoll-Rand announced a hostile, all-cash tender offer of \$77 per share for Clark's stock. The shares, which were selling for just over \$50 prior to the offer, immediately jumped to \$83 in anticipation of a competing bidder at a higher price. Clark's board rejected the offer, but in view of the high price set on the bid, the board came under intense pressure to negotiate a deal. Adding to the pressure was the fact that Clark, unlike most companies, elected all of its directors each year, so the entire seven-member board ran the risk of being ousted at the next shareholder meeting—only a month away. With the pressure mounting, Clark's board agreed to a sweetened \$86-per-share deal only one week after the hostile tender offer was launched.

The Clark acquisition illustrates three points. First, an all-cash offer that is high enough will generally overcome any resistance by the target firm's management. Second, and this appears to be a trend in the current merger wave—strategic buyers often begin the hostile bidding process with a "preemptive" or "blowout" bid. The idea here is to offer such a high premium over the preannouncement price that no other bidders will be willing to jump into the fray and the target company's board cannot simply reject the bid. Third, if a hostile bid is eventually accepted by the target's board, the deal ends up as "friendly," regardless of the acrimony during the hostile phase.

IBM is reported to have negotiated with Lotus for almost two years before launching its hostile tender offer. The week before the offer was announced, Lotus's stock sold for $30 per share. IBM offered $60 per share, a 100 percent premium. IBM decided to make a preemptive bid, one so high that Lotus's stockholders would tender their stock and that no "white knight" could match or exceed. IBM had a cash hoard in excess of $10 billion, so it was unlikely that its bid could be stopped. Lotus's board agreed to the takeover at a price of $64 per share, so again, a hostile offer ended up as a friendly merger.

Self-Test Question

What's the difference between a hostile and a friendly merger?

Merger Regulation

Prior to the mid-1960s, friendly acquisitions generally took place as simple exchange-of-stock mergers, and a proxy fight was the primary weapon used in hostile control battles. However, in the mid-1960s corporate raiders began to operate differently. First, it took a long time to mount a proxy fight—raiders had to first request a list of the target company's stockholders, be refused, and then get a court order forcing management to turn over the list. During that time, the target's management could think through and then implement a strategy to fend off the raider. As a result, management won most proxy fights.

Then raiders began saying to themselves, "If we could bring the decision to a head quickly, before management can take countermeasures, that would greatly increase our probability of success." That led the raiders to turn from proxy fights to tender offers, which had a much shorter response time. For example, the stockholders of a company whose stock was selling for $20 might be offered $27 per share and be given two weeks to accept. The raider, meanwhile, would have accumulated a substantial block of the shares in open market purchases, and additional shares might have been purchased by institutional friends of the raider who promised to tender their shares in exchange for the tip that a raid was to occur.

Faced with a well-planned raid, managements were generally overwhelmed. The stock might actually be worth more than the offered price, but management simply did not have time to get this message across to stockholders or to find a competing bidder. This situation seemed unfair, so Congress passed the Williams Act in 1968. This law had two main objectives: (1) to regulate the way acquiring firms can structure takeover offers and (2) to force acquiring firms to disclose more information about their offers. Basically, Congress wanted to put target managements in a better position to defend against hostile offers. Additionally, Congress believed that shareholders needed easier access to information about tender offers—including information on any securities that might be offered in lieu of cash—in order to make rational tender-versus-don't-tender decisions.

The Williams Act placed the following four restrictions on acquiring firms: (1) Acquirers must disclose their current holdings and future intentions within 10 days of amassing at least 5 percent of a company's stock. (2) Acquirers must disclose the source of the funds to be used in the acquisition. (3) The target firm's shareholders must be allowed at least 20 days to tender their shares; that is, the offer must be "open" for at least 20 days. (4) If the acquiring firm increases the offer price during the 20-day open period, all shareholders who tendered prior to the new offer must receive the higher price. In total, these restrictions were intended to reduce the acquiring firm's ability to surprise management and to stampede target shareholders into accepting an inadequate offer. Prior to the Williams Act, offers were generally made on a first-come, first-served basis, and they were often accompanied by an implicit threat to lower the bid price after 50 percent of the shares were in hand. The legislation also gave the target more time to mount a defense, and it gave rival bidders and white knights a chance to enter the fray and thus help a target's stockholders obtain a better price.

Many states have also passed laws designed to protect firms in their states from hostile takeovers. At first, these laws focused on disclosure requirements, but by the late 1970s several states had enacted takeover statutes so restrictive that they virtually precluded hostile takeovers. In 1979, MITE Corporation, a Delaware firm, made a hostile tender offer for Chicago Rivet and Machine Co., a publicly held Illinois corporation. Chicago Rivet sought protection under the Illinois Business Takeover Act. The constitutionality of the Illinois act was contested, and the U.S. Supreme Court found the law unconstitutional. The court ruled that the market for securities is a national market, and even though the issuing firm was incorporated in Illinois, the state of Illinois could not regulate interstate securities transactions.

The Illinois decision effectively eliminated the first generation of state merger regulations. However, the states kept trying to protect their state-headquartered companies, and in 1987 the U.S. Supreme Court upheld an Indiana law that radically changed the rules of the takeover game. Specifically, the Indiana law first defined "control shares" as enough shares to give an investor 20 percent of the vote. It went on to state that when an investor buys control shares, those shares can be voted only after approval by a majority of "disinterested shareholders," defined as those who are neither officers nor inside directors of the company, nor associates of the raider. The law also gives the buyer of control shares the right to insist that a shareholders' meeting be called within 50 days to decide whether the shares may be voted. The Indiana law dealt a major blow to raiders, mainly because it slows down the action. Delaware (the state in which most large companies are incorporated) later passed a similar bill, as did New York and a number of other important states.

The new state laws also have some features that protect target stockholders from their own managers. Included are limits on the use of golden parachutes, onerous debt-financing plans, and some types of takeover defenses. Because these laws do not regulate tender offers per se, but rather govern the practices of firms in the state, they have withstood all legal challenges to date. But when companies such as IBM offer 100 percent premiums for companies such as Lotus, it is hard for any defense to hold them off.

Self-Test Questions

Is there a need to regulate mergers? Explain.

Do the states play a role in merger regulation, or is it all done at the national level?

Merger Analysis

In theory, merger analysis is quite simple. The acquiring firm simply performs an analysis to value the target company and then determines whether the target can be bought at that value or, preferably, for less than the estimated value. The target company, on the other hand, should accept the offer only if the price exceeds either its value if it continued to operate independently or the price it can get from some other bidder. Theory aside, however, some difficult issues are involved. In this section, we first discuss valuing the target firm, which is the initial step in a merger analysis. Then we discuss setting the bid price and postmerger control. In the next section, we discuss structuring the takeover bid.

Valuing the Target Firm

Several methodologies are used to value target firms, but we will confine our discussion to the two most common: (1) the discounted cash flow approach and (2) the market multiple method. However, regardless of the valuation methodology, it is crucial to recognize two facts. First, the target company typically will not continue to operate as a separate entity, but will become part of the acquiring firm's portfolio of assets. Therefore, changes in operations will affect the value of the business and must be considered in the analysis. Second, the goal of merger valuation is to value the target firm's equity, because a firm is acquired from its owners, not from its creditors. Thus, although we use the phrase "valuing the firm," our focus is on the value of the equity rather than on total value.

Discounted Cash Flow Analysis To apply the discounted cash flow (DCF) method, two key items are needed: (1) pro forma statements that forecast the incremental equity cash flows expected to result from the merger and (2) a discount rate, or cost of capital, to apply to these projected cash flows.

See ***Ch 26 Tool Kit.xls*** for all calculations.

Pro Forma Cash Flow Statements Obtaining accurate postmerger cash flow forecasts is by far the most important task in the DCF approach. In a pure **financial merger,** in which no synergies are expected, the incremental postmerger cash flows are simply the expected cash flows of the target firm. In an **operating merger,** where the two firms' operations are to be integrated, forecasting future cash flows is more difficult.

Table 26-2 shows the projected cash flow statements for Apex Corporation, which is being considered as a target by Hightech, a large technology company. The projected data are for the postmerger period, and all synergistic effects have been included. Hightech would assume Apex's existing debt and would maintain its current capital structure. Both Hightech and Apex have a 40 percent marginal federal-plus-state tax rate.

Lines 1 through 4 of the table show the operating information that Hightech expects for the Apex subsidiary if the merger takes place, and Line 5 contains the earnings before interest and taxes (EBIT) for each year. Unlike a typical capital budgeting analysis, a merger analysis usually *does* incorporate interest expense into the cash flow forecast, as shown on Line 6. This is done for three reasons: (1) acquiring firms often assume the debt of the target firm, so old debt at different coupon rates is often part of the deal; (2) the acquisition is often financed partially by debt; and (3) if the subsidiary is to grow in the future, new debt will have to be issued over time to support the expansion. Thus, debt associated with a merger is typically more complex than the single issue of new debt associated with a normal capital project, and the easiest way to properly account for the complexities of merger debt is to specifically include each year's expected interest expense in the cash flow forecast. Therefore, we are using what is called the **equity residual method** to value the target firm. Here the estimated net cash flows are a residual that belongs solely to the acquiring firm's shareholders. Therefore, they should be discounted at the cost of equity. This is in contrast to the corporate valuation model of Chapter 12, where the free cash flows (which belong to all investors, not just shareholders) are discounted at the WACC. Both methods lead to the same estimate of equity value when applied correctly, but the equity residual method is used most often in mergers.

TABLE 26-2 Projected Postmerger Cash Flow Statements for the Apex Subsidiary as of December 31 (Millions of Dollars)

	2002	2003	2004	2005	2006
1. Net sales	$105.0	$126.0	$151.0	$174.0	$191.0
2. Cost of goods sold	80.0	94.0	111.0	127.0	136.0
3. Selling and administrative expenses	10.0	12.0	13.0	15.0	16.0
4. Depreciation	8.0	8.0	9.0	9.0	10.0
5. EBIT	$ 7.0	$ 12.0	$ 18.0	$ 23.0	$ 29.0
6. Interest[a]	3.0	4.0	5.0	6.0	7.0
7. EBT	$ 4.0	$ 8.0	$ 13.0	$ 17.0	$ 22.0
8. Taxes (40%)[b]	1.6	3.2	5.2	6.8	8.8
9. Net income	$ 2.4	$ 4.8	$ 7.8	$ 10.2	$ 13.2
10. Plus depreciation	8.0	8.0	9.0	9.0	10.0
11. Cash flow	$ 10.4	$ 12.8	$ 16.8	$ 19.2	$ 23.2
12. Less retentions needed for growth[c]	4.0	4.0	7.0	9.0	12.0
13. Plus horizon value[d]					126.3
14. Net cash flow to Hightech's shareholders[e]	$ 6.4	$ 8.8	$ 9.8	$ 10.2	$137.5

[a]Interest payments are estimates based on Apex's existing debt, plus additional debt required to finance growth.

[b]Hightech will file a consolidated tax return after the merger. Thus, the taxes shown here are the full corporate taxes attributable to Apex's operations: there will be no additional taxes on any cash flows passed from Apex to Hightech.

[c]Some of the cash flows generated by the Apex subsidiary after the merger must be retained to finance asset replacements and growth, while some will be transferred to Hightech to pay dividends on its stock or for redeployment within the corporation. These retentions are net of any additional debt used to help finance growth.

[d]Apex's available cash flows are expected to grow at a constant 6 percent rate after 2006. The value of all post-2006 cash flows as of December 31, 2006, is estimated by use of the constant growth model to be $126.3 million:

$$V_{2006} = \frac{CF_{2007}}{k_c - g} = \frac{(\$23.2 - \$12.0)(1.06)}{0.154 - 0.06} = \$126.3 \text{ million.}$$

In the next section, we discuss the estimated 15.4 percent cost of equity. The $126.3 million is the PV at the end of 2006 of the stream of cash flows for Year 2007 and thereafter.

[e]These are the net cash flows projected to be available to Hightech by virtue of the acquisition. The cash flows could be used for dividend payments to Hightech's stockholders, to finance asset expansion in Hightech's other divisions and subsidiaries, and so on.

Line 7 contains the earnings before taxes (EBT), and Line 8 gives taxes based on Hightech's 40 percent marginal rate. Line 9 lists each year's net income, and depreciation is added back on Line 10 to obtain each year's cash flow as shown on Line 11. Since some of Apex's assets will wear out or become obsolete, and since Hightech plans to expand the Apex subsidiary should the acquisition occur, some equity funds must be retained and reinvested in the business. These retentions, which are not available for transfer to the parent, are shown on Line 12. These retentions are net of any new debt raised to help finance the new assets. Finally, we have projected only five years of cash flows, but Hightech would likely operate the Apex subsidiary for many years—in theory, forever. Therefore, we applied the constant growth model to the 2006 cash flow to estimate the value of all cash flows beyond 2006. (See Note d to Table 26-2.) This horizon, or continuing, value represents Apex's projected value at the end of the explicit forecast horizon (2006), and it is shown on Line 13.

The net cash flows shown on Line 14 would be available to Hightech's stockholders, and they are the basis of the valuation.[8] Of course, the postmerger cash flows are

[8]We purposely kept the cash flows relatively simple to help focus on key issues. In an actual merger valuation, the cash flows would be much more complex, normally including such items as additional capital furnished by the acquiring firm, tax loss carry-forwards, tax effects of plant and equipment valuation adjustments, and cash flows from the sale of some of the subsidiary's assets.

extremely difficult to estimate, and in a complete merger valuation, just as in a complete capital budgeting analysis, sensitivity, scenario, and simulation analyses should be conducted. Indeed, in a friendly merger the acquiring firm would send a team consisting of literally dozens of financial analysts, accountants, engineers, and so forth, to the target firm's headquarters. They would go over its books, estimate required maintenance expenditures, set values on assets such as real estate and petroleum reserves, and the like. Such an investigation, which is called *due diligence*, is an essential part of any merger analysis.

Estimating the Discount Rate The bottom-line net cash flows shown on Line 14 are after interest and taxes, hence they accrue to equity. Therefore, they should be discounted at the cost of equity rather than at the overall cost of capital. Further, the discount rate used should reflect the riskiness of the cash flows in the table. The most appropriate discount rate is Apex's cost of equity, not that of either Hightech or the consolidated postmerger firm.

Apex is a publicly traded company, so we can assess directly its market risk. Apex's market-determined premerger beta was 1.20. Because the merger would not change Apex's capital structure or tax rate, its postmerger beta would remain at 1.20. Although we will not illustrate it here, Hightech could perform a risk analysis on the Table 26-2 cash flows just as it does on any set of capital budgeting flows. Sensitivity analysis, scenario analysis, and/or Monte Carlo simulation could be used to give Hightech's management a feel for the risks involved with the acquisition.

We use the Capital Asset Pricing Model to estimate Apex's postmerger cost of equity. If the risk-free rate is 7 percent and the market risk premium is 7 percent, then Apex's cost of equity, k_s, after the merger with Hightech, would be about 15.4 percent.[9]

$$k_s = k_{RF} + (RP_M)b = 7\% + (7\%)1.20 = 15.4\%.$$

Valuing the Cash Flows The current value of Apex to Hightech's shareholders is the present value of the cash flows expected from Apex, discounted at 15.4 percent (in millions of dollars):

$$V_{2001} = \frac{\$6.4}{(1.154)^1} + \frac{\$8.8}{(1.154)^2} + \frac{\$9.8}{(1.154)^3} + \frac{\$10.2}{(1.154)^4} + \frac{\$137.5}{(1.154)^5} \approx \$91.5.$$

Thus, the value to Hightech's shareholders is $91.5 million.

Note that in a merger analysis, the value of the target consists of the target's premerger value plus any value created by operating or financial synergies. In this example, we held the target's capital structure and tax rate constant. Therefore, the only synergies were operating synergies, and these effects were incorporated into the forecasted cash flows. If there had been financial synergies, the analysis would have to be modified to reflect this added value. We show such an example in a later section.

---

[9]In this example, we used the Capital Asset Pricing Model to estimate Apex's cost of equity, and thus we assumed that investors require a premium for market risk only. We could have also conducted a corporate risk analysis, in which the relevant risk would be the contribution of Apex's cash flows to the total risk of the postmerger firm.

In actual merger situations among large firms, companies almost always hire an investment banker to help develop valuation estimates. For example, when General Electric acquired Utah International, GE hired Morgan Stanley to determine Utah's value. We discussed the valuation process with the Morgan Stanley analyst in charge of the appraisal, and he confirmed that they applied all of the standard procedures discussed in this chapter. Note, though, that merger analysis, like the analysis of any other complex issue, requires judgment, and people's judgments differ as to how much weight to give to different methods in any given situation.

WWW

A video clip entitled "T. Boone Pickens on White Knights," which discusses mergers and takeovers, is available at Ohio State University's web site at **http:www.cob.ohio-state.edu/~fin/clips.htm**. The clip requires a QuickTime video player for either Windows or Macintosh machines (which you download for free over the Internet at **http:www.quicktime.apple.com/sw/**). One caveat is that the video clip is in excess of 5 MB in size and should therefore only be accessed with a rapid Internet connection.

Market Multiple Analysis The second method of valuing a target company is **market multiple analysis,** which applies a market-determined multiple to net income, earnings per share, sales, book value, or, for businesses such as cable TV or cellular telephone systems, the number of subscribers. While the DCF method applies valuation concepts in a precise manner, focusing on expected cash flows, market multiple analysis is more judgmental. To illustrate the concept, note that Apex's forecasted net income is \$2.4 million in 2002, and it rises to \$13.2 million in 2006, for an average of \$7.7 million over the five-year forecast period. The average P/E ratio for publicly traded companies similar to Apex is 12.

To estimate Apex's value using the market P/E multiple approach, simply multiply its \$7.7 million average net income by the market multiple of 12 to obtain the value of \$7.7(12) = \$92.4 million. This is the equity, or ownership, value of the firm. Note that we used the average net income over the coming five years to value Apex. The market P/E multiple of 12 is based on the current year's income of comparable companies, but Apex's current income does not reflect synergistic effects or managerial changes that will be made. By averaging future net income, we are attempting to capture the value added by Hightech to Apex's operations.

Note that measures other than net income can be used in the market multiple approach. For example, another commonly used measure is *earnings before interest, taxes, depreciation, and amortization (EBITDA)*. The EBITDA multiple is the total value of a company (the market value of equity plus debt) divided by EBITDA. This multiple is based on total value, since EBITDA measures the entire firm's performance. The EBITDA market multiple is the average EBITDA multiple for similar publicly traded companies. Multiplying the target company's EBITDA by the market multiple gives an estimate of the target's total value. To find the target's estimated stock price per share, subtract debt from total value, and then divide by the number of shares of stock.

As noted above, in some businesses such as cable TV and cellular telephone, an important element in the valuation process is the number of customers a company has. The acquirer has an idea of the cost required to obtain a new customer and the average cash flow per customer. For example, telephone companies have been paying about \$2,000 per customer for cellular operators. Managed care companies such as HMOs have applied similar logic in acquisitions, basing their valuations on the number of people insured. Some Internet companies have been valued by the number of "eyeballs," which is the number of hits on the site.

Setting the Bid Price

Under the acquisition plan, Hightech will assume Apex's debt, but it will not issue additional debt at the time of the acquisition. Using the DCF valuation results, \$91.5 million is the most Hightech should pay for Apex's stock. If it pays more, then Hightech's own value will be diluted. On the other hand, if Hightech can get Apex for less than \$91.5 million, Hightech's stockholders will gain value. Therefore, Hightech will bid something less than \$91.5 million when it makes an offer for Apex.

Figure 26-1 graphs the merger situation. The \$91.5 million is shown as a point on the horizontal axis, and it is the maximum price that Hightech can afford to pay. If Hightech pays less, say, \$81.5 million, then its stockholders will gain \$10 million from the merger, while if it pays more, its stockholders will lose. What we have, then, is a 45-degree line that cuts the X axis at \$91.5 million, and that line shows how much Hightech's stockholders can expect to gain or lose at different acquisition prices.

Now consider the target company, Apex. It has 10 million shares of stock that sell for \$6.25, so its equity value as an independent operating company is presumably \$62.5 million. [In making this statement, we assume (1) that the company is being operated as well as possible by its present management, and (2) that the \$6.25 market

FIGURE 26-1 A View of Merger Analysis (Millions of Dollars)

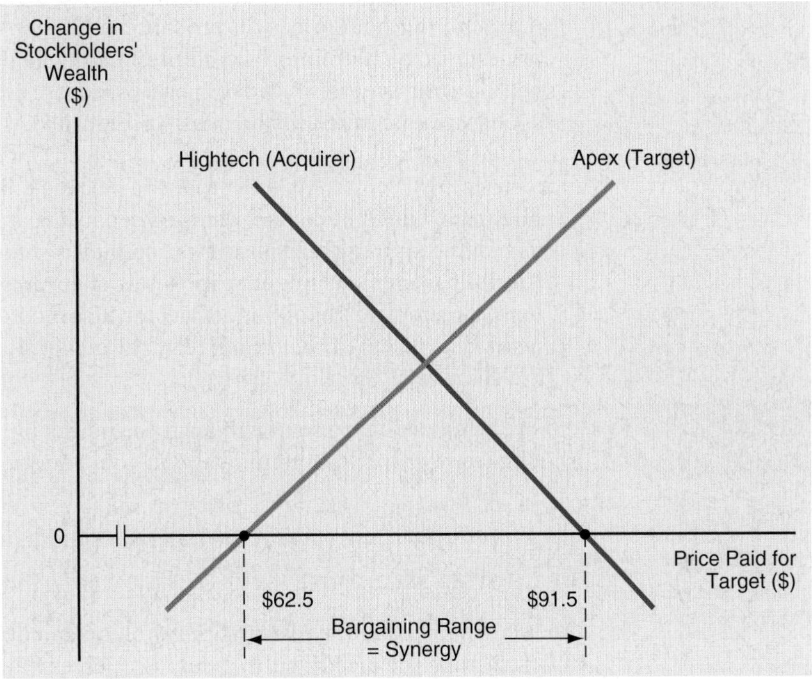

price per share does not include a "speculative merger premium" in addition to the PV of its operating cash flows.] If Apex is acquired at a price greater than $62.5 million, its stockholders will gain value, while they will lose value at any lower price. Thus, we can draw another 45-degree line, this one with an upward slope, to show how the merger price affects Apex's stockholders.

The difference between $62.5 and $91.5 million, or $29.0 million, represents synergistic benefits expected from the merger. Here are some points to note:

1. If there were no synergistic benefits, the maximum bid would be equal to the current value of the target company. The greater the synergistic gains, the greater the gap between the target's current price and the maximum the acquiring company could pay.
2. The greater the synergistic gains, the more likely a merger is to be consummated.
3. The issue of how to divide the synergistic benefits is critically important. Obviously, both parties will want to get as much as possible. In our example, if Apex's management knew the maximum price that Hightech could pay, it would argue for a price close to $91.5 million. Hightech, on the other hand, would try to get Apex at a price as close to $62.5 million as possible.
4. Where, within the $62.5 to $91.5 million range, will the actual price be set? The answer depends on a number of factors, including whether Hightech offers to pay with cash or securities, the negotiating skills of the two management teams, and, most importantly, the bargaining positions of the two parties as determined by fundamental economic conditions. To illustrate the latter point, suppose there are many companies similar to Apex that Hightech could acquire, but no company other than Hightech that could gain synergies by acquiring Apex. In this case, Hightech would probably make a relatively low, take-it-or-leave-it offer, and Apex would probably take it because some gain is better than none. On the other hand,

if Apex has some unique technology or other asset that many companies want, then once Hightech announces its offer, others will probably make competing bids, and the final price will probably be close to or even above \$91.5 million. A price above \$91.5 million would presumably be paid by some other company that had a better synergistic fit or, perhaps, whose management was more optimistic about Apex's cash flow potential. In Figure 26-1, this situation would be represented by a line parallel to that for Hightech but shifted to the right of the Hightech line.

5. Hightech would, of course, want to keep its maximum bid secret, and it would plan its bidding strategy carefully. If it thought that other bidders would emerge, or that Apex's management might resist in order to preserve their jobs, it might make a high "preemptive" bid in hopes of scaring off competing bids and/or management resistance. On the other hand, it might make a low-ball bid in hopes of "stealing" the company.

We will have more to say about these points in the sections that follow, and you should keep Figure 26-1 in mind as you go through the rest of the chapter.

Analysis of the Apex Acquisition with a Change in Capital Structure

Apex currently has equity worth \$62.5 million and debt of \$27 million, giving it a capital structure financed with about 30 percent debt: \$27.0/(\$62.5 + \$27.0) = 0.30 = 30%. If Hightech decides to increase Apex's capital structure to about 40 percent after the acquisition, this will change the cash flow, the discount rate, and the bid price.

The Effect on Cash Flows to Hightech's Shareholders With more debt, the interest payments will be higher than those shown in Table 26-2, which decreases the cash flows shown in Line 11. However, as the acquired Apex subsidiary grows, a larger proportion of the assets added each year will be financed with debt. Thus, the retentions needed for growth will be smaller than those in Line 12 of Table 26-2. Factoring in the higher interest payments and lower retentions, the annual net cash flows (in millions of dollars) to Hightech under the new capital structure are shown below:

	2002	2003	2004	2005	2006
Net cash flow to Hightech's shareholders	\$6.0	\$8.5	\$9.0	\$9.8	\$10.4

The Effect on the Discount Rate Because the post-acquisition Apex subsidiary will be financed with more debt, beta and (consequently) the cost of equity will increase. To find the new beta, we must first find the Apex's pre-acquisition unlevered beta, which is the beta Apex would have if it had no debt. Recall from Chapter 16 that the Hamada equation (Equation 16-2) expresses beta in terms of the unlevered beta, the tax rate, and the capital structure:

$$b = b_U [1 + (1 - T)(D/E)]. \qquad \textbf{(26-1)}$$

Here b_U is the unlevered beta, T is the tax rate, D is the value of debt, and E is the value of equity.

To express the unlevered beta in terms of the tax rate and the percent financed with debt, we rewrite the Hamada equation as follows:

$$b_U = b/[1 + (1 - T)(w_D/w_E)]. \qquad \textbf{(26-2)}$$

Here w_D is the percent financed with debt and w_E is the percent financed with equity. Using Equation 26-2, the unlevered beta of Apex is found to be 0.955:

$$b_U = 1.2/[1 + (1 - 0.4)(0.3/0.7)] = 0.955.$$

To estimate the postacquisition beta of Apex, we must use Equation 26-1 to "relever" the unlevered beta at the new capital structure:

$$b = 0.955[1 + (1 - 0.4)(0.4/0.6)] = 1.337.$$

Based on the new beta of 1.337, the post-acquisition cost of equity rises from 15.4 to 16.4 percent:

$$k_s = 7\% + 1.337(7\%) = 16.359\% \approx 16.4\%.$$

The Effect on the Bid Price The new capital structure has two effects on the bid price. The first is on the value of the firm and the second is on the price per share of Apex's stock that Hightech is willing to pay.

The estimated value of equity should now reflect the new cash flows and the new cost of equity. The horizon value is

$$V_{2006} = \frac{CF_{2007}}{k_s - g} = \frac{\$10.4(1 + 0.06)}{0.164 - 0.06} = \$106.0 \text{ million}.$$

Using the new cash flows, the new discount rate, and the new horizon value, the value of equity (in millions of dollars) is

$$V_{2001} = \frac{\$6.0}{(1.164)^1} + \frac{\$8.5}{(1.164)^2} + \frac{\$9.0}{(1.164)^3} + \frac{\$9.8}{(1.164)^4} + \frac{\$10.4 + \$106.0}{(1.164)^5} \approx \$76.9 \text{ million}.$$

One might be tempted to say that the change in capital structure has a negative effect on value, since the value of equity was \$91.5 million under the old capital structure and \$76.9 million under the new one. However, this is wrong. To see why, first note that the total value of Apex prior to the acquisition was \$89.5 million, the sum of \$62.5 million in equity and \$27 million in debt. In the original acquisition plan, where Apex's debt would be assumed, the total value was \$91.5 + \$27.0 = \$118.5 million. Under the alternative 40 percent capital structure, the Apex subidiary will have about \$51.3 million in debt: \$51.3/(\$51.37 + \$76.9) = 0.400 = 40%. Therefore, the Apex subsidiary is worth \$76.9 + \$51.3 = \$128.2 million. Table 26-3 summarizes these results.

The first column in Table 26-3 shows the total value of Apex as a separate company prior to the merger, \$89.5 million. The second column shows Apex's total value as a subsidiary with the same amount of debt, \$118.5 million. Because the debt remains the same, the increase in Column 2 value is due to the anticipated operating synergies.[10] The third column shows \$128.2 million value of the Apex subsidiary, reflecting operating synergies and capital structure effects.

The maximum amount that Hightech should be willing to pay for Apex's stock is the total post-acquisition value minus the pre-acquisition debt, and it is shown in the fourth row of Table 26-3. Note that with the change in capital structure, Hightech should be willing to pay more than \$76.9 million for Apex's stock. For example, Hightech could raise \$76.9 million in equity and \$24.3 million in debt, for a total of \$101.2 million. If Hightech paid this amount for Apex's stock and assumed Apex's debt, then Hightech's

[10]Note that our previous analysis assumed that the initial level of debt remained at \$27 million and that the percent of the firm financed with debt remained at 30 percent. However, given the increase in value due to operating synergies, if the initial level of debt remains at \$27 million, then the percent financed with debt actually is \$27/\$118.5 = 0.228 = 22.8%. We ignored this in our earlier analysis so that we could focus on the main points of merger valuation.

TABLE 26-3 Analysis of the Apex Acquisition with a Change in Capital Structure (Millions of Dollars)

		Apex as a	
	Separate Company Prior to the Acquisition	Subsidiary with No Change in Debt	Subsidiary with a 40% Debt Ratio
Value of equity	$62.5	$ 91.5	$ 76.9
Value of debt	27.0	27.0	51.3
Total value	$89.5	$118.5	$128.2
Maximum amount Hightech should pay for Apex's equity[a]		$91.5	$101.2
Maximum price per share Hightech should pay for Apex's equity[b]		$9.15	$10.12

Notes:
[a]Calculated as the total value as a subsidiary minus the amount of debt as a separate company.
[b]Calculated as the maximum amount divided by the 10 million shares of Apex stock.

stockholders would have a $76.9 million stake in an enterprise that is worth $128.2 million but that owes a total of $51.3 million. In other words, it is a zero NPV investment. But if Hightech can buy Apex's stock for less than $101.2 million, say, $95 million, then Hightech's stockholders could still borrow $24.3 million, contribute only $70.7 million of equity, buy Apex's equity, and assume its debt. In this case, Hightech's stockholders would own a company that is still worth $128.2 million and that owes $51.3 million, leaving them an equity stake worth $76.9 million. Note, however, that they only contributed $70.7 million, making this a $6.2 million NPV investment: $76.9 − $70.7 = $6.2 million. As this example shows, the maximum bid price for a target's equity is the total value of the post-acquisition target (which reflects operating synergies and capital structure effects) minus the target's pre-acquisition debt.

Postmerger Control

The employment/control situation is often of vital interest in a merger analysis. First, consider the situation in which a small, owner-managed firm sells out to a larger concern. The owner-manager may be anxious to retain a high-status position, and he or she may also have developed a camaraderie with the employees and thus be concerned about their retention after the merger. If so, these points would be stressed during the merger negotiations.[11] When a publicly owned firm that is not owned by its managers

[11]The acquiring firm may also be concerned about this point, especially if the target firm's management is quite good. Indeed, a condition of the merger may be that the management team agree to stay on for a period such as five years after the merger. In this case, the price paid may be contingent on the acquired firm's performance subsequent to the merger. For example, when International Holdings acquired Walker Products, the price paid was an immediate 100,000 shares of International Holdings stock worth $63 per share plus an additional 30,000 shares each year for the next three years, provided Walker Products earned at least $1 million during each of these years. Because Walker's managers owned the stock and would receive the bonus, they had a strong incentive to stay on and help the firm meet its targets.

Finally, if the managers of the target company are highly competent but do not wish to remain on after the merger, the acquiring firm may build into the merger contract a noncompete agreement with the old management. Typically, the acquired firm's principal officers must agree not to affiliate with a new business that is competitive with the one they sold for a specified period, say, five years. Such agreements are especially important with service-oriented businesses.

When You Merge You Combine More Than Just Financial Statements

When corporations merge, they combine more than just their financial statements. Mergers bring together two organizations with different histories and corporate cultures. Deals that look good on paper can fail if the individuals involved are unwilling or unable to work together to generate the potential synergies. Consequently, when analyzing a potential merger, it is important to determine whether the two companies are compatible.

Many deals fall apart because, during the "due diligence" phase, synergistic benefits are revealed to be less than was originally anticipated, so there is little economic rationale for the merger. Other negotiations break off because the two parties cannot agree on the price to be paid for the acquired firm's stock. In addition, merger talks often collapse because of "social issues." These social issues include both the "chemistry" of the companies and their personnel and such basic issues as these: What will be the name of the combined company? Where will headquarters be located? And, most important: Who will run the combined company? Robert Kindler, a partner at Cravath, Swaine & Moore, a prominent New York law firm that specializes in mergers, summarizes the importance of these issues as follows: "Even transactions that make absolute economic sense don't happen unless the social issues work."

Investment bankers, lawyers, and other professionals state that mergers tend to be most successful if there is a clear and well-arranged plan spelling out who will run the company. This issue is straightforward if one firm is clearly dominant and is acquiring the other. However, in cases where there is "a merger of equals," senior personnel issues often become sticky. This situation is made considerably easier if one of the chief executives is at or near the retirement age.

Some analysts believe that social issues often play too large a role, derailing mergers that should take place. In other cases where a merger occurs, concerns about social issues preclude managers from undertaking the necessary changes—like laying off redundant staff—for the deal to benefit shareholders.

Source: "In Many Merger Deals, Ego and Pride Play Big Roles in Which Way Talks Go," *The Wall Street Journal*, August 22, 1996, C1.

is merged into another company, the acquired firm's managers will be worried about their postmerger positions. If the acquiring firm agrees to retain the old management, then management may be willing to support the merger and to recommend its acceptance to the stockholders. If the old management is to be removed, then it will probably resist the merger.[12]

Self-Test Questions

What is the difference between an operating merger and a financial merger?

Describe the way postmerger cash flows are estimated in a DCF analysis.

What is the basis for the discount rate in a DCF analysis? Describe how this rate might be estimated.

Describe the market multiple approach.

What are some factors that acquiring firms consider when they set a bid price?

How do control issues affect mergers?

[12]Managements of firms that are thought to be attractive merger candidates often arrange *golden parachutes* for themselves. Golden parachutes are extremely lucrative retirement plans that take effect if a merger is consummated. Thus, when Bendix was acquired by Allied, Bill Agee, Bendix's chairman, "pulled the ripcord of his golden parachute" and walked away with $4 million. If a golden parachute is large enough, it can also function as a poison pill—for example, where the president of a firm worth $10 million would have to be paid $8 million if the firm is acquired, this will prevent a takeover. Stockholders are increasingly resisting such arrangements, but some still exist.

Taxes and the Structure of the Takeover Bid

In a merger, the acquiring firm can either buy the target's assets or buy shares of stock directly from the target's shareholders. If the offer is for the target's assets, the target's board of directors will make a recommendation to the shareholders, who will vote either to accept or reject the offer. If they accept the offer, the payment goes directly to the target corporation, which pays off any debt not assumed by the acquiring firm, pays any corporate taxes that are due, and then distributes the remainder of the payment to the shareholders, often in the form of a liquidating dividend. In this situation, the target firm is usually dissolved and no longer continues to exist as a separate legal entity, although its assets and work force may continue to function as a division or a wholly owned subsidiary of the acquiring firm. The acquisition of assets is a very common form of a takeover for small and medium-sized firms, especially those that are not publicly traded. A major advantage of this method relative to the acquisition of the target's stock is that the acquiring firm simply acquires assets and is not saddled with any hidden liabilities. In contrast, if the acquiring firm buys the target's stock, then it is responsible for any legal contingencies against the target, even for those that might have occurred prior to the takeover.

An offer for a target's stock rather than its assets can be made either directly to the shareholders, as is typical in a hostile takeover, or indirectly through the board of directors, who in a friendly deal make a recommendation to the shareholders to accept the offer. In a successful offer, the acquiring firm will end up owning a controlling interest, or perhaps even all of the target's stock. Sometimes the target retains its identity as a separate legal entity and is operated as a subsidiary of the acquiring firm, and sometimes its corporate status is dissolved and it is operated as one of the acquiring firm's divisions.

The payment offered by the acquiring firm can be in the form of cash, stock of the acquiring firm, debt of the acquiring firm, or some combination. The structure of the bid affects (1) the capital structure of the postmerger firm, (2) the tax treatment of both the acquiring firm and the target's stockholders, (3) the ability of the target firm's stockholders to benefit from future merger-related gains, and (4) the types of federal and state regulations to which the acquiring firm will be subjected. In this section, we discuss how acquiring firms structure their offers.

The tax consequences of the merger depend on whether it is classified as a *taxable offer* or a *nontaxable offer*.[13] In general, a nontaxable offer is one in which the form of payment is predominately stock, although the application of this simple principle is much more complicated in practice. The Internal Revenue Code views a mostly stock merger as an exchange rather than a sale, making it a nontaxable event. However, if the offer includes a significant amount of cash or bonds, then the IRS views it as a sale, and it is a taxable transaction, just like any other sale.

In a nontaxable deal, target shareholders who receive shares of the acquiring company's stock do not have to pay any taxes at the time of the merger. When they eventually sell their stock in the acquiring company, they must pay a tax on the gain. The amount of the gain is the sales price of their stock in the acquiring company minus the price at which they purchased their original stock in the target

---

[13]For more details, see J. Fred Weston, Juan A. Siu, and Brian A. Johnson, *Takeovers, Restructuring, & Corporate Governance* (Upper Saddle River, NJ: Prentice-Hall, 2001), especially Chapter 4. Also see Kenneth E. Anderson, Thomas R. Pope, and John L. Kramer, eds., *Prentice Hall's Federal Taxation: Corporations, Partnerships, Estates, and Trusts*, 2001 edition (Upper Saddle River, NJ: Prentice-Hall, 2001), especially Chapter 7.

company.[14] In a taxable offer, the gain between the offer price and the original purchase price of the target stock is taxed in the year of the merger.[15]

All other things equal, stockholders prefer nontaxable offers, since they may then postpone taxes on their gains. Furthermore, if the target firm's stockholders receive stock, they will benefit from any synergistic gains produced by the merger. Most target shareholders are thus willing to give up their stock for a lower price in a nontaxable offer than in a taxable one. As a result, one might expect nontaxable bids to dominate. However, this is not the case—roughly half of all mergers have been taxable. The reason for this is explained in the following paragraphs.

The form of the payment also has tax consequences for the acquiring and target firms. To illustrate, consider the following situation. The target firm has assets with a book value of \$100 million, but these assets have an appraised value of \$150 million. The offer by the acquiring firm is worth \$225 million. If it is a nontaxable offer, then after the merger the acquiring firm simply adds the \$100 million book value of the target's assets to its own assets and continues to depreciate them according to their previous depreciation schedules. To keep the example simple, we assume the target has no debt.

The situation is more complicated for a taxable offer, and the treatment is different depending on whether the offer is for the target's assets or for its stock. If the acquiring firm offers \$225 million for the target's assets, then the target firm must pay a tax on the gain of \$225 − \$100 = \$125 million. Assuming a corporate tax rate of 40 percent, this tax is 0.40(\$125) = \$50 million. This leaves the target with \$225 − \$50 = \$175 million to distribute to its shareholders upon liquidation. Adding insult to injury, the target's shareholders must also pay individual taxes on any of their own gains.[16] This is truly a taxable transaction, with taxes assessed at both the corporate and individual levels! In contrast to the tax disadvantages for the target and its shareholders, the acquiring firm receives two major tax advantages. First, it records the acquired assets at their appraised value and depreciates them accordingly. Thus, it will depreciate \$150 million of assets in this taxable transaction versus only \$100 million in a nontaxable transaction. Second, it will create \$75 million in a new asset account called "goodwill," which is the difference between the purchase price of \$225 million and the appraised value of \$150 million. Tax laws that took effect in 1993 permit companies to amortize this goodwill over 15 years using the straight-line method and deduct the amortization from taxable income. The net effect is that the full purchase price of \$225 million can be depreciated or amortized in a taxable merger versus only the original book value of \$100 million in a nontaxable transaction.

Now suppose the acquiring firm offers \$225 million for the target's stock in a taxable offer. After completing the merger, the acquiring firm must choose between two alternative tax treatments. Under the first alternative, it will record the assets at their book value of \$100 million and continue depreciating them using their current schedules. This treatment does not create any goodwill. Under the second alternative, it will record the assets at their appraised value of \$150 million and create \$75 million of goodwill. As described earlier for the asset purchase, this allows the acquiring firm to effectively depreciate the entire purchase price of \$225 million for tax purposes.

---

[14]This is a capital gain if it has been at least one year since they purchased their original stock in the target.

[15]Even in nontaxable deals, taxes must be paid in the year of the merger by any stockholders who receive cash.

[16]Our example assumes that the target is a publicly owned firm, which means that it must be a "C corporation" for tax purposes. However, if it is privately held, it might be an "S corporation," in which case only the stockholders would be taxed. This helps smaller firms use mergers as an exit strategy.

However, there will also be an immediate tax liability on the \$125 million gain, just as when the firm purchased assets.[17] Therefore, many companies choose not to mark up the assets.

If you think this is complicated, you are right! At this point you should know enough to talk with specialized accountants and lawyers, or be ready to delve into tax accounting texts, but merger taxation is too complex a subject to be covered thoroughly in a general finance textbook.

Securities laws also have an effect on the construction of the offer. The SEC has oversight over the issuance of new securities, including stock or debt issued in connection with a merger. Therefore, whenever a corporation bids for control of another firm through the exchange of equity or debt, the entire process must take place under the scrutiny of the Securities and Exchange Commission. The time required for such reviews allows target managements to implement defensive tactics and other firms to make competing offers, and as a result, nearly all hostile tender offers are for cash rather than securities.

Self-Test Questions

What are some alternative ways of structuring takeover bids?

How do taxes influence the payment structure?

How do securities laws affect the payment structure?

Financial Reporting for Mergers

Although a detailed discussion of financial reporting is best left to accounting courses, the accounting implications of mergers cannot be ignored. Currently, mergers are handled in either of two basic ways: (1) as a pooling of interests or (2) as a purchase.[18] The method used can have a significant effect on postmerger reported profits, and this, in turn, can influence the desirability of the merger.

Keep in mind, however, that all larger companies are required to keep two sets of books. The first is for the IRS, and it reflects the tax treatment of mergers as described in the previous section. The second is for financial reporting, and it reflects the treatment described below. As you will see, the rules for financial reporting often differ from those for the IRS.

Pooling of Interests Accounting

A **pooling of interests** is, in theory, a merger among equals, and hence the consolidated balance sheet is constructed by simply adding together the balance sheets of the merged companies. The top section of Table 26-4 shows the essential elements of the consolidated balance sheet after Firms A and B have merged under a pooling of interests. This final balance sheet holds regardless of how many shares Firm A (the survivor) gave up to acquire Firm B. (In a pooling, shares, not cash, must be exchanged.)

[17]Technically speaking, it is the target firm that is responsible for this tax on the write-up. Keep in mind, however, that the acquiring firm previously purchased the stock in the target, so it must in reality bear the brunt of the tax.

[18]At the time this was written, the Financial Accounting Standards Board (FASB) was expected to issue a final standard on business combinations by year-end 2000 that will permit only the purchase method of accounting for business combinations.

TABLE 26-4 Accounting for Mergers: A Acquires B

POOLING OF INTERESTS

	Firm A	Firm B	Postmerger: Firm A
Current assets	$ 50	$25	$ 75
Fixed assets	50	25	75
Total assets	$100	$50	$150
Debt	$ 40	$20	$ 60
Common equity	60	30	90
Total claims	$100	$50	$150

PURCHASE ACCOUNTING

			Postmerger: Firm A		
	Firm A (1)	Firm B (2)	$20 Paid[a] (3)	$30 Paid[a] (4)	$50 Paid[a] (5)
Current assets	$ 50	$25	$ 75	$ 75	$ 80[c]
Fixed assets	50	25	65[b]	75	80[c]
Goodwill[d]	0	0	0	0	10[d]
Total assets	$100	$50	$140	$150	$170
Debt	$ 40	$20	$ 60	$ 60	$ 60
Equity	60	30	80[e]	90	110[f]
Total claims	$100	$50	$140	$150	$170

[a]The price paid is the *net asset value*, that is, total assets minus debt.
[b]Here we assume that Firm B's fixed assets are written down from $25 to $15 before constructing the consolidated balance sheet.
[c]Here we assume that Firm B's current and fixed assets are both increased to $30.
[d]*Goodwill* refers to the excess paid for a firm above the appraised value of the physical assets purchased. Goodwill represents payment both for intangibles such as patents and for "organization value" such as that associated with having an effective sales force.
[e]Firm B's common equity is reduced by $10 prior to consolidation to reflect the fixed asset write-off.
[f]Firm B's equity is increased to $50 to reflect the above-book purchase price.

Purchase Accounting

The lower section of Table 26-4, which uses the same data as for the pooled companies, illustrates purchase accounting. Here Firm A is assumed to have "bought" Firm B in much the same way it would buy any capital asset, paying for it with cash, debt, or stock of the acquiring company. If the price paid is exactly equal to the acquired firm's *net asset value*, which is defined as its total assets minus its liabilities, then the consolidated balance sheet will be identical to that under pooling. Otherwise, there is an important difference. If the price paid exceeds the net asset value, then asset values will be increased to reflect the price actually paid, whereas if the price paid is less than the net asset value, then assets must be written down when preparing the consolidated balance sheet.

Note that Firm B's net asset value is $30, which is also its reported common equity value. This $30 book value could be equal to the market value (which is determined by investors based on the firm's earning power), but book value could also be more or less than the market value. Three situations are considered in the lower section of Table 26-4. First, in Column 3 we assume that Firm A gives cash or stock worth $20 for Firm B. Thus, B's assets as reported on its balance sheet were overvalued, and A pays less than B's net asset value. The overvaluation could be in either fixed or current assets; an appraisal would be made but we assume that it is fixed assets that are overvalued. Accordingly, we reduce B's fixed assets and also its common equity by $10 before constructing the consolidated balance sheet shown in Column 3. Next, in Column 4, we assume that A pays exactly the net asset value for B. In this case, pooling and purchase accounting would produce identical balance sheets.

Finally, in Column 5 we assume that A pays more than the net asset value for B: $50 is paid for $30 of net assets. This excess is assumed to be partly attributable to undervalued assets (land, buildings, machinery, and inventories), so to reflect this undervaluation, current and fixed assets are each increased by $5. In addition, we assume that $10 of the $20 excess of market value over book value is due to a superior sales organization, or some other intangible factor, and we post this excess as **goodwill.** B's common equity is increased by $20, the sum of the increases in current and fixed assets plus goodwill, and this markup is also reflected in A's postmerger equity account.[19]

Income Statement Effects

Significant differences can also arise in reported profits under the two accounting methods. If asset values are increased, as they often are under a purchase, this must be reflected in higher depreciation charges (and also in a higher cost of goods sold if inventories are written up). This, in turn, will further reduce reported profits. Also, goodwill represents the excess paid for a firm over its adjusted net asset value. This excess is presumably paid because of the acquired firm's superior earning power, which will probably be eroded over time as patents expire, as new firms enter the industry, and so forth. Thus, goodwill is written off, or "amortized," over a period corresponding to the expected life of the superior earning power, but in no case more than 40 years. Goodwill is certainly not a trivial issue. For example, when Philip Morris acquired Seven-Up for a price of $520 million, approximately $390 million of the purchase price represented goodwill.

See ***Ch 26 Tool Kit.xls*** for details.

Table 26-5 illustrates the income statement effects of the higher current and fixed assets, and also the write-off of goodwill, under pooling versus purchase. For the purchase, we assume that A purchased B for $50, creating $10 of goodwill and $10 of higher physical asset value. Further, we assume that this $20 will be written off over ten years.[20] As Column 4 indicates, the writing off of goodwill and asset markups under purchase accounting causes reported profits to be lower than they would be under pooling.

The write-off of goodwill is also reflected in earnings per share. In our hypothetical merger, we assume that nine shares exist in the consolidated firm. (Six of these shares went to A's stockholders, and three to B's.) Under pooling, EPS = $2.40, while under purchase, EPS = $2.22. Further, the greater the amount of goodwill, the larger is the write-off and the more significant is the dilution in reported earnings per share. This fact causes managers to prefer pooling to purchase accounting.

Several conditions must be met to use the pooling method, the most important of which is that the acquisition must be paid for with common stock of the acquiring

[19]This example assumes that additional debt was not issued to help finance the acquisition. If the acquisition were totally debt financed, the postmerger balance sheet would show increases in the debt account rather than increases in the equity account. If it were financed by a mix of debt and equity, both accounts would be changed.

[20]In financial reports, the write-off of goodwill is not a deduction for income tax purposes. However, purchased goodwill, as described in the previous section on the tax treatment of mergers, may be amortized for tax purposes in calculating the tax liability for the IRS, even though it may not be deducted when reporting the tax liability to investors.

TABLE 26-5 Income Effects of Pooling versus Purchase Accounting

	Premerger		Postmerger: Firm A	
	Firm A (1)	Firm B (2)	Pooling (3)	Purchase (4)
Sales	$100.0	$50.0	$150.0	$150.0
Operating costs	72.0	36.0	108.0	109.0[a]
Operating income	$ 28.0	$14.0	$ 42.0	$ 41.0[a]
Interest (10%)	4.0	2.0	6.0	6.0
Taxable income	$ 24.0	$12.0	$ 36.0	$ 35.0
Taxes (40%)	9.6	4.8	14.4	14.0
Earnings after taxes	$ 14.4	$ 7.2	$ 21.6	$ 21.0
Goodwill write-off	0	0	0	1.0[b]
Net income	$ 14.4	$ 7.2	$ 21.6	$ 20.0
EPS[c]	$ 2.40	$2.40	$ 2.40	$ 2.22

[a]Operating costs are $1 higher than they otherwise would be to reflect the higher reported costs (depreciation and cost of goods sold) caused by the physical asset markup at the time of purchase.
[b]($10 of increased goodwill)/10 years = $1 write-off per year.
[c]Firm A had six shares and Firm B had three shares before the merger. A gives one of its shares for each of B's, so A has nine shares outstanding after the merger.

firm.[21] This, coupled with other conditions, restricts the use of pooling in practice. Nevertheless, about 90 percent of all recent acquisitions over $100 million have used pooling, which does not lower the combined firm's reported earnings.

Self-Test Questions

What is the difference between pooling of interests and purchase accounting for mergers?

What is goodwill? What impact does goodwill have on the firm's balance sheet? On its income statement?

Analysis for a "True Consolidation"

Most of our analysis in the preceding sections assumed that one firm plans to acquire another. However, in many situations it is hard to identify an "acquirer" and a "target"—the merger appears to be a true "merger of equals," as was the case with the Citicorp/Travelers and NationsBank/BankAmerica mergers. In such cases, how is the analysis handled? Here are the steps one would go through:

1. Develop pro forma financial statements for the consolidated corporation. What are the projected sales, costs, interest charges, taxes, net income, and free cash flows, assuming the two firms merge? How will the consolidated balance sheets look? Such mergers are virtually always handled on a pooling of interests basis, so the balance sheets are combined, with no write-up or write-down. Synergies are generally expected to be important, so they must be worked into the pro forma income statements. If antitrust considerations require the disposal of certain assets (say,

[21]See Accounting Principles Board Opinions #16 and #17. Also, note that the Financial Accounting Standards Board is currently considering changes that would end pooling.

some branches if two banks with overlapping service areas merge), that must be reflected in the projected statements. The key set of figures is the projected consolidated free cash flows available to stockholders.

2. Estimate the new company's cost of equity, and use that rate to discount the equity flows of the consolidated company. This is the value of the equity of the consolidated company.
3. Decide how to allocate the new company's stock between the two sets of old stockholders. Normally, one would expect the consolidated value to exceed the sum of the pre-announcement values of the two companies because of synergy. For example, Company A might have had a premerger equity value of $10 billion, found as (Number of shares)(Price per share), and Company B might have had a premerger value of $15 billion. If the postmerger value of new Company AB is estimated to be $30 billion, then that value must be allocated. Company A's stockholders will have to receive enough shares to cause its stockholders to have a projected value of at least $10 billion, and Company B's stockholders will have to receive at least $15 billion. But how will the remaining $5 billion of synergistic-induced value be divided?

   This is a key issue, and one that the two management groups will negotiate long and hard over. There is no rule, or formula, that can be applied, but one basis for the allocation is the relative pre-announcement values of the two companies. For example, in our hypothetical merger of A and B to form AB, the companies might agree to give $10/$25 = 40% of the new stock to A's stockholders and 60% to B's stockholders. Unless a case could be made for giving a higher percentage of the shares to one of the companies because it was responsible for more of the synergistic value, then the premerger value proportions would seem to be a "fair" solution. In any event, the premerger proportions will probably be given the greatest weight in reaching the final decision.

It should also be noted that control of the consolidated company is always an issue in mergers such as the Citicorp/Travelers and NationsBank/BankAmerica deals. Generally, the companies hold a press conference and announce that the CEO of one firm will be chairman of the new company, that the other CEO will be president, that the new board will consist of directors from both old boards, and that power will be shared. With huge mergers such as those we have been seeing lately, there is plenty of power to be shared.

Self-Test Questions

How does merger analysis differ in the case of a large company acquiring a smaller one versus a "true merger of equals"?

Do you think the same guidelines for allocating synergistic gains would be used in both types of mergers?

The Role of Investment Bankers

Investment bankers are involved with mergers in a number of ways: (1) They help arrange mergers, (2) they help target companies develop and implement defensive tactics, (3) they help value target companies, (4) they help finance mergers, and (5) they invest in the stocks of potential merger candidates. These merger-related activities have been quite profitable. For example, the investment bankers and lawyers who arranged the Campeau-Federated merger earned fees of about $83 million—First Boston and Wasserstein Perella split $29 million from Campeau, and Goldman Sachs, Hellman & Friedman, and Shearson Lehman Hutton divided up $54 million for representing Federated. No wonder investment banking houses are able to make top offers to finance graduates!

Arranging Mergers

The major investment banking firms have merger and acquisition groups that operate within their corporate finance departments. (Corporate finance departments offer advice, as opposed to underwriting or brokerage services, to business firms.) Members of these groups identify firms with excess cash that might want to buy other firms, companies that might be willing to be bought, and firms that might, for a number of reasons, be attractive to others. Also, if an oil company, for instance, decided to expand into coal mining, then it might enlist the aid of an investment banker to help it acquire a coal company. Similarly, dissident stockholders of firms with poor track records might work with investment bankers to oust management by helping to arrange a merger. Investment bankers are reported to have offered packages of financing to corporate raiders, where the package includes both designing the securities to be used in the tender offer, plus lining up people and firms who will buy the target firm's stock now and then tender it once the final offer is made.

Investment bankers have occasionally taken illegal actions in the merger arena. For one thing, they are reported to have *parked stock*—purchasing it for a raider under a guaranteed buy-back agreement—to help the raider de facto accumulate more than 5 percent of the target's stock without disclosing the position. People have gone to jail for this.

Developing Defensive Tactics

Target firms that do not want to be acquired generally enlist the help of an investment banking firm, along with a law firm that specializes in mergers. Defenses include such tactics as (1) changing the bylaws so that only one-third of the directors are elected each year and/or so that a 75 percent approval (a *super-majority*) versus a simple majority is required to approve a merger; (2) trying to convince the target firm's stockholders that the price being offered is too low; (3) raising antitrust issues in the hope that the Justice Department will intervene; (4) repurchasing stock in the open market in an effort to push the price above that being offered by the potential acquirer; (5) getting a **white knight** who is acceptable to the target firm's management to compete with the potential acquirer; (6) getting a **white squire** who is friendly to current management to buy enough of the target firm's shares to block the merger; and (7) taking a poison pill, as described next.

Poison pills—which occasionally really do amount to committing economic suicide to avoid a takeover—are such tactics as borrowing on terms that require immediate repayment of all loans if the firm is acquired, selling off at bargain prices the assets that originally made the firm a desirable target, granting such lucrative **golden parachutes** to their executives that the cash drain from these payments would render the merger infeasible, and planning defensive mergers that would leave the firm with new assets of questionable value and a huge debt load. Currently, the most popular poison pill is for a company to give its stockholders *stock purchase rights* that allow them to buy at half-price the stock of an acquiring firm, should the firm be acquired. The blatant use of poison pills is constrained by directors' awareness that excessive use could trigger personal suits by stockholders against directors who voted for them, and, perhaps in the near future, by laws that would further limit management's use of pills. Still, investment bankers and antitakeover lawyers are busy thinking up new poison pill formulas, and others are just as busy trying to come up with antidotes.[22]

[22]It has become extremely difficult and expensive for companies to buy "directors' insurance," which protects the board from such contingencies as stockholders' suits, and even when insurance is available it often does not pay for losses if the directors have not exercised due caution and judgment. This exposure is making directors extremely leery of actions that might trigger stockholder suits.

Another takeover defense that is being used is the employee stock ownership plan (ESOP). ESOPs are designed to give lower-level employees an ownership stake in the firm, and current tax laws provide generous incentives for companies to establish such plans and fund them with the firm's common stock. As we discussed earlier, Polaroid used an ESOP to help fend off Shamrock Holdings's hostile takeover attempt. Also, Procter & Gamble recently set up an ESOP that, along with an existing profit-sharing plan, eventually will give employees a 20 percent ownership stake in the company. Since the trustees of ESOPs generally support current management in any takeover attempt, and since up to 85 percent of the votes is often required to complete a merger, an ESOP can provide an effective defense against a hostile tender offer. Procter & Gamble stated that its ESOP was designed primarily to lower its costs by utilizing the plan's tax advantages and to improve employees' retirement security. However, the company also noted that the ESOP would strengthen its defenses against a takeover.

Establishing a Fair Value

If a friendly merger is being worked out between two firms' managements, it is important to document that the agreed-upon price is a fair one; otherwise, the stockholders of either company may sue to block the merger. Therefore, in most large mergers each side will hire an investment banking firm to evaluate the target company and to help establish the fair price. For example, General Electric employed Morgan Stanley to determine a fair price for Utah International, as did Royal Dutch to help establish the price it paid for Shell Oil. Even if the merger is not friendly, investment bankers may still be asked to help establish a price. If a surprise tender offer is to be made, the acquiring firm will want to know the lowest price at which it might be able to acquire the stock, while the target firm may seek help in "proving" that the price being offered is too low.[23]

Financing Mergers

Many mergers are financed with the acquiring company's excess cash. However, if the acquiring company has no excess cash, it will require a source of funds. Perhaps the single most important factor behind the 1980s merger wave was the development of junk bonds for use in financing acquisitions.

Drexel Burnham Lambert was the primary developer of junk bonds, defined as bonds rated below investment grade (BBB/Baa). Prior to Drexel's actions, it was almost impossible to sell low-grade bonds to raise new capital. Drexel then pioneered a procedure under which a target firm's situation would be appraised very closely, and a cash flow projection similar to that in Table 26-2 (but much more detailed) would be developed.

With the cash flows having been forecasted, Drexel's analysts would figure out a debt structure—amount of debt, maturity structure, and interest rate—that could be serviced by the cash flows. With this information, Drexel's junk bond people,

[23]Such investigations must obviously be done in secret, for if someone knew that Company A was thinking of offering, say, $50 per share for Company T, which was currently selling at $35 per share, then huge profits could be made. One of the biggest scandals to hit Wall Street was the disclosure that Ivan Boesky was buying information from Dennis Levine, a senior member of the investment banking house of Drexel Burnham Lambert, about target companies that Drexel was analyzing for others. Purchases based on such insider information would, of course, raise the prices of the stocks and thus force Drexel's clients to pay more than they otherwise would have had to pay. Levine and Boesky, among others, went to jail for their improper use of insider information.

operating out of Beverly Hills, would approach financial institutions (savings and loans, insurance companies, pension funds, and mutual funds) with a financing plan, and they would offer a rate of return several percentage points above the rate on more conservative investments. Drexel's early deals worked out well, and the institutions that bought the bonds were quite pleased. These results enabled Drexel to expand its network of investors, which increased its ability to finance larger and larger mergers. T. Boone Pickens, who went after Phillips, Texaco, and several other oil giants, was an early Drexel customer, as was Ted Turner.

To be successful in the mergers and acquisitions (M&A) business, an investment banker must be able to offer a financing package to clients, whether they are acquirers who need capital to take over companies or target companies trying to finance stock repurchase plans or other defenses against takeovers. Drexel was the leading player in the merger financing game during the 1980s, but since Drexel's bankruptcy Merrill Lynch, Morgan Stanley Dean Witter, Salomon Smith Barney, and others are all vying for the title.

Arbitrage Operations

Arbitrage generally means simultaneously buying and selling the same commodity or security in two different markets at different prices, and pocketing a risk-free return. However, the major brokerage houses, as well as some wealthy private investors, are engaged in a different type of arbitrage called *risk arbitrage.* The *arbitrageurs,* or "arbs," speculate in the stocks of companies that are likely takeover targets. Vast amounts of capital are required to speculate in a large number of securities and thus reduce risk, and also to make money on narrow spreads. However, the large investment bankers have the wherewithal to play the game. To be successful, arbs need to be able to sniff out likely targets, assess the probability of offers reaching fruition, and move in and out of the market quickly and with low transactions costs.

The risk arbitrage business has been rocked by insider trading scandals. Indeed, the most famous arb of all, Ivan Boesky, was caught buying inside information from executives of some leading investment banking houses and law firms. The Boesky affair slowed risk arbitrage activity for awhile, but it is now back.

Self-Test Questions

What are some defensive tactics that firms can use to resist hostile takeovers?

What is the difference between pure arbitrage and risk arbitrage?

What role did junk bonds play in the merger wave of the 1980s?

Who Wins: The Empirical Evidence

All the recent merger activity has raised two questions: (1) Do corporate acquisitions create value, and, (2) if so, how is the value shared between the parties?

Most researchers agree that takeovers increase the wealth of the shareholders of target firms, for otherwise they would not agree to the offer. However, there is a debate as to whether mergers benefit the acquiring firm's shareholders. In particular, managements of acquiring firms may be motivated by factors other than shareholder wealth maximization. For example, they may want to merge merely to increase the size of the corporations they manage, because increased size usually brings larger salaries plus job security, perquisites, power, and prestige.

The question of who gains from corporate acquisitions can be tested by examining the stock price changes that occur around the time of a merger or takeover announcement. Changes in the stock prices of the acquiring and target firms represent market participants' beliefs about the value created by the merger, and about how that value will be divided between the target and acquiring firms' shareholders. So, examining a large sample of stock price movements can shed light on the issue of who gains from mergers.

One cannot simply examine stock prices around merger announcement dates, because other factors influence stock prices. For example, if a merger was announced on a day when the entire market advanced, the fact that the target firm's price rose would not necessarily signify that the merger was expected to create value. Hence, studies examine *abnormal returns* associated with merger announcements, where abnormal returns are defined as that part of a stock price change caused by factors other than changes in the general stock market.

These "event studies" have examined both acquiring and target firms' stock price responses to mergers and tender offers.[24] Jointly, they have covered nearly every acquisition involving publicly traded firms from the early 1960s to the present, and they are remarkably consistent in their results: on average, the stock prices of target firms increase by about 30 percent in hostile tender offers, while in friendly mergers the average increase is about 20 percent. However, for both hostile and friendly deals, the stock prices of acquiring firms, on average, remain constant. Thus, the event study evidence strongly indicates (1) that acquisitions do create value, but (2) that shareholders of target firms reap virtually all the benefits.

Although most empirical research indicates that target firms are the primary beneficiaries of mergers, it has been suggested that those studies are flawed, and that gains may in fact be more evenly distributed between targets and acquirers. The three primary reasons for this view are given below:

1. *Expectations.* If a firm has a history of making good capital budgeting decisions, i.e., ones where the NPV is positive, investors will come to expect this situation to continue, and those expectations will be built into the expected growth rate. Therefore, if such a firm takes on a positive NPV project, its stock price won't necessarily increase when the project is announced, because it had increased earlier in anticipation of this and other similar projects. The same situation may exist with mergers. A number of extraordinarily successful firms have gotten much of their growth through a series of well-conceived and well-executed mergers. Included would be such firms as Cisco, GE, Johnson and Johnson, and Microsoft. For these firms, merger-augmented growth rates are reflected in their stock prices, and investors have come to expect their merger-related growth to continue.

   Note, though, that these mergers could only benefit the acquiring firms if they capture some of the synergies. For example, suppose a given merger would create \$100 million of synergy, and the firms agree to a cash price that gives \$50 million to each party. The target firm's stock price will rise to reflect its share of the synergy, but the acquiring firm's stock price will not rise because investors have built expectations for such synergy-producing mergers into its price. An event study would suggest that the target firm got all the synergy, even though it was divided 50-50.
2. *Relative size.* The event studies look at changes in the target's and acquirer's stock price around the time of the merger. If the target is much smaller than the acquirer, then the merger will have a much more profound effect on the target's price, and making it appear that the target captured most of the synergy, even if that was not the case.

[24]For an excellent summary of the effects of mergers on value, see Michael C. Jensen and Richard S. Ruback, "The Market for Corporate Control: The Scientific Evidence," *Journal of Financial Economics,* April 1983, 5–50.

3. *The explanation for the event studies' results may be wrong.* The primary reasons given for the event studies' conclusion that targets get most of the benefits are (a) that many mergers are motivated by acquiring firms' managers' egos, which cause them to engage in mergers that make their firms larger even if stockholders don't benefit, and (b) that the targets can always find another buyer, so competition among buyers drives the price up to the point where the target captures the synergies. There is merit to these arguments, but they are not totally compelling. The ego argument assumes that managers want to and can get away with things that are not in their stockholders' best interests. That may or may not be correct. Regarding the competition issue, while some targets are attractive to a number of potential acquirers, in other cases the fit is far better with one acquirer than with others, and here the acquiring firm might be in the driver's seat.

The event study evidence suggests that mergers benefit targets but not acquirers, hence that acquiring firms' stockholders should be skeptical of their managers' plans for acquisitions. This evidence cannot be dismissed out of hand, but neither is it entirely convincing. There are undoubtedly many good mergers, just as there are many poorly conceived ones. Like most of finance, merger decisions should be studied carefully, and it is best not to judge the outcome of a specific merger until the actual results start to come in.

Self-Test Questions

Explain how researchers can study the effects of mergers on shareholder wealth.

Do mergers create value? If so, who profits from this value?

Do the research results discussed in this section seem logical? Explain.

Corporate Alliances

Mergers are one way for two companies to join forces, but many companies are striking cooperative deals, called **corporate,** or **strategic, alliances,** which stop far short of merging. Whereas mergers combine all of the assets of the firms involved, as well as their ownership and managerial expertise, alliances allow firms to create combinations that focus on specific business lines that offer the most potential synergies. These alliances take many forms, from simple marketing agreements to joint ownership of worldwide operations.

One form of corporate alliance is the **joint venture,** in which parts of companies are joined to achieve specific, limited objectives.[25] A joint venture is controlled by a management team consisting of representatives of the two (or more) parent companies. Joint ventures have been used often by U.S., Japanese, and European firms to share technology and/or marketing expertise. For example, Whirlpool announced a joint venture with the Dutch electronics giant Philips to produce appliances under Philips's brand names in five European countries. By joining with their foreign counterparts, U.S. firms are gaining a stronger foothold in Europe. Although alliances are new to some firms, they are established practices to others. For example, Corning Glass now obtains over half of its profits from 23 joint ventures, two-thirds of them with foreign companies representing almost all of Europe, as well as Japan, China, South Korea, and Australia.

---

[25]Cross-licensing, consortia, joint bidding, and franchising are still other ways for firms to combine resources. For more information on joint ventures, see Sanford V. Berg, Jerome Duncan, and Phillip Friedman, *Joint Venture Strategies and Corporate Innovation* (Cambridge, MA: Oelgeschlager, Gunn and Hain, 1982).

A recent study of 345 corporate alliances found that the stock prices of both partners in an alliance tended to increase when the alliance was announced, with an average abnormal return of about 0.64 percent on the day of the announcement.[26] About 43 percent of the alliances were marketing agreements, 14 percent were R&D agreements, 11 percent were for licensing technology, 7 percent for technology transfers, and 25 percent were for some combination of the four basic reasons. Although most alliances were for marketing agreements, the market reacted most favorably when the alliance was for technology sharing between two firms in the same industry. The study also found that the typical alliance lasted at least five years, and the allied firms had better operating performance than their industry peers during this period.

Self-Test Questions

What is the difference between a merger and a corporate alliance?

What is a joint venture? Give some reasons why joint ventures may be advantageous to the parties involved.

Leveraged Buyouts

In a **leveraged buyout (LBO)** a small group of investors, usually including current management, acquires a firm in a transaction financed largely by debt. The debt is serviced with funds generated by the acquired company's operations and, often, by the sale of some of its assets. Generally, the acquiring group plans to run the acquired company for a number of years, boost its sales and profits, and then take it public again as a stronger company. In other instances, the LBO firm plans to sell off divisions to other firms that can gain synergies. In either case, the acquiring group expects to make a substantial profit from the LBO, but the inherent risks are great due to the heavy use of financial leverage. To illustrate the profit potential, Kohlberg Kravis Roberts & Company (KKR), a leading LBO specialist firm, averaged a spectacular 50 percent annual return on its LBO investments during the 1980s. However, high stock prices for target firms have dampened the returns on recent LBO investments, so current activity is slower than in its heyday of the 1980s.

A good example of an LBO was KKR's buyout of RJR Nabisco. RJR, a leading producer of tobacco and food products with brands such as Winston, Camel, Planters, Ritz, Oreo, and Del Monte, was trading at about $55 a share in October 1988. Then, F. Ross Johnson, the company's chairman and CEO, announced a $75-a-share, or $17.6 billion, offer to outside stockholders in a plan to take the firm private. This deal, if completed, would have been the largest business transaction up to that time. After the announcement, RJR's stock price soared from $55 to $77.25, which indicated that investors thought the final price would be even higher than Johnson's bid. A few days later KKR offered $90 per share, or $20.6 billion. The battle between the two bidders raged until late November, when RJR's board accepted KKR's final bid of cash and securities worth about $106 a share, for a total value of about $25 billion. Of course, the investment bankers' fees reflected the record size of the deal—the bankers received almost $400 million, with Drexel Burnham Lambert alone getting over $200 million. Johnson lost his job, but he walked away with a multimillion-dollar golden parachute.

---

[26] See Su Han Chan, John W. Kensinger, Arthur J. Keown, and John D. Martin, "When Do Strategic Alliances Create Shareholder Value?" *Journal of Applied Corporate Finance*, Vol. 11, no. 4, Winter 1999, 82–87.

KKR wasted no time in restructuring the newly private RJR. In June 1989, RJR sold its five European businesses to France's BSN for $2.5 billion. Then, in September RJR sold the tropical fruit portion of its Del Monte foods unit to Polly Peck, a London-based food company, for $875 million. In the same month, RJR sold the Del Monte canned foods business to an LBO group led by Citicorp Venture Capital for $1.48 billion. Next, in October 1990 RJR sold its Baby Ruth, Butterfinger, and Pearson candy businesses to Nestlé, a Swiss company, for $370 million. In total, RJR sold off more than $5 billion worth of businesses in 1990 to help pay down the tremendous debt taken on in the LBO. In addition to asset sales, in 1991 RJR went public again by issuing more than $1 billion in new common stock, which placed about 25 percent of the firm's common stock in public hands. Also, as the firm's credit rating improved due to the retirement of some of its debt, RJR issued about $1 billion of new debt at significantly lower rates and used the proceeds to retire even more of its high-cost debt.

The RJR Nabisco story is the classic LBO tale—a company is taken private in a highly leveraged deal, the private firm's high-cost junk debt is reduced through asset sales, and finally the company again goes public, which gives the original LBO dealmakers the opportunity to "cash out." This story, however, did not have a fairytale ending. When KKR finally sold the last of its RJR shares in early 1995, it made a profit of about $60 million on a $3.1 billion investment, hardly a stellar return. The best a KKR spokesman could say about the deal was that "it preserved investors' equity." The transaction was largely financed by outside investors, with KKR putting up only $126 million of the original investment. Even though the return on their investment was the same as that received by outside investors, KKR earned an additional $500 million in transactions, advisor, management, and directors' fees.

Regardless of the outcome of the RJR Nabisco deal, there have been some spectacularly successful LBOs. For example, in an early deal that helped fuel the LBO wave, William Simon and Raymond Chambers bought Gibson Greeting Cards in 1982 for $1 million in equity and $79 million in debt. Less than 18 months later, Simon's personal investment of $330,000 was worth $66 million in cash and stock. However, there have also been some spectacular failures. For example, in 1988 Revco became the first large LBO to file for Chapter 11 bankruptcy. It turned out that sales were nearly $1 billion short of the $3.4 billion forecasted at the time of the drugstore chain's buyout.[27]

Self-Test Questions

What is an LBO?

Have LBOs been profitable in recent years?

What actions do companies typically take to meet the large debt burdens resulting from LBOs?

How do LBOs typically affect bondholders?

[27]For a more detailed discussion of the impact of the RJR LBO on the firm's different classes of investors, see Nancy Mohan and Carl R. Chen, "A Review of the RJR-Nabisco Buyout," *Journal of Applied Corporate Finance*, Summer 1990, 102–108. For interesting discussions of highly leveraged takeovers, see Martin S. Fridson, "What Went Wrong with the Highly Leveraged Deals? (Or, All Variety of Agency Costs)," *Journal of Applied Corporate Finance*, Fall 1991, 47–57; and "The Economic Consequences of High Leverage and Stock Market Pressures on Corporate Management: A Round Table Discussion," *Journal of Applied Corporate Finance*, Summer 1990, 6–57.

Divestitures

In this section, we briefly discuss the major types of divestitures, in which corporations sell divisions or other operating units. We then present some recent examples and rationales for divestitures.

Types of Divestitures

There are four types of **divestitures:** (1) sale of an operating unit to another firm, (2) setting up the business to be divested as a separate corporation and then "spinning it off" to the divesting firm's stockholders, (3) following the steps for a spin-off but selling only some of the shares, and (4) outright liquidation of assets.

Sale to another firm generally involves the sale of an entire division or unit, usually for cash but sometimes for stock of the acquiring firm. In a **spin-off,** the firm's existing stockholders are given new stock representing separate ownership rights in the division that was divested. The division establishes its own board of directors and officers, and it becomes a separate company. The stockholders end up owning shares of two firms instead of one, but no cash has been transferred. In a **carve-out,** a minority interest in a corporate subsidiary is sold to new shareholders, so the parent gains new equity financing yet retains control. Finally, in a **liquidation** the assets of a division are sold off piecemeal, rather than as an operating entity. To illustrate the different types of divestitures, we present some recent examples in the next section.

Divestiture Illustrations

1. Pepsi recently spun off its fast-food business, which included Pizza Hut, Taco Bell, and Kentucky Fried Chicken. The spun-off businesses now operate under the name Tricon Global Restaurants. Pepsi originally acquired the chains because it wanted to increase the distribution channels for its soft drinks. Over time, however, Pepsi began to realize that the soft-drink and restaurant businesses were quite different, and synergies between them were less than anticipated. The spin-off is part of Pepsi's attempt to once again focus on its core business. However, Pepsi tried to maintain these distribution channels by signing long-term contracts that ensure that Pepsi products will be sold exclusively in each of the three spun-off chains.
2. United Airlines sold its Hilton International Hotels subsidiary to Ladbroke Group PLC of Britain for $1.1 billion, and also sold its Hertz rental car unit and its Westin hotel group. The sales culminated a disastrous strategic move by United to build a full-service travel empire. The failed strategy resulted in the firing of Richard J. Ferris, the company's chairman. The move into nonairline travel-related businesses had been viewed by many analysts as a mistake, because there were few synergies to be gained. Further, analysts feared that United's managers, preoccupied by running hotels and rental car companies, would not maintain the company's focus in the highly competitive airline industry. The funds raised by the divestitures were paid out to United's shareholders as a special dividend.
3. General Motors (GM) spun off its Electronic Data Systems (EDS) subsidiary. EDS, a computer services company founded in 1962 by Ross Perot, prospered as an independent company until it was acquired by GM in 1984. The rationale for the acquisition was that EDS's expertise would help GM both operate better in the information age and build cars that encompassed leading-edge computer technology. However, the spread of desktop computers and the movement of companies to

Governments Are Divesting State-Owned Businesses to Spur Economic Efficiency

In many countries governments have traditionally owned or controlled a number of key businesses. When Margaret Thatcher became prime minister of Britain in 1979, she set out to reverse this trend, and soon her officials were devising methods for the government to divest state-owned enterprises. Thatcher coined the term "privatization" to describe the process of transferring productive operations and assets from the public sector to the private sector.

The privatization momentum picked up in the early and mid-1980s, expanding to other countries including France, Germany, Japan, and Singapore. Privatization accelerated further as the communist countries and authoritarian regimes across Eastern Europe, Asia, and Latin America shifted toward market-based economies.

Telecommunications, electric power, and airlines are examples of industries that have undergone extensive privatization throughout the world. These industries are vitally important to the economic infrastructure of every nation, and for this reason governments have historically been heavily involved in owning and regulating them within their national borders. Generally, the government-owned enterprise was granted monopoly power to supply the service in question and was subsidized in an effort to hold down costs to consumers. However, economists have long argued that government operations are inherently less efficient than are enterprises which are subject to competitive pressures and whose managers are guided by the profit motive. Thus, in recent years there have been numerous privatizations in these important industries, and as governments have sold their interests, competition has led to lower costs and improved service.

In Western Europe, privatizations in the telecommunications industry have been given an extra push by a European Union plan that opened markets to competition. Because most European telecoms were government owned, the resulting privatizations brought to market tens of billions of dollars of telecom stock. Globally, governments have raised hundreds of billions of dollars through privatizations.

The results are not all in, but it is clear that the removal of bureaucrats and politicians from the control of key enterprises often results in increased economic efficiency and a higher standard of living.

downsize their internal computer staffs caused EDS's non-GM business to soar. Ownership by GM hampered EDS's ability to strike alliances and, in some cases, to enter into business agreements. The best way for EDS to compete in its industry was as an independent, hence it was spun off.

4. AT&T was broken up in 1983 to settle a Justice Department antitrust suit filed in the 1970s.[28] For almost 100 years AT&T had operated as a holding company that owned Western Electric (its manufacturing subsidiary), Bell Labs (its research arm), a huge long-distance network that was operated as a division of the parent company, and 22 Bell operating companies, such as Pacific Telephone, New York Telephone, Southern Bell, and Southwestern Bell. In 1984, AT&T was reorganized into eight separate companies—a slimmed-down AT&T, which kept Western Electric, Bell Labs, and the long-distance operations, plus seven new regional telephone holding companies that were created from the 22 old operating telephone companies. The stock of the seven new telephone companies was then spun off to the old AT&T's stockholders. A person who held 100 shares of old AT&T stock owned, after the divestiture, 100 shares of the "new" AT&T plus 10 shares of each of the seven new operating companies. These 170 shares were backed by the same assets that had previously backed 100 shares of old AT&T common.

The AT&T divestiture resulted from a suit by the Justice Department, which wanted to divide the Bell System into a regulated monopoly segment (the seven

[28]Another forced divestiture involved Du Pont and General Motors. In 1921, GM was in serious financial trouble, and Du Pont supplied capital in exchange for 23 percent of the stock. In the 1950s, the Justice Department won an antitrust suit that required Du Pont to spin off (to Du Pont's stockholders) its GM stock.

regional telephone companies) and a manufacturing/ long-distance segment that would be exposed to competition. The breakup was designed to strengthen competition and thus speed up technological change in those parts of the telecommunications industry that are not natural monopolies.

5. After its forced breakup, AT&T lost little time in building itself up. In 1991 it acquired computer maker NCR, and in 1994 it bought McCaw Cellular Communications, a cellular phone operator. Then, in 1995, AT&T made a surprise announcement. Its massive combination of technology assets was not paying off, and AT&T's stock was in the doldrums. Then the company split itself into three parts. The surviving AT&T included the core $53 billion long-distance and cellular phone businesses. The division that makes the switching equipment used by local and long-distance companies was spun off under the name Lucent Technologies. AT&T also spun off its loss-plagued computer business (the former NCR). AT&T shares took off on the announcement, adding more than $6 to the share price and $11 billion to AT&T's total value—more than enough to make up for the purchase of NCR and the ensuing losses. One reason for the breakup was the fact that AT&T and the local telephone companies were entering one another's markets, and the locals were reluctant to buy equipment from a competitor (AT&T). Therefore, Lucent was losing business to other manufacturers. Also, the breakup permitted the managers of each entity to focus exclusively on the problems and opportunities of their own businesses. Then they could concentrate on those areas where they have the greatest expertise without distraction from events in other business lines.[29]
6. Some years ago, Woolworth liquidated all of its 336 Woolco discount stores. This made the company, which had had sales of $7.2 billion before the liquidation, 30 percent smaller. Woolco had posted operating losses of $19 million the year before the liquidation, and its losses in the latest six months had climbed to an alarming $21 million. Woolworth's CEO, Edward F. Gibbons, was quoted as saying, "How many losses can you take?" Woolco's problems necessitated a write-off of $325 million, but management believed it was better to go ahead and "bite the bullet" rather than let the losing stores bleed the company to death.
7. As a result of some imprudent loans to oil companies and to developing nations, Continental Illinois, one of the largest U.S. bank holding companies at the time, was threatened with bankruptcy. Continental then sold off several profitable divisions, such as its leasing and credit card operations, to raise funds to cover losses on bad loans. In effect, Continental sold assets in order to stay alive. Ultimately, Continental was bailed out by the Federal Deposit Insurance Corporation and the Federal Reserve, which arranged a $7.5 billion rescue package and provided a blanket guarantee for all of Continental's $40 billion of deposits, which kept deposits in excess of $100,000 from fleeing the bank because of their uninsured status.

As the preceding examples illustrate, the reasons for divestitures vary widely. Sometimes the market feels more comfortable when firms "stick to their knitting"; the Pepsi and United Airlines divestitures are examples. Other companies need cash either to finance expansion in their primary business lines or to reduce a large debt burden, and divestitures can be used to raise this cash; Continental Bank illustrates this point. The divestitures also show that running a business is a dynamic process—conditions change, corporate strategies change in response, and as a result firms alter their asset portfolios by acquisitions and/or divestitures. Some divestitures, such as

---

[29]AT&T has gone on with other large acquisitions and divestitures, but without much success. In early 2001, the stock was selling for about $17 per share, down from a 52-week high of $61, and the company announced plans for yet another break-up in which it would be divided into three separate companies.

Woolworth's liquidation of its Woolco stores, are to unload losing assets that would otherwise drag the company down. The first AT&T example is one of the many instances in which a divestiture is the result of an antitrust settlement. The AT&T and GM spin-offs illustrate situations in which parts of the business are thought to be able to operate more efficiently alone than together.

In general, the empirical evidence shows that the market reacts favorably to divestitures, with the divesting company typically having a small increase in stock price on the day of the announcement. The announcement-day returns are largest for companies that "undo" previous conglomerate mergers by divesting businesses in unrelated areas.[30] Studies also show that divestitures generally lead to superior operating performance for both the parent and the divested company.[31]

Self-Test Questions

What are some reasons companies divest assets?

What are four major motives for divestitures?

Holding Companies

Holding companies date from 1889, when New Jersey became the first state to pass a law permitting corporations to be formed for the sole purpose of owning the stocks of other companies. Many of the advantages and disadvantages of holding companies are identical to those of any large-scale organization. Whether a company is organized on a divisional basis or with subsidiaries kept as separate companies does not affect the basic reasons for conducting a large-scale, multiproduct, multiplant operation. However, as we show next, the use of holding companies to control large-scale operations has some distinct advantages and disadvantages.

Advantages of Holding Companies

1. **Control with fractional ownership.** Through a holding company operation, a firm may buy 5, 10, or 50 percent of the stock of another corporation. Such fractional ownership may be sufficient to give the holding company effective working control over the operations of the company in which it has acquired stock ownership. Working control is often considered to entail more than 25 percent of the common stock, but it can be as low as 10 percent if the stock is widely distributed. One financier says that the attitude of management is more important than the number of shares owned: "If management thinks you can control the company, then you do." In addition, control on a very slim margin can be held through relationships with large stockholders outside the holding company group.
2. **Isolation of risks.** Because the various **operating companies** in a holding company system are separate legal entities, the obligations of any one unit are separate from those of the other units. Therefore, catastrophic losses incurred by one unit of the holding company system may not be translatable into claims on the assets of the other units. However, we should note that while this is a customary generalization, it is not always valid. First, the **parent company** may feel obligated to make

[30]For details, see Jeffrey W. Allen, Scott L. Lummer, John J. McConnell, and Debra K. Reed, "Can Takeover Losses Explain Spin-Off Gains?" *Journal of Financial and Quantitative Analysis*, Vol. 30, no. 4, December 1995, 465–485.

[31]See Shane A. Johnson, Daniel P. Klein, and Verne L. Thibodeaux, "The Effects of Spin-Offs on Corporate Investment and Performance," *Journal of Financial Research*, Vol. 19, no. 2, Summer 1996, 293–307.

good on the subsidiary's debts, even though it is not legally bound to do so, in order to keep its good name and to retain customers. An example of this was American Express's payment of more than $100 million in connection with a swindle that was the responsibility of one of its subsidiaries. Second, a parent company may feel obligated to supply capital to an affiliate in order to protect its initial investment; General Public Utilities' continued support of its subsidiaries' Three Mile Island nuclear plant after the accident at that plant is an example. And, third, when lending to one of the units of a holding company system, an astute loan officer may require a guarantee by the parent holding company. To some degree, therefore, the assets in the various elements of a holding company are not really separate. Still, a catastrophic loss, as could occur if a drug company's subsidiary distributed a batch of toxic medicine, may be avoided.[32]

Disadvantages of Holding Companies

1. **Partial multiple taxation.** Provided the holding company owns at least 80 percent of a subsidiary's voting stock, the IRS permits the filing of consolidated returns, in which case dividends received by the parent are not taxed. However, if less than 80 percent of the stock is owned, then tax returns cannot be consolidated. Firms that own more than 20 percent but less than 80 percent of another corporation can deduct 80 percent of the dividends received, while firms that own less than 20 percent may deduct only 70 percent of the dividends received. This partial double taxation somewhat offsets the benefits of holding company control with limited ownership, but whether the tax penalty is sufficient to offset other possible advantages varies from case to case.
2. **Ease of enforced dissolution.** It is relatively easy to require dissolution by disposal of stock ownership of a holding company operation found guilty of antitrust violations. For instance, in the 1950s Du Pont was required to dispose of its 23 percent stock interest in General Motors Corporation, acquired in the early 1920s. Because there was no fusion between the corporations, there were no difficulties from an operating standpoint in requiring the separation of the two companies. However, if complete amalgamation had taken place, it would have been much more difficult to break up the company after so many years, and the likelihood of forced divestiture would have been reduced.

Holding Companies as a Leveraging Device

The holding company vehicle has been used to obtain huge degrees of financial leverage. In the 1920s, several tiers of holding companies were established in the electric utility, railroad, and other industries. In those days, an operating company at the bottom of the pyramid might have $100 million of assets, financed by $50 million of debt and $50 million of equity. Then, a first-tier holding company might own the stock of the operating firm as its only asset and be financed with $25 million of debt and $25 million of equity. A second-tier holding company, which owned the stock of the first-tier company, might be financed with $12.5 million of debt and $12.5 million of equity. Such systems were extended to five or six levels. With six holding companies, $100 million of operating assets could be controlled at the top by only $0.78 million of

[32]Note, though, that the parent company would still be held accountable for such losses if it were deemed to exercise operating control over the subsidiary. Thus, Union Carbide was held responsible for its subsidiary's Bhopal, India, disaster, and Dow Chemical may be held liable for Dow-Corning's multibillion-dollar silicone breast implant product liability judgment.

equity, and the operating assets would have to provide enough cash income to support \$99.22 million of debt. *Such a holding company system is highly leveraged—its consolidated debt ratio is 99.22 percent, even though each of the individual components shows only a 50 percent debt/assets ratio.* Because of this consolidated leverage, even a small decline in profits at the operating company level could bring the whole system down like a house of cards. This situation existed in the electric utility industry in the 1920s, and the Depression of the 1930s wreaked havoc with the holding companies and led to federal legislation which constrained holding companies in that industry.

Self-Test Questions

What is a holding company?

What are some of the advantages of holding companies? What are some of the disadvantages?

Summary

This chapter included discussions of mergers, divestitures, holding companies, and LBOs. The majority of the discussion in this chapter was on mergers. We discussed the rationale for mergers, different types of mergers, the level of merger activity, merger regulation, and merger analysis. We also showed how to use two different approaches to valuing the target firm: discounted cash flow and market multiple analyses. We also explained how the acquiring firm can structure its takeover bid, the different ways accountants treat mergers, and investment bankers' roles in arranging and financing mergers. In addition, we discussed two cooperative arrangements that fall short of mergers: corporate, or strategic, alliances and joint ventures. The key concepts covered are listed below:

- A **merger** occurs when two firms combine to form a single company. The primary motives for mergers are (1) synergy, (2) tax considerations, (3) purchase of assets below their replacement costs, (4) diversification, (5) gaining control over a larger enterprise, and (6) breakup value.
- Mergers can provide economic benefits through **economies of scale** and through putting assets in the hands of **more efficient managers.** However, mergers also have the potential for reducing competition, and for this reason they are carefully regulated by government agencies.
- In most mergers, one company (the **acquiring firm**) initiates action to take over another (the **target firm**).
- A **horizontal merger** occurs when two firms in the same line of business combine.
- A **vertical merger** combines a firm with one of its customers or suppliers.
- A **congeneric merger** involves firms in related industries, but where no customer-supplier relationship exists.
- A **conglomerate merger** occurs when firms in totally different industries combine.
- In a **friendly merger,** the managements of both firms approve the merger, whereas in a **hostile merger,** the target firm's management opposes it.
- An **operating merger** is one in which the operations of the two firms are combined. A **financial merger** is one in which the firms continue to operate separately hence, no operating economies are expected.
- In a typical **merger analysis,** the key issues to be resolved are (1) the price to be paid for the target firm and (2) the employment/control situation. If the merger is a consolidation of two relatively equal firms, an issue is, "What percentage of the ownership do each merger partner's shareholders receive?"
- Two methods are commonly used to determine the **value of the target firm:** (1) the **discounted cash flow (DCF)** method and (2) the **market multiple** method.

- For accounting purposes, mergers are handled in one of two ways: (1) as a **pooling of interests** or (2) as a **purchase.**
- A **joint venture** is a **corporate alliance** in which two or more companies combine some of their resources to achieve a specific, limited objective.
- A **leveraged buyout (LBO)** is a transaction in which a firm's publicly owned stock is acquired in a mostly debt-financed tender offer, and a privately owned, highly leveraged firm results. Often, the firm's own management initiates the LBO.
- A **divestiture** is the sale of some of a company's operating assets. A divestiture may involve (1) selling an operating unit to another firm, (2) **spinning off** a unit as a separate company, or (3) the outright **liquidation** of a unit's assets.
- The **reasons for divestiture** include to settle antitrust suits, to clarify what a company actually does, to enable management to concentrate on a particular type of activity, and to raise capital needed to strengthen the corporation's core business.
- A **holding company** is a corporation that owns sufficient stock in another firm to control it. The holding company is also known as the **parent company,** and the companies that it controls are called **subsidiaries,** or **operating companies.**
- Advantages to holding company operations include (1) control can often be obtained for a smaller cash outlay, (2) risks may be segregated, and (3) regulated companies can operate separate subsidiaries for their regulated and unregulated businesses.
- Disadvantages to holding company operations include (1) tax penalties and (2) the fact that incomplete ownership, if it exists, can lead to control problems.

Questions

26–1 Define each of the following terms:

a. Synergy; merger
b. Horizontal merger; vertical merger; congeneric merger; conglomerate merger
c. Friendly merger; hostile merger; defensive merger; tender offer; target company; breakup value; acquiring company
d. Operating merger; financial merger
e. Discounted cash flow method; market multiple method
f. Pooling of interests; purchase accounting
g. White knight; poison pill; golden parachute; proxy fight
h. Joint venture; corporate alliance
i. Divestiture; spin-off; leveraged buyout (LBO)
j. Holding company; operating company; parent company
k. Arbitrage; risk arbitrage

26–2 Four economic classifications of mergers are (1) horizontal, (2) vertical, (3) conglomerate, and (4) congeneric. Explain the significance of these terms in merger analysis with regard to (a) the likelihood of governmental intervention and (b) possibilities for operating synergy.

26–3 Firm A wants to acquire Firm B. Firm B's management agrees that the merger is a good idea. Might a tender offer be used?

26–4 Distinguish between operating mergers and financial mergers.

26–5 In the spring of 1984, Disney Productions' stock was selling for about \$3.125 per share (all prices have been adjusted for 4-for-1 splits in 1986 and 1992). Then Saul Steinberg, a New York financier, began acquiring it, and after he had 12 percent, he announced a tender offer for another 37 percent of the stock—which would bring his holdings up to 49 percent—at a price of \$4.22 per share. Disney's management then announced plans to buy Gibson Greeting Cards and Arvida Corporation, paying for them with stock. It also lined up bank credit and (according to Steinberg) was prepared to borrow up to \$2 billion and use the funds to repurchase shares at a higher price than Steinberg was offering. All of these efforts were designed to keep Steinberg from taking control. In June, Disney's management agreed to pay Steinberg \$4.84 per share, which gave him a gain of about \$60 million on a 2-month investment of about \$26.5 million.

When Disney's buy-back of Steinberg's shares was announced, the stock price fell almost instantly from \$4.25 to \$2.875. Many Disney stockholders were irate, and they sued to block the buyout. Also, the Disney affair added fuel to the fire in a Congressional committee that was holding hearings on proposed legislation that would (1) prohibit someone from acquiring more than 10 percent of a firm's stock without making a tender offer for all the remaining shares, (2) prohibit poison pill tactics such as those Disney's management had used to fight off Steinberg, (3) prohibit buy-backs such as the deal eventually offered to Steinberg (greenmail) unless there was an approving vote by stockholders, and (4) prohibit (or substantially curtail) the use of golden parachutes (the one thing Disney's management did not try).

Set forth the arguments for and against this type of legislation. What provisions, if any, should it contain? Also, look up Disney's current stock price to see how its stockholders have actually fared.

26-6 Two large, publicly owned firms are contemplating a merger. No operating synergy is expected. However, since returns on the 2 firms are not perfectly positively correlated, the standard deviation of earnings would be reduced for the combined corporation. One group of consultants argues that this risk reduction is sufficient grounds for the merger. Another group thinks this type of risk reduction is irrelevant because stockholders can themselves hold the stock of both companies and thus gain the risk-reduction benefits without all the hassles and expenses of the merger. Whose position is correct?

Problems

The following information is required to work Problems 26-1, 26-2, and 26-3.

Harrison Corporation is interested in acquiring Van Buren Corporation. Assume that the risk-free rate of interest is 5 percent and the market risk premium is 6 percent.

26-1 *VALUATION* Van Buren currently expects to pay a year-end dividend of \$2.00 a share (D_1 = \$2.00). Van Buren's dividend is expected to grow at a constant rate of 5 percent a year, and its beta is 0.9. What is the current price of Van Buren's stock?

26-2 *MERGER VALUATION* Harrison estimates that if it acquires Van Buren, the year-end dividend will remain at \$2.00 a share, but synergies will enable the dividend to grow at a constant rate of 7 percent a year (instead of the current 5 percent). Van Buren has no debt, and Harrison will not add any. What is the per-share value of Van Buren to Harrison Corporation?

26-3 *MERGER BID* On the basis of your answers to Problems 26-1 and 26-2, if Harrison were to acquire Van Buren, what would be the range of possible prices that it could bid for each share of Van Buren common stock?

26-4 *MERGER ANALYSIS* Apilado Appliance Corporation is considering a merger with the Vaccaro Vacuum Company. Vaccaro is a publicly traded company, and its current beta is 1.30. Vaccaro has been barely profitable, so it has paid an average of only 20 percent in taxes during the last several years. In addition, it uses little debt, having a debt ratio of just 25 percent.

If the acquisition were made, Apilado would operate Vaccaro as a separate, wholly owned subsidiary. Apilado would pay taxes on a consolidated basis, and the tax rate would therefore increase to 35 percent. Apilado also would increase the debt capitalization in the Vaccaro subsidiary to 40 percent of assets, which would increase its beta to 1.50. Apilado's acquisition department estimates that Vaccaro, if acquired, would produce the following net cash flows to Apilado's shareholders (in millions of dollars):

Year	Net Cash Flows
1	\$1.30
2	1.50
3	1.75
4	2.00
5 and beyond	Constant growth at 6%

These cash flows include all acquisition effects. Apilado's cost of equity is 14 percent, its beta is 1.0, and its cost of debt is 10 percent. The risk-free rate is 8 percent.

a. What discount rate should be used to discount the estimated cash flow? (Hint: Use Apilado's k_s to determine the market risk premium.)

b. What is the dollar value of Vaccaro to Apilado's shareholders?

26–5 *CAPITAL BUDGETING ANALYSIS*

The Stanley Stationery Shoppe wishes to acquire The Carlson Card Gallery for $400,000. Stanley expects the merger to provide incremental earnings of about $64,000 a year for 10 years. Ken Stanley has calculated the marginal cost of capital for this investment to be 10 percent. Conduct a capital budgeting analysis for Stanley to determine whether or not he should purchase The Carlson Card Gallery.

26–6 *MERGER ANALYSIS*

TransWorld Communications Inc., a large telecommunications company, is evaluating the possible acquisition of Georgia Cable Company (GCC), a regional cable company. TransWorld's analysts project the following postmerger data for GCC (in thousands of dollars, with a December 31 year-end):

		2002	2003	2004	2005
Net sales		$450	$518	$555	$600
Selling and administrative expense		45	53	60	68
Interest		18	21	24	27
Tax rate after merger	35%				
Cost of goods sold as a percent of sales	65%				
Beta after merger	1.50				
Risk-free rate	8%				
Market risk premium	4%				
Terminal growth rate of cash flow available to TransWorld's shareholders	7%				

If the acquisition is made, it will occur on January 1, 2002. All cash flows shown in the income statements are assumed to occur at the end of the year. GCC currently has a capital structure of 40 percent debt, but TransWorld would increase that to 50 percent if the acquisition were made. GCC, if independent, would pay taxes at 20 percent, but its income would be taxed at 35 percent if it were consolidated. GCC's current market-determined beta is 1.40, and its investment bankers think that its beta would rise to 1.50 if the debt ratio were increased to 50 percent. The cost of goods sold is expected to be 65 percent of sales, but it could vary somewhat. Depreciation-generated funds would be used to replace worn-out equipment, so they would not be available to TransWorld's shareholders. The risk-free rate is 8 percent, and the market risk premium is 4 percent.

a. What is the appropriate discount rate for valuing the acquisition?

b. What is the terminal value? What is the value of GCC to TransWorld's shareholders?

Spreadsheet Problems

26–7 *BUILD A MODEL: MERGER ANALYSIS*

Start with the partial model in the file ***Ch 26-7 Build a Model.xls*** on your textbook's CD-ROM. Wansley Portal Inc., a large Internet service provider, is evaluating the possible acquisition of Alabama Connections Company (ACC), a regional Internet service provider. Wansley's analysts project the following postmerger data for ACC (in thousands of dollars):

	2002	2003	2004	2005
Net sales	$500	$600	$700	$760
Selling and administrative expense	60	70	80	90
Interest	20	23	25	28

If the acquisition is made, it will occur on January 1, 2002. All cash flows shown in the income statements are assumed to occur at the end of the year. ACC currently has a capital structure of 30 percent debt, but Wansley would increase that to 40 percent if the acquisition were made. ACC, if independent, would pay taxes at 30 percent, but its income would be taxed at 35 percent if it were consolidated. ACC's current market-determined beta is 1.40. The cost of goods sold is expected to be 65 percent of sales, but it could vary somewhat. Depreciation-generated funds would be used to replace worn-out equipment, so they would not be available to Wansley's shareholders. The risk-free rate is 7 percent, and the market risk premium is 6.5 percent.

a. What is the appropriate discount rate for valuing the acquisition?

b. What is the horizon, or continuing, value? What is the value of ACC to Wansley's shareholders?

26–8 *WHAT IF ANALYSIS: MERGER ANALYSIS*

Use the model in the file ***Ch 26-8 What If Analysis.xls*** on your textbook's CD-ROM and answer the questions shown there.

Cyberproblem

The information related to this cyberproblem is likely to change over time, due to the release of new information and the ever-changing nature of the World Wide Web. Accordingly, we will periodically update the problem on the textbook's web site.

26–9 *MERGERS—EXXON MOBIL*

In 1882, John D. Rockefeller created a petroleum consortium under the name of Standard Oil Trust. The Standard Oil empire comprised several incorporated refining and marketing organizations, and among its divisions were Standard Oil Company of New Jersey and Standard Oil Company of New York, commonly known as Jersey Standard and Socony, respectively. In 1911, the U.S. Supreme Court ordered the disbanding of Standard Oil Trust, resulting in the spin-off of 34 companies. Among those 34 companies were Standard Oil of New Jersey and Standard Oil Company of New York, which would later assume the names of Exxon and Mobil, respectively. In 1998, nearly 90 years after the breakup of Standard Oil Trust, Exxon and Mobil announced that they would again unite in one of the biggest mergers of the year.

This cyberproblem looks at the Exxon/Mobil merger. Go to the textbook's web page, **www.harcourtcollege.com/finance/theory/student/resources/cyberprob/ch26.html** and answer the questions shown there.

Mini Case

See ***Ch 26 Show.ppt*** and ***Ch 26 Mini Case.xls***.

Smitty's Home Repair Company, a regional hardware chain that specializes in "do-it-yourself" materials and equipment rentals, is cash rich because of several consecutive good years. One of the alternative uses for the excess funds is an acquisition. Linda Wade, Smitty's treasurer and your boss, has been asked to place a value on a potential target, Hill's Hardware, a small chain that operates in an adjacent state, and she has enlisted your help.

The table below indicates Wade's estimates of Hill's earnings potential if it came under Smitty's management (in millions of dollars). The interest expense listed here includes the interest (1) on Hill's existing debt and (2) on new debt expected to be issued over time to help finance expansion within the new "H division," the code name given to the target firm. The retentions represent earnings that will be reinvested within the H division to help finance its growth.

Security analysts estimate Hill's beta to be 1.3. The acquisition would not change Hill's capital structure or tax rate. Wade realizes that Hill's Hardware also generates depreciation cash flows, but she believes that these funds would have to be reinvested within the division to replace worn-out equipment.

Wade estimates the risk-free rate to be 9 percent and the market risk premium to be 4 percent. She also estimates that net cash flows after 2005 will grow at a constant rate of 6 percent. Following are projections for sales and other items.

	2002	2003	2004	2005
Net sales	$60.0	$90.0	$112.5	$127.5
Cost of goods sold (60%)	36.0	54.0	67.5	76.5
Selling/administrative expense	4.5	6.0	7.5	9.0
Interest expense	3.0	4.5	4.5	6.0
Necessary retained earnings	0.0	7.5	6.0	4.5

Smitty's management is new to the merger game, so Wade has been asked to answer some basic questions about mergers as well as to perform the merger analysis. To structure the task, Wade has developed the following questions, which you must answer and then defend to Smitty's board.

a. Several reasons have been proposed to justify mergers. Among the more prominent are (1) tax considerations, (2) risk reduction, (3) control, (4) purchase of assets at below-replacement cost, (5) synergy, and (6) globalization. In general, which of the reasons are economically justifiable? Which are not? Which fit the situation at hand? Explain.
b. Briefly describe the differences between a hostile merger and a friendly merger.
c. Use the data developed in the table to construct the H division's cash flow statements for 2002 through 2005. Why is interest expense deducted in merger cash flow statements, whereas it is not normally deducted in a capital budgeting cash flow analysis? Why are earnings retentions deducted in the cash flow statement?
d. Conceptually, what is the appropriate discount rate to apply to the cash flows developed in part c? What is your actual estimate of this discount rate?
e. What is the estimated horizon, or continuing, value of the acquisition; that is, what is the estimated value of the H division's cash flows beyond 2005? What is Hill's value to Smitty's shareholders? Suppose another firm were evaluating Hill's as an acquisition candidate. Would they obtain the same value? Explain.
f. Assume that Hill's has 10 million shares outstanding. These shares are traded relatively infrequently, but the last trade, made several weeks ago, was at a price of $9 per share. Should Smitty's make an offer for Hill's? If so, how much should it offer per share?
g. Assume that publicly traded companies in Hill's line of business have stock prices in the range of 12 to 14 times earnings per share (EPS). Use the market multiple approach to value the target company.
h. There has been considerable research undertaken to determine whether mergers really create value and, if so, how this value is shared between the parties involved. What are the results of this research?
i. What are the two methods of accounting for mergers?
j. What merger-related activities are undertaken by investment bankers?
k. What is a leveraged buyout (LBO)? What are some of the advantages and disadvantages of going private?
l. What are the major types of divestitures? What motivates firms to divest assets?
m. What are holding companies? What are their advantages and disadvantages?

Selected Additional References and Cases

Considerable empirical investigation has been conducted to determine whether stockholders of acquiring or acquired companies benefit most from corporate mergers. Several excellent studies are

Black, Bernard S., and Joseph A. Grundfest, "Shareholder Gains from Takeovers and Restructurings between 1981 and 1986: $162 Billion Is a Lot of Money," *Journal of Applied Corporate Finance*, Spring 1988, 5–15.

Jarrell, Greg A., and Annettee B. Poulsen, "The Returns to Acquiring Firms in Tender Offers: Evidence from Three Decades," *Financial Management*, Autumn 1989, 12–19.

Mandelker, Gershon, "Risk and Return: The Case of Merging Firms," *Journal of Financial Economics*, December 1974, 303–335.

For some additional insights into merger returns, see

Elgers, Pieter T., and John J. Clark, "Merger Types and Shareholder Returns: Additional Evidence," *Financial Management*, Summer 1980, 66–72.

Mueller, Dennis C., "The Effects of Conglomerate Mergers," *Journal of Banking and Finance*, December 1977, 315–347.

Wansley, James W., William R. Lane, and Ho C. Yang, "Abnormal Returns to Acquired Firms by Type of Acquisition and Method of Payment," *Financial Management*, Autumn 1983, 16–22.

For an interesting test of the existence of synergy in mergers, see

Haugen, Robert A., and Terence C. Langetieg, "An Empirical Test for Synergism in Merger," *Journal of Finance*, September 1975, 1003–1014.

For more insights into the likelihood of acceptance of a cash tender offer, see

Hoffmeister, J. Ronald, and Edward A. Dyl, "Predicting Outcomes of Cash Tender Offers," *Financial Management*, Winter 1981, 50–58.

Some additional works on tender offers include

Dodd, Peter, and Richard Ruback, "Tender Offers and Stockholder Returns," *Journal of Financial Economics*, November 1977, 351–373.

Kummer, Donald R., and J. Ronald Hoffmeister, "Valuation Consequences of Cash Tender Offers," *Journal of Finance*, May 1978, 505–516.

The following articles examine the effect of merger accounting on stock price:

Davis, Michael L., "The Purchase versus Pooling Controversy: How the Stock Market Responds to Goodwill," *Journal of Applied Corporate Finance*, Spring 1996, 51–59.

Hong, Hai, Gershon Mandelker, and R. S. Kaplan, "Pooling versus Purchase: The Effects of Accounting for Mergers on Stock Prices," *Accounting Review*, January 1978, 31–47.

For a selection of articles on LBOs, see the Spring 1989 issue of the Journal of Applied Corporate Finance *and the Spring 1992 issue of* Financial Management.

The Summer 1989 issue of the Journal of Applied Corporate Finance *also focuses on mergers and acquisitions.*

For a selection of articles on LBOs, see the Spring 1989 issue of the Journal of Applied Corporate Finance.

For a very interesting discussion of many of the important merger issues, see

"A Discussion of Mergers and Acquisitions," *Midland Corporate Finance Journal*, Summer 1983, 21–47.

Other recent articles that pertain to this chapter include the following:

Allen, Jay R., "LBOs—The Evolution of Financial Strategies and Structures," *Journal of Applied Corporate Finance*, Winter 1996, 18–29.

Baker, George P., "Beatrice: A Study in the Creation and Destruction of Value," *Journal of Finance*, July 1992, 1081–1119.

Baker, George P., and Karen H. Wruck, "Lessons from a Middle Market LBO: The Case of O. M. Scott," *Journal of Applied Corporate Finance*, Spring 1991, 46–58.

Eckbo, B. Espen, "Mergers and the Value of Antitrust Deterrence," *Journal of Finance*, July 1992, 1005–1029.

Ezzell, John R., H. Christine Hsu, and James A. Miles, "An Analysis of Regulated Rates of Return for Wholly Owned Subsidiaries," *Journal of Financial Research*, Summer 1991, 167–180.

Kaplan, Steven, and Michael S. Weisbach, "The Success of Acquisitions: Evidence from Divestitures," *Journal of Finance*, March 1992, 107–138.

Mitchell, Mark L., and Kenneth Lehn, "Do Bad Bidders Become Good Targets?" *Journal of Applied Corporate Finance*, Summer 1990, 60–69.

Mohan, Nancy, M. Fall Ainina, Daniel Kaufman, and Bernard J. Winger, "Acquisition/ Divestiture Valuation Practices in Major U.S. Firms," *Financial Practice and Education*, Spring 1991, 73–81.

Morck, Randall, Andrei Shleifer, and Robert W. Vishny, "Do Managerial Objectives Drive Bad Acquisitions?" *Journal of Finance*, March 1990, 31–48.

Romano, Roberta, "Rethinking Takeover Regulations," *Journal of Applied Corporate Finance*, Fall 1992, 47–57.

Weaver, Samuel C., Robert S. Harris, Daniel W. Bielinski, and Kenneth F. MacKenzie, "Merger and Acquisition Valuation," *Financial Management*, Summer 1991, 85–96.

Wruck, Karen H., "What Really Went Wrong at Revco?" *Journal of Applied Corporate Finance*, Summer 1991, 79–92.

The following cases in the Cases in Financial Management: Dryden Request *series illustrate merger analysis:*

Case 40, "Nina's Fashions, Inc.," Case 40A, "Nero's Pasta, Inc.," and Case 40B, "Computer Concepts/CompuTech," which focus on merger valuation.

27

Multinational Financial Management[1]

From the end of World War II until the 1970s, the United States dominated the world economy. However, that situation no longer exists. Raw materials, finished goods, services, and money flow freely across most national boundaries, as do innovative ideas and new technologies. World-class U.S. companies are making breakthroughs in foreign labs, obtaining capital from foreign investors, and putting foreign employees on the fast track to the top. Dozens of top U.S. manufacturers, including Dow Chemical, Colgate-Palmolive, Gillette, Hewlett-Packard, and Xerox, sell more of their products outside the United States than they do at home. Service firms are not far behind, as Citigroup, Disney, McDonald's, and Time Warner all receive more than 20 percent of their revenues from foreign sales.

The trend is even more pronounced in profits. In recent years, Coca-Cola and many other companies have made more money in the Pacific Rim and Western Europe than in the United States. However, like other companies, Coke has found that global investing also presents unique challenges and risks. Recent weakness in the Asian economy, along with a contamination scare in Belgium, have hurt the bottom line and put Coke on the defensive. Still, most analysts believe that these are only temporary setbacks and that Coke will continue to generate huge profits from its overseas operations in the years ahead.

Successful global companies such as Coca-Cola must conduct business in different economies, and they must be sensitive to the many subtleties of different cultures and political systems. Accordingly, they find it useful to blend into the foreign landscape to win product acceptance and avoid political problems.

At the same time, foreign-based multinationals are arriving on American shores in ever greater numbers. Sweden's ABB, the Netherlands' Philips, France's Thomson, and Japan's Fujitsu and Honda are all waging campaigns to be identified as American companies that employ Americans, transfer technology to America, and help the U.S. trade balance. Few Americans know or care that Thomson owns the RCA and General Electric names in consumer electronics, or that Philips owns Magnavox.

The emergence of "world companies" raises a host of questions for governments. For example, should domestic firms be favored, or does it make no difference what a company's nationality is as long as it provides domestic jobs? Should a company make an effort to keep jobs in its home country, or should it produce where total production costs are lowest? What nation controls the technology developed by a multinational corporation, particularly if the technology can be used in military applications? Must a multinational company adhere to rules imposed in its home country with respect to its operations outside the home country? Keep these questions in mind as you read this chapter. When you finish it, you should have a better appreciation of both the problems facing governments and the difficult but profitable opportunities facing managers of multinational companies.

---

[1]This chapter was coauthored with Professor Roy Crum of the University of Florida and Subu Venkataraman with Morgan Stanley Dean Witter.

Managers of multinational companies must deal with a wide range of issues that are not present when a company operates in a single country. In this chapter, we highlight the key differences between multinational and domestic corporations, and we discuss the effect these differences have on the financial management of multinational businesses.

Multinational, or Global, Corporations

CD

The textbook's CD-ROM contains an *Excel* file that will guide you through the chapter's calculations. The file for this chapter is ***Ch 27 Tool Kit.xls,*** and we encourage you to open the file and follow along as you read the chapter.

The term **multinational,** or **global, corporation** is used to describe a firm that operates in an integrated fashion in a number of countries. During the past 20 years, a new and fundamentally different form of international commercial activity has developed, and this has greatly increased worldwide economic and political interdependence. Rather than merely buying resources from and selling goods to foreign nations, multinational firms now make direct investments in fully integrated operations, from extraction of raw materials, through the manufacturing process, to distribution to consumers throughout the world. Today, multinational corporate networks control a large and growing share of the world's technological, marketing, and productive resources.

Companies, both U.S. and foreign, "go global" for six primary reasons:

1. **To broaden their markets.** After a company has saturated its home market, growth opportunities are often better in foreign markets. Thus, such homegrown firms as Coca-Cola and McDonald's are aggressively expanding into overseas markets, and foreign firms such as Sony and Toshiba now dominate the U.S. consumer electronics market. Also, as products become more complex, and development becomes more expensive, it is necessary to sell more units to cover overhead costs, so larger markets are critical. Thus, movie companies have "gone global" to get the volume necessary to support pictures such as *Titanic.*
2. **To seek raw materials.** Many U.S. oil companies, such as Exxon, have major subsidiaries around the world to ensure access to the basic resources needed to sustain the companies' primary business line.
3. **To seek new technology.** No single nation holds a commanding advantage in all technologies, so companies are scouring the globe for leading scientific and design ideas. For example, Xerox has introduced more than 80 different office copiers in the United States that were engineered and built by its Japanese joint venture, Fuji Xerox. Similarly, versions of the superconcentrated detergent that Procter & Gamble first formulated in Japan in response to a rival's product are now being marketed in Europe and the United States.
4. **To seek production efficiency.** Companies in high-cost countries are shifting production to low-cost regions. For example, GE has production and assembly plants in Mexico, South Korea, and Singapore, and even Japanese manufacturers are shifting some of their production to lower-cost countries in the Pacific Rim. BMW, in response to high production costs in Germany, has built assembly plants in the United States. The ability to shift production from country to country has important implications for labor costs in all countries. For example, when Xerox threatened to move its copier rebuilding work to Mexico, its union in Rochester agreed to work rule changes and productivity improvements that kept the operation in the United States. Some multinational companies make decisions almost daily on where to shift production. When Dow Chemical saw European demand for a certain solvent declining, the company scaled back production at a German plant and shifted its production to another chemical that had previously been imported from the United States. Relying on complex computer models for making

such decisions, Dow runs its plants at peak capacity and thus keeps capital costs down.

5. **To avoid political and regulatory hurdles.** The primary reason Japanese auto companies moved production to the United States was to get around U.S. import quotas. Now Honda, Nissan, Toyota, Mazda, and Mitsubishi are all assembling vehicles in the United States. One of the factors that prompted U.S. pharmaceutical maker SmithKline and Britain's Beecham to merge was that they wanted to avoid licensing and regulatory delays in their largest markets, Western Europe and the United States. Now SmithKline Beecham can identify itself as an inside player in both Europe and the United States. Similarly, when Germany's BASF launched biotechnology research at home, it confronted legal and political challenges from the environmentally conscious Green movement. In response, BASF shifted its cancer and immune system research to two laboratories in Boston suburbs. This location is attractive not only because of its large number of engineers and scientists but also because the Boston area has resolved controversies involving safety, animal rights, and the environment. "We decided it would be better to have the laboratories located where we have fewer insecurities about what will happen in the future," said Rolf-Dieter Acker, BASF's director of biotechnology research.
6. **To diversify.** By establishing worldwide production facilities and markets, firms can cushion the impact of adverse economic trends in any single country. For example, General Motors softened the blow of poor sales in the United States during a recent recession with strong sales by its European subsidiaries. In general, geographic diversification works because the economic ups and downs of different countries are not perfectly correlated. Therefore, companies investing overseas benefit from diversification in the same way that individuals benefit from investing in a broad portfolio of stocks.

Over the past 10 to 15 years, there has been an increasing amount of investment in the United States by foreign corporations, and in foreign nations by U.S. corporations. This trend is shown in Figure 27-1, and it is important because of its implications for eroding the traditional doctrine of independence and self-reliance that has been a hallmark of U.S. policy. Just as U.S. corporations with extensive overseas operations are said to use their economic power to exert substantial economic and political influence over host governments in many parts of the world, it is feared that foreign corporations are gaining similar sway over U.S. policy. These developments suggest an increasing degree of mutual influence and interdependence among business enterprises and nations, to which the United States is not immune.

The world economy is quite fluid. Here are a few of the recent events that have dramatically changed the international financial environment:

WWW

The NAFTA (North American Free Trade Agreement) ensures that continued international investment will be made by U.S. corporations. An interesting report about the effect of NAFTA on the U.S. economy can be found on the United States Trade Representative's home page at **http://www.ustr.gov/reports/index.html**.

1. The disintegration of the former Soviet Union and the movement toward market economies in the newly formed countries have created a vast new market for international commerce.
2. The reunification of Germany, coupled with the collapse of communism in Eastern Europe, has created significant new opportunities for foreign investment.
3. The European Community and the European Free Trade Association have created a "borderless" region where people, capital, goods, and services move freely among the 19 nations without the burden of tariffs. This consolidation has led to the creation of a single "Eurocurrency" called the "Euro."
4. The North American Free Trade Agreement (NAFTA) has moved the economies of the United States, Canada, and Mexico much closer together, and made them more interdependent.
5. U.S. bank regulations have been loosened dramatically. One key deregulatory feature was the removal of interest rate ceilings, thus allowing banks to attract foreign

FIGURE 27-1 Direct Investment for the United States, 1982–1999

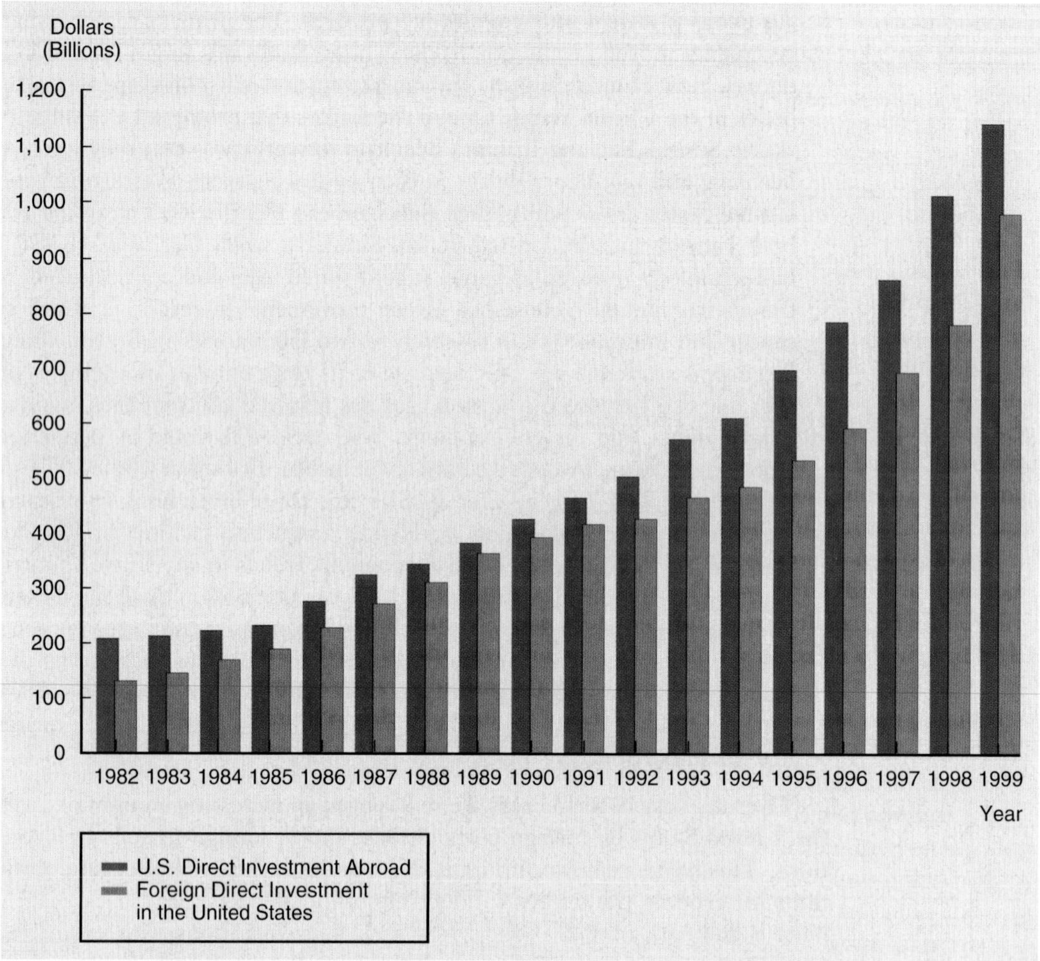

Source: S. Vargas, "Direct Investment Positions for 1999, Country and Industry Detail," *Survey of Current Business,* July 2000, 58–69.

deposits by raising rates. Another key feature was the removal of barriers to entry by foreign banks, which resulted in more cross-border banking transactions. Still, U.S. commercial and investment banks do not have as much freedom as foreign banks, which has led many U.S. banks to establish subsidiaries in Europe that can offer a wider range of services. All this has increased global competition in the financial services industry.

Self-Test Questions

What is a multinational corporation?

Why do companies "go global"?

Multinational versus Domestic Financial Management

In theory, the concepts and procedures discussed in the first 26 chapters are valid for both domestic and multinational operations. However, six major factors distinguish financial management in firms operating entirely within a single country from firms that operate globally:

1. **Different currency denominations.** Cash flows in various parts of a multinational corporate system will be denominated in different currencies. Hence, an analysis of exchange rates must be included in all financial analyses.
2. **Economic and legal ramifications.** Each country has its own unique economic and legal systems, and these differences can cause significant problems when a corporation tries to coordinate and control its worldwide operations. For example, differences in tax laws among countries can cause a given economic transaction to have strikingly different after-tax consequences, depending on where the transaction occurs. Similarly, differences in legal systems of host nations, such as the Common Law of Great Britain versus the French Civil Law, complicate matters ranging from the simple recording of business transactions to the role played by the judiciary in resolving conflicts. Such differences can restrict multinational corporations' flexibility in deploying resources, and can even make procedures that are required in one part of the company illegal in another part. These differences also make it difficult for executives trained in one country to move easily to another.
3. **Language differences.** The ability to communicate is critical in all business transactions, and here U.S. citizens are often at a disadvantage because we are generally fluent only in English, while European and Japanese businesspeople are usually fluent in several languages, including English. Thus, they can penetrate our markets more easily than we can penetrate theirs.
4. **Cultural differences.** Even within geographic regions that are considered relatively homogeneous, different countries have unique cultural heritages that shape values and influence the conduct of business. Multinational corporations find that matters such as defining the appropriate goals of the firm, attitudes toward risk, dealings with employees, and the ability to curtail unprofitable operations vary dramatically from one country to the next.
5. **Role of governments.** Most financial models assume the existence of a competitive marketplace in which the terms of trade are determined by the participants. The government, through its power to establish basic ground rules, is involved in the process, but its role is minimal. Thus, the market provides the primary barometer of success, and it gives the best clues about what must be done to remain competitive. This view of the process is reasonably correct for the United States and Western Europe, but it does not accurately describe the situation in most of the world. Frequently, the terms under which companies compete, the actions that must be taken or avoided, and the terms of trade on various transactions are determined not in the marketplace but by direct negotiation between host governments and multinational corporations. This is essentially a political process, and it must be treated as such. Thus, our traditional financial models have to be recast to include political and other noneconomic aspects of the decision.
6. **Political risk.** A nation is free to place constraints on the transfer of corporate resources and even to expropriate without compensation assets within their boundaries. This is *political risk*, and it tends to be largely a given rather than a variable that can be changed by negotiation. Political risk varies from country to country, and it must be addressed explicitly in any financial analysis. Another aspect of political risk is terrorism against U.S. firms or executives. For example, U.S. and Japanese executives have been kidnapped and held for ransom—with some killed to prove that the kidnappers were serious—in several South American countries.

These six factors complicate financial management, and they increase the risks faced by multinational firms. However, the prospects for high returns, diversification benefits, and other factors make it worthwhile for firms to accept these risks and learn how to manage them.

The Euro: What You Need to Know

In January 1999, many Europeans began making purchases using a new currency, the euro. This is one result of the Maastricht Treaty, signed in 1992, as part of a decades-long effort to form a tighter economic and monetary union (EMU) in Europe. Eleven countries adopted the euro: Belgium, Austria, Finland, France, Luxembourg, Italy, the Netherlands, Germany, Spain, Ireland, and Portugal. (Tip: You can remember them by the phrase BAFFLING SIP). Britain, Switzerland, and the Scandinavian countries chose not to join the union because they did not want to give up control of their currencies.

Euro bills and coins will not begin circulating until January 1, 2002. Before then, all cash transactions must be made with the country's national currency, but paperless transactions, such as those with a credit card, can be made in either euros or the national currency. For example, you could pay for a bottle of French champagne using either francs or euros (with your credit card). After euro bills and coins begin circulating, there will be a six-month phase-in period, and then all transactions must be made in euros. (You will still have 10 more years to convert remaining bills or coins at a bank.)

Each of the 11 currencies is tied to the euro at a permanently fixed exchange rate. For example, one euro is worth 6.56 French francs and 1.956 German marks. Because these rates don't change, the exchange rate between these countries is also fixed: 1 mark is worth 3.35 francs. However, the value of the euro will fluctuate relative to other currencies, such as the U.S. dollar. Finally, instead of each country having a central bank to manage its currency, the European Central Bank, located in Frankfurt, Germany, will set interest rates and manage monetary policy for the entire region.

Source: Helene Cooper, "Europe Unites: The Launch of the Euro; The Euro: What You Need to Know," *The Wall Street Journal*, January 4, 1999, A5.

Self-Test Question

Identify and briefly discuss six major factors that complicate financial management in multinational firms.

Exchange Rates

WWW

The Bloomberg World Currency Values site provides up-to-the-minute foreign currency values versus the U.S. dollar, as well as a cross-currency table similar to that found in *The Wall Street Journal* for the world's major currencies. The site can be accessed at **http://www.bloomberg.com/markets/fxc.html**.

An **exchange rate** specifies the number of units of a given currency that can be purchased with one unit of another currency. Exchange rates appear in the financial sections of newspapers each day. Selected rates from *The Wall Street Journal* are given in Table 27-1. The values shown in Column 1 are the number of U.S. dollars required to purchase one unit of foreign currency; this is called a *direct quotation.* Direct quotations have a dollar sign in their quotation. Thus, the direct U.S. dollar quotation for the German mark is \$0.4272, because one German mark could be bought for 42.72 cents. The exchange rates given in Column 2 represent the number of units of foreign currency that can be purchased for one U.S. dollar; these are called *indirect quotations.* Indirect quotations often begin with the foreign currency's equivalent to the dollar sign. Thus, the indirect quotation for the German mark is M2.3408. (The "M" stands for *Mark*, and it is analogous to the symbol "\$.") Normal practice in the United States is to use indirect quotations (Column 2) for all currencies other than British pounds, for which direct quotations are given. Thus, we speak of the pound as "selling at \$1.45" but of the mark as "being at 2.34."

It is also a universal convention on the world's foreign currency exchanges to state all exchange rates except British pounds on a "dollar basis"—that is, as the foreign currency price of one U.S. dollar as reported in Column 2 of Table 27-1. Thus, in all currency trading centers, whether in New York, Frankfurt, London, Tokyo, or anywhere else, the exchange rate for the German mark would be displayed as M2.3408. This

TABLE 27-1 Illustrative Exchange Rates

	Direct Quotation: U.S. Dollars Required to Buy One Unit of Foreign Currency (1)	Indirect Quotation: Number of Units of Foreign Currency per U.S. Dollar (2)
British pound	$1.4515	0.6889
Canadian dollar	0.6623	1.5100
Denmark krone	0.1123	8.9075
Euro	0.8356	1.1967
French franc	0.1274	7.8506
German mark	0.4272	2.3408
Italian lira	0.0004315	2,317.36
Japanese yen	0.009233	108.31
Mexican peso	0.1043	9.5890
Netherlands guilder	0.3792	2.6374
Spanish peseta	0.005022	199.13
Swedish krona	0.0985	10.1496
Swiss franc	0.5559	1.7990

Note: Column 2 equals 1.0 divided by Column 1. However, rounding differences do occur.

Source: *The Wall Street Journal*, October 24, 2000, C15.

convention eliminates confusion when comparing quotations from one trading center with those from another.

We can use the data in Table 27-1 to show how one works with exchange rates. Suppose a U.S. tourist on holiday flies from New York to London, then to Paris, then on to Munich, and finally back to New York. When she arrives at London's Heathrow Airport, she goes to the bank to check the foreign exchange listing. The rate she observes for U.S. dollars is $1.4515; this means that £1 will cost her $1.4515. Assume that she exchanges $2,000 for $2,000/$1.4515 = £1,377.88 and enjoys a week's vacation in London, spending £877.88 while there and saving £500.

At the end of the week she travels to Dover to catch the Hovercraft to Calais on the coast of France and realizes that she needs to exchange her 500 remaining British pounds for French francs. However, what she sees on the board is the direct quotation between pounds and dollars ($1.4515) and the indirect quotation between francs and dollars (FF7.8506). (For our purposes, we assume that the exchange rates in effect at the start of the trip remain in effect throughout our example. This is unrealistic for reasons explained later in this chapter.) The exchange rate between any two currencies is called a *cross rate.* Cross rates are actually calculated on the basis of various currencies relative to the U.S. dollar. For example, the cross rate between British pounds and French francs is computed as follows:

$$\begin{aligned}\text{Cross rate} &= \frac{\text{Dollars}}{\text{Pound}} \times \frac{\text{Francs}}{\text{Dollar}} = \frac{\text{Francs}}{\text{Pound}} \\ &= 1.4515 \text{ dollars per pound} \times 7.8506 \text{ francs per dollar} \\ &= 11.3951 \text{ francs per pound.}\end{aligned}$$

Therefore, for every British pound she would receive 11.3951 French francs, so she would receive 11.3951 × 500 = 5,697.55 ≈ 5,698 francs.

When she finishes touring in France and arrives in Germany, she again needs to determine a cross rate, this time between French francs and German marks. The dollar-basis quotes she sees, as shown in Table 27-1, are FF7.8506 per dollar and M2.3408 per dollar. To find the cross rate, she must divide the two dollar-basis rates:

$$\text{Cross rate} = \frac{\dfrac{\text{Marks}}{\text{Dollar}}}{\dfrac{\text{Francs}}{\text{Dollar}}} = \frac{\text{Marks}}{\text{Franc}}$$

$$= \frac{\text{M2.3408 per \$}}{\text{FF7.8506 per \$}} = 0.2982 \text{ mark per franc.}$$

Then, if she had FF3,000 remaining, she could exchange them for $0.2982 \times 3{,}000 =$ M894.51, or about 895 marks.

Finally, when her vacation ends and she returns to New York, the quotation she sees is M2.3408, which tells her that she can buy 2.3408 marks for a dollar. She now holds 50 marks, so she wants to know how many U.S. dollars she will receive for her marks. First, she must find the reciprocal of the quoted indirect rate,

$$\frac{1}{\text{M2.3408}} = \$0.4272$$

which is the direct quote shown in Table 27-1, Column 1. Then she will end up with

$$\$0.4272 \times 50 = \$21.36.$$

In this example, we made three very strong and generally incorrect assumptions. First, we assumed that our traveler had to calculate all the cross rates. For retail transactions, it is customary to display the cross rates directly instead of a series of dollar rates. Second, we assumed that exchange rates remain constant over time. Actually, exchange rates vary every day, often dramatically. We will have more to say about exchange rate fluctuations in the next section. Finally, we assumed that there were no transactions costs involved in exchanging currencies. In reality, small retail exchange transactions such as those in our example usually involve fixed and/or sliding scale fees that can easily consume 5 or more percent of the transaction amount. However, credit card purchases minimize these fees.

Major business publications such as *The Wall Street Journal* regularly report cross rates among key currencies. A set of cross rates is given in Table 27-2. When examining the table, note the following points:

1. Column 1 gives indirect quotes for dollars, that is, units of a foreign currency that can be bought with one U.S. dollar. Examples: $1 will buy 7.8506 French francs or 2.3408 German marks. Note the consistency with Table 27-1, Column 2.
2. Other columns show number of units of other currencies that can be bought with one pound, one Swiss franc, etc. For example, the D-mark column shows that 1 D-mark will buy 0.64508 Canadian dollar, 3.3538 French francs, or 0.42720 U.S. dollar.
3. The rows show direct quotes, that is, number of units of the currency of the country listed in the left column required to buy one unit of the currency listed in the top row. The bottom row is particularly important for U.S. companies, as it shows the direct quotes for the U.S. dollar. This row is consistent with Column 1 of Table 27-1. Note too that the values on the bottom row are reciprocals of the corresponding values in Column 1. For example, the United Kingdom row in Column 1

TABLE 27-2 Key Currency Cross Rates

	Dollar	Euro	Pound	SFranc	Guilder	Peso	Yen	Lira	D-Mark	FFranc	CdnDlr
Canada	1.5100	1.2618	2.1918	0.8394	.57253	.15747	.01394	.00065	.64508	.19234	—
France	7.8506	6.5600	11.3951	4.3639	2.9766	.81871	.07248	.00339	3.3538	—	5.1991
Germany	2.3408	1.9560	3.3977	1.3012	.88754	.24411	.02161	.00101	—	.29817	1.5502
Italy	2317.4	1936.4	3363.6	1288.1	878.64	241.67	21.395	—	989.98	295.18	1534.7
Japan	108.31	90.50	157.21	60.206	41.067	11.295	—	.04674	46.270	13.796	71.728
Mexico	9.5890	8.0126	13.918	5.3302	3.6358	—	.08853	.00414	4.0965	1.2214	6.3503
Netherlands	2.6374	2.2038	3.8282	1.4660	—	.27504	.02435	.00114	1.1267	.33595	1.7466
Switzerland	1.7990	1.5032	2.6112	—	.68211	.18761	.01661	.00078	.76854	.22915	1.1914
United Kingdom	.68890	.5757	—	.3830	.26122	.07185	.00636	.00030	.29432	.08776	.45625
Euro	1.19670	—	1.7371	.66523	.45376	.12480	.01105	.00052	.51125	.15244	.79255
United States	—	.8356	1.4515	.55586	.37916	.10429	.00923	.00043	.42720	.12738	.66225

Source: "Key Currency Cross Rates," *The Wall Street Journal*, October 24, 2000, C15.

shows 0.68890 pound per dollar, and the pound column in the bottom row shows 1/0.68890 = 1.4515 dollars per pound.

4. Now notice, by reading down the FFranc column, that one French franc was worth 0.29817 ≈ 0.2982 German mark. This is the same cross rate that we calculated for the U.S. tourist in our example.

The tie-in with the dollar ensures that all currencies are related to one another in a consistent manner. If this consistency did not exist, currency traders could profit by buying undervalued and selling overvalued currencies. This process, known as *arbitrage*, works to bring about an equilibrium wherein the same relationship described earlier would exist. Currency traders are constantly operating in the market, seeking small inconsistencies from which they can profit. The traders' existence enables the rest of us to assume that currency markets are in equilibrium and that, at any point in time cross rates are all internally consistent.

As a final point, you should recognize that the consolidation of the European market has had a profound impact on European exchange rates. The exchange rates for the currencies of each of the participating countries are now fixed relative to the **euro.** Consequently, the cross-exchange rates between the various participating currencies are also fixed. Note, however, that the value of the euro continues to fluctuate. Therefore, if the euro strengthens relative to the U.S. dollar, the value of the German mark and the French franc (and all other EMU countries' currencies) will also strengthen relative to the dollar. However, because the mark and the franc are fixed relative to the euro, each of the currencies will increase by the same proportion and the cross-exchange rate between the mark and the franc will remain constant. Recall that these individual currencies are scheduled to disappear after 2002, at which time the euro will be the sole currency for each of the participating countries. (See the box, "The Euro: What You Need to Know.") We will then have to revise Table 27-2 to show "Europe" and "euro" rather than list the individual European countries. However, until there is just one world currency (which is unlikely), there will continue to be exchange rates, cross rates, and the like.

Self-Test Questions

What is an exchange rate?

Explain the difference between direct and indirect quotations.

What is a cross rate?

The International Monetary System

Every nation has a monetary system and a monetary authority. In the United States, the Federal Reserve is our monetary authority, and its task is to hold down inflation while promoting economic growth and raising our national standard of living. Moreover, if countries are to trade with one another, we must have some sort of system designed to facilitate payments between nations.

From the end of World War II until August 1971, the world was on a **fixed exchange rate system** administered by the International Monetary Fund (IMF). Under this system, the U.S. dollar was linked to gold ($35 per ounce), and other currencies were then tied to the dollar. Exchange rates between other currencies and the dollar were controlled within narrow limits but then adjusted periodically. For example, in 1964 the British pound was adjusted to $2.80 for £1, with a 1 percent permissible fluctuation about this rate.

Fluctuations in exchange rates occur because of changes in the supply of and demand for dollars, pounds, and other currencies. These supply and demand changes have two primary sources. First, changes in the demand for currencies depend on changes in imports and exports of goods and services. For example, U.S. importers must buy British pounds to pay for British goods, whereas British importers must buy U.S. dollars to pay for U.S. goods. If U.S. imports from Great Britain exceeded U.S. exports to Great Britain, there would be a greater demand for pounds than for dollars, and this would drive up the price of the pound relative to that of the dollar. In terms of Table 27-1, the dollar cost of a pound might rise from $1.4515 to $2.0000. The U.S. dollar would be said to be *depreciating*, because a dollar would now be worth fewer pounds, whereas the pound would be *appreciating*. In this example, the root cause of the change would be the U.S. **trade deficit** with Great Britain. Of course, if U.S. exports to Great Britain were greater than U.S. imports from Great Britain, Great Britain would have a trade deficit with the United States.[2]

Changes in the demand for a currency, and the resulting exchange rate fluctuations, also depend on capital movements. For example, suppose interest rates in Great Britain were higher than those in the United States. To take advantage of the high British interest rates, U.S. banks, corporations, and sophisticated individuals would buy pounds with dollars and then use those pounds to purchase high-yielding British securities. This buying of pounds would tend to drive up their price.[3]

---

[2]If the dollar value of the pound moved up from $1.45 to $2.00, this increase in the value of the pound would mean that British goods would now be more expensive in the United States. For example, a box of candy costing £1 in England would rise in price in the United States from about $1.45 to $2.00. Conversely, U.S. goods would become cheaper in England. For example, the British could now buy goods worth $2.00 for £1, whereas before the exchange rate change £1 would buy merchandise worth only $1.45. These price changes would, of course, tend to *reduce* British exports and *increase* imports, and this, in turn, would lower the exchange rate, because people in the United States would be buying fewer pounds to pay for English goods.

[3]Such capital inflows would also tend to drive down British interest rates. If British rates were high in the first place because of efforts by the British monetary authorities to curb inflation, these international currency flows would tend to thwart that effort. This is one of the reasons domestic and international economies are so closely linked.

A good example of this occurred during the summer of 1981. In an effort to curb inflation, the Federal Reserve Board pushed U.S. interest rates to record levels. This, in turn, caused a flow of capital from European nations to the United States. The Europeans were suffering from a severe recession and wanted to keep interest rates down in order to stimulate investment, but U.S. policy made this difficult because of international capital flows. Just the opposite occurred in 1992, when the Fed drove short-term rates down to record lows in the United States to promote growth, while Germany and most other European countries pushed their rates higher to combat the inflationary pressures of reunification. Thus, investment in the United States was dampened as investors moved their money overseas to capture higher interest rates.

Before August 1971, exchange rate fluctuations were kept within a narrow 1 percent limit by regular intervention of the British government in the market. When the value of the pound was falling, the Bank of England would step in and buy pounds to push up their price, offering gold or foreign currencies in exchange. Conversely, when the pound rate was too high, the Bank of England would sell pounds. The central banks of other countries operated similarly.

Devaluations and **revaluations** occurred only rarely before 1971. They were usually accompanied by severe international financial repercussions, partly because nations tended to postpone needed measures until economic pressures had built up to explosive proportions. For this and other reasons, the old international monetary system came to a dramatic end in the early 1970s, when the U.S. dollar, the foundation upon which all other currencies were anchored, was cut loose from the gold standard and, in effect, allowed to "float."

The United States and other major trading nations currently operate under a system of **floating exchange rates,** whereby currency prices are allowed to seek their own levels without much governmental intervention. However, the central bank of each country does intervene to some extent, buying and selling its currency to smooth out exchange rate fluctuations.

Each central bank would like to keep its average exchange rate at a level deemed desirable by its government's economic policy. This is important, because exchange rates have a profound effect on the levels of imports and exports, which influence the level of domestic employment. For example, if a country is having a problem with unemployment, its central bank might try to lower interest rates, which would cause capital to flee the country to find higher rates, which would lead to the sale of the currency, which would cause a *decline* in the value of the currency. This would cause its goods to be cheaper in world markets and thus stimulate exports, production, and domestic employment. Conversely, the central bank of a country that is operating at full capacity and experiencing inflation might try to raise the value of its currency to reduce exports and increase imports. Under the current floating rate system, however, such intervention can affect the situation only temporarily, because market forces will prevail in the long run. In the case of the euro, each of the EMU currencies is fixed relative to the euro; however, the value of the euro still fluctuates. The 11 EMU countries have turned over control of their monetary policy to the new European Central Bank. Beginning in 2002, the national currencies of the countries in the EMU will be phased out, and only the euro will exist.

Exchange rate fluctuations can have a profound impact on international monetary transactions. For example, in 1985 it cost Honda Motors 2,380,000 yen to build a particular model in Japan and ship it to the United States. The model carried a U.S. sticker price of $12,000. Since the $12,000 sales price was the equivalent of (238 yen per dollar)($12,000) = 2,856,000 yen, which was 20 percent above the 2,380,000 yen cost, the automaker had built a 20 percent markup into the U.S. sales price. However, three years later the dollar had depreciated to 128 yen. Now if the model still sold for $12,000, the yen return to Honda would be only (128 yen per dollar)($12,000) = 1,536,000 yen, and the automaker would be losing about 35 percent on each auto sold. Therefore, the depreciation of the dollar against the yen turned a healthy profit into a huge loss. In fact, for Honda to maintain its 20 percent markup, the model would have to sell in the United States for 2,856,000 yen/128 yen per dollar = $22,312.50. This situation, which grew even worse, led Honda to build its most popular model, the Accord, in Marysville, Ohio.

The inherent volatility of exchange rates under a floating system increases the uncertainty of the cash flows for a multinational corporation. Because its cash flows are generated in many parts of the world, they are denominated in many different currencies. Since exchange rates can change, the dollar-equivalent value of the company's consolidated cash flows can also fluctuate. For example, Toyota estimates that each one-yen drop in the dollar reduces the company's annual net income by about 10 billion yen. This is known as *exchange rate risk*, and it is a major factor differentiating a global company from a purely domestic one.

Concerns about exchange rate risk have led to attempts to stabilize currency movements. Indeed, this concern was one of the motivating factors behind the European consolidation. As we indicated above, each participating country's currency is now pegged relative to the euro. Countries with **pegged exchange rates** establish a fixed exchange rate with some major currency, and then the values of the pegged currencies move together over time. Other countries have chosen to peg their currency to the U.S. dollar. For example, Venezuela pegs its currency to the U.S. dollar at a rate of 0.001444 dollar per Bolivar. Its reason for pegging its currency to the dollar is that a large portion of its revenues are linked to its oil exports, which are typically traded in dollars, and its trading partners feel more comfortable dealing with contracts that can, in essence, be stated in dollar terms. Similarly, Kuwait pegs its currency to a composite of currencies that roughly represents the mix of currencies used by its trading partners to purchase its oil. In other instances, currencies are pegged because of traditional ties—for example, Chad, a former French colony, still pegs its currency to the French franc.[4]

Before closing our discussion of the international monetary system, we should note that not all currencies are **convertible.** A currency is convertible when the nation that issued it allows it to be traded in the currency markets and is willing to redeem it at market rates. This means that, except for limited central bank influence, the issuing government loses control over the value of its currency. However, a lack of convertibility creates major problems for international trade. For example, consider the situation faced by Pepsico when it wanted to open a chain of Pizza Hut restaurants in the former Soviet Union. The Russian ruble is not convertible, so Pepsico could not take the profits from its restaurants out of the Soviet Union in the form of dollars. There was no mechanism to exchange the rubles it earned in Russia for dollars, so the investment in the Soviet Union was essentially worthless to the U.S. parent. However, Pepsico arranged to use the ruble profit from the restaurants to buy Russian vodka, which it then shipped to the United States and sold for dollars. Pepsico managed to work things out, but lack of convertibility significantly inhibits the ability of a country to attract foreign investment.

Self-Test Questions

What is the difference between a fixed exchange rate system and a floating rate system? What are the pros and cons of each system?

What are pegged exchange rates?

What does it mean to say that the dollar is depreciating with respect to the euro? For a U.S. consumer of European goods, would this be good or bad? How could changes in consumption arrest the decline of the dollar?

What is a convertible currency?

Trading in Foreign Exchange

Importers, exporters, tourists, and governments buy and sell currencies in the foreign exchange market. For example, when a U.S. trader imports automobiles from Japan,

[4]The International Monetary Fund reports each year a full listing of exchange rate arrangements in its *International Monetary Statistics.*

payment will probably be made in Japanese yen. The importer buys yen (through its bank) in the foreign exchange market, much as one buys common stocks on the New York Stock Exchange or pork bellies on the Chicago Mercantile Exchange. However, whereas stock and commodity exchanges have organized trading floors, the foreign exchange market consists of a network of brokers and banks based in New York, London, Tokyo, and other financial centers. Most buy and sell orders are conducted by computer and telephone.[5]

WWW

Current currency futures prices are available directly from the Chicago Mercantile Exchange (CME) on their web site at **http://www.cme.com/market/prices/currencies.html**. The quotes are updated every ten minutes throughout the trading session. Updated currency spot and forward rates (from 1 to 12 months) are also provided by the Bank of Montreal Treasury Group at **http://www.bmo.com/economic/fxrates.htm**.

Spot Rates and Forward Rates

The exchange rates shown earlier in Tables 27-1 and 27-2 are known as **spot rates,** which means the rate paid for delivery of the currency "on the spot" or, in reality, no more than two days after the day of the trade. For most of the world's major currencies, it is also possible to buy (or sell) currencies for delivery at some agreed-upon future date, usually 30, 90, or 180 days from the day the transaction is negotiated. This rate is known as the **forward exchange rate.**

For example, suppose a U.S. firm must pay 500 million yen to a Japanese firm in 30 days, and the current spot rate is 108.31 yen per dollar. Unless spot rates change, the U.S. firm will pay the Japanese firm the equivalent of $4.62 million (500 million yen divided by 108.31 yen per dollar) in 30 days. But if the spot rate falls to 100 yen per dollar, for example, the U.S. firm will have to pay the equivalent of $5 million. The treasurer of the U.S. firm can avoid this risk by entering into a 30-day forward exchange contract. This contract promises delivery of yen to the U.S. firm in 30 days at a guaranteed price of 107.69 yen per dollar. No cash changes hands at the time the treasurer signs the forward contract, although the U.S. firm might have to put some collateral down as a guarantee against default. Because the firm can use an interest-bearing instrument for the collateral, though, this requirement is not costly. The counterparty to the forward contract must deliver the yen to the U.S. firm in 30 days, and the U.S. firm is obligated to purchase the 500 million yen at the previously agreed-upon rate of 107.69 yen per dollar. Therefore, the treasurer of the U.S. firm is able to lock in a payment equivalent to $4.64 million, no matter what happens to spot rates. This technique, which is called "hedging," was discussed in more detail in Chapter 24.

Forward rates for 30-, 90-, and 180-day delivery, along with the current spot rates for some commonly traded currencies, are given in Table 27-3. If one can obtain *more* of the foreign currency for a dollar in the forward than in the spot market, the forward currency is less valuable than the spot currency, and the forward currency is said to be selling at a **discount.** Conversely, since a dollar would buy *fewer* yen and marks in the forward than in the spot market, the forward yen and marks are selling at a **premium.**

Self-Test Questions

Differentiate between spot and forward exchange rates.

Explain what it means for a forward currency to sell at a discount and at a premium.

Interest Rate Parity

Market forces determine whether a currency sells at a forward premium or discount, and the general relationship between spot and forward exchange rates is specified by a concept called "interest rate parity."

[5]For a more detailed explanation of exchange rate determination and operations of the foreign exchange market, see Mark Eaker, Frank Fabozzi, and Dwight Grant, *International Corporate Finance* (Fort Worth, TX: The Dryden Press, 1996).

TABLE 27-3 Selected Spot and Forward Exchange Rates (Number of Units of Foreign Currency per U.S. Dollar)

		Forward Rates			
	Spot Rate	**30 Days**	**90 Days**	**180 Days**	**Forward Rate at a Premium or Discount**
British pound	0.6889	0.6886	0.6878	0.6870	Premium
Canadian dollar	1.5100	1.5089	1.5066	1.5039	Premium
French franc	7.8506	7.8388	7.8191	7.7938	Premium
German mark	2.3408	2.3372	2.3314	2.3238	Premium
Japanese yen	108.31	107.69	106.62	105.04	Premium
Swiss franc	1.7990	1.7936	1.7846	1.7716	Premium

Notes:
a. These are representative quotes as provided by a sample of New York banks. Forward rates for other currencies and for other lengths of time can often be negotiated.
b. When it takes more units of a foreign currency to buy one dollar in the future, the value of the foreign currency is less in the forward market than in the spot market, hence the forward rate is at a *discount* to the spot rate.

Source: *The Wall Street Journal*, October 24, 2000.

Interest rate parity holds that investors should earn the same return on security investments in all countries after adjusting for risk. It recognizes that when you invest in a country other than your home country, you are affected by two forces—returns on the investment itself and changes in the exchange rate. It follows that your overall return will be higher than the investment's stated return if the currency in which your investment is denominated appreciates relative to your home currency. Likewise, your overall return will be lower if the foreign currency you receive declines in value.

Interest rate parity is expressed as follows:

$$\frac{\text{Forward exchange rate}}{\text{Spot exchange rate}} = \frac{(1 + k_h)}{(1 + k_f)}.$$

Here both the forward and spot rates are expressed in terms of the amount of home currency received per unit of foreign currency, and k_h and k_f are the periodic interest rates in the home country and the foreign country, respectively. If this relationship does not hold, then currency traders will buy and sell currencies—that is, engage in arbitrage—until it does hold.

To illustrate interest rate parity, consider the case of a U.S. investor who can buy default-free 90-day German bonds that promise a 4 percent nominal return. The 90-day interest rate, k_f, is $4\%/4 = 1\%$ because 90 days is 1/4 of a 360-day year. Assume also that the spot exchange rate is \$0.4272, which means that you can exchange 0.4272 dollar for one mark, or 2.3408 marks per dollar. Finally, assume that the 90-day forward exchange rate is \$0.4289, which means that you can exchange one mark for 0.4289 dollar, or receive 2.3314 marks per dollar exchanged, 90 days from now.

The U.S. investor can receive a 4 percent annualized return denominated in marks, but if he or she ultimately wants to consume goods in the United States, those marks must be converted to dollars. The dollar return on the investment depends, therefore, on what happens to exchange rates over the next three months. However, the investor can lock in the dollar return by selling the foreign currency in the forward market. For example, the investor could simultaneously

- Convert \$1,000 to 2,340.8 marks in the spot market.
- Invest the 2.340.8 marks in 90-day German bonds that have a 4 percent annualized

return or a 1 percent quarterly return, hence will pay (2,340.8)(1.01) = 2,364.21 marks in 90 days.

- Agree today to exchange these 2,364.21 marks 90 days from now at the 90-day forward exchange rate of 2.3314 marks per dollar, or for a total of $1,014.07.

This investment, therefore, has an expected 90-day return of $14.07/$1,000 = 1.41%, which translates into a nominal return of 4(1.41%) = 5.64%. In this case, 4 percent of the expected 5.64 percent return is coming from the bond itself, and 1.64 percent arises because the market believes the mark will strengthen relative to the dollar. Note that by locking in the forward rate today, the investor has eliminated any exchange rate risk. And, since the German bond is assumed to be default-free, the investor is assured of earning a 5.64 percent annual dollar rate of return.

Interest rate parity implies that an investment in the United States with the same risk as a German bond should have a return of 5.64 percent. Solving for k_h in the parity equation, we indeed find that the predicted interest rate in the United States is 5.64 percent.

Interest rate parity shows why a particular currency might be at a forward premium or discount. Note that a currency is at a forward premium whenever domestic interest rates are higher than foreign interest rates. Discounts prevail if domestic interest rates are lower than foreign interest rates. If these conditions do not hold, then arbitrage will soon force interest rates back to parity.

Self-Test Question

Briefly explain interest rate parity, illustrating it with an example.

Purchasing Power Parity

We have discussed exchange rates in some detail, and we have considered the relationship between spot and forward exchange rates. However, we have not yet addressed the fundamental question: What determines the spot level of exchange rates in each country? While exchange rates are influenced by a multitude of factors that are difficult to predict, particularly on a day-to-day basis, over the long run market forces work to ensure that similar goods sell for similar prices in different countries after taking exchange rates into account. This relationship is known as "purchasing power parity."

Purchasing power parity (PPP), sometimes referred to as the *law of one price,* implies that the level of exchange rates adjusts so as to cause identical goods to cost the same amount in different countries. For example, if a pair of tennis shoes costs $150 in the United States and 100 pounds in Britain, PPP implies that the exchange rate be $1.50 per pound. Consumers could purchase the shoes in Britain for 100 pounds, or they could exchange their 100 pounds for $150 and then purchase the same shoes in the United States at the same effective cost, assuming no transaction or transportation costs. Here is the equation for purchasing power parity:

$$P_h = (P_f)(\text{Spot rate}),$$

or

$$\text{Spot rate} = \frac{P_h}{P_f}.$$

Hungry for a Big Mac? Go to Malaysia!

Purchasing power parity (PPP) implies that the same product will sell for the same price in every country after adjusting for current exchange rates. One problem when testing to see if PPP holds is that it assumes that goods consumed in different countries are of the same quality. For example, if you find that a product is more expensive in Switzerland than it is in Canada, one explanation is that PPP fails to hold, but another explanation is that the product sold in Switzerland is of a higher quality and therefore deserves a higher price.

One way to test for PPP is to find goods that have the same quality worldwide. With this in mind, *The Economist* magazine occasionally compares the prices of a well-known good whose quality is the same in nearly 120 different countries: the McDonald's Big Mac hamburger.

The table on the next page provides information collected during 2000. The first column shows the price of a Big Mac in the local currency. Column 2 calculates the price of the Big Mac in terms of the U.S. dollar—this is obtained by dividing the local price by the actual exchange rate at that time. For example, a Big Mac costs 4.99 German marks in Munich. Given an exchange rate of 2.11 marks per dollar, this implies that the dollar price of a Big Mac is 4.99 marks/2.11 marks per dollar = $2.37.

The third column backs out the implied exchange rate that would hold under PPP. This is obtained by dividing the price of the Big Mac in each local currency by its U.S. price. For example, a Big Mac costs 39.5 rubles in Russia, and $2.51 in the United States. If PPP holds, the exchange rate should be 15.7 rubles per dollar (39.5 rubles/$2.51).

Comparing the implied exchange rate to the actual exchange rate in Column 4, we see the extent to which the local currency is under- or overvalued relative to the dollar. Given that the actual exchange rate at the time was 28.5 rubles per dollar, this implies that the ruble was 45 percent undervalued.

The evidence suggests that strict PPP does not hold, but the Big Mac test may shed some insights about where exchange rates are headed. The price of a Big Mac varies within the 11 countries of the EMU, but the average price within the EMU is 2.56 euros. Due to its recent decline, the euro is still undervalued by 5 percent. The table shows Big Mac prices for the EMU's biggest member countries—ranging from the equivalent of $2.62 in France to $2.09 in Spain. Because their currencies are fixed to the euro, this gap can be narrowed only if prices fall in France or rise in Spain.

The currencies of the European countries that decided to stay outside the EMU are all overvalued. For example, the British pound is overvalued by 20 percent against the dollar and 25 percent against the euro. In contrast, most of the emerging market currencies are significantly undervalued against the dollar. The Big Mac 2000 test suggests that the pound and other non-euro currencies will fall over the next year or so, but that China's yuan will rise.

One last benefit of the Big Mac test is that it tells us the cheapest places to find a Big Mac. According to the data, if you are looking for a Big Mac, head to Malaysia, and avoid Switzerland.

Source: Excerpted from "Big MacCurrencies," *The Economist*, April 29, 2000, 75. Reprinted by permission from *The Economist*.

Here

P_h = the price of the good in the home country ($150, assuming the United States is the home country).
P_f = the price of the good in the foreign country (100 pounds).

Note that the spot market exchange rate is expressed as the number of units of home currency that can be exchanged for one unit of foreign currency ($1.50 per pound).

	Big Mac Prices				
	In Local Currency (1)	In Dollars (2)	Implied Exchange Rate Based on PPP[a] (3)	Actual $ Exchange Rate 4/25/00 (4)	Local Currency Under(−)/Over(+) Valuation[b](%) (5)
United States[c]	$2.51	2.51	—	—	—
Argentina	Peso2.50	2.50	1.00	1.00	0
Australia	A$2.59	1.54	1.03	1.68	−38
Britain	£1.90	3.00	1.32[d]	1.58[d]	+20
Canada	C$2.85	1.94	1.14	1.47	−23
China	Yuan9.90	1.20	3.94	8.28	−52
Denmark	DKr24.75	3.08	9.86	8.04	+23
Euro area	Euro2.56	2.37	0.98[e]	0.93[e]	−5
France	FFr18.50	2.62	7.37	7.07	+4
Germany	DM4.99	2.37	1.99	2.11	−6
Hong Kong	HK$10.20	1.31	4.06	7.79	−48
Italy	Lire4,500	2.16	1,793.00	2,088.00	−14
Japan	¥294	2.78	117.00	106.00	+11
Malaysia	M$4.52	1.19	1.80	3.80	−53
Mexico	Peso20.90	2.22	8.33	9.41	−11
Russia	Ruble39.50	1.39	15.70	28.50	−45
Spain	Ptas375	2.09	149.00	179.00	−17
Switzerland	SFr5.90	3.48	2.35	1.70	+39
Thailand	Baht55.00	1.45	21.90	38.00	−42

Notes:
[a]Purchasing power parity: local price divided by price in the United States.
[b]Against dollar.
[c]Average of New York, Chicago, San Francisco, and Atlanta.
[d]Dollars per pound.
[e]Dollars per euro.

Source: McDonald's.

PPP assumes that market forces will eliminate situations in which the same product sells at a different price overseas. For example, if the shoes cost $140 in the United States, importers/exporters could purchase them in the United States for $140, sell them for 100 pounds in Britain, exchange the 100 pounds for $150 in the foreign exchange market, and earn a profit of $10 on every pair of shoes. Ultimately, this trading activity would increase the demand for shoes in the United States and thus raise P_h, increase the supply of shoes in Britain and thus reduce P_f, and increase the demand for dollars in the foreign exchange market and thus reduce the spot rate. Each of these actions works to restore PPP.

Note that PPP assumes that there are no transportation or transaction costs, or import restrictions, all of which limit the ability to ship goods between countries. In many cases, these assumptions are incorrect, which explains why PPP is often violated. An additional problem for empirical tests of the PPP theorem is that products in different countries are rarely identical. Frequently, there are real or perceived differences in quality, which can lead to price differences in different countries.

Still, the concepts of interest rate and purchasing power parity are critically important to those engaged in international activities. Companies and investors must anticipate changes in interest rates, inflation, and exchange rates, and they often try to hedge the risks of adverse movements in these factors. The parity relationships are extremely useful when anticipating future conditions.

Self-Test Question

What is meant by purchasing power parity? Illustrate it.

Inflation, Interest Rates, and Exchange Rates

Relative inflation rates, or the rates of inflation in foreign countries compared with that in the home country, have many implications for multinational financial decisions. Obviously, relative inflation rates will greatly influence future production costs at home and abroad. Equally important, inflation has a dominant influence on relative interest rates and exchange rates. Both of these factors influence decisions by multinational corporations for financing their foreign investments, and both have an important effect on the profitability of foreign investments.

The currencies of countries with higher inflation rates than that of the United States by definition *depreciate* over time against the dollar. Countries where this has occurred include Italy, Mexico, and all the South American nations. On the other hand, the currencies of Germany, Switzerland, and Japan, which have had less inflation than the United States, have generally *appreciated* against the dollar. *In fact, a foreign currency will, on average, depreciate or appreciate at a percentage rate approximately equal to the amount by which its inflation rate exceeds or is less than the U.S. rate.*

Relative inflation rates also affect interest rates. The interest rate in any country is largely determined by its inflation rate. Therefore, countries currently experiencing higher rates of inflation than the United States also tend to have higher interest rates. The reverse is true for countries with lower inflation rates.

It is tempting for a multinational corporation to borrow in countries with the lowest interest rates. However, this is not always a good strategy. Suppose, for example, that interest rates in Germany are lower than those in the United States because of Germany's lower inflation rate. A U.S. multinational firm could therefore save interest by borrowing in Germany. However, because of relative inflation rates, the mark will probably appreciate in the future, causing the dollar cost of annual interest and principal payments on German debt to rise over time. Thus, *the lower interest rate could be more than offset by losses from currency appreciation.* Similarly, multinational corporations should not necessarily avoid borrowing in a country such as Brazil, where interest rates have been very high, because future depreciation of the Brazilian cruzeiro could make such borrowing end up being relatively inexpensive.

Self-Test Questions

What effects do relative inflation rates have on relative interest rates?

What happens over time to the currencies of countries with higher inflation rates than that of the United States? To those with lower inflation rates?

Why might a multinational corporation decide to borrow in a country such as Brazil, where interest rates are high, rather than in a country like Germany, where interest rates are low?

International Money and Capital Markets

One way for U.S. citizens to invest in world markets is to buy the stocks of U.S. multinational corporations that invest directly in foreign countries. Another way is to purchase foreign securities—stocks, bonds, or money market instruments issued by foreign companies. Security investments are known as *portfolio investments*, and they are distinguished from *direct investments* in physical assets by U.S. corporations.

From World War II through the 1960s, the U.S. capital markets dominated world markets. Today, however, the value of U.S. securities represents less than one-fourth the value of all securities. Given this situation, it is important for both corporate managers and investors to have an understanding of international markets. Moreover, these markets often offer better opportunities for raising or investing capital than are available domestically.

Eurodollar Market

A **Eurodollar** is a U.S. dollar deposited in a bank outside the United States. (Although they are called Eurodollars because they originated in Europe, Eurodollars are really any dollars deposited in any part of the world other than the United States.) The bank in which the deposit is made may be a non-U.S. bank, such as Barclay's Bank in London; the foreign branch of a U.S. bank, such as Citibank's Paris branch; or even a foreign branch of a third-country bank, such as Barclay's Munich branch. Most Eurodollar deposits are for $500,000 or more, and they have maturities ranging from overnight to about one year.

The major difference between Eurodollar deposits and regular U.S. time deposits is their geographic locations. The two types of deposits do not involve different currencies—in both cases, dollars are on deposit. However, Eurodollars are outside the direct control of the U.S. monetary authorities, so U.S. banking regulations, including reserve requirements and FDIC insurance premiums, do not apply. The absence of these costs means that the interest rate paid on Eurodollar deposits can be higher than domestic U.S. rates on equivalent instruments.

Although the dollar is the leading international currency, British pounds, German marks, Swiss francs, Japanese yen, and other currencies are also deposited outside their home countries; these *Eurocurrencies* are handled in exactly the same way as Eurodollars.

Eurodollars are borrowed by U.S. and foreign corporations for various purposes, but especially to pay for goods exported from the United States and to invest in U.S. security markets. Also, U.S. dollars are used as an international currency, or international medium of exchange, and many Eurodollars are used for this purpose. It is interesting to note that Eurodollars were actually "invented" by the Soviets in 1946. International merchants did not trust the Soviets or their rubles, so the Soviets bought some dollars (for gold), deposited them in a Paris bank, and then used these dollars to buy goods in the world markets. Others found it convenient to use dollars this same way, and soon the Eurodollar market was in full swing.

Eurodollars are usually held in interest-bearing accounts. The interest rate paid on these deposits depends (1) on the bank's lending rate, as the interest a bank earns on loans determines its willingness and ability to pay interest on deposits, and (2) on rates of return available on U.S. money market instruments. If money market rates in the United States were above Eurodollar deposit rates, these dollars would be sent back and invested in the United States, whereas if Eurodollar deposit rates were significantly above U.S. rates, which is more often the case, more dollars would be sent out of the United States to become Eurodollars. Given the existence of the Eurodollar market and the electronic flow of dollars to and from the United States, it is easy to see why interest rates in the United States cannot be insulated from those in other parts of the world.

Interest rates on Eurodollar deposits (and loans) are tied to a standard rate known by the acronym *LIBOR*, which stands for *London Interbank Offer Rate*. LIBOR is the rate of interest offered by the largest and strongest London banks on dollar deposits of significant size. In October 2000, LIBOR rates were just a little above domestic U.S. bank rates on time deposits of the same maturity—6.65 percent for three-month CDs versus 6.76 percent for LIBOR CDs. The Eurodollar market is essentially a short-term market; most loans and deposits are for less than one year.

International Bond Markets

Any bond sold outside the country of the borrower is called an *international bond.* However, there are two important types of international bonds: foreign bonds and Eurobonds. **Foreign bonds** are bonds sold by a foreign borrower but denominated in the currency of the country in which the issue is sold. For instance, Northern Telcom (a Canadian company) may need U.S. dollars to finance the operations of its subsidiaries in the United States. If it decides to raise the needed capital in the United States, the bond will be underwritten by a syndicate of U.S. investment bankers, denominated in U.S. dollars, and sold to U.S. investors in accordance with SEC and applicable state regulations. Except for the foreign origin of the borrower, this bond will be indistinguishable from those issued by equivalent U.S. corporations. Since Northern Telcom is a foreign corporation, however, the bond would be a foreign bond. Furthermore, because it is denominated in dollars and sold in the United States under SEC regulations, it is also called a **Yankee bond.** In contrast, if Northern Telcom issued bonds in Mexico denominated in pesos, it would be a foreign bond, but not a Yankee bond.

The term **Eurobond** is used to designate any bond issued in one country but denominated in the currency of some other country. Examples include a Ford Motor Company issue denominated in dollars and sold in Germany, or a British firm's sale of mark-denominated bonds in Switzerland. The institutional arrangements by which Eurobonds are marketed are different than those for most other bond issues, with the most important distinction being a far lower level of required disclosure than is usually found for bonds issued in domestic markets, particularly in the United States. Governments tend to be less strict when regulating securities denominated in foreign currencies, because the bonds' purchasers are generally more "sophisticated." The lower disclosure requirements result in lower total transaction costs for Eurobonds.

Eurobonds appeal to investors for several reasons. Generally, they are issued in bearer form rather than as registered bonds, so the names and nationalities of investors are not recorded. Individuals who desire anonymity, whether for privacy reasons or for tax avoidance, like Eurobonds. Similarly, most governments do not withhold taxes on interest payments associated with Eurobonds. If the investor requires an effective yield of 10 percent, a Eurobond that is exempt from tax withholding would need a coupon rate of 10 percent. Another type of bond—for instance, a domestic issue subject to a 30 percent withholding tax on interest paid to foreigners—would need a coupon rate of 14.3 percent to yield an after-withholding rate of 10 percent. Investors who desire secrecy would not want to file for a refund of the tax, so they would prefer to hold the Eurobond.

More than half of all Eurobonds are denominated in dollars. Bonds in Japanese yen, German marks, and Dutch guilders account for most of the rest. Although centered in Europe, Eurobonds are truly international. Their underwriting syndicates include investment bankers from all parts of the world, and the bonds are sold to investors not only in Europe but also in such faraway places as Bahrain and Singapore. Up to a few years ago, Eurobonds were issued solely by multinational firms, by international financial institutions, or by national governments. Today, however, the Eurobond market is also being tapped by purely domestic U.S. firms, because they often find that by borrowing overseas they can lower their debt costs.

International Stock Markets

New issues of stock are sold in international markets for a variety of reasons. For example, a non-U.S. firm might sell an equity issue in the United States because it can tap a much larger source of capital than in its home country. Also, a U.S. firm might tap a foreign market because it wants to create an equity market presence to accompany its operations in that country. Large multinational companies also occasionally issue new stock simultaneously in multiple countries. For example, Alcan Aluminum, a Canadian company, recently issued new stock in Canada, Europe, and the United States simultaneously, using different underwriting syndicates in each market.

In addition to new issues, outstanding stocks of large multinational companies are increasingly being listed on multiple international exchanges. For example, Coca-Cola's stock is traded on six stock exchanges in the United States, four stock exchanges in Switzerland, and the Frankfurt stock exchange in Germany. Some 500 foreign stocks are listed in the United States—an example here is Royal Dutch Petroleum, which is listed on the NYSE. U.S. investors can also invest in foreign companies through *American Depository Receipts (ADRs)*, which are certificates representing ownership of foreign stock held in trust. About 1,700 ADRs are now available in the United States, with most of them traded on the over-the-counter (OTC) market. However, more and more ADRs are being listed on the New York Stock Exchange, including England's British Airways, Japan's Honda Motors, and Italy's Fiat Group.

Self-Test Questions

Differentiate between foreign portfolio investments and direct foreign investments.

What are Eurodollars?

Has the development of the Eurodollar market made it easier or more difficult for the Federal Reserve to control U.S. interest rates?

Differentiate between foreign bonds and Eurobonds.

Why do Eurobonds appeal to investors?

Multinational Capital Budgeting

Up to now, we have discussed the general environment in which multinational firms operate. In the remainder of the chapter, we will see how international factors affect key corporate decisions. We begin with capital budgeting. Although the same basic principles of capital budgeting analysis apply to both foreign and domestic operations,

Stock Market Indices Around the World

In Chapter 5, we described the major U.S. stock market indices. As discussed below, similar market indices also exist for each major world financial center. The accompanying figure compares five of the indices against the U.S. Dow Jones Industrial Average.

Hong Kong

In Hong Kong, the primary stock index is the Hang Seng. Created by HSI Services Limited, the Hang Seng index reflects the performance of the Hong Kong stock market. It is composed of 33 domestic stocks that account for about 70 percent of the market's capitalization. The largest stock in the index is HBSC Holdings, which alone accounts for 21 percent of the index's total market value.

Germany

The major indicator of the German stock market, the XETRA DAX, is comprised of 30 German blue chip stocks. These stocks are all listed on the Frankfurt exchange, and they are representative of the industrial structure of the German economy.

Great Britain

The FT-SE 100 Index (pronounced "footsie") is the most widely followed indicator of equity investments in Great Britain. It is a value-weighted index composed of the 100 largest companies on the London Stock Exchange whose value is calculated every minute of trading.

Japan

In Japan, the principal barometer of stock performance is the Nikkei 225 Index. The index's value, which is calculated every minute throughout daily trading, consists of a collection of highly liquid equity issues thought to be representative of the Japanese economy.

Chile

The Santiago Stock Exchange has three main share indices: the General Stock Price Index (IGPA), the Selective Stock Price Index (IPSA), and the INTER-10 Index. The IPSA, which reflects the price variations of the most active stocks, is composed of 40 of the most actively traded stocks on the exchange.

India

Of the 22 stock exchanges in India, the Bombay Stock Exchange (BSE) is the largest, with more than 6,000 listed stocks and approximately two-thirds of the country's total trading volume. Established in 1875, the exchange is also the oldest in Asia. Its yardstick is the BSE Sensex, an index of 30 publicly traded Indian stocks that account for one-fifth of the BSE's market capitalization.

Spain

In Spain, the IBEX 35 is the official index for measuring equity market performance for continuously traded stocks. This index is composed of the 35 most actively traded securities on the Joint Stock Exchange System (comprising the four Spanish stock exchanges).

International Stock Indices—Values Relative to December 31, 1991 (Starting Values = 100)

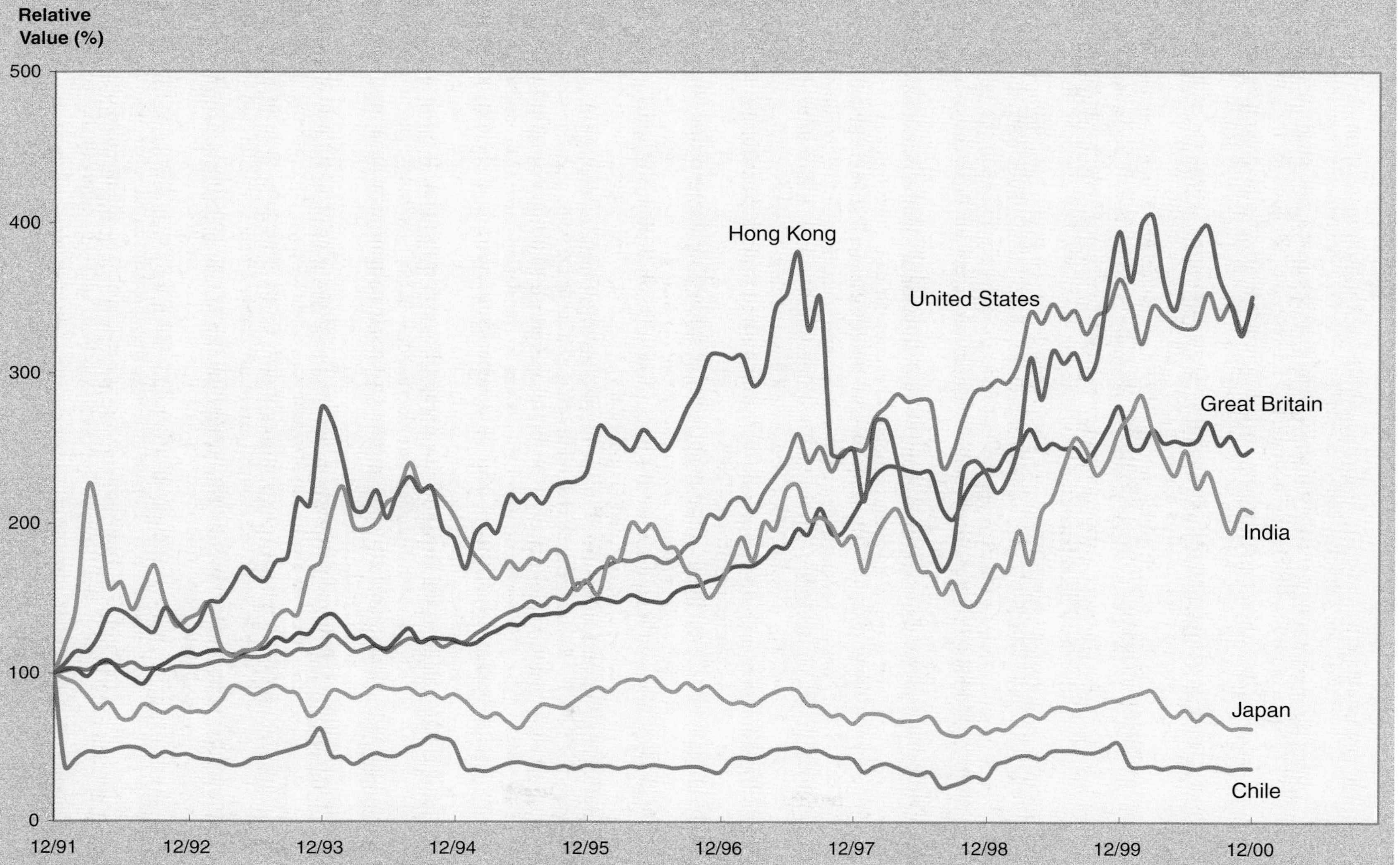

Source: Yahoo!, http://finance.yahoo.com.

there are some key differences. First, cash flow estimation is more complex for overseas investments. Most multinational firms set up separate subsidiaries in each foreign country in which they operate, and the relevant cash flows for the parent company are the dividends and royalties paid by the subsidiaries to the parent. Second, these cash flows must be converted into the parent company's currency, hence they are subject to exchange rate risk. For example, General Motors' German subsidiary may make a profit of 100 million marks in 2001, but the value of this profit to GM will depend on the dollar/mark exchange rate: How many *dollars* will 100 million marks buy?

Dividends and royalties are normally taxed by both foreign and home-country governments. Furthermore, a foreign government may restrict the amount of the cash that may be **repatriated** to the parent company. For example, some governments place a ceiling, stated as a percentage of the company's net worth, on the amount of cash dividends that a subsidiary can pay to its parent. Such restrictions are normally intended to force multinational firms to reinvest earnings in the foreign country, although restrictions are sometimes imposed to prevent large currency outflows, which might disrupt the exchange rate.

Whatever the host country's motivation for blocking repatriation of profits, the result is that the parent corporation cannot use cash flows blocked in the foreign country to pay dividends to its shareholders or to invest elsewhere in the business. Hence, from the perspective of the parent organization, *the cash flows relevant for foreign investment analysis are the cash flows that the subsidiary is actually expected to send back to the parent.* The present value of those cash flows is found by applying an appropriate discount rate, and this present value is then compared with the parent's required investment to determine the project's NPV.

In addition to the complexities of the cash flow analysis, *the cost of capital may be different for a foreign project than for an equivalent domestic project, because foreign projects may be more or less risky.* A higher risk could arise from two primary sources—(1) exchange rate risk and (2) political risk. A lower risk might result from international diversification.

Exchange rate risk relates to the value of the basic cash flows in the parent company's home currency. The foreign currency cash flows to be turned over to the parent must be converted into U.S. dollars by translating them at expected future exchange rates. An analysis should be conducted to ascertain the effects of exchange rate variations, and, on the basis of this analysis, an exchange rate risk premium should be added to the domestic cost of capital to reflect this risk. It is sometimes possible to hedge against exchange rate fluctuations, but it may not be possible to hedge completely, especially on long-term projects. If hedging is used, the costs of doing so must be subtracted from the project's cash flows.

Political risk refers to potential actions by a host government that would reduce the value of a company's investment. It includes at one extreme the expropriation without compensation of the subsidiary's assets, but it also includes less drastic actions that reduce the value of the parent firm's investment in the foreign subsidiary, including higher taxes, tighter repatriation or currency controls, and restrictions on prices charged. The risk of expropriation is small in traditionally friendly and stable countries such as Great Britain or Switzerland. However, in Latin America, Africa, the Far East, and Eastern Europe, the risk may be substantial. Past expropriations include those of ITT and Anaconda Copper in Chile, Gulf Oil in Bolivia, Occidental Petroleum in Libya, Enron Corporation in Peru, and the assets of many companies in Iraq, Iran, and Cuba.

Several organizations rate the political risk of countries. For example, The PRS Group, LLC, an independent company based in Syracuse, New York, publishes the

TABLE 27-4 Selected Countries Ranked by Composite Risk

Rank	Country	Political Risk	Financial Risk	Economic Risk	Composite Risk
1	Luxembourg	92.0	43.5	45.0	90.3
6	Switzerland	85.0	46.5	43.0	87.3
15	United States	88.0	36.5	41.0	82.8
15	Canada	86.0	38.0	41.5	82.8
57	Panama	74.0	32.5	38.0	72.3
79	Peru	61.0	37.5	34.0	66.3
86	Israel	56.0	36.5	37.0	64.8
96	Venezuela	63.0	36.5	26.0	62.8
115	Colombia	50.0	36.0	28.5	57.3
140	Sierra Leone	33.0	12.0	14.0	29.5

Note: A total of 140 countries are ranked, but only 10 are shown here.
Source: *International Country Risk Guide*, February 1999.

International Country Risk Guide, which contains individual ratings for political, financial, and economic risk, along with a composite rating for each country. Table 27-4 contains selected portions of its February 1999 report. The political variable—which is given 50 percent of the weight in the composite rating—includes factors such as government corruption and the gap between economic expectations and reality. The financial rating looks at such things as the likelihood of losses from exchange controls and loan defaults. The economic rating takes into account such factors as inflation and debt-service costs.

The best, or least risky, score is 100 for political factors and 50 each for the financial and economic factors, and the composite risk is a weighted average of the political, financial, and economic factors. The United States is ranked 15th, below Luxembourg, Norway, Netherlands, Ireland, Singapore, Switzerland, Finland, Denmark, Taiwan, Austria, Brunei, Sweden, Iceland, and Japan. Sierra Leone, as shown in Table 27-4, is ranked last.

Note that companies can take several steps to reduce the potential loss from expropriation: (1) finance the subsidiary with local capital, (2) structure operations so that the subsidiary has value only as a part of the integrated corporate system, and (3) obtain insurance against economic losses from expropriation from a source such as the Overseas Private Investment Corporation (OPIC). In the latter case, insurance premiums would have to be added to the project's cost.

Self-Test Questions

List some key differences in capital budgeting as applied to foreign versus domestic operations.

What are the relevant cash flows for an international investment—the cash flow produced by the subsidiary in the country where it operates or the cash flows in dollars that it sends to its parent company?

Why might the cost of capital for a foreign project differ from that of an equivalent domestic project? Could it be lower?

What adjustments might be made to the domestic cost of capital for a foreign investment due to exchange rate risk and political risk?

International Capital Structures

Companies' capital structures vary among countries. For example, the Organization for Economic Cooperation and Development (OECD) recently reported that, on average, Japanese firms use 85 percent debt to total assets (in book value terms), German firms use 64 percent, and U.S. firms use 55 percent. One problem, however, when interpreting these numbers is that different countries often use very different accounting conventions with regard to (1) reporting assets on a historical- versus a replacement-cost basis, (2) the treatment of leased assets, (3) pension plan funding, and (4) capitalizing versus expensing R&D costs. These differences make it difficult to compare capital structures.

A study by Raghuram Rajan and Luigi Zingales of the University of Chicago attempted to control for differences in accounting practices. In their study, Rajan and Zingales used a database that covered fewer firms than the OECD but that provided a more complete breakdown of balance sheet data. They concluded that differences in accounting practices can explain much of the cross-country variation in capital structures.

Rajan and Zingales' results are summarized in Table 27-5. There are a number of different ways to measure capital structure. One measure is the average ratio of total liabilities to total assets—this is similar to the measure used by the OECD, and it is reported in Column 1. Based on this measure, German and Japanese firms appear to be more highly levered than U.S. firms. However, if you look at Column 2, where capital structure is measured by interest-bearing debt to total assets, it appears that German firms use *less* leverage than U.S. and Japanese firms. What explains this difference? Rajan and Zingales argue that much of this difference is explained by the way German firms account for pension liabilities. German firms generally include all pension liabilities (and their offsetting assets) on the balance sheet, whereas firms in other countries

TABLE 27-5 Median Capital Structures among Large Industrialized Countries (Measured in Terms of Book Value)

Country	Total Liabilities to Total Assets (Unadjusted for Accounting Differences) (1)	Interest-Bearing Debt to Total Assets (Unadjusted for Accounting Differences) (2)	Total Liabilities to Total Assets (Adjusted for Accounting Differences) (3)	Debt to Total Assets (Adjusted for Accounting Differences) (4)	Times-Interest-Earned (TIE) Ratio (5)
Canada	56%	32%	48%	32%	1.55×
France	71	25	69	18	2.64
Germany	73	16	50	11	3.20
Italy	70	27	68	21	1.81
Japan	69	35	62	21	2.46
United Kingdom	54	18	47	10	4.79
United States	58	27	52	25	2.41
Mean	64%	26%	57%	20%	2.69×
Standard deviation	8%	7%	10%	8%	1.07×

Source: Raghuram Rajan and Luigi Zingales, "What Do We Know about Capital Structure? Some Evidence from International Data," *The Journal of Finance*, Vol. 50, no. 5, December 1995, 1421–1460. Used with permission.

(including the United States) generally "net out" pension assets and liabilities on their balance sheets. To see the importance of this difference, consider a firm with $10 million in liabilities (not including pension liabilities) and $20 million in assets (not including pension assets). Assume that the firm has $10 million in pension liabilities that are fully funded by $10 million in pension assets. Therefore, net pension liabilities are zero. If this firm were in the United States, it would report a ratio of total liabilities to total assets equal to 50 percent ($10 million/$20 million). By contrast, if this firm operated in Germany, both its pension assets and liabilities would be reported on the balance sheet. The firm would have $20 million in liabilities and $30 million in assets—or a 67 percent ($20 million/$30 million) ratio of total liabilities to total assets. Total debt is the sum of short-term debt and long-term debt and excludes other liabilities including pension liabilities. Therefore, the measure of total debt to total assets provides a more comparable measure of leverage across different countries.

Rajan and Zingales also make a variety of adjustments that attempt to control for other differences in accounting practices. The effect of these adjustments are reported in Columns 3 and 4. Overall, the evidence suggests that companies in Germany and the United Kingdom tend to have less leverage, whereas firms in Canada appear to have more leverage, relative to firms in the United States, France, Italy, and Japan. This conclusion is supported by data in the final column, which shows the average times-interest-earned ratio for firms in a number of different countries. Recall from Chapter 3 that the times-interest-earned ratio is the ratio of operating income (EBIT) to interest expense. This measure indicates how much cash the firm has available to service its interest expense. In general, firms with more leverage have a lower times-interest-earned ratio. The data indicate that this ratio is highest in the United Kingdom and Germany and lowest in Canada.

Self-Test Question

Do international differences in financial leverage exist? Explain.

Multinational Working Capital Management

Cash Management

The goals of cash management in a multinational corporation are similar to those in a purely domestic corporation: (1) to speed up collections, slow down disbursements, and thus maximize net float; (2) to shift cash as rapidly as possible from those parts of the business where it is not needed to those parts where it is needed; and (3) to maximize the risk-adjusted, after-tax rate of return on temporary cash balances. Multinational companies use the same general procedures for achieving these goals as domestic firms, but because of longer distances and more serious mail delays, such devices as lockbox systems and electronic funds transfers are especially important.

Although multinational and domestic corporations have the same objectives and use similar procedures, multinational corporations face a far more complex task. As noted earlier in our discussion of political risk, foreign governments often place restrictions on transfers of funds out of the country, so although IBM can transfer money from its Salt Lake City office to its New York concentration bank just by pressing a few buttons, a similar transfer from its Buenos Aires office is far more complex. Buenos Aires funds are denominated in australs (Argentina's equivalent of the dollar), so the australs must be converted to dollars before the transfer. If there is a shortage of dollars in Argentina, or if the Argentinean government wants to conserve dollars so they will be available for the purchase of strategic materials, then conversion, hence the transfer, may be blocked. Even if no dollar shortage exists in Argentina, the government may still restrict funds outflows if those funds represent profits or depreciation rather than payments for purchased materials or equipment, because many countries, especially those that are less developed, want profits reinvested in the country in order to stimulate economic growth.

Once it has been determined what funds can be transferred, the next task is to get those funds to locations where they will earn the highest returns. Whereas domestic corporations tend to think in terms of domestic securities, multinationals are more likely to be aware of investment opportunities all around the world. Most multinational corporations use one or more global concentration banks, located in money centers such as London, New York, Tokyo, Zurich, or Singapore, and their staffs in those cities, working with international bankers, are able to take advantage of the best rates available anywhere in the world.

Credit Management

Like most other aspects of finance, credit management in the multinational corporation is similar to but more complex than that in a purely domestic business. First, granting credit is more risky in an international context because, in addition to the normal risks of default, the multinational corporation must also worry about exchange rate fluctuations between the time a sale is made and the time a receivable is collected. For example, if IBM sold a computer to a Japanese customer for 90 million yen when the exchange rate was 90 yen to the dollar, IBM would obtain 90,000,000/90 = \$1,000,000 for the computer. However, if it sold the computer on terms of net/6 months, and if the yen fell against the dollar so that one dollar would now buy 112.5 yen, IBM would end up realizing only 90,000,000/112.5 = \$800,000 when it collected the receivable. Hedging can reduce this type of risk, but at a cost.

Offering credit is generally more important for multinational corporations than for purely domestic firms for two reasons. First, much U.S. trade is with poorer, less-developed nations, where granting credit is generally a necessary condition for doing business. Second, and in large part as a result of the first point, developed nations whose economic health depends on exports often help their manufacturing firms compete internationally by granting credit to foreign countries. In Japan, for example, the major manufacturing firms have direct ownership ties with large "trading companies" engaged in international trade, as well as with giant commercial banks. In addition, a government agency, the Ministry of International Trade and Industry (MITI), helps Japanese firms identify potential export markets and also helps potential customers arrange credit for purchases from Japanese firms. In effect, the huge Japanese trade surpluses are used to finance Japanese exports, thus helping to perpetuate their favorable trade balance. The United States has attempted to counter with the Export-Import Bank, which is funded by Congress, but the fact that the United States has a large balance of payments deficit is clear evidence that we have been less successful than others in world markets in recent years.

The huge debt that countries such as Korea and Thailand owe U.S. and other international banks is well known, and this situation illustrates how credit policy (by banks in this case) can go astray. The banks face a particularly sticky problem with these loans, because if a sovereign nation defaults, the banks cannot lay claim to the assets of the country as they could if a corporate customer defaulted. Note too that although the banks' loans to foreign governments often get most of the headlines, many

U.S. multinational corporations are also in trouble as a result of granting credit to business customers in the same countries where bank loans to governments are on shaky ground.

By pointing out the risks in granting credit internationally, we are not suggesting that such credit is bad. Quite the contrary, for the potential gains from international operations far outweigh the risks, at least for companies (and banks) that have the necessary expertise.

Inventory Management

As with most other aspects of finance, inventory management in a multinational setting is similar to but more complex than for a purely domestic firm. First, there is the matter of the physical location of inventories. For example, where should Exxon keep its stockpiles of crude oil and refined products? It has refineries and marketing centers located worldwide, and one alternative is to keep items concentrated in a few strategic spots from which they can then be shipped as needs arise. Such a strategy might minimize the total amount of inventories needed and thus might minimize the investment in inventories. Note, though, that consideration will have to be given to potential delays in getting goods from central storage locations to user locations all around the world. Both working stocks and safety stocks would have to be maintained at each user location, as well as at the strategic storage centers. Problems like the Iraqi occupation of Kuwait in 1990 and the subsequent trade embargo, which brought with it the potential for a shutdown of production of about 25 percent of the world's oil supply, complicate matters further.

Exchange rates also influence inventory policy. If a local currency, say, the Danish krone, were expected to rise in value against the dollar, a U.S. company operating in Denmark would want to increase stocks of local products before the rise in the krone, and vice versa if the krone were expected to fall.

Another factor that must be considered is the possibility of import or export quotas or tariffs. For example, Apple Computer Company was buying certain memory chips from Japanese suppliers at a bargain price. Then U.S. chipmakers accused the Japanese of dumping chips in the U.S. market at prices below cost, so they sought to force the Japanese to raise prices.[6] That led Apple to increase its chip inventory. Then computer sales slacked off, and Apple ended up with an oversupply of obsolete computer chips. As a result, Apple's profits were hurt and its stock price fell, demonstrating once more the importance of careful inventory management.

As mentioned earlier, another danger in certain countries is the threat of expropriation. If that threat is large, inventory holdings will be minimized, and goods will be brought in only as needed. Similarly, if the operation involves extraction of raw materials such as oil or bauxite, processing plants may be moved offshore rather than located close to the production site.

---

[6]The term "dumping" warrants explanation, because the practice is so potentially important in international markets. Suppose Japanese chipmakers have excess capacity. A particular chip has a variable cost of \$25, and its "fully allocated cost," which is the \$25 plus total fixed cost per unit of output, is \$40. Now suppose the Japanese firm can sell chips in the United States at \$35 per unit, but if it charges \$40, it will not make any sales because U.S. chipmakers sell for \$35.50. If the Japanese firm sells at \$35, it will cover variable cost plus make a contribution to fixed overhead, so selling at \$35 makes sense. Continuing, if the Japanese firm can sell in Japan at \$40, but U.S. firms are excluded from Japanese markets by import duties or other barriers, the Japanese will have a huge advantage over U.S. manufacturers. This practice of selling goods at lower prices in foreign markets than at home is called "dumping." U.S. firms are required by antitrust laws to offer the same price to all customers and, therefore, cannot engage in dumping.

Taxes have two effects on multinational inventory management. First, countries often impose property taxes on assets, including inventories, and when this is done, the tax is based on holdings as of a specific date, say, January 1 or March 1. Such rules make it advantageous for a multinational firm (1) to schedule production so that inventories are low on the assessment date, and (2) if assessment dates vary among countries in a region, to hold safety stocks in different countries at different times during the year.

Finally, multinational firms may consider the possibility of at-sea storage. Oil, chemical, grain, and other companies that deal in a bulk commodity that must be stored in some type of tank can often buy tankers at a cost not much greater—or perhaps even less, considering land cost—than land-based facilities. Loaded tankers can then be kept at sea or at anchor in some strategic location. This eliminates the danger of expropriation, minimizes the property tax problem, and maximizes flexibility with regard to shipping to areas where needs are greatest or prices highest.

This discussion has only scratched the surface of inventory management in the multinational corporation—the task is much more complex than for a purely domestic firm. However, the greater the degree of complexity, the greater the rewards from superior performance, so if you want challenge along with potentially high rewards, look to the international arena.

Self-Test Questions

What are some factors that make cash management especially complicated in a multinational corporation?

Why is granting credit especially risky in an international context?

Why is inventory management especially important for a multinational firm?

Summary

Over the past two decades, the global economy has become increasingly integrated, and more and more companies generate more and more of their profits from overseas operations. In many respects, the concepts developed in the first 26 chapters still apply to multinational firms. However, multinational companies have more opportunities but also face different risks than do companies that operate only in their home market. The chapter discussed many of the key trends affecting the global markets today, and it described the most important differences between multinational and domestic financial management. The key concepts are listed below:

- **International operations** are becoming increasingly important to individual firms and to the national economy. A **multinational,** or **global, corporation** is a firm that operates in an integrated fashion in a number of countries.
- Companies "go global" for six primary reasons: (1) **to expand their markets,** (2) **to obtain raw materials,** (3) **to seek new technology,** (4) **to lower production costs,** (5) **to avoid trade barriers,** and (6) **to diversify.**
- Six major factors distinguish financial management as practiced by domestic firms from that practiced by multinational corporations: (1) **different currency denominations,** (2) **different economic and legal structures,** (3) **languages,** (4) **cultural differences,** (5) **role of governments,** and (6) **political risk.**
- When discussing **exchange rates,** the number of U.S. dollars required to purchase one unit of a foreign currency is called a **direct quotation,** while the number of units of foreign currency that can be purchased for one U.S. dollar is an **indirect quotation.**

- **Exchange rate fluctuations** make it difficult to estimate the dollars that overseas operations will produce.
- Prior to August 1971, the world was on a **fixed exchange rate system** whereby the U.S. dollar was linked to gold, and other currencies were then tied to the dollar. After August 1971, the world monetary system changed to a **floating system** under which major world currency rates float with market forces, largely unrestricted by governmental intervention. The central bank of each country does operate in the foreign exchange market, buying and selling currencies to smooth out exchange rate fluctuations, but only to a limited extent.
- The consolidation of the European market has had a profound impact on European exchange rates. The exchange rates for the currencies of each of the participating countries are now fixed relative to the **euro.** Consequently, the cross rates between the various participating currencies are also fixed. However, the value of the euro continues to fluctuate.
- **Pegged exchange rates** occur when a country establishes a fixed exchange rate with a major currency. Consequently, the values of pegged currencies move together over time.
- A **convertible currency** is one that may be readily exchanged for other currencies.
- **Spot rates** are the rates paid for delivery of currency "on the spot," while the **forward exchange rate** is the rate paid for delivery at some agreed-upon future date, usually 30, 90, or 180 days from the day the transaction is negotiated. The forward rate can be at either a **premium** or a **discount** to the spot rate.
- **Interest rate parity** holds that investors should expect to earn the same return in all countries after adjusting for risk.
- **Purchasing power parity,** sometimes referred to as the *law of one price,* implies that the level of exchange rates adjusts so that identical goods cost the same in different countries.
- Granting credit is more risky in an international context because, in addition to the normal risks of default, the multinational firm must worry about **exchange rate changes** between the time a sale is made and the time a receivable is collected.
- Credit policy is important for a multinational firm for two reasons: (1) Much trade is with less-developed nations, and in such situations granting credit is a necessary condition for doing business. (2) The governments of nations such as Japan whose economic health depends upon exports often help their firms compete by granting credit to foreign customers.
- Foreign investments are similar to domestic investments, but political risk and exchange rate risk must be considered. **Political risk** is the risk that the foreign government will take some action that will decrease the value of the investment, while **exchange rate risk** is the risk of losses due to fluctuations in the value of the dollar relative to the values of foreign currencies.
- Investments in **international capital projects** expose firms to exchange rate risk and political risk. The relevant cash flows in international capital budgeting are the dollars that can be **repatriated** to the parent company.
- **Eurodollars** are U.S. dollars deposited in banks outside the United States. Interest rates on Eurodollars are tied to **LIBOR,** the London Interbank Offer Rate.
- U.S. firms often find that they can raise long-term capital at a lower cost outside the United States by selling bonds in the **international capital markets.** International bonds may be either **foreign bonds,** which are exactly like regular domestic bonds except that the issuer is a foreign company, or **Eurobonds,** which are bonds sold in a foreign country but denominated in the currency of the issuing company's home country.

Questions

27–1 Define each of the following terms:
- **a.** Multinational corporation
- **b.** Exchange rate
- **c.** Fixed exchange rate system; floating exchange rates
- **d.** Trade deficit
- **e.** Devaluation; revaluation
- **f.** Exchange rate risk; convertible currency
- **g.** Pegged exchange rates
- **h.** Interest rate parity; purchasing power parity
- **i.** Spot rate; forward exchange rate
- **j.** Discount on forward rate; premium on forward rate
- **k.** Repatriation of earnings; political risk
- **l.** Eurodollar; Eurobond; international bond; foreign bond
- **m.** The Euro

27–2 Under the fixed exchange rate system, what was the currency against which all other currency values were defined? Why?

27–3 Exchange rates fluctuate under both the fixed exchange rate and floating exchange rate systems. What, then, is the difference between the two systems?

27–4 If the French franc depreciates against the U.S. dollar, can a dollar buy more or fewer French francs as a result?

27–5 If the United States imports more goods from abroad than it exports, foreigners will tend to have a surplus of U.S. dollars. What will this do to the value of the dollar with respect to foreign currencies? What is the corresponding effect on foreign investments in the United States?

27–6 Why do U.S. corporations build manufacturing plants abroad when they could build them at home?

27–7 Should firms require higher rates of return on foreign projects than on identical projects located at home? Explain.

27–8 What is a Eurodollar? If a French citizen deposits $10,000 in Chase Manhattan Bank in New York, have Eurodollars been created? What if the deposit is made in Barclay's Bank in London? Chase Manhattan's Paris branch? Does the existence of the Eurodollar market make the Federal Reserve's job of controlling U.S. interest rates easier or more difficult? Explain.

27–9 Does interest rate parity imply that interest rates are the same in all countries?

27–10 Why might purchasing power parity fail to hold?

Self-Test Problem (Solution Appears in Appendix A)

ST–1 *CROSS RATES* Suppose the exchange rate between U.S. dollars and EMU euros is Euro 0.98 = $1.00, and the exchange rate between the U.S. dollar and the Canadian dollar is $1.00 = C$1.50. What is the cross rate of euros to Canadian dollars?

Problems

27–1 *CROSS RATES* A currency trader observes that in the spot exchange market, 1 U.S. dollar can be exchanged for 1,498.2 Italian lira or for 111.23 Japanese yen. What is the cross-exchange rate between the yen and the lira; that is, how many yen would you receive for every lira exchanged?

27–2 *INTEREST RATE PARITY* Six-month T-bills have a nominal rate of 7 percent, while default-free Japanese bonds that mature in 6 months have a nominal rate of 5.5 percent. In the spot exchange market, 1 yen equals \$0.009. If interest rate parity holds, what is the 6-month forward exchange rate?

27–3 *PURCHASING POWER PARITY* A television set costs \$500 in the United States. The same set costs 2,535 French francs. If purchasing power parity holds, what is the spot exchange rate between the franc and the dollar?

27–4 *EXCHANGE RATE* If British pounds sell for \$1.50 (U.S.) per pound, what should dollars sell for in pounds per dollar?

27–5 *CURRENCY APPRECIATION* Suppose that 1 French franc could be purchased in the foreign exchange market for 20 U.S. cents today. If the franc appreciated 10 percent tomorrow against the dollar, how many francs would a dollar buy tomorrow?

27–6 *CROSS EXCHANGE RATES* Suppose the exchange rate between U.S. dollars and the French franc was FF5.9 = \$1, and the exchange rate between the dollar and the British pound was £1 = \$1.50. What was the exchange rate between francs and pounds?

27–7 *CROSS EXCHANGE RATES* Look up the 3 currencies in Problem 27-6 in the foreign exchange section of a current issue of *The Wall Street Journal.* What is the current exchange rate between francs and pounds?

27–8 *FOREIGN INVESTMENT ANALYSIS* After all foreign and U.S. taxes, a U.S. corporation expects to receive 3 pounds of dividends per share from a British subsidiary this year. The exchange rate at the end of the year is expected to be \$1.60 per pound, and the pound is expected to depreciate 5 percent against the dollar each year for an indefinite period. The dividend (in pounds) is expected to grow at 10 percent a year indefinitely. The parent U.S. corporation owns 10 million shares of the subsidiary. What is the present value in dollars of its equity ownership of the subsidiary? Assume a cost of equity capital of 15 percent for the subsidiary.

27–9 *EXCHANGE GAINS AND LOSSES* You are the vice-president of International InfoXchange, headquartered in Chicago, Illinois. All shareholders of the firm live in the United States. Earlier this month, you obtained a loan of 5 million Canadian dollars from a bank in Toronto to finance the construction of a new plant in Montreal. At the time the loan was received, the exchange rate was 75 U.S. cents to the Canadian dollar. By the end of the month, it has unexpectedly dropped to 70 cents. Has your company made a gain or loss as a result, and by how much?

27–10 *EXCHANGE RATES* Table 27-1 lists foreign exchange rates for October 24, 2000. On that day, how many dollars would be required to purchase 1,000 units of each of the following: German marks, Italian lira, Japanese yen, Mexican pesos, and Swiss francs?

27–11 *EXCHANGE RATES* Look up the 5 currencies in Problem 27-10 in the foreign exchange section of a current issue of *The Wall Street Journal.*

a. What is the current exchange rate for changing dollars into 1,000 units of marks, lira, yen, pesos, and Swiss francs?

b. What is the percentage gain or loss between the October 24, 2000, exchange rate and the current exchange rate for each of the currencies in part a?

27–12 *RESULTS OF EXCHANGE RATE CHANGES* Early in September 1983, it took 245 Japanese yen to equal \$1. More than 17 years later that exchange rate had fallen to 108 yen to \$1. Assume the price of a Japanese-manufactured automobile was \$8,000 in September 1983 and that its price changes were in direct relation to exchange rates.

a. Has the price, in dollars, of the automobile increased or decreased during the 13-year period because of changes in the exchange rate?

b. What would the dollar price of the automobile be October 24, 2000, again assuming that the car's price changes only with exchange rates?

27–13 *SPOT AND FORWARD RATES*

Boisjoly French Imports has agreed to purchase 15,000 cases of French wine for 16 million francs at today's spot rate. The firm's financial manager, James Desreumaux, has noted the following current spot and forward rates:

	U.S. Dollar/Franc	Franc/U.S. Dollar
Spot	0.16933	5.9055
30-day forward	0.16890	5.9207
90-day forward	0.16807	5.9499
180-day forward	0.16719	5.9812

On the same day, Desreumaux agrees to purchase 15,000 more cases of wine in 3 months at the same price of 16 million francs.

a. What is the price of the wine, in U.S. dollars, if it is purchased at today's spot rate?

b. What is the cost, in dollars, of the second 15,000 cases if payment is made in 90 days and the spot rate at that time equals today's 90-day forward rate?

c. If the exchange rate for the French franc is 5.00 to $1 in 90 days, how much will he have to pay for the wine (in dollars)?

27–14 *INTEREST RATE PARITY*

Assume that interest rate parity holds and that 90-day risk-free securities yield 5 percent in the United States and 5.3 percent in Germany. In the spot market, 1 mark equals 0.63 dollar.

a. Is the 90-day forward rate trading at a premium or discount relative to the spot rate?

b. What is the 90-day forward rate?

27–15 *INTEREST RATE PARITY*

Assume that interest rate parity holds. In both the spot market and the 90-day forward market 1 Japanese yen equals 0.0086 dollar. The 90-day risk-free securities yield 4.6 percent in Japan. What is the yield on 90-day risk-free securities in the United States?

27–16 *PURCHASING POWER PARITY*

In the spot market 7.8 pesos can be exchanged for 1 U.S. dollar. A compact disk costs $15 in the United States. If purchasing power parity holds, what should be the price of the same disk in Mexico?

27–17 *PURCHASING POWER PARITY*

A chair costs 500 French francs. The same chair also costs 10,000 Japanese yen. If purchasing power parity holds, what should be the exchange rate between the yen and the French franc?

Spreadsheet Problem

27–18 *BUILD A MODEL: MULTINATIONAL FINANCIAL MANAGEMENT*

Start with the partial model in the file ***Ch 27-18 Build a Model.xls*** from the textbook's CD-ROM. Yohe Telecommunications is a multinational corporation that produces and distributes telecommunications technology. Although its corporate headquarters are located in Maitland, Florida, Yohe usually must buy its raw materials in several different foreign countries using several different foreign currencies. The matter is further complicated because Yohe usually sells its products in other foreign countries. One product in particular, the SY-20 radio transmitter, draws its principal components, Component X, Component Y, and Component Z, from Germany, France, and England, respectively. Specifically, Component X costs 165 German DM, Component Y costs 425 French francs, and Component Z costs 105 British pounds. The largest market for the SY-20 is in Japan, where it sells for 38,000 Japanese yen. Naturally, Yohe is intimately concerned with economic conditions that could adversely affect dollar exchange rates. You will find Tables 27-1, 27-2, and 27-3 useful for this problem.

a. How much, in dollars, does it cost for Yohe to produce the SY-20? What is the dollar sale price of the SY-20?

b. What is the dollar profit that Yohe makes on the sale of the SY-20? What is the percentage profit?

c. If the U.S. dollar were to weaken by 10 percent against all foreign currencies, what would be the dollar profit for the SY-20?

d. If the U.S. dollar were to weaken by 10 percent only against the Japanese yen and remained constant relative to all other foreign currencies, what would be the dollar and percentage profits for the SY-20?

e. Using the forward exchange information from Table 28-3, calculate the return on 1-year securities in Germany, if the rate of return on 1-year securities in the U.S. is 4.9 percent.

f. Assuming that purchasing power parity (PPP) holds, what would be the sale price of the SY-20 if it were sold in England rather than Japan?

Cyberproblem

The information related to this cyberproblem is likely to change over time, due to the release of new information and the ever-changing nature of the World Wide Web. Accordingly, we will periodically update the problem on the textbook's web site.

27–19
MULTINATIONAL FINANCIAL MANAGEMENT

With more than 25,000 restaurants in over 100 countries, McDonald's is the largest and best-known global foodservice retailer. Built upon the Dick and Mac McDonald's concept of a quick-service restaurant and pioneered by Ray Kroc, McDonald's has evolved from a simple restaurant to a cultural icon and global empire. McDonald's has effectively fostered innovation and established itself as the premier entity in the fast-food industry. This cyberproblem looks at McDonald's presence abroad and the strategies it employs to maintain stability in an always-evolving foreign market.

Go to the cyberproblem on the textbook's web site, **http://harcourtcollege.com/theory/student/resources/cyberprob/ch27.htm,** and answer the questions shown there.

Mini Case

CD

See **Ch 27 Show.ppt** and **Ch 27 Mini Case.xls**.

Citrus Products Inc. is a medium-sized producer of citrus juice drinks with groves in Indian River County, Florida. Until now, the company has confined its operations and sales to the United States, but its CEO, George Gaynor, wants to expand into Europe. The first step would be to set up sales subsidiaries in Spain and Sweden, then to set up a production plant in Spain, and, finally, to distribute the product throughout the European common market. The firm's financial manager, Ruth Schmidt, is enthusiastic about the plan, but she is worried about the implications of the foreign expansion on the firm's financial management process. She has asked you, the firm's most recently hired financial analyst, to develop a 1-hour tutorial package that explains the basics of multinational financial management. The tutorial will be presented at the next board of directors meeting. To get you started, Schmidt has supplied you with the following list of questions.

a. What is a multinational corporation? Why do firms expand into other countries?
b. What are the six major factors which distinguish multinational financial management from financial management as practiced by a purely domestic firm?
c. Consider the following illustrative exchange rates.

	U.S. Dollars Required to Buy One Unit of Foreign Currency
Spanish peseta	0.0050
Swedish krona	0.0985

(1) Are these currency prices direct quotations or indirect quotations?
(2) Calculate the indirect quotations for pesetas and kronas.
(3) What is a cross rate? Calculate the two cross rates between pesetas and kronas.
(4) Assume Citrus Products can produce a liter of orange juice and ship it to Spain for $1.75. If the firm wants a 50 percent markup on the product, what should the orange juice sell for in Spain?
(5) Now, assume Citrus Products begins producing the same liter of orange juice in Spain. The product costs 240 pesetas to produce and ship to Sweden, where it can be sold for 20 kronas. What is the dollar profit on the sale?
(6) What is exchange rate risk?

d. Briefly describe the current international monetary system. How does the current system differ from the system that was in place prior to August 1971?
e. What is a convertible currency? What problems arise when a multinational company operates in a country whose currency is not convertible?
f. What is the difference between spot rates and forward rates? When is the forward rate at a premium to the spot rate? At a discount?
g. What is interest rate parity? Currently, you can exchange 1 peseta for 0.00505 dollar in the 30-day forward market, and the risk-free rate on 30-day securities is 6 percent in the United States 4 percent in Spain. Does interest rate parity hold? If not, which securities offer the highest expected return?
h. What is purchasing power parity? If grapefruit juice costs $2.00 a liter in the United States and purchasing power parity holds, what should be the price of grapefruit juice in Spain?
i. What impact does relative inflation have on interest rates and exchange rates?
j. Briefly discuss the international capital markets.
k. To what extent do average capital structures vary across different countries?
l. What is the impact of multinational operations on each of the following financial management topics?

(1) Cash management.
(2) Capital budgeting decisions.
(3) Credit management.
(4) Inventory management.

Selected Additional References and Cases

Perhaps the best way to obtain more information on multinational financial management is to consult one of the many excellent textbooks on the subject. For example, see

Eaker, Mark R., Frank J. Fabozzi, and Dwight Grant, *International Corporate Finance* (Fort Worth, TX: The Dryden Press, 1996).

Levi, Maurice, *International Finance* (New York: McGraw-Hill, 1996).

Madura, Jeff, *International Financial Management* (St. Paul: West, 1995).

For some recent articles on multinational financial management, see

Black, Fischer, "Equilibrium Exchange Rate Hedging," *Journal of Finance*, July 1990, 899–907.

Carre, Herve, and Karen H. Johnson, "Progress Toward a European Monetary Union," *Federal Reserve Bulletin*, October 1991, 769–783.

Choi, Jongmoo Jay, and Anita Mehra Prasad, "Exchange Risk Sensitivity and Its Determinants: A Firm and Industry Analysis of U.S. Multinationals," *Financial Management*, Autumn 1995, 77–88.

Frankel, Jeffrey A., "The Japanese Cost of Finance," *Financial Management*, Spring 1991, 95–127.

Hammer, Jerry A., "Hedging Performance and Hedging Objectives: Tests of New Performance Measures in the Foreign Currency Market," *Journal of Financial Research*, Winter 1990, 307–323.

Hunter, William C., and Stephen G. Timme, "A Stochastic Dominance Approach to Evaluating Foreign Exchange Hedging Strategies," *Financial Management*, Autumn 1992, 104–112.

Kester, George W., Rosita P. Chang, and Kai-Chong Tsui, "Corporate Financial Policy in the Pacific Basin: Hong Kong and Singapore," *Financial Practice and Education*, Spring/Summer 1994, 117–127.

Lee, Insup, and Steve B. Wyatt, "The Effects of International Joint Ventures on Shareholder Wealth," *Financial Review*, November 1990.

Mahajan, Arvind, "Pricing Expropriation Risk," *Financial Management*, Winter 1990, 77–86.

Pauls, B. Dianne, "U.S. Exchange Rate Policy: Bretton Woods to Present," *Federal Reserve Bulletin*, November 1990, 891–908.

Two finance journals have devoted entire issues to multinational financial management. See Financial Management, *Winter 1991, and* Journal of Applied Corporate Finance, *Winter 1991, Winter 1994, Fall 1996, and Winter 1997.*

The following case from the Cases in Financial Management: Dryden Request *series focuses on multinational capital budgeting:*

Case 18, "Alaska Oil Corporation."

APPENDIX A

Solutions to Self-Test Problems

Chapter 2

ST-1 a.

EBIT	\$5,000,000
Interest	1,000,000
EBT	\$4,000,000
Taxes (40%)	1,600,000
Net income	\$2,400,000

b.

$$\begin{aligned} \text{NCF} &= \text{NI} + \text{DEP} \\ &= \$2{,}400{,}000 + \$1{,}000{,}000 = \$3{,}400{,}000. \end{aligned}$$

c.

$$\begin{aligned} \text{NOPAT} &= \text{EBIT}\,(1 - \text{T}) \\ &= \$5{,}000{,}000\,(0.6) \\ &= \$3{,}000{,}000. \end{aligned}$$

d.

$$\begin{aligned} \text{OCF} &= \text{EBIT}\,(1 - \text{T}) + \text{DEP} \\ &= \$5{,}000{,}000\,(0.6) + \$1{,}000{,}000 \\ &= \$4{,}000{,}000. \end{aligned}$$

e.

$$\begin{aligned} \text{FCF} &= \text{NOPAT} - \text{Net investment in operating capital} \\ &= \$3{,}000{,}000 - (\$25{,}000{,}000 - \$24{,}000{,}000) \\ &= \$2{,}000{,}000. \end{aligned}$$

f.

$$\begin{aligned} \text{EVA} &= \text{EBIT}\,(1 - \text{T}) - (\text{Total capital})\,(\text{After-tax cost of capital}) \\ &= \$5{,}000{,}000\,(0.6) - (\$25{,}000{,}000)\,(0.10) \\ &= \$3{,}000{,}000 - \$2{,}500{,}000 = \$500{,}000. \end{aligned}$$

ST-2

	2002	2003	2004
Henderson's Taxes as a Corporation			
Income before salary and taxes	\$52,700	\$90,000	\$150,000
Less: salary	(40,000)	(40,000)	(40,000)
Taxable income, corporate	\$12,700	\$50,000	\$110,000
Total corporate tax	1,905[a]	7,500	26,150
Salary	\$40,000	\$40,000	\$ 40,000
Less exemptions and deductions	(17,650)	(17,650)	(17,650)
Taxable personal income	\$21,900	\$21,900	\$ 21,900
Total personal tax	3,285[b]	3,285	3,285
Combined corporate and personal tax:	\$5,190	\$10,785	\$ 29,435

	2002	2003	2004
Henderson's Taxes as a Proprietorship			
Total Income	$52,700	$90,000	$150,000
Less: exemptions and deductions	(17,650)	(17,650)	(17,650)
Taxable personal income	$34,600	$71,900	$131,900
Tax liability of proprietorship	$ 5,190[c]	$14,432	$ 32,010
Advantage to being a corporation:	$ 0	$ 3,647	$ 2,575

[a]Corporate tax in 2002 = (0.15)($12,700) = $1,905.
[b]Personal tax (if Henderson incorporates) in 2002 = (0.15)($21,900) = $3,285.
[c]Proprietorship tax in 2002 = (0.15)($34,600) = $5,190.

Note that in 2002, both the corporate form of organization and the proprietorship form have the same tax liability; however, in 2003 and 2004, the corporate form has the lower tax liability. Thus, the corporate form of organization allows Henderson to pay the lowest taxes in each year. Therefore, on the basis of taxes over the 3-year period, Henderson should incorporate her business. However, note that to get additional money out of the corporation so she can spend it, Henderson will have to have the corporation pay dividends, which will be taxed to Henderson, and thus she will, sometime in the future, have to pay additional taxes.

Chapter 3

ST-1 Billingsworth paid $2 in dividends and retained $2 per share. Since total retained earnings rose by $12 million, there must be 6 million shares outstanding. With a book value of $40 per share, total common equity must be $40(6 million) = $240 million. Since Billingsworth has $120 million of debt, its debt ratio must be 33.3 percent:

$$\frac{\text{Debt}}{\text{Assets}} = \frac{\text{Debt}}{\text{Debt} + \text{Equity}} = \frac{\$120 \text{ million}}{\$120 \text{ million} + \$240 \text{ million}}$$
$$= 0.333 = 33.3\%.$$

ST-2 a. In answering questions such as this, always begin by writing down the relevant definitional equations, then start filling in numbers. Note that the extra zeros indicating millions have been deleted in the calculations below.

(1)
$$\text{DSO} = \frac{\text{Accounts receivable}}{\text{Sales}/360}$$
$$40 = \frac{\text{A/R}}{\$1{,}000/360}$$
$$\text{A/R} = 40(\$2.778) = \$111.1 \text{ million.}$$

(2)
$$\text{Quick ratio} = \frac{\text{Current assets} - \text{Inventories}}{\text{Current liabilities}} = 2.0$$
$$= \frac{\text{Cash and marketable securities} + \text{A/R}}{\text{Current liabilities}} = 2.0$$
$$2.0 = \frac{\$100 + \$111.1}{\text{Current liabilities}}$$
$$\text{Current liabilities} = (\$100 + \$111.1)/2 = \$105.5 \text{ million.}$$

(3)
$$\text{Current ratio} = \frac{\text{Current assets}}{\text{Current liabilities}} = 3.0$$
$$= \frac{\text{Current assets}}{\$105.5} = 3.0$$
$$\text{Current assets} = 3.0(\$105.5) = \$316.50 \text{ million.}$$

(4)

$$\text{Total assets} = \text{Current assets} + \text{Fixed assets} = \$316.5 + \$283.5 = \$600 \text{ million.}$$

(5)

$$\begin{aligned}\text{ROA} &= \text{Profit margin} \times \text{Total assets turnover}\\ &= \frac{\text{Net income}}{\text{Sales}} \times \frac{\text{Sales}}{\text{Total assets}}\\ &= \frac{\$50}{\$1{,}000} \times \frac{\$1{,}000}{\$600}\\ &= 0.05 \times 1.667 = 0.0833 = 8.33\%.\end{aligned}$$

(6)

$$\begin{aligned}\text{ROE} &= \text{ROA} \times \frac{\text{Assets}}{\text{Equity}}\\ 12.0\% &= 8.33\% \times \frac{\$600}{\text{Equity}}\\ \text{Equity} &= \frac{(8.33\%)(\$600)}{12.0\%}\\ &= \$416.50 \text{ million.}\end{aligned}$$

(7)

$$\begin{aligned}\text{Total assets} = \text{Total claims} &= \$600 \text{ million}\\ \text{Current liabilities} + \text{Long-term debt} + \text{Equity} &= \$600 \text{ million}\\ \$105.5 + \text{Long-term debt} + \$416.5 &= \$600 \text{ million}\\ \text{Long-term debt} = \$600 - \$105.5 - \$416.5 &= \$78 \text{ million.}\end{aligned}$$

Note: We could have found equity as follows:

$$\begin{aligned}\text{ROE} &= \frac{\text{Net income}}{\text{Equity}}\\ 12.0\% &= \frac{\$50}{\text{Equity}}\\ \text{Equity} &= \$50/0.12\\ &= \$416.67 \text{ million (rounding difference).}\end{aligned}$$

Then we could have gone on to find current liabilities and long-term debt.

b. Kaiser's average sales per day were \$1,000/360 = \$2.8 million. Its DSO was 40, so A/R = 40 (\$2.8) = \$111.1 million. Its new DSO of 30 would cause A/R = 30(\$2.8) = \$83.3 million. The reduction in receivables would be \$111.1 − \$83.3 = \$27.8 million, which would equal the amount of cash generated.

(1)

$$\begin{aligned}\text{New equity} &= \text{Old equity} - \text{Stock bought back}\\ &= \$416.5 - \$27.8\\ &= \$388.7 \text{ million.}\end{aligned}$$

Thus,

$$\begin{aligned}\text{New ROE} &= \frac{\text{Net income}}{\text{New equity}}\\ &= \frac{\$50}{\$388.7}\\ &= 12.86\% \text{ (versus old ROE of 12.0\%).}\end{aligned}$$

(2)

$$\begin{aligned}\text{New ROA} &= \frac{\text{Net income}}{\text{Total assets} - \text{Reduction in A/R}}\\ &= \frac{\$50}{\$600 - \$27.8}\\ &= 8.74\% \text{ (versus old ROA of 8.33\%).}\end{aligned}$$

(3) The old debt is the same as the new debt:

$$\begin{aligned}\text{Debt} &= \text{Total claims} - \text{Equity}\\ &= \$600 - \$416.5 = \$183.5 \text{ million.}\\ \text{Old total assets} &= \$600 \text{ million.}\\ \text{New total assets} &= \text{Old total assets} - \text{Reduction in A/R}\\ &= \$600 - \$27.8\\ &= \$572.2 \text{ million.}\end{aligned}$$

Therefore,

$$\frac{\text{Debt}}{\text{Old total assets}} = \frac{\$183.5}{\$600} = 30.6\%,$$

while

$$\frac{\text{New debt}}{\text{New total assets}} = \frac{\$183.5}{\$572.2} = 32.1\%.$$

Chapter 4

ST-1 To solve this problem, we will define ΔS as the change in sales and g as the growth rate in sales, and then we use the three following equations:

$$\begin{aligned}\Delta S &= S_0 g.\\ S_1 &= S_0(1 + g).\\ \text{AFN} &= (A^*/S_0)(\Delta S) - (L^*/S_0)(\Delta S) - MS_1(1 - d).\end{aligned}$$

Set AFN = 0, substitute in known values for A^*/S_0, L^*/S_0, M, d, and S_0, and then solve for g:

$$\begin{aligned}0 &= 1.6(\$100g) - 0.4(\$100g) - 0.10[\$100(1 + g)](0.55)\\ &= \$160g - \$40g - 0.055(\$100 + \$100g)\\ &= \$160g - \$40g - \$5.5 - \$5.5g\\ \$114.5g &= \$5.5\\ g &= \$5.5/\$114.5 = 0.048 = 4.8\%\\ &= \text{Maximum growth rate without external financing.}\end{aligned}$$

ST-2 Assets consist of cash, marketable securities, receivables, inventories, and fixed assets. Therefore, we can break the A^*/S_0 ratio into its components—cash/sales, inventories/sales, and so forth. Then,

$$\frac{A^*}{S_0} = \frac{A^* - \text{Inventories}}{S_0} + \frac{\text{Inventories}}{S_0} = 1.6.$$

We know that the inventory turnover ratio is sales/inventories = 3 times, so inventories/sales = 1/3 = 0.3333. Further, if the inventory turnover ratio can be increased to 4 times, then the inventory/sales ratio will fall to 1/4 = 0.25, a difference of 0.3333 − 0.2500 = 0.0833. This, in turn, causes the A^*/S_0 ratio to fall from $A^*/S_0 = 1.6$ to $A^*/S_0 = 1.6 - 0.0833 = 1.5167$.

This change has two effects: First, it changes the AFN equation, and second, it means that Weatherford currently has excessive inventories. Because it is costly to hold excess inventories, Weatherford will want to reduce its inventory holdings by not replacing inventories until the excess amounts have been used. We can account for this by setting up the revised AFN equation (using the new A^*/S_0 ratio), estimating the funds that will be needed next year if no excess inventories are currently on hand, and then subtracting out the excess inventories which are currently on hand:

Present Conditions:

$$\frac{\text{Sales}}{\text{Inventories}} = \frac{\$100}{\text{Inventories}} = 3,$$

so

$$\text{Inventories} = \$100/3 = \$33.3 \text{ million at present.}$$

New Conditions:

$$\frac{\text{Sales}}{\text{Inventories}} = \frac{\$100}{\text{Inventories}} = 4,$$

so

$$\text{New level of inventories} = \$100/4 = \$25 \text{ million.}$$

Therefore,

$$\text{Excess inventories} = \$33.3 - \$25 = \$8.3 \text{ million.}$$

Forecast of Funds Needed, First Year;

$$\begin{aligned} \Delta S \text{ in first year} &= 0.2(\$100 \text{ million}) = \$20 \text{ million.} \\ \text{AFN} &= 1.5167(\$20) - 0.4(\$20) - 0.1(0.55)(\$120) - \$8.3 \\ &= \$30.3 - \$8 - \$6.6 - \$8.3 \\ &= \$7.4 \text{ million.} \end{aligned}$$

Forecast of Funds Needed, Second Year:

$$\begin{aligned} \Delta S \text{ in second year} &= gS_1 = 0.2(\$120 \text{ million}) = \$24 \text{ million.} \\ \text{AFN} &= 1.5167(\$24) - 0.4(\$24) - 0.1(0.55)(\$144) \\ &= \$36.4 - \$9.6 - \$7.9 \\ &= \$18.9 \text{ million.} \end{aligned}$$

ST-3 a.

$$\text{Full capacity sales} = \frac{\text{Current sales}}{\text{Percentage of capacity at which FA were operated}} = \frac{\$36{,}000}{0.75} = \$48{,}000.$$

$$\text{Percentage increase} = \frac{\text{New sales} - \text{Old sales}}{\text{Old sales}} = \frac{\$48{,}000 - \$36{,}000}{\$36{,}000} = 0.33 = 33\%.$$

Therefore, sales could expand by 33 percent before Van Auken Lumber would need to add fixed assets.

b. Because none of the operating ratios are assumed to change, it is easier to let the appropriate items increase at the sales growth rate.

Van Auken Lumber: Pro Forma Income Statement for December 31, 2002 (Thousands of Dollars)

	2001	Forecast Basis	Pro Forma 2002
Sales	$36,000	1.25 (Sales_{01})	$45,000
Operating costs	30,783	85.508% (Sales_{02})	38,479
EBIT	$ 5,217		$ 6,521
Interest	1,017		1,017
EBT	$ 4,200		$ 5,504
Taxes (40%)	1,680		2,202
Net income	$ 2,520		$ 3,302
Dividends (60%)	$ 1,512		$ 1,981
Addition to RE	$ 1,008		$ 1,321

Van Auken Lumber: Pro Forma Balance Sheet for December 31, 2002 (Thousands of Dollars)

	2001	Percent of 2002 Sales	Additions	2002	AFN	2002 After AFN
Cash	$ 1,800	5.000%		$ 2,250		$ 2,250
Receivables	10,800	30.000		13,500		13,500
Inventories	12,600	35.000		15,750		15,750
Total current assets	$25,200			$31,500		$31,500
Net fixed assets	21,600			21,600[a]		21,600
Total assets	$46,800			$53,100		$53,100
Accounts payable	$ 7,200	20.000		$ 9,000		$ 9,000
Notes payable	3,472			3,472	+2,549	6,021
Accruals	2,520	7.000		3,150		3,150
Total current liabilities	$13,192			$15,622		$18,171
Mortgage bonds	5,000			5,000		5,000
Common stock	2,000			2,000		2,000
Retained earnings	26,608		1,321[b]	27,929		27,929
Total liabilities and equity	$46,800			$50,551		$53,100
AFN =				$ 2,549		

[a]From part a we know that sales can increase by 33% before additions to fixed assets are needed.
[b]See income statement.

c. Van Auken Lumber: Pro Forma Income Statement for December 31, 2002 (Thousands of Dollars)

	1st Pass 2002	Financing Feedback	2nd Pass 2002
Sales	$45,000		$45,000
Operating costs	38,479		38,479
EBIT	$ 6,521		$ 6,521
Interest	1,017	+306[a]	1,323
EBT	$ 5,504		$ 5,198
Taxes (40%)	2,202		2,079
Net income	$ 3,302		$ 3,119
Dividends (60%)	$ 1,981		$ 1,871
Addition to RE	$ 1,321		$ 1,248

[a]Δ in interest = \$2,549 × (0.12) = \$306.

Van Auken Lumber: Pro Forma Balance Sheet for December 31, 2002
(Thousands of Dollars)

	1st pass 2002	Financing Feedback	2nd Pass 2002
Total assets	$53,100		$53,100
Accounts payable	9,000		$ 9,000
Notes payable	6,021		6,021
Accruals	3,150		3,150
Total current liabilities	$18,171		$18,171
Mortgage bonds	5,000		5,000
Common stock	2,000		2,000
Retained earnings	27,929	−73[a]	27,856
Total liabilities and equity	$53,100		$53,027
AFN =			73

[a]Change in RE addition = $1,248 − $1,321 = −$73.
Note: The cumulative AFN for the first 2 passes = $2,549 + $73 = $2,622.

d. The rate of return projected for 2002 under the conditions in part c is (calculations in thousands):

$$\text{ROE} = \frac{\$3{,}119}{\$29{,}856} = 10.45\%.$$

If Van Auken Lumber attained the industry average DSO and inventory turnover ratio, this would mean a reduction in financial requirements of:

$$\text{Receivables: } \frac{\text{New A/R}}{\$45{,}000/360} = 90$$
$$\text{New A/R} = \$11{,}250.$$
$$\text{Change in A/R} = \$13{,}500 - \$11{,}250 = \$2{,}250.$$
$$\text{Inventory: } \frac{\$45{,}000}{\text{I}} = 3.33;\ \text{I} = \$13{,}500.$$
$$\text{Change in Inventory} = \$15{,}750 - \$13{,}500 = \$2{,}250.$$
$$\text{Total Change} = \$2{,}250 + \$2{,}250 = \$4{,}500.$$

If this freed capital was used to reduce equity, the new figures for common equity would be $29,856 − $4,500 = $25,356. Assuming no change in net income, the new ROE would be:

$$\text{ROE} = \frac{\$3{,}119}{\$25{,}356} = 12.3\%.$$

One would, in a real analysis, want to consider both the feasibility of maintaining sales if receivables and inventories were reduced and also other possible effects on the profit margin. Also, note that the current ratio was $25,200/$13,192 = 1.91 in 2001. It is projected to decline in part c to $31,500/$18,244 = 1.73, and the latest change would cause a further reduction to ($31,500 − $4,500)/$18,244 = 1.48. Creditors might not tolerate such a reduction in liquidity and might insist that at least some of the free capital be used to reduce notes payable. Still, this would reduce interest charges, which would increase the profit margin, which would in turn raise the ROE. Management should always consider the possibility of changing ratios as part of financial projections.

Chapter 5

ST-1 a. Average = (4% + 5% + 6% + 7%)/4 = 22%/4 = 5.5%.

b. $k_{T\text{-bond}} = k^* + IP = 2\% + 5.5\% = 7.5\%$.

c. If the 5-year T-bond rate is 8 percent, the inflation rate is expected to average approximately 8% − 2% = 6% during the next 5 years. Thus, the implied Year 5 inflation rate is 8 percent:

$$\begin{aligned} 6\% &= (4\% + 5\% + 6\% + 7\% + I_5)/5 \\ 30\% &= 22\% + I_5 \\ I_5 &= 8\%. \end{aligned}$$

Chapter 6

ST-1 a. The average rate of return for each stock is calculated simply by averaging the returns over the 5-year period. The average return for each stock is 18.90 percent, calculated for Stock A as follows:

$$\begin{aligned} k_{Avg} &= (-10.00\% + 18.50\% + 38.67\% + 14.33\% + 33.00\%)/5 \\ &= 18.90\%. \end{aligned}$$

The realized rate of return on a portfolio made up of Stock A and Stock B would be calculated by finding the average return in each year as k_A(% of Stock A) + k_B(% of Stock B) and then averaging these yearly returns:

Year	Portfolio AB's Return, k_{AB}
1997	(6.50%)
1998	19.90
1999	41.46
2000	9.00
2001	30.65
	k_{Avg} = 18.90%

b. The standard deviation of returns is estimated, using Equation 6-3a, as follows:

$$\text{Estimated } \sigma = S = \sqrt{\frac{\sum_{t=1}^{n}(\bar{k}_t - \bar{k}_{Avg})^2}{n-1}}. \tag{6-3a}$$

For Stock A, the estimated σ is 19.0 percent:

$$\begin{aligned} \sigma_A &= \sqrt{\frac{(-10.00 - 18.9)^2 + (18.50 - 18.9)^2 + \cdots + (33.00 - 18.9)^2}{5-1}} \\ &= \sqrt{\frac{1{,}445.92}{4}} = 19.0\%. \end{aligned}$$

The standard deviation of returns for Stock B and for the portfolio are similarly determined and they are as follows:

	Stock A	Stock B	Portfolio AB
Standard deviation	19.0	19.0	18.6

c. Because the risk reduction from diversification is small (σ_{AB} falls only from 19.0 to 18.6 percent), the most likely value of the correlation coefficient is 0.9. If the correlation coefficient were −0.9, the risk reduction would be much larger. In fact, the correlation coefficient between Stocks A and B is 0.92.

d. If more randomly selected stocks were added to a portfolio, σ_p would decline to somewhere in the vicinity of 20 percent; see Figure 6-8. σ_p would remain constant only if the correlation coefficient were +1.0, which is most unlikely. σ_p would decline to zero only if the correlation coefficient, r, were equal to zero and a large number of stocks were added to the portfolio, or if the proper proportions were held in a two-stock portfolio with r = −1.0.

ST-2 a.

$$\begin{aligned} b &= (0.6)(0.70) + (0.25)(0.90) + (0.1)(1.30) + (0.05)(1.50) \\ &= 0.42 + 0.225 + 0.13 + 0.075 = 0.85. \end{aligned}$$

b.

$$\begin{aligned} k_{RF} &= 6\%;\ RP_M = 5\%;\ b = 0.85. \\ k &= 6\% + (5\%)(0.85) \\ &= 10.25\%. \end{aligned}$$

c.

$$\begin{aligned} b_N &= (0.5)(0.70) + (0.25)(0.09) + (0.1)(1.30) + (0.15)(1.50) \\ &= 0.35 + 0.225 + 0.13 + 0.225 \\ &= 0.93. \\ k &= 6\% + (5\%)(0.93) \\ &= 10.65\%. \end{aligned}$$

Chapter 7

ST-1 a. For Security A:

P_A	k_A	$P_A k_A$	$(k_A - \hat{k}_A)$	$(k_A - \hat{k}_A)^2$	$P_A (k_A - \hat{k}_A)^2$
0.1	−10%	−1.0%	−25%	625	62.5
0.2	5	1.0	−10	100	20.0
0.4	15	6.0	0	0	0.0
0.2	25	5.0	10	100	20.0
0.1	40	4.0	25	625	62.5
		$\hat{k}_A = 15.\%$.			$\sigma_A = \sqrt{165.0} = 12.8\%$.

b.

$$\begin{aligned} w_A &= \frac{\sigma_B(\sigma_B - r_{AB}\sigma_A)}{\sigma_A^2 + \sigma_B^2 - 2r_{AB}\sigma_A\sigma_B} \\ &= \frac{25.7[25.7 - (-0.5)(12.8)]}{(12.8)^2 + (25.7)^2 - 2(-0.5)(12.8)(25.7)} \\ &= \frac{824.97}{1{,}153.29} = 0.7153. \end{aligned}$$

or 71.53% invested in A, 28.47% in B.

c.

$$\begin{aligned} \sigma_p &= \sqrt{(w_A\sigma_A)^2 + (1 - w_A)^2(\sigma_B)^2 + 2w_A(1 - w_A)r_{AB}\sigma_A\sigma_B} \\ &= \sqrt{(0.75)^2(12.8)^2 + (0.25)^2(25.7)^2 + 2(0.75)(0.25)(-0.5)(12.8)(25.7)} \\ &= \sqrt{92.16 + 41.28 - 61.68} \\ &= \sqrt{71.76} = 8.47\%, \text{ when } w_A = 75\%. \\ \sigma_p &= \sqrt{(0.7153)^2(12.8)^2 + (0.2847)^2(25.7)^2 + 2(0.7153)(0.2847)(-0.5)(12.8)(25.7)} \\ &= 8.38\%, \text{ when } w_A = 71.53\%. \text{ This is the minimum } \sigma_p. \\ \sigma_p &= \sqrt{(0.5)^2(12.8)^2 + (0.5)^2(25.7)^2 + 2(0.5)(0.5)(-0.5)(12.8)(25.7)} \\ &= 11.13\%, \text{ when } w_A = 50\%. \\ \sigma_p &= \sqrt{(0.25)^2(12.8)^2 + (0.75)^2(25.7)^2 + 2(0.25)(0.75)(-0.5)(12.8)(25.7)} \\ &= 17.89\%, \text{ when } w_A = 25\%. \end{aligned}$$

% in A	% in B	$\hat{k}_P$	σ_P
100%	0%	15.00%	12.8%
75	25	16.25	8.5
71.53	28.47	16.42	8.4
50	50	17.50	11.1
25	75	18.75	17.9
0	100	20.00	25.7

Calculations for preceding table:

$$\begin{aligned}
\hat{k}_p &= w_A(\hat{k}_A) + (1 - w_A)(\hat{k}_B) \\
&= 0.75(15) + (0.25)(20) &&= 16.25\% &&\text{when } w_A = 75\%. \\
&= 0.7153(15) + 0.2847(20) &&= 16.42\% &&\text{when } w_A = 71.53\%. \\
&= 0.5(15) + 0.5(20) &&= 17.50\% &&\text{when } w_A = 50\%. \\
&= 0.25(15) + 0.75(20) &&= 18.75\% &&\text{when } w_A = 25\%.
\end{aligned}$$

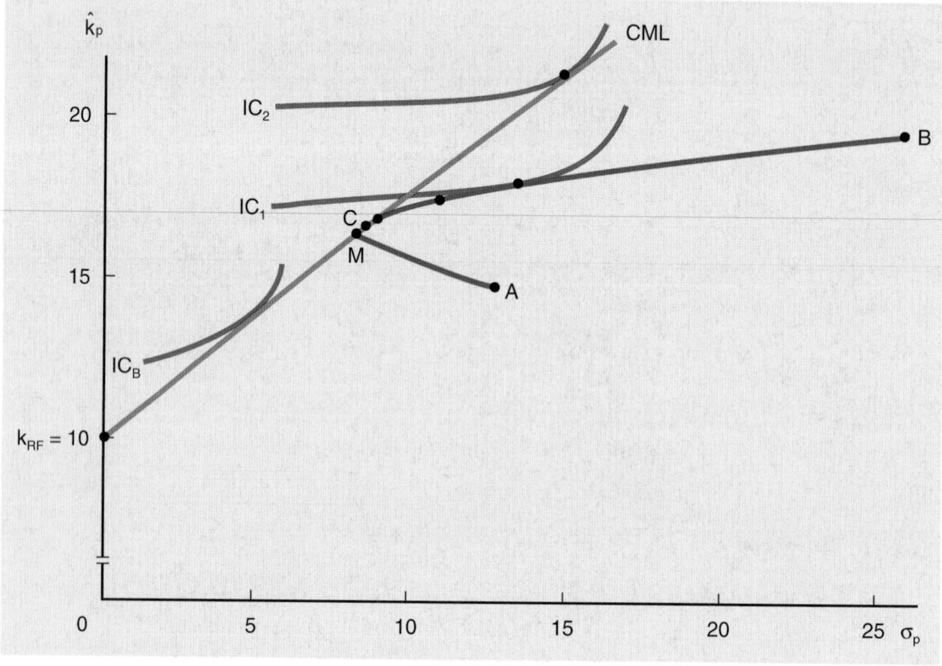

e. See indifference curve IC_1 above. At the point where $\hat{k}_p = 18\%$, $\sigma_p = 13.5\%$.

$$\begin{aligned}
\hat{k}_p &= w_A(\hat{k}_A) + (1 - w_A)(\hat{k}_B) \\
18 &= w_A(15) + (1 - w_A)(20) \\
&= 15w_A + 20 - 20w_A \\
5w_A &= 2 \\
w_A &= 0.4 \text{ or } 40\%.
\end{aligned}$$

Therefore, to an approximation, your optimal portfolio would have 40 percent in A, 60 percent in B, with $\hat{k}_p = 18\%$ and $\sigma_p = 13.5\%$. (We could get an exact σ_p by using x = 0.4 in the equation for σ_p.)

f. The existence of the riskless asset would enable you to go to the CAPM. We would draw in the CML as shown on the graph in Part d. Now you would hold a portfolio of stocks, borrowing on margin to hold more stocks than your net worth, and move to a higher indifference curve, IC_2.

You can put all of your money into the riskless asset, all in A, all in B, or some in each security. The most logical choices are (1) hold a portfolio of A and B plus some of the riskless asset, (2) hold only a portfolio of A and B, or (3) hold a portfolio of A and B and borrow to leverage the portfolio, assuming you can borrow at the riskless rate.

Reading from the graph, we see that your $\hat{k}_p$ at the point of tangency between your IC_2 and the CML is about 22 percent. We can use this information to find out how much you invest in the market portfolio and how much you invest in the riskless asset. (It will turn out that you have a *negative* investment in the riskless asset, which means that you borrow rather than lend at the risk-free rate.)

$$\begin{aligned}
\hat{k}_p &= w_{RF}(k_{RF}) + (1 - w_{RF})(\hat{k}_M) \\
22 &= w_{RF}(10) + (1 - w_{RF})(16.8) \\
&= 10w_{RF} + 16.8 - 16.8w_{RF} \\
-6.8w_{RF} &= 5.2 \\
w_{RF} &= -0.76 \text{ or } -76\%\text{, which means that you borrow.} \\
1 - w_{RF} &= 1.0 - (-0.76) \\
&= +1.76 \text{ or } 176\% \text{ in the market portfolio.}
\end{aligned}$$

This investor, with \$200,000 of net worth, thus buys stock with a value of \$200,000(1.76) = \$352,000 and borrows \$152,000.

The riskiness of this leveraged portfolio is

$$\begin{aligned}
\sigma_p &= \sqrt{(-0.76)^2(0)^2 + (1.76)^2(8.5)^2 + 2(-0.76)(1.76)(0)(8.5)(0)} \\
&= \sqrt{(1.76)^2(8.5)^2} \\
&= (1.76)(8.5) = 15\%.
\end{aligned}$$

Your indifference curve suggests that you are not very risk averse. A risk-averse investor would have a steep indifference curve (visualize a set of steep curves that were tangent to CML to the left of Point C). This investor would hold some of A and B, combined to form portfolio M, and some of the riskless asset.

g. Given your assumed indifference curve, you would, when the riskless asset becomes available, change your portfolio from the one found in part e (with $\hat{k}_p = 18\%$, $\sigma_p = 13.5\%$) to one with $\hat{k}_p \approx 22.0\%$ and $\sigma_p \approx 15.00\%$.

h.

$$\begin{aligned}
k_A &= k_{RF} + (k_M - k_{RF})\, b_A \\
15 &= 10 + (16.8 - 10)\, b_A \\
&= 10 + (6.8)\, b_A. \\
b_A &= 0.74. \\
20 &= 10 + (6.8)\, b_B \\
b_B &= 1.47.
\end{aligned}$$

Note that the 16.8 percent value for k_M was approximated from the graph. Also, note that this solution *assumes* that you can borrow at $k_{RF} = 10\%$. This is a basic—but questionable—CAPM assumption. If the borrowing rate is *above* k_{RF}, then CML would turn down to the right of Point M.

Chapter 8

ST-1 a.

1/1/02	8%	1/1/03	1/1/04	1/1/05	1/1/06
		−1,000			FV = ?

\$1,000 is being compounded for 3 years, so your balance on January 1, 2006 is \$1,259.71:

$$FV_n = PV(1 + i)^n = \$1{,}000(1 + 0.08)^3 = \$1{,}259.71.$$

Alternatively, using a financial calculator, input N = 3, I = 8, PV = −1000, PMT = 0, and FV = ? FV = \$1,259.71.

b. 1/1/02 1/1/03 1/1/04 1/1/05 1/1/06

2%

−1,000 FV = ?

Use FVIF for 2%, $3 \times 4 = 12$ periods:

$$FV_{12} = \$1{,}000(FVIF_{2\%,12}) = \$1{,}000(1 + 0.02)^{12} = \$1{,}000(1.2682) = \$1{,}268.20.$$

Alternatively, using a financial calculator, input N = 12, I = 2, PV = −1000, PMT = 0, and FV = ? FV = $1,268.24. (Note that a rounding difference occurs.)

c. 1/1/02 8% 1/1/03 1/1/04 1/1/05 1/1/06

250 250 250 250

FV = ?

As you work this problem, keep in mind that the tables assume that payments are made at the end of each period. Therefore, you may solve this problem by finding the future value of an annuity of $250 for 4 years at 8 percent:

$$FVA_4 = PMT(FVIFA_{i,n}) = \$250\left(\frac{(1 + 0.08)^4 - 1}{0.08}\right) = \$250(4.5061) = \$1{,}126.53.$$

Alternatively, using a financial calculator, input N = 4, I = 8, PV = 0, PMT = −250, and FV = ? FV = $1,126.53.

d. 1/1/02 8% 1/1/03 1/1/04 1/1/05 1/1/06

? ? ? ?

FV = 1,259.71

N = 4; I = 8; PV = 0; FV = 1259.71; PMT = ?; PMT = $279.56.

Alternatively,

$$PMT(FVIFA_{8\%,4}) = FVA_4$$
$$PMT\left(\frac{(1 + 0.08)^4 - 1}{0.08}\right) = \$1{,}259.71$$
$$PMT(4.5061) = \$1{,}259.71$$
$$PMT = \$1{,}259.71/4.5061 = \$279.56.$$

Therefore, you would have to make 4 payments of $279.56 each to have a balance of $1,259.71 on January 1, 2006.

ST-2 a. Set up a time line like the one in the preceeding problem:

1/1/02 8% 1/1/03 1/1/04 1/1/05 1/1/06

PV = ? 1,000

Note that your deposit will grow for 3 years at 8 percent. The fact that it is now January 1, 2002, is irrelevant. The deposit on January 1, 2003, is the PV, and the FV is $1,000. Here is the solution:

N = 3; I = 8; PMT = 0; FV = 1000; PV = ?; PV = $793.83.

Alternatively,

$$FV_3(PVIF_{8\%,3}) = PV$$
$$\$1000\left(\frac{1}{(1 + 0.08)^3}\right) = PV$$
$$PV = \$1{,}000(0.7938) = \$793.80 = \text{Initial deposit to accumulate } \$1{,}000.$$

(Difference due to rounding.)

b.

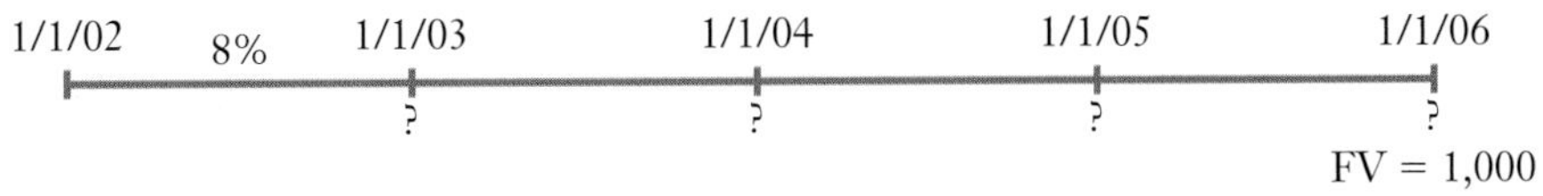

Here we are dealing with a 4-year annuity whose first payment occurs 1 year from today, on 1/1/03, and whose future value must equal \$1,000. You should modify the time line to help visualize the situation. Here is the solution:

N = 4; I = 8; PV = 0; FV = 1000; PMT = ?; PMT = \$221.92.

Alternatively,

$$\text{PMT}(\text{FVIFA}_{8\%,4}) = \text{FVA}_4$$

$$\text{PMT}\left(\frac{(1 + 0.08)^4 - 1}{0.08}\right) = \$1{,}000$$

$$= \frac{\$1{,}000}{4.5061} = \$221.92 = \begin{array}{c}\text{Payment necessary}\\ \text{to accumulate } \$1{,}000.\end{array}$$

c. This problem can be approached in several ways. Perhaps the simplest is to ask this question: "If I received \$750 on 1/1/03 and deposited it to earn 8 percent, would I have the required \$1,000 on 1/1/06?" The answer is no:

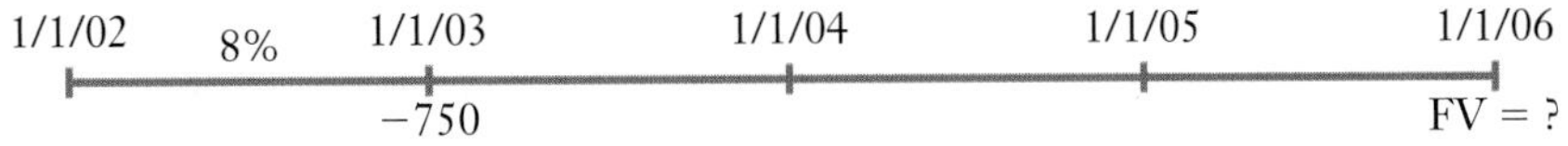

$$\text{FV}_3 = \$750(1.08)(1.08)(1.08) = \$944.78.$$

This indicates that you should let your father make the payments rather than accept the lump sum of \$750.

You could also compare the \$750 with the PV of the payments:

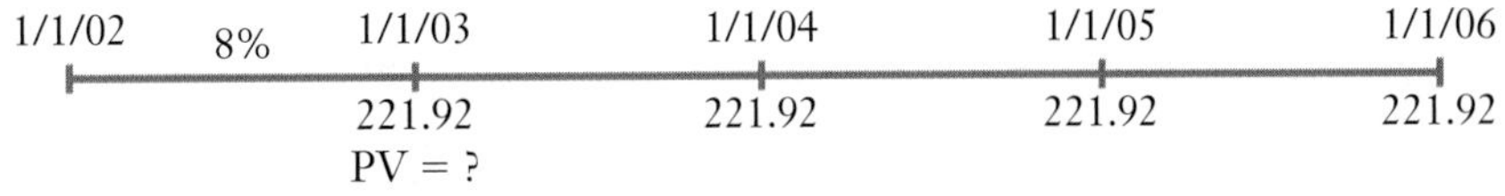

N = 4; I = 8; PMT = −221.92; FV = 0; PV = ?; PV = \$735.03.

Alternatively,

$$\text{PMT}(\text{PVIFA}_{8\%,4}) = \text{PVA}_4$$

$$\$221.92\left(\frac{1 - \dfrac{1}{(1 + 0.08)^4}}{0.08}\right) = \text{PVA}_4$$

$$\$221.92(3.3121) = \$735.02 = \begin{array}{c}\text{Present value}\\ \text{of the required payments.}\end{array}$$

(Difference due to rounding.)

This is less than the \$750 lump sum offer, so your initial reaction might be to accept the lump sum of \$750. However, this would be a mistake. The problem is that when you found the \$735.02 PV of the annuity, you were finding the value of the annuity *today*, on January 1, 2002. You were comparing \$735.02 today with the lump sum of \$750 1 year from now. This is, of course, invalid. What you should have done was take the \$735.02, recognize that this is the PV of an annuity as of January 1, 2002, multiply \$735.02 by 1.08 to get \$793.82, and compare \$793.82 with the lump sum of \$750. You would then take your father's offer to make the payments rather than take the lump sum on January 1, 2003.

d.

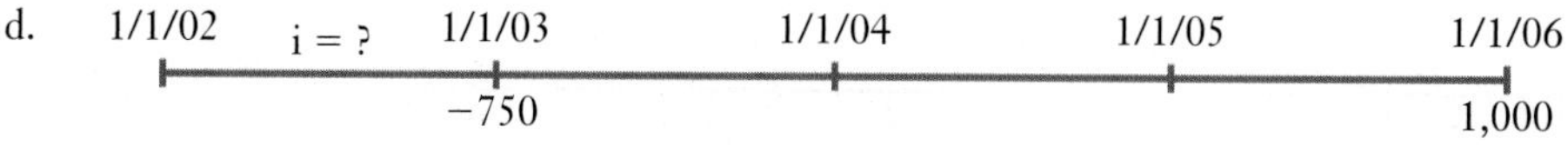

N = 3; PV = −750; PMT = 0; FV = 1000; I = ?; I = 10.0642%.

e.

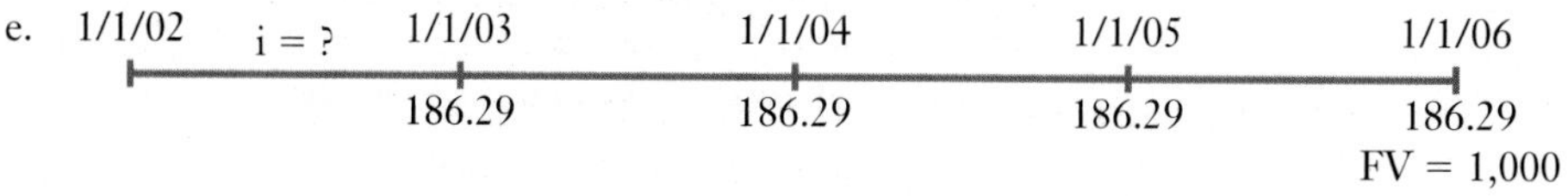

N = 4; PV = 0; PMT = −186.29; FV = 1000, I = ?; I = 19.9997%.

You might be able to find a borrower willing to offer you a 20 percent interest rate, but there would be some risk involved—he or she might not actually pay you your $1,000!

f.

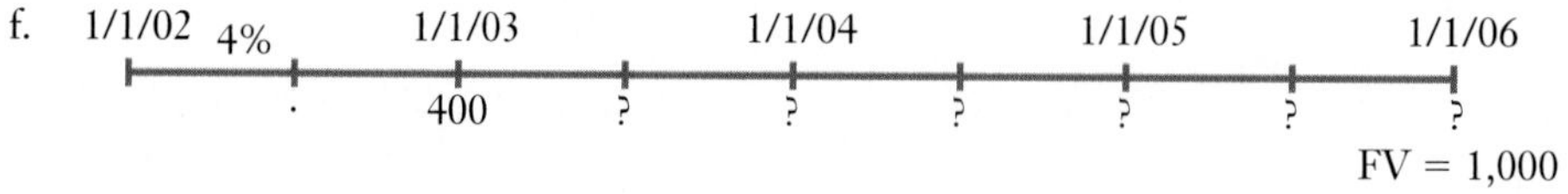

Find the future value of the original $400 deposit:

$$FV_6 = PV(FVIF_{4\%,6}) = \$400(1 + 0.04)^6 = \$400(1.2653) = \$506.12.$$

This means that on January 1, 2006, you need an additional sum of $493.88:

$$\$1{,}000.00 - \$506.12 = \$493.88.$$

This will be accumulated by making 6 equal payments which earn 8 percent compounded semiannually, or 4 percent each 6 months:

N = 6; I = 4; PV = 0; FV = 493.88; PMT = ?; PMT = $74.46.

Alternatively,

$$PMT(PVIFA_{4\%,6}) = FVA_6$$

$$PMT\left(\frac{(1 + 0.04)^6 - 1}{0.04}\right) = \$493.88$$

$$PMT = \frac{\$493.88}{6.6330} = \$74.46.$$

Alternatively, using a financial calculator, input N = 6, I = 4, PV = −400, FV = 1000, and PMT = ?; PMT = $74.46.

g.

$$\text{Effective annual rate} = \left(1 + \frac{i_{Nom}}{m}\right)^m - 1.0$$
$$= \left(1 + \frac{0.08}{2}\right)^2 - 1 = (1.04)^2 - 1$$
$$= 1.0816 - 1 = 0.0816 = 8.16\%.$$

h. There is a reinvestment rate risk here because we assumed that funds will earn an 8 percent return in the bank. In fact, if interest rates in the economy fall, the bank will lower its deposit rate because it will be earning less when it lends out the funds you deposited with it. If you buy certificates of deposit (CDs) that mature on the date you need the money (1/1/03), you will avoid the reinvestment risk, but that would work only if you were making the deposit today. Other ways of reducing reinvestment rate risk will be discussed later in the text.

ST-3 Bank A's effective annual rate is 8.24 percent:

$$\text{Effective annual rate} = \left(1 + \frac{0.08}{4}\right)^4 - 1.0$$
$$= (1.02)^4 - 1 = 1.0824 - 1$$
$$= 0.0824 = 8.24\%.$$

Now Bank B must have the same effective annual rate:

$$\left(1+\frac{i}{12}\right)^{12}-1.0=0.0824$$
$$\left(1+\frac{i}{12}\right)^{12}=1.0824$$
$$1+\frac{i}{12}=(1.0824)^{1/12}$$
$$1+\frac{i}{12}=1.00662$$
$$\frac{i}{12}=0.00662$$
$$i=0.07944=7.94\%.$$

Thus, the two banks have different quoted rates—Bank A's quoted rate is 8 percent, while Bank B's quoted rate is 7.94 percent; however, both banks have the same effective annual rate of 8.24 percent. The difference in their quoted rates is due to the difference in compounding frequency.

Chapter 9

ST-1 a. Pennington's bonds were sold at par; therefore, the original YTM equaled the coupon rate of 12%.

b.

$$V_B=\sum_{t=1}^{50}\frac{\$120/2}{\left(1+\frac{0.10}{2}\right)^t}+\frac{\$1{,}000}{\left(1+\frac{0.10}{2}\right)^{50}}$$
$$=\$60(PVIFA_{5\%,50})+\$1{,}000(PVIF_{5\%,50})$$
$$=\$60\left(\frac{1-\frac{1}{(1+0.05)^{50}}}{0.05}\right)+\$1{,}000\left(\frac{1}{(1+0.05)^{50}}\right)$$
$$=\$60(18.2559)+\$1{,}000(0.0872)$$
$$=\$1{,}095.35+\$87.20=\$1{,}182.55.$$

Alternatively, with a financial calculator, input the following: N = 50, I = 5, PMT = 60, FV = 1000, and PV = ? PV = −$1,182.56.

c.

$$\text{Current yield}=\text{Annual coupon payment/Price}$$
$$=\$120/\$1{,}182.55$$
$$=0.1015=10.15\%.$$
$$\text{Capital gains yield}=\text{Total yield}-\text{Current yield}$$
$$=10\%-10.15\%=-0.15\%.$$

d.

$$\$916.42=\sum_{t=1}^{13}\frac{\$60}{(1+k_d/2)^t}+\frac{\$1{,}000}{(1+k_d/2)^{13}}.$$

With a financial calculator, input the following: N = 13, PV = −916.42, PMT = 60, FV = 1000, and $k_d/2$ = I = ? Calculator solution = $k_d/2$ = 7.00%; therefore, k_d = 14.00%.

e.

$$\text{Current yield}=\$120/\$916.42=13.09\%.$$
$$\text{Capital gains yield}=14\%-13.09\%=0.91\%.$$

f. The following time line illustrates the years to maturity of the bond:

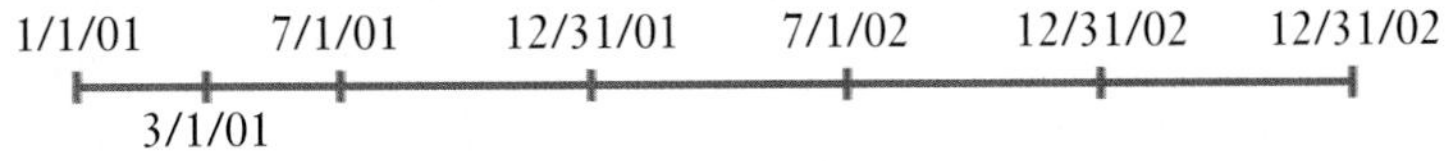

Thus, on March 1, 2001, there were 13⅔ periods left before the bond matured. Bond traders actually use the following procedure to determine the price of the bond:

(1) Find the price of the bond on the next coupon date, July 1, 2001.

$$
\begin{aligned}
V_{B\ 7/1/01} &= \$60(PVIFA_{7.75\%,13}) + \$1{,}000(PVIF_{7.75\%,13}) \\
&= \$60\left(\frac{1 - \frac{1}{(1+0.0775)^{13}}}{0.0775}\right) + \$1{,}000\left(\frac{1}{(1+0.0775)^{13}}\right) \\
&= \$60(8.0136) + \$1{,}000(0.3789) \\
&= \$859.72.
\end{aligned}
$$

With a financial calculator, N = 13, I = 7.75, PV = ?, PMT = 60, FV = 1000, and we get PV = −859.76.

(2) Add the coupon, \$60, to the bond price to get the total value, TV, of the bond on the next interest payment date: TV = \$859.72 + \$60.00 = \$919.72.

(3) Discount this total value back to the purchase date:

$$
\begin{aligned}
\text{Value at purchase date (March 1, 2001)} &= \$919.72(PVIF_{7.75\%,4/6}) \\
&= \$919.72\left(\frac{1}{(1+0.0775)^{(4/6)}}\right) \\
&= \$919.72(0.9515) \\
&= \$875.11.
\end{aligned}
$$

(4) Therefore, you would have written a check for \$875.11 to complete the transaction. Of this amount, \$20 = (⅓)(\$60) would represent accrued interest and \$855.11 would represent the bond's basic value. This breakdown would affect both your taxes and those of the seller.

(5) This problem could be solved *very* easily using a financial calculator with a bond valuation function, such as the HP-12C or the HP-17B. This is explained in the calculator manual under the heading, "Bond Calculations."

ST-2 a. \$100,000,000/10 = \$10,000,000 per year, or \$5 million each 6 months. Since the \$5 million will be used to retire bonds immediately, no interest will be earned on it.

b. The debt service requirements will decline. As the amount of bonds outstanding declines, so will the interest requirements (amounts given in millions of dollars):

Semiannual Payment Period (1)	Outstanding Bonds on Which Interest Is Paid (2)	Interest Payment[a] (3)	Sinking Fund Payment (4)	Total Bond Service (3) + (4) = (5)
1	\$100	\$6.0	\$5	\$11.0
2	95	5.7	5	10.7
3	90	5.4	5	10.4
.	.	.	.	.
.	.	.	.	.
.	.	.	.	.
20	5	0.3	5	5.3

[a]Interest is calculated as (0.5)(0.12)(Column 2); for example: interest in Period 2 = (0.5)(0.12)(\$95) = \$5.7.

The company's total cash bond service requirement will be \$21.7 million per year for the first year. The requirement will decline by 0.12 (\$10,000,000) = \$1,200,000 per year for the remaining years.

c. Here we have a 10-year, 9 percent annuity whose compound value is \$100 million, and we are seeking the annual payment, PMT. The solution can be obtained with a financial calculator. Input N = 10, I = 9, PV = 0, and FV = 100000000, and press the PMT key to obtain \$6,582,009.

We could also find the solution using this equation:

$$\begin{aligned}
\$100{,}000{,}000 &= \sum_{t=1}^{10} PMT(1 + k)^t \\
&= PMT(FVIFA_{9\%,10}) \\
&= PMT\left(\frac{(1 + 0.09)^{10} - 1}{0.09}\right) \\
&= PMT(15.193) \\
PMT &= \$6{,}581{,}979 = \text{Sinking fund payment.}
\end{aligned}$$

The difference is due to rounding.

d. Annual debt service costs will be \$100,000,000(0.12) + \$6,582,009 = \$18,582.009.

e. If interest rates rose, causing the bonds' price to fall, the company would use open market purchases. This would reduce its debt service requirements.

Chapter 10

ST-1 a. This is not necessarily true. Because G plows back two-thirds of its earnings, its growth rate should exceed that of D, but D pays higher dividends (\$6 versus \$2). We cannot say which stock should have the higher price.

b. Again, we just do not know which price would be higher.

c. This is false. The changes in k_d and k_s would have a greater effect on G; its price would decline more.

d. The total expected return for D is $\hat{k}_D = D_1/P_0 + g = 15\% + 0\% = 15\%$. The total expected return for G will have D_1/P_0 less than 15 percent and g greater than 0 percent, but $\hat{k}_G$ should be neither greater nor smaller than D's total expected return, 15 percent, because the two stocks are stated to be equally risky.

e. We have eliminated a, b, c, and d, so e should be correct. On the basis of the available information, D and G should sell at about the same price, \$40; thus, $\hat{k}_s = 15\%$ for both D and G. G's current dividend yield is \$2/\$40 = 5%. Therefore, g = 15% − 5% = 10%.

ST-2 The first step is to solve for g, the unknown variable, in the constant growth equation. Since D_1 is unknown but D_0 is known, substitute $D_0(1 + g)$ as follows:

$$\begin{aligned}
\hat{P}_0 = P_0 &= \frac{D_1}{k_s - g} = \frac{D_0(1 + g)}{k_s - g} \\
\$36 &= \frac{\$2.40(1 + g)}{0.12 - g}.
\end{aligned}$$

Solving for g, we find the growth rate to be 5 percent:

$$\begin{aligned}
\$4.32 - \$36g &= \$2.40 + \$2.40g \\
\$38.4g &= \$1.92 \\
g &= 0.05 = 5\%.
\end{aligned}$$

The next step is to use the growth rate to project the stock price 5 years hence:

$$\begin{aligned}
\hat{P}_5 &= \frac{D_0(1 + g)^6}{k_s - g} \\
&= \frac{\$2.40(1.05)^6}{0.12 - 0.05} \\
&= \$45.95.
\end{aligned}$$

[Alternatively, $\hat{P}_5 = \$36(1.05)^5 = \$45.95$.]

Therefore, Ewald Company's expected stock price 5 years from now, $\hat{P}_5$ is \$45.95.

ST-3 a. (1) Calculate the PV of the dividends paid during the supernormal growth period:

$$D_1 = \$1.1500(1.15) = \$1.3225.$$
$$D_2 = \$1.3225(1.15) = \$1.5209.$$
$$D_3 = \$1.5209(1.13) = \$1.7186.$$
$$\begin{aligned} \text{PV D} &= \$1.3225(0.8929) + \$1.5209(0.7972) + \$1.7186(0.7118) \\ &= \$1.1809 + \$1.2125 + \$1.2233 \\ &= \$3.6167 \approx \$3.62. \end{aligned}$$

(2) Find the PV of Snyder's stock price at the end of Year 3:

$$\begin{aligned} \hat{P}_3 = \frac{D_4}{k_s - g} &= \frac{D_3(1 + g)}{k_s - g} \\ &= \frac{\$1.7186(1.06)}{0.12 - 0.06} \\ &= \$30.36. \end{aligned}$$
$$\text{PV } \hat{P}_3 = \$30.36(0.7118) = \$21.61.$$

(3) Sum the two components to find the value of the stock today:

$$\hat{P}_0 = \$3.62 + \$21.61 = \$25.23.$$

Alternatively, the cash flows can be placed on a time line as follows:

0	1	2	3	4
12%; g = 15%		g = 13%	g = 6%	
	1.3225	1.5209	1.7186	1.8217
			30.3617 =	$\left(\frac{\$1.8217}{0.12 - 0.06}\right)$
			32.0803	

Enter the cash flows into the cash flow register, I = 12, and press the NPV key to obtain P_0 = \$25.23.

b.

$$\begin{aligned} \hat{P}_1 &= \$1.5209(0.8929) + \$1.7186(0.7972) + \$30.36(0.7972) \\ &= \$1.3580 + \$1.3701 + \$24.2030 \\ &= \$26.9311 \approx \$26.93. \end{aligned}$$
(Calculator solution: \$26.93.)

$$\begin{aligned} \hat{P}_2 &= \$1.7186(0.8929) + \$30.36(0.8929) \\ &= \$1.5345 + \$27.1084 \\ &= \$28.6429 \approx \$28.64. \end{aligned}$$
(Calculator solution: \$28.64.)

c.

Year	Dividend Yield	+	Capital Gains Yield	=	Total Return
1	$\frac{\$1.3225}{\$25.23} \approx 5.24\%$	+	$\frac{\$26.93 - \$25.23}{\$25.23} \approx 6.74\%$	≈	12%
2	$\frac{\$1.5209}{\$26.93} \approx 5.65\%$	+	$\frac{\$28.64 - \$26.93}{\$26.93} \approx 6.35\%$	≈	12%
3	$\frac{\$1.7186}{\$28.64} \approx 6.00\%$	+	$\frac{\$30.36 - \$28.64}{\$28.64} \approx 6.00\%$	≈	12%

Chapter 11

ST-1 a. Component costs are as follows:

Debt at k_d = 12%:

$$k_d(1 - T) = 12\%(0.6) = 7.2\%.$$

Preferred with F = 5%:

$$k_{ps} = \frac{\text{Preferred dividend}}{P_n} = \frac{\$11}{\$100(.95)} = 11.6\%.$$

Common with DCF:

$$k_s = \frac{D_1}{P_0} + g = \frac{\$3.924}{\$60} + 9\% = 15.5\%.$$

Common with CAPM:

$$k_s = 11\% + 1.51(14\% - 11\%) = 15.5\%$$

b.

$$\begin{aligned} \text{WACC} &= w_d k_d(1 - T) + w_{ps}k_{ps} + w_e k_s \\ &= 0.25(12\%)(1 - 0.4) + 0.15(11.6\%) + 0.60(15.5\%) \\ &= 12.8\%. \end{aligned}$$

Chapter 12

ST-1 a.

$$V_{Op} = \frac{\text{FCF}(1 + g)}{\text{WACC} - g} = \frac{\$100{,}000(1 + 0.07)}{0.11 - 0.07} = \$2{,}675{,}000.$$

b.

$$\begin{aligned} \text{Total value} &= \text{Value of operations} + \text{Value of nonoperating assets} \\ &= \$2{,}675{,}000 + \$325{,}000 = \$3{,}000{,}000. \end{aligned}$$

c.

$$\begin{aligned} \text{Value of equity} &= \text{Total value} - \text{Value of debt} \\ &= \$3{,}000{,}000 - \$1{,}000{,}000 = \$2{,}000{,}000. \end{aligned}$$

Chapter 13

ST-1 a. **Payback:**

To determine the payback, construct the cumulative cash flows for each project:

	Cumulative Cash Flows	
Year	**Project X**	**Project Y**
0	($10,000)	($10,000)
1	(3,500)	(6,500)
2	(500)	(3,000)
3	2,500	500
4	3,500	4,000

$$\text{Payback}_X = 2 + \frac{\$500}{\$3{,}000} = 2.17 \text{ years.}$$

$$\text{Payback}_Y = 2 + \frac{\$3{,}000}{\$3{,}500} = 2.86 \text{ years.}$$

Net Present Value (NPV):

$$\begin{aligned} \text{NPV}_X &= -\$10{,}000 + \frac{\$6{,}500}{(1.12)^1} + \frac{\$3{,}000}{(1.12)^2} + \frac{\$3{,}000}{(1.12)^3} + \frac{\$1{,}000}{(1.12)^4} \\ &= \$966.01. \end{aligned}$$

$$\begin{aligned} \text{NPV}_Y &= -\$10{,}000 + \frac{\$3{,}500}{(1.12)^1} + \frac{\$3{,}500}{(1.12)^2} + \frac{\$3{,}500}{(1.12)^3} + \frac{\$3{,}500}{(1.12)^4} \\ &= \$630.72. \end{aligned}$$

Alternatively, using a financial calculator, input the cash flows into the cash flow register, enter I = 12, and then press the NPV key to obtain NPV_X = \$966.01 and NPV_Y = \$630.72.

Internal Rate of Return (IRR):

To solve for each project's IRR, find the discount rates which equate each NPV to zero:

$$IRR_X = 18.0\%.$$
$$IRR_Y = 15.0\%.$$

Modified Internal Rate of Return (MIRR):

To obtain each project's MIRR, begin by finding each project's terminal value (TV) of cash inflows:

$$\begin{aligned} TV_X &= \$6{,}500(1.12)^3 + \$3{,}000(1.12)^2 \\ &\quad + 3{,}000(1.12)^1 + \$1{,}000 = \$17{,}255.23. \\ TV_Y &= \$3{,}500(1.12)^3 + \$3{,}500(1.12)^2 \\ &\quad + \$3{,}500(1.12)^1 + \$3{,}500 = \$16{,}727.65. \end{aligned}$$

Now, each project's MIRR is that discount rate which equates the PV of the TV to each project's cost, \$10,000:

$$MIRR_X = 14.61\%.$$
$$MIRR_Y = 13.73\%.$$

b. The following table summarizes the project rankings by each method:

	Project That Ranks Higher
Payback	X
NPV	X
IRR	X
MIRR	X

Note that all methods ranks Project X over Project Y. In addition, both projects are acceptable under the NPV, IRR, and MIRR criteria. Thus, both projects should be accepted if they are independent.

c. In this case, we would choose the project with the higher NPV at k = 12%, or Project X.

d. To determine the effects of changing the cost of capital, plot the NPV profiles of each project. The crossover rate occurs at about 6 to 7 percent (6.2%). See the graph on the next page.

If the firm's cost of capital is less than 6 percent, a conflict exists because $NPV_Y > NPV_X$, but $IRR_X > IRR_Y$. Therefore, if k were 5 percent, a conflict would exist. Note, however, that when k = 5.0%, $MIRR_X$ = 10.64% and $MIRR_Y$ = 10.83%; hence, the modified IRR ranks the projects correctly, even if k is to the left of the crossover point.

e. The basic cause of the conflict is differing reinvestment rate assumptions between NPV and IRR. NPV assumes that cash flows can be reinvested at the cost of capital, while IRR assumes reinvestment at the (generally) higher IRR. The high reinvestment rate assumption under IRR makes early cash flows especially valuable, and hence short-term projects look better under IRR.

NPV Profiles for Projects X and Y

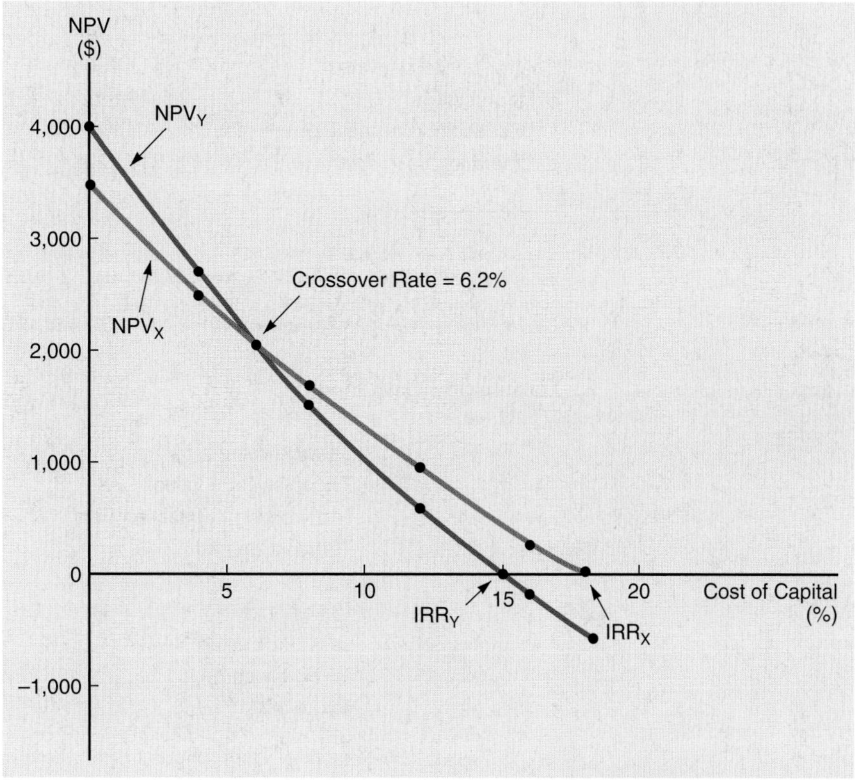

Cost of Capital	NPV_X	NPV_Y
0%	$3,500	$4,000
4	2,545	2,705
8	1,707	1,592
12	966	631
16	307	(206)
18	5	(585)

Chapter 14

ST-1 a. **Estimated Investment Requirements:**

Price	($50,000)
Modification	(10,000)
Change in net working capital	(2,000)
Total investment	($62,000)

b. **Operating Cash Flows:**

	Year 1	Year 2	Year 3
1. After-tax cost savings[a]	$12,000	$12,000	$12,000
2. Depreciation[b]	19,800	27,000	9,000
3. Depreciation tax savings[c]	7,920	10,800	3,600
Operating cash flow (1 + 3)	$19,920	$22,800	$15,600

[a]$20,000(1 − T).
[b]Depreciable basis = $60,000; the MACRS percentage allowances are 0.33, 0.45, and 0.15 in Years 1, 2, and 3, respectively; hence, depreciation in Year 1 = 0.33($60,000) = $19,800, and so on. There will remain $4,200, or 7 percent, undepreciated after Year 3; it would normally be taken in Year 4.
[c]Depreciation tax savings = T(Depreciation) = 0.4($19,800) = $7,920 in Year 1, and so on.

c. **Termination Cash Flow:**

Salvage value	$20,000
Tax on salvage value[a]	(6,320)
Net working capital recovery	2,000
Termination cash flow	$15,680

[a]Sales price	$20,000
Less book value	4,200
Taxable income	$15,800
Tax at 40%	$ 6,320

$$\text{Book value} = \text{Depreciation basis} - \text{Accumulated depreciation}$$
$$= \$60{,}000 - \$55{,}800 = \$4{,}200.$$

d. **Project NPV:**

0 (10%)	1	2	3
−62,000	19,920	22,800	31,280

$$\text{NPV} = -\$62{,}000 + \frac{\$19{,}920}{(1.10)^1} + \frac{\$22{,}800}{(1.10)^2} + \frac{\$31{,}280}{(1.10)^3}$$
$$= -\$1{,}547.$$

Alternatively, using a financial calculator, input the cash flows into the cash flow register, enter I = 10, and then press the NPV key to obtain NPV = −$1,547. Because the earthmover has a negative NPV, it should not be purchased.

ST-2 a. First, find the expected cash flows:

Year	Expected Cash Flows			
0	0.2(−$100,000)	+0.6(−$100,000)	+0.2(−$100,000)	= ($100,000)
1	0.2($20,000)	+0.6($30,000)	+0.2($40,000)	= $30,000
2				$30,000
3				$30,000
4				$30,000
5				$30,000
5*	0.2($0)	+0.6($20,000)	+0.2($30,000)	= $18,000

0 (10%)	1	2	3	4	5
−100,000	30,000	30,000	30,000	30,000	48,000

Next, determine the NPV based on the expected cash flows:

$$NPV = -\$100{,}000 + \frac{\$30{,}000}{(1.10)^1} + \frac{\$30{,}000}{(1.10)^2} + \frac{\$30{,}000}{(1.10)^3} + \frac{\$30{,}000}{(1.10)^4} + \frac{\$48{,}000}{(1.10)^5} = \$24{,}900.$$

Alternatively, using a financial calculator, input the cash flows in the cash flow register, enter I = 10, and then press the NPV key to obtain NPV = \$24,900.

b. For the worst case, the cash flow values from the cash flow column farthest on the left are used to calculate NPV:

0 (10%)	1	2	3	4	5
−100,000	20,000	20,000	20,000	20,000	20,000

$$NPV = -\$100{,}000 + \frac{\$20{,}000}{(1.10)^1} + \frac{\$20{,}000}{(1.10)^2} + \frac{\$20{,}000}{(1.10)^3} + \frac{\$20{,}000}{(1.10)^4} + \frac{\$20{,}000}{(1.10)^5} = -\$24{,}184.$$

Similarly, for the best case, use the values from the column farthest on the right. Here the NPV is \$70,259.

If the cash flows are perfectly dependent, then the low cash flow in the first year will mean a low cash flow in every year. Thus, the probability of the worst case occurring is the probability of getting the \$20,000 net cash flow in Year 1, or 20 percent. If the cash flows are independent, the cash flow in each year can be low, high, or average, and the probability of getting all low cash flows will be

$$0.2(0.2)(0.2)(0.2)(0.2) = 0.2^5 = 0.00032 = 0.032\%.$$

c. The base-case NPV is found using the most likely cash flows and is equal to \$26,142. This value differs from the expected NPV of \$24,900 because the Year 5 cash flows are not symmetric. Under these conditions, the NPV distribution is as follows:

P	NPV
0.2	(\$24,184)
0.6	26,142
0.2	70,259

Thus, the expected NPV is 0.2(−\$24,184) + 0.6(\$26,142) + 0.2(\$70,259) = \$24,900. As is generally the case, the expected NPV is the same as the NPV of the expected cash flows found in part a. The standard deviation is \$29,904:

$$\begin{aligned}\sigma^2_{NPV} &= 0.2(-\$24{,}184 - \$24{,}900)^2 + 0.6(\$26{,}142 - \$24{,}900)^2 \\ &\quad + 0.2(\$70{,}259 - \$24{,}900)^2 \\ &= \$894{,}261{,}126. \\ \sigma_{NPV} &= \sqrt{\$894{,}261{,}126} = \$29{,}904.\end{aligned}$$

The coefficient of variation, CV, is \$29,904/\$24,900 = 1.20.

d. Since the project's coefficient of variation is 1.20, the project is riskier than average, and hence the project's risk-adjusted cost of capital is 10% + 2% = 12%. The project now should be evaluated by finding the NPV of the expected cash flows, as in part a, but using a 12 percent discount rate. The risk-adjusted NPV is \$18,357, and, therefore, the project should be accepted.

Chapter 15

ST-1 a.

$$\text{Exercise value} = \text{Current stock price} - \text{Strike price} = \$30 - \$25 = \$5.$$

b.

$$\text{Premium} = \text{Option price} - \text{Exercise value} = \$7 - \$5 = \$2.$$

ST-2 a. An increase in stock price increases the value of a call option because it increases the size of the profit should the option be exercised.

b. An increase in volatility means that the stock price might become much higher or much lower than the strike price. Stock prices higher than the strike price lead to high exercise values, but the exercise value will never be less than zero, no matter how low the stock price. So volatility increases the upside potential without increasing the downside risk. Therefore, volatility increases the value of a call option.

c. As the risk-free rate increases, the present value of the cost of exercising the option in the future decreases, which causes the value of the call option to increase.

d. A decrease in the time remaining until expiration reduces the chance that the stock price will go up very much. Therefore, a decrease in time reduces the value of a call option.

Chapter 16

ST-1 a.

$$S = \frac{(\text{EBIT} - k_dD)(1 - T)}{k_s}$$

$$= \frac{[\$4,000,000 - 0.10(\$2,000,000)](0.65)}{0.15} = \$16,466,667.$$

$$P_0 = S/n = \frac{\$16,466,667}{600,000} = \$27.44.$$

$$V = D + S = \$2,000,000 + \$16,466,667 = \$18,466,667.$$

b.

$$\text{WACC} = (D/V)(k_d)(1 - T) + (S/V)(k_s)$$

$$= \left(\frac{\$2,000,000}{\$18,466,667}\right)(10\%)(0.65) + \left(\frac{\$16,466,667}{\$18,466,667}\right)(15\%)$$

$$= 14.08\%.$$

c. Under the new capital structure,

$$S = \frac{[\$4,000,000 - 0.12(\$10,000,000)](0.65)}{0.17} = \$10,705,882.$$

$$V = \$10,000,000 + \$10,705,882 = \$20,705,882.$$

The new value of the firm will thus be \$20,705,882. This value belongs to the *present* stockholders and bondholders, so we may calculate the new equilibrium price of the stock, P_1:

$$P_1 = \frac{V_1 - D_0}{n_0} = \frac{\$20,705,882 - \$2,000,000}{600,000} = \$31.18.$$

$$\text{Check: Shares repurchased} = \frac{\text{New debt}}{P_1} = \frac{\$8,000,000}{\$31.18} = \$256,575.$$

$$P_1 = \frac{S_1}{n_1} = \frac{\$10,705,882}{600,000 - 256,575} \approx \$31.18.$$

$$\text{WACC} = \left(\frac{\$10,000,000}{\$20,705,882}\right)(12\%)(0.65) + \left(\frac{\$10,705,882}{\$20,705,882}\right)(17\%) = 12.56\%.$$

Thus, the proposed capital structure change would increase the value of the firm and the price of its stock (from \$27.44 to \$31.18), and lower its cost of capital. Therefore, the firm should increase its use of financial leverage. Of course, it is possible that some amount of debt other than \$10 million would result in an even higher value, but we do not have enough information to make this determination.

ST-2 a. LIC's current cost of equity is 6% + 1.5(4%) = 12%.

b. LIC's unlevered beta is 1.5/[1 + (1 − 0.40)(25/75)] = 1.5/1.2 = 1.25.

c. LIC's levered beta at D/E = 60/40 = 1.5 is 1.25[1 + (1 − 0.40)(1.5)] = 2.375. LIC's new cost of capital will be 6% + (2.375)(4%) = 15.5%.

Chapter 17

ST-1 a. Value of unleveraged firm, $V_U = EBIT(1 - T)/k_{sU}$:

$$\$12 = \$2(1 - 0.4)k_{sU}$$
$$\$12 = \$1.2/k_{sU}$$
$$k_{sU} = \$1.2/\$12 = \$10.0\%.$$

Therefore, k_{sU} = WACC = 10.0%.

b. Value of leveraged firm according to MM mode with taxes:

$$V_L = V_U + TD.$$

As shown in the following table, value increases continuously with debt, and the optimal capital structure consists of 100 percent debt. Note: The table is not necessary to answer this question, but the data (in millions of dollars) are necessary for part c of this problem.

Debt, D	V_U	TD	$V_L = V_U + TD$
$ 0	$12.0	$ 0	$12.0
2.5	12.0	1.0	13.0
5.0	12.0	2.0	14.0
7.5	12.0	3.0	15.0
10.0	12.0	4.0	16.0
12.5	12.0	5.0	17.0
15.0	12.0	6.0	18.0
20.0	12.0	8.0	20.0

c. With financial distress costs included in the analysis, the value of the leveraged firm now is

$$V_L = V_U + TD - PC,$$

where

$V_U + TD$ = value according to MM after-tax model.
P = probability of financial distress.
C = present value of distress costs.

D	$V_U + TD$	P	PC = (P)$8	$V_L = V_U + TD - PC$
$ 0	$12.0	0	$ 0	$12.0
2.5	13.0	0	0	13.0
5.0	14.0	0.0125	0.10	13.9
7.5	15.0	0.0250	0.20	14.8
10.0	16.0	0.0625	0.50	15.5
12.5	17.0	0.1250	1.00	16.0
15.0	18.0	0.3125	2.50	15.5
20.0	20.0	0.7500	6.00	14.0

Note: All dollar amounts in table are in millions.

Optimal debt level: D = \$12.5 million.
Maximum value of firm: V = \$16.0 million.
Optimal debt/value ratio: D/V = \$12.5/\$16 = 78%.

d. The value of the firm versus debt value with and without financial distress costs is plotted next (millions of dollars):

V_L = Value without financial distress costs.
V_B = Value with financial distress costs.

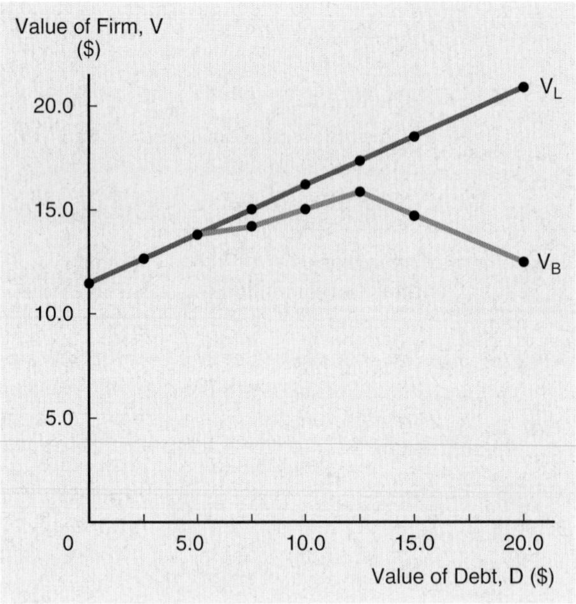

Chapter 18

ST-1 a.

Projected net income	\$2,000,000
Less projected capital investments	800,000
Available residual	\$1,200,000
Shares outstanding	200,000

DPS = \$1,200,000/200,000 shares = \$6 = D_1.

b. EPS = \$2,000,000/200,000 shares = \$10.
Payout ratio = DPS/EPS = \$6/\$10 = 60%, or
Total dividends/NI = \$1,200,000/\$2,000,000 = 60%.

c. $$\text{Currently, } P_0 = \frac{D_1}{k_s - g} = \frac{\$6}{0.14 - 0.05} = \frac{\$6}{0.09} = \$66.67.$$

Under the former circumstances, D_1 would be based on a 20 percent payout on \$10 EPS, or \$2. With k_s = 14% and g = 12%, we solve for P_0:

$$P_0 = \frac{D_1}{k_s - g} = \frac{\$2}{0.14 - 0.12} = \frac{\$2}{0.02} = \$100.$$

Although CMC has suffered a severe setback, its existing assets will continue to provide a good income stream. More of these earnings should now be passed on to the shareholders, as the slowed internal growth has reduced the need for funds. However, the net result is a 33 percent decrease in the value of the shares.

d. If the payout ratio were continued at 20 percent, even after internal investment opportunities had declined, the price of the stock would drop to \$2/(0.14 − 0.06) = \$25 rather than to \$66.67. Thus, an increase in the dividend payout is consistent with maximizing shareholder wealth.

Because of the diminishing nature of profitable investment opportunities, the greater the firm's level of investment, the lower the average ROE. Thus, the more money CMC retains and invests, the lower its average ROE will be. We can determine the average ROE under different conditions as follows:

Old Situation (With Founder Active and a 20 Percent Payout):

$$\begin{aligned} g &= (1.0 - \text{Payout ratio})(\text{Average ROE}) \\ 12\% &= (1.0 - 0.2)(\text{Average ROE}) \\ \text{Average ROE} &= 12\%/0.8 = 15\% > k_s = 14\%. \end{aligned}$$

Note that the *average* ROE is 15 percent, whereas the *marginal* ROE is presumably equal to 14 percent.

New Situation (With Founder Retired and a 60 Percent Payout):

$$\begin{aligned} g = 6\% &= (1.0 - 0.6)(\text{ROE}) \\ \text{ROE} &= 6\%/0.4 = 15\% > k_s = 14\%. \end{aligned}$$

This suggests that the new payout is appropriate and that the firm is taking on investments down to the point at which marginal returns are equal to the cost of capital. Note that if the 20 percent payout was maintained, the *average* ROE would be only 7.5 percent, which would imply a marginal ROE far below the 14 percent cost of capital.

Chapter 20

ST-1 a. **Cost of Leasing:**

	Year 0	Year 1	Year 2	Year 3	Year 4
Lease payment	(\$10,000)	(\$10,000)	(\$10,000)	(\$10,000)	\$0
Payment tax savings	4,000	4,000	4,000	4,000	0
Net cash flow	(\$ 6,000)	(\$ 6,000)	(\$ 6,000)	(\$ 6,000)	\$0

PV cost of leasing @ 6% = (\$22,038)

b. **Cost of Owning:**

In our solution, we will consider the \$40,000 cost as a Year 0 outflow rather than including all the financing cash flows. The net effect is the same since the PV of the financing flows, when discounted at the after-tax cost of debt, is the cost of the asset.

	Year 0	Year 1	Year 2	Year 3	Year 4
Net purchase price	(\$40,000)				
Maintenance cost		(\$1,000)	(\$1,000)	(\$1,000)	(\$1,000)
Maintenance tax savings		400	400	400	400
Depreciation tax savings		5,280	7,200	2,400	1,120
Residual value					10,000
Residual value tax					(4,000)
Net cash flow	(\$40,000)	\$4,680	\$6,600	\$1,800	\$6,520

PV cost of owning @ 6% = (\$23,035)

Since the present value of the cost of leasing is less than the present value of the cost of owning, the truck should be leased. Specifically, the NAL is \$23,035 − \$22,038 = \$997.

c. Use the cost of debt because most cash flows are fixed by contract and consequently are relatively certain; thus lease cash flows have about the same risk as the firm's debt. Also, leasing is considered as a substitute for debt. Use an after-tax cost rate to account for interest tax deductibility.

d. The firm could increase the discount rate on the residual value cash flow. Note that since the firm plans to replace the truck after 4 years, the residual value is treated as an inflow in the cost of owning analysis. This makes it reasonable to raise the discount rate for analysis purposes. However, had the firm planned to continue using the truck, then we would have had to place the estimated residual value as an additional Year 4 outflow in the leasing section, but without a tax adjustment. Then, higher risk would have been reflected in a *lower* discount rate. This is all very ad hoc, which is why analysts often prefer to use one discount rate throughout the analysis.

Chapter 22

ST-1 The Calgary Company: Alternative Balance Sheets

	Restricted (40%)	Moderate (50%)	Relaxed (60%)
Current assets	\$1,200,000	\$1,500,000	\$1,800,000
Fixed assets	600,000	600,000	600,000
Total assets	\$1,800,000	\$2,100,000	\$2,400,000
Debt	\$ 900,000	\$1,050,000	\$1,200,000
Equity	900,000	1,050,000	1,200,000
Total liabilities and equity	\$1,800,000	\$2,100,000	\$2,400,000

The Calgary Company: Alternative Income Statements

	Restricted	Moderate	Relaxed
Sales	\$3,000,000	\$3,000,000	\$3,000,000
EBIT	450,000	450,000	450,000
Interest (10%)	90,000	105,000	120,000
Earnings before taxes	\$ 360,000	\$ 345,000	\$ 330,000
Taxes (40%)	144,000	138,000	132,000
Net income	\$ 216,000	\$ 207,000	\$ 198,000
ROE	24.0%	19.7%	16.5%

ST-2 a. First, determine the balance on the firm's checkbook and the bank's records as follows:

	Firm's Checkbook	Bank's Records
Day 1: Deposit \$500,000; write check for \$1,000,000	(\$500,000)	\$500,000
Day 2: Write check for \$1,000,000	(\$1,500,000)	\$500,000
Day 3: Write check for \$1,000,000	(\$2,500,000)	\$500,000
Day 4: Write check for \$1,000,000; deposit \$1,000,000	(\$2,500,000)	\$500,000

After Upton has reached a steady state, it must deposit \$1,000,000 each day to cover the checks written 3 days earlier.

b. The firm has 3 days of float; not until Day 4 does the firm have to make any additional deposits.

c. As shown above, Upton should try to maintain a balance on the bank's records of \$500,000. On its own books it will have a balance of *minus* \$2,500,000.

Chapter 23

ST-1 a. and b.

Income Statements for Year Ended December 31, 2001 (Thousands of Dollars)

	Vanderheiden Press		Herrenhouse Publishing	
	a	b	a	b
EBIT	\$ 30,000	\$ 30,000	\$ 30,000	\$ 30,000
Interest	12,400	14,400	10,600	18,600
Taxable income	\$ 17,600	\$ 15,600	\$ 19,400	\$ 11,400
Taxes (40%)	7,040	6,240	7,760	4,560
Net income	\$ 10,560	\$ 9,360	\$ 11,640	\$ 6,840
Equity	\$100,000	\$100,000	\$100,000	\$100,000
Return on equity	10.56%	9.36%	11.64%	6.84%

The Vanderheiden Press has a higher ROE when short-term interest rates are high, whereas Herrenhouse Publishing does better when rates are lower.

c. Herrenhouse's position is riskier. First, its profits and return on equity are much more volatile than Vanderheiden's. Second, Herrenhouse must renew its large short-term loan every year, and if the renewal comes up at a time when money is very tight, when its business is depressed, or both, then Herrenhouse could be denied credit, which could put it out of business.

Chapter 24

ST-1 a. The underlying bond has an annual coupon of 6 percent (paid semiannually) and a maturity of 20 years. At a price of 97 17/32 (this is the percent of par), a \$1,000 par bond would have a price of \$974.0625. To find the yield, N = 40; PMT = 30; FV = 1000; PV = −974.0625; solve for I = 3.1143% per six months. The nominal annual yield is 2(3.1143%) = 6.229%.

b. In this situation, the firm would be hurt if interest rates were to rise by September, so it would use a short hedge or sell futures contracts. Because futures contracts are for \$100,000 in Treasury bonds, the firm must sell 50 contracts to cover the planned \$5,000,000 September bond issue. Because futures maturing in June are selling for 97 17/32 of par, the value of Wansley's futures is about 50(0.9740625) = 4,870,313. Should interest rates rise by September, Wansley will be able to repurchase the futures contracts at a lower cost, which will help offset their loss from financing at the higher interest rate. Thus, the firm has hedged against rising interest rates.

c. The firm would now pay 13 percent on the bonds. With a 12 percent coupon rate, the PV of the new issue is only N = 60; I = 13/2 = 6.5; PMT = 0.12/2 × 5000000 = 300000; FV = 5000000; and solve for PV = \$4,624,176. Therefore, the new bond issue would bring in only \$4,624,176, so the cost of the bond issue due to rising rates is \$5,000,000 − \$4,624,176 = \$375,824.

However, the value of the short futures position began at \$4,870,313. Now, if interest rates increased by 1 percentage point, the yield on the futures would go up to 7.229 percent (7.229 = 6.229 + 1). The value of the futures position is N = 40; I = 7.229/2 = 3.6143 (from part a); PMT = 150000; FV = 5000000; and solve for PV = \$4,355,552 (note: if you don't round in any previous calculations, the PV is \$4,355,557).

Because Wansley Company sold the futures contracts for \$4,870,313, and will, in effect, buy them back at \$4,355,552, the firm would make a profit of \$4,870,313 − \$4,355,552 = \$514,761 profit on the transaction ignoring transaction costs.

Thus, the firm gained \$514,761 on its futures position, but lost \$375,824 on its underlying bond issue. On net, it gained \$514,761 − \$375,824 = \$138,937.

Chapter 27

ST-1

$$\frac{\text{Euros}}{\text{C\$}} = \frac{\text{Euros}}{\text{US\$}} \times \frac{\text{US\$}}{\text{C\$}}$$

$$= \frac{0.98}{\$1} \times \frac{\$1}{1.5} = \frac{0.98}{1.5} = 0.6533 \text{ euro per Canadian dollar.}$$

APPENDIX B

Answers to End-of-Chapter Problems

We present here some intermediate steps and final answers to selected end-of-chapter problems. Please note that your answer may differ slightly from ours due to rounding differences. Also, although we hope not, some of the problems may have more than one correct solution, depending upon what assumptions are made in working the problem. Finally, many of the problems involve some verbal discussion as well as numerical calculations; this verbal material is not presented here.

2-1 \$1,000,000.

2-2 \$3,600,000.

2-3 5.76%.

2-4 \$21,459.50.

2-5 25%.

2-6 Tax = \$107,855; NI = \$222,145; Marginal tax rate = 39%; Average tax rate = 33.8%.

2-7 a. Tax = \$3,575,000.
b. Tax = \$350,000.
c. Tax = \$105,000.

2-8 AT&T preferred stock = 5.37%.

2-9 Municipal bond; yield = 7%.

2-10 NI = \$450,000; NCF = \$650,000; OCF = \$650,000.

2-11 a.

2-12 a. \$584.
c. \$1,520.

2-13 a. \$2,400,000.

2-14 \$2,500,000.

2-15 a. NOPAT = \$90,000,000.
b. $NOWC_{00}$ = \$210,000,000;
$NOWC_{01}$ = \$192,000,000.
c. Operating $capital_{00}$ = \$460,000,000;
Operating $capital_{01}$ = \$492,000,000.
d. FCF = \$58,000,000.

2-17 Tax_{2002} = \$0; Tax_{2003} = \$0; Tax_{2004} = \$12,000,000; Tax_{2005} = \$32,000,000; Tax_{2006} = \$0 and receive refund of \$44,000,000 for 2004 and 2005 taxes.

2-18 a. 2002 advantage as a corporation = \$825.50; 2003 advantage = \$4,075.50; 2004 advantage = \$5,225.50.

2-19 a. Personal tax = \$25,894.00.
b. Marginal rate = 31%; average rate = 24.6%.
c. Disney yield = 5.52%; choose FLA bonds.
d. 25%.

3-1 CL = \$2,000,000; Inv = \$1,000,000.

3-2 AR = \$800,000.

3-3 D/A = 58.33%.

3-4 TATO = 5; EM = 1.5.

3-5 $\frac{NI}{S} = 2\%; \frac{D}{A} = 40\%.$

3-6 \$262,500; 1.19×.

3-7 Sales = \$2,592,000; DSO = 36 days.

3-8 TIE = 3.86×.

3-9 ROE = 23.1%.

3-10 7.2%.

3-11 a.

3-12 a. +5.54%.
b(2). +3.21%.
(3). +2.50%.

3-13 a. Current ratio = 1.98×; DSO = 75 days; Total assets turnover = 1.7×; Debt ratio = 61.9%.

3-14 A/P = \$90,000; Inv = \$90,000; FA = \$138,000.

3-16 a. Quick ratio = 0.8×; DSO = 37 days; ROE = 13.1%; Debt ratio = 54.8%.

4-1 AFN = \$410,000.

4-2 AFN = \$610,000.

4-3 AFN = \$200,000.

4-4 ΔS = \$68,965.52.

4-5 a. \$13.44 million.
b. Notes payable = \$31.44 million.
c. Current ratio = 2.00×; ROE = 14.2%.
d(1). −\$14.28 million.
(2). Total assets = \$147 million; Notes payable = \$3.72 million.
(3). Current ratio = 4.25×; ROE = 10.84%.

4-6 a. Total assets = \$33,534; AFN = \$2,128.
b. Notes payable = \$4,228; AFN = \$70;
ΔInterest = \$213.

4-7 a. AFN = \$128,783.
b. Notes payable = \$220,392; ΔInterest = \$8,371; AFN = \$8,028.
c. 3.45%.

4-8 a. AFN = \$667.
b. Increase in notes payable = \$51; Increase in common stock = \$368.

4-9 a. \$480,000.
b. \$18,750.

4-10 AFN = \$360.

5-1 6%; 6.33%.

5-2 1.5%.

5-3 5.5%.

5-4 0.2%.

5-5 6.4%.

5-6 8.5%.

5-7 6.8%.

5-8 a. k_1 in Year 2 = 6%.

5-9 k_1 in Year 2 = 9%; Year 2 inflation = 7%.

5-10 1.5%.

5-11 6.0%.

5-12 a. $k_1 = 9.20\%$; $k_5 = 7.20\%$.

5-14 a. 8.20%.
b. 10.20%.
c. $k_5 = 10.70\%$.

6-1 $\hat{k} = 11.40\%$; $\sigma = 26.69\%$; CV = 2.34.

6-2 b = 1.12.

6-3 $k_M = 11\%$; k = 12.2%.

6-4 k = 10.90%.

6-5 a. $\hat{k}_M = 13.5\%$; $\hat{k}_j = 11.6\%$.
b. $\sigma_M = 3.85\%$; $\sigma_j = 6.22\%$.
c. $CV_M = 0.29$; $CV_j = 0.54$.

6-6 a. $\hat{k}_Y = 14\%$.
b. $\sigma_X = 12.20\%$.

6-7 a. $b_A = 1.40$.
b. $k_A = 15\%$.

6-8 a. $k_i = 15.5\%$.
b(1). $k_M = 15\%$; $k_i = 16.5\%$.
(2). $k_M = 13\%$; $k_i = 14.5\%$.
c(1). $k_i = 18.1\%$.
(2). $k_i = 14.2\%$.

6-9 $b_N = 1.16$.

6-10 $b_p = 0.7625$; $k_p = 12.1\%$.

6-11 $b_N = 1.1250$.

6-12 4.5%.

6-13 a. \$0.5 million.

6-14 a. $k_i = 6\% + (5\%)b_i$.
b. 15%.
c. Indifference rate = 16%.

6-15 a. $\bar{k}_A = 11.30\%$.
c. $\sigma_A = 20.8\%$; $\sigma_p = 20.1\%$.

6-16 a. $b_X = 1.3471$; $b_Y = 0.6508$.
b. $k_X = 12.7355\%$; $k_Y = 9.254\%$.
c. $k_p = 12.04\%$.

7-1 b. X: 10.6%; 13.1%.
M: 12.1%; 22.6%.
c. 8.6%.

8-1 a. \$530.
b. \$561.80.
c. \$471.70.
d. \$445.00.

8-2 a. \$895.40.
b. \$1,552.90.
c. \$279.20.
d. i = 12%; \$500.03.
i = 6%; \$867.14.

8-3 a. n ≈ 10 years.
b. n ≈ 7 years.
c. n ≈ 4 years.
d. n ≈ 1 year.

8-4 a. \$6,374.96.
b. \$1,105.12.
c. \$2,000.00.
d(1). \$7,012.46.
(2). \$1,160.38.
(3). \$2,000.00

8-5 a. \$2,457.84.
b. \$865.90.
c. \$2,000.00.
d(1). \$2,703.62.
(2). \$909.20.
(3). \$2,000.00.

8-6 a. PV_A = \$1,251.21.
PV_B = \$1,300.27.
b. PV_A = \$1,600.
PV_B = \$1,600.

8-7 a. 7%.
b. 7%.
c. 9%.
d. 15%.

8-8 a. \$881.15.
b. \$895.40.
c. \$903.05.
d. \$908.35.

8-9 a. \$279.20.
b. \$276.85.
c. \$443.70.

8-10 a. \$5,272.32.
b. \$5,374.07.

8-12 b. \$13,189.87.
c. \$8,137.27.

8-13 a. $I_Z = 9\%$; $I_B = 8\%$.

8-14 a. \$61,203.
b. \$11,020.
c. \$6,841.

8-15 \$1,000 today.

8-16 a. $i \approx 15\%$.

8-17 $i = 7.18\%$.

8-18 $i = 12\%$.

8-19 $i = 9\%$.

8-20 a. \$33,872.00.
b(1). \$26,243.04.
(2). \$0.

8-21 15 years.

8-22 6 years; \$1,106.01.

8-23 (1). \$1,428.57.
(2). \$714.29.

8-24 \$893.26.

8-25 \$984.88.

8-26 57.18%.

8-27 a. \$1,432.02.
b. \$93.07.

8-28 $i_{Nom} = 15.19\%$.

8-29 PMT = \$36,949.61.

9-1 \$935.82.

9-2 12.48%.

9-3 YTM = 6.62%; YTC = 6.49%.

9-4 8.55%.

9-5 \$1,028.60.

9-6 a. V_L at 5 percent = \$1,518.97; V_L at 8 percent = \$1,171.15; V_L at 12 percent = \$863.79.

9-7 a. YTM at \$829 ≈ 15%.

9-8 15.03%.

9-9 a. 10.37%.
b. 10.91%.
c. −0.54%.
d. 10.15%.

9-10 8.65%.

9-11 10.78%.

9-12 YTC = 6.47%.

9-13 a. \$1,251.26.
b. \$898.90.

9-15 a. YTM = 3.4%.
b. YTM ≈ 7%.
c. \$934.91.

9-16 a. YTM = 8%; YTC = 6.1%.

9-17 10-year, 10% coupon = 6.75%;
10-year zero = 9.75%;
5-year zero = 4.76%;
30-year zero = 32.19%;
\$100 perpetuity = 14.29%.

9-18 a. C_0 = \$1,012.79; Z_0 = \$693.04;
C_1 = \$1,010.02; Z_1 = \$759.57;
C_2 = \$1,006.98; Z_2 = \$832.49;
C_3 = \$1,003.65; Z_3 = \$912.41;
C_4 = \$1,000.00; Z_4 = \$1,000.00.

10-1 D_1 = \$1.5750; D_3 = \$1.7364; D_5 = \$2.1011.

10-2 P_0 = \$6.25.

10-3 P_1 = \$22.00; $k_s = 15.50\%$.

10-4 $k_{ps} = 8.33\%$.

10-5 \$50.50.

10-6 $g = 9\%$.

10-7 $\hat{P}_3$ = \$27.32.

10-8 a. 13.3%.
b. 10%.
c. 8%.
d. 5.7%.

10-9 \$23.75.

10-10 a. $k_C = 10.6\%$; $k_D = 7\%$.

10-11 \$25.03.

10-12 P_0 = \$19.89.

10-13 a. \$125.
b. \$83.33.

10-14 b. PV = \$5.29.
d. \$30.01.

10-15 a. 7%.
b. 5%.
c. 12%.

10-16 a(1). \$9.50.
(2). \$13.33.
b(1). Undefined.

10-18 a. Dividend 2004 = \$2.66.
b. P_0 = \$39.42.
c. Dividend yield 2002 = 5.10%; 2007 = 7.00%.

10-19 a. P_0 = \$54.11.

10-20 a. P_0 = \$21.43.
b. P_0 = \$26.47.
c. P_0 = \$40.54.

10-21 a. New price = \$31.34.
b. beta = 0.49865.

11-1 $k_s = 13\%$.

11-2 $k_{ps} = 8\%$.

11-3 $k_s = 15\%$.

11-4 a. 13%.
b. 10.4%.
c. 8.45%.

11-5 7.80%.

11-6 11.94%.

11-7 7.2%.

11-8 a. 16.3%.
b. 15.4%.
c. 16%.

11-9 a. 8%.
b. \$2.81.
c. 15.81%.

11-10 a. $g = 3\%$.
b. $EPS_1 = \$5.562$.

11-11 a. \$15,000,000.
b. 8.4%.

11-12 a. 4.8%; 12.3%.
b. 10.05%.

11-13 Short-term debt = 11.14%.
Long-term debt = 22.03%.
Common equity = 66.83%.

11-15 $w_{d(Short)} = 0\%$; $w_{d(Long)} = 20\%$; $w_{ps} = 4\%$; $w_{ce} = 76\%$. k_d (After-tax) = 7.2%; $k_{ps} = 11.6\%$; $k_s \approx 17.5\%$.

12-1 FCF = \$37.0.

12-2 $V_{op} = \$6,000,000$.

12-3 a. $V_{op2} = \$2,700,000$.
b. \$2,303,571.43.

12-4 a. \$713.33.
b. \$527.89.
c. \$43.79.

12-5 V_{op} at 2003 = \$15,000.

12-6 $V_{op} = \$160,000,000$.
MVA = −\$40,000,000.

12-7 \$259,375,000.

12-8 \$416 million.

12-9 \$46.90.

12-10 a. \$34.96 million.
b. \$741.152 million.
c. \$699.20 million.
d. \$749.10 million.
e. \$50.34.

13-1 4.34 years.

13-2 NPV = \$7,486.20.

13-3 IRR = 16%.

13-4 DPP = 6.51 years.

13-5 MIRR = 13.89%.

13-6 5%: $NPV_A = \$16,108,952$; $NPV_B = \$18,300,939$.
15%: $NPV_A = \$10,059,587$; $NPV_B = \$13,897,838$.

13-7 NPV = \$174.90.

13-8 $NPV_T = \$409$; $IRR_T = 15\%$; $MIRR_T = 14.54\%$; Accept: $NPV_P = \$3,318$; $IRR_P = 20\%$; $MIRR_P = 17.19\%$; Accept.

13-9 $NPV_E = \$3,861$; $IRR_E = 18\%$; $NPV_G = \$3,057$; $IRR_G = 18\%$; Purchase electric-powered forklift; it has a higher NPV.

13-10 $NPV_S = \$814.33$; $NPV_L = \$1,675.34$;
$IRR_S = 15.24\%$; $IRR_L = 14.67\%$;
$MIRR_S = 13.77\%$; $MIRR_L = 13.46\%$;
$PI_S = 1.081$; $PI_L = 1.067$.

13-11 b. $PV_C = -\$556,717$; $PV_F = -\$493,407$; Forklift should be chosen.

13-12 $MIRR_X = 13.59\%$.

13-13 $IRR_L = 11.74\%$.

13-14 MIRR = 10.93%.

13-15 a. NPV = \$136,578; IRR = 19.22%.

13-16 a. Payback = 0.33 year; NPV = \$81,062.35; IRR = 261.90%.

13-17 a. No; $PV_{Old} = -\$89,910.08$; $PV_{New} = -\$94,611.45$.
b. \$2,470.80.
c. 22.94%.

13-18 b. $IRR_A = 18.1\%$; $IRR_B = 24.0\%$.
d(1). $MIRR_A = 15.10\%$; $MIRR_B = 17.03\%$.
(2). $MIRR_A = 18.05\%$; $MIRR_B = 20.49\%$.

13-19 a. \$0; −\$10,250,000; \$1,750,000.
b. 16.07%.

13-20 a. $NPV_A = \$18,108,510$; $NPV_B = \$13,946,117$; $IRR_A = 15.03\%$; $IRR_B = 22.26\%$.
b. $NPV_\Delta = \$4,162,393$; $IRR_\Delta = 11.71\%$.

13-21 d. 7.61%; 15.58%.

13-23 a. Undefined.
b. $PV_C = -\$911,067$; $PV_F = -\$838,834$.

13-24 a. A = 2.67 years; B = 1.5 years.
b. A = 3.07 years; B = 1.825 years.
d. $NPV_A = \$18,243,813$; choose A.
e. $NPV_B = \$8,643,390$; choose B.
f. 13.53%.
g. $MIRR_A = 21.93\%$; $MIRR_B = 20.96\%$

13-25 Extended $NPV_A = \$12.76$ million.

13-26 Machine A; Extended $NPV_A = \$4.51$ million.

13-28 a. 3 years.
b. No.

14-1 \$12,000,000.

14-2 \$2,600,000.

14-3 \$4,600,000.

14-4 a. −\$126,000.
b. \$42,518; \$47,579; \$34,926.
c. \$50,702.
d. NPV = \$10,841; Purchase.

14-5 a. \$89,000.
b. \$26,220; \$30,300; \$20,100.
c. \$24,380.

14-7 a. NPV = \$106,537.

14-8 E(NPV) = \$3 million; $\sigma_{NPV} = \$23.622$ million; $CV_{NPV} = 7.874$.

14-9 a. Expected CF_A = \$6,750; Expected CF_B = \$7,650; CV_A = 0.0703.
b. NPV_A = \$10,037; NPV_B = \$11,624.

14-10 a. E(IRR) ≈ 15.3%.
b. \$38,589.

15-1 \$1.82.

15-2 \$27.00; \$37.00.

15-3 a. \$1.074 million.
b. \$2.96 million.

15-4 a. \$4.6795 million.
b. \$3.208 million.

15-5 a. −\$19 million.
b. \$9.0981 million.

15-6 a. −\$2.113 million.
b. \$1.973 million.
c. −\$70,222.
d. \$565,090.
e. \$1.116 million.

15-7 P = \$18.646 million; X = \$20 million; t = 1; k_{RF} = 0.08; σ^2 = 0.0687; V = \$2.028 million.

15-8 P = \$10.479 million; X = \$9 million; t = 2; k_{RF} = 0.06; σ^2 = 0.0111; V = \$2.514 million.

16-1 a. ROI = 21.25% > WACC = 15%.
b(1). OL_{Old} = 44.44%; OL_{New} = 47.17%.
(2). $Q_{BE_{Old}}$ = 40; $Q_{BE_{New}}$ = 45.45.

16-2 a. ROE_C = 15%; σ_C = 11%.

16-3 b. \$2 million.
c. \$20.28; \$17.96.

16-4 a. V = \$3,283,636.
b. \$16.42.
c. \$1.81.

16-5 a. 14.0%.
c. \$38.85.

16-7 a. 10.10%; 1.025.
b. 0.788; 9.153%.
c. At D = \$40 million: 1.261; 11.05%.
d. At D = \$40 million: \$64.6 million.

16-8 11.45%.

17-1 a. b_U = 1.13.
b. k_{sU} = 15.65%; 5.65%.
c. 1%; 2.42%; 4.62%.
d. 4.62%.

17-2 a. V_U = V_L = \$20 million.
b. k_{sU} = 10%; k_{sL} = 15%.
c. S_L = \$10 million.
d. $WACC_U$ = 10%; $WACC_L$ = 10%.

17-3 a. V_U = \$12 million; V_L = \$16 million.
b. k_{sU} = 10%; k_{sL} = 15%.
c. S_L = \$6 million.
d. $WACC_U$ = 10%; $WACC_L$ = 7.5%.

17-4 a. V_U = 9.6 million.
b. V_L = \$12.93 million.
c. \$3.33 million versus \$4 million.
d. V_L = \$20 million; \$0.
e. V_L = \$16 million; \$4 million.
f. V_L = \$12.64 million; \$4 million.

17-5 a. V_U = V_L = \$14,545,455.
b. At D = \$6 million: k_{sL} = 14.51%; WACC = 11.0%.
c. V_U = \$8,727,273; V_L = \$11,127,273.
d. At D = \$6 million: k_{sL} = 14.51%; WACC = 8.63%.
e. D = V = \$14,545,455.

17-6 a. A: \$32.5 million; B: \$30.0 million.
b. Project B.

17-7 a. Harris: \$10.0 million; Broske: \$10.0 million.

18-1 Payout = 55%.

18-2 P_0 = \$60.

18-3 P_0 = \$40.

18-4 \$3,250,000.

18-5 Payout = 20%.

18-6 Payout = 52%.

18-7 D_0 = \$3.44.

18-8 Payout = 31.39%.

18-9 a(1). \$3,960,000.
(2). \$4,800,000.
(3). \$9,360,000.
(4). Regular = \$3,960,000; Extra = \$5,400,000.
c. 15%.
d. 15%.

18-10 a. \$6,000,000.
b. DPS = \$2.00; Payout = 25%.
c. \$5,000,000.
d. No.
e. 50%.
f. \$1,000,000.
g. \$8,333,333.

19-1 a. \$700,000.
b. \$3,700,000.
c. −\$2,300,000.

19-2 964,115.

19-3 a. 2001: \$12,000; \$6,000; \$90,000.
b. Edelman: g_{EPS} = 8.0%; g_{DPS} = 7.4%.
e. 2001: \$3.00; \$1.50; \$22.50.
f. Kennedy: 15.00%; Strasburg: 13.64%.
g. 2001: Kennedy: 50%; Strasburg: 50%.
h. Kennedy: 43%; Strasburg: 37%.
i. Kennedy: 8×; Strasburg: 8.67×.

20-1 a(1). 50%.
(2). 60%.
(3). 50%.

20-2 Cost of owning = −\$127; cost of leasing = −\$128.

20-3 a. NAL = \$37,206.

21-1 \$196.36.

21-2 25 shares.

21-3 a(1). −\$5, or \$0.
(2). \$0.
(3). \$5.
(4). \$75.
d. 10%; \$100.

21-5 a. 14.1%.
b. \$12 million before tax.

21-6 b. Plan 1: 49%; Plan 2: 53%; Plan 3: 53%.
c. Plan 1: \$0.59; Plan 2: \$0.64; Plan 3: \$0.88.
d. Plan 1: 19%; Plan 2: 19%; Plan 3: 50%.

21-7 b. 11.65%.

22-1 a. 83 days.
b. 4.8×.

22-2 \$10,000.

22-3 \$3,000,000.

22-4 A/R = \$59,500.

22-5 a. \$103,350.
b. \$97,500.

22-6 a. DSO = 28 days.
b. A/R = \$70,000.

22-7 a. ROE_T = 11.75%; ROE_M = 10.80%; ROE_R = 9.16%.

22-8 a. \$1,600,000.
c. Bank = \$1,200,000; Books = −\$5,200,000.

22-9 b. \$420,000.
c. \$35,000.

22-10 a. Feb. surplus = \$2,000.

22-11 a. Oct. loan = \$22,800.

23-1 k_{Nom} = 74.23%; EAR = 107.72%.

23-2 EAR = 8.37%.

23-3 \$7,500,000.

23-4 \$233.56.

23-5 EAR = 21.60%.

23-6 b. 14.69%.
d. 20.99%.

23-7 a. 44.54%.

23-8 a. k_d = 12%.
b. k_d = 11.25%.
c. k_d = 11.48%.
d. k_d = 14.47%. Alternative b has lowest interest rate.

23-9 Nominal cost = 14.69%; Effective cost = 15.66%.

23-10 Bank loan = 13.64%.

23-11 d. 8.3723%.

23-12 a. \$100,000.
c(1). \$300,000.
(2). Nominal cost = 36.73%; Effective cost = 43.86%.

23-14 a. \$300,000.

23-15 a. 11.73%.
b. 12.09%.
c. 13.45%.

23-16 a. With discount = \$83.33.
Without = \$250.
b. With discount = \$641.03.
Without = \$384.62.
c. Nominal cost of trade credit = 18.18%.
Effective cost of trade credit = 19.83%.
Bank cost = 23.08%.
d. Cash = \$126.90; NP = \$434.60.

23-17 a(1). \$27,500.
(3). \$25,833.

24-1 k_d = 5.96%.

24-2 b. Futures = +\$1,859,117; Bond = −\$1,101,851; Net = +\$757,326.

24-3 Net to Carter = 9.95% fixed.
Net to Brence = LIBOR + 3.05% floating.

25-1 a. Total assets: \$327 million.
b. Income: \$7 million.
c. Before: \$15.6 million.
After: \$13.0 million.
d. Before: 35.7%.
After: 64.2%.

25-2 a. \$0.
b. First mortgage holders: \$300,000.
Second mortgage holders: \$100,000 plus \$12,700 as a general claimant.
c. Trustee's expenses: \$50,000.
Wages due: \$30,000.
Taxes due: \$40,000.

25-3 b. AP = 24%; NP = 100%; WP = 100%; TP = 100%; Mortgage = 85%.
Subordinated debentures = 9%; Trustee = 100%.

26-1 P_0 = \$37.04.

26-2 P_0 = \$43.48.

26-3 \$37.04 to \$43.48.

26-4 a. 17%.
b. V = \$14.65 million.

26-5 NPV = −\$6,747.71; Do not purchase.

26-6 a. 14%.
b. TV = \$1,143.4; V = \$877.2.

27-1 0.07425 yen per lira.

27-2 f_t = \$0.00907.

27-3 1 FF = \$0.19724 or \$1 = 5.07 FF.

27-4 0.6667 pound per dollar.

27-5 4.5455 FF.

27-6 8.85 francs per pound.

27-8 \$480,000,000.

27-9 +\$250,000.

27-10

Dollars per 1,000 Units of:				
Marks	Lira	Yen	Pesos	Swiss Francs
\$427.20	\$0.43	\$9.23	\$104.30	\$555.90

27-12 b. \$18,148.00.

27-13 a. \$2,709,339.
b. \$2,689,121.
c. \$3,200,000.

27-14 b. f_t = \$0.6295.

27-15 $k_{Nom\text{-}U.S.}$ = 4.6%.

27-16 117 pesos.

27-17 e_0 = 20 yen per 1 FF, or 0.05 FF per 1 yen.

APPENDIX C

Selected Equations and Data

Chapter 2

$$\text{Net operating working capital} = \frac{\text{All current assets that}}{\text{do not pay interest}} - \frac{\text{All current liabilities that}}{\text{do not charge interest}}$$

$$= \text{Operating current assets} - \text{operating current liabilities.}$$

$$\text{Operating capital} = (\text{Net operating working capital}) + (\text{Net plant and equipment}).$$

$$\text{NOPAT} = \text{Net operating profit after taxes} = \text{EBIT}(1 - \text{Tax rate}).$$

$$\text{Operating cash flow} = \text{NOPAT} + \text{Depreciation.}$$

$$\begin{array}{c}\text{Equivalent pre-tax yield}\\ \text{on taxable bond}\end{array} = \frac{\text{Yield on muni}}{1 - \text{Marginal tax rate}}.$$

$$\text{Free cash flow (FCF)} = \text{Operating cash flow} - \text{Gross investment in operating capital.}$$

$$= \text{NOPAT} - \text{Net investment in operating capital.}$$

$$\text{WACC} = \text{Weighted average cost of capital.}$$

$$\text{Return on invested capital (ROIC)} = \frac{\text{NOPAT}}{\text{Operating capital}}.$$

$$\text{MVA} = (\text{Market value of equity} + \text{Market value of debt}) - \text{Capital supplied by investors}$$

$$= \text{Market value of equity} - \text{Equity capital supplied by shareholders}$$

$$= (\text{Shares outstanding})(\text{Stock price}) - \text{Total common equity.}$$

$$\text{EVA} = \text{After-tax operating profit, or NOPAT} - \text{After-tax dollar cost of capital used to support operations.}$$

$$= \text{EBIT}(1 - \text{Tax rate}) - (\text{After-tax percentage cost of capital})(\text{Operating capital}).$$

$$= \text{Operating capital (ROIC} - \text{WACC).}$$

Individual Tax Rates for the 2000 Tax Year

SINGLE INDIVIDUALS

If Your Taxable Income Is	You Pay This Amount on the Base of the Bracket	Plus This Percentage on the Excess over the Base	Average Tax Rate at Top of Bracket
Up to \$26,250	\$ 0	15.0%	15.0%
\$26,250–\$63,550	3,937.50	28.0	22.6
\$63,550–\$132,600	14,381.50	31.0	27.0
\$132,600–\$288,350	35,787.00	36.0	31.9
Over \$288,350	91,857.00	39.6	39.6

MARRIED COUPLES FILING JOINT RETURNS

If Your Taxable Income Is	You Pay This Amount on the Base of the Bracket	Plus This Percentage on the Excess over the Base	Average Tax Rate at Top of Bracket
Up to \$43,850	\$ 0	15.0%	15.0%
\$43,850–\$105,950	6,577.50	28.0	22.6
\$105,950–\$161,450	23,965.50	31.0	25.5
\$161,450–\$288,350	41,170.50	36.0	30.1
Over \$288,350	86,854.50	39.6	39.6

Corporate Tax Rates

If a Corporation's Taxable Income Is	It Pays This Amount on the Base of the Bracket	Plus This Percentage on the Excess over the Base	Average Tax Rate at Top of Bracket
Up to \$50,000	\$ 0	15%	15.0%
\$50,000–\$75,000	7,500	25	18.3
\$75,000–\$100,000	13,750	34	22.3
\$100,000–\$335,000	22,250	39	34.0
\$335,000–\$10,000,000	113,900	34	34.0
\$10,000,000–\$15,000,000	3,400,000	35	34.3
\$15,000,000–\$18,333,333	5,150,000	38	35.0
Over \$18,333,333	6,416,667	35	35.0

Chapter 3

$$\text{Current ratio} = \frac{\text{Current assets}}{\text{Current liabilities}}.$$

$$\text{Quick, or acid test, ratio} = \frac{\text{Current assets} - \text{Inventories}}{\text{Current liabilities}}.$$

$$\text{Inventory turnover ratio} = \frac{\text{Sales}}{\text{Inventories}}.$$

$$\text{DSO} = \begin{matrix}\text{Days}\\ \text{sales}\\ \text{outstanding}\end{matrix} = \frac{\text{Receivables}}{\text{Average sales per day}} = \frac{\text{Receivables}}{\text{Annual sales/360}}.$$

$$\text{Fixed assets turnover ratio} = \frac{\text{Sales}}{\text{Net fixed assets}}.$$

$$\text{Total assets turnover ratio} = \frac{\text{Sales}}{\text{Total assets}}.$$

$$\text{Debt ratio} = \frac{\text{Total debt}}{\text{Total assets}}.$$

$$\text{D/E} = \frac{\text{D/A}}{1 - \text{D/A}}, \text{ and D/A} = \frac{\text{D/E}}{1 + \text{D/E}}.$$

$$\text{Equity multiplier} = \frac{\text{Total assets}}{\text{Equity}} = \frac{\text{A}}{\text{E}}.$$

$$\text{Debt ratio} = 1 - \frac{1}{\text{Equity multiplier}}.$$

$$\text{Times-interest-earned (TIE) ratio} = \frac{\text{EBIT}}{\text{Interest charges}}.$$

$$\begin{matrix}\text{EBITDA}\\ \text{coverage ratio}\end{matrix} = \frac{\text{EBITDA} + \text{Lease payments}}{\text{Interest charges} + \text{Principal payments} + \text{Lease payments}}.$$

$$\text{Profit margin on sales} = \frac{\begin{matrix}\text{Net income available to}\\ \text{common stockholders}\end{matrix}}{\text{Sales}}.$$

$$\text{Basic earning power ratio} = \frac{\text{EBIT}}{\text{Total assets}}.$$

$$\text{Return on total assets (ROA)} = \frac{\begin{matrix}\text{Net income available to}\\ \text{common stockholders}\end{matrix}}{\text{Total assets}}.$$

$$\text{ROA} = \left(\begin{matrix}\text{Profit}\\ \text{margin}\end{matrix}\right)(\text{Total assets turnover})$$

$$= \frac{\text{Net income}}{\text{Sales}} \times \frac{\text{Sales}}{\text{Total assets}}.$$

$$\text{Return on common equity (ROE)} = \frac{\text{Net income available to common stockholders}}{\text{Common equity}}.$$

$$\text{Price/earnings (P/E) ratio} = \frac{\text{Price per share}}{\text{Earnings per share}}.$$

$$\text{Book value per share} = \frac{\text{Common equity}}{\text{Shares outstanding}}.$$

$$\text{Market/book (M/B) ratio} = \frac{\text{Market price per share}}{\text{Book value per share}}.$$

$$\text{Price/cash flow ratio} = \frac{\text{Price per share}}{\text{Cash flow per share}}.$$

$$\begin{aligned}\text{ROE} &= \text{ROA} \times \text{Equity multiplier}\\ &= \left(\begin{matrix}\text{Profit}\\ \text{margin}\end{matrix}\right)\left(\begin{matrix}\text{Total assets}\\ \text{turnover}\end{matrix}\right)\left(\begin{matrix}\text{Equity}\\ \text{multiplier}\end{matrix}\right)\\ &= \left(\frac{\text{Net income}}{\text{Sales}}\right)\left(\frac{\text{Sales}}{\text{Total assets}}\right)\left(\frac{\text{Total assets}}{\text{Common equity}}\right)\\ &= \frac{\text{Net income}}{\text{Common equity}}.\end{aligned}$$

Chapter 4

$$\text{AFN} = (A^*/S_0)\Delta S - (L^*/S_0)\Delta S - MS_1(1 - d).$$

$$\text{Full capacity sales} = \frac{\text{Actual sales}}{\text{Percentage of capacity at which fixed assets were operated}}.$$

$$\text{Target FA/Sales ratio} = \frac{\text{Actual fixed assets}}{\text{Full capacity sales}}.$$

$$\text{Required level of FA} = (\text{Target FA/Sales ratio})(\text{Projected sales}).$$

Chapter 5

$$\text{Quoted interest rate} = k = k^* + IP + DRP + LP + MRP.$$

$$k_{\text{T-bill}} = k_{RF} = k^* + IP.$$

$$IP_n = \frac{I_1 + I_2 + \ldots + I_n}{n}.$$

Chapter 6

$$\text{Rate of return} = \frac{\text{Amount received} - \text{Amount invested}}{\text{Amount invested}}.$$

$$\text{Expected rate of return} = \hat{k} = \sum_{i=1}^{n} P_i k_i.$$

$$\text{Variance} = \sigma^2 = \sum_{i=1}^{n} (k_i - \hat{k})^2 P_i.$$

$$\text{Standard deviation} = \sigma = \sqrt{\sum_{i=1}^{n} (k_i - \hat{k})^2 P_i}.$$

$$CV = \frac{\sigma}{\hat{k}}.$$

$$\hat{k}_p = \sum_{i=1}^{n} w_i \hat{k}_i.$$

$$\sigma_p = \sqrt{\sum_{i=1}^{n} (k_{pi} - \hat{k}_p)^2 P_i}.$$

$$b_i = \left(\frac{r_i}{r_M}\right) r_{iM}.$$

$$b_p = \sum_{i=1}^{n} w_i b_i.$$

Required return on stock market $= k_M$.
Market risk premium $(RP_M) = k_M - k_{RF}$.
$RP_i = (k_M - k_{RF})b_i = (RP_M)b_i$.
SML: $k_i = k_{RF} + (k_M - k_{RF})b_i = k_{RF} + (RP_M)b_i$.

$$b_J = \frac{Y_2 - Y_1}{X_2 - X_1} = \text{slope coefficient in regression: } \bar{k}_J = a_J + b_J\bar{k}_M + e_J.$$

Chapter 7

$$\sigma_p = \sqrt{\sum_{i=1}^{n} (k_{pi} - \hat{k}_p)^2 P_i}.$$

$$\text{Cov(AB)} = \sum_{i=1}^{n} (k_{Ai} - \hat{k}_A)(k_{Bi} - \hat{k}_B)P_i.$$

$$r_{AB} = \frac{\text{Cov(AB)}}{\sigma_A\sigma_B}.$$

$$\sigma_p = \sqrt{w_A^2\sigma_A^2 + (1 - w_A)^2\sigma_B^2 + 2w_A(1 - w_A)r_{AB}\sigma_A\sigma_B}.$$

$$\hat{k}_p = w_A\hat{k}_A + (1 - w_A)\hat{k}_B.$$

$$\text{Minimum risk portfolio: } w_A = \frac{\sigma_B(\sigma_B - r_{AB}\sigma_A)}{\sigma_A^2 + \sigma_B^2 - 2r_{AB}\sigma_A\sigma_B}.$$

$$\text{Capital Market Line (CML): } \hat{k}_p = k_{RF} + \left(\frac{\hat{k}_M - k_{RF}}{\sigma_M}\right)\sigma_p.$$

Security Market Line (SML): $k_J = k_{RF} + (k_M - k_{RF})b_J = k_{RF} + (RP_M)b_J$.

$$b_i = \frac{\text{Cov}(\bar{k}_i, \bar{k}_M)}{\sigma_M^2} = \frac{r_{iM}\sigma_i\sigma_M}{\sigma_M^2} = r_{iM}\left(\frac{\sigma_i}{\sigma_M}\right).$$

Predicted future rate of return $= \hat{k}_J = a_J + b_J\hat{k}_M + e_J$.
$\sigma_J^2 = b_J^2\sigma_M^2 + \sigma_{eJ}^2$.
APT: $k_i = k_{RF} + (k_1 - k_{RF})b_{i1} + \cdots + (k_j - k_{RF})b_{ij}$.
Fama-French: $k_i = k_{RF} + a_i + b_i(k_M - k_{RF}) + c_i(k_{SMB}) + d_i(k_{HML})$.

Chapter 8

$$FV_n = PV(1 + i)^n = PV(FVIF_{i,n}).$$

$$PV = FV_n\left(\frac{1}{1 + i}\right)^n = FV_n(1 + i)^{-n} = FV_n(PVIF_{i,n}).$$

$$PVIF_{i,n} = \frac{1}{FVIF_{i,n}}.$$

$$FVIFA_{i,n} = \sum_{t=1}^{n} (1 + i)^{n-t} = \frac{(1 + i)^n - 1}{i}.$$

$$PVIFA_{i,n} = \sum_{t=1}^{n} \frac{1}{(1 + i)^t} = \frac{1 - \dfrac{1}{(1 + i)^n}}{i} = \frac{1}{i} - \frac{1}{i(1 + i)^n}.$$

$FVA_n = PMT(FVIFA_{i,n})$.
FVA_n(Annuity due) $= PMT(FVIFA_{i,n})(1 + i)$.

$$PVA_n = PMT(PVIFA_{i,n}).$$
$$PVA_n(\text{Annuity due}) = PMT(PVIFA_{i,n})(1 + i).$$
$$PV(\text{Perpetuity}) = \frac{\text{Payment}}{\text{Interest rate}} = \frac{PMT}{i}.$$
$$PV_{\text{Uneven stream}} = \sum_{t=1}^{n} CF_t\left(\frac{1}{1+i}\right)^t = \sum_{t=1}^{n} CF_t(PVIF_{i,t}).$$
$$FV_{\text{Uneven stream}} = \sum_{t=1}^{n} CF_t(1+i)^{n-t} = \sum_{t=1}^{n} CF_t(FVIF_{i,n-t}).$$
$$FV_n = PV\left(1 + \frac{i_{Nom}}{m}\right)^{mn}.$$
$$\text{Effective annual rate} = \left(1 + \frac{i_{Nom}}{m}\right)^m - 1.0.$$
$$\text{Periodic rate} = i_{Nom}/m.$$
$$i_{Nom} = APR = (\text{Periodic rate})(m).$$

Chapter 9

$$V_B = \sum_{t=1}^{N} \frac{INT}{(1+k_d)^t} + \frac{M}{(1+k_d)^N}$$
$$= INT(PVIFA_{k_d,N}) + M(PVIF_{k_d,N}).$$
$$V_B = \sum_{t=1}^{2N} \frac{INT/2}{(1+k_d/2)^t} + \frac{M}{(1+k_d/2)^{2N}} = \frac{INT}{2}(PVIFA_{k_d/2,2N}) + M(PVIF_{k_d/2,2N}).$$
$$\text{Price of callable bond} = \sum_{t=1}^{N} \frac{INT}{(1+k_d)^t} + \frac{\text{Call price}}{(1+k_d)^N}.$$

Chapter 10

$$\hat{P}_0 = \text{PV of expected future dividends} = \sum_{t=1}^{\infty} \frac{D_t}{(1+k_s)^t}.$$
$$\hat{P}_0 = \frac{D_0(1+g)}{k_s - g} = \frac{D_1}{k_s - g}.$$
$$\hat{k}_s = \frac{D_1}{P_0} + g.$$
$$\bar{k}_s = \text{Actual dividend yield} + \text{Actual capital gains yield}.$$
$$V_{ps} = \frac{D_{ps}}{k_{ps}}.$$
$$k_{ps} = \frac{D_{ps}}{V_{ps}}.$$

Chapter 11

$$\text{After-tax component cost of debt} = k_d(1 - T).$$
$$\text{Component cost of preferred stock} = k_{ps} = \frac{D_{ps}}{P_n}.$$
$$k_s = \hat{k}_s = k_{RF} + RP = D_1/P_0 + \text{expected } g.$$
$$k_s = k_{RF} + (k_M - k_{RF})b_i.$$

k_s = Bond yield + Risk premium.
g = (Retention rate)(ROE) = (1.0 − Payout rate)(ROE) = b(ROE).
$WACC = w_d k_d(1 - T) + w_{ps} k_{ps} + w_{ce} k_s$.

Chapter 12

$$V_{op} = \text{Value of operations}$$
$$= \text{PV of expected future free cash flows}$$
$$= \sum_{t=1}^{\infty} \frac{FCF_t}{(1 + WACC)^t}.$$

Horizon value (HV): $HV_T = \dfrac{FCF_T(1 + g)}{WACC - g} = \dfrac{FCF_{T+1}}{WACC - g}$.

Total value = V_{op} + Value of nonoperating assets.
Value of equity = Total value − Preferred stock − Debt.

Operating profitability (OP): $OP = \dfrac{NOPAT}{Sales}$.

Capital requirements (CR): $CR = \dfrac{\text{Operating capital}}{\text{Sales}}$.

For constant growth:
V_{op} at time N =

$$Capital_N + \left[\frac{Sales_N(1 + g)}{WACC - g}\right]\left[OP - WACC\left(\frac{CR}{1 + g}\right)\right].$$

Expected return on invested capital (EROIC): $EROIC_T = \dfrac{NOPAT_{T+1}}{Capital}$.

For constant growth: V_{op} at time N $= Capital_N + \dfrac{Capital_N(EROIC_N - WACC)}{WACC - g}$.

Chapter 13

Payback period = Year before full recovery + $\dfrac{\text{Unrecovered cost at start of year}}{\text{Cash flow during year}}$.

$$NPV = CF_0 + \frac{CF_1}{(1 + k)^1} + \frac{CF_2}{(1 + k)^2} + \cdots + \frac{CF_n}{(1 + k)^n}$$
$$= \sum_{t=0}^{n} \frac{CF}{(1 + k)^t}.$$

$$IRR: CF_0 + \frac{CF_1}{(1 + IRR)^1} + \frac{CF_2}{(1 + IRR)^2} + \cdots + \frac{CF_n}{(1 + IRR)^n} = 0.$$
$$\sum_{t=0}^{n} \frac{CF_t}{(1 + IRR)^t} = 0.$$

MIRR: PV costs = PV terminal value

$$\sum_{t=0}^{n} \frac{COF_t}{(1 + k)^t} = \frac{\sum_{t=0}^{n} CIF_t(1 + k)^{n-t}}{(1 + MIRR)^n}$$

$$\text{PV costs} = \frac{TV}{(1 + MIRR)^n}.$$

$$PI = \frac{\text{PV of future cash flows}}{\text{Initial cost}} = \frac{\sum_{t=0}^{n} \frac{CF_t}{(1 + k)^t}}{CF_0}.$$

Chapter 14

Recovery Allowance Percentage for Personal Property

Ownership Year	Class of Investment: 3-Year	5-Year	7-Year	10-Year
1	33%	20%	14%	10%
2	45	32	25	18
3	15	19	17	14
4	7	12	13	12
5		11	9	9
6		6	9	7
7			9	7
8			4	7
9				7
10				6
11				3
	100%	100%	100%	100%

$$\text{NPV(no inflation)} = \sum_{t=0}^{n} \frac{\text{RCF}_t}{(1 + k_r)^t} = \sum_{t=0}^{n} \frac{\text{NCF}_t}{(1 + k_n)^t}.$$

$$\text{NPV(with inflation)} = \sum_{t=0}^{n} \frac{\text{NCF}_t}{(1 + k_n)^t} = \sum_{t=0}^{n} \frac{\text{RCF}_t(1 + i)^t}{(1 + k_r)^t(1 + i)^t}.$$

$$\sigma_{NPV} = \sqrt{\sum_{i=1}^{n} P_i[\text{NPV}_i - \text{E(NPV)}]^2}.$$

$$\text{CV}_{NPV} = \frac{\sigma_{NPV}}{\text{E(NPV)}}.$$

Chapter 15

$$\text{Exercise value} = \frac{\text{Current price}}{\text{of stock}} - \text{Strike price}.$$

$$V = P[N(d_1)] - Xe^{-k_{RF}t}[N(d_2)].$$

$$d_1 = \frac{\ln(P/X) + [k_{RF} + (\sigma^2/2)]t}{\sigma\sqrt{t}}.$$

$$d_2 = d_1 = \sigma\sqrt{t}.$$

$$\text{Variance of a project's rate of return: } \sigma^2 = \frac{\ln(CV^2 + 1)}{t}.$$

Chapter 16

$$\text{Return on invested capital (ROIC)} = \frac{\text{NOPAT}}{\text{Capital}}.$$

$$\text{EBIT} = PQ - VQ - F.$$

$$Q_{BE} = \frac{F}{P - V}.$$

$$\text{EPS} = \frac{(S - FC - VC - I)(1 - T)}{\text{Shares outstanding}} = \frac{(\text{EBIT} - I)(1 - T)}{\text{Shares outstanding}}.$$

$$b = b_U[1 + (1 - T)(D/E)].$$

$$b_U = b/[1 + (1 - T)(D/E)].$$

$$D/E = \frac{D/A}{1 - D/A}.$$

$k_s = k_{RF}$ + Premium for business risk + Premium for financial risk.

Chapter 17

For no taxes:

$$V_L = V_U = \frac{EBIT}{WACC} = \frac{EBIT}{k_{sU}}.$$

$$k_{sL} = k_{sU} + (k_{sU} - k_d)(D/S).$$

For corporate taxes:

$$V_L = V_U + TD.$$

$$V_U = \frac{EBIT(1 - T)}{k_{sU}}.$$

$$k_{sL} = k_{sU} + (k_{sU} - k_d)(1 - T)(D/S).$$

$$V_L = V_U + TD - \begin{pmatrix}\text{PV of expected} \\ \text{financial distress} \\ \text{costs}\end{pmatrix} - \begin{pmatrix}\text{PV of} \\ \text{agency} \\ \text{costs}\end{pmatrix}.$$

$$CF_L = (EBIT - I)(1 - T_c)(1 - T_s) + I(1 - T_d).$$

$$V_L = V_U + \left[1 - \frac{(1 - T_c)(1 - T_s)}{(1 - T_d)}\right]D.$$

$$V_U = \frac{EBIT(1 - T_c)(1 - T_s)}{k_{sU}}.$$

Hamada equation: $k_{sL} = k_{RF} + (k_M - k_{RF})b_U + (k_M - k_{RF})b_U(1 - T)(D/S).$

$$b = b_U[1 + (1 - T)(D/S)].$$

$$b = b_U + b_U(P/S) + b_U(1 - T)(D/S).$$

Chapter 18

g = (Retention rate) (ROE) = (1 − Payout rate) (ROE).

Dividends = Net income − [(Target equity ratio) (Total capital budget)].

Chapter 20

NAL = PV cost of owning − PV cost of leasing.

Chapter 21

$$\begin{matrix}\text{Price paid for} \\ \text{bond with warrants}\end{matrix} = \begin{matrix}\text{Straight-debt} \\ \text{value of bonds}\end{matrix} + \begin{matrix}\text{Value of} \\ \text{warrants.}\end{matrix}$$

$$\text{Conversion price} = P_c = \frac{\text{Par value of bond given up}}{\text{Shares received}}$$

$$= \frac{\text{Par value of bond given up}}{CR}.$$

$$\text{Conversion ratio} = CR = \frac{\text{Par value of bond given up}}{P_c}.$$

Chapter 22

$$\begin{matrix}\text{Inventory conversion} \\ \text{period}\end{matrix} = \frac{\text{Inventory}}{\text{Sales}/360}.$$

$$\begin{matrix}\text{Receivables collection} \\ \text{period}\end{matrix} = DSO = \frac{\text{Receivables}}{\text{Sales}/360}.$$

$$\text{Payables deferral period} = \text{Payables/Credit purchases per day} = \text{Payables/(Cost of goods sold/360)}.$$

$$\begin{matrix}\text{Inventory} \\ \text{conversion} \\ \text{period}\end{matrix} + \begin{matrix}\text{Receivables} \\ \text{collection} \\ \text{period}\end{matrix} - \begin{matrix}\text{Payables} \\ \text{deferral} \\ \text{period}\end{matrix} = \begin{matrix}\text{Cash} \\ \text{conversion} \\ \text{cycle}\end{matrix}.$$

$$\text{A/R} = \begin{matrix}\text{Credit sales} \\ \text{per day}\end{matrix} \times \begin{matrix}\text{Length of} \\ \text{collection period}\end{matrix}.$$

$$\text{ADS} = \text{Annual sales/360} = \frac{\text{(Units sold)(Sales price)}}{360}.$$

$$\text{Receivables} = \text{(ADS)(DSO)}.$$

Chapter 23

$$\text{Nominal cost of payables} = \frac{\text{Discount percent}}{100 - \begin{matrix}\text{Discount} \\ \text{percent}\end{matrix}} \times \frac{360}{\begin{matrix}\text{Days credit is} \\ \text{outstanding}\end{matrix} - \begin{matrix}\text{Discount} \\ \text{period}\end{matrix}}.$$

$$\text{Simple interest rate per day} = \frac{\text{Nominal rate}}{\text{Days in year}}.$$

$$\text{Simple interest charge for period} = \text{(Days in period) (Rate per day) (Amount of loan)}.$$

$$\text{Face value}_{\text{Discount}} = \frac{\text{Funds received}}{1.0 - \text{Nominal rate (decimal)}}.$$

$$\text{APR} = \text{(Periods per year)(Rate per period)}.$$

Chapter 27

$$\frac{\text{Forward exchange rate}}{\text{Spot exchange rate}} = \frac{(1 + k_h)}{(1 + k_f)}.$$

$$P_h = (P_f)(\text{Spot rate}).$$

$$\text{Spot rate} = \frac{P_h}{P_f}.$$

APPENDIX D

Mathematical Table

TABLE D-1 Values of the Areas under the Standard Normal Distribution Function

z	0.00	0.01	0.02	0.03	0.04	0.05	0.06	0.07	0.08	0.09
0.0	.0000	.0040	.0080	.0120	.0160	.0199	.0239	.0279	.0319	.0359
0.1	.0398	.0438	.0478	.0517	.0557	.0596	.0636	.0675	.0714	.0753
0.2	.0793	.0832	.0871	.0910	.0948	.0987	.1026	.1064	.1103	.1141
0.3	.1179	.1217	.1255	.1293	.1331	.1368	.1406	.1443	.1480	.1517
0.4	.1554	.1591	.1628	.1664	.1700	.1736	.1772	.1808	.1844	.1879
0.5	.1915	.1950	.1985	.2019	.2054	.2088	.2123	.2157	.2190	.2224
0.6	.2257	.2291	.2324	.2357	.2389	.2422	.2454	.2486	.2517	.2549
0.7	.2580	.2611	.2642	.2673	.2704	.2734	.2764	.2794	.2823	.2852
0.8	.2881	.2910	.2939	.2967	.2995	.3023	.3051	.3078	.3106	.3133
0.9	.3159	.3186	.3212	.3238	.3264	.3289	.3315	.3340	.3365	.3389
1.0	.3413	.3438	.3461	.3485	.3508	.3531	.3554	.3577	.3599	.3621
1.1	.3643	.3665	.3686	.3708	.3729	.3749	.3770	.3790	.3810	.3830
1.2	.3849	.3869	.3888	.3907	.3925	.3944	.3962	.3980	.3997	.4015
1.3	.4032	.4049	.4066	.4082	.4099	.4115	.4131	.4147	.4162	.4177
1.4	.4192	.4207	.4222	.4236	.4251	.4265	.4279	.4292	.4306	.4319
1.5	.4332	.4345	.4357	.4370	.4382	.4394	.4406	.4418	.4429	.4441
1.6	.4452	.4463	.4474	.4484	.4495	.4505	.4515	.4525	.4535	.4545
1.7	.4554	.4564	.4573	.4582	.4591	.4599	.4608	.4616	.4625	.4633
1.8	.4641	.4649	.4656	.4664	.4671	.4678	.4686	.4693	.4699	.4706
1.9	.4713	.4719	.4726	.4732	.4738	.4744	.4750	.4756	.4761	.4767
2.0	.4773	.4778	.4783	.4788	.4793	.4798	.4803	.4808	.4812	.4817
2.1	.4821	.4826	.4830	.4834	.4838	.4842	.4846	.4850	.4854	.4857
2.2	.4861	.4864	.4868	.4871	.4875	.4878	.4881	.4884	.4887	.4890
2.3	.4893	.4896	.4898	.4901	.4904	.4906	.4909	.4911	.4913	.4916
2.4	.4918	.4920	.4922	.4925	.4927	.4929	.4931	.4932	.4934	.4936
2.5	.4938	.4940	.4941	.4943	.4945	.4946	.4948	.4949	.4951	.4952
2.6	.4953	.4955	.4956	.4957	.4959	.4960	.4961	.4962	.4963	.4964
2.7	.4965	.4966	.4967	.4968	.4969	.4970	.4971	.4972	.4973	.4974
2.8	.4974	.4975	.4976	.4977	.4977	.4978	.4979	.4979	.4980	.4981
2.9	.4981	.4982	.4982	.4982	.4984	.4984	.4985	.4985	.4986	.4986
3.0	.4987	.4987	.4987	.4988	.4988	.4989	.4989	.4989	.4990	.4990

Index